The Essential Writings of the American Black Church

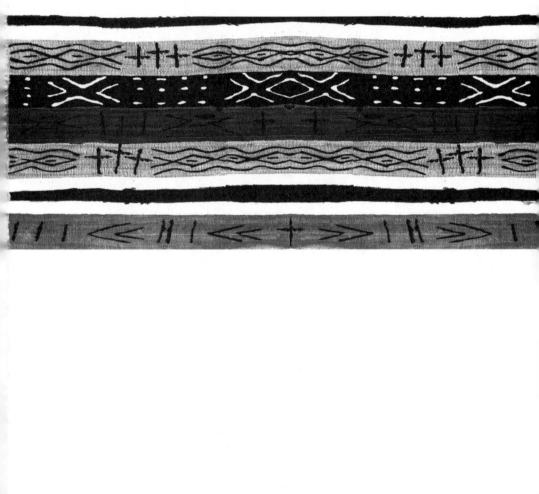

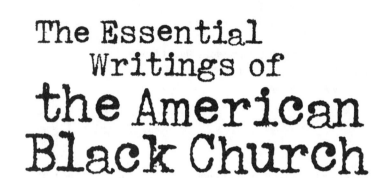

The Essential Writings of the American Black Church

COMPILED BY:

John Hunt

Advancing the Ministries of the Gospel

AMG *Publishers*

God's Word to you is our highest calling.

CONTENTS

INTRODUCTION

A rich heritage

According to Marcus Garvey, "A people without knowledge of their past history, origin or culture is like a tree without roots". *Essential Writings of the Black American Church* provides hundreds of glimpses into the many-faceted lives of African Americans over the centuries.

"Those who have no record of what their forebears have accomplished lose the inspiration which comes from the teaching of biography and history." These are the words of Dr. Carter Godwin Woodson, distinguished Black author, editor, publisher, and historian (December 1875—April 1950). Carter G. Woodson believed that,

> Blacks should know their past in order to participate intelligently in the affairs in our country. He strongly believed that Black history—which others have tried so diligently to erase—is a firm foundation for young Black Americans to build on in order to become productive citizens of our society.

Joseph C. Price, founder and President of Livingston College in North Carolina, who in 1890 delivered an address to the National Education Association annual convention held in Minneapolis put it this way,

> If I had a thousand tongues, and each tongue were a thousand thunderbolts, and each thunderbolt had a thousand voices, I would use them all today to help you understand a loyal and misrepresented and misjudged people.

Price's words reflect on the long tradition of African American oratory. *Essential Writings of the Black American Church* adds its voice to Price's "thousand voices" about African Americans and their faith in God.

The bondage of racism

Essential Writings of the Black American Church has scores of examples, sometimes in most graphic detail, of the bondage of racism which African Americans have endured.

Back in 1968 James Cone wrote the following words which are as relevant now as they were when first written:

> Theologically, Malcolm X was not far wrong when he called the white man "the devil." The white structure of this American society, personified in every racist, must be at least part of what the New Testament meant by demonic forces. ... Ironically, the man who enslaves another enslaves himself. ... To be free to do what I will in relation to another is to be in bondage to the law of least resistance. This is the bondage of racism. Racism is that bondage in which whites are free to beat, rape, or kill blacks. About thirty years ago it was acceptable to lynch a black man by hanging him from a tree; but today whites

destroy him by crowding him into a ghetto and letting filth and despair put the final touches on death.

Black Theology and Black Power

Writings
Included in "writings" are sermons, eulogies, confessions, letters, biographies, autobiographies, prayers, poems, lectures, and speeches. Among written items are extracts from books, diaries, journals and magazines.

The entries are, for the most part, arranged in chronological order, starting with Abraham Johnstone, a condemned man, and his *Letter to His Wife*, written on the eve of his execution. This is followed by Jupiter Hammon's *An Evening Thought: Salvation by Christ, With Penitential Cries*, the first published poem written by an African American. Short introductions to the writers and/or to their writing are also included in the entries.

Black
The terms "black" and "African American" are used interchangeably in *Essential Writings of the Black American Church*. It is vitally important that the rich heritage of African American Christian writings are not lost. A significant proportion of the entries in *Essential Writings of the Black American Church* are taken from old half-forgotten dusty volumes that have only recently been rescued from obscurity. As Vashti M. McKenzie once remarked, "Too much of the genius of African American preaching has gone to the grave with our brightest and best preachers."

In an attempt to help prevent this from happening William Blair founded his *Black Preachers Hall of Fame*. William Blair, a former Negro league baseball star, believes that just as we have halls of fame for sports and other areas of endeavor, so we should have one for the church and its strong leaders. His daughter, museum director Debra Blair Abron, says, "African-Americans sung and prayed our way to where we are today; that story needs to be told." She also explained that, "Preachers are the unsung heroes of the black community. And these honorees are the cream of the crop. These are the ones who made big contributions over many years."

Black church history is a big part of African-American history. Says Mr. Blair: "Go to just about any city, and the oldest building or the oldest institution is likely to be a black church. The church was part of the African-American experience from the very beginning."

"Many times, especially during the time of slavery, the church was all we had. It has literally been a lifesaver in the black community," said Earnestine Cole, the museum's public relations director. Cole continued, "And even today, the heart of the city for the African-American community is the black church." *Essential Writings of the Black American Church* seeks to ensure that the writings of past African American Christians are never forgotten.

Topics
Essential Writings of the Black American Church is not just a history of the African American church, although many of the longer entries give a detailed picture of the diabolic brutality of the slave trade and the excruciating suffering of the blacks. Ron Rhodes claims that,

Between 1517 and 1840 it is estimated that twenty million blacks were captured in Africa, transported to America, and brutally enslaved. The experience of these blacks—and their descendants—serves as the backdrop for understanding contemporary black liberation theology.

Essential Writings of the Black American Church also highlights their perseverance and faith in the one true God who would rescue them, just as he had done for Moses in the Exodus. Historical documents and first hand accounts of many of the barbaric acts of ill-treatment of blacks are recorded here, lest we forget this dreadful chapter in the history of America, and lest we fail to learn the relevant lessons from it.

Many of the entries focus on the comfort individuals received from the Lord in these horrific circumstances. They also record how the Black Church started and grew so rapidly.

Slave narratives

Essential Writings of the Black American Church includes a selection of the best slave narratives. The slave narratives were immensely popular with the public. Frederick Douglass' *Narrative of the Life of Frederick Douglass* sold 30,000 copies between 1845 and 1860, William Wells Brown's *Narrative* went through four editions in its first year, and Solomon Northups' *Twelve Years a Slave* sold 27,000 copies during its first two years in print. Many narratives were translated into French, German, Dutch and Russian.

One of the most gripping slave narratives in *Essential Writings of the Black American Church* was written by Smith H. Platt. It is called, *The Martyrs, and the Fugitive; or a Narrative of the Captivity, Sufferings, and Death of an African Family, and the Slavery and Escape of Their Son, 1859.* A gruesome extract from this follows:

> There, under the shed, hung by the thumbs the naked and writhing form of a beautiful quadroon girl of sixteen summers, and by her stood a burly, drunken villain, holding in one hand a bloody knife, and in the other the dripping cowskin, alternately swearing, maiming, and whipping, and she groaning, writhing, and almost dying. He had bought her for the basest of purposes, and when she refused his will and resisted his pollution, and then tried by running away to escape from his power, all the fiend was aroused within him. He pursued and captured her, then stripped her naked, and hung her, as has been stated, by her thumbs, and whipped her till her entire body, from her neck to her feet, was gored—cut off a toe from each foot, and both ears, and knocked out two front teeth, as marks, if she should ever run away again; and that maimed and bleeding girl was the object that they saw!

Challenge

There is a good deal of thought-provoking material in *Essential Writings of the Black American Church.* There are edifying didactic sermons as well as devotional and reflective poems and heart-warming Negro spirituals.

According to Walter B. Shurden everyone has a great deal to learn from the history of African Americans. In an address entitled, *"A Baptist Most of You Readers Have Never Heard Of"* Shurden spoke about the African American preacher Peter Randolph and stated:

> Peter Randolph … made me aware that white Baptists must take their place at the feet of their African American Baptist sisters and brothers. We white folk must learn a different kind of Baptist history in America, one that is laced with unspeakable suffering and buoyed by unimaginable hope.

Essential Writings of the Black American Church should challenge us wherever we are: in our classrooms, places of study, with our colleagues at work, among our families, and in our Christian fellowships. For the whole volume shrieks out at us, at the top of its voice, "How we treat one another is of paramount importance. We are all equal in the sight of God. Following God's agenda will transform us."

As Martin Luther King Jr. wrote in his *Paul's Letter to American Christians*, as far back as 4 November, 1956,

> In your struggle for justice, let your oppressor know that you are not attempting to defeat or humiliate him, or even to pay him back for injustices that he has heaped upon you. Let him know that you are merely seeking justice for him as well as yourself. Let him know that the festering sore of segregation debilitates the white man as well as the Negro. With this attitude you will be able to keep your struggle on high Christian standards.

Essential Writings of the Black American Church bears witness to two truths that are often present among African American Christians: the truths of justice and right Christian living.

As Martin Luther King Jr. wrote from his prison cell: "Injustice anywhere is a threat to justice everywhere." *Letter from Birmingham Jail*, April 16, 1963.

The following famous Old Testament verse, written by Amos, has been a rallying cry for the implementation of justice.

> But let justice roll on like a river,
> righteousness like a never-failing stream! Amos 5:24 NIV.

As for right Christian living, the words of Jesus himself have always been the yardstick for the African American church:

> "Love the Lord your God with all your heart and with all your soul and with all your mind and with all your strength." The second is this: "Love your neighbor as yourself." There is no commandment greater than these." Mark 12:30-31, NIV.

ABRAHAM JOHNSTONE (?-1797)

Introduction

In 1797 Abraham Johnstone, a former slave born in Delaware was convicted in Gloucester County, New Jersey of murdering Thomas Read, another free African American. Johnstone was to be hanged. When the court asked for a statement from Johnstone after his conviction was announced, he gave a long eloquent public address. Johnstone never admitted his guilt for the murder. The letter he wrote to his wife just before he was hanged follows.

Johnstone was hanged at Woodbury on Saturday 8th of July, 1797.

Abraham Johnstone's Letter to His Wife

My ever dear, ever beloved and adored Wife! My much regretted Sarah.

As there are but a few, very few! short fleeting moments to glide away ere I enter into the mansion, of bliss and tranquility, and take a final leave of this vain transitory and delusory world, wherein I have experienced nothing but crosses, vexations, and tribulations, from all of which, I in a few short, alas! swift passing moments will be delivered, and set free, my paying that general, and certain debt that mankind must pay to nature, and resign in peace this cumbrous load of mortality, this weak body which as yet is faintly animated with vital warmth; but whose soul is full of the spirit, and heart cheering presence of my God, and Redeemer, through the merits of whose sufferings I hope for salvation; to its kindred clay.

I declare my innocence

For of the crime that I am to die for, I most solemnly declare to you my ever dear, ever beloved wife; in the presence of God all just and omnipotent, and all the host of Heaven; That I am perfectly innocent, and therefore am perfectly resigned to death, and satisfied to quit this world, for like a lamb led to the slaughter house, shall I go in a few moments to my death, and have thoroughly resigned myself to the will of my heavenly father. I have fully weaned myself from this frail world and its gross affections, except what centers solely in you, on you now my beloved wife, all my earthly considerations rest, and all that in death appears unfriendly or unwelcome is the parting. The parting from a wife so beloved!— From you my beloved Sally; and leaving you behind in the world without husband to protect you, or friend to sooth, console, or alleviate, your distresses, miseries or wants, or support, and enable you to bear up under, and encounter misfortunes, with fortitude, such my dear Sally have I ever been to you. And tho' sometimes I went astray and lusted after other women, yet still my dear Sally, my true and fond heart rested with you, and love for you always brought your wanderer back: you were to me, my all! my every thing dear and beloved. From the first of our acquaintance, to this moment, I have loved you with unabated fervor, unceasing tenderness; and the purest attachment: and even at this so truly awful and solemn moment, all that seems terrible in death is the parting from you.—My God and redeemer, and him alone possesses the first part (a part pure and uncontaminated) in my affections; and you possess the next; I am sure you cannot be impious enough to expect to hold an equal share with God, it must suffice you to know that in you my all, and only earthly considerations or affections rest, at this moment so truly awful.

My final farewell

I did hope my dear wife to have seen you once more ere I departed this life. And to have obtained your pardon for all the transgressions I have committed against God, and our marriage bed during the time we have been united, and also to have given you such counsel as I thought best with respect to your future conduct; or as I should have deemed necessary, or expedient. And to have bestowed on you the blessing of a dying husband, and have bid you a final farewell, all which I must do by letter as you would not consent to come and see me tho,' I had the Sheriff's express permission for your coming, and nobody should have molested you. Indeed my dear Sally had it been your case as it was mine: no earthly consideration should or would have kept me from seeing you. Even was certain death to have been the consequence, and that I was sure I should suffer on the same gallows with you: All! all! I would have braved to have seen my Sally and would embrace you even in death. The cold phlegmatic remonstrance of disinterested persons; who under the sacred name of friend; But strangers to that and every nobler and better feeling and sentiment, are so often interposed under the mask of friendship, and is generally termed good reason; by which they so powerfully operate on the passions of the weak and timorous, as to leave them no will at all of their own, (of all such people my dear Sally beware in future) I say my dear wife that in spite of all such busy-bodies I should have gone to see you, but I will not wound your feelings by pursuing the subject farther, for I well know that your heart is already cankered with grief, and care worn on my account. And my wish is to alleviate and sooth the acute misery and poignant anguish and distress (I well know) at this moment endure: and to speak peace to your bleeding heart, rather than plant a dagger in the rankled wound. Which my unhappy fate and unmerited sufferings has given you, who possesses a mind replete with the tenderest and livest sensibility.

Christian resignation

And now my dear Sally, that you see me so thoroughly resigned to my fate, let me earnestly beg and exhort you to alike resigned on and endeavor to encounter this sad blow with fortitude, and true Christian resignation to the will of the Almighty. Call in religion to your aid, and take it as one of those way ward incidents directed by the Almighty to try the faith of us poor frail mortals, and if you consider it as such, you will and surely must think it just to murmur at the decrees of the Almighty God our creator: it is true my dear Sally. It is a shameful death to be suspended in the air between Heaven and earth like a dog that at first fight may hurt your feelings, but on reflection it must vanish and leave no trace behind. For in the first place, as nothing can take place, however trivial, without divine permission; so no manner of death can be unnatural: But in the second place, only give yourself time to reflect a moment, and then get a testament and read, the 22d, 23d, and 24th, Chapters of the Apostle Luke, you will there find sufficient matter to console, and prevent your tears flowing for me. You will see there how much more ignominious a death our Savior suffered; he was nailed to a cross crowned with thorns, arrayed in purple, lots cast for garments his sacred sides pierced with a spear by the hands of common garments his sacred sides pierced with a spear by the hands of common soldiers, crucified between thieves on Mount Calvary; All! every species of ignominy and infamy was heaped on the divine immaculate lambs, His life was taken away by false swearing, (Alas! so is mine,) He prayed for and forgive his enemies, (so do I most freely forgive mine,) the only and blessed person of the most high and omnipotent God shed his precious blood on the cross for the redemption of many; He offered himself up the accepted ransom for all mankind; What is my sufferings and death in comparison with his? What have I to fear in a future state, as I will die innocent of the crime I am to suffer for, and confidently but without presumption, hope a reward for all my sufferings, from him who has himself suffered by false witnesses? He who has said take up your cross and follow me, him will I follow with all my heart and soul, through and with all my crosses and trials. ...

My white hat
My dear Sally, my white Hat, that you were so fond of, I leave you with this injunction that you wear it yourself while it lasts and give it, to no other person, and two orders for a small sum of money I also leave you, besides all the cloths at Henry Cravers; Mr. Hughes, my good and esteemed friend, whom together with his family may God bless, prosper, and prolong their lives; will hand you my hat and the two orders, the rest of my things being useless to you, I have given them away to different people; the spinning wheel and little box I have given to the little girl that lived with us.

And having now settled my worldly affairs I shall close and prepare to depart in peace.

I've kissed this paper—and bid it convey the kiss to you my love: And now my dear Sally, I bid you—Oh—Heavens!—I bid you my dear wife!—not the farewell of a day month nor year—But an eternal—Farewell.

I earnestly beg your prayers for me; and may God protect preserve prosper and bless you; is the dying prayer of your dotingly fond husband.

Abraham Johnstone, Woodbury Jail, July 8th, 1797

JUPITER HAMMON (1711-1806)

Introduction

Settled blacks in the New World acquired a self-consciousness as a separate group through laws restricting racial intermarriage, as well as by racist portrayals in the press, and because of their involvement in evangelical Christianity that emerged following the Great Awakening.

Jupiter Hammon was well-placed to observe these trends and his writing reflects his efforts to evangelize his black brethren when most African-Americans were not Christians. Hammon writes as a traditional Calvinist.

Jupiter Hammon's *An Evening Thought* was the first work by an African-American to be published in the United States.

An Evening Thought: Salvation by Christ, With Penitential Cries

Salvation comes by Christ alone,
The only Son of God;
Redemption now to every one,
That love his holy Word.

Dear Jesus, we would fly to Thee,
And leave off every Sin,
Thy tender Mercy well agree;
Salvation from our King;

Salvation comes now from the Lord,
Our victorious King.
His holy Name be well ador'ed,
Salvation surely bring.

Dear Jesus, give thy Spirit now,
Thy Grace to every Nation,
That han't the Lord to whom we bow,
The Author of Salvation.

Dear Jesus, unto Thee we cry,
Give us the Preparation;
Turn not away thy tender Eye;
We seek thy true Salvation.

Salvation comes from God we know,
The true and only One;

It's well agreed and certain true,
He gave his only Son.

Lord, hear our penitential Cry:
Salvation from above;
It is the Lord that doth supply,
With his Redeeming Love.

Dear Jesus, by thy precious Blood,
The World Redemption have:
Salvation now comes from the Lord,
He being thy captive slave.

Dear Jesus, let the Nations cry,
And all the People say,
Salvation comes from Christ on high,
Haste on Tribunal Day.

We cry as Sinners to the Lord,
Salvation to obtain;
It is firmly fixt his holy Word,
Ye shall not cry in vain.

Dear Jesus, unto Thee we cry,
And make our Lamentation;
O let our Prayers ascend on high;
We felt thy Salvation.

Lord, turn our dark benighted Souls;
Give us a true Motion,
And let the Hearts of all the World,
Make Christ their Salvation.

Ten Thousand Angels cry to Thee,
Yea, louder than the Ocean.
Thou art the Lord, we plainly see;
Thou art the true Salvation.

Now is the Day, excepted Time;
The Day of Salvation;
Increase your Faith, do not repine:
Awake ye, every Nation.

Lord, unto whom now shall we go,
Or seek a safe Abode ?
Thou hast the Word Salvation Too,
The only Son of God.

Ho ! every one that hunger hath,
Or pineth after me,
Salvation be thy leading Staff,
To set the Sinner free.

Dear Jesus, unto Thee we fly;
Depart, depart from Sin,
Salvation doth at length supply,
The Glory of our King.

Come, ye Blessed of the Lord,
Salvation greatly given;
O turn your Hearts, accept the Word,
Your Souls are fit for Heaven.

Dear Jesus, we now turn to Thee,
Salvation to obtain;
Our hearts and souls do meet again,
To magnify thy Name.

Come holy Spirit, Heavenly Dove,
The Object of our Care;
Salvation doth increase our Love;
Our hearts hath felt thy fear.

Now Glory be to God on High,
Salvation high and low;
And thus the Soul on Christ rely,
To heaven surely go.

Come, Blessed Jesus, Heavenly Dove,
Accept repentance here;
Salvation give, with tender Love;
Let us with Angels share.

Jupiter Hammon

An Address to the Negroes in the State of New York
"Of a truth I perceive that God is no respecter of persons: But in every Nation, he that feareth him and worketh righteousness, is accepted with him." Acts 10:34, 35.

Link with the apostle Paul
When I am writing to you with a design to say something to you for your good, and with a view to promote your happiness, I can with truth and sincerity join with the apostle Paul, when speaking of his own nation the Jews, and say, "That I have great heaviness and continual sorrow in my heart for my brethren, my kinsmen according to the flesh."

1. Respecting obedience to masters
Now whether it is right, and lawful, in the sight of God, for them to make slaves of us or not, I am certain that while we are slaves, it is our duty to obey our masters, in all their lawful commands, and mind them unless we are bid to do that which we know to-be sin, or forbidden in God's word. The apostle Paul says, "Servants be obedient to them that are your masters according to the flesh, with fear and trembling in singleness in your heart as unto Christ: Not with eye service, as men pleasers, but as the servants of Christ doing the will of God from the heart: With good will doing service to the Lord, and not to men: Knowing that whatever thing a man doeth the same shall he receive of the Lord, whether he be bond or free." Here is a plain command of God for us to obey our masters. It may seem hard for us, if we think our masters wrong in holding us slaves, to obey in all things, but who of us dare dispute with God! He has commanded us to obey, and we ought to do it cheerfully, and freely. This should be done by us, not only because God commands, but because our own peace and comfort depend upon it. As we depend upon our masters, for what we eat and drink and wear, and for all our comfortable things in this world, we cannot be happy, unless we please them. This we cannot do without obeying them freely, without muttering or finding fault. If a servant strives to please his master and studies and takes pains to do it, I believe there are but few masters who would use such a servant cruelly. Good servants frequently make good masters. If your master is really hard, unreasonable and cruel, there is no way so likely for you to convince him of it, as always to obey his commands, and try to serve him, and take care of his interest, and try to promote it all in your power. If you are proud and stubborn and always finding fault, your master will think the fault lies wholly on your side, but if you are humble, and meek, and bear all things patiently, your master may think he is wrong, if he does not, his neighbors will be apt to see it, and will befriend you, and try to alter his conduct. If this does not do, you must cry to him, who has the hearts of all men in his hands, and turneth them as the rivers of waters are turned.

2: The particular I would mention, is honesty and faithfulness
You must suffer me now to deal plainly with you, my dear brethren, for I do not mean to flatter, or omit speaking the truth, whether it is for you, or against you. How many of you are there who allow yourselves in stealing from your masters. It is very wicked for you not to take care of your masters goods, but how much worse is it to pilfer and steal from them,

whenever you think you shall not be found out. This you must know is very wicked and provoking to God. There are none of you so ignorant, but that you must know that this is wrong. Though you may try to excuse yourselves, by saying that your masters are unjust to you, and though you may try to quiet your consciences in this way, yet if you are honest in owning the truth you must think it is as wicked, and on some accounts more wicked to steal from your masters, than from others.

We cannot certainly, have any excuse either for taking any thing that belongs to our masters without their leave, or for being unfaithful in their business. It is our duty to be faithful, not with eye service as men pleasers. We have no right to stay when we are sent on errands, any longer than to do the business we were sent upon. All the time spent idly, is spent wickedly, and is unfaithfulness to our masters. In these things I must say, that I think many of you are guilty. I know that many of you endeavor to excuse yourselves, and say that you have nothing that you can call your own, and that you are under great temptations to be unfaithful and take from your masters. But this will not do, God will certainly punish you for stealing and for being unfaithful. All that we have to mind is our own duty. If God has put us in bad circumstances that is not our fault and he will not punish us for it. If any are wicked in keeping us so, we cannot help it, they must answer to God for it. Nothing will serve as an excuse to us for not doing our duty. The same God will judge both them and us. Pray then my dear friends, fear to offend in this way, but be faithful to God, to your masters, and to your own souls.

Warning against profanity

The next thing I would mention, and warn you against, is profaneness. This you know is forbidden by God. Christ tells us, "swear not at all," and again it is said "thou shalt not take the name of the Lord thy God in vain, for the Lord will not hold him guiltless, that taketh his name in vain." Now though the great God has forbidden it, yet how dreadfully profane are many. How common is it to hear you take the terrible and awful name of the great God in vain. To swear by it, and by Jesus Christ, his Son—How common is it to hear yon wish damnation to your companions, and to your own souls—and to sport with in the name of Heaven and Hell, as if there were no such places for you to hope for, or to fear. Oh my friends, be warned to forsake this dreadful sin of profaneness. Pray my dear friends, believe and realize, that there is a God—that he is great and terrible beyond what you can think— that he keeps you in life every moment—and that he can send you to that awful Hell, that you laugh at, in an instant, and confine you there for ever, and that he will certainly do it, if you do not repent. You certainly do not believe, that there is a God, or that there is a Heaven or Hell, or you would never trifle with them. It would make you shudder, if you heard others do it, if you believe them as much, as you believe any thing you see with your bodily eyes.

I have heard some learned and good men say, that the heathen, and all that worshiped false Gods, never spoke lightly or irreverently of their Gods, they never took their names in vain, or jested with those things which they held sacred. Now why should the true God, who made all things, be treated worse in this respect, than those false Gods, that were made of wood and stone. I believe it is because Satan tempts men to do it. He tried to make them love their false Gods, and to speak well of them, but he wishes to have men think lightly of the true God, to take his holy name in vain, and to scoff at, and make a jest of all things that are really good. You may think that Satan has not power to do so much, and have so great influence on the minds of men: But the scripture says, "he goeth about like a roaring Lion, seeking whom he may devour—That he is the prince of the power of the air—and that he rules in the hearts of the children of disobedience,—and that wicked men are led captive by him, to do his will." All those of you who are profane, are serving the Devil. You are doing what he tempts and desires you to do. If you could see him with your bodily eyes, would you like to make an agreement with him, to serve him, and do as he bid you. I believe most of you would be shocked at this, but you may be certain that all of you who allow yourselves in this sin, are as really serving him, and to just as good purpose, as if you met him, and promised to dishonor God, and serve him with all your might. Do you believe this? It is true whether you believe it or not. Some of you to excuse yourselves, may plead the example of others, and say that you hear a great many white-people, who know more, than such poor ignorant Negroes, as you are, and some who are rich and great gentlemen, swear, and talk profanely; and some of you may say this of your masters, and say no more than is true. But all this is not a sufficient excuse for you. You know that murder is wicked. If you saw your master kill a man, do you suppose this would be any excuse for you, if you should commit the same crime? You must know it would not; nor will your hearing him curse and swear, and take the name of God in vain, or any other man, be he ever so great or rich, excuse you. God is greater than all other beings, and him we are bound to obey. To him we must give an account for every idle word that we speak. He will bring us all, rich and poor, white and black, to his judgment seat. If we are found among those who feared his name, and trembled at his word, we shall be called good and faithful servants. Our slavery will be at an end, and though ever so mean, low, and despised in this world, we shall sit with God in his kingdom as Kings and Priests, and rejoice forever, and ever. Do not then, my dear friends, take God's holy name in vain, or speak profanely in any way. Let not the example of others lead you into the sin, but reverence and fear that great and fearful name, the Lord our God. I might now caution you against other sins to which you are exposed; but as I meant only to mention those you were exposed to, more than others, by your being slaves, I will conclude what I have to say to you, by advising you to become religious, and to make religion the great business of your lives.

Should Negroes seek freedom?
Now I acknowledge that liberty is a great thing, and worth seeking for, if we can get it honestly, and by our good conduct, prevail on our masters to set us free: Though for my own part I do not wish to be free, yet I should be glad, if others, especially the young Negroes were to be free, for many of us, who are grown up slaves, and have always had masters to take care of us, should hardly know how to take care of ourselves; and it may be more for our own comfort to remain as we are. That liberty is a great thing we may know from our own feelings, and we may likewise judge so from the conduct of the white-people, in the late war. How much money has been spent, and how many lives has been lost, to defend their liberty. I must say that I have hoped that God would open their eyes, when they were so

much engaged for liberty, to think of the state of the poor blacks, and to pity us. He has done it in some measure, and has raised us up many friends, for which we have reason to be thankful, and to hope in his mercy. What may be done further, he only knows, for known unto God are all his ways from the beginning.

A greater concern

But this my dear brethren is by no means, the greatest thing we have to be concerned about. Getting our liberty in this world, is nothing to our having the liberty of the children of God. Now the Bible tells us that we are all by nature, sinners, that we are slaves to sin and Satan, and that unless we are converted, or born again, we must be miserable forever. Christ says, except a man be born again, he cannot see the kingdom of God, and all that do not see the kingdom of God, must be in the kingdom of darkness. There are but two places where all go after death, white and black, rich and poor; those places are Heaven and Hell. Heaven is a place made for those, who are born again, and who love God, and it is a place where they will be happy for ever. Hell is a place made for those who hate God, and are his enemies, and where they will be miserable to all eternity. Now you may think you are not enemies to God, and do not hate him: But if your heart has not been changed, and you have not become true Christians, you certainly are enemies to God, and have been opposed to him ever since you were born. Many of you, I suppose, never think of this, and are almost as ignorant as the beasts that perish.

Study the Bible

Those of you who can read I must beg you to read the Bible, and whenever you can get time, study the Bible, and if you can get no other time, spare some of your time from sleep, and learn what the mind and will of God is. But what shall I say to them who cannot read. This lay with great weight on my mind, when I thought of writing to my poor brethren, but I hope that those who can read will take pity on them and read what I have to say to them. In hopes of this I will beg of you to spare no pains in trying to learn to read. If you are once engaged you may learn. Let all the time you can get be spent in trying to learn to read. Get those who can read to learn you, but remember, that what you learn for, is to read the Bible. If there was no Bible, it would be no matter whether you could read or not. Reading other books would do you no good. But the Bible is the word of God, and tells you what you must do to please God; it tells you how you may escape misery, and be happy for ever. If you see most people neglect the Bible, and many that can read never look into it, let it not harden you and make you think lightly of it, and that it is a book of no worth. All those who are really good, love the Bible, and meditate on it day and night. In the Bible God has told us every thing it is necessary we should know, in order to be happy here and hereafter. The Bible is a revelation of the mind and will of God to men. Therein we may learn, what God is. That he made all things by the power of his word; and that he made all things for his own glory, and not for our glory. That he is over all, and above all his creatures, and more above them that we can think or conceive—that they can do nothing without him—that he upholds them all, and will over-rule all things for his own glory.

The nature of man

In the Bible likewise we are told what man is. That he was at first made holy, in the image of God, that he fell from that state of holiness, and became an enemy to God, and that since the fall, all the imaginations of the thoughts of his heart, are evil and only evil, and that continually. That the carnal mind is not subject to the law of God, neither indeed can be. And that all mankind, were under the wrath, and curse of God, and must have been for ever miserable, if they had been left to suffer what their sins deserved. It tells us that God, to save some of mankind, sent his Son into this world to die, in the room and stead of sinners, and that now God can save from eternal misery, all that believe in his Son, and take him for their savior, and that all are called upon to repent, and believe in Jesus Christ. It tells us that those who do repent, and believe, and are friends to Christ, shall have many trials and sufferings in this world, but that they shall be happy forever, after death, and reign with Christ to all eternity.

A place of trial

The Bible tells us that this world is a place of trial, and that there is no other time or place for us to alter, but in this life. If we are Christians when we die, we shall awake to the resurrection of life; if not, we shall awake to the resurrection of damnation. It tells us, we must all live in Heaven or Hell, be happy or miserable, and that without end. The Bible does not tell us of but two places, for all to go to. There is no place for innocent folks, that are not Christians. There is no place for ignorant folks, that did not know how to be Christians. What I mean is, that there is no place besides Heaven and Hell. These two places, will receive all mankind, for Christ says, there are but two sorts, he that is not with me is against me, and he that gathereth not with me, scattereth abroad.—The Bible likewise tells us that this world, and all things in it shall be burnt up—and that "God has appointed a day in which he will judge the world, and that he will bring every secret thing whether it be good or bad into judgment—that which is done in secret shall be declared on the house top." I do not know, nor do I think any can tell, but that the day of judgment may last a thousand years. God could tell the state of all his creatures in a moment, but then every thing that every one has done, through his whole life is to be told, before the whole world of angels, and men. There, Oh how solemn is the thought! You, and I, must stand, and hear every thing we have thought or done, however secret, however wicked and vile, told before all the men and women that ever have been, or ever will be, and before all the angels, good and bad.

God did not choose the rich

Now my dear friends seeing the Bible is the word of God, and every thing in it is true, and it reveals such awful and glorious things, what can be more important than that you should learn to read it; and when you have learned to read, that you should study it day and night. There are some things very encouraging in God's word for such ignorant creatures as we are; for God hath not chosen the rich of this world. Not many rich, not many noble are called, but God hath chosen the weak things of this world, and things which are not, to confound the things that are: And when the great and the rich refused coming to the gospel feast, the servant was told, to go into the highways, and hedges, and compel those poor creatures that he found there to come in. Now my brethren it seems to me, that there are no people that ought to attend to the hope of happiness in another world so much as we do. Most of us are cut off from comfort and happiness here in this world, and can expect nothing from it. Now seeing this is the case, why should we not take care to be happy after death. Why should we spend our whole lives in sinning against God: And be miserable in this world, and in the world to come. If we do thus, we shall certainly be the greatest fools. We shall be slaves here, and slaves forever. We cannot plead so great temptations to neglect religion as others. Riches and honors which drown the greater part of mankind, who have the gospel, in perdition, can be little or no temptations to us.

Reflect on eternal life

We live so little time in this world that it is no matter how wretched and miserable we are, if it prepares us for heaven. What is forty, fifty, or sixty years, when compared to eternity. When thousands and millions of years have rolled away, this eternity will be no nigher coming to an end. Oh how glorious is an eternal life of happiness! And how dreadful, an eternity of misery. Those of us who have had religious masters, and have been taught to read the Bible, and have been brought by their example and teaching to a sense of divine things, how happy shall we be to meet them in heaven, where we shall join them in praising God forever. But if any of us have had such masters, and yet have lived and died wicked, how will it add to our misery to think of our folly. If any of us, who have wicked and profane masters should become religious, how will our estates be changed in another world.

Oh my friends, let me entreat of you to think on these things, and to live as if you believed them to be true. If you become Christians you will have reason to bless God forever, that you have been brought into a land where you have heard the gospel, though you have been slaves. If we should ever get to Heaven, we shall find nobody to reproach us for being black, or for being slaves. Let me beg of you my dear African brethren, to think very little of your bondage in this life, for your thinking of it will do you no good. If God designs to set us free, he will do it, in his own time, and way; but think of your bondage to sin and Satan, and do not rest, until you are delivered from it. We cannot be happy if we are ever so free or ever so rich, while we are servants of sin, and slaves to Satan. We must be miserable here, and to all eternity.

To freed Negroes

I will conclude what I have to say with a few words to those Negroes who have their liberty. The most of what I have said to those who are slaves may be of use to you, but you have more advantages, on some accounts, if you will improve your freedom, as you may do, than they. You have more time to read God's holy word, and to take care of the salvation of your souls. Let me beg of you to spend your time in this way, or it will be better for you, if you had always been slaves. If you think seriously of the matter, you must conclude, that if you do not use your freedom, to promote the salvation of your souls, it will not be of any lasting good to you. Besides all this, if you are idle, and take to bad courses, you will hurt those of your brethren who are slaves, and do all in your power to prevent their being free. One great reason that is given by some for not freeing us, I understand is, that we should not know how to take care of ourselves, and should take to bad courses. That we should be lazy and idle, and get drunk and steal. Now all those of you, who follow any bad courses, and who do not take care to get an honest living by your labor and industry, are doing more to prevent our being free, than any body else. Let me beg of you then for the sake of your own good and happiness, in time, and for eternity, and for the sake of your poor brethren, who are still in bondage "to lead quiet and peaceable lives in all Godliness and honesty," and may God bless you, and bring you to his kingdom, for Christ's sake, Amen.

Jupiter Hammon, Queen's Village, 24th Sept. 1786.

BENJAMIN BANNEKER (1731-1806)

Introduction

Benjamin Banneker was born in Maryland on November 9, 1731, his father and grandfather being former slaves.

Although only a farmer of modest means, Banneker achieved a great deal in his life. In 1753, the young man borrowed a pocket watch from a well-to-do neighbor; he took it apart and made a drawing of each component, then reassembled the watch and returned it, fully functioning, to its owner. From his drawings Banneker then proceeded to carve, out of wood, enlarged replicas of each part. Calculating the proper number of teeth for each gear and the necessary relationships between the gears, he constructed a working wooden clock that kept accurate time and struck the hours for over 50 years.

Banneker started to study astronomy when he was 58 years old. He was soon able to predict future solar and lunar eclipses. He compiled the ephemeris, or information table, for annual almanacs that were published for the years 1792 through 1797. *Benjamin Banneker's Almanac* became a best seller.

The "Sable Astronomer", as Banneker was sometimes called, was used as proof that African Americans were not intellectually inferior to European Americans, as Thomas Jefferson noted in a letter to Banneker.

In 1980, the U.S. Postal Service issued a postage stamp in Banneker's honor.

Despite the popular prejudices of his times, Bannker was quite unwilling to let his race or his age hinder in any way his thirst for intellectual development.

Banneker's Letter to Thomas Jefferson

Sir,

I am fully sensible of the greatness of that freedom, which I take with you on the present occasion; a liberty which seemed to me scarcely allowable, when I reflected on that distinguished and dignified station in which you stand, and the almost general prejudice and prepossession, which is so prevalent in the world against those of my complexion.

I suppose it is a truth too well attested to you, to need a proof here, that we are a race of beings, who have long labored under the abuse and censure of the world; that we have long been looked upon with an eye of contempt; and that we have long been considered rather as brutish than human, and scarcely capable of mental endowments.

Sir, I hope I may safely admit, in consequence of that report which hath reached me, that you are a man far less inflexible in sentiments of this nature, than many others; that you are measurably friendly, and well disposed towards us; and that you are willing and ready to lend your aid and assistance to our relief, from those many distresses, and numerous calamities, to which we are reduced. Now Sir, if this is founded in truth, I apprehend you will embrace every opportunity, to eradicate that train of absurd and false ideas and opinions, which so generally prevails with respect to us; and that your sentiments are concurrent with mine, which are, that one universal Father hath given being to us all; and that he hath not only made us all of one flesh, but that he hath also, without partiality, afforded us all the same sensations and endowed us all with the same faculties; and that however variable we may be in society or religion, however diversified in situation or color, we are all of the same family, and stand in the same relation to him.

Sir, if these are sentiments of which you are fully persuaded, I hope you cannot but acknowledge, that it is the indispensable duty of those, who maintain for themselves the rights of human nature, and who possess the obligations of Christianity, to extend their power and influence to the relief of every part of the human race, from whatever burden or oppression they may unjustly labor under; and this, I apprehend, a full conviction of the truth and obligation of these principles should lead all to. Sir, I have long been convinced, that if your love for yourselves, and for those inestimable laws, which preserved to you the rights of human nature, was founded on sincerity, you could not but be solicitous, that every individual, of whatever rank or distinction, might with you equally enjoy the blessings thereof; neither could you rest satisfied short of the most active effusion of your exertions, in order to their promotion from any state of degradation, to which the unjustifiable cruelty and barbarism of men may have reduced them.

Sir, I freely and cheerfully acknowledge, that I am of the African race, and in that color which is natural to them of the deepest dye; and it is under a sense of the most profound gratitude to the Supreme Ruler of the Universe, that I now confess to you, that I am not under that state of tyrannical thralldom, and inhuman captivity, to which too many of my brethren are doomed, but that I have abundantly tasted of the fruition of those blessings, which proceed from that free and unequalled liberty with which you are favored; and which, I hope, you will willingly allow you have mercifully received, from the immediate hand of that Being, from whom proceedeth every good and perfect Gift.

Sir, suffer me to recall to your mind that time, in which the arms and tyranny of the British crown were exerted, with every powerful effort, in order to reduce you to a state of servitude : look back, I entreat you, on the variety of dangers to which you were exposed; reflect on that time, in which every human aid appeared unavailable, and in which even hope and fortitude wore the aspect of inability to the conflict, and you cannot but be led to a serious and grateful sense of your miraculous and providential preservation; you cannot but acknowledge, that the present freedom and tranquility which you enjoy you have merci-fully received, and that it is the peculiar blessing of Heaven.

This, Sir, was a time when you clearly saw into the injustice of a state of slavery, and in which you had just apprehensions of the horrors of its condition. It was now that your abhorrence thereof was so excited, that you publicly held forth this true and invaluable doctrine, which is worthy to be recorded and remembered in all succeeding ages : "We hold these truths to be self-evident, that all men are created equal; that they are endowed by their Creator with certain unalienable rights, and that among these are, life, liberty, and the pursuit of happiness" [Declaration of Independence]. Here was a time, in which your tender feelings for yourselves had engaged you thus to declare, you were then impressed with proper ideas of the great violation of liberty, and the free possession of those blessings, to which you were entitled by nature; but, Sir, how pitiable is it to reflect, that although you were so fully convinced of the benevolence of the Father of Mankind, and of his equal and impartial distribution of these rights and privileges, which he hath conferred upon them, that you should at the same time counteract his mercies, in detaining by fraud and violence so numerous a part of my brethren, under groaning captivity and cruel oppression, that you should at the same time be found guilty of that most criminal act, which you professedly detested in others, with respect to yourselves.

I suppose that your knowledge of the situation of my brethren, is too extensive to need a recital here; neither shall I presume to prescribe methods by which they may be relieved, otherwise than by recommending to you and all others, to wean yourselves from those narrow prejudices which you have imbibed with respect to them, and as Job proposed to his friends, ``put your soul in their souls' stead;'' thus shall your hearts be enlarged with kindness and benevolence towards them; and thus shall you need neither the direction of myself or others, in what manner to proceed herein. And now, Sir, although my sympathy and affection for my brethren hath caused my enlargement thus far, I ardently hope, that your candor and generosity will plead with you in my behalf, when I make known to you, that it was not originally my design; but having taken up my pen in order to direct to you, as a present, a copy of an Almanac, which I have calculated for the succeeding year, I was unexpectedly and unavoidably led thereto.

This calculation is the production of my arduous study, in this my advanced stage of life; for having long had unbounded desires to become acquainted with the secrets of nature, I have had to gratify my curiosity herein, through my own assiduous application to Astronomical Study, in which I need not recount to you the many difficulties and disadvantages, which I have had to encounter.

And although I had almost declined to make my calculation for the ensuing year, in consequence of that time which I had allotted therefore, being taken up at the Federal Territory, by the request of Mr. Andrew Ellicott, yet finding myself under several engagements to Printers of this state, to whom I had communicated my design, on my return to my place of residence, I industriously applied myself thereto, which I hope I have accomplished with correctness and accuracy; a copy of which I have taken the liberty to direct to you, and which I humbly request you will favorably receive; and although you may have the opportunity of perusing it after its publication, yet I choose to send it to you in manuscript previous thereto, that thereby you might not only have an earlier inspection, but that you might also view it in my own hand writing.

And now, Sir, I shall conclude, and subscribe myself, with the most profound respect,

Your most obedient humble servant,

Benjamin Banneker

Jefferson's Reply to Banneker's letter

To Mr. Benjamin Banneker

Philadelphia, August 30, 1791.

Sir,

I thank you, sincerely, for your letter of the 19th instant, and for the Almanac it contained. No body wishes more than I do, to see such proofs as you exhibit, that nature has given to our black brethren talents equal to those of the other colors of men; and that the appearance of the want of them, is owing merely to the degraded condition of their existence, both in Africa and America. I can add with truth, that no body wishes more ardently to see a good system commenced, for raising the condition, both of their body and mind, to what it ought to be, as far as the imbecility of their present existence, and other circumstances, which cannot be neglected, will admit.

I have taken the liberty of sending your Almanac to Monsieur de Condozett, Secretary of the Academy of Sciences at Paris, and Member of the Philanthropic Society, because I considered it as a document, to which your whole color had a right for their justification, against the doubts which have been entertained of them.

I am with great esteem, Sir, Your most obedient Humble Servant,

Thomas Jefferson

PHILLIS WHEATLEY (1753-84)

Introduction

Along with Jupiter Hammon, Phillis Wheatley is remembered as being the first or second published African-American poet. Born in Senegal in about 1753, Wheatley was captured by slave traders and brought to America in 1761. Purchased by John Wheatley, a prominent tailor from Boston, Phillis was taught to read by one of Wheatley's daughters and studied English, Latin and Greek. She starting writing poetry in 1767 and her first poem, *On the Death of George Whitefield*, was published in 1770. Her book of poems *Poems on Various Subjects, Religious and Moral* was published in London in 1773.

In an attempt to improve her poor health Wheatley was sent to London in 1774 and on leaving America she wrote *A Farewell to America*.

In her *Letter to Reverend Samson Occum*, March 11, 1774 Wheatley speaks of her frustration with the institution of slavery.

On the Death of George Whitefield (1770)

Hail, happy saint! on thine immortal throne,
Possest of glory, life, and bliss unknown;
We hear no more the music of thy tongue;
Thy wonted auditories cease to throng.
Thy sermons in unequalled accents flowed,
And ev'ry bosom with devotion glowed;
Thou didst, in strains of eloquence refined,
Inflame the heart, and captivate the mind.
Unhappy, we the setting sun deplore,
So glorious once, but ah! it shines no more.

Behold the prophet in his towering flight!
He leaves the earth for heaven's unmeasured height,
And worlds unknown receive him from our sight.
There Whitefield wings with rapid course his way,
And sails to Zion through vast seas of day.
Thy prayers, great saint, and thine incessant cries,
Have pierced the bosom of thy native skies.
Thou, moon, hast seen, and all the stars of light,
How he has wrestled with his God by night.
He prayed that grace in ev'ry heart might dwell;
He longed to see America excel;
He charged its youth that ev'ry grace divine
Should with full luster in their conduct shine.

That Savior, which his soul did first receive,
The greatest gift that ev'n God can give,
He freely offered to the num'rous throng,
That on his lips with list'ning pleasure hung.

"Take him, ye wretched, for your only good,
"Take him, ye starving sinners, for your food;
"Ye thirsty, come to this life-giving stream,
"Ye preachers, take him for your joyful theme;
"Take him, my dear Americans, he said,
"Be your complaints on his kind bosom laid:
"Take him, ye Africans, he longs for you;
"Impartial Savior is his title due:
"Washed in the fountain of redeeming blood,
"You shall be sons, and kings, and priests to God."

Great Countess*, we Americans revere
Thy name, and mingle in thy grief sincere;
New England deeply feels, the orphans mourn,
Their more than father will no more return.

But though arrested by the hand of death,
Whitefield no more exerts his lab'ring breath,
Yet let us view him in the eternal skies,
Let ev'ry heart to this bright vision rise;
While the tomb, safe, retains its sacred trust,
Till life divine re-animates the dust.

Phillis Wheatley

*Great Countess is a reference to the Lady Huntingdon who appointed George Whitefield as one of her chaplains. She established sixty-four Methodist meeting houses in England, and provided seminaries for the education of these ministers. Horace Walpole described Lady Huntingdon as, "The St. Teresa of the Methodists".

On Being Brought from Africa to America (1773)

'Twas mercy brought me from my pagan land,
Taught my benighted soul to understand
That there's a God—that there's a Savior too:
Once I redemption neither sought nor knew.
Some view our sable race with scornful eye—
'Their color is a diabolic dye.'
Remember, Christians, Negroes black as Cain

May be refined, and join th'angelic train.

Phillis Wheatley

Letter to Reverend Samson Occum (1774)

Rev'd and honor'd Sir,

I have this Day received your obliging kind Epistle, and am greatly satisfied with your Reasons respecting the Negroes, and think highly reasonable what you offer in Vindication of their natural Rights: Those that invade them cannot be insensible that the divine Light is chasing away the thick Darkness which broods over the Land of Africa; and the Chaos which has reign'd so long, is converting into beautiful Order, and reveals more and more clearly, the glorious Dispensation of civil and religious Liberty, which are so inseparably Limited, that there is little or no Enjoyment of one Without the other: Otherwise, perhaps, the Israelites had been less solicitous for their Freedom from Egyptian slavery; I do not say they would have been contented without it, by no means, for in every human Breast, God has implanted a Principle, which we call Love of Freedom; it is impatient of Oppression, and pants for Deliverance; and by the Leave of our modern Egyptians I will assert, that the same Principle lives in us. God grant Deliverance in his own Way and Time, and get him honor upon all those whose Avarice impels them to countenance and help forward the Calamities of their fellow Creatures. This I desire not for their Hurt, but to convince them of the strange Absurdity of their Conduct whose Words and Actions are so diametrically, opposite. How well the Cry for Liberty, and the reverse Disposition for the exercise of oppressive Power over others agree,—I humbly think it does not require the Penetration of a Philosopher to determine God.

Phillis Wheatley

LEMUEL HAYNES (1753-1833)

Introduction

Lemuel Haynes, an African-American minister, became pastor of several white churches in Rutland, Vermont. Although he received little formal education, Haynes immersed himself in the Bible and in the writings of Isaac Watts, Edward Young, and George Whitefield. In an era when few blacks achieved the literacy demanded for serious literary activity, Haynes, along with Jupiter Hammon and Phillis Weatley was one of the earliest African Americans to generate the first significant body of African American writing that emerged after the revival known as the Great Awakening.

In his sermon *Universal Salvation,* Haynes links the doctrine of universalism with the devil's assault upon godliness as part of a sustained characterization of the sinful will. Haynes' writings, "suggest the nexus of thought that grounded the evangelical Protestant and libertarian principles of early black writers in the late eighteenth and the early nineteenth century," according to Phillip M. Richards of Colgate University.

Universal Salvation

And the serpent said unto the woman, Ye shall not surely die. GENESIS 3:4.

She pluck'd, she ate;
Earth felt the wound;
nature from her seat,
Sighing through all her works,
gave signs of wo,
That all was lost.

Milton

I. As to the preacher, I would observe, he has many names given to him in the sacred writings; the most common is the Devil. That it was he that disturbed the felicity of our first parents, is evident from 2 Cor. 11:3, and many other passages of scripture. He was once an angel of light, and knew better than to teach such doctrine; he did violence to his own reason. But to be a little more particular, let it be observed,

1. He is an old preacher. He lived about two thousand years before Abraham—about four thousand four hundred years before Christ. It is now five thousand eight hundred years since he commenced preaching. By this time he must have acquired great skill in the art.

2. He is a very cunning, artful preacher. When Elymas, the sorcerer, came to turn away people from the faith, he is said to be "full of all subtlety, and a child of the devil,"—not only because he was an enemy of all righteousness, but on account of his carnal cunning and craftiness.

3. He is a very laborious, unwearied preacher. He has been in the ministry about six thousand years, and yet his zeal is not in the least abated. The Apostle Peter compares him

to a roaring lion, walking about, seeking whom he may devour. When God inquires of this persevering preacher, Job 2:2, "From whence comest thou?" he "answered the Lord and said, From going to and fro in the earth, and from walking up and down in it." He is far from being circumscribed within the narrow limits of parish, state, or continental lines; but his haunt and travel is very extensive.

4. He is a heterogeneous preacher, if I may so express myself. He makes use of a Bible, when he holds forth, as in his sermon to our Savior, Matt. 4:6. He mixes truth with error, in order to make it go well, or carry his point.

5. He is a very presumptuous preacher. Notwithstanding God had declared, in the most plain and positive terms, "Thou shalt surely die,"—or, "In dying thou shalt die,"—yet this audacious wretch had the impudence to confront Omnipotence, and say, "Ye shall not surely die!"

6. He is a very successful preacher. He draws a great number after him. No preacher can command hearers like him. He was successful with our first parents—with the old world. Noah once preached to those spirits that are now in the prison of hell, and told them from God that they should surely die; but this preacher came along, and declared the contrary— "Ye shall not surely die." The greater part, it seems, believed him, and went to destruction. So it was with Sodom and Gomorrah—Lot preached to them; the substance of which was, "Up, get ye out of this place; for the Lord will destroy this city." Gen. 19:14. But this old declaimer told them, No danger! no danger! "Ye shall not die." To which they generally gave heed; and Lot seemed to them as one who mocked—they believed the Universal preacher, and were consumed, agreeably to the declaration of the Apostle Jude, "Sodom and Gomorrah, and the cities about them, suffering the vengeance of eternal fire."

II. Let us attend to the doctrine inculcated by this preacher, "Ye shall not surely die." Bold assertion! without a single argument to support it. The death contained in the threatening was doubtless eternal death—as nothing but this would express God's feelings towards sin, or render an infinite atonement necessary. To suppose it to be spiritual death, is to blend crime and punishment together. To suppose temporal death to be the curse of the law, then believers are not delivered from it, according to Galatians 3:13. What Satan meant to preach was, that there is no hell; and that the wages of sin is not death, but eternal life.

III. We shall now take notice of the hearer addressed by the preacher. This we have in the text, "And the serpent said unto the *woman*, Ye shall not surely die." That Eve had not so much experience as Adam, is evident; and so not equally able to withstand temptation. This doubtless was a reason why the tempter chose her, with whom he might hope to be successful. Doubtless he took a time when she was separated from her husband. That this preacher has had the greatest success in the dark and ignorant paths of the earth, is evident; his kingdom is a kingdom of darkness. He is a great enemy to light. Paul gives us some account of him in his day,—2 Tim. 3:6, "For of this sort are they which creep into houses, and lead captive silly women, laden with sins, led away with divers lusts." The same apostle observes, Romans 16:17, "Now I beseech you, brethren, mark them which cause divisions and offences contrary to the doctrine which ye have learned, and avoid them. For they that are such serve not our Lord Jesus Christ, but their own belly; and by good words and fair speeches deceive the hearts of the simple."

IV. The instrument or medium made use of by the preacher will now be considered. This we have in the text, "And the *serpent* said unto the woman, Ye shall not surely die." But how came the devil to preach through the serpent?

1. To save his own character, and the better to carry his point. Had the devil come to our first parents personally and unmasked, they would have more easily seen the deception. The reality of a future punishment is at times so clearly impressed on the human mind, that even Satan is constrained to his own that there is a hell, although at other times he denies it. He does not wish to have it known that he is a liar; therefore he conceals himself, that he may the better accomplish his designs and save his own character.

2. The devil is an enemy to all good, to all happiness and excellence. He is opposed to the felicity of the brutes. He took delight in tormenting the swine. The serpent, before he set up preaching universal salvation, was a cunning, beautiful, and happy creature; but now his glory is departed. "And the Lord said unto the serpent, because thou hast done this art cursed above all cattle, and about every beast of the field; upon thy belly shalt thou go, and dust shalt thou eat all the days of thy life." There is therefore a king of duplicate cunning in the matter—Satan gets the preachers and hearers also.

"And is not this triumphant treachery, And more than simple conquest in the foe!" Young.

3. Another reason why Satan employs instruments in his service is, because his empire is large, and he cannot be everywhere himself.

4. He has a large number at his command, that love and approve of his work, delight in building up his kingdom, and stand ready to go at his call.

Inferences

1. The devil is not dead, but still lives, and is able to preach as well as ever, "Ye shall not surely die."

2. Universal salvation is no new-fangled scheme, but can boast of great antiquity.

3. See a reason why it ought to be rejected, because it is an ancient devised doctrine.

4. See one reason why it is that Satan is such a moral enemy to the Bible, and to all who preach the Gospel, because of that injunction, Mark 16:15, 16,—"And he said unto them, Go ye into all the world, and preach the Gospel to every creature. He that believeth and is baptized shall be saved; but he that believeth not shall be damned."

5. See whence it is that Satan exerted himself so much to convince our first parents that there was no hell, because the denunciation of the Almighty was true, and he was afraid that Adam and Eve would continue in the belief of it. Was there no truth in future punishment, or was it only a temporary evil, Satan would not be so busy in trying to convince men that there is none. It is his nature and element to lie. "When he speaketh a lie, he speaketh of his own; for he is a liar, and the father of it." John 7:44.

6. We infer that ministers should not be proud of their preaching. If they preach the true Gospel, they only in substance repeat Christ's sermons. If they preach, "Ye shall not surely die," they only make use of the devil's old notes that he delivered almost six thousand years ago.

7. It is probable that the doctrine of universal salvation will still prevail since this preacher is yet alive, and not in the least superannuated; and every effort against him only enrages him more, and excites him to new inventions and exertions to build up his cause.

To close the subject

As the author of the foregoing discourse has confined himself wholly to the character of Satan, he trusts no one will feel himself personally injured by this short sermon. But should any imbibe a degree of friendship for this aged divine, and think that I have not treated this universal preacher with that respect and veneration that he justly deserves, let him be so kind as to point it out, and I will most cheerfully retract; for it has ever been a maxim with me, "Render unto all their dues."

Lemuel Haynes

ABSALOM JONES (1746-1818)

Introduction

Absalom Jones, a Black minister and abolitionist, who became a force in Black spirituality, was a house slave from Delaware, where he taught himself to read from the New Testament, and other books. He bought his freedom in 1784. Then he served as lay minister for the black members of St. George's Methodist Episcopal.

This congregation grew to more than five hundred members in the first year and Jones became known as "the black Bishop of the Episcopal Church". Following the segregation of blacks in this church, in Philadelphia in 1786, Jones along with his friend Richard Allen founded a black congregation, St. Thomas African Episcopal Church. This was the mother church for what became, beginning in 1816, the African Methodist Episcopal Church movement.

Jones denounced slavery, and warned the oppressors to "clean their hands of slaves." To him, God was the Father who always acted on "behalf of the oppressed and distressed."

Jones' *Thanksgiving Sermon* preached on 1 January 1808 in St. Thomas African Episcopal Church in Philadelphia, commemorated the end of legal importation of slaves into the United States. This holiday became one of the central antislavery celebration days among free black communities in the North.

A Thanksgiving Sermon

Exodus, 3:7–8. And the Lord said, I have surely seen the affliction of my people which are in Egypt, and have heard their cry by reason of their task-masters; for I know their sorrows; and I am come down to deliver them out of the hand of the Egyptians.

These words, my brethren, contain a short account of some of the circumstances which preceded the deliverance of the children of Israel from their captivity and bondage in Egypt.

Their affliction

They mention, in the first place, their affliction. This consisted in their privation of liberty: they were slaves to the kings of Egypt, in common with their other subjects; and they were slaves to their fellow slaves. They were compelled to work in the open air, in one of the hottest climates in the world; and, probably, without a covering from the burning rays of the sun. Their work was of a laborious kind: it consisted of making bricks, and traveling, perhaps to a great distance, for the straw, or stubble, that was a component part of them. Their work was dealt out to them in tasks, and performed under the eye of vigilant and rigorous masters, who constantly upbraided them with idleness. The least deficiency, in the product of their labor, was punished by beating. Nor was this all. Their food was of the cheapest kind, and contained but little nourishment: it consisted only of leeks and onions, which grew almost spontaneously in the land of Egypt. Painful and distressing as these sufferings were, they constituted the smallest part of their misery. While the fields resounded with their cries in the day, their huts and hamlets were vocal at night with their lamentations over their sons; who were dragged from the arms of their mothers, and put to death by drowning, in order to prevent such an increase in their population, as to endanger the safety of the state by an insurrection. In this condition, thus degraded and oppressed, they passed nearly four hundred years. Ah! who can conceive of the measure of their sufferings, during that time? What tongue, or pen, can compute the number of their sorrows? To them no morning or evening sun ever disclosed a single charm: to them, the beauties of spring, and the plenty of autumn had no attractions: even domestic endearments were scarcely known to them: all was misery; all was grief; all was despair.

Not God-forsaken

Our text mentions, in the second place that, in this situation, they were not forgotten by the God of their fathers, and the Father of the human race. Though, for wise reasons, he delayed to appear in their behalf for several hundred years; yet he was not indifferent to their sufferings.

Our text tells us, that he saw their affliction, and heard their cry: his eye and his ear were constantly open to their complaint: every tear they shed, was preserved, and every groan they uttered, was recorded; in order to testify, at a future day, against the authors of their oppressions.

But our text goes further: it describes the Judge of the world to be so much moved, with what he saw and what he heard, that he rises from his throne—not to issue a command to the armies of angels that surrounded him to fly to the relief of his suffering children—but to come down from heaven, in his own person, in order to deliver them out of the hands of the Egyptians.

Glory to God for this precious record of his power and goodness: let all the nations of the earth praise him. "Clouds and darkness are round about him, but righteousness and judgment are the habitation of his throne" [Ps. 97:2]. "O sing unto the Lord a new song, for he hath done marvelous things: his right hand and his holy arm hath gotten him the victory" [Ps. 98:1]. "He hath remembered his mercy and truth toward the house of Israel, and all the ends of the earth shall see the salvation of God" [Ps. 98:3]. The history of the world shows us, that the deliverance of the children of Israel from their bondage, is not the only instance, in which it has pleased God to appear in behalf of oppressed and distressed nations, as the deliverer of the innocent, and of those who call upon his name. He is as unchangeable in his nature and character, as he is in his wisdom and power. The great and blessed event, which we have this day met to celebrate, is a striking proof, that the God of heaven and earth is the same, yesterday, and to-day, and for ever. Yes, my brethren, the nations from which most of us have descended, and the country in which some of us were born, have been visited by the tender mercy of the Common Father of the human race.

He has seen the affliction of our countrymen, with an eye of pity. He has seen the wicked arts, by which wars have been fomented among the different tribes of the Africans, in order to procure captives, for the purpose of selling them for slaves. He has seen ships fitted out from different ports in Europe and America, and freighted with trinkets to be exchanged for the bodies and souls of men. He has seen the anguish which has taken place, when parents have been torn from their children, and children from their parents, and conveyed, with their hands and feet bound in fetters, on board of ships prepared to receive them. He has seen them thrust in crowds into the holds of those ships, where many of them have perished from the want of air. He has seen such of them as have escaped from that noxious place of confinement, leap into the ocean; with a faint hope of swimming back to their native shore, or a determination to seek early retreat from their impending misery, in a watery grave. He has seen them exposed for sale, like horses and cattle, upon the wharves; or, like bales of goods, in warehouses of West India and American sea ports. He has seen the pangs of separation between members of the same family. He has seen them driven into the sugar; the rice, and the tobacco fields, and compelled to work—in spite of the habits of ease which they derived from the natural fertility of their own country in the open air, beneath a burning sun, with scarcely as much clothing upon them as modesty required. He has seen them faint beneath the pressure of their labors. He has seen them return to their smoky huts in the evening, with nothing to satisfy their hunger but a scanty allowance of roots; and these, cultivated for themselves, on that day only, which God ordained as a day of rest for man and beast. He has seen the neglect with which their masters have treated their immortal souls; not only in withholding religious instruction from them, but, in some instances, depriving them of access to the means of obtaining it. He has seen all the different modes of torture, by means of the whip, the screw, the pincers, and the red hot iron, which have been exercised upon their bodies, by inhuman overseers: overseers, did I say? Yes: but not by these only.

Our all-seeing God

Our God has seen masters and mistresses, educated in fashionable life, sometimes take the instruments of torture into their own hands, and, deaf to the cries and shrieks of their agonizing slaves, exceed even their overseers in cruelty. Inhuman wretches! though You have been deaf to their cries and shrieks, they have been heard in Heaven. The ears of Jehovah have been constantly open to them: He has heard the prayers that have ascended from the hearts of his people; and he has, as in the case of his ancient and chosen people the Jews, come down to deliver our suffering country-men from the hands of their oppressors. He came down into the United States, when they declared, in the constitution which they framed in 1788, that the trade in our African fellow-men, should cease in the year 1808: He came down into the British Parliament, when they passed a law to put an end to the same iniquitous trade in May, 1807: He came down into the Congress of the United States, the last winter, when they passed a similar law, the operation of which commences on this happy day. Dear land of our ancestors! thou shalt no more be stained with the blood of thy children, shed by British and American hands: the ocean shall no more afford a refuge to their bodies, from impending slavery: nor shall the shores of the British West India islands, and of the United States, any more witness the anguish of families, parted for ever by a public sale. For this signal interposition of the God of mercies, in behalf of our brethren, it becomes us this day to offer up our united thanks. Let the song of angels, which was first heard in the air at the birth of our Savior, be heard this day in our assembly: Glory to God in the highest, for these first fruits of peace upon earth, and good will to man: O! let us give thanks unto the Lord: let us call upon his name, and make known his deeds among the people. Let us sing psalms unto him and talk of all his wondrous works. [See Ps. 105:1-2.] Having enumerated the mercies of God to our nation, it becomes us to ask, what shall we render unto the Lord for them? Sacrifices and burnt offerings are no longer pleasing to him: the pomp of public worship, and the ceremonies of a festive day, will find no acceptance with him, unless they are accompanied with actions that correspond with them. The duties which are inculcated upon us, by the event we are now celebrating, divide themselves into five heads.

Thanksgiving every day

In the first place, Let not our expressions of gratitude to God for his late goodness and mercy to our countrymen, be confined to this day, nor to this house: let us carry grateful hearts with us to our places of abode, and to our daily occupations; and let praise and thanksgivings ascend daily to the throne of grace, in our families, and in our closets, for what God has done for our African brethren. Let us not forget to praise him for his mercies to such of our color as are inhabitants of this country; particularly, for disposing the hearts of the rulers of many of the states to pass laws for the abolition of slavery; for the number and zeal of the friends he has raised up to plead our cause; and for the privileges, we enjoy, of worshiping God, agreeably to our consciences, in churches of our own. This comely building, erected chiefly by the generosity of our friends, is a monument of God's goodness to us, and calls for our gratitude with all the other blessings that have been mentioned.

Pray for a humane spirit

Secondly, Let us unite, with our thanksgiving, prayer to Almighty God, for the completion of his begun goodness to our brethren in Africa. Let us beseech him to extend to all the nations in Europe, the same humane and just spirit towards them, which he has imparted to the British and American nations. Let us, further, implore the influence of his divine and holy Spirit, to dispose the hearts of our legislatures to pass laws, to ameliorate the condition of our brethren who are still in bondage; also, to dispose their masters to treat them with kindness and humanity; and, above all things, to favor them with the means of acquiring such parts of human knowledge, as will enable them to read the holy scriptures, and understand the doctrines of the Christian religion, whereby they may become, even while they are the slaves of men, the freemen of the Lord.

Correct behavior

Thirdly, Let us conduct ourselves in such a manner as to furnish no cause of regret to the deliverers of our nation, for their kindness to us. Let us constantly remember the rock whence we were hewn, and the pit whence we were digged. Pride was not made for man, in any situation; and, still less, for persons who have recently emerged from bondage. The Jews, after they entered the promised land, were commanded, when they offered sacrifices to the Lord, never to forget their humble origin; and hence, part of the worship that accompanied their sacrifices consisted in acknowledging, that a Syrian, ready to perish, was their father:

in like manner, it becomes us, publicly and privately, to acknowledge, that an African slave, ready to perish, was our father or our grandfather.

Let our conduct be regulated by the precepts of the gospel; let us be sober minded, humble, peaceable, temperate in our meats and drinks, frugal in our apparel and in the furniture of our houses, industrious in our occupations, just in all our dealings, and ever ready to honor all men. Let us teach our children the rudiments of the English language, in order to enable them to acquire a knowledge of useful trades; and, above all things, let us instruct them in the principles of the gospel of Jesus Christ, whereby they may become wise unto salvation. It has always been a mystery, Why the impartial Father of the human race should have permitted the transportation of so many millions of our fellow creatures to this country, to endure all the miseries of slavery. Perhaps his design was, that a knowledge of the gospel might be acquired by some of their descendants, in order that they might become qualified to be the messengers of it, to the land of their fathers. Let this thought animate us, when we are teaching our children to love and adore the name of our Redeemer. Who knows but that a Joseph may rise up among them, who shall be the instrument of feeding the African nations with the bread of life, and of saving them, not from earthly bondage, but from the more galling yoke of sin and Satan.

Our benefactors

Fourthly, Let us be grateful to our benefactors, who, by enlightening the minds of the rulers of the earth, by means of their publications and remonstrances against the trade in our countrymen, have produced the great event we are this day celebrating. Abolition societies and individuals have equal claims to our gratitude. It would be difficult to mention the names of any of our benefactors, without offending many whom we do not know. Some of them are gone to heaven, to receive the reward of their labors of love towards us; and the kindness and benevolence of the survivors, we hope, are recorded in the book of life, to be mentioned with honor when our Lord shall come to reward his faithful servants before an assembled world.

Fifthly, and lastly, Let the first of January, the day of the abolition of the slave trade in our country, be set apart in every year, as a day of public thanksgiving for that mercy. Let the history of the sufferings of our brethren, and of their deliverance, descend by this means to our children, to the remotest generations; and when they shall ask, in time to come, saying, What mean the lessons, the psalms, the prayers and the praises in the worship of this day? let us answer them, by saying, the Lord, on the day of which this is the anniversary, abolished the trade which dragged your fathers from their native country, and sold them as bondmen in the United States of America.

Absalom Jones

RICHARD ALLEN (1760-1831)

Introduction

Richard Allen, who was born a slave in Philadelphia, became a Black religious leader, and founder and first bishop of the African Methodist Episcopal (A.M.E.) Church.

In about 1777 he was converted to Methodism which stressed the virtues of honesty, modesty, and sobriety. From 1780 Allen preached at Methodist churches in Delaware and surrounding states. In 1786, Allen paid his last installment to his slave-master, Sturgis, and became free.

In 1786 Allen became pastor to a mixed race congregation at St. George's Church in Philadelphia. Because black members of the congregation increased dramatically white elders at St. George's enforced separate seating for whites and blacks. Allen's friend, Rev Absalom Jones, challenged St. George's segregated seating arrangement by sitting downstairs. Jones was ejected from the church and this caused other Black members to walk out. On August 12, 1794, The African Church of Philadelphia was founded, but because of the Methodists' discriminatory treatment of Blacks, the church was consecrated as part of the Protestant Episcopal Church and Jones became the denomination's first Black minister.

Allen bought land for and founded the Bethel African Church on April 9, 1794, to which he was ordained deacon. Many other Black Methodists formed African Methodist Churches in north-eastern cities. Out of this situation the leaders of these churches united under the name of the African Methodist Episcopal (A.M.E.) Church. The A.M.E. Church quickly became a center of Black institutional life.

Allen published articles attacking slavery and organizations such as the American Colonization Society. He wrote: "We will never separate ourselves voluntarily from the slave population in this country; they are our brethren and we feel there is more virtue in suffering privations with them than fancied advantage for a season."

The Life, Experience, and Gospel Labors of the Rt. Rev. Richard Allen

Mark the perfect man, and behold the upright: for the end of that man is peace.—Ps. 37:37

My background

I was born in the year of our Lord 1760, on February 14th, a slave to Benjamin Chew, of Philadelphia. My mother and father and four children of us were sold into Delaware State, near Dover, and I was a child and lived with him until I was upwards of twenty years of age, during which time I was awakened and brought to see myself poor, wretched and undone, and without the mercy of God must be lost. Shortly after I obtained mercy through the blood of Christ, and was constrained to exhort my old companions to seek the Lord. I went rejoicing for several days, and was happy in the Lord, in conversing with many old experienced Christians. I was brought under doubts, and was tempted to believe I was deceived, and was constrained to seek the Lord afresh. I went with my head bowed down for many days. My sins were a heavy burden. I was tempted to believe there was no mercy for me. I cried to the Lord both night and day. One night I thought hell would be my portion. I cried unto Him who delighteth to hear the prayers of a poor sinner; and all of a sudden my dungeon shook, my chains flew off, and glory to God, I cried. My soul was filled. I cried, enough for me—the Savior died. Now my confidence was strengthened that the Lord, for Christ's sake, had heard my prayers, and pardoned all my sins. I was constrained to go from house to house, exhorting my old companions, and telling to all around what a dear Savior I had found. I joined the Methodist society, and met in class at Benjamin Wells's, in the forest, Delaware State. John Gray was the class-leader. I met in his class for several years.

A good master

My master was an unconverted man, and all the family; but he was what the world called a good master. He was more like a father to his slaves than any thing else. He was a very tender, humane man. My mother and father lived with him for many years. He was brought into difficulty, not being able to pay for us; and mother having several children after he had bought us, he sold my mother and three children. My mother sought the Lord and found favor with him, and became a very pious woman. There were three children of us remained with our old master. My oldest brother embraced religion, and my sister. Our neighbors, seeing that our master indulged us with the privilege of attending meeting once in two weeks, said that Stokeley's Negroes would soon ruin him; and so my brother and myself held a council together that we would attend more faithfully to our master's business, so that it should not be said that religion made us worse servants, we would work night and day to get our crops forward, so that they should be disappointed. We frequently went to meeting on every other Thursday; but if we were likely to be backward with our crops we would refrain from going to meeting. When our master found we were making no provision to go to meeting, he would frequently ask us if it was not our meeting day, and if we were not going. We would frequently tell him, "no, sir, we would rather stay at home and get our work done." He would tell us, "Boys, I would rather you would go to your meeting: if I am not good myself, I like to see you striving yourselves to be good." Our reply would be, "Thank you, sir; but we would rather stay and get our crops forward." So we always continued to keep our crops more forward than our neighbors; and we would attend public preaching once in two weeks, and class meeting once a week. At length our master said he was convinced that religion made slaves better and not worse, and often boasted of his slaves for their honesty and industry.

Methodist preacher invited

Some time after I asked him if I might ask the preachers to come and preach at his house. He being old and infirm, my master and mistress cheerfully agreed for me to ask some of the Methodist preachers to come and preach at his house. I asked him for a note. He replied, if my word was not sufficient, he should send no note. I accordingly asked the preacher. He seemed somewhat backward at first, as my master did not send a written request; but the class-leader (John Gray) observed that my word was sufficient; so he preached at my old master's house on the next Wednesday. Preaching continued for some months; at length

Freeborn Garrison preached from these words, "Thou art weighed in the balance, and art found wanting." In pointing out and weighing the different characters, and among the rest weighed the slave-holders, my master believed himself to be one of that number, and after that he could not be satisfied to hold slaves, believing it to be wrong. And after that he proposed to me and my brother buying our times, to pay him sixty pounds gold and silver, or two thousand dollars continental money, which we complied with in the year 17—. ...

A traveling preacher

After peace was proclaimed I then traveled extensively, striving to preach the Gospel. My lot was cast in Wilmington. Shortly after I was taken sick with the fall fever and then the pleurisy. September the 3d, 1783, I left my native place. After leaving Wilmington, I went into New-Jersey, and there traveled and strove to preach the Gospel until the spring of 1784. I then became acquainted with Benjamin Abbot, that great and good apostle. He was one of the greatest men that ever I was acquainted with. He seldom preached but what there were souls added to his labor. He was a man of as great faith as any that ever I saw. The Lord was with him, and blessed his labors abundantly. He was as a friend and father to me. I was sorry when I had to leave West Jersey, knowing I had to leave a father. I was employed in cutting of wood for Captain Cruenkleton, although I preached the Gospel at nights and on Sundays. My dear Lord was with me, and blessed my labors—glory to God—and gave me souls for my hire. I then visited East Jersey, and labored for my dear Lord, and became acquainted with Joseph Budd, and made my home with him, near the new mills—a family, I trust, who loved and served the Lord. I labored some time there; but being much afflicted in body with the inflammatory rheumatism, was not so successful as in some other places.

I went from there to Jonathan Bunn's, near Bennington, East Jersey. There I labored in that neighborhood for some time. I found him and his family kind and affectionate, and he and his dear wife were a father and mother of Israel. In the year 1784 I left East Jersey, and labored in Pennsylvania. I walked until my feet became so sore and blistered the first day, that I scarcely could bear them to the ground. I found the people very humane and kind in Pennsylvania. I having but little money, I stopped at Cæsar Water's, at Radnor township, twelve miles from Philadelphia. I found him and his wife very kind and affectionate to me. In the evening they asked me if I would come and take tea with them; but after sitting awhile, my feet became so sore and painful that I could scarcely be able to put them to the floor. I told them that I would accept of their kind invitation, but my feet pained me so that I could not come to the table. They brought the table to me. Never was I more kindly received by strangers that I had never before seen, than by them. She bathed my feet with warm water and bran; the next morning my feet were better and free from pain. They asked me if I would preach for them. I preached for them the next evening. We had a glorious meeting. They invited me to stay till Sabbath day, and preach for them. I agreed to do so, and preached on Sabbath day to a large congregation of different persuasions, and my dear Lord was with me, and I believe there were many souls cut to the heart, and were added to the ministry. They insisted on me to stay longer with them. I stayed and labored in Radnor several weeks. ...

Persecution

We bore much persecution from many of the Methodist connexion; but we have reason to be thankful to Almighty God, who was our deliverer. The day was appointed to go and dig the cellar. I arose early in the morning and addressed the throne of grace, praying that the Lord would bless our endeavors. Having by this time two or three teams of my own—as I was the first proposer of the African church, I put the first spade in the ground to dig a cellar for the same. This was the first African church or meeting house that was erected in the United States of America. We intended it for the African preaching house or church; but finding that the elder stationed in this city was such an opposer to our proceedings of erecting a place of worship; though the principal part of the directors of this church belonged to the Methodist connexion, the elder stationed here would neither preach for us, nor have any thing to do with us. We then held an election, to know what religious denomination we should unite with. At the election it was determined—there were two in favor of the Methodist, the Rev. Absalom Jones and myself, and a large majority in favor of the Church of England. The majority carried. Notwithstanding we had been so violently persecuted by the elder, we were in favor of being attached to the Methodist connexion; for I was confident that there was no religious sect or denomination would suit the capacity of the colored people as well as the Methodist; for the plain and simple gospel suits best for any people, for the unlearned can understand, and the learned are sure to understand; and the reason that the Methodist is so successful in the awakening and conversion of the colored people, the plain doctrine and having a good discipline. But in many cases the preachers would act to please their own fancy, without discipline, till some of them became such tyrants, and more especially to the colored people. They would turn them out of society, giving them no trial, for the smallest offence, perhaps only hearsay. They would frequently, in meeting the class, impeach some of the members of whom they had heard an ill report, and turn them out, saying, "I have heard thus and thus of you, and you are no more a member of society"—without witnesses on either side. This has been frequently done, notwithstanding in the first rise and progress in Delaware State, and elsewhere, the colored people were their greatest support; for there were but few of us free; but the slaves would toil in their little patches many a night until midnight to raise their little truck and sell to get something to support them more than what their masters gave them, but we used often to divide our little support among the white preachers of the Gospel. This was once a quarter. It was in the time of the old revolutionary war between Great Britain and the United States. The Methodists were the first people that brought glad tidings to the colored people. I feel thankful that ever I heard a Methodist preach. We are beholden to the Methodists, under God, for the light of the Gospel we enjoy; for all other denominations preached so high-flown that we were not able to comprehend their doctrine. Sure am I that reading sermons will never prove so beneficial to the colored people as spiritual or extempore preaching. I am well convinced that the Methodist has proved beneficial to thousands and ten times thousands. It is to be awfully feared that the simplicity of the Gospel that was among them fifty years ago, and that they conform more to the world and the fashions thereof, they would fare very little better than the people of the world. The discipline is altered considerably from what it was. We would ask for the good old way, and desire to walk therein. ...

Spiritual despotism

Many of the colored people in other places were in a situation nearly like those of Philadelphia and Baltimore, which induced us in April 1816 to call a general meeting, by way of Conference. Delegates from Baltimore and other places which met those of Philadelphia, and taking into consideration their grievances, and in order to secure the privileges, promote union and harmony among themselves, it was resolved, "That the people of Philadelphia, Baltimore, &c. &c., should become one body, under the name of the African Methodist Episcopal Church." We deemed it expedient to have a form of discipline, whereby we may guide our people in the fear of God, in the unity of the Spirit, and in the bonds of peace, and preserve us from that spiritual despotism which we have so recently experienced—remembering that we are not to lord it over God's heritage, as greedy dogs that can never have enough. But with long suffering, and bowels of compassion to bear each other's burdens, and so fulfill the Law of Christ, praying that our mutual striving together for the promulgation of the Gospel may be crowned with abundant success.

Articles of Association

Extracts from the Articles of Association, of the African Methodist Episcopal Church, commonly called, and known by the name of "Bethel Church" of the City of Philadelphia

Acts of faith

I believe, O God, that thou art an eternal, incomprehensible spirit, infinite in all perfections, who didst make all things out of nothing, and dost govern them all by thy wise providence.

Let me always adore thee with profound humility, as my Sovereign Lord; and help me to love and praise thee with godlike affections, and suitable devotion.

I believe that in the unity of the Godhead there is a trinity of persons, that thou art perfectly one and perfectly three; one essence and three persons. I believe O blessed Jesus, that thou art of one substance with the father, the very and eternal God, that thou didst take upon thee our frail nature, that thou didst truly suffer, and wert crucified, dead and buried, to reconcile us to thy Father, and to be a sacrifice for sin.

I believe, that according to the types and prophecies which went before of thee, and according to thy own infallible prediction, thou didst by thy own power rise from the dead the third day, that thou didst ascend into Heaven, that there thou sittest on thy throne of glory adored by angels, and interceding for sinners.

I believe, that thou hast instituted and ordained holy mysteries as pledges of thy love, and for a continual commemoration of thy death; that thou hast not only given thyself to die for me, but to be my spiritual food and sustenance in that holy sacrament, to my great and endless comfort. O may I frequently approach thy altar with humility and devotion, and work in me all those holy and Heavenly affections, which become the remembrance of a crucified Savior.

I believe, O Lord, that thou hast not abandoned me to the dim light of my own reason, to conduct me to happiness; but that thou hast revealed in the holy Scriptures whatever is necessary for me to believe and practice, in order to my eternal salvation.

O how noble and excellent are the precepts; how sublime and enlightening the truth; how persuasive and strong the motives; how powerful the assistances of thy holy religion, in which thou hast instructed me; my delight shall be in thy statutes, and I will not forget thy word.

I believe, it is my greatest honor and happiness to be thy disciple: how miserable and blind are those that live without God in the world, who despise the light of thy holy faith. Make me to part with all the enjoyments of life; nay, even life itself, rather than forfeit this jewel of great price. Blessed are the sufferings which are endured, happy is the death which is undergone for Heavenly and immortal truth! I believe that thou hast prepared for those that love thee, everlasting mansions of glory; if I believe thee, O eternal happiness; Why does any thing appear difficult that leads to thee? Why should I not willingly resist unto blood to obtain thee? Why do the vain and empty employments of life take such fast hold of us? O perishing time! Why doest thou thus bewitch and deceive me? O blessed eternity! When shalt thou be my portion for ever?

Acts of hope

O, my God! in all my dangers temporal and spiritual I will hope in thee who art Almighty power, and therefore able to relieve me; who art infinite goodness, and therefore ready and willing to assist me.

O precious blood of my dear Redeemer! O gaping wounds of my crucified Savior! Who can contemplate the sufferings of God incarnate, and not raise his hope, and not put his trust in him. What though my body be crumbled into dust, and that dust blown over the face of the earth, yet I undoubtedly know my Redeemer lives, and shall raise me up at the last day [Job 19:25-27]; whether I am comforted or left desolate; whether I enjoy peace or am afflicted with temptations, whether I am healthful or sickly, succored or abandoned by the good things of this life, I will always hope in thee, O my chiefest, infinite good.

Although the fig-tree shall not blossom, neither shall fruit be in the vines; although the labor of the olive shall fail, and the fields yield no meat; although the flock shall be cut off from the fold, and there shall be no herd in the stalls, yet I will rejoice in the Lord, I will joy in the God of my salvation [Hab 3:17-19].

What though I mourn and am afflicted here, and sigh under the miseries of this world for a time, I am sure that my tears shall one day be turned into joy, and that joy none shall take from me. Whoever hopes for the great things in this world, takes pains to attain them; how can my hopes of everlasting life be well ground, if I do not strive and labor for that eternal inheritance? I will never refuse the meanest labors, while I look to receive such glorious wages; I will never repine at any temporal loss, while I expect to gain such eternal rewards. Blessed hope! be thou my chief delight in life, and then I shall be steadfast and immoveable, always abounding in the work of the Lord, be thou my comfort and support at the hour of death, and then I shall contentedly leave this world, as a captive that is released from his imprisonment.

Acts of love

O infinite amiableness! When shall I love thee without bounds, without coldness or interruption which, alas! so often seize me here below? Let me never suffer any creature to be thy rival, or to share my heart with thee; let me have no other God, no other love, but only thee.

Whoever loves, desires to please the beloved object; and according to the degree of love is the greatness of desire; make me O God diligent and earnest in pleasing thee; let me cheerfully discharge the most painful and costly duties; and forsake friends, riches, ease and life itself, rather than disobey thee.

Whoever loves, desires the welfare and happiness of the beloved object; but thou, O dear Jesus, can'st receive no addition from my imperfect services; what shall I do to express my affection towards thee? I will relieve the necessities of my poor brethren, who are members of thy body; for he that loveth not his brother whom he has seen, how can he love God whom he hath not seen?

O crucified Jesus in whom I live, and without whom I die; mortify in me all sensual desires, inflame my heart with thy holy love, that I may no longer esteem the vanities of this world, but place my affections entirely on thee.

Let my last breath, when my soul shall leave my body, breathe forth love to thee, my God; I entered into life without acknowledging thee, let me therefore finish it in loving thee; O let the last act of life be love, remembering that God is love.

Richard Allen

An Address to Those Who Keep Slaves and Approve the Practice

The judicious part of mankind, will think it unreasonable, that a superior good conduct is looked for from our race, by those who stigmatize us as men, whose baseness is incurable, and may therefore be held in a state of servitude, that a merciful man would not doom a beast to; yet you try what you can, to prevent our rising from a state of barbarism you represent us to be in, but we can tell you from a degree of experience, that a black man, although reduced to the most abject state human nature is capable of, short of real madness, can think, reflect, and feel injuries, although it may not be with the same degree of keen resentment and revenge, that you who have been, and are our great oppressors would manifest, if reduced to the pitiable condition of a slave. We believe if you would try the experiment of taking a few black children, and cultivate their minds with the same care, and let them have the same prospect in view as to living in the world, as you would wish for your own children, you would find upon the trial, they were not inferior in mental endowments. I do not wish to make you angry, but excite attention to consider how hateful slavery is, in the sight of that God who hath destroyed kings and princes, for their oppression of the poor slaves. Pharaoh and his princes with the posterity of king Saul, were destroyed by the protector and avenger of slaves. Would you not suppose the Israelites to be utterly unfit for freedom, and that it was impossible for them, to obtain to any degree of excellence? Their history shews how slavery had debased their spirits. Men must be willfully blind, and extremely partial, that cannot see the contrary effects of liberty and slavery upon the mind of man; I truly confess the vile habits often acquired in a state of servitude, are not easily thrown off; the example of the Israelites shews, who with all that Moses could do to reclaim them from it, still continued in their habits more or less; and why will you look for better from us, why will you look for grapes from thorns, or figs from thistles? it is in our posterity enjoying the same priviledges with your own, that you ought to look for better things.

When you are pleaded with, do not you reply as Pharaoh did, "Wherefore do ye Moses and Aaron let the people from their work, behold the people of the land now are many, and you make them rest from their burdens." We wish you to consider, that God himself was the first pleader of the cause of slaves.

That God who knows the hearts of all men, and the propensity of a slave to hate his oppressor, hath strictly forbidden it to his chosen people, "Thou shalt not abhor an Egyptian, because thou wast a stranger in his land." Deut. 23. 7. The meek and humble Jesus, the great pattern of humanity, and every other virtue that can adorn and dignify men, hath commanded to love our enemies, to do good to them that hate and despitefully use us [Matt. 5:44; Luke 6:27, 33]. I feel the obligations, I wish to impress them on the minds of our colored brethren, and that we may all forgive you, as we wish to be forgiven, we think it a great mercy to have all anger and bitterness removed from our minds; I appeal to your own feelings, if it is not very disquieting to feel yourselves under dominion of wrathful disposition.

If you love your children, if you love your country, if you love the God of love, clear your hands from slaves, burthen not your children or your country with them, my heart has been sorry for the blood shed of the oppressors, as well as the oppressed, both appear guilty of each others blood, in the sight of him who hath said, he that sheddeth man's blood, by man shall his blood be shed [Gen. 9:6].

Will you, because you have reduced us to the unhappy condition our color is in, plead our incapacity for freedom, and our contented condition under oppression, as a sufficient cause for keeping us under the grievous yoke. I have shown the cause,—I will also shew why they appear contented as they can in your sight, but the dreadful insurrections they have made when opportunity has offered, is enough to convince a reasonable man, that great uneasiness and not contentment, is the inhabitant of their hearts. God himself hath pleaded their cause, he hath from time to time raised up instruments for that purpose, sometimes mean and contemptible in your sight, at other times he hath used such as it hath pleased him, with whom you have not thought it beneath your dignity to contend. Many have been convinced of their error, condemned their former conduct, and become zealous advocates for the cause of those, whom you will not suffer to plead for themselves.

Richard Allen

To the People of Color

Feeling an engagement of mind for your welfare, I address you with an affectionate sympathy, having been a slave, and as desirous of freedom as any of you; yet the bands of bondage were so strong that no way appeared for my release; yet at times a hope arose in my heart that a way would open for it; and when my mind was mercifully visited with the feeling of the love of God, then these hopes increased, and a confidence arose that he would make way for my enlargement; and as a patient waiting was necessary, I was sometimes favored with it; at other times I was very impatient. Then the prospect of liberty almost vanished away, and I was in darkness and perplexity.

I mention experience to you, that your hearts may not sink at the discouraging prospects you may have, and that you may put your trust in God, who sees your condition; and as a merciful father pitieth his children, so doth God pity them that love him; and as your hearts are inclined to serve God, you will feel an affectionate regard towards your masters and mistresses, so called, and the whole family in which you live. This will be seen by them, and tend to promote your liberty, especially with such as have feeling masters; and if they are otherwise, you will have the favor and love of God dwelling in your hearts, which you will value more than any thing else, which will be a consolation in the worst condition you can be in, and no master can deprive you of it, and as life is short and uncertain, and the chief end of our having a being in this world is to be prepared for a better, I wish you to think of this more than any thing else; then you will have a view of that freedom which the sons of God enjoy; and if the troubles of your condition end with your lives, you will be admitted to the freedom which God hath prepared for those of all colors that love him. Here the power of the most cruel master ends, and all sorrow and tears are wiped away.

To you who are favored with freedom—let your conduct manifest your gratitude toward the compassionate masters who have set you free; and let no rancor or ill-will lodge in your breast for any bad treatment you may have received from any. If you do, you transgress against God, who will not hold you guiltless. He would not suffer it even in his beloved people Israel [Deut. 23:7]; and you think he will allow it unto us? Many of the white people have been instruments in the hands of God for our good; even such as have held us in captivity, are now pleading our cause with earnestness and zeal; and I am sorry to say, that too many think more of the evil than of the good they have received, and instead of taking the advice of their friends, turn from it with indifference. Much depends upon us for the help of our color—more than many are aware. If we are lazy and idle, the enemies of freedom plead it as a cause why we ought not to be free, and say we are better in a state of servitude, and that giving us our liberty would be an injury to us, and by such conduct we strengthen the bands of oppression, and keep many in bondage who are more worthy than ourselves. I entreat you to consider the obligations we lie under to help forward the cause of freedom. We who know how bitter the cup is of which the slave hath to drink, O how ought we to feel for those who yet remain in bondage! will even our friends excuse—will God pardon us—for the part we act in making strong the hands of the enemies of our color?

Richard Allen

A Short Address to the Friends of Him Who Hath No Helper
I feel an inexpressible gratitude towards you who have engaged in the cause of the African race; you have wrought a deliverance for many from more than Egyptian bondage; your labors are unremitted for their complete redemption from the cruel subjection they are in. You feel our afflictions—you sympathize with us in the heart-rending distress, when the husband is separated from the wife, and the parents from the children, who are never more to meet in this world. The tear of sensibility trickles from your eye to see the sufferings that

keep us from increasing. Your righteous indignation is roused at the means taken to supply the place of the murdered babe; you see our race more effectually destroyed than was in Pharaoh's power to effect upon Israel's sons; you blow the trumpet against the mighty evil; you make the tyrants tremble; you strive to raise the slave to the dignity of a man; you take our children by the hand to lead them in the path of virtue, by your care of our education; you are not ashamed to call the most abject of our race brethren, children of one Father, who hath made of one blood all the nations of the earth. You ask for this, nothing for yourselves, nothing but what is worthy the cause you are engaged in; nothing but that we would be friends to ourselves, and not strengthen the bands of oppression by an evil conduct, when led out of the house of bondage. May He who hath arisen to plead our cause, and engaged you as volunteers in the service, add to your numbers, until the princes shall come forth from Egypt, and Ethiopia stretch out her hands unto God.

Our Savior's first and great work was that of the salvation of men's souls; yet we find that of the multitudes who came or were brought to him laboring under sickness and disorders, he never omitted one opportunity of doing good to their bodies, or sent away one that applied to him without a perfect cure; though sometimes, for the trial of their faith, he suffered himself to be importuned. And that he also often administered to the necessities of the poor in money, is plain from several passages of his life, one of which may suffice for the present, viz. When Satan had entered into Judas, and our blessed Savior had said, "That thou doest do quickly;" [John 13:27] none of the other disciples knew for what intent he had so spoken; for some of them thought, because Judas had the bag or common purse, that either he had ordered him to buy what was necessary against the feast, or (as was usual, no doubt, otherwise they could not have supposed it) that he should give something to the poor.

Our Savior's exhortations

To this unanswerable proof from our Savior's practice maybe added his repeated precepts and exhortations; for his examples and doctrines were always of a piece. A new commandment, says he, I give unto you, that ye love one another. By this shall all men know that ye are my disciples, if ye have love one to another [John 13:34, 35]. This is my commandment, that ye love one another as I have loved you. Greater love hath no man than this, that a man lay down his life for his friends [John 15:12, 13]. I say unto you which hear, love your enemies, and do good to them which hate you; bless them that curse you, and pray for them which despitefully use you [Matt 5:44]. Love your enemies, and do good and lend, hoping for nothing again; and your reward shall be great, and ye shall be the children of the Highest; for he is kind to the unthankful and to the evil. Be ye therefore merciful as your father also is merciful [Luke 6:35, 36]. From these few passages may be collected the nature, extent, and necessity of Christian charity. In its nature it is pure and disinterested, remote from all hopes or views of worldly return or recompense from the persons we relieve. We are to do good and lend, hoping for nothing again. In its extent it is unlimited and universal; and though it requires that an especial regard be had to our fellow Christians, is confined to no persons, countries, or places, but takes in all mankind, strangers as well as relations or acquaintances, enemies as well as friends, the evil and unthankful, as well as the good and grateful. It has no other measure than the love of God to us, who gave his only begotten Son, and the love of our Savior, who laid down his life for us, even whilst we were his enemies. It reaches not only to the good of the soul, but also to such assistance as may be necessary for the supply of the bodily wants of our fellow creatures.

And the absolute necessity of practicing this duty is the very same with that of being Christians; this being the only sure mark by which we may be known and distinguished from such as are not Christians or disciples of Christ. By this shall all men know that ye are my disciples, if ye have love one to another.

St. Paul

Hearken to St. Paul, speaking of this most excellent way or duty, and then judge ye, my brethren, of the necessity of putting it in practice. Though I speak with the tongue of men and angels, and have not charity, I am become as a sounding brass or a tinkling cymbal. And though I have the gift of prophecy, and understand all mysteries, and all knowledge, and though I have all faith, so that I could remove mountains, and have not charity, I am nothing. And though I bestow all my goods to feed the poor, and though I give my body to be burned, and have not charity, it profiteth nothing [1Cor. 13:1-3].

But these articles will receive a considerable light from the consideration of the second point, viz. the benefits and advantages arising from the practice of Christian charity.

In which, as the present occasion more especially points out to us, we may take a short general view of the advantages and benefits attending the exercise of that particular branch of Christian charity, which consists in the applying and bestowing some part of our substance, or the produce of our labors, towards the relief and support of the poor and needy; or in contributing towards such works of piety and mercy as are intended and contrived for the real good and bettering the condition of our indigent brethren, either by public or private ways of charity. And by this we improve our talents to the glory of God and the welfare of our own immortal souls.

Everything is from the Almighty

Consider, my brethren, that all we have and are is entrusted to us by Almighty God. In him we live, move, and have our being [Acts 17:28]. The earth is the Lord's, and the fullness (or plenty) thereof [Ps. 24:1]. We are consequently no more than his servants or stewards; the talents are all his; it is his substance that is distributed by him among us, to some more, to some less, as it has pleased him to entrust us with our own several portions or dividends; and to him we must give an account at the great day of reckoning, for every penny—for the improvement as well as for the principal.

Our blessed Lord has not committed his goods to us as a dead stock, to be boarded up, or to lie unprofitably in our own hands. He expects that we shall put them out to proper and beneficial uses, and raise them to an advanced value by doing good with them, as often as we have opportunity of laying them out upon the real interest and welfare of his poor children and subjects. By doing acts of mercy and charity we acknowledge our dependence upon God and his absolute right to whatever we possess through his bounty and goodness;

we glorify him in his creatures, and reverence him by a due and cheerful obedience to his commands. By applying our substance to the pomps and vanities of this wicked world or the gratification of the sinful lusts of the flesh, we deny God's right to what he hath thought fit to place in our hands; and disown him as our master by laying out his substance in ways expressly contrary to his orders; we thereby glorify Satan, whom we renounced at our baptism, and most shamefully dishonor our Maker by the abuse of his talents. When, therefore, we are called to a reckoning at that awful tribunal before which the most wealthy and powerful upon earth shall appear as naked and friendless as the poorest beggar, and when nothing but the goodness of our cause, and the mercy of our judge, can afford us the least support, if in that strict and solemn examination we have no better accounts to give in, than—so much laid out in luxury and extravagance, rapine and oppression; so much in a vexatious, litigious law-suit, or other idle, useless diversions, but little or nothing in charity. Shillings and pounds upon our vanity and folly, but scarce a few pence upon doing good! With what shame and confusion shall we hang down our heads, and wish for rocks and mountains to cover us, not only from the view of our justly offended master, but from the eyes of angels and men, all witnesses of our disgrace!

Have you shown love?

Some may perhaps say, "Well, I have refrained from debauchery, folly, and idleness; I have earned my honest penny, and kept it, and laid up a comfortable provision for my family." Be it so—this is laudable and praiseworthy, and it were to be wished that many more in this country would do so much. But may not such a one be asked, have you been charitable withal? have you been as industrious in laying up treasures in heaven, as you have been in hoarding up the perishable riches of this world? Have you stretched out your hand, as you had opportunity, beyond the circle of your own house and family? Have your poorer neighbors cause to bless you for your kind and charitable assistance? Have you dedicated any portion of your labors to God who blessed them, by doing good to any besides your own? Has the stranger, the widow, or the fatherless ever tasted of your bounty? If you have never done things of this kind, but have hitherto slighted, overlooked, or put off occasions of this sort, your talent is as yet hid in a napkin, it lies yet buried in the ground, huddled up within yourself. And consider farther, that the real poor and needy are Christ's representatives.

We cannot, surely, doubt of this, if we look into our Savior's own account of the last judgment, 25th chap. of St. Matthew's Gospel, which plainly shows us that the inquiry at that great and solemn day will be very particular about our works of mercy and charity: "Inasmuch as ye have done, or inasmuch as ye have not done it to the least of these my brethren, ye have done, or ye have not done it to me." When, therefore, an object of charity, or an opportunity of doing good, presents itself, the prudent Christian will not once deliberate, shall I relieve this man or this woman? shall I assist this widow, this orphan, or this poor child? No: he rather considers it as a demand made upon him by Christ himself, and would be as much afraid to delay or refuse payment in such case, as if he saw his Lord and Savior to ask it of him in person. The question, therefore, with him is this: Do not the holy Scriptures expressly teach me that whatsoever I do to my brethren who stand in need, will be reckoned to me as if I had done it to Christ himself? Can I relieve them without relieving him, or can I neglect them without slighting him? What hope could I have of being received and accepted of him at the last day, or that he will then hearken to my cries for mercy and forgiveness, should I be regardless of the requests he now makes to me by his members and representatives? I earnestly desire my Lord may have mercy upon me; therefore will I cheerfully show mercy to this his brother, however little or contemptible he may appear. I ardently wish my Lord may show goodness to me at the great day of reckoning; therefore will I seize the present opportunity of doing good, which he, in his good will towards me, now offers to my acceptance.

The accustoming ourselves to those acts, separates our affections from earthly things, learns us to sit loose to the world, and secures us treasures in heaven.

To people who are heartily in love with this world, who can see no greater happiness than wealth or power upon earth can afford them, such advantages, I own, are in no sort alluring. To talk of placing their affections upon possessions beyond the grave, or of lessening their present gains, in hopes of future benefits, is much to the same purpose as setting a most beautiful prospect before a blind man, or the most delicate meats before one who has lost his palate.

Love of the world

The person who has a due regard to his eternal salvation; who knows by experience how apt the love of earthly things is to draw off his affections from those of a heavenly nature; who remembers that he ought not to love the world, nor the things that are in the world, because the friendship of this world is enmity with God, and that whosoever will be a friend (or lover) of the world is the enemy of God [James 4:4]; who reflects that a time will come when he must part with all that is dear to him here: how necessary it is, therefore, to wean his mind from these perishable things, that they may give him no pain or uneasiness in quitting them, and is convinced that the whole world is of infinitely less value than the least inheritance in the kingdom of heaven. Such a one is always prepared to exercise himself in acts of mercy and charity; giving up a part, whenever opportunity offers of doing good, in token of his readiness to give up the whole whensoever God shall please to call upon him for it; and rejoices in the means afforded him of laying up treasures subject to no waste, rapine, or corruption, at the small expense of a trifling sum here; nay, is ready, should it appear necessary, to follow the advice of our Savior to his little flock, "Sell that ye have, and give alms; provide yourselves bags which wax not old, a treasure in the heavens which faileth not" [Luke 12:33].

In short, the love of this world is a heavy weight upon the soul, which chains her down, and prevents her flight towards heaven. Habitual acts of charity loosen her from it by degrees, and help her in her struggle to disengage herself and mount upwards.

A dying person would give the whole world, were it in his possession, for any rational assurance of acceptance with God, and an inheritance in the kingdom of heaven; why then will any man, who knows he must one day die, neglect the insuring it to himself by such works of mercy in his health and strength, as he may be assured will help him to mercy in a dying hour? Blessed are the merciful, saith our dear Redeemer, for they shall obtain mercy [Matt. 5:7].

Another advantage arising from acts of mercy and charity is, that they secure us the blessing and protection of heaven.

Care for the poor

Blessed is he, saith King David, who considereth the poor and the needy; the Lord will deliver him in the time of trouble. The Lord will preserve him and keep him alive, and he shall be blessed upon the earth, and thou wilt not deliver him into the will of his enemies. The Lord will strengthen him upon the bed of languishing: thou wilt make all his bed in his sickness [Ps. 41:1-3]. To be slow and uneasy at almsgiving, argues a strong distrust in providence, either that God cannot or will not make up to us what we thus bestow. To suppose he cannot, is to deny his Almighty power, and consequently that he is God. To imagine he will not, is to suspect his truth, who has not only promised eternal treasures in heaven, but has also engaged his sure word that he will repay it, even upon earth, as if it were lent to himself. He that hath pity upon the poor lendeth to the Lord; and that which he hath borrowed, he will repay him again.

Covetousness

With how great reason did our Savior so solemnly charge his disciples to beware of covetousness, since we see it borders so nearly upon infidelity? How strangely inconsistent is the narrow-hearted man with himself, with his own settled principles! He desires a blessing upon all that he has; he earnestly wishes for wealth and prosperity, yet cannot find in his heart to lay out a little of what he has to secure that blessing, that prosperity he aims at for himself and family, in doing these good and charitable actions which Providence throws in his way, and which God has assured him will purchase it! How much more rationally does the open-hearted benevolent Christian act, and upon what sure and steady principles does he proceed! This trifle, says he to himself, which I now bestow, may possibly be of some small present inconvenience to me; but it is given to God, and he will never suffer me to feel the want of it. My Savior has kindly insured to me whatever is necessary in this world, by promising, that if I first seek the kingdom of God and his righteousness, and these things, which others are toiling and sweating after, often to no purpose but vexation and disappointment, shall be added unto me. Here are both earthly and heavenly blessings laid before me, so that I cannot fail of a return from God, though he hath expressly ordered me to hope for nothing again from those I give to. I shall therefore assuredly reap according to my sowing—in this world, if God sees it good for me, but most certainly in the blessings of the next, if I grow not faint or impatient. My alms will ascend up before God for a memorial; and as he has taken the payment upon himself, I am convinced that even a cup of cold water thus bestowed, by those who have no more to give, will not lose its reward; for Jesus has promised, and in him all the promises of God are yea and amen.

Objections

Having thus gone through the proposed heads, and shewn the nature, the extent, and necessity of Christian charity; having pointed out the benefits and advantages arising from the practice of it, and how it secures to us the blessings both of this world and the world to come, it now remains that some common objections be considered, with a short application to the present design. Objections, I know, are many; and each person unwilling to contribute towards a charitable proposal will find out one of some kind or other, to ward off the blow that seems to aim at his very heart. Numerous, however, as they are, they appear so trifling, as to deserve little particular consideration, and might well enough be examined in bulk.

All objections to charitable contributions may well be supposed to arise from covetousness, or an unwillingness to part with the present penny. Covetousness is indeed a Goliath, a giant of the first magnitude, which is always ready to defy and set at naught the best formed arguments and motives drawn from reason and Scripture, all the armies of the living God. All the common pretences to prudence in the manner or time of giving charity, all hints of reserving it for better purposes, generally center in covetousness, in the love of money: and how wretched a fruit is to be expected from the root of all evil [1 Tim. 6:10], as St. Paul expressly calls it, let every one judge for himself.

Intentions matter

But the answer to all such pretences of prudence in bestowing, in short, is this: you may be deceived in the object, but you never can be deceived in your intention of charity, be the object ever go undeserving; nay, should I bestow money upon one in apparent necessity, who might abuse it to ill purposes, yet the good intention sanctifies my gift, consecrates it to God, and insures me a blessing, because it was done in his name and for his sake; while the whole abuse of it rests upon the guilty head of the vile person who thus basely misapplies my good deed. It may indeed be a reasonable objection against my giving a second time to that same person, but can be no excuse to me for withholding my hand from the relief of any other object which may appear another time to be in real want of charity.

And O! consider what a joyful thing it must be for a person in a dying hour to have a conscience free from offence, and to see their blessed Savior, with his arms stretched out, ready to receive them when their breath leaves the body, and saying, "Well done, thou good and faithful servant; thou hast been faithful over a few things, I will make thee ruler over many things; enter thou into the joy of thy Lord" [Matt. 25:21]. Are not these, my brethren and sisters, pleasures worth seeking after? are not these privileges, this freedom, and these possessions of far more value than thousands of worlds like this we live in, which we must all leave in a short time, and cannot carry with us into another life? And can you ever sufficiently admire the goodness of God, or ever be thankful enough to him for his loving kindness, who hath set these glories and these enjoyments as much within the reach of the poorest slave as of the greatest prince alive? For it is not power and high station that can purchase these heavenly possessions: they are only to be gained by goodness and serving of God; and the lowest of us can serve God as well as the richest person here below, and, by that means may adorn the doctrine of the Lord your God in all things, and bring more honor to Christ than many of higher rank and condition, who are not so careful of their souls as you may be.

When, therefore, we shall leave this impertinent and unsociable world, and all our good old friends that are gone to heaven before us, shall meet us as soon as we are landed upon the shore of eternity, and with infinite congratulations for our safe arrival, shall conduct us into the company of patriarchs, prophets, apostles and martyrs, and introduce us into an intimate acquaintance with them, and with all those brave and generous souls, who, by their glorious examples, have recommended themselves to the world; when we shall be familiar friends with angels and archangels; and all the courtiers of heaven shall call us brethren, and bid us welcome to their master's joy, and we shall be received into their glorious society with all the tender endearments and caresses of those heavenly lovers. What a mighty addition to our happiness will this be! There are indeed some other additions to the happiness of heaven, such as the glory and magnificence of the place, which is the highest heaven, or the upper and purer tracts of the ether, which our Savior calls Paradise.

Antipathy towards the heavenly life

In the temper of every wicked mind there is a strong antipathy to the pleasures of Heaven, which being all chaste, pure and spiritual, can never agree with the vitiated palate of a base and degenerate soul. For what concord can there be between a spiteful and devilish spirit, and the fountain of all love and goodness? between a sensual and carnalized one, that understands no other pleasures but only those of the flesh, and those pure and virgin spirits that neither eat nor drink but live forever upon wisdom, holiness, love and contemplation? Certainly till our mind is contempered to the Heavenly state, and we are of the same disposition with God and angels and saints, there is no pleasure in Heaven that can be agreeable to us. For as in the main we shall be of the same temper and disposition when we come into the other life as we are when we leave this, it being unimaginable how a total change should be wrought in us merely by passing out of one world into another, and therefore as in this world it is likeness that does congregate and associate beings together, so doubtless it is in the other world too, so that if we carry with us thither our wicked and devilish dispositions, (as we shall certainly do, unless we subdue and mortify them here) there will be no company fit for us to associate with, but only the devilish and damned ghost of wicked men, with whom our wretched spirits being already joined by a likeness of nature, will mingle themselves as soon as ever they are excommunicated from the society of mortals.

Heaven or hell?

For whither should they flock but to the birds of their own feather, with whom should they associate but with those malignant spirits, to whom they are already joined by a community of nature? So that supposing that when they land in eternity? it were left to their own choice to go to Heaven or hell, into the society of the blessed or the damned, it is plain that Heaven would be no place for them; that the air of that bright region of eternal day, would never agree with their black and hellish natures, for alas! what should they do among those blessed beings that inhabit it? To whose godlike natures divine contemplation and Heavenly employments, they have so great a repugnancy and aversion? So that, besides the having a right to Heaven, it is necessary to our enjoying it, that we should be antecedently disposed and qualified for it. And it being thus, God hath been graciously pleased to make those very virtues, the condition of our right to Heaven, which are the proper dispositions and qualifications of our spirits for it, that so, with one and the same labor, we might entitle ourselves, and qualify ourselves to enjoy it.

Richard Allen

JAMES FORTEN (1766-1842)

Introduction

James Forten was born in 1766 as a free Black man in Philadelphia, Pennsylvania. The son of Thomas and Sarah Forten and the grandson of slaves, Forten was raised in Philadelphia and educated in Anthony Benezet's Quaker school for colored children. James, aged eight, began working for Robert Bridges in his sail loft. Later, Forten invented a new type of sail, and so became very rich. He spent his amassed wealth on others as well as on himself and his family. More than half of his fortune was devoted towards abolitionist causes. He often purchased slaves their freedom, helped to finance William Garrison's newspaper, the *Libertarian*, opened his home on Lombard Street as an Underground Railroad depot, (the Underground Railroad was a vast network of people who helped fugitive slaves escape to the North and to Canada) and opened a school for Black children.

Put On the Armour of Righteousness
On the evening of April 14, 1836, the nineteen-year-old Forten presented an address to the Ladies' Anti-Slavery Society in Philadelphia which now follows.

Ladies
There is nothing that could more forcibly induce me to express my humble sentiments at all times, than an entire consciousness that is the duty of every individual who would wish to see the foul curse of slavery swept forever from the land—who wishes to become one amongst the undaunted advocates of the oppressed—who wishes to deal amongst the undaunted advocates of the oppressed—who wishes to deal justly and love mercy. In a word, it is my indispensable duty, in view of the wretched, the helpless, the friendless condition of my countrymen in chains, to raise my voice, feeble though it be, in their behalf; to plead for the restoration of their inalienable rights.

Pure motives
As to the character of the Anti-Slavery Society, it requires but one glance from an impartial eye, to discover the purity of its motives—the great strength of its moral energies; its high and benevolent-its holy and life giving principles. These are the foundations, the very architecture of Abolition, and prove its sovereignty. In fact, all associated bodies which have for their great aim the destruction of tyranny, and the moral and intellectual improvement of mankind, have been, and ever will, considered as bearing a decided superiority over all others. And how well may this Association, before which I now have the honor to appear, be deemed one of that description; and still more is its superiority increased from a knowledge of the truth that it is composed entirely of your sex.

A Christian perspective
It stands aloof from the storms of passion and political tumult, exhibiting in its extended

and Christian views a disposition to produce an immediate reformation of the heart and soul. Never before has there been a subject brought into the arena of public investigation, so fraught with humanity—so alive to the best interest of our country—so dear to all those for whose benefit it was intended, as the one which now calls you together. How varied and abundant—how eloquent and soul-thrilling have been the arguments advanced in its defense, by the greatest and best of the land; and yet, so boundless is the theme—so inexhaustible the fountain, that even the infant may be heard lisping a prayer for the redemption of the perishing captive.

A vitally important movement
Ladies. The task you are called upon to perform is certainly of vital importance. Great is the responsibility which this association imposes upon you; however, I need scarcely remind you of it, feeling confident that long before this you have made a practical and familiar acquaintance with all its bearings, and with every sentence contained in your society's sacred declaration; ever remembering that in it is concentrated one of the noblest objects that ever animated the breast of a highly favored people—the immediate and unconditional abolition of Slavery. It is the acknowledgement of a broad principle like this, and recommending it to a prejudiced public, who have been all along accustomed to reason upon the dangerous doctrine of gradualism, viewing it as the only safe and efficient remedy for this monstrous evil which has brought about such an excitement, and convulsed our country from North to South; an excitement which I have every reason to believe will prove a powerful engine towards the furtherance of your noble cause.

Opposition
As to this opposition now arrayed against you, terrible as it appears, it is no more than what you might anticipate; it is a fate which, in this age of iniquity, must inevitably follow such a change as your society proposes to effect. For what else is to be expected for a measure the tendency of which is to check the tide of corruption—to make narrower the limits of tyrannical power—to unite liberty and law—to save the body of the oppressed from the blood-stained lash of the oppressor—and to secure a greater respect and obedience to Him who wills the happiness of all mankind, and who endowed them with life, and liberty, as conducive to that happiness? What else, I repeat, can be expected but opposition, at a time like this, when brute force reigns supreme; when ministers of the Gospel, commissioned to spread the light of Christianity among all nations are overleaping the pale of the church, forsaking the holy path, and sowing the seeds of discord where they should plant the "olive branch of peace."

Loss of freedom
When liberty has dwindled into a mere shadow, its vitality being lost, shrouded in darkness, swallowed up as it were in the eternal dumbness of the grave. This, my friends, is the present situation of things, and warns you that the desperate struggle has commenced between freedom and despotism—light and darkness. This is the hour you are called upon to move with a bold and fearless step; there must be no luke-warmness, no shrinking from the pointed

finger of scorn, or the contemptuous vociferation of the enemy; no withholding your aid, or concealing your mighty influence behind the screen of timidity; no receding from the foothold you have already gained. To falter now, would be to surrender your pure and unsullied principles into the hands of a vicious and perverted portion of the community, who are anxiously waiting to see you grow weak and fainthearted; you would be casting the whole spirit and genius of patriotism into that polluted current just described. To falter now would retard the glorious day of emancipation which is now dawning, for years, perhaps forever.

But why should you pause? It is true that public opinion is bitter against you, and exercises a powerful influence over the minds of many; it is also true that you are frustrated in nearly every attempt to procure a place to hold your meetings, and the hue and cry is raised, "Down with the incendiaries—hang all who dare to open their mouths in vindication of equal rights;" still, this would be no excuse for a dereliction of duty; you are not bound to follow public opinion constantly and lose sight of the demands of justice; for it is plain to be seen that public opinion, in its present state, is greatly at fault; it affixes the seal of condemnation upon you without giving you an opportunity to be fairly heard; therefore I think the obligation ought to cease, and you pursue a more natural course by looking to your own thoughts and feeling as a guide, and not to the words of others. Again—in order to promote your antislavery principles you should make it the topic of your conversation amidst your acquaintances, in every family circle, and in the shades of private life. Be assured that by acting thus, hundreds will rise up to your aid. ...

An anti-Christian spirit

I rejoice to see you engaged in this mighty cause; it befits you; it is your province; your aid and influence is greatly to be desired in this hour of peril; it never was, never can be insignificant. Examine the records of history, and you will find that woman has been called upon in the severest trials of public emergency. That your efforts will stimulate the men to renewed exertion I have not the slightest doubt; for, in general, the pride of man's heart is such, that while he is willing to grant unto woman exclusively many conspicuous and dignified privileges, he at the same time feels an innate disposition to check the modest ardor of her zeal and ambition, and revolts at the idea of her managing the reins of improvement. Therefore, you have only to be constantly exhibiting some new proof of your interest in the cause of the oppressed, and shame, if not duty, will urge our sex on the march. It has often been said by anti-abolitionists that the females have no right to interfere with the question of slavery, or petition for its overthrow; that they had better be at home attending to their domestic affairs, &c. What a gross error-what an anti-Christian spirit this bespeaks. Were not the only commands, "Remember them that are in bonds, as bound with them," and "Do unto others as ye would they should do unto you," intended for women to obey as well as man? Most assuredly they were.

Devils incarnate

But from whom does this attack upon your rights come? Not, I am confident, from the respectable portion of our citizens, but invariably from men alienated by avarice and self-importance from the courtesy and respect which is due to your sex on all occasions; such "men of property and standing" as mingled with the rank, breath, and maniac spirit, of the mob at Boston, men (I am sorry to say) like the Representative from Virginia, Mr. Henry Wise, who, lost to all shame, openly declared you to be devils incarnate. And for what? Why, because the ladies in the several states north of the Potomac, in the magnitude of their philanthropy, with hearts filled with mercy, choose to raise their voices in behalf of the suffering and the dumb—because they choose to raise their voices in behalf of the suffering and the dumb—because they choose to exercise their legal privileges, and offer their time and talents as a sacrifice, in order that the District of Columbia may be freed, and washed clean from the stains of blood, cruelty and crime. It is for acting thus that you received so refined a compliment. Truly, some of our great men at the South are hand and hand in inequity: they are men after the heart of the tyrant Nero, who wished that all the Romans had but one neck that he might destroy them all at a single blow. This is just the position in which these Neros of a modern mould would like to place all who dare to utter one syllable against the sin of slavery—that is if they had the power.

Thought, feeling and action

But, Ladies, I verily believe that the time is fast approaching when thought, feeling and action, the three principal elements of public opinion, will be so revolutionized as to turn the scale in your favor; when the prejudice and contumely of your foes will be held in the utmost contempt by an enlightened community. You have already been the means of awakening hundreds from the deep slumber into which they have fallen; they have arisen, and put on the armor of righteousness, and gone forth to battle. Yours is the cause of Truth, and must prevail over error; it is the cause of sympathy, and therefore it calls aloud for the aid of woman.

Yours is the cause of Christianity; for it pleads that the mental and physical powers of millions may not be wasted—buried forever in ruins; that virtue may not be sacrificed at the altar of lasciviousness; making the South but one vast gulf of infamy; that the affections of a parent may not be sundered; that hearts may not be broken; that souls, bearing the impress of the Deity-the proof of their celestial origin and eternal duration—may not be lost. It is for all these you plead, and you must be victorious; never was there a contest commenced on more hallowed principles. Yes, my friends, from the height of your holy cause, as from a mountain, I see already rising the new glory and grandeur of regenerated—Free-—America!
. . .

James Forten

GEORGE LAWRENCE

Introduction

Little is known about George Lawrence, who delivered this New Year's Day oration. Lawrence was not among the early leaders of the African Methodist Episcopal Church in New York City, which was chartered in 1801 by black members of the John Street Methodist Church. There are no further known publications by George Lawrence. Abraham Thompson, who offered a prayer at the beginning of this service, was one of the founders of the church and, together with James Varick and Leven Smith, one of the first three ordained ministers of this new congregation.

This oration is an example of the New Year's antislavery sermon tradition within the early African Methodist Episcopal Church.

An Oration on the Abolition of the Slave Trade
This oration was delivered on January 1, 1813, in the African Methodist Episcopal Church.

Respected Audience,

We have again assembled with warm and grateful hearts, to celebrate our annual anniversary. It presents a period rendered venerable by the wise and humane fathers of our liberties, who laid the foundation of the happiness we now enjoy, and plucked from the very jaws of destruction, our devoted mother country. Gratitude then towards that veteran band of patriots, whose patriotism was crowned with justice, and shod with humanity, calls aloud. And shall we be backward in showing it? No, God forbid! The name of a Sharp, a Pitt, and a Fox, as the strong tower of our defense, cemented and made still stronger by the aid of many others, shall ever dwell with delight on our memories, and be treasured up in our hearts as the choicest gifts of heaven; for heaven gave them and heaven again shall receive them.

In our behalf they struggled long against a host of powerful and malignant enemies, who being supplied with the wisdom of Satan, and bound by the impulse of avarice, made an almost impenetrable defense: but that great and alwise being who holds the reigns of justice and destiny of nations, using them as arrows of his divine will, they passed the brazen walls of their opponents, and brought to light the august era of this thrice blessed and ever memorable day. Animated by the reverse of our hard fortunes, my brethren, and beholding the many blessings incident to our present situations: anticipating the advantages necessarily arising from the good work already begun, as we verge towards the summit of our happiness, it becomes us to make public our joy, for which purpose we are convened. We now celebrate the fifth anniversary of the Abolition of the Slave Trade, and a partial restoration of one of those rights most congenial to the human heart, it becomes the grand epoch of our boast; a day joyful to every bosom through whose veins our noble blood does flow, we hail it as the birth day of justice and triumph over atrocious vice; we rejoice for a nation rising from the dark and dreary gulf of desponding servitude and shining forth conspicuously as she ascends the lofty mount of arts and sciences, giving presages of future greatness; and should we not rejoice when we consider that we make a part of this nation, although we were never exposed to all the piercing blasts of adversity that they were, yet does the refulgent beams of prosperity, dilate our hearts with joy. We rejoice for the abolition of the slave trade; and our joy overflows when we reflect that this heaven born plant shall bring forth the full fruits of emancipation, and divulge that bright genius so long smothered in slavery.

Restoration of lost rights
The subject of this day calls for our serious attention; at the recurrence of this season we rejoice, not because we have gained a victory over our enemies by the arts of war, or that we have become rich and opulent, no, but it is the epoch that has restored to us our long lost rights. It is a subject congenial with my heart, and I cannot but regret my inability to do it justice, although confident, that was my talents equal to the most eloquent and profound orator that ever graced the world, I could not fully expound it. The task is arduous—even experience might shrink before its magnitude. The field is very extensive, presenting to view various objects of infinite magnitude; such as past sufferings, present mitigation, and future happiness.

Justice usurped
All buoyed up to sign on the sea of reflection, the first forms a melancholy spectacle; a scene fraught with misery and horror. We behold Asia, Europe and America, claiming an authority, as far distant from moral rectitude, or the laws of nature, as heaven is from hell. They usurp the throne of justice, and she takes her flight from off the face of the earth. They commence their traffic in the innocent sons and daughters of Africa. View them divide their spoils dragged from our mother country, a country once rich in the enjoyments of liberty and all the glory nature could afford. Nature there caused the wild desert to be more fruitful and fragrant than the best cultivated gardens, the inventions of men, ever could produce. Her inhabitants was happy seated in the very temples of bliss and with nature for their guide, their employments were innocent, neither did they seek evil, contented in the enjoyments of their native sports; they sued not for the blood of their fellow men; they arose in the morning with cheerfulness before their God, and bowed down their heads at night, fully sensible of his goodness. But ah, my friends! the scene changes. Alas! the rose was nipped in the bud, and too soon did the canker worm enter the trunk of its support. Africa! thou was once free, and enjoyed all the blessings a land and people could. Once help up as the ornament of the world, on they golden shores strayed Liberty, Peace and Equality; but the usurping power of accursed demagogues, brought desolation within thy borders, thy populous cities are laid waste, thy mourning millions loaded with chains, are driven from their native homes, and far and wide does the ravages of merciless power, extend like the besom of destruction, sweeping off thy inhabitants without regard to age or sex. Thus did the baneful deed of avaricious power pierce the hearts of our ancestors, separated and dashed asunder the most sacred ties of nature, and hurled them, my brethren, not only from their native country, but to enhance

their misery, separated them from their dearest relatives; the aged parent from the tender child; the loving husband from the affectionate wife.

The sufferings of our ancestors
We cast the eye of retrospection, and behold the field crimsoned with the blood of those slain; and the earth drinks deeply of the tears of those that yet live, but to meet a worse fate, [slavery] while the heavens reverberate with their shrieks, and nature stands amazed! Yet the scene does not end here; misery is still pouring in like a deluge; we view them hurried on board some floating dungeons, whose rules, more like fiends, were never in the shape of men. Tis here our ancestors drank the wormwood and the gall!—Tis here they even died for lack of that care, which is due to the most inferior of the brute creation!—Tis here some noble spirits fired with indignation, and disdaining to submit to savage rules, sought an asylum in the bosom of the sea!—Tis here death that grim monster, so dreaded by the nations of the earth, at whose approach crowned monarchs quake and tremble; at whose sight the countenance once flushed with the crimson vigor of health, turns pale, the vivid eye that flashed with cheerfulness, sinks dimly back in its sockets, not willing to meet this ghastly visage. But view the contrast: Here injured innocence leaps to meet him, and receives him as a bosom friend. Yet death is their only alternative, from a set of beings, who through various customs, and the impulse of avarice, had trampled under foot, the most sacred rights of their nature. They who commenced and supported a trade begun in savage wars, prosecuted by unheard of barbarity, and ended in perpetual exile and slavery.

But to harangue you on the sufferings of our ancestors I know is excruciatingly painful, yet bear with me a little, although it rends the tender heart, or forces the silent tear, it is expedient. In reflecting on their situation, our celebration demonstrates itself, to be fully sensible of ours; we need but view theirs. They were pressed down beneath the surface of nature; we soar aloft as the towering eagle to an eminence commanding a view of the world, and three fourths we behold drenched in human gore, and the loud clarion of war is foreboding their total destruction; thus while the dark clouds of strife and contention are encompassing them in, we enjoy the perpetual sunshine of peace and happiness. ...

Love shall never fail: the man of love shall be held in everlasting remembrance, his memory shall be blessed; no spices can so embalm a man, no monument can so preserve his name, as works of love. Love gives worth to all its apparent virtues, in so much that without it, no quality of the heart, no action of the life is valuable in itself, or pleasing to God. Without love, what is courage but the boldness of a lion, or the fierceness of a tiger? What is power but merciless oppression? What is justice but passion or policy? What is wisdom but craft and subtlety? Without love what is riches but a barren shore or congealed stream? And what is man, that noble structure, but the ravenous wolf, or more subtle viper? What is devotion but mockery of God? What is any practice, how auspicious soever in itself, or beneficial to others, but the effect of pride? For says one of the ancient worthies, though I had faith that I could remove mountains, and had not love, I am nothing. Though I give all my goods to feed the poor, and have not love, it profiteth me nothing [1Cor. 13:2, 3]. Love is the crystal fountain from whence flows all human happiness; its golden mines shall never be exhausted, its silver brooks shall never run dry. Let this then be our rallying point, for this shall ward against animosities and contentions—this shall bring down the blessings of heaven upon our heads—this shall cause our society to flourish, and this shall break the chain that still holds thousands of our brethren in bondage.

Advance the cause of freedom

My brethren, the land in which we live gives us the opportunity rapidly to advance the prosperity of liberty. This government founded upon the principles of liberty and equality, and declaring them to be the free gift of God, if not ignorant of their declaration, must enforce it; I am confident she wills it, and strong forebodings of it is discernable. The northern sections of the union is fast conceding, and the southern must comply, although so biased by interest, that they have become callous to the voice of reason and justice; yet as the continual droppings of water has a tendency to wear away the hardest and most flinty substance, so likewise shall we, abounding in good works, and causing our examples to shine forth as the sun at noon day, melt their callous hearts, and render sinewless the arm of sore oppression. My brethren, you who are enrolled and proudly march under the banners of the Mutual Relief, and Wilberforce Societies, consider your important standings as incorporated bodies, and walk worthy of the name you bear, cling closely to the paths of virtue and morality, cherish the plants of peace and temperance; by doing this you shall not only shine as the first stars in the firmament, and do honor to your worthy patrons, but immortalize your names. Be zealous and vigilant, be always on the alert to promote the welfare of your injured brethren; then shall providence shower down her blessings upon your heads, and crown your labors with success. It has been said by your enemies, that your minds were not calculated to receive a sufficient store of knowledge, to fit you for beneficial or social societies; but your incorporation drowned that assertion in contempt; and now let shame cover their heads, and blushes crimson their countenances. In vain they fostered a hope that our unfavorable circumstances would bear them out in their profane insinuations. But is that hope yet alive? No; or do we know where to find it? If it is to be found, it must be in the dark abysses of ignorance and folly, too little, too trifling for our notice.

Africans are not inferior

There could be many reasons given, to prove that the mind of an African is not inferior to that of an European; yet to do so would be superfluous. It would be like adding hardness to the diamond, or lustre to the sun. There was a time whilst shrouded in ignorance, the African was estimated no higher than beasts of burthen, and while their minds were condensed within the narrow compass of slavery, and all their genius damped by the merciless power of cruel masters, they moved in no higher sphere. Their nature was cramped in infancy, and depraved in riper years, vice was showed them for virtue, and for their labor and industry, the scourge was their only reward. Then did they seem dead to a better state, but it was because they were subject to arbitrary power; and then did their proud oppressors assert, though against their better judgment, that they were destined by nature to no better inheritance. But their most prominent arguments are lighter than vanity, for vacuous must the reasons of that man have been, who dared to assert that genius is confined to complexion, or that nature knows difference in the immortal soul of man: No! the noble mind of a Newton could find room, and to spare, within the tenement of many an injured African.

Our day star has risen

My brethren, the time is fast approaching when the iron hand of oppression must cease to tyrannize over injured innocence, and very different are the days that we see, from those that our ancestors did; yet I know that there are thousands of our enemies who had rather see us exterminated from off the earth, than partake of the blessings that they enjoy; but their malice shall not be gratified; they will, though it blast their eyes, still see us in prosperity. Our day star is arisen, and shall perform its diurnal revolutions, until nature herself shall change; and my heart glows with the idea, and kindles with joy, as my eye catches its radiant beams dispersing the dark clouds of ignorance and superstition. The spring is come, and the autumn nigh at hand, when the rich fruits of liberty shall be strewed in the paths of every African, or descendant, and the olive hedge of peace encompass them in from their enemies.

Some of the most profound historians inform us, that if there is any truth fully ascertained by reason or revelation, it is this; that man is but to be happy. Then it is evident that the human being never was formed for slavery; for between no two things in existence does there exist so irreconcilable opposition, as between the human mind and slavery. Water and oil, fire and snow, may, by the powerful arts of chemistry, be taught to forget their friendly antipathies, and rush together into friendly embraces; but by no arts can human nature, even in the earliest stage of action, be taught to salute slavery as a friend—no! Take the child of three days old, confine him in some obscure cell; and at once you behold anxiety and misery fixed on his countenance, square his life there agreeable to your own rule, with all the tenderness that state will afford, but teach him not to crave liberty if you can. No, there is a something within him, tells him liberty is his own, and to have it is all his study; his noble mind without the help of arts and sciences, soars aloft and beholds throughout creation to liberty all lay claim, from the almost indiscernible plant to the stately oak their liberty, commands, the brute creation through their train enjoying all the liberty they are capable of and shall man who God created free and pronounced lord of his creation be enslaved by his fellow man, heaven forbid; man was made to be happy, therefore liberty is his undoubted right.

A willing sacrifice

In all the ages of the world, whether we take the present or retrospective view, we behold mankind worshiping at the shrine of liberty, and willingly sacrificing their all in pursuit of that fair goddess. We behold the rational man walk undauntedly in the very jaws of death to retain his liberty; he surmounts all difficulties; wades through all danger; he industriously climbs the rough and craggy mount, and undauntedly leaps forth from its lofty and dangerous precipice if he but beholds the most distant gleams of liberty; so attractive, so congenial is liberty with the human heart: from the crowned monarch down to the lowest miscreant the world affords, all sue for this; yes, that particle of creation cannot be found that either by words or actions does not lay strong claim to this celestial good, and it is evident that all creation, both animal and vegetable, were destined for liberty, for neither can thrive or come to perfection without it, and he who called this world to light from the dark and loathsome abodes of chaos, caused liberty to be the golden pillars on which alone can happiness dwell secure.

Then Fathers, Brethren and Friends, although depressed under many grievances, yet the strong fibers of that pressure must give way, and the time is not far distant when our tree of liberty shall reach the sun, and its branches spread from pool to pool. Then let us stand firm in union, let us transmit to ages yet to come, deeds that shall bear record with time and not find their rival; let us cultivate the minds of youth; let your examples clothed with wisdom be strewed in their paths; by you let their tender minds be impressed with human principles; let your virtues shine conspicuously before them, as lamps that shall light them to a glorious victory over their enemies, and conduct them to the haven of immortal bliss; let malice and hatred be far from your doors; let your hearts be linked in the chain that bids defiance to the intrigues of your enemies; let not the cries of the widow and orphan pass you unnoticed: although this happy land abounds with humane institutions, yet has your individual aid, opportunities to alleviate the miseries of thousands; many are the miseries of our exiled race in this land, and dark are the clouds that shrouds them in woe. O! then, let us call forth our every power, arrayed in wisdom and ornamented with virtue, such as shall gain the applause of men and be sanctioned by God; these shall alleviate their present miseries and finally burst with the refulgent beams of liberty on their devoted heads.

George Lawrence

JOHN JEA (1773-?)

The Life, History, and Unparalleled Sufferings of John Jea, the African Preacher

I John Jea, the subject of this narrative, was born in the town of Old Callabar, in Africa, in the year 1773. My father's name was Hambleton Robert Jea, my mother's name Margaret Jea; they were of poor, but industrious parents. At two years and a half old, I and my father, mother, brothers, and sisters, were stolen, and conveyed to North America, and sold for slaves; we were then sent to New York, the man who purchased us was very cruel, and used us in a manner, almost too shocking to relate; my master and mistress's names were Oliver and Angelika Triebuen, they had seven children—three sons and four daughters; he gave us a very little food or raiment, scarcely enough to satisfy us in any measure whatever; our food was what is called Indian corn pounded or bruised and boiled with water, the same way burgo is made, and about a quart of sour butter-milk poured on it; for one person two quarts of this mixture, and about three ounces of dark bread, per day, the bread was darker than that usually allowed to convicts, and greased over with very indifferent hog's lard; at other times when he was better pleased, he would allow us about half-a-pound of beef for a week, and about half-a-gallon of potatoes; but that was very seldom the case, and yet we esteemed ourselves better used than many of our neighbors.

Hard labor

Our labor was extremely hard, being obliged to work in the summer from about two o'clock in the morning, till about ten or eleven o'clock at night, and in the winter from four in the morning, till ten at night. The horses usually rested about five hours in the day, while we were at work; thus did the beasts enjoy greater privileges than we did. We dared not murmur, for if we did we were corrected with a weapon an inch and-a-half thick, and that without mercy, striking us in the most tender parts, and if we complained of this usage, they then took four large poles, placed them in the ground, tied us up to them, and flogged us in a manner too dreadful to behold; and when taken down, if we offered to lift up our hand or foot against our master or mistress, they used us in a most cruel manner; and often they treated the slaves in such a manner as caused their death, shooting them with a gun, or beating their brains out with some weapon, in order to appease their wrath, and thought no more of it than if they had been brutes: this was the general treatment which slaves experienced. After our master had been treating us in this cruel manner, we were obliged to thank him for the punishment he had been inflicting on us, quoting that Scripture which saith, "Bless the rod, and him that hath appointed it." But, though he was a professor of religion, he forgot that passage which saith "God is love, and whoso dwelleth in love dwelleth in God, and God in him." And, again, we are commanded to love our enemies; but it appeared evident that his wretched heart was hardened; which led us to look up unto him as our god, for we did not know him who is able to deliver and save all who call upon him in truth and sincerity. Conscience, that faithful monitor, (which either excuses or accuses) caused us to groan, cry, and sigh, in a manner which cannot be uttered.

Masters acted as gods

We were often led away with the idea that our masters were our gods; and at other times we placed our ideas on the sun, moon, and stars, looking unto them, as if they could save us; at length we found, to our great disappointment, that these were nothing else but the works of the Supreme Being; this caused me to wonder how my master frequently expressed that all his houses, land, cattle, servants, and every thing which he possessed was his own; not considering that it was the Lord of Hosts, who has said that the gold and the silver, the earth, and the fullness thereof, belong to him.

Our master told us, that when we died, we should be like the beasts that perish; not informing us of God, heaven, or eternal punishments, and that God hath promised to bring the secrets of every heart into judgment, and to judge every man according to his works.

God's judgments

From the following instances of the judgments of God, I was taught that he is God, and there is none besides him, neither in the heavens above, nor in the earth beneath, nor in the waters under the earth; for he doth with the armies of heaven and the inhabitants of the earth as seemeth him good; and there is none that can stay his hand, nor say unto him, with a prevailing voice, what dost thou?

My master was often disappointed in his attempts to increase the produce of his lands; for oftentimes he would command us to carry out more seed into the field to insure a good crop, but when it sprang up and promised to yield plentifully, the Almighty caused the worms to eat it at the root, and destroyed nearly the whole produce; God thus showing him his own inability to preserve the fruits of the earth.

At another time he ordered the trees to be pruned, that they might have brought forth more fruit, to have increased his worldly riches, but God, who doth not as man pleaseth, sent the caterpillar, the canker worm, and the locust, when the trees bore a promising appearance, and his fond hopes were blasted, by the fruits being all destroyed. Thus was he again disappointed, but still remained ignorant of the hand of God being in these judgments.

Notwithstanding he still went on in his wickedness until another calamity befell him; for when the harvest was fully ripe, the corn cut down, and standing in shocks ready to be carried into the barn, it pleased God to send a dreadful storm of thunder and lightning, hail and rain, which compelled them to leave it out, till it rotted on the ground. Often were his cattle destroyed by distempers of various kinds; yet he hearkened not unto the voice of the Lord. ...

Seeing them act in such a wicked manner, I was encouraged to go on in my sins, being subject to all manner of iniquity that could be mentioned, not knowing there was a God, for they told us that we poor slaves had no God. As I grew up, my desire to know who their God was increased, but I did not know who to apply to, not being allowed to be taught by any one whatever, which caused me to watch their actions very closely; and in so doing, I, at one time, perceived that something was going forward which I could not comprehend, at last I found out that they were burying a slave master, who was very rich; they appeared to mourn and lament for his death, as though he had been a good man, and I asked them why they let him die; they said they could not help it, for God killed him: I said unto them, what, could you not have taken him away from God? They said, no for he killed whomsoever he pleased. I then said he must be a dreadful God, and was led to fear least he should kill me also; although I had never seen death, but at a distance. But this fear did not last long, for seeing others full of mirth, I became so too.

Defeated Indians

A short time after this, there were great rejoicings on account of a great victory obtained by the Americans over the poor Indians, who had been so unfortunate as to lose their possessions, and they strove against the Americans, but they over-powered and killed thousands of them, and numbers were taken prisoners, and for this cause they greatly rejoiced They expressed their joy by the ringing of bells, firing of guns, dancing and singing, while we poor slaves were hard at work. When I was informed of the cause of these rejoicings, I thought, these people made a great mourning when God killed one man, but they rejoice when they kill so many. I was thus taught that though they talked much about their God, they did not regard him as they ought. They had forgotten that sermon of our blessed Savior's on the mount, which you find in St. Matthew's gospel, chapter 5, verses 43, 44; and I had reason to think their hearts were disobedient, not obeying the truth, though it was read and preached to them; their hearts being carnal, as the Scriptures saith, were at enmity with God, not subject to the law of God, neither indeed could be, for they gave themselves up to the works of the flesh, to fulfill it in the lusts thereof. ...

Black devils

Our masters often told us we were made by, and like the devil, and commonly called us black devils; not considering what the Scriptures saith in the Songs of Solomon, "I am black, but comely. Look not upon me, because I am black, because the sun hath looked upon me; my mother's children were angry with me; they made me keeper of the vineyards; but mine own vineyard have I not kept." This latter sentence was verified in the case of us poor slaves, for our master would make us work, and neglect the concerns of our souls.

I hated Christians

From my observations of the conduct and conversation of my master and his sons, I was led to hate those who professed themselves Christians, and to look upon them as devils; which made me neglect my work, and I told them what I thought of their ways. On this they did beat me in a most dreadful manner; but, instead of making me obedient, it made me the more stubborn, not caring whether I lived or died, thinking that after I was dead I should be at rest, and that I should go back again to my native country, Africa (an idea generally entertained by slaves); but when I told them this, they chastised me seven times the more, and kept me short of food. In addition to this punishment, they made me go to a place of worship, while the other slaves enjoyed a rest for an hour or two; I could not bear to be where the word of God was mentioned, for I had seen so much deception in the people that professed to know God, that I could not endure being where there were, nor yet to hear them call upon the name of the Lord; but I was still sent in order to punish me, for when I entered the place I had such malice against God and his people, as showed the depravity of my heart, and verified that Scripture which saith, "That the natural man understandeth not the things which are of God, for they are foolishness unto him; neither doth he know them, because he is not spiritually discerned."

My rage and malice against every person that was religious was so very great that I would have destroyed them all, had it been in my power; my indignation was so increased on my entering the place of worship, that, "the form of my visage was changed," like Nebuchadnezzar's, when he ordered Shadrach, Meshach, and Abednego, to be cast into the fiery furnace. My fury was more particularly kindled against the minister, and I should have killed him, had I not feared the people, it not being in my power to kill him, grieved me very much; and I went home and told my master what the minister had said, and what lies he had told, as I imagined, in hopes that he would send me no more; but he knowing this was a punishment to me, he made me go the more, for it was evident it was not for the good of my soul; this pained me exceedingly, so that I laid the blame to the minister, thinking that it was through his preaching so many lies, as I thought in my foolish opinion, that I was obliged to attend, not knowing that he spoke the truth, and I told the lies. The more I went to hear him preach, the more I wished to lay in wait to take away his life; but, as when the preaching was over, I was forced to return home to my master, and tell him what I had heard, I had no opportunity. At one time, the minister said that God was in the midst of them, which astonished me very much, and I looked all about to see if I could see him, but I could not, and I thought I had as good eyes as any one; not having any idea that "God is a spirit, and they that worship him, must worship him in spirit and in truth," John iv. 24; and only to be seen by a spiritual mind in the exercise of faith. ...

My dear reader, consider the state I was in, I was nearly naked, and had scarcely food to eat, and when I complained, I was tied up, both hands and feet, or put in chains, and flogged, so that the blood would run from my back to the ground; at one time he broke two of my ribs, by stamping and jumping upon me. Consider what a great deliverance I experienced, being released from the bondage of sin and Satan, and delivered from the misery in which I was in, surely none else but the eternal God could effect so great a change.

I had sinned against God with an high hand and an out-stretched arm, and had said in my heart, who is God, or the Almighty, that I should fear him, and what profit is it that we have kept his ordinances, or that we have walked mournfully before the Lord of Hosts, Mal. iii. chap. part of the 14th verse. But for ever-blessed be the Lord God Almighty, who heareth the prayers and supplications of poor unworthy sinful creatures, for when I humbled myself, and walked mournfully before the Lord God Almighty, and kept his ordinances and his commandments, he sent his Spirit into my heart, which convinced me "Of sin, of righteousness, and of judgment to come." John xvi 8. This made me confess my sins and my wickedness, with shame and confusion of face; and when I had confessed my sins and my wickedness to God, with grief and sorrow in heart, "He was faithful and just to forgive me my sins, and to cleanse me from all unrighteousness." I John i. 13.

Deliverance

I was about fifteen years of age when the Lord was pleased to remove gross darkness, super-stition, and idolatry, from my heart, and shined upon me with the glorious reconciliation and light of his countenance, and turned my darkness into day, and created a clean heart within me, and renewed a right spirit within me, and said unto my soul, "Let there be light, (Gen. i. 3.) "and there was light." This "was the true Light, which lighteth every man that cometh into the [spiritual] world." John i. 9. He was in my heart, and my heart was made by him a clean, new, and fleshy heart, and the heart of stone he took away, as says the prophet Ezekiel, and he renewed a right spirit within me, and gave me a broken spirit, and a humble and contrite heart, which God wilt not despise. Jesus Christ now revealed himself to me, and appeared as, "The altogether lovely, and the chiefest among ten thousands," as he did to the church of old; and for my sorrow and sadness, he gave me joy and gladness in my heart: he also bound up my broken heart, and strengthened my feeble knees, and lifted up my hanging down hands, and comforted my mourning soul; as says the prophet Isaiah; yea, he also poured out the ointment of his grace, and to my sin-sick soul he made his strength perfect in my weakness; and found his grace sufficient for me, and caused me to exclaim in the language of the Psalmist, in the 103rd Psalm, "Bless the Lord, O my soul: and all that is within me, bless his holy name, &c."

This was the language of my heart, day and night, for his goodness and mercy, in deliv-ering me from a wounded conscience, and from a broken spirit, and from all the enemies that rose up against me. Yea, he delivered me from the temptations of the world, the flesh, and the devil; and drew my feet out of the miry clay and horrible pit; hewed me out of the rock of unbelief; and brought me through the waste howling wilderness of sin and iniquity, where my enemies laid in wait to destroy my soul, and watched to take away my life; doing every thing to prevent my rest; yet, they hooted, laughed, and scoffed at me; my master beating me to keep me from attending the house of God, but all this did not hinder me, for I blessed and praised his holy name that I was counted worthy to suffer with my blessed Jesus; and in all my sufferings I found the presence of God with me, and the Spirit of the Lord to comfort me. I found the hand of the Lord in every thing, for when I was beaten it seemed that the Spirit of the Lord was so great on me, that I did not regard the pain and trouble which I felt.... At other times when they gave me any refreshment, I acknowledged that it came from the immediate hand of God, and rendered unto him humble and hearty thanks in the best manner I could, as the Spirit gave me utterance, which provoked my master greatly, for his desire was that I should render him thanks, and not God, for he said that he gave me the things, but I said, no, it all came from God, for all was his; that the Spirit of God taught me so; for I was led, guided, and directed by the Spirit, who taught me all things which are of God, and opened them unto my understanding.

Thus I could join with John in the Revelations, saying, "Thou art worthy, O Lord, to receive glory, and honor, and power: for thou hast created all things, and for thy pleasure they are and were created." Rev. iv. 9. For I then viewed all the things upon the earth as coming from God, and I asked my master where the earth came from; from God or man, and who had made it. He answered, that God made it. Then said I unto him, if God made the earth, he made the things on the earth, and the things in the earth, and the waters under the earth, Exodus xx. 4. Yea, and besides this, he made the heaven also, and the things in heaven, and in the firmament of heaven, Gen. i. See Rev. v. 12, to the end. ...

Seek the Lord

I would therefore advise you, my dear reader, to endeavor, if you have not, to seek the Lord, to attain this blessing, and to shun that dreadful place of punishment which you have heard of. Consider the multitude of sins which thou hast committed, and remember, that "One leak will sink a ship," and one single sin will sink thy soul into everlasting perdition; or, in plainer terms, into that lake which burneth with fire and brimstone, where the worm dieth not, and the fire is not quenched. Read the ixth chapter of the gospel by St. Mark. Matthew xvi. 28 xvii. 1, 22. xviii. It Luke xi. 49. 1 Cor. xii. 3 Matthew x 42. xviii. 6 v. 29. xviii. 8. Isaiah lxvi. 24. Leviticus ii. 13. Matthew v. 13.

There are many, it is to be lamented, in our day that profess religion, but by their life and conduct they betray themselves, and crucify their Lord and Master, by putting him to an open shame; but a true Christian is merciful to all, endeavoring always to do good. But this was not the case with me, for before I knew God, it was always my delight to do evil in persecuting the people of God, and committing all manner of sin and wickedness, to my own shame and confusion; "Wherefore I give you to understand, that no man speaking by the Spirit of God calleth Jesus accursed: and that no man can say that Jesus is the Lord, but by the Holy Ghost." 1 Cor. xii. 3. "And whosoever shall give to drink unto one of these little ones a cup of cold water, only in the name of a disciple, verily I say unto you, He shall in no wise lose his reward." Matthew x. 42. "But whoso shall offend one of these little ones which believe in me, it were better for him that a millstone were hanged about his neck, and that he were drowned in the depth of the sea." Matthew xviii. 6. But I did not think while I was persecuting the people of God, that he was able to cast me, both soul and body, into hell, where the worm dieth not, and the fire is not quenched. My dear reader, if you cannot do the followers of Jesus any good, do not injure them; consider what a solemn assertion is made in their behalf. ...

Like a little child

But, to resume my narrative, when my heart was changed by divine grace, and I became regenerated and born again of the water and of the spirit, and became as a little child, I began to speak the language of Canaan to my master and mistress, and to my own friends, but it seemed to them as if I was mad, or like one that was mocking them, when I bid them leave off their sins and wickedness, by the aid of God's divine Spirit, and be saved by grace, through faith in the Lord Jesus Christ, and said that they must be regenerated and born again of the water and of the Spirit, or else they could not enter into the kingdom of heaven; showing them the necessity of that important doctrine by the conversation of Jesus Christ with Nicodemus, John iii. But, though they professed Christianity, they knew nothing of what it meant; which surprised me exceedingly, and I exclaimed, "Are ye Christians, and know not these things?" And when I had thus exclaimed unto them, they thought I had lost my reason; yea, my dear mother and sisters, my master and his family, in particular, thought so of me; thus, "My foes were those of my own house."

But being taught and directed by the Spirit of God, I told my master, mistress, my mother, sisters, and brothers, that there was nothing too hard for the Almighty God to do, for he would deliver me from their hands, and from their tyrannical power; for he had began the work of grace in my heart, and he would not leave it unfinished, for whatsoever grace had begun, glory would end. He gave me to see the first approach of evil; and he gave me power over my besetting sins, to cast them from me, and to despise them as deadly poison. He armed me with the whole armor of divine grace, whereby I quenched all the fiery darts of the wicked, and compelled Satan to retreat; and put him to flight by faithful and fervent prayer.

No fear of death

In addition to these he gave me power over the last enemy, which is death; that is, I could look at it without any fear or dread; though it is the most terrible of all other things. There is nothing in the world that we can imagine, so dreadful and frightful as death. It is possible to escape the edge of the sword—to close the lions' mouths—to quench the fiery darts;—but when death shoots its poisoned arrows—when it opens its infernal pit—and when it sends forth its devouring flames—it is altogether impossible to secure ourselves, to guard ourselves from its merciless fury. There is an infinite number of warlike inventions, by which we defeat the evil designs of the most powerful and dreadful enemies; but there is no stratagem of the most renowned general, no fortification, ever so regular or artificial, no army, ever so victorious, that can but for a moment retard the approaches of death; this last enemy, in the twinkling of an eye, flies through the strongest bulwarks, the thickest walls, the most prodigious towers, the highest castles, and the most inaccessible rocks; makes its way through the strongest barricades, passes over trenches, pierces the impenetrable armor, and through the best-tempered breast-plates it strikes the proudest hearts, it enters the darkest dungeon, and snatches the prisoners out of the hands of the most trusty and watchful guards. Nature and art can furnish us with nothing able to protect us from death's cruel and insatiable hands. There are none so barbarous, but they are sometimes overcome by the prayers and tears of such as implore their mercy; nay, such as have lost all sense of humanity and goodness, commonly spare in their rage, the weakest age and sex; but unmerciful death hath no more regard to such as are humble, than to those that resist and defy it; it takes no notice of infants' tears and cries, it plucks them from the breasts of their tender-hearted mothers; it stops its ears to the requests of trembling old age, and casts to the ground the gray heads as so many withered oaks. At a battle, when princes and generals of the enemy's are taken prisoners, they are not treated as common soldiers; but unmerciful death treads under feet as audaciously the prince as the subject, the master as the servant, the noble as the vassal, the rich Dives and the begging Lazarus; together it blows out with the same blast, the most glorious luminaries and the most loathsome lamps. It hath no more respect for the crowns of kings, the pope's miter, and the cardinal's cap, than for the shepherd's crook, or the poor slave's chains; it heaps them all together, and shuts them in the same dungeon.

There is no war, though ever so furious and bloody, but it is interrupted with some days, or at least some hours, of cessation or truce; nay, the most inhuman minds are at last tired with bloody conquests; but insatiable death never saith it is enough, at every hour and moment it cuts down multitudes of the human race; the flesh of all the animals that have died since the creation of the world, has not been able to glut this devouring monster. All warfare is doubtful, he that gains the victory to day, may soon after be put to flight; he that at present is in a triumphant chariot may become the footstool of his enemy; but death is always victorious, it triumphs with an insufferable insolence over all the kings and nations of the earth; it never returns to its den, but when loaded with spoils, and glutted with blood, the strongest Samson and the most victorious David, who have torn in pieces, and have overcome lions and bears, and have cut off the heads of giants, have at last yielded themselves, and been cut off by death. The great Alexanders and the triumphing Cæsars, who have made all the world to tremble before them, and conquered the most part of the habitable earth, could never find any thing that might protect them from death's power; when magnificent statues and stately trophies were raised to their honor, death laughed at their vanity, and made sport with their rich marbles, where so many proud titles are engraved, which cover nothing but a little rotten flesh and a few bones, which death had broken and reduced to ashes. ...

From the fear of death it pleased the Lord to deliver me by his blessed Spirit; and gave me the witness of his Spirit to bear witness with my spirit, that I was passed from death unto life, and caused me to love the brethren. At the time I received this full evidence and witness within me, I was about seventeen years of age, then I began to love all men, women, and children, and began to speak boldly in the name of the living God, and to preach as the oracles of God, as the Spirit and love of God constrained me.

For I beheld them wandering away from God, like lost sheep, which caused me to exhort them to turn unto the shepherd and bishop of their souls, from whom they had so greatly revolted, and to fly from the wrath to come. When they reviled me, I told them of Christ's example: "Who did no sin, neither was guile found in his mouth: Who, when he was reviled, reviled not again; when he suffered, he threatened not; but committed himself to him that judgeth righteously." I Peter ii. 22 23. And I endeavored to follow his steps, by exhorting and praying for them to turn from their evil ways, although they were so inveterated against me, and strove to the utmost of their power to make me suffer as an evil-doer. But, blessed be God, that I counted it all joy that I was worthy to suffer for the glory of God, and for the good of my soul. See I Peter iii. 14—17.

Public testimony

I was sold to three masters, all of whom spoke ill of me, and said that I should spoil the rest of the slaves, by my talking and preaching. The last master I was sold to, I ran from to the house of God, and was baptized unknown to him; and when the minister made it known to him, he was like a man that had lost his reason, and swore that I should not belong to any society; but the minister informed him it was too late, for the work was already finished, and according to the spiritual law of liberty, I was considered a worthy member of society. My master then beat me most cruelly, and threatened to beat the minister over the head with a cane. He then took me before the magistrates, who examined me, and inquired what I knew about God and the Lord Jesus Christ. Upon this I made a public acknowledgment before the magistrates, that God, for Christ's sake, had pardoned my sins and blotted out all mine iniquities, through our Lord Jesus Christ, whereby he was become my defense and deliverer; and that there is no other name under heaven, given to man, whereby he shall be saved, but only in the name of our Lord Jesus Christ. On hearing this, the magistrates told me I was free from my master, and at liberty to leave him; but my cruel master was very unwilling to part with me, because he was of the world. "They are of the world: therefore speak they of the world, and the world heareth them." I John iv. 5. This was evident, for if my master had been of God he would have instructed me in the Scriptures, as God had given him ability, and according to the oracles of the living God; for we have all one father, and if any man teach let him do it as God gives him ability; so saith the Scriptures. But my master strove to baffle me, and to prevent me from understanding the Scriptures: so he used to tell me that there was a time to every purpose under the sun, to do all manner of work, that slaves were in duty bound to do whatever their masters commanded them, whether it was right or wrong; so that they must be obedient to a hard spiteful master as to a good one. He then took the bible and showed it to me, and said that the book talked with him. Thus he talked with me endeavoring to convince me that I ought not to leave him, although I had received my full liberty from the magistrates, and was fully determined, by the grace of God, to leave him; yet he strove to the uttermost to prevent me; but thanks be to God, his strivings were all in vain. ...

Illumination

The Lord heard my groans and cries at the end of six weeks, and sent the blessed angel of the covenant to my heart and soul, to release me from all my distress and troubles, and delivered me from all mine enemies, which were ready to destroy me; thus the Lord was pleased in his in finite mercy, to send an angel, in a vision, in shining raiment, and his countenance shining as the sun, with a large bible in his hands, and brought it unto me, and said, "I am come to bless thee, and to grant thee thy request," as you read in the Scriptures. Thus my eyes were opened at the end of six weeks, while I was praying, in the place where I slept; although the place was as dark as a dungeon, I awoke, as the Scripture saith, and found it illuminated with the light of the glory of God, and the angel standing by me, with the large book open, which was the Holy Bible, and said unto me, "Thou hast desired to read and understand this book, and to speak the language of it both in English and in Dutch; I will therefore teach thee, and now read;" and then he taught me to read the first chapter of the gospel according to St. John; and when I had read the whole chapter, the angel and the book were both gone in the twinkling of an eye, which astonished me very much, for the place was dark immediately; being about four o'clock in the morning in the winter season. After my astonishment had a little subsided, I began to think whether it was a fact that an angel had taught me to read, or only a dream; for I was in such a strait, like Peter was in the prison, when the angel smote him on the side, and said unto Peter, "Arise, Peter, and take thy garment, and spread it around thee, and follow me." And Peter knew not whether it was a dream or not; and when the angel touched him the second time, Peter arose, took his garment, folded it around him, and followed the angel, and the gates opened unto him of their own accord. So it was with me when the room was darkened again, that I wondered within myself whether I could read or not, but the Spirit of the Lord convinced me that I could; I then went out of the house to a secret place, and there rendered thanksgivings and praises unto God's holy name, for his goodness in showing me to read his holy word, to understand it, and to speak it, both in the English and Dutch languages.

I tarried at a distance from the house, blessing and praising God, until the dawning of the day, and by that time the rest of the slaves were called to their labor; they were all very much surprised to see me there so early in the morning, rejoicing as if I had found a pearl of great price, for they used to see me very sad and grieved on other mornings, but now rejoicing, and they asked me what was the reason of my rejoicing more now than at other times, but I answered I would not tell them. After I had finished my day's work I went to the minister's house, and told him that I could read, but he doubted greatly of it, and said unto me, "How is it possible that you can read? For when you were a slave your master would not suffer any one, whatever, to come near you to teach you, nor any of the slaves, to read; and it is not long since you had your liberty, not long enough to learn to read." But I told him, that the Lord had learnt me to read last night. He said it was impossible. I said, "Nothing is impossible with God, for all things are possible with him; but the thing impossible with man is possible with God: for he doth with the host of heaven, and with the inhabitants of the earth, as he pleaseth, and there is none that can withstay his hand, nor dare to say what dost thou? And so did the Lord with me as it pleased him, in shewing me to read his word, and to speak it, and if you have a large bible, as the Lord showed me last night, I can read it." But he said, "No, it is not possible that you can read." This grieved me greatly, which caused me to cry. His wife then spoke in my behalf, and said unto him, "You have a large bible, fetch it, and let him try and see whether he can read it or not, and you will then be convinced." The minister then brought the bible to me, in order that I should read; and as he opened the Bible for me to read, it appeared unto me, that a person said, "That is the place, read it." Which was the first chapter of the gospel of St. John, the same Lord had taught me to read. So I read to the minister; and he said to me, "You read very well and very distinct;" and asked me who had learnt me. I said the Lord had learnt me last night. He said that it was impossible; but, if it were so, he should find it out. On saying this he went and got other books, to see whether I could read them; I tried, but could not. He then brought a spelling book, to see if I could spell; but he found to his great astonishment, that I could not. This convinced him and his wife that it was the Lord's work, and it was marvelous in their eyes. ...

From that hour, in which the Lord taught me to read, until the present, I have not been able to read in any book, nor any reading whatever, but such as contain the word of God. ...

Preaching

I was now enabled, by the assistance of the Holy Spirit, to go from house to house, and from plantation to plantation, warning sinners, in the name of Jesus, to flee from the wrath to come; teaching and admonishing them to turn from their evil course of life; whilst some mocked and others scoffed at me, many said that I was mad, others pointed at me, and said there goes "the preacher," in a mocking and jeering manner. Sometimes after I had been preaching in a house, and was leaving it, some of the people, who were assembled together, without the door, would beat and use me in a very cruel manner, saying, as the Jews of old did to Jesus Christ, when they smote him with the palms of their hands, "Prophesy unto us who it was that smote thee?"

One soul

But, for ever blessed be the Lord, he was pleased to give me one soul for my hire, and one seal to my ministry; which caused me to bless the Lord, and ascribe all the honor and glory to his name, for not having let my labors been in vain. This poor, soul to whom the Lord was pleased to bless my feeble endeavors, was a poor black slave, the same as I had been; the Lord in infinite mercy, was pleased to liberate his soul from the bondage of sin and Satan, and afterwards from his cruel master.

It was a law of the state of the city of New York, that if any slave could give a satisfactorily account of what he knew of the work of the Lord on his soul he was free from slavery, by the Act of Congress, that was governed by the good people the Quakers, who were made the happy instruments, in the hands of God, of releasing some thousands of us poor black slaves from the galling chains of slavery.

After this poor man had received his liberty from slavery, he joined me in hand and heart, willing "To follow the Lamb of God whithersoever he goeth." His employment while with his master, was sweeping chimneys; but now his master, who was God, had given him his labor to endeavor to sweep the evils out of the hearts of poor slaves. He and I used to go from house to house, and in barns and under hedges, preaching the gospel of Christ, as the Spirit of God gave us utterance; and God added unto our number such as should be saved. In the course of about nineteen months, it pleased the Lord to add to our number about five hundred souls; and when we could not find room enough in the houses, we used to preach out of doors in the fields and woods, which we used to call our large chapel, and there we assembled together on Saturday evenings about eleven o'clock, after the slaves had done their masters' work, and continued until Sunday evening about ten or eleven o'clock. The other black man and myself used to go fourteen miles of a night to preach, and to instruct our poor fellow brethren, and thought ourselves well paid for our trouble in having a congregation together in the name of the Lord.

Take care

My dear reader, take care what company you keep, and take care whom you eat and drink with; for many would almost persuade you that they were saints, but by their gluttonness way of living, their hearts are like a knife to your throat. See Proverbs xxiii. 1-12.

Teaching slaves

We told the poor slaves that God had promised to deliver them that call upon him in time of trouble, out of all their distress; for "He would be with them in six troubles, and in the seventh he would not forsake them." We encouraged them to be angry with, and not to commit, sin, as the Scripture saith, "Be ye angry, and sin not;" For sin brought all their punishment upon them, whatever they suffered; therefore, I exhorted them to hate sin, and to fly from it as from the face of a serpent; and to remember that our blessed Lord had said, that we should have persecution in the world, but in him we should have peace; for the world hated him, and the world knew him not, and therefore they would hate us, because they hated him first; for they knew him not, neither do they know us, because he has chosen us out of the world; therefore our Lord has said, "It is through many tribulations that you shall enter the kingdom of heaven: for ye shall be hated of all men for my name's sake, and they shall cast out your name as evil, and they that kill you will think that they do God service; and they shall say all manner of evil against you falsely, for my sake. Rejoice, and be exceeding glad: for great is your reward in heaven: for so persecuted they the prophets and apostles that were before you." We encouraged them in the Christian life, and said to them "Finally, be ye all of one mind, having compassion one of another, love as brethren, be pitiful, be courteous: Not rendering evil for evil, or railing for railing: but contrariwise blessing; knowing that ye are thereunto called, that ye should inherit a blessing. For he that will love life, and see good days, let him refrain his tongue from evil, and his lips that they speak no guile: Let him eschew evil, and do good; let him seek peace, and ensue it. For the eyes of the Lord are over the righteous, and his ears are open unto their prayers; but the face of the Lord is against them that do evil." 1 Peter iii. 8-12.

Thus we went on preaching in the name of the Lord, and it pleased God to bless our feeble efforts, by adding unto our number such as should be saved.

White friends

At this time the Lord was pleased to raise up some white friends, who were benevolent and kind to us, when they saw our simpleness, and that God prospered us in our manner and way of worship; who joined their mites with ours, and purchased a piece of ground, and built upon it a meeting-house, in the city of New York, for us poor black Africans to worship in, which held about fifteen hundred people! They also procured white preachers twice a week to preach, to assist the other black man and myself.

Being thus highly favored, we now had preaching three times on the Sabbath-day, and every night in the week; and the number of them that were added unto the society, was about nine hundred and fifty souls!

I continued at this place four years after that, preaching with the other preachers; for we were appointed to preach in rotation. The word of the Lord grew and multiplied exceedingly, for it pleased the Lord, sometimes at one service, to add to our number fifteen souls! and, sometimes more! At our watch nights and camp meetings, I have known one hundred and fifty, or two hundred, awakened at one time; by which it was evident that the time was like the day of Pentecost; which you have an account of in the second chapter of Acts.

The Lord's converting spirit

Thus, when we were assembled together with one accord, the Lord was pleased to send down his convincing and converting spirit, to convince and convert the congregation, and they were filled with the spirit of prayer, which caused them to groan and cry unto God, begging him to have mercy upon their never-dying souls, to such a degree, that it caused some to say, that the people were drunk, others said they were possessed with devils, many said they were mad, and others laughing, mocking, and scoffing at them; while the people came running in out of the streets and houses to see what was the matter; and many of them were convinced of sin, and of righteousness, and of judgment to come; crying out with the jailor of old, "What shall we do to be saved?" We still continued speaking as the Spirit gave us utterance.

It was our heart's desire, and prayer to God, that every sinner might be saved; so we went on in the strength of God, by the aid of his Spirit, warning sinners every where to repent and believe the gospel, that their souls might be saved through grace, by faith in the Lord Jesus Christ. When the congregation grew numerous, and there were enough preachers besides myself, I was then constrained by the Spirit, and the love of God, to go about four hundred miles from thence, to preach the everlasting gospel to the people there, at a place called Boston, in North America. I continued preaching there about three years and a half, and the Lord crowned my feeble endeavors with great success, and gave me souls for my hire, and seals to my ministry. ...

I cannot write

My dear reader, I would now inform you, that I have stated this in the best manner I am able, for I cannot write, therefore it is not quite so correct as if I had been able to have written it myself; not being able to notice the time and date when I left several places, in my travels from time to time, as many do when they are traveling; nor would I allow alterations to be made by the person whom I employed to print this Narrative.

Now, dear reader, I trust by the grace of God, that the small house in Hawk Street, which the Lord hath been pleased to open unto me, for the public worship of his great and glorious name, will be filled with converts, and that my feeble labors will be crowned with abundant success.

John Jea

PETER WILLIAMS (1780-1840)

Introduction

The Rev. Peter Williams was born in New Brunswick, New Jersey, and died in New York city, on 18 October, 1840. His Negro father, also called Peter, was born a slave, but became sexton of the 1st Methodist Episcopal church in New York in 1796, before becoming a merchant. His son Peter Williams, a Protestant Episcopalian, was ordained in 1820 by Bishop John H. Hobart.

On March 2, 1807 Congress enacted a law that banned the external slave trade beginning January 1, 1808. After this enslaved people could no longer be brought to the United States. Although the law would be frequently violated until the eve of the Civil War, many black and white anti-slavery activists hailed it as the first major step toward banning slavery itself. To celebrate the passing of this act, one of those activists, the young Rev. Peter Williams, Jr. delivered this address in the New York African Church in New York City on January 1, 1808.

An Oration on the Abolition of the Slave Trade

Fathers, Brethren, and Fellow Citizens: At this auspicious moment I felicitate you on the abolition of the Slave Trade. This inhuman branch of commerce, which, for some centuries past, has been carried on to a considerable extent, is, by the singular interposition of Divine Providence, this day extinguished. An event so important, so pregnant with happy consequences, must be extremely consonant to every philanthropic heart.

But to us, Africans and descendants of Africans, this period is deeply interesting. We have felt, sensibly felt, the sad effects of this abominable traffic. It has made, if not ourselves, our forefathers and kinsmen its unhappy victims; and pronounced on them, and their posterity, the sentence of perpetual slavery. But benevolent men have voluntarily stepped forward to obviate the consequences of this injustice and barbarity. They have striven assiduously, to restore our natural rights; to guaranty them from fresh innovations; to furnish us with necessary information; and to stop the source from whence our evils have flowed.

The fruits of these laudable endeavors have long been visible; each moment they appear more conspicuous; and this day has produced an event which shall ever be memorable and glorious in the annals of history. We are now assembled to celebrate this momentous era; to recognize the beneficial influences of humane exertions; and by suitable demonstrations of joy, thanksgiving, and gratitude, to return to our heavenly Father, and to our earthly benefactors, our sincere acknowledgments.

This history of the Slave Trade

Review, for a moment, my brethren, the history of the Slave Trade. Engendered in the foul recesses of the sordid mind, the unnatural monster inflicted gross evils on the human race. Its baneful footsteps are marked with blood; its infectious breath spreads war and desolation; and its train is composed of the complicated miseries of cruel and unceasing bondage.

Before the enterprising spirit of European genius explored the western coast of Africa, the state of our forefathers was a state of simplicity, innocence, and contentment. Unskilled in the arts of dissimulation, their bosoms were the seats of confidence; and their lips were the organs of truth. Strangers to the refinements of civilized society, they followed with implicit obedience the (simple) dictates of nature. Peculiarly observant of hospitality, they offered a place of refreshment to the weary, and an asylum to the unfortunate. Ardent in their affections, their minds were susceptible of the warmest emotions of love, friendship, and gratitude.

Although unacquainted with the diversified luxuries and amusements of civilized nations, they enjoyed some singular advantages from the bountiful hand of nature and from their own innocent and amiable manners, which rendered them a happy people. But alas! this delightful picture has long since vanished; the angel of bliss has deserted their dwelling; and the demon of indescribable misery has rioted, uncontrolled, on the fair fields of our ancestors.

After Columbus unfolded to civilized man the vast treasures of this western world, the desire of gain, which had chiefly induced the first colonists of America to cross the waters of the Atlantic, surpassing the bounds of reasonable acquisition, violated the sacred injunctions of the gospel, frustrated the designs of the pious and humane, and enslaving the harmless aborigines, compelled them to drudge in the mines.

The severities of this employment was so insupportable to men who were unaccustomed to fatigue that, according to Robertson's "History of America," upwards of nine hundred thousand were destroyed in the space of fifteen years on the island of Hispaniola. A consumption so rapid must, in a short period, have deprived them of the instruments of labor, had not the same genius which first produced it found out another method to obtain them. This was no other than the importation of slaves from the coast of Africa.

The Genoese made the first regular importation, in the year 1517, by virtue of a patent granted by Charles of Austria to a Flemish favorite; since which, this commerce has increased to an astonishing and almost incredible degree.

After the manner of ancient piracy, descents were first made on the African coast; the towns bordering on the ocean were surprised, and a number of the inhabitants carried into slavery.

Alarmed at these depredations, the natives fled to the interior, and there united to secure themselves from the common foe. But the subtle invaders were not easily deterred from their purpose. Their experience, corroborated by historical testimony, convinced them that this spirit of unity would baffle every violent attempt; and that the most powerful method to dissolve it would be to diffuse in them the same avaricious disposition which they themselves possessed; and to afford them the means of gratifying it, by ruining each other. Fatal engine: fatal thou hast proved to man in all ages: where the greatest violence has proved ineffectual, their undermining principles have wrought destruction. By the deadly power, the strong Grecian arm, which bid the world defiance, fell nerveless; by thy potent attacks, the solid pillars of Roman grandeur shook to their base; and, Oh! Africans! by this parent of the Slave Trade, this grandsire of misery, the mortal blow was struck which crushed the peace and happiness of our country. Affairs now assumed a different aspect; the appearances of war were changed into the most amicable pretensions; presents apparently inestimable were made; and all the bewitching and alluring wiles of the seducer were practiced. The harmless African, taught to believe a friendly countenance, the sure token of a corresponding heart, soon disbanded his fears and evinced a favorable disposition towards his flattering enemies.

Thus the foe, obtaining an intercourse by a dazzling display of European finery, bewildered their simple understandings and corrupted their morals. Mutual agreements were then made; the Europeans were to supply the Africans with those gaudy trifles which so strongly affected them; and the Africans in return were to grant the Europeans their prisoners of war and convicts as slaves. These stipulations, naturally tending to delude the mind, answered the twofold purpose of enlarging their criminal code and of exciting incessant war at the same time that it furnished a specious pretext for the prosecution of this inhuman traffic. Bad as this may appear, had it prescribed the bounds of injustice, millions of unhappy victims might have still been spared. But, extending widely beyond measure and without control, large additions of slaves were made by kidnapping and the most unpalliated seizures.

Violation of human rights

Trace the past scenes of Africa and you will manifestly perceive these flagrant violations of human rights. The prince who once delighted in the happiness of his people, who felt himself bound by a sacred contract to defend their persons and property, was turned into their tyrant and scourge: he, who once strove to preserve peace and good understanding with the different nations, who never unsheathed his sword but in the cause of justice, at the signal of a slave ship assembled his warriors and rushed furiously upon his unsuspecting friends. What a scene does that town now present, which a few moments past was the abode of tranquility. At the approach of the foe, alarm and confusion pervade every part; horror and dismay are depicted on every countenance; the aged chief, starting from his couch, calls forth his men to repulse the hostile invader: all ages obey the summons; feeble youth and decrepit age join the standard; while the foe, to effect his purpose, fires the town.

Now, with unimaginable terror the battle commences: hear now the shrieks of the women, the cries of the children, the shouts of the warriors, and the groans of the dying. See with what desperation the inhabitants fight in defense of their darling joys. But, alas! overpowered by a superior foe, their force is broken; their ablest warriors fall; and the wretched remnant are taken captives.

Where are now those pleasant dwellings, where peace and harmony reigned incessant? where those beautiful fields, whose smiling crops and enchanting verdure enlivened the heart of every beholder? Alas! those tenements are now enveloped in destructive flames; those fair fields are now bedewed with blood and covered with mangled carcasses. Where are now those sounds of mirth and gladness, which loudly rang throughout the village? where those darling youth, those venerable aged, who mutually animated the festive throng? Alas! those exhilarating peals are now changed into the dismal groans of inconceivable distress;

the survivors of those happy people are now carried into cruel captivity. Ah! driven from their native soil, they cast their languishing eyes behind, and with aching hearts bid adieu to every prospect of joy and comfort.

A spectacle so truly distressing is sufficient to blow into a blaze the most latent spark of humanity; but, the adamantine heart of avarice, dead to every sensation of pity, regards not the voice of the sufferers, but hastily drives them to market for sale.

Horrid inhumanities

Oh Africa, Africa! to what horrid inhumanities have thy shores been witness; thy shores, which were once the garden of the world, the seat of almost paradisiacal joys, have been transformed into regions of woe; thy sons, who were once the happiest of mortals, are reduced to slavery, and bound in weighty shackles, now fill the trader's ship. But, though defeated in the contest for liberty, their magnanimous souls scorn the gross indignity, and choose death in preference to slavery. Painful; ah! painful, must be that existence which the rational mind can deliberately doom to self destruction. Thus the poor Africans, robbed of every joy, while they see not the most transient, glimmering, ray of hope to cheer their saddened hearts, sink into the abyss of consummate misery. Their lives, embittered by reflection, anticipation, and present sorrows, they feel burthensome; and death (whose dreary mansions appall the stoutest hearts) they view as their only shelter.

You, my brethren, beloved Africans, who had passed the days of infancy when you left your country, you best can tell the aggravated sufferings of our unfortunate race; your memories can bring to view these scenes of bitter grief. What, my brethren, when dragged from your native land on board the slave ship, what was the anguish which you saw, which you felt? what the pain, what the dreadful forebodings which filled your throbbing bosoms?

But you, my brethren, descendants of African forefathers, I call upon you to view a scene of unfathomable distress. Let your imagination carry you back to former days. Behold a vessel, bearing our forefathers and brethren from the place of their nativity to a distant and inhospitable clime; behold their dejected countenances, their streaming eyes, their fettered limbs; hear them, with piercing cries, and pitiful moans, deploring their wretched fate. After their arrival in port, see them separated without regard to the ties of blood or friendship: husband from wife; parent from child; brother from sister; friend from friend. See the parting tear rolling down their fallen cheeks; hear the parting sigh die on their quivering lips.

Africans rejoice

But let us no longer pursue a theme of boundless affliction. An enchanting sound now demands your attention. Hail! hail! glorious day, whose resplendent rising disperseth the clouds which have hovered with destruction over the land of Africa, and illumines it by the most brilliant rays of future prosperity. Rejoice, Oh! Africans! No longer shall tyranny, war, and injustice, with irresistible sway, desolate your native country; no longer shall torrents of human blood deluge its delightful plains; no longer shall it witness your countrymen wielding among each other the instruments of death; nor the insidious kidnapper, darting from his midnight haunt, on the feeble and unprotected; no longer shall its shores resound with the awful howlings of infatuated warriors, the deathlike groans of vanquished innocents, nor the clanking fetters of woe doomed captives. Rejoice, Oh, ye descendants of Africans! No longer shall the United States of America, nor the extensive colonies of Great Britain, admit the degrading commerce of the human species; no longer shall they swell the tide of African misery by the importation of slaves. Rejoice, my brethren, that the channels are obstructed through which slavery, and its direful concomitants, have been entailed on the African race. But let incessant strains of gratitude be mingled with your expressions of joy. Through the infinite mercy of the great Jehovah, this day announces the abolition of the Slave Trade. Let, therefore, the heart that is warmed by the smallest drop of African blood glow in grateful transports, and cause the lofty arches of the sky to reverberate eternal praise to his boundless goodness.

Peter Williams. First published in New York by Samuel Wood, 1808

DAVID WALKER (1785-1830)

Introduction

David Walker was a black abolitionist, most famous for his pamphlet *Walker's Appeal*, which called for black pride, demanded the immediate and universal emancipation of the slaves, and defended violent rebellion as a means for the slaves to gain their freedom.

Walker was born as a freeman in Wilmington, North Carolina, to an enslaved father and a free mother. Although he was free, Walker witnessed the cruelty of slavery during his childhood in North Carolina: later in life he remembered watching as a black slave was forced to whip his own mother to death. As an adult, he left the South and traveled the country, eventually settling in Boston, where he supported himself by opening a used clothing store on the waterfront during the 1820s.

In Boston, Walker made friends with black rights activists and began to write and speak against slavery and racism. He wrote many articles for *Freedom's Journal*, an early African American newspaper based out of New York City, and, in 1828, he played a major role in organizing the Massachusetts General Colored Association.

Before his death in 1830, Walker worked to circulate his Appeal to blacks in both the North and the South. Copies found in the possession of slaves led to stronger laws against teaching slaves to read and distributing inflammatory writing in a number of southern states.

Walker's Appeal consisted of the following Four Articles.
Article 1: Our wretchedness in consequence of slavery
Article 2: Our wretchedness in consequence of ignorance
Article 3: Our wretchedness in consequence of the preachers of the religion of Jesus Christ
Article 4: Our wretchedness in consequence of the colonizing plan

His third Article follows. It was written in Boston on September 28, 1829.

Walker's Appeal

Article 3
Our wretchedness in consequence of the preachers of the religion of Jesus Christ.

Religion, my brethren, is a substance of deep consideration among all nations of the earth. The Pagans have a kind, as well as the Muslims, the Jews and the Christians. But pure and undefiled religion, such as was preached by Jesus Christ and his apostles, is hard to be found in all the earth. God, through his instrument, Moses, handed a dispensation of his divine will to the children of Israel after they had left Egypt for the land of Canaan, or of Promise, who through hypocrisy, oppression, and unbelief, departed from the faith. He then, by his apostles handed a dispensation of his, together with the will of Jesus Christ, to the Europeans in Europe, who, in open violation of which, have made merchandize of us, and it does appear as though they take this very dispensation to aid them in their infernal depredations upon us. Indeed, the way in which religion was and is conducted by the Europeans and their descendants, one might believe it was a plan fabricated by themselves and the devils to oppress us. But hark! my master has taught me better than to believe it— he has taught me that his gospel as it was preached by himself and his apostles remains the same, notwithstanding Europe has tried to mingle blood and oppression with it.

Bartholomew Las Cassas

It is well known to the Christian world that Bartholomew Las Casas, that very notoriously avaricious Catholic priest or preacher, and adventurer with Columbus in his second voyage, proposed to his countrymen, the Spaniards in Hispaniola, to import the Africans from the Portuguese settlement in Africa, to dig up gold and silver, and work their plantations for them, to effect which, he made a voyage thence to Spain, and opened the subject to his master, Ferdinand, then in declining health, who listened to the plan; but who died soon after, and left it in the hands of his successor, Charles V. This wretch, ("Las Cassas, the Preacher,") succeeded so well in his plans of oppression, that in 1503, the first blacks had been imported into the new world. Elated with this success, and stimulated by sordid avarice only, he importuned Charles V. in 1511, to grant permission to a Flemish merchant to import 4000 blacks at one time. Thus we see, through the instrumentality of a pretended preacher of the gospel of Jesus Christ our common master, our wretchedness first commenced in America—where it has been continued from 1503 to this day, 1829. A period of three hundred and twenty-six years. But two hundred and nine, from 1620—when twenty of our fathers were brought into Jamestown, Virginia, by a Dutch man-of-war, and sold off like brutes to the highest bidders; and there is not a doubt in my mind, but that tyrants are in hopes to perpetuate our miseries under them and their children until the final consummation of all things. But if they do not get dreadfully, deceived, it will be because God has forgotten them.

Christian Americans

The Pagans, Jews and Muslims try to make proselytes to their religions, and whatever human beings adopt their religions, they extend to them their protection. But Christian Americans not only hinder their fellow creatures, the Africans, but thousands of them will absolutely beat a colored person nearly to death, if they catch him on his knees, supplicating the throne of grace. This barbarous cruelty was by all the heathen nations of antiquity, and is by the Pagans, Jews and Muslims of the present day, left entirely to Christian Americans to inflict on the Africans and their descendants that their cup which is nearly full may be completed. I have known tyrants or usurpers of human liberty in different parts of this country take their fellow creatures, the colored people, and beat them until they would scarcely leave life in them; what for? Why they say, "The black devils had the audacity to be found making prayers and supplications to the God who made them!!!"

Yes, I have known small collections of colored people to have convened together, for no other purpose than to worship God Almighty, in spirit and in truth, to the best of their knowledge; when tyrants, calling themselves patrols, would also convene and wait almost in breathless silence for the poor colored people to commence singing and praying to the Lord our God, and as soon as they had commenced the wretches would burst in upon them and drag them out and commence beating them as they would rattle-snakes—many of whom, they would beat so unmercifully, that they would hardly be able to crawl for weeks and sometimes for months.—Yet the American ministers send out missionaries to convert the heathen, while they keep us and our children sunk at their feet in the most abject ignorance and wretchedness that ever a people was afflicted with since the world began. Will the Lord suffer this people to proceed much longer? Will he not stop them in their career? Does he regard the heathens abroad, more than the heathens among the Americans? Surely the Americans must believe that God is partial, notwithstanding his Apostle Peter, declared before Cornelius and others that he has no respect to persons, but in every nation he that feareth God and worketh righteousness is accepted with him. "The word," said he, "which God sent unto the children of Israel, preaching peace, by Jesus Christ, (he is the Lord of all.")

Do Americans believe the Bible?
Have not the Americans the Bible in their hands? Do they believe it? Surely they do not. See how they treat us in open violation of the Bible!! They no doubt will be greatly offended with me, but if God does not awaken them, it will be, because they are superior to other men, as they have represented themselves to be. Our divine Lord and Master said: "all things whatsoever ye would that men should do unto you, do ye even so unto them."

But an American minister, with the Bible in his hand, holds us and our children in the most abject slavery and wretchedness. Now I ask them, would they like for us to hold them and their children in abject slavery and wretchedness? No says one, that never can be done— you are too abject and ignorant to do it—you are not men—you were made to be slaves to us, to dig up gold and silver for us and our children. Know this, my dear sirs, that although you treat us and our children now, as you do your domestic beasts—yet the final result of all future events are known but to God Almighty alone, who rules in the armies of heaven and among the inhabitants of the earth, and who dethrones one earthly king and sits up another, as it seemeth good in his holy sight. We may attribute these vicissitudes to what we please, but the God of armies and of justice rules in heaven and in earth, and the whole American people shall see and know it yet, to their satisfaction. I have known pretended preachers of the gospel of my Master, who not only held us as their natural inheritance, but treated us with as much rigor as any Infidel or Deist in the world—just as though they were intent only on taking our blood and groans to glorify the Lord Jesus Christ. The wicked and ungodly, seeing their preachers treat us with so much cruelty, they say: our preachers, who must be right, if any body are, treat them like brutes, and why cannot we?—They think it is no harm to keep them in slavery and put the whip to them, and why cannot we do the same!—They being preachers of the gospel of Jesus Christ, if it were any harm, they would surely preach against their oppression and do their utmost to erase it from the country; not only in one or two cities, but one continual cry would be raised in all parts of this confederacy, and would cease only with the complete overthrow of the system of slavery, in every part of the country. But how far the American preachers are from preaching against slavery and oppression, which have carried their country to the brink of a precipice; to save them from plunging down the side of which, will hardly be effected, will appear in the sequel of this paragraph, which I shall narrate just as it transpired.

A Camp Meeting

I remember a Camp Meeting in South Carolina, for which I embarked in a Steam Boat at Charleston, and having been five or six hours on the water, we at last arrived at the place of hearing, where was a very great concourse of people, who were no doubt, collected together to hear the word of God, (that some had collected barely as spectators to the scene, I will not here pretend to doubt, however, that is left to themselves and their God.) Myself and boat companions, having been there a little while, we were all called up to hear; I among the rest, went up and took my seat—being seated, I fixed myself in a complete position to hear the word of my Savior and to receive such as I thought was authenticated by the Holy Scriptures; but to my no ordinary astonishment, our Reverend gentleman got up and told us (colored people) that slaves must be obedient to their masters—must do their duty to their masters or be whipped—the whip was made for the backs of fools, &c. Here I pause for a moment, to give the world time to consider what was my surprise, to hear such preaching from a minister of my Master, whose very gospel is that of peace and not of blood and whips, as this pretended preacher tried to make us believe. What the American preachers can think of us, I aver this day before my God, I have never been able to define. They have newspapers and monthly periodicals, which they receive in continual succession, but on the pages of which, you will scarcely ever find a paragraph respecting slavery, which is ten thousand times more injurious to this country than all the other evils put together; and which will be the final overthrow of its government, unless something is very speedily done; for their cup is nearly full.—Perhaps they will laugh at, or make light of this; but I tell you Americans! that unless you speedily alter your course, you and your Country are gone!!!!!! For God Almighty will tear up the very face of the earth!!!! Will not that very remarkable passage of Scripture be fulfilled on Christian Americans? Hear it Americans!!

"He that is unjust, let him be unjust still:—and be which is filthy, let him be filthy still: and he that is righteous, let him be righteous still; and he that is holy, let him be holy still."

Hard hearts

I hope that the Americans may hear, but I am afraid that they have done us so much injury, and are so firm in the belief that our Creator made us to be an inheritance to them forever, that their hearts will be hardened, so that their destruction may be sure.—This language, perhaps is too harsh for the American's delicate ears. But Oh Americans! Americans!! I warn you in the name of the Lord, (whether you will hear, or forbear,) to repent and reform, or you are ruined!!!!!! Do you think that our blood is hidden from the Lord, because you can hide it from the rest of the world by sending out missionaries, and by your charitable deeds to the Greeks, Irish, &c.? Will he not publish your secret crimes on the house top? Even here in Boston, pride and prejudice have got to such a pitch, that in the very houses erected to the Lord, they have built little places for the reception of colored people, where they must sit during meeting, or keep away from the house of God; and the preachers say nothing about it—much less, go into the hedges and highways seeking the lost sheep of the house of Israel, and try to bring them in, to their Lord and Master. There are hardly a more wretched, ignorant, miserable, and abject set of beings in all the world, than the blacks in the Southern and Western sections of this country, under tyrants and devils. The preachers of America cannot see them, but they can send out missionaries to convert the heathens, notwithstanding. Americans! unless you speedily alter your course of proceeding, if God Almighty does not stop you, I say it in his name, that you may go on and do as you please for ever, both in time and eternity—never fear any evil at all!!!!!!!!

The preachers and people of the United States form societies against Free Masonry and Intemperance, and write against Sabbath breaking, Sabbath mails, Infidelity, &c. &c. But the fountain head, compared with which all those other evils are comparatively nothing, and from the bloody and murderous head of which, they receive no trifling support, is hardly noticed by the Americans. This is a fair illustration of the state of society in this country— it shows what a bearing avarice has upon a people, when they are nearly given up by the Lord to a hard heart and a reprobate mind, in consequence of afflicting their fellow creatures. God suffers some to go on until they are ruined for ever!! Will it be the case with our brethren the whites of the United States of America? We hope not—we would not wish to see them destroyed, notwithstanding they have and do now treat us more cruel than any people have treated another, on this earth since it came from the hands of its creator (with the exception of the French and the Dutch, they treat us nearly as bad as the Americans of the United States.) The will of God must however, in spite of us, be done.

The English

The English are the best friends the colored people have upon earth. Tho' they have oppressed us a little, and have colonies now in the West Indies, which oppress us sorely,—Yet notwithstanding they (the English) have done one hundred times more for the melioration of our condition, than all the other nations of the earth put together. The blacks cannot but respect the English as a nation, notwithstanding they have treated us a little cruel.

There is no intelligent black man who knows any thing, but esteems a real English man, let him see him in what part of the world he will—for they are the greatest benefactors we have upon earth. We have here and there, in other nations, good friends. But as a nation, the English are our friends. ?

How can the preachers and people of America believe the Bible? Does it teach them any distinction on account of a man's color? Hearken, Americans! to the injunctions of our Lord and Master, to his humble followers.

"And Jesus came and spake unto them saying, all power is given unto me in heaven and in earth. "Go ye, therefore, and teach all nations, baptizing them in the name of the Father, and of the Son, and of the Holy Ghost, Teaching them to observe all things whatsoever I have commanded you; and lo, I am with you alway, even unto the end of the world. Amen.'"

I declare, that the very face of these injunctions appears to be of God and not of man. They do not show the slightest degree of distinction.

"Go ye, therefore," (says my divine Master) "and teach all nations," (or in other words, all people) "baptizing them in the name of the Father, and of the Son, and of the Holy Ghost."

Do you understand the above, Americans? We are a people, notwithstanding many of you doubt it. You have the Bible in your hands, with this very injunction. Have you been to Africa, teaching the inhabitants thereof the words of the Lord Jesus?

"Baptizing them in the name of the Father, and of the Son, and of the Holy Ghost."

American preachers

Have you not, on the contrary, entered among us, and learnt us the art of throat-cutting, by setting us to fight, one against another, to take each other as prisoners of war, and sell to you for small bits of calicoes, old swords, knives, &c. to make slaves for you and your children? This being done, have you not brought us among you, in chains and handcuffs, like brutes, and treated us with all the cruelties and rigor your ingenuity could invent, consistent with the laws of your country, which (for the blacks) are tyrannical enough? Can the American preachers appeal unto God, the Maker and Searcher of hearts, and tell him, with the Bible in their hands, that they make no distinction on account of men's color? Can they say, O God! thou knowest all things—thou knowest that we make no distinction between thy creatures to whom we have to preach thy Word? Let them answer the Lord; and if they cannot do it in the affirmative, have they not departed from the Lord Jesus Christ, their master? But some may say, that they never had or were in possession of a religion, which makes no distinction, and of course they could not have departed from it. I ask you then, in the name of the Lord, of what kind can your religion be? Can it be that which was preached by our Lord Jesus Christ from Heaven? I believe you cannot be so wicked as to tell him that his Gospel was that of distinction. What can the American preachers and people take God to be?—Do they believe his words? If they do, do they believe that he will be mocked? Or do they believe because they are whites and we blacks, that God will have respect to them? Did not God make us as it seemed best to himself? What right, then, has one of us, to despise another and to treat him cruel, on account of his color, which none but the God who made it can alter? Can there be a greater absurdity in nature, and particularly in a free republican country? But the Americans, having introduced slavery among them, their hearts have become almost seared, as with an hot iron, and God has nearly given them up to believe a lie in preference to the truth!!! and I am awfully afraid that pride, prejudice, avarice and blood, will, before long, prove the final ruin of this happy republic, or land of liberty!!! Can any thing be a greater mockery of religion than the way in which it is conducted by the Americans? It appears as though they are bent only on daring God Almighty to do his best—they chain and handcuff us and our children and drive us around the country like brutes, and go into the house of the God of justice to return Him thanks for having aided him in their infernal cruelties inflicted upon us. Will the Lord suffer this people to go on much longer, taking his holy name in vain? Will he not stop them, preachers and all? O Americans! Americans!! I call God—I call angels—I call men, to witness, that your destruction is at hand, and will be speedily consummated unless you REPENT.

Revised and Published by David Walker, 1830

JOSIAH HENSON (1789-1883)

Introduction

Josiah Henson was born into slavery in Charles County, Maryland. Henson, with his wife, and their four children escaped from their slavery in 1830 and went to Canada. On their journey to freedom the Henson family struggled through sickness, wolves, and starvation. The Underground Railroad (the Underground Railroad was a vast network of people who helped fugitive slaves escape to the North and to Canada), and a tribe of Native Americans assisted the family on their journeys.

Henson stayed in Canada for a short time before he decided to get involved with the Underground. Henson made several trips and led over two hundred slaves to Canada. During his time in Canada, Josiah Henson started the Dawn Institute in Chatham, Ontario, a refuge for fugitive slaves where they were taught trades to support themselves and their families. When Henson went to the World's Fair in London, he became the first ex-slave to be granted an audience with Queen Victoria.

Henson's autobiography, *The Life of Josiah Henson, Formerly a Slave, Now an Inhabitant of Canada, as Narrated by Himself* (1849), is widely believed to have inspired the title character of Harriet Beecher Stowe's novel, *Uncle Tom's Cabin* (1852).

"Uncle Tom's Story of His Life"
An Autobiography of the Rev. Josiah Henson (Mrs. Harriet Beecher Stowe's "Uncle Tom"). From 1789 to 1876. With a Preface by Mrs. Harriet Beecher Stowe Edited by John Lobb, 1840-1921

Preface

The numerous friends of the author of this work will need no greater recommendation than his name to make it welcome. Among all the singular and interesting records to which the institution of American slavery has given rise, we know of none more striking, more characteristic and instructive, than that of Josiah Henson.

Born a slave—a slave in effect in a heathen land—and under a heathen master, he grew up without Christian light or knowledge, and like the Gentiles spoken of by St. Paul, "without the law did by nature the things that are written in the law." One sermon, one offer of salvation by Christ, was sufficient for him, as for the Ethiopian eunuch, to make him at once a believer from the heart and a preacher of Jesus.

To the great Christian doctrine of forgiveness of enemies and the returning of good for evil, he was by God's grace made a faithful witness, under circumstances that try men's souls and make us all who read it say, "Lead us not into such temptation." We earnestly commend this portion of his narrative to those who, under much smaller temptations, think themselves entitled to render evil for evil.

The African race appear as yet to have been companions only of the sufferings of Christ. In the melancholy scene of His death—while Europe in the person of the Roman delivered Him unto death, and Asia in the person of the Jew clamored for His execution—Africa was represented in the person of Simon the Cyrenean, who came patiently bearing after Him the load of the cross; and ever since then poor Africa has been toiling on, bearing the weary cross of contempt and oppression after Jesus. But they who suffer with Him shall also reign; and when the unwritten annals of slavery shall appear in the judgment, many Simons who have gone meekly bearing their cross after Jesus to unknown graves, shall rise to thrones and crowns! Verily a day shall come when He shall appear for these His hidden ones, and then "many that are last shall be first, and the first shall be last."

Harriet Beecher Stowe

Chapter 1

My birth and childhood

The story of my life, which I am about to record, is one full of striking incident. Keener pangs, deeper joys, more singular vicissitudes, few have been led in God's providence to experience. As I look back on it through the vista of more than eighty years, and scene after scene rises before me, an ever fresh wonder fills my mind. I delight to recall it. I dwell on it as did the Jews on the marvelous history of their rescue from the bondage of Egypt. Time has touched with its mellowing fingers its sterner features. The sufferings of the past are now like a dream, and the enduring lessons left behind, make me to praise God that my soul has been tempered by Him in so fiery a furnace and under such heavy blows.

I was born June 15th, 1789, in Charles county, Maryland, on a farm belonging to Mr. Francis Newman, about a mile from Port Tobacco. My mother was a slave of Dr. Josiah McPherson, but hired to Mr. Newman, to whom my father belonged. The only incident I can remember which occurred while my mother continued on Mr. Newman's farm, was the appearance one day of my father with his head bloody and his back lacerated. He was beside himself with mingled rage and suffering. The overseer had brutally assaulted my mother, when my father sprang upon him like a tiger. In a moment the overseer was down, and, mastered by rage, my father would have killed him but for the entreaties of my mother, and the overseer's own promise that nothing should ever be said of the matter. The promise was kept—like most promises of the cowardly and debased—as long as the danger lasted.

The laws of slave states provide means and opportunities for revenge so ample, that miscreants like him never fail to improve them. "A nigger has struck a white man;" that is enough to set a whole county on fire; no question is asked about the provocation. The authorities were soon in pursuit of my father. The penalty was one hundred lashes on the bare back, and to have the right ear nailed to the whipping-post, and then severed from the body. For a time my father kept out of the way, hiding in the woods, and at night venturing into some cabin in search of food. But at length the strict watch set baffled all his efforts. His supplies cut off, he was fairly starved out, and compelled by hunger to come back and give himself up.

The day for the execution of the penalty was appointed. The Negroes from the neighboring plantations were summoned to witness the scene. A powerful blacksmith named Hewes laid on the stripes. Fifty were given, during which the cries of my father might be heard a mile, and then a pause ensued. True, he had struck a white man, but as valuable property he must not be damaged. Judicious men felt his pulse. Oh! he could stand the whole. Again and again the thong fell on his lacerated back. His cries grew fainter and fainter, till a feeble groan was the only response to the final blows. His head was then thrust against the post, and his right ear fastened to it with a tack; a swift pass of a knife, and the bleeding member was left sticking to the place. Then came a hurrah from the degraded crowd, and the exclamation, "That's what he's got for striking a white man."

In the estimation of the illiterate, besotted poor whites who constituted the witnesses of such scenes in Charles county, Maryland, the man who did not feel rage enough at hearing of "a nigger" striking a white, to be ready to burn him alive, was only fit to be lynched out of the neighborhood.

Previous to this affair, my father, from all I can learn, had been a good-humored and light-hearted man, the ringleader in all fun at corn-huskings and Christmas buffoonery. His banjo was the life of the farm, and all night long at a merry-making would he play on it while the other Negroes danced. But from this hour he became utterly changed. Sullen, morose, and dogged, nothing could be done with him. The milk of human kindness in his heart was turned to gall. He brooded over his wrongs. No fear or threats of being sold to the far south—the greatest of all terrors to the Maryland slave—would render him tractable. So off he was sent to Alabama. What was his after-fate neither my mother nor I have ever learned; the great day will reveal all. This was the first chapter in my history.

Chapter 2

My first great trial

After the sale of my father by Newman, Dr. McPherson would no longer hire out my mother to him. She returned, accordingly, to his estate. He was far kinder to his slaves than the planters generally were, never suffering them to be struck by any one. He was a man of good, kind impulses, liberal, jovial, hearty. No degree of arbitrary power could ever lead him to cruelty. As the first Negro child ever born to him, I was his especial pet. He gave me his own Christian name, Josiah, and with that he also gave me my last name, Henson, after an uncle of his, who was an officer in the revolutionary war. A bright spot in my childhood was my residence with him—bright, but, alas! fleeting. Events were rapidly maturing which were to change the whole aspect of my life. The kind doctor was not exempt from that failing which too often besets easy, social natures in a dissipated community. He could not restrain his convivial propensities. Although he maintained a high reputation for goodness of heart and an almost saint-like benevolence, the habit of intemperance steadily gained ground, and finally occasioned his death. Two Negroes on the plantation found him one morning lying dead in the middle of a narrow stream, not a foot in depth. He had been away the night previous at a social party, and when returning home had fallen from his horse, probably, and being too intoxicated to stagger through the stream, fell and was drowned. "There's the place where massa got drowned at;" how well I remember having it pointed out to me in those very words.

For two or three years my mother and her young family of six children had resided on the doctor's estate, and we had been in the main very happy. She was a good mother to us, a woman of deep piety, anxious above all things to touch our hearts with a sense of religion.

How or where she acquired her knowledge of God, or her acquaintance with the Lord's Prayer, which she so frequently taught us to repeat, I am unable to say. I remember seeing her often on her knees, and hearing her pray by repeating constant ejaculations, and short phrases which were within my infant comprehension, and have remained in my memory to this hour.

Our term of happy union as one family was now, alas! at an end. The doctor's death was a great calamity to us, for the estate and the slaves were to be sold and the proceeds divided among the heirs. The first sad announcement that the sale was to be; the knowledge that all ties of the past were to be sundered; the frantic terror at the idea of being sent "down south;" the almost certainty that one member of a family will be torn from another; the anxious scanning of purchasers' faces; the agony at parting, often for ever, with husband, wife, child—these must be seen and felt to be fully understood. Young as I was then, the iron entered into my soul. The remembrance of the breaking up of McPherson's estate is photographed in its minutest features in my mind. The crowd collected round the stand, the huddling group of Negroes, the examination of muscle, teeth, the exhibition of agility, the look of the auctioneer, the agony of my mother—I can shut my eyes and see them all.

My brothers and sisters were bid off first, and one by one, while my mother, paralyzed by grief, held me by the hand. Her turn came, and she was bought by Isaac Riley, of Montgomery county. Then I was offered to the assembled purchasers. My mother, half-distracted with the thought of parting for ever from all her children, pushed through the crowd, while the bidding for me was going on, to the spot where Riley was standing. She fell at his feet, and clung to his knees, entreating him in tones that a mother only could command, to buy her baby as well as herself, and spare to her one, at least, of her little ones. Will it, can it be believed that this man, thus appealed to, was capable not merely of turning a deaf ear to her supplication, but of disengaging himself from her with such violent blows and kicks, as to reduce her to the necessity of creeping out of his reach, and mingling the groan of bodily suffering with the sob of a breaking heart? As she crawled away from the brutal man, I heard her sob out, "Oh, Lord Jesus, how long, how long shall I suffer this way?" I must have been then between five and six years old.

I was bought by a stranger named Robb, and truly a robber he was to me. He took me to his home, about forty miles distant, and put me into his Negro quarters with about forty others, of all ages, colors, and conditions, all strangers to me. Of course nobody cared for me. The slaves were brutalized by this degradation, and had no sympathy for me. I soon fell sick, and lay for some days almost dead on the ground. Sometimes a slave would give me a piece of corn-bread, or a bit of herring. Finally I became so feeble that I could not move. This, however, was fortunate for me; for in the course of a few weeks, Robb met Riley, who had bought my mother, and offered to sell me to him cheap. Riley said he was afraid "the little nigger would die;" but he agreed, finally, to pay a small sum for me in horse-shoeing if I lived, and nothing if I died. Robb was a tavern-keeper, and owned a line of stages with the horses, and lived near Montgomery Court House; Riley carried on blacksmithing about five miles from that place. This clenched the bargain, and I was soon sent to my mother. A blessed change it was. I had been lying on a lot of rags, thrown on a dirt floor. All day long I had been left alone, crying for water, crying for mother; the slaves, who left at daylight, when they returned cared nothing for me. Now, I was once more with my best friend on earth, and under her care; destitute as she was of the proper means of nursing me, I recovered my health, and grew to be an uncommonly vigorous boy and man.

I faithfully served Riley for many years. He was coarse and vulgar in his habits, and unprincipled and cruel in his general deportment. His slaves had little opportunity for relaxation from wearying labor, were supplied with the scantiest means of sustaining their toil by necessary food, and had no security for personal rights. When such a master is a tyrant, the slaves often become cringing, treacherous, false, and thieving. Riley and his slaves were no exception to the general rule, but might be cited as apt illustrations of the nature of the relation. ...

Chapter 4

My conversion

I remember being torn from a dear and affectionate mother; I saw her tears and heard her groans; I remember all the particulars. From a little boy up I have remembered my mother; I remember what the prayers of my dear mother were; I have heard her pray for me; for she was a good Christian woman before I was born; and I thank God that I was born of a good Christian mother, a mother whose prayers fell on my ear. Of all earthly blessings there is none can approach to a good mother. I remember her entreaties; I remember her prayers to God for me. Blessed is the child, the son or daughter, that has the prayers of a mother. I remember well the feeling that those prayers wrought upon my heart, though I was but a boy.

My heart exults with gratitude when I mention the name of a good man who first taught me the blessedness of religion. His name was John McKenny. He lived at Georgetown, a few miles only from Riley's plantation; his business was that of a baker, and his character was that of an upright, benevolent Christian. He was noted especially for his detestation of slavery, and his resolute avoidance of the employment of slave-labor in his business. He would not even hire a slave, the price of whose toil must be paid to his master, but contented himself with the work of his own hands, and with such free labor as he could procure. His reputation was high, not only for this almost singular abstinence from what no one about him thought wrong, but for his general probity and excellence. This man occasionally served as a minister of the Gospel, and preached in a neighborhood where preachers were somewhat rare at that period. One Sunday when he was to officiate in this way, at a place three or four miles distant, my mother urged me to ask master's permission to go and hear him. I had so often been beaten for making such a request that I refused to make it. My mother came to me and said: "Now, my son, I want you to go and ask master to let you go down and hear Mr. McKenny preach." I said to my mother: "I do not want to go; I am afraid he will beat me." She said: "Go and ask him." I turned round, like many other boys, and said I would not go. She was standing against a rail; she dropped her head down and shed a tear. I stood and looked at her and was touched at her sorrow. I said: "I will go, mother." She said: "That is right." I went up to the house, and just before I got to the door, master saw my shadow. He turned round and asked what I wanted. I said; "I want to ask you if I can go to the meeting." "Where?" "Down at Newport Mill." "Who is going to preach?" "Mr. McKenny." "What do you want to hear him preach for?" Here I was in a difficulty; I did not know what I wanted to go for, and I told him so. "What good will it do for you?" Here I was at another point. "Who put that into your head?" There was another thing; I did not want to get my poor old mother into trouble. But she had always told me to tell the truth. So I answered: "My mother." "Ah," said he, "I thought it was your mother. I suppose she wants to have you spoilt. When will you come back?" "As soon as meeting is over." Well, I went to the meeting, I heard the preacher, but I could not see him. They would not let niggers go into the meeting. I went all round the house; I could hear him, and at last I got in front of the door. I saw him with his hands raised, looking up to heaven, and he said, with emphasis: "Jesus Christ, the Son of God, tasted death for every man; for the high, for the low, for the rich, for the poor, the bond, the free, the Negro in his chains, the man in gold and diamonds." His heart was filled with the love of Christ, and by the power of the Spirit of God he preached a universal salvation through Jesus Christ. I stood and heard it. It touched my heart, and I cried out: "I wonder if Jesus Christ died for me." And then I wondered what could have induced Him to die for me. I was then eighteen years old, I had never heard a sermon, nor any conversation whatever, upon religious topics, except what I had heard from my mother, on the responsibility of all to a Supreme Being. This was Heb. ii. 9, the first text of the Bible to which I had ever listened, knowing it to be such. I have never forgotten it, and scarcely a day has passed since, in which I have not recalled it, and the sermon that was preached from it.

The divine character of Jesus Christ, His tender love for mankind, His forgiving spirit, His compassion for the outcast and despised, His cruel crucifixion and glorious ascension, were all depicted, and some of the points were dwelt on with great power; great, at least, to me, who then heard of these things for the first time in my life. Again and again did the preacher reiterate the words "for every man." These glad tidings, this salvation, were not for the benefit of a select few only. They were for the slave as well as the master, the poor as well as the rich, for the persecuted, the distressed, the heavy-laden, the captive; even for me among the rest, a poor, despised, abused creature, deemed by others fit for nothing but unrequited toil—but mental and bodily degradation. Oh, the blessedness and sweetness of feeling that I was LOVED! I would have died that moment with joy, and I kept repeating to myself, "The compassionate Savior about whom I have heard "loves me," "He looks down in compassion from heaven on me," "He died to save my soul," and "He'll welcome me to the skies." " I was transported with delicious joy. I seemed to see a glorious being, in a cloud of splendor, smiling down from on high. In sharp contrast with the experience I had felt of the contempt and brutality of my earthly master, I basked, as it were, in the benign smiles of this Heavenly Being. I thought, "He'll be my clear refuge—He'll wipe any all tears from my eyes." "Now I can bear all things, nothing will seem hard after this." I felt sure that if "Massa Riley" only knew Him, he would not live such a coarse, wicked, cruel life. Swallowed up in the beauty of the divine love, I "loved my enemies, and prayed for them that did despitefully use and entreat me."

Revolving the things which I had heard in my mind as I went home. I became so excited that I turned aside from the road into the woods, and prayed to God for light and for aid with an earnestness, which, however unenlightened, was at least sincere and heartfelt; and which the subsequent course of my life has led me to imagine was acceptable to Him who heareth prayer. At all events, I date my conversion, and my awakening to a new life—a consciousness of power and a destiny superior to anything I had before conceived of—from this day, so memorable to me. I used every means and opportunity of inquiry into religious matters; and so deep was my conviction of their superior importance to everything else, so clear my perception of my own faults, and so undoubting my observation of the darkness and sin that surrounded me, that I could not help talking much on these subjects with those about me; and it was not long before I began to pray with them, exhort them, and impart to the poor slaves those little glimmerings of light from another world, which had reached my own eye. In a few years I became quite an esteemed preacher among them, and I believe that, through the grace of God, I was useful to many.

I must return, however, for the present, to the course of my life in secular affairs, the facts of which it is my principal object to relate.

Chapter 5
Maimed for life

The difference between the manner in which it was designed that all men should regard one another as children of the same Father, and the manner in which men of different color actually treated each other, is well exemplified by an incident that happened to me within a year or two from this period; that is, when I was nineteen or twenty years old. My master's habits were such as were common enough among the dissipated planters of the neighborhood; and one of their frequent practices was to assemble on Saturday or Sunday, which were their holidays, and gamble, run horses, or fight game-cocks, discuss politics, and drink whisky and brandy-and-water all day long. Perfectly aware that they would not be able to find their own way home at night, each one ordered his body-servant to come after him and help him home. I was chosen for this confidential duty by my master; and many were the times I have held him on his horse, when he could not hold himself in the saddle, and walked by his side in darkness and mud from the tavern to his house. Quarrels and brawls of the most violent description were frequent consequences of these meetings; and whenever they became especially dangerous, and glasses were thrown, dirks drawn, and pistols fired, it was the duty of the slaves to rush in, and each one drag his master from the fight, and carry him home. To tell the truth, this was a part of my business for which I felt no reluctance. I was young, remarkably athletic and self-relying, and in such affrays I carried it with a high hand, and would elbow my way among the whites,—whom it would have been almost death for me to strike,—seize my master and drag him out, mount him on his horse, or crowd him into his buggy, with the ease with which I would handle a bag of corn. I knew that I was doing for him what he could not do for himself, showing my superiority to others, and acquiring their respect in some degree, at the same time.

On one of these occasions my master got into a quarrel with his brother's overseer, Bryce Litton. All present sided with Litton against him, and soon there was a general row. I was sitting, at the time, out on the front steps of the tavern, and, hearing the scuffle, rushed in to look after my charge. My master, a stout man and a terrible bruiser, could generally hold his own in an ordinary general fight, and clear a handsome space around him; but now he was cornered, and a dozen were striking at him with fists, crockery, chairs, and anything that came handy. The moment he saw me, he hallooed, "That's it, Sie! pitch in! show me fair play." It was a rough business, and I went in roughly, shoving, tripping, and doing my best for the rescue. With infinite trouble, and many a bruise on my own head and shoulders, I at length got him out of the room. He was crazy with drink and rage, and struggled hard with me to get back and renew the fight. But I managed to force him into his wagon, jump in, and drive off.

By ill-luck, in the height of the scuffle, Bryce Litton got a severe fall. Whether the whisky he had drunk, or a chance-shove from me, was the cause, I am unable to say. He, however, attributed it to me, and treasured up his vengeance for the first favorable opportunity. The opportunity soon came.

About a week afterwards, I was sent by my master to a place a few miles distant, on horseback, with some letters. I took a short cut through a lane, separated by gates from the high road, and bounded by a fence on each side. This lane passed through a part of the farm owned by my master's brother, and his overseer was in the adjoining field, with three Negroes, when I went by. On my return, half an hour afterwards, the overseer was sitting on the fence, but I could see nothing of the black fellows. I rode on, utterly unsuspicious of any trouble; but as I approached, he jumped off the fence, and at the same moment two of the Negroes sprang up from under the bushes where they had been concealed, and stood with him immediately in front of me, while the third sprang over the fence just behind me. I was thus enclosed between what I could no longer doubt were hostile forces. The overseer seized my horse's bridle and ordered me to alight, in the usual elegant phraseology addressed by such men to slaves. I asked what I was to alight for. "To take the worst flogging you ever had in your life, you black scoundrel." He added many oaths that I will not repeat. "But what am I to be flogged for, Mr. L.?" I asked. "Not a word," said he, "but 'light at once, and take off your jacket." I saw there was nothing else to be done, and slipped off the horse on the opposite side from him. "Now take off your shirt," cried he; and as I demurred at this he lifted a stick he had in his hand to strike me, but so suddenly and violently that he frightened the horse, which broke away from him and ran home. I was thus left without means of escape to sustain the attacks of four men as well as I might. In avoiding Mr. L.'s blow, I had accidentally got into a corner of the fence where I could not be approached except in front. The overseer called upon the Negroes to seize me; but they, knowing something of my physical power, were slow to obey. At length they did their best, and as they brought themselves within my reach I knocked them down successively; and I gave one of them, who tried to trip up my feet, when he was down, a kick with my heavy shoe, which knocked out several teeth, and sent him howling away.

Meanwhile Bryce Litton beat my head with a stick, not heavy enough to knock me down, but it drew blood freely. He shouted all the while, "Won't you give up! Won't you give up!" adding oath after oath. Exasperated at my defense, he suddenly seized a heavy fence-rail and rushed at me with rage. The ponderous blow fell; I lifted my arm to ward it off, the bone cracked like a pipe-stem, and I fell headlong to the ground. Repeated blows then rained on my back till both shoulder-blades were broken, and the blood gushed copiously from my mouth. In vain the Negroes interposed. "Didn't you see the nigger strike me?" Of course they must say "Yes," although the lying coward had avoided close quarters, and fought with his stick alone. At length, his vengeance satisfied, he desisted, telling me "to remember what it was to strike a white man."

Meanwhile an alarm had been raised at the house by the return of the horse without his rider, and my master started off with a small party to learn what the trouble was. When he first saw me he swore with rage. "You've been fighting, you mean nigger!" I told him Bryce Litton had been beating me, because he said I shoved him the other night at the tavern, when they had a fuss. Seeing how much I was injured, he became still more fearfully mad; and after having me carried home, mounted his horse and rode over to Montgomery Court House to enter a complaint. Little good came of it. Litton swore that when he spoke to me in the lane I "sassed" him, jumped off my horse, attacked him, and would have killed him but for the help of his Negroes. Of course no Negro's testimony was admitted against a white man, and he was acquitted. My master was obliged to pay all the costs of court; and although he had the satisfaction of calling Litton a liar and scoundrel, and giving him a tremendous bruising, still even this partial compensation was rendered less gratifying by what followed, which was a suit for damages and a heavy fine.

My sufferings after this cruel treatment were intense. Besides my broken arm and the wounds on my head, I could feel and hear the pieces of my shoulder-blades grate against each other with every breath. No physician or surgeon was called to dress my wounds, and I never knew one to be called on Riley's estate on any occasion whatever. "A nigger will get well anyway," was a fixed principle of faith, and facts seemed to justify it. The robust, physical health produced by a life of outdoor labor, made our wounds heal with as little inflammation as they do in the case of cattle. I was attended by my master's sister, Miss Patty, as we called her, the Esculapius of the plantation. She was a powerful, big-boned woman, who flinched at no responsibility, from wrenching out teeth to setting bones. I have seen her go into the house and get a rifle to shoot a furious ox that the Negroes were in vain trying to butcher. She splintered my arm and bound up my back as well as she knew how. Alas! it was but cobbler's work. From that day to this I have been unable to raise my hands as high as my head. It was five months before I could work at all, and the first time I tried to plough, a hard knock of the coulter against a stone shattered my shoulder-blades again, and gave me even greater agony than at first. And so I have gone through life maimed and mutilated. Practice in time enabled me to perform many of the farm labors with considerable efficiency; but the free, vigorous play of the muscles of my arm was gone for ever.

I retained my situation as overseer, together with the especial favor of my master, who was pleased with saving the expense of a large salary for a white superintendent, and with the superior crops I was able to raise for him. I will not deny that I used his property more freely than he would have done himself, in supplying his people with better food; but if I cheated him in this way, in small matters, it was unequivocally for his own benefit in more important ones; and I accounted, with the strictest honesty, for every dollar I received in the sale of the property entrusted to me. Gradually the disposal of everything raised on the farm,—the wheat, oats, hay, fruit, butter, and whatever else there might be,—was confided to me, as it was quite evident that I could and did sell for better prices than any one else he could employ, and he was quite incompetent to attend to the business himself. For many years I was his factotum, and supplied him with all his means for all his purposes, whether they were good or bad. I had no reason to think highly of his moral character; but it was my duty to be faithful to him in the position in which he placed me; and I can boldly declare, before God and man, that I was so. I forgave him the causeless blows and injuries he had inflicted on me in childhood and youth, and was proud of the favor he now showed me, and of the character and reputation I had earned by strenuous and persevering efforts. ...

Chapter 7

A new home

I arrived at Davis county, Kentucky, about the middle of April, 1825, and delivered myself and my companions to my owner's brother, Mr. Amos Riley, who had a large plantation with from eighty to one hundred Negroes. His house was situated about five miles south of the Ohio River, and fifteen miles above the Yellow Banks, on Big Blackfords Creek. There I remained three years, and was employed meantime on the farm, of which I had the general management, in consequence of the recommendation for ability and honesty which I brought with me from Maryland. The situation was, in many respects, more comfortable than the one I had left. The farm was larger and more fertile, and there was a greater abundance of food, which is, of course, one of the principal sources of the comfort of a slave, debarred as he is from so many enjoyments which other men can obtain. Sufficiency of food is an important item in any man's account of life; it is tenfold more so in that of the slave, whose appetite is always stimulated by his arduous labor, and whose mind is little occupied by thought on subjects of deeper interest. My post of superintendent gave me some advantages, of which I did not fail to avail myself, particularly with regard to those religious privileges, which, since I first heard of Christ and Christianity, had greatly occupied my mind. In Kentucky the opportunities of attending the preaching of whites, as well as of blacks, were more numerous; and partly by attending them, and the camp-meetings which occurred from time to time, and partly from studying carefully my own heart, and observing the developments of character around me, in all the stations of life which I could watch, I became better acquainted with those religious feelings which are deeply implanted in the breast of every human being, and learned by practice how best to arouse them, and keep them excited, how to stir up the callous and indifferent, and, in general, to produce some good religious impressions on the ignorant and thoughtless community by which I was surrounded.

No great amount of theological knowledge is requisite for the purpose. If it had been, it is manifest enough that preaching never could have been my vocation; but I am persuaded that, speaking from the fullness of a heart deeply impressed with its own sinfulness and imperfection, and with the mercy of God, in Christ Jesus, my humble ministrations have not been entirely useless to those who have had less opportunity than myself to reflect upon these all-important subjects. It is certain that I could not refrain from the endeavor to do what I saw others doing in this field; and I labored at once to improve myself and those about me in the cultivation of the harvests which ripen only in eternity. I cannot but derive some satisfaction, too, from the proofs I have had that my services have been acceptable to those to whom they have been rendered. In the course of three years, from 1825 to 1828, I availed myself of all the opportunities of improvement which occurred, and was admitted as a preacher by a Quarterly Conference of the Methodist Episcopal Church.

In the spring of the year 1828, news arrived from my master that he was unable to induce his wife to accompany him to Kentucky, and that he must therefore remain where he was. He sent out an agent to sell all his slaves, except me and my family, and to carry back the proceeds to him. And now another of those heartrending scenes was to be witnessed, which had impressed itself so deeply on my childish soul. Husbands and wives, parents and children, were to be separated for ever. Affections, which are as strong in the African as in the European, were to be cruelly disregarded; and the iron selfishness generated by the hateful "institution," was to be exhibited in its most odious and naked deformity. I was exempted from a personal share in the dreadful calamity; but I could not see without the deepest grief, the agony of my associates. It was like that my own mother had once manifested, when I was separated from her for a time. I could not refrain from feeling the bitterest hatred of the system, and of those who sustained it. What else, indeed, could be the feeling of a slave, liable at every moment of his life to these frightful and unnecessary calamities, which might be caused by the caprice, or the supposed necessities of the slave-holders, and inflicted upon him without sympathy or redress, under the sanction of the laws which upheld the institution?

As I surveyed this scene, and listened to the groans and outcries of my afflicted companions, my eyes were opened, and I lamented that I had prevented them from availing themselves of the opportunity for acquiring freedom which offered itself at Cincinnati. I had only thought of being faithful to my master's interests, and nothing of the welfare of the slaves. Oh! what would I not have given to have had the chance offered once more! But now, through me, were they doomed to wear out life miserably in the hot and pestilential climate of the far south. Death would have been welcome to me in my agony. From that hour I saw through, hated, and cursed the whole system of slavery. One absorbing purpose occupied my soul—to gain freedom, self-assertion, and deliverance from the cruel caprices and fortunes of dissolute tyrants. Once to get away, with my wife and children, to some spot where I could feel that they were indeed mine—where no grasping master could stand between me and them, as arbiter of their destiny—was a heaven yearned after with insatiable longing. For it I stood ready to pray, toil, dissemble, plot like a fox, and fight like a tiger. All the noble instincts of my soul, and all the ferocious passions of my animal nature, were aroused and quickened into vigorous action.

The object of my old master Riley in directing that I and my family should be exempted from the sale, was a desire on his part to get me back to Maryland, and employ me in his own service. His best farms had been taken away from him, and but a few tracts of poor land remained, which he cultivated with hired labor after I took his slaves, and month by month he grew poorer and more desperate. He had written to his brother Amos to give me a pass and let me travel back; but this his brother was reluctant to do, as I saved him the expense of an overseer, and he moreover was aware that no legal steps could be taken to force him to comply. I knew of all this, but dared not seem anxious to return, for fear of exciting suspicion.

In the course of the summer of 1828, a Methodist preacher, a most excellent white man, visited our neighborhood, and I became acquainted with him. He was soon interested in me, and visited me frequently, and one day talked to me in a confidential manner about my position. He said, "You ought to be free. You have too much capacity to be confined to the limited and comparatively useless sphere of a slave, and though it must not be known that I have spoken to you on this subject, yet, if you will obtain Mr. Amos's consent to go to see your old master in Maryland, I will try and put you in a way by which I think you may succeed in buying yourself." He said this to me more than once; and as it was in harmony with all my aspirations and wishes, was flattering to my self-esteem, and gratified my impatience to bring matters to a direct issue, I now resolved to make the attempt to get the necessary leave. The autumn work was over, I was no longer needed in the fields, and a better chance would never offer itself. Still I dreaded to make the proposal. So much hung on it, such fond hopes were bound up with it, that I trembled for the result.

I opened the subject one Sunday morning while shaving Mr. Amos, and adroitly managed, by bringing the shaving brush close into his mouth whenever he was disposed to interrupt me, to "get a good say" first. Of course, I made no allusion to my plan of buying myself, but urged my request on the sole ground of a desire to see my old master. To my surprise, he made little objection. I had been faithful to him, and gained, in his rude way of showing it, his regard. Long before spring I would be back again. He even told me I had earned such a privilege.

The certificate he gave me, allowed me to pass and repass between Kentucky and Maryland as servant of Amos Riley. Furnished with this, and with a letter of recommendation from my Methodist friend to a brother preacher in Cincinnati, I started about the middle of September, 1828, for the east.

A new era in my history now opened upon me. A letter I carried with me to a kind-hearted man in Cincinnati, procured me a number of invaluable friends, who entered heart and soul into my plans. They procured me an opportunity to preach in two or three of the pulpits of the city, and I made my appeal with that eloquence which spontaneously breaks forth from a breast all alive and fanned into a glow by an inspiring project. Contact with those who were free themselves, and a proud sense of exultation in taking my destiny into my own hands, gave me the sacred "gift of tongues." I was pleading an issue of life and death, of heaven and hell, and such as heard me felt this in their hearts. In three or four days I left the city with no less a sum than one hundred and sixty dollars in my pockets, and with a soul jubilant with thanksgiving, and high in hope, directed my steps towards Chillicothe, to attend the session of the Ohio Conference of the Methodist Episcopal Church. My kind friend accompanied me, and, by his influence and exertions, still further success attended me.

By his advice, I then purchased a decent suit of clothes and an excellent horse, and traveled from town to town, preaching as I went. Everywhere I met with kindness. The contrast between the respect with which I was treated and the ordinary abuse of plantation life, gratified me in the extreme, as it must any one who has within him one spark of personal dignity as a man. The sweet enjoyment of sympathy, moreover, and the hearty "God speed you, brother!" which accompanied every dollar I received, were to my long-starved heart a celestial repast, and angels' food. Liberty was a glorious hope in my mind; not as an escape from toil, for I rejoiced in toil when my heart was in it, but as the avenue to a sense of self-respect, to ennobling occupation, and to association with superior minds. Still, dear as was the thought of liberty, I still clung to my determination to gain it in one way only—by purchase. The cup of my affliction was not yet full enough to lead me to disregard all terms with my master. ...

Chapter 9

Taken south, away from wife and children

Things went on in this way about a year. From time to time Master Amos joked me about the six hundred and fifty dollars, and said his brother kept writing to know why I did not send something. It was "diamond cut diamond" with the two brothers. Mr. Amos had no desire to play into the hands of Mr. Isaac. He was glad enough to secure my services to take care of his stock and his people.

One day my master suddenly informed me that his son Amos, a young man about twenty-one years of age, was going down the river to New Orleans, with a flat-boat loaded with produce from the farm, and that I was to go with him. He was to start the next day, and I was to accompany him and help him dispose of his cargo to the best advantage.

This intimation was enough. Though it was not distinctly stated, yet I well knew what was intended, and my heart sunk within me at the prospect of this fatal blight to all my long-cherished hopes. There was no alternative but death itself; still I thought that there was hope as long as there was life, and I would not despair even yet. The expectation of my fate, however, produced the degree of misery nearest to that of despair, and it is in vain for me to attempt to describe the wretchedness I experienced as I made ready to go on board the flat-boat. I had little preparation to make, to be sure; but there was one thing that seemed to me important. I asked my wife to sew my manumission-paper securely in a piece of cloth, and to sew that again round my person. I thought that its possession might be the means of saving me yet, and I would not neglect anything that offered the smallest chance of escape from the frightful servitude with which I was threatened.

The immediate cause of this movement on the part of Master Amos I never fully understood. It grew out of a frequent exchange of letters, which had been kept up between him and his brother in Maryland. Whether as a compromise between their rival claims it was agreed to sell me and divide the proceeds, or that Master Amos, in fear of my running away, had resolved to turn me into riches without wings, for his own profit, I never knew. The fact of his intention, however, was clear enough; and God knows it was a fearful blow.

My wife and children accompanied me to the landing, where I bade them an adieu which might be for life, and then stepped into the boat, manned by three white men, who had been hired for the trip. Mr. Amos and myself were the only other persons on board. The load consisted of beef-cattle, pigs, poultry, corn, whisky, and other articles which were to be sold as we dropped down the river, wherever they could be disposed of to the greatest advantage. It was a common trading-voyage to New Orleans, the interest of which consisted not in the incidents that occurred, not in storms, shipwreck, or external disaster of any sort; but in the storm of passions contending within me, and the imminent risk of the shipwreck of my soul, which was impending over me nearly the whole period of the voyage. One circumstance, only, I will mention, illustrating, as other events in my life have often clone, the counsel of the Savior, "He that will be chief among you, let him be your servant."

We were all bound to take our turn at the helm, sometimes under direction of the captain, and sometimes on our own responsibility, as he could not be always awake. In the daytime there was less difficulty than at night, when it required some one who knew how to avoid sandbars and snags in the river; the captain was the only person on board who had this knowledge. But whether by day or by night, as I was the only Negro in the boat, I was compelled to stand at least three turns at the helm to any other person's one; so that, from being much with the captain, and frequently thrown upon my own exertions, I learned the art of steering and managing the boat far better than the rest. I watched the maneuvers necessary to shoot by a "sawyer," to land on a bank, avoid a snag, or a steamboat, in the rapid current of the Mississippi, till I could do it as well as the captain. After a while, he was attacked by a disease of the eyes; they became very much inflamed and swollen. He was soon rendered totally blind, and unable to perform his share of duty. I was the person who could best take his place, and I was in fact master of the boat from that time till our arrival at New Orleans.

After the captain became blind, we were obliged to lie by at night, as none of the rest of us had been down the river before; and it was necessary to keep watch all night, to prevent depredations by the Negroes on shore, who used frequently to attack such boats as ours, for the sake of the provisions on board.

On our way down the river we stopped at Vicksburg, and I got permission to visit a plantation a few miles from the town, where some of my old companions whom I had brought from Kentucky were living. It was the saddest visit I ever made. Four years in an unhealthy climate and under a hard master had done the ordinary work of twenty. Their cheeks were literally caved in with starvation and disease. They described their daily life, which was to toil half-naked in malarious marshes, under a burning, maddening sun, exposed to poison of mosquitoes and black gnats, and they said they looked forward to death as their only deliverance. Some of them fairly cried at seeing me there, and at the thought of the fate which they felt awaited me. Their worst fears of being sold down South had been more than realized. I went away sick at heart, and to this day the remembrance of that wretched group haunts me. ...

Chapter 11
Providential deliverance
In a few days after this trying crisis in my life, we arrived at New Orleans. The little that

remained of our cargo was soon sold, the men were discharged, and nothing was left but to dispose of me, and break up the boat, and then Master Amos intended to take passage on a steamboat, and go home. There was no longer any disguise about the disposition which was to be made of me. Master Amos acknowledged that such were his instructions, and he set about fulfilling them. Several planters came to the boat to look at me; I was sent on some hasty errand that they might see how I could run; my points were canvassed as those of a horse would have been; and, doubtless, some account of my various faculties entered into the discussion of the bargain, that my value as a domestic animal might be enhanced. Master Amos had talked, with apparent kindness, about getting me a good master who would employ me as a coachman, or as a house-servant; but as time passed on I could discern no particular effort of the kind.

In our intervals of leisure I tried every possible means to move his heart. With tears and groans I besought him not to sell me away from my wife and children. I dwelt on my past services to his father, and called to his remembrance a thousand things I had done for him personally. I told him about the wretched condition of the slaves I had seen near Vicksburg. Sometimes he would shed tears himself, and say he was sorry for me. But still I saw his purpose was unchanged. He now kept out of my way as much as possible, and forestalled every effort I made to talk with him. His conscience evidently troubled him. He know he was doing a cruel and wicked thing, and wanted to escape from thinking about it. I followed him up hard, for I was supplicating for my life. I fell down and clung to his knees in entreaties. Sometimes when too closely pressed, he would curse and strike me. May God forgive him! And yet it was not all his fault; he was made so by the accursed relation of slave-master and slave. I was property,—not a man, not a father, not a husband. And the laws of property and self-interest, not of humanity and love, bore sway.

At length everything was wound up but this single affair. I was to be sold the next day, and. Master Amos was to set off on his return in a steamboat at six o'clock in the afternoon. I could not sleep that night; its hours seemed interminably long, though it was one of the shortest of the year. The slow way in which we had come down had brought us to the long days and heats of June; and everybody knows what the climate of New Orleans is at that period of the year.

And now occurred one of those sudden, marked interpositions of Providence, by which in a moment, the whole current of a human being's life is changed; one of those slight and, at first, unappreciated contingencies, by which the faith that man's extremity is God's opportunity is kept alive. Little did I think, when just before daylight Master Amos called me and told me he felt sick, how much my future was bound up in those few words. His stomach was disordered, and I advised him to lie down again, thinking it would soon pass off. Before long he felt worse, and it was soon evident that the river-fever was upon him. He became rapidly ill, and by eight o'clock in the morning was utterly prostrate. The tables were now turned. I was no longer property, no longer a brute-beast to be bought and sold, but his only friend in the midst of strangers. Oh, how different was his tone from what it had been the day before! He was now the supplicant, a poor, terrified object, afraid of death, and writhing with pain; there lay the late arbiter of my destiny. How he besought me to forgive him! "Stick to me, Sie!

Stick to me, Sie! Don't leave me, don't leave me. I'm sorry I was going to sell you." Sometimes he would say he had only been joking, and never intended to part with me. Yes, the tables were utterly turned. He entreated me to dispatch matters, sell the flat-boat in which we had been living, and get him and his trunk, containing the proceeds of the trip, on board the steamer as quickly as possible. I attended to all his requests, and by twelve o'clock that day, he was in one of the cabins of the steamer appropriated to sick passengers.

O my God! how my heart sang jubilees of praise to Thee, as the steamboat swung loose from the levee and breasted the mighty tide of the Mississippi! Away from this land of bondage and death! Away from misery and despair! Once more exulting hope possessed me, and I thought, if I do not now find my way to freedom, may God never give me a chance again!

Before we had proceeded many hours on our voyage, my young master appeared to be better. The change of air in a measure revived him; and well it was for him that such was the case. Short as his illness had been, the fever had raged like a fire, and he was already near death. I watched and nursed him like a mother; for all remembrance of personal wrong was obliterated at the sight of his peril. His eyes followed me in entreaty wherever I went. His strength was so entirely gone, that he could neither speak nor move a limb, and could only indicate his wish for a teaspoonful of gruel, or something to moisten his throat, by a feeble motion of his lips. I nursed him carefully and constantly. Nothing else could have saved his life. It hung by a thread for a long time. We were twelve days in reaching home, for the water was low at that season, particularly in the Ohio River; and when we arrived at our landing, he was still unable to speak, and could only be moved on a litter. Something of this sort was fixed up at the landing, on which he could be carried to the house, which was five miles off; and I got a party of the slaves belonging to the estate to form relays for the purpose. As we approached the house, the surprise at seeing me back again, and the perplexity to imagine what I was bringing along, with such a party, were extreme; but the discovery was soon made which explained the strange appearance; and the grief of father and mother, brothers and sisters, made itself seen and heard. Loud and long were the lamentations over poor Amos; and when the family came a little to themselves, great were the commendations bestowed upon me for my care of him and of the property.

Although we reached home by the 10th of July, it was not until the middle of August that Master Amos was well enough to leave his chamber. To do him justice, he manifested strong gratitude towards me. Almost his first words after recovering his strength sufficiently to talk, were in commendation of my conduct. "If I had sold him I should have died." On the rest of the family no permanent impression seemed to have been made. The first few words of praise were all I ever received. I was set at my old work. My merits, whatever they were, instead of exciting sympathy or any feeling of attachment to me, seemed only to enhance my market-value in their eyes. I saw that my master's only thought was to render me profitable to himself. From him I had nothing to hope, and I turned my thoughts to myself and my own energies.

Before long I felt assured another attempt would be made to dispose of me. Providence seemed to have interfered once to defeat the scheme, but I could not expect such extraordinary circumstances to be repeated; and I was bound to do everything in my power to secure myself and my family from the wicked conspiracy of Isaac and Amos Riley against my life, as well as against my natural rights, and those which I had acquired, even under the barbarous laws of slavery, by the money I had paid for myself. If Isaac had only been honest enough to adhere to his bargain, I would have adhered to mine, and paid him all I had promised. But his attempt to kidnap me again, after having pocketed three-fourths of my market value, in my opinion, absolved me from all obligation to pay him any more, or to continue in a position which exposed me to his machinations. ...

Chapter 13

Journey to Canada

I now felt comparatively at home. Before entering the town I hid my wife and children in the woods, and then walked on alone in search of my friends. They welcomed me warmly, and just after dusk my wife and children were brought in, and we found ourselves hospitably cheered and refreshed. Two weeks of exposure to incessant fatigue, anxiety, rain, and chill, made it indescribably sweet to enjoy once more the comfort of rest and shelter.

I have sometimes heard harsh and bitter words spoken of those devoted men who were banded together to succor and bid God speed to the hunted fugitive; men who, through pity for the suffering, voluntarily exposed themselves to hatred, fines, and imprisonment. If there be a God who will have mercy on the merciful, great will be their reward. In the great day when men shall stand in judgment before the Divine Master, crowds of the outcast and forsaken of earth, will gather around them, and in joyful tones bear witness, "We were hungry and ye gave us meat, thirsty and ye gave us drink, naked and ye clothed us, sick and ye visited us." And He Who has declared that, "inasmuch as ye have done it unto the least of these My brethren, ye have done it unto Me," will accept the attestation, and hail them with His welcome, "Come ye blessed of My Father." Their glory shall yet be proclaimed from the house-tops, and may that "peace of God which the world can neither give nor take away" dwell richly in their hearts!

Among such as those—good Samaritans, of whom the Lord would say, "Go ye and do likewise,"—our lot was now cast. Carefully they provided for our welfare until our strength was recruited, and then they set us thirty miles on our way by wagon.

We followed the same course as before—traveling by night and resting by day—till we arrived at the Scioto, where we had been told we should strike the military road of General Hull, made in the last war with Great Britain, and might then safely travel by day. We found the road, according by the large sycamore and elms which marked its beginning, and entered upon it with fresh spirits early in the day. Nobody had told us that it was cut through the wilderness, and I had neglected to provide any food, thinking we should soon come to some habitation, where we could be supplied. But we traveled on all day without seeing one, and lay down at night, hungry and weary enough. The wolves were howling around us, and though too cowardly to approach, their noise terrified my poor wife and children. Nothing remained to us in the morning but a little piece of dried beef, too little, indeed, to satisfy our cravings, but enough to afflict us with intolerable thirst. I divided most of this amongst us, and then we started for a second day's tramp in the wilderness. A painful day it was to us. The road was rough, the underbrush tore our clothes and exhausted our strength; trees that had been blown down, blocked the way; we were faint with hunger, and no prospect of relief opened up before us. We spoke little, but steadily struggled along; I with my babes on my back, my wife aiding the two other children to climb over the fallen trunks and force themselves through the briers. Suddenly, as I was plodding along a little ahead of my wife and the boys, I heard them call me, and turning round saw my wife prostrate on the ground. "Mother's dying," cried Tom; and when I reached her, it seemed really so. From sheer exhaustion she had fallen in surmounting a log. Distracted with anxiety, I feared she was gone. For some minutes no sign of life was manifest; but after a time she opened her eyes, and finally recovering enough to take a few mouthfuls of the beef, her strength returned, and we once more went bravely on our way. I cheered the sad group with hopes I was far from sharing myself. For the first time I was nearly ready to abandon myself to despair. Starvation in the wilderness was the doom that stared me and mine in the face. But again, "man's extremity was God's opportunity."

We had not gone far, and I suppose it was about three o'clock in the afternoon, when we discerned some persons approaching us at no great distance. We were instantly on the alert, as we could hardly expect them to be friends. The advance of a few paces showed me they were Indians, with packs on their shoulders; and they were so near that if they were hostile it would be useless to try to escape. So I walked along boldly, till we came close upon them. They were bent down with their burdens, and had not raised their eyes till now; and when they did so, and saw me coming towards them, they looked at me in a frightened sort of a way for a moment, and then, setting up a peculiar howl, turned round, and ran as fast as they could. There were three or four of them, and what they were afraid of I could not imagine. There was no doubt they were frightened, and we heard their wild and prolonged howl, as they ran, for a mile or more. My wife was alarmed, too, and thought they were merely running back to collect more of a party, and then would come and murder us; and she wanted to turn back. I told her they were numerous enough to do that, if they wanted to, without help; and that as for turning back, I had had quite too much of the road behind us, and that it would be a ridiculous thing that both parties should run away. If they were disposed to run, I would follow. We did follow, and the noise soon ceased. As we advanced, we could discover Indians peeping at us from behind the trees, and dodging out of sight if they thought we were looking at them. Presently we came upon their wigwams, and saw a fine-looking, stately Indian, with his arms folded, waiting for us to approach. He was, apparently, the chief; and, saluting us civilly, he soon discovered we were human beings, and spoke to his young men, who were scattered about, and made them come in and give up their foolish fears. And now curiosity seemed to prevail. Each one wanted to touch the children, who were as shy as partridges with their long life in the woods; and as they shrunk away, and uttered a little cry of alarm, the Indian would jump back too, as if he thought they would bite him. However, a little while sufficed to make them understand whither we were going, and what we needed; and then they supplied our wants, fed us bountifully, and gave us a comfortable wigwam for our night's rest. The next day we resumed our march, having ascertained from the Indians that we were only about twenty-five miles from the lake. They sent some of their young men to point out the place where we were to turn off, and parted from us with as much kindness as possible.

In passing over the part of Ohio near the lake, where such an extensive plain is found, we came to a spot overflowed by a stream, across which the road passed. I forded it first, with the help of a sounding-pole, and then taking the children on my back, first the two little ones, and then the others, one at a time, and, lastly, my wife, I succeeded in getting them safely across. At this time the skin was worn from my back to an extent almost equal to the size of the knapsack.

One night more was passed in the woods, and in the course of the next forenoon, we came out upon the wide, treeless plain which lies south and West of Sandusky city. The houses of the village were in plain sight. About a mile from the lake I hid my wife and children in the bushes, and pushed forward. I was attracted by a house on the left, between which and a small coasting vessel, a number of men were passing and repassing with great activity. Promptly deciding to approach them, I drew near, and scarcely had I come within hailing distance, when the captain of the schooner cried out, "Hollo there, man! you want to work?" "Yes, sir!" shouted I. "Come along, come along; I'll give you a shilling an hour. Must get off with this wind." As I came near, he said, "Oh, you can't work; you're crippled." "Can't I?" said I; and in a minute I had hold of a bag of corn, and followed the gang in emptying it into the hold. I took my place in the line of laborers next to a colored man, and soon got into conversation with him. "How far is it to Canada?" He gave me a peculiar look, and in a minute I saw he knew all. "Want to go to Canada? Come along with us, then. Our captain's a fine fellow. We're going to Buffalo." "Buffalo; how far is that from Canada?" "Don't you know, man? Just across the river." I now opened my mind frankly to him, and told him about my wife and children. "I'll speak to the captain," said he. He did so, and in a moment the captain took me aside, and said, "The Doctor says you want to go to Buffalo with your family." "Yes, sir." "Well, why not go with me?" was his frank reply. "Doctor says you've got a family." "Yes, sir." "Where do you stop?" "About a mile back." "How long have you been here?" "No time," I answered, after a moment's hesitation. "Come, my good fellow, tell us all about it. You're running away, ain't you?" I saw he was a friend, and opened my heart to him. "How long will it take you to get ready?" "Be here in half an hour, sir." "Well, go along and get them." Off I started; but, before I had run fifty feet, he called me back. "Stop," said he; "you go on getting the grain in. When we get off, I'll lay to over opposite that island, and send a boat back. There's a lot of regular nigger-catchers in the town below, and they might suspect if you brought your party out of the bush by daylight." I worked away with a will. Soon the two or three hundred bushels of corn were aboard, the batches fastened down, the anchor raised, and the sails hoisted.

I watched the vessel with intense interest as she left her moorings. Away she went before the free breeze. Already she seemed beyond the spot at which the captain agreed to lay to, and still she flew along. My heart sank within me; so near deliverance, and again to have my hopes blasted, again to be cast on my own resources! I felt that they had been making sport of my misery. The sun had sunk to rest, and the purple and gold of the west were fading away into gray. Suddenly, however, as I gazed with a weary heart, the vessel swung round into the wind, the sails flapped, and she stood motionless. A moment more, and a boat was lowered from her stern, and with a steady stroke made for the point at which I stood. I felt that my hour of release had come. On she came, and in ten minutes she rode up handsomely on to the beach.

My black friend and two sailors jumped out, and we started off at once for my wife and children. To my horror, they were gone from the place where I left them. Overpowered with fear, I supposed they bad been found and carried off. There was no time to lose, and the men told me I would have to go alone. Just at the point of despair, however, I stumbled on one of the children. My wife, it seemed, alarmed at my long absence, had given up all for lost, and supposed I had fallen into the hands of the enemy. When she heard my voice, mingled with those of the others, she thought my captors were leading me back to make me discover my family, and in the extremity of her terror she had tried to hide herself. I had hard work to satisfy her. Our long habits of concealment and anxiety had rendered her suspicious of every one; and her agitation was so great that for a time she was incapable of understanding what I said, and went on in a sort of paroxysm of distress and fear. This, however, was soon over, and the kindness of my companions did much to facilitate the matter.

And now we were off for the boat. It required little time to embark our baggage—one convenience, at least, of having nothing. The men bent their backs with a will, and headed steadily for a light hung from the vessel's mast. I was praising God in my soul. Three hearty cheers welcomed us as we reached the schooner, and never till my dying day shall I forget the shout of the captain—he was a Scotchman—"Coom up on deck, and clop your wings and craw like a rooster; you're a free nigger as sure as you're a live mon." Round went the vessel, the wind plunged into her sails as though inoculated with the common feeling—the water seethed and hissed past her sides. Man and nature, and, more than all, I felt the God of man and nature, who breathes love into the heart and maketh the winds His ministers, were with us. My happiness that night rose at times to positive pain. Unnerved by so sudden a change from destitution and danger to such kindness and blessed security, I wept like a child.

The next evening we reached Buffalo, but it was too late to cross the river that night. "You see those trees," said the noble-hearted captain, next morning, pointing to a group in the distance; "they grow on free soil, and as soon as your feet touch that, you're a mon. I want to see you go and be a freeman. I'm poor myself, and have nothing to give you; I only sail the boat for wages; but I'll see you across. Here, Green," said he to a ferryman, "what will you take this man and his family over for—he's got no money?" "Three shillings." He then took a dollar out of his pocket and gave it to me. Never shall I forget the spirit in which he spoke. He put his hand on my head and said, "Be a good fellow, won't you?" I felt streams of emotion running down in electric courses from head to foot. "Yes," said I; "I'll use my freedom well; I'll give my soul to God." He stood waving his hat as we pushed off for the opposite shore. God bless him! God bless him eternally! Amen!

It was the 28th of October, 1830, in the morning, when my feet first touched the Canada shore. I threw myself on the ground, rolled in the sand, seized handfuls of it and kissed them, and danced around, till, in the eyes of several who were present, I passed for a madman. "He's some crazy fellow," said a Colonel Warren, who happened to be there. "Oh no, master! don't you know? I'm free!" He burst into a shout of laughter. "Well, I never knew freedom make a man roll in the sand in such a fashion." Still I could not control myself. I hugged and kissed my wife and children, and, until the first exuberant burst of feeling was over, went on as before.

Chapter 14
New scenes and a new home

There was not much time to be lost, though, in frolic even, at this extraordinary moment. I was a stranger in a strange land, and had to look about me at once for refuge and resource. I found a lodging for the night, and the next morning set about exploring the interior for the means of support. I knew nothing about the country or the people, but kept my eyes and ears open, and made such inquiries as opportunity afforded. I heard, in the course of the day, of a Mr. Hibbard, who lived some six or seven miles off. He was a rich man, as riches were counted there, had a large farm, and several small tenements on it, which he was in the habit of letting to his laborers. To him I went immediately, though the character given him by his neighbors was not, by any means, unexceptionably good. But I thought he was not, probably, any worse than those I had been accustomed to serve, and that I could get along with him, if honest and faithful work would satisfy him. In the afternoon I found him, and soon struck a bargain with him for employment. I asked him if there was any house where he would let me live. He said, "Yes," and led the way to an old two-story sort of shanty, into the lower story of which the pigs had broken, and had apparently made it their resting-place for some time. Still, it was a house, and I forthwith expelled the pigs, and set about cleaning it for the occupancy of a better sort of tenants. With the aid of hoe and shovel, hot water and a mop, I got the floor into a tolerable condition by midnight, and only then did I rest from my labor. The next day I brought the rest of the Hensons, the only furniture I had, to my house, and though there was nothing there but bare walls, and floors, we were all in a state of great delight, and my wife laughed and acknowledged that it was better than a log cabin with an earth-floor. I begged some straw of Mr. Hibbard, and confining it by logs in the corners of the room, I made beds of it three feet thick, upon which we reposed luxuriously after our long fatigues.

Another trial awaited me which I had not anticipated. In consequence of the great exposures we had been through, my wife and all the children fell sick; and it was not without extreme peril that they escaped with their lives.

My employer soon found that my labor was of more value to him than that of those he was accustomed to hire; and as I consequently gained his favor, and his wife took quite a fancy to mine, we soon procured some of the comforts of life, while the necessaries of life, food and fuel, were abundant. I remained with Mr. Hibbard three years, sometimes working on shares, and sometimes for wages; and I managed in that time to procure some pigs, a cow, and a horse. Thus my condition gradually improved, and I felt that my toils and sacrifices for freedom had not been in vain. Nor were my labors for the improvement of myself and others, in more important things than food and clothing, without effect. It so happened that one of my Maryland friends arrived in this neighborhood, and hearing of my being here, inquired if I ever preached now, and spread the reputation I had acquired elsewhere for my gifts in the pulpit. I had said nothing myself, and had not intended to say anything of my having ever officiated in that way. I went to meeting with others, when I had an opportunity, and enjoyed the quiet of the Sabbath when there was no assembly. I could not refuse to labor in this field, however, when afterwards desired to do so; and I was from this time frequently called upon, not by blacks alone, but by all classes in my vicinity—the comparatively educated, as well as the lamentably ignorant—to speak to them on their duty, responsibility, and immortality, on their obligations to themselves, their Savior, and their Maker.

I am aware it must seem strange to many that a man so ignorant, unable to read, and having heard so little as I had of religion, natural or revealed, should be able to preach acceptably to persons who had enjoyed greater advantages than myself. I can explain it only by reference to our Savior's comparison of the kingdom of heaven to a plant which may spring from a seed no bigger than a mustard-seed, and may yet reach such a size, that the birds of the air may take shelter therein. Religion is not so much knowledge as wisdom; and observation upon what passes without, and reflection upon what passes within a man's heart, will give him a larger growth in grace than is imagined by the devoted adherents of creeds, or the confident followers of Christ, who call Him "Lord, Lord," but do not the things which He says.

Mr. Hibbard was good enough to give my eldest boy, Tom, two quarters' schooling, to which the schoolmaster added more, of his own kindness, so that my boy learned to read fluently and well. It was a great advantage, not only to him, but to me; for I used to got him to read much to me in the Bible, especially on Sunday mornings, when I was going to preach; and I could easily commit to memory a few verses, or a chapter, from hearing him read it over.

One beautiful summer Sabbath I rose early, and called him to come and read to me. "Where shall I read, father?" "Anywhere, my son," I answered, for I knew not how to direct him. He opened upon Psalm ciii., "Bless the Lord, O my soul: and all that is within me, bless His holy name;" and as he read this beautiful outpouring of gratitude, which I now first heard, my heart melted within me. I recalled, with all the rapidity of which thought is capable, the whole current of my life; and, as I remembered the dangers and afflictions from which the Lord had delivered me, and compared my present condition with what it had been, not only my heart but my eyes overflowed, and I could neither check nor conceal the emotion which overpowered me. The words, "Bless the Lord, O my soul," with which the Psalm begins and ends, were all I needed, or could use, to express the fullness of my thankful heart. When he had finished, Tom turned to me and asked, "Father, who was David?" He had observed my excitement, and added, "He writes pretty, don't he?" and then repeated his question. It was a question I was utterly unable to answer. I had never heard of David, but could not bear to acknowledge my ignorance to my own child. So I answered, evasively, "He was a man of God, my son." "I suppose so," said he, "but I want to know something more about him. Where did he live? What did he do?" As he went on questioning me, I saw it was in vain to attempt to escape, and so I told him frankly I did not know. "Why, father," said he, "can't you read?" This was a worse question than the other, and, if I had any pride in me at the moment, it took it all out of me pretty quick. It was a direct question, and must have a direct answer; so I told him at once I could not. "Why not?" said he. "Because I never had an opportunity to learn, nor anybody to teach me." "Well, you can learn now, father." "No, my son, I am too old, and have not time enough. I must work all day, or you would not have enough to eat." "Then you might do it at night." "But still there is nobody to teach me. I can't afford to pay anybody for it, and, of course, no one can do it for nothing." "Why, father, I'll teach you. I can do it, I know. And then you'll know so much more that you will be able to talk better, and preach better." The little fellow was so earnest, there was no resisting him; but it is hard to describe the conflicting feelings within me at such a proposition from such a quarter. I was delighted with the conviction that my children would have advantages I had never enjoyed; but it was no slight mortification to think of being instructed by my young son. Yet ambition, and a true desire to learn, for the good it would do my own mind, conquered the shame, and I agreed to try. But I did not reach this state of mind instantly.

I was greatly moved by the conversation I had with Tom, so much so, that I could not undertake to preach that day. The congregation were disappointed, and I passed the Sunday in solitary reflection in the woods. I was too much engrossed with the multitude of my thoughts to return home to dinner, and spent the whole day in secret meditation and prayer, trying to compose myself, and ascertain my true position. It was not difficult to see that my predicament was one of profound ignorance, and that I ought to use every opportunity of enlightening it. I began to take lessons of Tom, therefore, immediately, and followed it up every evening, by the light of a pine knot, or some hickory bark, which was the only light I could afford. Weeks passed, and my progress was so slow that poor Tom was almost discouraged, and used to drop asleep sometimes, and whine a little over my dullness, and talk to me very much as a schoolmaster talks to a stupid boy, till I began to be afraid that my age, nearly fifty, my want of practice in looking at such little scratches, the daily fatigue, and the dim light, would be effectual preventives of my ever acquiring the art of reading. But Tom's perseverance and mine conquered at last, and in the course of the winter I did really learn to read a little.

It was, and has been ever since, a great comfort to me to have made this acquisition; though it has made me comprehend better the terrible abyss of ignorance into which I had been plunged all my previous life. It made me also feel more deeply and bitterly the oppression under which I had toiled and groaned, the crushing and cruel nature of which I had not appreciated, till I found out, in some slight degree, from what I had been debarred. At the same time it made me more anxious than before, to do something for the rescue and the elevation of those who were suffering the same evils I had endured, and who did not know how degraded and ignorant they really were.

Chapter 16

Conducting slaves to Canada

The degraded and hopeless condition of a slave can never be properly felt by him while he remains in such a position. After I had tasted the blessings of freedom, my mind reverted to those whom I knew were groaning in captivity, and I at once proceeded to take measures to free as many as I could. I thought that, by using exertion, numbers might make their escape as I did, if they had some practical advice how to proceed.

I was once attending a very large meeting at Fort Erie, at which a great many colored people were present. In the course of my preaching, I tried to impress upon them the importance of the obligations they were under; first, to God, for their deliverance; and then, secondly, to their fellow-men, to do all that was in their power to bring others out of bondage. In the congregation was a man named James Lightfoot, who was of a very active temperament, and had obtained his freedom by fleeing to Canada, but had never thought of his family and friends whom he had left behind, until the time he heard me speaking, although he himself had been free for some five years. However, that day the cause was brought home to his heart. When the service was concluded, he begged to have an interview with me, to which I gladly acceded, and an arrangement was made for further conversation on the same subject one week from that time. He then informed me where he came from, also to whom he belonged, and that he had left behind a dear father and mother, three sisters and four brothers; and that they lived on the Ohio River, not far from the city of Maysville. He said that he never saw his duty towards them to be so clear and unmistakable as be did at that time, and professed himself ready to co-operate in any measures that might be devised for their release. During the short period of his freedom he had accumulated some little property, the whole of which, he stated, he would cheerfully devote to carrying out those measures; for he had no rest, night nor day, since the meeting above mentioned.

I was not able at that time to propose what was best to be done, and thus we parted; but in a few days he came to see me again on the same errand. Seeing the agony of his heart in behalf of his kindred, I consented to commence the painful and dangerous task of endeavoring to free those whom he so much loved. I left my own family in the hands of no other save God, and commenced the journey alone, on foot, and traveled thus about four hundred miles. But the Lord furnished me with strength sufficient for the undertaking. I passed through the States of New York, Pennsylvania, and Ohio—free States, so called— crossed the Ohio River into Kentucky, and ultimately found his friends in the place he had described.

I was an entire stranger to them, but I took with me a small token of their brother who was gone, which they at once recognized; and this was to let them know that he had gone to Canada, the land of freedom, and had now sent a friend to assist them in making their escape. This created no little excitement. But his parents had become so far advanced in years that the could not undertake the fatigue; his sisters had a number of children, and they could not travel; his four brothers and a nephew were young men, and sufficiently able for the journey, but the thought of leaving their father, and mother, and sisters, was too painful; and they also considered it unsafe to make the attempt then, for fear that the excitement and grief of their friends might betray them; so they declined going at that time, but promised that they would go in a year if I would return for them.

To this I assented, and then went between forty and fifty miles into the interior of Kentucky, having heard that there was a large party ready to attempt their escape if they had a leader to direct their movements. I traveled by night, resting by day, and at length reached Bourbon county, the place where I expected to find these people. After a delay of about a week, spent in discussing plans, making arrangements, and other matters, I found that there were about thirty collected from different States, who were disposed to make the attempt. At length, on a Saturday night, we started. The agony of parting can be better conceived than described; as, in their case, husbands were leaving their wives, mothers their children, and children their parents. This, at first sight, will appear strange, and even incredible; but, when we take into consideration the fact, that at any time they were liable to be separated, by being sold to what are termed "nigger traders," and the probability that such an event would take place, it will, I think, cease to excite any surprise.

We succeeded in crossing the Ohio River in safety, and arrived in Cincinnati the third night after our departure. Here we procured assistance; and, after stopping a short time to rest, we started for Richmond, Indiana. This is a town which had been settled by Quakers, and there we found friends indeed, who at once helped us on our way, without loss of time; and after a difficult journey of two weeks, through the wilderness, we reached Toledo, Ohio, a town on the south-western shore of Lake Erie, and there we took passage for Canada, which we reached in safety. I then went home to my family, taking with me a part of this large party, the rest finding their friends scattered in other towns, perfectly satisfied with my conduct in the matter, in being permitted to be the instrument of freeing such a number of my fellow-creatures.

Chapter 17
Second journey on the Underground Railroad
I remained at home, working on my farm, until the next autumn, about the time I had promised to assist in the restoring to liberty the friends of James Lightfoot, the individual who had excited my sympathy at the meeting at Fort Erie. In pursuance of this promise, I again started on my long journey into Kentucky.

On my way, that strange occurrence happened, called the great meteoric shower. The heavens seemed broken up into streaks of light and falling stars. I reached Lancaster, Ohio, at three o'clock in the morning, found the village aroused, the bells ringing, and the people exclaiming, "The day of judgment is come!" I thought it was probably so; but felt that I was in the right business, and walked on through the village, leaving the terrified people behind. The stars continued to fall till the light of the sun appeared.

On arriving at Portsmouth, in the State of Ohio, I had a very narrow escape from being detected. The place was frequented by a number of Kentuckians, who were quite ready to suspect a colored man, if they saw anything unusual about him. I reached Portsmouth in the morning, and waited until two in the afternoon for the steamboat, so that I might not arrive in Maysville till after dark. While in the town I was obliged to resort to a stratagem, in order to avoid being questioned by the Kentuckians I saw in the place. To this end I procured some dried leaves, put them into a cloth and bound it all round my face, reaching nearly to my eyes, and pretended to be so seriously affected in my head and teeth as not to be able to speak. I then hung around the village till the time for the evening boat, so as to arrive at

Maysville in the night. I was accosted by several during my short stay in Portsmouth, who appeared very anxious to get some particulars from me as to who I was, where I was going, and to whom I belonged. To all their numerous inquiries I merely shook my head, mumbled out indistinct answers, and acted so that they could not get anything out of me; and, by this artifice, I succeeded in avoiding any unpleasant consequences. I got on board the boat and reached Maysville, Kentucky, in the evening, about a fortnight from the time I had left Canada.

On landing, a wonderful providence happened to me. The second person I met in the street was Jefferson Lightfoot, brother of the James Lightfoot previously mentioned, and one of the party who had promised to escape if I would assist them. He stated that they were still determined to make the attempt, decided to put it into execution the following Saturday night, and preparations for the journey were at once commenced. The reason why Saturday night was chosen on this and the previous occasion was, that from not having to labor the next day, and being allowed to visit their families, they would not be missed until the time came for their usual appearance in the field, at which period they would be some eighty or a hundred miles away. During the interval I had to keep myself concealed by day, and used to meet them by night to make the necessary arrangements.

From fear of being detected, they started of without bidding their father or mother farewell, and then, in order to prevent the bloodhounds from following on our trail, we seized a skiff, a little below the city, and made our way down the river. It was not the shortest way, but it was the surest.

It was sixty-five miles from Maysville to Cincinnati, and we thought we could reach that city before daylight, and then take the stage for Sandusky. Our boat sprung a leak before we had got half way, and we narrowly escaped being drowned; providentially, however, we got to the shore before the boat sunk. We then took another boat, but this detention prevented us from arriving at Cincinnati in time for the stage. Day broke upon us when we were about ten miles above the city, and we were compelled to leave our boat from fear of being apprehended. This was an anxious time. However, we had got so far away that we knew there was no danger of being discovered by the hounds, and we thought we would go on foot. When we got within seven miles of Cincinnati, we came to the Miami River, and we could not reach the city without crossing it.

This was a great barrier to us, for the water appeared to be deep, and we were afraid to ask the loan of a boat, being apprehensive it might lead to our detection. We went first up and then down the river, trying to find a convenient crossing-place, but failed. I then said to my company, "Boys, let us go up the river and try again." We started, and after going about a mile we saw a cow coming out of a wood, and going to the river as though she intended to drink. Then said I, "Boys, let us go and see what the cow is about, it may be that she will tell us some news." I said this in order to cheer them up. One of them replied, in rather a peevish way, "Oh, that cow can't talk;" but I again urged them to come on. The cow remained until we approached her within a rod or two; she then walked into the river, and went straight across without swimming, which caused me to remark, "The Lord sent that cow to show us where to cross the river!" This has always seemed to me to be a very wonderful event.

Having urged our way with considerable haste, we were literally saturated with perspiration, though it was snowing at the time, and my companions thought that it would be highly dangerous for us to proceed through the water, especially as there was a large quantify of ice in the river. But as it was a question of life or death with us, there was no time left for reasoning; I therefore advanced—they reluctantly following. The youngest of the Lightfoots, ere we reached halfway over the river, was seized with violent contraction of the limbs, which prevented further self-exertion on his part; he was, therefore, carried the remainder of the distance. After resorting to continued friction, he partially recovered, and we proceeded on our journey.

We reached Cincinnati about eleven on Sunday morning, too late for the stage that day; but having found some friends, we hid ourselves until Monday evening, when we recommenced our long and toilsome journey, through mud, rain, and snow, towards Canada. We had increased our distance about one hundred miles, by going out of our road to get among the Quakers. During our passage through the woods, the boy before referred to was taken alarmingly ill, and we were compelled to proceed with him on our backs; but finding this mode of conveying him exceedingly irksome, we constructed a kind of litter with our shirts and handkerchiefs laid across poles. By this time we got into the State of Indiana, so that we could travel by day as long as we kept to the woods. Our patient continued to get worse, and it appeared, both to himself and to us, that death would soon release him from his sufferings. He therefore begged to be left in some secluded spot, to die alone, as he feared that the delay occasioned by his having to be carried through the bush, might lead to the capture of the whole company. With very considerable reluctance we acceded to his request, and laid him in a sheltered place, with a full expectation that death would soon put an end to his sufferings. The poor fellow expressed his readiness to meet the last struggle in hope of eternal life. Sad, indeed, was the parting; and it was with difficulty we tore ourselves away.

We had not, however, proceeded more than two miles on our journey, when one of the brothers of the dying man made a sudden stop, and expressed his inability to proceed whilst he had the consciousness that he had left his brother to perish, in all probability, a prey to the devouring wolves. His grief was so great that we determined to return, and at length reached the spot, where we found the poor fellow apparently dying, moaning out with every breath a prayer to heaven. Words cannot describe the joyousness experienced by the Lightfoots when they saw their poor afflicted brother once more; they literally danced for joy. We at once prepared to resume our journey as we best could, and once more penetrated the bush. After making some progress, we saw, at a little distance on the road, a wagon approaching, and I immediately determined to ascertain whether some assistance could not be obtained.

I at length circumvented the road, so as to make it appear that I had been journeying in an opposite direction to that which the wagon was taking. When I came up with the driver, I bade him good day. He said, "Where is thee going?" "To Canada." I saw his coat, heard his thee and thou, and set him down for a Quaker. I therefore plainly told him our circumstances. He at once stopped his horses, and expressed his willingness to assist us. I returned to the place where my companions were in waiting for me, and soon had them in the presence of the Quaker. Immediately on viewing the sufferer he was moved to tears, and without delay turned his horses' heads, to proceed in the direction of his home, although he had intended to go to a distant market with a load of produce for sale. The reception we met with from the Quaker's family overjoyed our hearts, and the transports with which the poor men looked upon their brother, now so favorably circumstanced, cannot be described.

We remained with this happy family for the night, and received from them every kindness. It was arranged that the boy should remain behind, until, through the blessing of God, he should recover. We were kindly provided by them with a sack of biscuit and a joint of meat, and once more set our faces in the direction of Lake Erie.

After proceeding some distance on our road, we perceived a white man approaching, but as he was traveling alone, and on foot, we were not alarmed at his presence. It turned out that he had been residing for some time in the South, and although a free white man, his employers had attempted to castigate him; in return for which he had used violence, which made it necessary that he should at once escape. We traveled in company, and found that his presence was of signal service to us in delivering us out of the hands of the slave-hunters who were now on our track, and eagerly grasping after their prey. We had resolved on reaching the lake, a distance of forty miles, by the following morning; we, therefore, walked all night.

Just as the day was breaking, we reached a wayside tavern, immediately contiguous to the lake, and our white companion having knocked up the landlord, ordered breakfast for six. Whilst our breakfast was in course of preparation, we dosed off into slumber, wearied with our long-continued exertion.

Just as our breakfast was ready, whilst half-asleep and half-awake, an impression came forcibly upon me that danger was nigh, and that I must at once leave the house. I immediately urged my companions to follow me out, which they were exceedingly unwilling to do; but as they had promised me submission, they at length yielded to my request. We retired to the yard at the side of the house, and commenced washing ourselves with the snow, which was now up to our knees. Presently we heard the tramping of horses, and were at once warned of the necessity of secreting ourselves. We crept beneath a pile of bushes, close at hand, which permitted a full view of the road. The horsemen came to a dead stop at the door of the house, and commenced their inquiries; my companions at once recognized the parties on horseback, and whispered their names to me. This was a critical moment, and the loud beatings of their hearts testified the dreadful alarm with which they viewed the scene. Had we been within doors, we should have been inevitably sacrificed. Our white friend proceeded to the door in advance of the landlord, and maintained his position. He was at once interrogated by the slave-hunters whether he had seen any Negroes pass that way. He said, yes, he thought he had. Their number was demanded, and they were told about six, and that they were proceeding in the direction of Detroit; and that they might be some few miles on the road. They at once reigned their horses, which were greatly fatigued, through having been ridden all night, and were soon out of sight. We at length ventured into the house, and devoured breakfast in an incredibly short space of time. After what had transpired, the landlord became acquainted with our circumstances, and at once offered to sail us in his boat across to Canada. We were happy enough to have such an offer, and soon the white sail of our little bark was laying to the wind, and we were gliding along on our way, with the land of liberty in full view. Words cannot describe the feelings experienced by my companions as they neared the shore—their bosoms were swelling with inexpressible joy as they mounted the seats of the boat, ready, eagerly, to spring forward, that they might touch the soil of the freeman. And when they reached the shore, they danced and wept for joy, and kissed the earth on which they first stepped, no longer the SLAVE—but the FREE.

After the lapse of a few months, on one joyous Sabbath morning, I had the happiness of clasping the poor boy we had left in the kind care of the Quaker, no longer attenuated in frame, but robust and healthy, and surrounded by his family. Thus my joy was consummated, and superadded were the blessings of those who were ready to perish, which came upon me. It is one of the greatest sources of my happiness to know, that by similar means to those above narrated, I have been instrumental in delivering one hundred and eighteen human beings out of the cruel and merciless grasp of the slaveholder.

Mr. Frank Taylor, the owner of the Lightfoots, whose escape I have just narrated, soon after he missed his slaves, fell ill, and became quite deranged; on recovering, he was persuaded by his friends to free the remainder of the family of the Lightfoots, which he at length did, and after a short lapse of time, they all met each other in Canada, where they are now living.

Chapter 18

Home at dawn

I did not find that our prosperity increased with our numbers. The mere delight the slaves took in their freedom, rendered them, at first, contented with a lot far inferior to that to which they might have attained. Their ignorance often led them to make unprofitable bargains, and they would often hire wild land on short terms, and bind themselves to clear a certain number of acres. But by the time they were cleared and fitted for cultivation, and the lease was out, the landlords would take possession of the cleared land and raise a splendid crop on it. The tenants would, very likely, start again on just such another bargain, and be no better off at the end of ten years than at the beginning. Another way in which they lost the profits of their labor was by raising nothing but tobacco, the high price of which was very tempting, and the cultivation of which was a monopoly in their hands, as no white man understood it, or could compete with them at all. The consequence was, however, that the had nothing but tobacco to sell, and soon there was rather too much of it in the market, and the price of wheat rose, while their commodity was depressed; hence they lost all they should have saved, in the profit they gave the trader for his corn and stores.

I saw the effect of these things so clearly, that I could not help trying to make my friends and neighbors see it too; and I set seriously about the business of lecturing upon the subject of crops, wages, and profit, just as if I had been brought up to it. I insisted on the necessity of their raising their own crops, saving their own wages, and securing the profits of their own labor, using such plain arguments as occurred to me, and were as clear to their comprehension as to mine. I did this very openly; and, frequently, my audience consisted in part of the very traders whose inordinate profits upon individuals I was trying to diminish, but whose balance of profit would not be ultimately lessened, because they would have so many more persons to trade with, who would be able to pay them a reasonable advance in cash, or its equivalent, on all their purchases. The purse is a tender part of the system; but I handled it so gently, that the sensible portion of my natural opponents were not, I believe, offended; while those whom I wished to benefit, saw, for the most part, the propriety of my advice, and took it. At least, there are now great numbers of colored fugitives, in this region of Canada, who own their farms, are training up their children in true independence, and giving them a good elementary education, who had not taken a single step towards such a result before I began to talk to them.

While I remained at Colchester, I became acquainted with a Congregational missionary from Massachusetts, by the name of Hiram Wilson, who took an interest in our people, and was disposed to do what he could to promote the cause of improvement which I had so much at heart. He co-operated with me in many efforts, and I have been associated with him for over thirty years. He has been a faithful friend, and still continues his important labors of love in our behalf. Among other things, he wrote to a Quaker friend of his, an Englishman, by the name of James C. Fuller, residing at Skeneateles, New York, and endeavored to interest him in the welfare of our struggling population.

He succeeded so far, that Mr. Fuller, who was going on a visit to England, promised to interest his friends there, to induce them to aid us. He came back with fifteen hundred dollars which had been subscribed for our benefit. It was a great question how this sum, which sounded vast to many of my brethren, should be appropriated. I had my own decided opinion as to what it was best for us all to do with it. But, in order to come to a satisfactory conclusion, it was thought expedient to call a convention of delegates from every settlement of blacks that was within reach; that all might see that the ultimate decision was sanctioned by the disinterested votes of those who were thought by their companions best able to judge what would meet the wants of our community. Mr. Wilson and myself, therefore, called such a convention, to meet in London, Upper Canada, and it was held in June, 1838.

I urged the appropriation of the money to the establishment of a manual-labor school, at which our children could gain those elements of knowledge which are usually taught in a grammar-school. I urged that the boys should be taught, in addition, the practice of some mechanical art, and the girls should be instructed in those domestic arts which are the proper occupation and ornament of their sex; and that such an establishment would not only train up those who would afterwards instruct others, but that it would gradually enable us to become independent of the white man for our intellectual progress, as we could be for our physical prosperity. It was the more necessary, as in many districts, owing to the insurmountable prejudices of the inhabitants, the children of the blacks were not allowed to share the advantages of the common school. There was some opposition to this plan in the convention; but in the course of the discussion, which continued for three days, it appeared so obviously for the advantage of all to husband this donation, so as to preserve it for a purpose of permanent utility, that the proposal was, at last, unanimously adopted; and a committee of three was appointed to select and purchase a site for the establishment. Mr.

Wilson and myself were the active members of this committee, and after traversing the country for several months, we could find no place more suitable than that upon which I had had my eye for three or four years, for a permanent settlement, in the town of Dawn.

We therefore bought two hundred acres of fine rich land, on the River Sydenham, covered with a heavy growth of black walnut and white wood, at four dollars the acre. I had made a bargain for two hundred acres adjoining this lot, on my own account; and circumstances favored me so, that the man of whom I purchased, was glad to let me have them at a large discount from the price I had agreed to pay, if I would give him cash for the balance I owed him. I transferred a portion of the advantage of this bargain to the institution, by selling to it one hundred acres more, at the low price at which I obtained them.

In 1842 I removed with my family to Dawn, and as a considerable number of my friends were soon there about me, and the school was permanently fixed there, as we thought, the future importance of this settlement seemed to be decided. There are many other settlements which are prosperous; indeed, the colored population is scattered over a territory which does not fall far short of three hundred miles in extent, in each direction, and probably numbers not less than twenty thousand persons in all. We looked to the school, and the possession of landed property by individuals, as two great means by which our oppressed and degraded race could be elevated to enjoy a participation in the blessings of civilization, whereas they had hitherto been permitted to share only its miseries and vices.

My efforts to aid them, in every way in my power, and to procure the aid of others for them, have been constant. I have made many journeys into New York, Connecticut, Massachusetts, and Maine, in all of which States I have found or made many friends to the cause, as well as personal friends. I have received many liberal gifts for my people, and experienced much kindness of treatment; but I must be allowed to allude particularly to the donations received from Boston—by which we were enabled to erect a sawmill, and thus to begin in good earnest the clearing of our lands, and to secure a profitable return for the support of our school—as among those which have been most welcome and valuable to us. ...

Chapter 21

The World's Fair in London

I have already mentioned that the first idea which suggested to me the plan of going to England, was to exhibit, at the World's Great Fair, in London, some of the best specimens of our black walnut-lumber, in the hope that it might lead to sales in England. For this purpose, I selected some of the best boards out of the cargo which I had brought to Boston, which Mr. Chickering was kind enough to have properly packed in boxes, and sent to England in the American ship which carried the American products for exhibition. The boards which I selected were four in number, excellent specimens, about seven feet in length and four feet in width, of beautiful grain and texture. On their arrival in England, I had them planed and perfectly polished, in French style, so that they actually shone like a mirror.

The history of my connection with the World's Fair is a little amusing. Because my boards happened to be carried over in the American ship, the superintendent of the

American Department, who was from Boston, insisted that my lumber should be exhibited in the American department. To this I objected. I was a citizen of Canada, my boards were from Canada, and there was an apartment of the building appropriated to Canadian products. I therefore insisted that my boards should be removed from the American department to the Canadian. But, said the American, "You cannot do it. All these things are under my control. You can exhibit what belongs to you if you please, but not a single thing here must be moved an inch without my consent."

This was quite a damper to me. I thought his position was rather absurd, and for the time it seemed impossible to move him or my boards.

A happy suggestion, however, occurred to me. Thought I, if this Yankee wants to retain my furniture, the world shall know who owns it. I accordingly hired a painter to paint in large white letters on the tops of my boards:

This is the product of the industry of a fugitive slave from the United States, whose residence is Dawn, Canada.

This was done early in the morning. In due time, the American superintendent came around, and found me at my post. The gaze of astonishment with which he read my inscription, was laughable to witness. His face was as black as a thunder-cloud.

"Look here, sir," said he. "What, under heaven, have you got up there?"

"Oh, that is only a little information to let the people know who am."

"But don't you know better than that? Do you suppose I am going to have that insult up there?"

The English gentlemen began to gather around, chuckling with half-suppressed delight, to see the wrath of the Yankee. This only added fuel to the fire.

"Well, sir," said he, "do you suppose brought that stuff across the Atlantic for nothing?"

"I never asked you to bring it for nothing. I am ready to pay you, and have been from the beginning"

"Well, sir, you may take it away, and carry it where you please."

"Oh," said I, "I think, as you wanted it very much, I will not disturb it. You can have it now."

"No, sir; take it away!"

"I beg your pardon, sir," said I, "when I wanted to remove it, you would not allow it, and now, for all me, it shall remain."

In the meantime the crowd enjoyed it and so did I. The result was, that by the next day, the boards were removed to their proper place at no expense to me, and no bill was ever presented to me for carrying the lumber across the Atlantic.

In that immense exhibition, my humble contribution received its due share of attention. I had many interesting conversations with individuals among that almost innumerable multitude from every nation under heaven. Perhaps my complexion attracted attention, but nearly all who passed, paused to look at me, and at themselves, as reflected in my large black walnut mirrors.

Among others, the Queen of England, Victoria, preceded by her guide, and attended by her cortège, paused to view me and my property. I uncovered my head and saluted her as respectfully as I could, and she was pleased with perfect grace to return my salutation. "Is he indeed a fugitive slave?" I heard her inquire; and the answer was, "He is indeed, and that is his work."

But notwithstanding such pleasant occurrences, the time wore heavily away. The immense crowd, kept in as perfect order as a single family, became wearisome to me, and I was not sorry, as related in a preceding chapter, to go back to Canada, leaving my boards on exhibition.

On returning to England the exhibition was still in progress. There seemed no diminution of the crowd. Like the waters of the great Mississippi, the channel was still full, though the individuals were changed.

But among all the exhibitors from every nation in Europe, and from Asia, America, and the Isles of the Sea, there was not a single black man but myself. There were Negroes there from Africa, brought to be exhibited, but no exhibitors-exhibitors but myself. Though my condition was wonderfully changed from what it was in my childhood and youth, yet it was a little saddening to reflect that my people were not more largely represented there. The time will yet come, I trust, when such a state of things will no longer exist.

At the close of the exhibition, on my return to Canada, I received from England a large quarto bound volume containing a full description of all the objects presented at the exhibition, the names of the officers of all the committees, juries, exhibitors, prizes, &c., &c. Among others, I found my own name recorded; and in addition a bronze medal was awarded to me. I also received a beautiful picture of the Queen and royal family, of the size of life, and several other objects of interest.

These testimonials of honor I greatly prize. I fully succeeded in my mission to England, and released myself from the voluntarily-assumed debt in behalf of the manual-labor school. While in England, I was permitted to enjoy some excellent opportunities to witness its best society, which I propose to relate in the following chapter.

Chapter 22

Visits to the ragged schools

While in England I was frequently called upon to speak at public meetings of various kinds. I was deeply interested in the Ragged School enterprise, and frequently addressed the schools, and also public meetings held in their behalf. I attended most of the great anniversaries held in May, and was called upon to speak at many of them. On several occasions I did what I could, to make known the true condition of slaves, in Exeter Hall and other places. On one occasion, I recollect, an eminent man from Pennsylvania was addressing the anniversary of a Sabbath School Union. He boasted of the great benefits of Sunday schools in the United States, and asserted that all classes indiscriminately enjoyed their blessings. I felt bound to contradict him, and after putting to the speaker a few questions, which he stammeringly answered, I told the immense meeting that in the Southern States, the great body of the colored people were almost entirely neglected, and in many places they were excluded altogether; and that in the majority of the Northern States, the great mass of the colored children were not sought out and gathered into Sunday schools. This created some little storm, but my own personal observation and experience carried conviction to the people.

Being thus introduced to the public, I became well acquainted with many of the leading men of England. Lord Grey made a proposition to me, which, if circumstances had permitted, I should have been glad to have accepted. It was to go to India, and there super-intend some great efforts made by the government to introduce the culture of cotton on the American plan. He promised to appoint me to an office, with a good salary. Had it not been for my warm interest in my Canadian enterprise, I should have accepted his proposal.

One of the most pleasing incidents for me now to look back upon, was a long interview which I was permitted to enjoy with the Archbishop of Canterbury. The elevated social position of this man, the highest beneath the crown, is well known to all those acquainted with English society. Samuel Gurney, the noted philanthropist, introduced me, by a note and his family-card, to his grace the archbishop. The latter received me kindly in his palace. I immediately entered into a conversation with him upon the condition of my people, and the plans I had in view. He expressed the strongest interest in me, and after about a half-hour's conversation, he inquired, "At what university, sir, did you graduate?"

"I graduated, your grace," said I, in reply, "at the university of adversity."

"The university of adversity," said he, looking up with astonishment; "where is that?"

I saw his surprise, and explained. "It was my lot, your grace," said I, "to be born a slave, and to pass my boyhood and all the former part of my life as a slave. I never entered a school, never read the Bible in my youth, and received all of my training under the most adverse circumstances. This is what I mean by graduating in the university of adversity."

"I understand you, sir," said he. "But is it possible that you are not a scholar?"

"I am not," said I.

"But I should never have suspected that you were not a liberally educated man. I have heard many Negroes talk, but have never seen one that could use such language as you. Will you tell me, sir, how you learned our language?"

I then explained to him, as well as I could, my early life; that it had always been my custom to observe good speakers, and to imitate only those who seemed to speak most correctly.

"It is astonishing," said the archbishop. "And is it possible that you were brought up ignorant of religion? How did you attain to the knowledge of Christ?"

I explained to him, in reply, "that a poor ignorant slave mother had taught me to say the Lord's Prayer, though I did not then know how, truly, to pray."

"And how were you led to a better knowledge of the Savior?" I answered by the hearing of the Gospel preached. He then asked me to repeat the text, and to explain all the circum-stances. I told him the text of the first sermon I had heard, was, "He, by the grace of God, tasted death for every man."

"A beautiful text was that," said the archbishop, and so affected was he by my simple story, that he shed tears freely. ...

Chapter 23

Closing up my London agency

The dinner at Lord John Russell's, as detailed in the previous chapter, was in the Month of June, 1852; from that time to the 1st of August, I was busily employed in finishing up all matters connected with my agency, in which I was very successful, having accomplished the objects of my mission. During the month of August, I was engaged in publishing a narrative of incidents in my slave-life, which I had been urgently requested to do by some of the noblest men and women in England. Just as I had completed the work, I received, on the 3rd of September, a letter from my family in Canada, stating that my beloved wife, the companion of my life, the sharer of my joys and sorrows, was at the point of death, and that she earnestly desired me to return immediately, that she might see me once more before she bade adieu to earth. This was a trying hour for me. I was in England, four thousand miles from my home. I was not long in deciding to go home. On the morning of the 4th of September, having received the letter from home at four o'clock on the afternoon of the 3rd, I was on my way from London to Liverpool, and embarked from Liverpool on the 5th, in the steamer Canada, bound for Boston. On the 20th of the same month I arrived at my own Canadian home. Those who have been placed in similar situations, can realize what must have been my feelings as I drew near my humble dwelling. I had heard nothing since the information contained in the letter which reached me at Liverpool. I knew not whether my dear wife, the mother of my children, she who had traveled with me, sad, solitary, and footsore, from the land of bondage, who had been to me a kind, affectionate, and dutiful wife for forty years, was still alive, or whether she had entered into her rest.

A merciful Father had, however, kindly prolonged her life, and we were permitted once more to meet. And oh! such a meeting! I was met in the yard by four of my daughters, who rushed to my arms, delighted at my unexpected return. They begged me not to go in to see mother, until they should first go and prepare her for it, thinking very wisely that the shock would be too great for her poor shattered nerves to bear. I consented that they should precede me. They gradually prepared her mind for our meeting. When I went to her bedside, she received and embraced me with the calmness and fortitude of a Christian, and even chided me for the strong emotions of sorrow which I found it utterly impossible to suppress. I found her perfectly calm and resigned to the will of God, awaiting with Christian firmness the hour for her summons. She was rejoiced to see me once more, while at the same time she said that perhaps she had done wrong in allowing me to leave England when my business-prospects were so flattering. I told her that I was more than satisfied, that I was truly thankful to my Heavenly Father for granting us this interview, no matter what the pecuniary sacrifice might be. We talked over our whole past life as far as her strength would permit, reviewing the many scenes of sorrow and trouble, as well as the many bright and happy days of our pilgrimage, until exhausted nature sought repose, and she sunk into a quiet sleep.

The day following she revived; my return seemed to inspire her with the hope that possibly she might again be restored to health. It was not, however, so to be; but God in His mercy granted her a reprieve, and her life was prolonged a few weeks. I thus had the melancholy satisfaction of watching day and night by her bed of languishing and pain, and was permitted to close her eyes when the final summons came. She blessed me, and blessed her children, commending us to the ever-watchful care of that Savior who had sustained her in so many hours of trial; and finally, after kissing me and each one of the children, she passed from earth to heaven without a pang or a groan, as gently as the falling to sleep of an infant on its mother's breast.

> Who would not wish to die like those
> Whom God's own Spirit deigns to bless?
> To sink into that soft repose,
> Then wake to perfect happiness?

I can truly and from an overflowing heart say, that she was a sincere and devoted Christian, a faithful and kind wife to me, even to the day of her death arranging all our domestic matters, in such a manner as to contribute as largely as possible to my comfort and happiness.

Chapter 24

My brother's freedom

I received numerous tokens of regard from many philanthropic gentlemen while I was in London, which I shall never forget; but I was particularly touched by the special kindness of Samuel Morley, Esq., and George Hitchcock, Esq., of St. Paul's Churchyard. These two gentlemen invited me to dine with them every day at half-past one. I gratefully accepted their invitation, and dined alternately with these gentlemen, always receiving a very warm welcome from them. The spirit of manhood, one of the strongest elements of my mind, was in no instance wounded, for I was invariably received and entertained as a respected guest. One day I was sitting at Mr. Morley's table, and was about to partake of his bountiful supply of nourishing food, when suddenly my mind reverted to the past. I remembered the trying scenes of my eventful life, and that my only brother was still bound in the iron chains of slavery, deprived of all the comforts of life, dragging out an abject, miserable existence, while I was surrounded with luxuries, and sitting at the sumptuous table of one of the first men in the kingdom. I could almost hear the clanking of his chains, and, in my mind's eye, see him with scarcely a crust of bread to satisfy his hunger, or a glass of water to quench his thirst. I was so forcibly impressed with my vision, that I rose from the table without eating a mouthful of food.

Struck with my unusual appearance, for I had always been cheerful and happy, Mr. Morley said, "What is the matter, Josiah? Has anything occurred to disturb your peace of mind?"

At first I could not control my emotions sufficiently, to reply. He added, "Come, come, Josiah, do help yourself and make yourself at home."

Soon I summoned the courage to tell him the cause of my agitation, and asked him "to excuse me from eating my dinner on that day, for I had no appetite."

I then and there resolved in my own mind, that as soon as I returned to America, I would make every possible effort to secure to my brother the blessed freedom I enjoyed.

Slavery had no power to eradicate the social ties that bound the different members of a family together, and though families were often torn asunder, yet memory generally kept the affections warm and abiding.

I had made several efforts to induce my brother to run away previous to my going to England. Mr. William L. Chaplain, of New York, saw him in his southern home, and tried to induce him to take the Underground Railroad—that is, to run away. But he found my brother's mind so demoralized or stultified by slavery, that he would not risk his life in the attempt to gain his freedom, and he informed me of this fact. Still I could not rest contented, and Mr. Chaplain promised to make another effort, as he intended to visit the neighborhood again. He labored with my brother the second time, with no good result, and then he endeavored to assist Mr. Toomb's slaves, who had resolved to escape from Georgia to Canada. Mr. Chaplain was detected, and thrown into prison to await a trial. He was released on bail, three times the amount of the value of the slaves. The Hathaways, benevolent Quakers of Farmington, New York, Asa B. Smith, and William R. Smith, his son, of the same town, paid the bail, which they desired Mr. Chaplain to forfeit, as they knew that the result of a trial would be that he would be hung. I will here add that the Smiths had to sell their farms, and were pecuniarily ruined for the time, and it is with pleasure that I make this record of their generosity in the Anti-Slavery cause.

On my return to Canada, the release of my brother was my uppermost thought. Whenever I have adopted the language of the prodigal son, who said, "I will arise, and go to my father,"—that is, when I have uttered in my heart the words, "God helping me, I will,"—I have somehow had the ability to accomplish my undertaking. Though I may have been obliged to change my plans and course of action, and pursue others more feasible, yet, ultimately, the end has been most marvelously attained. All my previous plans to rescue my brother had failed, but I was not at all disposed to relinquish the project. By the aid of friends, I learned that the mistress to whom my brother belonged would give him his freedom-papers for 400 dollars, and I concluded that I must raise 550 dollars, or about £110, so that I should be able to take him to my home in Canada. I consulted some of the Anti-Slavery friends in Boston, particularly Amos Lawrence, Esq., and they agreed to publish the story of my life, as I had suggested to them, that I might be able, from its sale, to raise a sufficient sum of money to buy my brother's freedom. I took a package of the books on my back and traveled in the New England States, and succeeded in interesting the people, so that I was enabled to raise the money I required. Then, through the negotiation of Mr. Charles C. Berry, cashier of the City Bank in Boston, Massachusetts, who had friends at the South, I joyfully sent the ransom. Soon my brother came from Maryland to Baltimore; thence by sea to Boston, where I met him and took him to my home in Canada, and kept him there for fifteen years. When President Lincoln's Proclamation of Emancipation gave freedom to all the slaves in America, my brother's eldest son came to Canada to see his father, and the meeting would have done President Lincoln's heart good if he had witnessed it.

The son went back and remained with his mother and brothers for three years. Then he came to Canada to take my brother to rejoin his wife and family in New Jersey; for after the

Emancipation Act was enforced, my brother's mistress removed from Maryland to New Jersey, where her husband bought a large dairy-farm. She had in vain endeavored to suit herself with ordinary white servants. Then she persuaded my brother to bring his family to her farm, and they have remained with her to this day as hired servants, receiving excellent wages for their faithful services. My brother's eldest son superintends her dairy, and is the head-man, in whom great confidence is placed. My brother is now ninety-one years of age, and is the only living relative I have, excepting my wife and children.

Chapter 25

Mrs. Stowe's characters

After my successful visit to England, I traveled in Canada, and in Maine, New Hampshire, Vermont, Massachusetts, Connecticut, and Rhode Island. In all these states I was cordially welcomed as a speaker in the pulpits of the Congregationalists, Presbyterians, Methodists, Baptists, and Universalists. I held many meetings, and discussed the subject of slavery in all its bearings on society. At that time, slavery was considered to be a permanent institution of the South, and it was supposed that nothing but an earthquake would have the power to break up the foundations of the system. It is a mistaken idea that the majority of the slave-holders would have sold their slaves if the government had offered to buy them. They liked the system, had grown up with it, and were not disposed to part with it without a struggle. Anti-slavery ideas were not popular at the South, nor generally at the North. On this account, those who had sufficient moral courage to discuss the merits and demerits of the system, were accustomed to hold meetings and conventions for this purpose. I was constantly traveling and doing all I could to help to change the public sentiment at the North. I was in the vicinity of Andover, Mass., where Mrs. Harriet Beecher Stowe resided. She sent for me and my traveling companion, Mr. George Clark, a white gentleman, who had a fine voice for singing, and usually sang at my meetings to add to their interest. We went to Mrs. Stowe's house, and she was deeply interested in the story of my life and misfortunes, and had me narrate its details to her. She said she was glad it had been published, and hoped it would be of great service, and would open the eyes of the people to the enormity of the crime of holding men in bondage. She manifested so much interest in me, that I told her about the peculiarities of many slaveholders, and the slaves in the region where I had lived for forty-two years. My experiences had been more varied than those of the majority of slaves, for I was not only my master's overseer, but a market-man for twenty-five years in the market at Washington, going there to sell the produce from my master's plantation.

Soon after, Mrs. Stowe's remarkable book, "Uncle Tom's Cabin," was published, and circulated in all parts of America, and read openly at the North, stealthily at the South. Many thought that her statements were exaggerations. She then published the key to the book to prove that it was impossible to exaggerate the enormities of slavery, and she therein gave many parallel cases, and referred to my published life-story, as an exemplification of the truth of the character of her Uncle Tom. From that time to the present, I have been called "Uncle Tom," and I feel proud of the title. If my humble words in any way inspired that gifted lady to write such a plaintive story that the whole community has been touched with pity for the sufferings of the poor slave, I have not lived in vain; for I believe that her book was the beginning of the glorious end. It was a wedge that finally rent asunder that gigantic fabric with a fearful crash.

Though she made her hero die, it was fit that she did this to complete her story; and if God had not given to me a giant's constitution, I should have died over and over again long before I reached Canada. I regard it as one of the most remarkable features of my life that I have rallied after so many exposures to all kinds of hardships. I am grateful to God for His abundant mercies to me in bringing me out of Egypt into the promised land, and I hope to be His faithful servant to my dying hour. ...

Chapter 31
My third and last visit to London
After the lapse of twenty-five years I was delighted to be in London again. Many of the friends whom I had known during my former visit have passed away. I found that Samuel Morley, Esq., and George Sturge, Esq., remembered me most kindly, and that they were disposed to be my staunch, steadfast friends; they have been genuine friends to me during all these long years that have passed, and I hope to greet them when we have all passed over the River Jordan. They at once promised to aid me in removing the weight that was pressing down my spirits and embarrassing my declining years when I could not labor as formerly. They started a fund, and generously headed it, not only with their influential names, but each gave £50 towards it. May God bless them for their generosity, and for their abiding friendship to me. Sir Thomas Fowell Buxton, Bart., and R. C. L. Bevan, added £25 each to the fund, and many belonging to the Society of Friends added their subscriptions. I should like to record that I have always received the most generous treatment, both in America and England, from the members of the Friends' Society, and specially from George Sturge, Esq., who has interested himself to the extent of assuring me he would send me back to my Canadian home with a light heart. I am certain my heart will be heavy with gratitude, for it will be full of that emotion, and I shall pray to my dying day for blessings to rest upon one who has afforded me so much relief.

Among the new friends I have made are Professor and Mrs. Fowler, formerly of New York, now residing in London, and I have always felt at home in their pleasant office.

Professor Fowler, with his remarkable skill, gave me an analysis of my character from my head. I told him "I should have supposed my old master had beaten out all my brains," but he humorously remarked "that perhaps my skull was so thick, the blows did not penetrate."

The description he gave of me was published, with my portrait, in the Christian Age, a weekly paper, and notwithstanding there were 80,000 copies of this number circulated, a third edition had to be printed to meet the demand. I am sure Professor Fowler's description will be of interest, and therefore give it insertion here.

"The organization of 'Uncle Tom' is as remarkable as his life and labors have been. His father was six feet in height, and was a very powerful, muscular man. He had a strong sense of justice and virtue, and an unflinching will. His son, Uncle Tom, is five feet seven inches in height.

"From his father he inherited a very strong osseous, muscular system, and a powerful constitution, as his physiology indicates and his most laborious life has proved. He has a large brain, twenty-three inches in circumference, with a predominance of brain in the superior coronal region, indicating great mental vigor, compass of mind, and availability of talent. His head is narrow, long, and high. The strength of his social nature centers in love to his wife and children, especially the latter, which he has proved to be intense, by his carrying two of his children on his back 600 miles, traveling on foot during the night, while fleeing from slavery and seeking his freedom on British soil in Canada. His head is very high in the crown and above the ears. No white man has a greater sense of liberty, love of freedom, manliness of feeling, and independence of mind, joined to a degree of firmness, perseverance, and determination of mind, not exceeded by a Cromwell or a Wellington, than Uncle Tom. His sense of moral obligations and love of truth are very strong.

"He is scrupulously honest, and his mind is as transparent as daylight. He is not inclined to double dealing, deception, and hypocrisy, undue selfishness or greed in his disposition, but he is cautious, looks ahead, and prepares for the future.

"He has by organization, as well as by grace, a strong feeling of devotion, worship, and sense of dependence. As a Christian, some of his strongest religious feelings are his love of prayer and thankfulness, and his disposition to seek aid and consolation from a higher source than man in the hour of trouble. The exercise of his veneration was his comfort when a slave, and it has been a comfort to him through all the vicissitudes of life. Benevolence is also very large; he is full of the missionary element, delights to do good, and many years of his life have been spent in labors of love. He is liable to forget his own interests when he can make himself useful to others. In his mind, "faith without works is dead." He does not expect an answer to his prayers without he makes an effort in the right direction. He is active, industrious, and delights to be occupied; is always busy in one way or another; and is not afraid of hard work if necessary. His mind works slowly but quite safely. When he has an object he holds on to it till his end is accomplished. He is one of the real plodding kind. He has not the qualities to render him showy and imaginative, but he has good powers of imitation, and can easily adapt himself to a change of situation and circumstances. He has a vast amount of dry humor, and is very direct, practical, natural, and truthful in his style of talking. His intellectual faculties are of the most practical and common-sense kind.

"He has superior powers to draw correct conclusions and inferences, as he understands them. He deals mostly in facts, conditions, qualities, and bearings of things, and turns all his knowledge into useful channels. He has a remarkable gift for observing everything that is transpiring around him; has a superior memory of persons he sees, facts he hears, of places, events, and anecdotes; and his mind is like a great storehouse, in which he has collected a vast amount of interesting incidents. He has a good capacity to arrange, systematize, organize, and plan, with reference to definite results.

"He is a great lover of simple truths; acts and speaks just as he feels, and thinks instinctively; cannot assume a character and appear differently from what he really feels, and has a thorough abhorrence of hypocrisy or falsehood. He has great courage in times of danger, also great presence of mind and great self-control in the midst of excitement and opposition.

"He is not revengeful, but has any amount of contemptuous feeling towards those who act meanly. He is more direct in his style of talking than copious or wordy; yet, having but little restraint from secretiveness, and so much varied knowledge and experience, he finds it easy to talk when he has attentive listeners.

"Though in his eighty-eighth year, he appears to be at least fifteen years younger, for he is firm in step, erect in form, disposed to wait on himself, and prefers to walk rather than ride; is positive in his manner of speaking, social in his disposition, emotional in his feelings, tender in his sympathies, distinct in his intellectual operations, humorous in his conversation, and apt in his illustrations. While many at fifty years of age consider that there is no opportunity left for them to improve their condition, Uncle Tom, at eighty-eight, is buoyant, elastic, and still anxious to make improvements.

"I have been much gratified in making the acquaintance of 'Uncle Tom,' and hope the friends of the colored race in England will send him back to Canada with sufficient means to enable him to live in comfort the remainder of his days."...

Josiah Henson, edited by John Lobb

SOJOURNER TRUTH (1797-1833)

Introduction

Sojourner Truth was a slave, social reformer, abolitionist, evangelist, counselor, suffragist and lecturer. And, like many of her contemporaries, she spent the majority of her public speaking years in churches, halls and podiums throughout the nation: relying on the kindness of friends to provide room, board and the basic necessities of life.

According to Margaret Washington, associate professor of history at Cornell University and editor of the 1993 edition of the *Narrative of Sojourner Truth*, Truth was among the most quoted activists of her time: a time which included the likes of Frederick Douglass, Susan B. Anthony, and countless other orators.

"Her penetrating one-line comments captured the heart of moral, social, political and religious issues," wrote Washington in her introduction to Truth's Narrative.

Washington said Truth inserted parables from everyday life into her speeches, sermons, and lectures to explain important political and social issues.

"Her words were peppered with biblical metaphors, symbols, and quotations," she wrote. "In the extemporaneous, spontaneous 'stump' speaker tradition popular to antebellum America, few could match Sojourner Truth: Whether trying to persuade farmers in western states on antislavery, communing with her eastern abolitionist friends, detailing her own bondage experience with other blacks, or addressing her favorite audience....the children, who often flocked around her."

Sojourner Truth wrote the following paragraph *On Heaven and Hell* in an address to the Michigan state legislature in June 1881.

The newspapers of my childhood used to have pictures of hell. I bought one once in New York, and there was one whole side covered with such a picture. On one side there was a narrow stair leading to heaven and the rest of the picture was a terrible abyss, with smoke rising up out of it, and numberless human beings swimming around in the flames. Then there was the old Evil One, with a long snout and a tail, stirring the others up with a pitchfork and I gazed upon that picture, I said, "My God, that is hell, sure 'nuff." There are probably persons here who can remember these things. As I got older I found out that there wasn't no such thing as hell, and that the narrow stairs only showed the narrowness of the mind that conceived the picture. I have found out and know that God's brightness and goodness and glory is hot enough to scorch all the sinners in the world.

Empowered by her religious faith, the former slave worked tirelessly for many years to transform national attitudes and institutions. According to Nell Painter, Princeton professor and Truth biographer, "No other woman who had gone through the ordeal of slavery managed to survive with sufficient strength, poise and self-confidence to become a public presence over the long term." (Painter, *Sojourner Truth: A Life, A Symbol*, page 4).

Sojourner Truth is often identified as a women's rights advocate and abolitionist. Such assessments overlook is the source of Sojourner's fiery devotion to human rights: That was her commitment to Jesus Christ. "The Lord gave me the name Sojourner," she declared, "because I was to travel up and down the land, showing people their sins, and being a sign unto them." At age eighty-eight, her dying words were, "Follow the Lord Jesus."

"Ain't I a Woman?"

Well, children, where there is so much racket there must be something out of kilter. I think that 'twixt the Negroes of the South and the women at the North, all talking about rights, the white men will be in a fix pretty soon. But what's all this here talking about? That man over there says that women need to be helped into carriages, and lifted over ditches, and to have the best place everywhere. Nobody ever helps me into carriages, or over mud-puddles, or gives me any best place! And ain't I a woman? Look at me! Look at my arm! I have ploughed and planted, and gathered into barns, and no man could head me! And ain't I a woman? I could work as much and eat as much as a man—when I could get it—and bear the lash as well! And ain't I a woman? I have borne thirteen children, and seen most all sold off to slavery, and when I cried out with my mother's grief, none but Jesus heard me! And ain't I a woman? Then they talk about this thing in the head; what's this they call it? [member of audience whispers, "intellect"] That's it, honey. What's that got to do with women's rights or Negroes' rights? If my cup won't hold but a pint, and yours holds a quart, wouldn't you be mean not to let me have my little half measure full? Then that little man in black there, he says women can't have as much rights as men, 'cause Christ wasn't a woman! Where did your Christ come from? Where did your Christ come from? From God and a woman! Man had nothing to do with Him. If the first woman God ever made was strong enough to turn the world upside down all alone, these women together ought to be able to turn it back, and get it right side up again! And now they is asking to do it, the men better let them. Obliged to you for hearing me, and now old Sojourner ain't got nothing more to say.

Sojourner Truth, Women's Convention, Akron, Ohio. Delivered 1851

Interview with Lincoln

Truth's account of her meeting with President Abraham Lincoln on October 29, 1864, is taken from a letter dictated by her to Rowland Johnson.

Dear friend,

It was about 8 o'clock a.m., when I called on the president. Upon entering his reception room we found about a dozen persons in waiting, among them two colored women. I had quite a pleasant time waiting until he was disengaged, and enjoying his conversation with others; he showed as much kindness and consideration to the colored persons as to the whites—if there was any difference, more. One case was that of a colored woman who was sick and likely to be turned out of her house on account of her inability to pay her rent. The president listened to with much attention, and spoke to her with kindness and tenderness.

He said he had given so much he could give no more, but told her where to go and get the money, and asked Mrs. C——-to assist her, which she did.

The president was seated at his desk. Mrs. C. said to him, "This is Sojourner Truth, who has come all the way from Michigan to see you."

He then arose, gave me his hand, made a bow, and said, "I am pleased to see you."

I said to him, Mr. President, when you first took your seat I feared you would be torn to pieces, for I likened you unto Daniel, who was thrown into the lion's den; and if the lions did not tear you into pieces, I knew that it would be God that had saved you; and I said, if he spared me I would see you before the four years expired, and he has done so, and now I am here to see you for myself.

He then congratulated me upon having been spared.

Then I said, I appreciate you, for you are the best president who has ever taken the seat.

He replied: "I expect you have reference to my having emancipated the slaves in my proclamation. But," said he, mentioning the names of several of his predecessors (and among them emphatically that of Washington), "they were all just as good, and would have done just as I have done if the time had come. If the people over the river [pointing across the Potomac] had behaved themselves, I could not have done what I have; but they did not, which gave the opportunity to do those things.'

I then said, I thank God that you were the instrument selected by him and the people to do it. I told him that I had never heard of him before he was talked of for president.

He smilingly replied, "I had heard of you many times before that." He then showed me the Bible presented to him by the colored people of Baltimore, of which you have no doubt seen a description. I have seen it for myself and it is beautiful beyond description.

After I had looked it over, I said to him, "This is beautiful indeed; the colored people have given this to the head of the government, and that government once sanctioned laws that would not permit its people to learn enough to enable them to read this book. And for what? Let them answer who can.'

I must say, and I am proud to say, that I never was treated by any one with more kindness and cordiality than were shown to me by that great and good man, Abraham Lincoln, by the grace of God president of the United States for four years more. He took my little book, and with the same hand that signed the death-warrant of slavery, wrote as follows:

For Aunty Sojourner Truth October 29, 1864 A. Lincoln

As I was taking my leave, he arose and took my hand, and said he would be pleased to have me call again. I felt that I was in the presence of a friend, and now I thank God from the bottom of my heart that I always have advocated his cause, and have done it openly and boldly. I shall feel still more in duty bound to do so in time to come. May God assist me.

Sojourner Truth

THEODORE S. WRIGHT (1797-1847)

Introduction

Rev. Theodore S. Wright, was born to free parents in Providence, Rhode Island. By the 1830s Wright had become pastor of the First Presbyterian Church in New York City and a conductor on the Underground Railroad. Wright, a dedicated abolitionist, attended the New York State Anti-Slavery Society convention held in Utica, on September 20, 1837. However, he also recognized the growing racial prejudice directed against free blacks in the North. In his speech, *Prejudice Against the Colored Man* Wright supported a resolution introduced into the convention which said anti-black prejudice was "nefarious and wicked and should be practically reprobated and discountenanced."

Prejudice Against the Colored Man

Mr. President, with much feeling do I rise to address the society on this resolution, and I should hardly have been induced to have done it had I not been requested. I confess I am personally interested in this resolution. But were it not for the fact that none can feel the lash but those who have it upon them, that none know where the chain galls but those who wear it, I would not address you.

This is a serious business, sir. The prejudice which exists against the colored man, the free man is like the atmosphere, everywhere felt by him. It is true that in these United States and in this State, there are men, like myself, colored with the skin like my own, who are not subjected to the lash, who are not liable to have their wives and their infants torn from them; from whose hand the Bible is not taken. It is true that we may walk abroad; we may enjoy our domestic comforts, our families; retire to the closet; visit the sanctuary, and may be permitted to urge on our children and our neighbors in well doing. But sir, still we are slaves—every where we feel the chain galling us. It is by that prejudice which the resolution condemns, the spirit of slavery, the law which has been enacted here, by a corrupt public sentiment, through the influence of slavery which treats moral agents different from the rule of God, which treats them irrespective of their morals or intellectual cultivation. This spirit is withering all our hopes, and ofttimes causes the colored parent as he looks upon his child, to wish he had never been born. Often is the heart of the colored mother, as she presses her child to her bosom, filled with sorrow to think that, by reason of this prejudice, it is cut off from all hopes of usefulness in this land. Sir, this prejudice is wicked.

This killing influence

If the nation and church understood this matter, I would not speak a word about that killing influence that destroys the colored man's reputation. This influence cuts us off from every-thing; it follows us up from childhood to manhood; it excludes us from all stations of profit, usefulness and honor; takes away from us all motive for pressing forward in enterprises, useful and important to the world and to ourselves.

In the first place, it cuts us off from the advantages of the mechanic arts almost entirely.

A colored man can hardly learn a trade, and if he does it is difficult for him to find any one who will employ him to work at that trade, in any part of the State. In most of our large cities there are associations of mechanics who legislate out of their society colored men. And in many cases where our young men have learned trades, they have had to come to low employments for want of encouragement in those trades.

It must be a matter of rejoicing to know that in this vicinity colored fathers and mothers have the privileges of education. It must be a matter of rejoicing that in this vicinity colored parents can have their children trained up in schools.—At present, we find the colleges barred against them.

I will say nothing about the inconvenience which I have experienced myself, and which every man of color experiences, though made in the image of God. I will say nothing about the inconvenience of traveling; how we are frowned upon and despised. No matter how we may demean ourselves, we find embarrassments everywhere.

Debarred from heaven

But sir, this prejudice goes further. It debars men from heaven. While sir, slavery cuts off the colored portion of the community from religious privileges, men are made infidels. What, they demand, is your Christianity? How do you regard your brethren? How do you treat them at the Lord's table? Where is your consistency in talking about the heathen, transversing the ocean to circulate the Bible everywhere, while you frown upon them at the door? These things meet us and weigh down our spirits.

And, sir, the constitution of society, molded by this prejudice, destroys souls. I have known extensively, that in revivals which have been blessed and enjoyed in this part of the country, the colored population were overlooked. I recollect an instance. The Lord God was pouring out His Spirit. He was entering every house, and sinners were converted. I asked, Where is the colored man? who is weeping for them? who is endeavoring to pull them out of the fire? No reply was made.—I was asked to go round with one of the elders and visit them. We went and they humbled themselves. The Church commenced efficient efforts, and God blessed them as soon as they began to act for these people as though they had souls.

And sir, the manner in which our churches are regulated destroys souls. Whilst the church is thrown open to everybody, and one says come, come in and share the blessings of the sanctuary, this is the gate of heaven—he says to the colored man, be careful where you take your stand. I know an efficient church in this State, where a respectable colored man went to the house of God, and was going to take a seat in the gallery, and one of the officers contended with him, and said, "you cannot go there, sir."

In one place the people had come together to the house of the Lord. The sermon was preached—the emblems were about to be administered—and all at once the person who managed the church thought the value of the pews would be diminished if the colored people sat in them. They objected to their sitting there, and the colored people left and went into the gallery, and that, too, when they were thinking of handling the memorials of the broken body and shed blood of the Savior! And, sir, this prejudice follows the colored man everywhere, and depresses his spirits.

A buoyant principle

Thanks be to God, there is a buoyant principle which elevates the poor down-trodden colored man above all this:—It is that there is society which regards man according to his worth; it is the fact, that when he looks up to Heaven he knows that God treats him like a moral agent, irrespective of caste or the circumstances in which he may be placed. Amid the embarrassments which he has to meet, and the scorn and contempt that is heaped upon him, he is cheered by the hope that he will be disenthralled, and soon, like a bird set forth from its cage, wing his flight to Jesus, where he can be happy, and look down with pity on the man who despises the poor slave for being what God made him, and who despises him because he is identified with the poor slave. Blessed be God for the principles of the Gospel. Were it not for these, and for the fact that a better day is dawning, I would not wish to live.— Blessed be God for the antislavery movement. Blessed be God there is a war waging with slavery, that the granite rock is about to be rolled from its base. But as long as the colored man is to be looked upon as an inferior caste, so long will they disregard his cries, his groans, his shrieks.

I rejoice, sir, in this Society; and I deem the day when I joined this Society as one of the proudest days of my life. And I know I can die better, in more peace to-day, to know there are men who will plead the cause of my children.

Let me, through you, sir, request this delegation to take hold of this subject. This will silence the slave holder, when he says where is your love for the slave? Where is your love for the colored man who is crushed at your feet? Talking to us about emancipating our slaves when you are enslaving them by your feelings, and doing more violence to them by your prejudice, than we are to our slaves by our treatment. They call on us to evince our love for the slave, by treating man as man, the colored man as a man, according to his worth.

Theodore S. Wright, Liberator, October 2, 1837

WILLIAM SPOTISWOOD WHITE (1800-1873)

The African Preacher. An Authentic Narrative

The prominence given in the Scriptures to the characters and lives of such persons as Ruth, Esther, and Nehemiah, proves, that "God hath chosen the poor of this world, rich in faith, and heirs of the kingdom which he hath promised to them that love him"—that he hath moreover "chosen the foolish things of the world, to confound the wise, and the weak things of the world, to confound the things that are mighty." Since the days of inspiration ended, the dealings of God's providence and the dispensations of his grace, have beautifully harmonized with the revelations of his word. Hence, in all ages of the world, down to the present hour, many of the loveliest specimens of true piety, have been found in the humblest walks of life. Here, God's wisdom, love, and mercy shine with a lustre all their own; and here, religion displays its richest fruits.

A native of Africa

The narrative now to be given is designed to illustrate these remarks. The subject of it was a native of Africa. When about seven years of age, he was kidnapped, brought to this country, and enslaved. He was supposed to belong to one of the last cargoes of this sort, ever landed on the shores of Virginia. He was purchased at Osborne's, on James' river, by a Mr. Stewart, and was subsequently taken to the county of Nottoway, Virginia, where the whole of his long and interesting life was spent.

He grew to manhood, ignorant of letters, and a stranger to God; engaged in the occupations common to those in a state of bondage. The region of country in which he lived, was, at this period, deplorably destitute of the means of grace. The gospel was seldom preached, the Sabbath scarcely known as a "day of sacred rest," and few were found willing to incur the odium of a public profession of religion.

"Uncle Jack"

Before we proceed further with our narrative it is important to state, that "Uncle Jack," for so he was universally called, possessed great acuteness of mind, and understood and spoke the English language far better than any native of Africa we have ever known. His pronunciation was not only distinct and accurate, but his style was chaste and forcible. His great superiority in this respect must be ascribed to the following causes:—First, to his having left his native land at so early an age. Next, to the freedom with which he was permitted and encouraged to mingle in the best society the country afforded; and above all, to the familiar acquaintance he soon formed with the language of the Bible. The reader must not be surprised, therefore, that nothing occurs in what we quote from his own lips, of the jargon peculiar to the African race. Nobody ever heard the good old preacher say *massa* for *master* or *me* for *I*.

It was during the period of intellectual and moral darkness already referred to, and when he had probably reached the fortieth year of his age, that he became anxious on the subject of religion. The account he gave of his early religious impressions, was very simple. He said nothing of dreams and visions, as is so common with persons of his color. His attention was first arrested, and his fears excited, by hearing from a white man that the world would probably be destroyed in a few days. On hearing this, he asked his informant what he must do to prepare for an event so awful. He was told to pray. "This," he said, "I knew nothing about. I could not pray." At length he was enabled to recall some portions of the Lord's prayer, which he continued to repeat for a considerable time. But these efforts brought him no relief.

That which thus commenced in mere alarm, soon led to a deep and thorough conviction of his guilt, helplessness, and misery, in the sight of God. He now exerted himself in various ways, and with untiring zeal, to obtain a knowledge of the truth as it is in Jesus. There were literally none in his vicinity, either in the ministry, or among the private members of the church, qualified to teach and to guide an inquiring mind like his. The Presbyterian church, then recently established in Prince Edward, was within thirty miles of his residence. The ministers of the gospel from that county, made occasional excursions into Nottoway. From these he soon obtained the help he needed. His own statement on this subject is as follows:

> I had a very wicked heart, and every thing I did, to make it better, seemed to make it worse. At length a preacher passed along; they called him Mr. President Smith. [The Rev. John Blair Smith, D. D., then President of Hampden Sidney College.] He turned my heart inside out. The preacher talked so directly to me, and about me, that I thought the whole sermon was meant for me. I wondered much, who could have told him what a sinner I was. But after a while there came along a young man they called Mr. Hill; [The Rev. Wm. Hill, D. D., of Winchester, Va. Alexander] and about the same time another, with a sweet voice. These were powerful preachers too, and told me all about my troubles; and brought me to see, that there was nothing for a poor, helpless sinner to do, but to go to the Lord Jesus Christ, and trust in him alone for salvation. Since that time, I have had many ups and downs; but hitherto the Lord has helped me, and I hope he will help me to the end.

He now became deeply interested in hearing the Scriptures read. As his knowledge of the Bible increased, he found, to use his own language, "that it knew all that was in his heart." He wondered how "a book should know so much."

Learning to read

He was still unable to read, but now determined to learn. To this end he applied to his master's children for assistance; promising to reward them for their pains with nuts and other fruits, as tuition fees. By the aid of his youthful instructors, his object was soon attained, and he read the word of God with ease. The sacred volume now became the constant companion of his leisure hours. So rapid was his progress in divine knowledge, and such his prudence, good sense, and zeal, that many of the most intelligent and pious people of his neighborhood expressed the desire to have him duly authorized to preach the gospel.

The Baptist church, of which he had become a member, took this matter into serious consideration; and after subjecting him to the trials usually imposed by that denomination, licensed him to labor as a herald of the cross.

Abundant labors

Upon the duties of his new and responsible office, he entered with a truly apostolic spirit. His labors were abundant and faithful. He was often called to preach at a distance of more than thirty miles from his home. He was still a slave, and never seemed to think of any better state, until his attention was called to it by others. He belonged to the undivided estate of his original purchaser, who was now dead. Some of the legatees of this estate were willing to emancipate him, but others were not. This, however, constituted no serious obstacle. He had rendered himself so useful, and had gained the confidence and good will of the community to so great an extent, that a sum of money was soon raised by subscription, quite sufficient to satisfy the demands of those who were unwilling to liberate him. Some idea may be formed of the estimation in which he was held, when it is known that many contributed liberally to the fund thus created, who were not professors of religion. Having thus secured his freedom, he settled on a small tract of land, of which he became the proprietor, chiefly through the munificence of others, and lived in a way which satisfied his humble wishes. Here he literally earned his bread with the sweat of his brow, while he faithfully dispensed to others the bread of life, with scarcely any compensation, except the consciousness of doing good.

The late Rev. John H. Rice, D. D., had a brief interview with our preacher, in which he was deeply interested. This occurred during the summer of 1826, when the old man had nearly reached the 80th year of his age, and one year before our acquaintance with him commenced.

Referring to this interview afterwards, Dr. Rice said, "The acquaintance of this African preacher with the Scriptures is wonderful. Many of his interpretations of obscure passages are singularly just and striking. In many respects, indeed, he is one of the most remarkable men I have ever known."

At this period, Dr. Rice was editor of the *Virginia Literary and Evangelical Magazine*; and entertaining the views expressed above, it is not surprising that the pages of this valuable periodical should contain a brief but interesting memoir of "Uncle Jack.":

There lives in a neighboring county, an old African, named Jack, whose history is more worthy of record than that of many a man whose name has held a conspicuous place in the annals of the world. There is a book which, I have no doubt, contains the name of Old Jack, but not those, I fear, of many great men and nobles of this world. It is "the Lamb's book of life."

Jack possesses the entire confidence of the whole neighborhood in which he lives. No man doubts his integrity or the sincerity of his piety. All classes treat him with marked respect. Everybody gives unequivocal testimony to the excellence of his character.

He possesses a strong mind, and, for a man in his situation, has acquired considerable religious knowledge. His influence among people of his own color is very extensive and beneficial.

Old Jack is as entirely free from all bigotry and party spirit, as any Christian I have ever seen. He acknowledges every man to be a brother, whom he believes to be a Christian. A very striking proof of his humble, teachable, catholic spirit, is given in his conduct towards two Presbyterian missionaries, who were successively sent to the part of the country where he resides. On their arrival, he seemed very cautiously to investigate their character. The result was a conviction that they were pious and devoted men; and a hearty recognition of them as ambassadors of Christ. He found, too, that they knew a great deal more than he did, and resolved to employ his influence in bringing the black people in his neighborhood under their instruction. He also frequently consulted them in regard to matters of difficulty with himself, and used their attainments for the increase of his own knowledge, and for enabling him the better to instruct the numerous blacks who looked up to him as their only teacher.

It has before been said, that the conduct of this old Christian had secured the respect and confidence of the white people. As evidence of this, some time ago a lawless white man attempted to deprive him of his land, under a plea that his title was not good. As soon as the design was known, a number of the first men in the neighborhood volunteered to assist him in maintaining his right, and a lawyer of some distinction, not then a believer, rendered gratuitous service on the occasion, because everybody said, Uncle Jack was a good man.

But while the white people respect, the blacks love, fear, and obey him. His influence among them is unbounded. His authority over the members of his own church is greater than that of the master, or the overseer. And if one of them commits an offence of any magnitude, he never ceases dealing with him, until the offender is brought to repentance, or excluded from the society. The gentlemen of the vicinity freely acknowledge, that this influence is highly beneficial. Accordingly, he has permission to hold meetings on the neighboring plantations whenever he thinks proper. He often visits the sick of his own color, and preaches at all the funerals of the blacks who die any where within his reach.

The high source from whence this extract is taken, and the extent to which it must sustain and enforce the subsequent portion of our narrative, is a sufficient excuse for its introduction.

One of the most gifted and honored sons of old Virginia, Dr. James Jones, of Mountain Hall, who resided for more than forty years within one mile of the subject of this narrative, who was thoroughly acquainted with his public and private life, and who even acknowledged himself under obligations to this humble preacher of righteousness as a spiritual instructor, furnished the following just and beautiful delineation of his character.

I regard this old African as a burning and shining light, raised up by Christian principles alone, to a degree of moral purity seldom equaled, and never exceeded in any country.

Think of him as an African boy, kidnapped at seven years of age, torn away from his heathen parents, thrust into a slave-ship among hundreds of the most degraded beings, transported across the Atlantic, landed on our coast, bought by a very obscure planter in what was then the back-woods of Virginia, here kept in bondage at the usual occupation of slaves, under circumstances but little calculated to improve the mind, or mend the heart; without letters, without instruction, until a glimpse of divine truth, caught by hearing the Bible read, arrested his attention. Seizing on the truth thus obtained, and appreciating its excellence, almost without assistance, he soon learns to read the sacred volume. His researches are now pursued with growing zeal, and signal success, until he is enabled to penetrate into some of its most sublime mysteries, to feel the force of its obligations, to enjoy its consolations, and to become an able and successful expounder of its doctrines to others.

As a preacher of the gospel, he gained the good will and secured the confidence of all who were capable of appreciating true excellence of character, gained admittance into the best families, and was there permitted to enjoy a freedom of intercourse that I never witnessed in any other similar case.

All these views of this old man's character, have excited in my mind somewhat of an enthusiastic admiration seldom felt by me for any member of the human family, of any rank or station. Such effects under all the circumstances of the case, must be traced up to a cause altogether superhuman, and set the seal to the superlative excellence, the divine authenticity of the Christian system.

A lady, whose rank, intelligence and piety, place her among the first of her sex, and who still lives to bear testimony to the literal truth of this narrative, has kindly furnished the following statement written more than ten years ago.

My acquaintance with the old man commenced about thirty years since, when there was scarcely a vestige of piety, especially among the higher classes in this community. The Baptist church to which he belonged was in this region nearly extinct. The few members who remained, he regularly visited and instructed. His first visit at our house was intended for a Baptist lady who was spending some time with us. In his conversation with this lady, I was surprised at the readiness and propriety with which he quoted the Scriptures; and especially at the sound sense which characterized his practical reflections on the passages quoted. This induced me to seek a more intimate acquaintance with him; and as he found I was interested in his conversation, he often called on me.

He has been eminently useful to many persons of my acquaintance. When under spiritual concern, they would apply to no other teacher. During the period of dreadful darkness, to which I have already alluded, he went from house to house, doing good. About this time, he became signally instrumental in the conversion of his former master's youngest son. This youth gave abundant evidence of vital piety, both in his life and his death.

I think the most prominent traits in his character, are meekness, humility and rigid integrity. He possesses naturally a strong mind, a very retentive memory, with the happiest talent for illustrating important truth, by the objects of sense, and the ordinary employments of life. I trust, dear sir, you will be able to furnish the public with an instructive account of this humble and obscure, but interesting and useful old man.

This communication was designed to aid in the preparation of a series of biographical sketches of "The African Preacher," which appeared in the columns of the Watchman of the South in 1839; and was so used. The writer still lives, and would doubtless acknowledge that in her transition from darkness to light, and from the power of Satan unto God, she was mainly indebted, through divine grace, to the visits and the conversations of the good old African, referred to in her letter.

Thoroughly evangelical views

Jack's views of the fundamental doctrines of the Bible, were thoroughly evangelical. He was particularly fond, to use his own words, of "that preaching which makes God everything, and man nothing." The total depravity of man—the absolute sovereignty of God in electing him to salvation through the imputed righteousness of Christ—the necessity of regeneration by the Spirit, through the belief of the truth—the growth in grace and final salvation of all who truly repent and believe the gospel; these were his favorite themes, both in his sermons and conversation. And these, with all their kindred topics, he could illustrate by allusions to nature and art, with a clearness which left no obscurity about his real sentiments. He was particularly fond of the Epistle to the Romans, and often spoke of it, as containing "the very marrow of the gospel." He often bestowed much time on a single passage. On one occasion, he called our attention to the third verse of the eighth chapter of Romans, saying, "Master C. and I have been studying a great deal over that verse for the last three weeks, and we do not fully understand it yet. Do tell me all about it."

Anxious to know what his own construction was, we insisted that he should give us his opinion, promising to give him ours when he had concluded. With this proposition he was very reluctant to comply, but finally consenting, he proceeded as follows. We give the exposition in his own order, and almost verbatim as he gave it to us.

Romans 8:3

"Well," said he, "I will do the best I can. The verse begins thus: "For what the law could not do." And what is it the law can't do? Why, it can't justify us in the sight of God. Why not? Because "it was weak through the flesh." There is no weakness in the law. That is as strong as its Author. But the weakness is in man's flesh. Observe, this is a weakness "through the flesh." That is, the weakness is in man's corrupt nature. Now, what is to be done for man in his helplessness and guilt? The text tells us plainly, "God sending his own Son'—for what? Why, to do for ruined man what the law could not do on account of his sinfully weak nature. And when God sent his Son, how did he come? "In the likeness of sinful flesh." I suppose that means, he came as a man, though not a sinful man; for he knew no sin. And why did he come? The text answers, "and for sin, condemned sin in the flesh." That is, on account of sin in man, he suffered the condemnation due to that sin in his own person. So," says the old

African—his dark visage brightening with the emotions within—"what God's law cannot do, his own Son can do. Thanks be to God for his unspeakable gift!"

We could only join in his closing exclamation, assuring him that, according to our best judgment, he had adopted the true interpretation of the passage, and we left him, blessing God, as we shook his hand, for bestowing such grace and knowledge upon one so humble and so unpretending. His knowledge of human nature was profound, because it was derived wholly from the Bible, confirmed by his own observation. Hence his extensive usefulness, not only among those of his own color, but also in a large circle of whites, embracing many of the most intelligent, wealthy, and refined people of the county.

In the familiar intercourse to which he was admitted by the latter class, he was never known to offend by any thing like forwardness. Says one who knew him well: "His humility has always been of the most rational kind—entirely removed from all cant and grimace. Before he became superannuated, the great field of his operations as a preacher was the funeral sermons called for by the owners of deceased slaves. He was universally employed in this way, with the hearty consent of persons of all descriptions in this community. I have known him to be sent for to a distance of more than thirty miles to attend to a service of this kind. In every instance he would receive the most polite and friendly attentions of the white portion of the family and even by the irreligious, was frequently remunerated in money for his services."

Thirst for knowledge

Through life, he manifested a surprising thirst for knowledge. He embraced with avidity every opportunity of getting instruction, both in public and in private. Nothing pleased him more than the opportunity of conversing, with ministers of the gospel. Mountain Hall, the delightful residence of the late Dr. Jones, was a home for Christ's ministering servants as they journeyed through that part of the country. The African Preacher lived at the distance of a mile from this place. He seemed to know, almost by intuition, when a minister called to spend the night with the good doctor and his lady. And however dark or even stormy the night might be, when the bell rang for evening family worship, the good old African would be seen with tremulous steps slowly entering, and with deep solemnity, seating himself in a retired part of the room to attend upon the service. A stranger would not be likely to observe him, unless indeed the person conducting the worship should happen to sing Windham, or Mear, or Old Hundred, to some appropriate psalm or hymn. Then his attention would very probably be arrested by a voice, not remarkable for its melody, nor yet remarkable for its strength—but a voice so solemn, so tremulous with the emotions which seemed to accompany it from the depths of a heart all alive to God's praise, that he could no longer remain unobserved. ...

His view on revivals

The reader will be interested also in knowing something of his sentiments in regard to revivals of religion. More mistaken views on this subject could hardly prevail any where, or at any time, than prevailed in the region of country in which the African Preacher lived, and during the time of his ministry. His sentiments may be fairly and fully learned from the following incident.

On a certain occasion, he attended a protracted meeting, conducted by some of the best white preachers in that part of the country; at which "the new measures" were used, and at which there was a great deal of excitement and no little noise. On his return, he called to see me, and, during his visit, gave me the following account of the meeting. "There were a great many people, and a great deal of talking, and singing, and praying. They call it a revival; and if by a revival, they mean a great increase of confusion and noise, they are right. But so it is, I had no enjoyment at the meeting. I heard very little of what I call real preaching. I was constantly thinking, and it may be, this was a temptation of the devil—any how, I was constantly thinking Of what I have sometimes noticed in new grounds. If a man clears up a piece of land in the summer, and has not time to cut down and take away all the trees, but belts a good many, and leaves them standing about in the field, the leaves die, but don't fall. Now, when winter comes, and the wind blows hard, I always noticed that one of these belted trees made more noise in the wind, than a half dozen green, living trees. These noisy Christians look to me so much like belted trees with the leaves on, in a windy day, that I could not enjoy the meeting at all. And yet the fault might have been in me."

Progressive piety

He was fond of considering piety, both internal and external, as progressive in its developments. He opposed with the utmost firmness and faithfulness, the idea of one's getting religion, as the phrase is, and then folding his hands in utter idleness. He was fully aware that this error prevailed to a deplorable extent, among those of his own color, and he spared no pains to resist and eradicate it. He was accustomed to say, "I have no notion of that religion which is better at first than it ever is afterwards. When Christians hear a sermon on the text, "Turn ye, turn ye, for why will ye die?" they are apt to conclude that it don't suit them, because they have turned long ago. Now, the truth is, to be the real children of God, we must continue to turn as long as we live. For my own part, I often feel as if I had as much turning to do now, as I had when I first set out."

His views on this subject were unusually enlarged and scriptural. They reached into eternity. Nothing less than the expectation of an eternal progression, in knowledge, holiness, and usefulness satisfied his desires. Of this, we are furnished with a striking illustration, in the following incident. A pious young man, of considerable intelligence, conversing with him on growth in grace, said, "We should strive to grow until we die." "Yes," replied our preacher, "and hope to grow after we die. I trust in God I shall grow for ever."

Standing one day in sight of a field of tobacco, he said to me, "Some fifty years ago, I expected the time would come, when I should be of some account in the Lord's vineyard. But now, I am very old, and have given up this hope." Then pointing to the tobacco, which grew near us, he said, "That is very promising tobacco, but it must be cut and cured, before it will be of any service to its owner. And so it is with me. All that now comforts me on this subject, is the hope that God will make some good use of me in another and better world.

The redeemed of the Lord are said to serve him in heaven. What a service that must be! How unlike any thing seen or known on earth!"

The school of Christ
Here let the reader pause and consider, that this old African could barely read, and never learned to write. He was taught in the school of Christ, and only there. We never knew him read, nor do we think he cared to read, any book except the Bible, or something of a kindred character. He was literally taught of God, and thus became wise unto salvation. With the jet black color, and all the features of the African race fully developed, such were the beauties of his mind and heart, as to render him an object worthy of the highest respect—the most profound veneration. Often have we rejoiced to sit at his feet and learn, and with no little delight do we anticipate the day when we shall walk, side by side, along the banks of the river of life, and partake together of the fruits of that tree, whose leaves are for the healing of the nations.

Another very striking characteristic of the African Preacher was solicitude for the prevalence of pure and undefiled religion He sought, in every legitimate way, the advancement of Christ's cause. Most truly could he say, "If I forget thee, 0 Jerusalem, let my right hand forget her cunning." . . .

When he prayed, as we know he did with unusual faith and fervor, "Thy kingdom come, thy will be done on earth, as it is in heaven," his far reaching mind and heart extended to every nation and kindred and tribe, upon the whole earth. He had known what it was to live amidst the darkness of heathenism, and what it is to enjoy the genial light of the Sun of righteousness.

On one occasion, after listening with fixed attention and deep feeling to a statement of a discouraging character respecting the state of religion in a neighboring county, he said, "There seems to be great coldness and deadness on the subject of religion every where. The fire has almost gone out, and nothing is left, but a few smoking chunks lying about in places." How striking is the thought of one's having just religion enough "to smoke," but not enough to burn. No light, no beat—only a little smoke. Who that has the fire of divine love in his heart, can be content to lead such a life? Indeed it is extremely doubtful, whether a principle of such potency can exist, and yet exert no more influence. Let the inactive, useless member of the church, ponder the homely but expressive language of the good old African, and hang his head for shame, that he should hold no higher place, and act no better part in the vineyard of his Master, than that of a "smoking chunk" lying by the way-side.

Speaking of the causes of a low state of piety, he said, "Christians don't love each other enough. They don't keep close enough together. They are too much like fire-coals, scattered over a large hearth. Coals in that condition, you know, soon die out. Only gather them up, and bring them close together, and they soon become bright and warm again. So it is with Christians. They must be often and close together—in the church—at the prayer meeting, and thus help one another along." . . .

Humility

Perhaps no Christian grace shone more brightly in his character, than humility. The attentions bestowed upon him by persons of the highest standing, were remarkable. He was invited into their houses—sat with their families—took part in their social worship, sometimes leading in prayer at the family altar. Many of the most intelligent people attended upon his ministry, and listened to his sermons with great delight. Indeed, previous to the year 1825, he was considered by the best judges the best preacher in that county. His opinions were respected, his advice followed, and yet he never betrayed the least symptom of arrogance or self-conceit. When in the presence of white people, he seldom introduced conversation, and when he did, it was invariably done by modestly asking some very pertinent question on some very important subject. He was perpetually employed either in seeking or communicating information, and when no opportunity presented itself of doing either, he was habitually silent.

His dwelling was a rude log cabin; his apparel of the plainest and even coarsest materials, and yet no one ever heard him utter one "murmuring word." Like the shepherd of Salisbury Plain, his gratitude for what he had, precluded all anxiety for what he had not.

The tones of his voice, the expression of his countenance, together with every word, and every action, proclaimed that, in true lowliness of mind, he esteemed others better than himself.

An illustration of his meekness and humility is furnished by the fact, that when asked his opinion respecting the law, then recently enacted by the State Legislature, prohibiting colored men from preaching, he very promptly expressed his approbation of the law; adding, "It is altogether wrong for such as have not been taught themselves, to undertake to teach others. As to my preaching, I have long thought it was no better than the ringing of an old cowbell, and ought to be stopped." He accordingly bowed to the authority of this law; and although often told, that the penalty for its violation would not be inflicted on him, he never preached afterwards; but became a constant and devout worshipper in a neighboring Presbyterian congregation, which had been recently organized, and over which the first pastor of that denomination ever settled in the county of Nottoway, had been recently installed.

Another incident, illustrating his humble and contented disposition, must not be omitted Previous to the cessation of his public ministry, a pious and wealthy lady, feeling grieved to see him so rudely clad, presented him with a well made suit of black cloth. This suit, he wore but once, and then returned it to his kind friend, begging that she would not be displeased at his doing so, and justified his conduct thus: "These clothes are a great deal better than are generally worn by people of my color. And besides, if I wear them, I find I shall be obliged to think about them even at meeting." . . .

Suffering

The life of the African Preacher was one of no little toil and suffering. Perhaps the most imprudent step he ever took, was marrying a woman who was in no respect "a help meet for him." Without mental culture, without religion, encumbered with a large family of children, the fruits of a former marriage, and surrounded by an extensive circle of other relatives, she only served to burden him with domestic cares, sufficient to have crushed the spirit of any ordinary man. These people were idle and profligate; he, industrious and economical. They hung, around and imposed upon him in the most shameful manner. Often would they filch from him the products of his own daily labor, and then add insult to injury, by the grossest personal unkindness, and even cruelty. But all this only served to give additional brightness and purity to his piety. Some metals become the more brilliant on being rubbed, and some flowers are all the more fragrant when trodden upon. So with pure and undefiled religion, and so it was with this good old African Preacher.

His thoughts, his affections, his aims, were all lifted so far above the din of domestic strife, that it seldom or never disturbed his equanimity even for a moment. The dreariness of his home on earth only served to make him sigh more deeply for "that house not made with hands, eternal in the heavens." He rarely alluded to these things, and whenever he did, he never failed to say all he could in extenuation of the guilt of those who had injured him. To the writer, he never alluded to these trials but once, and then he said, "I am such a hard-headed, disobedient child, that I need a whipping every day." At another time, referring to his poverty, and also to the fact that he had no descendants, he said, "I left nothing in Africa, and I brought nothing to this country. When I die, I shall leave nothing behind me, and shall carry nothing with me, but the merits of my Savior's obedience and death."

The simplicity of faith, and the self-application with which our good preacher was accustomed to attend upon the ministrations of the sanctuary, were truly remarkable. "A day in thy courts is better than a thousand," was not only the language of his lips, but of his heart and of his life. When more than ninety years of age, we have known him to walk two, and sometimes four miles to reach the house of God. And this he would sometimes do in very inclement weather. Nor was he a forgetful hearer, but a doer of the word. We have often been surprised at the accuracy with which he could give the outlines of a sermon many days, and even weeks, after he had heard it. Under faithful and pungent exhibitions of the truth, he was often very deeply affected. After hearing a very lucid and impressive sermon on the resurrection of the dead, we found him, when the service had ended, in the rear of the church, leaning against the side of the house, bathed in tears. On asking him why he wept, he replied, "I am afraid, sir, that after all, I shall never realize what that young preacher talked about today. The glories of the resurrection unto life are too high for me." He was reminded of what the preacher had said about the changes which annually occur in nature, as to some extent illustrative of the resurrection. He was told to recollect the astonishing difference in the appearance of the trees in winter and spring; and was then asked, if the God who caused this difference, who, in the spring thus adorned the forest, could not, with perfect ease, beautify and adorn his body in an infinitely higher degree. To this he said, "I do not doubt the power or the love of God; but that which troubles me is this. If the tree has not a good root, God will never make it bloom. And so it is with me. If I have not the root of the matter in me, I shall never know any thing of the resurrection unto life."

Pastoral care

The next thing deserving of consideration in the character of this excellent old man, was his method of dealing with persons awakened to a sense of their sinfulness in the sight of God.

He was very often consulted by persons in this state of mind, of every grade in society; as also by those who, having hope in Christ, were asking what step they should take next, to honor Christ and do good. Here, as in other matters, his course was characterized by good sense and discretion.

On one occasion, a lady of great respectability told him that she considered herself a Christian, but at the same time avowed the purpose of not making a profession of religion by connecting herself with the Church. At this he expressed great surprise—reminded her of what our Savior said of those who "confessed," and of those who "denied" him, and then added, "Mistress, if you should suddenly come in possession of a large sum of money, would you lock it up in your house, and try to keep it a great secret? It would neither do you nor any body else much good, to take that course with it."

At another time, one gave him a long account of a remarkable dream she had had, and desired his opinion on the subject. To this he replied, "The Scriptures do tell us something about dreams, but no where that I remember, of any one converted by a dream or converted when he was asleep. I can understand people a great deal better when they tell me of what they say and do when they are awake, and when they talk about a work of grace in their hearts."

There lived in his immediate vicinity, a very respectable man who had become interested on the subject of religion, and who, with some earnestness, had begun to "search the Scriptures." He had been thus employed but a short time when he became greatly perplexed with some of those passages which even an inspired apostle has said, are "hard to be understood." In this state of mind he repaired to our preacher for instruction, and found him at noon, on a sultry day in summer, occupied in his field, hoeing corn. As the man approached, the preacher saluted him with his accustomed politeness; and then with patriarchal simplicity, leaning upon the handle of his hoe, listened to his story.

"Uncle Jack," said he, "I have discovered lately that I am a great sinner, and I have commenced reading the Bible that I may learn. I have discovered lately that I am a great sinner and what I must do to be saved. But I have met with a passage here," holding up his Bible, "which I cannot understand, and which greatly perplexes me. It is this, 'God, will have mercy on whom he will have mercy, and whom he will he hardeneth;' what does this mean?"

A short pause intervened, and the old African answered as follows: "Master, if I have been rightly informed, it has only been a short time since you commenced reading the Bible, and I think the passage you have just read is in the Epistle to the Romans. Long before you get to that, at the very beginning of the gospel it is said, "Repent, for the kingdom of heaven is at hand." Now, have you done with that? The truth is, you read entirely too fast. You must begin again, and learn the lesson as God has been pleased to give it to you. When you have done what you are told to do in Matthew, come to see me, and we will talk about that passage in Romans." Having thus answered, he resumed his work, and left the visitor to his own reflections.

Who does not admire the simplicity and good sense displayed in thus dealing with a person of this description ? Could the most learned polemic more effectually have met and disposed of such a difficulty? The gentleman particularly interested in this incident gave the foregoing account of it to the writer, and, if he still lives, will joyfully say now, as he did when he first spoke of it, "It convinced me fully of the mistake into which I had fallen. I took the old man's advice, soon saw its propriety and wisdom, and hope to bless God for ever for sending me to him." The consequence was, that he soon became an intelligent, consistent Christian, connected himself with the Church, and contributed in no small degree to the promotion of a cause he had once hated and opposed. ...

Knowing that the African Preacher was now very old, and evidently near the end of his earthly pilgrimage and our personal intercourse with him having for several years ceased, we addressed a letter, early in the winter of 1838, to our best earthly friend and his, Dr. James Jones, asking for information of his state, now that the shadows were lengthening, and his end supposed to be near. To this letter, the good Doctor promptly sent us the following reply:

Mountain Hall, Nottoway, Dec. 31,1838.

My Dear Sir—There are very few persons either among the living or the dead, with whom I have had so long personal intercourse, as with Uncle Jack. I found him among my nearest neighbors, when I first settled at my present residence. His deportment, under all circumstances, has never varied; always modest, unassuming and humble. His serene and placid countenance is seldom without a smile, if engaged in conversation, or great gravity, if disengaged. Ever prone to enter into conversation, where he thinks it not disagreeable, he scarcely ever fails to make religion the topic before it ends. He visits my family with the utmost freedom, on all sorts of business and occasions which are legitimate, and I think I cannot be mistaken in the assertion just made. His visits are now, perhaps, more frequent than ever; and seem to be made almost exclusively for the purpose of getting information on some text or parable or narrative in the Bible. When this is his object, he announces it immediately on his arrival, asks to have it read from the Bible, and frequently inquires what our commentators say on the subject.

It is proper here to state, that while his memory is greatly impaired on all matters of secular concern, it is retentive and ready on every thing relating to the Scriptures, in connection with his own experience of the influence of divine truth. On propounding his questions for information, he invariably quotes, most accurately, the chapter and verse; not infrequently, the words themselves. Very frequently he will refer to the occasion on which he first heard it read or spoken of; perhaps thirty or forty years ago, in some sermon or private conversation.

Both his physical and mental powers are evidently on the wane. He exhibits no little debility by his unsteady gait, his head inclining forwards, so that his chin almost rests upon his breast; and he complains much of rheumatism. Still, he manifests great reluctance to confinement, so long as he can use the organs of motion. He gives his personal attention to every branch of business on his little establishment, and is, at this time, in a most comfortable situation, as respects his supplies of the necessaries of life. I perceive no alteration at all in the temper and disposition of his mind The same equanimity which has so long distinguished him, still prevails; and so remarkable has his character been, in this respect, that I have never yet seen an individual who has known him to be put out of temper, or to show any thing like petulance, or irritation, or resentment, on any occasion whatever, throughout his whole life.

Weak and feeble as he is at this time, he seems to have been most highly excited, both in mind and body, by the revival of religion which has been for some time past in progress in the churches around him. He is unable to attend distant meetings, but frequently walks to those near at hand. He takes special care, however, to get to very many of the families in which conversions have been reported, let them be far or near. I am often surprised to hear from him an account of what passed between him and certain families, in recent conversations. Upon inquiry, I find he has walked all the way expressly to see them. He would say, "I could not resist. I was obliged to try and get to them, that I might tell them all I knew to help them on their way."

I can only add the assurance of the undiminished esteem and affection of

Yours truly,

James Jones

It must not be forgotten, that the subject of this narrative was supposed to be nearly eighty years of age when the writer first made his acquaintance. Both in mind and body he was already on the wane. Little or nothing, is remembered of what he was in the vigor of mature age. There were none at that period, whose feelings and habits prompted them to preserve for future use the incidents of a life so unpretending and so humble. They who have rendered us so much assistance, were not then professors of religion; and few, if any, of those who were, could be considered capable of appreciating the old man's real worth. We have therefore only called the attention of the reader to the rays of a luminary near the horizon. For any adequate, conceptions of his noon-day brilliancy, we are left wholly to conjecture. We have, moreover, sketched the lineaments of a mind almost entirely destitute of cultivation. With thorough training, may we not reasonably suppose that our African Preacher would have attained to the intellectual stature of an Augustine or a Cyprian—those distinguished sons of his father-land?

Illness

But we must resume our narrative. Shortly after the foregoing letter was written, he became extremely ill. He thought the time of his departure had arrived, and so thought all his friends. Dr. Jones, who attended him as his physician, during this illness, has kindly furnished us with the following account of the old man's views and feelings at this trying time.

"During his illness, I often listened with intense interest to the views and feelings he expressed, as he lay upon what he supposed to be his death-bed. And views more rational and scriptural I never heard from any one. The most perfect calmness, as to his future destiny, pervaded his bosom. Gratitude to God for all his merciful dealings towards him, was the prominent exercise of his mind. The neighbors vied with each other in acts of kindness in that crisis. In view of this he said to me, 'What have I done to deserve all this? I came, a stranger to all, thousands of miles across the great water, and as long as I have lived, I have never wanted a friend. And now, when I am about to die, I am loaded with kindness beyond any thing that I deserve.'" The Doctor closes his statement thus: "Whenever this venerable African departs hence, it may be truly said, that a purer spirit than his never escaped its clay tenement on earth, to its house not made with hands, eternal in the heavens."

From this attack, however, he recovered, and lived about four years longer. During this period, his hearing, sight, and speech were all impaired. Still he enjoyed surprising health for one of his advanced age. Nor did his interest in the cause of Christ suffer the least abatement. His path was emphatically that of the just, "which shineth more and more to the perfect day." The truth is, when every thing else failed to arrest his attention and excite his feelings, the bare mention of that name which "is above every name," imparted, in no small degree, the lustre of youth to his almost sightless eyes, and the animation and vigor of mature age to his emaciated frame.

In July, 1842, we saw him for the last time. On reaching Mountain Hall, we soon learned from the family that Uncle Jack was then with them. He had recently come on one of his accustomed visits, and was taken suddenly so ill that be could not return to his own cottage. This was very favorable to his comfort. For here he was supplied with every thing necessary to check his disease or to cheer his spirit. On proposing to go to his room, we were told that he had been for some days in a stupor; that he could scarcely be induced to say any thing, or to notice any body; and that it would be painful to see him. But we determined to go, not doubting that he could be roused. He had no fever, and suffered no pain. The candle had sunk in the socket, and only needed raising, to make it shine as brilliantly as ever. And there was a way by which this might be done. Accordingly, we went to his room, accompanied by the good friend, whose guests both Uncle Jack and we were, as we had often been before. We found him, on entering his apartment, surrounded with as many conveniences and comforts as any one could reasonably have desired. He lay calm and tranquil, with his eyes fixed on the ceiling. Approaching his bedside, we took his black and bony hand in ours, but he spoke not, nor moved his eyes.

We then saluted him in the usual style of ordinary civility, inquiring, in a very distinct voice, after his health. Perceiving that he scarcely noticed what we said to him, Dr. Jones advanced and said, "Old man, don't you know who this is?"

He replied, "My hearing is better than my eye-sight. I don't know the face, but I am sure I have heard the voice before. I think I have heard that voice in the pulpit,"

We then determined to try the experiment of rousing him, by merely quoting passage after passage of Scripture in his hearing; and soon succeeded, far beyond our most sanguine expectations. When the passage, commencing, "For God so loved the world, that he gave his only begotten Son," was mentioned, he responded with great animation, "That he did—that he did; and there rests all my hope."

He now expressed great pleasure in recognizing an old acquaintance, and said, "Sometimes I hear of you in one place, and sometimes in another; but go where you may, the Lord takes care of you."

On being asked how he felt in prospect of death, he replied: "Every thing I call my own will soon be dissolved and pass away. Without Christ, I am but as sounding brass and a tinkling cymbal." After a short pause, he proceeded to speak, substantially as follows: "Some years ago I heard you preach a sermon on the text, "Behold, I stand at the door and knock!' That text, I think, is in Revelations. I have thought of that day and that sermon a great many times since. You seemed to be much in earnest, but I was sorry to see how little interest the people took in it. They seemed to go away unconcerned. Then I thought, what will all our knocking come to, unless the Lord adds his blessing?" After another pause, during which he seemed to be asleep, he opened his eyes and said, "We have had a revival here lately. Some call it a revival, and some say it is all trash. Any how, the Lord can take even trash, and make a real fire, if he chooses."

Having joined with him in prayer and praise, we left him for the night, greatly revived both in body and spirit. We had seen and heard that over which the soul of man might well rejoice, and we could but utter in silent ejaculation, thanksgiving to Him who not only came into our world "to seek and to save" the rich publican, Zaccheus, but also to provide that the poor should have the gospel preached to them.

On the ensuing morning we found him improved in health, but depressed in spirit. "I have lived a long time," he said, "but all to no purpose. I do not see the least fruit of any thing I ever did; and I suppose it would be no better if I should live as long again. For a long time I have tried to get a new heart and a right spirit, but fear I never succeeded. Such thoughts and feelings as trouble me, would never disturb a real Christian." Here he was reminded of the Christian warfare, and particularly of what the Apostle says about "wrestling." He replied, "That is all true. I have many a time gone into the woods and wrestled in prayer, until my enemies would all flee, and I would think they were gone for ever; but they soon came back and worried me worse than ever."

His attention was next called to our Savior's interview with the woman of Samaria; and particularly to this expression: "If thou knewest the gift of God, and who it is that saith to thee, Give me to drink, thou wouldest have asked of him and he would have given thee living water." In this he was deeply interested, and made many pertinent remarks about the water of life, and concluded as follows: "This water springeth up: it don't run down like common water. It is very pleasant and refreshing water. Sometimes we suffer the trash of this world to get into it, and then it is not so good. But it is our own fault. The fountain is in heaven, but there are streams of this water now running about almost every where. I am nearly done with the stream, and hope soon to be at the fountain."

Speaking of prayer he said, "Wherever there is a praying heart, there is the throne of grace."

He was next told that a missionary had recently returned from Africa, his native land, and brought the pleasing intelligence that many of his countrymen had received the gospel. At this announcement he clasped his withered hands, and with much emotion said, "Every word that cometh out of the mouth of the Lord is true. He said that his word should be a witness among all nations—that it should have free course, run and be glorified—and so the gospel has gone across the great sea all the way to Africa. When the Lord works, none can hinder. Then, I suppose, I shall meet some of my countrymen in heaven. Bless the Lord! As we shall all sing one song, I suppose we shall all speak one language."

When we rose to leave him, he said, smiling, "You have given me a snack upon which I can feed for some time; such talk is meat and drink to me. You must not go away to-day. I wish you to say and do all you can before you leave, to keep me from wandering away any more. It is no wonder that God's child, when he leaves his father's side, should get crippled; and when he does, he has nobody to blame but himself." Shortly after we had left his apartment, one of his attendants came to me, saying, "Uncle Jack has sent me to tell you that his doubts and fears and difficulties are all gone; that he is now very peaceful and happy, and has nothing more to do but to die and be at rest."

To the surprise of every one, he lingered for several months, but never fully regained his health. We left him, never expecting to see his face in the flesh again. Nor did we. All that we subsequently learned of his state was, that he so far recovered as to be carried to his own humble home, where he lingered a little longer, and then rested from his labors, and now his works follow him.

William Spotiswood White

The Night Funeral of a Slave

Traveling recently on business, in the interior of Georgia, I reached, just at sunset, the mansion of the proprietor through whose estate, for the last half hour of my journey, I had pursued my way. My tired companion pricked his ears, and with a low whinny indicated his pleasure, as I turned up the broad avenue leading to the house. Calling to a black boy in view, I made him inquire of his owner if I could be accommodated with lodgings for the night.

My request brought the proprietor himself to the door, and from thence to the gate, when, after a scrutinizing glance at my person and equipments, he inquired my name, business, and destination. I promptly responded to his questions, and he invited me to alight and enter the house, in the true spirit of Southern hospitality.

He was apparently thirty years of age, and evidently a man of education and refinement. I soon observed an air of gloomy abstraction about him. He said but little, and even that little seemed the result of an effort to obviate the seeming want of civility to a stranger. At supper, the mistress of the mansion appeared, and did the honors of the table, in her particular department. She was exceedingly lady-like and beautiful. She retired immediately after supper, and a servant handing some splendid habanas on a small silver tray, we had seated ourselves comfortably before the enormous fire of oak wood, when a servant appeared at the end door near my host, hat in hand, and uttered, in subdued but distinct tones, the, to me, startling words:

"Master, de coffin hab come."

"Very well," was the only reply, and the servant disappeared.

My host remarked my gaze of inquisitive wonder, and replied to it—

"I have been sad, sad," said he, "to-day. I have had a greater misfortune than I have experienced since my father's death. I lost this morning the truest and most reliable friend I had in the world—one whom I have been accustomed to honor and respect since my earliest recollection. He was the playmate of my father's youth, and the mentor of mine; a faithful servant, an honest man, and sincere Christian. I stood by his bedside to-day, and with his hands clasped in mine, I heard the last words he uttered; they were, 'Master, meet me in heaven.'"

His voice faltered a moment, and he continued, after a pause, with increased excitement:

"His loss is a melancholy one to me. If I left my home, I said to him, 'John, see that all things are taken care of,' and I knew that my wife and child, property and all, were as safe as though they were guarded by a hundred soldiers. I never spoke a harsh word to him in all my life, for he never merited it. I have a hundred others, many of them faithful and true, but his loss is irreparable."

I came from a section of the Union where slavery does not exist; and I brought with me all the prejudices which so generally prevail in the free States in regard to this "institution." I had already seen much to soften these, but the observation of years would have failed to give me so clear an insight into the relation between master and servant as this simple incident. It was not the haughty planter, the lordly tyrant, talking of his dead slave as of his dead horse, but the kind-hearted gentleman, lamenting the loss and eulogizing the virtues of his good old friend.

After an interval of silence, my host resumed:

"There are," said he, "many of the old man's relatives and friends who would wish to attend his funeral. To afford them opportunity, several plantations have been notified that he will be buried to-night. Some, I presume, have already arrived; and desiring to see that all things are properly prepared for his interment, I trust you will excuse my absence a few moments."

"Most certainly, sir; but," I added, "if there is no impropriety, I would be pleased to accompany you."

"There is none," he replied; and I followed him to one of a long row of cabins, situated at the distance of some three hundred yards from the mansion. The house was crowded with Negroes. All arose on our entrance, and many of them exchanged greeting with my host, in tones that convinced me that they felt that he was an object of sympathy from them! The corpse was deposited in the coffin, attired in a shroud of the finest cotton materials, and the coffin itself painted black.

The master stopped at its head, and laying his hand upon the cold brow of his faithful bondsman, gazed long and intently upon features with which he had been so long familiar, and which he now looked upon for the last time on earth. Raising his eyes at length, and glancing at the serious countenances now bent upon his, he said solemnly, and with much feeling—

"He was a faithful servant and true Christian. If you follow his example, and live as he lived, none of you need fear when the time comes for you to lie here."

A patriarch, with the snow of eighty winters on his head, answered,

"Master, it is true, and we will try to live like him."

There was a murmur of general assent, and after giving some instructions relative to the burial, we returned to the building.

About nine o'clock a servant appeared with the notice that they were ready to move, and to know if further instructions were necessary. My host remarked to me that, by stepping into the piazza, I would probably behold, to me, a novel scene. The procession had moved, and its route led within a few yards of the mansion. There were one hundred and fifty Negroes, arranged four deep, and following a wagon in which was placed the coffin. Down the entire length of the line, at intervals of a few feet on each side, were carried torches of the resinous pine, here called light-wood. About the center was stationed the black preacher, a man of gigantic frame and stentorian lungs, who gave out from memory the words of a hymn suitable to the occasion. The Southern Negroes are proverbial for the melody and compass of their voices, and I thought that hymn, mellowed by distance, the most solemn, and yet the sweetest music that had ever fallen upon my ear. The stillness of the night, and strength of their voices, enabled me to distinguish the air at the distance of half a mile.

It was to me a strange and solemn scene, and no incident of my life has impressed me with more powerful emotions than the night funeral of the poor Negro. For this reason I have hastily and most imperfectly sketched its leading features.

William Spotiswood White

BIBLE AGAINST SLAVEHOLDERS, 1840

Introduction

This anonymous tract was published twice, in 1840 and again in 1849, in Buffalo, New York. "Friend of Freedom and the Perpetuity of the Union," the unknown author of *Bible Against Slaveholders*, paid for the printing of the tract at the *Buffalo Republican*, a newspaper that existed under various names during the 1840s and beyond.

Bible Against Slaveholders

My doctrine is:

"That God hath made of one blood, all Nations of men, for to dwell on all the face of the earth."

That the Negro is a man, and that which is the inalienable right of one man is also the right of all men,

That Freedom and Slavery are antagonistical principles; both cannot be right

That Freedom is right and Slavery wrong, therefore Slavery ought not to exist.

SLAVES BOUGHT AND SOLD!
READ AND EXAMINE

As we were passing through your city we saw the above sign, and a man came out and accosted us, "Have you slaves to sell? or do you wish to buy?"

Ardent. Neither; we abhor all such business.

Man. There is no need to speak reproachfully of it. It is a legal business, carried on under the sanction of the public authorities. I claim to have just as much right to buy men, women and children, as my neighbor has to buy horses and cattle.

Thoughtful. The laws of the land may protect you in so doing; but they do not make it right, unless it is authorized by the laws of God, which we suppose you will scarcely claim.

Man. I believe that slaveholding is authorized by the Bible; and that, consequently, the buying and selling of slaves is authorized also. Was not Abraham a slaveholder?

Ard. I think not. But, perhaps we shall need to define our terms. What is a slave?

Man. He is a "chattel personal." He is not regarded as a person, but a thing. He has no rights and can have no property. Whatever he has in his possession belongs to his master.

Th. I believe that is a correct definition of modern slavery, and nearly so of the ancient Roman slavery. The fundamental idea is that *slaves are not persons but things*, (thereby all the rights of property attach, even to the selling of men, women, children, and even babies by the pound, as is said to have been done.) In this case I deny that slavery was authorized in the Old Testament or the New.

Man. You take bold ground. Had not Abraham bondman and bondwomen, born in his house, and bought with his money?

Th. Yes; but, what was a *bondman in* Abraham's house? Was he considered as a *person,* having rights, like the white servants among us, capable of making contracts, capable of acquiring and holding property, and the like? If so, he was not a slave. For a slave is a *thing,* and not *a person.* A slave has no rights.

Man. But I suppose the word *bondman* meant slave.

Th. The Hebrew word is *ebed,* which is commonly rendered *servant.* David was the *Ebed of* Saul, not his slave. Ziba was the *ebed* of Mephibosheth, but a man of wealth and importance. Jeroboam was the *ebed* of Solomon. It is used just as we use the word *servant,* to denote subordination and dependence, but not the degradation of *persons* to *things,* in which the essence of slavery consists.

Man. But Abraham's servants were *bought* with his money.

Th. The word signifies, *acquired, got, procured.* Abraham procured them with his money. And this is the way we procure white servants. The usual way to obtain a servant in patriarchal times is brought into view in that very ancient composition, the Book of Job, where, in respect to the leviathan, it is asked, "Will he make a covenant with thee? wilt thou take him for a servant forever?" The servant was bought, indeed, but he was bought of himself, and became a servant by contract. So it seems to be contemplated it might be among the Israelites. "If a sojourner or stranger wax rich by thee, and thy brother that dwelleth by him wax poor, and *sell himself* unto the stranger." *Slaves* are never bought of themselves, but of some other. Abraham might also have procured servants of his heathen neighbors, by way of redeeming captives taken in war, on the easy condition of their becoming permanent members of his family, and there enjoying the substantial benefits of freedom, which they could not hope to do among their enemies. Wives also were *bought.* Jacob gave fourteen years' personal service for his. David bought his wife of the king her father, by his military services. To betroth a wife among the Israelites was to *buy* her, by paying a sum of money, or goods to her father. Joseph bought the people with food to be servants unto Pharaoh. But they were not made slaves. They were only to pay Pharaoh a large rent for their land.

Ard. Would any slaveholder now treat his slaves as Abraham did his servants? He put arms into their hands, and entrusted them with the guardianship of his person. They were to be his heirs, in case of the failure of children, in preference to other relations. The oldest servant of Abraham's house was a person of great consideration, to whom Isaac was in some respects subordinate, even at the age of forty years. And Abraham thought it necessary to bind him by an oath that *he* would not marry Isaac to any of the daughters of the land. There is no evidence that Abraham sold any of them, or gave them away, or treated them in any respect like slaves.

Th. If Abraham's service was slavery, his servants had an easy method of emancipating themselves. It was but to refuse a compliance with some of the religious obligations which his family were required to observe, and they would at once be excluded from his family, and turned out of his house. No, they must have been substantially like the servants of whom the apostle' speaks. "Now I say that the heir, as long as he is a child, differeth nothing from a servant, though he be lord of all." Of course, the servant differs nothing from a child in his minority. But as a child in his minority is very different from a slave, so also the servitude which is authorized by the Scriptures is very different from slavery.

Man. But Moses found slavery in existence, and made laws to regulate it.

Th. Moses found a system of servitude in existence, not slavery, and made laws to regulate it which are not found in modern slave countries. Servants could make intermarriages with other members of the family, and become heirs with the children. "A wise servant shall have rule over a son that causeth shame, and shall have part of the inheritance among the brethren." Servants were not allowed to be separated from their wives and children; they were invited guests at all the national and family festivals of the household in which they resided; they were under the same religious instruction, and under the same civil laws with their masters. There was not one law for the master, and another for the servant, as in all slave countries. Servants might be parties to a suit at law for the recovery of their rights; and they could give testimony in courts of justice where masters were concerned.

Man. But Moses says: "Both thy bondmen and thy bondmaids, which thou shalt have, shall be of the heathen that are round about you; of them shall ye buy bondmen and bondmaids-they shall be your bondmen forever." Is not that authority to buy slaves?

Th. The word rendered, *bondmen* signifies *servants*; the word rendered *buy* signifies *procure.* — And we are not obliged by the language, when divested of the wrong ideas derived from our familiarity with slavery, to understand it as meaning any more than this: "Both thy male and female" servants, which thou shalt have, shall be of the heathen that are round about you; (and not of your Hebrew brethren;) of them shall ye procure men servants and maid servants-of such shall be your permanent servants in all ages."

Ard. Did Moses authorize the buying and selling of slaves?

Th. The institutions of Moses provide for persons selling themselves to be servants, that is, hiring themselves out to be permanent servants, for a sum paid in advance; and also for fathers selling their daughters to be wives, and thus providing them with a dowry. But there seems to be no trace of any toleration of slave trading. The possibility that such a thing might be attempted appears to be provided for. "He that stealeth a man, and selleth him, or if he be found in his hand, he shall surely be put to death."

Man. Were not the Israelites slaves in Egypt?"

Th. They were under great oppression there, for which their oppressors were severely punished; but not slaves according to your definition. They resided by themselves in the land of Goshen, in permanent dwellings, in their own distinct and separate families. They held their possessions independently, and owned a large amount of property, which does not appear to have been claimed by their masters. They kept arms, and were fully equipped when they left Egypt. They had their own government, and laws, and magistrates. They appear to have been called out, a given portion of the men at a time, to labor in the public works. And the great oppression consisted in their being required to perform too much labor for the king. They appear to have had time to learn and practice several of the fine arts. There is no complaint that their women were subject to any personal outrages, nor to any species of cruel treatment, save that which Pharaoh judged to be necessary for his own safety, the destruction of their male children. They were abundantly supplied with the necessaries and comforts of life, as they afterwards alleged in their complaints when in the wilderness. Instead of being allowed "a quart of corn a day," as some slave-holding states now provide, they "sat by the flesh pots, and did eat bread to the full." They also did "eat fish freely, and cucumbers, and melons, and leeks, and onions, and garlic." No restrictions seem to have been placed on their intellectual and moral improvement, or the free exercise of their religion, till they asked leave to go away in a body three days' journey into the wilderness, with all they possessed. And then the king seems to have refused chiefly from the fear that they would not return. If such was the bondage of Egypt, so decidedly condemned and so severely punished; if it was so mild, compared with modern slavery; is it credible that God would authorize any thing like modern slavery, among a people whom he so abundantly enjoins not to oppress the stranger, nor to forget that they had been strangers in the land of Egypt? I cannot think it credible.

Ard. And then, there was a year of jubilee, of which it is said: "And ye shall hallow the fiftieth *year,* and proclaim liberty throughout all the land, unto *all* the inhabitants thereof."

Th. And there was another direction, which the modern advocates of slavery do not like to have us obey. "Thou shalt not deliver unto his master the servant which is escaped from his master unto thee."

Man. You had better take care what you do, when you are within the reach of slave-holders.

Th. We mean to obey God, in relation to this matter, as well as all others; and bear testimony against oppression and cruelty. And we do not think you have any right to complain of us for doing so.

Man. "Slavery was prevalent at the coming of Christ; but he issued no command with regard to it; the apostles nowhere assailed it; the Gospel does not proclaim liberty to the slave."

Th. I cannot but wonder that you should use such language, if you have read the New Testament. It brings to mind the annunciation of the object of his coming, which is put into the mouth of our Lord, by the prophet: "The Spirit of the Lord God is upon me; because the Lord hath anointed me to preach good tidings unto to the meek; he hath sent me to bind up the broken-hearted, *to proclaim liberty to the captives,* and the opening of the prison to them that are bound; to proclaim the acceptable year of the Lord, and the day of vengeance of our God; to comfort all that mourn."

Man. But I cannot think it a sin to hold slaves, because the New Testament gives precepts to regulate the conduct both of masters and slaves. "Servants, be obedient to them that are your masters according to the flesh." "Exhort servants to be obedient unto their own masters, and to please them well in all things."

Th. With reference to these precepts, I have two remarks to make. One is that nothing is here said about *slaves.* The Greek word is *doaloi,* servants. The relation of *master* and *servant* may be, very proper, and the relation of *master* and *slave* not be sanctioned at all. The proper Greek for *slave is andrapodon. Doulos,* servant, is used in the New Testament, very much as the Hebrew *ebed,* (servant,) is in the Old. It is evident, to any who examine the New Testament, that those who are called *douloi* were regarded as *persons,* and not as *things;* they possessed property of their own, were capable of making contracts, of owing debts to others, and having debts due to them; their wives and children were theirs, and not their masters. None of these things apply to modern slaves. Paul called himself a *doulos, servant,* of Jesus Christ, which was a title of honor. But his declaring it to be the same condition in which the heir is, during his minority, shows that it meant a man in a subordinate station, and not a mere chattel. But there is another remark to be made respecting these commands: They mention the duty of the servant, without deciding whether it is right for him to be held in that condition. It is the duty of those who are held as slaves; to be obedient to the lawful commands of those to whom, in the providence of God, they are subordinate. But that does not prove it right for them to be held in that condition. Christianity found Nero exercising the most cruel tyranny at Rome; and it says, to the Christians of that city: "Let every soul be subject unto the higher powers; for there is no power but of God; the powers that be are ordained of God." Did this prove that the government of Nero was right and no sin?

Man. But Christianity gives precepts to masters also; and thus recognizes that relation.

Th. It gives precepts for, the treatment of *servants.* But I do not

admit that it therefore recognizes slave-holding as no sin. It says, indeed, "Masters, give unto your servants that which is just and equal; knowing that ye also have a master in heaven." *Just* and *equal;* what is that, but a fair equivalent for their service? Can it be just and equal to compel them to labor without wages, and refuse to pay them for their work?

Man. I consider the case of Onesimus as good proof. When Paul sent him, back to Philemon, he practically recognized the right of taking up runaway slaves, and sending them back to their masters.

Th. This case seems to be strangely misunderstood. Philemon had embraced the Gospel. His servant Onesimus had run away, apparently in his debt. By the preaching of Paul, Onesimus was converted to Christianity. Paul speaks as if he might have retained him for the service of the Gospel; but he chose to have Philemon do his duty in discharging him, of his own accord, and not by compulsion. He sends him therefore, and exhorts Philemon to receive him, *"not now as a servant,* but above a servant, a brother beloved, especially to me; but how much more unto thee." Was that to receive him as a slave? He said, "If thou count me, therefore, a partner, receive him as myself," that is receive him as a partner, a companion, not as a slave. And he expresses the greatest confidence that he would do his duty in the case: "Having confidence in thy obedience, I wrote unto thee, knowing that thou wilt also do more than I say." If all men, now held as slaves, were treated as Paul asks Onesimus might be, the reproach of slavery would no longer rest upon our country.

Ard. How do you pretend to reconcile slave-holding with our Savior's golden rule, "Whatsoever ye would that men should do to you, do ye even so them; for this is the law and the prophets!"

Man. That means, I suppose, that we should do what is best for others, considering their situation, character, and circumstances. And it is clearly best for most slaves to be kept in that condition; for they cannot take care of themselves.

Ard. They prove that they can, by taking care of themselves and their masters, too, in many cases. But that would acknowledge that all who would be better off in freedom, should be set free.

Man. I doubt whether any would be better off.

Ard. Suppose you test the sincerity of your principles by changing places with them. Would you be willing to be shut up for a season, and then be sold to the highest bidder? Would you be willing to be chained in a company, and be driven with a whip to the sugar plantations, and there be worked, as those you sell are worked, till they are exhausted, and die? Just put the case to yourself; and put yourself in their place, and see what you ought to do.

Man. "Slavery is the corner-stone of our republican edifice."

Ard. Out upon such republicanism. The republican edifice erected by our revolutionary fathers, has the contrary as its foundation. They say: "We hold these truths to be self-evident, that all men are created equal, that they are endowed by their Creator with certain inalienable rights; that among these are life, liberty, and the pursuit of happiness." If these truths are self-evident, in the light of nature, they are equally clear according to the word of God. That affirms that God "hath made of one blood all nations of men, for to dwell on the face of the earth." Here, then, we, take our stand, with the Bible in one hand, and the declaration of our fathers in the other; and we fearlessly affirm, that every pretended grant of the right of property in human beings, is self-evidently null and void; and every assertion of such a right is usurpation and robbery.

Man. Such declarations are mere rhetorical flourishes. Nobody believed them at the time.

Th. I am not willing to think that it was so. I believe them to be true, according to the natural import of their language, and I honor the patriots who put forth such a declaration before the world; and I think it eminently disgraceful for their posterity to maintain the contrary now.

Man. We must have slaves in our warm regions to perform the labor necessary to support human life. If they were free, they could not be hired to do it, and the land would become desolate.

Th. Better so, than live in the continual violation of the laws of God and man. "Woe unto him that buildeth his house by unrighteousness, and his chambers by wrong; that useth his neighbor's service without wages, and giveth him not for his work" "Rob not the poor because he is poor; neither oppress the afflicted in the gate; for the Lord will plead their cause, and spoil the soul of those that spoiled them." I should suppose you would sometimes think as Mr. Jefferson, himself a slaveholder, said: "I tremble for my country, when I reflect that God is just, and that his justice cannot sleep forever. The Almighty has no attribute which can take sides with us."

Man. I am astonished at such sentiments. *Slaveholders* will not tolerate them; secession, rebellion, and division of the Union will be the result, if persevered in.

Ard. Away with your threats of rebellion, secession, and disunion — remember the Whisky Rebellion and Shay's War — in later times, Nullification. Will not freemen, now as then, stand by the union. Try it.

Th. Hold, hold, brother! "In meekness admonish those that oppose themselves."

Although I admit that slaveholding, in these United States *is sin*; the vilest transgression of the laws of God, and the principles of the constitution of. these United States, that ever had a legal existence, yet we must remember the slaveholding mind is darkened by reason of its existence, therefore we must bear with their taunts and threats. But as you love your country, your fellow men and our free institutions, do nothing to extend or perpetuate the system of slaveholding; or in any way be partaker of its iniquity. — The love you bear your fellow men at the south, and their children yet unborn, — Demand it at your hands!

Author unknown

NAT TURNER (1800-1831)

Introduction

Nat Turner was born in Southampton County, Virginia on October 2, 1800. As a young man, he began having visions that he believed were from God. Turner had three visions prior to the rebellion in 1831. His first vision occurred in 1821, after he had run away. While hiding out in the woods, he was prompted by a vision to return to his master. After thirty days in the woods, he returned.

His second vision came in 1825 after seeing lights in the sky. He prayed to find out what it meant. He believed that his prayers were answered when he saw " …drops of blood on the corn, as though it were dew from heaven." He believed that this was a sign that Jesus was returning to earth as dew and judgment day approached.

On May 12, 1828, he had his third vision. He believed that the Spirit spoke to him and told him to fight the "Serpent." According to his vision, a sign from heaven would reveal when the revolt should take place. In February 1831, an eclipse of the sun occurred, and Turner believed that this was a sign to begin planning. He told four other slaves, and they planned the attack for July 4. However, Turner became ill so the rebellion was canceled.

The plans were postponed until August 20, 1831. On that evening, Turner and six other men met in the woods. At 2:00 a.m., they went to the home of Turner's master. They killed his master's entire family. Then they went house-to-house, killing other whites.

To the white residents of Southampton County, it came as a surprise that a slave named Nat Turner was the leader of a slave rebellion that resulted in the deaths of 55 white people. This rebellion, which Turner believed was directed by God, became one of the most famous slave insurrections in U.S. history.

The rebellion ended when the militia began pursuing Turner and the other slaves. During the pursuit, some slaves were captured and about 15 were hanged. Turner escaped and hid out for about six weeks until he was captured. He was imprisoned and on November 5, 1831, he was sentenced to execution. While in prison, he dictated his confession to Thomas R. Gray. On November 11, 1831 he was hanged and skinned.

The following text is Nat Turner's confession, as it was dictated to Thomas R. Gray and published in 1831 in *The Confessions of Nat Turner, The Leader of the Late Insurrection, in Southampton, VA.*

Thomas R. Gray published *The Confessions of Nat Turner* (1831) to satisfy public curiosity and provide an account of the events leading up to, during, and following a slave insurrection in Southampton, Virginia that was led by Nat Turner. Gray recorded Turner's confession in a jail cell shortly after Turner's capture and arrest. According to Gray's account, which he asserts contains little or no variation from Turner's words, Nat Turner was called by the Holy Spirit to commit his crimes.

The Confessions of Nat Turner

Introduction

I was thirty-one years of age the 2nd of October last, and born the property of Benj. Turner, of this county. In my childhood a circumstance occurred which made an indelible impression on my mind, and laid the ground work of that enthusiasm, which has terminated so fatally to many, both white and black, and for which I am about to atone at the gallows. It is here necessary to relate this circumstance—trifling as it may seem, it was the commencement of that belief which has grown with time, and even now, sir, in this dungeon, helpless and forsaken as I am, I cannot divest myself of.

Early signs of divine election

Being at play with other children, when three or four years old, I was telling them something, which my mother overhearing, said it had happened before I was born—I stuck to my story, however, and related something which went, in her opinion, to confirm it— others being called on were greatly astonished, knowing that these things had happened, and caused them to say in my hearing, I surely would be a prophet, as the Lord had shewn me things that had happened before my birth. And my father and mother strengthened me in this my first impression, saying in my presence, I was intended for some great purpose, which they had always thought from certain marks on my head and breast—[a parcel of excrescences which I believe are not at all uncommon, particularly among Negroes, as I have seen several with the same. In this case he has either cut them off or they have nearly disappeared]—

My grand mother, who was very religious, and to whom I was much attached—my master, who belonged to the church, and other religion persons who visited the house, and whom I often saw at prayers, noticing the singularity of my manners, I suppose, and my uncommon intelligence for a child, remarked I had too much sense to be raised, and if I was, I would never be of any service to any one as a slave—To a mind like mine, restless, inquisitive and observant of every thing that was passing, it is easy to suppose that religion was the subject to which it would be directed, and although this subject principally occupied my thoughts—there was nothing that I saw or heard of to which my attention was not directed—

The manner in which I learned to read and write, not only had great influence on my own mind, as I acquired it with the most perfect ease, so much so that I have no recollection whatever of learning the alphabet—but to the astonishment of the family, one day, when a book was shewn me to keep me from crying, I began spelling the names of different objects—this was a source of wonder to all in the neighborhood, particularly the blacks— and this learning was constantly improved at all opportunities— when I got large enough to go to work, while employed, I was reflecting on many things that would present themselves to my imagination, and whenever an opportunity occurred of looking at a book, when the school children were getting their lessons, I would find many things that the fertility of my own imagination had depicted to me before; all my time, not devoted to my master's service, was spent either in prayer, or in making experiments in casting different things in moulds made of earth, in attempting to make paper, gun powder, and many other experiments, that although I could not perfect, yet convinced me of its practicability if I had the means.

I was not addicted to stealing in my youth, nor have ever been—Yet such was the confidence of the Negroes in the neighborhood, even at this early period of my life, in my superior judgment, that they would often carry me with them when they were going on any roguery, to plan for them. Growing up among them, with this confidence in my superior judgment, and when this, in their opinions, was perfected by Divine inspiration, from the circumstances already alluded to in my infancy, and which belief was ever afterwards zealously inculcated by the austerity of my life and manners, which became the subject of remark by white and black.—

Having soon discovered to be great, I must appear so, and therefore studiously avoided mixing in society, and wrapped myself in mystery, devoting my time to fasting and prayer.—

By this time, having arrived to man's estate, and hearing the scriptures commented on at meetings, I was struck with that particular passage which says: "Seek ye the kingdom of Heaven and all things shall be added unto you." I reflected much on this passage, and prayed daily for light on this subject—As I was praying one day at my plough, the spirit spoke to me, saying "Seek ye the kingdom of Heaven and all things shall be added unto you.

Question—what do you mean by the Spirit. Ans. The Spirit that spoke to the prophets in former days— and I was greatly astonished, and for two years prayed continually, whenever my duty would permit—and then again I had the same revelation, which fully confirmed me in the impression that I was ordained for some great purpose in the hands of the Almighty.

Several years rolled round, in which many events occurred to strengthen me in this my belief. At this time I reverted in my mind to the remarks made of me in my childhood, and the things that had been shewn me—and as it had been said of me in my childhood by those by whom I had been taught to pray, both white and black, and in whom I had the greatest confidence, that I had too much sense to be raised. and if I was, I would never be of any use to any one as a slave. Now finding I had arrived to man's estate, and was a slave, and these revelations being made known to me, I began to direct my attention to this great object, to fulfill the purpose for which, by this time, I felt assured I was intended.

Knowing the influence I had obtained over the minds of my fellow servants, (not by the means of conjuring and such like tricks—for to them I always spoke of such things with contempt) but by the communion of the Spirit whose revelations I often communicated to them, and they believed and said my wisdom came from God. I now began to prepare them for my purpose, by telling them something was about to happen that would terminate in fulfilling the great promise that had been made to me.

Escape and voluntary return as first prophetic act
About this time I was placed under an overseer, from whom I ran away—and after remaining in the woods thirty days, I returned, to the astonishment of the Negroes on the plantation, who thought I had made my escape to some other part of the country, as my father had done before. But the reason of my return was, that the Spirit appeared to me and

said I had my wishes directed to the things of this world, and not to the kingdom of Heaven, and that I should return to the service of my earthly master—"For he who knoweth his Master's will, and doeth it not, shall be beaten with many stripes, and thus have I chastened you." And the Negroes found fault, and murmured against me, saying that if they had my sense they would not serve any master in the world.

Prophetic call and vision sequence
And about this time I had a vision—and I saw white spirits and black spirits engaged in battle, and the sun was darkened—the thunder rolled in the Heavens, and blood flowed in streams—and I heard a voice saying, "Such is your luck, such you are called to see, and let it come rough or smooth, you must surely bare it." I now withdrew myself as much as my situation would permit, from the intercourse of my fellow servants, for the avowed purpose of serving the Spirit more fully—and it appeared to me, and reminded me of the things it had already shown me, and that it would then reveal to me the knowledge of the elements, the revolution of the planets, the operation of tides, and changes of the seasons.

After this revelation in the year 1825, and the knowledge of the elements being made known to me, I sought more than ever to obtain true holiness before the great day of judgment should appear, and then I began to receive the true knowledge of faith.

And from the first steps of righteousness until the last, was I made perfect; and the Holy Ghost was with me, and said, "Behold me as I stand in the Heavens"—and I looked and saw the forms of men in different attitudes—and there were lights in the sky to which the children of darkness gave other names than what they really were—for they were the lights of the Savior's hands, stretched forth from east to west, even as they were extended on the cross on Calvary for the redemption of sinners.

And I wondered greatly at these miracles, and prayed to be informed of a certainty of the meaning thereof— and shortly afterwards, while laboring in the field, I discovered drops of blood on the corn as though it were dew from heaven—and I communicated it to many, both white and black, in the neighborhood— and I then found on the leaves in the woods hieroglyphic characters, and numbers, with the forms of men in different attitudes, portrayed in blood, and representing the figures I had seen before in the heavens.

Meaning of the visions revealed
And now the Holy Ghost had revealed itself to me, and made plain the miracles it had shown me—For as the blood of Christ had been shed on this earth, and had ascended to heaven for the salvation of sinners, and was now returning to earth again in the form of dew—and as the leaves on the trees bore the impression of the figures I had seen in the heavens, it was plain to me that the Savior was about to lay down the yoke he had borne for the sins of men, and the great day of judgment was at hand.

Miraculous confirmation
About this time I told these things to a white man, (Ethelred T. Brantley) on whom it had a wonderful effect—and he ceased from his wickedness, and was attacked immediately with a

cutaneous eruption, and blood oozed from the pores of his skin, and after praying and fasting nine days, he was healed, and the Spirit appeared to me again, and said, as the Savior had been baptized so should we be also—and when the white people would not let us be baptized by the church, we went down into the water together, in the sight of many who reviled us, and were baptized by the Spirit—after this I rejoiced greatly, and gave thanks to God.

Vision of revolt

And on the 12th of May, 1828, I heard a loud noise in the heavens, and the Spirit was loosened, and Christ had laid down the yoke he had borne for the sins of men, and that I should take it on and fight against the Serpent, for the time was fast approaching when the first should be last and the last should be first.

Question. Do you not find yourself mistaken now?
Answer. Was not Christ crucified.

And by signs in the heavens that it would make known to me when I should commence the great work—and until the first sign appeared, I should conceal it from the knowledge of men—And on the appearance of the sign, (the eclipse of the sun last February) I should arise and prepare myself, and slay my enemies with their own weapons.

Preparations

And immediately on the sign appearing in the heavens, the seal was removed from my lips, and I communicated the great work laid out for me to do, to four in whom I had the greatest confidence, (Henry, Hark, Nelson, and Sam)—

It was intended by us to have begun the work of death on the 4th July last—Many were the plans formed and rejected by us, and it affected my mind to such a degree, that I fell sick, and the time passed without our coming to any determination how to commence—Still forming new schemes and rejecting them, when the sign appeared again, which determined me not to wait longer.

The rebellion

Since the commencement of 1830, I had been living with Mr. Joseph Travis, who was to me a kind master, and placed the greatest confidence in me; in fact, I had no cause to complain of his treatment to me.

On Saturday evening, the 20th of August, it was agreed between Henry, Hark and myself, to prepare a dinner the next day for the men we expected, and then to concert a plan, as we had not yet determined on any. Hark, on the following morning, brought a pig, and Henry brandy, and being joined by Sam, Nelson, Will and Jack, they prepared in the woods a dinner, where, about three o'clock, I joined them.

Q. Why were you so backward in joining them.
A. The same reason that had caused me not to mix with them for years before.

I saluted them on coming up, and asked Will how came he there, he answered, his life was worth no more than others, and his liberty as dear to him. I asked him if he thought to obtain it? He said he would, or loose his life. This was enough to put him in full confidence. . Jack, I knew, was only a tool in the hands of Hark, it was quickly agreed we should commence at home (Mr. J. Travis') on that night, and until we had armed and equipped ourselves, and gathered sufficient force, neither age nor sex was to be spared, (which was invariably adhered to.)

We remained at the feast, until about two hours in the night, when we went to the house and found Austin; they all went to the cider press and drank, except myself.

On returning to the house, Hark went to the door with an axe, for the purpose of breaking it open, as we knew we were strong enough to murder the family, if they were awaked by the noise; but reflecting that it might create an alarm in the neighborhood, we determined to enter the house secretly, and murder them whilst sleeping. Hark got a ladder and set it against the chimney, on which I ascended, and hoisting a window, entered and came down stairs, unbarred the door and removed the guns from their places.

First blood

It was then observed that I must spill the first blood. On which, armed with a hatchet, and accompanied by Will, I entered my master's chamber, it being dark, I could not give a death blow, the hatchet glanced from his head, he sprang from the bed and called his wife, it was his last word, Will laid him dead, with a blow of his axe, and Mrs. Travis shared the same fate, as she lay in bed.

The murder of this family, five in number, was the work of a moment, not one of them awoke; there was a little infant sleeping in a cradle, that was forgotten, until we had left the house and gone same distance, when Henry and Will returned and killed it; we got here, four guns that would shoot, and several old muskets, with a pound or two of powder.

Path of destruction

We remained some time at the barn, where we paraded; I formed them in a line as soldiers, and after carrying them through all the maneuvers I was master of, marched them off to Mr. Salathul Francis', about six hundred yards distant.

Sam and Will went to the door and knocked. M. Francis asked who was there, Sam replied it was him, and he had a letter for him, on which he got up and came to the door; they immediately seized him, and dragging him out a little from the door, he was dispatched by repeated blows on the head; there was no other white person in the family.

We started from there for Mrs. Reese's, maintaining the most perfect silence on our march, where finding the door unlocked, we entered, and murdered Mrs. Reese in her bed, while sleeping: her son awoke, but it was only to sleep the sleep of death, he had only time to say who is that, and he was no more.

From Mrs. Reese's we went to Mrs. Turner's, a mile distant, which we reached about sunrise, on Monday morning. Henry, Austin, and Sam, went to the still, where, finding Mr. Peebles, Austin shot him, and the rest of us went to the house; as we approached, the family discovered us, and shut the door. Vain hope! Will, with one stroke of his axe, opened it, and we entered and found Mrs. Turner and Mrs. Newsome in the middle of a room, almost frightened to death. Will immediately killed Mrs. Turner, with one blow of his axe. I took Mrs. Newsome by the hand, and with the sword I had when I was apprehended, I struck her several blows over the head, but not being able to kill her, as the sword was dull. Will turning around and discovering it, dispatched her also.

A general destruction of property and search for money and ammunition, always succeeded the murders. By this time my company amounted to fifteen, and nine men mounted, who started for Mrs. Whitehead's, (the other six were to go through a by way to Mr. Bryant's, and rejoin us at Mrs. Whitehead's,) as we approached the house we discovered Mr. Richard Whitehead standing in the cotton patch, near the lane fence: we called him over into the lane, and Will, the executioner, was near at hand, with his fatal axe, to send him to an untimely grave. As we pushed on to the house, I discovered some one run round the garden, and thinking it was some of the white family, I pursued them, but finding it was a servant girl belonging to the house, I returned to commence the work of death, but they whom I left, had not been idle; all the family were already murdered, but Mrs. Whitehead and her daughter Margaret.

As I came round to the door I saw Will pulling Mrs. Whitehead out of the house, and at the step he nearly severed her head from her body, with his broad axe. Miss Margaret, when I discovered her, had concealed herself in the corner, formed by the projection of the cellar cap from the house; on my approach she fled, but was soon overtaken, and after repeated blows with a sword, I killed her by a blow on the head, with a fence rail.

By this time, the six who had gone by Mr. Bryant's, rejoined us, and informed me they had done the work of death assigned them. We again divided, part going to Mr. Richard Porter's, and from thence to Nathaniel Francis', the others to Mr. Howell Harris'; and Mr. T. Doyles.

The alarm spreads

On my reaching Mr. Porter's, he had escaped with his family. I understood there, that the alarm had already spread, and I immediately returned to bring up those sent to Mr. Doyles, and Mr. Howell Harris'; the party I left going on to Mr. Francis', having told them I would join them in that neighborhood. I met these sent to Mr. Doyles' and Mr. Harris' returning, having met Mr. Doyle on the road and killed him; and learning from some who joined them, that Mr. Harris was from home, I immediately pursued the course taken by the party gone on before; but knowing they would complete the work of death and pillage, at Mr. Francis' before I could get there, I went to Mr. Peter Edwards', expecting to find them there, but they had been here also.

I then went to Mr. John T. Barrow's, they had been here and murdered him. I pursued on their track to Capt. Newit Harris', where I found the greater part mounted, and ready to start; the men now amounting to about forty, shouted and hurried as I rode up, some were in the yard, loading their guns, others drinking. They said Captain Harris and his family had escaped, the property in the house they destroyed, robbing him of money and other valuables. I ordered them to mount and march instantly, this was about nine or ten o'clock, Monday morning.

I proceeded to Mr. Levi Waller's, two or three miles distant. I took my station in the rear, and as it 'twas my object to carry terror and devastation wherever we went, I placed fifteen or twenty of the best armed and most to be relied on, in front, who generally approached the houses as fast as their horses could run; this was for two purposes, to prevent their escape arid strike terror to the inhabitants—on this account I never got to the houses, after leaving Mrs. Whitehead's, until the murders were committed, except in one case. I sometimes got in sight in time to see the work of death completed, viewed the mangled bodies as they lay, in silent satisfaction, and immediately started in quest of other victims—having murdered Mrs. Waller and ten children, we started for Mr. William Williams'—Having killed him and two little boys that were there; while engaged in this, Mrs. Williams fled and got some distance from the house, but she was pursued, overtaken, and compelled to get up behind one of the company, who brought her back, and after showing her the mangled body of her lifeless husband, she was told to get down and lay by his side, where she was shot dead.

I then started for Mr. Jacob Williams, where the family were murdered—Here we found a young man named Drury, who had come on business with Mr. Williams—he was pursued, overtaken and shot.

Mrs. Vaughan was the next place we visited—and after murdering the family here, I determined on starting for Jerusalem—Our number amounted now to fifty or sixty, all mounted and armed with guns, axes, swords and clubs—

On reaching Mr. James W. Parkers' gate, immediately on the road leading to Jerusalem, and about three miles distant, it was proposed to me to call there, but I objected, as I knew he was gone to Jerusalem, and my object was to reach there as soon as possible; but some of the men having relations at Mr. Parker's it was agreed that they might call and get his people.

White men retaliate

After waiting some time for them, I became impatient, and started to the house for them, and on our return we were met by a party of white men, who had pursued our blood-stained track, and who had fired on those at the gate, and dispersed them, which I new nothing of, not having been at that time rejoined by any of them—

Immediately on discovering the whites, I ordered my men to halt and form, as they appeared to be alarmed—The white men, eighteen in number, approached us in about one hundred yards, when one of them fired, (this was against the positive orders of Captain Alexander P. Peete, who commanded, and who had directed the men to reserve their fire until within thirty paces)

And I discovered about half of them retreating, I then ordered my men to fire and rush on them; the few remaining stood their ground until we approached within fifty yards, when they fired and retreated. We pursued and overtook some of them who we thought we left dead; (they were not killed) after pursuing them about two hundred yards, and rising a little hill, I discovered they were met by another party, and had halted, and were reloading their guns, (this was a small party from Jerusalem who knew the Negroes were in the field, and had just tied their horses to await their return to the road, knowing that Mr. Parker and family were in Jerusalem, but knew nothing of the party that had gone in with Captain Peete; on hearing the firing they immediately rushed to the spot and arrived just in time to arrest the progress of these barbarous villains, and save the lives of their friends and fellow citizens.) Thinking that those who retreated first, and the party who fired on us at fifty or sixty yards distant, had all only fallen back to meet others with ammunition.

Panic sets in

As I saw them re-loading their guns, and more coming up than I saw at first, and several of my bravest men being wounded, the others became panic struck and squandered over the field; the white men pursued and fired on us several times.

Hark had his horse shot under him, and I caught another for him as it was running by me; five or six of my men were wounded, but none left on the field; finding myself defeated here I instantly determined to go through a private way, and cross the Nottoway river at the Cypress Bridge, three miles below Jerusalem, and attack that place in the rear, as I expected they would look for me on the other road, and I had a great desire to get there to procure arms and ammunition.

After going a short distance in this private way, accompanied by about twenty men, I overtook two or three; who told me the others were dispersed in every direction. After trying in vain to collect a sufficient force to proceed to Jerusalem, I determined to return, as I was sure they would make back to their old neighborhood, where they would rejoin me, make new recruits, and come down again.

They regroup

On my way back, I called at Mrs. Thomas's, Mrs. Spencer's, and several other places, the white families having fled, we found no more victims to gratify our thirst for blood, we stopped at Major. Ridley's quarter for the night, and being joined by four of his men, with the recruits made since my defeat, we mustered now about forty strong.

After placing our sentinels, I laid down to sleep, but was quickly roused by a great racket; starting up, I found some mounted, and others in great confusion; one of the sentinels having given the alarm that we mere about to be attacked, I ordered some to ride round and reconnoiter, and on their return the others being more alarmed, not knowing who they were, fled in different ways, so that I was reduced to about twenty again; with this I determined to attempt to recruit, and proceed on to rally in the neighborhood, I had left.

Dr. Blunt's was the nearest house, which we reached just before day; on riding up the yard, Hark fired a gun. We expected Dr. Blunt and his family were at Maj. Ridley's, as I knew there was a company of men there; the gun was fired to ascertain if any of the family was at home; we were immediately fired upon and retreated, leaving several of my men. I do not know what became of them, as I never saw them afterwards.

Desertion

Pursuing our course back and coming in sight of Captain Harris' where we had been the day before, we discovered a party of white men at the house, on which all deserted me but two, (Jacob and Nat,) we concealed ourselves in the woods until near night, when I sent them in search of Henry, Sam, Nelson, and Hark, and directed them to rally all they could, at the place we had had our dinner the Sunday before, where they would find me, and I accordingly returned there as soon as it was dark and remained until Wednesday evening, when discovering white men riding around the place as though they were looking for some one, and none of my men joining me, I concluded Jacob and Nat had been taken, and compelled to betray me.

Fugitive life

On this I gave up all hope for the present; and on Thursday night after having supplied myself with provisions from Mr. Travis's, I scratched a hole under a pile of fence rails in a field where I concealed myself for six weeks, never leaving my hiding place but for a few minutes in the dead of night to get water which was very near; thinking by this time I could venture out, I began to go about in the night and eaves drop the houses in the neighborhood; pursuing this course for about a fortnight and gathering little or no intelligence, afraid of speaking to any human being, and returning every morning to my cave before the dawn of day.

Discovery

I know not how long I might have led this life, if accident had not betrayed me, a dog in the neighborhood passing by my hiding place one night while I was out, was attracted by some meat I had in my cave, and crawled in and stole it, and was coming out just as I returned. A few nights after, two Negroes having started to go hunting with the same dog, and passed that way, the dog came again to the place, and having just gone out to walk about, discovered me and barked, on which thinking myself discovered, I spoke to them to beg concealment. On making myself known they fled from me.

Knowing then they would betray me, I immediately left my hiding place and was pursued almost incessantly until I was taken a fortnight afterwards by Mr.: Benjamin Phipps, in a little hole I had dug out with my sword, for the purpose of concealment, under the top of a fallen tree. On Mr. Phipps' discovering the place of my concealment, he cocked his gun and aimed at me. I requested him not to shoot and I would give up, upon which he demanded my sword. I delivered it to him, and he brought me to prison.

Conclusion

During the time I was pursued, I had many hair breadth escapes, which your time will not permit you to relate. I am here loaded with chains, and willing to suffer the fate that awaits me.

Cross examination

I here proceeded to make some inquiries of him, after assuring him of the certain death that awaited him, and that concealment would only bring destruction on the innocent as well as guilty, of his own color, if he knew of any extensive or concerted plan. His answer was, I do not.

When I questioned him as to the insurrection in North Carolina happening about the same time, he denied any knowledge of it; and when I looked him in the face as though I would search his inmost thoughts, he replied, "I see sir, you doubt my word; but can you not think the same ideas, and strange appearances about this time in the heaven's might prompt others, as well as myself, to this undertaking."

I now had much conversation with and asked him many questions, having forborne to do so previously, except in the cases noted in parenthesis; but during his statement, I had, unnoticed by him, taken notes as to some particular circumstances, and having the advantage of his statement before me in writing, on the evening of the third day that I had been with him, I began a cross examination, and found his statement corroborated by every circumstance coming within my own knowledge or the confessions of others whom had been either killed or executed, and whom he had not seen nor had any knowledge since 22nd of August last, he expressed himself fully satisfied as to the impracticability of his attempt.

Impressions of Turner

It has been said he was ignorant and cowardly, and that his object was to murder and rob for the purpose of obtaining money to make his escape. It is notorious, that he was never known to have a dollar in his life; to swear an oath, or drink a drop of spirits.

As to his ignorance, he certainly never had the advantages of education, but he can read and write, (it was taught him by his parents,) and for natural intelligence and quickness of apprehension, is surpassed by few men I have ever seen.

As to his being a coward, his reason as given for not resisting Mr. Phipps, shows the decision of his character. When he saw Mr. Phipps present his gun, he said he knew it was impossible for him to escape as the woods were full of men; he therefore thought it was better to surrender, and trust to fortune for his escape.

He is a complete fanatic, or plays his part most admirably. On other subjects he possesses an uncommon share of intelligence, with a mind capable of attaining anything; but warped and perverted by, the influence of early impressions.

He is below the ordinary stature, though strong and active, having the true Negro face, every feature of which is strongly marked.

I shall not attempt to describe the effect of his narrative, as told and commented on by himself, in the condemned hole of the prison. The calm, deliberate composure with which he spoke of his late deeds and intentions, the expression of his fiend-like face when excited by enthusiasm, still bearing the stains of the blood of helpless innocence about him; clothed with rags and covered with chains; yet daring to raise his manacled hands to heaven, with a spirit soaring above the attributes of man; I looked on him and my blood curdled in my veins.

Providential escapes

I will not shock the feelings of humanity, nor wound afresh the bosoms of the disconsolate sufferers in this unparalleled and inhuman massacre, by detailing the deeds of their fiend-like barbarity. There were two or three who were in the power of these wretches, had they known it, and who escaped in the most providential manner.

There were two whom they thought they left dead on the field at Mr. Parker's, but who were only stunned by the blows of guns, as they did not take time to reload when they charged on them.

The escape of a little girl who went to school at Mr. Waller's, and where the children were collecting for that purpose, excited general sympathy. As their teacher had not arrived, they were at play in the yard, and seeing the Negroes approach, she ran up on a dirt chimney, (such as are common to log houses,) and remained there unnoticed during the massacre of the eleven that were killed at this place. She remained on her hiding place till just before the arrival of a party, who were in pursuit of the murderers, when she came down and fled to a swamp, where, a mere child as she was, with the horrors of the late scene before her, she lay concealed until the next day, when seeing a party go up to the house, she came up, and on being asked how she escaped, replied with the utmost simplicity, "The Lord helped her." She was taken up behind a gentleman of the party, and returned to the arms of her weeping mother.

Miss Whitehead concealed herself between the bed and the mat that supported it, while they murdered her sister in the same room, without discovering her. She was afterwards carried off, and concealed for protection by a slave of the family, who gave evidence against several of them on their trial.

Mrs. Nathaniel Francis, while concealed in a closet heard their blows, and the shrieks of the victims of these ruthless savages; they then entered the closet where she was concealed, and went out without discovering her. While in this hiding place, she heard two of her women in a quarrel about the division of her clothes.

Mr. John T. Baron, discovering them approaching his house, told his wife to make her escape, and scorning to fly, fell fighting on his own threshold. After firing his rifle, he discharged his gun at them, and then broke it over the villain who first approached him, but he was overpowered and slain. His bravery, however, saved from the hands of these monsters, his lovely and amiable wife, who will long lament a husband so deserving of her love. As directed by him, she attempted to escape through the garden, when she was caught and held by one of her servant girls, but another coming to her rescue, she fled to the woods, and concealed herself.

The hand of justice

Few indeed, were those who escaped their work of death. But fortunate for society, the hand of retributive justice has overtaken them, and not one that was known to be concerned has escaped.

Nat Turner

NOAH DAVIS (1803-59?)

Introduction

Noah Davis, a former slave, was pastor of the Saratoga Street African Baptist Church, Baltimore. His book, *A Narrative of the Life of Rev. Noah Davis, a Colored Man (1859)* was a nonprofit book was printed solely for the purpose of raising money to buy two of Davis' children out of slavery.

A Narrative of the Life of Rev. Noah Davis, A Colored Man
Chapter 1
Early Life in Virginia—Example of Pious Parents

I was born a slave, in Madison county, Virginia, March, 1804. My father, John Davis, and his family, belonged to Robert Patten, Esq., a wealthy merchant, residing in Fredericksburg—who was also owner, in connection with Mr. John Thom, of a large merchant mill, located on "Crooked Run," a stream running between Madison and Culpepper counties. My father was the head miller in that large establishment, in which responsible station he was much respected.

There I was born, and remained until I was twelve years old. Mr. Patten was always considered one of the best of masters, allowing his servants many privileges; but my father enjoyed more than many others. Both he and my mother were pious members of a Baptist church, and from their godly example, I formed a determination, before I had reached my twelfth year, that if I was spared to become a man, I would try to be as good as my parents. My father could read a little, and make figures, but could scarcely write at all. His custom, on those Sabbaths when we remained at home, was to spend his time in instructing his children, or the neighboring servants, out of a New Testament, sent him from Fredericksburg by one of his older sons. I fancy I can see him now, sitting under his bush arbor, reading that precious book to many attentive hearers around him.

Such was the esteem I had for my pious father, that I have kept that blessed book ever since his death, for his sake; and it was the first New Testament I read, after I felt the pardoning love of God in my soul.

My father died, August 20, 1826, aged 60 years. My mother, Jane Davis, at the death of my father, removed from the farm, where my father died, and spent the remainder of her days in Fredericksburg, with her children. She lived to good old age, and fell asleep in Jesus, Dec. 24, 1831.

My father had been allowed to keep a cow and horse, for his own use; and to raise and feed his hogs and poultry from the mill.—He had the privilege of keeping his children with him, until they were old enough to put out to such trades as they might choose. I had several brothers and one sister. Two of my brothers, one older, the other younger than myself, lived with our parents, at this place. My oldest brother worked in the mill, with my father, while my youngest brother and I did little else than play about home, and wait upon our mother. I had several playmates, besides my brothers, and among them were the sons of Col. Thom, and the servant boys who stayed at his house. Although many years have passed away since, it gives me pleasure, even now, to recollect the happy seasons I enjoyed with the playmates of my childhood.

But this pleasant state of things was not to continue long. The owners of the mill and farm concluded to sell out the whole concern. My father and his family then removed to another farm, belonging to our owner, located in Culpeper county, near Stevensburg. Here I remained nearly two years, working, part of the time, with a carpenter, who was building a summer residence for my master; and the rest of the time, assisting my father to cultivate as much ground as he and his family could tend. Here I learned something of a farmer's life. The overseer, Mr. Daniel Brown, had the reputation of being one of the best overseers in the county. But my father's family was not put under him further than for his protection; for after our owner sold the mill, he set my parents free, and allowed them to maintain themselves, by cultivating as much ground on the farm as they needed.

Sometimes my father would leave his little place in charge of my brother Robert and myself, and would hire himself to work in some mill, or go peddling poultry, vegetables, &c., at some of the market places around.

Chapter 2
Apprenticed to the shoe-making—Learns housework—Intemperance—"A Negro can't be trusted"—Learning how to write and cipher

In December, 1818, for the first time in my life, I left my parents, to go a distance from home; and I was sad at the thought of parting with those whom I loved and reverenced more than any persons on earth. But the expectation of seeing Fredericksburg, a place which, from all I had then learned, I supposed must be the greatest place in the world, reconciled me somewhat with the necessity of saying Good-bye to the dear ones at home. I arrived at Fredericksburg, after a day and a half's travel, in a wagon—a distance of some fifty miles. Having arrived in town, a boy green from the country, I was astonished and delighted at what appeared to me the splendor and beauty of the place. I spent a merry Christmas at my old master's stately mansion, along with my older brother, and for a while forgot the home on the farm.

But soon, another home was selected for me, where I might learn a trade, and as I preferred the boot and shoe-making, I was put to Mr. Thomas Wright, a man of sterling integrity, who was considered the best workman in the whole town. Here I had an older brother living, which was some inducement for my going to live with Mr. Wright. I was bound, to serve until I should be twenty-one years old. This was in January, 1819.

Upon entering with Mr. Wright, I learned that the colored boys had to serve one year with Mrs. Wright, in the house and kitchen. The object of this was to train them for future usefulness, when called from the shop, to serve as waiters or cooks. Mrs. Wright was a good manager, and a very particular housekeeper. I used to think she was too particular. But I have learned better since. I have often wished, when I have been seeking homes for my children, that I could find one like Mrs. Wright. She would spare no pains to teach her servants how she wanted her work done; and then she would spare no pains to make them do it. I have often looked back, with feelings of gratitude and veneration, to that pious lady, for her untiring perseverance in training me up in the way I should go. But she is gone, as I trust, to receive the reward of righteousness, in a better world.

After I had been under Mrs. Wright's special charge the first year, she could leave me to cook a dinner, or clean the house, or do anything she might set me at, without her being present. I was now considered fit to take my seat among the hands in the shop.

Here I found quite a new state of things. The shoemakers, at that time, in Fredericksburg were considered the most intemperate of any class of men in the place; and as the apprentice-boys had always to be very obliging to the journeymen, in order to get along pleasantly with them, it was my duty to be runner for the shop; and I was soon trained how to bring liquor among the men with such secrecy as to prevent the boss, who had forbidden it to come on the premises, from knowing it.

But, in those days, the drinking of ardent spirits was a common practice, even among Christians. With such examples all around, I soon learned the habit of drinking, along with every other vile habit to which my companions were addicted. It was true in my case, that "evil communications corrupt good manners;" and had it not been for the strictness with which my boss and his amiable lady watched over me, I should in all probability have become a confirmed drunkard, before my time was out. But they held the reins over me, and kept me in, until I had served out my apprenticeship.

I can say, however, that, much as I was inclined to other vices and sins, Mr. Wright readily gave me a recommendation for honesty, truthfulness, and goodness of character. In fact, he had felt such confidence in me, that he would often leave his shoe store in my care, when he would have to go to the north, for a supply of stock. And I can truly say, that I never deceived him, when he thus trusted me. Nothing would mortify me as much, as to hear it said, "A Negro can't be trusted." This saying would always nerve me with a determination to be trustworthy.—If I was trusted, I would deserve to be trusted. I wanted to show that principle was not confined to color. But I have been led to look at it since, and have thought that perhaps it was more pride than principle in me, at that time, for I was a wicked sinner.

The first idea I ever got of writing, was from trying to imitate my employer, who used to write the names of his customers on the lining of the boots and shoes, as he gave them out to be made. So I tried to make letters, and soon succeeded in writing my name, and then the word Fredericksburg, and so on. My father had previously taught me the alphabet, in the spelling book, before I had left the mill. After I became religious, I would carry my father's New Testament to church, and always try to get to meeting in time to hear the preacher read a chapter before sermon. If he named the chapter before reading it, I would soon find it. In this way, I gathered much information in pronouncing many hard words in the Scriptures.

It was a long time before I learned the meaning of the numeral letters put in the Bible over the chapters. I had often seen them in the spelling book running alongside a column of figures; but no one ever told me that they were put there for the same use as the figures.

Chapter 3

Religious Experience—Conviction—Conversion

Just about the close of my apprenticeship, and as I began to feel myself a man, I commenced to visit the girls, which induced me go still more frequently to church.

At that time, there were four churches in Fredericksburg. The colored people had apartments for worship with the white people, at each of these churches. They were Methodist, Presbyterian, Episcopalian and Baptist.

I had no particular preference for any one of these denominations, more than another; but, went wherever my favorites went. One night a young lady invited me to go to the Methodist church, where a prayer-meeting was to be held. During the meeting, a venerable old gentleman rose to his feet, and related an account of the sudden death of a young lady, which he had read in a newspapers. When he related that solemn circumstance, it so affected me, that I felt as if I was about to die, in a sudden manner also.

Having always, from parental training, purposed in my mind to become religious before I died, I thought that now was the time to begin to pray. But I could not try to pray in the church, for I was afraid that the girls would laugh at me. Yet I became so troubled, that I left the house, girls and all, intending to seek some place where I might pray. But to my horror and surprise, when I got out of the church, this reflection occurred to me, "God is in heaven, and you are on earth:—how can He hear you?" O, what distress of mind I now felt! I began to wonder how God could hear my prayer;. for, sure enough, He was in heaven, and I on the earth. In my perplexity, I started for home.

Just before I reached the shop, where I slept, this thought struck me, if possible with more force than the former reflection: "God does see you!" It really appeared to me as if I could see that God was indeed looking at me; and not only so, but I felt that He had been looking at me all my life. I now said to myself, "It is of no use for me to pray.—If God has seen all my wickedness, as I feel that He has, then there is no mercy for me."

So I ran to my lodging-place, and tried to hide myself in a dark room. But this was useless; for it appeared that God could see me in the dark, as well as in the light.

I now felt constrained to beg for mercy, and spent the time in trying to obtain pardon for my sins. But the morning came, and the hour drew near for the hands to go to work, and I was still unhappy.

I felt so very different to what I had always felt, that I tried to examine my impressions of the previous night, to learn if it was true that God did see me or not; for I thought my imagination might have deceived me.

Up to this time, I was not fully convinced that God knew all about me. So I began to study about the matter. As I sat on the shoe-bench, I picked up a bunch of bristles, and selecting one of the smallest, I began to wonder, if God could see an object so small as that. No sooner had this inquiry arose in my heart, than it appeared to me, that the Lord could not only see the bristle, but that He beheld me, as, plainly as I saw the little object in my hand; and not only so, but that God was then looking through me, just as I would hold up a tumbler of clear water to the sun and look through it. This was enough. I felt that I must pray, or perish; and now I began to pray.

But it really seemed, that the more I prayed the less hope there was for me. Still I could not stop praying; for I felt that God was angry with me. I had sinned against his holy laws; and now, if He should cut me off, and send me to hell, it was but right. These thoughts followed me day and night, for five weeks, before I felt relief. At length, one day, while sitting on my shoe bench, I felt that my time had come when I must die. What troubled me most, was that I should have to appear before God, in all my sins;—O, what horror filled my soul at the thought!

I began to wonder what I must do. I knew I was not prepared for death and the Judgment. It is true that two of my shopmates, at that time, were members of the church; but they did not seem to care for my soul. All the rest of the hands were as wicked as myself. "What shall I do?" was in my mind, all the time I sat at work.

The reflection occurred to me, "Your mother is a Christian; it may be she can save you." But this suggestion appeared to be offensive to God. Then came another thought,—"As my master was a rich man, could he not do something to help me?" But I found no relief in either … . and while I sat thus, hoping and praying, light broke into my mind—all my trouble left me in an instant.

I felt such a love and peace flowing in my soul, that I could not sit longer; I sprang to my feet, and cried out, "Glory to God!" It seemed to me, that God, whom I had beheld, a few seconds previously, angry with me, was now well-pleased. I could not tell why this great change had taken place in me; and my shopmates were surprised at my conduct, saying, that I must be getting crazy. But, just at this moment, the thought came into my mind, that I was converted; still, as I felt so very different from what I had expected to feel, I could not see how that could be. I concluded to run and see my mother, and ask her how people felt, when they got converted. So I went, right away, to my mother's house, some five or six squares from the shop.

When I reached the door of her house, it appeared to me that everything was new and bright. I went in, and sat down. Mother asked me how I was. I told her, I felt right smart. This was a new sound from me; for my answers to this question had long been—"poorly." But now came the trial; to ask mother how people felt, when they were converted. I felt ashamed to ask the question; so I went into another room; and seeing a hymn book lying on the table, I took it up. The first hymn that struck my sight began with these words:

When converts first begin to sing,
Their happy souls are on the wing—
Their theme is all redeeming love;
Fain would they be with Christ above.
With admiration they behold
The love of Christ, which can't be told, &c.

These lines expressed my feelings precisely, and being encouraged from them, I went to my mother, and asked her the question—"How do people feel, when they get converted?" She replied, "Do you think you are converted?" Now, this was a severe trial; for, although I felt that

I was really changed, yet I wanted to hear from her, before I could decide whether I was actually converted, or not. I replied, "No." Then she said, "My son, the devil makes people think themselves converted, sometimes." I arose, and left immediately, believing that the devil had made a fool of me. I returned to my shop, more determined to pray than ever before.

I arrived, and took my seat, and tried to get under that same weight, that I had felt pressing me down, but a short while before. But it seemed to me that I could not; and, instead of feeling sad, I felt joyful in my heart; and while trying to pray, I thought the Savior appeared to me. I thought I saw God smiling upon me, through Christ, His Son. My soul was filled with love to God and Jesus Christ. It appeared to me, I saw a fullness in Jesus Christ, to save every sinner who would come to Him. And I felt, that if I was only converted, I would tell all sinners how precious the Savior was. But I could not think myself converted yet, because I could not see what I had done, for God to pardon my sins. Still I felt a love to Him for what He had done for my soul.

Then I began to think upon my shopmates—and, O what pity ran through my soul for them. I wished to pray for them; but I felt so unworthy, that I could not do it. At last I promised the Lord that if He would convert my soul, I would talk to them.

It was several months after that, before I was made to realize this to be the work of God; and when it was made plain, O what joy it did bring to my poor soul!

I shortly became a member of the Baptist church, and was baptized, in company with some twenty others, by Rev. Geo. F. Adams, who was then pastor of the Baptist church in Fredericksburg—September 19,1831. This then contained about three hundred colored members.

Chapter 4
Marriage—License to Preach—Purchase of Freedom—A Call to Baltimore

I had not been a member of the church a great while, before I formed an attachment to a young woman, who ultimately became my wife. I have ever regarded her as the special gift of God to me. She embraced religion about the same time that I did. We had been acquainted with each other for several years previous, and although we associated frequently in the same social circle together; yet nothing of a special liking had manifested itself until the day she was baptized.

But we were both slaves, and of course had to get the consent of our owners, before we went further. My wife belonged to the late Carter L. Stephenson, Esq., who was a brother to Hon. Andrew Stephenson, of Va. My wife's master was quite indulgent to the servants about the house. He never restrained visitors from coming on his premises to visit his domestics. It was said he had the likeliest set of servant girls in the town; and though I cannot say I got the prettiest, yet I think I got the best one among them. We have lived happily together, as husband and wife, for the last twenty-eight years. We have had nine children—seven born in slavery, and two since my wife's freedom. Five out of the seven in slavery I have bought—two are still in bondage.

Before long, the brethren chose me to fill the office of a deacon. But it never seemed to me to be the place that God designed for me; though I felt willing to do whatever lay in my power for God's glory and the good of His people. The impression made upon my at my conversion, to talk to sinners, increased on me, until I could wait no longer.

I related my convictions of duty to my brethren, and particularly to one who was always held in high esteem for his piety and excellent character—a colored brother, Armistead Walker. My case was first brought by him before the colored portion of the church; and after a full hearing of my statement, by the white brethren, with regard to my call to preach, &c., I was licensed to preach the gospel, and exhort sinners to repentance, opportunity might be afforded. I had ample opportunities at that time, for doing good, by preaching to my fellow men, both in town and country.

Several other colored brethren, about this time, gave evidence of having been called of God, to the work of preaching the gospel. Among these was a dear brother, named Alexander Daniel. He was a bright and shining light, among our people, and everything considered, I think he was the best preacher of color I ever heard. But alas, he is no more! He was esteemed as a Christian minister, and his friends, both white and colored, united in erecting a monument over his grave.

In my attempts to preach the gospel to my fellow sinners, I often felt embarrassed, not knowing how to read a chapter in the Bible correctly. My desires now increased for such a knowledge of the sacred Scriptures, as would enable me to read a chapter publicly to my hearers. I thought that if I had all my time at my own command, I would devote it all to divine things. This desire I think, led me more than anything else, to ask permission of my master, Dr. F. Patten, to purchase my freedom. I made this a subject of prayer, both night and day, that God would show me what he would have me do. I felt encouraged to hope that I should find favor with my owner, as he had always treated me kindly. But how shall I get the purchase money, provided he grants my request?—This appeared a difficult matter, but I thought if my master would give me a chance, that I should be able to raise the money.

I went to him and stated my wishes, informing him why I wanted to be free—that I had been led to believe the Lord had converted my soul, and had called me to talk to sinners. He granted my request, without a single objection, fixing my price at five hundred dollars.

But now I had to tell him that I had no Money, and that I desired him to grant me another request; which was, to let me travel and find friends, who would give me the money. After learning my wishes fully, he consented, and told me, when I got ready to start, he would give me a pass, to go where I pleased.

I thanked him sincerely for this privilege, and after making arrangements, in the way of obtaining suitable letters of recommendation, I left Fredericksburg, in June, 1845, for Philadelphia, New York, Boston, &c.

After spending nearly four months in visiting the northern cities, I returned home, with about one hundred and fifty dollars, greatly disheartened.

Previous to going north, I had raised about a hundred and fifty dollars, which I had already paid on my debt.

The cause of my failure to raise all the money, I believe, was that I was unaccustomed to addressing large congregations of strangers; and often, when I was favored with an opportunity of presenting my case to the people, I would feel such embarrassment that I could scarcely say anything. And I met another obstacle, which discouraged me very much; which was, that some persons would tell me they sympathized with me, in my efforts to get free; but they said it was against their principles to give money, to buy slaves. I confess, this was new to me, and would cut me down much in my spirits—still I found generous and noble-hearted friends, who treated me with every mark of kindness.

I began to wonder to myself, whether God was in this matter, or not; and if so, why I had not succeeded. However, having returned home, I went to work at my trade, for the purpose of earning the remainder of the money. Having paid what I was able, toward my debt, and reserving enough to open a shop, upon my own account, my old boss, Mr. Wright, my true and constant friend, became my protector, so that I might carry on my business lawfully. In this, however, I was not very successful; but I had not been long engaged at it, before I received a communication from my white Baptist friends in Baltimore, through my pastor, Rev. Sam'l Smith, informing me that if I would come to Baltimore, and accept an appointment as missionary to the colored people of that city, they would assist me in raising the balance of the money then due upon myself.

This was indeed an unexpected, and to me an undesired call. I began to think, how can I leave my wife and seven small children, to go to Baltimore to live, a distance of more than a hundred miles from them. This, I thought, could not be. I thought my children would need my watchful care, more now than at any other time. It is true, they were all slaves, belonging to a rich widow lady. But she had always given me the entire control of my family. Now, if I should leave them at their tender age, mischief might befall them. Still, as the letter from Baltimore was from gentlemen of the best standing, it became me to give them an answer. This I could not do, without first consulting my master. I did so, and after giving the matter a careful consideration, he thought I had better go and see those gentlemen—he was perfectly willing to leave the matter to me.

The result was, that I accepted the offer of the brethren in Baltimore; and by them I was enabled to pay the debt I owed; and I have never had cause to repent it—though I had misgivings sometimes, when I would get into trouble.

But I have found those who were my friends at first, are my friends still. In a few weeks after I had arrived in Baltimore, (1847,) the white Baptists who were favorable to the mission in behalf of the colored people, secured for me an appointment as missionary of the Domestic Board of the Southern Baptist Convention, in connection with the Maryland Baptist Union Association. I now felt a debt of gratitude to these dear friends, that I could not show more acceptably to them, than by engaging heartily in the work to which I had been thus called. I went to work, first, by hiring a room in a private house, where I would collect what few children I could get together, in a Sabbath school. I continued in this place for nearly a year, teaching the little children, and preaching to a few grown persons, who would come in at times to hear what this Baptist man had to say; and who, after satisfying their curiosity, would generally leave me. During my stay in this locality I could not find half a dozen colored Baptists, who would take hold with me in this missionary enterprise. There were some few attached to the white churches; but only two of those showed any disposition to help me in this great and good work. I found that everybody loved to go with the multitude, and it was truly up-hill work with me. I found some who are called Anti-Mission, or Old School Baptists, who, when I called upon them, would ask of what faith I was,—and when I would reply, that I belonged to what I understood to be the Regular Baptists, they would answer, "Then you are not of our faith," &c.

Now I felt lonely indeed, separated far from home, from family, from dear brethren and friends; thrown among strangers in a strange place. Those I came to benefit, stood aloof from me, and seemed to look upon all my movements with distrust and suspicion, and opposed to all I was trying to do for the moral and spiritual benefit of our degraded race. But, thanks be to God, all I found in Baltimore were not of this stamp. Those of the white Baptists who had been the means of calling me to this field, adhered to me like brethren, indeed. Could I feel at liberty to mention names, I would bring to notice some dear friends who have ever stood by me, in all my efforts to do good, and whose acts of disinterested benevolence have been rarely equaled. But their labors of love are recorded on high, and I must forbear.

Chapter 5

Experience in Baltimore—Education—Purchase of a Wife and Two Children—Great Distress of Mind—Generous Assistance—Church Matters

When I came among the colored people of Baltimore, I found, to my surprise, that they were advanced in education, quite beyond what I had conceived of. Of course, as I never had such advantages, I was far behind the people; and as this did not appear well in a preacher, I felt very small, when comparing my abilities with others of a superior stamp. I found that the great mass of colored professors of religion were Methodists, whose piety and zeal seemed to carry all before them. There were, at that time, some ten or eleven colored Methodist churches, one Episcopalian, one Presbyterian; and one little Baptist church, located upon the outskirts of the city. The most of the Methodist churches were large and influential; and the Presbyterian church had one of the best Sabbath schools for colored children in the city.

But the Baptist colored membership was looked upon as the smallest; and under these circumstances, I was surrounded with discouragements; although the ministers and brethren of other denominations have always treated me with marked Christian kindness.

I had never had a day's schooling; and coming to one of the first cities in the Union, where the colored people had the advantages of schools, and where their pulpits were occupied, Sabbath after Sabbath, by comparatively intelligent colored ministers—what could I expect, but that the people would turn away from one who was trying to preach in the room of a private house, some fifteen by twenty feet? Yet, there was no turning back: God had called me to the work, and it was His cause I was advocating.

I found, that to preach, like other preachers, I must improve my mind, by reading the Bible and other good books, and by studying my own language. I started afresh—I got a small stock of books, and the white brethren loaned and gave me other useful volumes, to which they added a word of instruction and encouragement, whenever an opportunity offered; and the ministers cordially invited me to attend their Monday ministerial conference meeting, which was very useful to me.

I had now been in Baltimore more than a year. My wife and seven children were still in Virginia. I went to see them as often as my circumstances permitted—three or four times a year. About this time, my wife's mistress agreed to sell to me my wife and our two youngest children. The price fixed, was eight hundred dollars cash, and she gave me twelve months to raise the money. The sun rose bright in my sky that day; but before the year was out, my prospects were again in darkness. Now I had two great burdens upon my mind: one to attend properly to my missionary duty, the other to raise eight hundred dollars. During this time we succeeded in getting a better place for the Sabbath school, and there was a larger attendance upon my preaching, which demanded reading and study, and also visiting, and increased my daily labors. On the other hand, the year was running away, in which I had to raise eight hundred dollars. So that I found myself at times in a great strait.

My plan to raise the money was, to secure the amount, first, by pledges, before I collected any. Finally, the year was more than passed away, and I had upon my subscription list about one half of the money needed. It was now considered that the children had increased in value one hundred dollars, and I was told that I could have them, by paying in cash six hundred dollars, and giving a bond, with good security, for three hundred more, payable in twelve months. I had six weeks, in which to consummate this matter. I felt deeply, that this was a time to pray the Lord to help me, and for this my wife's prayers were fervently offered with my own. I had left my wife in Virginia, and come to Baltimore, a distance of over a hundred miles; I had been separated thus for nearly three years; I had been trying to make arrangements to have her with me, for over twelve months, and as yet had failed. We were oppressed with the most gloomy forebodings, and could only kneel down together and pray for God's direction and help.

I was in Fredericksburg, and had but one day longer to stay, and spend with my wife. What could be done, must be done quickly. I went to my old friend, Mr. Wright, and stated my case to him. After hearing of all I had done, and the conditions I had to comply with, he told me that if I would raise the six hundred dollars cash, he would endorse my bond for the remaining three hundred.—This promise inspired me with new life. The next thing was, how could the six hundred dollars be obtained in six weeks. I had upon my subscription list and in pledges nearly four hundred dollars. But this had to be collected from friends living in Fredericksburg, Washington city, Baltimore, and Philadelphia.

I left Fredericksburg, and spent a few days in Washington, to collect what I could of the money promised to me there; and met much encouragement, several friends doubling their subscriptions. When I arrived in Baltimore, and made known the peculiar strait I was in, to my joyful surprise, some of the friends who had pledged five dollars, gave me ten; and one dear friend who had promised me ten dollars, for this object, and who had previously contributed largely in the purchase of myself, now gave me fifty. I began to count up, and in two weeks from the time I commenced collecting, I had in hand four hundred dollars. Presently, another very dear friend enquired of me how I was getting along; and when I told him, he said, "Bring your money to me." I did so. It lacked two hundred dollars to make the purchase. This, the best friend I ever had in the world, made up the six hundred dollars, and said, "Go, get your wife; and you can keep on collecting, and repay the two hundred dollars when you get able."

I was now overcome with, gratitude and joy, and knew not what to say; and when I began to speak, he would not have any of my thanks. I went to my boarding house, and shut myself up in my room, where I might give vent to the gratitude of my heart: and, O, what a melting time I had! It was to me a day of thanksgiving.

Having now in band the six hundred dollars, and the promise of Mr. Wright's security for three hundred more, I was, by twelve o'clock, next day in Fredericksburg.

At first sight, my wife was surprised that I had come back so soon; for it was only two weeks since I had left her; and when I informed her that I had come after her and the children, she could hardly believe me. In a few days, having duly arranged all things relative to the purchase and removal, we left for Baltimore, with feelings commingled with joy and sorrow—sorrow at parting with five of our older children, and our many friends; and rejoicing in the prospect of remaining together permanently in the missionary field, where God had called me to labor. I arrived in Baltimore, with my wife and two little ones, November 5th, 1851, and stopped with sister Hester Ann Hughes, a worthy member of the M. E. Church, with whom I had been boarding for four years. ...

This year was a joyful one to me—my little church increasing, and the Sabbath school flourishing, under the superintendence of the late truly excellent brother James C. Crane, though he was with us but for a short season. My wife and little ones were also with me, both in the church and Sabbath school. I was a happy man, and felt more than ever inclined to give thanks to God, and serve Him to the best of my ability.

My salary was only three hundred dollars a year; but with hard exertion and close economy, together with my wife's taking in washing and going out at day's work, we were enabled by the first of the year, to pay the two hundred dollars our dear friend had loaned us, in raising, the six hundred dollars before spoken of. But the bond for three hundred dollars was now due, and how must this be met? I studied out a plan; which was to get some gentleman who might want a little servant girl, to take my child, and advance me three hundred dollars for the purpose of paying my note, which was now due in Virginia. In this plan I succeeded; and had my own life insured for seven years for five hundred dollars, and made it over to this gentleman, as security; until I ultimately paid him the whole amount; though I was several years in paying it.

Among the number that joined our little church, was a young brother, Jos. M. Harden, who was baptized by Dr. Fuller, but soon became a valuable member with us, both in the church and Sunday school. He was born in Baltimore, and had been early taught to read, and though he had been at ten years old bound out, till he was twenty-one, his love of books had made him far superior to colored people generally, and he was very valuable to me. Things had gone on hopefully with me, and my little church, though our progress was very slow. But we had to suffer a loss in brother Harden's leaving us for the great missionary field in Africa, where I trust the Lord has sent him for a great and happy work. But God has blessed us in the person of brother Samuel W. Madden, whose labors as a licensed preacher for several years have been invaluable to us. ...

Chapter 7
Conclusion—Object of this Book

I now left the north, for home, and arrived there safely. My friends greeted me cordially on my success in collecting money.

I still lacked, however, one hundred and forty-two dollars of the needed eleven hundred. I had used every effort in my power to prevent the necessity of having to call on my generous friend in Providence. But in spite of all my endeavors, I had to make known to him this deficiency, which he immediately and generously supplied, by remitting me a check for the full amount.

I was now prepared to go after my daughter, which I did, December 1st, 1858; thus releasing her within one year from the time she was sold. She is now with me, and doing well.

I received a promise from the young master of my two sons, at the time he purchased them, that if I should succeed in paying for my daughter during that year, he would let me know what I might have my two boys for. At the time, my boys were about returning to Richmond, where they had been hired out for several years. I charged them to let me hear a good report of their conduct; and if I could do anything for them, after I had got through with the purchase of their sister, I would do it. This. pledge I made to the boys, in the presence of their master's agent.

Having, through the aid of a kind Providence, been enabled to pay for my daughter, I have felt it my duty to turn my attention toward redeeming my word to my last children now in bondage.

But this, of course, has called up anxious thought and prayerful meditation. I have also considered the peculiar condition of my church—the large outlay of money in the erection of the building, and the heavy debt hanging upon it, which is increased every year by the interest. I have also considered how long I have been supported in this field of labor by the Missionary Board of the Southern Baptist Convention and the Maryland Baptist Union Association.

The question then occurred to me, Could I not, by making a book, do something to relieve myself and my children, and ultimately, by the same means, help my church, under its heavy debt, and also relieve the Missionary Board from helping me. This idea struck me with so, much force, that I have yielded to it—that is, to write a short Narrative of my own life, setting forth the trials and difficulties the Lord has brought me through to this day, and offer it for sale to my friends generally, as well as to the public at large; and, I hope it may not only aid me, but may serve to encourage others, who meet with similar difficulties, to put their trust in God.

Noah Davis

Sermon on 1 Timothy 5:8
"But if any provide not for his own, and especially for those of his own house, he hath denied the faith, and is worse than an infidel."—1 Tim. 5: 8.

In this chapter, we have several Christian duties set forth by the apostle Paul, to Timothy, a young preacher of the gospel, who was to teach other Christians to observe them, as evidences of the genuineness of their faith in Christ.

That faith which does not produce obedience to the commands of Jesus must be regarded as defective. Religion requires us to love God, and all men, and we must show our faith, by a life consistent with our profession.

If human nature, fallen as it is, prompts men of the world to labor zealously to supply their own temporal necessities and the wants of those whom Providence has made to depend upon them, how much more will it be expected of those who profess to have drank of that pure Fountain of love, the Spirit of our blessed Lord and Savior, Jesus Christ. God has indeed doomed man to eat his bread in the sweat of his face; but as if to reward him, he has connected with it a pleasure in the labor, and especially, in our efforts to do good to others.

In speaking from these words, let us first consider what is here meant by "providing" for "his own;" secondly, "and especially for those of his own house;" thirdly, what it is to "deny the faith;" and lastly, draw a comparison between the one who "hath denied the faith" and the "infidel."

1. In the first place, we are to consider the duty enjoined in the text, to provide for our own.

This we understand to mean our own temporal wants, such as food and raiment and every temporal benefit. Every man is bound by the laws of nature to provide for himself the necessaries of life, honestly in the sight of God and men, as far as in him lieth. This both reason and common sense dictate. This religion inspires. "He that will not work, shall not eat," is the teaching of the Word of God. "Provide things honest in the sight of all men," is the instruction of the great apostle to the Gentiles; at the same time giving them an example, by working with his own hands, to supply his necessities, and the wants of those who were with him. I have heard it said that a lazy person cannot be a Christian, and the same idea seems to be supported in my text.

"But if any provide not for his own." Religion benefits those who possess it, by regulating their appetite for temporal things, as well as giving them a relish for spiritual ones. While we are in love with sin, we labor hard to enjoy its pleasures. How industriously do wicked men labor for what they can eat, drink and wear. And shall a Christian be less active to secure for himself the necessaries of life?—he would prove himself indeed to be worse than the infidel. But we have other wants to be supplied, beside those of the body. God has given to all men an intellectual nature—a mind, which distinguishes them from the brutes. These minds are capable of improvement; and every man is under obligation to make use of the means and opportunities which God has given him for cultivating his mind, by educating himself, that he may be useful to himself and those around him. But man is a social being as well as an intellectual one. "God hath made of one blood, all nations of men, for to dwell on all the face of the earth.—(Acts 17: 26.) Much of our happiness, and usefulness in this world arises from this quality which man possesses over the animal creation. And just in proportion, as we shall cultivate, and refine our social and intellectual natures, just in that proportion, shall we rise above the level of the savage and the heathen.

But man has a soul, which must be fitted for the enjoyment of God, here and hereafter. Now to provide for the wants of the soul, is our highest duty on earth.—Sin has unclothed us of that innocence in which our Creator first made us, and the responsibility now rests upon every soul, to provide a clothing which will stand the inspection of God himself. This clothing, Christ has prepared through His sufferings, and death, and it is given to all them that believe in Him. And surely, if it be our duty to provide temporal things for ourselves, and for those of our own house, how much more are we bound to seek and secure the one thing needful.

2. But we will consider in the second place, what is meant by providing for our own house?—"and especially for those of his own house?"

House here means family. First, we will consider the duty devolving upon a Christian parent, in making suitable provision for his own house, or family. This embraces all we have urged as his duty to himself. It is the duty of all parents, to provide for their families every temporal good which adds to their own comfort or usefulness in life. And it is no less the duty of parents to provide for the spiritual necessities of their own families. And first—we shall consider the duty of parents, to provide suitable training for their children. This is a duty which God has enjoined and approves. He said of Abraham, "For I know him, that he will command his children and his household after him, and they shall keep the way of the Lord, to do justice and judgment, that the Lord may bring upon Abraham, that which He hath spoken of him." The duty of parents to train their children religiously, is clearly taught under the gospel dispensation.

"And ye fathers, provoke not your children to wrath, but bring them up in the nurture and admonition of the Lord." Here, we have divine authority, for teaching our children, the things, which make for their good, both in this life and that which is to come. But it may be asked, to what extent are parents bound to comply with these high and solemn obligations? We answer, to the utmost of their ability. To whom much is given, of him much is required, and to whom little is given, of him little is required.—But all are bound to train up their children "in the way they should go, that when they are old, they may not depart from it." This duty is seen in the judgments which God has visited upon those parents and children who have neglected to obey the Lord in this particular.—(1 Samuel 2: 34.)

3. We are, in the third place, to enquire what it is to "deny the faith." Much is said in the Scriptures about faith.

Much depends upon it. We are said to be "justified by faith," and "saved by faith;" we "live by faith." And inasmuch, as such as are spoken of in the text are said to be worse than an infidel, because they provide not for themselves and families, thereby showing that they have denied the faith, therefore let us try to consider what genuine faith is, and what it is to deny it. This is the most important point in the subject now before us. "Without faith it is impossible to please God."

We will consider some of the effects of this distinguishing grace. There are several kinds of faith spoken of in the Bible. In one case, men are said to "believe for a while." This faith is shown us in the parable taught by our blessed Savior, in the characters represented by the seed sown upon the rock, "which for a while believe, and in time of temptation fall away."—(Luke 8: 33.)

There is a faith which is called dead.—"Even so faith, if it hath not works, is dead, being alone."—(James 2: 17.) But the faith which enables the Christian to obey the Savior in all things, is said to "work by love."—(Gal. 5: 6.) Now we say that those who have this faith, will never deny it. The counterfeit may deceive, but the genuine cannot. We say this faith cannot deny itself. All who are spoken of in the Old Testament as having this faith never denied it. By it Abel made a more excellent sacrifice to God than Cain. By it, Enoch walked with God, when the other portion of mankind walked in the vain wicked imaginations of their own hearts. "By faith Noah, being warned of God of things not seen as yet, moved with fear, prepared an ark for the saving of his house." "Abraham believed God, and it was counted unto him for righteousness."

This is the grace which enables believers to renounce the pleasures of sin, which are but for a season. It gives them a complete victory over the world. It abideth with hope and charity. Now, whosoever professes this faith, and then by his unholy life denies it, by neglecting to provide for his own, and especially for those of his own house, makes it manifest that he never had it. It is as unchangeable as its Author, for it is the gift of God. It prompted Noah to labor over a hundred years, to build an ark, to save his house. And what it has done, it will continue to do, for those who have it. This is the principle in religion which purifies the heart, overcomes the world, and causes Christians to love one another, whatever may be their circumstances, or color or rank in life.

4. We are now in the fourth and last place to draw a comparison between those who deny the faith, and an infidel.

Now an infidel, is an unbeliever in the religion of Christ.—Yet he provides for his own, and especially for those of his own house. In this he is consistent with himself. Here he acts from reason, and principles of nature. But the individual who denies the faith, is one, who has taken upon himself the solemn vow before God and men, that he will act out what his profession supposes him to be in possession of, which is superior in its influence, to the infidel's principles, yet he fails to do as much.

But again, an infidel is a bad man, and makes no pretensions to hide it. But he who contradicts his profession, by denying it in the manner here set forth, is worse for attempting to cover up a character, which in itself is no better. But consider the effect produced by a false faith, (and we have shown, that such a faith, as does not come up with the infidel's, is false,) it does the greatest harm. Many persons, when they make a profession of faith, suppose it is the true faith, but after a while, they find that their faith does not work by love, it does not purify their hearts. They love sin secretly, as much as before. They love worldly company as well as ever. And they find the employments, which their profession enjoins upon them, irksome and dry. Such persons are greatly deceived, yet they are ashamed to confess it, and throw off the mask of profession. And such persons are often the greatest fault-finders with those, whose true faith inspires them to endure hardness, afflictions and deny themselves and take up their cross, so that they may glorify their Savior in their bodies and spirits which are the Lord's.

In conclusion, dear brethren, let us, who have made a profession of faith, examine ourselves, whether we be in the faith of the gospel, or not. "Know ye not your own selves how that Jesus Christ is in you, except ye be reprobates." AMEN.

Noah Davis

MARIA W. STEWART (1803-1879)

Introduction

Maria W. Stewart was one of the first American women to leave copies of her speeches. The address below is her second public lecture. It was given on September 21, 1832 in Franklin Hall in Boston, the meeting site of the new England Anti-Slavery Society. Although as an abolitionist, she usually attacked slavery, in this address she condemns the attitude that denied black women education and prohibited their occupational advancement. She argues that Northern African American women, in terms of treatment, were only slightly better off than slaves.

"Why Sit Ye Here and Die?"

Why sit ye here and die? If we say we will go to a foreign land, the famine and the pestilence are there, and there we shall die. If we sit here, we shall die. Come let us plead our cause before the whites: if they save us alive, we shall live—and if they kill us, we shall but die.

Methinks I heard a spiritual interrogation—'Who shall go forward, and take off the reproach that is cast upon the people of color? Shall it be a woman? And my heart made this reply —'If it is thy will, be it even so, Lord Jesus!'

I have heard much respecting the horrors of slavery; but may Heaven forbid that the generality of my color throughout these United States should experience any more of its horrors than to be a servant of servants, or hewers of wood and drawers of water! Tell us no more of southern slavery; for with few exceptions, although I may be very erroneous in my opinion, yet I consider our condition but little better than that. Yet, after all, methinks there are no chains so galling as the chains of ignorance—no fetters so binding as those that bind the soul, and exclude it from the vast field of useful and scientific knowledge. O, had I received the advantages of early education, my ideas would, ere now, have expanded far and wide; but, alas! I possess nothing but moral capability—no teachings but the teachings of the Holy spirit.

I have asked several individuals of my sex, who transact business for themselves, if providing our girls were to give them the most satisfactory references, they would not be willing to grant them an equal opportunity with others? Their reply has been—for their own part, they had no objection; but as it was not the custom, were they to take them into their employ, they would be in danger of losing the public patronage.

And such is the powerful force of prejudice. Let our girls possess what amiable qualities of soul they may; let their characters be fair and spotless as innocence itself; let their natural taste and ingenuity be what they may; it is impossible for scarce an individual of them to rise above the condition of servants. Ah! why is this cruel and unfeeling distinction? Is it merely because God has made our complexion to vary? If it be, O shame to soft, relenting humanity! "Tell it not in Gath! publish it not in the streets of Askelon!" Yet, after all, methinks were the American free people of color to turn their attention more assiduously to moral worth and intellectual improvement, this would be the result:

prejudice would gradually diminish, and the whites would be compelled to say, unloose those fetters!

> Though black their skins as shades of night,
> Their hearts are pure, their souls are white.

Few white persons of either sex, who are calculated for any thing else, are willing to spend their lives and bury their talents in performing mean, servile labor. And such is the horrible idea that I entertain respecting a life of servitude, that if I conceived of there being no possibility of my rising above the condition of a servant, I would gladly hail death as a welcome messenger. O, horrible idea, indeed! to possess noble souls aspiring after high and honorable acquirements, yet confined by the chains of ignorance and poverty to lives of continual drudgery and toil. Neither do I know of any who have enriched themselves by spending their lives as house-domestics, washing windows, shaking carpets, brushing boots, or tending upon gentlemen's tables. I can but die for expressing my sentiments; and I am as willing to die by the sword as the pestilence; for I and a true born American; your blood flows in my veins, and your spirit fires my breast.

I observed a piece in the Liberator a few months since, stating that the colonizationists had published a work respecting us, asserting that we were lazy and idle. I confute them on that point. Take us generally as a people, we are neither lazy nor idle; and considering how little we have to excite or stimulate us, I am almost astonished that there are so many industrious and ambitious ones to be found; although I acknowledge, with extreme sorrow, that there are some who never were and never will be serviceable to society. And have you not a similar class among yourselves?

Again. It was asserted that we were "a ragged set, crying for liberty." I reply to it, the whites have so long and so loudly proclaimed the theme of equal rights and privileges, that our souls have caught the flame also, ragged as we are. As far as our merit deserves, we feel a common desire to rise above the condition of servants and drudges. I have learnt, by bitter experience, that continual hard labor deadens the energies of the soul, and benumbs the faculties of the mind; the ideas become confined, the mind barren, and, like the scorching sands of Arabia, produces nothing; or, like the uncultivated soil, brings forth thorns and thistles.

Again, continual hard labor irritates our tempers and sours our dispositions; the whole system becomes worn out with toil and failure; nature herself becomes almost exhausted, and we care but little whether we live or die. It is true, that the free people of color throughout these United States are neither bought nor sold, nor under the lash of the cruel driver; many obtain a comfortable support; but few, if any, have an opportunity of becoming rich and independent; and the employments we most pursue are as unprofitable to us as the spider's web or the floating bubbles that vanish into air. As servants, we are respected; but let us presume to aspire any higher, our employer regards us no longer. And where it not that the King eternal has declared that Ethiopia shall stretch forth her hands unto God, I should indeed despair.

I do not consider it derogatory, my friends, for persons to live out to service. There are many whose inclination leads them to aspire no higher; and I would highly commend the performance of almost any thing for an honest livelihood; but where constitutional strength is wanting, labor of this kind, in its mildest form, is painful. And doubtless many are the prayers that have ascended to Heaven from Africa's daughters for strength to perform their work. Oh, many are the tears that have been shed for the want of that strength! Most of our color have dragged out a miserable existence of servitude from the cradle to the grave. And what literary acquirements can be made, or useful knowledge derived, from either maps, books or charm, by those who continually drudge from Monday morning until Sunday noon? O, ye fairer sisters, whose hands are never soiled, whose nerves and muscles are never strained, go learn by experience! Had we had the opportunity that you have had, to improve our moral and mental faculties, what would have hindered our intellects from being as bright, and our manners from being as dignified as yours? Had it been our lot to have been nursed in the lap of affluence and ease, and to have basked beneath the smiles and sunshine of fortune, should we not have naturally supposed that we were never made to toil? And why are not our forms as delicate, and our constitutions as slender, as yours? Is not the workmanship as curious and complete? Have pity upon us, have pity upon us, O ye who have hearts to feel for other's woes; for the hand of God has touched us. Owing to the disadvantages under which we labor, there are many flowers among us that are

...born to bloom unseen,

And waste their fragrance on the desert air.

My beloved brethren, as Christ has died in vain for those who will not accept of offered mercy, so will it be vain for the advocates of freedom to spend their breath in our behalf, unless with united hearts and souls you make some mighty efforts to raise your sons, and daughters from the horrible state of servitude and degradation in which they are placed. It is upon you that woman depends; she can do but little besides using her influence; and it is for her sake and yours that I have come forward and made myself a hissing and a reproach among the people; for I am also one of the wretched and miserable daughters of the descendants of fallen Africa. Do you ask, why are you wretched and miserable? I reply, look at many of the most worthy and interesting of us doomed to spend our lives in gentlemen's kitchens. Look at our young men, smart, active and energetic, with souls filled with ambitious fire; if they look forward, alas! what are their prospects? They can be nothing but the humblest laborers, on account of their dark complexions; hence many of them lose their ambition, and become worthless. Look at our middle-aged men, clad in their rusty plaids and coats; in winter, every cent they earn goes to buy their wood and pay their rents; their poor wives also toil beyond their strength, to help support their families. Look at our aged sires, whose heads are whitened with the front of seventy winters, with their old wood-saws on their backs. Alas, what keeps us so? Prejudice, ignorance and poverty. But ah! methinks our oppression is soon to come to an end; yes, before the Majesty of heaven, our groans and cries have reached the ears of the Lord of Sabaoth [James 5:4]. As the prayers and tears of Christians will avail the finally impenitent nothing; neither will the prayers and tears of the friends of humanity avail us any thing, unless we possess a spirit of virtuous emulation within our breasts. Did the pilgrims, when they first landed on these shores, quietly compose themselves, and say, "the Britons have all the money and all the power, and we must continue their servants forever?" Did they sluggishly sigh and say, "our lot is hard, the Indians own the soil, and we cannot cultivate it?" No; they first made powerful efforts to raise themselves and then God raised up those illustrious patriots Washington and Lafayette, to assist and defend them. And, my brethren, have you made a powerful effort? Have you prayed the Legislature for mercy's sake to grant you all the rights and privileges of free citizens, that your daughters may raise to that degree of respectability which true merit deserves, and your sons above the servile situations which most of them fill?

Maria W. Stewart, speech delivered at Franklin Hall,
Boston, September 21, 1832.

WILLIAM WHIPPER (1804–1876)

Introduction

William Whipper was an African American abolitionist and businessman. He advocated nonviolence and co-founded the American Moral Reform Society, an early African American abolitionist organization.

Peace activism in the African American community have very deep roots. Benjamin Banneker, the 18th Century mathematician and astronomer, recommended that a "Secretary of Peace" should be added to the President's cabinet. His chief function would be to craft measures to prevent international conflict. Other leaders such as William Whipper called on abolitionists and other reformers to seek change through model behavior and by appealing to humanity's rationality rather than by force. Whipper argues in his speech that non-violence and non-resistance could effect change.

Non-Resistance to Offensive Aggression, 1837

Mr. President

The above resolution presupposes, that if there were no God, to guide, and govern, the destinies of man on this planet, no Bible to light his path through the wilds of sin, darkness and error, and no religion to give him a glorious, and lasting consolation, while traversing the gloomy vale of despondency, and to light up his soul anew, with fresh influence, from the fountain of Divine grace,—that mankind might enjoy an exalted state of civilization, peace, and quietude, in their social, civil, and international relations, far beyond that which Christians now enjoy, who profess to be guided, guarded and protected by the great Author of all good, and the doctrines of the Prince of Peace.

But, sir, while I am assuming the position, that the cause of peace amongst mankind, may be promoted without the scriptures, I would not, for a single moment, sanction the often made assertion, that the doctrines of the holy scriptures justify war—for they are in my humble opinion its greatest enemy. And I further believe, that as soon as they become fully understood, and practically adopted, wars, and strife will cease. I believe that every argument urged in favor of what is termed a "just and necessary war," or physical self-defense, is at enmity with the letter, and spirit of the scriptures, and when they emanate from its professed advocates should be repudiated, as inimical to the principles they profess, and a reproach to Christianity itself.

I have said this much in favor of the influence of the scriptures, on the subject of peace. It is neither my intention, nor my province, under the present resolution, to give proofs for my belief by quotations from holy writ. That portion of the discussion, I shall leave to the minister to the altar, and the learned and biblical theologian. Though I may make a few incidental quotations hereafter, I shall now pass on for a few brief moments to the resolution under consideration, viz.:

The resolution asserts that the practice of non-resistance to physical aggression is consistent with reason.

Non-resistance

A very distinguished man asserts, "that reason is that distinguishing characteristic that separates man from the brute creation," and that this power was bestowed upon him by his Maker, that he might be capable of subduing all subordinate intelligences to his will." It is this power when exerted in its full force, that enables him to conquer the animals of the forest, and which makes him lord of creation. There is a right, and a wrong method of reasoning. The latter is governed by our animal impulses, and wicked desires, without regard to the end to be attained. The former fixes its premises, in great fundamental, and unalterable truths—surveys the magnitude of the objects, and the difficulties to be surmounted, and calls to its aid the resources of enlightened wisdom, as a landmark by which to conduct its operations.

It is self-evident, that when the greatest difficulties surround us, we should summon our noblest powers. "Man is a being formed for action as well as contemplation"; for this purpose there are interwoven in his constitution, powers, instincts, feelings and affections, which have a reference to his improvement in virtue, and which excite him to promote the happiness of others. When we behold them by their noble sentiments, exhibiting sublime virtues and performing illustrious actions, we ascribe the same to the goodness of their hearts, their great reasoning powers and intellectual abilities. For were it not for these high human endowments we should never behold men in seasons of calamity, displaying tranquility and fortitude in the midst of difficulties and dangers, enduring poverty and distress with a noble heroism, suffering injuries and affronts with patience and serenity—stifling resentment when they have it in their power to inflict vengeance—displaying kindness and generosity towards enemies and slanderers—submitting to pain and disgrace in order to promote the prosperity of their friends and relatives, or the great interests of the human race.

Such acts may be considered by persons of influence and rank as the offspring of pusillanimity, because they themselves are either incapable of conceiving the purity of the motives from which they emanate, or are too deeply engulfed in the ruder passions of our nature, to allow them to bestow a just tribute to the efforts of enlightened reason.

It is happy for us to contemplate, that every age, both of the pagan and the Christian world, has been blessed, that they always have fastened their attention on the noblest gifts of our nature, and that they now still shine as ornaments to the human race, connecting the interests of one generation with that of another. Rollin, in speaking of Aristides and Just, says "that an extraordinary greatness of souls made him superior to every passion. Interest, pleasure, ambition, resentment and judgment, were extinguished in him by the love of virtue and his country," and just in proportion as we cultivate our intellectual faculties, we shall strengthen our reasoning powers, and be prepared to become his imitators.

The savage custom of war

Our country and the world have become the munificent patron of many powerful, existing evils, that have spread their devastating influence over the best interests of the human race. One of which is the adopting of the savage custom of wars, and fighting as a redress of grievances, instead of some means more consistent with reason and civilization.

The great law of love forbids our doing aught against the interests of our fellow men. It is altogether inconsistent with reason and common sense, for persons when they deem themselves insulted, by the vulgar aspersions of others, to maltreat their bodies for the acts of their minds. Yet how frequently do we observe those that are blest by nature and education, (and if they would but aspire to acts that bear a parallel to their dignified minds, they would shine as illustrious stars, in the created throngs,) that degrade themselves by practicing this barbarous custom, suited only to tyrants—because in this they may be justly ranked with the untutored savages of the animals of the forest, that are impelled only by instinct.

Another fatal error arises from the belief that the only method of maintaining peace, is always to be ready for war. The spirit of war can never be destroyed by all the butcheries and persecutions the human mind can invent. The history of all the "bloody tragedies," by which the earth has been drenched by human blood, cannot be justified in the conclusion, for it is the spirit of conquest that feeds it—Thomas Dick, after collecting the general statistics of those that have perished by the all desolating pestilence of war, says "it will not be overrating the destruction of human life, if we affirm, that one tenth of the human race has been destroyed by the ravages of war,"—and if this estimate be admitted, it will follow that more than fourteen thousand millions of beings have been slaughtered in war since the beginning of the world, which is about eighteen times the number of its present inhabitants. This calculation proceeds from a geographical estimate, "that since the Mosaic creation one hundred and forty-five thousand millions of being have existed."

But, sir, it is not my intention to give a dissertation, on the subject of national wars, although it appropriately belongs to my subject. I decline it only for the simple reason, that it would be inapplicable to us as a people, while we may be more profitably employed in inveighing against the same evil as practiced by ourselves, although it exists under another form, but equally obnoxious to the principles of reason and Christianity. My reason for referring to national wars was to exhibit by plain demonstration that the war principle, which is the production of human passions, has never been, nor can ever be, conquered by its own elements. Hence, if we ever expect the word of prophecy to be fulfilled— "when the swords shall be turned into plough-shares, and the spears into pruning-hooks, and that the nations of the earth shall learn war no more," we must seek the destruction of the principle that animates, quickens, and feeds it, by the elevation of another more powerful, and omnipotent, and preservative; or mankind will continue, age after age, to march on in their made career, until the mighty current of time will doubtless sweep thousands of millions more into endless perdition, beyond the reach of mercy, and the hope of future bliss. Thus the very bones, sinews, muscles, and immortal mind, that God, in his infinite mercy has bestowed on man, that he might work out his own glory, and extend the principles of "Righteousness, justice, peace on earth, and good-will to their fellow men," are constantly employed in protracting the period when the glorious millennium shall illumine our world, "and righteousness cover the earth as the water of the great deep."

Now let us solemnly ask ourselves is it reasonable, that for the real or supposed injuries that have been inflicted on mankind from the beginning to the present day, that the attempted redress of the same should have cost so much misery, pain, sweat, blood, and tears, and treasure? Most certainly not; since the very means used has measurably entailed the evil a thousand fold, on coming generations. If man's superiority over the brute creation consists only in his reasoning powers and rationality of mind; his various methods of practicing violence towards his fellow creatures, has in many cases placed him on a level with, and sometimes below many species of the quadruped race. We search in vain amongst the animal race to find a parallel, for their cruelties to each other on their own species, that is faithfully recorded in history of wars and bloodshed, that have devoured empires, desolated kingdoms, overthrown government, and well nigh aimed at the total annihilation of the human race. There are many species of animals that are so amiable in their disposition to each other, that they might well be considered an eminent pattern for mankind in their present rude condition. The sheep, the ox, the horse, and many other animals exist in a state of comparative quietude, both among themselves, and the other races of animals when compared with man. And if it were possible for them to know the will of their Author, and enjoy that communion all with the Creator of all worlds, all men and all animals, they might justly be entitled to a distinction above all other species of creation, that had made greater departures from the will of the divine government.

It is evidently necessary that man should at all times bear in mind his origin and his end. That it is not because he was born a ruler, and superior to all other orders of creation, that he continually reigns above them—it is because he has made a right use of the powers that God has given him or rising in the scale of existence. The rich bequest of Heaven to man, was a natural body, a reasonable soul, and an immortal mind. With these he is rendered capable through wisdom of Providence, or ascending to the throne of angels, or descending to the abyss of devils. Hence there seems to be a relation between man and the animal creation, that subsists, neither in their origin nor their end, but satisfactorily exhibits that man may exist in a state of purity, as far superior to their, as future happiness is to this world, and as far inferior, as we are distant from future misery.

This history of wars
There is scarcely a single fact more worthy of indelible record, that the utter inefficiency of human punishments, to cure human evils. The history of wars, exhibits a hopeless, as well as a fatal lesson, to all such enterprises. All the associated powers of human governments have been placed in requisition to quell and subdue the spirit of passion; without improving the condition of the human family. Human bodies have been lacerated with whips and scourges—prisons and penitentiaries have been erected for the immolation of human victims—the gibbet and halter have performed their office—while the increase of crime has kept pace with the genius of punishment, and the whole march of mind seems to have been employed in evading penal enactments, and inventing new methods of destroying the blessings of the social state, not recognized by human codes.

If mankind ever expects to enjoy a state of peace and quietude, they must at all times be ready to sacrifice on the altar of principle, the rude passions that animate them. This they can only perform by exerting their reasoning powers. If there be those that desire to overlook the offences of others, and rise above those inflictions that are the offspring of passion, they must seek for protection in something higher than human power. They must place their faith in Him who is able to protect them from danger, or they will soon fall prey to the wicked artifices of their wicked enemies.

Human passion is the hallucination of a distempered mind. It renders the subject of it like a ship upon the ocean, without ballast, or cargo, always in danger of being wrecked by every breeze. Phrenologically speaking, a mind that is subject to he fluctuating whims of passion, is without the organ of order, "which is nature's first law." Our reasoning powers ought to be the helm that should guide us through the shoals and quicksands of life.

Wholly impracticable?

I am aware that there are those who consider the non-resistance wholly impracticable. But I trust that but few such can be found, that have adopted the injunction of the Messiah for their guide and future hope, for he commands us to "love our enemies, bless them that curse you, pray for them that despitefully use you, and persecute you." These words were peculiarly applicable at the period they were uttered, and had a direct reference to the wars and strifes that then convulsed the world, and they are equally applicable at this moment. If the Christian church had at her beginning made herself the enemy of war, the evil would doubtless have been abolished throughout Christendom. The Christians of the present day do not seem to regard the principles of peace as binding, or they are unwilling to become subject to the Divine government. Human governments then, as well as now, were too feeble to stay the ravages of passion and crime, and hence there was an evident necessity for the imperious command, "Whomsoever shall smite thee on thy right cheek, turn unto him the other also."

Scripture is reasonable

And now, Mr. President, I rest my argument on the ground, that whatever is Scriptural is right, and that whatever is right, is reasonable, and from this invulnerable position I mean not to stray, for the sake of any expediency whatever. The doctrine evidently taught by the scriptural quotation, evidently instructs us that resistance to physical aggression is wholly unnecessary as well as unrighteous, and subjects the transgressor to the penalty due from a willful departure from the moral and Divine law. Therefore every act of disobedience to the commands of Christian duty, in relation to our fellow men, may fairly be deemed unreasonable, as it is at enmity with our true interests and the welfare of human society. We are further instructed to turn away from the evil one, rather than waste our strength, influence and passions, in a conflict that must in the end prove very injurious to both.

But some one perhaps is ready to raise an objection against this method of brooking the insults of others; and believes it right to refer to the maxim "that self- defense is the first law of nature." I will readily agree that it is the unbounded duty of every individual to defend himself against both the vulgar and false aspersions of a wicked world. But then I contend that his weapons should be his reasoning powers. That since a kind Providence has bestowed on him the power of speech, and the ability to reason, he degrades his Creator by engulfing himself in the turmoils of passion, and physical conflict. A mode of warfare practiced by barbarous tribes in their native forests, and suited only to those animals that are alone endowed with the powers of instinct. Nor is it possible to suppose that men can pursue such a course, without first parting with their reason. We often see men, while under the reigning influence of passion, as fit subjects for the lunatic asylum, as any that are confined in the lunatic asylum on account of insanity.

The weakness of physical conflict
In every possible and impartial view we take of the subject, we find that physical conflict militates against the interest of the parties in collision. If I, in conflict with mine enemy, overcome him by my superior physical powers, or my skill in battle, I neither wholly subdue him, nor convince him or the justice of my cause. His spirit becomes still more enraged, and he will seek retaliation and conquest on some future occasion, that may seem to him more propitious. If I intimidate him I have made him a slave, while I reign a despot; and our relation will continue unnatural, as well as dangerous to each other, until our friendship has become fully restored. And what has been gained by this barbarous method of warfare, when both parties become losers thereby? Yet this single case illustrates the value of all personal conflicts.

But let us pursue this subject in a more dignified view, I mean as it respects the moral and Divine government. Is it possible that any Christian man or woman, that will flog and maltreat their fellow beings, can be in earnest, when they with apparent devotion; ask their heavenly Father to "forgive their trespass as they forgive others?" Surely they must be asking God to punish them—or when they say "lead us not into temptation, but deliver us from evil," do they mean that they should run headlong into both, with all their infuriated madness? Certainly not. Who would not be more willing to apply to them insincerity of motive, and that they knew not what they were doing, rather than suppose that intelligent minds would be capable of such gross inconsistency. Would it not prove infinitely better in times of trials and difficulties, to leave the temper, and temptation behind, and pursue our course onward? But says the objector, there will be no safety nor security in this method from the insults of the vulgar and the brutal attacks of the assassin. I am inclined to believe to the contrary, and will be borne out in that belief by the evidence, of those that have pursued this Christian course of conduct.

A writer under the signature of Philopacificus, while "taking a solemn view of the custom of war," says, "There are two sets of professed Christians in this country, which, as sects, are peculiar in their opinions respecting the lawfulness of war, and the right of repelling injury by violence." These are the Quakers and Shakers. They are remarkably pacific. Now we ask, does it appear from experience, that their forbearing spirit brings on them a greater portion of injury and insults, than what is experienced by people of other sects? Is not the reverse of this true in fact? There may indeed be some such instances of gross depravity as a person taking advantage of their pacific character, to do them an injury with the hope of impunity. But in general it is believed their pacific principles and spirit command the esteem, even of the vicious, and operate as a shield from insult and abuse.

The question may be brought home to every society. How seldom do children of a mild and forbearing temper experience insults or injury, compared with the waspish, who will sting if they are touched? The same inquiry may be made in respect to persons of these opposite descriptions of every age, and in every situation of life, and the result will prove favorable to the point in question.

Quakers

When William Penn took the government of Pennsylvania, he distinctly avowed to the Indians, his forbearing and pacific principles, and his benevolent wishes for uninterrupted peace with them. On these principles the government was administered while it remained in the hands of the Quakers. This was an illustrious example of government on religious principles, worthy of imitation by all the nations of the earth.

I am happy to state, that there are various incidents related by travelers, both among the native Africans and Indians, where lives have been saved by the presentation of a pacific attitude, when they would have otherwise fallen prey to savage barbarity.

It has been my purpose to exhibit reason as a great safeguard, at all times capable of dethroning passion and alleviating our condition in periods of the greatest trouble and difficulty, and of being a powerful handmaid in achieving a triumph of the principles of universal peace. I have also thus far treated the subject as a grand fundamental principle, universal in its nature, and binding alike on every member of the human family. But if there be a single class of people in these United States, on which these duties are more imperative and binding, than another, that class is the colored population of this country, both free and enslaved. Situated as we are, among a people that recognize the lawfulness of slavery, and more of whom sympathize with the oppressor than the oppressed, it requires us to pursue our course calmly onward, with much self-denial, patience and perseverance.

Meeting prejudice

We must be prepared at all times, to meet the scoffs and scorns of the vulgar and indecent— the contemptible frowns of haughty tyrants, and the blighting mildew of a popular and sinful prejudice. If amidst these difficulties we can but possess our souls in patience, we shall finally triumph over our enemies. But among the various duties that devolve on us, not the least is that which relates to ourselves. We must learn on all occasions to rebuke the spirit of violence, both in sentiment and practice. God has said, "Vengeance is mine, and I will repay it." The laws of the land guarantee the protection of our persons from personal violence, and whoever for any cause, inflicts a single blow on a fellow being, violates the laws of God and of his country, and has no just claim to being regarded as a Christian or a good citizen.

As a people we have suffered much from the pestilential influence of mob violence that has spread its devastating influence over our country. And it is to me no matter of astonishment that they continue to exist. They do but put in practice a common every day theory that pervades every neighborhood, and almost every family, viz.: That it is right, under certain circumstances, to violate all law, both civil and national, and abuse, kick and cuff your fellow man, when they deem that he has offended or insulted the community in which he resides.

Whenever the passions of individuals rise above all laws, human and divine, then they are in the first stages of anarchy, and then every act prosecuted under the influence of this spirit, necessarily extends itself beyond the boundary of our laws. The act of the multitude is carried out on the principle of combination, which is the grand lever by which machinery as well as man is impelled in this fruitful age. There is no difference in principle between the acts of a few individuals, and those of a thousand, while actuated by the spirit of passion, dethroning reason, the laws of our country and the liberty of man. Hence every individual that either aids or abets an act of personal violence towards the humblest individual is guilty of sustaining the detestable practice of mobocratic violence. Yet such is the general spirit that pervades our common country, and receives its sanction from places of high honor and trust, that it is patriotism to disregard the laws. It is but reasonable to suppose the individuals, guided by like views and motives, will on some occasions concentrate their power, and carry on their operations on a large scale. Unless the hearts and reasoning powers of man become improved, it is impossible for the most sagacious mind to augur the consequences. The spirit of passion has become so implanted in human bosoms, that the laws of our country give countenance to the same, by exhibiting lenity for those who are under its influence.

Error in legislation
This is doubtless a great error in legislation, because it not only pre-supposes the irrationality of man, but gives him a plea of innocence, in behalf of his idiotism. The only sure method of conquering these evils is to commend a reform in ourselves, and then the spirit of passion will soon be destroyed in individuals, and communities, and governments, and then the ground-work will be fully laid for a speedy triumph of the principles of universal peace.

The love of power is one of the greatest human infirmities, and with it comes the usurping influence of despotism, the mother of slavery. Show me any country or people where despotism reigns triumphant, and I will exhibit to your view the spirit of slavery, whether the same be incorporated in the government or not. It is this demon-like spirit of passion that sends forth its poignant influence over professedly civilized nations, as well as the more barbarous tribes. Its effects on the human interest is the same, whether it emanates from the subjugator of Poland—the throne of Britain—the torrid zone of the South, or the genial clime of Pennsylvania; from the white, the red, or the black man—whether he be of European or African descent—or the native Indian that resides in the wilds of the forest, their combined action is at war with the principles of peace, and the liberty of the world.

How different is the exercise of this love of power, when exercised by man, or enforced by human governments, to the exercise of Him who holds all "power over the heavens, earth, and seas, and all that in them is." With God, all is in order—with man, all confusion. The planets perform their annual revolutions —the tides ebb and flow—the seas obey. His command—the whole government of universal worlds are sustained by His wisdom and power—each invariably performing the course marked out by their great Author, because they are impelled by His love. But with man, governments are impelled by the law of force; hence despotism becomes an ingredient in all human governments.

Power of reason

The power of reason is the noblest gift of Heaven to man, because it assimilates man to his Maker. And were he to improve his mind by cultivating his reasoning powers, his acts of life would bear the impress of Deity, indelibly stamped upon them. If human governments bore any direct resemblance to the government of God, they would be mild in their operation, and the principles of universal peace would become implanted in every mind. Wars, fighting, and strifes would cease —there would be a signal triumph of truth over error—the principles of peace, justice, righteousness, and universal love would guide and direct mankind onward in that sublime path marked out by the great Prince of Peace.

And now my friends, let us cease to be guided by the influence of a wild and beguiling passion—the wicked and foolish fantasies of pride, folly and lustful ambition—the alluring the detestable examples of despotism and governments—the sickly sensibility of those who from false notions of honor, attempt to promote the ends of justice, by placing "righteousness under their feet," and are at all times ready to imbue their hands in a fellow creature's blood, for the purpose of satisfying their voracious appetites for crime, murder and revenge. I say from them let us turn away, for a terrible retaliation must shortly await them, even in this life. The moral powers of this nation and the world is fast wakening from the sleep of ages, and wielding a swift besom, that will sweep from the fact of the earth error and iniquity with the power of a whirlwind. But a few years ago and dueling was considered necessary to personal honor, and the professional Christian, or the most upright citizen might barter away the lives and happiness of a nation with his guilty traffic in ardent spirits, with impunity. But now a regenerated public sentiment not only repudiates their conduct, but consigns them with "body and soul murderers." Though the right to be free has been deemed inalienable by this nation, from a period antecedent to the declaration of American Independence, yet a mental fog hovered over this nation on the subject of slavery that had well nigh sealed her doom, were it not that in the Providence of God a few noble spirits arose in the might of moral power to her rescue. They girded on the power of truth, for their shield, and the principles of peace for their buckler and thus boldly pierced through the incrustations of a false and fatal philosophy, and from the incision, sprang forth the light of glorious liberty, disseminating its delectable rays over the dark chasms of slavery, and lighting up the vision of the vision of a ruined world. And the effect has been to awaken the nation to her duty with regard to the rights of man—to render slaveholders despicable and guilty of robbery and murder—and in many places, those that profess Christianity have been unchurched, denied the privilege of Christian fellowship. And the same moral power is now awakening in the cause of peace, and will bring disgrace and dishonor on all who engage in wars and fighting.

The period is fast approaching when the church, as at present constituted, must undergo one of the severest contests she has met with since her foundation, because in so many cases she has refused to sustain her own principles. The moral warfare that is now commenced will not cease if the issue should be a dissolution of both church and state. The time has already come when those believe that intemperance, slavery, war and fighting is sinful, and it will soon arrive when those who practice either their rights to enjoy Christian fellowship will be questioned.

Practical examples

And now, Mr. President, I shall give a few practical illustrations, and then I shall have done. It appears by history that there have been many faithful advocates of peace since the apostolic age, but none have ever given a more powerful impetus to the cause of peace, than the modern abolitionists. They have been beater and stoned, mobbed and persecuted from city to city, and never returned evil for evil, but submissively, as a sheep brought before the shearer have they endured scoffings and scourges for the cause's sake, while they prayed for their prosecutors. And how miraculously they have been preserved in the midst of a thousand dangers from without and within. Up to the present moment not the life of a single individual has been sacrificed on the altar of popular fury. Had they have set out in this glorious undertaking of freeing 2,500,000 human beings, with the war-cry of "liberty or death," they would have been long since demolished, or a civil war would have ensued; thus would have dyed the national soil with human blood. And now let me ask you, was not their method of attacking the system of human slavery the most reasonable? And would not their policy have been correct, even if we were to lay aside their Christian motives? Their weapons were reason and moral truth, and on them they desired to stand or fall—and so it will be in all causes that are sustained form just and Christian principles, they will ultimately triumph. Now let us suppose for a single moment what would have been our case, if they had started on the principle, that "resistance to tyrants is obedience to God"?—what would have been our condition, together with that of the slave population? Why, we should have doubtless perished by the sword, or been praying for the destruction of our enemies, and probably engaged in the same bloody warfare.

And now we are indebted to the modern abolitionists more than to any other class of men for the instructions we have received from the dissemination of their principles, or we would not at this moment be associated here to advocate the cause of moral reform—of temperance, education, peace and universal liberty. Therefore let us, like them, obliterate from our minds the idea of revenge, and from our hearts all wicked intentions towards each other and the world, and we shall b able through the blessing of Almighty God, to so much to establish the principles of universal peace. Let us not think the world has no regard for our efforts—they are looking forward to them with intense interest and anxiety. The enemies of the abolitionists are exhibiting a regard for the power of their principles that they are unwilling to acknowledge, although it is every where known over the country, that abolitionists "will not fight," yet they distrust their own strength so much, that they frequently muster a whole neighborhood of from 50 to 300 men, with sticks, stones, rotten eggs and bowie knives, to mob and beat a single individual probably in his "teens," whose heart's law is non-resistance. There is another way in which they do us honor—they admit the right of all people to fight for their liberty, but colored people and abolitionists—plainly inferring that they are too good for the performance of such unchristian acts—and lastly, while we endeavor to control our own passions and keep them in subjection, let us be mindful of the weakness of others; and for acts of wickedness of others; and for acts of wickedness committed against us, let us reciprocate in the spirit of kindness. If they continue their injustice towards us, let us always decide that their reasoning powers are defective, and that it is with men as the laws of mechanics —large bodies move slowly, while smaller ones are easily propelled with swift velocity. In every case of passion that presents itself, the subject is one of pity rather than derision, and in his cooler moments let us earnestly advise him to improve his understanding, by cultivating his intellectual powers, and thus exhibit his close alliance with God, who is the author of all wisdom, peace, justice, righteousness and truth. And in conclusion, felt it always be our aim to live in a spirit of unity with each other, supporting one common cause, by spreading our influence for the good of mankind, with the hope that the period will ultimately arrive when the principles of universal peace will triumph throughout the world.

William Whipper. The Colored American, *September 9, 16, 23, 30, 1837*

JAMES W. C. PENNINGTON (1807-1870)

Introduction

James Pennington was born a slave in Maryland. He worked as a stonemason and black-smith but when he was about twenty he escaped to Pennsylvania. He was looked after by a Quaker who taught him to read and write.

In 1828 Pennington moved to New York where he worked as a blacksmith. He joined the campaign against slavery and during this period became friends with William Lloyd Garrison and Lewis Tappan. He continued with his education and worked as a schoolteacher in Newtown, Long Island, before becoming pastor of the Temple Street Congregational Church.

In 1839 Pennington joined with Lewis Tappan in organizing help for Joseph Cinque and his fellow Africans who had been arrested as a result of the Amistad Mutiny. Eventually the Supreme Court ruled that the Africans had been kidnapped and had the right to use violence to escape from captivity.

Pennington's *The Origin and History of the Colored People* was published in 1841. Two years later he represented Connecticut at the World's Anti-Slavery Convention in London.

His autobiography, *The Fugitive Blacksmith,* one of the most important of the American Antebellum slave narratives, was serialized in the magazine *Afro-American* in 1859.

James Pennington continued to work for black civil rights until his death in 1870.

The Fugitive Blacksmith
Chapter 1

My birth and parentage—The treatment of slaves generally in Maryland

I was born in the state of Maryland, which is one of the smallest and most northern of the slave-holding states; the products of this state are wheat, rye, Indian corn, tobacco, with some hemp, flax, &c. By looking at the map, it will be seen that Maryland, like Virginia her neighbor, is divided by the Chesapeake Bay into eastern and western shores. My birthplace was on the eastern shore, where there are seven or eight small counties; the farms are small, and tobacco is mostly raised.

At an early period in the history of Maryland, her lands began to be exhausted by the bad cultivation peculiar to slave states; and hence she soon commenced the business of breeding slaves for the more southern states. This has given an enormity to slavery, in Maryland, differing from that which attaches to the system in Louisiana, and equaled by none of the kind, except Virginia and Kentucky, and not by either of these in extent.

My parents did not both belong to the same owner: my father belonged to a man named ——; my mother belonged to a man named ——. This not only made me a slave, but made me the slave of him to whom my mother belonged; as the primary law of slavery is, that the child shall follow the condition of the mother.

When I was about four years of age, my mother, an older brother and myself, were given to a son of my master, who had studied for the medical profession, but who had now married wealthy, and was about to settle as a wheat planter in Washington County, on the western shore. This began the first of our family troubles that I knew anything about, as it occasioned a separation between my mother and the only two children she then had, and my father, to a distance of about two hundred miles. But this separation did not continue long; my father being a valuable slave, my master was glad to purchase him.

About this time, I began to feel another evil of slavery—I mean the want of parental care and attention. My parents were not able to give any attention to their children during the day. I often suffered much from hunger and other similar causes. To estimate the sad state of a slave child, you must look at it as a helpless human being thrown upon the world without the benefit of its natural guardians. It is thrown into the world without a social circle to flee to for hope, shelter, comfort, or instruction. The social circle, with all its heaven-ordained blessings, is of the utmost importance to the tender child; but of this, the slave child, however tender and delicate, is robbed.

There is another source of evil to slave children, which I cannot forbear to mention here, as one which early embittered my life,—I mean the tyranny of the master's children. My master had two sons, about the ages and sizes of my older brother and myself. We were not only required to recognize these young sirs as our young masters, but they felt themselves to be such; and, in consequence of this feeling, they sought to treat us with the same air of authority that their father did the older slaves.

Another evil of slavery that I felt severely about this time, was the tyranny and abuse of the overseers. These men seem to look with an evil eye upon children. I was once visiting a menagerie, and being struck with the fact, that the lion was comparatively indifferent to every one around his cage, while he eyed with peculiar keenness a little boy I had; the keeper informed me that such was always the case Such is true of those human beings in the slave states, called overseers. They seem to take pleasure in torturing the children of slaves, long before they are large enough to be put at the hoe, and consequently under the whip.

We had an overseer, named Blackstone; he was an extremely cruel man to the working hands. He always carried a long hickory whip, a kind of pole. He kept three or four of these in order, that he might not at any time be without one.

I once found one of these hickories lying in the yard, and supposing that he had thrown it away, I picked it up, and boy-like, was using it for a horse; he came along from the field, and seeing me with it, fell upon me with the one he then had in his hand, and flogged me most cruelly. From that, I lived in constant dread of that man; and he would show how much he delighted in cruelty by chasing me from my play with threats and imprecations. I have lain for hours in a wood, or behind a fence, to hide from his eye.

At this time my days were extremely dreary. When I was nine years of age, myself and my brother were hired out from home; my brother was placed with a pump-maker, and I was placed with a stone mason. We were both in a town some six miles from home. As the men with whom we lived were not slaveholders, we enjoyed some relief from the peculiar evils of slavery. Each of us lived in a family where there was no other Negro.

The slaveholders in that state often hire the children of their slaves out to non-slave-holders, not only because they save themselves the expense of taking care of them, but in this way they get among their slaves useful trades. They put a bright slave-boy with a tradesman, until he gets such a knowledge of the trade as to be able to do his own work, and then he takes him home. I remained with the stonemason until I was eleven years of age: at this time I was taken home. This was another serious period in my childhood; I was separated from my older brother, to whom I was much attached; he continued at his place, and not only learned the trade to great perfection, but finally became the property of the man with whom he lived, so that our separation was permanent, as we never lived nearer after, than six miles. My master owned an excellent blacksmith, who had obtained his trade in the way I have mentioned above. When I returned home at the age of eleven, I was set about assisting to do the mason-work of a new smith's shop. This being done, I was placed at the business, which I soon learned, so as to be called a "first-rate blacksmith." I continued to work at this business for nine years, or until I was twenty-one, with the exception of the last seven months.

In the spring of 1828, my master sold me to a Methodist man, named ——, for the sum of seven hundred dollars. It soon proved that he had not work enough to keep me employed as a smith, and he offered me for sale again. On hearing of this, my old master re-purchased. me, and proposed to me to undertake the carpentering business. I had been working at this trade six months with a white workman, who was building a large barn when I left. I will now relate the abuses which occasioned me to fly.

Three or four of our farm hands had their wives and families on other plantations. In such cases, it is the custom in Maryland to allow the men to go on Saturday evening to see their families, stay over the Sabbath, and return on Monday morning, not later than "half-an-hour by sun." To overstay their time is a grave fault, for which, especially at busy seasons, they are punished.

One Monday morning, two of these men had not been so fortunate as to get home at the required time: one of them was an uncle of mine. Besides these, two young men who had no families, and for whom no such provision of time was made, having gone somewhere to spend the Sabbath, were absent. My master was greatly irritated, and had resolved to have, as he said, "a general whipping-match among them."

Preparatory to this, he had a rope in his pocket, and a cowhide in his hand, walking about the premises, and speaking to every one he met in a very insolent manner, and finding fault with some without just cause. My father, among other numerous and responsible duties, discharged that of shepherd to a large and valuable flock of Merino sheep. This morning he was engaged in the tenderest of a shepherd's duties;—a little lamb, not able to go alone, lost its mother; he was feeding it by hand. He had been keeping it in the house for several days. As he stooped over it in the yard, with a vessel of new milk he had obtained, with which to feed it, my master came along, and without the least provocation, began by asking, "Bazil, have you fed the flock?"

"Yes, sir."

"Were you away yesterday?"

"No, sir."

"Do you know why these boys have not got home this morning yet?"

"No, sir, I have not seen any of them since Saturday night."

"By the Eternal, I'll make them know their hour. The fact is, I have too many of you; my people are getting to be the most careless, lazy, and worthless in the country."

"Master," said my father, "I am always at my post; Monday morning never finds me off the plantation."

"Hush, Bazil! I shall have to sell some of you; and then the rest will have enough to do; I have not work enough to keep you all tightly employed; I have too many of you."

All this was said in an angry, threatening, and exceedingly insulting tone. My father was a high-spirited man, and feeling deeply the insult, replied to the last expression,—"If I am one too many, sir, give me a chance to get a purchaser, and I am willing to be sold when it may suit you."

"Bazil, I told you to hush!" and suiting the action to the word, he drew forth the "cowhide" from under his arm, fell upon him with most savage cruelty, and inflicted fifteen or twenty severe stripes with all his strength, over his shoulders and the small of his back. As he raised himself upon his toes, and gave the last stripe, he said, "I will make you know that I am master of your tongue as well as of your time!"

Being a tradesman, and just at that time getting my breakfast, I was near enough to hear the insolent words that were spoken to my father, and to hear, see, and even count the savage stripes inflicted upon him.

Let me ask any one of Anglo-Saxon blood and spirit, how would you expect a son to feel at such a sight?

This act created an open rupture with our family—each member felt the deep insult that had been inflicted upon our head; the spirit of the whole family was roused; we talked of it in our nightly gatherings, and showed it in our daily melancholy aspect. The oppressor saw this, and with the heartlessness that was in perfect keeping with the first insult, commenced a series of tauntings, threatenings, and insinuations, with a view to crush the spirit of the whole family.

Although it was sometime after this event before I took the decisive step, yet in my mind and spirit, I never was a Slave after it.

Whenever I thought of the great contrast between my father's employment on that memorable Monday morning, (feeding the little lamb,) and the barbarous conduct of my master, I could not help cordially despising the proud abuser of my sire; and I believe he discovered it, for he seemed to have diligently sought an occasion against me. Many incidents occurred to convince me of this, too tedious to mention; but there is one I will mention, because it will serve to show the state of feeling that existed between us, and how it served to widen the already open breach.

I was one day shoeing a horse in the shop yard. I had been stooping for some time under the weight of the horse, which was large, and was very tired; meanwhile, my master had taken his position on a little hill just in front of me, and stood leaning back on his cane, with his hat drawn over his eyes. I put down the horse's foot, and straightened myself up to rest a moment, and without knowing that he was there, my eye caught his. This threw him into a panic of rage; he would have it that I was watching him. "What are you rolling your white eyes at me for, you lazy rascal?" He came down upon me with his cane, and laid on over my shoulders, arms, and legs, about a dozen severe blows, so that my limbs and flesh were sore for several weeks; and then after several other offensive epithets, left me.

This affair my mother saw from her cottage, which was near; I being one of the oldest sons of my parents, our family was now mortified to the lowest degree. I had always aimed to be trustworthy; and feeling a high degree of mechanical pride, I had aimed to do my work with dispatch and skill, my blacksmith's pride and taste was one thing that had reconciled me so long to remain a slave. I sought to distinguish myself in the finer branches of the business by invention and finish; I frequently tried my hand at making guns and pistols, putting blades in penknives, making fancy hammers, hatchets, sword-canes, &c., &c. Besides I used to assist my father at night in making straw-hats and willow-baskets, by which means we supplied our family with little articles of food, clothing and luxury, which slaves in the mildest form of the system never get from the master; but after this, I found that my mechanic's pleasure and pride were gone. I thought of nothing but the family disgrace under which we were smarting, and how to get out of it.

Perhaps I may as well extend this note a little. The reader will observe that I have not said much about my master's cruel treatment; I have aimed rather to shew the cruelties incident to the system. I have no disposition to attempt to convict him of having been one of the most cruel masters—that would not be true—his prevailing temper was kind, but he was a perpetualist. He was opposed to emancipation; thought free Negroes a great nuisance, and was, as respects discipline, a thorough slaveholder. He would not tolerate a look or a word from a slave like insubordination. He would suppress it at once, and at any risk. When he thought it necessary to secure unqualified obedience, he would strike a slave with any weapon, flog him on the bare back, and sell. And this was the kind of discipline he also empowered his overseers and sons to use.

I have seen children go from our plantations to join the chained-gang on its way from Washington to Louisiana; and I have seen men and women flogged—I have seen the overseers strike a man with a hayfork—nay more, men have been maimed by shooting! Some dispute arose one morning between the overseer and one of the farm hands, when the former made at the slave with a hickory club; the slave taking to his heels, started for the woods; as he was crossing the yard, the overseer turned, snatched his gun which was near, and fired at the flying slave, lodging several shots in the calf of one leg. The poor fellow continued his flight, and got into the woods; but he was in so much pain that he was compelled to come out in the evening, and give himself up to his master, thinking he would not allow him to be punished he had been shot. He was locked up that night; the next morning the overseer was allowed to tie him up and flog him; his master then took his instruments and picked the shot out of his leg, and told him, it served him just right.

My master had a deeply pious and exemplary slave, an elderly man, who one day had a misunderstanding with the overseer, when the latter attempted to flog him. He fled to the woods; it was noon; at evening he came home orderly. The next morning, my master, taking one of his sons with him, a rope and cowhide in his hand, led the poor old man away into the stable; tied him up, and ordered the son to lay on thirty-nine lashes, which he did, making the keen end of the cowhide lap around and strike him in the tenderest part of his side, till the blood sped out, as if a lance had been used.

While my master's son was thus engaged, the sufferer's little daughter, a child six years of age, stood at the door, weeping in agony for the fate of her father. I heard the old man articulating in a low tone of voice; I listened at the intervals between the stripes, and lo! he was praying!

When the last lash was laid on, he was let down; and leaving him to put on his clothes, they passed out of the door, and drove the man's weeping child away! I was mending a hinge to one of the barn doors; I saw and heard what I have stated. Six months after, this same man's eldest daughter, a girl fifteen years old, was sold to slave-traders, where he never saw her more.

This poor slave and his wife were both Methodists, so was the wife of the young master who flogged him. My old master was an Episcopalian.

These are only a few of the instances which came under my own notice during my childhood and youth on our plantations; as to those which occurred on other plantations in the neighborhood, I could state any number.

I have stated that my master was watching the movements of our family very closely. Sometime after the difficulties began, we found that he also had a confidential slave assisting him in the business. This wretched fellow, who was nearly white, and of Irish descent, informed our master of the movements of each member of the family by day and by night, and on Sundays. This stirred the spirit of my mother, who spoke to our fellow-slave, and told him he ought to be ashamed to be engaged in such low business.

Master hearing of this, called my father, mother, and myself before him, and accused us of an attempt to resist and intimidate his "confidential servant." Finding that only my mother had spoken to him, he swore that if she ever spoke another word to him, he would flog her.

I knew my mother's spirit and my master's temper as well. Our social state was now perfectly intolerable. We were on the eve of a general fracas. This last scene occurred on Tuesday; and on Saturday evening following, without counsel or advice from any one, I determined to fly.

Chapter 2
The flight

It was the Sabbath: the holy day which God in his infinite wisdom gave for the rest of both man and beast. In the state of Maryland, the slaves generally have the Sabbath, except in those districts where the evil weed, tobacco, is cultivated; and then, when it is the season for setting the plant, they are liable to be robbed of this only rest.

It was in the month of November, somewhat past the middle of the month. It was a bright day, and all was quiet. Most of the slaves were resting about their quarters; others had leave to visit their friends on other plantations, and were absent. The evening previous I had arranged my little bundle of clothing, and had secreted it at some distance from the house. I had spent most of the forenoon in my workshop engaged in deep and solemn thought.

It is impossible for me now to recollect all the perplexing thoughts that passed through my mind during that forenoon; it was a day of heart aching to me. But I distinctly remember the two great difficulties that stood in the way of my flight: I had a father and mother whom I dearly loved,—I had also six sisters and four brothers on the plantation. The question was, shall I hide my purpose from them? moreover, how will my flight affect them when I am gone? Will they not be suspected? Will not the whole family be sold off as a disaffected family, as is generally the case when one of its members flies? But a still more trying question was, how can I expect to succeed, I have no knowledge of distance or direction. I know that Pennsylvania is a free state, but I know not where its soil begins, or where that of Maryland ends? Indeed, at this time there was no safety in Pennsylvania, New Jersey, or New York, for a fugitive, except in lurking-places, or under the care of judicious friends, who could be entrusted not only with liberty, but also with life itself.

With such difficulties before my mind, the day had rapidly worn away; and it was just past noon. One of my perplexing questions I had settled—I had resolved to let no one into my secret; but the other difficulty was now to be met. It was to be met without the least knowledge of its magnitude, except by imagination. Yet of one thing there could be no mistake, that the consequences of a failure would be most serious. Within my recollection no one had attempted to escape from my master; but I had many cases in my mind's eye, of slaves of other planters who had failed, and who had been made examples of the most cruel treatment, by flogging and selling to the far South, where they were never to see their friends more. I was not without serious apprehension that such would be my fate. The bare possibility was impressively solemn; but the hour was now come, and the man must act and be free, or remain a slave for ever. How the impression came to be upon my mind I cannot tell; but there was a strange and horrifying belief, that if I did not meet the crisis that day, I should be self-doomed—that my ear would be nailed to the door-post for ever. The emotions of that moment I cannot fully depict. Hope, fear, dread, terror, love, sorrow, and deep melancholy were mingled in my mind together; my mental state was one of most painful distraction. When I looked at my numerous family—a beloved father and mother, eleven brothers and sisters, &c.; but when I looked at slavery as such; when I looked at it in its mildest form, with all its annoyances; and above all, when I remembered that one of the chief annoyances of slavery, in the most mild form, is the liability of being at any moment sold into the worst form; it seemed that no consideration, not even that of life itself, could tempt me to give up the thought of flight. And then when I considered the difficulties of the way—the reward that would be offered—the human blood-hounds that would be set upon my track—the weariness—the hunger—the gloomy thought, of not only losing all one's friends in one day, but of having to seek and to make new friends in a strange world. But, as I have said, the hour was come, and the man must act, or for ever be a slave.

It was now two o'clock. I stepped into the quarter; there was a strange and melancholy silence mingled with the destitution that was apparent in every part of the house. The only morsel I could see in the shape of food, was a piece of Indian flour bread, it might be half-a-pound in weight. This I placed in my pocket, and giving a last look at the aspect of the house, and at a few small children who were playing at the door, I sallied forth thoughtfully and melancholy, and after crossing the barn-yard, a few moments' walk brought me to a small cave, near the mouth of which lay a pile of stones, and into which I had deposited my clothes. From this, my course lay through thick and heavy woods and back lands to—town, where my brother lived. This town was six miles distance. It was now near three o'clock, but my object was neither to be seen on the road, or to approach the town by daylight, as I was well-known there, and as any intelligence of my having been seen there would at once put the pursuers on my track. This first six miles of my flight, I not only traveled very slowly, therefore, so as to avoid carrying any daylight to this town; but during this walk another very perplexing question was agitating my mind. Shall I call on my brother as I pass through, and shew him what I am about? My brother was older than I, we were much attached; I had been in the habit of looking to him for counsel.

I entered the town about dark, resolved, all things in view, not to shew myself to my brother. Having passed through the town without being recognized, I now found myself under cover of night, a solitary wanderer from home and friends; my only guide was the north star, by this I knew my general course northward, but at what point I should strike Penn, or when and where I should find a friend, I knew not. Another feeling now occupied my mind,—I felt like a mariner who has gotten his ship outside of the harbor and has spread his sails to the breeze. The cargo is on board—the ship is cleared—and the voyage I must make; besides, this being my first night, almost every thing will depend upon my clearing the coast before the day dawns. In order to do this my flight must be rapid. I therefore set forth in sorrowful earnest, only now and then I was cheered by the wild hope, that I should somewhere and at sometime be free.

The night was fine for the season, and passed on with little interruption for want of strength, until, about three o'clock in the morning, I began to feel the chilling effects of the dew.

At this moment, gloom and melancholy again spread through my whole soul. The prospect of utter destitution which threatened me was more than I could bear, and my heart began to melt. What substance is there in a piece of dry Indian bread; what nourishment is there in it to warm the nerves of one already chilled to the heart? Will this afford a sufficient sustenance after the toil of the night? But while these thoughts were agitating my mind, the day dawned upon me, in the midst of an open extent of country, where the only shelter I could find, without risking my travel by daylight, was a corn shock, but a few hundred yards from the road, and here I must pass my first day out. The day was an unhappy one; my hiding-place was extremely precarious. I had to sit in a squatting position the whole day, without the least chance to rest. But, besides this, my scanty pittance did not afford me that nourishment which my hard night's travel needed. Night came again to my relief, and I sallied forth to pursue my journey. By this time, not a crumb of my crust remained, and I was hungry and began to feel the desperation of distress.

As I traveled I felt my strength failing and my spirits wavered; my mind was in a deep and melancholy dream. It was cloudy; I could not see my star, and had serious misgivings about my course.

In this way the night passed away, and just at the dawn of day I found a few sour apples, and took my shelter under the arch of a small bridge that crossed the road. Here I passed the second day in ambush.

This day would have been more pleasant than the previous, but the sour apples, and a draught of cold water, had produced anything but a favorable effect; indeed, I suffered most of the day with severe symptoms of cramp. The day passed away again without any further incident, and as I set out at nightfall, I felt quite satisfied that I could not pass another twenty-four hours without nourishment. I made but little progress during the night, and often sat down, and slept frequently fifteen or twenty minutes. At the dawn of the third day I continued my travel. As I had found my way to a public turnpike road during the night, I came very early in the morning to a toll-gate, where the only person I saw, was a lad about twelve years of age. I inquired of him where the road led to. He informed me it led to Baltimore. I asked him the distance, he said it was eighteen miles.

This intelligence was perfectly astounding to me. My master lived eighty miles from Baltimore. I was now sixty-two miles from home. That distance in the right direction, would have placed me several miles across Mason and Dixon's line, but I was evidently yet in the state of Maryland.

I ventured to ask the lad at the gate another question—Which is the best way to Philadelphia? Said he, you can take a road which turns off about half-a-mile below this, and goes to Getsburgh, or you can go on to Baltimore and take the packet.

I made no reply, but my thought was, that I was as near Baltimore and Baltimore-packets as would answer my purpose.

In a few moments I came to the road to which the lad had referred, and felt some relief when I had gotten out of that great public highway, "The National Turnpike," which I found it to be.

When I had walked a mile on this road, and when it had now gotten to be about nine o'clock, I met a young man with a load of hay. He drew up his horses, and addressed me in a very kind tone, when the following dialogue took place between us.

"Are you traveling any distance, my friend?"

"I am on my way to Philadelphia."

"Are you free?"

"Yes, sir."

"I suppose, then, you are provided with free papers?"

"No, sir. I have no papers."

"Well, my friend, you should not travel on this road: you will be taken up before you have gone three miles. There are men living on this road who are constantly on the look-out for your people; and it is seldom that one escapes them who attempts to pass by day."

He then very kindly gave me advice where to turn off the road at a certain point, and how to find my way to a certain house, where I would meet with an old gentleman who would further advise me whether I had better remain till night, or go on.

I left this interesting young man; and such was my surprise and chagrin at the thought of having so widely missed my way, and my alarm at being in such a dangerous position, that in ten minutes I had so far forgotten his directions as to deem it unwise to attempt to follow them, lest I should miss my way, and get into evil hands.

I, however, left the road, and went into a small piece of wood, but not finding a sufficient hiding-place, and it being a busy part of the day, when persons were at work about the fields, I thought I should excite less suspicion by keeping in the road, so I returned to the road; but the events of the next few moments proved that I committed a serious mistake.

I went about a mile, making in all two miles from the spot where I met my young friend, and about five miles from the toll-gate to which I have referred, and I found myself at the twenty-four miles' stone from Baltimore. It was now about ten o'clock in the forenoon; my strength was greatly exhausted by reason of the want of suitable food; but the excitement that was then going on in my mind, left me little time to think of my need of food. Under ordinary circumstances as a traveler, I should have been glad to see the "Tavern," which was near the mile-stone; but as the case stood with me, I deemed it a dangerous place to pass, much less to stop at. I was therefore passing it as quietly and as rapidly as possible, when from the lot just opposite the house, or sign-post, I heard a coarse stern voice cry, "Halloo!"

I turned my face to the left, the direction from which the voice came, and observed that it proceeded from a man who was digging potatoes. I answered him politely; when the following occurred:—

"Who do you belong to?"

"I am free, sir."

"Have you got papers?"

"No, sir."

"Well, you must stop here."

By this time he had got astride the fence, making his way into the road. I said,

"My business is onward, sir, and I do not wish to stop."

"I will see then if you don't stop, you black rascal."

He was now in the middle of the road, making after me in a brisk walk.

I saw that a crisis was at hand; I had no weapons of any kind, not even a pocket-knife; but I asked myself, shall I surrender without a struggle. The instinctive answer was "No." What will you do? continue to walk; if he runs after you, run; get him as far from the house as you can, then turn suddenly and smite him on the knee with a stone; that will render him, at least, unable to pursue you.

This was a desperate scheme, but I could think of no other, and my habits as a blacksmith had given my eye and hand such mechanical skill, that I felt quite sure that if I could only get a stone in my hand, and have time to wield it, I should not miss his knee-pan.

He began to breathe short. He was evidently vexed because I did not halt, and I felt more and more provoked at the idea of being thus pursued by a man to whom I had not done the least injury. I had just began to glance my eye about for a stone to grasp, when he made a tiger-like leap at me. This of course brought us to running. At this moment he yelled out "Jake Shouster!" and at the next moment the door of a small house standing to the left was opened, and out jumped a shoemaker girded up in his leather apron, with his knife in hand. He sprang forward and seized me by the collar, while the other seized my arms behind. I was now in the grasp of two men, either of whom were larger bodied than myself, and one of whom was armed with a dangerous weapon.

Standing in the door of the shoemaker's shop, was a third man; and in the potato lot I had passed, was still a fourth man. Thus surrounded by superior physical force, the fortune of the day it seemed to me was gone.

My heart melted away, I sunk resistlessly into the hands of my captors, who dragged me immediately into the tavern which was near. I ask my reader to go in with me, and see how the case goes.

Great moral dilemma

A few moments after I was taken into the bar-room, the news having gone as by electricity, the house and yard were crowded with gossipers, who had left their business to come and see "the runaway nigger." This hastily assembled congregation consisted of men, women, and children, each one had a look to give at, and a word to say about, the "nigger."

But among the whole, there stood one whose name I have never known, but who evidently wore the garb of a man whose profession bound him to speak for the dumb, but he, standing head and shoulders above all that were round about, spoke the first hard sentence against me. Said he, "That fellow is a runaway I know; put him in jail a few days, and you will soon hear where he came from." And then fixing a fiend-like gaze upon me, he continued, "if I lived on this road, you fellows would not find such clear running as you do, I'd trap more of you."

But now comes the pinch of the case, the case of conscience to me even at this moment. Emboldened by the cruel speech just recited, my captors enclosed me, and said, "Come now, this matter may easily be settled without you going to jail; who do you belong to, and where did you come from?"

The facts here demanded were in my breast. I knew according to the law of slavery, who I belonged to and where I came from, and I must now do one of there things—I must refuse to speak at all, or I must communicate the fact, or I must tell an untruth. How would an untutored slave, who had never heard of such a writer as Archdeacon Paley, be likely to act in such a dilemma? The first point decided, was, the facts in this case are my private property. These men have no more right to them than a highway robber has to my purse. What will be the consequence if I put them in possession of the facts. In forty-eight hours, I shall have received perhaps one hundred lashes, and be on my way to the Louisiana cotton fields. Of what service will it be to them. They will get a paltry sum of two hundred dollars. Is not my liberty worth more to me than two hundred dollars are to them?

I resolved therefore, to insist that I was free. This not being satisfactory without other evidence, they tied my hands and set out, and went to a magistrate who lived about half a mile distant. It so happened, that when we arrived at his house he was not at home. This was to them a disappointment, but to me it was a relief; but I soon learned by their conversation, that there was still another magistrate in the neighborhood, and that they would go to him. In about twenty minutes, and after climbing fences and jumping ditches, we, captors and captive, stood before his door, but it was after the same manner as before—he was not at home. By this time the day had worn away to one or two o'clock, and my captors evidently began to feel somewhat impatient of the loss of time. We were about a mile and a quarter from the tavern. As we set out on our return, they began to parley. Finding it was difficult for me to get over fences with my hands tied, they untied me, and said, "New John," that being the name they had given me, "if you have run away from any one, it would be much better for you to tell us!" but I continued to affirm that I was free. I knew, however, that my situation was very critical, owing to the shortness of the distance I must be from home: my advertisement might overtake me at any moment.

On our way back to the tavern, we passed through a small skirt of wood, where I resolved to make an effort to escape again. One of my captors was walking on either side of me; I made a sudden turn, with my left arm sweeping the legs of one of my captors from under him; I left him nearly standing on his head, and took to my heels. As soon as they could recover they both took after me. We had to mount a fence. This I did most success-fully, and making across an open field towards another wood; one of my captors being a long-logged man, was in advance of the other, and consequently nearing me. We had a hill to rise, and during the ascent he gained on me. Once more I thought of self-defense. I am trying to escape peaceably, but this man is determined that I shall not.

My case was now desperate; and I took this desperate thought: "I will run him a little farther from his coadjutor; I will then suddenly catch a stone, and wound him in the breast." This was my fixed purpose, and I had arrived near the point on the top of the hill, where I expected to do the act, when to my surprise and dismay, I saw the other side of the hill was not only all ploughed up, but we came suddenly upon a man ploughing, who as suddenly left his plough and cut off my flight, by seizing me by the collar, when at the same moment my pursuer seized my arms behind. Here I was again in a sad fix. By this time the other pursuer had come up; I was most savagely thrown down on the ploughed ground with my face downward, the ploughman placed his knee upon my shoulders, one of my captors put his upon my legs, while the other tied my arms behind me. I was then dragged up, and marched off with kicks, punches and imprecations.

We got to the tavern at three o'clock. Here they again cooled down, and made an appeal to me to make a disclosure. I saw that my attempt to escape strengthened their belief that I was a fugitive. I said to them, "If you will not put me in jail, I will now tell you where I am from." They promised. "Well," said I, "a few weeks ago, I was sold from the eastern shore to a slave-trader, who had a large gang, and set out for Georgia, but when he got to a town in Virginia, he was taken sick, and died with the small-pox. Several of his gang also died with it, so that the people in the town became alarmed, and did not wish the gang to remain among them. No one claimed us, or wished to have anything to do with us; I left the rest, and thought I would go somewhere and get work."

When I said this, it was evidently believed by those who were present, and notwith-standing the unkind feeling that had existed, there was a murmur of approbation. At the same time I perceived that a panic began to seize some, at the idea that I was one of a small-pox gang. Several who had clustered near me, moved off to a respectful distance. One or two left the bar-room, and murmured, "better let the small-pox nigger go."

I was then asked what was the name of the slave-trader. Without premeditation, I said, "John Henderson."

"John Henderson!" said one of my captors, "I knew him; I took up a yaller boy for him about two years ago, and got fifty dollars. He passed out with a gang about that time, and the boy ran away from him at Frederickstown. What kind of a man was he?"

At a venture, I gave a description of him. "Yes," said he, "that is the man." By this time, all the gossipers had cleared the coast; our friend, "Jake Shouster," had also gone back to his bench to finish his custom work, after having "lost nearly the whole day, trotting about with a nigger tied," as I heard his wife say as she called him home to his dinner. I was now left alone with the man who first called to me in the morning. In a sober manner, he made this proposal to me: "John, I have a brother living in Risterstown, four miles off, who keeps a tavern; I think you had better go and live with him, till we see what will turn up. He wants an ostler." I at once assented to this. "Well," said he, "take something to eat, and I will go with you."

Although I had so completely frustrated their designs for the moment, I knew that it would by no means answer for me to go into that town, where there were prisons, handbills, newspapers, and travelers. My intention was, to start with him, but not to enter the town alive.

I sat down to eat; it was Wednesday, four o'clock, and this was the first regular meal I had since Sunday morning. This over, we set out, and to my surprise, he proposed to walk. We had gone about a mile and a half, and were approaching a wood through which the road passed with a bend. I fixed upon that as the spot where I would either free myself from this man, or die in his arms. I had resolved upon a plan of operation—it was this: to stop short, face about, and commence action; and neither ask or give quarters, until I was free or dead!

We had got within six rods of the spot, when a gentleman turned the corner, meeting us on horse-back. He came up, and entered into conversation with my captor, both of them speaking in Dutch, so that I knew not what they said. After a few moments, this gentleman addressed himself to me in English, and I then learned that he was one of the magistrates on whom we had called in the morning; I felt that another crisis was at hand. Using his saddle as his bench, he put on an extremely stern and magisterial-like face, holding up his horse not unlike a field-marshal in the act of reviewing troops, and carried me through a most rigid examination in reference to the statement I had made. I repeated carefully all I had said; at the close, he said, "Well, you had better stay among us a few months, until we see what is to be done with you." It was then agreed that we should go back to the tavern, and there settle upon some further plan. When we arrived at the tavern, the magistrate alighted from his horse, and went into the bar-room. He took another close glance at me, and went over some points of the former examination. He seemed quite satisfied of the correctness of my statement, and made the following proposition: that I should go and live with him for a short time, stating that he had a few acres of corn and potatoes to get in, and that he would give me twenty-five cents per day. I most cheerfully assented to this proposal. It was also agreed that I should remain at the tavern with my captor that night, and that he would accompany me in the morning. This part of the arrangement I did not like, but of course I could not say so. Things being thus arranged, the magistrate mounted his horse, and went on his way home.

It had been cloudy and rainy during the afternoon, but the western sky having partially cleared at this moment, I perceived that it was near the setting of the sun.

My captor had left his hired man most of the day to dig potatoes alone; but the wagon being now loaded, it being time to convey the potatoes into the barn, and the horses being all ready for that purpose, he was obliged to go into the potato field and give assistance.

I should say here, that his wife had been driven away by the small-pox panic about three o'clock, and had not yet returned; this left no one in the house, but a boy, about nine years of age.

As he went out, he spoke to the boy in Dutch, which I supposed, from the little fellow's conduct, to be instructions to watch me closely, which he certainly did.

The potato lot was across the public road, directly in front of the house; at the back of the house, and about 300 yards distant, there was a thick wood. The circumstances of the case would not allow me to think for one moment of remaining there for the night—the time had come for another effort—but there were two serious difficulties. One was, that I must either deceive or dispatch this boy who is watching me with intense vigilance. I am glad to say, that the latter did not for a moment seriously enter my mind. To deceive him effectually, I left my coat and went to the back door, from which my course would be direct to the wood. When I got to the door, I found that the barn, to which the wagon must soon come, lay just to the right, and overlooking the path I must take to the wood. In front of me lay a garden surrounded by a picket fence, to the left of me was a small gate, and that by passing through that gate would throw me into an open field, and give me clear running to the wood; but on looking through the gate, I saw that my captor, being with the team, would see me if I attempted to start before he moved from the position he then occupied. To add to my difficulty the horses had baulked; while waiting for the decisive moment, the boy came to the door and asked me why I did not come in. I told him I felt unwell, and wished him to be so kind as to hand me a glass of water; expecting while he was gone to get it, the team would clear, so that I could start. While he was gone, another attempt was made to start the team but failed; he came with the water and I quickly used it up by gargling my throat and by drinking a part. I asked him to serve me by giving me another glass: he gave me a look of close scrutiny, but went in for the water. I heard him fill the glass, and start to return with it; when the hind end of the wagon cleared the corner of the house, which stood in a range with the fence along which I was to pass in getting to the wood. As I passed out the gate, I "squared my main yard," and laid my course up the line of fence, I cast a last glance over my right shoulder, and saw the boy just perch his head above the garden picket to look after me; I heard at the same time great confusion with the team, the rain having made the ground slippery, and the horses having to cross the road with a slant and rise to get into the barn, it required great effort after they started to prevent their baulking. I felt some assurance that although the boy might give the alarm, my captor could not leave the team until it was in the barn. I heard the horses' feet on the barn-floor, just as I leaped the fence, and darted into the wood.

The sun was now quite down behind the western horizon, and just at this time a heavy dark curtain of clouds was let down, which seemed to usher in haste the night shade. I have never before or since seen anything which seemed to me to compare in sublimity with the spreading of the night shades at the close of that day. My reflections upon the events of that day, and upon the close of it, since I became acquainted with the Bible, have frequently brought to my mind that beautiful passage in the Book of Job, "He holdeth back the face of His throne, and spreadeth a cloud before it."

Before I proceed to the critical events and final deliverance of the next chapter, I cannot forbear to pause a moment here for reflection. The reader may well imagine how the events of the past day affected my mind. You have seen what was done to me; you have heard what was said to me—you have also seen what I have done, and heard what I have said. If you ask me whether I had expected before I left home, to gain my liberty by shedding men's blood, or breaking their limbs? I answer, no! and as evidence of this, I had provided no weapon whatever; not so much as a penknife—it never once entered my mind. I cannot say that I expected to have the ill fortune of meeting with any human being who would attempt to impede my flight.

If you ask me if I expected when I left home to gain my liberty by fabrications and untruths? I answer, no! my parents, slaves as they were, had always taught me, when they could, that "truth may be blamed but cannot be shamed;" so far as their example was concerned, I had no habits of untruth. I was arrested, and the demand made upon me, "Who do you belong to?" knowing the fatal use these men would make of my truth, I at once concluded that they had no more right to it than a highwayman has to a traveler's purse.

If you ask me whether I now really believe that I gained my liberty by those lies? I answer, no! I now believe that I should be free, had I told the truth; but, at that moment, I could not see any other way to baffle my enemies, and escape their clutches.

The history of that day has never ceased to inspire me with a deeper hatred of slavery; I never recur to it but with the most intense horror at a system which can put a man not only in peril of liberty, limb, and life itself, but which may even send him in haste to the bar of God with a lie upon his lips.

Whatever my readers may think, therefore, of the history of events of the day, do not admire in it the fabrications; but see in it the impediments that often fall into the pathway of the flying bondman. See how human bloodhounds gratuitously chase, catch, and tempt him to shed blood and lie; how, when he would do good, evil is thrust upon him.

Chapter 3

A dreary night in the woods—critical situation the next day

Almost immediately on entering the wood, I not only found myself embosomed in the darkness of the night, but I also found myself entangled in a thick forest of undergrowth, which had been quite thoroughly wetted by the afternoon rain.

I penetrated through the wood, thick and thin, and more or less wet, to the distance I should think of three miles. By this time my clothes were all thoroughly soaked through, and I felt once more a gloom and wretchedness; the recollection of which makes me shudder at this distant day. My young friends in this highly favored Christian country, surrounded with all the comforts of home and parental care, visited by pastors and Sabbath-school teachers, think of the dreary condition of the blacksmith boy in the dark wood that night; and then consider that thousands of his brethren have had to undergo much greater hardships in their flight from slavery.

I was now out of the hands of those who had so cruelly teased me during the day; but a number of fearful thoughts rushed into my mind to alarm me. It was dark and cloudy, so that I could not see the north star. How do I know what ravenous beasts are in this wood? How do I know what precipices may be within its bounds? I cannot rest in this wood to-morrow, for it will be searched by those men from whom I have escaped; but how shall I regain the road? How shall I know when I am on the right road again?

These are some of the thoughts that filled my mind with gloom and alarm.

At a venture I struck an angle northward in search of the road. After several hours of zigzag and laborious travel, dragging through briars, thorns and running vines, I emerged from the wood and found myself wading marshy ground and over ditches.

I can form no correct idea of the distance I traveled, but I came to a road, I should think about three o'clock in the morning. It so happened that I came out near where there was a fork in the road of three prongs.

Now arose a serious query—which is the right prong for me? I was reminded by the circumstance of a superstitious proverb among the slaves, that "the left-hand turning was unlucky," but as I had never been in the habit of placing faith in this or any similar super-stition, I am not aware that it had the least weight upon my mind, as I had the same diffi-culty with reference to the right-hand turning. After a few moments parley with myself, I took the central prong of the road and pushed on with all my speed.

It had not cleared off, but a fresh wind had sprung up; it was chilly and searching. This with my wet clothing made me very uncomfortable; my nerves began to quiver before the searching wind. The barking of mastiffs, the crowing of fowls, and the distant rattling of market wagons, warned me that the day was approaching.

My British reader must remember that in the region where I was, we know nothing of the long hours of twilight you enjoy here. With us the day is measured more by the immediate presence of the sun, and the night by the prevalence of actual darkness.

The day dawned upon me when I was near a small house and barn, situate close to the road side. The barn was too near the road, and too small to afford secure shelter for the day; but as I cast my eye around by the dim light, I could see no wood, and no larger barn. It seemed to be an open country to a wide extent. The sun was traveling so rapidly from his eastern chamber, that ten or fifteen minutes would spread broad daylight over my track. Whether my deed was evil, you may judge, but I freely confess that I did then prefer darkness rather than light; I therefore took to the mow of the little barn at a great risk, as the events of the day will show. It so happened that the barn was filled with corn fodder, newly cured and lately gotten in. You are aware that however quietly one may crawl into such a bed, he is compelled to make much more noise than if it were a feather-bed; and also considerably more than if it were hay or straw. Besides inflicting upon my own excited imagination the belief that I made noise enough to be heard by the inmates of the house who were likely to be rising at the time, I had the misfortune to attract the notice of a little house-dog, such as we call in that part of the world a "fice," on account of its being not only the smallest species of the canine race, but also, because it is the most saucy, noisy, and teasing of all dogs. This little creature commenced a fierce barking. I had at once great fears that the mischievous little thing would betray me; I fully apprehended that as soon as the man of the house arose, he would come and make search in the barn. It now being entirely daylight, it was too late to retreat from this shelter, even if I could have found another; I, therefore, bedded myself down into the fodder as best I could, and entered upon the annoyances of the day, with the frail hope to sustain my mind.

It was Thursday morning; the clouds that had veiled the sky during the latter part of the previous day and the previous night were gone. It was not until about an hour after the sun rose that I heard any out-door movements about the house. As soon as I heard those movements, I was satisfied there was but one man about the house, and that he was preparing to go some distance to work for the day. This was fortunate for me; the busy movements about the yard, and especially the active preparations in the house for breakfast, silenced my unwelcome little annoyer, the fice, until after the man had gone, when he commenced afresh, and continued with occasional intermissions through the day. He made regular sallies from the house to the barn, and after smelling about, would fly back to the house, barking furiously; thus he strove most skillfully throughout the entire day to raise an alarm. There seemed to be no one about the house but one or two small children and the mother, after the man was gone. About ten o'clock my attention was gravely directed to another trial: how I could pass the day without food. The reader will remember it is Thursday, and the only regular meal I have taken since Sunday, was yesterday, in the midst of great agitation, about four o'clock; that since that I have performed my arduous night's travel. At one moment, I had nearly concluded to go and present myself at the door, and ask the woman of the house to have compassion and give me food; but then I feared the consequences might be fatal, and I resolved to suffer the day out. The wind sprang up fresh and cool; the barn being small and the crevices large, my wet clothes were dried by it, and chilled me through and through.

I cannot now, with pen or tongue, give a correct idea of the feeling of wretchedness I experienced; every nerve in my system quivered, so that not a particle of my flesh was at rest. In this way I passed the day till about the middle of the afternoon, when there seemed to be an unusual stir about the public road, which passed close by the barn. Men seemed to be passing in parties on horseback, and talking anxiously. From a word which I now and then overheard, I had not a shadow of doubt that they were in search of me. One I heard say, "I ought to catch such a fellow, the only liberty he should have for one fortnight, would be ten feet of rope." Another I heard say, "I reckon he is in that wood now." Another said, "Who would have thought that rascal was so'cute?" All this while the little fice was mingling his voice with those of the horsemen, and the noise of the horses' feet. I listened and trembled.

Just before the setting of the sun, the laboring man of the house returned, and commenced his evening duties about the house and barn; chopping wood, getting up his cow, feeding his pigs, &c., attended by the little brute, who continued barking at short intervals. He came several times into the barn below. While matters were passing thus, I heard the approach of horses again, and as they came up nearer, I was led to believe that all I had heard pass, were returning in one party. They passed the barn and halted at the house, when I recognized the voice of my old captor; addressing the laborer, he asked, "Have you seen a runaway nigger pass here to-day?"

LABOURER.—"No; I have not been at home since early this morning. Where did he come from?"

CAPTOR.—"I caught him down below here yesterday morning. I had him all day, and just at night he fooled me and got away. A party of us have been after him all day; we have been up to the line, but can't hear or see anything of him. I heard this morning where he came from. He is a blacksmith, and a stiff reward is out for him, two hundred dollars."

LAB.—"He is worth looking for."

CAP.—"I reckon so. If I get my clutches on him again, I'll mosey him down to—before I eat or sleep."

Reader, you may if you can, imagine what the state of my mind was at this moment. I shall make no attempt to describe it to you; to my great relief, however, the party rode off, and the laborer after finishing his work went into the house. Hope seemed now to dawn for me once more; darkness was rapidly approaching, but the moments of twilight seemed much longer than they did the evening before. At length the sable covering had spread itself over the earth. About eight o'clock, I ventured to descend from the mow of the barn into the road. The little dog the while began a furious fit of barking, so much so, that I was sure that with what his master had learned about me, he could not fail to believe I was about his premises. I quickly crossed the road, and got into an open field opposite. After stepping lightly about two hundred yards, I halted, and on listening, I heard the door open. Feeling about on the ground, I picked up two stones, and one in each hand I made off as fast as I could, but I heard nothing more that indicated pursuit, and after going some distance I discharged my encumbrance, as from the reduced state of my bodily strength, I could not afford to carry ballast.

This incident had the effect to start me under great disadvantage to make a good night's journey, as it threw me at once off the road, and compelled me to encounter at once the tedious and laborious task of beating my way across marshy fields, and to drag through woods and thickets where there were no paths.

After several hours I found my way back to the road, but the hope of making anything like clever speed was out of the question. All I could do was to keep my legs in motion, and this I continued to do with the utmost difficulty. The latter part of the night I suffered extremely from cold. There came a heavy frost; I expected at every moment to fall on the road and perish. I came to a corn-field covered with heavy shocks of Indian corn that had been cut; I went into this and got an ear, and then crept into one of the shocks; eat as much of it as I could, and thought I would rest a little and start again, but weary nature could not sustain the operation of grinding hard corn for its own nourishment, and I sunk to sleep.

When I awoke, the sun was shining around; I started with alarm, but it was too late to think of seeking any other shelter; I therefore nestled myself down, and concealed myself as best I could from the light of day. After recovering a little from my fright, I commenced again eating my whole corn. Grain by grain I worked away at it; when my jaws grew tired, as they often did, I would rest, and then begin afresh. Thus, although I began an early breakfast, I was nearly the whole of the forenoon before I had done.

Nothing of importance occurred during the day, until about the middle of the afternoon, when I was thrown into a panic by the appearance of a party of gunners, who passed near me with their dogs. After shooting one or two birds, however, and passing within a few rods of my frail covering, they went on, and left me once more in hope. Friday night came without any other incident worth naming. As I sallied out, I felt evident benefit from the ear of corn I had nibbled away. My strength was considerably renewed; though I was far from being nourished, I felt that my life was at least safe from death by hunger. Thus encouraged, I set out with better speed than I had made since Sunday and Monday night. I had a presentiment, too, that I must be near free soil. I had not yet the least idea where I should find a home or a friend, still my spirits were so highly elated, that I took the whole of the road to myself; I ran, hopped, skipped, jumped, clapped my hands, and talked to myself. But to the old slaveholder I had left, I said, "Ah! ha! old fellow, I told you I'd fix you."

After an hour or two of such freaks of joy, a gloom would come over me in connexion with these questions, "But where are you going? What are you going to do? What will you do with freedom without father, mother, sisters, and brothers? What will you say when you are asked where you were born? You know nothing of the world; how will you explain the fact of your ignorance?"

These questions made me feel deeply the magnitude of the difficulties yet before me.

Saturday morning dawned upon me; and although my strength seemed yet considerably fresh, I began to feel a hunger somewhat more destructive and pinching, if possible, than I had before. I resolved, at all risk, to continue my travel by day-light, and to ask information of the first person I met.

The events of the next chapter will shew what fortune followed this resolve.

Chapter 4

The good woman of the toll-gate directs me to W. W.—my reception by him

The resolution of which I informed the reader at the close of the last chapter, being put into practice, I continued my flight on the public road; and a little after the sun rose, I came in sight of a toll-gate again. For a moment all the events which followed my passing a toll-gate on Wednesday morning, came fresh to my recollection, and produced some hesitation; but at all events, said I, I will try again.

On arriving at the gate, I found it attended by an elderly woman, whom I afterwards learned was a widow, and an excellent Christian woman. I asked her if I was in Pennsylvania. On being informed that I was, I asked her if she knew where I could get employ? She said she did not; but advised me to go to W. W., a Quaker, who lived about three miles from her, whom I would find to take an interest in me. She gave me directions which way to take; I thanked her, and bade her good morning, and was very careful to follow her directions.

In about half an hour I stood trembling at the door of W. W. After knocking, the door opened upon a comfortably spread table; the sight of which seemed at once to increase my hunger sevenfold. Not daring to enter, I said I had been sent to him in search of employ. "Well," said he, "Come in and take thy breakfast, and get warm, and we will talk about it; thee must be cold without any coat." "Come in and take thy breakfast, and get warm!," These words spoken by a stranger, but with such an air of simple sincerity and fatherly kindness, made an overwhelming impression upon my mind. They made me feel, spite of all my fear and timidity, that I had, in the providence of God, found a friend and a home. He at once gained my confidence; and I felt that I might confide to him a fact which I had, as yet, confided to no one.

From that day to this, whenever I discover the least disposition in my heart to disregard the wretched condition of any poor or distressed persons with whom I meet, I call to mind these words—"Come in and take thy breakfast, and get warm." They invariably remind me of what I was at that time; my condition was as wretched as that of any human being can possibly be, with the exception of the loss of health or reason. I had but four pieces of clothing about my person, having left all the rest in the hands of my captors. I was a starving fugitive, without home or friends—a reward offered for my person in the public papers— pursued by cruel man hunters, and no claim upon him to whose door I went. Had he turned me away, I must have perished. Nay, he took me in, and gave me of his food, and shared with me his own garments. Such treatment I had never before received at the hands of any white man.

A few such men in slaveholding America, have stood, and even now stand, like Abrahams and Lots, to stay its forthcoming and well-earned and just judgment.

The limits of this work compel me to pass over many interesting incidents which occurred during my six months' concealment in that family. I must confine myself only to those which will show the striking providence of God, in directing my steps to the door of W. W., and how great an influence the incidents of that six months has had upon all my subsequent history. My friend kindly gave me employ to saw and split a number of cords of wood, then lying in his yard, for which he agreed with me for liberal pay and board. This inspired me with great encouragement. The idea of beginning to earn something was very pleasant. Next; we confidentially agreed upon the way and means of avoiding surprise, in case any one should come to the house as a spy, or with intention to arrest me. This afforded still further relief, as it convinced me that the whole family would now be on the look out for such persons.

The next theme of conversation was with reference to my education.

"Can thee read or write any, James?" was the question put to me the morning after my arrival, by W. W.

"No, sir, I cannot; my duties as a blacksmith have made me acquainted with the figures on the common mechanics' square. There was a day-book kept in the shop, in which the overseer usually charged the smithwork we did for the neighbors. I have spent entire

Sabbaths looking over the pages of that book; knowing the names of persons to whom certain pieces of work were charged, together with their prices, I strove anxiously to learn to write in this way. I got paper, and picked up feathers about the yard, and made ink of— berries. My quills being too soft, and my skill in making a pen so poor, that I undertook some years ago to make a steel pen.

In this way I have learnt to make a few of the letters, but I cannot write my own name, nor do I know the letters of the alphabet."

W. W., (handing a slate and pencil.)—"Let me see how thee makes letters; try such as thou hast been able to make easily."

A. B. C. L. G.

P. W., (wife of W. W.)—"Why, those are better than I can make."

W. W.—"Oh, we can soon get thee in the way, James."

Arithmetic and astronomy became my favorite studies. W. W. was an accomplished scholar; he had been a teacher for some years, and was cultivating a small farm on account of ill-health, which had compelled him to leave teaching. He is one of the most far-sighted and practical men I ever met with. He taught me by familiar conversations, illustrating his themes by diagrams on the slate, so that I caught his ideas with ease and rapidity.

I now began to see, for the first time, the extent of the mischief slavery had done to me. Twenty-one years of my life were gone, never again to return, and I was as profoundly ignorant, comparatively, as a child five years old. This was painful, annoying, and humiliating in the extreme. Up to this time, I recollected to have seen one copy of the New Testament, but the entire Bible I had never seen, and had never heard of the Patriarchs, or of the Lord Jesus Christ. I recollected to have heard two sermons, but had heard no mention in them of Christ, or the way of life by Him. It is quite easy to imagine, then, what was the state of my mind, having been reared in total moral midnight; it was a sad picture of mental and spiritual darkness.

As my friend poured light into my mind, I saw the darkness; it amazed and grieved me beyond description. Sometimes I sank down under the load, and became discouraged, and dared not hope that I could ever succeed in acquiring knowledge enough to make me happy, or useful to my fellow-beings.

My dear friend, W. W., however, had a happy tact to inspire me with confidence; and he, perceiving my state of mind, exerted himself, not without success, to encourage me. He cited to me various instances of colored persons, of whom I had not heard before, and who had distinguished themselves for learning, such as Bannicker, Wheatley, and Francis Williams.

How often have I regretted that the six months I spent in the family of W. W., could not have been six years. The danger of recapture, however, rendered it utterly imprudent that I should remain longer; and early in the month of March, while the ground was covered with the winter's snow, I left the bosom of this excellent family, and went forth once more to try my fortune among strangers.

My dear reader, if I could describe to you the emotions I felt when I left the threshold of W. W.'s door, you could not fail to see how deplorable is the condition of the fugitive slave, often for months and years after he has escaped the immediate grasp of the tyrant. When I left my parents, the trial was great, but I had now to leave a friend who had done more for me than parents could have done as slaves; and hence I felt an endearment to that friend which was heightened by a sense of the important relief he had afforded me in the greatest need, and hours of pleasant and highly profitable intercourse.

About a month previous to leaving the house of W. W., a small circumstance occurred one evening, which I only name to shew the harassing fears and dread in which I lived during most of the time I was there. He had a brother-in-law living some ten miles distant—he was a friend to the slave; he often came unexpectedly and spent a few hours—sometimes a day and a night. I had not, however, ever known him to come at night. One night about nine o'clock, after I had gone to bed, (my lodging being just over the room in which W. W. and his wife were sitting,) I heard the door open and a voice ask, "Where is the boy?" The voice sounded to me like the voice of my master; I was sure it must be his. I sprang and listened for a moment—it seemed to be silent; I heard nothing, and then it seemed to me there was a confusion. There was a window at the head of my bed, which I could reach without getting upon the floor: it was a single sash and opened upon hinges. I quickly opened this window and waited in a perfect tremor of dread for further development. There was a door at the foot of the stairs; as I heard that door open, I sprang for the window, and my head was just out, when the gentle voice of my friend W. W. said, "James?"

"Here," said I, "——has come, and he would like to have thee put up his horse." I drew a breath of relief, but my strength and presence of mind did not return for some hours. I slept none that night; for a moment I could doze away, but the voice would sound in my ears, "Where is that boy?" and it would seem to me it must be the tyrant in quest of his weary prey, and would find myself starting again.

From that time the agitation of my mind became so great that I could not feel myself safe. Every day seemed to increase my fear, till I was unfit for work, study or rest. My friend endeavored, but in vain, to get me to stay a week longer.

The events of the spring proved that I had not left too soon. As soon as the season for traveling fairly opened, active search was made, and my master was seen in a town, twenty miles in advance of where I had spent my six months.

The following curious fact also came out. That same brother-in-law who frightened me, was putting up one evening at a hotel some miles off, and while sitting quietly by himself in one part of the room, he overheard a conversation between a traveling peddler and several gossipers of the neighborhood, who were lounging away the evening at the hotel.

PEDLER.—"Do you know one W. W. somewhere about here?"

GOSSIPER.—"Yes, he lives —— miles off."

PED.—"I understand he had a black boy with him last winter, I wonder if he is there yet?"

GOS.—"I don't know, he most always has a runaway nigger with him."

PED.—"I should like to find out whether that fellow is there yet."

BROTHER-IN-LAW, (turning about.)—"What does thee know about that boy?"

PED.—"Well he is a runaway."

BROTHER-IN-LAW.—"Who did he run away from?"

PED.—"From Col—— in ——."

BROTHER-IN-LAW.—"How did thee find out that fact?"

PED.—"Well, I have been over there peddling."

BROTHER-IN-LAW.—"Where art thou from?"

PED.—"I belong in Conn."

BROTHER-IN-LAW.—"Did thee see the boy's master?"

PED.—"Yes."

BROTHER-IN-LAW.—"What did he offer thee to find the boy?"

PED.—"I agreed to find out where he was, and let him know, and if he got him, I was to receive ——."

BROTHER-IN-LAW.—"How didst thou hear the boy had been with W. W."

PED.—"Oh, he is known to be a notorious rascal for enticing away, and concealing slaves; he'll get himself into trouble yet, the slaveholders are on the look out for him."

BROTHER-IN-LAW.—"W. W. is my brother-in-law; the boy of whom thou speakest is not with him, and to save thee the trouble of abusing him, I can moreover say, he is no rascal."

PED.—"He may not be there now, but it is because he has sent him off. His master heard of him, and from the description, he is sure it must have been his boy. He could tell me pretty nigh where he was; he said he was a fine healthy boy, twenty-one, a first-rate blacksmith; he would not have taken a thousand dollars for him."

BROTHER-IN-LAW.—"I know not where the boy is, but I have no doubt he is worth more to himself than he ever was to his master, high as he fixes the price on him; and I have no doubt thee will do better to pursue thy peddling honestly, than to neglect it for the sake of serving hunters-hunters at a venture."

All this happened within a month or two after I left my friend. One fact which makes this part of the story deeply interesting to my own mind, is, that some years elapsed before it came to my knowledge.

Chapter 5

Seven months' residence in the family of J. K., a member of the society of friends, in Chester county, Pennsylvania.—removal to New York—becomes a convert to religion—becomes a teacher

On leaving W. W., I wended my way in deep sorrow and melancholy, onward towards Philadelphia, and after traveling two days and a night, I found shelter and employ in the family of J. K., another member of the Society of Friends, a farmer.

The religious atmosphere in this family was excellent. Mrs. K. gave me the first copy of the Holy Scriptures I ever possessed, she also gave me much excellent counsel. She was a preacher in the Society of Friends; this occasioned her with her husband to be much of their time from home. This left the charge of the farm upon me, and besides put it out of their power to render me that aid in my studies which my former friend had. I, however, kept myself closely concealed, by confining myself to the limits of the farm, and using all my leisure time in study. This place was more secluded, and I felt less of dread and fear of discovery than I had before, and although seriously embarrassed for want of an instructor, I realized some pleasure and profit in my studies. I often employed myself in drawing rude maps of the solar system, and diagrams illustrating the theory of solar eclipses. I felt also a fondness for reading the

Bible, and committing chapters, and verse of hymns to memory. Often on the Sabbath when alone in the barn, I would break the monotony of the hours by endeavoring to speak, as if I was addressing an audience. My mind was constantly struggling for thought, and I was still more grieved and alarmed at its barrenness; I found it gradually freed from the darkness entailed by slavery, but I was deeply and anxiously concerned how I should fill it with useful knowledge. I had a few books, and no tutor.

In this way I spent seven months with J. K., and should have continued longer, agreeably to his urgent solicitation, but I felt that life was fast wearing, and that as I was now free, I must adventure in search of knowledge. On leaving J. K., he kindly gave me the following certificate,—

East Nautmeal, Chester County, Pennsylvania,
Tenth Month 5th, 1828
I hereby certify, that the bearer, J. W. C. Pennington, has been in my employ seven months, during most of which time I have been from home, leaving my entire business in his trust, and that he has proved a highly trustworthy and industrious young man. He leaves with the sincere regret of myself and family; but as he feels it to be his duty to go where he can obtain education, so as to fit him to be more useful, I cordially commend him to the warm sympathy of the friends of humanity wherever a wise providence may appoint him a home.
Signed, J. K.

Passing through Philadelphia, I went to New York, and in a short time found employ on Long Island, near the city. At this time, the state of things was extremely critical in New York. It was just two years after the general emancipation in that state. In the city it was a daily occurrence for slaveholders from the southern states to catch their slaves, and by certificate from Recorder Riker take them back. I often felt serious apprehensions of danger, and yet I felt also that I must begin the world somewhere.

I was earning respectable wages, and by means of evening schools and private tuition, was making encouraging progress in my studies.

Up to this time, it had never occurred to me that I was a slave in another and a more serious sense. All my serious impression of mind had been with reference to the slavery from which I had escaped. Slavery had been my theme of thought day and night.

In the spring of 1829, I found my mind unusually perplexed about the state of the slave. I was enjoying rare privileges in attending a Sabbath school; the great value of Christian knowledge began to be impressed upon my mind to an extent I had not been conscious of before. I began to contrast my condition with that of ten brothers and sisters I had left in slavery, and the condition of children I saw sitting around me on the Sabbath, with their pious teachers, with that of 700,000, now 800,440 slave children, who had no means of Christian instruction.

The theme was more powerful than any my mind had ever encountered before. It entered into the deep chambers of my soul, and stirred the most agitating emotions I had ever felt. The question was, what can I do for that vast body of suffering brotherhood I have left behind. To add to the weight and magnitude of the theme, I learnt for the first time how many slaves there were. The question completely staggered my mind; and finding myself more and more borne down with it, until I was in an agony; I thought I would make it a subject of prayer to God, although prayer had not been my habit, having never attempted it but once.

I not only prayed, but also fasted. It was while engaged thus, that my attention was seriously drawn to the fact that I was a lost sinner, and a slave to Satan; and soon I saw that I must make another escape from another tyrant. I did not by any means forget my fellow-bondmen, of whom I had been sorrowing so deeply, and travailing in spirit so earnestly; but I now saw that while man had been injuring me, I had been offending God; and that unless I ceased to offend him, I could not expect to have his sympathy in my wrongs; and moreover, that I could not be instrumental in eliciting his powerful aid in behalf of those for whom I mourned so deeply.

This may provoke a smile from some who profess to be the friends of the slave, but who have a lower estimate of experimental Christianity than I believe is due to it; but I am not the less confident that sincere prayer to God, proceeding from a few hearts deeply imbued with experimental Christianity about that time, has had much to do with subsequent happy results. At that time the 800,000 bondmen in the British Isles had not seen the beginning of the end of their sufferings—at that time, 20,000 who are now free in Canada, were in bonds—at that time, there was no Vigilance Committee to aid the flying slave—at that time, the two powerful Anti-Slavery Societies of America had no being.

I distinctly remember that I felt the need of enlisting the sympathy of God, in behalf of my enslaved brethren; but when I attempted it day after day, and night after night, I was made to feel, that whatever else I might do, I was not qualified to do that, as I was myself alienated from him by wicked works. In short, I felt that I needed the powerful aid of some in my behalf with God, just as much as I did that of my dear friend in Pennsylvania, when flying from man. "If one man sin against another, the judge shall judge him, but if a man sin against God, who shall entreat for him?"

Day after day, for about two weeks, I found myself more deeply convicted of personal guilt before God. My heart, soul and body were in the greatest distress; I thought of neither food, drink or rest, for days and nights together. Burning with a recollection of the wrongs man had done me—mourning for the injuries my brethren were still enduring, and deeply convicted of the guilt of my own sins against God. One evening, in the third week of the struggle, while alone in my chamber, and after solemn reflection for several hours, I concluded that I could never be happy or useful in that state of mind, and resolved that I would try to become reconciled to God. I was then living in the family of an Elder of the Presbyterian Church. I had not made known my feelings to any one, either in the family or out of it; and I did not suppose that any one had discovered my feelings. To my surprise, however, I found that the family had not only been aware of my state for several days, but were deeply anxious on my behalf. The following Sabbath, Dr. Cox was on a visit in Brooklyn to preach, and was a guest in the family; hearing of my case, he expressed a wish to converse with me, and without out knowing the plan, I was invited into a room and left alone with him. He entered skillfully and kindly into my feelings, and after considerable conversation he invited me to attend his service that afternoon. I did so, and was deeply interested.

Without detaining the reader with too many particulars, I will only state that I heard the doctor once or twice after this, at his own place of worship in New York City, and had several personal interviews with him, as the result of which, I hope, I was brought to a saving acquaintance with Him, of whom Moses in the Law and the Prophets did write; and soon connected myself with the church under his pastoral care.

I now returned with all my renewed powers to the great theme—slavery. It seemed now as I looked at it, to be more hideous than ever. I saw it now as an evil under the moral government of God—as a sin not only against man, but also against God. The great and engrossing thought with me was, how shall I now employ my time and my talents so as to tell most effectually upon this system of wrong! As I have stated, there was no Anti-Slavery Society then—there was no Vigilance Committee. I had, therefore, to select a course of action, without counsel or advice from any one who professed to sympathize with the slave. Many, many lonely hours of deep meditation have I passed during the years 1828 and 1829, before the great anti-slavery movement. On the questions, What shall I do for the slave? How shall I act so that he will reap the benefit of my time and talents? At one time I had resolved to go to Africa, and to react from there; but without bias or advice from any mortal, I soon gave up that, as looking too much like feeding a hungry man with a long spoon.

At length, finding that the misery, ignorance, and wretchedness of the free colored people was by the whites tortured into an argument for slavery; finding myself now among the free people of color in New York, where slavery was so recently abolished; and finding much to do for their elevation, I resolved to give my strength in that direction. And well do I remember the great movement which commenced among us about this time, for the holding of General Conventions, to devise ways and means for their elevation, which continued with happy influence up to 1834, when we gave way to anti-slavery friends, who had then taken up the laboring oar. And well do I remember that the first time I ever saw those tried friends, Garrison, Jocelyn, and Tappan, was in one of those Conventions, where they came to make our acquaintance, and to secure our confidence in some of their preliminary labors.

My particular mode of labor was still a subject of deep reflection; and from time to time I carried it to the Throne of Grace. Eventually my mind fixed upon the ministry as the desire of my whole heart. I had mastered the preliminary branches of English education, and was engaged in studying logic, rhetoric, and the Greek Testament, without a master. While thus struggling in my laudable work, an opening presented itself which was not less surprising than gratifying. Walking on the street one day, I met a friend, who said to me, "I have just had an application to supply a teacher for a school, and I have recommended you." I said,

"My dear friend, I am obliged to you for the kindness; but I fear I cannot sustain an examination for that station." "Oh," said he, "try." I said, "I will," and we separated. Two weeks afterwards, I met the trustees of the school, was examined, accepted, and agreed with them for a salary of two hundred dollars per annum; commenced my school, and succeeded. This was five years, three months, and thirteen days after I came from the South.

As the events of my life since that have been of a public professional nature, I will say no more about it. My object in writing this tract is now completed. It has been to shew the reader the hand of God with a slave; and to elicit your sympathy in behalf of the fugitive slave, by shewing some of the untold dangers and hardships through which he has to pass to gain liberty, and how much he needs friends on free soil; and that men who have felt the yoke of slavery, even in its mildest form, cannot be expected to speak of the system otherwise than in terms of the most unqualified condemnation.

There is one sin that slavery committed against me, which I never can forgive. It robbed me of my education; the injury is irreparable; I feel the embarrassment more seriously now than I ever did before. It cost me two years' hard labor, after I fled, to unshackle my mind; it was three years before I had purged my language of slavery's idioms; it was four years before I had thrown off the crouching aspect of slavery; and now the evil that besets me is a great lack of that general information, the foundation of which is most effectually laid in that part of life which I served as a slave. When I consider how much now, more than ever, depends upon sound and thorough education among colored men, I am grievously overwhelmed with a sense of my deficiency, and more especially as I can never hope now to make it up. If I know my own heart, I have no ambition but to serve the cause of suffering humanity; all that I have desired or sought, has been to make me more efficient for good. So far I have some consciousness that I have done my utmost; and should my future days be few or many, I am reconciled to meet the last account, hoping to be acquitted of any willful neglect of duty; but I shall have to go to my last account with this charge against the system of slavery, "Vile monster! thou hast hindered my usefulness, by robbing me of my early education."

Oh! what might I have been now, but for this robbery perpetrated upon me as soon as I saw the light. When the monster heard that a man child was born, he laughed, and said, "It is mine." When I was laid in the cradle, he came and looked on my face, and wrote down my name upon his barbarous list of chattels personal, on the same list where he registered his horses, hogs, cows, sheep, and even his dogs! Gracious Heaven, is there no repentance for the misguided men who do these things!

The only harm I wish to slaveholders is, that they may be speedily delivered from the guilt of a sin, which, if not repented of, must bring down the judgment of Almighty God upon their devoted heads. The least I desire for the slave is, that he may be speedily released from the pain of drinking a cup whose bitterness I have sufficiently tasted, to know that it is insufferable.

Chapter 6
Some account of the family I left in slavery—Proposal to purchase myself and parents—How met by my old master

It is but natural that the reader should wish to hear a word about the family I left behind.

There are frequently large slave families with whom God seems to deal in a remarkable manner. I believe my family is an instance.

I have already stated that when I fled, I left a father, mother, and eleven brothers and sisters. These were all, except my oldest brother, owned by the man from whom I fled. It will be seen at once then how the fear of implicating them embarrassed me in the outset. They suffered nothing, however, but a strong suspicion, until about six months after I had left; when the following circumstance took place:—

When I left my friend W. W. in Pennsylvania to go on north, I ventured to write a letter back to one of my brothers, informing him how I was; and this letter was directed to the care of a white man who was hired on the plantation, who worked in the garden with my father, and who professed a warm friendship to our family; but instead of acting in good faith, he handed the letter to my master. I am sorry that truth compels me to say that that man was an Englishman.

From that day the family were handled most strangely. The history begins thus: they were all sold into Virginia, the adjoining state. This was done lest I should have some plan to get them off; but God so ordered that they fell into kinder hands. After a few years, however, their master became much embarrassed, so that he was obliged to pass them into other hands, at least for a term of years. By this change the family was divided, and my parents, with the greater part of their children, were taken to New Orleans. After remaining there several years at hard labor,—my father being in a situation of considerable trust, they were again taken back to Virginia; and by this means became entitled by the laws of that state to their freedom. Before justice, however, could take its course, their old master in Maryland, as if intent to doom them for ever to bondage, repurchased them; and in order to defeat a similar law in Maryland, by which they would have been entitled to liberty, he obtained from the General Assembly of that state the following special act. This will show not only something of his character as a slaveholder, but also his political influence in the state. It is often urged in the behalf of slaveholders, that the law interposes an obstacle in the way of emancipating their slaves when they wish to do so, but here is an instance which lays open the real philosophy of the whole case. They make the law themselves, and when they find the laws operate more in favor of the slaves than themselves, they can easily evade or change it. Maryland being a slave-exporting state, you will see why they need a law to prohibit the importation of slaves; it is a protection to that sort of trade. This law he wished to evade.

An act for the Relief of —— of —— County. Passed January 17th, 1842.

Whereas it is represented to this General Assembly that —— of —— county, brought into this state from the state of Virginia, sometime in the month of March last, two Negro slaves, to wit, —— and —— his wife, who are slaves for life, and who were acquired by the said —— by purchase, and whereas, the said —— is desirous of retaining said slaves in this state. THEREFORE, BE IT ENACTED, by the General Assembly of Maryland, that the said —— be, and he is hereby authorized to retain said

Negroes as slaves for life within this state, provided that the said —— shall within thirty days after the passage of this act, file with the clerk of the —— county court, a list of said slaves so brought into this state, stating their ages, with an affidavit thereto attached, that the same is a true and faithful list of the slaves so removed, and that they were not brought into this state for the purpose of sale, and that they are slaves for life. And provided also, that the sum of fifteen dollars for each slave, between the ages of twelve and forty-five years, and the sum of five dollars for each slave above the age of forty-five years and under twelve years of age, so brought into this state, shall be paid to the said clerk of —— county court: to be paid over by him to the treasurer of the western shore, for the use and benefit of the Colonization Society of this state.

State of Connecticut.

Office of Secretary of State.

I hereby certify, that the foregoing is a true copy of an act passed by the General Assembly of Maryland, January 17th, 1842, as it appears in the printed acts of the said Maryland, in the Library of the state.

In testimony whereof, I have hereunto set my hand and seal of said state, at Hartford, this 17th day of August, 1846.

(SEAL.) CHARLES W. BEADLEY, Secretary of State.

Thus, the whole family after being twice fairly entitled to their liberty, even by the laws of two slave states, had the mortification of finding themselves again, not only recorded as slaves for life, but also a premium paid upon them, professedly to aid in establishing others of their fellow-beings in a free republic on the coast of Africa; but the hand of God seems to have been heavy upon the man who could plan such a stratagem to wrong his fellows.

The immense fortune he possessed when I left him, (bating one thousand dollars I brought with me in my own body,) and which he seems to have retained till that time, began to fly, and in a few years he was insolvent, so that he was unable to hold the family, and was compelled to think of selling them again. About this time I heard of their state by an Underground Railroad passenger, who came from that neighborhood, and resolved to make an effort to obtain the freedom of my parents, and to relieve myself from liability. For this purpose, after arranging for the means to purchase, I employed counsel to make a definite offer for my parents and myself. To his proposal, the following evasive and offensive answer was returned.

January 12th, 1846.

J. H.—, Esq.

Sir,—Your letter is before me. The ungrateful servant in whose behalf you write, merits no clemency from me. He was guilty of theft when he departed, for which I hope he has made due amends. I have heard he was a respectable man, and calculated to do some good to his fellow-beings. Servants are selling from five hundred and fifty to seven hundred dollars. I will take five hundred and fifty dollars, and liberate him. If my proposition is acceded to, and the money lodged in Baltimore, I will execute the necessary instrument, and deliver it in Baltimore, to be given up on payment being made.

Yours, &c.,

Here he not only refuses to account for my parents, by including them in his return and proposition, but he at the same time attempts to intimidate me by mooting the charge of theft.

I confess I was not only surprised, but mortified, at this result. The hope of being once more united to parents whom I had not seen for sixteen years, and whom I still loved dearly, had so excited my mind, that I disarranged my business relations, disposed of a valuable library of four hundred volumes, and by additional aid obtained among the liberal people of Jamaica, I was prepared to give the extravagant sum of five hundred dollars each for myself, and my father and mother. This I was willing to do, not because I approve of the principle involved as a general rule. But supposing that, as my former master was now an old man not far from his grave, (about which I was not mistaken) and as he knew, by his own shewing, that I was able to do some good, he would be inclined, whatever might have been our former relations and misunderstandings, to meet my reasonable desire to see my parents, and to part this world in reconciliation with each other, as well as with God. I should have rejoiced had his temper permitted him to accede to my offer. But I thought it too bad, a free man of Jesus Christ, living on "free soil," to give a man five hundred dollars for the privilege of being let alone, and to be branded as a thief into the bargain, and that too after I had served him twenty prime years, without the benefit of being taught so much as the alphabet.

I wrote him with my own hand, sometime after this, stating that no proposition would be acceded to by me, which did not include my parents; and likewise fix the sum for myself more reasonable, and also retract the offensive charge; to this he maintained a dignified silence. The means I had acquired by the contributions of kind friends to redeem myself, I laid by, in case the worst should come; and that designed for the purchase of my parents, I used in another kind of operation, as the result of which, my father and two brothers are now in Canada. My mother was sold a second time, south, but she was eventually found. Several of my sisters married free men, who purchased their liberty; and three brothers are owned, by what may be called conscience slaveholders, who hold slaves only for a term of years. My old master has since died; my mother and he are now in the other world together, she is at rest from him. Sometime after his death, I received information from a gentleman, intimate with his heirs, (who are principally females) that the reduced state of the family, afforded not only a good opportunity to obtain a release upon reasonable terms, but also to render the children of my oppressor some pecuniary aid; and much as I had suffered, I must confess this latter was the stronger motive with me, for acceding to their offer made by him.

I have many other deeply interesting particulars touching our family history, but I have detailed as many as prudence will permit, on account of those members who are yet south of Mason and Dixon's line.

I have faith in the hand that has dealt with us so strangely, that all our remaining members will in time be brought together; and then the case may merit a reviewed and enlarged edition of this tract, when other important matter will be inserted.

Chapter 7

The feeding and clothing of the slaves in the part of Maryland where I lived, &c.

The slaves are generally fed upon salt pork, herrings and Indian corn. The manner of dealing it out to them is as follows:—Each working man, on Monday morning, goes to the cellar of the master where the provisions are kept, and where the overseer takes his stand with some one to assist him, when he, with a pair of steel-yards, weighs out to every man the amount of three-and-a-half pounds, to last him till the ensuing Monday—allowing him just half-a-pound per day. Once in a few weeks there is a change made, by which, instead of the three-and-a-half pounds of pork, each man receives twelve herrings, allowing two a-day. The only bread kind the slaves have is that made of Indian meal. In some of the lower counties, the masters usually give their slaves the corn in the ear; and they have to grind it for themselves by night at hand-mills. But my master had a quantity sent to the grist mill at a time, to be ground into coarse meal, and kept it in a large chest in his cellar, where the woman who cooked for the boys could get it daily. This was baked in large loaves, called "steel poun bread." Sometimes as a change it was made into "Johnny Cake," and then at others into mush.

The slaves had no butter, coffee, tea, or sugar; occasionally they were allowed milk; the only exception to this statement was the "harvest provisions." In harvest, when cutting the grain, which lasted from two to three weeks in the heat of summer, they were allowed some fresh meat, rice, sugar, and coffee; and also their allowance of whiskey.

At the beginning of winter, each slave had one pair of coarse shoes and stockings, one pair of pantaloons, and a jacket.

At the beginning of summer, he had two pair of coarse linen pantaloons and two shirts.

Once in a number of years, each slave, or each man and his wife, had one coarse blanket and enough coarse linen for a "bed-tick." He never had any bedstead or other furniture kind. The men had no hats, waistcoats or handkerchiefs given them, or the women any bonnets. These they had to contrive for themselves. Each laboring man had a small "patch" of ground allowed him; from this he was expected to furnish himself and his boys hats, &c. These patches they had to work by night; from these, also, they had to raise their own provisions, as no potatoes, cabbage, &c., were allowed them from the plantation. Years ago the slaves were in the habit of raising broom-corn, and making brooms to supply the market in the towns; but now of later years great quantities of these and other articles, such as scrubbing-brushes, wooden trays, mats, baskets, and straw hats which the slaves made, are furnished by the shakers and other small manufacturers, from the free states of the north.

Neither my master or any other master, within my acquaintance, made any provisions for the religious instruction of his slaves. They were not worked on the Sabbath. One of the "boys" was required to stay at home and, "feed," that is, take care of the stock, every

Sabbath; the rest went to see their friends. Those men whose families were on other planta-tions usually spent the Sabbath with them; some would lie about at home and rest themselves.

When it was pleasant weather my master would ride "into town" to church, but I never knew him to say a word to one of us about going to church, or about our obligations to God, or a future state. But there were a number of pious slaves in our neighborhood, and several of these my master owned; one of these was an exhorter. He was not connected with a religious body, but used to speak every Sabbath in some part of the neighborhood. When slaves died, their remains were usually consigned to the grave without any ceremony, but this old gentleman, wherever he heard of a slave having been buried in that way, would send notice from plantation to plantation, calling the slaves together at the grave on the Sabbath, where he'd sing, pray, and exhort. I have known him to go ten or fifteen miles voluntarily to attend these services. He could not read, and I never heard him refer to any Scripture, and state and discourse upon any fundamental doctrine of the gospel; but he knew a number of "spiritual songs by heart," of these he would give two lines at a time very exact, set and lead the tune himself; he would pray with great fervor and his exhortations were amongst the most impressive I have heard.

The Methodists at one time attempted to evangelize the slaves in our neighborhood, but the effort was sternly resisted by the masters. They held a Camp Meeting in the neigh-borhood, where many of the slaves attended. But one of their preachers for addressing words of comfort to the slaves, was arrested and tried for his life.

My master was very active in this disgraceful affair, but the excellent man, Rev. Mr. G., was acquitted and escaped out of their hands. Still, it was deemed by his brethren to be imprudent for him to preach any more in the place, as some of the more reckless masters swore violence against him. This good man's name is remembered dearly, till this day, by slaves in that county. I met with a fugitive about a year ago, who remembered distinctly the words spoken by Mr. G., and by which his own mind was awakened to a sense of the value of his soul. He said, in the course of his preaching, addressing himself to the slaves, "You have precious immortal souls, that are worth far more to you than your bodies are to your masters;" or words to that effect. But while these words interested many slaves, they also made many masters exceedingly angry, and they tortured his words into an attempt to excite the slaves to rebellion.

Some of my master's slaves who had families, were regularly married, and others were not; the law makes no provision for such marriages, and the only provision made by the master was, that they should obtain his leave. In some cases, after obtaining leave to take his wife, the slave would ask further leave to go to a minister and be married. I never knew him to deny such a request, and yet, in those cases where the slave did not ask it, he never required him to be married by a minister. Of course, no Bibles, Tracts, or religious books of any kind, were ever given to the slaves; and no ministers or religious instructors were ever known to visit our plantation at any time, either in sickness or in health. When a slave was sick, my master being himself a physician, sometimes attended, and sometimes he called other physicians. Slaves frequently sickened and died, but I never knew any provision made to administer to them the comforts, or to offer to them the hopes of the gospel, or to their friends after their death.

There is no one feature of slavery to which the mind recurs with more gloomy impressions, than to its disastrous influence upon the families of the masters, physically, pecuniarily, and mentally.

It seems to destroy families as by a powerful blight, large and opulent slave-holding families, often vanish like a group of shadows at the third or fourth generation. This fact arrested my attention some years before I escaped from slavery, and of course before I had any enlightened views of the moral character of the system. As far back as I can recollect, indeed, it was a remark among slaves, that every generation of slaveholders are more and more inferior. There were several large and powerful families in our county, including that of my master, which affords to my mind a melancholy illustration of this remark. One of the wealthiest slaveholders in the county, was General R., a brother-in-law to my master. This man owned a large and highly valuable tract of land, called R.'s Manor. I do not know how many slaves he owned, but the number was large. He lived in a splendid mansion, and drove his coach and four. He was for some years a member of Congress. He had a numerous family of children.

The family showed no particular signs of decay until he had married a second time, and had considerably increased his number of children. It then became evident that his older children were not educated for active business, and were only destined to be a charge. Of sons, (seven or eight,) not one of them reached the eminence once occupied by the father. The only one that approached to it, was the eldest, who became an officer in the navy, and obtained the doubtful glory of being killed in the Mexican war.

General R. himself ran through his vast estate, died intemperate, and left a widow and large number of daughters, some minors, destitute, and none of his sons fitted for any employment but in the army and navy.

Slaves have a superstitious dread of passing the dilapidated dwelling of a man who has been guilty of great cruelties to his slaves, and who is dead, or moved away. I never felt this dread deeply but once, and that was one Sabbath about sunset, as I crossed the yard of General R.'s residence, which was about two miles from us, after he had been compelled to leave it.

To see the once fine smooth gravel walks, overgrown with grass—the redundancies of the shrubbery neglected—the once finely painted pricket fences, rusted and fallen down—a fine garden in splendid ruins—the lofty ceiling of the mansion thickly curtained with cobwebs—the spacious apartments abandoned, while the only music heard within as a substitute for the voices of family glee that once filled it, was the crying cricket and cockroaches! Ignorant slave as I was at that time, I could but pause for a moment, and recur in silent horror to the fact that, a strange reverse of fortune, had lately driven from that proud mansion, a large and once opulent family. What advantage was it now to the members of that family, that the father and head had for near half a century stood high in the counsels of the state, and had the benefit of the unrequited toil of hundreds of his fellowmen, when they were already grappling with the annoyances of that poverty, which he had entailed upon others.

My master's family, in wealth and influence, was not inferior to General R.'s originally. His father was a member of the convention that framed the present constitution of the state; he was, also, for some years chief justice of the state.

My master was never equal to his father, although he stood high at one time. He once lacked but a few votes of being elected Governor of the state: he once sat in the Assembly, and was generally a leading man in his own county. His influence was found to be greatest when exerted in favor of any measure in regard to the control of slaves. He was the first mover in several cruel and rigid municipal regulations in the county, which prohibited slaves from going over a certain number of miles from their master's places on the Sabbath, and from being seen about the town. He once instigated the authorities of the town where he attended service, to break up a Sabbath-school some humane members of the Methodist and Lutheran denominations had set up to teach the free Negroes, lest the slaves should get some benefit of it.

But there was a still wider contrast between my master and his own children, eight in number, when I left him. His eldest daughter, the flower of the family, married a miserable and reckless gambler. His eldest son was kind-hearted, and rather a favorite with the slaves on that account; but he had no strength of mind or weight of character. His education was limited, and he had no disposition or tact for business of any kind. He died at thirty-six, intestate; leaving his second wife (a sister to his father's second wife) with several orphan children, a widow with a small estate deeply embarrassed. The second son was once sent to West Point to fit for an officer. After being there a short time, however, he became unsteady, and commenced the study of medicine, but he soon gave that up and preferred to live at home and flog the slaves; and by them was cordially dreaded and disliked, and among themselves he was vulgarly nicknamed on account of his cruel and filthy habits.

These two families will afford a fair illustration of the gloomy history of many others that I could name. This decline of slaveholding families is a subject of observation and daily remark among slaves; they are led to observe every change in the pecuniary, moral, and social state of the families they belong to, from the fact, that as the old master declines, or as his children are married off, they are expecting to fall into their hands, or in case of insolvency on the part of the old master, they expect to be sold; in either case, it involves a change of master—a subject to which they cannot be indifferent. And it is very rarely the case that a slave's condition is benefited by passing from the old master into the hands of one of his children. Owing to the causes I have mentioned, the decline is so rapid and marked, in almost every point of view, that the children of slaveholders are universally inferior to themselves, mentally, morally, physically, as well as pecuniarily, especially so in the latter point of view; and this is a matter of most vital concern to the slaves. The young master not being able to own as many slaves as his father, usually works what he has more severely, and being more liable to embarrassment, the slaves' liability to be sold at an early day is much greater. For the same reason, slaves have a deep interest, generally, in the marriage of a young mistress. Very generally the daughters of slaveholders marry inferior men; men who seek to better their own condition by a wealthy connection. The slaves who pass into the hands of the young master has had some chance to become acquainted with his character, bad as it may be; but the young mistress brings her slaves a new, and sometimes an unknown master. Sometimes these are the sons of already broken down slaveholders. In other cases they are adventurers from the north who remove to the south, and who readily become the most cruel masters.

James W. C. Pennington

SOLOMON NORTHUP (1808-?)

Introduction

In 1841, Solomon Northup was an educated, free black man and a respected resident of Saratoga, New York. *Twelve Years a Slave*, originally published in 1853, is the true account of one man's harrowing experiences under slavery.

A couple of white strangers noticed Northup's talent for playing the fiddle and paid him to play for them. Northup followed the two men to Washington, D.C.—and soon found himself drugged, beaten senseless, and confined in a slave mart in the shadow of the nation's Capitol.

Northup describes his purchase by a slave trader and his journey to the swamps of Louisiana, where he became a slave on the cotton plantations of the notorious "Bayou Boeuf." For twelve years he labored for a succession of masters, some cruel and some kind. Overwhelmed with the hopelessness of his plight, Northup sometimes despaired of ever seeing his family again. However, he refused to relinquish his status as a man, and once thrashed his master with a bullwhip in an astonishing display of defiance that almost cost him his life.

The story of Northup's rescue and return to his family in 1853 is compelling, as is the thoughtful way he relates the details of his ordeal. Writing about the condition of slavery, Northup states:

> There may be humane masters, as there certainly are inhuman ones. Men may … discourse flippantly from arm chairs on the pleasures of slave life. But let them toil with him in the field—sleep with him in the cabin—feed with him on husks; let them behold him scourged, hunted, trampled on, and they will come back with another story in their mouths.

Twelve Years a Slave

To Harriet Beecher Stowe:

Whose name, throughout the world, is identified with the great reform; this narrative, affording another key to Uncle Tom's Cabin, is respectfully dedicated.

Chapter 2

One morning, towards the latter part of the month of March, 1841, having at that time no particular business to engage my attention, I was walking about the village of Saratoga Springs, thinking to myself where I might obtain some present employment, until the busy season should arrive. Anne, as was her usual custom, had gone over to Sandy Hill, a distance of some twenty miles, to take charge of the Culinary department at Sherrill's Coffee House, during the session of the court. Elizabeth, I think, had accompanied her. Margaret and Alonzo were with their aunt at Saratoga.

On the corner of Congress street and Broadway near the tavern, then, and for aught I know to the contrary, still kept by Mr. Moon, I was met by two gentlemen of respectable appearance, both of whom were entirely unknown to me. I have the impression that they were introduced to me by some one of my acquaintances, but who, I have in vain endeavored to recall, with the remark that I was an expert player on the violin.

At any rate, they immediately entered into conversation on that subject, making numerous inquiries touching my proficiency in that respect. My responses being to all appearances satisfactory, they proposed to engage my services for a short period, stating, at the same time, I was just such a person as their business required. Their names, as they afterwards gave them to me, were Merrill Brown and Abram Hamilton, though whether these were their true appellations, I have strong reasons to doubt. The former was a man apparently forty years of age, somewhat short and thick-set, with a countenance indicating shrewdness and intelligence. He wore a black frock coat and black hat, and said he resided either at Rochester or at Syracuse. The latter was a young man of fair complexion and light eyes, and, I should judge, had not passed the age of twenty-five. He was tall and slender, dressed in a snuff-colored coat, with glossy hat, and vest of elegant pattern. His whole apparel was in the extreme of fashion. His appearance was somewhat effeminate, but prepossessing and there was about him an easy air, that showed he had mingled with the world. They were connected, as they informed me, with a circus company, then in the city of Washington; that they were on their way thither to rejoin it, having left it for a short time to make an excursion northward, for the purpose of seeing the country, and were paying their expenses by an occasional exhibition. They also remarked that they had found much difficulty in procuring music for their entertainments, and that if I would accompany them as far as New-York, they would give me one dollar for each day's services, and three dollars in addition for every night I played at their performances, besides sufficient to pay the expenses of my return from New-York to Saratoga.

I at once accepted the tempting offer, both for the reward it promised, and from a desire to visit the metropolis. They were anxious to leave immediately. Thinking my absence would be brief, I did not deem it necessary to write to Anne whither I had gone; in fact supposing that my return, perhaps, would be as soon as hers. So taking a change of linen and my violin, I was ready to depart. The carriage was brought round—a covered one, drawn by a pair of noble bays, altogether forming an elegant establishment. Their baggage, consisting of three large trunks, was fastened on the rack, and mounting to the driver's seat, while they took their places in the rear, I drove away from Saratoga on the road to Albany, elated with my new position, and happy as I had ever been, on any day in all my life.

We passed through Ballston, and striking the ridge road, as it is called, if my memory correctly serves me, followed it direct to Albany. We reached that city before dark, and stopped at a hotel southward from the Museum. This night I had an opportunity of witnessing one of their performances—the only one, during the whole period I was with them. Hamilton was stationed at the door; I formed the orchestra, while Brown provided the entertainment. It consisted in throwing balls, dancing on the rope, frying pancakes in a hat, causing invisible pigs to squeal, and other like feats of ventriloquism and legerdemain. The audience was extraordinarily sparse, and not of the selectest character at that, and Hamilton's report of the proceeds but a "beggarly account of empty boxes."

Early next morning we renewed our journey. The burden of their conversation now was the expression of an anxiety to reach the circus without delay. They hurried forward, without again stopping to exhibit, and in due course of time, we reached New-York, taking lodgings at a house on the west side of the city, in a street running from Broadway to the river. I supposed my journey was at an end, and expected in a day or two at least, to return to my friends and family at Saratoga. Brown and Hamilton, however, began to importune me to continue with them to Washington. They alleged that immediately on their arrival, now that the summer season was approaching, the circus would set out for the north. They promised me a situation and high wages if I would accompany them. Largely did they expatiate on the advantages that would result to me, and such were the flattering representations they made, that I finally concluded to accept the offer.

The next morning they suggested that, inasmuch as we were about entering a slave State, it would be well, before leaving New-York, to procure free papers. The idea struck me as a prudent one, though I think it would scarcely have occurred to me, had they not proposed it. We proceeded at once to what I understood to be the Custom House. They made oath to certain facts showing I was a free man. A paper was drawn up and handed us, with the direction to take it to the clerk's office. We did so, and the clerk having added something to it, for which he was paid six shillings, we returned again to the Custom House. Some further formalities were gone through with before it was completed, when, paying the officer two dollars, I placed the papers in my pocket, and started with my two friends to our hotel. I thought at the time I must confess, that the papers were scarcely worth the cost of obtaining them—the apprehension of danger to my personal safety never having suggested itself to me in the remotest manner. The clerk, to whom we were directed, I remember, made a memorandum in a large book, which, I presume, is in the office yet. A reference to the entries during the latter part of March, or first of April, 1841, I have no doubt will satisfy the incredulous, at least so far as this particular transaction is concerned.

With the evidence of freedom in my possession, the next day after our arrival in New-York, we crossed the ferry to Jersey City, and took the road to Philadelphia. Here we remained one night, continuing our journey towards Baltimore early in the morning. In due time, we arrived in the latter city, and stopped at a hotel near the railroad depot, either kept by a Mr. Rathbone, or known as the Rathbone House. All the way from New-York, their anxiety to reach the circus seemed to grow more and more intense. We left the carriage at Baltimore, and entering the cars, proceeded to Washington, at which place we arrived just at nightfall, the evening previous to the funeral of General Harrison, and stopped at Gadsby's Hotel, on Pennsylvania Avenue.

After supper they called me to their apartments, and paid me forty-three dollars, a sum greater than my wages amounted to, Which act of generosity was in consequence, they said, of their not having exhibited as often as they had given me to anticipate, during our trip from Saratoga. They moreover informed me that it had been the intention of the circus company to leave Washington the next morning, but that on account of the funeral, they had concluded to remain another day. They were then, as they had been from the time of our first meeting, extremely kind. No opportunity was omitted of addressing me in the language of approbation; while, on the other hand, I was certainly much prepossessed in their favor. I gave them my confidence without reserve, and would freely have trusted them to almost any extent. Their constant conversation and manner towards me—their foresight in suggesting the idea of free papers, and a hundred other little acts, unnecessary to be repeated— all indicated that they were friends indeed, sincerely solicitous for my welfare. I know not but they were. I know not but they were innocent of the great wickedness of which I now believe them guilty. Whether they were accessory to my misfortunes—subtle and inhuman monsters in the shape of men—designedly luring me away from home and family, and liberty, for the sake of gold—those these read these pages will have the same means of determining as myself If they were innocent, my sudden disappearance must have been unaccountable indeed; but revolving in my mind all the attending circumstances, I never yet could indulge, towards them, so charitable a supposition.

After receiving the money from them, of which they appeared to have an abundance, they advised me not to go into the streets that night, inasmuch as I was unacquainted with the customs of the city. Promising to remember their advice, I left them together, and soon after was shown by a colored servant to a sleeping room in the back part of the hotel, on the ground floor. I laid down to rest, thinking of home and wife, and children, and the long distance that stretched between us, until I fell asleep. But no good angel of pity came to my bedside, bidding me to fly—no voice of mercy forewarned me in my dreams of the trials that were just at hand.

The next day there was a great pageant in Washington. The roar of cannon and the tolling of bells filled the air, while many houses were shrouded with crape, and the streets were black with people. As the day advanced, the procession made its appearance, coming slowly through the Avenue, carriage after carriage, in long succession, while thousands upon thousands followed on foot—all moving to the sound of melancholy music. They were bearing the dead body of Harrison to the grave.

From early in the morning, I was constantly in the company of Hamilton and Brown. They were the only persons I knew in Washington. We stood together as the funeral pomp passed by. I remember distinctly how the window glass would break and rattle to the ground, after each report of the cannon they were firing in the burial ground. We went to the Capitol, and walked a long time about the grounds. In the afternoon, they strolled towards the President's House, all the time keeping me near to them, and pointing out various places of interest. As yet, I had seen nothing of the circus. In fact, I had thought of it but little, if at all, amidst the excitement of the day.

My friends, several times during the afternoon, entered drinking saloons, and called for liquor. They were by no means in the habit, however, so far as I knew them, of indulging to excess. On these occasions, after serving themselves, they would pour out a glass and hand it to me. I did not become intoxicated, as may be inferred from what subsequently occurred. Towards evening, and soon after partaking of one of these potations, I began to experience most unpleasant sensations. I felt extremely ill. My head commenced aching—a dull, heavy pain, inexpressibly disagreeable. At the supper table, I was without appetite; the sight and flavor of food was nauseous. About dark the same servant conducted me to the room I had occupied the previous night. Brown and Hamilton advised me to retire, commiserating me kindly, and expressing hopes that I would be better in the morning. Divesting myself of coat and boots merely, I threw myself upon the bed. It was impossible to sleep. The pain in my head continued to increase, until it became almost unbearable.

In a short time I became thirsty. My lips were parched. I could think of nothing but water—of lakes and flowing rivers, of brooks where I had stooped to drink, and of the dripping bucket, rising with its cool and overflowing nectar, from the bottom of the well. Towards midnight, as near as I could judge, I arose, unable longer to bear such intensity of thirst. I was a stranger in the house, and knew nothing of its apartments. There was no one up, as I could observe. Groping about at random, I knew not where, I found the way at last to a kitchen in the basement. Two or three colored servants were moving through it, one of whom, a woman, gave me two glasses of water. It afforded momentary relief, but by the time I had reached my room again, the same burning desire of drink, the same tormenting thirst, had again returned. It was even more torturing than before, as was also the wild pain in my head, if such a thing could be. I was in sore distress—in most excruciating agony! I seemed to stand on the brink of madness! The memory of that night of horrible suffering will follow me to the grave.

In the course of an hour or more after my return from the kitchen, I was conscious of some one entering my room. There seemed to be several—a mingling of various voices,— but how many, or who they were, I cannot tell. Whether Brown and Hamilton were among them, is a mere matter of conjecture. I only remember with any degree of distinctness, that I was told it was necessary to go to a physician and procure medicine, and that pulling on my boots, without coat or hat, I followed them through a long passage-way, or alley, into the open street. It ran out at right angles from Pennsylvania Avenue. On the opposite side there was a light burning in a window. My impression is there were then three persons with me, but it is altogether indefinite and vague, and like the memory of a painful dream. Going towards the light, which I imagined proceeded from a physician's office, and which seemed to recede as I advanced, is the last glimmering recollection I can now recall.

From that moment I was insensible. How long I remained in that condition— whether only that night, or many days and nights— I do not know; but when consciousness returned I found myself alone, in utter darkness, and in chains.

The pain in my head had subsided in a measure, but I was very faint and weak. I was sitting upon a low bench, made of rough boards, and without coat or hat. I was hand cuffed. Around my ankles also were a pair of heavy fetters. One end of a chain was fastened to a large ring in the floor, the other to the fetters on my ankles. I tried in vain to stand upon my feet. Waking from such a painful trance, it was some time before I could collect my thoughts. Where was I? What was the meaning of these chains? Where were Brown and Hamilton? What had I done to deserve imprisonment in such a dungeon? I could not comprehend. There was a blank of some indefinite period, preceding my awakening in that lonely place, the events of which the utmost stretch of memory was unable to recall. I listened intently for some sign or sound of life, but nothing broke the oppressive silence, save the clinking of my chains, whenever I chanced to move. I spoke aloud, but the sound of my voice startled me. I felt of my pockets, so far as the fetters would allow—far enough, indeed, to ascertain that I had not only been robbed of liberty, but that my money and free papers were also gone! Then did the idea begin to break upon my mind, at first dim and confused, that I had been kidnapped. But that I thought was incredible. There must have been some misapprehension—some unfortunate mistake. It could not be that a free citizen of New-York, who had wronged no man, nor violated any law, should be dealt with thus inhumanly. The more I contemplated my situation, however, the more I became confirmed in my suspicions. It was a desolate thought, indeed. I felt there was no trust or mercy in unfeeling man; and commending myself to the God of the oppressed, bowed my head upon my fettered hands, and wept most bitterly.

Chapter 3

Some three hours elapsed, during which time I remained seated on the low bench, absorbed in painful meditations. At length I heard the crowing of a cock, and soon a distant rumbling sound, as of carriages hurrying through the streets, came to my ears, and I knew that it was day. No ray of light, however, penetrated my prison. :Finally, I heard footsteps immediately overhead, as of some one walking to and fro. It occurred to me then that I must be in an underground apartment, and the damp, moldy odors of the place confirmed the supposition. The noise above continued for at least an hour, when, at last, I heard footsteps approaching from without. A key rattled in the lock—a strong door swung back upon its hinges, admitting a flood of light, and two men entered and stood before me. One of them was a large, powerful man, forty years of age, perhaps, with dark, chestnut-colored hair, slightly interspersed with gray. His face was full, his complexion flush, his features grossly coarse, expressive of nothing but cruelty and cunning. He was about five feet ten inches high, of full habit, and, without prejudice, I must be allowed to say, was a man whose whole appearance was sinister and repugnant. His name was James H. Burch, as I learned afterwards—a well-known slave-dealer in Washington; and then, or lately connected in business, as a partner, with Theophilus Freeman, of New-Orleans. The person who accompanied him was a simple lackey, named Ebenezer Radburn, who acted merely in the capacity of turnkey. Both of these men still live in Washington, or did, at the time of my return through that city from slavery in January last.

The light admitted through the open door enabled me to observe the room in which I was confined. It was about twelve feet square—the walls of solid masonry. The floor was of heavy plank. There was one small window, crossed with great iron bars, with an outside shutter, securely fastened.

An iron-bound door led into an adjoining cell, or vault, wholly destitute of windows, or any means of admitting light. The furniture of the room in which I was, consisted of the wooden bench on which I sat, an old-fashioned, dirty box stove, and besides these, in either cell, there was neither bed, nor blanket, nor any other thing whatever. The door, through which Burch and Radburn entered, led through a small passage, up a flight of steps into a yard, surrounded by a brick wall ten or twelve feet high, immediately in rear of a building of the same width as itself. The yard extended rearward from the house about thirty feet. In one part of the wall there was a strongly ironed door, opening into a narrow, covered passage, leading along one side of the house into the street. The doom of the colored man, upon whom the door leading out of that narrow passage closed, was sealed. The top of the wall supported one end of a roof, which ascended inwards, forming a kind of open shed. Underneath the roof there was a crazy loft all round, where slaves, if so disposed, might sleep at night, or in inclement weather seek shelter from the storm. It was like a farmer's barnyard in most respects, save it was so constructed that the outside world could never see the human cattle that were herded there.

The building to which the yard was attached, was two stories high, fronting on one of the public streets of Washington. Its outside presented only the appearance of a quiet private residence. A stranger looking at it, would never have dreamed of its execrable uses. Strange as it may seem, within plain sight of this same house, looking down from its commanding height upon it, was the Capitol. The voices of patriotic representatives boasting of freedom and equality, and the rattling of the poor slave's chains, almost commingled. A slave pen within the very shadow of the Capitol!

Such is a correct description as it was in 1841, of Williams' slave pen in Washington, in one of the cellars of which I found myself so unaccountably confined.

"Well, my boy, how do you feel now?" said Burch, as he entered through the open door. I replied that I was sick, and inquired the cause of my imprisonment. He answered that I was his slave— that he had bought me, and that he was about to send me to New-Orleans. I asserted, aloud and boldly, that I was a freeman—a resident of Saratoga, where I had a wife and children, who were also free, and that my name was Northup. I complained bitterly of the strange treatment I had received, and threatened, upon my liberation, to have satisfaction for the wrong. He denied that I was free, and with an emphatic oath, declared that I came from Georgia. Again and again I asserted I was no man's slave, and insisted upon his taking off my chains at once. He endeavored to hush me, as if he feared my voice would be overheard. But I would not be silent, and denounced the authors of my imprisonment, whoever they might be, as unmitigated villains. Finding he could not quiet me, he flew into a towering passion. With blasphemous oaths, he called me a black liar, a runaway from Georgia, and every other profane and vulgar epithet that the most indecent fancy could conceive.

During this time Radburn was standing silently by. His business was, to oversee this human, or rather inhuman stable, receiving slaves, feeding, and whipping them, at the rate of two shillings a head per day. Turning to him, Burch ordered the paddle and cat-o'-ninetails to be brought in. He disappeared, and in a few moments returned with these instruments of torture. The paddle, as it is termed in slave-beating parlance, or at least the one with which I first became acquainted, and of which I now speak, was a piece of hard-wood board, eighteen or twenty inches long, molded to the shape of an old-fashioned pudding stick, or ordinary oar The flattened portion, which was about the size in circumference of two open hands, was bored with a small auger in numerous places. The cat was a large rope of many strands— the strands unraveled, and a knot tied at the extremity of each.

As soon as these formidable whips appeared, I was seized by both of them, and roughly divested of my clothing. My feet, as has been stated, were fastened to the floor. Drawing me over the bench, face downwards, Radburn placed his heavy foot upon the fetters, between my wrists, holding them painfully to the floor. With the paddle, Burch commenced beating me. Blow after blow was inflicted upon my naked body. When his unrelenting arm grew tired, he stopped and asked if I still insisted I was a free man. I did insist upon it, and then the blows were renewed, faster and more energetically, if possible, than before. When again tired, he would repeat the same question, and receiving the same answer, continue his cruel labor. All this time, the incarnate devil was uttering most fiendish oaths. At length the paddle broke, leaving the useless handle in his hand. Still I would not yield. All his brutal blows could not force from my lips the foul lie that I was a slave. Casting madly on the floor the handle of the broken paddle, he seized the rope. This was far more painful than the other. I struggled with all my power, but it was in vain. I prayed for mercy, but my prayer was only answered with imprecations and with stripes. I thought I must die beneath the lashes of the accursed brute. Even now the flesh crawls upon my bones, as I recall the scene. I was all on fire. My sufferings I can compare to nothing else than the burning agonies of hell!

At last I became silent to his repeated questions. I would make no reply. In fact, I was becoming almost unable to speak. Still he plied the lash without stint upon my poor body, until it seemed that the lacerated flesh was stripped from my bones at every stroke. A man with a particle of mercy in his soul would not have beaten even a dog so cruelly. At length Radburn said that it was useless to whip me any more—that I would be sore enough. Thereupon Burch desisted, saying, with an admonitory shake of his fist in my face, and hissing the words through his firm-set teeth, that if ever I dared to utter again that I was entitled to my freedom, that I had been kidnapped, or any thing whatever of the kind, the castigation I had just received was nothing in comparison with what would follow. He swore that he would either conquer or kill me. With these consolatory words, the fetters were taken from my wrists, my feet still remaining fastened to the ring; the shutter of the little barred window, which had been opened, was again closed, and going out, locking the great door behind them, I was left in darkness as before.

In an hour, perhaps two, my heart leaped to my throat, as the key rattled in the door again. I, who had been so lonely, and who had longed so ardently to see some one, I cared not who, now shuddered at the thought of man's approach. A human face was fearful to me, especially a white one. Radburn entered, bringing with him, on a tin plate, a piece of shriveled fried pork, a slice of bread and a cup of water. He asked me how I felt, and remarked that I had received a pretty severe flogging. He remonstrated with me against the propriety of asserting my freedom. In rather a patronizing and confidential manner, he gave it to me as his advice, that the less I said on that subject the better it would be for me. The man evidently endeavored to appear kind—whether touched at the sight of my sad condition, or with the view of silencing, on my part, any further expression of my rights, it is not necessary now to conjecture. He unlocked the festers from my ankles, opened the shutters of the little window, and departed, leaving me again alone.

By this time I had become stiff and sore; my body was covered with blisters, and it was with great pain and difficulty that I could move. From the window I could observe nothing but the roof resting on the adjacent wall. At night I laid down upon the damp, hard floor, without any pillow or covering whatever. Punctually, twice a day, Radburn came in, with his pork, and bread, and water. I had but little appetite, though I was tormented with continual thirst. My wounds would not permit me to remain but a few minutes in any one position; so, sitting, or standing, or moving slowly round, I passed the days and nights. I was heart sick and discouraged. Thoughts of my family, of my wife and children, continually occupied my mind. When sleep overpowered me I dreamed of them—dreamed I was again in Saratoga—that I could see their faces, and hear their voices calling me. Awakening from the pleasant phantasms of sleep to the bitter realities around me, I could but groan and weep. Still my spirit was not broken. I indulged the anticipation of escape, and that speedily. It was impossible, I reasoned, that men could be so unjust as to detain me as a slave, when the truth of my case was known. Burch, ascertaining I was no runaway from Georgia, would certainly let me go. Though suspicions of Brown and Hamilton were not infrequent, I could not reconcile myself to the idea that they were instrumental to my imprisonment. Surely they would seek me out—they would deliver me from thralldom. Alas! I had not then learned the measure of "man's inhumanity to man," nor to what limitless extent of wickedness he will go for the love of gain.

In the course of several days the outer door was thrown open, allowing me the liberty of the yard. There I found three slaves—one of them a lad of ten years, the others young men of about twenty and twenty-five. I was not long in forming an acquaintance, and learning their names and the particulars of their history.

The eldest was a colored man named Clemens Ray. He had lived in Washington; had driven a hack, and worked in a livery stable there for a long time. He was very intelligent, and fully comprehended his situation. The thought of going south overwhelmed him with grief. Burch had purchased him a few days before, and had placed him there until such time as he was ready to send him to the New-Orleans market. From him I learned for the first time that I was in William's Slave Pen., a place I had never heard of previously. He described to me the uses for which it was designed. I repeated to him the particulars of my unhappy story, but he could only give me the consolation of his sympathy. He also advised me to be silent henceforth on the subject of my freedom for, knowing, the character of Burch, he assured me that it would only be attended with renewed whip-ping. The next eldest was named John Williams. He was raised in Virginia, not far from Washington. Burch had taken him in payment of a debt, and he constantly entertained the hope that his master would redeem him—a hope that was subsequently realized. The lad was a sprightly child, that answered to the name of Randall. Most of the time he was playing about the yard, but occasionally would cry, calling for his mother, and wondering when she would come. His mother's absence seemed to be the great and only grief in his little heart. He was too young to realize his condition, and when the memory of his mother was not in his mind, he amused us with his pleasant pranks.

At night, Ray, Williams, and the boy, slept in the loft of the shed, while I was locked in the cell. Finally we were each provided with blankets, such as are used upon horses—the only bedding I was allowed to have for twelve years afterwards. Ray and Williams asked me many questions about New-York —how colored people were treated there; how they could have homes and families of their own, with none to disturb and oppress them; and Ray, especially, sighed continually for freedom. Such conversations, however, were not in the hearing of Burch, or the keeper Radburn. Aspirations such as these would have brought down the lash upon our backs.

It is necessary in this narrative, in order to present a full and truthful statement of all the principal events in the history of my life, and to portray the institution of Slavery as I have seen and known it, to speak of well-known places, and of many persons who are yet living. I am, and always was, an entire stranger in Washington and its vicinity—aside from Burch and Radburn, knowing no man there, except as I have heard of them through my enslaved companions What I am about to say, if false, can be easily contradicted.

I remained in Williams, slave pen about two weeks. The night previous to my departure a woman was brought in, weeping bitterly, and leading by the hand a little child. They were Randall's mother and half-sister. On meeting them he was overjoyed, clinging to her dress, kissing the child, and exhibiting every demonstration of delight. The mother also clasped him in her arms, embraced him tenderly, and gazed at him fondly through her tears, calling him by many an endearing name.

Emily, the child, was seven or eight years old, of light complexion, and with a face of admirable beauty. Her hair fell in curls around her neck, while the style and richness of her dress, and the neatness of her whole appearance indicated she had been brought up in the midst of wealth. She was a sweet child indeed. The woman also was arrayed in silk, with rings upon her fingers, and golden ornaments suspended from her ears. Her air and manners, the correctness and propriety of her language—all showed evidently, that she had sometime stood above the common level of a slave. She seemed to be amazed at finding herself in such a place as that. It was plainly a sudden and unexpected turn of fortune that had brought her there. Filling the air with her complaining she was hustled, with the children and myself, into the cell. Language can convey but an inadequate impression of the lamentations to which she gave incessant utterance. Throwing herself upon the floor, and encircling the children in her arms, she poured forth such touching words as only maternal love and kindness can suggest. They nestled closely to her, as if there only was there any safety or protection. At last they slept, their heads resting upon her lap. While they slumbered, she smoothed the hair back from their little foreheads, and talked to them all night long. She called them her darlings —her sweet babes—poor innocent things, that knew not the misery they were destined to endure. Soon they would have no mother to comfort them—they would be taken from her. What would become of them? Oh! she could not live away from her little Emmy and her dear boy. They had always been good children, and had such loving ways. It would break her heart, God knew, she said, if they were taken from her; and yet she knew they meant to sell them, and, may be, they would be separated, and could never see each other any more. It was enough to melt heart of stone to listen to the pitiful expressions of that desolate and distracted mother. Her name was Eliza; and this was the story of her life, as she afterwards related it:

She was the slave of a rich man, living in the neighborhood of Washington. She was born, I think she said, on his plantation. Years before, he had fallen into dissipated habits, and quarreled with his wife. In fact, soon after the birth of Randall, they separated. Leaving his wife and daughter in the house they had always occupied, he erected a new one nearby, on the estate. Into this house he brought Eliza; and, on condition of her living with him, she and her children were to be emancipated. She resided with him there nine years, with servants to attend upon her, and provided with every comfort and luxury of life. Emily was his child! Finally, her young mistress, who had always remained with her mother at the homestead, married a Mr. Jacob Brooks. At length, for some cause, (as I gathered from her relation,) beyond Berry's control, a division of his property was made. She and her children fell to the share of Mr. Brooks. During the nine years she had lived with Berry, in consequence of the position she was compelled to occupy, she and Emily had become the object of Mrs. Berry and her daughter's hatred and dislike. Berry himself she represented as a man of naturally a kind heart, who always promised her that she should have her freedom, and who, she had no doubt, would arrant it to her then, if it were only in his power. As soon as they thus came into the possession and control of the daughter, it became very manifest they would not live long together. The sight of Eliza seemed to be odious to Mrs. Brooks; neither could she bear to look upon the child, half-sister, and beautiful as she was!

The day she was led into the pen, Brooks had brought her from the estate into the city, under pretence that the time had come when her free papers were to be executed, in fulfillment of her master's promise. Elated at the prospect of immediate liberty, she decked herself and little Emmy in their best apparel, and accompanied him with a joyful heart. On their arrival in the city, instead of being baptized into the family of freemen, she was delivered to the trader Burch. The paper that was executed was a bill of sale. The hope of years was blasted in a moment. From the height of most exulting happiness to the utmost depths of wretchedness, she had that day descended. No wonder that she wept, and filled the pen with wailings and expressions of heart-rending woe.

Eliza is now dead. Far up the Red River, where it pours its waters sluggishly through the unhealthy low lands of Louisiana, she rests in the grave at last— the only resting place of the poor slave! ...

Chapter 21

The letter written-by Bass, directed to Parker and Perry, and which was deposited in the post-office in Marksville on the 15th day of August, 1852, arrived at Saratoga in the early part of September. Some time previous to this, Anne had removed to Glens Falls, Warren county, where she had charge of the kitchen in Carpenter's Hotel. She kept house, however, lodging with our children, and was only absent from them during such time as the discharge of her duties in the hotel required.

Messrs. Parker and Perry, on receipt of the letter, forwarded it immediately to Anne. On reading it the children were all excitement, and without delay hastened to the neighboring village of Sandy Hill, to consult Henry B. Northup, and obtain his advice and assistance in the matter.

Upon examination, that gentleman found among the statutes of the State an act providing for the recovery of free citizens from slavery. It was passed May 14, 1840, and is entitled "An act more effectually to protect the free citizens of this State from being kidnapped or reduced to slavery." It provides that it shall be the duty of the Governor, upon the receipt of satisfactory information that any free citizen or inhabitant of this State, is wrongfully held in another State or Territory of the United States, upon the allegation or pretence that such person is a slave, or by color of any usage or rule of law is deemed or taken to be a slave, to take such measures to procure the restoration of such person to liberty, as he shall deem necessary. And to that end, he is authorized to appoint and employ an agent, and directed to furnish him with such credentials and instructions as will be likely to accomplish the object of his appointment. It requires the agent so appointed to proceed to collect the proper proof to establish the right of such person to his freedom; to perform such journeys, take such measures, institute such legal proceedings, &c., as may be necessary to return such person to this State, and charges all expenses incurred in carrying the act into effect, upon moneys not otherwise appropriated in the treasury.

It was necessary to establish two facts to the satisfaction of the Governor: First, that I was a free citizen of New-York; and secondly, that I was wrongfully held in bondage. As to the first point, there was no difficulty, all the older inhabitants in the vicinity being ready to testify to it. The second point rested entirely upon the letter to Parker and Perry, written in an unknown hand, and upon the letter penned on board the brig Orleans, which, unfortunately, had been mislaid or lost.

A memorial was prepared, directed to his excellency, Governor Hunt, setting forth her marriage, my departure to Washington city; the receipt of the letters; that I was a free citizen, and such other facts as were deemed important, and was signed and verified by Anne. Accompanying this memorial were several affidavits of prominent citizens of Sandy Hill and Fort Edward, corroborating fully the statements it contained, and also a request of several well known gentlemen to the Governor, that Henry B. Northup be appointed agent under the legislative act.

On reading the memorial and affidavits, his excellency took a lively interest in the matter, and on the 23d day of November, 1852, under the seal of the State, "constituted, appointed and employed Henry B. Northup, Esq., an agent, with full power to effect" my restoration, and to take such measures as would be most likely to accomplish it, and instructing him to proceed to Louisiana with all convenient dispatch.

The pressing nature of Mr. Northup's professional and political engagements delayed his departure until December. On the fourteenth day of that month he left Sandy Hill, and proceeded to Washington. The Hon. Pierre Soule, Senator in Congress from Louisiana, Hon. Mr. Conrad, Secretary of War, and Judge Nelson, of the Supreme Court of the United States, upon hearing a statement of the facts, and examining his commission, and certified copies of the memorial and affidavits, furnished him with open letters to gentlemen in Louisiana, strongly urging their assistance in accomplishing the object of his appointment.

Senator Soule especially interested himself in the matter, insisting, in forcible language, that it was the duty and interest of every planter in his State to aid in restoring me to freedom, and trusted the sentiments of honor and justice in the bosom of every citizen of the commonwealth would enlist him at once in my behalf. Having obtained these valuable letters, Mr. Northup returned to Baltimore, and proceeded from thence to Pittsburgh. It was his original intention, under advice of friends at Washington, to go directly to New Orleans, and consult the authorities of that city. Providentially, however, on arriving at the mouth of Red River, he changed his mind. Had he continued on, he would not have met with Bass, in which case the search for me would probably have been fruitless.

Taking passage on the first steamer that arrived, he pursued his journey up Red River, a sluggish, winding stream, flowing through a vast region of primitive forests and impenetrable swamps, almost wholly destitute of inhabitants. About nine o'clock in the forenoon, January 1st, 1853, he left the steamboat at Marksville, and proceeded directly to Marksville Court House, a small village four miles in the interior.

From the fact that the letter to Messrs. Parker and Perry was post-marked at Marksville, it was supposed by him that I was in that place or its immediate vicinity. On reaching this town, he at once laid his business before the Hon. John P. Waddill, a legal gentleman of distinction, and a man of fine genius and most noble impulses. After reading the letters and documents presented him, and listening to a representation of the circumstances under which I had been carried away into captivity, Mr. Waddill at once proffered his services, and entered into the affair with great zeal and earnestness. He, in common with others of like elevated character, looked upon the kidnapped with abhorrence. The title of his fellow parishioners and clients to the property which constituted the larger proportion of their wealth, not only depended upon the good faith in which slave sales were transacted, but he was a man in whose honorable heart emotions of indignation were aroused by such an instance of injustice.

Marksville, although occupying a prominent position, and standing out in impressive italics on the map of Louisiana, is, in fact, but a small and insignificant hamlet. Aside from the tavern, kept by a jolly and generous boniface, the court house, inhabited by lawless cows and swine in the seasons of vacation, and a high gallows, with its dissevered rope dangling in the air, there is little to attract the attention of the stranger.

Solomon Northup was a name Mr. Waddill had never heard, but he was confident that if there was a slave bearing that appellation in Marksville or vicinity, his black boy Tom would know him. Tom was accordingly called, but in all his extensive circle of acquaintants there was no such personage.

The letter to Parker and Perry was dated at Bayou Boeuf. At this place, therefore, the conclusion was, I must be sought. But here a difficulty suggested itself, of a very grave character indeed. Bayou Boeuf, at its nearest point, was twenty-three miles distant, and was the name applied to the section of country extending between fifty and a hundred miles, on both sides of that stream. Thousands and thousands of slaves resided upon its shores, the remarkable richness and fertility of the soil having attracted thither a great number of planters. The information in the letter was so vague and indefinite as to render it difficult to conclude upon any specific course of proceeding. It was finally determined, however, as the only plan that presented any prospect of success, that Northup and the brother of Waddill, a student in the office of the latter, should repair to the Bayou, and traveling up one side and down the other its whole length, inquire at each plantation for me. Mr. Waddill tendered the use of his carriage, and it was definitely arranged that they should start upon the excursion early Monday morning.

It will be seen at once that this course, in all probability, would have resulted unsuccessfully. It would have been impossible for them to have gone into the fields and examine all the gangs at work. They were not aware that I was known only as Platt; and had they inquired of Epps himself, he would have stated truly that he knew nothing of Solomon Northup.

The arrangement being adopted however , there was nothing further to be done until Sunday had elapsed. The conversation between Messrs. Northup and Waddill, in the course of the afternoon, turned upon New-York politics.

"I can scarcely comprehend the nice distinctions and shades of political parties in your State," observed Mr. Waddill. "I read of soft-shells and hard-shells, hunkers and barnburners, woolly-heads and silver-grays, and am unable to understand the precise difference between them. Pray, what is it?"

Mr. Northup, re-filling his pipe, entered into quite an elaborate narrative of the origin of the various reactions of parties, and concluded by saying there was another party in New-York, known as free-soilers or abolitionists. "You have seen none of those in this part of the country, I presume?" Mr. Northup remarked.

"Never, but one," answered Waddill, laughingly. "We have one here in Marksville, an eccentric creature, who preaches abolitionism as vehemently as any fanatic at the North. He is a generous, inoffensive man, but always maintaining the wrong side of an argument. It affords us a deal of amusement. He is an excellent mechanic, and almost indispensable in this community. He is a carpenter. His name is Bass."

Some further good-natured conversation was had at the expense of Bass' peculiarities, when Waddill all at once fell into a reflective mood, and asked for the mysterious letter again.

"Let me see—l-e-t m-e s-e-e!" he repeated, thoughtfully to himself, running his eyes over the letter once more. "'Bayou Boeuf, August 15.' August 15—post-marked here. 'He that is writing for me—' Where did Bass work last summer?" he inquired, turning suddenly to his brother. His brother was unable to inform him, but rising, left the office, and soon returned with the intelligence that "Bass worked last summer somewhere on Bayou Boeuf."

"He is the man who can tell us all about Solomon Northup," exclaimed Waddill.

Bass was immediately searched for, but could not be found. After some inquiry, it was ascertained he was at the landing on Red River. Procuring a conveyance, young Waddill and Northup were not long in traversing the few miles to the latter place. On their arrival, Bass was found, just on the point of leaving, to be absent a fortnight or more. After an introduction, Northup begged the privilege of speaking to him privately a moment. They walked together towards the river, when the following conversation ensued:

"Mr. Bass," said Northup, "allow me to ask you if you were on Bayou Boeuf last August?"

"Yes, sir, I was there in August," was the reply.

"Did you write a letter for a colored man as that place to some gentleman in Saratoga Springs?"

"Excuse me, sir, if I say that is none of your business," answered Bass, stopping and looking his interrogator searchingly in the face.

"Perhaps I am rather hasty, Mr. Bass; I beg your pardon; but I have come from the State of New-York to accomplish the purpose the writer of a letter dated the 15th of August, post-marked at Marksville, had in view. Circumstances have led me to think that you are perhaps the man who wrote it. I am in search of Solomon Northup. If you know him, I beg you to inform me frankly where he is, and I assure you the source of any information you may give me shall not be divulged, if you desire it not to be."

A long time Bass looked his new acquaintance steadily in the eyes, without opening his lips. He seemed to be doubting in his own mind if there was not an attempt to practice some deception upon him. Finally he said, deliberately—

"I have done nothing to be ashamed of I am the man who wrote the letter. If you have come to rescue Solomon Northup, I am glad to see you."

"When did you last see him, and where is he?" Northup inquired.

"I last saw him Christmas, a week ago to-day. He is the slave of Edwin Epps, a planter on Bayou Boeuf, near Holmesville. He is not known as Solomon Northup; he is called Platt."

The secret was out—the mystery was unraveled. Through the thick, black cloud, amid whose dark and dismal shadows I had walked twelve years, broke the star that was to light me back to liberty. All mistrust and hesitation were soon thrown aside, and the two men conversed long and freely upon the subject uppermost in their thoughts. Bass expressed the interest he had taken in my behalf—his intention of going north in the Spring, and declaring that he had resolved to accomplish my emancipation, if it were in his power. He described the commencement and progress of his acquaintance with me, and listened with eager curiosity to the account given him of my family, and the history of my early life. Before separating, he drew a map of the bayou on a strip of paper with a piece of red chalk, showing the locality of Epps' plantation, and the road leading most directly to it.

Northup and his young companion returned to Marksville, where it was determined to commence legal proceedings to test the question of my right to freedom. I was made plaintiff, Mr. Northup acting as my guardian, and Edwin Epps defendant. The process to be issued was in the nature of replevin, directed to the sheriff of the parish, commanding him to take me into custody, and detain me until the decision of the court. By the time the papers were duly drawn up, it was twelve o'clock at night—too late to obtain the necessary signature of the Judge, who resided some distance out of town. Further business was therefore suspended until Monday morning.

Everything, apparently, was moving along swimmingly, until Sunday afternoon, when Waddill called at Northup's room to express his apprehension of difficulties they had not expected to encounter. Bass had become alarmed, and had placed his affairs in the hands of a person at the landing, communicating to him his intention of leaving the State. This person had betrayed the confidence reposed in him to a certain extent, and a rumor began to float about the town, that the stranger at the hotel, who had been observed in the company of lawyer Waddill, was after one of old Epps, slaves, over on the bayou. Epps was known at Marksville, having frequent occasion to visit that place during the session of the courts, and the fear entertained by Mr. Northup's adviser was, that intelligence would be conveyed to him in the night, giving him an opportunity of secreting me before the arrival of the sheriff.

This apprehension had the effect of expediting matters considerably. The sheriff, who lived in one direction from the village, was requested to hold himself in readiness immediately after midnight, while the Judge was informed he would be called upon at the same time. It is but justice to say, that the authorities at Marksville cheerfully rendered all the assistance in their power.

As soon after midnight as bail could be perfected, and the Judge's signature obtained, a carriage, containing Mr. Northup and the sheriff, driven by the landlord's son, rolled rapidly out of the village of Marksville, on the road towards Bayou Boeuf.

It was supposed that Epps would contest the issue involving my right to liberty, and it therefore suggested itself to Mr. Northup, that the testimony of the sheriff, describing my first meeting with the former, might perhaps become material on the trial. It was accordingly arranged during the ride, that, before I had an opportunity of speaking to Mr. Northup, the sheriff should propound to me certain questions agreed upon, such as the number and names of my children, the name of my wife before marriage, of places I knew at the North, and so forth. If my answers corresponded with the statements given him, the evidence must necessarily be considered conclusive.

At length, shortly after Epps had left the field, with the consoling assurance that he would soon return and warm us, as was stated in the conclusion of the preceding chapter, they came in sight of the plantation, and discovered us at work. Alighting from the carriage, and directing the driver to proceed to the great house, with instructions not to mention to any one the object of their errand until they met again, Northup and the sheriff turned from the highway, and came towards us across the cotton field. We observed them, on looking up at the carriage—one several rods in advance of the other. It was a singular and unusual thing to see white men approaching us in that manner, and especially at that early hour in the morning, and Uncle Abram and Patsey made some remarks, expressive of their astonishment. Walking up to Bob, the sheriff inquired:

"Where's the boy they call Platt?"

"Thar he is, massa," answered Bob, pointing to me, and twitching off his hat.

I wondered to myself what business he could possibly have with me, and turning round, gazed at him until he had approached within a step. During my long residence on the bayou, I had become familiar with the face of every planter within many miles; but this man was an utter stranger—certainly I had never seen him before.

"Your name is Platt, is it?" he asked.

"Yes, master," I responded.

Pointing towards Northup, standing a few rods distant, he demanded—"Do you know that man?"

I looked in the direction indicated, and as my eyes rested on his countenance, a world of images thronged my brain; a multitude of well-known faces—Anne's, and the dear children's, and my old dead father's; all the scenes and associations of childhood and youth; all the friends of other and happier days, appeared and disappeared, flitting and floating like dissolving shadows before the vision of my imagination, until at last the perfect memory of the man recurred to me, and throwing up my hands towards Heaven, I exclaimed, in a voice louder than I could utter in a less exciting moment—

"Henry B. Northup! Thank God—thank God!"

In an instant I comprehended the nature of his business, and felt that the hour of my deliverance was at hand. I started towards him, but the sheriff stepped before me.

"Stop a moment," said he; "have you any other name than Platt?"

"Solomon Northup is my name, master," I replied.

"Have you a family?" he inquired.

"I had a wife and three children."

"What were your children's names?"

"Elizabeth, Margaret and Alonzo."

"And your wife's name before her marriage?"

"Anne Hampton."

"Who married you?"

"Timothy Eddy, of Fort Edward."

"Where does that gentleman live?" again pointing to Northup, who remained standing in the same place where I had first recognized him.

"He lives in Sandy Hill, Washington county, New York," was the reply.

He was proceeding to ask further questions, but I pushed past him, unable longer to restrain myself. I seized my old acquaintance by both hands. I could not speak. I could not refrain from tears.

"Sol," he said at length, "I'm glad to see you."

I essayed to make some answer, but emotion choked all utterance, and I was silent. The slaves, utterly confounded, stood gazing upon the scene, their open mouths and rolling eyes indicating the utmost wonder and astonishment. For ten years I had dwelt among them, in the field and in the cabin, borne the same hardships, partaken the same fare, mingled my griefs with theirs, participated in the same scanty joys; nevertheless, not until this hour, the last I was to remain among them, had the remotest suspicion of my true name, or the slightest knowledge of my real history been entertained by any one of them.

Not a word was spoken for several minutes, during which time I clung fast to Northup, looking up into his face, fearful I should awake and find it all a dream.

"Throw down that sack," Northup added, finally; "your cotton-picking days are over. Come with us to the man you live with."

I obeyed him, and walking between him and the sheriff, we moved towards the great house. It was not until we had proceeded some distance that I had recovered my voice sufficiently to ask if my family were all living. He informed me he had seen Anne, Margaret and Elizabeth but a short time previously; that Alonzo was also living, and all were well. My mother, however, I could never see again. As I began to recover in some measure from the sudden and great excitement which so overwhelmed me, I grew faint and weak, insomuch it was with difficulty I could walk. The sheriff took hold of my arm and assisted me, or I think I should have fallen. As we entered the yard, Epps stood by the gate, conversing with the driver. That young man, faithful to his instructions, was entirely unable to give him the least information in answer to his repeated inquiries of what was going on. By the time we reached him he was almost as much amazed and puzzled as Bob or Uncle Abram.

Shaking hands with the sheriff, and receiving an introduction to Mr. Northup, he invited them into house, ordering me, at the same time, to bring in some wood. It was some time before I succeeded in cutting an armful, having, somehow, unaccountably lost the power of wielding the axe with any manner of precision. When I entered with it at last, the table was strewn with papers, from one of which Northup was reading. I was probably longer than necessity required, in placing the sticks upon the fire, being particular as to the exact position of each individual one of them. I heard the words, "the said Solomon Northup," and "the deponent further says," and "free citizen of New-York," repeated frequently, and from these expressions understood that the secret I had so long retained from Master and Mistress Epps, was finally developing. I lingered as long as prudence permitted, and was about leaving the room, when Epps inquired,

"Platt, do you know this gentleman?"

"Yes, master," I replied, "I have known him as long as I can remember."

"Where does he live?"

"He lives in New-York."

"Did you ever live there?"

"Yes, master—born and bred there."

"You was free, then. Now you d—d nigger," he exclaimed, "why did you not tell me that when I bought you?"

"Master Epps," I answered, in a somewhat different tone than the one in which I had been accustomed to address him "Master Epps, you did not take the trouble to ask me; besides, I told one of my owners— the man that kidnapped me—that I was free, and was whipped almost to death for it."

"It seems there has been a letter written for you by somebody. Now, who is it?" he demanded, authoritatively. I made no reply.

"I say, who wrote that letter?" he demanded again.

"Perhaps I wrote it myself", I said.

"You haven't been to Marksville post-office and back before light, I know."

He insisted upon my informing him, and I insisted I would not. He made many vehement threats against the man, whoever he might be, and intimated the bloody and savage vengeance he would wreak upon him, when he found him out. his whole manner and language exhibited a feeling of anger towards the unknown person who had written for me, and of fretfulness at the idea of losing so much property. Addressing Mr. Northup he swore if he had only had an hour's notice of his coming, he would have saved him the trouble of taking me back to New-York; that he would have run me into the swamp, or some other place out of the way, where all the sheriffs on earth couldn't have found me.

I walked out into the yard, and was entering the kitchen door, when something struck me in the back. Aunt Phebe, emerging from the back door of the great house with a pan of potatoes, had thrown one of them with unnecessary violence, thereby giving me to understand that she wished to speak to me a moment confidentially. Running up to me, she whispered in my ear with great earnestness,

"Lor a' mity, Platt! what d'ye think? Dem two men come after ye. Heard 'em tell masse you free— got wife and tree children back thar whar you come from. Goin' wid 'em? Fool if ye don't—wish I could go," and Aunt Phebe ran on in this manner at a rapid rate.

Presently Mistress Epps made her appearance in the kitchen. She said many things to me, and wondered why I had not told her who I was. She expressed her regret, complimenting me by saying she had rather lose any other servant on the plantation. Had Patsey that day stood in my place, the measure of my mistress' joy would have overflowed. Now there was no one left who could mend a chair or a piece of furniture—no one who was of any use about the house—no one who could play for her on the violin —and Mistress Epps was actually affected to tears.

Epps had called to Bob to bring up his saddle horse. The other slaves, also, overcoming their fear of the penalty, had left their work and come to the yard. They were standing behind the cabins, out of sight of Epps. They beckoned me to come to them, and with all the eagerness of curiosity, excited to the highest pitch, conversed with and questioned me. If I could repeat the exact words they uttered, with the same emphasis—if I could paint their several attitudes, and the expression of their countenances—it would be indeed an interesting picture. In their estimation, I had suddenly arisen to an immeasurable height—had become a being of immense importance.

The legal papers having been served, and arrangements made with Epps to meet them the next day at Marksville, Northup and the sheriff entered the carriage to return to the latter place. As I was about mounting to the driver's seat, the sheriff said I ought to bid Mr. and Mrs. Epps good bye. I ran back to the piazza where they were standing, and taking off my hat, said,

"Good-bye, missis."

"Good-bye, Platt," said Mrs. Epps, kindly.

"Good-bye, master."

"Ah! you d—d nigger," muttered Epps, in a surly, malicious tone of voice, "you needn't feel so cussed tickled—you ain't gone yet—I'll see about this business at Marksville to-morrow."

I was only a "nigger" and knew my place, but felt as strongly as if I had been a white man, that it would have been an inward comfort, had I dared to have given him a parting kick. On my way back toward the carriage, Patsey ran from behind a cabin and threw her arms about my neck.

"Oh! Platt," she cried, tears streaming down her face, "you're goin' to be free—you're goin' way off yonder where we'll neber see ye any more. You've saved me a good many whipping, Platt; I'm glad you're goin' to be free—but oh! de Lord, de Lord! what'll become of me?"

I disengaged myself from her, and entered the carriage. The driver cracked his whip and away we rolled. I looked back and saw Patsey, with drooping head, half reclining on the ground; Mrs. Epps was on the piazza; Uncle Abram, and Bob, and Wiley, and Aunt Phebe stood by the gate, gazing after me. I waved my hand, but the carriage turned a bend of the bayou, hiding them from my eyes forever.

We stopped a moment at Carey's sugar house, where a great number of slaves were at work, such an establishment being a curiosity to a Northern man. Epps dashed by us on horseback at full speed—on the way, as we learned next day, to the "Pine Woods," to see William Ford, who had brought me into the country.

Tuesday, the fourth of January, Epps and his counsel, the Hon. E. Taylor, Northup, Waddill, the Judge and sheriff of Avoyelles, and myself, met in a room in the village of Marksville. Mr. Northup stated the facts in regard to me, and presented his commission, and the affidavits accompanying it. The sheriff described the scene in the cotton field. I was also interrogated at great length. Finally, Mr. Taylor assured his client that he was satisfied, and that litigation would not only be expensive, but utterly useless. In accordance with his advice, a paper was drawn up and signed by the proper parties, wherein Epps acknowledged he was satisfied of my right to freedom, and formally surrendered me to the authorities of New-York. It was also stipulated that it be entered of record in the recorder's office of Avoyelles.

Mr. Northup and myself immediately hastened to the landing, and taking passage on the first steamer that arrived, were soon floating down Red River, up which, with such desponding thoughts, I had been borne twelve years before.

Chapter 22

As the steamer glided on its way towards New-Orleans, perhaps I was not happy—perhaps there was no difficulty in restraining myself from dancing round the deck—perhaps I did not feel grateful to the man who had come so many hundred miles for me—perhaps I did not light his pipe, and wait and watch his word, and run at his slightest bidding. If I didn't— well, no matter.

We tarried at New-Orleans two days. During that time I pointed out the locality of Freeman's slave pen, and the room in which Ford purchased me. We happened to meet Theophilus in the street, but I did not think it worth while to renew acquaintance with him. From respectable citizens we ascertained he had become a low, miserable rowdy—a broken-down, disreputable man.

We also visited the recorder, Mr. Genois, to whom Senator Soule's letter was directed, and found him a man well deserving the wide and honorable reputation that he bears. He very generously furnished us with a sort of legal pass, over his signature and seal of office, and as it contains the recorder's description of my personal appearance, it may not be amiss to insert it here. The following is a copy:

State of Louisiana—City of New-Orleans:

Recorder's Office, Second District.

To all to whom these presents shall come:—

This is to certify that Henry B. Northup, Esquire, of the county of Washington, New-York, has produced before me due evidence of the freedom of Solomon, a mulatto man, aged about forty-two years, five feet, seven inches and six lines, woolly hair, and chestnut eyes, who is a native born of the State of New-York. That the said Northup, being about bringing the said Solomon to his native place, through the southern routes, the civil authorities are requested to let the aforesaid colored man Solomon pass unmolested, he demeaning well and properly.

Given under my hand and the seal of the city of New-Orleans this 7th January, 1853. [L. S.] "TH. GENOIS, Recorder.

On the 8th we came to Lake Pontchartrain, by railroad, and, in due time, following the usual route, reached Charleston. After going on board the steamboat, and paying our passage at this city, Mr. Northup was called upon by a custom-house officer to explain why he had not registered his servant. He replied that he had no servant—that, as the agent of New-York, he was accompanying a free citizen of that State from slavery to freedom, and did not desire nor intend to make any registry whatever. I conceived from his conversation and manner, though I may perhaps be entirely mistaken, that no great pains would be taken to avoid whatever difficulty the Charleston officials. might deem proper to create. At length, however, we were permitted to proceed, and, passing through Richmond, where I caught a glimpse of Goodin's pen, arrived in Washington January 17th, 1853.

We ascertained that both Burch and Radburn were still residing in that city. Immediately a complaint was entered with a police magistrate of Washington, against James H. Burch, for kidnapping and selling me into slavery. He was arrested upon a warrant issued by Justice Goddard, and returned before Justice Mansel, and held to bail in the sum of three thousand dollars. When first arrested, Burch was much excited, exhibiting the utmost fear and alarm, and before reaching the justice's office on Louisiana Avenue, and before knowing the precise nature of the complaint, begged the police to permit him to consult Benjamin O. Shekels, a slave trader of seventeen years, standing, and his former partner. The latter became his bail.

At ten o'clock, the 18th of January, both parties appeared before the magistrate. Senator Chase, of Ohio, Hon. Orville Clark, of Sandy Hill, and Mr. Northup acted as counsel for the prosecution, and Joseph H. Bradley for the defense.

Gen. Orville Clark was called and sworn as a witness, and testified that he had known me from childhood, and that I was a free man, as was my father before me. Mr. Northup then testified to the same, and proved the facts connected with his mission to Avoyelles.

Ebenezer Radburn was then sworn for the prosecution, and testified he was forty-eight years old; that he was a resident of Washington, and had known Burch fourteen years; that in 1841 he was keeper of Williams' slave pen; that he remembered the fact of my confinement in the pen that year. At this point it was admitted by the defendant's counsel, that I had been placed in the pen by Burch in the spring of 1841, and hereupon the prosecution rested.

Benjamin O. Shekels was then offered as a witness by the prisoner. Benjamin is a large, coarse-featured man, and the reader may perhaps get a somewhat correct conception of him by reading the exact language he used in answer to the first question of defendant's lawyer. He was asked the place of his nativity, and his reply, uttered in a sort of rowdyish way, was in these very words—

"I was born in Ontario county, New-York, and weighed fourteen pounds!"

Benjamin was a prodigious baby! He further testified that he kept the Steamboat Hotel in Washington in 1841, and saw me there in the spring of that year. He was proceeding to state what he had heard two men say, when Senator Chase raised a legal objection, to wit, that the sayings of third persons, being hearsay, was improper evidence. The objection was overruled by the Justice, and Shekels continued, stating that two men came to his hotel and represented they had a colored man for sale; that they had an interview with Burch; that they stated they came from Georgia, but he did not remember the county; that they gave a full history of the boy, saying he was a bricklayer, and played on the violin; that Burch remarked he would purchase if they could agree; that they went out and brought the boy in, and that I was the same person. He further testified, with as much unconcern as if it was the truth, that I represented I was born and bred in Georgia; that one of the young men with me was my master; that I exhibited a great deal of regret at parting with him, and he believed "got into tears!"—nevertheless, that I insisted my master had a right to sell me; that he ought to sell me; and the remarkable reason I gave was, according to Shekels, because he, my master, "had been gambling and on a spree!"

He continued, in these words, copied from the minutes taken on the examination: "Burch interrogated the boy in the usual manner, told him if he purchased him he should send him south. The boy said he had no objection, that in fact he would like to go south. Burch paid $650 for him, to my knowledge. I don't know what name was given him, but think it was not Solomon. Did not know the name of either of the two men. They were in my tavern two or three hours, during which time the boy played on the violin. The bill of sale was signed in my bar-room. It was a printed blank, filled up by Burch. Before 1838 Burch was my partner. Our business was buying and selling slaves. After that time he was a partner of Theophilus Freeman, of New-Orleans. Burch bought here—Freeman sold there!"

Shekels, before testifying, had heard my relation of the circumstances connected with the visit to Washington with Brown and Hamilton, and therefore, it was, undoubtedly, he spoke of "two men," and of my playing on the violin. Such was his fabrication, utterly untrue, and yet there was found in Washington a man who endeavored to corroborate him.

Benjamin A. Thorn testified he was at Shekels' in 1841, and saw a colored boy playing on a fiddle. "Shekels said he was for sale. Heard his master tell him he should sell him. The boy acknowledged to me he was a slave. I was not present when the money was paid. Will not swear positively this is the boy. The master came near shedding tears: I think the boy did! I have been engaged in the business of taking slaves south, off and on, for twenty years. When I can't do that I do something else."

I was then offered as a witness, but, objection being made, the court decided my evidence inadmissible. It was rejected solely on the ground that I was a colored man—the fact of my being a free citizen of New-York not being disputed.

Shekels having testified there was a bill of sale executed, Burch was called upon by the prosecution to produce it, inasmuch as such a paper would corroborate the testimony of Thorn and Shekels. The prisoner's counsel saw the necessity of exhibiting it, or giving some reasonable explanation for its non-production. To effect the latter, Burch himself was offer- as a witness in his own behalf It was contended by counsel for the people, that such testimony should not be allowed—that it was in contravention of every rule of evidence, and if permitted would defeat the ends of justice. His testimony, however, was received by the court! He made oath that such a bill of sale had been drawn up and signed, but he had lost it, and did not know what had become of it! Thereupon the magistrate was requested to dispatch a police officer to Burch's residence, with directions to bring his books, containing his bills of sales for the year 1841. The request was granted, and before any measure could be taken to prevent it, the officer had obtained possession of the books, and brought them into court. The sales for the year 1841 were found, and carefully examined, but no sale of myself, by any name, was discovered!

Upon this testimony the court held the fact to be established, that Burch came innocently and honestly by me, and accordingly he was discharged.

An attempt was then made by Burch and his satellites, to fasten upon me the charge that I had conspired with the two white men to defraud him—with what success, appears in an extract taken from an article in the New-York Times, published a day or two subsequent to the trial: "The counsel for the defendant had drawn up, before the defendant was discharged; an affidavit, signed by Burch, and had a warrant out against the colored man for a conspiracy with the two white men before referred to, to defraud Burch out of six hundred and twenty-five dollars. The warrant was served, and the colored man arrested and brought before officer Goddard. Burch and his witnesses appeared in court, and H. B. Northup appeared as counsel for the colored man, stating he was ready to proceed as counsel on the part of the defendant, and asking no delay whatever. Burch, after consulting privately a short time with Shekels, stated to the magistrate that he wished him to dismiss the complaint, as he would not proceed farther with it. Defendant's counsel stated to the magistrate that if the complaint was withdrawn, it must be without the request or consent of the defendant. Burch then asked the magistrate to let him have the complaint and the warrant, and he took them. The counsel for the defendant objected to his receiving them, and insisted they should remain as part of the records of the court, and that the court should endorse the proceedings which had been had under the process. Burch delivered them up, and the court rendered a judgment. of discontinuance by the request of the prosecutor, and filed it in his office."

There may be those who will affect to believe the statement of the slave-trader—those, in whose minds his allegations will weigh heavier than mine. I am a poor colored man—one of a down-trodden and degraded race, whose humble voice may not be heeded by the oppressor—but knowing the truth, and with a full sense of my accountability, I do solemnly declare before men, and before God, that any charge or assertion, that I conspired directly or indirectly with any person or persons to sell myself; that any other account of my visit to Washington, my capture and imprisonment in Williams, slave pen, shall is contained in these pages, is utterly and absolutely false. I never played on the violin in Washington. I never was in the Steamboat Hotel, and never saw Thorn or Shekels, to my knowledge, in my life, until last January. The story of the trio of slave-traders is a fabrication as absurd as it is base and unfounded. Were it true, I should not have turned aside on my way back to liberty for the purpose of prosecuting Burch. I should have avoided rather than sought him. I should have known that such a step would have resulted in rendering me infamous. Under the circumstances —longing as I did to behold my family, and elated with the prospect of returning home—it is an outrage upon probability to suppose I would have run the hazard, not only of exposure, but of a criminal prosecution and conviction, by voluntarily placing myself in the position I did, if the statements of Burch and his confederates contain a particle of truth. I took pains to seek him out, to confront him in a court of law, charging him with the crime of kidnapping; and the only motive that impelled me to this step, was a burning sense of the wrong he had inflicted upon me, and a desire to bring him to justice. He was acquitted, in the manner, and by such means as have been described. A human tribunal has permitted him to escape; but there is another and a higher tribunal, where false testimony will not prevail, and where I am willing, so far at least as these statements are concerned, to be judged at last.

We left Washington on the 20th of January, and proceeding by the way of Philadelphia, New-York, and Albany, reached Sandy Hill in the night of the 21st. My heart overflowed with happiness as I looked around upon old familiar scenes, and found myself in the midst of friends of other days. The following morning I started, in company with several acquaintances, for Glens Falls, the residence of Anne and our children.

As I entered their comfortable cottage, Margaret was the first that met me. She did not recognize me. When I left her, she was but seven years old, a little prattling girl, playing with her toys. Now she was grown to womanhood—was married, with a bright-eyed boy standing by her side. Not forgetful of his enslaved, unfortunate grand-father, she had named the child Solomon Northup Staunton. When told who I was, she was overcome with emotion, and unable to speak. Presently Elizabeth entered the room, and Anne came running from the hotel, having been informed of my arrival. They embraced me, and with tears flowing down their cheeks, hung upon my neck. But I draw a veil over a scene which can better be imagined than described.

When the violence of our emotions had subsided to a sacred joy—when the household gathered round the fire, that sent out its warm and crackling comfort through the room, we conversed of the thousand events that had occurred—the hopes and fears, the joys and sorrows, the trials and troubles we had each experienced during the long separation. Alonzo was absent in the western part of the State. The boy had written to his mother a short time previous, of the prospect of his obtaining sufficient money to purchase my freedom. From his earliest years, that had been the chief object of his thoughts and his ambition. They knew I was in bondage. The letter written on board the brig, and Clem Ray himself , had given them that information. But where I was, until the arrival of Bass' letter, was a matter of conjecture. Elizabeth and Margaret once returned from school— so Anne informed me— weeping bitterly. On inquiring the cause of the children's sorrow, it was found that, while studying geography, their attention had been attracted to the picture of slaves working in the cotton-field, and an overseer following them with his whip. It reminded them of the sufferings father might be, and, as it happened, actually was, enduring in the South. Numerous incidents, such as these, were related—incidents showing they still held me in constant remembrance, but not, perhaps, of sufficient interest to the reader, to be recounted.

My narrative is at an end. I have no comments to make upon the subject of Slavery. Those who read this book may form their own opinions of the "peculiar institution." What it may be in other States, I do not profess to know; what it is in the region of Red River, is truly and faithfully delineated in these pages. This is no fiction, no exaggeration. If I have failed in anything, it has been in presenting to the reader too prominently the bright side of the picture. I doubt not hundreds have been as unfortunate as myself; that hundreds of free citizens have been kidnapped and sold into slavery, and are at this moment wearing out their lives on plantations in Texas and Louisiana. But I forbear. Chastened and subdued in spirit by the sufferings I have borne, and thankful to that good Being through whose mercy I have been restored to happiness and liberty, I hope henceforward to lead an upright though lowly life, and rest at last in the church yard where my father sleeps.

Solomon Northup

DANIEL A. PAYNE (1811-1893)

Introduction

Bishop Daniel A. Payne was an historian, educator and A.M.E. (African Methodist Episcopal) minister.

Daniel A. Payne, born in Charleston, South Carolina, the son of free blacks, attended a private school in Charleston, South Carolina and Gettysburg Seminary in Pennsylvania. Payne was the first Bishop to have formal theological seminary training. He, more than any other individual, is responsible for the A.M.E. church's interest in trained ministry.

Payne was ordained an elder in the Lutheran Church in 1837. He was the first Black president of a Black college in the western world, (Wilberforce University), where he was president for sixteen years.

He was elected the Historiographer of the A.M.E. Church in 1848. Payne was elected a Bishop at the General Conference in New York City on May 7, 1852. He was an accomplished author of important books. His *History of the A.M.E. Church*, 1891, and *Recollections of Seventy Years*, 1888, were his greatest writings and were an authoritative source of history of the first 75 years of the A.M.E. church.

A deep vein of genuine piety pervades nearly all the productions of Bishop Payne. As a pulpit orator, he stands deservedly high. In stature, he is rather under the medium size, about three fourths African, rather sharper features than the average of his race, and appears to be about fifty years of age. He is very popular, both as a writer and a speaker, with his own color. The moral, social, and political standard of the black man has been much elevated by the influence of Bishop Payne.

William Wells Brown

American Slavery Brutalizes Man, 1839

Introduction

In June 1839, Payne delivered the oration *American Slavery Brutalizes Man* at Fordsboro, New York, when he was ordained by the Franckean Synod of the Lutheran Church. The speech was delivered in support of a synodical report to end slavery in America. The speech helped persuade the synod leadership to support the report.

Mr President: I move the adoption of the Report, because it is based upon the following propositions:

American Slavery brutalizes man—destroys his moral agency, and subverts the moral government of God.

Sir, I am opposed to slavery, not because it enslaves the black man, but because it enslaves man. And were all the slaveholders in this land men of color, and the slaves white men, I would be as thorough and uncompromising an abolitionist as I now am; for whatever and whenever I may see a being in the form of a man, enslaved by his fellow man, without respect to his complexion, I shall lift up my voice to plead his cause, against all the claims of his proud oppressor; and I shall do it not merely from the sympathy which man feels towards suffering man, but because God, the living God, whom I dare not disobey, has commanded me to open my mouth for the dumb, and to plead the cause of the oppressed.

Slavery brutalizes man. We know that the word man, in its primitive sense, signifies. But the intellectual and moral structure of man, and the august relations which he sustains to the Deity, have thrown around the name, and being designated by it, a halo of glory, brightened by all the ideas, that are ennobling on earth, and blessed in eternity. This being God created but a little lower than the angels, and crowned him with glory and honor; but slavery hurls him down from his elevated position, to the level of brutes, strikes this crown of glory from his head and fastens upon his neck the galling yoke, and compels him to labor like an ox, through summer's sun and winter's snow, without remuneration. Does a man take the calf from the cow and sell it to the butcher? So slavery tears the child from the arms of the reluctant mother, and barters it to the soul trader for a young colt, or some other commodity! Does the bird catcher tear away the dove from his mate? So slavery separates the groaning husband from the embraces of his distracted and weeping wife! And are the beasts of the forest hunted, tortured and slain at the pleasure of the cruel hunter? So are the slaves hunted, tortured and slain by the cruel monster slavery! To treat a man like a brute is to brutalize him. We have seen that slavery treats man like a brute, therefore slavery brutalizes man! But does slavery stop here? Is it content with merely treating the external man like a brute? No, sir, it goes further, and with a heart as brazen as that of Belshazzar and hands still more sacrilegious, it lays hold of the immortal mind, seizes the will, and binds that which Jehovah did not bind—fetters that which the Eternal made as free to move and act as the breath of Heaven. "It destroys moral agency!" To destroy moral agency is to fetter or obstruct the will of man. Now let us see if slavery is innocent of this. The very moment that a man conceives the diabolic design of enslaving his brother's body, that very moment does he also conceive the still more heinous design of fettering his will, for well does he know that in order to make his dominion supreme over the body, he must fetter the living spring of all its motions. Hence, the first lesson the slave is taught is to yield his will unreservedly and exclusively to the dictates of his master. And if a slave desire to educate himself or his children, in obedience to the dictates of reason or the laws of God, he does not, he cannot do it without the consent of his master. Does reason and circumstances and the Bible command a slave to preach the gospel of his brethren? Slavery arises, and with a frown, an oath and a whip, fetters or obstructs the holy volition of his soul! I knew a pious slave in Charleston who was a licensed exhorter in the Methodist Episcopal Church; this good man was in the habit of spending his Saturday nights on the surrounding plantations, preaching to the slaves. One night, as usual, he got into a canoe, sailed upon James' Island. While in the very act of preaching the unsearchable riches of Christ to dying men, the patrols seized him and whipped him in the most cruel manner, and compelled him to promise that he would never return to preach again to those slaves. In the year 1834, several colored brethren, who were also exhorters in the Methodist Episcopal Church commenced preaching to several destitute white families, who gained a subsistence by cultivating some poor lands about three or four miles from Charleston. The first Sunday I was present; the house was nearly filled with these poor white farmers. The master of the house was awakened to a sense of his lost condition. During the following week he was converted. On the third Sunday from the day he was convinced of sin he died in the triumphs of faith, and went to heaven. On the fourth Sunday from the time the dear brethren began to preach, the patrols scented their tract, and put them to chase. Thus, an end was put to their labors. Their willing souls were fettered, and the poor whites constrained to go without the preaching of the gospel. In a word, it is in view of man's moral agency that God commands him to shun vice, and practice virtue. But what female slave can do this? I lived twenty-four years in the midst of slavery and never knew but six female slaves who were reputedly virtuous! What profit is to the female slave that she is disposed to be virtuous? Her will, like her body, is not her own; they are both at the pleasure of her master; and he brands them at his will. So it subverts the moral government of God.

In view of the moral agency of man, God hath most wisely and graciously given him a code of laws, and certain positive precepts, to control and regulate moral actions. This code of laws, and these positive precepts, with the divine influence which they are naturally calculated to exert on the mind of man, constitutes his moral government.

Now, to nullify these laws—to weaken or destroy their legitimate influence on the human mind, or to hinder man from yielding universal and entire obedience to them is to subvert the moral government of God.

Now, slavery nullifies these laws and precepts—weakens and destroys their influence over the human mind, and hinders men from yielding universal and entire obedience to them; therefore slavery subverts the moral government of God. This is the climax of the sin of slavery! This is the blackest, foulest, and most horrid feature of the heaven-daring Monster! He stretcheth out his hand against God, and strengtheneth himself against the Almighty-he runneth on him, even on his neck, upon the thick bosses of his buckler. Thus saith the Lord, "Thou shalt not commit adultery." But does the man who owns a hundred females obey the law? Does he not nullify it and compel the helpless woman to disobey God? Concerning the religious instruction of children, thus saith the Lord, "Bring them up in the nurture and admonition of the Lord." But what saith slavery? "They are my property, and shall be brought up to serve me." They shall not even learn to read his word, in order that they may be brought up in his nurture and admonition. If any man doubts this, let him read the slave code of Louisiana and see if it is not death to teach slaves. Thus saith the Lord, "Remember the Sabbath day, to keep it holy." Does not slavery nullify this law, and compel the slave to work on the Sabbath? Thus saith the Lord, "Obey thy father and thy mother." Can the slave children obey this command of God? Does not slavery command the children to obey the master and let him alone? Thus saith the Son of God, "What God hath joined together let no man put asunder." Does not slavery nullify this law, by breaking the sacred bands of wedlock, and separating the husband and wife forever? Thus saith the Son of God, "Search the Scriptures." Does not slavery seal up the word of God and make it criminal for the slave to read it? In 1834, the legislature of South Carolina enacted a law prohibiting the instruction of any slave; and Mr. Lawrence in a pamphlet which he published in 1835, to defend this law, declared that if the slaves were permitted to read the Bible, ninety of them would become infidels, like Voltaire, where ten would become Christians. "Go ye into all the world, and preach the Gospel unto every creature," saith the Son of God. Does slavery permit it? In 1835, a minister of the Episcopal Church, in the city of Charleston, appealed to the civil authority for permission to preach to the free population of an evening, but they would not permit him.

The objector may reply, that at the present moment there are four Methodist missionaries, and one Lutheran, laboring among the slave population of South Carolina. We answer, that this is true, and we are glad of it; but this fact does not overthrow our proposition, nor falsify what we have stated, for although a few planters have permitted the Gospel to be preached to their slaves, the majority of them prohibit it, and this permission is extraneous to slavery and is no part of its creed or code. Slavery never legislates for the religious instruction of slaves, but, on the contrary, legislates to perpetuate their ignorance; and there are laws this very moment in the statute books of South Carolina and other states, prohibiting the religious instruction of slaves. But this is not all that slavery does to subvert the moral government of God. The slaves are sensible of the oppression exercised by their masters; and they see these masters on the Lord's day worshiping in his holy Sanctuary. They hear their masters professing Christianity; they see their masters preaching the Gospel; they hear these masters praying in their families, and they know that oppression and slavery are inconsistent with the Christian religion; therefore they scoff at religion itself-mock their masters, and distrust both the goodness and justice of God. Yes, I have known them even to question His existence. I speak not of what others have told me, but of what I have both seen and heard from the slaves themselves. I have heard the mistress ring the bell for family prayer, and I have seen the servants immediately begin to sneer and laugh; and have heard them declare they would not go in to prayers, adding, if I go in she will only just read, "Servants obey your masters"; but she will not read, "Break every yoke, and let the oppressed go free." I have seen colored men at the church door, scoffing at the ministers, while they were preaching, and saying, you had better go home, and set your slaves free. A few nights ago between ten and eleven o'clock a runaway slave came to the house where I live for safety and succor. I asked him if he was a Christian. "No sir," said he, "white men treat us so bad in Mississippi that we can't be Christians."

Sir, I taught school in Charleston five years. In 1834 the legislature of our state enacted a law to prohibit colored teachers. My school was filled with children and youth of the most promising talents; and when I looked upon them and remembered that in a few more weeks this school shall be closed and I be permitted no more to teach them, notwithstanding I had been a professor seven years, I began to question the existence of the Almighty and to say, if indeed there is a God, does he deal justly? Is he a just God? Is he a holy Being? If so, why does he permit a handful of dying men thus to oppress us? Why does he permit them to hinder me from teaching these children, when nature, reason and Revelation command me to teach them? Thus I began to question the divine government and to murmur at the administration of His providence. And could I do otherwise, while slavery's cruelties were pressing and grinding my soul in the dust, and robbing me and my people of those privileges which it was hugging to its breast, and giving thousands to perpetuate the blessing which it was tearing away from us? Sir, the very man who made the law alluded to, did that very year, increase the property of South Carolina College.

In a word, slavery tramples the laws of the living God under its unhallowed feet—weakens and destroys the influence which those laws are calculated to exert over the mind of man, and constrains the oppressed to blaspheme the name of the Almighty. For I have often heard them sneeringly say, that "The Almighty made Charleston on Saturday night, when he was weary, and in a great hurry." O, Brethren of the Franckean Synod! awake! Awake to the battle and hurl the hottest thunders of divine truth at the head of this cruel monster, until he shall fall to rise no more, and the groans of the enslaved are converted into the songs of the free!

Daniel A. Payne. Lutheran Herald and Journal of the
Fort Plain, N.Y., Franckean Synod, August 1, 1839

To the Colored People of the United States

Men, brethren, sisters: A crisis is upon us which no one can enable us to meet, conquer, and convert into blessings for all concerned, but that God who builds up one nation and breaks down another.

For more than one generation, associations of white men, entitled Colonization Societies, have been engaged in plans and efforts for our expatriation; these have been met sometimes by denunciations, sometimes by ridicule, often by argument; but now the American government has assumed the work and responsibility of colonizing us in some foreign land within the torrid zone, and is now maturing measures to consummate this scheme of expatriation.

But let us never forget that there is a vast difference between voluntary associations of men and the legally constituted authorities of a country; while the former may be held in utter contempt, the latter must always be respected. To do so is a moral and religious, as well as a political duty.

The opinions of the government are based upon the ideas, that white men and colored men cannot live together as equals in the same country; and that unless a voluntary and peaceable separation is effected now, the time must come when there will be a war of extermination between the two races.

Now, in view of these opinions and purposes of the government, what shall we do? My humble advice is, before all, and first of all,—even before we say yea or nay,—let us seek from the mouth of God. Let every heart be humbled, and every knee bent in prayer before him. Throughout all this land of our captivity, in all this house of our bondage, let our cries ascend perpetually to Heaven for aid and direction.

To your knees, I say, O ye oppressed and enslaved ones of this Christian republic, to your knees, and be there.

Before the throne of God, if nowhere else, the black man can meet his white brother as an equal, and be heard.

It has been said that he is the God of the white man, and not of the black. This is horrible blasphemy—a lie from the pit that is bottomless—believe it not—no—never. Murmur not against the Lord on account of the cruelty and injustice of man. His almighty arm is already stretched out against slavery—against every man, every constitution, and every union that upholds it. His avenging chariot is now moving over the bloody fields of the doomed south, crushing beneath its massive wheels the very foundations of the blasphemous system. Soon slavery shall sink like Pharaoh—even like that brazen-hearted tyrant, it shall sink to rise no more forever.

Haste ye, then, O, hasten to your God; pour the sorrows of your crushed and bleeding hearts into his sympathizing bosom. It is true that "on the side of the oppressor there is power'—the power of the purse and the power of the sword. That is terrible. But listen to what is still more terrible: on the side of the oppressed there is the strong arm of the Lord, the Almighty God of Abraham, and Isaac, and Jacob—before his redeeming power the two contending armies, hostile to each other, and hostile to you, are like chaff before the whirlwind.

Fear not, but believe. He who is for you is more than they who are against you. Trust in him—hang upon his arm—go, hide beneath the shadow of his wings.

O God! Jehovah-jireh! wilt thou not hear us? We are poor, helpless, unarmed, despised. Is it not time for thee to hear the cry of the needy—to judge the poor of the people—to break in pieces the oppressor.

Be, O, be unto us what thou wast unto Israel in the land of Egypt, our Counselor and Guide—our Shield and Buckler—our Great Deliverer—our Pillar of cloud by day—our Pillar of fire by night!

Stand between us and our enemies, O thou angel of the Lord! Be unto us a shining light—to our enemies, confusion and impenetrable darkness. Stand between us till this Red Sea be crossed, and thy redeemed, now sighing, bleeding, weeping, shall shout and sing, for joy, the bold anthem of the free.

Daniel A. Payne, Weekly Anglo-African

SMITH H. PLATT

Introduction

In April, 1868, the Rev. S. H. Platt became the incumbent of Fleet Street M.E. Church, Booklyn, which had been founded in 1850.

He was author of several books, including, *The Gift of Power*, and *Christ and Adornments*.

The Martyrs, and the Fugitive; or a Narrative of the Captivity, Sufferings, and Death of an African Family, and the Slavery and Escape of Their Son

Preface

The reader may wish to know whether the following pages are fictitious or historical. They are both. The chief personages, with their "sentiments, virtues, vices, follies, and peculiarities, surroundings," etc. are historical. The connections in which they are placed are sometimes supposed, and when true, are in some places changed from their real relations to prevent the exposure of the parties, who are still living; yet in no case are they so changed as to distort the facts of the slave system. It is admitted that the heroes of the story are extreme cases, and that it was their misfortune to be such; but the author does not present their experience as an average sample of the sufferings of slave life; he simply vouches for the accuracy of the story as illustrative of the liabilities of their life.

If this feeble effort may avail to stir up the minds of some to a more active hatred of the system, and afford some pecuniary aid to the suffering fugitive, the object in sending it forth will be accomplished.

S. H. P., Brooklyn, April, 1859.

Chapter 1

"Why are you so sad?" exclaimed the playful Molly Myrtle, as her brother laid aside his pen.

"I have just finished writing out the notes that I took the other evening while conversing with the colored man whom you saw at church, and who narrated his experience there."

"What; have you written his history? O, I shall be delighted to read it. Poor man! he must have suffered a great deal, judging from his appearance. But was he not afraid to give you all the facts? How did he know that you would not betray him?"

"He was fearful, and it was a long time before I could persuade him to confide in me. Poor fellow! he seems to distrust everybody. His enjoyment of freedom must be sadly disturbed by his suspicions. I could only get his story by solemnly promising to so disguise it that there would be no danger to him from it."

"But can you rely upon his statement?"

"O yes. He gave so many dates and names of persons and places, and I cross-questioned him so closely, that what he says must be true. Besides, I have independent proof from other sources."

"O! do let me hear it, brother; wont you?"

"This is only the outline that I now have; but if you wish, I will relate the history from this sketch."

"Well, I am all attention; but you must allow me to ask questions if I wish."

"Certainly; that is one of the privileges conceded to such attractive listeners."

About five hundred miles toward the interior of South-Western Africa, was a beautiful valley some miles in length, entirely covered with coarse grass several feet in height, and drained by a small stream, which, running slowly through, marked its course by the tall rushes which lined its banks.

An unusually hot season had dried all the streams in the vicinity but this, and the valley was now a scene of no ordinary activity. The huge and unwieldy hippopotamus wallowed in the stream, and herds of wild animals, such as elands, koodoos, and antelopes, were gathered beneath the shade of the forests that bounded the neighboring hills, or threading their way through the high grass, in the narrow path of the elephant or buffalo, toward the water.

There in that secluded vale lived Bobah, with his wife, Mabowah, their two children, and her aged parents.

Their little hut of reeds was sheltered from the sun and rain by an almost impenetrable grove of banana-trees and shrubs of manioc, interlaced with vines and creepers, and situated upon an elevation near the stream. In a small opening was his patch of manioc (a species of plant used for food, from which cassava and tapioca are prepared) and maize, with here and there beans and ground-nuts interspersed, which, together with the game he took in hunting, furnished them a comfortable support.

The day had been one of extreme heat, and Bobah and his wife were sitting, in the cool of the evening, singing a native song, and watching the gambols of their children as they sported by the door, when suddenly a rustling sound, proceeding from the narrow path that led to his hut, attracted his attention, and before he could rise, several soldiers of his tribe from the village of his chief, several miles distant, rushed upon him, and saying that the chief wanted a talk with him, bound his hands, and ordered him, with his wife and children, to start at once. He obeyed; when, just as they were passing into the shadow of the grove, a succession of dull, heavy sounds caused him to turn, and the scene transfixed him with horror.

Mabowah uttered a shriek of anguish, tore away from her captors, and threw herself upon the bodies of her murdered parents, from which she was driven a moment after by the flames of her burning house.

A short pole was then laid upon the shoulder of Bobah, and firmly lashed round his neck by a tough vine, and Mabowah was bound in the same way to the opposite end, while the children, a boy of thirteen and a girl of eleven, were placed between the two, and fastened by longer pieces to the same pole; then, with some of the captors before and some behind, they began their sad march through the narrow path to the distant village. The silence of their journey was only broken by the sobs of the heart-stricken captives.

Their loss they knew, for none could reverence parents more than they; but what to fear they could not tell.

Had they been subject to some other chief, they knew that this would prove but the beginning of the life-long doom of slavery. But their chief had never sold his people, and to be convicted of some fearful but unknown crime seemed now their fate. Arrived at the village, they were taken at once before the chief, where the presence of a savage half-blood Portuguese revealed their destiny. Their minds instinctively strove to penetrate the dark future before them, but the very hopelessness of the effort threw them back upon the past, and the images of murdered parents, and burning home, and captive children, rose with appalling distinctness before them, till the strong man writhed in agony, and the mother lifted up her voice in the long, low wail of hopeless despair.

Already the chieftain's heart was beginning to relent, when the practiced eye of the trader discovered his hesitation, and another dram from his ready flask, accompanied with a significant glance at a pile of coveted "cloths," decided the question. They were accused of some trifling crime, and condemned, without a hearing, to be sold as slaves.

"The wretch!" exclaimed the indignant Molly, "why did he treat them so?"

"Because the trader had exhibited his cloths, beads, etc, and refused to trade except for slaves and ivory. The chief had but little ivory, and could not then make war for slaves; so the trader made him drunk, and then incited him to sell some of his own people, as was frequently done in similar cases."

"Then why did they kill the old people?"

"Because they were not fit for slaves; and the Africans believe that the relatives of those whom they have greatly injured may bewitch them in revenge; so they kill them, to avoid the power of their supposed witchcraft."

"How horrid! Do they do so all over Africa?"

"No—only where the slave-traders go: it is a result of their business. In those places where the slave trade is not practiced, the people are hospitable and possess many of the virtues of humanity. True, they are heathen, but they have no vice, aside from their idolatry, so sinful and degrading as the slave-holding of their Christian oppressors."

The next day they were marched to another village, from which they were to commence their long and dreary journey to the coast.

When once on the way, the younger slaves were allowed to run free, as there was then little danger of losing them. The older ones were tied as before described, and loaded with ivory and such other articles as the trader had procured, and with the goods still reserved with which to pay for passing through the country.

For several days they proceeded slowly along, sweltering in the heat and parched with thirst, when late one evening they reached a place where they expected to find water and spend the night; but, to their dismay, the bed of the stream was dry, and nothing but a little slimy moisture oozing from the boggy banks could be found. The sultry march, the unavailing cries of the thirsty children for water, with all the increasing tortures of their condition, wrought fearfully upon the mother's mind. The stupid gaze of despair had been succeeded by the wild flashing of an eye that looked upon a purpose too desperate to be told. The deep, mournful shadows of a night of gloom were fast creeping over them.

Great rolling masses of black clouds were scattered like withered leaves in an autumn tempest around the heavens, while through their riven forms the gray moonbeams struggled, and the light and shade chased each other like mad phantoms o'er the earth.

It was just the time to awaken all the fears or arouse all the phrenzy of the superstitious soul, and from one dark and bewildered mind the response arose full and free. As the night deepened, Mabowah called her little girl to her side, and folding her in her arms, she lay down and fixed her eyes upon her child in the long, searching, yet fitful gaze of a mother's love burning through a tottering reason, and mingling with the revengeful flame of a crushed and wounded heart. Nor long did she smother that consuming fire. "Me child a slave! me child a slave!" she uttered through her fevered, trembling lips; "No—no slave!" and her eye flashed and her hands clenched, and all the mother was lost in the maniac. Yet who shall say that her act then was not the most motherly one of her whole life? Slowly and quietly she laid her child upon the ground; then cautiously glanced around upon the sleeping slaves, to make sure that no eye beheld her, then quickly unwound the fibers of a short piece of rope that she had found, twisted it into a strong cord with a running noose around the neck of the innocent sleeper, and then with one hand over her mouth to suppress her cries, with the other she drew the noose tighter and tighter till the sufferer ceased to struggle; then bending low over the form of her dead, while her reeling mind chuckled over her successful cheat of the trader and the doom of slavery, she gazed till the delirious joy burst forth, "Me child no slave—no slave!" And then, as the rushing tide rolled back upon her heart, she uttered one wild shriek of woe, and fell swooning upon her child.

Her accents of triumph, followed so suddenly by her unearthly screech of agony, brought the trader to the spot; and when he saw his loss, his anger vented itself in kicks and blows upon the insensible form before him. The blood flowed freely and relieved her over-charged brain, and she returned to consciousness only to sink into the sleep of exhaustion. When she was aroused by the brutal kicks of the trader, in the morning, the body of her child had been dragged away to be devoured by beasts and fowls, and her own bruised and swollen limbs increased the thirst that was fast drying up the fountain of her life. With tottering steps and haggard looks she was compelled to resume the march; and though again and again did she attempt to throw herself down to die, the lash of the trader drove her on, till, exasperated by her repeated efforts, he resolved to give her to the next chief who should demand a slave, a tooth, (of ivory,) a gun, or cloth, for permission to pass through his territory. After the most terrible sufferings, the party arrived at a place where water was abundant, and there rested a few days to recruit their strength, having lost several on the way by heat and thirst, and many others being scarcely able to stand. The son of Bobah had suffered intensely from the heat, and on the fourth day of their stay at the place, was permitted, with others of his age, to sport in the waters of the stream. Before they were aware of it, they had worked themselves to a greater distance from the camp than was allowed, when the approach of one of the drivers caused them to scamper toward it. In the noise and confusion of their flight they did not observe an immense alligator that plunged into the stream, close in their rear, but in front of young Bobah, and effectually cut off his retreat. A sudden bend in the stream concealed him from the driver, and before his loss was discovered he had disappeared, but whether he had gained the shore and been lost in the high grass, or had become food for the alligator, none could tell.

In either case it was now over with the poor boy. He had gone where no slave-gangs swelter, and no traders drive.

Soon after leaving this place they entered the territory of another chief, and halted while he made the usual demand for a gun, or a slave, etc. and Mabowah was sent to "shake his hand."

"What do you mean, brother, by 'shaking his hand?'"

"In some parts of Africa, when any one wishes to see the chief, or pass through his country, a present is sent to him, which is called 'shaking his hand.' If the present is accepted, the chief returns a much smaller one, and then the parties are friends."

We must here leave them until another evening; but let us not forget that He who has stamped His image within a casing of ebony, is as mindful of their sorrows as He is of ours; and that our duty is to repair, as far as we can, the wrongs done to the parents, by breaking off the yoke from the children and training them for their immortal destiny.

Chapter 2

"I have been thinking, brother," said Molly, at their next interview, "of poor Mabowah, and I wonder how men could be so cruel."

"The heart is deceitful above all things and desperately wicked." If its wickedness can impel to such deeds of blood as midnight assassinations and wholesale piracy for gold, its deceitfulness will furnish some fancied justification of a system which civilization and religion have apparently sanctioned. It is stated that some Greek pirates captured a vessel and murdered all the crew, during Lent, but recoiled with horror at the very thought of eating meat, during the fast of their church, from a well-spread table in the cabin. They could murder without scruple, but to break a fast, was a crime of which they could not be guilty.

"How strange!" said Molly, "and so I suppose that inhuman monster, the trader, persuaded himself that he was not doing a very great wrong."

Very likely. But let us proceed with the story. The mind of the African may not be as gifted in intellect as ours, but his heart glows with a fervor of attachment unknown to us. The powers of his nature running in the channel of affection intensify its action, and he lives in what he loves.

You can imagine some of the feelings of the broken-hearted Bobah, as he started on the next morning with the troop, but with no wife—no boy—no girl—no parents—no home; to go, he knew not whither, and to suffer, he knew not what. Sadly that day he bore his burden on; and the tender flowers looked up and caught his falling tear-drops and treasured them away, while a voice came in the moaning of the breeze, calling him to join his loved and lost in the land of shades.

The trader had learned, at his cost, that with many of his captives liberty was dearer than life, and he could not drive the conviction from their minds, that death was the gateway to the path that would lead them back to their own country; hence he was constantly watching to discover the first indication of a suicidal wish, that he might anticipate the act by giving the slave to the first chief who might demand one.

Bobah was selected that eve, and sent to the village of the chief. This revived his hopes, for he knew that he was but two days' journey from Mabowah, and he might possibly escape to her.

The rainy season now set in, and the village in which he was held, being bounded on three sides by a gloomy forest of impenetrable thickness, and on the other by a small stream, which, when flooded, covered the adjacent plain to the depth of two or three feet, precluded all access during the wet season, except by boats. Here he remained while the rain fell and the water rose; and day after day his stricken heart would speed across the watery waste to lay itself in fancy's dreams beside the pining one who alone bound him to earth, and each time it would return to the bitter consciousness of its misery, all the more painful from the mockery of its hope. Aside from this, his condition was not hard; for, like other slaves there, he was treated more as a dependent than a slave. The belief in witchcraft is so strong, and slaves are supposed to have so much of that dreaded gift, that fear of their supernatural powers secures them better treatment than they might otherwise receive. The slave often owns other slaves, and sometimes a greater number than his master.

But no treatment, however kind, could banish from his mind the recollection of his shaded hut and its loved inmates; and each day of continued rain fell upon him like the dull sound that echoes from the grave when the first clod strikes the coffin of our shrouded joys, and crashes upon our hearts like an avalanche of woe.

Little did he think that the time of their meeting was so nigh.

A day of pouring rain had passed, and the gloomy shadows of twilight seemed rolled along upon the bosom of the wind, that sighed and moaned through the tall palm-trees and died away in the dense forest growth; and the poor people, as if instinctively interpreting the prophetic voices of the breeze, were huddled together, regarding their fetishes with superstitious awe, when a wild shout burst from the outskirts of the village, and before the panic-stricken people could fight or fly, the foe was upon them.

"Who were the foe?" asked Molly.

"A party from far off to the north-west, near the river Congo."

"But why did they fight these people—had they been injured by them?"

"No; but a strong party from a slave ship had sailed far up the Congo, lying in wait near some village, under cover of the thick overhanging bushes by day, and in the night darting out, firing the huts, killing the old, capturing the others, and then pushing on to the next village before the news of their approach could precede them."

They had thus succeeded in securing nearly the desired number, which they hoped to complete by one more attack.

But the village next assaulted proved much stronger than they had supposed, and made a desperate resistance; and though the men were driven from the huts, they seized the boats, which had been left poorly guarded, and spread the alarm.

The position of the slavers now became perilous in the extreme. Their only safety lay in the women and children whom they had captured in the fight. By their means a parley was held; and as the natives still looked upon them with unaffected dread, a "peace palaver" was concluded on condition that the slavers should deliver up the captive villagers, each with a "cloth" for herself and for each of her family, and never disturb them again, and the natives should restore the boats and give a certain number of slaves within a specified time. Hence the war and the surprise, as described.

"How cruel," exclaimed Molly, "to make slaves of their own countrymen in order to buy a peace with their enemies! It would have been good enough for them if they had been captured."

"But you should remember, sister, that the trade has made them what they are. Now, if a chief wants slaves, and his fear of witchcraft or love for his people prevents his taking them, he sends a war-party to burn the first village they can find, and bring away all they can catch."

This warlike tribe sent their party several days' journey to the south-east, where they fell upon the village in which Bobah was kept, and he, with others, was carefully guarded, while the kidnappers rested, and sent a portion of their number to take more captives from a hut which, from the light gleaming faintly through the fog, they supposed stood across the plain upon the hillside. They returned toward morning with a number of prisoners, and, without bringing them on shore, Bobah and his companions were ordered to join them in the boats.

They were soon crowded in; and Bobah, who, in his utter despair, had not even raised his eyes to behold the new captives, had just been thrust, bound, into the bottom of a huge canoe, when, with a scream of frantic joy, a female captive sprang from the boat alongside and clasped him in her arms, her eyes upturned to heaven, and the big tear-drops pouring down her dusky cheeks.

It was his own Mabowah. The hard hearts of their cruel captors were touched, and they were permitted to sit together and tell to each other their tale of suffering and sorrow. A few days after Mabowah was left, as before narrated, another trader passed, who bought her, and on his journey to the coast he had encamped at the edge of the valley just in time to be intercepted by the party, who had mistaken his camp-fire for a village.

After a tedious journey in open boats, and through paths covered with water and hedged in by tall, overhanging grass, adding its showers to the pouring rain whenever shaken by the wind or by the passing traveler, and wallowing through mire and fording streams, and sleeping unsheltered save by some friendly boughs or rushes, they arrived weary, heart-sick, and hopeless, where a boat was waiting to take them to the coast.

They were soon put aboard, shackled and crowded; and, after days and nights of anxious foreboding, were taken to the ship, which proved to be an American of 320 tons' burden, with a Portuguese captain, and a crew of desperate ruffians from different nations.

When once on board, a scene occurred which utterly defies description. Each party, as they were brought upon deck, were made secure, and then each person was thrown into such a position as was best suited to the purpose, and branded by the inhuman villains, on some part of the person, by having a red-hot iron in the form of certain letters or signs dipped into an oily preparation, and then pressed against the naked body till it burnt a deep and ineffaceable scar, to show who was the owner. The screams of the poor children were heart-rending, but a fiend in human shape stood over them with a cat-o'-nine-tails, (a whip of nine lashes with fine wire braided in the end of each lash, and attached to a short, stout handle,) and whenever their outcries or resistance became irksome, they were lashed without mercy on the bare back, breasts, thighs, or wherever the cruelty of the inhuman slaver chose to inflict the wounds, every blow bringing with the returning lash pieces of quivering flesh. Mothers with babes at their breasts were basely branded and lashed, hewed and scarred, till it would seem as if the very heavens must smite the infernal tormentors with the doom that they so richly merited. They were then chained two and two, the right arm and leg of one to the left arm and leg of another, and crowded into the slave rooms between decks. The women were stowed in without being shackled.

Allowing six feet by one foot and four inches for each man, five feet ten inches by one foot four inches for each woman, five feet by one foot two inches for each boy, and four feet six inches by one foot for each girl, the vessel could carry in that crowded state four hundred and fifty-one persons; but in that space were jammed six hundred and two men, women, and children,—all naked and compelled to stow themselves away, by the lash, for a voyage of eight or ten weeks under a tropical sun, and where they could not sit upright,—the space between decks being only two feet ten inches in height. Their sufferings in that confined place, (where they had not as much room, either in length or breadth, as a man in his coffin,) especially when the tarpaulins were accidentally thrown over the gratings, or when the scuttles were closed in foul weather, were utterly indescribable.

When Bobah was shackled for the voyage, his astonishment may be imagined when he found that his fellow-captive was the identical trader who had induced his chief to sell him.

"How singular!" exclaimed Molly. "But how came he to be a slave?"

He had brought his slaves on board, and succeeded in making a better bargain than two rival traders, who at once resolved to be revenged upon him and get him out of their way in the future. They accordingly watched his departure from the ship, pursued and overtook him, when one of them knocked him down with an oar and the other bound him.

They then returned to the ship and sold him. His remonstrances were only answered by the captain with the taunt, "That it mattered not who his slaves were, so long as they were paid for; and as he had been paid for, he might now go along with his gang." But the perfidious traders met with a speedy retribution; for in their glee at the success of their trick, they did not observe the speedy effect of the mixed brandy potations with which the captain had treated them after inviting them below, where their friendly chat soon ended in a stupid, drunken sleep.

The sails were immediately set, and the terrible voyage begun. They had run several hours along the coast, when a boat full of provisions put off from the shore and made signs to trade. The ship was at once hauled to, and the company received on board with tempting offers; but no sooner were they within the power of the slaver than the course was resumed, and the poor deluded people seized and ironed as slaves. Their bitter wails aroused the two sleepers, who, yet half dreaming, stumbled upon deck, and were met with the derisive laugh of the captain, who ordered them shackled and stowed away with the others.

On each fair day, between eight and nine o'clock in the morning, they were all permitted to come on deck, which was surrounded with high nettings to prevent them from jumping overboard.

For their additional security a ring was attached to the shackles of each pair, through which a large chain was reeved, which locked them all in a body to ring-bolts in the deck. About three or four in the afternoon they were again put below, to remain till morning. In the interval, while on deck, they were fed twice with rice, yams, horse-beans, and occasionally a little beef and bread, and allowed a pint of water each during the day, which was served to them after their meals. They were then made to jump in their irons for exercise, which was called dancing, and they were compelled by the "cat" to do it, even though their irons wore to the bones, and though sick with flux or scurvy, or with limbs swollen so that it was painful to move at all.

The groans and suffocating cries of the poor victims for air and water sickened the soul of humanity into a loathing of the horrid traffic, which was deepened by the frequent howling, melancholy sound of anguish caused by their thoughts or dreams of their own country, often followed by hysteric fits of the women and the most desperate imprecations of the men. Their sorrows, confinement, and want of water, caused many to pine away, till a sudden attack of dysentery released them from their sufferings. Many were brought up every morning dead, suffocated by the heat, which was so great between decks, that when the surgeon went below, his shirt was as wet with perspiration in five minutes as if dipped in water, and he could rarely remain more than thirty minutes at a time. Yet those poor creatures were there compelled to moan the long hours of night away, with no water to quench their tormenting thirst, and just air enough to prolong their misery: sick or well, lying naked upon the bare boards till often their bones would wear through the skin, and no kind and sympathizing hand to relieve or friendly heart to feel for them. [Yet, through such sufferings, during the ten years preceding 1856, about 36,000 slaves per year were brought to America.]

Yes; there was One who noticed all their cries and bottled all their tears; and though they knew not his precious name, his angel of compassion moved amid that sweltering multitude, and whispered (so low that the slaver could not hear it, yet in accents that even those dark minds comprehended) of a rest somewhere—of running streams, and untainted breezes, and unshackled limbs; and many a poor African raised his eyes imploringly toward heaven, and gasped his soul out thither. Yes, and there was at least one human heart that had not lost its impress of humanity.

When some time out, a fearful storm broke upon the ship, and raged for four hours with such fury that an ocean-grave seemed their inevitable fate. However, by the skill of the captain they were kept afloat, and, though somewhat disabled, continued their voyage. During the storm, while the vessel was pitching and rolling, now in a mad endeavor to scale the sky, then in a reckless plunge to fathom ocean's depths, the poor Africans were so awe-stricken, that though suffering intensely from the closed scuttles, not a sound was heard save the muffled groans that would involuntarily burst forth; and when at last the tempest ceased, the dead were many, and fear and confinement had sown dysentery broad-cast among the remainder.

While the sea was yet heavily rolling, the look-out sang out from the cross-trees—

"Ship ahoy! boat to the windward!"

"Where away?" asked the captain through his trumpet.

"About a mile off the larboard quarter, sir."

The captain sprang up the mast, and pointing his glass in the direction indicated, saw what seemed to be a boat with her side stove in, and a single person clinging to her.

"Helm hard down! Brace back the maintopsail! Haul down the jib and mainsail! Lay her to! Man the long boat! Shove off!" thundered from him in such quick succession, that none but a practiced sailor could remember half.

"Ay, ay, sir!" was the response, and in less time than it has taken us to tell it, the ship was laid to, and the nimble boat, impelled by half a dozen as fearless hands as ever swung an oar, was dashing through the sea like a thing of life.

It was a desperate chance: they could only see the object of their search when both rose on the waves at once, and a moment's delay might prove fatal to the exhausted mariner. But, guided by occasional glimpses of him and by signs from the ship, they soon reached him and drew him in, more dead than alive, and hastened back to the ship, when a few cordials and rest soon restored him sufficiently to tell his story. He was a young surgeon aboard of a merchantman returning from India, which had been wrecked in the gale, and all had perished.

An American by birth, he had graduated from a northern medical college with distinction, and then, to enlarge his knowledge and gratify his ardent love of adventure, he had wandered away to the eastern world, and was on his return when wrecked, as before stated.

He met with the hearty welcome which the sailor, however hardened, always extends to a shipwrecked brother, and, when sufficiently restored, was offered and accepted the post of surgeon, which had been made vacant by the previous death of that officer while on the coast.

Although himself a slaveholder, he was a man of nature's noblest pattern.

To a keen and searching intellect was added a disposition as mild and tranquil as it was benevolent and sympathizing. Having been all his life absorbed in his studies, and a great part of the time not in immediate contact with the system of slavery, he knew little of it, and far less of the foreign trade.

When he saw it in all its horrors before him, his soul sickened, and he regretted for the moment that he had not found his grave upon the sea-weed's bed, rather than live to behold such utter wretchedness, and such heaven-defying iniquity.

Then, when he thought—"All this for paltry gold!" the noble instincts of his nature rose in indignant reprobation of the sin. He remonstrated, entreated, did everything that he could do in his dependent position to induce the captain to remit the rigors of their condition. The captain at first listened respectfully, and answered that self-preservation drove them to such severity; that if they should relax their discipline, the slaves would rise and kill them all. But as this did not satisfy the humane surgeon, he raved and swore, and at last told him if he did not like their conduct he might return where they found him. Finding entreaties unavailing, he turned his whole attention to ministering to the wants of the unfortunate victims as best he could.

In each slave-room two or three large tubs were placed for their convenience. But often one of a shackled couple would be attacked with the dysentery while his fellow would be unable or disinclined to move, especially as they must drag themselves over the bodies of others; and thus the deck was soon covered with blood and mucous, emitting the most horrid stench, and breeding death continually. Yet into that living hell the noble martyr would plunge barefoot that he might not tread upon them—often before they had learned his kindness, to be scratched, and bitten, and pinched, till his feet and legs were scarred, and frequently, as he leaned over some poor gasping sufferer, would he find him shackled to a corpse! O how earnestly did he long to tell them of the Savior; but ignorance of their language forbade it.

Yet death to them had no terrors. The lingering one would look down upon the cold body beside him, and with sorrow that he had been left, mournfully repeat, "Gone to he own country! Gone to he own friends!"

Then, in their wild agony, crowds would rush to the scuttles as fast as their manacled limbs would go, some dragging the dead with them in their desperate madness, and cry for air and water, till they fell fainting beneath the throng that pressed for their places, only to repeat their unavailing cries. O, it would have melted the heart of a brute to behold them! Yet the cruel sailors would curse them in their rage, and perhaps lash them for their impudence. Good God! was it thy wind that sped them on their course? Was it thy ocean that bore them on its bosom? Was it thy image that they scathed, and peeled, and smothered? Yes; and judgment belongeth unto thee!

The companion of Bobah now realized the full iniquity of his horrid traffic, and, goaded by the pangs of remorse, he resolved to die. But as no violent means of self-destruction were within his reach, he determined to starve himself to death. His design was soon detected and he was commanded to eat, and upon refusal, was lashed till he fainted, and then dragged back to the slave-room, and told that he would be whipped every day until he yielded. For three successive days he was lashed, until his entire body was one mass of raw and quivering fiber. After each whipping he was washed off in salt brine to prevent mortification, and the last time red pepper was added to increase his tortures.

Nature sank beneath the repeated inflictions, and the night after his fourth whipping he breathed his last. Poor Bobah envied him his fate, but from the terrible process of delivery he shrank in fear, till the dripping perspiration and raging thirst, which could only be gratified by a single paltry pint of water during all the long hours of sun-hot days and the longer ones of suffocating nights, drove him to the desperate resolution to die, cost what pain it might.

Our tongue refuses to tell all the awful scourgings he received, or how cruelly his jaws were forced open by the speculum-oris, (an instrument used by surgeons in the treatment of lock-jaw,) and his mouth crammed so full that he was nearly choked. A record so much like that which devils might cause to be made, is only here given in part with deepest loathing. It was all in vain. Yet what pain could not extort, the persuasions of kindness effected. The sympathy of the noble surgeon melted the heart that would not bend to force, and he yielded.

Both Bobah and Mabowah, each ignorant of the fate of the other, comforted themselves with the hope that when the voyage was over they might meet again; yet that hope was faint indeed, for all around them their fellow-captives were dying nightly by dozens, and were pitched into the sea as unceremoniously as so many brute carcasses, often before the last breath was drawn.

As they drew near the termination of their voyage, the ceaseless watchfulness and untiring exertions of the noble surgeon, together with the constant strain upon his sympathies, wore fearfully upon his strength. But once more he felt that he must explore the horrors of that living tomb between decks.

His weakness had increased his nervous sensibility to such an extent that he lost his usual self-possession, and, overcome with the scene, he fell upon his knees, and then, amidst that wondering, stricken throng, he prayed—prayed only as the strong man in agony can pray, till, stifled by the fumes and exhausted by the excitement, he fainted and was hauled up nearly dead.

The captain had passed the hatchway during the prayer, and his quick ear caught the hated sounds that were even then bearing his guilty soul with all its enormities before the throne of mercy, and he gnashed his teeth in rage. Suddenly all the demon seemed roused within him, and he ran for his pistols, determined to shoot the rash pleader on the spot.

When he returned he found him insensible upon the deck, and, ashamed to maim him then, he turned to wreak his vengeance upon a babe. There was a child on board, of nine months' age, which had refused to eat, and the captain had taken it in his hand and flogged it with the 'cat,' saying with an oath, "——you; I'll make you eat, or I'll kill you." The poor child having swollen feet, he ordered them to be put into water, although the cook told him it was too hot. This brought off the skin and nails. He then ordered sweet-oil and cloths to be applied; and as the child again refused to eat, he again flogged it, and then tied a piece of mango-wood, weighing some twelve or fourteen pounds, to its neck as a punishment." He had flogged it three times, when he became so enraged at the surgeon. He now took it and repeated the scourging, then dropped it from his arms upon the deck, and in a few moments it ceased to breathe. Then, with a barbarous refinement of cruelty, he called its own mother to heave it overboard, and beat her for refusing till she was forced to take it to the ship's side, where, with her head averted that she might not see it, she dropped it overboard, and then shrank away and wept the night's long hours through.

"O the cruel monster!" exclaimed Molly, how could he treat it so, and then call its own dear mother to throw her darling overboard! I am sure there are few such men in the world."

"It may seem to you like an extreme case, and so no doubt it is; yet it is the natural result of the system, to destroy sympathy and even create an unnatural love of cruelty."

None but hard-hearted men will be captains of slavers; and their crew, if engaged with a knowledge of their business, will be like themselves, or if engaged on some other pretext and forced into the business, so abhorrent to all their better feelings, they will be morose and undutiful except from fear of the lash; so that the crew itself tends to make the captain still worse. Then he becomes so much accustomed to regard Negroes only as so much property to make money on, that he loses all thought that they are his fellow-creatures. It would be singular, indeed, if his natural hardness should not deepen under such circumstances to utter callousness, and make him only an intelligent and malicious tiger.

The good surgeon's hours were numbered. He revived but in part, and knowing that his moments were fast passing, he called the incensed captain, and before he had time to speak or strike, poured upon him such a flood of sublime and holy rebuke, rising to the grandeur of prophetic denunciation, and mingled with such melting pathos of entreaty, that the crime-steeped man was overwhelmed and fled from the scene.

Then, turning to the hardened crew, he preached salvation through Christ with such power, that had a bolt of heaven's wrath been speeding towards that sin-laden vessel, it must have turned aside, at least till that dying exhortation was over.

Its last accents fell upon hearts from which the tear of penitence had not been wrung before, but now they wept! Yes, they wept; for the march of death was upon those words, and an unseen power clothed them with a spell-binding might. He ceased; the chin quivered, the head dropped, and the noble Astern was no more. He had done his work, and had reached his reward. Solemnly, and with more respect than ever before, the human clay was committed to the deep from that ship's side—did they lay him upon the bosom of the sea to await the resurrection of the just.

Nearly three hundred of the slaves had died on the passage, and when at last they arrived in port, many were sick and numbers died—some after landing. The healthy ones, except a few reserved for the owners of the ship, were sold by scramble; i. e. the ship was covered and darkened with sails, the men placed on the main deck, and the women on the quarter deck. When all was ready, the purchasers on shore came on board, each with cards bearing his own name, and rushed through the barricade door, some with handkerchiefs tied together to encircle all they thought fit. The sick and disabled ones were sold at auction for whatever they might bring; some selling for a single dollar. Col. Halman, a wealthy planter in Georgia, owned one-eighth of the vessel, and was therefore entitled to some of the slaves. Bobah and Mabowah were among the number which fell to him, and thus they met.

They were at once sent off to his large cotton and rice plantation near Savannah, where he employed between seven and eight hundred slaves.

Their names were changed to Jacob and Ruth Welden, and they were shown a miserable hut, which was to be their future home.

But in their joy at being released from the terrible slave-ship, it seemed for a time, in comparison, a palace. It was eight feet by ten, and eight feet high, with a hole in the top to let the smoke out—put up without a nail, and totally destitute of window-glass, chairs, table, and bedstead. Their only bedding was a blanket, and wrapping themselves in that, on the cold ground they were compelled to sleep. Their food consisted of one peck of corn meal each, per week, which they were obliged to grind for themselves after the day's toil, and which, from the insufficient accommodations for so many, often brought the labor late in the night.

They were allowed an hour and a half or two hours to prepare and eat their first meal, at about eleven o'clock, and the second was taken after the day's work was over.

They had not been here long when Ruth became a mother. The birth of her child was followed by a painful illness of some three weeks' duration, in which her utter loneliness seemed almost as hard to be borne as the suffocating tortures of the middle passage.

With no kind hand to soothe her, and no one to supply her wants during all the long fifteen hours of Jacob's daily toil, she would often lie, with the tears streaming down her cheeks, and trace in each feature of her boy some resemblance to those whom she had so fondly loved yet lost in her fatherland.

The vigor of a good constitution at length triumphed, and as soon as she recovered so that her master thought she could bear it without a relapse, he ordered the babe to be taken from her and sent a few miles away to a cotton-cleaning establishment which he owned, to be cared for by the old and infirm slaves at work there. There he was named Cæsar. This separation opened all poor Ruth's wounds afresh; and in the bitterness of her spirit she cursed the white man, and sobbed, and implored heaven—and sobbed, and cursed, and implored again, till Jacob entered, after his day's toil, and found her rolling in anguish, smiting her breast, and tearing her hair in a phrensy of unutterable and uncontrollable grief. To all his anxious inquiries she could only answer, "Me child—me child—me child!" Overwhelmed with sorrow and dread, he rushed to every corner of the hut, then out, around and in again, madly seeking for his child.

"Why, Lor, now, what yer goin' on so fur?" exclaimed a fat, bustling negress, with eyes half starting from their sockets.

"Me child—me child—me child!" in slow, broken, mournful tones, as if embittered woe had found an utterance, fell upon her ear from the darkness of the hut; to which she answered, "Wal, now, I 'spect yer takin' on so 'bout yer baby, what Mas'r sent off. 'Taint no use, yer may's well gin in. Yer baby aint killed, nor sold. He's jist goin' out a piece to grow up light, to ride Mas'rs hosses."

This utterance, though they scarcely understood its meaning, served to quiet them for the moment, and the old woman went on to explain that the child was taken away in order to stunt his growth, that he might become a rider of his master's race-horses. Comforted with the hope of seeing him again, Ruth and Jacob settled themselves for the night's sleep. But the burden lay too heavily upon their hearts; and, locked in each other's embrace, they lay sighing those deep heart-sighs which succeed the tumultuous outburst of impassioned woe.

We will now leave them, and glance at their master and his family. Col. Halman was a short, fleshy, stout-built, red-faced, gray-headed, hard-drinking man of about two hundred pounds' weight, naturally pleasant and good-natured, but rendered irritable by his vices, till he had become exceedingly passionate, overbearing, and cruel.

Mrs. Halman was a tall, slim, rather sharp-featured, though handsome Spanish Creole, nearly twenty years younger than her husband, with an ungovernable temper, goaded by her ill-starred position into constant fretfulness, which made her both cruel and revengeful.

They had two children, of which he was extremely fond—particularly the daughter—his two former wives having died childless, and the son being subject to fits of derangement.

The daughter was a beautiful, kind-hearted child of three years, with eyes and hair of jet black, but complexion lighter than her mother's.

The overseer was a spare but stout-built, wiry, full-faced, black-haired Irishman called McCabe. He had been found trustworthy, and, committing the oversight of the plantation to him, the Colonel had given himself up to a life of ease and pleasure. Hunting, horse-racing, and drinking were his principal amusements.

Chapter 3

We will now pass over four years, marked by no special incident, other than the occasional scourgings and constant hard usage which they had learned to regard as their ordinary lot. Col. Halman had been away on a racing tour, and had lost several races, and involved himself so deeply that upon his return he was unable to meet a payment which was then due.

The sale of one of his slaves was the only alternative. A New-Orleans trader was in the neighborhood, who, upon being informed of the Colonel's wishes, immediately repaired to the plantation and selected Jacob, offering a large price, and refusing any other. Accordingly, he was ordered to go to the quarters upon some trifling errand, where he was at once shackled and marched off to the trader's coffle. Poor Jacob begged earnestly to be allowed to say at least one farewell word to Ruth, but a "scene" was not to be endured just then, and he was compelled to go. When the coffle was made up, they were driven to a distant market. While on their way, they stopped one night at a tavern where Jacob and his fellow-prisoner were unbound, to assist in some slight repairs about the driver's wagon, when they heard groans, as of some one in distress, issuing from an adjoining shed.

The driver walked carelessly toward the place, stood a moment surveying the scene, and with an oath turned away.

Not so with Jacob and his companion. With the curiosity natural to the race, and thoughtless of the consequences, they followed the driver, and when he turned they stood transfixed with horror. There, under the shed, hung by the thumbs the naked and writhing form of a beautiful quadroon girl of sixteen summers, and by her stood a burly, drunken villain, holding in one hand a bloody knife, and in the other the dripping cowskin, alternately swearing, maiming, and whipping, and she groaning, writhing, and almost dying. He had bought her for the basest of purposes, and when she refused his will and resisted his pollution, and then tried by running away to escape from his power, all the fiend was aroused within him. He pursued and captured her, then stripped her naked, and hung her, as has been stated, by her thumbs, and whipped her till her entire body, from her neck to her feet, was gored—cut off a toe from each foot, and both ears, and knocked out two front teeth, as marks, if she should ever run away again; and that maimed and bleeding girl was the object that they saw!

As the trader turned and saw them, he raised his whip to strike, when the horrified expression of their countenances arrested the blow, and ere he could repeat the effort they had dashed forward, and Jacob, snatching the knife from the monster's grasp, had severed the cords that bound the bleeding victim, while his companion knocked him down, and then both lifted the poor creature in their arms and bore her out.

They had scarcely reached the open space, when the infuriated villain sprang up, drew a pistol from his pocket and fired. The ball passed through Jacob's neck, severing the jugular vein, and lodged against the skull of the miserable girl. She drew one convulsive gasp and all was over. Jacob fell forward upon her, and his companion was about to feel the force of the clubbed pistol, when the trader interfered and the slave retreated to the coffle. The trader raised Jacob's head upon his knee, examined the wound attentively, and seeing that he was almost gone, laid him down, and with a desperate oath demanded nine hundred dollars of the murderer. But he in turn looked upon the corpse before him, and demanded fifteen hundred of the trader for his slave's act in occasioning her death. The dispute ran high, and was only decided by appealing to the law.

A jury of slave-holders was called the next day,—the boon companions of the murderer,—and the slave, Jacob's companion, arraigned for assaulting a white man!

No other proof was needed than the oath of the person thus assaulted, and the case was clear. He was condemned to "receive five hundred lashes, and (to make the cruel torture more keen) not more than thirty-nine at any one time; and the physician of the jail was instructed to see that they should not be administered too frequently, and only when in his opinion he could bear them." Most infernal decision! Five hundred blows for one! And yet this is law! Good God, save us from its protecting shadow! [Yet under such laws more than 600,000 slaves are held by men professing to be Christians.]

The trader was now fairly aroused. He had lost nine hundred dollars already, and now seven hundred more were to lie in jail till they could bear five hundred lashes; because, forsooth, it would be cruel and a crime to kill him outright for his guilt. So Christian mercy ordains that he shall die thirteen times over!

The trader at once instituted a suit against his enemy for cruelly and maliciously punishing his slave girl with unlawful severity, and another for the unjustifiable killing of the slave Jacob.

On the trial of the first case it was decided that "The end of the law respecting the slave is the profit of the master and his security, not the good of the slave; and to secure this end, the power of the master must be absolute, to render the submission of the slave perfect. That the slave, to remain a slave, must be sensible that there is no appeal from his master." "Therefore it is the policy of the law, in respect to the relation of master and slave, and for the purpose of securing subordination and obedience on the part of the slave, to protect the master from prosecution in all such cases, even if the whipping and punishment be malicious, cruel, and excessive." Again: "All colored testimony is excluded; and no white man saw the punishment except the trader, who only saw two or three blows, and could not tell whether the punishment was of 'unusual severity' or not—not knowing for what she was punished; and as obedience was absolutely necessary, she was in a state of insurrection until she obeyed him, and a slave in insurrection might be killed by any person." Case decided for defendant.

As to the second case, it was decreed that "When the slave of one party is killed, or his property value diminished by another party, the person thus doing is liable for damages to the owner of the slave thus injured, to the full amount of the loss sustained, except the slave be outlawed, or offers resistance when running away, or assaults a white man. In the case in question, the slave was killed while aiding and abetting a rebel slave, and after assaulting the defendant; therefore, the case is ruled for defendant." O, even-handed justice, is this thy ruling? Is it rebellion to the death, for the innocent and pure to turn with loathing from the wretch whose very touch is pollution?

Is it outlawry, and crime, and life-blood, to pity the maimed, quivering, gasping, dying, stainless maiden, whom lust, and passion, and power (cursed trio!) had striped, and gored, and mutilated? And this in a Christian land, where the symbol of liberty proudly floats on every flag, and a falsified Constitution declares that all men are born free and equal, but black men are chattels personal!

Yet, thank God! there are men better than their laws, although, from the more numerous class of the uncultivated in manners and morals in the community, they are in a small minority; still, the bare fact that some, in the exercise of their irresponsible power, are better than the laws, goes far to redeem humanity from the utter stigma that must otherwise attach to it.

"But, brother!" exclaimed Molly, "that must have been an extreme case; all masters cannot certainly be so cruel."

"They are not, and I believe but few are; but every one has it in his power to be, and the slave has no redress. True, the law professes to protect him, but the testimony of colored witnesses,—slave or free,—cannot be received; so that all the master has to do, is to perpetrate his barbarities where no white person can see him, and he is safe."

And should he be prosecuted on suspicion, his own oath clears him, in spite of any amount of circumstantial evidence. Besides, ordinarily, no friend of the slave will prosecute the master for ill-treatment; because, if proved, (as a southern judge has himself said,) "No man can anticipate the many and aggravated provocations of the master, which the slave would be constantly stimulated, by his own passions or the instigations of others, to give; or the consequent wrath of the master, prompting him to bloody vengeance upon the turbulent traitor—a vengeance generally practiced with impunity, by reason of its privacy." Hence, says another judge, "There have been no prosecutions of the sort. The established and uniform practice of the country, in this respect, is the best evidence of the portion of power deemed by the whole community requisite to the preservation of the master's dominion."

"But would not their own interest lead them to avoid inhuman punishment?"

If interest were always superior to passion it might; but that it is not, is seen everywhere in the passionate cruelty to animals, which diminishes their value; and you should remember that the whole slave system is one great nursing mother of passion, as Jefferson wrote:

The whole commerce between master and slave is a perpetual exercise of the most boisterous passions; the most unremitting despotism on the one part, and degrading submission on the other. Our children see this, and learn to imitate it; for man is an imitative animal. The parent storms; the child looks on, catches the lineaments of wrath, puts on the same airs in a circle of smaller slaves, gives loose to the worst of passions; and thus nursed, educated, and daily exercised in tyranny, cannot but be stamped by it with odious peculiarities. The man must be a prodigy who can retain his morals and manners undepraved in such circumstances.

Besides, it is often more for the master's interest to overwork and subject his slaves to murderous hardship, than to treat them well, because of the increased pecuniary gain. Thus, on the southern sugar plantations it is an established custom to task the hands so as to kill them in from five to seven years, and then re-stock; it being cheaper to purchase new hands, than to keep a sufficient number to do the work without injury to themselves. And again, it is for the master's interest to exact obedience at all hazards; and if the poor slave girl has been so unfortunate as to inherit the female slave's greatest curse, personal beauty, and then to save her honor dares to resist, she must be compelled to yield, or the master's authority is at an end; and to whatever extremity the punishment may be carried, the law and public sentiment will uphold it, and interest demands it; for it then sustains the most essential and necessary right of the master's relation—one without which the relation itself must cease.

Some other mode of exacting obedience might be preferred, but obedience itself to any and every mandate of the master must be enforced, come life or death.

And every slaveholder is compelled, by the necessities of the case, virtually to act upon this principle, whether he approves it or not. Hence, many of the hardships of the slave's life are chargeable not so much upon the disposition of the master, as upon the requirements of the system. And when, in the case of the stubbornly refractory all other measures fail,—and he is sold to the southern driver instead of being whipped to death,—it is only a refinement of the torture and protraction of the agony. No wonder that the moral sentiment in regard to the Negro is so blunted and paralyzed. It would be so with us were we exposed to the direct educational influence of the slave system. Says a southern paper: "There are many persons—and we regret to say it—who think they have the same right to shoot a Negro, if he insults them, or even runs from them, that they have to shoot down a dog." And why should they not think so? Their papers are filled with advertisements of rewards for runaways,—"dead or alive,"—described as having "lost toes," "fingers," or "ears," having "front teeth knocked out," "branded on the cheek," "breast," "back," "marks of severe cuttings with the whip," "sores caused by the wearing of irons," "scars from the bite of hounds," "lame from broken limbs," "having only one eye," etc., etc., etc.

What can such things suggest, but the treatment that has caused them—a treatment familiarized by observation and perhaps experience, till it would be strange indeed if their rights and feelings as men should not be totally disregarded.

In South Carolina, for killing a slave outright a man may be put to death, (if convicted;) but if he tortures him to death with the lash, or otherwise, he may pay $500 and possibly be imprisoned six months.

Hence we should be the deadly foes of the accursed system, spurning compromises as infamous bargains with the devil and compacts with hell, all the more dangerous as they profess to be "constitutional!"

"Why, brother, you are getting excited."

"So I am, Molly; and shame on the detestable cowardice that fears to become excited upon such a question as this! But we must leave it till to-morrow."

Chapter 4

When Ruth came from the field, after the sale of Jacob, and learned her loss from the old negress, who was her comforter before, her cheek blanched, her frame quivered for a moment like an aspen-leaf, and then, without a groan or a sigh, she fell heavily upon the ground.

The old woman was accustomed to strange sights, and could bear any ordinary scene with a stoical indifference that clearly belied the goodness of her nature. But this awful silence of woe, this chilling despair that settled with such frigid coldness upon the heart, and looked its calm iciness through the half-closed eyes, this was something she had never seen before. "Good Lor e massa! ded an' gone! O, marcy! marcy! gone off in an eberlastin' fit! Fetch de water! Here, yer lazy niggers, tell massa! O Lor! what kin a poor creetur du?" And old Chloe, once overcome, fairly crazy with excitement, danced about, uttering such wild, disconnected sentences that the hubbub soon brought scores of blacks and the overseer to the spot. As soon as the trouble could be ascertained,—for poor Chloe was too much excited to tell,—Ruth was borne away from the confusion, and a few restoratives administered with success. She partially revived, then sank away again, then revived to a state of sleepy, muttering delirium, or wild, staring, speechless mania.

Weeks passed away, and she slowly recovered her strength till she was able to sit on a bench outside the sick-quarters. While sitting there, one day, sadly musing upon the past, little May chanced to stray by, and, with the quick perception of childhood, saw at once that something more than common ailed her. She instantly ran to her, and not knowing her name, stood before her, and for a moment looked upon her with the unaffected tenderness and sympathy of her years, then in the soft and subdued tones which the presence of a great sorrow elicits, asked, "What's the matter, Aunty?" The words fell like the voice of an angel upon the o'erfraught heart, and it welled up afresh, as grief's fountain does when the hand of rare kindness is laid upon it. The burst of tears only deepened Mary's sympathy, and she laid her little face upon Ruth's lap and wept with her.

O, it was a lovely sight, to see that young unburdened heart bend itself beneath the weight of woes that the strength of years could scarcely stagger under; and it eased for a brief moment the cankering heart-ache of stricken Ruth, and she clasped her to her bosom and wept again.

When the tumult of her feelings had somewhat subsided, she answered the inquiries of her little comforter, till she had told her the whole story of her life.

From that hour Ruth found a friend, and from that same hour the thoughtful mind of Mary took a new channel; and if her light-hearted gayety was chastened, and her vivacity diminished, it could easily be seen that a richer harvest of heart-treasure was ripening within for the garner. She was not allowed to associate with the plantation-slaves, but she often found an opportunity to slip away to see Ruth, whose only desire now seemed to be to see her boy. It was preying upon her life, and the sympathies of Mary could not rest till her desires were gratified.

The guileless artlessness of her manner, and the tears of unaffected sympathy with which she plead with the overseer, soon prevailed, and Ruth was permitted to go to see her boy, and remain with him until able to work in the fields again. Her recovery was slow, so slow that all the native affection of her heart had time to warm into a fervid glow of love for her child, the intensity of which only embittered her existence the more. It would be useless to describe all the pangs she felt when compelled to return to the plantation, and resume the dreary life of toil from which even her painful sickness had been a recreation.

We will leave her in her loneliness and sorrow, and pass on to the time when Cæsar commenced his active life. He was put to knitting when about three years old, and then hemming cotton handkerchiefs. When between five and six he was sent to the plantation, and put under the care of one Dick Burley, his master's principal jockey and trainer, to be trained for a race-horse rider. Col. Halman kept a number of horses, and prided himself upon keeping some of the fleetest in the country.

Dick was of about middling height, sharp features, sandy hair, quick-tempered, and given to drink.

His method of training was to first put the boy on a well-trained horse, and instruct him how to sit and rein. After becoming somewhat accustomed to this, he tied him upon a young unbroken horse, gave him the bridle, and then turned him loose. Just before Cæsar was tied on, he was very much frightened by an awful scene in the training of two boys, who were a little farther advanced than himself. The two boys were tied on at the same time, and for a few moments managed bravely, but by a sudden turn of one of the horses, his rider slipped around under him, and hung head downwards; this frightened the timid colt so much, that in his frantic plunges to rid himself of the boy, before any one could interfere he was a bruised and mangled corpse. The terrific bounds of this horse so terrified the other, that he too began to rear and plunge, and the poor little rider, seeing the fate of his companion and losing all presence of mind, jerked with all his strength upon the reins just as the animal reared, and brought him over, and was crushed to death in an instant. This scene did not greatly strengthen the nerves of Cæsar, when, a few days after, he was tied on in the same manner. He too would have shared their fate, had not two old slave women noticed his slipping, and caught the horse just in time to prevent his going under.

Col. Halman owned a plantation and stables in Virginia; and Cæsar was employed, after his tenth year, as a rider and a body-servant, that is, to wait upon his master. In this capacity he came to Virginia, and while there ran his first race for money near the James River, where he won $2,000, and a few days after ran again and lost $2,500. They then went to Norfolk, and took a steamer to New-York, and put up in Cherry-street. While there the Colonel made arrangements for a race on the Long Island Course, and meantime went to Hunting Park Course in Pennsylvania, where he won $3,000.

Burley was a notorious scoundrel, and taught Cæsar all sorts of tricks to balk his adversaries' horses, which he often used successfully. Thence they went to New-Jersey, and in Hoboken won another purse of $2,500.

While traveling, especially in free States, Cæsar was well used; but not knowing that he was then free, he could not take advantage of the fact. Major J—, of Cold Spring was the competitor in the race on the Long Island Course. The first heat Cæsar's horse won with ease, when the Colonel took Cæsar aside, and ordered him not to do his best, but let the Major win, so that he would be induced to bet higher. The purse of $2,000 was then again lost, but the Major would not bet again, so they then returned to Georgia. The next season they went to Mobile, in Alabama, and ran four races and lost them all. Colonel Halman was in liquor most of the time; and the more bad luck he had, the harder he drank, and the worse poor Cæsar fared, being whipped after every race, if unsuccessful. His usual punishment was twenty-five lashes on the bare back, and then rubbed down with salt brine, and left standing in the sun from fifteen minutes to half an hour—which was often worse than the whipping. The Colonel resolved to try once more; and after a rainy week, when the track was slippery, he ordered him to "win or catch it." The horse made tremendous exertions under the goadings of his almost despairing rider, but slipped and fell broadside, breaking Cæsar's arm and leg.

The Colonel was watching the race with much anxiety, when the fall aroused all his drunken wrath. He rushed to the spot, and instantly ordered him to be stripped and receive twenty-five lashes. A physician, who chanced to be present, now came forward and examined his wounds, and decidedly objected to any punishment in that condition. The master raved and swore; the doctor stood firm and objected. At length the dispute ran so high that they drew pistols over his body, when others interfered and prevented any further mischief. He was then carried to the hospital, where he lay nearly five months. His master would occasionally call to see him,—always in a passion,—and generally, before leaving, wish him dead.

Before his recovery he was sent home, and while his arm was still weak he was forced to ride again. The horse was young and not well trained, and his arm not being strong, the horse ran and threw him, his head struck a post, and he was taken up for dead with a broken skull. He then lay two or three months, most of the time delirious, and, after recovering sufficiently, traveled with his master as body-servant. They visited Niagara Falls and other places, and he was treated better than he ever was at any other time, except when on a subsequent journey to England. They returned by way of St. Louis, New-Orleans, and Mobile; and while at Mobile his master, while in a drunken spree, sold him to a southern trader named Jim Wallace, who intended taking him to New-Orleans where he lived. The morning before he was to start, Col. Halman came to him and wished to buy Cæsar back. The trader replied: "You have not money enough to do it." But the Colonel remonstrated—said it was not a fair trade—was done when intoxicated, etc.; and at last bought him back for $1,000, losing $500 by the trade, but swearing that he would have it out of him before a year passed.

While there he witnessed one of those thrilling scenes that not infrequently transpires in slave markets. An old woman and her daughter were put up to be sold for debt. They had lived with a kind mistress, and were struck off to different persons. The old woman cried aloud, when the cruel trader stepped up to her, and cut her two or three times with his whip, saying at the same time, "Shut up, you old wench, or I'll whip you till the blood runs into your shoes!" The mistress then came forward and begged to buy her back; but he would not sell, and the mother and daughter were parted, never to meet again till that day when the slave and the free shall alike "be judged according to the deeds done in the body."

When Cæsar was well, his master was accustomed to order him to attack any Negro that chanced to pass, that the fight might afford amusement to the spectators. He became very skillful in these "rough and tumble" encounters, for he was stimulated by his love of applause if successful, and fear of blows from his master if unsuccessful.

After spending some time at home, the Colonel resolved to visit England to try his Grey against the English trotting-horses. He accordingly sailed for Liverpool; but the passage was very rough, and the horse was so bruised that he was unfit to run upon their arrival.

Hence the match was postponed, and finally won. Thence they went to Ireland, and ran on the Curragh of Kildare, and after an unsuccessful season returned home. While in Dublin, Cæsar was offered $40 per month by a sportsman to stay with him as jockey and rider. But poor Cæsar knew not that he was free; and fearing that his master might hear of the offer and whip him for it, according to previous instructions he replied he "was not out of his time." After his return he was employed as body and house servant. His mistress would sit in a large rocking-chair in the middle of the room, with her cowskin in her hand; and whenever he or her two female servants came within her reach, if she was displeased at anything, she would vent her spite in blows upon their necks. One of her female servants had been so injured in early life that her intellect was blunted, and she became the special object of aversion. Her neck was kept a raw and bleeding sore constantly, by the stripes of her tormentor. Of course, such treatment roused all the hateful and vindictive feelings of Cæsar's heart, and his whole delight was to study out some means to tease her, and yet escape chastisement.

One day, while drawing water for his horses, he observed some nice apple-dumplings just taken from the fire. At that moment the room was left vacant, and he dodged in and seized a large one, with which he was about to make his escape, when his mistress entered; but quickly turning, he dropped the scalding dumpling into the pocket of his thin tow pants, and catching up his pail, ran for the stables; but before he had reached there his thigh was burned to a blister.

A short time after, the family were all away, and he resolved to revenge himself upon his mistress. Accordingly he went to the kitchen, and there found her favorite cat. He then heated the poker, and with it burned her nose and paws till she became desperate. Having cornered her where there was no escape, he plied his iron with increasing zeal, when she suddenly sprang upon him, and fixing her claws in his breast, fought and tore like a tigress. Poor Cæsar had now found more than he had bargained for, and roared aloud with pain; but before he could open the door and release himself his bosom was terribly lacerated. His wounds made him weak and sick; and as he dare not tell of them for fear of worse ones on his back, he had to dress them with his horse-liniment and endure the pain.

While yet lame and dull from their effects, his mistress frequently gave him passing blows, and finally sent him to the quarters to receive a dozen lashes there. When he returned to the house she ordered him to take a pitcher, and go to the spring-run, and get some milk that was kept there. He went and kicked the milk-pot into the spring, then filled his pitcher with the water and took it to her, saying that "some one had upset the pot." She saw the trick at once, and accused him of it, but he denied it. She then ordered him to follow her; and taking her cowskin, led the way to the spring, where she whipped him till she was tired, then told him if he did not confess it she would drown him in the spring. She accordingly seized him; but he contrived to so entangle himself with her, that as she made an effort to put him in, she fell backwards and struck her head against the stone side, and lay insensible in the run. He resolved to let her drown; but before she was quite gone, some other member of the family discovered her and carried her to the house.

When his master returned, a few days after, he called for Cæsar, and gave him a note to take to the quarters. He took it, suspecting something of its import, when the overseer ordered him to strip, tied him up, gave him twenty-five lashes, and brined him as usual.

He was unable to work for two weeks after this, and it taught him to be more prudent in his plans of revenge.

"Well," said Molly, "he deserved some punishment that time."

"Very true, and no doubt slaves often deserve it; for a more vexatious life can scarcely be imagined, than to be obliged to control a lot of lazy, stubborn, and revengeful Negroes. Yet it is this very fact that makes the system the more repulsive; because it is a vast educational establishment, in which the worst passions are developed as a principle, and iniquity is studied as a science! Instead of training them for usefulness and the high destiny of immortality, they are constantly educated in the development of passions of which it would be slander to accuse the brute, and to which devils never could sink.

And yet men say that the very God who has redeemed them, authorizes such an educational influence. If I believed it, I would burn my Bible as the most despicable humbug on earth, and reprobate its God as I now hate the devil. But more of this at our next interview.

Chapter 5

I will now attempt to show the educational influence of the slave system, as it operates upon both classes, in the incidents that follow.

The father of Col. Halman had a female house-servant by whom he had a child, a handsome mulatto girl, who grew up with Col. H., and by whom she had a beautiful quadroon child. This child's mother the Colonel had been compelled to sell, in consequence of the constant reproaches of a former wife; and the present Mrs. Halman could not brook seeing the beautiful quadroon upon the premises, rivaling her own charms, and a constant reminder of her husband's shame. She occasionally wreaked her ill-humor upon her, till the Colonel sent her to his plantation in Virginia, to save her from further severity and himself from merited reproaches.

While on one of his northern tours, he fell in company with Mr. De Alembert, of one of the proudest and most aristocratic families of southern Virginia, and invited him to visit him at his Longfield plantation.

Alembert had just succeeded, by the death of his widowed mother, to the inheritance of the old family homestead; and as he desired to increase his patrimony, he sold all the house-slaves, and with the avails re-stocked his plantation with a sufficiency of good healthy hands, mostly young females, and set out to visit Col. Halman. One article in his inventory of goods he had purposely left unsupplied, until one to his taste should fall in his way. The condition was quickly met, for at the Colonel's he saw Rosette, the beautiful quadroon, and at once unfolded his plans and made an offer.

"You see, Colonel," said he, "if I marry I shall have to keep two or three house-servants, which will cost me $3,000, beside all the expense of a wife; so I have concluded to buy me a right sort of a girl, and manage without a wife. Now, there is that quadroon there—what will you take for her?"

"Don't want to sell!" gruffly replied the Colonel, as the recollection of her near relationship forced itself upon him.

"But would'nt $1,500 be something of an inducement?" urged Alembert.

"Lord knows I need the money bad enough, but ye see I don't just like to sell her."

They sat some time in silence, each watching the graceful movements of Rosette, one thinking of the past, the other of the future.

The past was not a very pleasant theme for the Colonel's meditations, and he sat uneasily, hitching, hemming, and spitting, till he unconsciously thrust his hand into his pocket, and it rested upon a letter that he had received the day before, challenging him to a race. He had thought little of it, because the want of funds prevented his acceptance of the offer. But now a new idea struck him.

"I tell you what, young fellow, if you will give me $2,000 for her, she's yours, sure as fate; but not a picayune less."

"Two thousand dollars! two thousand dollars! that's a heap for one girl! But then she's mighty handsome (and she'll raise splendid young ones, too,") mused Alembert, and then spoke out: "Well, Colonel, that's a high figure; but I'll take her."

And the papers were made out and signed, and Alembert, with his property-mistress, started for his plantation.

In due time she bore her chaste bachelor lord a beautiful, flaxen-haired boy, who grew in interest and beauty as he did in stature, and moreover so favored his master's features, that even strangers were at no loss to divine his paternity. Meantime a strange bleaching process was going on in the somewhat numerous children of the plantation-slaves. They—particularly the children of the younger mothers—were a great part of them mulattoes, or quadroons, according as the mothers were black or mulattoes; and as the value of the children increased in the ratio of their whiteness, the master, of course, would not trouble himself to ascertain the cause.

Nearly three years passed away, and Rosette's child grew more and more like "master," till it could be endured no longer, and one day he was sold to go off south. His mother had left him to step out for a few moments, and when she returned he was gone. The trader had taken him and rode away.

We will not attempt to describe poor Rosette's feelings. She had seen the children of other slaves sold thus, but she fondly hoped that hers would be spared to her. Alembert at once told her that if she cheered up and behaved herself, she would be treated the same as before; but if she "moped and whimpered" around in that way, he would sell her to the first New-Orleans trader. She saw the hopelessness of her lot, and though her heart buried itself in anguish, she assumed a cheerful aspect in his presence and was retained in his favor. Not long after, she found herself exposed to the same fearful trial again; and rather than endure the suspense that must always hang over her, she resolved to secure her freedom or perish in the attempt.

She had learned enough to know that her only hope was in reaching the mountains without discovery, which she had been told lay towards the setting sun, and then following the north star till she came to a land of freedom. Animated by the hope of escape, and not knowing the dangers of the way, she assumed a cheerful guise and waited for an opportunity. Alembert had gone on some business to the sea-shore, and would not return before three days, when the favorable time came. A lowery day was succeeded by a night of pitchy darkness and rain, with a strong wind from the south-east; when late in the eve she emerged from the mansion, with a small bundle containing such food as she had been able to secure, and a few little articles, among others, a dress which had been worn by her little boy.

Placing her back to the wind, she stumbled on through the darkness, falling over various obstructions, and into holes and gullies; but still she kept on till the light began to break in the east, when weary, faint, bruised, and hungry, she crawled into a thick hedge, ate her morning meal, and slept—the dreamy, disturbed, and fitful sleep of anxious fatigue. The next night she continued the same course, with the north star for her pilot, instead of the wind, keeping it constantly upon her right. Thus she proceeded till she reached the mountains and struck for the north.

Great was the commotion at the mansion on the morning after her escape. The heavy rain of the night had completely obliterated every trace of her course, hence all was doubt and uncertainty respecting it. However, no time was to be lost, and the energetic overseer at once caused the following advertisement to be inserted in the county papers, and sent off for a notorious catcher-catcher to come with his hounds, and, if possible, trace her:

$200 REWARD!!

Ran away from the subscriber, living near Barksdale, Halifax Co., a very light quadroon woman, of medium size, very handsome, and about 20 years old; has long, straight, auburn hair, which she usually keeps in good order. When she left, she had on either a white dress or a striped muslin, and a pink sun-bonnet. She dresses very neatly, wears one or two rings, is very intelligent, converses well, and can spell out print. Her name is Rosette, and the above reward will be paid for her if taken out of the State, and $100 if taken within the State.

De Alembert

But notwithstanding all the efforts of dogs and men, the rain had so effectually befriended her, that they were compelled to relinquish the search.

We will now continue the narrative of Cæsar. We left him—

"If you please, brother, I would like to ask if it is the custom in Virginia to raise slaves to sell, and if what you have intimated is really true—that they increase in value as they are white in color?"

"I have heard that they do not separate families; but I should think if they raise them to sell, they must do so."

Your inquiry includes so much, that I shall have to answer each point separately.

In regard to the raising of slaves for the southern market, nothing is more common in the papers of Mississippi, Louisiana, etc., than to find advertisements from dealers closing with such an assurance as this, viz: "The subscriber will continue to receive fresh supplies from Richmond, Va., during the season, and will be able to furnish to order any description of Negroes sold in Richmond."

In 1836 Virginia exported forty thousand slaves. During the same year the four States of Louisiana, Mississippi, Alabama, and Arkansas, imported from the more northern States two hundred and fifty thousand. At least one-third of these (over 80,000) were sold, and the remainder immigrated with their masters. In reference to these facts, a southern writer (Professor Dow, of the University of William and Mary, in Virginia) says: "A full equivalent being left in the place of the slave, (the purchase money,) this emigration becomes an advantage to the State, and does not check the black population as much as at first view we might imagine; because it furnishes every inducement to the master to attend to the Negroes, to encourage breeding, and to cause the greatest number possible to be raised."

"Virginia is, in fact, a raising-raising State for the other States."

From 1817 to 1837, from Virginia and North Carolina alone, 300,000 slaves were sent to the south.

From January 1st, 1851, to November 20th, 1852, were sent from the single port of Baltimore to southern ports 1,033 slaves, mostly between the ages of ten and thirty.

I presume these facts will be sufficient to show the truth in regard to raising.

Now how can all these young slaves be sent away without a separation of families? Look at such advertisements as this: "I have just returned to my stand, at the forks of the road, with fifty likely young Negroes for sale."

Were they all of one family? Where were the fathers and mothers, and young brothers and sisters? Sixty-four southern papers report, during the last two weeks of the month of November, 1852, the sale of 4,100 slaves, besides 30 lots of various numbers, and 92 runaways. We do not accuse slaveholders of wishing to separate families, but simply assert the utter impossibility of doing otherwise, as a common thing, as long as they foster such a trade with such a market.

As to the increased value of mixed blood, the simple fact that the 350,000 slaveholders of the south own 800,000 mulattoes, is fearfully suggestive of that—and another fact of the slave system also, viz: its constant temptations to the indulgence of the passions.

Able field-hands now bring from $600 to $1,500; but beautiful young mulatto girls bring from $1,000 to $2,500, and one was sold at public auction to a rich young planter for $7,500. A rich admixture of white blood is a great improvement of the breed, and many of the best and most valued slaves of the south are as white as their masters!

Chapter 6

After Cæsar's return from England, he lived about three years in much the same way as before his journey. He slept in the stables, and had trained one of the horses so that he could lie in the stall with him; and if the horse wished to move, he would shove Cæsar across the stall with his nose, and never tread on him, however soundly he might sleep. When in the stall, the horse would allow no person, not even Col. Halman, to enter. In the faithful attachment of this horse Cæsar found his greatest comfort. But the carefulness of his horse proved, upon one occasion, a serious misfortune. They were in the stable, in the midst of the racing season, and it often happened when several races came off in quick succession, that the care of the horses and the riding took most of Cæsar's time, so that he had little opportunity for sleep. At one time he had been up two entire nights, and was busily rubbing down his horse, with the animal's hind leg across his knees, when, overcome with fatigue, he fell asleep in that position. Thus his master found him, and seizing a large bar of wood which was used as a fastening to the door, struck him a severe blow across the arm and ordered him to go to work.

"I can't, master, my arm is broke."

"Your arm is broke, is it—pity it was'nt your head! Come out and I'll break your neck, you lazy, sleepy nigger, if you don't mind my orders and keep your eyes open!"

An examination showed that the limb was really broken, and he was sent to the overseer to be cared for.

Some time after his recovery his master resolved upon a tour through France and Spain, and concluded to take two of his best horses along, and Cæsar to groom them.

One horse died on the passage, but the other landed in good condition. They ran one race in France for $20,000 and lost, and then proceeded to Spain. There was to be a great race for $40,000, and Col. Halman determined to compete for the purse. As they were proceeding towards the place, and within two or three days' journey, Cæsar ran a scrub-race with a young Spaniard, and then disputed with him about the race, when the Spaniard drew a dirk and threw it, intending it to strike his heart; but by a sudden movement he dodged the weapon, and received it in his arm. He at once drew it out, and knocked his assailant down with his riding-whip, and beat him "till he lay quiet;" then bound up his arm with his handkerchief and rode as quickly as possible to his master, when they both mounted and rode nearly all night to avoid pursuit. At the great race the Colonel's horse won the purse, but again poor Cæsar suffered. In endeavoring to pull up his horse the bits parted, and he was thrown and three ribs broken.

On their return they had a stormy passage, and Cæsar was so knocked about that his imperfectly healed ribs were displaced, and for fourteen months he was disabled, and has never entirely recovered. Even now they gather and discharge during every long storm.

Just previous to his return, a number of the plantation-slaves, who were experienced, were sent up to Virginia to the Longfield farm, and exchanged for those less accustomed to their work.

Ruth was among the number. But the progress of years and sorrows had wrought their change. A deep melancholy had settled upon her: she seldom smiled, and when she did, it was quickly followed by a sigh. But the time of her redemption drew nigh: a new destiny was awaiting her.

In the shade of a thick wood near the Longfield farm stood an old deserted hut, in which the Negroes of the adjoining plantations were accustomed, whenever they could steal away, to assemble for religious services. In spite of their secrecy, however, the place and employment was known. But the overseers were shrewd men, and as long as no treasonable designs were entertained, they cared not how many of the slaves experienced religion, nor how much they obtained; for real genuine piety enhanced a Negro's value full a hundred dollars, by making him honest and obedient. They therefore allowed the meetings to continue, in spite of the law, and Ruth was invited to attend them. She did so, and her mournful expression soon elicited all the sympathies of the African heart. She was instructed, prayed for, exhorted, etc., till by the Divine Spirit's agency she was led to the Savior, of whom she now for the first time definitely heard. Her joy then equaled her ignorance and darkness before, and she prayed and sang from morning till night. Thus her mistress found her on her return from a visit to the north. At first she was confounded, then her wrath was kindled. She could not endure to see any one happier than herself; especially that a slave woman like Ruth should presume to such an experience, was a transgression of propriety closely bordering upon insolence. Then, when she remembered May's early interest in her, she resolved to watch. May was now with her, just returning after a long absence to complete her education, but had not as yet recognized Ruth in her transient glimpses of her among the other slaves. Mrs. Halman requested her own waiting-maid to be exchanged for a time for Ruth.

When May and Ruth first met, it was when Mrs. Halman was absent; and well for Ruth that it was so, for had her mistress have seen that meeting, Ruth would have suffered for her temerity.

In the fullness of her heart she had forgotten that the little tender-hearted May, who once wept with her, had now become the queenly belle of twenty-one summers, and she unburdened her heart in the same simple and undisguised manner that she did before the quarters in her earlier sorrows. But the story was now very different. For a time May listened with mechanical attention; for though the looks, the voice, and the gestures of the speaker were strangely new and touching, her memory was busy in recalling that scene of her infant years. When it stood before her in all its proportions, the contrast of the present pressed with overwhelming power upon her heart.

With melting pathos Ruth told of her long years of darkness, her troubled seeking after something that should satisfy her soul, and then her joyful finding; and as she knelt before May and clasped her arms around her, and with flowing tears exclaimed, "O, missus May! de Lor he be berry good! O, he my song all de day, an', me joy in de night time!" May could refrain no longer, and bending over, she buried her head upon the shoulder of Ruth and sobbed like an infant. Her apparent sympathy only called out a fresh burst of praise from Ruth: "O, bress de Lor! bress de Lor! me be ready to go up in de charyat ob fire!" Little did she know the terrible storm that was raging within the fair bosom that to her seemed the shrine of all innocence and loveliness.

But One saw it, and his angels rejoiced. May had always been thoughtful, but she now, for the first time, saw her sinfulness and felt her need of a Savior. Not long did she struggle; for the native trustfulness of her heart seemed instinctively to fly toward Him, and she was soon at peace. The external change was not great, yet the keen observer—such as her mother was—could detect a quiet peacefulness, and a more radiant loveliness than ever before.

Mrs. Halman soon discovered the cause, and, true to the instincts of her depraved heart, she resolved to whip the foolishness out of Ruth. When she found her efforts vain, she wrote to the Colonel, requesting him to order Ruth back to Georgia and cure her of her fanaticism. He accordingly had her sent back to the plantation, and ordered her to stop singing and praying. She refused, and was whipped; still she persisted, and again was whipped, but still refused. The Colonel then swore that no nigger on his plantation should break his orders, and she must yield or die. He then ordered her to have twenty-five lashes every day till she stopped her "——nonsense." But the more she was whipped the more obstinate she became, declaring that she would die rather than give up her religion.

May had meantime arrived, and having heard of the punishment, interceded for Ruth with all the powers of persuasion which she could command; and gladly would the Colonel have granted her desire, but the thing was too well known upon the plantation to allow it to pass. So, with a seeming compliance, he sent her off upon a short excursion, promising to follow in a few hours.

He then ordered Ruth to be brought out, and a large number of the slaves collected, among whom was Cæsar, to witness her submission. She was tied up and stripped, then told that she must yield or die. The Colonel had at that time two overseers—the Irishman before described, and a stout, large-fisted Scotchman, named Anderson. She saw that her hour had come, and turning her eyes toward heaven, she prayed for strength to persevere. Anderson at once laid on the lash with all his strength, mangling her body with every stroke. Her screams and screeches for a time were perfectly heart-rending; then they subsided into low moans, mingled with ejaculatory prayers for strength, for her boy, for her master, and for her overseer. Anderson could endure it no longer. He threw the whip down, and swore he would never strike her another blow. But McCabe seized it, and for one hour, with occasional intermissions, he plied the lash, till the master ordered him to desist. They then untied her, and she fell dead at their feet!

On the adjoining plantation lived Dr. Whitlow, a kind and Christian man. Cæsar had been sent there occasionally upon errands, and had heard the Doctor read the Bible to his slaves, and pray with them. He knew, too, that they were contented and happy, and that no inducement would prove sufficient to cause them to run away.

He became interested, and often stole away and listened, about the time the Doctor usually read, and thus had learned considerable about the Bible and his soul. When he saw his mother martyred, and listened to her exhortation and prayers, his seriousness was deepened. Soon after, he went with his master to Virginia to groom the horses there, as he was no longer of any service as a rider. The Colonel supposed that there would be no danger of his learning to pray, after seeing his mother's fate. He was soon invited to the meetings, and was prayed for. The third time he went he fell prostrate and senseless, and lay all night and the most of the next day in that condition. The slaves hid him, and the master searched for him. His feelings while in that state are given in his own words, thus:

"I seemed to be in a great meeting in a large house, and wanted to get out, but the door was fast. I then tried to leap from the window, but under it was a great gulf of fire, into which

I was falling, when I cried for mercy. Then a tall person with white hair appeared, and asked, "Dost thou believe?" I answered, "Yes, Lord,' and was at once lifted away and carried into another room, brilliantly lighted, from which a door opened into another which seemed filled with singers and harpers, singing, "This is the place of holiness." Then two angels appeared, singing, "Great is the Lord and greatly to be praised in the city of our God and in the mountain of his holiness." When I recovered I was happy, and I exclaimed, "As my mother died praying, so will I." Soon after, master found me in a back room praying.

"'What are you doing here?' said he.

"'seeking the salvation of my soul.'

"'I'll give you salvation, when I get you home! These —— niggers are getting you into the same way that your mother was. You saw what became of her, and if you don't give up this cursed foolishness, I'll whip the heart out of you!'

"Said I, 'Master, I mean to serve you just as well as I can, but I must save my soul.'

"'soul! What do you know about soul? Niggers have no more souls than horses. Now go about your business; and mind, let me hear no more of this.'"

He was at once sent back to Georgia, where he deliberated some time as to the best plan to pursue; but he at length determined to pray on, and suffer the consequences. ...

He now endeavored, in every possible way, to do his duty to his master, hoping thus to show that religion had not injured him, and for several weeks he was permitted to enjoy himself. But he soon grew bolder, and instead of praying softly, his voice could be heard at some distance from the stables; and his master came in a tearing passion and ordered him to be whipped, and never pray again, commanding every one upon the premises to report to him if they knew of his attempting it. Poor Cæsar begged for mercy, promised to do anything, day or night, but said he must escape the punishment of hell. His master told him there was "no future for a nigger—when he died it was the end of him," etc.

But all this was poor consolation for Cæsar, amid his stripes. Again and again he was scored, till the very mention of the whip sent a tremor through his frame. Again and again did the lovely May plead with tears for him, till she was compelled to fly like an angel of purity from the presence of her enraged and maddened father. But all the scourgings could not lash out the manhood from the patient Cæsar. ...

In his voyages to Europe he had heard the sailors talk about the stars, till he could shape his course by them. While in Virginia, too, he had learned that if he could reach Pennsylvania safely, he need fear no more. He at once commenced making preparations, by digging a hole under the stable floor, in which to put whatever he might collect.

He had a brace of pistols which he always carried at races, and his master kept a large quantity of powder and balls in his cellar for sporting purposes, of which he contrived to secure a sufficient amount. He also had the dirk that he took from the Spaniard who stabbed him. He then removed a board from the stable and replaced it, so that he could go out and in at pleasure, when locked in during the night. He was allowed for food a pound of crackers per day, and occasionally a quarter of a pound of cheese, during the racing season, and about the same substance in other things at other times. Out of that he saved one meal each day and stored it away in his cellar; also, twenty-eight boxes of matches. He then gathered pitch, and with some rosin which was in the stables he made three or four hundred torches, about 2½ inches long by an inch in diameter, by melting the ingredients together over a little furnace near the stables, which he used to heat water with for the horses. Then, with a large, round-bottomed, canvass union bag, his preparations were completed.

He knew that an overseer of an adjacent plantation was in the habit of crossing the Ogeechee river every night, and leaving his boat on the bank. His plan was to wait until some night when the wind would blow directly across the river, so as to drive the boat back, after he had crossed.

After some time the favorable moment came, and shouldering his bag, with pistols and dirk in his pocket, he made his way out of the stables late in the evening, and struck for the river, which he crossed, and shoved the boat off, and the wind took it back to the other shore. His object in this was to escape the dogs. His dress consisted of tow-cloth, and thin riding-slippers. He traveled all that night, and in the morning, after wading in a small brook several miles so that the hounds might not track him, he climbed a thick tree, and remained throughout the day, eating but one meal and trembling at every sound.

Thus he went on several days, till one time he heard the hounds, and gave up all for lost. A short distance from the place on which he stood he saw a large stream, and started for it, with the intention of drowning himself in it rather than be captured. But the sound suddenly receded, and he then concluded it was only the baying of huntsmen's dogs. Then, with safety from that danger, came the overwhelming sense of his loneliness and wretchedness. Alone in the vast forest, with hundreds of miles of weary travel before him, and every man a foe, he sat down and wept. Then he thought he would return, and perhaps his master would not be hard with him. Then he thought he would feign himself lost. But prayer soon brought relief, and he traveled on. His food was soon exhausted and his slippers worn out, and he was compelled to bear hunger and pain as he had never anticipated. Still, he found a poor subsistence upon nuts, wild oranges, persimmons, and such small game as he could shoot.

After being out a few weeks, he slept within a circle of fire, his strength being too much exhausted to climb trees. Often, as the gloomy shades of night hung around him, did the loneliness of his condition force itself upon him with such resistless power, that he threw himself upon the cold, wet ground and sobbed his strength away, and longed to find his grave. And anon, as some trembling starlight would penetrate the dense overhanging branches, it would seem to lift the sense of utter desolation from his heart, and a whispered prayer for protection and strength would compose him for his weary slumbers.

One day, as he was looking around for a convenient place to collect his bed of leaves and circle of brush, he was suddenly confronted by a large wolf. He dare not fire upon her for fear of only wounding her, and thus rendering his position still more dangerous; but he had heard hunters say that if a man fixed his eye steadily upon a wild animal without quailing, the beast would shrink away. Nerving himself by a mental prayer, he fastened his eyes upon her while he struck a match, kindled a torch, and hurled it at her, upon which she turned and slowly galloped off.

Some days after, he came to a large river, which he swam with his bag tied upon his head. But the effort had nearly proved fatal. He had reached the middle of the stream, when his strength failed and the current began to sweep him down. Again prayer was his refuge, and animated by a faith that he should yet escape, he cast his eyes down the stream, and saw that just below him a point jutted out into the river, making a bend in the current. Towards that point he directed his exertions, when the current swept him past, and he yielded in despair and sunk; but his feet touched the bottom, and he gained the shore.

Thirteen weeks and four days was that poor slave wandering thus, an exile and a criminal, for daring to wish to own himself. During the eleventh week of his journey, while in the Blue Mountains of Virginia, threading a deep and gloomy gorge, he suddenly came to the body of a female slave. He had found several before, some in different stages of decay, and some with only the bleaching bones to tell how vainly they had sought for earthly freedom. But this one was but recently dead. He drew near with the solemn awe that any man would feel after a separation of eleven weeks from everything human, and then to find himself in the presence of the dead. Alone with the dead! Not in lighted rooms, and with the corpse robed for its long rest, but in the deep gloom of forest trees and mountain gorges, and the dead robed for flight, and beautiful in death.

He stooped over the prostrate form, as it lay with its face turned towards heaven, and hands clasped across the bosom, and a smile still lingering upon the lips, and with the exclamation, "O God, 'tis Rosette!" fell upon his knees beside the corpse. Her flight and exposure had overcome her, and she had died alone and apparently without a struggle, but with joy that Alembert could claim her no longer.

At last he reached ——, Penn. and just in the edge of evening made his way towards the house of a Quaker, and asked for help. The good man took him in, and his family nursed him for many weeks, before he recovered from the long exposure and hardships of that fearful forest journey.

He then found work at a place toward the interior of the State, as hostler, where he remained till observed by a gentleman from New-Jersey, who induced him to leave and go to —— to live. There he had a fellow-laborer, a colored man who professed to be very pious, and who succeeded by his apparent friendship in drawing from him his whole history, and saw his brand.

A few days after, this man wrote several letters, and in due time received others. He then professed to have business to Philadelphia. A day or two after, as Cæsar was sitting in the kitchen eating supper, a loud knock was heard at the front door of the kitchen, which his employer opened, and some one asked, "Have you a nigger working for you?" Cæsar knew the voice as his old master's, and seizing his cap from a chair by his side, he darted through the rear door and ran for a large wood about a quarter of a mile from the house. His pursuers saw his movements, and immediately gave chase. They were Col. Halman, a constable from the south, and the sheriff of the place. The constable was a small man and a fleet runner, and just before they reached the wood he had his hand almost upon poor Cæsar's shoulder, when he drew his pistol and snapped it over his shoulder. The weapon missed fire, but it checked the pursuer so that he reached the shade in safety. The officers halted at the edge of the pines till Col. Halman came up, puffing and blowing, and seeing that they had not secured him, he raved like a madman. He swore that he "would have him, dead or alive, if he had to go through perdition for him."

The sheriff proposed surrounding the woods, but the Colonel answered,—

"May as well chase a deer through ——, as to hunt him there."

They then started for the village for help, and he struck for New-Brunswick, which he reached just in time to take the six o'clock boat for New-York, where he arrived and placed himself in the care of a colored minister's family, the minister himself being on a journey to Canada with some fugitives; and by their influence he was provided with a temporary home.

Thus the Colonel's $500 reward, his long journey, and the execrable perfidy of the black hypocrite who betrayed him, (may he long live to repent of his cowardly villainy!) all failed.

He has since met his master in a railroad depot, but was not recognized, and, to use his own phrase, he "did not care to be introduced to him." Now the old man sleeps his last sleep, and it is not for us to say bow much or how little of his cruel and tyrannical life is chargeable upon his early associations, and the distorting influence of the accursed system which blights both master and slave for time and eternity. The Judge of all the earth will do right. Be it ours to spread the mantle of a Christian charity as far as possible over the actors in the dark scene, while we abate not one jot or tittle of the deep and eradicable hatred which we cherish toward the abominable system.

A few more pages will now complete our record. Col. Halman had sold to Dr. Whitlow a mulatto man, his own son, who by his intelligence and faithfulness won the regard of his master, and was rewarded by emancipation and a free passage to a northern port; and soon after, the good doctor died and emancipated all his slaves by will. In order to prepare the mulatto for freedom, he taught him to read and write. The Colonel being informed of these things, and incensed at what Cæsar had told him about hearing the Doctor read the Bible, induced a low, scurrilous white resident to institute two suits against the Doctor—one for teaching his slave to read and write, for which he was fined one hundred dollars; the other suit, for emancipating the same slave, was commenced on the day of his death, and was unknown to him, but continued against his heirs, who were fined two hundred dollars, (one-half to the informer,) and the Negro remanded to a state of slavery. The last part of the decree came too late—he was beyond pursuit. Not so fortunate, however, were the other slaves. For attempting to execute the will of the Doctor, his heirs were fined one thousand dollars, and every slave being convicted of being the subject of such merciful intentions was sold at public auction to southern drivers.

These things had been transpiring during the last three months of Cæsar's captivity, and May had heard of them till her very soul loathed the system which created such abominations, and she longed to flee from it for ever.

While reflecting upon them her heart turned towards the land of freedom, and she sought relief from her sad thoughts in re-perusing some letters from her northern friends. As she was seeking them, she accidentally discovered a tract which had been given her by one of her friends, on the "Rights of Conscience," and which in the hurry of her departure she had thrown into her trunk, and had not thought of since. She now read it with the deepest interest. It was founded on the words, "We ought to obey God rather than men," and illustrated the truth in clear and forcible terms.

Taking the tract in her hand, she had gone to encourage Cæsar to remain faithful, hoping yet to overcome the opposition of her father, when she found him in tears and covered with blood from a recent whipping. In the agitation of the moment she laid down the tract, consoled him as well as she could, and returned to her room. A moment after, he discovered the tract and took it to carry to her. But unfortunately for him, he had learned to spell out the names of horses on their blankets, and he stopped a short time to spell out a few words through his tears. While thus engaged, the Colonel came upon him, and snatching it from his hand, demanded angrily, "What he had there?" Then glancing over a page or two, he thought he discovered a conspiracy of his daughter's, whose pious feelings he derided, and instantly ordered a most unmerciful lashing for poor Cæsar, (utterly regardless of his protestations of innocence,) and a general branding of some two hundred of his slaves, (Cæsar among the number, whose brand had nearly grown out,) as soon as the plantation-work would permit. He then commanded his daughter before him, and demanded an explanation. The appearance of her father for a moment overcame her, and without waiting for her reply, he proceeded in a storm of invective against "religion, northern sentiment, her insurrectionary folly," etc. Shame, pride, and indignation struggled in the poor girl's heart for the mastery, and with a violent effort she controlled her emotion, drew herself up to her full height, and with a withering glance of firm and scornful determination, checked his tirade.

"Father, if you have anything to say to me, say it as a gentleman and a parent, or excuse me from your presence."

The old man stood abashed. There was a spirit of which he had never dreamed, and he quailed before her stern look of virtuous indignation; then suddenly turning, he requested her to remain till his return, which was in a few moments, with a ponderous law-book in his hand.

"I wish you to see to what you have exposed yourself," said he, pointing to the open page. She took it and read:

"The publishing or circulating any pamphlet or paper, having an evident tendency to excite slaves or free persons of color to insurrection or resistance," (Cæsar was resisting,) "shall be punished with imprisonment for not less than one year, and standing in the pillory, and whipping, at the discretion of the court," (even if it be within an inch of death,) "for the first offense, and death for the second."

"Father, are such laws necessary to sustain the slave system?"

"Yes."

"Then farewell to them and it together! I will not longer breathe the air that is tainted by the horrid thing! I shall soon depart for the north!"

The look and the voice proclaimed the earnestness of feeling and decision of will that prompted the words. The father well knew that beneath the lovely and gentle exterior of his daughter there lay, in her instinctive abhorrence of wrong, the elements of a conflict, which if once aroused would impel her to any sacrifice; and hard as it was for his domineering spirit to yield, he saw its necessity now. Still his hatred of her principles must find vent.

"So your self-sacrificing religion leads you to run away from what you don't like?" Then, in a mournful tone he added:

"I am an old man now, and shall not stay here long. Your brother will never be fit for anything, and who then will take care of all these niggers?"

She had never viewed the subject in this light before, but now her course was clear.

"Father, forgive my hasty resolution; I will remain, and show you by my life that the religion of Christ, while it abhors the traffic in the souls of men, can nerve its possessor to endure association with it, to some extent, for the good of the oppressed."

And while Cæsar was threading the lonely wilds of Virginia, she was an angel of compassion to many a sorrowing heart in the place where he had borne his last stripes, and which he had left for ever.

Cæsar still lives, has a wife and children, and retains his Christian integrity; and though his hardships have been great in the past, they have purchased for him but slight exemption in the present. He is yet a child of sorrow; and as he treads his thorny way toward the grave, his uncomplaining spirit, pressed beneath a load of poverty, and sickness, and trial, looks up amid its tears and anticipates a rest in heaven. Since he gained his freedom, one leg has been broken by the kick of a horse, and he has been confined more than a year from the effects of a dose of poison administered for some unknown cause in a glass of beer, by a dastardly scoundrel with a white skin. Probably it was not designed to affect him so seriously, but his early sufferings had so undermined his constitution, that there was little strength to resist its influence.

He is every year confined from two to six or eight months by sickness, and supported by the labors of his wife, with assistance from sympathizing friends, and the little that he can earn (from five to ten dollars per month) when able to work. His mind, naturally superior to most of his race, has inclined to song, and he has composed a number of homely, uncouth "ballads," as he calls them.—poor enough according to our standard of judgment, but which, sung in his melodious but now broken voice, sound really pleasing. He has thus earned some small change from time to time, and is now soliciting the aid of the benevolent to secure a small old house, that he may die a freeman and leave a shelter for his family. Heaven prosper his efforts! If the sufferings of the unfortunate merit sympathy, he has surely earned success.

Now, kind reader, if you have had patience to follow us through this somewhat disguised narrative thus far, and your heart now prompts to some act of kindness to this son of misfortune, lend your aid in the circulation of this book, as its profits will be sacredly devoted to his use. ...

Smith H. Platt

MARTIN R. DELANY (1812-1885)

Introduction

Martin Robinson Delany was an African American abolitionist, arguably the first proponent of American black nationalism and the first African American field officer in the United States Army. Martin Delany has been called, "The Malcolm X of the 19th century," and "The Father of Black Nationalism." His personal life motto was "Act, Act in the Living Present, But Act."

The Condition, Elevation, Emigration, and Destiny of the Colored People of the United States, 1852

Chapter 4

Our elevation in the United States

We believe in the universal equality of man, and believe in that declaration of God's word in which it is there positively said that "God has made of one blood all the nations that dwell on the face of the earth." Now of "the nations that dwell on the face of the earth," that is, all the people, there are one thousand millions of souls, and of this vast number of human beings, two thirds are colored, from black tending in complexion to the olive, or that of the Chinese with all the intermediate and admixtures of black and white, with the various "crosses" as they are physiologically, but erroneously termed, to white. We are thus explicit in stating these points because we are determined to be understood by all. We have then: two colored to one white person throughout the earth, and yet, singular as it may appear, according to the present geographical and political history of the world, the white race predominates over the colored; or in other words, wherever there is one white person, that one rules and governs two colored persons.

The justice of God is impartial

This is a living undeniable truth to which we call the especial attention of the colored reader in particular. Now there is cause for this, as there is no effect without a cause, a comprehensible remediable cause. We all believe in the justice of God, that he is impartial, "looking upon his children with an eye of care," dealing out to them all the measure of his goodness; yet, how can we reconcile ourselves to the difference that exists between the colored and the white races, as they truthfully present themselves before our eyes? To solve this problem is to know the remedy; and to know it is but necessary, in order successfully to apply it. And we shall but take the colored people of the United States, as a fair sample of the colored races everywhere of the present age, as the arguments that apply to the one will apply to the other, whether Christians, Mohammedans or pagans.

The colored races are highly susceptible of religion, it is a constituent principle of their nature, and an excellent trait in their character. But unfortunately for them they carry it too far. Their hope is largely developed and consequently they usually stand still, hope in God, and really expect Him to do that for them which it is necessary they should do themselves. This is their great mistake, and arises from a misconception of the character and ways of Deity. We must know God, that is understand His Nature and purposes, in order to serve Him; and to serve Him well is but to know Him rightly. To depend for assistance upon God, is a duty and right, but to know when, how, and in what manner to obtain it, is the key to this great Bulwark of Strength, and Depository of Aid.

God has a means for every end
God himself is perfect; perfect in all his works and ways. He had means for every end; and every means used must be adequate to the end to be gained. God's means are laws, fixed laws of nature, a part of His own being, and as immutable, as unchangeable as Himself. Nothing can be accomplished but through the medium of, and conformable to these laws.

They are three, and like God himself, represented in the three persons in the Godhead, the Spiritual, Moral, and Physical Laws.

The Spiritual, Moral, and Physical Laws
That which is Spiritual can only be accomplished through the medium of the Spiritual law,; that which is Moral, through the medium of the Moral law; and that which is Physical, through the medium of Physical law. Otherwise than this, it is useless to expect anything. Should a person want a spiritual blessing, he must apply through the medium of the spiritual law: pray for it in order to obtain it. If they desire to do a moral good, they must apply through the medium of the moral law: exercise their sense and feeling of right and justice, in order to effect it. Do they want to attain a physical end, they can only do so through the medium of the physical law: go to work with muscles, hands, limbs, might, and strength and this, and nothing else will attain it.

The argument that man must pray for what he receives is a mistake, and one that is doing the colored people, especially, incalculable injury. That man must pray in order to get to Heaven every Christian will admit, but a great truth we have yet got to learn is that he can live on earth whether he is religious or not, so that he conforms to the great law of God, regulating the things of earth; the great physical laws. It is only necessary, in order to convince our people of their error and palpable mistake in this matter to call their attention to the fact that there are no people more religious in the Country, than the colored people, and none so poor and miserable as they. That prosperity and wealth smile upon the efforts of wicked white men, whom we know to utter the name of God with curses, instead of praises; that among the slaves, there are thousands of them religious, continually raising their voices, sending up their prayers to God, invoking His aid in their behalf, asking for a speedy deliverance; but they are still in chains, although they have thrice suffered out their three score years and ten. That "God send the rain upon the just and unjust," should be sufficient to convince us that our success in life does not depend upon our religious character, but that the physical laws governing all earthly and temporary affairs benefit equally the just and the unjust. Any other doctrine than this is downright delusion unworthy of a free people, and only intended for slaves. That all men and women should be moral, upright, good, and religious, (we mean Christians), we would not utter a word against, and could only wish that it were so; but, what we here desire to do is to correct the long standing error among a large body of the colored people in this country that the cause of our oppression and degradation is the displeasure of God towards us; because if God is just, and He is, there could be no justice in prospering white men with his fostering care, for more than two thousand years, in all their wickedness while dealing out to the colored people, the measure of his displeasure, for not half the wickedness as that of the whites. Here then is our mistake, and let it forever henceforth be corrected. We are no longer slaves, believing any interpretation that our oppressors may give the word of God, for the purpose of deluding us to the more easy subjugation; but freemen, comprising some of the first minds of intelligence and rudimental qualifications in the country. What then is the remedy for our degradation and oppression? This appears now to be the only remaining question, the means of successful elevation in this our own native land? This depends entirely upon the application of the means of Elevation.

Martin Delany

JOHN JASPER (1812-1901)

Introduction

John Jasper was an African American preacher, philosopher, and orator.

Jasper was born in Fluvanna County, Virginia, the youngest of 24 children. He became a Christian on July 4th 1839 in Capital Square of Richmond, Virginia. He was baptized in 1849 and on the same day, he preached at a funeral, and immediately became famous because of his eulogy. He taught himself to read and write, and although he delivered his sermons in the dialect of the southern slave, more educated ministers said that Jasper's vivid and dramatic sermons transcended "mere grammar." Jasper is known for being one of the great Slave preachers. Every Sunday he led new converts from the Sixth Mount Zion Baptist Church to be baptized in the James River. He once baptized as many as three hundred people in four hours. He became known nationally when he first preached his sermon, "De Sun Do Move" sermon, in which he tried to prove through biblical references that the sun revolves around the earth.

John Jasper: The Unmatched Negro Philosopher and Preacher

Introduction

Reader; stay a moment. A word with you before you begin to sample this book. We will tell you some things in advance, which may help you to decide whether it is worth while to read any further. These pages deal with a Negro, and are not designed either to help or to hurt the Negro race. They have only to do with one man. He was one of a class,—without pedigree, and really without successors, except that he was so dominant and infectious that numbers of people affected his ways and dreamed that they were one of his sort. As a fact, they were simply of another and of a baser sort.

The man in question was a Negro, and if you cannot appreciate greatness in a black skin you would do well to turn your thoughts into some other channel. Moreover, he was a Negro covered over with ante bellum habits and ways of doing. He lived forty years before the war and for about forty years after it. He grew wonderfully as a freeman; but he never grew away from the tastes, dialects, and manners of the bondage times. He was a man left over from the old régime and never got infected with the new order. The air of the educated Negro preacher didn't set well upon him. The raw scholarship of the new "ish," as he called it, was sounding brass to him. As a fact, the new generation of Negro preachers sent out by the schools drew back from this man. They branded him as an anachronism, and felt that his presence in the pulpit was a shock to religion and an offense to the ministry; and yet not one of them ever attained the celebrity or achieved the results which came to this unlettered and grievously ungrammatical son of Africa.

But do not be afraid that you are to be fooled into the fanatical camp. This story comes from the pen of a Virginian who claims no exemption from Southern prejudices and feels no call to sound the praises of the Negro race. Indeed, he never intended to write what is contained within the covers of this book. It grew up spontaneously and most of the contents were written before the book was thought of.

It is, perhaps, too much to expect that the meddlers with books will take the ipse dixitof an unaccredited stranger. They ought not to do it: they are not asked to do it. They can go on about their business, if they prefer; but if they do, they will miss the story of the incomparable Negro of the South. This is said with sobriety and after a half century spent in close observation of the Negro race.

More than that, the writer of this never had any intention of bothering with this man when he first loomed up into notoriety. He got drawn in unexpectedly. He heard that there was a marvel of a man "over in Africa," a not too savory portion of Richmond, Virginia,— and one Sunday afternoon in company with a Scot-Irishman, who was a scholar and a critic, with a strong leaning towards ridicule, he went to hear him preach. Shades of our Anglo-Saxon fathers! Did mortal lips ever gush with such torrents of horrible English! Hardly a word came out clothed and in its right mind. And gestures! He circled around the pulpit with his ankle in his hand; and laughed and sang and shouted and acted about a dozen characters within the space of three minutes. Meanwhile, in spite of these things, he was pouring out a gospel sermon, red hot, full of love, full of invective, full of tenderness, full of bitterness, full of tears, full of every passion that ever flamed in the human breast. He was a theatre within himself, with the stage crowded with actors. He was a battle-field;—himself the general, the staff, the officers, the common soldiery, the thundering artillery and the rattling musketry. He was the preacher; likewise the church and the choir and the deacons and the congregation. The Scot-Irishman surrendered in fifteen minutes after the affair commenced, but the other man was hard-hearted and stubborn and refused to commit himself. He preferred to wait until he got out of doors and let the wind blow on him and see what was left. He determined to go again; and he went and kept going, off and on, for twenty years. That was before the Negro became a national figure. It was before he startled his race with his philosophy as to the rotation of the sun. It was before he became a lecturer and a sensation, sought after from all parts of the country. Then it was that he captured the Scot-Irish and the other man also. What is written here constitutes the gatherings of nearly a quarter of a century, and, frankly speaking, is a tribute to the brother in black,—the one unmatched, unapproachable, and wonderful brother.

But possibly the reader is of the practical sort. He would like to get the worldly view of this African genius and to find out of what stuff he was made. Very well; he will be gratified! Newspapers are heartlessly practical. They are grudging of editorial commendation, and in Richmond, at the period, they were sparing of references of any kind to Negroes. You could hardly expect them to say anything commendatory of a Negro, if he was a Negro, with odd and impossible notions. Now this man was of that very sort. He got it into his big skull that the earth was flat, and that the sun rotated;—a scientific absurdity! But you see he proved it by the Bible. He ransacked the whole book and got up ever so many passages. He took them just as he found them. It never occurred to him that the Bible was not dealing with natural science, and that it was written in an age and country when astronomy was unknown and therefore written in the language of the time. Intelligent people understand this very well, but this miracle of his race was behind his era. He took the Bible literally, and, with it in hand, he fought his battles about the sun. Literally, but not scientifically, he proved his position, and he gave some of his devout antagonists a world of botheration by the tenacity with which he held to his views and the power with which he stated his case. Scientifically, he was one of the ancients, but that did not interfere with his piety and did not at all eclipse his views. His perfect honesty was most apparent in all of his contentions; and, while some laughed at what they called his vagaries, those who knew him best respected him none the less, but rather the more, for his astronomical combat. There was something in his love of the Bible, his faith in every letter of it, and his courage, that drew to him the good will and lofty respect of uncounted thousands and, probably, it might be said, of uncounted millions.

Now when this man died it was as the fall of a tower. It was a crash, heard and felt farther than was the collapse of the famous tower at Venice. If the dubious, undecided reader has not broken down on the road but has come this far, he is invited to look at the subjoined editorial from The Richmond Dispatch, the leading morning paper of Richmond, Va., which published at the time an article on this lofty figure, now national in its proportions and imperishable in its fame, when it bowed to the solemn edict of death.

It is a sad coincidence that the destruction of the Jefferson Hotel and the death of the Rev. John Jasper should have fallen upon the same day. John Jasper was a Richmond Institution, as surely so as was Major Ginter's fine hotel. He was a national character, and he and his philosophy were known from one end of the land to the other. Some people have the impression that John Jasper was famous simply because he flew in the face of the scientists and declared that the sun moved. In one sense, that is true, but it is also true that his fame was due, in great measure, to a strong personality, to a deep, earnest conviction, as well as to a devout Christian character. Some preachers might have made this assertion about the sun's motion without having attracted any special attention. The people would have laughed over it, and the incident would have passed by as a summer breeze. But John Jasper made an impression upon his generation, because he was sincerely and deeply in earnest in all that he said. No man could talk with him in private, or listen to him from the pulpit, without being thoroughly convinced of that fact. His implicit trust in the Bible and everything in it, was beautiful and impressive. He had no other lamp by which his feet were guided. He had no other science, no other philosophy. He took the Bible in its literal significance; he accepted it as the inspired word of God; he trusted it with all his heart and soul and mind; he believed nothing that was in conflict with the teachings of the Bible—scientists and philosophers and theologians to the contrary notwithstanding.

"They tried to make it appear," said he, in the last talk we had with him on the subject, "that John Jasper was a fool and a liar when he said that the sun moved. I paid no attention to it at first, because I did not believe that the so-called scientists were in earnest. I did not think that there was any man in the world fool enough to believe that the sun did not move, for everybody had seen it move. But when I found that these so-called scientists were in earnest I took down my old Bible and proved that they, and not

John Jasper, were the fools and the liars." And there was no more doubt in his mind on that subject than there was of his existence. John Jasper had the faith that removed mountains. He knew the literal Bible as well as Bible scholars did. He did not understand it from the scientific point of view, but he knew its teachings and understood its spirit, and he believed in it. He accepted it as the true word of God, and he preached it with unction and with power.

John Jasper became famous by accident, but he was a most interesting man apart from his solar theory. He was a man of deep convictions, a man with a purpose in life, a man who earnestly desired to save souls for heaven. He followed his divine calling with faithfulness, with a determination, as far as he could, to make the ways of his God known unto men, His saving health among all nations. And the Lord poured upon His servant, Jasper, "the continual dew of His blessing."

The Richmond Dispatch

Chapter 1
Jasper presented

John Jasper, the Negro preacher of Richmond, Virginia, stands preeminent among the preachers of the Negro race in the South. He was for fifty years a slave, and a preacher during twenty-five years of his slavery, and distinctly of the old plantation type. Freedom came full-handed to him, but it did not in any notable degree change him in his style, language, or manner of preaching. He was the ante bellum preacher until eighty-nine years of age, when he preached his last sermon on "Regeneration," and with quiet dignity laid off his mortal coil and entered the world invisible. He was the last of his type, and we shall not look upon his like again. It has been my cherished purpose for some time to embalm the memory of this extraordinary genius in some form that would preserve it from oblivion. I would give to the American people a picture of the God-made preacher who was great in his bondage and became immortal in his freedom.

This is not to be done in biographic form, but rather in vagrant articles which find their kinship only in the fact that they present some distinct view of a man, hampered by early limitations, denied the graces of culture, and cut off even from the advantages of a common education, but who was munificently endowed by nature, filled with vigor and self-reliance, and who achieved greatness in spite of almost limitless adversities. I account him genuinely great among the sons of men, but I am quite sure that the public can never apprehend the force and gist of his rare manhood without first being made acquainted with certain facts appertaining to his early life.

Born a slave

Jasper was born a slave. He grew up on a plantation and was a toiler in the fields up to his manhood. When he came to Richmond, now grown to a man, he was untutored, full of dangerous energies, almost gigantic in his muscle, set on pleasure, and without the fear of God before his eyes. From his own account of himself, he was fond of display, a gay coxcomb among the women of his race, a fun-maker by nature, with a self-assertion that made him a leader within the circles of his freedom.

We meet him first as one of the "hands" in the tobacco factory of Mr. Samuel Hargrove, an enterprising and prosperous manufacturer in the city of Richmond. Jasper occupied the obscure position of "a stemmer,"—which means that his part was to take the well-cured tobacco leaf and eliminate the stem, with a view to preparing what was left to be worked into "the plug" which is the glory of the tobacco-chewer. This position had one advantage for this quick-witted and alert young slave. It threw him into contact with a multitude of his own race, and as nature had made him a lover of his kind his social qualities found ample scope for exercise. In his early days he went at a perilous pace and found in the path of the sinful many fountains of common joy. Indeed, he made evil things fearfully fascinating by the zestful and remorseless way in which he indulged them.

It was always a joy renewed for him to tell the story of his conversion. As described by him, his initial religious experiences, while awfully mystical and solemn to him, were grotesque and ludicrous enough. They partook of the extravagances of the times, yet were so honest in their nature, and so soundly Scriptural in their doctrines, and so reverential in their tone, that not even the most captious skeptic could hear him tell of them, in his moments of exalted inspiration, without feeling profoundly moved by them.

It ought to be borne in mind that this odd and forcible man was a preacher in Richmond for a half century, and that during all that time, whether in slavery or in freedom, he lived up to his religion, maintaining his integrity, defying the unscrupulous efforts of jealous foes to destroy him, and walking the high path of spotless and incorruptible honor. Not that he was always popular among his race. He was too decided, too aggressive, too intolerant towards meanness, and too unpitying in his castigation of vice, to be popular. His life, in the nature of the case, had to be a warfare, and it may be truly said that he slept with his sword buckled on.

Emancipated

Emancipation did not turn his head. He was the same high-minded, isolated, thoughtful Jasper. His way of preaching became an offense to the "edicated" preachers of the new order, and with their new sense of power these double-breasted, Prince-Albert-coated, high hat and kid-gloved clergymen needed telescopes to look as far down as Jasper was, to get a sight of him. They verily thought that it would be a simple process to transfix him with their sneers, and flaunt their new grandeurs before him, in order to annihilate him. Many of these new-fledged preachers, who came from the schools to be pastors in Richmond, resented Jasper's prominence and fame. They felt that he was a reproach to the race, and they did not fail to fling at him their flippant sneers.

But Jasper's mountain stood strong. He looked this new tribe of his adversaries over and marked them as a calcimined and fictitious type of culture. To him they were shop-made and unworthy of respect. They called forth the storm of his indignant wrath. He opened his batteries upon them, and, for quite a while, the thunder of his guns fairly shook the steeples on the other Negro churches of Richmond. And yet it will never do to think of him as the incarnation of a vindictive and malevolent spirit. He dealt terrific blows, and it is hardly too much to say that many of his adversaries found it necessary to get out of the range of his guns. But, after all, there was a predominant good nature about him. His humor was inexhaustible, and irresistible as well. If by his fiery denunciations he made his people ready to "fight Philip," he was quite apt before he finished to let fly some of his odd comparisons, his laughable stories, or his humorous mimicries. He could laugh off his own grievances, and could make his own people "take the same medicine."

Jasper was something of a hermit, given to seclusion, imperturbably calm in his manner, quite ascetic in his tastes, and a cormorant in his devouring study of the Bible. Naturally, Jasper was as proud as Lucifer,—too proud to be egotistic and too candid and self-assertive to affect a humility which he did not feel. He walked heights where company was scarce, and seemed to love his solitude. Jasper was as brave as a lion and possibly not a little proud of his bravery. He fought in the open and set no traps for his adversaries. He believed in himself,—felt the dignity of his position, and never let himself down to what was little or unseemly.

The Sun Do Move

The most remarkable fact in Jasper's history is connected with his extraordinary performances in connection with his tersely expressed theory,—THE SUN DO MOVE! We would think in advance that any man who would come forward to champion that view would be hooted out of court. It was not so with Jasper. His bearing through all that excitement was so dignified, so sincere, so consistent and heroic, that he actually did win the rank of a true philosopher. This result, so surprising, is possibly the most handsome tribute to his inherent excellence and nobility of character. One could not fail to see that his fight on a technical question was so manifestly devout, so filled with zeal for the honor of religion, and so courageous in the presence of overwhelming odds, that those who did not agree with him learned to love and honor him.

The sensation which he awakened fairly flew around the country. It is said that he preached the sermon 250 times, and it would be hard to estimate how many thousands of people heard him. The papers, religious and secular, had much to say about him. Many of them published his sermons, some of them at first plying him with derision, but about all of them rounding up with the admission of a good deal of faith in Jasper. So vast was his popularity that a mercenary syndicate once undertook to traffic on his popularity by sending him forth as a public lecturer. The movement proved weak on its feet, and after a little travel he hobbled back richer in experience than in purse.

As seen in the pulpit or in the street Jasper was an odd picture to look upon. His figure was uncouth; he was rather loosely put together; his limbs were fearfully long and his body strikingly short,—a sort of nexus to hold his head and limbs in place. He was black, but his face saved him. It was open, luminous, thoughtful, and in moments of animation it glowed with a radiance and exultation that was most attractive.

Jasper's career as a preacher after the war was a poem. The story is found later on and marks him as a man of rare originality, and of patience born of a better world. He left a church almost entirely the creation of his own productive life, that holds a high rank in Richmond and that time will find it hard to estrange from his spirit and influence. For quite a while he was hardly on cooperative terms with the neighboring churches, and it is possible that he ought to share somewhat in the responsibility for the estrangement which so long existed;—though it might be safely said that if they had left Jasper alone he would not have bothered them. Let it be said that the animosities of those days gradually gave away to the gracious and softening influence of time, and, when his end came, all the churches and ministers of the city most cordially and lovingly united in honoring his memory.

It may betoken the regard in which Jasper was held by the white people if I should be frank enough to say that I was the pastor of the Grace Street Baptist Church, one of the largest ecclesiastical bodies in the city at the time of Jasper's death, and the simple announcement in the morning papers that I would deliver an address in honor of this Negro preacher who had been carried to his grave during the previous week brought together a representative and deeply sympathetic audience which overflowed the largest church auditorium in the city. With the utmost affection and warmth I put forth my lofty appreci-ation of this wonderful prince of his tribe, and so far as known there was never an adverse criticism offered as to the propriety or justice of the tribute which was paid him.

It is of this unusual man, this prodigy of his race, and this eminent type of the Christian Negro, that the somewhat random articles of this volume are to treat. His life jumped the common grooves and ran on heights not often trod. His life went by bounds and gave surprises with each succeeding leap.

Chapter 2
Jasper has a thrilling conversion

Let us bear in mind that at the time of his conversion John Jasper was a slave, illiterate and working in a tobacco factory in Richmond. It need hardly be said that he shared the superstitions and indulged in the extravagances of his race, and these in many cases have been so blatant and unreasonable that they have caused some to doubt the Negro's capacity for true religion. But from the beginning Jasper's religious experiences showed forth the Lord Jesus as their source and center. His thoughts went to the Cross. His hope was founded on the sacrificial blood, and his noisy and rhapsodic demonstrations sounded a distinct note in honor of his Redeemer.

Call to the ministry

Jasper's conviction as to his call to the ministry was clear-cut and intense. He believed that his call came straight from God. His boast and glory was that he was a God-made preacher. In his fierce warfares with the educated preachers of his race,—"the new issue," as he contemptuously called them—he rested his claim on the ground that God had put him into the ministry; and so reverential, so full of noble assertion and so irresistibly eloquent was he in setting forth his ministerial authority that even his most skeptical critics were constrained to admit that, like John the Baptist, he was "a man sent from God." . . .

His homely way of putting the Gospel came home to them. Let me add that his allusions to his old master were in keeping with his kindly and conciliatory tone in all that he had to say about the white people after the emancipation of the slaves. He loved the white people, and among them his friends and lovers were counted by the thousand.

Chapter 3

How Jasper got his schooling

These chapters disclaim outright any pretension to biography. They deal with a weird, indescribable and mysterious genius, standing out in gloomy grandeur, and not needing the setting forth of ordinary incidents. At the same time, when an extraordinary man comes along and does masterful things, there be some who are ready to ask questions. Was he educated? Well, yes, he was. He had rare educational advantages, not in the schools; but what of that? A genius has no use for a school, except so far as it teaches him the art of thinking. If we run back to the boyhood of Jasper and look him over we find that he had, after all, distinct educational advantages.

Mother Nina

It is another case of a good mother. We know that her name was Nina, and that she was the wife of Philip Jasper, and if tradition tells the truth she was the mother of twenty-four children—a premature applicant for the Rooseveltian prize. John was the last, and was not born until two months after his father's death. Truly grace as well as genius was needed in his case, or he would have struck the wrong road.

That mother was the head of the working women on the Fluvanna farm and learned to govern by reason of the position she held. Her appointment bespoke her character, and her work improved it. Later on, she became in another home the chief of the servant force in a rich family. It was quite a good place. It brought her in contact with cultivated people and the imitative quality in the Negro helped her to learn the manners and to imbibe the spirit of the lady. Later on still, she became a nurse to look after the sick at the Negro Quarters. There she had to do with doctors, medicines and counselors and helpers. Add to all this, she was a sober, thoughtful, godly woman, and you will quite soon reach the conclusion that she was a very excellent teacher for John; and John coming latest in the domestic procession found her rich in experience, matured in motherliness, and enlarged in her outlook of life.

Preacher-father

John's father was a preacher. Harsh things, and some of them needlessly false, are said of the fact that there were no Negro preachers in the times of the slaveholding. It is true, that the laws of the country did not allow independent organizations of Negroes, and Negro preachers were not allowed, except by the consent of their masters, to go abroad preaching the Gospel. They could not accept pastoral charges, and were hampered, as all must admit, by grievous restrictions, but there were Negro preachers in that day just the same,—scores of them, and in one way and another they had many privileges and did good and effective service. One thing about the Negro preacher of the ante bellum era was his high character. It is true that the owner of slaves was not in all cases adapted to determine the moral character of the slave who wanted to preach, and too often, it may be admitted, his prejudices and self-interest may have ruled out some men who ought to have been allowed to preach. It is a pity if this were true. But this strictness had one advantage. When the master of a Negro man allowed him to preach it was an endorsement, acceptable and satisfactory, wherever the man went. If they thought he was all right at home, he could pass muster elsewhere. ...

Varied slave experience

John Jasper was himself an aristocrat. His mode of dress, his manner of walking, his lofty dignity, all told the story. He received an aristocratic education, and he never lost it. Besides this, he had a most varied experience as a slave. He grew up on the farm, and knew what it was to be a plantation hand. He learned to work in the tobacco factory. He worked also in the foundries, and also served around the houses of the families with whom he lived; for it must be understood that after the breaking up of the Peachy family he changed owners and lived in different places. These things enlarged his scope, and with that keen desire to know things he learned at every turn of life.

Keen student

After his conversion he became a passionate student. He acknowledges one who sought to teach him to read, and after hc became a preacher he spelled out the Bible for himself. He was eager to hear other men preach and to talk with those who were wiser than he. And so he kept on learning as long as he lived, though of course he missed the help of the schools, and never crossed the threshold of worldly science in his pursuit of knowledge.

It may be well to say here that Jasper never lost his pride in white people. He delighted to be with them. Thousands upon thousands went to hear him, and while there was a strain of curiosity in many of them there was an under-note of respect and kindliness which always thrilled his heart and did him good. Time and again he spoke to me personally of white people, and always with a beautiful appreciation. It is noteworthy that the old man rode his high horse when his house was partly filled with white people, and it would be no exaggeration to say that not since the end of the war has any Negro been so much loved or so thoroughly believed in as John Jasper.

Chapter 4

The slave preacher

It is as a preacher that John Jasper is most interesting. His personality was notable and full of force anywhere, but the pulpit was the stage of his chief performance. It is worth while to bear in mind that he began to preach in 1839 and that was twenty-five years before the coming of freedom. For a quarter of a century, therefore, he was a preacher while yet a slave. His time, of course, under the law belonged to his master, and under the laws of the period, he could preach only under very serious limitations. He could go only when his master said he might, and he could preach only when some white minister or committee was present to see that things were conducted in an orderly way. This is the hard way of stating the case, but there are many ways of getting around such regulations. The man who could preach, though a Negro, rarely failed of an opportunity to preach. The man who was fit for the work had friends who enabled him to "shy around" his limitations.

The importance of funerals

There was one thing which the Negro greatly insisted upon, and which not even the most hard-hearted masters were ever quite willing to deny them. They could never bear that their dead should be put away without a funeral. Not that they expected, at the time of the burial, to have the funeral service. Indeed, they did not desire it, and it was never according to their notions. A funeral to them was a pageant. It was a thing to be arranged for a long time ahead. It was to be marked by the gathering of the kindred and friends from far and wide. It was not satisfactory unless there was a vast and excitable crowd. It usually meant an all-day meeting, and often a meeting in a grove, and it drew white and black alike, sometimes almost in equal numbers. Another demand in the case,—for the slaves knew how to make their demands,—was that the Negro preacher "should preach the funeral," as they called it. In things like this, the wishes of the slaves generally prevailed. "The funeral" loomed up weeks in advance, and although marked by sable garments, mournful manners and sorrowful outcries, it had about it hints of an elaborate social function with festive accompaniments. There was much staked on the fame of the officiating brother. He must be one of their own color, and a man of reputation. They must have a man to plough up their emotional depths, and they must have freedom to indulge in the extravagancies of their sorrow. These demonstrations were their tribute to their dead and were expected to be fully adequate to do honor to the family.

It was in this way that Jasper's fame began. At first, his tempestuous, ungrammatical eloquence was restricted to Richmond, and there it was hedged in with many humbling limitations. But gradually the news concerning this fiery and thrilling orator sifted itself into the country, and many invitations came for him to officiate at country funerals.

A funeral preacher

He was preeminently a funeral preacher. A Negro funeral without an uproar, without shouts and groans, without fainting women and shouting men, without pictures of triumphant deathbeds and the judgment day, and without the gates of heaven wide open and the subjects of the funeral dressed in white and rejoicing around the throne of the Lamb, was no funeral at all. Jasper was a master from the outset at this work. One of his favorite texts, as a young preacher, was that which was recorded in Revelations, sixth chapter, and second verse: "And I saw and beheld a white horse; and he that sat upon him had a bow, and a crown was given unto him, and he went forth conquering and to conquer." Before the torrent of his florid and spectacular eloquence the people were swept down to the ground, and sometimes for hours many seemed to be in trances, not a few lying as if they were dead.

Hanover Country

Jasper's first visit to the country as a preacher of which we have any account was to Hanover County. A prominent and wealthy slaveholder had the custom of allowing his servants to have imposing funerals, when their kindred and friends died; but those services were always conducted by a white minister. In some way the fame of Jasper had penetrated that community, and one of the slaves asked his master to let Jasper come and attend the funeral. But to this the master made an objection. He knew nothing about Jasper, and did not believe that any Negro was capable of preaching the Gospel with good effect. This Negro was not discouraged by the refusal of the proprietor of the great plantation to grant his request. He went out and collected a number of most trustworthy and influential Negro men and they came in a body to his master and renewed the plea. They told him in their way about what a great man Jasper was, how anxious they were to hear him, what a comfort his presence would be to the afflicted family, and how thankful they would be to have their request honored. They won their point in part. He said to them, as if yielding reluctantly, "very well, let him come." They however had something more to say. They knew Jasper would need to have a good reason in order to get his master's consent for him to come, and they knew that Jasper would not come unless he came under the invitation and protection of the white people, and therefore they asked the gentleman if he would not write a letter inviting him to come. Accordingly, in a spirit of compromise and courtesy very pleasing to the colored people, the letter was written and Jasper came.

The news of his expected coming spread like a flame. Not only the country people in large numbers, but quite a few of the Richmond people, made ready to attend the great occasion. Jasper went out in a private conveyance, the distance not being great, and, in his kind wish to take along as many friends as possible, he overloaded the wagon and had a breakdown. The delay in his arrival was very long and unexplained; but still the people lingered and beguiled the time with informal religious services.

At length the Richmond celebrity appeared on the scene late in the day. The desire to hear him was imperative, and John Jasper was equal to the occasion. Late as the hour was, and wearied as were the people, he spoke with overmastering power. The owner of the great company of slaves on that plantation was among his hearers, and he could not resist the spell of devout eloquence which poured from the lips of the unscholared Jasper. It was a sermon from the heart, full of personal passion and hot with gospel fervor, and the heart of the lord of the plantation was powerfully moved. He undertook to engage Jasper to preach on the succeeding Sunday and handed the blushing preacher quite a substantial monetary token of his appreciation.

The day was accounted memorable by reason of the impression which Jasper made. Indeed, Jasper was a master of assemblies. No politician could handle a crowd with more consummate tact than he. He was the king of hearts and could sway throngs as the wind shakes the trees. ...

Petersburg

Another fact should be referred to here. Jasper was a pastor in the City of Petersburg even before the breaking out of the Civil War. He had charge of one of the less prominent Negro churches and went over from Richmond for two Sundays in each month. This, of course, showed the enlargement of his liberty, that he could take the time to leave the city so often in pursuance of his ministerial work.

It need hardly be mentioned that his presence in Petersburg brought unusual agitation. He fairly depopulated the other Negro churches and drew crowds that could not be accommodated. When it was rumored that Jasper was to preach for the first time on Sunday afternoon, the Rev. Dr. Keene, of the First Baptist Church, and many other white people attended. They were much concerned lest his coming should produce a disturbance, and they went with the idea of preventing any undue excitement. Jasper, flaming with fervid zeal and exhilarated with the freedom of the truth, carried everything before him. He had not preached long before the critical white people were stirred to the depths of their souls and their emotion showed in their weeping.

They beheld and felt the wonderful power of the man. It is said that Dr. Keene was completely captivated, and recognized in Jasper a man whom God had called. ...

Chapter 6

Jasper set free

Jasper came to the verge of his greatness after he had passed the half century line. Freedom had come and to him brought nothing except the opportunity to carve out his own fortune. His ministry had been migratory, restricted and chiefly of ungathered fruit. He found himself in Richmond without money and without a home. By daily toil he was picking up his bread. He was dead set on doing something in the way he wanted to do it. He was of the constructive sort, and never had done well when building on another man's foundation.

His ambition was to build a church. Down on the James River, where the big furnaces were run, there was a little island, and on the island a little house, and scattered along the canal and river were many of the newly liberated and uncared for people of his race.

He began to hold religious services on the island,—said by some to have been held in a private house, and by others in a deserted stable, which was fitted up to accommodate the increasing crowds. Things went well with him. The joy of building flamed his soul, and beneath the tide of the river he baptized many converts. Happy days they were! The people were wild with enthusiasm, and the shouts of his congregation mingled with the noise of the James River Falls. It was to Jasper as the gate of heaven, and he walked as the King's ambassador among his admiring flock.

But it could not be that way long. There was not room enough to contain the people, and yet the church was poverty itself, and what could they do? Happily they found a deserted building beyond the canal and accessible to the growing company of his lovers in the city. There things went with a snap and a roar. From every quarter the people came to hear this African Boanerges. The crowds and songs and riotous shouts of his young church filled the neighborhood. Constant processions, with Jasper at the head, visited the river or canal, to give baptism to the multiplying converts.

The Africa of Richmond

Meanwhile, however, the northern part of the city was fast becoming the Africa of Richmond. Into its meaner outskirts at first the tide began to roll, but in a little while the white people began to retreat, street after street, until a vast area was given up to the colored people. Jasper's people, also, as they prospered, began to settle in this new Africa, and Jasper found once more that he was simply dwelling in tents, when the time was coming for the building of the temple.

Jasper was on the outlook for a new location. Finally he hit upon an old brick church building, at the corner of Duval and St. John Streets. The Presbyterians, who had started this mission years before, had despaired of success under the changed conditions and they offered the house for sale, the price being $2,025. The sense of growth and progress fairly maddened this unique and fascinating preacher with enthusiasm. He had found a home for his people at last, and yet, in point of fact, he had not. The house was a magnificent gain on their old quarters, and yet Sunday afternoon found most of his crowd every on the outside. Quite soon his people had to enlarge and remodel the house, and this they did at a cost of $6,000. By that time the membership was well on towards 2,000. There they dwelt for a number of years until the church became the center of the religious life in that part of the town. "John Jasper," as he was universally called, had easily become the most attractive and popular minister of his race in the city. By this time he was over sixty years of age, and it would have taken much to have quenched the yet unwasted buoyancy and vitality of his ministry. Necessity demanded another building, and in the later prime of his kingly manhood, and very largely by his personal forcefulness and intrepid leadership, he led a movement for a house of worship that would be respectable in almost any part of Richmond. What was more to his purpose, it was very capacious, wisely adapted to the wants of his people and a fitting monument to his constructive resource and enthusiasm. It is said that he, out of his own slender resources, gave $3,000 to the building fund, and this was probably in addition to great sums of money given him by white people who went to hear him preach and who delighted to honor and cheer the old man. I suppose that thousands of dollars were given him from no motive save that of kindness towards him, and the donors would just as soon have given the money directly to him and for his own use. They helped to build the church simply to please the old man whose eloquence and honesty had won their hearts. His love for his church amounted to devotion. He had seen it grow from the most insignificant beginning, had watched the tottering steps of its childhood, and with pride natural and affectionate had gloried in its prosperity.

But be it said to the old man's honor that he was too great to be conceited. He had no sense of boastfulness or self-glorification about the church. He had the frankness to tell the truth about things when it was necessary, but he had too much manly modesty to claim distinction for the part he had borne in the building up of the church. Indeed, he was strangely silent about his relations with the church, and his dominant feeling was one of affectionate solicitude for the future of the church rather than of self-satisfaction on account of its history.

Severity

There was a strain of severity in Jasper. He had some of the temper of the reformer. He was quick,—often too quick—in condemning those who criticized him. The fact is, he was so unfeignedly honest that he could not be patient towards those whose sincerity or honesty he doubted. For those who plotted against the church or gave trouble in other ways he had little charity. Those that would not work in harness, and help to move things along, he was quite willing to show to the church door. For his part, he could not love those very warmly who did not love the "Sixth Mount Zion."

This may be the right place to say a word or two as to Jasper's enemies. He was a man of war, and it may be that his prejudices sometimes got in the saddle. But not very often. Possibly, his most striking characteristic was his bottom sense of justice. He told the truth by instinct, and it never occurred to him to take an undue advantage. If, however, a man wronged him, he was simply terrible in bringing the fellow to book. There was a case, in which it is better not to mention names, in which an insidious and grievous accusation was brought against this sturdy old friend of the faith. The charge sought to fasten falsehood upon Jasper. That was enough for him,—it amounted to a declaration of war, and at once he entered upon the conflict. Never did he cease the strife until the charge was unsaid. Nothing, in short, could terrify him.

It must not be inferred that those who assailed him with questions and arguments were put into the category of personal enemies. Controversy was exactly to his taste. All he asked of the other man was to state his proposition, and he was ready for the contest. Not that he went into it pell-mell. By no means; he took time for preparation, and when he spoke it was hard to answer him. This, of course, applies when the questions were theological and Scriptural, and not scientific. His knowledge of the Scriptures was remarkable, and his spiritual insight into the doctrines of the Bible was extraordinary. When he preached, he supported every point with Scriptural quotations, invariably giving the chapter and verse, and often adding, "Ef yer don' find it jes' ezackly ez I tells yer, yer kin meet me on de street nex' week an' say ter me: 'John Jasper, you ar er lier,' an' I won' say er wurd."

A God-sent man

What gave to Jasper an exalted and impressive presence was his insistent claim that he was a God-sent man. This he asserted in almost every sermon, and with such evident conviction that he forced other people to believe it. Even those who differed with him were constrained to own his sincerity and Godliness. It was impossible to be with him much without being impressed that he was anointed of God for his work. It was in this that his people gloried. Their faith in him was preeminent,—far above every question— and he was also full of inspiration. You may talk with his disciples now, wherever you meet them, and they are quick to tell you that "Brer Jasper was certinly aninted uv God," and even the more intelligent of the people ascribed his greatness to the fact that he was under the power of the Holy Ghost. Many wicked people heard him preach, and some of them still went their wicked way, but they felt that the power of God was with Jasper, and they were always ready to say so. In many points, John Jasper was strikingly like John the Baptist,—a just man and holy, and the people revered him in a way I never met with in any other man.

Chapter 7

The picture-maker

In the circle of Jasper's gifts his imagination was preeminent. It was the mammoth lamp in the tower of his being. A matchless painter was he. He could flash out a scene, coloring every feature, defining every incident and unveiling every detail. Time played no part in the performance,—it was done before you knew it. Language itself was of second moment. His vocabulary was poverty itself, his grammar a riot of errors, his pronunciation a dialectic wreck, his gestures wild and unmeaning, his grunts and heavings terrible to hear. At times he hardly talked but simply emitted; his pictures were simply himself in flame. His entire frame seemed to glow with living light, and almost wordlessly he wrought his miracles. But do not misunderstand. Some insisted on saying that education would have stripped John of his genius by subduing the riot of his power and chastening the fierceness of his imagination. I think not, for John in a good sense was educated. He was a reverential and laborious student for half-a-century. He worked on his sermons with a marked assiduity and acquired the skill and mastership of faithful struggle. Even his imagination had to work, and its products were the fruit of toil. There was no mark of the abnormal or disproportionate in his sky, but all the stars were big and bright. He was well ballasted in his mental make-up, and in his most radiant pictures there was an ethical regard for facts, and an instinctive respect for the truth. Moreover, his ministrations fairly covered the theological field, were strongly doctrinal, and he grappled with honest vigor the deepest principles of the Gospel. He was also intensely practical, scourging sin, lashing neglect, and with lofty authority demanding high and faithful living.

A series of pictures

Think not of Jasper merely as a pictorial preacher. There were wrought into his pictures great principles and rich lessons. But now and then he would present a sermon which was largely a series of pictures from beginning to end. His imagination would be on duty all the time and yet never flag. I cannot forget his sermon on Joseph and his Brethren. It was a stirring presentation of the varied scenes in that memorable piece of history. He opened on the favoritism of Jacob, and was exceedingly strong in condemning partiality, as unhappily expressed in the coat of many colors. That brief part was a sermon itself for parents. From that he passed quickly to the envy of his brothers. jealousy was a demon creeping in among them, inflicting poisonous stings, and spreading his malignant power, until murder rankled in every heart. Then came Joseph, innocent and ignorant of offending, to fall a victim to their conspiracy, with the casting of him into the pit, the selling of him to the traveling tradesmen, the showing to Jacob of the blood-stained coat, with scene after scene until the happy meeting at last between Jacob and his long lost son.

One almost lived a lifetime under the spell of that sermon. It was eloquent, pathetic, terrific in its denunciations, rich in homely piety, and with strains of sweetness that was as balm to sorrowing souls. The effects were as varied as human thoughts and sentiments. The audience went through all moods. Now they were bent down as if crushed with burdens; now they were laughing in tumults at the surprises and charms of heavenly truth; anon they were sobbing as if all hearts were broken, and in a moment hundreds were on their feet shaking hands, shouting, and giving forth snatches of jubilant song. This all seems extravagant, without sobriety entirely, but those that were there, perhaps without an exception, felt that it was the veritable house of God and the gate of heaven.

At other times, Jasper's sermons were sober and deliberate, sometimes even dull; but rarely did the end come without a burst of eloquence or an attractive, entertaining picture. But, remember, that his pictures were never foreign to his theme. They were not lugged in to fill up. They had in them the might of destiny and fitted their places, and fitted them well. Often they came unheralded, but they were evidently born for their part. On one occasion his sermon was on Enoch. It started out at a plodding gait and seemed for a time doomed to dullness, for Jasper could be dull sometimes. At one time he brought a smile to the faces of the audience, in speaking of Enoch's age, by the remark: "Dem ole folks back dar cud beat de presunt ginerashun livin' all ter pieces."

As he approached the end of his sermon, his face lighted up and took on a new grace and passion, and he went out with Enoch on his last walk. That walk bore him away to the border of things visible; earthly scenes were lost to view; light from the higher hills gilded the plains. Enoch caught sight of the face of God, heard the music and the shouting of a great host, and saw the Lamb of God seated on the throne. The scene was too fair to lose, and Enoch's walk quickened into a run which landed him in his father's house. It was a quick, short story, told in soft and mellow tones, and lifted the audience up so far that the people shouted and sang as if they were themselves entering the gates of heaven.

One of his more elaborate descriptions, far too rich to be reproduced, celebrated the ascension of Elijah. There was the oppressive unworldliness of the old prophet, his efforts to shake off Elisha, and Elisha's wise persistence in clamoring for a blessing from his spiritual father. But it was when the old prophet began to ascend that Jasper, standing off like one apart from the scene, described it so thrillingly that everything was as plain as open day. To the people, the prophet was actually and visibly going away. They saw him quit the earth, saw him rise above the mountain tops, sweeping grandly over the vast fields of space, and finally saw him as he passed the moon and stars. Then something happened. In the fraction of a second Jasper was transmuted into Elijah and was actually in the chariot and singing with extraordinary power the old chorus: "Going up to heaven in a chariot of fire." The scene was overmastering! For a time I thought that Jasper was the real Elijah, and my distinct feeling was that the song which he sang could be heard around the world. Of course, it was not so; but there was something in the experience of the moment that has abided with me ever since.

Dialogue with death

At a funeral one Sunday I saw Jasper attempt a dialogue with death, himself speaking for both. The line of thought brought him face to face with death and the grave. The scene was solemnized by a dead body in a coffin. He put his hands over his mouth and stooped down and addressed death. Oh, death—death, speak to me. Where is thy sting? And then with the effect of a clairvoyant he made reply: "Once my sting was keen and bitter, but now it is gone. Christ Jesus has plucked it out, and I have no more power to hurt His children. I am only the gatekeeper to open the gateway to let His children pass." In closing this chapter an incident will largely justify my seemingly extraordinary statements as to the platform power of this unschooled Negro preacher in Virginia.

Listen to Jasper for yourself

In company with a friend I went very often Sunday afternoons to hear Jasper and the fact was bruited about quite extensively, and somewhat to the chagrin of some of my church-members. Two of them, a professor in Richmond College and a lawyer well-known in the city, took me to task about it They told me in somewhat decided tones that my action was advertising a man to his injury, and other things of a similar sort. I cared but little for their criticism, but told them that if they would go to hear him when he was at his best, and if afterwards they felt about him as they then felt, I would consider their complaints. They went the next Sunday. The house was overflowing, and Jasper walked the mountain tops that day. His theme was "The raising of Lazarus" and by steps majestic he took us along until he began to describe the act of raising Lazarus from the dead. It happened that the good professor was accompanied by his son, a sprightly lad of about ten, who was sitting between his father and myself. Suddenly the boy, evidently agitated, turned to me and begged that we go home at once. I sought to soothe him, but all in vain, for as he proceeded the boy urgently renewed his request to go home. His father observed his disquietude and putting an arm around him restored him to calmness. After the service ended and we had reached the street, I said to him: "Look here, boy, what put you into such a fidget to quit the church before the end of the service?" "Oh, doctor, I thought he had a dead man under the pulpit and was going to take him out," he said. My lawyer brother heard the sermon and with profound feeling said, "Hear that, and let me say to you that in a lifetime I have heard nothing like it, and you ought to hear that man whenever you can."

I heard no later criticisms from any man concerning my conduct in evincing such cordial interest in this eloquent son of Fluvanna.

It was only necessary to persuade Jasper's critics to hear him, to remove all question as to his genuine character and effective spiritual ministry.

Chapter 8

Jasper's star witness

The domestic history of this rare and gifted man was not without its tragic incidents. One of the worst features of slavery, as an institution in the South, was the inevitable legislation which it necessitated, and under which many grievous wrongs were perpetrated. The right of the slave owner to the person of the slave carried with it the authority to separate man and wife at the dictate of self-interest, and that was often done, though it ought to be said that thousands of kindhearted men and women did their utmost to mitigate the wrongs which such legislation legalized. In the sale of the Negroes regard was often had for the marriage relation, and it was arranged so that the man and wife might not be tom asunder. But it was not always this way. Too often the sanctity of marriage and the laws of God concerning it were sacrificed to the greed of the slaveholder.

Untimely marriage

If the tradition of Mr. Jasper's first marriage is to be accepted as history, then he was the victim of the cruel laws under which the institution of slavery was governed. In the changes which came to him in the breaking up of the family to which he belonged his lot was cast for a while in the city of Williamsburg. The story is that he became enamored of a maiden bearing the name of Elvy Weaden, and he was successful in his suit. It chanced, however, that on the very day set for his marriage, he was required to go to Richmond to live. The marriage was duly solemnized and he was compelled to leave his bride abruptly, but was buoyed with the hope that fairer days would come when their lot would be cast together. The fleeting days quenched the hope and chilled the ardor of the bride, and in course of time the impatient woman notified Jasper that unless he would come to see her and they could live together, she would account herself free to seek another husband. He was not a man to brook mistreatment, and he made short work of the matter. He wrote her that he saw no hope of returning to Williamsburg, and that she must go ahead and work out her own fate. Naturally enough, the difficulties under which the married life had to be maintained served to weaken seriously the marital tie and to imperil the virtue of the slaves. But this remark ought not to be made without recalling the fact that there were thousands and tens of thousands of happy and well-governed families among the slaves of the South.

Second marriage and divorce

Jasper felt seriously the blight of this untimely marriage and he seems to have remained unmarried until after he united with the church and became a preacher. In time, his thoughts turned again to marriage. He was then a member of the First African Baptist Church of Richmond. He took the letter which his wife had written him some time before and presented it to the church and asked what was his duty under the circumstances. It was a complex and vexing question, but his brethren, after soberly weighing the matter, passed a resolution expressing the conviction that it would be entirely proper for him to marry again. Accordingly, about five years after his conversion, he married a woman bearing the unusual name of Candus Jordan. According to all reports, this marriage was far more fruitful in children than in the matter of connubial peace and bliss for the high-strung and ambitious Jasper. It seems that the case must have had some revolting features, as in due time Jasper secured a divorce and was fully justified by his brethren and friends in taking this action. Evidently this separation from his wife, which was purely voluntary, in no way weakened him in the confidence and good-will of the people.

Years after his divorce, Jasper married Mrs. Mary Anne Cole. There were no children by this marriage, but his wife had a daughter by her former marriage who took the name of Jasper, and was adopted in fact and in heart as the daughter of this now eminent and beloved minister. This wife died in 1874, and Jasper married once more. His widow survived him and still lives, a worthy and honored woman whose highest earthly joy is the recollection of having been the wife of Elder John Jasper, and also the solace and cheer of his old age. This is a checkered story of a matrimonial career, but justice loudly demands the statement that through it all John Jasper walked the lofty path of virtue and honor. It was impossible, however, for a man like Jasper to escape the arrows of the archer. Jealousy, envy, and slander were often busy with his name, and if foul charges could have befouled him none could have been fouler than he. But his daily life was a clean and unanswerable story. Reproaches would not stick to him, and the deadliest darts fell harmless at his feet. His noble seriousness, his absorption in the study of the Bible, his enthusiasm in the ministry, and, most of all, his quiet walk with God, saved him from the grosser temptations of life.

Perhaps the finest incident in all the story of his life was the perfect faith of the people in Jasper. This was true everywhere that he was known, but it was most powerfully true among those who stood nearest to him and knew him best. Jasper, to them, was the incarnation of goodness. They felt his goodness, reveled in it, and lived on it. Their best earthly inspirations sprang out of the fair and incorruptible character of their pastor. If his enemies sought to under mine and defame him, they rallied around him and fought his battles. Little cared he for the ill things said about him personally. Conscious of his rectitude, and, embosomed in the love of his great church, he walked serenely and triumphantly in the way of the Lord. He believed in the sanctity of his home, and he hallowed it by the purity, honesty, and charity of his brethren. ...

Chapter 13
The sun do move

In presenting John Jasper's celebrated sermon on "De Sun Do Move," I beg to introduce it with several explanatory words. It is of a dual character. It includes an extended discussion, after his peculiar fashion, of the text, "The Lord God is a man of war; the Lord is His name." Much that he said in that part of his sermon is omitted, only so much being retained as indicates his view of the rotation of the sun. It was really when he came into this part of his sermon that he showed to such great advantage, even though so manifestly in error as to the position which he tried so manfully to antagonize. It was of that combative type of public speech which always put him before the people at his best. I never heard this sermon but once, but I have been amply aided in reproducing it by an elaborate and altogether friendly report of the sermon published at the time by *The Richmond Dispatch*. Jasper opened his discourse with a tender reminiscence and quite an ingenious exordium.

"Low me ter say," he spoke with an outward composure which revealed an inward but mastered swell of emotion, "dat when I wuz a young man and a slave, I knowed nuthin' wuth talkin' 'bout consarnin' books. Dey wuz sealed mysteries ter me, but I tell yer I longed ter break de seal. I thusted fer de bread uv learnin'. When I seen books I ached ter git in ter um, fur I knowed dat dey had de stuff fer me, an' I wanted ter taste dere contents, but most of de time dey wuz bar'd aginst me.

"By de mursy of de Lord a thing happened. I got er room-feller—he wuz a slave, too, an' he had learn'd ter read. In de dead uv de night he giv me lessons outen de New York Spellin' book. It wuz hard pullin', I tell yer; harder on him, fur he know'd jes' a leetle, an' it made him sweat ter try ter beat sumthin' inter my hard haid. It wuz wuss wid me. Up de hill ev'ry step, but when I got de light uv de less'n into my noodle I farly shouted, but I kno'd I wuz not a scholur. De consequens wuz I crep 'long mighty tejus, gittin' a crum here an' dar untel I cud read de Bible by skippin' de long words, tolerable well. Dat wuz de start uv my eddicashun—dat is, wat little I got. I mek menshun uv dat young man. De years hev fled erway sense den, but I ain't furgot my teachur, an' nevur shall. I thank mer Lord fur him, an' I carries his mem'ry in my heart.

"'Bout seben months after my gittin' ter readin', Gord cunverted my soul, an' I reckin 'bout de fust an' main thing dat I begged de Lord ter give me wuz de power ter und'stan' His Word. I ain' braggin', an' I hates self-praise, but I boun' ter speak de thankful word. I b'lieves in mer heart dat mer pra'r ter und'stand de Scripshur wuz heard. Sence dat time I ain't keerd 'bout nuthin' 'cept ter study an' preach de Word uv God.

"Not, my bruthrin, dat I'z de fool ter think I knows it all. Oh, mer Father, no! Fur frum it. I don' hardly und'stan myse'f, nor ha'f uv de things roun' me, an' dar is milyuns uv things in de Bible too deep fur Jasper, an' sum uv 'em too deep fur ev'rybody. I doan't cerry de' keys ter de Lord's closet, an' He ain' tell me ter peep in, an' ef I did I'm so stupid I wouldn't know it when I see it. No, frens, I knows my place at de feet uv my Marster, an' dar I stays.

"But I kin read de Bible and git de things whar lay on de top uv de soil. Out'n de Bible I knows nuthin' extry 'bout de sun. I sees 'is courses as he rides up dar so gran' an' mighty in de sky, but dar is heaps 'bout dat flamin' orb dat is too much fer me. I know dat de sun shines powerfly an' po's down its light in floods, an' yet dat is nuthin' compared wid de light dat flashes in my min' frum de pages of Gord's book. But you knows all dat. I knows dat de sun burns—oh, how it did burn in dem July days. I tell yer he cooked de skin on my back many er day when I wuz hoein' in de corn feil'. But you knows all dat, an' yet dat is nuthin' der to de divine fire dat burns in der souls uv Gord's chil'n. Can't yer feel it, bruthrin?

"But 'bout de courses uv de sun, I have got dat. I hev dun rang'd thru de whole blessed book an' scode down de las' thing de Bible has ter say 'bout de' movements uv de sun. I got all dat pat an' safe. An' lemme say dat if I doan't giv it ter you straight, if I gits one word crooked or wrong, you jes' holler out, 'Hol' on dar, Jasper, yer ain't got dat straight,' an' I'll beg pardon. If I doan't tell de truf, march up on dese steps here an' tell me I'z a liar, an' I'll take it. I fears I do lie sometimes—I'm so sinful, I find it hard ter do right; but my Gord doan't lie an' He ain' put no lie in de Book uv eternal truf, an' if I giv you wat de Bible say, den I boun' ter tell de truf.

"I got ter take yer all dis arternoon on er skershun ter a great bat'l feil'. Mos' folks like ter see fights—some is mighty fon' er gittin' inter fights, an' some is mighty quick ter run down de back alley when dar is a bat'l goin' on, fer de right. Dis time I'll 'scort yer ter a scene whar you shall witness a curus bat'l. It tuk place soon arter Isrel got in de Promus Lan'. Yer 'member de people uv Gibyun mak frens wid Gord's people when dey fust entered Canum an' dey wuz monsus smart ter do it. But, jes' de same, it got 'em in ter an orful fuss. De cities roun' 'bout dar flar'd up at dat, an' dey all jined dere forces and say dey gwine ter mop de Gibyun people orf uv de groun', an' dey bunched all dar armies tergedder an' went up fer ter do it. Wen dey kum up so bol' an' brave de Giby'nites wuz skeer'd out'n dere senses, an' dey saunt word ter Joshwer dat dey wuz in troubl' an' he mus' run up dar an' git 'em out. Joshwer had de heart uv a lion an' he wuz up dar d'reckly. Dey had an orful fight, sharp an' bitter, but yer might know dat Ginr'l Joshwer wuz not up dar ter git whip't. He prayed an' he fought, an' de hours got erway too peart fer him, an' so he ask'd de Lord ter issure a speshul ordur dat de sun hol' up erwhile an' dat de moon furnish plenty uv moonshine down on de lowes' part uv de fightin' groun's. As a fac', Joshwer wuz so drunk wid de bat'l, so thursty fer de blood uv de en'mies uv de Lord, an' so wild wid de vict'ry dat he tell de sun ter stan' still tel he cud finish his job. Wat did de sun do? Did he glar down in fi'ry wrath an' say, 'What you talkin' 'bout my stoppin' for, Joshwer; I ain't navur startid yit. Bin here all de time, an' it wud smash up ev'rything if I wuz ter start'? Naw, he ain' say dat. But wat de Bible say? Dat's wat I ax ter know. It say dat it wuz at de voice uv Joshwer dat it stopped. I don' say it stopt; tain't fer Jasper ter say dat, but de Bible, de Book uv Gord, say so. But I say dis; nuthin' kin stop untel it hez fust startid. So I knows wat I'm talkin' 'bout. De sun wuz travlin' long dar thru de sky wen de order come. He hitched his red ponies and made quite a call on de lan' uv Gibyun. He purch up dar in de skies jes' as frenly as a naibur whar comes ter borrer sumthin', an' he stan' up dar an' he look lak he enjoyed de way Joshwer waxes dem wicked armies. An' de moon, she wait down in de low groun's dar, an' pours out her light and look jes' as ca'm an' happy as if she wuz waitin' fer her 'scort. Dey nevur budg'd, neither uv 'em, long as de Lord's army needed er light to kerry on de bat'l.

"I doan't read when it wuz dat Joshwer hitch up an' drove on, but I 'spose it wuz when de Lord toll him ter go. Ennybody knows dat de sun didn' stay dar all de time. It stopt fur bizniz, an' went on when it got thru. Dis is 'bout all dat I has ter do wid dis perticl'r case. I dun show'd yer dat dis part uv de Lord's word teaches yer dat de sun stopt, which show dat he wuz movin' befo' dat, an' dat he went on art'rwuds. I toll yer dat I wud prove dis an' I's dun it, an' I derfies ennybody to say dat my p'int ain't made.

"I tol' yer in de fust part uv dis discose dat de Lord Gord is a man uv war. I 'spec by now yer begin ter see it is so. Doan't yer admit it?

When de Lord cum ter see Joshwer in de day uv his feers an' warfar, an' actu'ly mek de sun stop stone still in de heavuns, so de fight kin rage on tel all de foes is slain, yer bleeged ter und'rstan' dat de Gord uv peace is also de man uv war. He kin use bofe peace an' war ter hep de reichus, an' ter scattur de host uv de ailyuns. A man talked ter me las' week 'bout de laws uv nature, an' he say dey carn't poss'bly be upsot, an' I had ter laugh right in his face. As if de laws uv ennythin' wuz greater dan my Gord who is de lawgiver fer ev'rything. My Lord is great; He rules in de heavuns, in de earth, an' doun und'r de groun'. He is great, an' greatly ter be praised. Let all de people bow doun an' wurship befo' Him!

"But let us git erlong, for dar is quite a big lot mo' comin' on. Let us take nex' de case of Hezekier. He wuz one of dem kings of Juder—er mighty sorry lot I mus' say dem kings wuz, fur de mos' part. I inclines ter think Hezekier wuz 'bout de highes' in de gin'ral avrig, an' he war no mighty man hisse'f. Well, Hezekier he got sick. I dar say dat a king when he gits his crown an' fin'ry off, an' when he is posterated wid mortal sickness, he gits 'bout es commun lookin' an' grunts an' rolls, an' is 'bout es skeery as de res' of us po' mortals. We know dat Hezekier wuz in er low state uv min'; full uv fears, an' in a tur'ble trub'le. De fac' is, de Lord strip him uv all his glory an' landed him in de dust. He tol' him dat his hour had come, an' dat he had bettur squar up his affaars, fur death wuz at de do'. Den it wuz dat de king fell low befo' Gord; he turn his face ter de wall; he cry, he moan, he beg'd de Lord not ter take him out'n de worl' yit. Oh, how good is our Gord! De cry uv de king moved his heart, an' he tell him he gwine ter give him anudder show. Tain't only de kings dat de Lord hears. De cry uv de pris'nur, de wail uv de bondsman, de tears uv de dyin' robber, de prars uv de backslider, de sobs uv de womun dat wuz a sinner, mighty apt to tech de heart uv de Lord. It look lik it's hard fer de sinner ter git so fur orf or so fur down in de pit dat his cry can't reach de yere uv de mussiful Savior.

"But de Lord do evun better den dis fur Hezekier—He tell him He gwine ter give him a sign by which he'd know dat what He sed wuz cummin' ter pars. I ain't erquainted wid dem sun diuls dat de Lord toll Hezekier 'bout, but ennybody dat hes got a grain uv sense knows dat dey wuz de clocks uv dem ole times an' dey marked de travuls uv de sun by dem diuls. When, darfo' Gord tol' de king dat He wud mek de shadder go backwud, it mus' hev bin jes' lak puttin' de han's uv de clock back, but, mark yer, Izaer 'spressly say dat de sun return'd ten dergrees. Thar yer are! Ain't dat de movement uv de sun? Bless my soul. Hezekier's case beat Joshwer. Joshwer stop de sun, but heer de Lord mek de sun walk back ten dergrees; an' yet dey say dat de sun stan' stone still an' nevur move er peg. It look ter me he move roun' mighty brisk an' is ready ter go ennyway dat de Lord ordurs him ter go. I wonder if enny uv dem furloserfers is roun' here dis arternoon. I'd lik ter take a squar' look at one uv dem an' ax him to 'splain dis mattur. He carn't do it, my bruthr'n. He knows a heap 'bout books, maps, figgers an' long distunces, but I derfy him ter take up Hezekier's case an' 'splain it orf. He carn't do' it. De Word uv de Lord is my defense an' bulwurk, an' I fears not what men can say nor do; my Gord gives me de vict'ry.

"'Low me, my frens, ter put mysef squar 'bout dis movement uv de sun. It ain't no bizniss uv mine wedder de sun move or stan' still, or wedder it stop or go back or rise or set. All dat is out er my han's 'tirely, an' I got nuthin' ter say. I got no the-o-ry on de subjik. All I ax is dat we will take wat de Lord say 'bout it an' let His will be dun 'bout ev'rything. Wat dat will is I karn't know 'cept He whisper inter my soul or write it in a book. Here's de Book. Dis is 'nough fer me, and wid it ter pilut me, I karn't git fur erstray.

"But I ain't dun wid yer yit. As de song says, dere's mo' ter foller. I envite yer ter heer de fust vers in de sev'nth chaptur uv de book uv Reverlashuns. What do John, und'r de pow'r uv de Spirit, say? He say he saw fo' anguls standin' on de fo' corners uv de earth, holdin' de fo' win's uv de earth, an' so fo'th. 'Low me ter ax ef de earth is roun', whar do it keep its corners? Er flat, squar thing has corners, but tell me where is de cornur uv er appul, ur a marbul, ur a cannun ball, ur a silver dollar. Ef dar is enny one uv dem furloserfurs whar's been takin' so many cracks at my ole haid 'bout here, he is korjully envited ter step for'd an' squar up dis vexin' bizniss. I here tell you dat yer karn't squar a circul, but it looks lak dese great scolurs dun learn how ter circul de squar. Ef dey kin do it, let 'em step ter de front an' do de trick. But, mer brutherin, in my po' judmint, dey karn't do it; tain't in 'em ter do it. Dey is on der wrong side of de Bible; dat's on de outside of de Bible, an' dar's whar de trubbul comes in wid 'em. Dey dun got out uv de bres'wuks uv de truf, an' ez long ez dey stay dar de light uv de Lord will not shine on der path. I ain't keer'n so much 'bout de sun, tho' it's mighty kunveenyunt ter hav it, but my trus' is in de Word uv de Lord. Long ez my feet is flat on de solid rock, no man kin move me. I'se gittin' my order f'um de Gord of my salvashun.

"Tother day er man wid er hi coler and side whisk'rs cum ter my house. He was one nice North'rn gemman wat think a heap of us col'rd people in de Souf. Da ar luvly folks and I honors 'em very much. He seem from de start kinder strictly an' cross wid me, and arter while, he brake out furi'us and frettid, an' he say: 'Erlow me Mister Jasper ter gib you sum plain advise. Dis nonsans 'bout de sun movin' whar you ar gettin' is disgracin' yer race all ober de kuntry, an' as a fren of yer peopul, I cum ter say it's got ter stop.' Ha! Ha! Ha! Mars' Sam Hargrove nuvur hardly smash me dat way. It was equl to one ov dem ole overseurs way bac yondur. I tel him dat ef he'll sho me I'se wrong, I giv it all up.

"My! My! Ha! Ha! He sail in on me an' such er storm about science, nu 'scuv'ries, an' de Lord only knos wat all, I ner hur befo', an' den he tel me my race is ergin me an' po ole Jasper mus shet up 'is fule mouf.

"Wen he got thru—it look lak he nuvur wud, I tel him John Jasper ain' set up to be no scholur, an' doant kno de ferlosophiz, an' ain' tryin' ter hurt his peopul, but is wurkin' day an' night ter lif 'em up, but his foot is on de rock uv eternal truff. Dar he stan' and dar he is goin' ter stan' til Gabrul soun's de judgment note. So er say to de gemman wat scol'd me up so dat I hur him mek his remarks, but I ain' hur whar he get his Scriptu' from, an' dat 'tween him an' de wurd of de Lord I tek my stan' by de Word of Gord ebery time. Jasper ain' mad: he ain' fightin' nobody; he ain' bin 'pinted janitur to run de sun: he nothin' but de servunt of Gord and a luver of de Everlasting Word. What I keer about de sun? De day comes on wen de sun will be called frum his race-trac, and his light squincked out foruvur; de moon shall turn ter blood, and this yearth be konsoomed wid fier. Let um go; dat wont skeer me nor trubble Gord's erlect'd peopul, for de word uv de Lord shell aindu furivur, an' on dat Solid Rock we stan' an' shall not be muved.

"Is I got yer satisfied yit? Has I prooven my p'int? Oh, ye whose hearts is full uv unberlief! Is yer still hol'in' out? I reckun de reason yer say de sun don' move is 'cause yer are so hard ter move yerse'f. You is a reel triul ter me, but, nevur min'; I ain't gi'n yer up yit, an' nevur will. Truf is mighty; it kin break de heart uv stone, an' I mus' fire anudder arrur uv truf out'n de quivur uv de Lord. If yer haz er copy uv God's Word 'bout yer pussun, please tu'n ter dat miner profit, Malerki, wat writ der las' book in der ole Bible, an' look at chaptur de fust, vurs 'leben; what do it say? I bet'r read it, fur I got er noshun yer critics doan't kerry enny Bible in thar pockits ev'ry day in de week. Here is wat it says: 'Fur from de risin' uv de sun evun unter de goin' doun uv de same My name shall be great 'mong de Gentiles. My name shall be great 'mong de heathun, sez de Lord uv hosts.' How do dat suit yer? It look lak dat ort ter fix it. Dis time it is de Lord uv hosts Hisse'f dat is doin' de talkin', an' He is talkin' on er wonderful an' glorious subjik. He is tellin' uv de spredin' uv His Gorspel, uv de kummin' uv His larst vict'ry ovur de Gentiles, an' de wurldwide glories dat at de las' He is ter git. Oh, my bruddrin, wat er time dat will be. My soul teks wing es I erticipate wid joy dat merlenium day! De glories as dey shine befo' my eyes blin's me, an' I furgits de sun an' moon an' stars. I jes' 'members dat 'long 'bout dose las' days dat de sun an moon will go out uv bizniss, fur dey won' be needed no mo'. Den will King Jesus come back ter see His people, an' He will be de suffishunt light uv de wurl'. Joshwer's bat'ls will be ovur. Hezekier woan't need no sun diul, an' de sun an' moon will fade out befo' de glorius splendurs uv de New Jerruslem.

"But wat der mattur wid Jasper. I mos' furgit my bizniss, an' mos' gon' ter shoutin' ovur de far away glories uv de secun' cummin' uv my Lord. I beg pardun, an' will try ter git back ter my subjik. I hev ter do as de sun in Hezekier's case—fall back er few dergrees. In dat part uv de Word dat I gin yer frum Malerki—dat de Lord Hisse'f spoke—He klars dat His glory is gwine ter spred. Spred? Whar? Frum de risin' uv de sun ter de goin' down uv de same. Wat? Doan't say dat, duz it? Dat's edzakly wat it sez. Ain't dat cleer 'nuff fer yer? De Lord pity dese doubtin' Tommusses. Here is 'nuff ter settul it all an' kure de wuss cases. Walk up yere, wise folks, an' git yer med'sin. Whar is dem high collar'd furloserfurs now? Wat dey skulkin' roun' in de brush fer? Why doan't yer git out in der broad arternoon light an' fight fer yer cullurs? Ah, I un'stans it; yer got no answer. De Bible is agin yer, an' in yer konshunses yer are convictid.

"But I hears yer back dar. Wat yer wisprin' 'bout? I know; yer say yer sont me sum papurs an' I nevur answer dem. Ha, ha, ha! I got 'em. De differkulty 'bout dem papurs yer sont me is dat dey did not answer me. Dey nevur menshun de Bible one time. Yer think so much uv yoursef's an' so little uv de Lord Gord an' thinks wat yer say is so smart dat yer karn't even speak uv de Word uv de Lord. When yer ax me ter stop believin' in de Lord's Word an' ter pin my faith ter yo words, I ain't er gwine ter do it. I take my stan' by de Bible an' res' my case on wat it says. I take wat de Lord says 'bout my sins, 'bout my Savior, 'bout life, 'bout death, 'bout de wurl' ter come, an' I take wat de Lord say 'bout de sun an' moon, an' I cares little wat de haters of mer Gord chooses ter say. Think dat I will fursake de Bible? It is my only Book, my hope, de arsnel uv my soul's surplies, an' I wants nuthin' else.

"But I got ernudder wurd fur yer yit. I done wuk ovur dem. papurs dat yer sont me widout date an' widout yer name. Yer deals in figgurs an' thinks yer are biggur dan de arkanjuls. Lemme see wat yer dun say. Yer set yerse'f up ter tell me how fur it is frum here ter de sun. Yer think yer got it down ter er nice p'int. Yer say it is 3,339,002 miles frum de earth ter de sun. Dat's wat yer say. Nudder one say dat de distuns is 12,000,000; nudder got it ter 27,000,000. I hers dat de great Isuk Nutun wuk't it up ter 28,000,000, an' later on de furloserfurs gin ernudder rippin' raze to 50,000,000. De las' one gits it bigger' dan all de yuthers, up to 90,000,000. Doan't enny uv 'em ergree edzakly an' so dey runs a guess game, an' de las' guess is always de bigges'. Now, wen dese guessers kin hav a kunvenshun in Richmun' an' all ergree 'pun de same thing, I'd be glad ter hear frum yer ag'in, an' I duz hope dat by dat time yer won't be ershamed uv yer name.

"Heeps uv railroads hes bin built sense I saw de fust one wen I wuz fifteen yeers ole, but I ain't hear tell uv er railroad built yit ter de sun. I doan' see why ef dey kin meshur de distuns ter de sun, dey might not git up er railroad er a telurgraf an' enabul us ter fin' sumthin' else 'bout it den merely how fur orf de sun is. Dey tell me dat a kannun ball cu'd mek de trep ter de sun in twelve years. Why doan' dey send it? It might be rig'd up wid quarturs fur a few furloserfers on de inside an' fixed up fur er kumfurterble ride. Dey wud need twelve years' rashuns an' a heep uv changes uv ramint—mighty thick clo'es wen dey start and mighty thin uns wen dey git dar.

"Oh, mer bruthrin, dese things mek yer laugh, an' I doan' blem yer fer laughin', 'cept it's always sad ter laugh at der follies uv fools. If we cu'd laugh 'em out'n kount'nens, we might well laugh day an' night. Wat cuts inter my soul is, dat all dese men seem ter me dat dey is hittin' at de Bible. Dat's wat sturs my soul an' fills me wid reichus wrath. Leetle keers I wat dey says 'bout de sun, purvided dey let de Word uv de Lord erlone. But nevur min'. Let de heethun rage an' de people 'madgin er vain thing. Our King shall break 'em in pieces an' dash 'em down. But blessed be de name uv our Gord, de Word uv de Lord indurith furivur. Stars may fall, moons may turn ter blood, an' de sun set ter rise no mo', but Thy kingdom, oh, Lord, is frum evurlastin' ter evurlastin'.

"But I has er word dis arternoon fer my own brutherin. Dey is de people fer whose souls I got ter watch—fur dem I got ter stan' an' report at de last—dey is my sheep an' I'se der shepherd, an' my soul is knit ter dem forever. 'Tain fer me ter be troublin' yer wid dese questions erbout dem heb'nly bodies. Our eyes goes far beyon' de smaller stars; our home is clean outer sight uv dem twinklin' orbs; de chariot dat will cum ter take us to our Father's mansion will sweep out by dem flickerin' lights an' never halt till it brings us in clar view uv de throne uv de Lamb. Doan't hitch yer hopes to no sun nor stars; yer home is got Jesus fer its light, an' yer hopes mus' trabel up dat way. I preach dis sermon jest fer ter settle de min's uv my few brutherin, an' repeats it 'cause kin' frens wish ter hear it, an' I hopes it will do honor ter de Lord's Word. But nuthin' short of de purly gates can satisfy me, an' I charge, my people, fix yer feet on de solid Rock, yer hearts on Calv'ry, an' yer eyes on de throne uv de Lamb. Dese strifes an' griefs 'll soon git ober; we shall see de King in His glory an' be at ease. Go on, go on, ye ransom uv de Lord; shout His praises as yer go, an' I shall meet yer in de city uv de New Jeruserlum, whar we shan't need the light uv de sun, fer de Lam' uv de Lord is de light uv de saints." . . .

Chapter 15

Jasper's picture of heaven

I never heard Jasper preach a sermon on heaven, nor did I ever hear of his doing so. So far as my observation goes, sermons on heaven have failed to edify the thoughtful—sometimes proving distinctly disappointing. It was not to Jasper's taste to argue on heaven as a doctrine. With him it was as if he were camping outside of a beautiful city, knowing much of its history and inhabitants, and in joyous expectation of soon moving into it. The immediate things of the kingdom chiefly occupied his attention; but when his sermons took him into the neighborhood of heaven, he took fire at once and the glory of the celestial city lit his face and cheered his soul. This chapter deals only with one of his sermons which, while not on heaven, reveals his heart-belief in it, and its vital effect upon his character.

Two funerals

Imagine a Sunday afternoon at his church—a fair, inspiring day. His house was thronged to overflowing. It was the funeral of two persons—William Ellyson and Mary Barnes. The text is forgotten, but the sermon is vividly recalled.

From the start Jasper showed a burden and a boldness that promised rich things for his people. At the beginning he betrayed some hesitation—unusual for him. "Lemme say," he said, "a word about dis William Ellersin. I say it de fust an' git it orf mer min'. William

Ellersin was no good man—he didn't say he wus; he didn't try to be good, an' de tell me he die as he live, 'out Gord an' 'out hope in de worl'. It's a bad tale to tell on 'im, but he fix de story hissef. As de tree falls dar mus it lay. Ef you wants folks who live wrong to be preached and sung to glory, don' bring 'em to Jasper. Gord comfut de monur and warn de onruly.

"But, my bruthrin," he brightened as he spoke, "Mary Barnes wus difrunt. She wer wash'd in de blood of de Lam' and walk'd in white; her r'ligion was of Gord. Yer could trust Mary anywhar; nuvr cotch 'er in dem playhouses ner friskin' in dem dances; she wan' no street-walk'r trapsin' roun' at night. She love de house of de Lord; her feet clung to de straight and narrer path; I know'd her. I seen her at de prarmeetin'—seed her at de supper— seed her at de preachin', an' seed her tendin' de sick an' helpin' de mounin' sinn'rs. Our Sister Mary, good-bye. Yer race is run, but yer crown is shure."

From this Jasper shot quite apart. He was full of fire, humor gleamed in his eye, and freedom was the bread of his soul. By degrees he approached the realm of death, and he went as an invader. A note of defiant challenge rang in his voice and almost blazed on his lips. He escorted the Christian to the court of death, and demanded of the monster king to exhibit his power to hurt. It was wonderful to see how he pictured the high courage of the child of God, marching up to the very face of the king of terrors and demanding that he come forth and do his worst. Death, on the other hand, was subdued, slow of speech, admitted his defeat, and proclaimed his readiness to serve the children of Immanuel. Then he affected to put his mouth to the grave and cried aloud: "Grave! Grave! Er Grave!" he cried as if addressing a real person, "Whar's yer vict'ry? I hur you got a mighty banner down dar, an' you turrurizes ev'rybody wat comes long dis way. Bring out your armies an' furl fo'th your bann'rs of vict'ry. Show your han' an' let 'em see wat you kin do." Then he made the grave reply: "Ain't got no vict'ry now; had vict'ry, but King Jesus pars'd through dis country an' tord my banners down. He says His peopl' shan't be troubled no mo' forev'r; an' He tell me ter op'n de gates an' let 'um pass on dar way to glory."

"Oh, my Gord," Jasper exclaimed in thrilling voice, "did yer hur dat? My Master Jesus done jerk'd de sting of death, done broke de scept'r of de king of tur'rs, an' He dun gone inter de grave an' rob it uv its victorous banners, an' fix'd nice an' smooth for His people ter pass through. Mo' en dat, He has writ a song, a shoutin' anthim for us to sing when we go thur, passin' suns an' stars, an' singin' dat song, 'Thanks be onter Gord—be onter Gord who give us de vict'ry thru de Lord Jesus Christ.'" Too well I know that I do scant justice to the greatness of Jasper by this outline of his transcendent eloquence. The whole scene, distinct in every detail, was before the audience, and his responsive hearers were stirred into uncontrollable excitement.

"My bruthrin," Jasper resumed very soberly, "I oft'n ax myself how I'd behave myself ef I was ter git to heav'n. I tell you I would tremble fo' de consequinces. Eben now when I gits er glimpse—jist a peep into de palis of de King, it farly runs me ravin' 'stracted. What will I do ef I gits thar? I 'spec I'll make er fool of myself, 'cause I ain't got de pritty ways an' nice manners my ole Mars' Sam Hargrove used to have, but ef I git thar they ain't goin' to put me out. Mars' Sam'll speak fur me an' tell 'em to teach me how to do. I sometimes thinks if I's 'lowed to go free—I 'specs to be free dar, I tell you, b'leve I'll jest do de town—walkin' an' runnin' all roun' to see de home which Jesus dun built for His people.

"Fust of all, I'd go down an' see de river of life. I lov's to go down to de ole muddy Jemes—mighty red an' muddy, but it goes 'long so gran' an' quiet like 'twas 'tendin' to ' business—but dat ain't nothin' to the river which flows by de throne. I longs fer its crystal waves, an' de trees on de banks, an' de all mann'rs of fruits. Dis old head of mine oft'n gits hot with fever, aches all night an' rolls on de piller, an' I has many times desired to cool it in that blessed stream as it kisses de banks of dat upper Canaan. Bl'ssed be de Lord! De thought of seein' dat river, drinkin' its water an' restin' un'r dose trees—" Then suddenly Jasper began to intone a chorus in a most affecting way, no part of which I can recall except the last line: "Oh, what mus' it be to be thar?" "Aft'r dat," Jasper continued with quickened note, I'd turn out an' view de beauties of de city—de home of my Father. I'd stroll up dem abenuse whar de children of Gord dwell an' view dar mansions. Father Abraham, I'm sure he got a grate pallis, an' Moses, what 'scorted de children of Israel out of bondige thru' de wilderness an' to de aidge of de promised lan', he must be pow'rful set up being sich er man as he is; an' David, de king dat made pritty songs, I'd like to see 'is home, an' Paul, de mighty scholar who got struck down out in de 'Mascus road, I want to see his mansion, an' all of 'em. Den I would cut roun' to de back streets an' look for de little home whar my Savior set my mother up to housekeepin' when she got thar. I 'spec to know de house by de roses in de yard an' de vine on de poch." As Jasper was moving at feeling pace along the path of his thoughts, he stopped and cried: "Look dar; mighty sweet house, ain't it lovely?" Suddenly he sprang back and began to shout with joyous clapping of hands. "Look dar; see dat on de do; hallelujah, it's John Jasper. Said He was gwine to prepar a place for me; dar it is. Too good for a po' sinner like me, but He built it for me, a turn-key job, an' mine forev'r." Instantly he was singing his mellow chorus ending as before with: "Oh, what mus' it be to be thar!"

From that scene, he moved off to see the angelic host. There were the white plains of the heavenly Canaan—a vast army of angels with their bands of music, their different ranks and grades, their worship before the throne and their pealing shouts as they broke around the throne of God. The charm of the scene was irresistible; it lifted everybody to a sight of heaven, and it was all real to Jasper. He seemed entranced. As the picture began to fade up rose his inimitable chorus, closing as always: "Oh, what mus' it be to be thar!"

Then there was a long wait. But for the subdued and unworldly air of the old preacher— full seventy years old then—the delay would have dissolved the spell. "An' now, frenz," he said, still panting and seeking to be calm, "ef yer'll 'scuse me, I'll take er trip to de throne an' see de King in 'is roy'l garmints." It was an event to study him at this point. His earnestness and reverence passed all speech, and grew as he went. The light from the throne dazzled him from afar. There was the great white throne—there, the elders bowing in adoring wonder— there, the archangels waiting in silence for the commands of the King—there the King in His resplendent glory—there in hosts innumerable were the ransomed. In point of vivid description it surpassed all I had heard or read. By this time the old Negro orator seemed glorified. Earth could hardly hold him. He sprang about the platform with a boy's alertness; he was unconsciously waving his handkerchief as if greeting a conqueror; his face was streaming with tears; he was bowing before the Redeemer; he was clapping his hands, laughing, shouting and wiping the blinding tears out of his eyes. It was a moment of transport and unmatched wonder to every one, and I felt as if it could never cease, when suddenly in a new note he broke into his chorus, ending with the soul-melting words: "Oh, what mus' it be to be thar!"

It was a climax of climaxes. I supposed nothing else could follow. We had been up so often and so high we could not be carried up again. But there stood Jasper, fully seeing the situation. He had seen it in advance and was ready. "My bruthrin," said he as if in apology, "I dun fergot somethin'. I got ter tek anuth'r trip. I ain't visit'd de ransum of de Lord. I can't slight dem. I knows heap ov 'em, an' I'm boun' to see 'em." In a moment he had us out on the celestial plains with the saints in line. There they were—countless and glorious! We walked the whole line and had a sort of universal handshake in which no note of time was taken. "Here's Brer Abul, de fust man whar got here; here's Brer Enoch whar took er stroll and straggled inter glory; here's ole Ligie, whar had er carriage sent fur 'im an' comed a nigher way to de city." Thus he went on greeting patriarchs, prophets, apostles, martyrs, his brethren and loved ones gone before until suddenly he sprang back and raised a shout that fairly shook the roof. "Here she is; I know'd sh'd git here; why, Mary Barnes, you got home, did yer?" A great handshake he gave her and for a moment it looked as if the newly-glorified Mary Barnes was the center of Jasper's thoughts; but, as if by magic, things again changed and he was singing at the top of his voice the chorus which died away amid the shrieks and shouts of his crowd with his plaintive note: "Oh, what mus' it be to be thar!"

When Death Shall Shake My Frame

Jasper dropped exhausted into a chair and some chief singer of the old-time sort, in noble scorn of all choirs, struck that wondrous old song, *When Death Shall Shake My Frame*, and in a moment the great building throbbed and trembled with the mighty old melody. It was sung only as Jasper's race can sing, and especially as only Jasper's emotional and impassioned church could sing it. This was Jasper's greatest sermon. In length it was not short of an hour and a half—maybe it was longer than that. He lifted things far above all thought of time, and not one sign of impatience was seen. The above sketch is all unworthy of the man or the sermon. As for the venerable old orator himself he was in his loftiest mood—free in soul, alert as a boy, his imagination rioting, his action far outwent his words, and his pictures of celestial scenes glowed with unworldly lustre. He was in heaven that day, and took us around in his excursion wagon, and turning on the lights showed us the City of the Glorified.

What is reported here very dimly hints at what he made us see. Not a few of Richmond's most thoughtful people, though some of them laid no claim to piety, were present and not one of them escaped the profound spiritual eloquence of this simple-hearted old soldier of the cross.

Valiant, heroic old man! He stood in his place and was not afraid. He gave his message in no uncertain words—scourged error wherever it exposed its front stood sentinel over the word of God and was never caught sleeping at his post.

When his work ended, he was ready to go up and see his Master face to face.

The stern old orator, brave as a lion, rich in humor, grim, and a dreamer whose dreams were full of heaven, has uttered his last message and gone within the veil to see the wonders of the unseen. If the grapes of Eschol were so luscious to him here, "Oh, what must it be for him to be there."

William Eldridge, John Jasper: The Unmatched Negro
Philosopher and Preacher, *Fleming H. Revell Company, 1908*

HARRIET ANN JACOBS (1813-1897)

Introduction

Harriott Ann Jacobs, an American abolitionist and writer, was born in Edenton, North Carolina to Daniel Jacobs and Delilah. Her father was a mulatto slave owned by Dr. Andrew Knox. Her mother was a mulatto slave owned by John Horniblow, a tavern owner. Harriet inherited the status of both her parents as a slave by birth. She was raised by Delilah until the latter died around 1819. She then was raised by her mother's mistress, Margaret Horniblow. Margaret taught Harriet to read, write, and sew.

Harriet Ann Jacobs eventually escaped to the North, where she wrote a narrative about her ordeal of slavery. The book, *Incidents in the Life of a Slave Girl*, recounts how Jacobs was hidden in the crawl space of her grandmother's house for seven years in order to escape the sexual advances of her master. In chapter nine, Jacobs describes the torture and death of a slave on a neighboring plantation, sometime in the 1820s. In 1861, she published *Incidents in the Life of a Slave Girl* under the pseudonym Linda Brent.

Incidents in the Life of a Slave Girl
Chapter 9
A Slave Is Tortured

In my childhood I knew a valuable slave, named Charity, and loved her, as all children did. Her young mistress married, and took her to Louisiana. Her little boy, James, was sold to a good sort of master. He became involved in debt, and James was sold again to a wealthy slaveholder, noted for his cruelty. With this man he grew up to manhood, receiving the treatment of a dog. After a severe whipping, to save himself from further infliction of the lash, with which he was threatened, he took to the woods. He was in a most miserable condition—cut by the cowskin, half naked, half starved, and without the means of procuring a crust of bread.

Some weeks after his escape, he was captured, tied, and carried back to his master's plantation. This man considered punishment in his jail, on bread and water, after receiving hundreds of lashes, too mild for the poor slave's offence. Therefore he decided, after the overseer should have whipped him to his satisfaction, to have him placed between the screws of the cotton gin, to stay as long as he had been in the woods. This wretched creature was cut with the whip from his head to his foot, then washed with strong brine, to prevent the flesh from mortifying, and make it heal sooner than it otherwise would. He was then put into the cotton gin, which was screwed down, only allowing him room to turn on his side when he could not lie on his back. Every morning a slave was sent with a piece of bread and bowl of water, which were placed within reach of the poor fellow. The slave was charged, under penalty of severe punishment, not to speak to him.

Four days passed, and the slave continued to carry the bread and water. On the second morning, he found the bread gone, but the water untouched.

When he had been in the press four days and five nights, the slave informed his master that the water had not been used for four mornings, and that a horrible stench came from the gin house. The overseer was sent to examine into it. When the press was unscrewed, the dead body was found partly eaten by rats and vermin. Perhaps the rats that devoured his bread had gnawed him before life was extinct. Poor Charity! Grandmother and I often asked each other how her affectionate heart would bear the news, if she should ever hear of the murder of her son. We had known her husband, and knew that James was like him in manliness and intelligence. These were the qualities that made it so hard for him to be a plantation slave. They put him into a rough box, and buried him with less feeling than would have been manifested for an old house dog. Nobody asked any questions. He was a slave; and the feeling was that the master had a right to do what he pleased with his own property. And what did he care for the value of a slave? He had hundreds of them. When they had finished their daily toil, they must hurry to eat their little morsels, and be ready to extinguish their pine knots before nine o'clock, when the overseer went his patrol rounds. He entered every cabin, to see that men and their wives had gone to bed together, lest the men, from over-fatigue, should fall asleep in the chimney corner, and remain there till the morning horn called them to their daily task. Women are considered of no value, unless they continually increase their owner's stock. They are put on a par with animals. This same master shot a woman through the head, who had run away and been brought back to him. No one called him to account for it. If a slave resisted being whipped, the bloodhounds were unpacked, and set upon him, to tear his flesh from his bones. The master who did these things was highly educated, and styled a perfect gentleman. He also boasted the name and standing of a Christian, though Satan never had a truer follower.

I could tell of more slaveholders as cruel as those I have described. They are not exceptions to the general rule. I do not say there are no humane slaveholders. Such characters do exist, notwithstanding the hardening influences around them. But they are "like angels' visits—few and far between."

Harriott Ann Jacobs

WILLIAM WELLS BROWN (1814-1884)

Introduction

William Wells Brown was born near Lexington, Kentucky, in 1814. His father was George Higgins, a white plantation owner, but his mother was a black slave. His mother had seven children, all with different fathers. William served several slave-masters before escaping in 1834. He adopted the name of his friend, Wells Brown, a Quaker who had helped him obtain his freedom.

Brown became a conductor on the Underground Railroad and worked on a Lake Erie steamer ferrying slaves to freedom in Canada.

In 1843 Brown became a lecturing agent for the New York Anti-Slavery Society. After obtaining a reputation as one of the movement's best orators, Brown was employed by the American Anti-Slavery Society where he worked closely with William Lloyd Garrison and Wendell Phillips.

Brown, who settled in Boston, published his autobiography, *Narrative of William W. Brown, a Fugitive Slave*, in 1847.

In 1853 Brown published *Clotel*, a story about Thomas Jefferson's relationship with a slave mistress Sally Hemings. The book is believed to be the first novel to be published by an African-American.

Narrative of William W. Brown, an American Slave, 1849
Chapter 1

I was born in Lexington, Ky. The man who stole me as soon as I was born, recorded the births of all the infants which he claimed to be born his property, in a book which he kept for that purpose. My mother's name was Elizabeth. She had seven children, viz.: Solomon, Leander, Benjamin, Joseph, Millford, Elizabeth, and myself. No two of us were children of the same father. My father's name, as I learned from my mother, was George Higgins. He was a white man, a relative of my master, and connected with some of the first families in Kentucky.

My master owned about forty slaves, twenty-five of whom were field hands. He removed from Kentucky to Missouri when I was quite young, and settled thirty or forty miles above St. Charles, on the Missouri, where, in addition to his practice as a physician, he carried on milling, merchandizing and farming. He had a large farm, the principal productions of which were tobacco and hemp. The slave cabins were situated on the back part of the farm, with the house of the overseer, whose name was Grove Cook, in their midst. He had the entire charge of the farm, and having no family, was allowed a woman to keep house for him, whose business it was to deal out the provisions for the hands.

A woman was also kept at the quarters to do the cooking for the field hands, who were summoned to their unrequited toil every morning, at four o'clock, by the ringing of a bell, hung on a post near the house of the overseer. They were allowed half an hour to eat their breakfast, and get to the field. At half past four a horn was blown by the overseer, which was the signal to commence work; and every one that was not on the spot at the time, had to receive ten lashes from the whip-whip, with which the overseer always went armed. The handle was about three feet long, with the butt-end filled with lead, and the lash, six or seven feet in length, made of cow-hide, with platted wire on the end of it. This whip was put in requisition very frequently and freely, and a small offence on the part of a slave furnished an occasion for its use. During the time that Mr. Cook was overseer, I was a house servant—a situation preferable to that of a field hand, as I was better fed, better clothed, and not obliged to rise at the ringing of the bell, but about half an hour after. I have often laid and heard the crack of the whip, and the screams of the slave.

My mother and sister tortured

My mother was a field hand, and one morning was ten or fifteen minutes behind the others in getting into the field. As soon as she reached the spot where they were at work, the overseer commenced whipping her. She cried, "Oh! pray—Oh! pray—Oh! pray"—these are generally the words of slaves, when imploring mercy at the hands of their oppressors. I heard her voice, and knew it, and jumped out of my bunk, and went to the door. Though the field was some distance from the house, I could hear every crack of the whip, and every groan and cry of my poor mother. I remained at the door, not daring to venture any further. The cold chills ran over me, and I wept aloud. After giving her ten lashes, the sound of the whip ceased, and I returned to my bed, and found no consolation but in my tears. Experience has taught me that nothing can be more heart-rending than for one to see a dear and beloved mother or sister tortured, and to hear their cries, and not be able to render them assistance. But such is the position which an American slave occupies.

My master, being a politician, soon found those who were ready to put him into office, for the favors he could render them; and a few years after his arrival in Missouri he was elected to a seat in the legislature. In his absence from home everything was left in charge of Mr. Cook, the overseer, and he soon became more tyrannical and cruel. Among the slaves on the plantation was one by the name of Randall. He was a man about six feet high, and well-proportioned, and known as a man of great strength and power. He was considered the most valuable and able-bodied slave on the plantation; but no matter how good or useful a slave may be, he seldom escapes the lash. But it was not so with Randall. He had been on the plantation since my earliest recollection, and I had never known of his being flogged. No thanks were due to the master or overseer for this. I have often heard him declare that no white man should ever whip him—that he would die first.

Cook, from the time that he came upon the plantation, had frequently declared that he could and would flog any nigger that was put into the field to work under him. My master had repeatedly told him not to attempt to whip Randall, but he was determined to try it. As soon as he was left sole dictator, he thought the time had come to put his threats into execution. He soon began to find fault with Randall, and threatened to whip him if he did not do better. One day he gave him a very hard task—more than he could possibly do; and at night, the task not being performed, he told Randall that he should remember him the next morning. On the following morning, after the hands had taken breakfast, Cook called out to Randall, and told him that he intended to whip him; and ordered him to cross his hands and be tied. Randall asked why he wished to whip him. He answered, because he had not finished his task the day before. Randall said that the task was too great, or he should have done it. Cook said it made no difference—he should whip him. Randall stood silent for a moment, and then said, "Mr. Cook, I have always tried to please you since you have been on the plantation, and I find you are determined not to be satisfied with my work, let me do as well as I may. No man has laid hands on me, to whip me, for the last ten years, and I have long since come to the conclusion not to be whipped by any man living." Cook, finding by Randall's determined look and gestures, that he would resist, called three of the hands from their work, and commanded them to seize Randall, and tie him. The hands stood still;—they knew Randall—and they also knew him to be a powerful man, and were afraid to grapple with him. As soon as Cook had ordered the men to seize him, Randall turned to them, and said—"Boys, you all know me; you know that I can handle any three of you, and the man that lays hands on me shall die. This white man can't whip me himself, and therefore he has called you to help him." The overseer was unable to prevail upon them to seize and secure Randall, and finally ordered them all to go to their work together.

Over one hundred lashes

Nothing was said to Randall by the overseer for more than a week. One morning, however, while the hands were at work in the field, he came into it, accompanied by three friends of his, Thompson, Woodbridge and Jones. They came up to where Randall was at work, and Cook ordered him to leave his work, and go with them to the barn. He refused to go; whereupon he was attacked by the overseer and his companions, when he turned upon them, and laid them, one after another, prostrate on the ground. Woodbridge drew out his pistol, and fired at him, and brought him to the ground by a pistol ball. The others rushed upon him with their clubs, and beat him over the head and face, until they succeeded in tying him. He was then taken to the barn, and tied to a beam. Cook gave him over one hundred lashes with a heavy cow-hide, had him washed with salt and water, and left him tied during the day. The next day he was untied, and taken to a blacksmith's shop, and had a ball and chain attached to his leg. He was compelled to labor in the field, and perform the same amount of work that the other hands did. When his master returned home, he was much pleased to find that Randall had been subdued in his absence.

Chapter 2

Soon afterwards, my master removed to the city of St. Louis, and purchased a farm four miles from there, which he placed under the charge of an overseer by the name of Friend Haskell. He was a regular Yankee from New England. The Yankees are noted for making the most cruel overseers.

My mother was hired out in the city, and I was also hired out there to Major Freeland, who kept a public house. He was formerly from Virginia, and was a horse-racer, cock-fighter, gambler, and withal an inveterate drunkard. There were ten or twelve servants in the house, and when he was present, it was cut and slash—knock down and drag out. In his fits of anger, he would take up a chair, and throw it at a servant; and in his more rational moments, when he wished to chastise one, he would tie them up in the smoke-house, and whip them; after which, he would cause a fire to be made of tobacco stems, and smoke them. This he called "Virginia play."

I complained to my master of the treatment which I received from Major Freeland; but it made no difference. He cared nothing about it, so long as he received the money for my labor. After living with Major Freeland five or six months, I ran away, and went into the woods back of the city; and when night came on, I made my way to my master's farm, but was afraid to be seen, knowing that if Mr. Haskell, the overseer, should discover me, I should be again carried back to Major Freeland; so I kept in the woods. One day, while in the woods, I heard the barking and howling of dogs, and in a short time they came so near that I knew them to be the bloodhounds of Major Benjamin O'Fallon. He kept five or six, to hunt runaway slaves with.

Very severely whipped

As soon as I was convinced that it was them, I knew there was no chance of escape. I took refuge in the top of a tree, and the hounds were soon at its base, and there remained until the hunters came up in a half or three quarters of an hour afterwards. There were two men with the dogs, who, as soon as they came up, ordered me to descend. I came down, was tied, and taken to St. Louis jail. Major Freeland soon made his appearance, and took me out, and ordered me to follow him, which I did. After we returned home, I was tied up in the smoke-house, and was very severely whipped. After the major had flogged me to his satisfaction, he sent out his son Robert, a young man eighteen or twenty years of age, to see that I was well smoked. He made a fire of tobacco stems, which soon set me to coughing and sneezing. This, Robert told me, was the way his father used to do to his slaves in Virginia. After giving me what they conceived to be a decent smoking, I was untied and again set to work.

Robert Freeland was a "chip of the old block." Though quite young, it was not infrequently that he came home in a state of intoxication. He is now, I believe, a popular commander of a steam-boat on the Mississippi river. Major Freeland soon after failed in business, and I was put on board the steamboat Missouri, which plied between St. Louis and Galena. The commander of the boat was William B. Culver. I remained on her during the sailing season, which was the most pleasant time for me that I had ever experienced. At the close of navigation I was hired to Mr. John Colburn, keeper of the Missouri Hotel. He was from one of the free states; but a more inveterate hater of the Negro I do not believe ever walked God's green earth. This hotel was at that time one of the largest in the city, and there were employed in it twenty or thirty servants, mostly slaves.

Cut to pieces

Mr. Colburn was very abusive, not only to the servants, but to his wife also, who was an excellent woman, and one from whom I never knew a servant to receive a harsh word; but never did I know a kind one to a servant from her husband. Among the slaves employed in the hotel was one by the name of Aaron, who belonged to Mr. John F. Darby, a lawyer. Aaron was the knife-cleaner. One day, one of the knives was put on the table, not as clean as it might have been. Mr. Colburn, for this offence, tied Aaron up in the wood-house, and gave him over fifty lashes on the bare back with a cow-hide, after which, he made me wash him down with rum. This seemed to put him into more agony than the whipping. After being untied he went home to his master, and complained of the treatment which he had received. Mr. Darby would give no heed to anything he had to say, but sent him directly back. Colburn, learning that he had been to his master with complaints, tied him up again, and gave him a more severe whipping than before. The poor fellow's back was literally cut to pieces; so much so, that he was not able to work for ten or twelve days.

There was, also, among the servants, a girl whose master resided in the country. Her name was Patsey. Mr. Colburn tied her up one evening, and whipped her until several of the boarders came out and begged him to desist. The reason for whipping her was this. She was engaged to be married to a man belonging to Major William Christy, who resided four or five miles north of the city. Mr. Colburn had forbid her to see John Christy. The reason of this was said to be the regard which he himself had for Patsey. She went to meeting that evening, and John returned home with her. Mr. Colburn had intended to flog John, if he came within the enclosure; but John knew too well the temper of his rival, and kept at a safe distance:—so he took vengeance on the poor girl. If all the slave-drivers had been called together, I do not think a more cruel man than John Colburn—and he too a northern man—could have been found among them.

While living at the Missouri hotel, a circumstance occurred which caused me great unhappiness. My master sold my mother, and all her children, except myself. They were sold to different persons in the city of St. Louis.

Chapter 3

I was soon after taken from Mr. Colburn's, and hired to Elijah P. Lovejoy, who was at that time publisher and editor of the "St. Louis Times." My work, while with him, was mainly in the printing office, waiting on the hands, working the press, &c. Mr. Lovejoy was a very good man, and decidedly the best master that I had ever had. I am chiefly indebted to him, and to my employment in the printing office, for what little learning I obtained while in slavery.

St. Louis barbarity

Though slavery is thought, by some, to be mild in Missouri, when compared with the cotton, sugar and rice growing states, yet no part of our slave-holding country is more noted for the barbarity of its inhabitants than St. Louis. It was here that Col. Harney, a United States officer, whipped a slave woman to death. It was here that Francis McIntosh, a free colored man from Pittsburg, was taken from the steamboat Flora and burned at the stake. During a residence of eight years in this city, numerous cases of extreme cruelty came under my own observation;—to record them all would occupy more space than could possibly be allowed in this little volume. I shall, therefore, give but a few more in addition to what I have already related.

Capt. J. B. Brant, who resided near my master, had a slave named John. He was his body servant, carriage driver, &c. On one occasion, while driving his master through the city—

the streets being very muddy, and the horses going at a rapid rate—some mud spattered upon a gentleman by the name of Robert More. More was determined to be revenged. Some three or four months after this occurrence, he purchased John, for the express purpose, as he said, " to tame the d —- d nigger." After the purchase he took him to a black-smith's shop, and had a ball and chain fastened to his leg, and then put him to driving a yoke of oxen, and kept him at hard labor, until the iron around his leg was so worn into the flesh, that it was thought mortification would ensue. In addition to this, John told me that his master whipped him regularly three times a week for the first two months:—and all this to "tame him." A more noble-looking man than he was not to be found in all St. Louis, before he fell into the hands of More; and a more degraded and spirit-crushed looking being was never seen on a southern plantation, after he had been subjected to this "taming" process for three months. The last time that I saw him, he had nearly lost the entire use of his limbs.

While living with Mr. Lovejoy, I was often sent on errands to the office of the "Missouri Republican," published by Mr. Edward Charless. Once, while returning to the office with type, I was attacked by several large boys, sons of slave-holders, who pelted me with snow-balls. Having the heavy form of type in my hands, I could not make my escape by running; so I laid down the type and gave them battle. They gathered around me, pelting me with stones and sticks, until they overpowered me, and would have captured me, if I had not resorted to my heels. Upon my retreat they took possession of the type; and what to do to regain it I could not devise. Knowing Mr. Lovejoy to be a very humane man, I went to the office and laid the case before him. He told me to remain in the office. He took one of the apprentices with him and went after the type, and soon returned with it; but on his return informed me that Samuel McKinney had told him he would whip me, because I had hurt his boy. Soon after, McKinney was seen making his way to the office by one of the printers, who informed me of the fact, and I made my escape through the back door.

McKinney not being able to find me on his arrival, left the office in a great rage, swearing that he would whip me to death. A few days after, as I was walking along Main street, he seized me by the collar, and struck me over the head five or six times with a large cane, which caused the blood to gush from my nose and ears in such a manner that my clothes were completely saturated with blood. After beating me to his satisfaction he let me go, and I returned to the office so weak from the loss of blood that Mr. Lovejoy sent me home to my master. It was five weeks before I was able to walk again. During this time it was necessary to have some one to supply my place at the office. and I lost the situation.

After my recovery, I was hired to Capt. Otis Reynolds as a waiter on board the steamboat Enterprise, owned by Messrs. John and Edward Walsh, commission merchants at St. Louis. This boat was then running on the upper Mississippi. My employment on board was to wait on gentlemen, and the captain being a good man, the situation was a pleasant one to me;— but in passing from place to place, and seeing new faces every day, and knowing that they could go where they pleased, I soon became unhappy, and several times thought of leaving the boat at some landing-place, and trying to make my escape to Canada, which I had heard much about as a place where the slave might live, be free, and be protected.

I would never leave my mother in slavery

But whenever such thoughts would come into my mind, my resolution would soon be shaken by the remembrance that my dear mother was a slave in St. Louis, and I could not bear the idea of leaving her in that condition. She had often taken me upon her knee, and told me how she had carried me upon her back to the field when I was an infant—how often she had been whipped for leaving her work to nurse me—and how happy I would appear when she would take me into her arms. When these thoughts came over me, I would resolve never to leave the land of slavery without my mother. I thought that to leave her in slavery, after she had undergone and suffered so much for me, would be proving recreant to the duty which I owed to her. Besides this, I had three brothers and a sister there—two of my brothers having died.

My mother, my brothers Joseph and Millford, and my sister Elizabeth, belonged to Mr. Isaac Mansfield, formerly from one of the free states, (Massachusetts, I believe.) He was a tinner by trade, and carried on a large manufacturing establishment. Of all my relatives, mother was first, and sister next. One evening, while visiting them, I made some allusion to a proposed journey to Canada, and sister took her seat by my side, and taking my hand in hers, said, with tears in her eyes—

"Brother, you are not going to leave mother and your dear sister here without a friend, are you?"

I looked into her face, as the tears coursed swiftly down her cheeks, and bursting into tears myself, said—

"No, I will never desert you and mother!"

She clasped my hand in hers, and said—

"Brother, you have often declared that you would not end your days in slavery. I see no possible way in which you can escape with us; and now, brother, you are on a steamboat where there is some chance for you to escape to a land of liberty. I beseech you not to let us hinder you. If we cannot get our liberty, we do not wish to be the means of keeping you from a land of freedom."

I could restrain my feelings no longer, and an outburst of my own feelings caused her to cease speaking upon that subject. In opposition to their wishes, I pledged myself not to leave them in the hand of the oppressor. I took leave of them, and returned to the boat, and laid down in my bunk; but "sleep departed from mine eyes, and slumber from mine eyelids."

A beautiful girl

A few weeks after, on our downward passage, the boat took on board, at Hannibal, a drove of slaves, bound for the New Orleans market. They numbered from fifty to sixty, consisting of men and women from eighteen to forty years of age. A drove of slaves on a southern steamboat, bound for the cotton or sugar regions, is an occurrence so common, that no one, not even the passengers, appear to notice it, though they clank their chains at every step. There was, however, one in this gang that attracted the attention of the passengers and crew. It was a beautiful girl, apparently about twenty years of age, perfectly white, with straight light hair and blue eyes. But it was not the whiteness of her skin that created such a sensation among those who gazed upon her—it was her almost unparalleled beauty. She had been on the boat but a short time, before the attention of all the passengers, including the ladies, had been called to her, and the common topic of conversation was about the beautiful slave-girl. She was not in chains. The man who claimed this article of human merchandise was a Mr. Walker—a well known slave-trader, residing in St. Louis. There was a general anxiety among the passengers and crew to learn the history of the girl. Her master kept close by her side, and it would have been considered impudent for any of the passengers to have spoken to her, and the crew were not allowed to have any conversation with them. When we reached St. Louis, the slaves were removed to a boat bound for New Orleans, and the history of the beautiful slave-girl remained a mystery.

I remained on the boat during the season, and it was not an infrequent occurrence to have on board gangs of slaves on their way to the cotton, sugar and rice plantations of the south.

Toward the latter part of the summer Captain Reynolds left the boat, and I was sent home. I was then placed on the farm, under Mr. Haskell, the overseer. As I had been some time out of the field, and not accustomed to work in the burning sun, it was very hard; but I was compelled to keep up with the best of the hands.

I found a great difference between the work in a steamboat cabin and that in a corn-field.

My master, who was then living in the city, soon after removed to the farm, when I was taken out of the field to work in the house as a waiter. Though his wife was very peevish, and hard to please, I much preferred to be under her control than the overseer's. They brought with them Mr. Sloane, a Presbyterian minister; Miss Martha Tulley, a niece of theirs from Kentucky; and their nephew William. The latter had been in the family a number of years, but the others were all new comers.

My master "got religion"

Mr. Sloane was a young minister, who had been at the South but a short time, and it seemed as if his whole aim was to please the slaveholders, especially my master and mistress. He was intending to make a visit during the winter, and he not only tried to please them, but I think he succeeded admirably. When they wanted singing, he sung; when they wanted praying, he prayed; when they wanted a story told, he told a story. Instead of his teaching my master theology, my master taught theology to him. While I was with Captain Reynolds my master "got religion," and new laws were made on the plantation. Formerly we had the privilege of hunting, fishing, making splint brooms, baskets, &c., on Sunday; but this was all stopped. Every Sunday we were all compelled to attend meeting. Master was so religious that he induced some others to join him in hiring preacher to preach to the slaves.

Chapter 4

My master had family worship, night and morning. At night the slaves were called in to attend; but in the mornings they had to be at their work, and master did all the praying. My master and mistress were great lovers of mint julep, and every morning, a pitcher-full was made, of which they all partook freely, not excepting little master William. After drinking freely all round, they would have family worship, and then breakfast. I cannot say but I loved the julep as well as any of them, and during prayer was always careful to seat myself close to the table where it stood, so as to help myself when they were all busily engaged in their devotions. By the time prayer was over, I was about as happy as any of them. A sad accident happened one morning. In helping myself, and at the same time keeping an eye on my old mistress, I accidentally let the pitcher fall upon the floor, breaking it in pieces, and spilling the contents. This was a bad affair for me; for as soon as prayer was over, I was taken and severely chastised.

My master's family consisted of himself, his wife, and their nephew, William Moore. He was taken into the family when only a few weeks of age. His name being that of my own, mine was changed for the purpose of giving precedence to his, though I was his senior by ten or twelve years. The plantation being four miles from the city, I had to drive the family to church. I always dreaded the approach of the Sabbath; for, during service, I was obliged to stand by the horses in the hot, broiling sun, or in the rain, just as it happened.

One Sabbath, as we were driving past the house of D. D. Page, a gentleman who owned a large baking establishment, as I was sitting upon the box of the carriage, which was very much elevated, I saw Mr. Page pursuing a slave around the yard with a long whip, cutting him at every jump. The man soon escaped from the yard, and was followed by Mr. Page. They came running past us, and the slave, perceiving that he would be overtaken, stopped suddenly, and Page stumbled over him, and falling on the stone pavement, fractured one of his legs, which crippled him for life. The same gentleman, but a short time previous, tied up a woman of his, by the name of Delphia, and whipped her nearly to death; yet he was a deacon in the Baptist church, in good and regular standing. Poor Delphia! I was well acquainted with her, and called to see her while upon her sick bed; and I shall never forget her appearance. She was a member of the same church with her master.

Soon after this, I was hired out to Mr. Walker, the same man whom I have mentioned as having carried a gang of slaves down the river on the steamboat Enterprise. Seeing me in the capacity of a steward on the boat, and thinking that I would make a good hand to take care of slaves, he determined to have me for that purpose; and finding that my master would not sell me, he hired me for the term of one year.

Soul driver

When I learned the fact of my having been hired to a Negro speculator, or a "soul driver," as they are generally called among slaves, no one can tell my emotions. Mr. Walker had offered a high price for me, as I afterwards learned, but I suppose my master was restrained from selling me by the fact that I was a near relative of his. On entering the service of Mr. Walker, I found that my opportunity of getting to a land of liberty was gone, at least for the time being. He had a gang of slaves in readiness to start for New Orleans, and in a few days we were on our journey. I am at a loss for language to express my feelings on that occasion. Although my master had told me that he had not sold me, and Mr. Walker had told me that he had not purchased me, I did not believe them; and not until I had been to New Orleans, and was on my return, did I believe that I was not sold.

There was on the boat a large room on the lower deck, in which the slaves were kept, men and women, promiscuously—all chained two and two, and a strict watch kept that they did not get loose; for cases have occurred in which slaves have got off their chains, and made their escape at landing- places, while the boats were taking in wood;—and with all our care, we lost one woman who had been taken from her husband and children, and having no desire to live without them, in the agony of her soul jumped overboard, and drowned herself. She was not chained.

It was almost impossible to keep that part of the boat clean.

On landing at Natchez, the slaves were all carried to the slave-pen, and there kept one week, during which time several of them were sold. Mr. Walker fed his slaves well. We took on board at St. Louis several hundred pounds of bacon (smoked meat) and corn-meal, and his slaves were better fed than slaves generally were in Natchez, so far as my observation extended.

At the end of a week, we left for New Orleans, the place of our final destination, which we reached in two days. Here the slaves were placed in a pen-pen, where those who wished to purchase could call and examine them. The pen-pen is a small yard, surrounded by buildings, from fifteen to twenty feet wide, with the exception of a large gate with iron bars. The slaves are kept in the buildings during the night, and turned out into the yard during the day. After the best of the stock was sold at private sale at the pen, the balance were taken to the Exchange Coffee-House Auction Rooms, kept by Isaac L. McCoy, and sold at public auction. After the sale of this lot of slaves, we left New Orleans for St. Louis.

Chapter 5

On our arrival at St. Louis I went to Dr. Young, and told him that I did not wish to live with Mr. Walker any longer. I was heart-sick at seeing my fellow-creatures bought and sold. But the Dr. had hired me for the year, and stay I must. Mr. Walker again commenced purchasing another gang of slaves. He bought a man of Colonel John O'Fallon, who resided in the suburbs of the city. This man had a wife and three children. As soon as the purchase was made, he was put in jail for safe keeping, until we should be ready to start for New Orleans. His wife visited him while there, several times, and several times when she went for that purpose was refused admittance.

In the course of eight or nine weeks Mr. Walker had his cargo of human flesh made up. There was in this lot a number of old men and women, some of them with gray locks. We left St. Louis in the steamboat Carlton, Captain Swan, bound for New Orleans. On our way down, and before we reached Rodney, the place where we made our first stop, I had to prepare the old slaves for market. I was ordered to have the old men's whiskers shaved off, and the gray hairs plucked out where they were not too numerous, in which case he had a preparation of blacking to color it, and with a blacking brush we would put it on. This was new business to me, and was performed in a room where the passengers could not see us. These slaves were also taught how old they were by Mr. Walker, and after going through the blacking process they looked ten or fifteen years younger; and I am sure that some of those who purchased slaves of Mr. Walker were dreadfully cheated, especially in the ages of the slaves which they bought.

We landed at Rodney, and the slaves were driven to the pen in the back part of the village. Several were sold at this place, during our stay of four or five days, when we proceeded to Natchez. There we landed at night, and the gang were put in the warehouse until morning, when they were driven to the pen. As soon as the slaves are put in these pens, swarms of planters may be seen in and about them. They knew when Walker was expected, as he always had the time advertised beforehand when he would be in Rodney, Natchez, and New Orleans. These were the principal places where he offered his slaves for sale.

A slave very cruelly whipped

When at Natchez the second time, I saw a slave very cruelly whipped. He belonged to a Mr. Broadwell, a merchant who kept a store on the wharf. The slave's name was Lewis. I had known him several years, as he was formerly from St. Louis. We were expecting a steamboat down the river, in which we were to take passage for New Orleans. Mr. Walker sent me to the landing to watch for the boat, ordering me to inform him on its arrival. While there I went into the store to see Lewis. I saw a slave in the store, and asked him where Lewis was. Said he, "They have got Lewis hanging between the heavens and the earth." I asked him what he meant by that. He told me to go into the warehouse and see. I went in, and found Lewis there. He was tied up to a beam, with his toes just touching the floor. As there was no one in the warehouse but himself, I inquired the reason of his being in that situation. He said Mr. Broadwell had sold his wife to a planter six miles from the city, and that he had been to visit her—that he went in the night, expecting to return before daylight, and went without his master's permission. The patrol had taken him up before he reached his wife. He was put in jail, and his master had to pay for his catching and keeping, and that was what he was tied up for.

Just as he finished his story, Mr. Broadwell came in, and inquired what I was doing there. I knew not what to say, and while I was thinking what reply to make he struck me over the head with the cowhide, the end of which struck me over my right eye, sinking deep into the flesh, leaving a scar which I carry to this day. Before I visited Lewis he had received fifty lashes. Mr. Broadwell gave him fifty lashes more after I came out, as I was afterwards informed by Lewis himself.

New Orleans

The next day we proceeded to New Orleans, and put the gang in the same pen-pen which we occupied before. In a short time the planters came flocking to the pen to purchase slaves. Before the slaves were exhibited for sale, they were dressed and driven out into the yard. Some were set to dancing, some to jumping, some to singing, and some to playing cards. This was done to make them appear cheerful and happy. My business was to see that they were placed in those situations before the arrival of the purchasers, and I have often set them to dancing when their cheeks were wet with tears. As slaves were in good demand at that time, they were all soon disposed of, and we again set out for St. Louis.

On our arrival, Mr. Walker purchased a farm five or six miles from the city. He had no family, but made a housekeeper of one of his female slaves. Poor Cynthia! I knew her well.

She was a quadroon, and one of the most beautiful women I ever saw. She was a native of St. Lewis, and bore an irreproachable character for virtue and propriety of conduct. Mr. Walker bought her for the New Orleans market, and took her down with him on one of the trips that I made with him. Never shall I forget the circumstances of that voyage! On the first night that we were on board the steamboat, he directed me to put her into a state-room he had provided for her, apart from the other slaves. I had seen too much of the workings of slavery not to know what this meant. I accordingly watched him into the state-room, and listened to hear what passed between them. I heard him make his base offers, and her reject them. He told her that if she would accept his vile proposals, he would take her back with him to St. Louis, and establish her as his housekeeper on his farm. But if she persisted in rejecting them, he would sell her as a field hand on the worst plantation on the river. Neither threats nor bribes prevailed, however, and he retired, disappointed of his prey.

Poor Cynthia

The next morning poor Cynthia told me what had passed, and bewailed her sad fate with floods of tears. I comforted and encouraged her all I could; but I foresaw but too well what the result must be. Without entering into any further particulars, suffice it to say that Walker performed his part of the contract at that time. He took her back to St. Louis, established her as his mistress and housekeeper at his farm, and before I left, he had two children by her. But, mark the end! Since I have been at the North, I have been credibly informed that Walker has been married, and, as a previous measure, sold poor Cynthia and her four children (she having had two more since I came away) into hopeless bondage!

He soon commenced purchasing to make up the third gang. We took steamboat, and went to Jefferson City, a town on the Missouri river. Here landed, and took stage for the interior of the state. He bought a number of slaves as he passed the different farms and villages. After getting twenty-two or twenty-three men and women, we arrived at St. Charles, a village on the banks of the Missouri. Here he purchased a woman who had a child in her arms, appearing to be four or five weeks old.

We had been traveling by land for some days, and were in hopes to have found a boat at this place for St. Louis, but were disappointed. As no boat was expected for some days, we started for St. Louis by land. Mr. Walker had purchased two horses. He rode one, and I the other. The slaves were chained together, and we took up our line of march, Mr. Walker taking the lead, and I bringing up the rear. Though the distance was not more than twenty miles, we did not reach it the first day. The road was worse than any that I have ever traveled.

Soon after we left St. Charles the young child grew very cross, and kept up a noise during the greater part of the day. Mr. Walker complained of its crying several times, and told the mother to stop the child's d——d noise, or he would. The woman tried to keep the child from crying, but could not. We put up at night with an acquaintance of Mr. Walker, and in the morning, just as we were about to start, the child again commenced crying. Walker stepped up to her, and told her to give the child to him. The mother tremblingly obeyed. He took the child by one arm, as you would a cat by the leg, walked into the house, and said to the lady,

"Madam, I will make you a present of this little nigger; it keeps such a noise that I can't bear it."

"Thank you, sir," said the lady.

Crying for her child

The mother, as soon as she saw that her child was to be left, ran up to Mr. Walker, and falling upon her knees, begged him to let her have her child; she clung around his legs, and cried, "Oh, my child! my child! master, do let me have my child! oh, do, do, do! I will stop its crying if you will only let me have it again." When I saw this woman crying for her child so piteously, a shudder—a feeling akin to horror—shot through my frame. I have often since in imagination heard her crying for her child.

None but those who have been in a slave state, and who have seen the American slave-trader engaged in his nefarious traffic, can estimate the sufferings their victims undergo. If there is one feature of American slavery more abominable than another; it is that which sanctions the buying and selling of human beings. The African slave-trade was abolished by the American Congress some twenty years since; and now, by the laws of the country, if an American is found engaged in the African slave-trade, he is considered a pirate; and if found guilty of such, the penalty would be death.

Although the African slave-trader has been branded as a pirate, men are engaged in the traffic in slaves in this country, who occupy high positions in society, and hold offices of honor in the councils of the nation; and not a few have made their fortunes by this business.

After the woman's child had been given away, Mr. Walker commanded her to return into the ranks with the other slaves. Women who had children were not chained, but those that had none were. As soon as her child was disposed of she was chained in the gang.

We finally arrived at Mr. Walker's farm. He had a house built during our absence to put slaves in. It was a kind of domestic jail. The slaves were put in the jail at night, and worked on the farm during the day. They were kept here until the gang was completed, when we again started for New Orleans, on board the steamboat North America, Capt. Alexander Scott. We had a large number of slaves in this gang. One, by the name of Joe, Mr. Walker was training up to take my place, as my time was nearly out, and glad was I. We made our first stop at Vicksburg, where we remained one week and sold several slaves.

Kept in a pen

Mr. Walker, though not a good master, had not flogged a slave since I had been with him, though he had threatened me. The slaves were kept in the pen, and he always put up at the best hotel, and kept his wines in his room, for the accommodation of those who called to negotiate with him for the purchase of slaves. One day, while we were at Vicksburg, several gentlemen came to see him for that purpose, and as usual the wine was called for. I took the tray and started around with it, and having accidentally filled some of the glasses too full, the gentlemen spilled the wine on their clothes as they went to drink. Mr. Walker apologized to them for my carelessness, but looked at me as though he would see me again on this subject.

After the gentlemen had left the room, he asked me what I meant by my carelessness, and said that he would attend to me. The next morning he gave me a note to carry to the jailer, and a dollar in money to give to him. I suspected that all was not right; so I went down near the landing, where I met with a sailor, and, walking up to him, asked him if he would be so kind as to read the note for me. He read it over, and then looked at me. I asked him to tell me what was in it. Said he,

"They are going to give you hell."

"Why?" said I.

He said, "This is a note to have you whipped, and says that you have a dollar to pay for it."

He handed me back the note, and off I started. I knew not what to do, but was determined not to be whipped. I went up to the jail—took a look at it, and walked off again. As Mr. Walker was acquainted with the jailer, I feared that I should be found out if I did not go, and be treated in consequence of it still worse.

Deception

While I was meditating on the subject, I saw a colored man about my size walk up, and the thought struck me in a moment to send him with my note. I walked up to him, and asked him who he belonged to. He said he was a free man, and had been in the city but a short time. I told him I had a note to go into the jail, and get a trunk to carry to one of the steamboats; but was so busily engaged that I could not do it, although I had a dollar to pay for it. He asked me if I would not give him the job. I handed him the note and the dollar, and off he started for the jail.

I watched to see that he went in, and as soon as I saw the door close behind him, I walked around the corner, and took my station, intending to see how my friend looked when he came out. I had been there but a short time, when a colored man came around the corner, and said to another colored man with whom he was acquainted—

"They are giving a nigger scissors in the jail."

"What for?" said the other. The man continued,

"A nigger came into the jail, and asked for the jailer. The jailer came out, and he handed him a note, and said he wanted to get a trunk. The jailer told him to go with him, and he would give him the trunk. So he took him into the room, and told the nigger to give up the dollar. He said a man had given him the dollar to pay for getting the trunk. But that lie would not answer. So they made him strip himself, and then they tied him down, and are now whipping him."

I stood by all the while listening to their talk, and soon found out that the person alluded to was my customer. I went into the street opposite the jail, and concealed myself in such a manner that I could not be seen by any one coming out. I had been there but a short time; when the young man made his appearance, and looked around for me. I, unobserved, came forth from my hiding-place, behind a pile of brick, and he pretty soon saw me, and came up to me complaining bitterly, saying that I had played a trick upon him. I denied any knowledge of what the note contained, and asked him what they had done to him. He told me in substance what I heard the man tell who had come out of the jail.

"Yes," said he, "they whipped me and took my dollar, and gave me this note."

He showed me the note which the jailer had given him, telling him to give it to his master. I told him I would give him fifty cents for it—that being all the money I had. He gave it to me and took his money. He had received twenty lashes on his bare back, with the whip-whip.

I took the note and started for the hotel where I had left Mr. Walker. Upon reaching the hotel, I handed it to a stranger whom I had not seen before, and requested him to read it to me. As near as I can recollect, it was as follows:

"Dear Sir:—By your direction, I have given your boy twenty lashes. He is a very saucy boy, and tried to make me believe that he did not belong to you, and I put it on to him well for lying to me.

"I remain

"Your obedient servant."

It is true that in most of the slave-holding cities, when a gentleman wishes his servants whipped, he can send him to the jail and have it done. Before I went in where Mr. Walker was, I wet my cheeks a little, as though I had been crying. He looked at me, and inquired what was the matter. I told him that I had never had such a whipping in my life, and handed him the note. He looked at it and laughed;—"And so you told him that you did not belong to me?" "Yes, sir;" said I. "I did not know that there was any harm in that." He told me I must behave myself, if I did not want to be whipped again.

This incident shows how it is that slavery makes its victims lying and mean; for which vices it afterwards reproaches them, and uses them as arguments to prove that they deserve no better fate. Had I entertained the same views of right and wrong which I now do, I am sure I should never have practiced the deception upon that poor fellow which I did. I know of no act committed by me while in slavery which I have regretted more than that; and I heartily desire that it may be at some time or other in my power to make him amends for his vicarious sufferings in my behalf.

Chapter 6

In a few days we reached New Orleans, and arriving there in the night, remained on board until morning.

I saw a slave killed

While at New Orleans this time, I saw a slave killed; an account of which has been published by Theodore D. Weld, in his book entitled "Slavery as it is." The circumstances were as follows. In the evening, between seven and eight o'clock, a slave came running down the levee, followed by several men and boys. The whites were crying out, "Stop that nigger! stop that nigger!" while the poor panting slave, in almost breathless accents, was repeating, "I did not steal the meat—I did not steal the meat." The poor man at last took refuge in the river. The whites who were in pursuit of him, run on board of one of the boats to see if they could discover him. They finally espied him under the bow of the steamboat Trenton. They got a pike-pole, and tried to drive him from his hiding place. When they would strike at him he would dive under the water. The water was so cold, that it soon became evident that he must come out or be drowned.

While they were trying to drive him from under the bow of the boat or drown him, he would in broken and imploring accents say, "I did not steal the meat; I did not steal the meat. My master lives up the river. I want to see my master. I did not steal the meat. Do let me go home to master." After punching him, and striking him over the head for some time, he at last sunk in the water, to rise no more alive.

On the end of the pike-pole with which they were striking him was a hook, which caught in his clothing, and they hauled him up on the bow of the boat. Some said he was dead; others said he was "playing possum;" while others kicked him to make him get up; but it was of no use—he was dead.

As soon as they became satisfied of this, they commenced leaving, one after another. One of the hands on the boat informed the captain that they had killed the man, and that the dead body was lying on the deck. The captain came on deck, and said to those who were remaining, "You have killed this nigger; now take him off of my boat." The captain's name was Hart. The dead body was dragged on shore and left there. I went on board of the boat where our gang of slaves were, and during the whole night my mind was occupied with what I had seen. Early in the morning I went on shore to see if the dead body remained there. I found it in the same position that it was left the night before. I watched to see what they would do with it. It was left there until between eight and nine o'clock, when a cart, which takes up the trash out of the streets, came along, and the body was thrown in, and in a few minutes more was covered over with dirt which they were removing from the streets. During the whole time, I did not see more than six or seven persons around it, who, from their manner, evidently regarded it as no uncommon occurrence.

During our stay in the city I met with a young white man with whom I was well acquainted in St. Louis. He had been sold into slavery, under the following circumstances. His father was a drunkard, and very poor, with a family of five or six children. The father died, and left the mother to take care of and provide for the children as best she might. The eldest was a boy, named Burrill, about thirteen years of age, who did chores in a store kept by Mr. Riley, to assist his mother in procuring a living for the family. After working with him two years, Mr. Riley took him to New Orleans to wait on him while in that city on a visit, and when he returned to St. Louis, he told the mother of the boy that he had died with the yellow fever. Nothing more was heard from him, no one supposing him to be alive. I was much astonished when Burrill told me his history. Though I sympathized with him I could not assist him. We were both slaves. He was poor, uneducated, and without friends; and, if living, is, I presume, still held as a slave.

After selling out this cargo of human flesh, we returned to St. Louis, and my time was up with Mr. Walker. I had served him one year, and it was the longest year I ever lived.

Chapter 7

I was sent home, and was glad enough to leave the service of one who was tearing the husband from the wife, the child from the mother, and the sister from the brother—but a trial more severe and heart-rending than any which I had yet met with awaited me. My dear sister had been sold to a man who was going to Natchez, and was lying in jail awaiting the hour of his departure. She had expressed her determination to die, rather than go to the far south, and she was put in jail for safekeeping. I went to the jail the same day that I arrived, but as the jailer was not in I could not see her.

I went home to my master, in the country, and the first day after my return he came where I was at work, and spoke to me very politely. I knew from his appearance that something was the matter. After talking to me about my several journeys to New Orleans with Mr. Walker, he told me that he was hard pressed for money, and as he

had sold my mother and all her children except me, he thought it would be better to sell me than any other one, and that as I had been used to living in the city, he thought it probable that I would prefer it to a country life. I raised up my head, and looked him full in the face. When my eyes caught his he immediately looked to the ground. After a short pause, I said,

"Master, mother has often told me that you are a near relative of mine, and I have often heard you admit the fact; and after you have hired me out, and received, as I once heard you say, nine hundred dollars for my service—after receiving this large sum, will you sell me to be carried to New Orleans or some other place?"

"No," said he, "I do not intend to sell you to a Negro trader. If I had wished to have done that, I might have sold you to Mr. Walker for a large sum, but I would not sell you to a Negro trader. You may go to the city, and find you a good master."

"But," said I, "I cannot find a good master in the whole city of St. Louis."

"Why?" said he.

"Because there are no good masters in the state."

"Do you not call me a good master?"

"If you were you would not sell me."

"Now I will give you one week to find a master in, and surely you can do it in that time."

The price set by my evangelical master upon my soul and body was the trifling sum of five hundred dollars. I tried to enter into some arrangement by which I might purchase my freedom; but he would enter into no such arrangement.

I set out for the city with the understanding that I was to return in a week with some one to become my new master. Soon after reaching the city, I went to the jail, to learn if I could once more see my sister; but could not gain admission. I then went to mother, and learned from her that the owner of my sister intended to start for Natchez in a few days.

Visiting my sister in jail

I went to the jail again the next day, and Mr. Simonds, the keeper, allowed me to see my sister for the last time. I cannot give a just description of the scene at that parting interview. Never, never can be erased from my heart the occurrences of that day! When I entered the room where she was, she was seated in one corner, alone. There were four other women in the same room, belonging to the same man. He had purchased them, he said, for his own use. She was seated with her face towards the door where I entered, yet she did not look up until

I walked up to her. As soon as she observed me she sprung up, threw her arms around my neck, leaned her head upon my breast, and, without uttering a word, burst into tears. As soon as she recovered herself sufficiently to speak, she advised me to take mother, and try to get out of slavery. She said there was no hope for herself—that she must live and die a slave. After giving her some advice, and taking from my finger a ring and placing it upon hers, I bade her farewell forever, and returned to my mother, and then and there made up my mind to leave for Canada as soon as possible.

I had been in the city nearly two days, and as I was to be absent only a week, I thought best to get on my journey as soon as possible. In conversing with mother, I found her unwilling to make the attempt to reach a land of liberty, but she counseled me to get my liberty if I could. She said, as all her children were in slavery, she did not wish to leave them. I could not bear the idea of leaving her among those pirates, when there was a prospect of being able to get away from them. After much persuasion I succeeded in inducing her to make the attempt to get away.

The escape

The time fixed for our departure was the next night. I had with me a little money that I had received, from time to time, from gentlemen for whom I had done errands. I took my scanty means and purchased some dried beef, crackers and cheese, which I carried to mother, who had provided herself with a bag to carry it in. I occasionally thought of my old master, and of my mission to the city to find a new one. I waited with the most intense anxiety for the appointed time to leave the land of slavery, in search of a land of liberty.

The time at length arrived, and we left the city just as the clock struck nine. We proceeded to the upper part of the city, where I had been two or three times during the day, and selected a skiff to carry us across the river. The boat was not mine, nor did I know to whom it did belong; neither did I care. The boat was fastened with a small pole, which, with the aid of a rail, I soon loosened from its moorings. After hunting round and finding a board to use as an oar, I turned to the city, and bidding it a long farewell, pushed off my boat. The current running very swift, we had not reached the middle of the stream before we were directly opposite the city.

We were soon upon the Illinois shore, and, leaping from the boat, turned it adrift, and the last I saw of it was going down the river at good speed. We took the main road to Alton, and passed through just at daylight, when we made for the woods, where we remained during the day. Our reason for going into the woods was, that we expected that Mr. Mansfield (the man who owned my mother) would start in pursuit of her as soon as he discovered that she was missing. He also new that I had been in the city looking for a new master, and we thought probably he would go out to my master's to see if he could find my mother, and in so doing, Dr. Young might be led to suspect that I had gone to Canada to find a purchaser.

We remained in the woods during the day, and as soon as darkness overshadowed the earth, we started again on our gloomy way, having no guide but the north star. We continued to travel by night, and secrete ourselves in the woods by day; and every night, before emerging from our hiding-place, we would anxiously look for our friend and leader—the north star. ...

Chapter 8

As we traveled towards a land of liberty, my heart would at times leap for joy. At other times, being, as I was, almost constantly on my feet, I felt as though I could travel no further. But when I thought of slavery, with its democratic whips—its republican chains—its evangelical blood-hounds, and its religious slave-holders—when I thought of all this paraphernalia of American democracy and religion behind me, and the prospect of liberty before me, I was encouraged to press forward, my heart was strengthened, and I forgot that I was tired or hungry.

No food left

On the eighth day of our journey, we had a very heavy rain, and in a few hours after it commenced we had not a dry thread upon our bodies. This made our journey still more unpleasant. On the tenth day, we found ourselves entirely destitute of provisions, and how to obtain any we could not tell. We finally resolved to stop at some farm-house, and try to get something to eat. We had no sooner determined to do this, than we went to a house, and asked them for some food. We were treated with great kindness, and they not only gave us something to eat, but gave us provisions to carry with us. They advised us to travel by day and lie by at night. Finding ourselves about one hundred and fifty miles from St. Louis, we concluded that it would be safe to travel by daylight, and did not leave the house until the next morning. We traveled on that day through a thickly settled country, and through one small village. Though we were fleeing from a land of oppression, our hearts were still there. My dear sister and two beloved brothers were behind us, and the idea of giving them up, and leaving them forever, made us feel sad. But with all this depression of heart, the thought that I should one day be free, and call my body my own, buoyed me up, and made my heart leap for joy. I had just been telling my mother how I should try to get employment as soon as we reached Canada, and how I intended to purchase us a little farm, and how I would earn money enough to buy sister and brothers, and how happy we would be in our own free home—when three men came up on horseback, and ordered us to stop.

I turned to the one who appeared to be the principal man, and asked him what he wanted. He said he had a warrant to take us up. The three immediately dismounted, and one took from his pocket a handbill, advertising us as runaways, and offering a reward of two hundred dollars for our apprehension and delivery in the city of St. Louis. The advertisement had been put out by Isaac Mansfield and John Young.

Captured

While they were reading the advertisement, mother looked me in the face, and burst into tears. A cold chill ran over me, and such a sensation I never experienced before, and I hope never to again. They took out a rope and tied me, and we were taken back about six miles, to the house of the individual who appeared to be the leader. We reached there about seven o'clock in the evening, had supper, and were separated for the night. Two men remained in the room during the night. Before the family retired to rest, they were all called together to attend prayers. The man who but a few hours before had bound my hands together with a strong cord, read a chapter from the Bible, and then offered up prayer, just as though God had sanctioned the act he had just committed upon a poor, panting, fugitive slave.

The land of whips, chains and Bibles

The next morning a blacksmith came in, and put a pair of handcuffs on me, and we started on our journey back to the land of whips, chains and Bibles. Mother was not tied, but was closely watched at night. We were carried back in a wagon, and after four days' travel, we came in sight of St. Louis. I cannot describe my feelings upon approaching the city.

As we were crossing the ferry, Mr. Wiggins, the owner of the ferry, came up to me, and inquired what I had been doing that I was in chains. He had not heard that I had run away. In a few minutes we were on the Missouri side, and were taken directly to the jail. On the way thither, I saw several of my friends, who gave me a nod of recognition as I passed them. After reaching the jail, we were locked up in different apartments.

Chapter 9

I had been in jail but a short time when I heard that my master was sick, and nothing brought more joy to my heart than that intelligence. I prayed fervently for him—not for his recovery, but for his death. I knew he would be exasperated at having to pay for my apprehension, and knowing his cruelty, I feared him. While in jail, I learned that my sister Elizabeth, who was in prison when we left the city, had been carried off four days before our arrival.

I had been in jail but a few hours when three traders-traders, learning that I was secured thus for running away, came to my prison-house and looked at me, expecting that I would be offered for sale. Mr. Mansfield, the man who owned mother, came into the jail as soon as Mr. Jones, the man who arrested us, informed him that he had brought her back. He told her that he would not whip her, but would sell her to a trader-trader, or take her to New Orleans himself. After being in jail about one week, master sent a man to take me our of jail, and send me home. I was taken out and carried home, and the old man was well enough to sit up. He had me brought into the room where he was, and as I entered, he asked me where I had been? I told him I had acted according to his orders. He had told me to look for a master, and I had been to look for one. He answered that he did not tell me to go to Canada to look for a master. I told him that as I had served him faithfully, and had been the means of putting a number of hundreds of dollars into his pocket, I thought I had a right to my liberty. He said he had promised my father that I should not be sold to supply the New Orleans market, or he would sell me to a trader-trader.

I was ordered to go into the field to work, and was closely watched by the overseer during the day, and locked up at night. The overseer gave me a severe whipping on the second day that I was in the field. I had been at home but a short time, when master was able to ride to the city; and on his return he informed me that he had sold me to Samuel Willi, a merchant tailor. I knew Mr. Willi. I had lived with him three or four months some years before, when he hired me of my master.

Mr. Willi was not considered by his servants as a very bad man, nor was he the best of masters. I went to my new home, and found my new mistress very glad to see me. Mr. Willi owned two servants before he purchased me—Robert and Charlotte. Robert was an excellent white-washer, and hired his time from his master, paying him one dollar per day, besides taking care of himself. He was known in the city by the name of Bob Music. Charlotte was an old woman, who attended to the cooking, washing, &c. Mr. Willi was not a wealthy man, and did not feel able to keep many servants around his house; so he soon decided to hire me out, and as I had been accustomed to service in steamboats, he gave me the privilege of finding such employment.

On board a steamship

I soon secured a situation on board the steamer Otto, Capt. J. B. Hill, which sailed from St. Louis to Independence, Missouri. My former master, Dr. Young, did not let Mr. Willi know that I had run away, or he would not have permitted me to go on board a steamboat. The boat was not quite ready to commence running, and therefore I had to remain with Mr. Willi. But during this time, I had to undergo a trial for which I was entirely unprepared. My mother, who had been in jail since her return until the present time, was now about being carried to New Orleans, to die on a cotton, sugar, or rice plantation!

I had been several times to the jail, but could obtain no interview with her. I ascertained, however, the time the boat in which she was to embark would sail, and as I had not seen mother since her being thrown into prison, I felt anxious for the hour of sailing to come. At last, the day arrived when I was to see her for the first time after our painful separation, and, for aught that I knew, for the last time in this world!

At about ten o'clock in the morning I went on board of the boat, and found her there in company with fifty or sixty other slaves. She was chained to another woman. On seeing me, she immediately dropped her head upon her heaving bosom. She moved not, neither did she weep. Her emotions were too deep for tears. I approached, threw my arms around her neck, kissed her, and fell upon my knees, begging her forgiveness, for I thought myself to blame for her sad condition; for if I had not persuaded her to accompany me, she would not then have been in chains.

"Do not weep for me"

She finally raised her head, looked me in the face, (and such a look none but an angel can give!) and said," My dear son, you are not to blame for my being here. You have done nothing more nor less than your duty. Do not, I pray you, weep for me. I cannot last long upon a cotton plantation. I feel that my heavenly Master will soon call me home, and then I shall be out of the hands of the slave-holders!"

I could bear no more—my heart struggled to free itself from the human form. In a moment she saw Mr. Mansfield coming toward that part of the boat, and she whispered into my ear, "My child, we must soon part to meet no more this side of the grave. You have ever said that you would not die a slave; that you would be a freeman. Now try to get your liberty! You will soon have no one to look after but yourself!" and just as she whispered the last sentence into my ear, Mansfield came up to me, and with an oath, said, "Leave here this instant; you have been the means of my losing one hundred dollars to get this wench back"—at the same time kicking me with a heavy pair of boots. As I left her, she gave one shriek, saying, "God be with you!" It was the last time that I saw her, and the last word I heard her utter. ...

I walked on shore. The bell was tolling. The boat was about to start. I stood with a heavy heart, waiting to see her leave the wharf. The love of liberty that had been burning in my bosom had well-nigh gone out. I felt as though I was ready to die. The boat moved gently from the wharf, and while she glided down the river, I realized that my mother was indeed gone. ...

After the boat was out of sight I returned home; but my thoughts were so absorbed in what I had witnessed, that I knew not what I was about half of the time. Night came, but it brought no sleep to my eyes.

In a few days, the boat upon which I was to work being ready, I went on board to commence. This employment suited me better than living in the city, and I remained until the close of navigation; though it proved anything but pleasant. The captain was a drunken, profligate, hard-hearted creature, not knowing how to treat himself, or any other person.

The boat, on its second trip, brought down Mr. Walker, the man of whom I have spoken in a previous chapter, as hiring my time. He had between one and two hundred slaves, chained and manacled. Among them was a man that formerly belonged to my old master's brother, Aaron Young. His name was Solomon. He was a preacher, and belonged to the same church with his master. I was glad to see the old man. He wept like a child when he told me how he had been sold from his wife and children.

The boat carried down, while I remained on board, four or five gangs of slaves. Missouri, though a comparatively new state, is very much engaged in raising slaves to supply the southern market. In a former chapter, I have mentioned that I was once in the employ of a slave-trader, or driver, as he is called at the south. For fear that some may think that I have misrepresented a slave-driver, I will here give an extract from a paper published in a slave-holding state, Tennessee, called the "Millennial Trumpeter."

Droves of Negroes, chained together in dozens and scores, and hand-cuffed, have been driven through our country in numbers far surpassing any previous year, and these vile slave-drivers and dealers are swarming like buzzards around a carrion. Through this county, you cannot pass a few miles in the great roads without having every feeling of humanity insulted and lacerated by this spectacle, nor can you go into any county or any neighborhood, scarcely, without seeing or hearing of some of these despicable creatures, called drivers-drivers.

Who is a driver-driver? One whose eyes dwell with delight on lacerated bodies of helpless men, women and children; whose soul feels diabolical raptures at the chains, and hand-cuffs, and cart-whips, for inflicting tortures on weeping mothers torn from helpless babes, and on husbands and wives torn asunder forever!

Dark and revolting as is the picture here drawn, it is from the pen of one living in the midst of slavery. But though these men may cant about drivers-drivers, and tell what despicable creatures they are, who is it, I ask, that supplies them with the human beings that they are tearing asunder? I answer, as far as I have any knowledge of the state where I came from, that those who raise slaves for the market are to be found among all classes, from Thomas H. Benton down to the lowest political demagogue who may be able to purchase a woman for the purpose of raising stock, and from the doctor of divinity down to the most humble lay member in the church.

The auction-block

It was not uncommon in St. Louis to pass by an auction-stand, and behold a woman upon the auction-block, and hear the seller crying out, "How much is offered for this woman? She is a good cook, good washer, a good, obedient servant. She has got religion!" Why should this man tell the purchasers that she has religion? I answer, because in Missouri, and as far as I have any knowledge of slavery in the other states, the religious teaching consists in teaching the slave that he must never strike a white man; that God made him for a slave; and that, when whipped, he must not find fault—for the Bible says, "He that knoweth his master's will and doeth it not, shall be beaten with many stripes!" And slave- holders find such religion very profitable to them.

After leaving the steamer Otto, I resided at home, in Mr. Willi's family, and again began to lay plans for making my escape from slavery. The anxiety to be a freeman would not let me rest day or night. I would think of the northern cities that had heard so much about;— of Canada, where so many of my acquaintances had found a refuge. I would dream at night that I was in Canada, a freeman, and on waking in the morning, weep to find myself so sadly mistaken.

Mr. Willi treated me better than Dr. Young ever had; but instead of making me contented and happy, it only rendered me the more miserable, for it enabled me better to appreciate liberty. Mr. Willi was a man who loved money as most men do, and without looking for an opportunity to sell me, he found one in the offer of Captain Enoch Price, a steamboat owner and commission merchant, living in the city of St. Louis. Captain Price tendered seven hundred dollars, which was two hundred more than Mr. Willi had paid. He therefore thought best to accept the offer. I was wanted for a carriage driver, and Mrs. Price was very much pleased with the captain's bargain. His family consisted of himself, wife, one child, and three servants, besides myself,—one man and two women.

Mrs. Price was very proud of her servants, always keeping them well dressed, and as soon as I had been purchased, she resolved to have a new carriage. And soon one was procured, and all preparations were made for a turn-out in grand style, I being the driver.

Maria or Eliza?

One of the female servants was a girl some eighteen or twenty years of age, named Maria. Mrs. Price was very soon determined to have us united, if she could so arrange matters. She would often urge upon me the necessity of having a wife, saying that it would be so pleasant for me to take one in the same family! But getting married, while in slavery, was the last of my thoughts; and had I been ever so inclined, I should not have married Maria, as my love had already gone in another quarter. Mrs. Price soon found out that her efforts at this match-making between Maria and myself would not prove successful. She also discovered (or thought she had) that I was rather partial to a girl named Eliza, who was owned by Dr. Mills. This induced her at once to endeavor the purchase of Eliza, so great was her desire to get me a wife!

Before making the attempt, however, she deemed it best to talk to me a little upon the subject of love, courtship, and marriage. Accordingly, one afternoon she called me into her room—telling me to take a chair and sit down. I did so, thinking it rather strange, for servants are not very often asked thus to sit down in the same room with the master or mistress. She said that she had found out that I did not care enough about Maria to marry her. I told her that was true. She then asked me if there was not a girl in the city that I loved. Well, now, this was coming into too close quarters with me! People, generally, don't like to tell their love stories to everybody that may think fit to ask about them, and it was so with me. But, after blushing a while and recovering myself, I told her that I did not want a wife. She then asked me if I did not think something of Eliza. I told her that I did. She then said that if I wished to marry Eliza, she would purchase her if she could.

I gave but little encouragement to this proposition, as I was determined to make another trial to get my liberty, and I knew that if I should have a wife, I should not be willing to leave her behind; and if I should attempt to bring her with me, the chances would be difficult for success. However, Eliza was purchased, and brought into the family.

Chapter 10

But the more I thought of the trap laid by Mrs. Price to make me satisfied with my new home, by getting me a wife, the more I determined never to marry any woman on earth until I should get my liberty. But this secret I was compelled to keep to myself, which placed me in a very critical position. I must keep upon good terms with Mrs. Price and Eliza. I therefore promised Mrs. Price that I would marry Eliza; but said that I was not then ready. And I had to keep upon good terms with Eliza, for fear that Mrs. Price would find out that I did not intend to get married.

I have here spoken of marriage, and it is very common among slaves themselves to talk of it. And it is common for slaves to be married; or at least to have the marriage ceremony performed. But there is no such thing as slaves being lawfully married. There has never yet a case occurred where a slave has been tried for bigamy. The man may have as many women as he wishes, and the women as many men; and the law takes no cognizance of such acts among slaves. And in fact some masters, when they have sold the husband from the wife, compel her to take another.

There lived opposite Captain Price's, Doctor Farrar, well known in St. Louis. He sold a man named Ben, to one of the traders. He also owned Ben's wife, and in a few days he compelled Sally (that was her name) to marry Peter, another man belonging to him. I asked Sally "why she married Peter so soon after Ben was sold." She said, "because master made her do it."

Mr. John Calvert, who resided near our place, had a woman named Lavinia. She was quite young, and a man to whom she was about to be married was sold, and carried into the country near St. Charles, about twenty miles from St. Louis. Mr. Calvert wanted her to get a husband; but she had resolved not to marry any other man, and she refused. Mr. Calvert whipped her in such a manner that it was thought she would die. Some of the citizens had him arrested, but it was soon hushed up. And that was the last of it. The woman did not die, but it would have been the same if she had.

Captain Price purchased me in the month of October, and I remained with him until December, when the family made a voyage to New Orleans, in a boat owned by himself, and named the "Chester." I served on board as one of the stewards. On arriving at New Orleans, about the middle of the month, the boat took in freight for Cincinnati; and it was decided that the family should go up the river in her, and what was of more interest to me, I was to accompany them.

Opportunity to escape

The long looked for opportunity to make my escape from slavery was near at hand.

Captain Price had some fears as to the propriety of taking me near a free state, or a place where it was likely I could run away, with a prospect of liberty. He asked me if I had ever been in a free state. "Oh yes," said I, "I have been in Ohio; my master carried me into that state once, but I never liked a free state."

It was soon decided that it would be safe to take me with them, and what made it more safe, Eliza was on the boat with us, and Mrs. Price, to try me, asked if I thought as much as ever of Eliza. I told her that Eliza was very dear to me indeed, and that nothing but death should part us. It was the same as if we were married. This had the desired effect. The boat left New Orleans, and proceeded up the river.

I had at different times obtained little sums of money, which I had reserved for a "rainy day." I procured some cotton cloth, and made me a bag to carry provisions in. The trials of the past were all lost in hopes for the future. The love of liberty, that had been burning in my bosom for years, and had been well-nigh extinguished, was now resuscitated. At night, when all around was peaceful, I would walk the decks, meditating upon my happy prospects.

An old man named Frank

I should have stated, that, before leaving St. Louis, I went to an old man named Frank, a slave, owned by a Mr. Sarpee. This old man was very distinguished (not only among the slave population, but also the whites) as a fortune-teller. He was about seventy years of age, something over six feet high, and very slender. Indeed, he was so small around his body, that it looked as though it was not strong enough to hold up his head.

Uncle Frank was a very great favorite with the young ladies, who would go to him in great numbers to get their fortunes told. And it was generally believed that he could really penetrate into the mysteries of futurity. Whether true or not, he had the name, and that is about half of what one needs in this gullible age. I found Uncle Frank seated in the chimney corner, about ten o'clock at night. As soon as I entered, the old man left his seat. I watched his movement as well as I could by the dim light of the fire. He soon lit a lamp, and coming up, looked me full in the face, saying, "Well, my son, you have come to get uncle to tell your fortune, have you?" "Yes," said I. But how the old man should know what I came for, I could not tell. However, I paid the fee of twenty-five cents, and he commenced by looking into a gourd, filled with water. Whether the old man was a prophet, or the son of a prophet, I cannot say; but there is one thing certain, many of his predictions were verified.

I am no believer in soothsaying; yet I am sometimes at a loss to know how Uncle Frank could tell so accurately what would occur in the future. Among the many things he told was one which was enough to pay me for all the trouble of hunting him up. It was that I should be free! He further said, that in trying to get my liberty I would meet with many severe trials. I thought to myself any fool could tell me that!

The first place in which we landed in a free state was Cairo, a small village at the mouth of the Ohio river. We remained here but a few hours, when we proceeded to Louisville. After unloading some of the cargo, the boat started on her upward trip. The next day was the first of January. I had looked forward to New Year's day as the commencement of a new era in the history of my life. I had decided upon leaving the peculiar institution that day.

Intense agony

During the last night that I served in slavery I did not close my eyes a single moment. When not thinking of the future, my mind dwelt on the past. The love of a dear mother, a dear sister, and three dear brothers, yet living, caused me to shed many tears. If I could only have been assured of their being dead, I should have felt satisfied; but I imagined I saw my dear mother in the cotton-field, followed by a merciless task-master, and no one to speak a consoling word to her! I beheld my dear sister in the hands of a slave-driver, and compelled to submit to his cruelty! None but one placed in such a situation can for a moment imagine the intense agony to which these reflections subjected me.

Chapter 11

Time for action

At last the time for action arrived. The boat landed at a point which appeared to me the place of all others to start from. I found that it would be impossible to carry anything with me but what was upon my person. I had some provisions, and a single suit of clothes, about half worn. When the boat was discharging her cargo, and the passengers engaged carrying their baggage on and off shore, I improved the opportunity to convey myself with my little effects on land. Taking up a trunk, I went up the wharf, and was soon out of the crowd. I made directly for the woods, where I remained until night, knowing well that I could not travel, even in the state of Ohio, during the day, without danger of being arrested.

The slave's friend: the North Star

I had long since made up my mind that I would not trust myself in the hands of any man, white or colored. The slave is brought up to look upon every white man as an enemy to him and his race; and twenty-one years in slavery had taught me that there were traitors, even among colored people. After dark, I emerged from the woods into a narrow path, which led me into the main traveled road. But I knew not which way to go. I did not know north from south, east from west. I looked in vain for the North Star; a heavy cloud hid it from my view. I walked up and down the road until near midnight, when the clouds disappeared, and I welcomed the sight of my friend—truly the slave's friend—the North Star!

As soon as I saw it, I knew my course, and before daylight I traveled twenty or twenty-five miles. It being in the winter, I suffered intensely from the cold; being without an overcoat, and my other clothes rather thin for the season. I was provided with a tinder-box, so that I could make up a fire when necessary. And but for this, I should certainly have frozen to death; for I was determined not to go to any house for shelter. I knew of a man belonging to Gen. Ashly, of St. Louis, who had run away near Cincinnati, on the way to Washington, but had been caught and carried back into slavery; and I felt that a similar fate awaited me, should I be seen by any one. I traveled at night, and lay by during the day.

On the fourth day my provisions gave out, and then what to do I could not tell. Have something to eat I must; but how to get it was the question! On the first night after my food was gone, I went to a barn on the road-side and there found some ears of corn. I took ten or twelve of them, and kept on my journey. During the next day, while in the woods, I roasted my corn and feasted upon it, thanking God that I was so well provided for.

My name

My escape to a land of freedom now appeared certain, and the prospects of the future occupied a great part of my thoughts. What should be my occupation, was a subject of much anxiety to me; and the next thing what should be my name? I have before stated that my old master, Dr. Young, had no children of his own, but had with him a nephew, the son of his brother, Benjamin Young. When this boy was brought to Dr. Young, his name being William, the same as mine, my mother was ordered to change mine to something else. This, at the time, I thought to be one of the most cruel acts that could be committed upon my rights; and I received several very severe whippings for telling people that my name was William, after orders were given to change it. Though young, I was old enough to place a high appreciation upon my name. It was decided, however, to call me "Sandford," and this name I was known by, not only upon my master's plantation, but up to the time that I made my escape. I was sold under the name of Sandford.

But as soon as the subject came to my mind, I resolved on adopting my old name of William, and let Sandford go by the board, for I always hated it. Not because there was anything peculiar in the name; but because it had been forced upon me. It is sometimes common, at the south, for slaves to take the name of their masters. Some have a legitimate right to do so. But I always detested the idea of being called by the name of either of my masters. And as for my father, I would rather have adopted the name of "Friday," and been known as the servant of some Robinson Crusoe, than to have taken his name. So I was not only hunting for my liberty, but also hunting for a name; though I regarded the latter as of little consequence, if I could but gain the former. Traveling along the road, I would sometimes speak to myself, sounding my name over, by way of getting used to it, before I should arrive among civilized human beings. On the fifth or six day, it rained very fast, and froze about as fast as it fell, so that my clothes were one glare of ice. I traveled on at night until I became so chilled and benumbed—the wind blowing into my face—that I found it impossible to go any further, and accordingly took shelter in a barn, where I was obliged to walk about to keep from freezing.

Frostbite

I have ever looked upon that night as the most eventful part of my escape from slavery. Nothing but the providence of God, and that old barn, saved me from freezing to death. I received a very severe cold, which settled upon my lungs, and from time to time my feet had been frost-bitten, so that it was with difficulty I could walk. In this situation I traveled two days, when I found that I must seek shelter somewhere, or die.

The thought of death was nothing frightful to me, compared with that of being caught, and again carried back into slavery. Nothing but the prospect of enjoying liberty could have induced me to undergo such trials. This, and this alone, cheered me onward. But I at last resolved to seek protection from the inclemency of the weather, and therefore I secured myself behind some logs and brush, intending to wait there until some one should pass by; for I thought it probable that I might see some colored person, or, if not, some one who was not a slave holder; for I had an idea that I should know a slaveholder as far as I could see him.

The first person that passed was a man in a buggy-wagon. He looked too genteel for me to hail him. Very soon another passed by on horseback. I attempted to speak to him, but fear made my voice fail me. As he passed, I left my hiding- place, and was approaching the road, when I observed an old man walking towards me, leading a white horse. He had on a broad-brimmed hat and a very long coat, and was evidently walking for exercise. As soon as I saw him, and observed his dress, I thought to myself, "You are the man that I have been looking for!" Nor was I mistaken. He was the very man!

A covered wagon

On approaching me, he asked me, "if I was not a slave." I looked at him some time, and then asked him "if he knew of any one who would help me as I was sick." He answered that he would; but again asked, if I was not a slave. I told him I was. He then said that I was in a very pro-slavery neighborhood, and if I would wait until he went home, he would get a covered wagon for me. I promised to remain. He mounted his horse, and was soon out of sight.

After he was gone, I meditated whether to wait or not; being apprehensive that he had gone for some one to arrest me. But I finally concluded to remain until he should return; removing some few rods to watch his movements. After a suspense of an hour and a half or more, he returned with a two-horse covered wagon, such as are usually seen under the shed of a Quaker meeting-house on Sundays and Thursdays; for the old man proved to be a Quaker of the George Fox stamp.

A Quaker of the George Fox stamp

He took me to his house, but it was some time before I could be induced to enter it; not until the old lady came out, did I venture into the house. I thought I saw something in the old lady's cap that told me I was not only safe, but welcome, in her house. I was not, however, prepared to receive their hospitalities. The only fault I found with them was their being too kind. I had never had a white man to treat me as an equal, and the idea of a white lady waiting on me at the table was still worse! Though the table was loaded with the good things of this life, I could not eat. I thought if I could only be allowed the privilege of eating in the kitchen I should be more than satisfied!

Finding that I could not eat, the old lady, who was a "Thompsonian," made me a cup of "composition," or "number six;" but it was so strong and hot, that I called it "number seven!" However, I soon found myself at home in this family. On different occasions, when telling these facts, I have been asked how I felt upon finding myself regarded as a man by a white family; especially just having run away from one. I cannot say that I have ever answered the question yet.

The fact that I was in all probability a freeman, sounded in my ears like a charm. I am satisfied that none but a slave could place such an appreciation upon liberty as I did at that time. I wanted to see mother and sister, that I might tell them "I was free!" I wanted to see my fellow-slaves in St. Louis, and let them know that the chains were no longer upon my limbs. I wanted to see Captain Price, and let him learn from my own lips that I was no more a chattel, but a man! I was anxious, too, thus to inform Mrs. Price that she must get another coachman. And I wanted to see Eliza more than I did either Mr. or Mrs. Price!

The fact that I was a freeman—could walk, talk, eat and sleep, as a man, and no one to stand over me with the blood-clotted cow-hide—all this made me feel that I was not myself.

A devoted friend of the slave

The kind friend that had taken me in was named Wells Brown. He was a devoted friend of the slave; but was very old, and not in the enjoyment of good health. After being by the fire awhile, I found that my feet had been very much frozen. I was seized with a fever, which threatened to confine me to my bed. But my Thompsonian friends soon raised me, treating me as kindly as if I had been one of their own children. I remained with them twelve or fifteen days, during which time they made me some clothing, and the old gentleman purchased me a pair of boots.

I found that I was about fifty or sixty miles from Dayton, in the State of Ohio, and between one and two hundred miles from Cleaveland, on Lake Erie, a place I was desirous of reaching on my way to Canada. This I know will sound strangely to the ears of people in foreign lands, but it is nevertheless true. An American citizen was fleeing from a democratic, republican, Christian government, to receive protection under the monarchy of Great Britain. While the people of the United States boast of their freedom, they at the same time keep three millions of their own citizens in chains; and while I am seated here in sight of Bunker Hill Monument, writing this narrative, I am a slave, and no law, not even in Massachusetts, can protect me from the hands of the slave- holder!

Wells William Brown

Before leaving this good Quaker friend, he inquired what my name was besides William. I told him that I had no other name. "Well," said he, "thee must have another name. Since thee has got out of slavery, thee has become a man, and men always have two names."

I told him that he was the first man to extend the hand of friendship to me, and I would give him the privilege of naming me.

"If I name thee," said he, "I shall call thee Wells Brown, after myself."

"But," said I, "I am not willing to lose my name of William. As it was taken from me once against my will, I am not willing to part with it again upon any terms."

"Then," said he, "I will call thee William Wells Brown."

"So be it," said I; and I have been known by that name ever since I left the house of my first white friend, Wells Brown.

After giving me some little change, I again started for Canada. In four days I reached a public house, and went into warm myself. I there learned that some fugitive slaves had just passed through the place. The men in the bar-room were talking about it, and I thought that it must have been myself they referred to, and I was therefore afraid to start, fearing they would seize me; but I finally mustered courage enough, and took my leave. As soon as I was out of sight, I went into the woods, and remained there until night, when I again regained the road, and traveled on until next day.

Not having had any food for nearly two days; I was faint with hunger, and was in a dilemma what to do, as the little cash supplied me by my adopted father, and which had contributed to my comfort, was now all gone. I however concluded to go to a farm-house, and ask for something to eat. On approaching the door of the first one presenting itself, I knocked, and was soon met by a man who asked me what I wanted. I told him that I would like something to eat. He asked me where I was from, and where I was going. I replied that I had come some way, and was going to Cleaveland.

After hesitating a moment or two, he told me that he could give me nothing to eat, adding, "that if I would work, I could get something to eat."

I felt bad, being thus refused something to sustain nature, but did not dare tell him that I was a slave.

Just as I was leaving the door, with a heavy heart, a woman, who proved to be the wife of this gentleman, came to the door, and asked her husband what I wanted. He did not seem inclined to inform her. She therefore asked me herself. I told her that I had asked for something to eat. After a few other questions, she told me to come in, and that she would give me something to eat.

I walked up to the door, but the husband remained in the passage, as if unwilling to let me enter.

An angel of mercy

She asked him two or three times to get out of the way, and let me in. But as he did not move, she pushed him on one side, bidding me walk in! I was never before so glad to see a woman push a man aside! Ever since that act, I have been in favor of "woman's rights!"

After giving me as much food as I could eat, she presented me with ten cents, all the money then at her disposal, accompanied with a note to a friend, a few miles further on the road. Thanking this angel of mercy from an overflowing heart, I pushed on my way, and in three days arrived at Cleaveland, Ohio.

Being an entire stranger in this place, it was difficult for me to find where to stop. I had no money, and the lake being frozen, I saw that I must remain until the opening of the navigation, or go to Canada by way of Buffalo. But believing myself to be somewhat out of danger, I secured an engagement at the Mansion House, as a table waiter, in payment for my board. The proprietor, however, whose name was E. M. Segur, in a short time, hired me for twelve dollars a month; on which terms I remained until spring, when I found good employment on board a lake steamboat.

I purchased some books, and at leisure moments perused them with considerable advantage to myself. While at Cleaveland, I saw, for the first time, an anti-slavery newspaper. It was the "Genius of Universal Emancipation," published by Benjamin Lundy; and though I had no home, I subscribed for the paper. It was my great desire, being out of slavery myself, to do what I could for the emancipation of my brethren yet in chains, and while on Lake Erie, I found many opportunities of "helping their cause along."

It is well known that a great number of fugitives make their escape to Canada, by way of Cleaveland; and while on the lakes, I always made arrangement to carry them on the boat to Buffalo or Detroit, and thus effect their escape to the "promised land." The friends of the slave, knowing that I would transport them without charge, never failed to have a delegation when the boat arrived at Cleaveland. I have sometimes had four or five on board at one time.

I conveyed sixty-nine fugitives
In the year 1842, I conveyed, from the first of May to the first of December, sixty-nine fugitives over Lake Erie to Canada. In 1843, I visited Malden, in Upper Canada, and counted seventeen in that small village, whom I had assisted in reaching Canada. Soon after coming north I subscribed for the Liberator, edited by that champion of freedom, William Lloyd Garrison. I had heard nothing of the anti-slavery movement while in slavery, and as soon as I found that my enslaved countrymen had friends who were laboring for their liberation, I felt anxious to join them, and give what aid I could to the cause.

I early embraced the temperance cause, and found that a temperance reformation was needed among my colored brethren. In company with a few friends, I commenced a temperance reformation among the colored people in the city of Buffalo, and labored three years, in which time a society was built up, numbering over five hundred out of a population of less than seven hundred.

In the autumn, 1843, impressed with the importance of spreading anti-slavery truth, as a means to bring about the abolition of slavery, I commenced lecturing as an agent of the western New York Anti-Slavery Society, and have ever since devoted my time to the cause of my enslaved countrymen.

Chapter 12

During the autumn of 1836, a slaveholder by the name of Bacon Tate, from the State of Tennessee, came to the north in search of fugitives from slavery. On his arrival at Buffalo he heard of two of the most valuable of the slaves that he was in pursuit of. They were residing in St. Catharine's, in Upper Canada, some twenty-five miles from Buffalo. After hearing that they were in Canada, one would have supposed that Tate would have given up all hope of getting them. But not so. Bacon Tate was a man who had long been engaged in the slave-trade, and previous to that had been employed as a driver-driver. In these two situations he had gained the name of being the most complete "breaker-breaker" in that part of Tennessee where he resided. He was as unfeeling and as devoid of principle as a man could possibly be. This made him the person, above all others, to be selected to be put on the track of the fugitive slave. He had not only been commissioned to catch Stanford and his wife, the two valuable slaves already alluded to, but he had the names of some twenty others.

The slave-catcher

Many slaves had made their escape from the vicinity of Nashville, and the slaveholders were anxious to have some caught, that they might make an example of them. And Tate, anxious to sustain his high reputation as a catcher-catcher, left no stone unturned to carry out his nefarious objects.

Stanford and his little family were as happily situated as fugitives can be, who make their escape to Canada in the cold season of the year. Tate, on his arrival at Buffalo, took lodgings at the Eagle Tavern, the best house at that time in the city. And here he began to lay his plans to catch and carry back into slavery those men and women who had undergone so much to get their freedom. He soon became acquainted with a profligate colored woman, who was a servant in the hotel, and who was as unprincipled as himself. This woman was sent to St. Catharine's, to spy out the situation of Stanford's family. Under the pretence of wishing to get board in the family, and at the same time offering to pay a week's board in advance, she was taken in. After remaining with them three or four days, the spy returned to Buffalo, and informed Tate how they were situated. By the liberal use of money, Tate soon found those who were willing to do his bidding. A carriage was hired, and four men employed to go with it to St. Catharine's, and to secure their victims during the night.

The kidnappers

The carriage, with the kidnappers, crossed the Niagara river at Black Rock, on Saturday evening, about seven o'clock, and went on its way towards St. Catharine's; no one suspecting in the least that they were after fugitive slaves. About twelve o'clock that night they attacked Stanford's dwelling by breaking in the door. They found the family asleep, and of course met with no obstacle whatever in tying, gagging, and forcing them into the carriage.

The family had one child about six weeks old. That was kept at its mother's breast, to keep it quiet. The carriage re-crossed the river, at the same place, the next morning at sunrise, and proceeded to Buffalo, where it remained a short time, and after changing horses and leaving some of its company, it proceeded on its journey. The carriage being closely covered, no one had made the least discovery as to its contents. But some time during the morning, a man, who was neighbor to Stanford, and who resided but a short distance from him, came on an errand; and finding the house deserted, and seeing the most of the family's clothes lying on the floor, and seeing here and there stains of blood, soon gave the alarm, and the neighbors started in every direction, to see if they could find the kidnappers. One man got on the track of the carriage, and followed it to the ferry at Black Rock, where he heard that it had crossed some three hours before. He went on to Buffalo, and gave the alarm to the colored people of that place. The colored people of Buffalo are noted for their promptness in giving aid to the fugitive slave. The alarm was given just as the bells were ringing for church. I was in company with five or six others, when I heard that a brother slave with his family had been seized and dragged from his home during the night previous. We started on a run for the livery-stable, where we found as many more of our own color trying to hire horses to go in search of the fugitives. There were two roads which the kidnappers could take, and we were at some loss to know which to take ourselves. But we soon determined to be on the right track, and so divided our company,—one half taking the road to Erie, the other taking the road leading to Hamburgh. I was among those who took the latter.

The rescue

We traveled on at a rapid rate, until we came within half a mile of Hamburgh Corners, when we met a man on the side of the road on foot, who made signs to us to stop. We halted for a moment, when he informed us that the carriage that we were in pursuit of was at the public house, and that he was then in search of some of his neighbors, to assemble and to demand of the kidnappers the authority by which they were taking these people into slavery.

We proceeded to the tavern, where we found the carriage standing in front of the door, with a pair of fresh horses ready to proceed on their journey. The kidnappers, seeing us coming, took their victims into a room, and locked the door and fastened down the windows. We all dismounted, fastened our horses, and entered the house. We found four or five persons in the bar-room, who seemed to rejoice as we entered.

One of our company demanded the opening of the door, while others went out and surrounded the house. The kidnappers stationed one of their number at the door, and another at the window. They refused to let us enter the room, and the tavern-keeper, who was more favorable to us than we had anticipated, said to us, "Boys, get into the room in any way that you can; the house is mine, and I give you the liberty to break in through the door or window." This was all that we wanted, and we were soon making preparations to enter the room at all hazards. Those within had warned us that if we should attempt to enter, they would "shoot the first one." One of our company, who had obtained a crow-bar, went to the window, and succeeded in getting it under the sash, and soon we had the window up, and the kidnappers, together with their victims, in full view.

One of the kidnappers, while we were raising the window, kept crying at the top of his voice, "I'll shoot, I'll shoot!" but no one seemed to mind him. As soon as they saw that we were determined to rescue the slaves at all hazards, they gave up, one of their number telling us that we might "come in."

The door was thrown open, and we entered, and there found Stanford seated in one corner of the room, with his hands tied behind him, and his clothing, what little he had on, much stained with blood. Near him was his wife, with her child, but a few weeks old, in her arms. Neither of them had anything on except their night-clothes. They had both been gagged, to keep them from alarming the people, and had been much beaten and bruised when first attacked by the kidnappers. Their countenances lighted up the moment we entered the room.

The most of those who made up our company were persons who had made their escape from slavery, and who knew its horrors from personal experience, and who had left near and dear relatives behind them. And we knew how to "feel for those in bonds as bound with them."

The woman who had betrayed them, and who was in the house at the time they were taken, had been persuaded by Tate to go on with him to Tennessee. She had accompanied them from Canada, and we found her in the same room with Stanford and his wife. As soon as she found that we were about to enter the room, she ran under the bed. We knew nothing of her being in the room until Stanford pointed to the bed and said, "Under there is our betrayer." She was soon hauled out, and it was as much as some of us could do to keep the others from lynching her upon the spot. The curses came thick and fast from a majority of the company. But nothing attracted my attention at the time more than the look of Mrs. Stanford at the betrayer, as she sat before her. She did not say a word to her, but her countenance told the feelings of her inmost soul, and we could but think, that had she spoken to her, she would have said, "May the world deny thee a shelter! earth a home! the dust a grave! the sun his light! and Heaven her God!"

The betrayer begged us to let her go. I was somewhat disposed to comply with her request, but I found many to oppose me; in fact, I was entirely alone. My main reason for wishing to let her escape was that I was afraid that her life would be in danger. I knew that, if she was taken back to Buffalo or Canada, she would fall into the hands of an excited people, the most of whom had themselves been slaves. And they, being comparatively ignorant of the laws, would be likely to take the law into their own hands.

The sheriff
However, the woman was not allowed to escape, but was put into the coach, together with Stanford and his wife; and after an hour and a half's drive, we found ourselves in the city of Buffalo. The excitement which the alarm had created in the morning had broken up the meetings of the colored people for that day; and on our arrival in the city we were met by some forty or fifty colored persons. The kidnappers had not been inactive; for, on our arrival in the city, we learned that the man who had charge of the carriage and fugitives when we caught up with them, returned to the city immediately after giving the slaves up to us, and had informed Tate, who had remained behind, of what had occurred. Tate immediately employed the sheriff and his posse to re-take the slaves. So, on our arrival in Buffalo, we found that the main battle had yet to be fought. Stanford and his wife and child were soon provided with clothing and some refreshment, while we were preparing ourselves with

clubs, pistols, knives, and other weapons of defense. News soon come to us that the sheriff, with his under officers, together with some sixty or seventy men who were at work on the canal, were on the road between Buffalo and Black Rock, and that they intended to re-take the slaves when we should attempt to take them to the ferry to convey them to Canada. This news was anything but pleasant to us, but we prepared for the worst.

We returned to the city about two o'clock in the afternoon, and about four we started for Black Rock ferry, which is about three miles below Buffalo. We had in our company some fifty or more able-bodied, resolute men, who were determined to stand by the slaves, and who had resolved, before they left the city, that if the sheriff and his men took the slaves, they should first pass over their dead bodies.

We started, and when about a mile below the city, the sheriff and his men came upon us, and surrounded us. The slaves were in a carriage, and the horses were soon stopped, and we found it advisable to take them out of the carriage, and we did so. The sheriff came forward, and read something purporting to be a "Riot Act," and at the same time called upon all good citizens to aid him in keeping the "peace." This was a trick of his, to get possession of the slaves. His men rushed upon us with their clubs and stones and a general fight ensued. Our company had surrounded the slaves, and had succeeded in keeping the sheriff and his men off. We fought, and at the same time kept pushing on towards the ferry.

Pepper

In the midst of the fight, a little white man made his appearance among us, and proved to be a valuable friend. His name was Pepper; and he proved himself a pepper to the sheriff and his posse that day. He was a lawyer; and as the officers would arrest any of our company, he would step up and ask the officer if he had a "warrant to take that man;" and as none of them had warrants, and could not answer affirmatively, he would say to the colored man, "He has no right to take you; knock him down." The command was no sooner given than the man would fall. If the one who had been arrested was not able to knock him down, some who were close by, and who were armed with a club or other weapon, would come to his assistance.

After it became generally known in our company that the "little man" was a lawyer, he had a tremendous influence with them. You could hear them cry out occasionally, "That's right, knock him down; the little man told you to do it, and he is a lawyer; he knows all about the law; that's right,—hit him again! he is a white man, and he has done our color enough."

Such is but a poor representation of what was said by those who were engaged in the fight. After a hard-fought battle, of nearly two hours, we arrived at the ferry, the slaves still in our possession. On arriving at the ferry, we found that some of the sheriff's gang had taken possession of the ferry-boat. Here another battle was to be fought, before the slaves could reach Canada. The boat was fastened at each end by a chain, and in the scuffle for the ascendancy, one party took charge of one end of the boat, while the other took the other end. The blacks were commanding the ferryman to carry them over, while the whites were commanding him not to. While each party was contending for power, the slaves were pushed on board, and the boat shoved from the wharf. Many of the blacks jumped on board of the boat, while the whites jumped on shore. And the swift current of the Niagara soon carried them off, amid the shouts of the blacks, and the oaths and imprecations of the whites. We on shore swung our hats and gave three cheers, just as a reinforcement came to the whites. Seeing the odds entirely against us in numbers, and having gained the great victory, we gave up without resistance, and suffered ourselves to be arrested by the sheriff's posse. However, we all remained on the shore until the ferry-boat had landed on the Canada side. As the boat landed, Stanford leaped on shore, and rolled over in the sand, and even rubbed it into his hair.

I did not accompany the boat over, but those who did informed us that Mrs. Stanford, as she stepped on the shore, with her child in her arms, exclaimed, "I thank God that I am again in Canada!" We returned to the city, and some forty of our company were lodged in jail, to await their trial the next morning.

The betrayer

And now I will return to the betrayer. On our return to Buffalo, she was given over to a committee of women, who put her in a room, and put a guard over her. Tate, who had been very active from the time that he heard that we had recaptured the carriage with the slaves, was still in the city. He was not with the slaves when we caught up with them at Hamburgh, nor was he to be found in the fight. He sent his hirelings, while he remained at the hotel drinking champagne. As soon as he found the slaves were out of his reach, he then made an offer of fifty dollars to any person who would find the betrayer. He pretended that he wished to save her from the indignation of the colored people. But the fact is, he had promised her that if she would accompany him to the south, that he would put her in a situation where she would be a lady. Poor woman! She was foolish enough to believe him; and now that the people had lost all sympathy for her, on account of her traitorous act, he still thought that, by pretending to be her friend, he could induce her to go to the south, that he might sell her. But those who had her in charge were determined that she should be punished for being engaged in this villainous transaction.

Several meetings were held to determine what should be done with her. Some were in favor of hanging her, others for burning her, but a majority were for taking her to the Niagara river, tying a fifty-six pound weight to her, and throwing her in. There seemed to be no way in which she could be reached by the civil law. She was kept in confinement three days, being removed to different places each night.

So conflicting were the views of those who had her in charge, that they could not decide upon what should be done with her. However, there seemed to be such a vast majority in favor of throwing her into the Niagara river, that some of us, who were opposed to taking life, succeeded in having her given over to another committee, who, after reprimanding her, let her go.

Tate, in the mean time, hearing that the colored people had resolved to take vengeance on him, thought it best to leave the city. On Monday, at ten o'clock, we were all carried before Justice Grosvenor; and of the forty who had been committed the evening before, twenty-five were held to bail to answer to a higher court. When the trials came on, we were fined more or less, from five to fifty dollars each.

During the fight no one was killed, though there were many broken noses and black eyes; one young man, who was attached to a theatrical corps, was so badly injured in the conflict that he died some three months after.

Thus ended one of the most fearful fights for human freedom that I ever witnessed. The reader will observe that this conflict took place on the Sabbath, and that those who were foremost in getting it up were officers of justice. The plea of the sheriff and his posse was, that we were breaking the Sabbath by assembling in such large numbers to protect a brother slave and his wife and child from being dragged back into slavery, which is far worse than death itself.

William Wells Brown

HENRY H. GARNET (1815-1882)

Introduction

Rev. Henry H. Garnet, militant abolitionist, was born a slave in Kent County, MD. He escaped from his slavery in 1824 and made his way to New York where he studied at the Oneida Theological Institute in Whitesboro before becoming a Presbyterian minister in Troy, New York.

Garnet joined the Anti-Slavery Society and became one of the leading lecturers in the organization. However, in 1843, he was disowned by the society when he called upon slaves to murder their masters.

Address to the Slaves of the United States of America

This speech was d delivered to the National Convention of Colored Citizens Buffalo, New York on 16 August 1843.

Brethren and fellow citizens

Your brethren of the north, east, and west have been accustomed to meet together in National Conventions, to sympathize with each other, and to weep over your unhappy condition. In these meetings we have addressed all classes of the free, but we have never until this time, sent a word of consolation and advice to you. We have been contented in sitting still and mourning over your sorrows, earnestly hoping that before this day, your sacred Liberties would have been restored. But, we have hoped in vain. Years have rolled on, and tens of thousands have been borne on streams of blood, and tears, to the shores of eternity. While you have been oppressed, we have also been partakers with you; nor can we be free while you are enslaved. We therefore write to you as being bound with you.

Many of you are bound to us, not only by the ties of common humanity, but we are connected by the more tender relations of parents, wives, husbands, children, brothers, and sisters, and friends. As such we most affectionately address you.

A deep gulf

Slavery has fixed a deep gulf between you and us, and while it shuts out from you the relief and consolation which your friends would willingly render, it afflicts and persecutes you with a fierceness which we might not expect to see in the fiends of hell. But still the Almighty Father of Mercies has left to us a glimmering ray of hope, which shines out like a lone star in a cloudy sky. Mankind are becoming wiser, and better—the oppressor's power is fading, and you, every day, are becoming better informed, and more numerous. Your grievances, brethren, are many. We shall not attempt, in this short address, to present to the world, all the dark catalogue of this nation's sins, which have been committed upon an innocent people. Nor is it indeed, necessary, for you feel them from day to day, and all the civilized world look upon them with amazement.

History of slavery in America

Two hundred and twenty-seven years ago, the first of our injured race were brought to the shores of America. They came not with glad spirits to select their homes, in the New World. They came not with their own consent, to find an unmolested enjoyment of the blessings of this fruitful soil. The first dealings which they had with men calling themselves Christians, exhibited to them the worst features of corrupt and sordid hearts; and convinced them that no cruelty is too great, no villainy, and no robbery too abhorrent for even enlightened men to perform, when influenced by avarice, and lust. Neither did they come flying upon the wings of Liberty, to a land of freedom. But, they came with broken hearts, from their beloved native land, and were doomed to unrequited toil, and deep degradation. Nor did the evil of the bondage end at their emancipation by death. Succeeding generations inherited their chains, and millions have come from eternity into time, and have returned again to the world of spirits, cursed and ruined by American Slavery.

The propagators of the system, or their immediate ancestors very soon discovered its growing evil, and its tremendous wickedness and secret promises were made to destroy it. The gross inconsistency of a people holding slaves, who had themselves "ferried o'er the wave," for freedom's sake, was too apparent to be entirely overlooked. The voice of Freedom cried, "emancipate your Slaves." Humanity supplicated with tears, for the deliverance of the children of Africa. Wisdom urged her solemn plea. The bleeding captive plead his innocence, and pointed to Christianity who stood weeping at the cross. Jehovah frowned upon the nefarious institution, and thunderbolts, red with vengeance, struggled to leap forth to blast the guilty wretches who maintained it. But all was vain. Slavery had stretched its dark wings of death over the land, the Church stood silently by—the priests prophesied falsely, and the people loved to have it so. Its throne is established, and now it reigns triumphantly.

Forbidden to read the Bible

Nearly three millions of your fellow citizens, are prohibited by law, and public opinion (which in this country is stronger than law), from reading the Book of Life. Your intellect has been destroyed as much as possible, and every ray of light they have attempted to shut out from your minds. The oppressors themselves have become involved in the ruin. They have become weak, sensual, and rapacious. They have cursed you—they have cursed themselves—they have cursed the earth which they have trod. In the language of a Southern statesman, we can truly say "even the wolf, driven back long since by the approach of man now returns after a lapse of a hundred years, and howls amid the desolation of slavery."

The colonists threw the blame upon England. They said that the mother country entailed the evil upon them, and that they would rid themselves of it if they could. The world thought they were sincere, and the philanthropic pitied them. But time soon tested their sincerity. In a few years, the colonists grew strong and severed themselves from the British Government. Their independence was declared, and they took their station among the sovereign powers of the earth. The declaration was a glorious document. Sages admired it, and the patriotic of every nation reverenced the Godlike sentiments which it contained.

When the power of Government returned to their hands, did they emancipate the slaves? No, they rather added new links to our chains. Were they ignorant to the principles of Liberty? Certainly they were not. The sentiments of their revolutionary orators fell in burning eloquence upon their hearts, and with one voice they cried, liberty or death. O, what a sentence was that! It ran from soul to soul like electric fire, and nerved the arm of thousands to fight in the holy cause of Freedom. Among the diversity of opinions that are entertained in regard to physical resistance, there are but a few found to gainsay that stern declaration. We are among those who do not.

Misery

Slavery! How much misery is comprehended in that single word. What mind is there that does not shrink from its direful effects? Unless the image of God is obliterated from the soul, all men cherish the love of Liberty. The nice discerning political economist does not regard the sacred right, more than the untutored African who roams in the wilds of Congo. Nor has the one more right to the full enjoyment of his freedom than the other. In every man's mind the good seeds of Liberty are planted, and he who brings his fellow down so low, as to make him contented with a condition of slavery, commits the highest crime against God and man. Brethren, your oppressors aim to do this. They endeavor to make you as much like brutes as possible. When they have blinded the eyes of your mind—when they have embittered the sweet waters of life—when they have shut out the light which shines from the word of God—then, and not till then has American slavery done its perfect work.

No voluntary submission

To such degradation it is sinful in the extreme for you to make voluntary submission. The divine commandments, you are in duty bound to reverence, and obey. If you do not obey them you will surely meet with the displeasure of the Almighty. He requires you to love him supremely, and your neighbor as yourself—to keep the Sabbath day holy—to search the Scriptures—and bring up your children with respect for his laws, and to worship no other God but him. But slavery sets all these at naught, and hurls defiance in the face of Jehovah. The forlorn condition in which you are placed does not destroy your moral obligation to God. You are not certain of Heaven, because you suffer yourselves to remain in a state of slavery, where you cannot obey the commandments of the Sovereign of the universe. If the ignorance of slavery is a passport to heaven, then it is a blessing, and a curse, and you should rather desire its perpetuity than its abolition. God will not receive slavery, nor ignorance, nor any other state of mind, for love, and obedience to him. Your condition does not absolve you from your moral obligation. The diabolical injustice by which your Liberties are cloven down, neither God, nor angels, or just men command you to suffer for a single moment. therefore it is your solemn and imperative duty to use every means, both moral, intellectual, and physical, that promise success. If a band of heathen men should attempt to enslave a race of Christians, and to place their children under the influence of some false religion, surely, heaven would frown upon the men who would not resist such aggression, even to death. If, on the other hand, a band of Christians should attempt to enslave a race of heathen men and to entail slavery upon them, and to keep them in heathenism in the midst of Christianity, the God of heaven would smile upon every effort which the injured might make to disenthrall themselves.

Brethren, it is as wrong for your lordly oppressors to keep you in slavery, as it was for the man thief to steal our ancestors from the coast of Africa. You should therefore now use the same manner of resistance, as would have been just in our ancestors, when the bloody footprints of the first remorseless soul-thief was placed upon the shores of our fatherland. The humblest peasant is as free in the sight of God, as the proudest monarch that ever swayed a scepter. Liberty is a spirit sent out from God, and like its great Author, is no respecter of persons.

Act for yourselves

Brethren, the time has come when you must act for yourselves. It is an old and true saying, that "if hereditary bondsmen would be free, they must themselves strike the blow." You can plead your own cause, and do the work of emancipation better than any other. The nations of the old world are moving in the great cause of universal freedom, and some of them at least, will ere long, do you justice. The combined powers of Europe have placed their broad seal of disapprobation upon the African slave trade. But in the slave holding parts of the United States, the trade is as brisk as ever. They buy and sell you as though you were brute beasts. The North has done much—her opinion of slavery in the abstract is known. But in regard to the South, we adopt the opinion of the *New York Evangelist*—"We have advanced so far, that the cause apparently waits for a more effectual door to be thrown open than has been yet." We are about to point you to that more effectual door. Look around you, and behold the bosoms of your loving wives, heaving with untold agonies! Hear the cries of your poor children! Remember the stripes your fathers bore. Think of the torture and disgrace of your noble mothers. Think of your wretched sisters, loving virtue and purity, as they are driven into concubinage, and are exposed to the unbridled lusts of incarnate devils. Think of the undying glory that hangs around the ancient name of Africa—and forget not that you are native-born American citizens, and as such, you are justly entitled to all the rights that are granted to the freest. Think how many tears you have poured out upon the soil which you have cultivated with unrequited toil, and enriched with your blood; and then go to your lordly enslavers, and tell them plainly, that you are determined to be free. Appeal to their sense of justice, and tell them that they have no more right to oppress you, than you have to enslave them. Entreat them to remove the grievous burdens which they have imposed upon you, and to remunerate you for your labor. Promise them renewed diligence in the cultivation of the soil, if they will render to you an equivalent for your services. Point them to the increase of happiness and prosperity in the British West Indies, since the act of Emancipation.

Tell them in language which they cannot misunderstand, of the exceeding sinfulness of slavery, and of a future judgment, and of the righteous retributions of an indignant God. Inform them that all you desire, is freedom, and that nothing else will suffice. Do this, and forever after cease to toil for the heartless tyrants, who give you no other reward but stripes and abuse. If they then commence the work of death, they, and not you, will be responsible for the consequences. You had far better all die—die immediately, than live slaves, and entail your wretchedness upon your posterity. If you would be free in this generation, here is your only hope. However much you and all of us may desire it, there is not much hope of Redemption without the shedding of blood. If you must bleed, let it all come at once— rather, die freemen, than live to be slaves. It is impossible, like the children of Israel, to make a grand Exodus from the land of bondage. The pharoes are on both sides of the blood-red waters! You cannot remove en masse, to the dominions of the British Queen— nor can you pass through Florida, and overrun Texas, and at last find peace in Mexico. The propagators of American slavery are spending their blood and treasure, that they may plant the black flag in the heart of Mexico, and riot in the halls of the Montezumas. In the language of the Rev. Robert Hall, when addressing the volunteers of Bristol, who were rushing forth to repel the invasion of Napoleon, who threatened to lay waste the fair homes of England, "Religion is too much interested in your behalf, not to shed over you her most gracious influences."

You will not be compelled to spend much time in order to become inured to hardships. From the first moment that you breathed the air of heaven, you have been accustomed to nothing else but hardships. The heroes of the American Revolution were never put upon harder fare, than a peck of corn, and a few herrings per week. You have not become enervated by the luxuries of life. Your sternest energies have been beaten out upon the anvil of severe trial. Slavery has done this, to make you subservient to its own purposes; but it has done more than this, it has prepared you for any emergency. If you receive good treatment, it is what you could hardly expect; if you meet with pain, sorrow, and even death, these are the common lot of the slaves.

Fellow men! patient sufferers! behold your dearest rights crushed to the earth! See your sons murdered, and your wives, mothers, and sisters, doomed to prostitution! In the name of the merciful God! and by all that life is worth, let it no longer be a debatable question, whether it is better to choose liberty or death!

A plan for liberation

In 1822, Denmark Vesey, of South Carolina, formed a plan for the liberation of his fellow men. In the whole history of human efforts to overthrow slavery, a more complicated and tremendous plan was never formed. He was betrayed by the treachery of his own people, and died a martyr to freedom. Many a brave hero fell, but History, faithful to her high trust, will transcribe his name on the same monument with Moses, Hampden, Tell, Bruce, and Wallace, Toussaint L'Ouverture, Lafayette and Washington. That tremendous movement shook the whole empire of slavery. The guilty soul-thieves were overwhelmed with fear. It is a matter of fact, that at that time, and in consequence of the threatened revolution, the slave states talked strongly of emancipation. But they blew but one blast of the trumpet of freedom, and then laid it aside. As these men became quiet, the slaveholders ceased to talk about emancipation; and now, behold your condition today! Angels sigh over it, and humanity has long since exhausted her tears in weeping on your account!

The patriotic Nathaniel Turner followed Denmark Vesey. He was goaded to desperation by wrong and injustice. By Despotism, his name has been recorded on the list of infamy, but future generations will number him upon the noble and brave.

Next arose the immortal Joseph Cinque, the hero of the Amistad. He was a native African, and by the help of God he emancipated a whole ship-load of his fellow men on the high seas. And he now sings of Liberty on the sunny hills of Africa, and beneath his native palm trees, where he hears the lion roar, and feels himself as free as that king of the forest. Next arose Madison Washington, that bright star of freedom, and took his station in the constellation of freedom. He was a slave on board the brig Creole, of Richmond, bound to New Orleans, that great slave mart, with a hundred and four others. Nineteen struck for Liberty or death. But one life was taken, and the whole were emancipated, and the vessel was carried into Nassau, New Providence. Noble men! Those who have fallen in freedom's conflict, their memories will be cherished by the true hearted, and the God-fearing, in all future generations; those who are living, their names are surrounded by a halo of glory.

We do not advise you to attempt a revolution with the sword, because it would be inexpedient. Your numbers are too small, and moreover the rising spirit of the age, and the spirit of the gospel, are opposed to war and bloodshed. But from this moment cease to labor for tyrants who will not remunerate you. Let every slave throughout the land do this, and the days of slavery are numbered. You cannot be more oppressed than you have been—you cannot suffer greater cruelties than you have already. Rather die freemen, than live to be slaves. Remember that you are three millions.

It is in your power so to torment the God-cursed slaveholders, that they will be glad to let you go free. If the scale was turned and black men were the masters, and white men the slaves, every destructive agent and element would be employed to lay the oppressor low. Danger and death would hang over their heads day and night. Yes, the tyrants would meet with plagues more terrible than those of Pharaoh. But you are a patient people. You act as though you were made for the special use of these devils. You act as though your daughters were born to pamper the lusts of your masters and overseers. And worse than all, you tamely submit, while your lords tear your wives from your embraces, and defile them before your eyes. In the name of God we ask, are you men? Where is the blood of your fathers? Has it all run out of your veins? Awake, awake; millions of voices are calling you! Your dead fathers speak to you from their graves. Heaven, as with a voice of thunder, calls on you to arise from the dust.

Resistance

Let your motto be resistance! Resistance! Resistance! No oppressed people have ever secured their Liberty without resistance. What kind of resistance you had better make, you must decide by the circumstances that surround you, and according to the suggestion of expediency. Brethren, adieu. Trust in the living God. Labor for the peace of the human race, and remember that you are three millions.

Henry H Garnet

FREDERICK DOUGLASS (1818-1895)

Introduction

Frederick Douglass, an American slave, was an abolitionist, women's rights advocate, journalist and newspaper editor, social reformer and race leader. He became one of the most prominent black leaders of the nineteenth century and one of the most eloquent orators in American public life.

Douglass, the most famous escaped slave of his day, records how it felt to be a slave and how the Bible was used to justify the slave trade in his *Frederick Douglass, Narrative of the Life of Frederick Douglass: An American Slave*. He speaks from the heart in this book and is most critical of "religious slaveholders".

> We have men sold to build churches, women sold to support the gospel, and babes sold to purchase Bibles for the poor heathen, all for the glory of God and the good of souls. The slave auctioneer's bell and the church-going bell chime in with each other, and the bitter cries of the heart-broken slave are drowned in the religious shouts of his pious master. Revivals of religion and revivals of the slave trade go hand in hand. ... Were I to be again reduced to the chains of slavery, next to the enslavement, I should regard being the slave of a religious master the greatest calamity that could befall me. For of all slave-holders with whom I have ever met, religious slaveholders are the worst. I have ever found them the meanest and basest, the most cruel and cowardly, of all others.
> *Frederick Douglass, Narrative of the Life of Frederick Douglass: An American Slave*

Along with *Uncle Tom's Cabin*, *The Narrative of the Life of Frederick Douglass* was one of the most influential pieces of literature to fuel the abolitionist movement of the early 19th Century in the United States. The opening and closing chapters from this book are set out below.

The Narrative of the Life of Frederick Douglass: An American Slave
Chapter 1

I was born in Tuckahoe, near Hillsborough, and about twelve miles from Easton, in Talbot county, Maryland. I have no accurate knowledge of my age, never having seen any authentic record containing it. By far the larger part of the slaves know as little of their ages as horses know of theirs, and it is the wish of most masters within my knowledge to keep their slaves thus ignorant. I do not remember to have ever met a slave who could tell of his birthday. They seldom come nearer to it than planting-time, harvest- time, cherry-time, spring-time, or fall-time. A want of information concerning my own was a source of unhappiness to me even during childhood. The white children could tell their ages. I could not tell why I ought to be deprived of the same privilege. I was not allowed to make any inquiries of my master concerning it. He deemed all such inquiries on the part of a slave improper and impertinent, and evidence of a restless spirit. The nearest estimate I can give makes me now between twenty-seven and twenty- eight years of age. I come to this, from hearing my master say, some time during 1835, I was about seventeen years old.

My mother

My mother was named Harriet Bailey. She was the daughter of Isaac and Betsey Bailey, both colored, and quite dark. My mother was of a darker complexion than either my grand-mother or grandfather.

My father

My father was a white man. He was admitted to be such by all I ever heard speak of my parentage. The opinion was also whispered that my master was my father; but of the correctness of this opinion, I know nothing; the means of knowing was withheld from me. My mother and I were separated when I was but an infant—before I knew her as my mother. It is a common custom, in the part of Maryland from which I ran away, to part children from their mothers at a very early age. Frequently, before the child has reached its twelfth month, its mother is taken from it, and hired out on some farm a considerable distance off, and the child is placed under the care of an old woman, too old for field labor. For what this separation is done, I do not know, unless it be to hinder the development of the child's affection toward its mother, and to blunt and destroy the natural affection of the mother for the child. This is the inevitable result.

I hardly knew my mother

I never saw my mother, to know her as such, more than four or five times in my life; and each of these times was very short in duration, and at night. She was hired by a Mr. Stewart, who lived about twelve miles from my home. She made her journeys to see me in the night, traveling the whole distance on foot, after the performance of her day's work. She was a field hand, and a whipping is the penalty of not being in the field at sunrise, unless a slave has special permission from his or her master to the contrary—a permission which they seldom get, and one that gives to him that gives it the proud name of being a kind master. I do not recollect of ever seeing my mother by the light of day. She was with me in the night. She would lie down with me, and get me to sleep, but long before I waked she was gone. Very little communication ever took place between us. Death soon ended what little we could have while she lived, and with it her hardships and suffering. She died when I was about seven years old, on one of my master's farms, near Lee's Mill. I was not allowed to be present during her illness, at her death, or burial. She was gone long before I knew any thing about it. Never having enjoyed, to any considerable extent, her soothing presence, her tender and watchful care, I received the tidings of her death with much the same emotions I should have probably felt at the death of a stranger.

Called thus suddenly away, she left me without the slightest intimation of who my father was. The whisper that my master was my father, may or may not be true; and, true or false, it is of but little consequence to my purpose whilst the fact remains, in all its glaring odiousness, that slaveholders have ordained, and by law established, that the children of slave women shall in all cases follow the condition of their mothers; and this is done too obviously to administer to their own lusts, and make a gratification of their wicked desires profitable as well as pleasurable; for by this cunning arrangement, the slaveholder, in cases not a few, sustains to his slaves the double relation of master and father.

I know of such cases; and it is worthy of remark that such slaves invariably suffer greater hardships, and have more to contend with, than others. They are, in the first place, a constant offence to their mistress. She is ever disposed to find fault with them; they can seldom do any thing to please her; she is never better pleased than when she sees them under the lash, especially when she suspects her husband of showing to his mulatto children favors which he withholds from his black slaves. The master is frequently compelled to sell this class of his slaves, out of deference to the feelings of his white wife; and, cruel as the deed may strike any one to be, for a man to sell his own children to human flesh-mongers, it is often the dictate of humanity for him to do so; for, unless he does this, he must not only whip them himself, but must stand by and see one white son tie up his brother, of but few shades darker complexion than himself, and ply the gory lash to his naked back; and if he lisp one word of disapproval, it is set down to his parental partiality, and only makes a bad matter worse, both for himself and the slave whom he would protect and defend.

Every year brings with it multitudes of this class of slaves. It was doubtless in consequence of a knowledge of this fact, that one great statesman of the south predicted the downfall of slavery by the inevitable laws of population. Whether this prophecy is ever fulfilled or not, it is nevertheless plain that a very different-looking class of people are springing up at the south, and are now held in slavery, from those originally brought to this country from Africa; and if their increase do no other good, it will do away the force of the argument, that God cursed Ham, and therefore American slavery is right. If the lineal descendants of Ham are alone to be scripturally enslaved, it is certain that slavery at the south must soon become unscriptural; for thousands are ushered into the world, annually, who, like myself, owe their existence to white fathers, and those fathers most frequently their own masters.

Two masters

I have had two masters. My first master's name was Anthony. I do not remember his first name. He was generally called Captain Anthony—a title which, I presume, he acquired by sailing a craft on the Chesapeake Bay. He was not considered a rich slaveholder. He owned two or three farms, and about thirty slaves. His farms and slaves were under the care of an overseer. The overseer's name was Plummer. Mr. Plummer was a miserable drunkard, a profane swearer, and a savage monster. He always went armed with a cowskin and a heavy cudgel. I have known him to cut and slash the women's heads so horribly, that even master would be enraged at his cruelty, and would threaten to whip him if he did not mind himself. Master, however, was not a humane slaveholder. It required extraordinary barbarity on the part of an overseer to affect him. He was a cruel man, hardened by a long life of slave-holding. He would at times seem to take great pleasure in whipping a slave. I have often been awakened at the dawn of day by the most heart-rending shrieks of an own aunt of mine, whom he used to tie up to a joist, and whip upon her naked back till she was literally covered with blood. No words, no tears, no prayers, from his gory victim, seemed to move his iron heart from its bloody purpose. The louder she screamed, the harder he whipped; and where the blood ran fastest, there he whipped longest. He would whip her to make her scream, and whip her to make her hush; and not until overcome by fatigue, would he cease to swing the blood-clotted cowskin. I remember the first time I ever witnessed this horrible exhibition. I was quite a child, but I well remember it. I never shall forget it whilst I remember any thing. It was the first of a long series of such outrages, of which I was doomed to be a witness and a participant. It struck me with awful force. It was the blood-stained gate, the entrance to the hell of slavery, through which I was about to pass. It was a most terrible spectacle. I wish I could commit to paper the feelings with which I beheld it.

Aunt Hester
This occurrence took place very soon after I went to live with my old master, and under the following circumstances. Aunt Hester went out one night,—where or for what I do not know,—and happened to be absent when my master desired her presence. He had ordered her not to go out evenings, and warned her that she must never let him catch her in company with a young man, who was paying attention to her belonging to Colonel Lloyd. The young man's name was Ned Roberts, generally called Lloyd's Ned. Why master was so careful of her, may be safely left to conjecture. She was a woman of noble form, and of graceful proportions, having very few equals, and fewer superiors, in personal appearance, among the colored or white women of our neighborhood.

Warm, red blood, dripping to the floor
Aunt Hester had not only disobeyed his orders in going out, but had been found in company with Lloyd's Ned; which circumstance, I found, from what he said while whipping her, was the chief offence. Had he been a man of pure morals himself, he might have been thought interested in protecting the innocence of my aunt; but those who knew him will not suspect him of any such virtue. Before he commenced whipping Aunt Hester, he took her into the kitchen, and stripped her from neck to waist, leaving her neck, shoulders, and back, entirely naked. He then told her to cross her hands, calling her at the same time a d——d b——h. After crossing her hands, he tied them with a strong rope, and led her to a stool under a large hook in the joist, put in for the purpose. He made her get upon the stool, and tied her hands to the hook. She now stood fair for his infernal purpose. Her arms were stretched up at their full length, so that she stood upon the ends of her toes. He then said to her, "Now, you d——d b——h, I'll learn you how to disobey my orders!" and after rolling up his sleeves, he commenced to lay on the heavy cowskin, and soon the warm, red blood (amid heart-rending shrieks from her, and horrid oaths from him) came dripping to the floor. I was so terrified and horror-stricken at the sight, that I hid myself in a closet, and dared not venture out till long after the bloody transaction was over. I expected it would be my turn next. It was all new to me. I had never seen any thing like it before. I had always lived with my grandmother on the outskirts of the plantation, where she was put to raise the children of the younger

women. I had therefore been, until now, out of the way of the bloody scenes that often occurred on the plantation. ...

Chapter 11

I now come to that part of my life during which I planned, and finally succeeded in making, my escape from slavery. But before narrating any of the peculiar circumstances, I deem it proper to make known my intention not to state all the facts connected with the transaction. My reasons for pursuing this course may be understood from the following: First, were I to give a minute statement of all the facts, it is not only possible, but quite probable, that others would thereby be involved in the most embarrassing difficulties. Secondly, such a statement would most undoubtedly induce greater vigilance on the part of slaveholders than has existed heretofore among them; which would, of course, be the means of guarding a door whereby some dear brother bondman might escape his galling chains. I deeply regret the necessity that impels me to suppress any thing of importance connected with my experience in slavery. It would afford me great pleasure indeed, as well as materially add to the interest of my narrative, were I at liberty to gratify a curiosity, which I know exists in the minds of many, by an accurate statement of all the facts pertaining to my most fortunate escape. But I must deprive myself of this pleasure, and the curious of the gratification which such a statement would afford. I would allow myself to suffer under the greatest imputations which evil-minded men might suggest, rather than exculpate myself, and thereby run the hazard of closing the slightest avenue by which a brother slave might clear himself of the chains and fetters of slavery.

Upperground railroad

I have never approved of the very public manner in which some of our western friends have conducted what they call the Underground Railroad, but which I think, by their open declarations, has been made most emphatically the upperground railroad. I honor those good men and women for their noble daring, and applaud them for willingly subjecting themselves to bloody persecution, by openly avowing their participation in the escape of slaves. I, however, can see very little good resulting from such a course, either to themselves or the slaves escaping; while, upon the other hand, I see and feel assured that those open declarations are a positive evil to the slaves remaining, who are seeking to escape. They do nothing towards enlightening the slave, whilst they do much towards enlightening the master. They stimulate him to greater watchfulness, and enhance his power to capture his slave. We owe something to the slave south of the line as well as to those north of it; and in aiding the latter on their way to freedom, we should be careful to do nothing which would be likely to hinder the former from escaping from slavery. I would keep the merciless slaveholder profoundly ignorant of the means of flight adopted by the slave. I would leave him to imagine himself surrounded by myriads of invisible tormentors, ever ready to snatch from his infernal grasp his trembling prey. Let him be left to feel his way in the dark; let darkness commensurate with his crime hover over him; and let him feel that at every step he takes, in pursuit of the flying bondman, he is running the frightful risk of having his hot brains dashed out by an invisible agency. Let us render the tyrant no aid; let us not hold the light by which he can trace the footprints of our flying brother. But enough of this. I will now proceed to the statement of those facts, connected with my escape, for which I am alone responsible, and for which no one can be made to suffer but myself.

In the early part of the year 1838, I became quite restless. I could see no reason why I should, at the end of each week, pour the reward of my toil into the purse of my master. When I carried to him my weekly wages, he would, after counting the money, look me in the face with a robber-like fierceness, and ask, "Is this all?" He was satisfied with nothing less than the last cent. He would, however, when I made him six dollars, sometimes give me six cents, to encourage me. It had the opposite effect. I regarded it as a sort of admission of my right to the whole. The fact that he gave me any part of my wages was proof, to my mind, that he believed me entitled to the whole of them. I always felt worse for having received any thing; for I feared that the giving me a few cents would ease his conscience, and make him feel himself to be a pretty honorable sort of robber. My discontent grew upon me. I was ever on the look-out for means of escape; and, finding no direct means, I determined to try to hire my time, with a view of getting money with which to make my escape. In the spring of 1838, when Master Thomas came to Baltimore to purchase his spring goods, I got an opportunity, and applied to him to allow me to hire my time. He unhesitatingly refused my request, and told me this was another stratagem by which to escape. He told me I could go nowhere but that he could get me; and that, in the event of my running away, he should spare no pains in his efforts to catch me. He exhorted me to content myself, and be obedient. He told me, if I would be happy, I must lay out no plans for the future. He said, if I behaved myself properly, he would take care of me. Indeed, he advised me to complete thoughtlessness of the future, and taught me to depend solely upon him for happiness. He seemed to see fully the pressing necessity of setting aside my intellectual nature, in order to contentment in slavery. But in spite of him, and even in spite of myself, I continued to think, and to think about the injustice of my enslavement, and the means of escape.

About two months after this, I applied to Master Hugh for the privilege of hiring my time. He was not acquainted with the fact that I had applied to Master Thomas, and had been refused. He too, at first, seemed disposed to refuse; but, after some reflection, he granted me the privilege, and proposed the following terms: I was to be allowed all my time, make all contracts with those for whom I worked, and find my own employment; and, in return for this liberty, I was to pay him three dollars at the end of each week; find myself in calking tools, and in board and clothing. My board was two dollars and a half per week. This, with the wear and tear of clothing and calking tools, made my regular expenses about six dollars per week. This amount I was compelled to make up, or relinquish the privilege of hiring my time. Rain or shine, work or no work, at the end of each week the money must be forthcoming, or I must give up my privilege. This arrangement, it will be perceived, was decidedly in my master's favor. It relieved him of all need of looking after me. His money was sure. He received all the benefits of slaveholding without its evils; while I endured all the evils of a slave, and suffered all the care and anxiety of a freeman. I found it a hard bargain.

But, hard as it was, I thought it better than the old mode of getting along. It was a step towards freedom to be allowed to bear the responsibilities of a freeman, and I was determined to hold on upon it. I bent myself to the work of making money. I was ready to work at night as well as day, and by the most untiring perseverance and industry, I made enough to meet my expenses, and lay up a little money every week. I went on thus from May till August. Master Hugh then refused to allow me to hire my time longer.

I did no work

The ground for his refusal was a failure on my part, one Saturday night, to pay him for my week's time. This failure was occasioned by my attending a camp meeting about ten miles from Baltimore. During the week, I had entered into an engagement with a number of young friends to start from Baltimore to the camp ground early Saturday evening; and being detained by my employer, I was unable to get down to Master Hugh's without disappointing the company. I knew that Master Hugh was in no special need of the money that night. I therefore decided to go to camp meeting, and upon my return pay him the three dollars. I staid at the camp meeting one day longer than I intended when I left. But as soon as I returned, I called upon him to pay him what he considered his due. I found him very angry; he could scarce restrain his wrath. He said he had a great mind to give me a severe whipping. He wished to know how I dared go out of the city without asking his permission. I told him I hired my time and while I paid him the price which he asked for it, I did not know that I was bound to ask him when and where I should go. This reply troubled him; and, after reflecting a few moments, he turned to me, and said I should hire my time no longer; that the next thing he should know of, I would be running away. Upon the same plea, he told me to bring my tools and clothing home forthwith. I did so; but instead of seeking work, as I had been accustomed to do previously to hiring my time, I spent the whole week without the performance of a single stroke of work. I did this in retaliation. Saturday night, he called upon me as usual for my week's wages. I told him I had no wages; I had done no work that week. Here we were upon the point of coming to blows. He raved, and swore his determination to get hold of me. I did not allow myself a single word; but was resolved, if he laid the weight of his hand upon me, it should be blow for blow. He did not strike me, but told me that he would find me in constant employment in future. I thought the matter over during the next day, Sunday, and finally resolved upon the third day of September, as the day upon which I would make a second attempt to secure my freedom. I now had three weeks during which to prepare for my journey. Early on Monday morning, before Master Hugh had time to make any engagement for me, I went out and got employment of Mr. Butler, at his ship-yard near the drawbridge, upon what is called the City Block, thus making it unnecessary for him to seek employment for me. At the end of the week, I brought him between eight and nine dollars. He seemed very well pleased, and asked why I did not do the same the week before. He little knew what my plans were. My object in working steadily was to remove any suspicion he might entertain of my intent to run away; and in this I succeeded admirably. I suppose he thought I was never better satisfied with my condition than at the very time during which I was planning my escape. The second week passed, and again I carried him my full wages; and so well pleased was he, that he gave me twenty-five cents, (quite a large sum for a slaveholder to give a slave,) and bade me to make a good use of it. I told him I would.

Second bid for freedom

Things went on without very smoothly indeed, but within there was trouble. It is impossible for me to describe my feelings as the time of my contemplated start drew near. I had a number of warm-hearted friends in Baltimore,—friends that I loved almost as I did my life,—and the thought of being separated from them forever was painful beyond expression. It is my opinion that thousands would escape from slavery, who now remain, but for the strong cords of affection that bind them to their friends. The thought of leaving my friends was decidedly the most painful thought with which I had to contend. The love of them was my tender point, and shook my decision more than all things else. Besides the pain of separation, the dread and apprehension of a failure exceeded what I had experienced at my first attempt. The appalling defeat I then sustained returned to torment me. I felt assured that, if I failed in this attempt, my case would be a hopeless one—it would seal my fate as a slave forever. I could not hope to get off with any thing less than the severest punishment, and being placed beyond the means of escape. It required no very vivid imagination to depict the most frightful scenes through which I should have to pass, in case I failed. The wretchedness of slavery, and the blessedness of freedom, were perpetually before me. It was life and death with me. But I remained firm, and, according to my resolution, on the third day of September, 1838, I left my chains, and succeeded in reaching New York without the slightest interruption of any kind. How I did so,—what means I adopted,—what direction I traveled, and by what mode of conveyance,—I must leave unexplained, for the reasons before mentioned.

Trust no man

I have been frequently asked how I felt when I found myself in a free State. I have never been able to answer the question with any satisfaction to myself. It was a moment of the highest excitement I ever experienced. I suppose I felt as one may imagine the unarmed mariner to feel when he is rescued by a friendly man-of-war from the pursuit of a pirate. In writing to a dear friend, immediately after my arrival at New York, I said I felt like one who had escaped a den of hungry lions. This state of mind, however, very soon subsided; and I was again seized with a feeling of great insecurity and loneliness. I was yet liable to be taken back, and subjected to all the tortures of slavery. This in itself was enough to damp the ardor of my enthusiasm. But the loneliness overcame me. There I was in the midst of thousands, and yet a perfect stranger; without home and without friends, in the midst of thousands of my own brethren—children of a common Father, and yet I dared not to unfold to any one of them my sad condition. I was afraid to speak to any one for fear of speaking to the wrong one, and thereby falling into the hands of money-loving kidnappers, whose business it was to lie in wait for the panting fugitive, as the ferocious beasts of the forest lie in wait for their prey. The motto which I adopted when I started from slavery was this—"Trust no man!" I saw in every white man an enemy, and in almost every colored man cause for distrust. It was a most painful situation; and, to understand it, one must needs experience it, or imagine himself in similar circumstances. Let him be a fugitive slave in a strange land—a land given up to be the hunting- ground for slaveholders—whose inhabitants are legalized kidnappers—where he is every moment subjected to the terrible liability of being seized upon by his fellowmen, as the hideous crocodile seizes upon his prey!—I say, let him place himself in my situation— without home or friends—without money or credit—wanting shelter, and no one to give it—wanting bread, and no money to buy it,—and at the same time let him feel that he is pursued by merciless men-hunters, and in total darkness as to what to do, where to go, or where to stay,—perfectly helpless both as to the means of defense and means of escape,—in the midst of plenty, yet suffering the terrible gnawings of hunger,—in the midst of houses, yet having no home,—among fellow-men, yet feeling as if in the midst of wild beasts, whose greediness to swallow up the trembling and half-famished fugitive is only equaled by that with which the monsters of the deep swallow up the helpless fish upon which they subsist,— I say, let him be placed in this most trying situation,—the situation in which I was placed,— then, and not till then, will he fully appreciate the hardships of, and know how to sympa- thize with, the toil-worn and whip-scarred fugitive slave.

David Ruggles

Thank Heaven, I remained but a short time in this distressed situation. I was relieved from it by the humane hand of Mr. David Ruggles, whose vigilance, kindness, and perseverance, I shall never forget. I am glad of an opportunity to express, as far as words can, the love and gratitude I bear him. Mr. Ruggles is now afflicted with blindness, and is himself in need of the same kind offices which he was once so forward in the performance of toward others. I had been in New York but a few days, when Mr. Ruggles sought me out, and very kindly took me to his boarding-house at the corner of Church and Lespenard Streets. Mr. Ruggles was then very deeply engaged in the memorable Darg case, as well as attending to a number of other fugitive slaves, devising ways and means for their successful escape; and, though watched and hemmed in on almost every side, he seemed to be more than a match for his enemies.

Very soon after I went to Mr. Ruggles, he wished to know of me where I wanted to go; as he deemed it unsafe for me to remain in New York. I told him I was a calker, and should like to go where I could get work. I thought of going to Canada; but he decided against it, and in favor of my going to New Bedford, thinking I should be able to get work there at my trade. At this time, Anna, [She was free] my intended wife, came on; for I wrote to her immediately after my arrival at New York, (notwithstanding my homeless, houseless, and helpless condition,) informing her of my successful flight, and wishing her to come on forthwith. In a few days after her arrival, Mr. Ruggles called in the Rev. J. W. C. Pennington, who, in the presence of Mr. Ruggles, Mrs. Michaels, and two or three others, performed the marriage ceremony, and gave us a certificate, of which the following is an exact copy:—

This may certify, that I joined together in holy matrimony Frederick
Johnson and Anna Murray, as man and wife, in the presence of Mr.
David Ruggles and Mrs. Michaels.
James W. C. Pennington
New York, Sept. 15, 1838

I had changed my name from Frederick Bailey to that of Johnaon.

Upon receiving this certificate, and a five-dollar bill from Mr. Ruggles, I shouldered one part of our baggage, and Anna took up the other, and we set out forthwith to take passage on board of the steamboat John W. Richmond for Newport, on our way to New Bedford. Mr. Ruggles gave me a letter to a Mr. Shaw in Newport, and told me, in case my money did not serve me to New Bedford, to stop in Newport and obtain further assistance; but upon our arrival at Newport, we were so anxious to get to a place of safety, that, notwithstanding we lacked the necessary money to pay our fare, we decided to take seats in the stage, and promise to pay when we got to New Bedford. We were encouraged to do this by two excellent gentlemen, residents of New Bedford, whose names I afterward ascertained to be Joseph Ricketson and William C. Taber. They seemed at once to understand our circumstances, and gave us such assurance of their friendliness as put us fully at ease in their presence. It was good indeed to meet with such friends, at such a time. Upon reaching New Bedford, we were directed to the house of Mr. Nathan Johnson, by whom we were kindly received, and hospitably provided for. Both Mr. and Mrs. Johnson took a deep and lively interest in our welfare. They proved themselves quite worthy of the name of abolitionists. When the stage-driver found us unable to pay our fare, he held on upon our baggage as security for the debt. I had but to mention the fact to Mr. Johnson, and he forthwith advanced the money.

Frederick Douglass

We now began to feel a degree of safety, and to prepare ourselves for the duties and respon-sibilities of a life of freedom. On the morning after our arrival at New Bedford, while at the breakfast-table, the question arose as to what name I should be called by. The name given me by my mother was, "Frederick Augustus Washington Bailey." I, however, had dispensed with the two middle names long before I left Maryland so that I was generally known by the name of "Frederick Bailey." I started from Baltimore bearing the name of "Stanley." When I got to New York, I again changed my name to "Frederick Johnson," and thought that would be the last change. But when I got to New Bedford, I found it necessary again to change my name. The reason of this necessity was, that there were so many Johnsons in New Bedford, it was already quite difficult to distinguish between them. I gave Mr. Johnson the privilege of choosing me a name, but told him he must not take from me the name of "Frederick." I must hold on to that, to preserve a sense of my identity. Mr. Johnson had just been reading the "Lady of the Lake," and at once suggested that my name be "Douglass." From that time until now I have been called "Frederick Douglass;" and as I am more widely known by that name than by either of the others, I shall continue to use it as my own.

New Bedford

I was quite disappointed at the general appearance of things in New Bedford. The impression which I had received respecting the character and condition of the people of the north, I found to be singularly erroneous. I had very strangely supposed, while in slavery, that few of the comforts, and scarcely any of the luxuries, of life were enjoyed at the north, compared with what were enjoyed by the slaveholders of the south. I probably came to this conclusion from the fact that northern people owned no slaves. I supposed that they were about upon a level with the non-slaveholding population of the south. I knew they were exceedingly poor, and I had been accustomed to regard their poverty as the necessary consequence of their being non-slaveholders. I had somehow imbibed the opinion that, in the absence of slaves, there could be no wealth, and very little refinement. And upon coming to the north, I expected to meet with a rough, hard-handed, and uncultivated population, living in the most Spartan-like simplicity, knowing nothing of the ease, luxury, pomp, and grandeur of southern slaveholders. Such being my conjectures, any one acquainted with the appearance of New Bedford may very readily infer how palpably I must have seen my mistake.

In the afternoon of the day when I reached New Bedford, I visited the wharves, to take a view of the shipping. Here I found myself surrounded with the strongest proofs of wealth. Lying at the wharves, and riding in the stream, I saw many ships of the finest model, in the best order, and of the largest size. Upon the right and left, I was walled in by granite warehouses of the widest dimensions, stowed to their utmost capacity with the necessaries and comforts of life. Added to this, almost every body seemed to be at work, but noiselessly so, compared with what I had been accustomed to in Baltimore. There were no loud songs heard from those engaged in loading and unloading ships. I heard no deep oaths or horrid curses on the laborer. I saw no whipping of men; but all seemed to go smoothly on. Every man appeared to understand his work, and went at it with a sober, yet cheerful earnestness, which betokened the deep interest which he felt in what he was doing, as well as a sense of his own dignity as a man. To me this looked exceedingly strange. From the wharves I strolled around and over the town, gazing with wonder and admiration at the splendid churches, beautiful dwellings, and finely-cultivated gardens; evincing an amount of wealth, comfort, taste, and refinement, such as I had never seen in any part of slaveholding Maryland.

Every thing looked clean, new, and beautiful. I saw few or no dilapidated houses, with poverty-stricken inmates; no half-naked children and bare-footed women, such as I had been accustomed to see in Hillsborough, Easton, St. Michael's, and Baltimore. The people looked more able, stronger, healthier, and happier, than those of Maryland. I was for once made glad by a view of extreme wealth, without being saddened by seeing extreme poverty. But the most astonishing as well as the most interesting thing to me was the condition of the colored people, a great many of whom, like myself, had escaped thither as a refuge from the hunters of men. I found many, who had not been seven years out of their chains, living in finer houses, and evidently enjoying more of the comforts of life, than the average of slaveholders in Maryland. I will venture to assert, that my friend Mr. Nathan Johnson (of whom I can say with a grateful heart, "I was hungry, and he gave me meat; I was thirsty, and he gave me drink; I was a stranger, and he took me in") lived in a neater house; dined at a better table; took, paid for, and read, more newspapers; better understood the moral, religious, and political character of the nation,—than nine tenths of the slaveholders in Talbot county Maryland. Yet Mr. Johnson was a working man. His hands were hardened by toil, and not his alone, but those also of Mrs. Johnson. I found the colored people much more spirited than I had supposed they would be. I found among them a determination to protect each other from the blood-thirsty kidnapper, at all hazards. Soon after my arrival, I was told of a circumstance which illustrated their spirit. A colored man and a fugitive slave were on unfriendly terms. The former was heard to threaten the latter with informing his master of his whereabouts. Straightway a meeting was called among the colored people, under the stereotyped notice, "Business of importance!" The betrayer was invited to attend. The people came at the appointed hour, and organized the meeting by appointing a very religious old gentleman as president, who, I believe, made a prayer, after which he addressed the meeting as follows: "Friends, we have got him here, and I would recommend that you young men just take him outside the door, and kill him!" With this, a number of them bolted at him; but they were intercepted by some more timid than themselves, and the betrayer escaped their vengeance, and has not been seen in New Bedford since. I believe there have been no more such threats, and should there be hereafter, I doubt not that death would be the consequence.

New work

I found employment, the third day after my arrival, in stowing a sloop with a load of oil. It was new, dirty, and hard work for me; but I went at it with a glad heart and a willing hand. I was now my own master. It was a happy moment, the rapture of which can be understood only by those who have been slaves. It was the first work, the reward of which was to be entirely my own. There was no Master Hugh standing ready, the moment I earned the money, to rob me of it. I worked that day with a pleasure I had never before experienced. I was at work for myself and newly-married wife. It was to me the starting-point of a new existence. When I got through with that job, I went in pursuit of a job of calking; but such was the strength of prejudice against color, among the white calkers, that they refused to work with me, and of course I could get no employment. [I am told that colored persons can now get employment at calking in New Bedford—a result of anti-slavery effort. did for nearly three years in New Bedford, before I became known to the anti-slavery world.] Finding my trade of no immediate benefit, I threw off my calking habiliments, and prepared myself to do any kind of work I could get to do. Mr. Johnson kindly let me have his wood-horse and saw, and I very soon found myself a plenty of work. There was no work too hard—none too dirty. I was ready to saw wood, shovel coal, carry wood, sweep the chimney, or roll oil casks,—all of which I did.

The *Liberator*

In about four months after I went to New Bedford, there came a young man to me, and inquired if I did not wish to take the "Liberator." I told him I did; but, just having made my escape from slavery, I remarked that I was unable to pay for it then. I, however, finally became a subscriber to it. The paper came, and I read it from week to week with such feelings as it would be quite idle for me to attempt to describe. The paper became my meat and my drink. My soul was set all on fire. Its sympathy for my brethren in bonds—its scathing denunciations of slaveholders—its faithful exposures of slavery—and its powerful attacks upon the upholders of the institution—sent a thrill of joy through my soul, such as I had never felt before!

I had not long been a reader of the "Liberator," before I got a pretty correct idea of the principles, measures and spirit of the anti-slavery reform. I took right hold of the cause. I could do but little; but what I could, I did with a joyful heart, and never felt happier than when in an anti-slavery meeting. I seldom had much to say at the meetings, because what I wanted to say was said so much better by others. But, while attending an anti-slavery convention at Nantucket, on the 11th of August, 1841, I felt strongly moved to speak, and was at the same time much urged to do so by Mr. William C. Coffin, a gentleman who had heard me speak in the colored people's meeting at New Bedford. It was a severe cross, and I took it up reluctantly. The truth was, I felt myself a slave, and the idea of speaking to white people weighed me down. I spoke but a few moments, when I felt a degree of freedom, and said what I desired with considerable ease. From that time until now, I have been engaged in pleading the cause of my brethren—with what success, and with what devotion, I leave those acquainted with my labors to decide.

Frederick Douglass

My Bondage and My Freedom
Chapter 12
Religious Nature Awakened

Whilst in the painful state of mind described in the foregoing chapter, almost regretting my very existence, because doomed to a life of bondage, so goaded and so wretched, at times, that I was even tempted to destroy my own life, I was keenly sensitive and eager to know any, and every thing that transpired, having any relation to the subject of slavery. I was all ears, all eyes, whenever the words —slave, slavery—, dropped from the lips of any white person, and the occasions were not infrequent when these words became leading ones, in high, social debate, at our house. Every little while, I could hear Master Hugh, or some of his company, speaking with much warmth and excitement about —"abolitionists."— Of — who— or —what— these were, I was totally ignorant. I found, however, that whatever they might be, they were most cordially hated and soundly abused by slaveholders, of every grade. I very soon discovered, too, that slavery was, in some sort, under consideration, whenever the abolitionists were alluded to. This made the term a very interesting one to me. If a slave, for instance, had made good his escape from slavery, it was generally alleged, that he had been persuaded and assisted by the abolitionists. If, also, a slave killed his master— as was sometimes the case—or struck down his overseer, or set fire to his master's dwelling, or committed any violence or crime, out of the common way, it was certain to be said, that such a crime was the legitimate fruits of the abolition movement. Hearing such charges often repeated, I, naturally enough, received the impression that abolition—whatever else it might be—could not be unfriendly to the slave, nor very friendly to the slaveholder. I therefore set about finding out, if possible, —who— and —what— the abolitionists were, and —why— they were so obnoxious to the slaveholders. The dictionary afforded me very little help. It taught me that abolition was the "act of abolishing;" but it left me in ignorance at the very point where I most wanted information—and that was, as to the —thing— to be abolished. A city newspaper, the —Baltimore American—, gave me the incendiary information denied me by the dictionary. In its columns I found, that, on a certain day, a vast number of petitions and memorials had been presented to congress, praying for the abolition of slavery in the District of Columbia, and for the abolition of the slave trade between the states of the Union. This was enough. The vindictive bitterness, the marked caution, the studied reverse, and the cumbrous ambiguity, practiced by our white folks, when alluding to this subject, was now fully explained. Ever, after that, when I heard the words "abolition," or "abolition movement," mentioned, I felt the matter one of a personal concern; and I drew near to listen, when I could do so, without seeming too solicitous and prying. There was HOPE in those words. Ever and anon, too, I could see some terrible denunciation of slavery, in our papers—copied from abolition papers at the north—and the injustice of such denunciation commented on. These I read with avidity.

Abolitionism—the enigma solved

I had a deep satisfaction in the thought, that the rascality of slaveholders was not concealed from the eyes of the world, and that I was not alone in abhorring the cruelty and brutality of slavery. A still deeper train of thought was stirred. I saw that there was —fear—, as well as —rage—, in the manner of speaking of the abolitionists. The latter, therefore, I was compelled to regard as having some power in the country; and I felt that they might, possibly, succeed in their designs. When I met with a slave to whom I deemed it safe to talk on the subject, I would impart to him so much of the mystery as I had been able to penetrate. Thus, the light of this grand movement broke in upon my mind, by degrees; and I must say, that, ignorant as I then was of the philosophy of that movement, I believe in it from the first—and I believed in it, partly, because I saw that it alarmed the consciences of slaveholders. The insurrection of Nathaniel Turner had been quelled, but the alarm and terror had not subsided. The cholera was on its way, and the thought was present, that God was angry with the white people because of their slaveholding wickedness, and, therefore, his judgments were abroad in the land. It was impossible for me not to hope much from the abolition movement, when I saw it supported by the Almighty, and armed with death!

Religious awakening

Previous to my contemplation of the anti-slavery movement, and its probable results, my mind had been seriously awakened to the subject of religion. I was not more than thirteen years old, when I felt the need of God, as a father and protector. My religious nature was awakened by the preaching of a white Methodist minister, named Hanson. He thought that all men, great and small, bond and free, were sinners in the sight of God; that they were, by nature, rebels against His government; and that they must repent of their sins, and be reconciled to God, through Christ. I cannot say that I had a very distinct notion of what was required of me; but one thing I knew very well—I was wretched, and had no means of making myself otherwise. Moreover, I knew that I could pray for light. I consulted a good colored man, named Charles Johnson; and, in tones of holy affection, he told me to pray, and what to pray for. I was, for weeks, a poor, brokenhearted mourner, traveling through the darkness and misery of doubts and fears. I finally found that change of heart which comes by "casting all one's care" upon God, and by having faith in Jesus Christ, as the Redeemer, Friend, and Savior of those who diligently seek Him.

A new light

After this, I saw the world in a new light. I seemed to live in a new world, surrounded by new objects, and to be animated by new hopes and desires. I loved all mankind—slaveholders not excepted; though I abhorred slavery more than ever. My great concern was, now, to have the world converted. The desire for knowledge increased, and especially did I want a thorough acquaintance with the contents of the bible. I have gathered scattered pages from this holy book, from the filthy street gutters of Baltimore, and washed and dried them, that in the moments of my leisure, I might get a word or two of wisdom from them. While thus religiously seeking knowledge, I became acquainted with a good old colored man, named Lawson. A more devout man than he, I never saw. He drove a dray for Mr. James Ramsey, the owner of a rope-walk on Fell's Point, Baltimore. This man not only prayed three time a day, but he prayed as he walked through the streets, at his work—on his dray everywhere. His life was a life of prayer, and his words (when he spoke to his friends,) were about a better world. Uncle Lawson lived near Master Hugh's house; and, becoming deeply attached to the old man, I went often with him to prayer-meeting, and spent much of my leisure time with him on Sunday. The old man could read a little, and I was a great help to him, in making out the hard words, for I was a better reader than he. I could teach him —"the letter,"— but he could teach me —"the spirit;"— and high, refreshing times we had together, in singing, praying and glorifying God. These meetings with Uncle Lawson went on for a long time, without the knowledge of Master Hugh or my mistress. Both knew, however, that I had become religious, and they seemed to respect my conscientious piety. My mistress was still a professor of religion, and belonged to class. Her leader was no less a person than the Rev. Beverly Waugh, the presiding elder, and now one of the bishops of the Methodist Episcopal church. Mr. Waugh was then stationed over Wilk street church. I am careful to state these facts, that the reader may be able to form an idea of the precise influences which had to do with shaping and directing my mind.

In view of the cares and anxieties incident to the life she was then leading, and, especially, in view of the separation from religious associations to which she was subjected, my mistress had, as I have before stated, become lukewarm, and needed to be looked up by her leader. This brought Mr. Waugh to our house, and gave me an opportunity to hear him exhort and pray. But my chief instructor, in matters of religion, was Uncle Lawson. He was my spiritual father; and I loved him intensely, and was at his house every chance I got.

This pleasure was not long allowed me. Master Hugh became averse to my going to Father Lawson's, and threatened to whip me if I ever went there again. I now felt myself persecuted by a wicked man; and I would go to Father Lawson's, notwithstanding the threat. The good old man had told me, that the "Lord had a great work for me to do;" and I must prepare to do it; and that he had been shown that I must preach the gospel. His words made a deep impression on my mind, and I verily felt that some such work was before me, though I could not see —how— I should ever engage in its performance. "The good Lord," he said, "would bring it to pass in his own good time," and that I must go on reading and studying the scriptures. The advice and the suggestions of Uncle Lawson, were not without their influence upon my character and destiny. He threw my thoughts into a channel from which they have never entirely diverged. He fanned my already intense love of knowledge into a flame, by assuring me that I was to be a useful man in the world. When I would say to him, "How can these things be and what can —I— do?" his simple reply was, —"Trust in the Lord."— When I told him that "I was a slave, and a slave FOR LIFE," he said, "the Lord can make you free, my dear. All things are possible with him, only —have faith in God."— "Ask, and it shall be given." "If you want liberty," said the good old man, "ask the Lord for it, —in faith—, AND HE WILL GIVE IT TO YOU."

Thus assured, and cheered on, under the inspiration of hope, I worked and prayed with a light heart, believing that my life was under the guidance of a wisdom higher than my own. With all other blessings sought at the mercy seat, I always prayed that God would, of His great mercy, and in His own good time, deliver me from my bondage.

How I learned to write

I went, one day, on the wharf of Mr. Waters; and seeing two Irishmen unloading a large scow of stone, or ballast I went on board, unasked, and helped them. When we had finished the work, one of the men came to me, aside, and asked me a number of questions, and among them, if I were a slave. I told him "I was a slave, and a slave for life." The good Irishman gave his shoulders a shrug, and seemed deeply affected by the statement. He said, "it was a pity so fine a little fellow as myself should be a slave for life." They both had much to say about the matter, and expressed the deepest sympathy with me, and the most decided hatred of slavery. They went so far as to tell me that I ought to run away, and go to the north; that I should find friends there, and that I would be as free as anybody. I, however, pretended not to be interested in what they said, for I feared they might be treacherous. White men have been known to encourage slaves to escape, and then—to get the reward—they have kidnapped them, and returned them to their masters. And while I mainly inclined to the notion that these men were honest and meant me no ill, I feared it might be otherwise. I nevertheless remembered their words and their advice, and looked forward to an escape to the north, as a possible means of gaining the liberty for which my heart panted. It was not my enslavement, at the then present time, that most affected me; the being a slave —for life—, was the saddest thought. I was too young to think of running away immediately; besides, I wished to learn how to write, before going, as I might have occasion to write my own pass. I now not only had the hope of freedom, but a foreshadowing of the means by which I might, some day, gain that inestimable boon. Meanwhile, I resolved to add to my educational attainments the art of writing.

After this manner I began to learn to write: I was much in the ship yard—Master Hugh's, and that of Durgan & Bailey—and I observed that the carpenters, after hewing and getting a piece of timber ready for use, wrote on it the initials of the name of that part of the ship for which it was intended. When, for instance, a piece of timber was ready for the starboard side, it was marked with a capital "S." A piece for the larboard side was marked "L;" larboard forward, "L. F.;" larboard aft, was marked "L. A.;" starboard aft, "S. A.;" and starboard forward "S. F." I soon learned these letters, and for what they were placed on the timbers.

My work was now, to keep fire under the steam box, and to watch the ship yard while the carpenters had gone to dinner. This interval gave me a fine opportunity for copying the letters named. I soon astonished myself with the ease with which I made the letters; and the thought was soon present, "if I can make four, I can make more." But having made these easily, when I met boys about Bethel church, or any of our play-grounds, I entered the lists with them in the art of writing, and would make the letters which I had been so fortunate as to learn, and ask them to "beat that if they could." With playmates for my teachers, fences and pavements for my copy books, and chalk for my pen and ink, I learned the art of writing. I, however, afterward adopted various methods of improving my hand. The most successful, was copying the —italics— in Webster's spelling book, until I could make them all without looking on the book. By this time, my little "Master Tommy" had grown to be a big boy, and had written over a number of copy books, and brought them home. They had been shown to the neighbors, had elicited due praise, and were now laid carefully away. Spending my time between the ship yard and house, I was as often the lone keeper of the latter as of the former. When my mistress left me in charge of the house, I had a grand time; I got Master Tommy's copy books and a pen and ink, and, in the ample spaces between the lines, I wrote other lines, as nearly like his as possible. The process was a tedious one, and I ran the risk of getting a flogging for marring the highly prized copy books of the oldest son. In addition to those opportunities, sleeping, as I did, in the kitchen loft—a room seldom visited by any of the family—I got a flour barrel up there, and a chair; and upon the head of that barrel I have written (or endeavored to write) copying from the bible and the Methodist hymn book, and other books which had accumulated on my hands, till late at night, and when all the family were in bed and asleep. I was supported in my endeavors by renewed advice, and by holy promises from the good Father Lawson, with whom I continued to meet, and pray, and read the scriptures. Although Master Hugh was aware of my going there, I must say, for his credit, that he never executed his threat to whip me, for having thus, innocently, employed-my leisure time.

Frederick Douglass

The Church and Prejudice
Douglass delivered this speech at the Plymouth County Anti-Slavery Society, November 4, 1841.

At the South I was a member of the Methodist Church. When I came north, I thought one Sunday I would attend communion, at one of the churches of my denomination, in the town

I was staying. The white people gathered round the altar, the blacks clustered by the door. After the good minister had served out the bread and wine to one portion of those near him, he said, "These may withdraw, and others come forward;" thus he proceeded till all the white members had been served. Then he took a long breath, and looking out towards the door, exclaimed, "Come up, colored friends, come up! for you know God is no respecter of persons!" I haven't been there to see the sacraments taken since.

At New Bedford, where I live, there was a great revival of religion not long ago—many were converted and "received" as they said, "into the kingdom of heaven." But it seems, the kingdom of heaven is like a net; at least so it was according to the practice of these pious Christians; and when the net was drawn ashore, they had to set down and cull out the fish. Well, it happened now that some of the fish had rather black scales; so these were sorted out and packed by themselves. But among those who experienced religion at this time was a colored girl; she was baptized in the same water as the rest; so she thought she might sit at the Lord's table and partake of the same sacramental elements with the others. The deacon handed round the cup, and when he came to the black girl, he could not pass her, for there was the minister looking right at him, and as he was a kind of abolitionist, the deacon was rather afraid of giving him offense; so he handed the girl the cup, and she tasted. Now it so happened that next to her sat a young lady who had been converted at the same time, baptized in the same water, and put her trust in the same blessed Savior; yet when the cup containing the precious blood which had been shed for all, came to her, she rose in disdain, and walked out of the church. Such was the religion she had experienced!

Another young lady fell into a trance. When she awoke, she declared she had been to heaven. Her friends were all anxious to know what and whom she had seen there; so she told the whole story. But there was one good old lady whose curiosity went beyond that of all the others—and she inquired of the girl that had the vision, if she saw any black folks in heaven? After some hesitation, the reply was, "Oh! I didn't go into the kitchen!"

Thus you see, my hearers, this prejudice goes even into the church of God. And there are those who carry it so far that it is disagreeable to them even to think of going to heaven, if colored people are going there too. And whence comes it? The grand cause is slavery; but there are others less prominent; one of them is the way in which children in this part of the country are instructed to regard the blacks.

"Yes!" exclaimed an old gentleman, interrupting him—"when they behave wrong, they are told, 'black man come catch you.'"

Yet people in general will say they like colored men as well as any other, but in their proper place! They assign us that place; they don't let us do it for ourselves, nor will they allow us a voice in the decision. They will not allow that we have a head to think, and a heart to feel, and a soul to aspire. They treat us not as men, but as dogs—they cry "Stu-boy!" and expect us to run and do their bidding. That's the way we are liked. You degrade us, and then ask why we are degraded—you shut our mouths, and then ask why we don't speak—you close our colleges and seminaries against us, and then ask why we don't know more.

But all this prejudice sinks into insignificance in my mind, when compared with the enormous iniquity of the system which is its cause—the system that sold my four sisters and my brothers into bondage—and which calls in its priests to defend it even from the Bible! The slaveholding ministers preach up the divine right of the slaveholders to property in their fellow- men. The southern preachers say to the poor slave, "Oh! if you wish to be happy in time, happy in eternity, you must be obedient to your masters; their interest is yours. God made one portion of men to do the working, and another to do the thinking; how good God is! Now, you have no trouble or anxiety; but ah! you can't imagine how perplexing it is to your masters and mistresses to have so much thinking to do in your behalf! You cannot appreciate your blessings; you know not how happy a thing it is for you, that you were born of that portion of the human family which has the working, instead of the thinking to do! Oh! how grateful and obedient you ought to be to your masters! How beautiful are the arrangements of Providence! Look at your hard, horny hands—see how nicely they are adapted to the labor you have to perform! Look at our delicate fingers, so exactly fitted for our station, and see how manifest it is that God designed us to be His thinkers, and you the workers—Oh! the wisdom of God!"—I used to attend a Methodist church, in which my master was a class leader; he would talk most sanctimoniously about the dear Redeemer, who was sent "to preach deliverance to the captives, and set at liberty them that are bruised"—he could pray at morning, pray at noon, and pray at night; yet he could lash up my poor cousin by his two thumbs, and inflict stripes and blows upon his bare back, till the blood streamed to the ground! all the time quoting scripture, for his authority, and appealing to that passage of the Holy Bible which says, "He that knoweth his master's will, and doeth it not, shall be beaten with many stripes!" Such was the amount of this good Methodist's piety.

Frederick Douglass

Fighting Rebels with Only One Hand

What on earth is the matter with the American Government and people? Do they really covet the world's ridicule as well as their own social and political ruin? What are they thinking about, or don't they condescend to think at all? So, indeed, it would seem from their blindness in dealing with the tremendous issue now upon them. Was there ever anything like it before? They are sorely pressed on every hand by a vast army of slaveholding rebels, flushed with success, and infuriated by the darkest inspirations of a deadly hate, bound to rule or ruin. Washington, the seat of Government, after ten thousand assurances to the contrary, is now positively in danger of falling before the rebel army. Maryland, a little while ago considered safe for the Union, is now admitted to be studded with the materials for insurrection, and which may flame forth at any moment.—Every resource of the nation, whether of men or money, whether of wisdom or strength, could be well employed to avert the impending ruin. Yet most evidently the demands of the hour are not comprehended by the Cabinet or the crowd. Our Presidents, Governors, Generals and Secretaries are calling, with almost frantic vehemence, for men.—"Men! men! send us men!" they scream, or the cause of the Union is gone, the life of a great nation is ruthlessly sacrificed, and the hopes of a great nation go out in darkness; and yet these very officers, representing the people and Government, steadily and persistently refuse to receive the very class of men which have a deeper interest in the defeat and humiliation of the rebels, than all others.—Men are wanted in Missouri—wanted in Western Virginia, to hold and defend what has been already gained; they are wanted in Texas, and all along the sea coast, and though the Government has at its command a class in the country deeply interested in suppressing the insurrection, it sternly refuses to summon from among the vast multitude a single man, and degrades and insults the whole class by refusing to allow any of their number to defend with their strong arms and brave hearts the national cause. What a spectacle of blind, unreasoning prejudice and pusillanimity is this! The national edifice is on fire. Every man who can carry a bucket of water, or remove a brick, is wanted; but those who have the care of the building, having a profound respect for the feeling of the national burglars who set the building on fire, are determined that the flames shall only be extinguished by Indo-Caucasian hands, and to have the building burnt rather than save it by means of any other. Such is the pride, the stupid prejudice and folly that rules the hour.

Why does the Government reject the Negro? Is he not a man? Can he not wield a sword, fire a gun, march and countermarch, and obey orders like any other? Is there the least reason to believe that a regiment of well-drilled Negroes would deport themselves less soldier-like on the battlefield than the raw troops gathered up generally from the towns and cities of the State of New York? We do believe that such soldiers, if allowed to take up arms in defense of the Government, and made to feel that they are hereafter to be recognized as persons having rights, would set the highest example of order and general good behavior to their fellow soldiers, and in every way add to the national power.

If persons so humble as we can be allowed to speak to the President of the United States, we should ask him if this dark and terrible hour of the nation's extremity is a time for consulting a mere vulgar and unnatural prejudice? We should ask him if national preservation and necessity were not better guides in this emergency than either the tastes of the rebels, or the pride and prejudices of the vulgar? We would tell him that General Jackson in a slave state fought side by side with Negroes at New Orleans, and like a true man, despising meanness, he bore testimony to their bravery at the close of the war. We would tell him that colored men in Rhode Island and Connecticut performed their full share in the war of the Revolution, and that men of the same color, such as the noble Shields Green, Nathaniel Turner and Denmark Vesey stand ready to peril everything at the command of the Government. We would tell him that this is no time to fight with one hand, when both are needed; that this is no time to fight only with your white hand, and allow your black hand to remain tied.

Whatever may be the folly and absurdity of the North, the South at least is true and wise. The Southern papers no longer indulge in the vulgar expression, "free n——rs." That class of bipeds are now called "colored residents." The Charleston papers say:

> The colored residents of this city can challenge comparison with their class, in any city or town, in loyalty or devotion to the cause of the South. Many of them individually, and without ostentation, have been contributing liberally, and on Wednesday evening, the 7th inst., a very large meeting was held by them, and a committee appointed to provide

for more efficient aid. The proceedings of the meeting will appear in results hereinafter to be reported.

It is now pretty well established, that there are at the present moment many colored men in the Confederate army doing duty not only as cooks, servants and laborers, but as real soldiers, having muskets on their shoulders, and bullets in their pockets, ready to shoot down loyal troops, and do all that soldiers may to destroy the Federal Government and build up that of the traitors and rebels. There were such soldiers at Manassas, and they are probably there still. There is a Negro in the army as well as in the fence, and our Government is likely to find it out before the war comes to an end. That the Negroes are numerous in the rebel army, and do for that army its heaviest work, is beyond question. They have been the chief laborers upon those temporary defenses in which the rebels have been able to mow down our men. Negroes helped to build the batteries at Charleston. They relieve their gentlemanly and military masters from the stiffening drudgery of the camp, and devote them to the nimble and dexterous use of arms. Rising above vulgar prejudice, the slave-holding rebel accepts the aid of the black man as readily as that of any other. If a bad cause can do this, why should a good cause be less wisely conducted? We insist upon it, that one black regiment in such a war as this is, without being any more brave and orderly, would be worth to the Government more than two of any other; and that, while the Government continues to refuse the aid of colored men, thus alienating them from the national cause, and giving the rebels the advantage of them, it will not deserve better fortunes than it has thus far experienced.—Men in earnest don't fight with one hand, when they might fight with two, and a man drowning would not refuse to be saved even by a colored hand.

Frederick Douglass, Douglass' Monthly, *September 186*

What the Black Man Wants
Introduction
Douglass delivered this speech at the Annual Meeting of the Massachusetts Anti-Slavery Society in Boston, on April, 1865. His theme was, The Equality of all men in the eyes of the law. This address was given a few days after the end of the Civil War and the assassination of President Lincoln.

I came here, as I come always to the meetings in New England, as a listener, and not as a speaker; and one of the reasons why I have not been more frequently to the meetings of this society, has been because of the disposition on the part of some of my friends to call me out upon the platform, even when they knew that there was some difference of opinion and of feeling between those who rightfully belong to this platform and myself; and for fear of being misconstrued, as desiring to interrupt or disturb the proceedings of these meetings, I have usually kept away, and have thus been deprived of that educating influence, which I am always free to confess is of the highest order, descending from this platform. I have felt, since I have lived out West [Douglass means west of Boston, in Rochester, NY], that in going there I parted from a great deal that was valuable; and I feel, every time I come to these meetings, that I have lost a great deal by making my home west of Boston, west of Massachusetts; for, if anywhere in the country there is to be found the highest sense of justice, or the truest demands for my race, I look for it in the East, I look for it here. The ablest discussions of the whole question of our rights occur here, and to be deprived of the privilege of listening to those discussions is a great deprivation.

I do not know, from what has been said, that there is any difference of opinion as to the duty of abolitionists, at the present moment. How can we get up any difference at this point, or any point, where we are so united, so agreed? I went especially, however, with that word of Mr. Phillips, which is the criticism of Gen. Banks and Gen. Banks' policy. [Gen. Banks instituted a labor policy in Louisiana that was discriminatory of blacks, claiming that it was to help prepare them to better handle freedom. Wendell Phillips countered by saying, "If there is anything patent in the whole history of our thirty years' struggle, it is that the Negro no more needs to be prepared for liberty than the white man."] I hold that that policy is our chief danger at the present moment; that it practically enslaves the Negro, and makes the Proclamation [the Emancipation Proclamation] of 1863 a mockery and delusion. What is freedom? It is the right to choose one's own employment. Certainly it means that, if it means anything; and when any individual or combination of individuals undertakes to decide for any man when he shall work, where he shall work, at what he shall work, and for what he shall work, he or they practically reduce him to slavery. [Applause.] He is a slave. That I understand Gen. Banks to do—to determine for the so-called freedman, when, and where, and at what, and for how much he shall work, when he shall be punished, and by whom punished. It is absolute slavery. It defeats the beneficent intention of the Government, if it has beneficent intentions, in regards to the freedom of our people.

I have had but one idea for the last three years to present to the American people, and the phraseology in which I clothe it is the old abolition phraseology. I am for the "immediate, unconditional, and universal" enfranchisement of the black man, in every State in the Union. [Loud applause.] Without this, his liberty is a mockery; without this, you might as well almost retain the old name of slavery for his condition; for in fact, if he is not the slave of the individual master, he is the slave of society, and holds his liberty as a privilege, not as a right. He is at the mercy of the mob, and has no means of protecting himself.

It may be objected, however, that this pressing of the Negro's right to suffrage is premature. Let us have slavery abolished, it may be said, let us have labor organized, and then, in the natural course of events, the right of suffrage will be extended to the Negro. I do not agree with this. The constitution of the human mind is such, that if it once disregards the conviction forced upon it by a revelation of truth, it requires the exercise of a higher power to produce the same conviction afterwards. The American people are now in tears. The Shenandoah has run blood—the best blood of the North. All around Richmond, the blood of New England and of the North has been shed—of your sons, your brothers and your fathers. We all feel, in the existence of this Rebellion, that judgments terrible, wide-spread, far-reaching, overwhelming, are abroad in the land; and we feel, in view of these judgments, just now, a disposition to learn righteousness. This is the hour. Our streets are in mourning, tears are falling at every fireside, and under the chastisement of this Rebellion we have almost come up to the point of conceding this great, this all-important right of suffrage. I fear that if we fail to do it now, if abolitionists fail to press it now, we may not see, for centuries to come, the same disposition that exists at this moment. [Applause.] Hence, I say, now is the time to press this right.

It may be asked, "Why do you want it? Some men have got along very well without it. Women have not this right." Shall we justify one wrong by another? This is the sufficient answer. Shall we at this moment justify the deprivation of the Negro of the right to vote, because some one else is deprived of that privilege? I hold that women, as well as men, have the right to vote [applause], and my heart and voice go with the movement to extend suffrage to woman; but that question rests upon another basis than which our right rests. We may be asked, I say, why we want it. I will tell you why we want it. We want it because it is our right, first of all. No class of men can, without insulting their own nature, be content with any deprivation of their rights. We want it again, as a means for educating our race. Men are so constituted that they derive their conviction of their own possibilities largely by the estimate formed of them by others. If nothing is expected of a people, that people will find it difficult to contradict that expectation. By depriving us of suffrage, you affirm our incapacity to form an intelligent judgment respecting public men and public measures; you declare before the world that we are unfit to exercise the elective franchise, and by this means lead us to undervalue ourselves, to put a low estimate upon ourselves, and to feel that we have no possibilities like other men. Again, I want the elective franchise, for one, as a colored man, because ours is a peculiar government, based upon a peculiar idea, and that idea is universal suffrage. If I were in a monarchial government, or an autocratic or aristocratic government, where the few bore rule and the many were subject, there would be no special stigma resting upon me, because I did not exercise the elective franchise. It would do me no great violence. Mingling with the mass I should partake of the strength of the mass; I should be supported by the mass, and I should have the same incentives to endeavor with the mass of my fellow-men; it would be no particular burden, no particular deprivation; but here where universal suffrage is the rule, where that is the fundamental idea of the Government, to rule us out is to make us an exception, to brand us with the stigma of inferiority, and to invite to our heads the missiles of those about us; therefore, I want the franchise for the black man.

There are, however, other reasons, not derived from any consideration merely of our rights, but arising out of the conditions of the South, and of the country—considerations which have already been referred to by Mr. Phillips—considerations which must arrest the attention of statesmen. I believe that when the tall heads of this Rebellion shall have been swept down, as they will be swept down, when the Davises and Toombses and Stephenses, and others who are leading this Rebellion shall have been blotted out, there will be this rank undergrowth of treason, to which reference has been made, growing up there, and interfering with, and thwarting the quiet operation of the Federal Government in those states. You will se those traitors, handing down, from sire to son, the same malignant spirit which they have manifested and which they are now exhibiting, with malicious hearts, broad blades, and bloody hands in the field, against our sons and brothers. That spirit will still remain; and whoever sees the Federal Government extended over those Southern States will see that Government in a strange land, and not only in a strange land, but in an enemy's land. A post-master of the United States in the South will find himself surrounded by a hostile spirit; a collector in a Southern port will find himself surrounded by a hostile spirit; a United States marshal or United States judge will be surrounded there by a hostile element. That enmity will not die out in a year, will not die out in an age. The Federal Government will be looked upon in those States precisely as the Governments of Austria and France are looked upon in Italy at the present moment. They will endeavor to circumvent, they will endeavor to destroy, the peaceful operation of this Government. Now, where will you find the strength to counterbalance this spirit, if you do not find it in the Negroes of the South? They are your friends, and have always been your friends. They were your friends even when the Government did not regard them as such. They comprehended the genius of this war before you did. It is a significant fact, it is a marvelous fact, it seems almost to imply a direct interposition of Providence, that this war, which began in the interest of slavery on both sides, bids fair to end in the interest of liberty on both sides. [Applause.] It was begun, I say, in the interest of slavery on both sides. The South was fighting to take slavery out of the Union, and the North was fighting to keep it in the Union; the South fighting to get it beyond the limits of the United States Constitution, and the North fighting to retain it within those limits; the South fighting for new guarantees, and the North fighting for the old guarantees;—both despising the Negro, both insulting the Negro. Yet, the Negro, apparently endowed with wisdom from on high, saw more clearly the end from the beginning than we did. When Seward said the status of no man in the country would be changed by the war, the Negro did not believe him. [Applause.] When our generals sent their underlings in shoulder-straps to hunt the flying Negro back from our lines into the jaws of slavery, from which he had escaped, the Negroes thought that a mistake had been made, and that the intentions of the Government had not been rightly understood by our officers in shoulder-straps, and they continued to come into our lines, threading their way through bogs and fens, over briers and thorns, fording streams, swimming rivers, bringing us tidings as to the safe path to march, and pointing out the dangers that threatened us. They are our only friends in the South, and we should be true to them in this their trial hour, and see to it that they have the elective franchise.

I know that we are inferior to you in some things—virtually inferior. We walk about you like dwarfs among giants. Our heads are scarcely seen above the great sea of humanity. The Germans are superior to us; the Irish are superior to us; the Yankees are superior to us [Laughter]; they can do what we cannot, that is, what we have not hitherto been allowed to do. But while I make this admission, I utterly deny, that we are originally, or naturally, or practically, or in any way, or in any important sense, inferior to anybody on this globe. [Loud applause.] This charge of inferiority is an old dodge. It has been made available for oppression on many occasions. It is only about six centuries since the blue-eyed and fair-haired Anglo-Saxons were considered inferior by the haughty Normans, who once trampled upon them. If you read the history of the Norman Conquest, you will find that this proud

Anglo-Saxon was once looked upon as of coarser clay than his Norman master, and might be found in the highways and byways of Old England laboring with a brass collar on his neck, and the name of his master marked upon it. You were down then! [Laughter and applause.] You are up now. I am glad you are up, and I want you to be glad to help us up also. [Applause.]

The story of our inferiority is an old dodge, as I have said; for wherever men oppress their fellows, wherever they enslave them, they will endeavor to find the needed apology for such enslavement and oppression in the character of the people oppressed and enslaved. When we wanted, a few years ago, a slice of Mexico, it was hinted that the Mexicans were an inferior race, that the old Castilian blood had become so weak that it would scarcely run down hill, and that Mexico needed the long, strong and beneficent arm of the Anglo-Saxon care extended over it. We said that it was necessary to its salvation, and a part of the "manifest destiny" of this Republic, to extend our arm over that dilapidated government. So, too, when Russia wanted to take possession of a part of the Ottoman Empire, the Turks were an "inferior race." So, too, when England wants to set the heel of her power more firmly in the quivering heart of old Ireland, the Celts are an "inferior race." So, too, the Negro, when he is to be robbed of any right which is justly his, is an "inferior man." It is said that we are ignorant; I admit it. But if we know enough to be hung, we know enough to vote. If the Negro knows enough to pay taxes to support the government, he knows enough to vote; taxation and representation should go together. If he knows enough to shoulder a musket and fight for the flag, fight for the government, he knows enough to vote. If he knows as much when he is sober as an Irishman knows when drunk, he knows enough to vote, on good American principles. [Laughter and applause.]

But I was saying that you needed a counterpoise in the persons of the slaves to the enmity that would exist at the South after the Rebellion is put down. I hold that the American people are bound, not only in self-defense, to extend this right to the freedmen of the South, but they are bound by their love of country, and by all their regard for the future safety of those Southern States, to do this—to do it as a measure essential to the preservation of peace there. But I will not dwell upon this. I put it to the American sense of honor. The honor of a nation is an important thing. It is said in the Scriptures, "What doth it profit a man if he gain the whole world, and lose his own soul?" It may be said, also, What doth it profit a nation if it gain the whole world, but lose its honor? I hold that the American government has taken upon itself a solemn obligation of honor, to see that this war—let it be long or short, let it cost much or let it cost little—that this war shall not cease until every freedman at the South has the right to vote. [Applause.] It has bound itself to it. What have you asked the black men of the South, the black men of the whole country to do? Why, you have asked them to incur the enmity of their masters, in order to befriend you and to befriend this Government. You have asked us to call down, not only upon ourselves, but upon our children's children, the deadly hate of the entire Southern people. You have called upon us to turn our backs upon our masters, to abandon their cause and espouse yours; to turn against the South and in favor of the North; to shoot down the Confederacy and uphold the flag—the American flag. You have called upon us to expose ourselves to all the subtle machinations of their malignity for all time. And now, what do you propose to do when you come to make peace? To reward your enemies, and trample in the dust your friends? Do you intend to sacrifice the very men who have come to the rescue of your banner in the South, and incurred the lasting displeasure of their masters thereby? Do you intend to sacrifice them and reward your enemies? Do you mean to give your enemies the right to vote, and take it away from your friends? Is that wise policy? Is that honorable? Could American honor withstand such a blow? I do not believe you will do it. I think you will see to it that we have the right to vote. There is something too mean in looking upon the Negro, when you are in trouble, as a citizen, and when you are free from trouble, as an alien. When this nation was in trouble, in its early struggles, it looked upon the Negro as a citizen. In 1776 he was a citizen. At the time of the formation of the Constitution the Negro had the right to vote in eleven States out of the old thirteen. In your trouble you have made us citizens. In 1812 Gen. Jackson addressed us as citizens—"fellow-citizens." He wanted us to fight. We were citizens then! And now, when you come to frame a conscription bill, the Negro is a citizen again. He has been a citizen just three times in the history of this government, and it has always been in time of trouble. In time of trouble we are citizens. Shall we be citizens in war, and aliens in peace? Would that be just?

I ask my friends who are apologizing for not insisting upon this right, where can the black man look, in this country, for the assertion of his right, if he may not look to the Massachusetts Anti-Slavery Society? Where under the whole heavens can he look for sympathy, in asserting this right, if he may not look to this platform? Have you lifted us up to a certain height to see that we are men, and then are any disposed to leave us there, without seeing that we are put in possession of all our rights? We look naturally to this platform for the assertion of all our rights, and for this one especially. I understand the anti-slavery societies of this country to be based on two principles,—first, the freedom of the blacks of this country; and, second, the elevation of them. Let me not be misunderstood here. I am not asking for sympathy at the hands of abolitionists, sympathy at the hands of any. I think the American people are disposed often to be generous rather than just. I look over this country at the present time, and I see Educational Societies, Sanitary Commissions, Freedmen's Associations, and the like,—all very good: but in regard to the colored people there is always more that is benevolent, I perceive, than just, manifested towards us. What I ask for the Negro is not benevolence, not pity, not sympathy, but simply justice. [Applause.] The American people have always been anxious to know what they shall do with us. Gen. Banks was distressed with solicitude as to what he should do with the Negro. Everybody has asked the question, and they learned to ask it early of the abolitionists, "What shall we do with the Negro?" I have had but one answer from the beginning. Do nothing with us! Your doing with us has already played the mischief with us. Do nothing with us! If the apples will not remain on the tree of their own strength, if they are worm-eaten at the core, if they are early ripe and disposed to fall, let them fall! I am not for tying or fastening them on the tree in any way, except by nature's plan, and if they will not stay there, let them fall. And if the Negro cannot stand on his own legs, let him fall also. All I ask is, give him a chance to stand on his own legs! Let him alone! If you see him on his way to school, let him alone, don't disturb him! If you see him going to the dinner table at a hotel, let him go! If you see him going to the ballot- box, let him alone, don't disturb him! [Applause.] If you see him going into a work-shop, just let him alone,—your interference is doing him a positive injury. Gen. Banks' "preparation" is of a piece with this attempt to prop up the Negro. Let him fall if he cannot stand alone! If the Negro cannot live by the line of eternal justice, so beautifully pictured to you in the illustration used by Mr. Phillips, the fault will not be yours, it will be his who made the Negro, and established that line for his government. [Applause.] Let him live or die by that. If you will only untie his hands, and give him a chance, I think he will live. He will work as readily for himself as the white man. A great many delusions have been swept away by this war. One was, that the Negro would not work; he has proved his ability to work. Another was, that the Negro would not fight; that he possessed only the most sheepish attributes of humanity; was a perfect lamb, or an "Uncle Tom;" disposed to take off his coat whenever required, fold his hands, and be whipped by anybody who wanted to whip him. But the war has proved that there is a great deal of human nature in the Negro, and that "he will fight," as Mr. Quincy, our President, said, in earlier days than these, "when there is reasonable probability of his whipping anybody." [Laughter and applause.]

Frederick Douglass

Inhumanity of Slavery

Tucked away in the appendix of Frederick Douglass's My Bondage and My Freedom *is the following extract from a lecture on slavery, given at Rochester on December 8, 1850*

The relation of master and slave has been called patriarchal, and only second in benignity and tenderness to that of the parent and child. This representation is doubtless believed by many northern people; and this may account, in part, for the lack of interest which we find among persons whom we are bound to believe to be honest and humane. What, then, are the facts? Here I will not quote my own experience in slavery; for this you might call one-sided testimony. I will not cite the declarations of abolitionists; for these you might pronounce exaggerations. I will not rely upon advertisements cut from newspapers; for these you might call isolated cases. But I will refer you to the laws adopted by the legislatures of the slave states. I give you such evidence, because it cannot be invalidated nor denied. I hold in my hand sundry extracts from the slave codes of our country, from which I will quote.

Now, if the foregoing be an indication of kindness, what is cruelty? If this be parental affection, what is bitter malignity? A more atrocious and blood-thirsty string of laws could not well be conceived of. And yet I am bound to say that they fall short of indicating the horrible cruelties constantly practiced in the slave states.

I admit that there are individual slaveholders less cruel and barbarous than is allowed by law; but these form the exception.

The majority of slaveholders find it necessary, to insure obedience, at times, to avail themselves of the utmost extent of the law, and many go beyond it. If kindness were the rule, we should not see advertisements filling the columns of almost every

southern newspaper, offering large rewards for fugitive slaves, and describing them as being branded with irons, loaded with chains, and scarred by the whip. One of the most telling testimonies against the pretended kindness of slaveholders, is the fact that uncounted numbers of fugitives are now inhabiting the Dismal Swamp, preferring the untamed wilderness to their cultivated homes—choosing rather to encounter hunger and thirst, and to roam with the wild beasts of the forest, running the hazard of being hunted and shot down, than to submit to the authority of kind masters.

I tell you, my friends, humanity is never driven to such an unnatural course of life, without great wrong. The slave finds more of the milk of human kindness in the bosom of the savage Indian, than in the heart of his Christian master. He leaves the man of the bible, and takes refuge with the man of the tomahawk. He rushes from the praying slaveholder into the paws of the bear. He quits the homes of men for the haunts of wolves. He prefers to encounter a life of trial, however bitter, or death, however terrible, to dragging out his existence under the dominion of these kind masters.

The apologists for slavery often speak of the abuses of slavery; and they tell us that they are as much opposed to those abuses as we are; and that they would go as far to correct those abuses and to ameliorate the condition of the slave as anybody. The answer to that view is, that slavery is itself an abuse; that it lives by abuse; and dies by the absence of abuse. Grant that slavery is right; grant that the relations of master and slave may innocently exist; and there is not a single outrage which was ever committed against the slave but what finds an apology in the very necessity of the case. As we said by a slaveholder (the Rev. A. G. Few) to the Methodist conference, "If the relation be right, the means to maintain it are also right;" for without those means slavery could not exist. Remove the dreadful scourge—the plaited thong—the galling fetter—the accursed chain—and let the slaveholder rely solely upon moral and religious power, by which to secure obedience to his orders, and how long do you suppose a slave would remain on his plantation?"

The case only needs to be stated; it carries its own refutation with it.

Absolute and arbitrary power can never be maintained by one man over the body and soul of another man, without brutal chastisement and enormous cruelty.

To talk of kindness entering into a relation in which one party is robbed of wife, of children, of his hard earnings, of home, of friends, of society, of knowledge, and of all that makes this life desirable, is most absurd, wicked, and preposterous.

I have shown that slavery is wicked—wicked, in that it violates the great law of liberty, written on every human heart—wicked, in that it violates the first command of the Decalogue—wicked, in that it fosters the most disgusting licentiousness—wicked, in that it mars and defaces the image of God by cruel and barbarous inflictions—wicked, in that it contravenes the laws of eternal justice, and tramples in the dust all the humane and heavenly precepts of the New Testament.

The evils resulting from this huge system of iniquity are not confined to the states south of Mason and Dixon's line. Its noxious influence can easily be traced throughout our northern borders. It comes even as far north as the state of New York.

Traces of it may be seen even in Rochester; and travelers have told me it casts its gloomy shadows across the lake, approaching the very shores of Queen Victoria's dominions.

The presence of slavery may be explained by—as it is the explanation of—the mobocratic violence which lately disgraced New York, and which still more recently disgraced the city of Boston. These violent demonstrations, these outrageous invasions of human rights, faintly indicate the presence and power of slavery here. It is a significant fact, that while meetings for almost any purpose under heaven may be held unmolested in the city of Boston, that in the same city, a meeting cannot be peaceably held for the purpose of preaching the doctrine of the American Declaration of Independence, "that all men are created equal." The pestiferous breath of slavery taints the whole moral atmosphere of the north, and enervates the moral energies of the whole people.

The moment a foreigner ventures upon our soil, and utters a natural repugnance to oppression, that moment he is made to feel that there is little sympathy in this land for him. If he were greeted with smiles before, he meets with frowns now; and it shall go well with him if he be not subjected to that peculiarly

fining method of showing fealty to slavery, the assaults of a mob.

Now, will any man tell me that such a state of things is natural, and that such conduct on the part of the people of the north, springs from a consciousness of rectitude? No! every fiber of the human heart unites in detestation of tyranny, and it is only when the human mind has become familiarized with slavery, is accustomed to its injustice, and corrupted by its selfishness, that it fails to record its abhorrence of slavery, and does not exult in the triumphs of liberty.

The northern people have been long connected with slavery; they have been linked to a decaying corpse, which has destroyed the moral health. The union of the government; the union of the north and south, in the political parties; the union in the

religious organizations of the land, have all served to deaden the moral sense of the northern people, and to impregnate them with sentiments and ideas forever in conflict with what as a nation we call genius of American institutions. Rightly viewed, this is an alarming fact, and ought to rally all that is pure, just, and holy in one determined effort to crush the monster of corruption, and to scatter "its guilty profits" to the winds. In a high moral sense, as well as in a national sense, the whole American people are responsible for slavery, and must share, in its guilt and shame, with the most obdurate men-stealers of the south.

While slavery exists, and the union of these states endures, every American citizen must bear the chagrin of hearing his country branded before the world as a nation of liars and hypocrites; and behold his cherished flag pointed at with the utmost scorn and derision. Even now an American abroad is pointed out in the crowd, as coming from a land where men gain their fortunes by "the blood of souls," from a land of slave markets, of blood-hounds, and slave-hunters; and, in some circles, such a man is shunned altogether, as a moral pest. Is it not time, then, for every American to awake, and inquire into his duty with respect to this subject?

Wendell Phillips—the eloquent New England orator—on his return from Europe, in 1842, said, "As I stood upon the shores of Genoa, and saw floating on the placid waters of the Mediterranean, the beautiful American war ship Ohio, with her masts tapering proportionately aloft, and an eastern sun reflecting her noble form upon the sparkling waters, attracting the gaze of the multitude, my first impulse was of pride, to think myself an American; but when I thought that the first time that gallant ship would gird on her gorgeous apparel, and wake from beneath her sides her dormant thunders, it would be in defense of the African slave trade, I blushed in utter shame for my country."

Let me say again, slavery is alike the sin and the shame of the American people; it is a blot upon the American name, and the only national reproach which need make an American hang his head in shame, in the presence of monarchical governments.

With this gigantic evil in the land, we are constantly told to look at home; if we say ought against crowned heads, we are pointed to our enslaved millions; if we talk of sending missionaries and bibles abroad, we are pointed to three millions now lying in worse than heathen darkness; if we express a word of sympathy for Kossuth and his Hungarian fugitive brethren, we are pointed to that horrible and hell-black enactment, "the fugitive slave bill."

Slavery blunts the edge of all our rebukes of tyranny abroad—the criticisms that we make upon other nations, only call forth ridicule, contempt, and scorn. In a word, we are made a reproach and a by-word to a mocking earth, and we must continue to be so made, so long as slavery continues to pollute our soil.

We have heard much of late of the virtue of patriotism, the love of country, &c., and this sentiment, so natural and so strong, has been impiously appealed to, by all the powers of human selfishness, to cherish the viper which is stinging our national

life away. In its name, we have been called upon to deepen our infamy before the world, to rivet the fetter more firmly on the limbs of the enslaved, and to become utterly insensible to the voice of human woe that is wafted to us on every southern gale. We have been called upon, in its name, to desecrate our whole land by the footprints of slave-hunters, and even to engage ourselves in the horrible business of kidnapping.

I, too, would invoke the spirit of patriotism; not in a narrow and restricted sense, but, I trust, with a broad and manly signification; not to cover up our national sins, but to inspire us with sincere repentance; not to hide our shame from the world's gaze, but utterly to abolish the cause of that shame; not to explain away our gross inconsistencies as a nation, but to remove the hateful, jarring, and incongruous elements from the land; not to sustain an egregious wrong, but to unite all our energies in the grand effort to remedy that wrong.

I would invoke the spirit of patriotism, in the name of the law of the living God, natural and revealed, and in the full belief that "righteousness exalteth a nation, while sin is a reproach to any people." "He that walketh righteously, and speaketh uprightly; he that despiseth the gain of oppressions, that shaketh his hands from the holding of bribes, he shall dwell on high, his place of defense shall be the munitions of rocks, bread shall be given him, his water shall be sure."

We have not only heard much lately of patriotism, and of its aid being invoked on the side of slavery and injustice, but the very prosperity of this people has been called in to deafen them to the voice of duty, and to lead them onward in the pathway of sin. Thus has the blessing of God been converted into a curse. In the spirit of genuine patriotism, I warn the American people, by all that is just and honorable, to beware!

I warn them that, strong, proud, and prosperous though we be, there is a power above us that can "bring down high looks; at the breath of whose mouth our wealth may take wings; and before whom every knee shall bow;" and who can tell how soon the avenging angel may pass over our land, and the sable bondmen now in chains, may become the instruments of our nation's chastisement!

Without appealing to any higher feeling, I would warn the American people, and the American government, to be wise in their day and generation. I exhort them to remember the history of other nations; and I remind them that America cannot always sit "as a queen," in peace and repose; that prouder and stronger governments than this have been shattered by the bolts of a just God; that the time may come when those they now despise and hate, may be needed; when those whom they now compel by oppression to be enemies, may be wanted as friends. What has been, may be again. There is a point beyond which human endurance cannot go. The crushed worm may yet turn under the heel of the oppressor. I warn them, then, with all solemnity, and in the name of retributive justice, to look to their ways; for in an evil hour, those sable arms that have, for the last two centuries, been engaged in cultivating and adorning the fair fields of our country, may yet become the instruments of terror, desolation, and death, throughout our borders.

It was the sage of the Old Dominion that said—while speaking of the possibility of a conflict between the slaves and the slaveholders—"God has no attribute that could take sides with the oppressor in such a contest. I tremble for my country when I reflect that God is just, and that his justice cannot sleep forever." Such is the warning voice of Thomas Jefferson; and every day's experience since its utterance until now, confirms its wisdom, and commends its truth.

Frederick Douglass

HARRIET TUBMAN (1820-1913)

Introduction

Harriet Tubman was one of the most well-known Underground Railroad conductors. For ten years she made nineteen trips to the South and escorted over three hundred slaves to freedom. She once pointed out to Frederick Douglass that in all of her journeys she, "never lost a single passenger."

Tubman devised clever techniques to ensure her success in these rescues. She used the master's horse and buggy for the first leg of the journey. She often left on a Saturday night, since runaway notices could not be placed in newspapers until Monday morning. If she encountered slave hunters she turned south to evade them. She even took with her a special medicine to give to babies if their crying endangered the fleeing. Tubman also carried a gun so that she could threaten any the fugitives who might being thinking of turning back when they became very tired. Such people were confronted with this choice from the gun brandishing Tubman: "You'll be free or die."

Frederick Douglass once said of Tubman, "Excepting John Brown—of sacred memory— I know of no one who has willingly encountered more perils and hardships to serve our enslaved people than [Harriet Tubman]." John Brown once said that Tubman was, "one of the bravest persons on this continent."

Scenes in the Life of Harriet Tubman

Harriet Tubman, known at various times, and in various places, by many different names, such as "Moses," in allusion to her being the leader and guide to so many of her people in their exodus from the Land of Bondage; "the Conductor of the Underground Railroad;" and "Moll Pitcher," for the energy and daring by which she delivered a fugitive slave who was about to be dragged back to the South; was for the first twenty-five years of her life a slave on the eastern shore of Maryland. Her own master she represents as never unnecessarily cruel; but as was common among slaveholders, he often hired out his slaves to others, some of whom proved to be tyrannical and brutal to the utmost limit of their power.

Powerful muscles

She had worked only as a field-hand for many years, following the oxen, loading and unloading wood, and carrying heavy burdens, by which her naturally remarkable power of muscle was so developed that her feats of strength often called forth the wonder of strong laboring men. Thus was she preparing for the life of hardship and endurance which lay before her, for the deeds of daring she was to do, and of which her ignorant and darkened mind at that time never dreamed.

Miss Susan

The first person by whom she was hired was a woman who, though married and the mother of a family, was still "Miss Susan" to her slaves, as is customary at the South. This woman was possessed of the good things of this life, and provided liberally for her slaves—so far as food and clothing went. But she had been brought up to believe, and to act upon the belief, that a slave could be taught to do nothing, and would do nothing but under the sting of the whip. Harriet, then a young girl, was taken from her life in the field, and having never seen the inside of a house better than a cabin in the Negro quarters, was put to house-work without being told how to do anything. The first thing was to put a parlor in order. "Move these chairs and tables into the middle of the room, sweep the carpet clean, then dust everything, and put them back in their places!" These were the directions given, and Harriet was left alone to do her work. The whip was in sight on the mantel-piece, as a reminder of what was to be expected if the work was not done well. Harriet fixed the furniture as she was told to do, and swept with all her strength, raising a tremendous dust. The moment she had finished sweeping, she took her dusting cloth, and wiped everything "so you could see your face in 'em, de shone so," in haste to go and set the table for breakfast, and do her other work. The dust which she had set flying only settled down again on chairs, tables, and the piano. "Miss Susan" came in and looked around. Then came the call for "Minty"—Harriet's name was Araminta at the South.

She drew her up to the table, saying, "What do you mean by doing my work this way, you—!" and passing her finger on the table and piano, she showed her the mark it made through the dust. "Miss Susan, I done sweep and dust jus' as you tole me." But the whip was already taken down, and the strokes were falling on head and face and neck. Four times this scene was repeated before breakfast, when, during the fifth whipping, the door opened, and "Miss Emily" came in. She was a married sister of "Miss Susan," and was making her a visit, and though brought up with the same associations as her sister, seems to have been a person of more gentle and reasonable nature. Not being able to endure the screams of the child any longer, she came in, took her sister by the arm, and said, "If you do not stop whipping that child, I will leave your house, and never come back!" Miss Susan declared that "she would not mind, and she slighted her work on purpose." Miss Emily said, "Leave her to me a few moments;" and Miss Susan left the room, indignant. As soon as they were alone, Miss Emily said: "Now, Minty, show me how you do your work." For the sixth time Harriet removed all the furniture into the middle of the room; then she swept; and the moment she had done sweeping, she took the dusting cloth to wipe off the furniture. "Now stop there," said Miss Emily; "go away now, and do some of your other work, and when it is time to dust, I will call you." When the time came she called her, and explained to her how the dust had now settled, and that if she wiped it off now, the furniture would remain bright and clean. These few words an hour or two before, would have saved Harriet her whippings for that day, as they probably did for many a day after.

While with this woman, after working from early morning till late at night, she was obliged to sit up all night to rock a cross, sick child. Her mistress laid upon her bed with a whip under her pillow, and slept; but if the tired nurse forgot herself for a moment, if her weary head dropped, and her hand ceased to rock the cradle, the child would cry out, and then down would come the whip upon the neck and face of the poor weary creature. The scars are still plainly visible where the whip cut into the flesh. Perhaps her mistress was preparing her, though she did not know it then, by this enforced habit of wakefulness, for the many long nights of travel, when she was the leader and guide of the weary and hunted ones who were escaping from bondage.

Lifelong injury

"Miss Susan" got tired of Harriet, as Harriet was determined she should do, and so abandoned intention of buying her, and sent her back to her master. She was next hired out to the man who inflicted upon her the lifelong injury from which she is suffering now, by breaking her skull with a weight from the scales. The injury thus inflicted causes her often to fall into a state of somnolency from which it is almost impossible to rouse her. Disabled and sick, her flesh all wasted away, she was returned to her owner. He tried to sell her, but no one would buy her. "Dey said dey wouldn't give a sixpence for me," she said.

"And so," she said, "from Christmas till March I worked as I could, and I prayed through all the long nights—I groaned and prayed for ole master: 'Oh Lord, convert master!' 'Oh Lord, change dat man's heart!' 'Pears like I prayed all de time," said Harriet; "'bout my work, everywhere, I prayed an' I groaned to de Lord. When I went to de horse-trough to wash my face, I took up de water in my han' an' I said, 'Oh Lord, wash me, make me clean!' Den I take up something to wipe my face, an' I say, 'Oh Lord, wipe away all my sin!' When I took de broom and began to sweep, I groaned, 'Oh Lord, wha'soebber sin dere be in my heart, sweep it out, Lord, clar an' clean!'" No words can describe the pathos of her tones, as she broke out into these words of prayer, after the manner of her people. "An' so," said she, "I prayed all night long for master, till the first of March; an' all the time he was bringing people to look at me, an' trying to sell me. Den we heard dat some of us was gwine to be sole to go wid de chain-gang down to de cotton an' rice fields, and dey said I was gwine, an' my brudders, an' sisters. Den I changed my prayer. Fust of March I began to pray, 'Oh Lord, if you ant nebber gwine to change dat man's heart, kill him, Lord, an' take him out ob de way.'

"Nex' ting I heard old master was dead, an' he died jus' as he libed. Oh, then, it 'peared like I'd give all de world full ob gold, if I had it, to bring dat poor soul back. But I couldn't pray for him no longer."

Dreams and visions

The slaves were told that their master's will provided that none of them should be sold out of the State. This satisfied most of them, and they were very happy. But Harriet was not satisfied; she never closed her eyes that she did not imagine she saw the horsemen coming, and heard the screams of women and children, as they were being dragged away to a far worse slavery than that they were enduring there. Harriet was married at this time to a free Negro, who not only did not trouble himself about her fears, but did his best to betray her, and bring her back after she escaped. She would start up at night with the cry, "Oh, dey're comin', dey're comin', I mus' go!"

Her husband called her a fool, and said she was like old Cudjo, who when a joke went round, never laughed till half an hour after everybody else got through, and so just as all danger was past she began to be frightened. But still Harriet in fancy saw the horsemen coming, and heard the screams of terrified women and children. "And all that time, in my dreams and visions," she said, "I seemed to see a line, and on the other side of that line were green fields, and lovely flowers, and beautiful white ladies, who stretched out their arms to me over the line, but I couldn't reach them nohow. I always fell before I got to the line."

Messages in their songs

One Saturday it was whispered in the quarters that two of Harriet's sisters had been sent off with the chain-gang. That morning she started, having persuaded three of her brothers to accompany her, but they had not gone far when the brothers, appalled by the dangers before and behind them, determined to go back, and in spite of her remonstrances dragged her with them. In fear and terror, she remained over Sunday, and on Monday night a Negro from another part of the plantation came privately to tell Harriet that herself and brothers were to be carried off that night. The poor old mother, who belonged to the same mistress, was just going to milk. Harriet wanted to get away without letting her know, because she knew that she would raise an uproar and prevent her going, or insist upon going with her, and the time for this was not yet. But she must give some intimation to those she was going to leave of her intention, and send such a farewell as she might to the friends and relations on the plantation. Those communications were generally made by singing. They sang as they walked along the country roads, and the chorus was taken up by others, and the uninitiated knew not the hidden meaning of the words—

> When dat ar ole chariot comes,
> I'm gwine to lebe you;
> I'm boun' for de promised land,
> I'm gwine to lebe you.

These words meant something more than a journey to the Heavenly Canaan. Harriet said, "Here, mother, go 'long; I'll do the milkin' to-night and bring it in." The old woman went to her cabin. Harriet took down her sun-bonnet, and went on to the "big house," where some of her relatives lived as house servants. She thought she could trust Mary, but there were others in the kitchen, and she could say nothing. Mary began to frolic with her. She threw her across the kitchen, and ran out, knowing that Mary would follow her. But just as they turned the corner of the house, the master to whom Harriet was now hired, came riding up on his horse. Mary darted back, and Harriet thought there was no way now but to sing. But "the Doctor," as the master was called, was regarded with special awe by his slaves; if they were singing or talking together in the field, or on the road, and "the Doctor" appeared, all was hushed till he passed. But Harriet had no time for ceremony; her friends must have a warning; and whether the Doctor thought her "imperent " or not, she must sing him farewell. So on she went to meet him, singing:

> I'm sorry I'm gwine to lebe you,
> Farewell, oh farewell;

But I'll meet you in the mornin',
Farewell, oh farewell.

The Doctor passed, and she bowed as she went on, still singing:

I'll meet you in the mornin',
I'm boun' for de promised land,
On the oder side of Jordan,
Boun' for de promised land.

She reached the gate and looked round; the Doctor had stopped his horse, and had turned around in the saddle, and was looking at her as if there might be more in this than "met the ear." Harriet closed the gate, went on a little way, came back, the Doctor still gazing at her. She lifted up the gate as if she had not latched it properly, waved her hand to him, and burst out again:

I'll meet you in the mornin',
Safe in de promised land,
On the oder side of Jordan,
Boun' for de promised land.

And she started on her journey, "not knowing whither she went," except that she was going to follow the north star, till it led her to liberty. Cautiously and by night she traveled, cunningly feeling her way, and finding out who were friends; till after a long and painful journey she found, in answer to careful inquiries, that she had at last crossed that magic "line" which then separated the land of bondage from the land of freedom; for this was before we were commanded by law to take part in the iniquity of slavery, and aid in taking and sending back those poor hunted fugitives who had manhood and intelligence enough to enable them to make their way thus far towards freedom.

Crossed the line
"When I found I had crossed dat line," she said, "I looked at my hands to see if I was de same pusson. There was such a glory ober ebery ting; de sun came like gold through the trees, and ober the fields, and I felt like I was in Heaben."

But then came the bitter drop in the cup of joy. She said she felt like a man who was put in State Prison for twenty-five years. All these twenty-five years he was thinking of his home, and longing for the time when he would see it again. At last the day comes—he leaves the prison gates—he makes his way to his old home, but his old home is not there. The house has been pulled down, and a new one has been put up in its place; his family and friends are gone nobody knows where; there is no one to take him by the hand, no one to welcome him.

"So it was with me," she said. "I had crossed the line. I was free; but there was no one to welcome me to the land of freedom. I was a stranger in a strange land; and my home, after all, was down in Maryland; because my father, my mother, my brothers, and sisters, and friends were there. But I was free, and they should be free. I would make a home in the North and bring them there, God helping me. Oh, how I prayed then," she said; "I said to de Lord, 'I'm gwine to hole stiddy on to you, an' I know you'll see me through.'"

She came to Philadelphia, and worked in hotels, in club houses, and afterwards at Cape May. Whenever she had raised money enough to pay expenses, she would make her way back, hide herself, and in various ways give notice to those who were ready to strike for freedom. When her party was made up, they would start always on Saturday night, because advertisements could not be sent out on Sunday, which gave them one day in advance.

Pursuers

Then the pursuers would start after them. Advertisements would be posted everywhere. There was one reward of $12,000 offered for the head of the woman who was constantly appearing and enticing away parties of slaves from their master. She had traveled in the cars when these posters were put up over her head, and she heard them read by those about her—for she could not read herself. Fearlessly she went on, trusting in the Lord. She said, "I started with this idea in my head, 'Dere's two things I've got a right to, and dese are, Death or Liberty—one or tother I mean to have. No one will take me back alive; I shall fight for my liberty, and when de time has come for me to go, de Lord will let dem kill me." And acting upon this simple creed, and firm in this trusting faith, she went back and forth nineteen times, according to the reckoning of her friends. She remembers that she went eleven times from Canada, but of the other journeys she kept no reckoning.

While Harriet was working as cook in one of the large hotels in Philadelphia, the play of "Uncle Tom's Cabin" was being performed for many weeks every night. Some of her fellow-servants wanted her to I go and see it. "No," said Harriet, "I haint got no heart to go and see the sufferings of my people played on de stage. I've heard 'Uncle Tom's Cabin' read, and I tell you Mrs. Stowe's pen hasn't begun to paint what slavery is as I have seen it at the far South. I've seen de real ting, and I don't want to see it on no stage or in no teater."

Reward promised

I will give here an article from a paper published nearly a year ago, which mentions that the price set upon the head of Harriet was much higher than I have stated it to be. When asked about this, Harriet said she did not know whether it was so, but she heard them read from one paper that the reward offered was $12,000.

"Among American women," says the article referred to, "who has shown a courage and self-devotion to the welfare of others, equal to Harriet Tubman? Hear her story of going down again and again into the very jaws of slavery, to rescue her suffering people, bringing them off through perils and dangers enough to appall the stoutest heart, till she was known among them as 'Moses.'

"Forty thousand dollars was not too great a reward for the Maryland slaveholders to offer for her.

"Think of her brave spirit, as strong as Daniel's of old, in its fearless purpose to serve God, even though the fiery furnace should be her portion. I have looked into her dark face, and wondered and admired as I listened to the thrilling deeds her lion heart had prompted her to dare. 'I have heard their groans and sighs, and seen their tears, and I would give every drop of blood in my veins to free them,' she said.

"The other day, at Gerrit Smith's, I saw this heroic woman, whom the pen of genius will yet make famous, as one of the noblest Christian hearts ever inspired to lift the burdens of the wronged and oppressed, and what do you think she said to me? She had been tending and caring for our Union black (and white) soldiers in hospital during the war, and at the end of her labors was on her way home, coming in a car through New Jersey. A white man, the conductor, thrust her out of the car with such violence that she has not been able to work scarcely any since; and as she told me of the pain she had and still suffered, she said she did not know what she should have done for herself, and the old father and mother she takes care of, if Mr. Wendell Phillips had not sent her $60, that kept them warm through the winter. She had a letter from W. H. Seward to Maj.-Gen. Hunter, in which he says, 'I have known her long, and a nobler, higher spirit, or truer, seldom dwells in the human form.'"

It will be impossible to give any connected account of the different journeys taken by Harriet for the rescue of her people, as she herself has no idea of the dates connected with them, or of the order in which they were made. She thinks she was about 25 when she made her own escape, and this was in the last year of James K. Polk's administration. From that time till the beginning of the war, her years were spent in these journeyings back and forth, with intervals between, in which she worked only to spend the avails of her labor in providing for the wants of her next party of fugitives. By night she traveled, many times on foot, over mountains, through forests, across rivers, mid perils by land, perils by water, perils from enemies, "perils among false brethren." Sometimes members of her party would become exhausted, foot-sore, and bleeding, and declare they could not go on, they must stay where they dropped down, and die; others would think a voluntary return to slavery better than being overtaken and carried back, and would insist upon returning; then there was no remedy but force; the revolver carried by this bold and daring pioneer would be pointed at their heads. "Dead niggers tell no tales," said Harriet; "Go on or die;" and so she compelled them to drag their weary limbs on their northward journey.

At one time she collected and sent on a gang of thirty-nine fugitives in the care of others, as from some cause she was prevented from accompanying them. Sometimes, when she and her party were concealed in the woods, they saw their pursuers pass, on their horses, down the high road, tacking up the advertisements for them on the fences and trees.

Stations of the Underground Railway
"And den how we laughed," said she. "We was de fools, and dey was de wise men; but we wasn't fools enough to go down de high road in de broad daylight." At one time she left her party in the woods, and went by a long and roundabout way to one of the "stations of the

Underground Railway," as she called them. Here she procured food for her famished party, often paying out of her hardly-gained earnings, five dollars a day for food for them. But she dared not go back to them till night, for fear of being watched, and thus revealing their hiding-place. After nightfall, the sound of a hymn sung at a distance comes upon the ears of the concealed and famished fugitives in the woods, and they know that their deliverer is at hand.

Listening carefully to the songs
They listen eagerly for the words she sings, for by them they are to be warned of danger, or informed of safety. Nearer and nearer comes the unseen singer, and the words are wafted to their ears:

> Hail, oh hail ye happy spirits,
> Death no more shall make you fear,
> No grief nor sorrow, pain nor anger (anguish)
> Shall no more distress you there.
>
> Around him are ten thousan' angels,
> Always ready to 'bey comman'.
> Dey are always hobring round you,
> Till you reach the hebbenly lan'.
>
> Jesus, Jesus will go wid you;
> He will lead you to his throne;
> He who died has gone before you,
> Trod de wine-press all alone.
>
> He whose thunders shake creation;
> He who bids the planets roll;
> He who rides upon the temple, (tempest)
> An' his scepter sways de whole.
>
> Dark and thorny is de desert,
> Through de pilgrim makes his ways,
> Yet beyon' dis vale of sorrow,
> Lies de fiel's of endless days.

I give these words exactly as Harriet sang them to me to a sweet and simple Methodist air. "De first time I go by singing dis hymn, dey don't come out to me," she said, "till I listen if de coast is clar; den when I go back and sing it again, dey come out. But if I sing:

> Moses go down in Egypt,
> Till ole Pharo' let me go;

Hadn't been for Adam's fall,
Shouldn't hab to died at all,

den dey don't come out, for dere's danger in de way."
And so by night travel, by hiding, by signals, by threatening, she brought the people safely to the land of liberty. But after the passage of the Fugitive Slave law, she said, "I wouldn't trust Uncle Sam wid my people no longer; I brought 'em all clar off to Canada."

Joe

Of the very many interesting stories told me by Harriet, I cannot refrain from telling to my readers that of Joe, who accompanied her upon her seventh or eighth journey from Maryland to Canada.

Joe was a noble specimen of a Negro, and was hired out by his master to a man for whom he worked faithfully for six years, saving him the expense of an overseer, and taking all trouble off his hands. At length this man found him so absolutely necessary to him, that he determined to buy him at any cost. His master held him proportionably high. However, by paying a thousand dollars down for him, and promising to pay another thousand in a certain time, Joe passed into the hands of his new master.

As may be imagined, Joe was somewhat surprised when the first order issued from his master's lips, was, "Now, Joe, strip and take a whipping!" Joe's experience of whippings, as he had seen them inflicted upon others, was not such as to cause him particularly to desire to go through the same operation on his own account; and he, naturally enough, demurred, and at first thought of resisting. But he called to mind a scene which he had witnessed a few days before, in the field, the particulars of which are too horrible and too harassing to the feelings to be given to my readers, and he thought it best to submit; but first he tried remonstrance.

"Mas'r," said he, "habn't I always been faithful to you? Habn't I worked through sun an' rain, early in de mornin', and late at night; habn't I saved you an oberseer by doin' his work; hab you anyting to complain of agin me?"

"No, Joe; "I've no complaint to make of you; you're a good nigger, and you've always worked well; but the first lesson my niggers have to learn is that I am master, and that they are not to resist or refuse to obey anything I tell 'em to do. So the first thing they've got to do, is to be whipped; if they resist, they got it all the harder; and so I'll go on, till I kill 'em, but they've got to give up at last, and learn that I'm master."

Joe thought it best to submit. He stripped off his upper clothing, and took his whipping, without a word; but as he drew his clothes up over his torn and bleeding back, he said, "Dis is de last!" That night he took a boat and went a long distance to the cabin of Harriet's father, and said, "Next time Moses comes, let me know." It was only a week or two after that, that the mysterious woman whom no one could lay their finger on appeared, and men, women, and children began to disappear from the plantations. One fine morning Joe was missing, and his brother William, from another plantation; Peter and Eliza, too, were gone; and these made part of Harriet's next party, who began their pilgrimage from Maryland to Canada, or as they expressed it, from "Egypt to de land of Canaan."

Their adventures were enough to fill a volume; they were pursued; they were hidden in "potato holes," while their pursuers passed within a few feet of them; they were passed along by friends in various disguises; they scattered and separated, to be led by guides by a round-about way, to a meeting-place again. They were taken in by Sam Green, the man who was afterwards sent to State Prison for ten years for having a copy of "Uncle Tom's Cabin" in his house; and so, hunted and hiding and wandering, they came at last to the long bridge at the entrance of the city of Wilmington, Delaware. The rewards posted up everywhere had been at first five hundred dollars for Joe, if taken within the limits of the United States; then a thousand, and then fifteen hundred dollars, "an' all expenses clar an' clean, for his body in Easton Jail," Eight hundred for William, and four hundred for Peter, and twelve thousand for the woman who enticed them away. The long Wilmington Bridge was guarded by police officers, and the advertisements were everywhere.

Thomas Garrett

The party were scattered, and taken to the houses of different colored friends, and word was sent secretly to Thomas Garrett, of Wilmington, of their condition, and the necessity of their being taken across the bridge. Thomas Garrett is a Quaker, and a man of a wonderfully large and generous heart, through whose hands, Harriet tells me, two thousand self-emancipated slaves passed on their way to freedom. He was always ready, heart and hand and means, in aiding these poor fugitives, and rendered most efficient help to Harriet on many of her journeys back and forth. A letter received a few days since by the writer, from this noble-hearted philanthropist, will be given presently.

As soon as Thomas Garrett heard of the condition of these poor people, his plan was formed. He engaged two wagons, filled them with bricklayers, whom of course he paid well for their share in the enterprise, and sent them across the bridge. They went as if on a frolic, singing and shouting. The guards saw them pass, and of course expected them to re-cross the bridge. After nightfall (and fortunately it was a dark night) the same wagons went back, but with an addition to their party. The fugitives were on the bottom of the wagons, the bricklayers on the seats, still singing and shouting; and so they passed by the guards, who were entirely unsuspicious of the nature of the load the wagons contained, or of the amount of property thus escaping their hands. And so they made their way to New York. When they entered the anti-slavery office there, Joe was recognized at once by the description in the advertisement. "Well," said Mr. Oliver Johnson, "I am glad to see the man whose head is worth fifteen hundred dollars." At this Joe's heart sank. If the adver-tisement had got to New York, that place which it had taken them so many days and nights to reach, he thought he was in danger still. "And how far is it now to Canada?" he asked. When told how many miles, for they were to come through New York State, and cross the Suspension Bridge, he was ready to give up. "From dat time Joe was silent," said Harriet; "he sang no more, he talked no more; he sat wid his head on his hand, and nobody could 'muse him or make him take any interest in anyting." They passed along in safety, and at length found themselves in the cars, approaching Suspension Bridge. The rest were very joyous and happy, but Joe sat silent and sad. Their fellow-passengers all seemed interested in and for them, and listened with tears, as Harriet and all their party lifted up their voices and sang:

> I'm on my way to Canada,
> That cold and dreary land;
> The sad effects of slavery,
> I can't no longer stand.
> I've served my master all my days,
> Widout a dime's reward;
> And now I'm forced to run away,
> To flee the lash abroad.
> Farewell, ole master, don't think hard of me,
> I'll travel on to Canada, where all the slaves are free.
>
> The hounds are baying on my track,
> Ole master comes behind.
> Resolved that he will bring me back,
> Before I cross de line;
> I'm now embarked for yonder shore,
> There a man's a man by law;
> The iron horse will bear me o'er,
> To shake de lion's paw.
> Oh, righteous Father, wilt thou not pity me,
> And aid me on to Canada where all the slaves are free.
>
> Oh, I heard Queen Victoria say,
> That if we would forsake
> Our native land of slavery,
> And come across the lake;
> That she was standin' on de shore,
> Wid arms extended wide,
> To give us all a peaceful home
> Beyond de rolling tide.
> Farewell, ole master, etc.

The cars began to cross the bridge. Harriet was very anxious to have her companions see the Falls. William, Peter, and Eliza came eagerly to look at the wonderful sight; but Joe sat still, with his head upon his hand.

"Joe, come look at de Falls! Joe, you fool you, come see de Falls! its your last chance." But Joe sat still and never raised his head. At length Harriet knew by the rise in the center of the bridge, and the descent on the other side, that they had crossed "the line." She sprang across to Joe's seat, shook him with all her might, and shouted, "Joe, you've shook de lion's paw!"

Joe did not know what she meant. "Joe, you're free!" shouted Harriet. Then Joe's head went up, he raised his hands on high, and his face, streaming with tears, to heaven, and broke out in loud and thrilling tones:

> Glory to God and Jesus too,
> One more soul is safe!
> Oh, go and carry de news,
> One more soul got safe."

"Joe, come and look at de Falls!" called Harriet.

> Glory to God and Jesus too,
> One more soul got safe.

was all the answer. The cars stopped on the other side. Joe's feet were the first to touch British soil, after those of the conductor.

Loud roared the waters of Niagara, but louder still ascended the anthem of praise from the overflowing heart of the freeman. And can we doubt that the strain was taken up by angel voices, and that through the arches of Heaven echoed and reechoed the strain:

> Glory to God in the Highest,
> Glory to God and Jesus too,
> One more soul is safe.

"The ladies and gentlemen gathered round him," said Harriet, "till I couldn't see Joe for the crowd, only I heard 'Glory to God and Jesus too!' louder than ever." William went after him, and pulled him, saying, "Joe, stop your noise! you act like a fool!" Then Peter ran it, and jerked him mos' off his feet,—"Joe, stop your hollerin'! Folks 'll think you're crazy!" But Joe gave no heed. The ladies were crying, and the tears like rain ran down Joe's sable cheeks. A lady reached over her fine cambric handkerchief to him. Joe wiped his face, and then he spoke.

"Oh! if I'd felt like dis down South, it would hab taken nine men to take me; only one more journey for me now, and dat is to Hebben!" "Well, you ole fool you," said Harriet, with whom there seems but one step from the sublime to the ridiculous, "you might a' looked at de Falls fust, and den gone to Hebben afterwards." She has seen Joe several times since, a happy and industrious freeman in Canada.

"'Twas the Lord"

When asked, as she often is, how it was possible that she was not afraid to go back, with that tremendous price upon her head, Harriet always answers, "Why, don't I tell you, Missus, t'wan't me, 'twas de Lord! I always tole him, 'I trust to you. I don't know where to go or what to do, but I expect you to lead me,' an' he always did." At one time she was going down, watched for everywhere, after there had been a meeting of slaveholders in the court-house of one of the large cities of Maryland, and an added reward had been put upon her head, with various threats of the different cruel devices by which she should be tortured and put to death; friends gathered round her, imploring her not to go on directly in the face of danger and death, and this was Harriet's answer to them:

"Now look yer! John saw the city, didn't he? Yes, John saw the city. Well, what did he see? He saw twelve gates—three of dose gates was on de north—three of 'em was on de east—and three of 'em was on de west—but dere was three of 'em on de South too; an' I reckon if dey kill me down dere, I'll git into one of dem gates, don't you?"

Whether Harriet's ideas of the geographical bearings of the gates of the Celestial City, as seen in the Apocalyptic vision, were correct or not, we cannot doubt that she was right in the deduction her faith drew from them; and that somewhere, whether north, south, east, or west, to our dim vision, there is a gate to be opened for Harriet, where the welcome will be given, "Come in thou blessed of my Father." . . .

Harriet's hospital work

I find among her papers, many of which are defaced by being carried about with her for years, portions of letters addressed to myself, by persons at the South, and speaking of the valuable assistance Harriet was rendering our soldiers in the hospital, and our armies in the field. At this time her manner of life, as related by herself, was this:

"Well, Missus, I'd go to de hospital, I would, early eb'ry mornin'. I'd get a big chunk of ice, I would, and put it in a basin, and fill it with water; den I'd take a sponge and begin. Fust man I'd come to, I'd thrash away de flies, an' dey'd rise, dey would, like bees roun' a hive. Den I'd begin to bathe der wounds, an' by de time I'd bathed off three or four, de fire and heat would have melted de ice and made de water warm, an' it would be as red as clar blood. Den I'd go an' git more ice, I would, an' by de time I got to de nex' ones, de flies would be roun' de fust ones, black an' thick as eber." In this way she worked, day after day, till late at night; then she went home to her little cabin, and made about fifty pies, a great quantity of ginger-bread, and two casks of root beer. These she would hire some contraband to sell for her through the camps, and thus she would provide her support for another day; for this woman never received pay or pension, and never drew for herself but twenty days' rations during the four years of her labors. At one time she was called away from Hilton Head, by one of our officers, to come to Fernandina, where the men were "dying off like sheep," from dysentery. Harriet had acquired quite a reputation for her skill in curing this disease, by a medicine which she prepared from roots which grew near the waters which gave the disease. Here she found thousands of sick soldiers and contrabands, and immediately gave up her time and attention to them. At another time, we find her nursing those who were down by hundreds with small-pox and malignant fevers. She had never had these diseases, but she seems to have no more fear of death in one form than another. "De Lord would take keer of her till her time came, an' den she was ready to go." . . .

"Pitch the nagur out!"

The last time Harriet was returning from the war, with her pass as hospital nurse, she bought a half-fare ticket, as she was told she must do; and missing the other train, she got into an emigrant train on the Amboy Railroad. When the conductor looked at her ticket, he said, "Come, hustle out of here! We don't carry niggers for half-fare." Harriet explained to him that she was in the employ of Government, and was entitled to transportation as the soldiers were. But the conductor took her forcibly by the arm, and said, "I'll make you tired of trying to stay here." She resisted, and being very strong, she could probably have got the better of the conductor, had he not called three men to his assistance. The car was filled with emigrants, and no one seemed to take her part. The only word, she heard, accompanied with fearful oaths, were, "Pitch the nagur out!" They nearly wrenched her arm off, and at length threw her, with all their strength, into a baggage-car. She supposed her arm was broken, and in intense suffering she came on to New York. As she left the car, a delicate-looking young man came up to her, and, handing her a card, said, "You ought to sue that conductor, and if you want a witness, call on me." Harriet remained all winter under the care of a physician in New York; he advised her to sue the Railroad company, and said that he would willingly testify as to her injuries. But the card the young man had given her was only a visiting card, and she did not know where to find him, and so she let the matter go. ...

Harriet's parents

It was a wise plan of our sagacious heroine to leave her old parents till the last to be brought away. They were pensioned off as too old to work, had a cabin, and a horse and cow, and were quite comfortable. If Harriet had taken them away before the young people, these last would have been sold into Southern slavery, to keep them out of her way. But at length Harriet heard that the old man had been betrayed by a slave whom he had assisted, but who had turned back, and when questioned by his wife, told her the story of his intended escape, and of the aid he had received from "Old Ben." This woman, hoping to curry favor with her master, revealed the whole to him, and "Old Ben" was arrested. He was to be tried the next week, when Harriet appeared upon the scene and, as she says, "saved dem de expense ob de trial," and removed her father to a higher court, by taking him off to Canada.

Old Ben's escape

The manner of their escape is detailed in the following letter from Thomas Garrett, the *Wilmington Quaker*: Wilminton 6th Mo., 1868.

> My friend: Thy favor of the 12th reached me yesterday, requesting such reminiscences as I could give respecting the remarkable labors of Harriet Tubman, in aiding her colored friends from bondage. I may begin by saying, living as I have in a slave State, and the laws being very severe where my proof could be made of any one aiding slaves on their way to freedom, I have not felt at liberty to keep any written word of Harriet's or my own labors, except in numbering those whom I have aided. For that reason I cannot furnish so interesting an account of Harriet's labors as I otherwise could, and now would be glad

to do; for in truth I never met with any person, of any color, who had more confidence in the voice of God, as spoken direct to her soul. She has frequently told me that she talked with God, and he talked with her every day of her life, and she has declared to me that she felt no more fear of being arrested by her former master, or any other person, when in his immediate neighborhood, than she did in the State of New York, or Canada, for she said she never ventured only where God sent her, and her faith in a Supreme Power truly was great.

I have now been confined to my room with indisposition more than four weeks, and cannot sit to write much; but I feel so much interested in Harriet that I will try to give some of the most remarkable incidents that now present themselves to my mind. The date of the commencement of her labors, I cannot certainly give; but I think it must have been about 1845; from that time till 1860, I think she must have brought from the neighborhood where she had been held as a slave, from 60 to 80 persons, from Maryland, some 80 miles from here. No slave who placed himself under her care, was ever arrested that I have heard of; she mostly had her regular stopping places on her route; but in one instance, when she had two stout men with her, some 30 miles below here, she said that God told her to stop, which she did; and then asked him what she must do. He told her to leave the road, and turn to the left; she obeyed, and soon came to a small stream of tide water; there was no boat, no bridge; she again inquired of her Guide what she was to do. She was told to go through. It was cold, in the month of March; but having confidence in her Guide, she went in; the water came up to her arm-pits; the men refused to follow till they saw her safe on the opposite shore.

They then followed, and if I mistake not, she had soon to wade a second stream; soon after which she came to a cabin of colored people, who took them all in, put them to bed, and dried their clothes, ready to proceed next night on their journey. Harriet had run out of money, and gave them some of her underclothing to pay for their kindness. When she called on me two days after, she was so hoarse she could hardly speak, and was also suffering with violent toothache. The strange part of the story we found to be, that the master of these two men had put up the previous day, at the railroad station near where she left, an advertisement for them, offering a large reward for their apprehension; but they made a safe exit. She at one time brought as many as seven or eight, several of whom were women and children. She was well known here in Chester County and Philadelphia, and respected by all true abolitionists. I had been in the habit of furnishing her and those that accompanied her, as she returned from her acts of mercy, with new shoes; and on one occasion when I had not seen her for three months, she came into my store.

I said, "Harriet, I am glad to see thee! I suppose thee wants a pair of new shoes."

Her reply was "I want more than that."

I, in jest, said, "I have always been liberal with thee, and wish to be; but I am not rich, and cannot afford to give much."

Her reply was: "God tells me you have money for me."

I asked her "if God never deceived her?"

She said, "No!"

"Well! how much does thee want?"

After studying a moment, she said: "About twenty-three dollars."

I then gave her twenty-four dollars and some odd cents, the net proceeds of five pounds sterling, received through Eliza Wigham, of Scotland, for her. I had given some accounts of Harriet's labor to the Anti-Slavery Society of Edinburgh, of which Eliza Wigham was Secretary. On the reading of my letter, a gentleman present said he would send Harriet four pounds if he knew of any way to get it to her. Eliza Wigham offered to forward it to me for her, and that was the first money ever received by me for her. Some twelve months after, she called on me again, and said that God told her I had some money for her, but not so much as before. I had, a few days previous, received the net proceeds of one pound ten shillings from Europe for her.

To say the least, there was something remarkable in these facts, whether clairvoyance, or the divine impression on her mind from the source of all power, I cannot tell; but certain it was she had a guide within herself other than the written word, for she never had any education. She brought away her aged parents in a singular manner. They started with an old horse, fitted out in primitive style with a straw collar, a pair of old chaise wheels, with a board on the axle to sit on, another board swung with ropes, fastened to the axle, to rest their feet on. She got her parents, who were both slaves belonging to different masters, on this rude vehicle to the railroad, put them in the cars, turned Jehu herself, and drove to town in a style that no human being ever did before or since; but she was happy at having arrived safe. Next day, I furnished her with money to take them all to Canada. I afterwards sold their horse, and sent them the balance of the proceeds. I believe that Harriet succeeded in freeing all her relatives but one sister and her three children. Etc., etc.

Thy friend,

Thos. Garrett

Friend Garrett probably refers here to those who passed through his hands. Harriet was obliged to come by many different routes on her different journeys, and though she never counted those whom she brought away with her, it would seem, by the computation of others, that there must have been somewhere near three hundred brought by her to the Northern States and Canada.

Sarah H. Bradford

JOSEPH BAYSMORE (1823-?)

Introduction

Joseph Baysmore was born a slave in Bertie County, N.C. He was baptized in 1851 in Halifax County, N.C. Baysmore, where he became a licensed minister and temporary pastor until 1866. In 1866 he was ordained. Baysmore acted as pastor and minister of the first African-American Baptist church in Weldon, N.C. from 1865 through 1883.

In his preface to, *A Historical Sketch of the First Colored Baptist Church Weldon, N. C., With the Life and Labor of Elder Joseph Baysmore, with Four Collected Sermons,* published in 1887, Baysmore states:

> I began the church with only five members and I preached as a Licensed minister, and temporary pastor until 1866, then I was ordained to the work of the ministry, November the 22d, 1866, and became the pastor in charge and served the church as pastor 18 years. This is from 1865 to 1883.
>
> I was born in 1823 in Bertie County, N. C., and when I was but a youth my mother taught me to be a good boy, and she said a bad boy would come to a bad end, and she taught me the Lord's Prayer, and I was brought up in the fear of the Lord, and I began to seek the salvation of my soul at 12 years of age, but was off and on but could not depart from the presence of the Lord, so I professed hope in Christ and was baptized in the year 1851, in the county of Halifax where I then resided. I was a slave and was brought by my owner into Halifax county in the year 1846. My owner was good to me and when I was baptized they give me the liberty of holding prayer meetings by which the whole people of the place were convicted from their evil way and returned to the Lord and it was by the providence of God that I possessed a little share of education and by studying and practicing it the same I growed more and more in the light of literature, by which I was able to read the Bible.
>
> I organized eight Baptist Churches, and baptized nine hundred converts.

Joseph Baysmore's ministry is considered one of the important highlights of the African American history in North Carolina.

Falling from Grace

"Whosoever of you are justified by the law; ye are fallen from Grace."—Galatians 5th chap, part 4th verse.

And now, my dear brethren and congregation, the first proposition of the text treats upon the subject of justification, and I wish to give a clear explanation upon the subject, so that the eyes of your understanding may be enlightened; that you may know the hope of your calling; for some have not had the knowledge of justification;—hearken and hear what justification is: Justification is to be made free from sin and become reconciled to God through the atoning merits of Jesus Christ, which made a perfect reconciliation between God and man, and not by any work which we have done; for we are saved by Grace through faith in the Redeemer's blood. Therefore, if any of you think that you have done good enough to free you from sin without faith in the Redeemer's blood, ye are yet under the penalty of the law. And again, the law cannot have any compassion upon sin. Why? For sin is the transgression of the law. Hark! And again, the holy law saith, "The soul that sinneth shall die." And again, the Holy Scripture saith we all have sinned and the law has assumed the debt for sin, and it was death; and Christ our Savior paid our debt by His own blood, and has redeemed all who will believe on the only begotten Son of God, for by one offering he hath perfected forever them that are sanctified. And again, He saith: "This is the covenant that I will make with them after those days; I will put my laws into their hearts, and in their minds I will write them; and their sins and iniquities will I remember no more." And again, "Whom the Son setteth free are free indeed;" but "whomsoever of you are justified by the law, ye are fallen from Grace." And the word fallen means going down through the depths of God's favor and mercy. But the Apostles did not say that they had received the Grace of God and had lost it. And again, the Apostles did not say that they were children of God by faith in our Lord Jesus Christ, and had lost their faith; but the Apostles prove that their faith is in the law which cannot save them that putteth their trust therein; and again, as long as men trust in their own deeds for salvation they are fallen from grace. When they deny themselves and trust Christ for salvation He will catch the fallen sinner in the arms of His love. For the law was given by Moses, but grace and truth came by Jesus Christ; the law is the author of death because of sin, but grace is the author of life because of righteousness; therefore after the law has slain the sinner the law has finished its work, and then grace gives life again.

Whosoever of you that are justified by the law, ye are fallen from grace. But the text did not say that they had fell from grace, but that they are falling from grace; and again it is very important to know what the grace of God is before you can declare that you have fell from grace, for grace is God's favor and mercy. Again, the text declares, "Ye that are justified by the law ye are fallen from grace," but the text did not say that they had not fell from grace, but the text saith you that are justified by the law ye are fallen from grace. But some will say, How can you fall from grace before you receive it. I fancy to say ye that are fallen are fallen because you have not received the grace of God that is offered in the word of life. The Apostle saith, "the word is nigh them even in thy mouth and in thy heart, and this is the word of faith which we preach." Therefore, if grace is in thy heart and then ye will not receive it what shall I more say but cry in the language of the text, ye that are justified by the law ye are fallen. Oh, hearken and look and see by faith one Jesus upon the cross with open arms; hark, his love and mercy is deeper than the depth of death, and his arms are extended and he saith believe on me and you shall be saved; although ye are fallen I will catch your soul before it falls through Mercy's last depth, yea before it falls through Mercy's last depth.

Again, another Scripture saith, "I am he that liveth and was dead; and, behold, I am alive evermore; and have the keys of hell and of death." Therefore, if Christ has got the keys of death and hell, and he saith "because I live ye shall live," and, again "whosoever drinketh of the water that I shall give him shall never thirst, but the water that I shall give him shall be in him as a well of water springing up into everlasting life;" and again, another scripture saith, "whosoever abideth in Him sinneth not, and whosoever sinneth hath not seen him and neither know him now." There is another scriptural evidence, that "whosoever is born of the new birth in Christ cannot fall from grace," but "ye that are justified by the law ye are fallen from grace," and will continue to fall until you fall into the arms of Jesus. If you fall from his arms then I am sure you have fallen from grace and must enter hell, and there without remedy.

He that committeth sin is of the devil, for whosoever is born of God does not sin, for his seed remaineth in him and he cannot sin, because he is born of God; and again, ye are saved by grace through faith, and that not of yourselves, it is the gift of God, not of works, lest any man should boast, for men by nature are children of divine wrath, but the law is holy, just and good. Whoever of you that are justified by the law ye are fallen from grace.

And now my dear brethren and congregation, we plainly see that those who are justified by the law are the fallen subjects, because the law is just and holy, and whosoever counts themselves holy by their own good deeds are deceived and are overcome by their sinfulness of the flesh and are convinced of the law that they are sinners, and then they say that they have fell from grace. But I fancy to say that those that are fallen from grace have never been risen unto a new life in Christ Jesus our Lord; and they are not with us who believe in God through Christ, for we that believe are built upon the foundation of the apostles and prophets; and Jesus Christ is the chief foundation, and we cannot fall because he saith he that believes in me, "I am in him and he is in me and I am in the father," and again "the law is our witness that we have passed from death unto life; for as in Adam all died even so in Christ shall all be made alive."

Again, if the grace of God is mercy and favor, as the Doctors of Divinity of the different denominations have agreed upon, I shall prove that Adam did not fall from grace but that he fell from holiness and happiness, and when he fell from his holy state he fell into the arms of death; but we give God thanks that there was a foundation deeper than the depths of death, and this foundation is God's favor and mercy, which is the gift of Jesus.

Hark, I hear the Gospel's cheering sound,
The dead's alive and the lost is found.

Jesus is alive, he lives to die no more; and again, another Scripture saith, "My sheep hear my voice. I give them eternal life that they may never perish;" and again, "the law is our witness that we are built upon the foundation of the apostles and the prophets, and Jesus Christ is our chief foundation, sure and steadfast;" and again "we are more than conquerors through Him that loves us;" and the apostle saith, "neither death, nor life, nor angels, nor principalities, nor things present, nor things to come, shall be able to separate us from the love of God that is in Christ Jesus our Lord."

Whosoever of you that are justified by the law, ye are fallen from grace, but the arms of mercy are able to catch the falling sinner before he falls through the depth of mercy, and save him from the flames of fire. And again, when a sinner has fallen from grace he is a child of that wicked one, and has never known Christ in the pardon of his sins, for the scripture saith, "by their works ye shall know them;" and again, I John 2: 3, "and hereby we do know that we know him, if we keep his commandments;" and see chap. 3: 10, "In this the children of God are manifest, and the children of the devil: whosoever doeth not righteousness is not of God, neither he that loveth not his brother." Hark, Paul in his epistle to the Romans, chap. 14: 4, says, "Who art thou that judgest another man's servant? to his own master he standeth or falleth; yea, he shall be holden up: for God is able to make him stand."

And again, I wish to ask this question: "Can Satan blot out the blood of Christ which restores us to the new fellowship with God? (and 'by faith we are made heirs and joint heirs with Christ,'). If ye are so weak as to believe that Satan can overrule God and blot out the image of his Son ye are not a fit subject for the Kingdom of God; for he that esteemeth Satan equal with God he has denied the Father and the Son, for Jesus saith "whom the Son shall set free are free indeed."

And now may the Grace of God and the fellowship of the Holy Ghost be with you all now and forever. Amen.

Joseph Baysmore, Raleigh Edwards, Broughton & Co., 1878

Baptism

"Go ye into all the world and preach the gospel to every creature: he that believeth and is baptized shall be saved, but he that believeth not shall be damned." Mark 16th Chapter, 15th and 16th Verses.

And now I wish to give a clear explanation upon the subject of Baptism, for there has been so much said upon this matter, and it is so hard to be understood by those that believe not. Now my dear brethren and congregation and all that will hear this, I call your attention to this important subject, for it is worthy of our notice, for it is the commission of our Lord and Savior Jesus Christ. I fancy to say, according to the gospel, "he that believeth and is baptized shall be saved." This cannot be truthfully denied. "He that believeth not shall be damned." The text saith "go into all the world and preach the gospel to every creature." Every human being that can hear and understand, for "faith cometh by hearing and hearing by the word of God."

Again, our Savior saith, "when any one heareth the word of the kingdom and under-standeth not, then cometh the wicked one and taketh away that which is in his heart," catcheth away that which is sown in his heart, that is, to hinder him from obeying the truth of the gospel, for the word of the kingdom is the truth of the gospel which shall be preached in all the world for a witness unto all nations. Again, the Scripture saith, "whoso readeth let him understand." So then I fancy to say that the Messiah did not leave His Apostles without understanding, when He said unto them "go ye into all the world and preach the gospel to every creature: he that believeth and is baptized shall be saved." For I am persuaded that the Apostles understood the meaning of this word baptize; but some men say there are more ways than one to administer baptism, but I fancy to say that this is the doctrine of men, for the Scripture saith, "if the trumpet give an uncertain sound, who shall prepare himself for battle," and if the Messiah give an uncertain way to administer baptism, how shall the people or how shall the minister know when he has baptized those that believe? I am fully persuaded that believers are the proper subjects for baptism, and this is that which I shall prove by the evidence of the apostolic doctrine, for the Scripture declares that "when they believed they were baptized both men and women," but not before they believed, and it is evident that they could not believe until they heard the Word of Life and understood it. And again some men teach this false doctrine which do not bear witness with Scripture, and that is this, they say "be baptized first and then believe," but I fancy to say that is contrary to the doctrine of the apostles; and we are taught by the Scriptures to "mark them which cause dissensions and offences contrary to the doctrine which you have learned, and avoid them." Avoid them, believe them not, because their doctrine and practice are not Scriptural. The Holy Scripture is the voice of God, speaking through his Son Jesus Christ, our Lord, and "he that believeth not shall be damned."

"He that believeth not shall be damned," because they received not the love of the truth that they might be saved, and for this cause shall God send them strong delusion that they should believe a lie, that they all might be condemned that believe not the truth, but had pleasure in unrighteousness. Paul to the Thessalonians, 2d chapter, 11-12 verses: "Therefore, brethren, stand fast in the doctrine of the Apostles which you have been taught, for the wicked shall not stand in judgment, for the Lord shall consume them with the spirit of his mouth and he shall shine them away by the brightness of his coming. Go ye into all the world and preach the gospel to every creature, he that believeth and is baptized shall be saved, but he that believeth not shall be damned." All the world where men are found preach the gospel—proclaim the glad tidings of salvation through Jesus Christ. He that believes; he that receives the testimony of God and is baptized, (that is, dipping or immersing the believer in water in the name of the Holy Trinity,) he shall be saved, he shall be set apart for Heaven.

Baptism did not come in the place of circumcision, but was ordained for the new Covenant, for if baptism came in the place of circumcision, what was Jesus baptized for? He had received circumcision and then He was baptized. Circumcision was of the old Covenant and the old Covenant was of the law, but the new covenant is the Gospel system. Again, "go ye therefore and teach all nations, baptizing them in the name of the Father, and of the Son, and of the Holy Ghost, teaching them to observe all things whatsoever I have commanded you, and ye are witnesses of these things." And again: "behold I send the promise of my Father upon you, but tarry ye in the city of Jerusalem until ye be imbued with power from on high." When the day of Pentecost was fully come "they were all with one accord in one place, and there came a sound from Heaven as of a rushing mighty wind, and they were all filled with the Holy Ghost and began to speak with other tongues as the Spirit gave them utterance." And again: "when they heard this they were pricked to their hearts and said unto Peter and the other Apostles, 'what shall we do?' Then Peter said unto them, 'repent and be baptized, every one of you,' and they that gladly received the word were baptized." Receive the word, believe the word. Again: "when they believed Philip preaching the things concerning the kingdom of God and the name of Jesus Christ, they were baptized;" and again: "Philip preached Jesus unto the Eunuch, and the Eunuch said, 'see here is water, what doth hinder me to be baptized?' and Philip said, 'if thou believe with all thy heart thou mayest,' and he said, 'I do believe that Jesus Christ is the Son of God.' And they went both down into the water, and Philip baptized him with water, and not with the Holy Ghost; for Peter said, "who can deny water that these should be baptized which have received the Holy Ghost, as well as we, and he commanded them to be baptized in the name of Jesus." I am certain the Apostles could not be deceived, for I fancy to say that God did send John to baptize with water, but He sent His Son to baptize with the Holy Ghost and with fire. He that believeth and is baptized with water in the name of the Holy Trinity, he shall receive the gift of the Holy Ghost. Again: he that believeth not shall be baptized with fire, that is, he shall receive the fiery wrath of God's avenging law, for Christ did not promise to baptize his apostles with fire, but He said unto them, "ye shall be baptized with the Holy Ghost not many days hence." Hark again. Paul to Romans, 13 chap. 2d verse: "Whosoever therefore resisteth the power, resisteth the ordinance of God; and they that resist shall receive unto themselves damnation." And again we must confess that baptism is the ordinance of God; and again: ministers of all denominations that wish to save souls, must be wise enough to put their knowledge into the knowledge of God, and then they will clothe themselves with Godliness. And again: "John was baptizing in Enon, near Salem, because there was much water there, and they came and were baptized;" but these that John baptized were baptized unto repentance, yea, to prove that they confessed their sins, and they that would not confess their sins, he would not baptize them with water. And again: he that does not believe cannot be scripturally baptized; and again, he that doth believe the gospel, cannot renounce the water baptism. "What doth hinder me to be baptized?" "If thou believe with all thy heart thou mayest," and he said, "I do believe that Jesus Christ is the Son of God, and he baptized him." "He that believeth and is baptized shall be saved."

Scriptural baptism is the outward sign of the inward faith in Jesus' blood, and that leads us that do believe to confess the Lord Jesus by the water baptism. But whosoever renounces the water baptism, and then saith they are baptized with the Holy Ghost, they are deceived. "Go ye into all the world and preach the Gospel to every creature: he that believeth and is baptized shall be saved, but he that believeth not shall be damned." He that hears and has the ability to understand, and does understand, but will not obey the gospel, he shall be damned. And again, scriptural baptism is essential to salvation, for baptism professes to hate sin and corruptions, and professes a new life in Christ Jesus. "Arise and be baptized and wash away your sins." Infants are not charged with sin until they can understand, therefore they are not proper subjects for baptism; and if we baptize them before they can renounce their sin, their baptism is nothing, for their sins are dead and their baptism is dead; his baptism was put on him over his sin, before he renounced his sin, and of course when he renounces his sin, he must renounce his baptism, which was put on him over his sin; for his sin was put on him by Adam, and he must pull it off by the knowledge of Jesus, and then put on Christ by baptism, and he shall receive the gift of the Holy Ghost.

Again: all true religious practice is based upon the doctrine of the Bible, and all religious practice which is not found in the Bible is utterly false, and it is not the worship of God, but it is the worship of men, for all true religion can find rest in the Bible. Again: some saith that baptism is not essential to salvation, but the Scriptures declare that "men shall live by every word of God," and if believers are baptized in the name of the Holy Trinity, it is essential to salvation, for God commands us what to do through Christ, and Christ commands us to believe and be baptized in the name of the Father, and the Son, and the Holy Ghost.

And now may the God of peace and the fellowship of the Holy Ghost be with you all. Amen.

Joseph Baysmore, Raleigh Edwards, Broughton & Co., 1878

Predestination

"For whom he did foreknow, he also did predestinate to be conformed to the image of his Son,"—Romans, 8: 29.

The first proposition of the text treats of the foreknowledge of God, which is an important subject. We are taught by the Scriptures that the invisible things of Him from the creation of the world are clearly seen, being understood by the things that are made—even his eternal power and Godhead—even his eternal power to make what we see; and that the visible things of Him teaches us of His power, yea, His everlasting power, yea and His Godhead, His foreknowledge to know all His people whom He chose to dwell in the light of His countenance. And now I will illustrate upon the foreknowledge of men—for men do have a future thought of things to suit the wishes of their minds, and men do have a foreknowledge even in constructing their farms, and their buildings, and all other things that are connected with the pleasures of this life. And now, my dear brethren, we must acknowledge that God did foreknow what subjects would please him. And again, I fancy to say that predestination does not destroy the free will of men to act as agents for themselves; for when the employer hires his tenants he first intends to pay them, and that should make them more willing to work that they may be paid, and then predestination and free agency is united together.

Hark; God speaks by Isaiah in chapter 55th, 8th and 9th verses, in language like this: "For my thoughts are not your thoughts, neither are your ways my ways, saith the Lord; for as the heavens are higher than the earth, so are my ways higher than your ways, and my thoughts than your thoughts." Then let us express our highest gratitude to God who did foreknow what was his pleasure, and also what was his displeasure. O, hearken, before God created the visible things—the sun, and the moon, and the stars, and all the created objects—He did foreknow that His word was the purest of all the created objects and He glorified it; and God's Word is His only begotten Son, and it pleased God that in his Word all fullness should dwell. And again, we beheld His glory—the glory of the Only Begotten of the Father, full of grace and truth—and he was clothed with vesture dipped in blood, and His name was called the Word of God. And again, "For whom He did foreknow, He also did predestinate to be conformed to the image of His Son," for God did foreknow the objects of his choice. And again," whom He did predestinate them He also called" to partake of His divine nature: he also called us by His Son, that we should return from sin's destructive ways to perform the services of his own will, and again, this is the will of the Fattier that we might know Him and Jesus Christ whom He has sent to call us with a holy calling; and again; this is the call of His Son, "except ye repent ye shall all likewise perish."

But some do not understand this being chosen in God before the foundation of the world; but this was God's choice in His son, and His son came down from heaven to do his Father's will, and to make his glory known, yea the glory that was hid in the Father before the world was created. But some men say if they were chosen in God before the world was, that they will be saved whether they exercise faith or not, or whether they pray or not; but all such men will see that they had lost their first fellowship with God by the sins of their forefathers, and that Christ came down and bore the cross and shame to restore them to the fellowship of the Father by the gift of His divine nature, which is the love that was in God before the foundation of the world. And again, the love of God that is in Christ has the power, through faith, to re-make all the attributes of God's choice of that same love that was in God before the world was created. But these objects are not re-made or regenerated without faith in God. And again, I wish it to be understood that the scripture saith that without faith it is impossible to please God; and again, God has commanded all men every where to repent that they may partake of his divine nature; and again, before God did lay the foundation of the earth and the heavens he looked to see who could hold them up, but in the midst of all the created objects He saw none but His own Word, and He did make a vessel of honor and put His word therein, and He made it low into the form of a man that it might be near unto us, even in us, that we by obeying the truth might be stamped into the image of the only begotten of the Father. And again, Jesus did not sit still and say "my Father can save the people whether I die for them or not," but he said "it is meet that I should be about my Father's business;" and he should be our example. But these men that sit still and will not exercise faith in Christ are yet in darkness. Let us cast off the works of darkness by exercising faith in the Lord Jesus Christ, that we may receive his gracious promise of eternal life, even in his Son; and again, "behold what manner of love the Father hath bestowed upon us that we should be called the sons of God, and it doth not yet appear what we shall be, but we know that when he shall appear we shall be like him."

Now I fancy to say that in this I do see three creations of men, and that is this: the first Adam was made a living soul, and the second Adam was the Lord from heaven, and was the new man which was made by God's own word; and again, of His own will he hath begotten us again by the word of truth. For God does change the work of His hands, but God is the same, and his love changes not; but we shall be changed from glory to glory, for our last creation shall take place when Christ shall appear.

And now may the God of peace be with you all. Amen.

Joseph Baysmore, Raleigh Edwards, Broughton & Co., 1878

PETER RANDOLPH (1825-1897)

Introduction

In an address entitled, "A Baptist Most of You Readers Have Never Heard Of" Walter B. Shurden stated: "Peter Randolph ... made me aware that white Baptists must take their place at the feet of their African American Baptist sisters and brothers. We white folk must learn a different kind of Baptist history in America, one that is laced with unspeakable suffering and buoyed by unimaginable hope."

Details of Peter's life are found in the following account.

Sketches of Slave Life: Or, *Illustrations of the "Peculiar Institution"*
Preface

... The writer ... has known what it is to be a slave; and now that he has been set free, it is the ruling desire of his heart to do something, however feeble it may be, towards effecting the emancipation of the millions of his afflicted brethren, who are still held in the galling chains of bondage at the South. Remembering that he has never had any education, except such as he has been able to pick up for himself, the readers of this little work (especially in view of its object) will kindly overlook such errors of style as may be found in it.

The writer was formerly owned as a slave by one C. H. Edloe, of Prince George's County, Virginia, who also owned eighty others. His plantation was located on James River, in what was called upper Brandon. He always seemed to have some conscientious scruples in regard to holding slaves, and would not join any church, because "he did not believe he could be a Christian, and yet be a slaveholder." Six years before he died, he made his will, in which he set all his slaves free at his death, which took place July 29, 1844. This was truly a Christian act. More than three years passed away, however, before we obtained our liberty, when, being compelled to leave the State of Virginia, we came to Boston, (sixty-six in number,) Sept. 15, 1847, where we were received with Christian sympathy and kindness. Men, women and children, from twelve months to seventy-five years old, constituted our happy company. Some of these have gone the way of all the earth: the remainder continue in Massachusetts, and are proving to the world, by their conduct, that slaves, when liberated, can take care of themselves, and need no master or overseer to drive them to their toil. All that they need is— first, freedom—next, encouragement and a fair reward for their labor, and a suitable opportunity to improve themselves—without which, no people, black or white, can reasonably be expected to be industrious laborers or enlightened citizens.

May God hasten the day when not a slave shall be found in America, to water her soil with his tears, or stain it with his blood!

Peter Randolph, Boston, May 10, 1855

The blood of the slave

The blood of the slave cries unto God from the ground, and it calls loudly for vengeance on his adversaries.

The blood of the slave cries unto God from the rice swamps.

The blood of the slave cries unto God from the cotton plantations.

The blood of the slave cries unto God from the tobacco farms.

The blood of the slave cries unto God from the sugar fields.

The blood of the slave cries unto God from the corn fields.

The blood of the slave cries unto God from the whipping-post.

The blood of the slave cries unto God from the auction-block.

The blood of the slave cries unto God from the gallows.

The blood of the slave cries unto God from the hunting-dogs that run down the poor fugitive.

The blood of men, women and babes cries unto God from Texas to Maine. Wherever the Fugitive Slave Law reaches, the voice of its victims is heard.

The mighty God, the great Jehovah, speaks to the consciences of men, and says, "Let my people go free!"

And the slaveholder answers, "Who is Jehovah, that we should obey him?"

Then the Anti-Slavery voice is heard, calling, Awake! Awake! and cry aloud against this great evil; lift up your voice like a trumpet, and show the people their sins, and the nation its guilt. Pray that God may have mercy upon us. O, forgive us this great evil,—the evil of selling, whipping, and killing men, women and children! O, God of justice! give us hearts and consciences to feel the deep sorrows of this great evil that we have so long indulged in! Lo! we have sinned against Heaven; we have sinned against light,—against the civilized world. We have sinned against that declaration which our fathers put forth to the world, "All men are created equal."

O God! forgive us this great sin! O let this prayer be heard!

Slaves on the auction block

The auctioneer is crying the slave to the highest bidder. "Gentlemen, here is a very fine boy for sale. He is worth twelve hundred dollars. His name is Emanuel. He belongs to Dea. William Harrison, who wants to sell him because his overseer don't like him. How much, gentlemen—how much for this boy? He's a fine, hearty nigger. Bid up, bid up, gentlemen; he must be sold." Some come up to look at him, pull open his mouth to examine his teeth, and see if they are good. Poor fellow! he is handled and examined like any piece of merchandize; but he must bear it. Neither tongue nor hand, nor any other member, is his own,—why should he attempt to use another's property?

Again the bidding goes on: "I will give one thousand dollars for that boy." The auctioneer says, "Sir, he is worth twelve hundred at the lowest. Bid up, gentlemen, bid up; going, going—are you all done?—once, twice, three times—all done?—GONE!"

See the slaveholder, who just bought the image of God, come to his victim, and take possession of him. Poor Emanuel must go away from his wife, never to see her again. All the ties of love are severed; the declaration of the Almighty, which said, "What God hath joined together, let not man put asunder," is unheeded, and he must leave all to follow his Christian master,—a member of the Episcopal Church,—a partaker, from time to time, of the Lord's sacrament! Such men mock religion and insult God. O that God would rend the heavens, and appear unto these heartless men!

Next come Jenny and her five children. Her husband was sold and gone. The oldest of her children is a girl seventeen years old,—her name, Lucy.

Auctioneer—"Here, gentlemen, is a fine girl for sale: how much for her? Gentlemen, she will be a fortune for any one who buys her that wants to raise niggers. Bid up gentlemen, bid up! Fine girl; very hearty; good health; only seventeen years old; she's worth fifteen hundred dollars to any one who wants to raise niggers. Here's her mother; she's had nine children; the rest of them are sold. How much, gentlemen,—how much? Bid up! bid up!"

Poor Lucy is sold away from all the loved ones, and goes to receive the worst of insults from her cruel taskmaster. Her poor mother stands by heart-broken, with tears streaming down her face. O! is there a heart not all brutish, that can witness such a scene without falling to the earth with shame, that the rights of his fellow-creatures are so basely trampled upon? The seller or buyer of a human being, for purposes of slavery, is not human, and has no right to the name.

Harry

The next "article" sold is Harry, a boy of fifteen.

Auctioneer—"Gentlemen, how much for this boy? He is an honest boy, can be trusted with any thing you wish; how much for him?"

Harry is sold from his mother, who is standing watching for her turn. She began to scream out, "O, my child! my child!" Here the old slaveholder said, "Ah my girl, if you do not stop that hollering, I will give you something to holler for." Poor Jenny, the mother, tried to suppress her grief, but all in vain. Harry was gone, and the children cried out, "Good by, Harry; good by!" The broken-hearted mother sobbed forth, "Farewell, my boy; try to meet me in heaven."

The next of the children was Mary. She was put upon the block and sold. Then the mother became so much affected that she seemed like one crazy. So the old rough slaveholder went to the mother, and began to lay the lash upon her; but it mattered not to her—her little Mary was gone, and now her turn had come. O, mothers, who sit in your comfortable homes, surrounded by your happy children, think of the poor slave mother, robbed so cruelly of her all by a fate worse than death! O, think of her, pray for her, toil for her, even; teach your blooming daughters to think with compassion of their far-off colored sisters, and train them up anti-slavery women! Teach your sons the woes and burning wrongs of slavery; make them grow up earnest, hard-working anti-slavery men. When mothers all do this, we may hope yet to live in a free country.

Wretched, childless, widowed Jenny was placed upon the block for sale.

Auctioneer—"Gentlemen, here is Jenny,—how much for her? She can do good work. Now, gentlemen, her master says he believes her to be a Christian, a very pious old woman; and she will keep every thing straight around her. You may depend on her. She will neither lie nor steal: what she says may be believed. Just let her pray, and she will keep right."

Here Jesus Christ was sold to the highest bidder; sold in Jenny to keep her honest, to bring gold to the slaveholder. Jenny was sold away from all her little children, never to see them again. Poor mother! who had toiled day and night to raise her little children, feeling all a mother's affection for them, she must see them no more in this world! She feels like great mourning,—"like Rachel weeping for her children, and would not be comforted, because they were not." So she commends them to the care of the God of the widow and the fatherless, by bathing her bosom in tears, and giving them the last affectionate embrace, with the advice to meet her in heaven. O, the tears of the poor slave that are in bottles, to be poured out upon this blood- stained nation, as soon as the cup of wrath of the almighty Avenger is full, when He shall say, "I have heard the groanings of my people, and I will deliver them from the oppressor!"

Slaveholders carry the price of blood upon their backs and in their pockets; the very bread they eat is the price of blood; the houses they live in are bought with blood; all the education they have is paid for by the blood and sorrows of the poor slaves.

In parting with their friends at the auction-block, the poor blacks have the anticipation of meeting them again in the heavenly Canaan, and sing—

O fare you well, O fare you well,
God bless you until me meet again;
Hope to meet you in heaven, to part no more.

Chorus
Sisters fare you well; sisters, fare you well;
God Almighty bless you, until we meet again.

Among the slaves, there is a great amount of talent, given by the hand of inspiration; talent, too, which, if cultivated, would be of great benefit to the world of mankind. If these large minds are kept sealed up, so that they cannot answer the end for which they were made, somebody must answer for it on the great day of account. O think of this, my readers! Think of that great day when it shall be said to all the world, "Give an account of thy stewardship!" Among the slaves may be found talents which, if improved, would be instrumental in carrying the blessed Gospel of truth to distant lands, and in bringing the people to acknowledge the true and living God. But all has been crushed down by a Christian world, and by the Christian Church. With these solemn facts written against this nation, see to it, my readers, before this iniquity overthrow you, and it be too late to repent.

The sin of holding slaves is not only against one nation, but against the whole world, because we are here to do one another good, in treating each other well; and this is to be done by having right ideas of God and his religion. But this privilege is denied to three millions and a half of the people of this our own "free" land. The slaveholders say we have not a true knowledge of religion; but the great Teacher said, when he came on his mission, "The spirit of the Lord is upon me, because he hath anointed me to preach the gospel to the poor. He hath sent me to heal the broken-hearted; to preach deliverance to the captive, and recovering of sight to the blind; to set at liberty them that are bruised, and to preach the acceptable year of the Lord." This ought to be the work of the ministers and the churches. Any thing short of this is not the true religion of Jesus.

This is the great command of the New Testament—"Love the Lord thy God with all thy heart, and thy neighbor as thyself." "Do unto others as ye would that they should do to you," is the golden rule for all men to follow. By this rule shall all men be judged. We have got to hear, "Come, ye blessed; depart, ye cursed!" These are my convictions, and my belief of the religion of Jesus, the wonderful Counselor of the children of the created Adam, our great progenitor.

This I respectfully submit to my readers, and earnestly beg of them to renew their interest in the anti-slavery cause, never turning a deaf ear to the pleadings of the poor slave, or to those who speak, however feebly, for him. The antislavery cause is the cause of humanity, the cause of religion, the cause of God!

Slaves on the plantation: colored drivers

The colored overseers are not over the slaves because they wish it, but are made so against their will. When they first commence to lash the backs of their fellows, they are like soldiers when they first go to the battle-field; they dread and fear the contest, until they hear the roaring of the cannon, and smell the powder, and mark the whizzing ball; then they rush into the battle, forgetful of all human sympathy while in the fight. So it is with the slave-drivers. They bear the angry tones of the slaveholder's voice, admonishing them that if they refuse to whip, they must take it themselves. After receiving the instructions of their owners, they must forget even their own wives and children, and do all they can for "Master." If they do not do this, they must receive all that would be given the others. In this manner, their hearts and consciences are hardened, and they become educated to whipping, and lose all human feeling.

This is the way the slaveholders take to hide their own wickedness. They say the colored driver is more cruel than the white overseer, and use this as an argument against the poor colored man, to show how cruelly they would treat each other if they had the power. Pardon me, my readers, if I say this is an insult to God; since my own experience teaches me better. Reader, when they say that colored drivers are worse than white, the question may well be asked, Why is this? Is it the fault of the colored people, or is it the fault of the white man? Good sense answers to every thinking mind, and says the poor Negro is not the greatest transgressor here, but the white men are the tyrannical instigators of this wrong.

It is said that the slaves love their masters so much, it is a sin to disturb their peace and harmony. This is as false as the institution itself. To illustrate, let me name one fact, and you will see how the slaves love their masters. There was my uncle Tom, who was owned by Mr. George Harrison, the owner of—Brandon. Uncle Tom, being his head plougher, ploughed wrong one day; so Harrison came to Uncle Tom, and began to beat him very brutally. To escape the whipping, Uncle Tom cried out, (it showed his love for his master!) "Do, pray, my master, don't fret so; I am afraid you will be sick." It is said the slaves will not leave their masters, they are treated so well. All I have to say is, give them an opportunity, and then see how close they will stick to their beloved masters.

It is also said, that they have the true gospel preached to them. If this were true, all slaves would be free, and think and act for themselves. Sail on, sail on, sweet times, and let the poor slaves go free!

Customs of the slaves, when one of their number dies
They go to the overseer, and obtain leave to sit up all night with their dead, and sing and pray. This is a very solemn season. First, one sings and another prays, and this they continue every night until the dead body is buried. One of the slaves makes the coffin,—and a very bad one it generally is. Some wheat straw is put in the coffin, and if they can get it, they wrap the body in a piece of white cloth; if they cannot get it, they put the body in the coffin without anything around it. Then they nail up the coffin, and put it in a cart, which is drawn by oxen or mules, and carried to the grave. As they have no tombs, they put all the slaves in the earth. If the slave who died was a Christian, the rest of the Christians among them feel very glad, and thank God that brother Charles, or brother Ned, or sister Betsey, is at last free, and gone home to heaven,—where bondage is never known. Some, who are left behind, cry and grieve that they, too, cannot die, and throw off their yoke of slavery, and join the company of the brother or sister who has just gone.

When the overseer is in good humor, he will let all the people go to look the last time upon their relative; if he is ill-tempered, he will not let the slaves go at all; so it all depends upon the state of mind the overseer is in, whether the child is permitted to look upon the remains of its parent, the husband upon his wife, the mother upon her child, or any other dear relative. Ah! my readers! think of this, and see the cruelty of the "peculiar institution." Slaves have tender human feelings,—very warm and tender they are; but it matters not how sorrowful and heavy a heart the poor Negro may have, he cannot see his lifeless friends, unless the slaveholder wills it.

When several of the slaves die together, the others go to their owner, and ask him to let them have a funeral. Most of the owners will grant their slaves this privilege. When the owner and overseer give their consent, the slaveholder sends a note to a white preacher; then they set the day, and then the slaves make ready for the funeral services over their friends.

The slaves go to the woods, and make seats to sit upon, (this is done Saturday night.) When the seats are prepared, they are left till the slaves take their seats upon them, and sit until about ten o'clock, when the slaveholding minister comes, and preaches about one hour and a half Then he gives the Negroes liberty to sing and pray, and he stands by them. This is to keep the slaves from their master, because they are not allowed to meet together, except a white man be present. At the funeral, all the slaves from the adjoining plantations obtain passes from their overseers, and come; so this is really a great day for the poor blacks to see each other. If their hearts are sad, they are happy to see their friends, and they all go to some place, and their friends receive such entertainment as it is in their power to give. They stay together till night draws on, and then each leaves for his home. As soon as possible after the funeral, the slaves must go to their work. They have no person to speak a word of comfort to them, to cheer their heavy hearts; but they must go on working and mourning all the day and night. If they had some one to sympathize with them, their burden would be lightened;

but no one cares for the tears of the widow, the sighs of the disconsolate husband, the sobbing cries of the mother, whose little son or daughter has been taken from her. No one pities the widow's son, that his mother (who labored all her life for the slaveholder, and for her son, when she could get an opportunity) is gone to the grave, leaving her only one behind, to toil on yet longer beneath the lash of tyrant overseers, and at the mercy of unfeeling slaveholders. Ah! my readers! even in the grave there is more comfort to the sad ones afflicted, than in the prison-house of hopeless slavery. Once, oh Northern reader! visit the auction-block, and all that is human within your soul will be aroused, and you will feel and know what American slavery is.

House slaves

When the slave-master owns a great many slaves, ten or a dozen are always employed to wait on himself and family. These are not treated as cruelly as the field slaves; they are better fed and wear better clothing, because the master and his family always expect to have strangers visit them, and they want their servants to look well. These slaves eat from their master's table, wear broadcloth and calico; they wear ruffled-bosomed shirts, too,—such as Doctor Nehemiah Adams declares he saw while on his visit to the South, where he became so much in love with the "peculiar institution." These slaves, although dressed and fed better than others, have to suffer alike with those whose outward condition is worse. They are much to be compared to galvanized watches, which shine and resemble gold, but are far from being the true metal; so with these slaves who wait upon their masters at table—their broadcloth and calico look fine, but you may examine their persons, and find many a lash upon their flesh. They are sure of their whippings, and are sold the same as others.

Sometimes their masters change, and put them on the farm, that the overseers may whip them. Among those who wait upon the master, there is always one to watch the others, and report them to him. This slave is treated as well as his master, because it is for the master's interest that be does this. This slave he always carries with him, when he visits the North; particularly, such slaves as cannot be made to leave their master, because they are their master's watch-dog at home. So master can trust them. Before leaving, master always talks very kindly to them, and promises something very great for a present, if they are true to him until his return.

These slaves know what they must say when asked as to their treatment at home, and of the treatment of their fellows. They leave their wives, their mothers, brothers and sisters, and children, toiling and being driven and whipped by the overseer, and tortured and insulted on every occasion.

Deception of the slaveholder

All the slaves, as well as their owners, are addicted to drinking; so when the slaveholder wants to make a show of his niggers, (as he calls them,) he gives them rum to drink.

When the master knows a Northern man is to visit him, he gives orders to the overseer, and the overseer orders every slave to dress himself, and appear on the field. If the slaves have any best, they must put it on. Perhaps a man has worked hard, extra times all the year, and got his wife a fourpenny gown,—she must put it on, and go to the field to work. About the time the stranger is expected, a jug of rum is sent to the field, and every slave has just enough given him to have him act as if he was crazy.

When such a stranger as the Reverend Doctor Adams appears with the master, he does not see the Negroes, but the rum that is in them; and when he hears their hurrah, and sees their Jim-Crow actions, he takes it for granted that they are as happy as need be, and their condition could not be bettered.

The owner gives the visitor liberty to ask his "niggers" questions. He will ask them if they love their master, or wish to leave him. Poor slave will say, he would not leave his master for the world; but O, my reader! just let the poor slave get off and he would be in Canada very soon, where the slaveholder dare not venture.

The slaves do not speak for themselves. The slave-holding master and his rum are working in their heads, speaking for slavery; and this is the way the slaveholder deceives his friend from the North.

Food and clothing

I shall now show what the slaves have to eat and wear. They have one pair of shoes for the year; if these are worn out in two months, they get no more that year, but must go barefooted the rest of the year, through cold and heat. The shoes are very poor ones, made by one of the slaves, and do not last more than two or three months. One pair of stockings is allowed them for the year; when these are gone, they have no more, although it is cold in Virginia for five months. They have one suit of clothes for the year. This is very poor, indeed; and made by the slaves themselves on the plantation. It will not last more than three months, and then the poor slave gets no more from the slaveholder, if he go naked. This suit consists of one shirt, one pair of pants, one pair of socks, one pair of shoes, and no vest at all. The slave has a hat given him once in two years; when this is worn out, he gets no more from the slaveholder, but must go bareheaded till he can get one somewhere else. Perhaps the slave will get him a skin of some kind, and make him a hat.

The food of the slave is this: Every Saturday night they receive two pounds of bacon, and one peck and a half of corn meal, to last the men through the week. The women have one half pound of meat, and one peck of meal, and the children one half peck each. When this is gone, they can have no more till the end of the week. This is very little food for the slaves. They have to beg when they can; when they cannot, they must suffer. They are not allowed to go off the plantation; if they do, and are caught, they are whipped very severely, and what they have begged is taken from them.

The hours for work

The slave goes to his work when he sees the daybreak in the morning, and works until dark at night. The slaves have their food carried to them in the field; they have one half hour to eat it in, in the winter, and one hour in the summer. Their time for eating is about eight in the morning, and one in the afternoon. Sometimes, they have not so much time given to them. The overseer stands by them until they have eaten, and then he orders them to work

The slaves return to their huts at night, make their little fires, and lie down until they are awakened for another day of toil. No beds are given them to sleep on; if they have any, they find themselves. The women and the men all have to work on the farms together; they must fare alike in slavery. Husbands and wives must see all that happens to each other, and witness the sufferings of each. They must see their children polluted, without the power to prevent it.

How the slaves contrive to get food

There are some animals in Virginia called raccoons, possums, old hares, and squirrels. The best of these is the possum, which lives in old trees and in the earth. The slave sets his traps in the swamps, where the possum usually lives. The traps are made by cutting down trees, and cutting them in short pieces about five feet long; then they raise the log on three pieces of sticks, like the figure four. These traps are made on the Sabbath. One slave will sometimes have fifteen or twenty of them, and will go at night, with his torch of pitch-pine, and see if his traps have caught anything for him to eat. Sometimes he finds a possum and a raccoon; and sometimes a squirrel and old hare. This old hare is something like a rabbit. All of these little animals are good food for the poor slave, and make him feel very glad that he has them to eat. Some of the slaves hunt these animals with dogs, trained for the purpose. They run them up the trees in the forest, where, as they are a harmless animal, they can be taken very easily. They do not fight very hard when caught, but are very easily overcome; but they are a very deceitful little animal. They will lie on the ground, and make you think they are dead; but if you leave them, they will creep off so soon, that you cannot conceive how the little animal got away so cute. The only way they can be kept safely is to be put in a bag, or in a basket with a cover. The slave knows best when to hunt these creatures. The best time is just at the rise of the tide in the rivers. There is another method that the slave takes to get his food. He makes what is called a fish-trap. This is made by cutting white oak wood into very small strips, which are tied together with a great deal of ingenuity. This trap is put in very deep water, and attended by the slaves at night, and on the Sabbath, (this being all the time they have to attend to their traps;) and very glad are they of this opportunity of getting some nice fish. Oftentimes the overseer will take what he wants for his own use, and the slaves must submit.

There are some little fruits in Virginia, that are called "simmons"; they grow very plentifully, and are sweet and good. The slaves get them in the fall of the year, then they get a barrel and put the "simmons" into it, and put water there too, and something else that grow on trees, that they call "locusses," which are about ten inches long, and two across. They put the "locusses" and "simmons" into the water together, and let them stand for two or three days. Then the water is drained off, and the leaves are used as you would use coffee. The slaves put the liquid in gourds, and carry it to the field with them, and drink out of the gourds while they eat their bread.

Flogging

For whipping the slaves in Virginia, there are no rules. The slave receives from the slaveholder from fifty to five hundred lashes. The slave-owner would think fifty stripes an insult to the slave. If the slave is let off with fifty lashes, he must show a very good temper. Men, women, and children must be whipped alike on their bare backs, it being considered an honor to whip them over their clothes. The slaves are placed in a certain position when they are flogged, with sufficient management to hold them very still, so they cannot work their hands or feet, while they are "wooding them up," as they call it in Virginia.

Some of the slaves have to lie down on their stomachs, flat on the ground, and be stretched out so as to keep their skin tight for the lash, and thus lie until they receive as much as they choose to put on; if they move, they must receive so many lashes extra. When the slaveholder expects to give his slave five hundred lashes, he gives him about half at a time; then washes him down with salt and water, and then gives him the remainder of what he is to have. At such times, the slave-owner has his different liquors to drink, while he is engaged in draining the blood of the slave. So he continues to drink his rum and whip his victim. When he does not flog his victims on the ground, they are tied by their hands, and swung up to a great tree, just so the end of their toes may touch the ground. In this way, they receive what number of lashes they are destined to. The master has straw brought, that the blood may not touch his shoes. Ah, reader! this is true, every word of it:—the poor slave is whipped till the blood runs down to the earth, and then he must work. all the day, cold or hot, from week's end to week's end. There are hundreds of slaves that have not the same skin they were born with.

Overseers

The first overseer I served under was Henry Hallingwork, a cruel and a bad man. He often whipped my mother and the children, and worked the slaves almost day and night, in all weather. The men had no comfort with their wives, for any of the latter who pleased him, he would take from their husbands, and use himself. If any refused his lewd embraces, he treated them with the utmost barbarity. At night, he watched their huts, to find out if the slaves said anything against him, or had any food except what he had allowed them; and he if discovered anything he disliked, they were severely whipped. He continued this conduct for about three years, when Mr. Edloe discovered it, and discharged him.

The next overseer who lived on the plantation did not treat the people so badly as did Hallingwork, but he drove them very hard, and watched them very closely, to see that they took nothing but their allowance. He only lived there two years, when he was discharged for misconduct.

The next overseer, a man named Harris, only remained about six months; his cruelty was so great, it came to Mr. Edloe's ear, and he was discharged.

The successor of Harris was L. Hobbs. He was very cruel to the people, especially to all women who would not submit to him. He used to bind women hand and foot, and whip them until the blood run down to the earth, and then wash them down in salt and water, and keep them tied all day, when Edloe was not at home. He used to take my cousin, and tie her up and whip her so she could not lie down to rest at night until her back got well. All this was done on Edloe's plantation, the good slaveholder who owned me; and the other slaveholders used to say to him that he "spoiled his niggers;"—but this was the way he spoiled them. Hobbs continued this ill-treatment for the space of three years, then he was turned off. Thus ends the history of Hobbs on Edloe's plantation, with the exception of leaving what are termed "mulattoes" in Virginia.

The fifth overseer was B. F. Buship. He came to the plantation as a tyrant, and proved himself such to men, women and children. He reigned tyrannically for one year, and did many things which decency will not permit me to speak of. He, and all of the overseers, were in the habit of stealing from their employer, and the colored people knew it, but their informing Edloe would have done no good, for he could not believe a slave. According to the laws of Virginia, the testimony of a slave against an overseer could not be taken. This Benj. Buship reigned "monarch of all he surveyed" (doing as he chose in every thing—cruel as cruel could be) one year, when he was discharged.

The sixth overseer was R. Lacy, a native of Charles City, Va. He reigned seven years. I cannot describe to my readers the malice and madness with which this being treated Edloe's slaves. You cannot find his parallel in history, except it be in Nero or Caligula. Indeed, he was a very wicked man, and a great hypocrite. I cannot point to one good deed he ever performed. He would enter the houses, and bind men and women, and inflict torture upon them, whether innocent or guilty. The blood of innocent slaves is yet crying to the God of justice to avenge their sufferings, and pour out deserved judgment upon the head of Lacy.

The seventh overseer was P. Vaughn. He was cruel, but not so much so as some of the others had been. He was too fond of rum and the females, so Edloe gave him his walking ticket.

The eighth overseer was J. G. Harrison. He was with Mr. Edloe at the time of his decease. Harrison was, like others in his station, hard and unmerciful. He made his dogs tear and bite my mother very badly. She died soon after, and was freed from her tormentors, at rest from her labors, and rejoicing in heaven.

This same Harrison shot one of Edloe's men, because he would not submit to the lash; but no one said anything to Harrison about his conduct. (He did not kill the man. Although shot, he is now living in Charlestown, Mass. His name is Wyatt Lee. He is well known in Boston.)

About this time, Edloe died, leaving a will by which all his slaves were to receive their freedom. His death took place the 29th of July, 1844. He appointed an executor to settle his estate, but he did not act in accordance with the wilt of Edloe. He kept the people on the plantation three years and thirty-five days after the death of the owner. He was very unjust. All the slaves earned was taken away by him; some of them he put in jail, and some were obliged to run away from the plantation.

At this period, some friend advised us to sue for our freedom, and we commenced the suit against the estate, but, like everything else, it went very hard with us. Our lawyer deceived us, and got our money, but did not get our freedom. We were at a loss what to do, but finally we went to Mr. Wm. B. Harrison, the owner of L. Brandon. This man owned a great many slaves, but he got our free papers for us. This was on Sept. 5th, 1847,—more than three years after the death of Edloe. A vessel was employed to bring sixty-six of us to Boston. Some went to Philadelphia, and some were kept on the plantation, where they remain, the victims of cruel slavery. Such bad reports were made respecting the free States, that they were afraid to come here, even to be free.

My own history

Having briefly given the history of the overseers, I will now give my own, and how I, a slave, learned to read and write. Edloe owned eighty-one slaves, and among them all, only myself could either read or write. When I was a child, my mother used to tell me to look to Jesus, and that he who protected the widow and fatherless would take care of me also. At that time, my ideas of Jesus were the same as those of the other slaves. I thought he would talk with me, if I wished it, and give me what I asked for. Being very sickly, my greatest wish was to live with Christ in heaven, and so I used to go into the woods and lie upon my back, and pray that he would come and take me to himself,—really expecting to see Him with my bodily eyes. I was then between ten and eleven years old, and I continued to look for Him until I began to feel very sorry that He would not come and talk with me; and then I felt that I was the worst little boy that ever lived, and that was the reason Jesus would not talk to me. I felt so about it, I wanted to die, and thought it would be just in God to kill me, and I prayed that he would kill me, for I did not want to live to sin against him any more. I felt so for many days and nights. At last, I gave myself up to the Lord, to do what he would with me, for I was a great sinner. I began to see the offended justice of God. O! my readers, the anguish of my heart! I thought the whole world was on me, and I must die and be lost. In the midst of my troubles, I felt that if God would have mercy on me, I should never sin again. When I had come to this, I felt my guilt give way, and thought that I was a new being. Now, instead of looking with my real eyes to see my Savior, I felt him in me, and I was happy. The eyes of my mind were open, and I saw things as I never did before. With my mind's eye, I could see my Redeemer hanging upon the cross for me.

I wanted all the other slaves to see him thus, and feel as happy as I did. I used to talk to others, and tell them of the friend they would have in Jesus, and show them by my experience how I was brought to Christ, and felt his love within my heart,—and love it was, in God's adapting himself to my capacity.

After receiving this revelation from the Lord, I became impressed that I was called of God to preach to the other slaves. I labored under this impression for seven years, but then I could not read the Bible, and I thought I could never preach unless I learned to read the Bible, but I had no one to teach me how to read. A friend showed me the letters, and how to spell words of three letters. Then I continued, until I got so as to read the Bible,—the great book of God,—the source of all knowledge. It was my great desire to read easily this book. I thought it was written by the Almighty himself. I loved this book, and prayed over it and labored until I could read it. I used to go to the church to hear the white preacher. When I heard him read his text, I would read mine when I got borne. This is the way, my readers, I learned to read the Word of God when I was a slave. Thus did I labor eleven years under the impression that I was called to preach the gospel of Jesus Christ, the ever-blessed God.

Then I learned to write. Here I had no teaching; but I obtained a book with the writing alphabet in it. I copied the letters until I could write. I had no slate, so I used to write on the ground. All by myself I learned the art of writing. Then I used to do my own letter-writing, and write my own pass. When the slave wants to go from one plantation to another, he must have a pass from the overseer. I could do my own writing unbeknown to the overseer, and carry my own pass.

My oldest brother's name was Benjamin. He was owned by C. H. Edloe, the same person who owned me. Benjamin was a very bright young man, and very active about his work. He was fond of laughing and frolicking with the young women on the plantation. This Lacy, the overseer, did not like; and therefore was always watching Benjamin, seeking an occasion to have him whipped. At one time, a pig had been found dead. The little pig could not tell why he was dead, and no one confessed a knowledge of his death; consequently, Lacy thought so great a calamity, so important a death, should be revenged. He advised Edloe to have every slave whipped. Edloe consented, expecting, probably, to prevent, by such cruelty, any other pig from dying a natural death. Lacy, the tender-hearted overseer, with a heart overflowing with sorrow at the great loss and sad bereavement of Edloe's plantation, took his rawhide, with a wire attached to the end of it, and gave each man twenty lashes on the bare back. O, monster! the blood was seen upon the side of the barn where these slaves were whipped for days and months. The wounds of these poor creatures prevented them from performing their daily tasks. They were, indeed, so cut up, that pieces came out of the backs of some of them, so that a child twelve or thirteen years old could lay his fist in the cruel place, My brother Benjamin was one of the slaves so savagely beaten. One morning, Lacy—perhaps thinking piggy's death not wholly avenged—proposed again to whip my brother; but Benjamin did not agree with him as to the necessity of such proceedings, and determined not to submit; therefore, he turned his back upon Lacy, and his face to the woods, making all possible speed towards the latter. Lacy fired upon him, but only sent a few shot into his flesh, which did not in the least frighten Benjamin; it only served to make him run as fast as if he himself had been shot from the overseer's gun. For seven months, he lived in the swamps of Virginia, while every effort was made to catch him, but without success. He once ventured on board a vessel on James River. There he was caught, but soon made his escape again to the swamp, where my mother and myself used to carry him such food as we could procure to keep him alive. My poor broken-hearted mother was always weeping and praying about Benjamin, for the overseer had threatened that if he ever saw him, he would shoot him, as quick as he would a wild deer. All the other overseers had made the same threats.

Edloe, not thinking it best to take Benjamin on to his plantation, (provided be could catch him,) sold him to another man, who, after he bad succeeded in his sham plan of buying my poor brother, sent for him to come out of the swamp and go with him. Benjamin went home to his new master, and went faithfully to work for him,—smart young man that he was!

Sometimes, Benjamin would steal over at night to see mother, (a distance of ten miles.) He could not come in the day-time, because Lacy still declared he would kill him the first time he saw him. He did see him one Sabbath, but having no gun or pistol with him, my brother again escaped him, thanks to the mercies of God. Benjamin continued to serve his new master, until he was suddenly bound and carried to Petersburgh, Virginia, and sold to a trader-trader, who put him in a slave-pen, until a large number of slaves were bought up by him, to be carried into bondage further South, there to lead miserable lives on the cotton and sugar plantations. Benjamin, my dear brother, left Petersburgh, and I have not seen him since. Thanks be unto God, prayer can ascend, and will be listened to by Him who answereth prayer! To him who crieth unto Him day and night, he will listen, and send His angel of peace to quiet his troubled heart, with the assurance that the down-trodden shall be lifted up, the oppressed shall be delivered from his oppressor, all captives set free, and all oppressors destroyed, as in ancient times. I know that God heard the prayers of my praying mother, because she was a Christian, and a widow, such as feared God and loved his commandments. She used often to sing the following hymn:—

Our days began with trouble here,
Our lives are but a span,
While cruel death is always near—
What a feeble thing is man!

Then sow the seed of grace while young,
That when you come to die,
You may sing the triumphant song,
Death! where's thy victory?

With the above lines has my mother often soothed, for a time, her own sorrows, when she thought of her poor son, so far away from her, she knew not where, neither could she know of his sufferings; and again, she would become a prey to bitter grief. Her only hope was to meet her son in heaven, where slaveholders could not come with their purchase-money, where Lacy could not come with his dogs, his guns, or his pistols, with powder or balls; neither would she have to steal away to see him, with a little food well concealed. Neither will Benjamin be obliged to crouch in the forest, hearing the midnight cry of wild beasts around him, while he seeks repose upon the cold, bare ground. No, she will meet him at the right hand of the Redeemer, who will wipe the briny tears from the eyes of the poor slave, and feed him with the hidden treasures of His love.

Sabbath and religious meetings
After doing their morning work, and breakfast over, (such as it is,) that portion of them belonging to the church ask of the overseer permission to attend meeting. If he is in the mood to grant their request, he writes them a pass, as follows:—

Permit the bearer to pass and repass to—, this evening, unmolested.

Should a pass not be granted, the slave lies down, and sleeps for the day—the only way to drown his sorrow and disappointment.

Others of the slaves, who do not belong to the church, spend their Sabbath in playing with marbles, and other games, for each other's food, &c.

Some occupy the time in dancing to the music of a banjo, made out of a large gourd. This is continued till the after part of the day, when they separate, and gather wood for their log-cabin fires the ensuing week.

Not being allowed to hold meetings on the plantation, the slaves assemble in the swamps, out of reach of the patrols. They have an understanding among themselves as to the time and place of getting together. This is often done by the first one arriving breaking boughs from the trees, and bending them in the direction of the selected spot. Arrangements are then made for conducting the exercises. They first ask each other how they feel, the state of their minds, &c. The male members then select a certain space, in separate groups, for their division of the meeting. Preaching in order, by the brethren; then praying and singing all round, until they generally feel quite happy. The speaker usually commences by calling himself unworthy, and talks very slowly, until, feeling the spirit, he grows excited, and in a short time, there fall to the ground twenty or thirty men and women under its influence. Enlightened people call it excitement; but I wish the same was felt by everybody, so far as they are sincere.

The slave forgets all his sufferings, except to remind others of the trials during the past week, exclaiming: "Thank God, I shall not live here always!" Then they pass from one to another, shaking hands, and bidding each other farewell, promising, should they meet no more on earth, to strive and meet in heaven, where all is joy, happiness and liberty. As they separate, they sing a parting hymn of praise.

Sometimes the slaves meet in an old log-cabin, when they find it necessary to keep a watch. If discovered, they escape, if possible; but those who are caught often get whipped. Some are willing to be punished thus for Jesus' sake. Most of the songs used in worship are composed by the slaves themselves, and describe. their own sufferings. Thus:—

O, that I had a bosom friend,
To tell my secrets to,
One always to depend upon
In everything I do!
How I do wander, up and down;
I seem a stranger, quite undone;
None to lend an ear to my complaint,
No one to cheer me, though I faint.

Some of the slaves sing—

No more rain, no more snow,
No more cowskin on my back;

then they change it by singing—

Glory be to God that rules on high.

In some places, if the slaves are caught praying to God, they are whipped more than if they had committed a great crime. The slaveholders will allow the slaves to dance, but do not want them to pray to God. Sometimes, when a slave, on being whipped, calls upon God, he is forbidden to do so, under threat of having his throat cut, or brains blown out. O, reader! this seems very hard,—that slaves cannot call on their Maker, when the case most needs it. Sometimes the poor slave takes courage to ask his master to let him pray, and is driven away with the answer, that if discovered praying, his back will pay the bill.

Mr. James L. Goltney was a Baptist preacher, and was employed by Mr. M. B. Harrison to give religious instruction to his slaves. He often used the common text: "Servants, obey your masters." He would try to make it appear that he knew what the slaves were thinking of,—telling them they thought they had a right to be free, but he could tell them better,— referring them to some passages of Scripture. "It is the devil," he would say, "who tells you to try and be free." And again he bid them be patient at work, warning them that it would be his duty to whip them, if they appeared dissatisfied,—all which would be pleasing to God! "If you run away, you will be turned out of God's church, until you repent, return, and ask God and your master's pardon." In this way he would continue to preach his slave-holding gospel.

This same Goltney used to administer the Lord's Supper to the slaves. After such preaching, let no one say that the slaves have the Gospel of Jesus preached to them.

One of the Baptist ministers was named B. Harrison. He owned slaves, and was very cruel to them. He came to an untimely end. While he was riding out one afternoon, the report of a gun was heard, and he was found dead,—his brains being blown out. It could never be found who killed him, and so he went to judgment, with all his sins on his head.

Mr. L. Hanner was a Christian preacher, selecting texts like the following: "The Spirit of the Lord is upon me, because he hath anointed me to preach deliverance to the captives, he hath sent me to bind up the broken-hearted." But Hanner was soon mobbed out of Prince George's County, and had to flee for his life, and all for preaching a true Gospel to colored people.

I did not know of any other denomination where I lived in Virginia, than the Baptists and Presbyterians. Most of the colored people, and many of the poorer class of whites, are Baptists.

My parents

When my father died, he left my mother with five children. We were all young at the time, and mother had no one to help take care or us. Her lot was very hard indeed. She had to work all the day for her owner, and at night for those who were dearer to her than life; for what was allowed her by Edloe was not sufficient for our wants. She used to get a little corn, without his knowledge, and boil it for us to satisfy our hunger. As for clothing, Edloe would give us a coarse suit once in three years; mother sometimes would beg the cast-off garments from the neighbors, to cover our nakedness; and when they had none to give, she would sit and cry over us, and pray to the God of the widow and fatherless for help and succor. At last, my oldest brother was sold from her, and carried where she never saw him again. She went mourning for him all her days, like a bird robbed of her young,—like Rachel bereft of her children, who would not be comforted, because they were not. She departed this life on the 27th of September, 1847, for that world "where the wicked cease from troubling, and the weary tire at rest."

My father did not belong to Edloe, but was owned by a Mr. George Harrison, whose plantation adjoined that of my master. Harrison made my father a slave-driver, placing an overseer over him. He was allowed to visit my mother every Wednesday and every Saturday night. This was the time usually given to the slaves to see their wives. My father would often tell my mother how the white overseer had made him cruelly whip his fellows, until the blood ran down to the ground. All his days he had to follow this dreadful employment of flogging men, women and children, being placed in this helpless condition by the tyranny of his master. I used to think very hard of my father, and that he was a very cruel man; but when I knew that he could not help himself, I could not but alter my views and feelings in regard to his conduct. I was ten years old when he died.

The sufferings of Christ

The slaves talk much of the sufferings of Christ; and oftentimes, when they are called to suffer at the hands of their cruel overseers, they think of what he endured, and derive patience and consolation from his example. Their ideas of him, however, are not very clear. They think that He is standing somewhere, looking at them with pitying eyes, and He knows all about what is going on. They conceive of God as a very large man, with feet and hands, and eyes and ears, whose house is somewhere in the skies, and that He has books, and is always writing down what takes place on the earth. They expect to see Him as a man; and that He will talk to them, if they will look for Him. They think Jesus to be inferior to God in size; and that the reason why He is so small, that He once dwelt in the flesh, and was so badly treated as to hinder his growing large!

Peter Randolph

BENJAMIN TUCKER TANNER (1835-1923)

Introduction

Benjamin Tucker Tanner was a Black minister and bishop who greatly influenced the African Methodist Episcopal (A.M.E.) Church. He served as an A.M.E. minister in Washington, DC, and Baltimore, Md., as principal of an A.M.E. school in Frederick, Md., and later as an A.M.E. bishop. He was editor of *The Christian Recorder* (1868-84) and the A.M.E. *Church Review* (1884-88). Thinking of the A.M.E. Tanner wrote: "the Founders of the African Methodist Episcopal Church ... dared to organize a Church of men, men to think for themselves, men to talk for themselves, men to act for themselves." Tanner was also one such person.

In *An Apology for African Methodism* Tanner defends the African Methodist Episcopal Church. He also includes a history of conferences and districts, and profiles of local ministers, as well as information about influential women. Three chapters from *An Apology for African Methodism* follow.

An Apology for African Methodism
Chapter 7
The determinately religious
"For they have driven me out this day from abiding in the inheritance of the Lord, saying, Go serve other gods."—David [1 Sam. 26:19]

What It Is
What is African Methodism, but an outburst of all that is manly in the Negro—manly political, manly ecclesiastical.

Politically Bound
Politically, impossible to be free, he embraced his first and only opportunity to make manifest his love of liberty with other peoples.

At the bottom of the great political fabric he lay buried, as the mighty stones in a foundation wall; and each was cemented to the other by mutual blood. Like the stone he was quiet, and the fabric seemed to have a sure foundation—so seemingly, indeed, that at home and abroad, we began to hear preached the doctrine of Free races, and Slave races, that is, races who will be free, and races who may be made slaves; and the Negro, of course, is one of the Slave races—meaning by this ignoble logic that the Negro is unfit for freedom. But to a mind unbiased, that logic vanishes like the morning dew, in the presence of the African M. E. Church: So reasons the astute Alexander Crummel, Esq.

The Negro then was bound politically, and he lay helpless on the earth, and over him stood the stalwart Saxon, the Saxon of the South, and of the North as well, with sword, and bayonet, and lash; and while now and then a Negro of over-daring spirit would rise, and despite all, strike for liberty—strike but to fall, the sturdy good sense, and Christian faith of the millions, told them to trust in God and be still. But when in addition to the political yoke, it was essayed by the ruling race, to bind on the ecclesiastical yoke likewise, almost to a man, the free Negroes of the Republic cried out, No! And though coaxed and threatened, and threatened and coaxed in turn, their determined, No! only increased in volume, till Philadelphia had echoed to Wilmington, and Wilmington to Philadelphia; while from the far South, Charleston whispered, for she dared not speak, No!

Whilst bound, to be patient is heroic; when free, to be led into bondage is cowardly. So thought the Negro, politically bound, I will be patient, ecclesiastically free, I will not be a slave. He had heard his Parson read: "Art thou called being a servant, care not for it; but if thou mayst be free, use it rather."

And who can tell what the world would have thought, had the Negro, not only worn his political chains, but had permitted ecclesiastical ones to have been forged, and riveted upon him, and all without a murmur, without an effort! Surely while peoples of every land were striking for religious liberty, the Quakers, the Baptists, the Pilgrims, the Methodists, the class of men that would have stood still, would have presented a strange anomaly to the ages. We repeat: Had Allen and his religious brethren, treated as they were, and as dissatisfied, had they not caught the contagious fever of liberty, the fever that burns and consumes, it would have proved them unworthy of their times and opportunities.

The Negro's Condition

As diseases, physical, are contagious among men, even so, are thoughts, moral and religious; and he who escapes, in that same proportion ceases to be as his kind. By taking the disease, Allen proved his manhood. But African Methodism was not only an upheaval of all that was manly in the Negro, but also, of all that was religious—it was the outburst of his religious nature, which like the fires of Vesuvius, or Ætna, had long been pent up. In the Church the most partial regulations had been made in regard to him; cruel laws had been enacted, and more cruelly enforced. Whilst he longed for the "Bread that cometh down from heaven," he was forbidden to enter consecrated places for it, nor would the Priests bring it to him. He dare not carry his child to the baptismal Font, nor would these Priests bring salvation to his house.

Like Ephraim

In short, he found himself well nigh like Ephraim, "feeding on the wind," and his soul revolted from a fate so terrible. Those pent up feelings—those longings after God broke forth, and the Negro resolved to take the matter in his own hands!

Methodism a Clear Gain

Indeed, Methodism, both among White and Black people, is but a demonstration of man's religious nature; so mighty, indeed, that it overrode all antiquated maxims, save those only which flow from the Bible.

Methodism, in short, is an uprising of the religious manhood of the Christian world against the slights and negligences, the oppressions and burden-some rituals of its religious teachers—it is a living protest against priestly injustice and disobedience.

As such, it is a clear gain to God, over and above; that which the Church as ruled by an Episcopally ordained clergy, would have brought and laid upon the Altar. It is the uncared for multitude, the dwellers in the wilderness, led on by a few Priests who loved piety more than ceremonies, charity more than creeds, taking the matter of their salvation in their own hands. Uncared for, and unsaved by those whom sacred history declares, that God appointed to be the Saviors of the world—those Cures of the soul, they arose in their might, and assumed the right of saving themselves—assumed the privilege of being religious!

The Appeal

And now grown to a mighty host, these determinately religious men, white and black, religious in defiance of Priests and orders—these men, who would not be pagans in a Christian land, aye, these men who would not be sinners, appeal from man to God, from earth to heaven. And their plea is, We were thirsty, even for thy Word, and thy Priests would not give us to drink; we were hungry, even for thy Bread, and they would not give us to eat; we were naked, and they would not clothe us; and turning from them, we fled to thy Word, and to Thee, O God, trusting that thou wouldst not turn us away, lest we faint by the wayside.

Chapter 11
The A.M.E. Preacher

An Ideal Picture

How shall I describe the above character? Avoiding alike flattery on the one hand, and uncharitable criticism on the other. That he is worthy of notice, is apparent from the stir he has made in the world. For fifty years has he toiled, not deigning to reply to those who challenged him; while plying the trowel, he ever and anon repeated the words, "Why should the work cease, while I come down?" Neh. vi: 3.

No Idler

But by the strength of his own brawny arm, with a good degree of the Lord's blessing, the work has advanced nobly—the walls of a complete organization are up, many temples are finished; and while the voice of thanksgiving is heard to re-echo through them—while scores of Priests are at the altar, performing the Divine service, a single one, a few, would step aside and hold controversy with her foes.

The African Methodist Preacher! Who is he? What the attainments of his head? What the qualities of his heart? What the animus of his spirit?

A first look at the material of which the Methodist ministry is composed, will give us an idea as to what it is. The A.M.E. Church, like a Joseph beloved, has been given, as it were a many-colored coat, to protect it from the blasts, even a ministry of almost every orthodox view. Men who have been educated to the strictest Presbyterianism, the most independent Congregationalism, have met at the Methodist shrine, the men of Lutheran and Episcopalian culture, and these, having joined hands, with the convert from Catholicism, all have buried in a common grave, their heads, their hearts, have buried themselves; and Paul like, "know only Jesus, and him crucified."

Few have a Sheep Skin

Few of them, however, can boast of a "sheepskin." They are as a whole, self-made men. But let it not be supposed that all are paupers, though they be not worth that sheepskin—let not "Numskull," be written on the foreheads of all those whose heads have not dozed against some college wall; for a born fool was never thus made wise.

What are Schools?

And what are schools and colleges after all, but places of convenience. It were a question, if the human intellect, would not be stronger, possessing more of its native vigor and individuality, if the coming generations of youth, were to have father and mother for abecedarians, and then given to understand that they must study at home, and advance themselves. We say not, let schools and colleges be abolished, but we do lift up our voice against the opinion that would account every man an irredeemable ignoramus, if he have not graduated.

At college the intellectual forces are developed; but the query we raise is, could not that development be done as well, and as effectually, if every fireside should be converted into a school room, and father be pedagogue, and mother be schoolmam. Admit then, replies one, that it could be done as well, then indeed would the two modes be balanced.

A Cloud

Nay, nay, for not stopping to weigh the superior home training which the child would receive, a cloud would be dispersed, that is dwarfing thousands of intellects, as the shade dwarfs the flower—the cloud—"Father aint able to send me to school, and I can't learn anything"—a cloud that millions follow with the same confidence that Israel followed the cloud of old; but it leads not to Canaan, but to Egypt.

The Methodist Preacher

But there is one character, who has mother wit enough, and courage enough to believe that he can learn something outside the walls of a college, even the Methodist Preacher. He believes colleges are splendid things, and according to present arrangements, are to be placed in the same catalogue with fine houses, rich coaches, and dashing steeds, and are to be accepted, if offered—attained, if possible. But he believes, if a man cannot live in a fine brick, let him live in a frame, or a cabin, or anything rather than be out in the snow; if he cannot ride in a fine coach, let him ride in a wagon; if not behind steeds of Arab worth, let him ride behind the honest ox. So in regard to colleges, if you can go, he says, "Go, and with all your might." But as he would not have you live out doors, for want of a fine brick, nor walk for want of a splendid coach; so he would not want you to be a fool for want of a college. He believes there is sufficient native power in the soul, to advance step by step, if not frowned back by false maxims and opinions. Acting up to his impressions, he puts his book in his pocket, and as he goes round his circuit he reads, reads in the buggy, reads in the

Railcar, reads at home, reads abroad. The moments which most men pass in idle gazing, he employs in reading.

His Morality

What the qualities of his heart? His traducers say: He is terribly impure, a wretch who has continual occasion to repeat Psalm 51.

There is a saying going the rounds, in which the head of his offense is told, it is: That were a Baptist preacher to get drowned, throw a demijohn in the water, and it would float until it came quite over his body, and sink! if a Presbyterian, throw a pocket-book in the water, and it would float, till it came over the body, and sink! but if a Methodist preacher got drowned, throw a lady's garment in, and it would sink immediately, on coming over his dead body!

We are quite as willing to take a hearty laugh at this clever remark as any, conceding that in the Methodist ministry there is as much impurity as any; but we do contend strenuously that there is no more, in proportion to numbers. The active ministry of our Church, will not fall short of five hundred itinerants, and yet, few indeed have been the cases where preachers have been expelled for the damning sin. Writing from memory, we can recall but a single instance, in which the Brother made an acknowledgment, and quietly withdrew. In the Conference, over which Bishop Payne has presided for twelve years, not a single instance of expulsion has occurred.

The Facts

Until the General Conference of 1864, the A.M.E. Church, was the only one of the Protestant Churches, that forbade second marriages, even for crime of proved fornication, and where a legal divorce had been obtained. So much for the sinking of the lady's garment.

His Disinterestedness

But let us take another view of the moral qualities of our Preachers.

What class of ministers can compare with him in disinterested labor, and self-sacrifice? The Roman Priest, has the assurance that his wants will ever be supplied, not only while strength endures, but when it fails. The Episcopalian Rector, the Presbyterian Pastor, even all the ministers of churches, save the Methodist, have the moral pledge of the members, whom they serve through life, that they will not beforgotten in old age; neither their widows and or phans. Not only thus, the usual support allowed to these ministers is generally so liberal, that a portion can uniformly be laid by for days of cloud and rain.

But how is it with the Methodist Preacher? To which, of the many congregations he has served, shall he turn in the winter of age, and find comfort? and as to support, not a mite can be pinched from it, for in the vast majority of cases, it is already too small, to give that easy living which a minister should have.

But on our preacher goes in the discharge of his duty, looking not to the right, nor to the left, but committing his wife and his little ones, to the kind providence of God, he offers himself a sacrifice to the interests of the Master's kingdom.

This general disinterestedness is exhibited by all the A.M.E. preachers, but there is a peculiar disinterestedness which a few exhibit, and still fewer appreciate.

The disinterestedness of a man like Bishop Payne, is peculiar, and he will pardon me for putting him between two fires. The ability of Bishop Payne, and others whose names might be mentioned, are such, that they have but to say the word, and easy positions could be attained. In fact they are constantly accosted with the words, "Why do you stay with those ignorant Methodists? Come with us, and your company will be made more congenial to you." This whole class of noble Methodist preachers, have ever made but one answer to these importunities, the answer, "It is mean to let go your blind brother's hand."

His Animus

What the animus of the spirit of our Methodist preacher?

He is a true American, possessing all that frankness, characteristic of his country. Of all nationalities, the American is the frankest. See the Methodist preacher, when you will, or where, and of whatever race he may be, he is the same, free-hearted, jovial soul. In the Church meeting, he is unreserved, handling the Word with a freedom, that shows that true friends have met; and in the social circle, none is more entertaining. Would you see a recess hour from school, dramatized? Visit a Methodist Preacher's social meeting.

Noble man, may he long live.

Chapter 12

The Methodist Brethren

"For the people had a mind to work."—Nehemiah [4:6]

An Ideal Picture

It were hard to find in any age of the Church, a more devoted company of Christian men. Poor as the early Christians, yet are they as liberal; and many a one of them, with the utmost fitness can be called Barnabas.

Of what class in society come these Brethren, but the laboring? and does not history and experience stamp poverty upon all such? But few of these Brethren have attained to easy positions in life, comparatively few count their treasures by the thousands; and yet thus poor, and getting their little monies, too, at such an outlay of muscle and sweat, still have they nobly contributed to erect those religious Temples, which ornament the land.

The Liberality

It costs something to be ranked among the Methodist Brethren. Membership may be held cheaply, in other branches of the Christian Church; but we proclaim it here, that no man can be a Brother in repute without great charity. He must be prepared to give largely of his substance.

Household Expenses

And why? The reason is plain,—the ambitious little body has set up housekeeping herself!

Dissatisfied with the treatment at home, and being of age, she concluded to commence life herself; and the result is, that all the household fixtures must be got.

Mother was Displeased

Mother was displeased, and would give her nothing, not even a change; so she was compelled to buy everything from her own slim purse; compelled to keep up the wear and tear of independent life. Bishops and preachers are to be supported, with many missionaries; churches are to be built and rebuilt; a Book Concern is to be sustained; a Paper to be kept afloat; Book Steward, Editor, and Clerks have to be fed, with ten thousand other little expenses in the catalogue of housekeeping; and every cent must come from the one pocket, and the ready cash at that!

It is true that Mother became somewhat reconciled, after two score and eight years had passed, and promised to help the aspiring daughter to bear her fast increasing expenses; for the little responsibilities, always attendant upon happy matches, had really increased so fact, that shoes and stockings were wanting to hide the toes, as well as dresses, and attirement for children, in general; but somehow, Mother failed to keep that very kind promise, and daughter, in the words of the poet Bell,

"Must paddle her own canoe."

The Methodist Brethren are the very men to do it, of strong muscles, a strength not to be resisted, with a will that recognizes no impossibilities, they are just the men to work at the oar, and work they do! A drone cannot well stay among them. The result is that our house is getting fixed up quite snugly—our house, be it remembered, and no one's else; every nail we drive belongs to the firm; and though our house is not as fine as somebody else's house, yet is it ours, and we are getting it fixed up. One by one the children are hiding their toes, and the patched trousers will soon be exchanged for whole ones. In fact we will be fixed up after a while in good style.

Alexander Crummell, an Episcopalian, thus speaks of the liberality of the Methodist Brethren: "In some cases they have been known to collect, that is, in Philadelphia and Baltimore, at one collection, over $1,000."

We stop not here to debate the principle of finance, which the Methodist Brethren have adopted, the principle that Paul ordained; for it is not exactly the principle which some people oppose, as the manner of executing that principle. Very many, within and without the pales of the A.M.E. Church, object to the "everlasting begging," which is done. We ask such objectors, and wherever found, not to take a one-side view, but to "walk around Zion," to view every side of the question.

Let me hold up to their gaze this view of the matter.

(a) The A.M.E. Church is perfectly independent of every other Church organization. She is her own master, responsible only to the great Head. This being true, she has no rich Presbytery or Diocese, or Association unto which she can appeal for help—appeal and be heard. Accounting to none, she can appeal to none. Not only has she no right to expect aid, other than in the general way of giving and receiving charities, but it would be dishonorable for her to send her Bishops, or any other of her officers, abroad to get their support.

Receiving the blessings of their labor, she, and she alone, must bear the burden of their wants. It would neither be right, nor honorable for President Benson, howsoever poor his little Republic may be, to draw on Secretary McCullough, of the American Treasury, for his support.

(b) The A.M.E. Church, then, must meet and pay her ordinary expenses, or resign her independency. Honor requires it, as well as the right. Here, then, thousands must be raised—thousands for ordinary expenses alone.

(c) Look also at the extraordinary expenses devolving upon all the richer Societies of our connexion. Ours is a community of burdens, as well as of joys, we are but one family. The older, and larger, and stronger Brothers, feel under obligations to the younger and weaker Brothers; they feel that it devolves on them to take them by the hand and help them along. Actuated by this feeling, numerous, indeed, are the calls made upon the large churches, for the younger and helpless children. But what brother would be without a little sister, because at times he must help her cross the mud? or provide a pair of shoes to keep the snow out, and the heat in?

Tell us not that other colored Churches, do not have these incessant calls, they have no little sisters and brothers; or if they have, their white father has provided for them.

These, then, are the requirements made upon us—requirements that honor and religion require us to meet and cash. How can this be done?

Our objectors say, "We should not coax or plead." As well may they object to human nature!

Shall not plead! A man's heart-strings are his purse-strings as well; loosen them, and the purse flies open; let them be stiff and cold, and the "Greenback," secure in his castle, will laugh at the cry of the widow. And how loosen the heart-strings, chilled by Arctic selfishness? Let burning words, like cannon-balls of white hotness, be hurled against them, let the balls fall thick and heavy, and soon they will melt and break. We apologize not for every incident which may occur, at every collection, for it is the high characteristic of man always to blunder a little! But to ask us not to lift collections, not a few, is to ask us to do one of two things, both of which every Methodist Brother abhors,—either to relinquish our independency, and come under some white organization as beggars, or to starve the little children and the weak, in the African M. E. family.

We are sick of the stale talk of these collections driving away our people! They may drive away some, some who prefer vanity to piety, the shadow to the substance—but never a Methodist Brother will they drive away. He knows nothing else, but to divide his bread; nothing else but to help the weak and lead the blind.

There is a work which these complaining brethren may do, more honorable to them, and of absolute benefit to the Church. Instead of railing out against these continued collections, let them go to work and devise a good, practicable plan, whereby the absolute demands of the Church will be met, and the Brethren, the bone and sinew of the Church, will accept it. But let them not ask us to leave the plan we have, until another and better is provided.

The Methodist Brethren are not only liberal, but they are, what I scarcely need mention here, a zealous body. Their worship is marked by all the warmth of their hopeful natures.

After one has visited a class meeting, or a prayer meeting, especially a Band of these Brethren, he will cease to wonder at the carnage of Fort Wagner and Miliken's Bend. What enthusiasm they have! what defiance! To see them worship, is to be convinced that they will fight.

Hence, we throw in the remark here, that they should be educated. The fervor of their nature demands it. The cold-blooded, unenthusiastic Saxon may do without education, but not the Negro: he is too rushing, and demands a pilot, else he will smash things! Such are the Methodist Brethren, whose offering to the world is the A.M.E. Church. May their generations increase in the land.

Benjamin Tucker Tanner, Baltimore, 1867

LUCIUS HENRY HOLSEY (1842-1920)

Introduction

Holsey was senior bishop of the Colored Methodist Episcopal Church in his home state of Georgia. He saw his congregation grow in a remarkable way. He also took advantage of his father being white and encouraged cooperation between black and white southern Methodists.

Holsey established churches that also served as sites for discussions of black political, economic, and social rights. Today the Christian Methodist Episcopal Church looks back to pioneers such as Holsey as part of their Christian heritage. In the opening editorial of the *Gospel Trumpet* published in 1897, Bishop Lucius H. Holsey stated that its purpose would be to "discuss without hesitation, any phase of the civic, social, and those economic and political questions that may affect the well-being of the Church and race."

Two sermons which Holsey included in his book, *Autobiography, Sermons, Addresses, and Essays of Bishop L. H. Holsey, D. D.* follow.

Life and Death

"Who hath abolished death, and hath brought life and immortality to light through the Gospel."—2 Tim. 1:10.

In the wide realm of human thought there cannot be any questions of profounder concern than those involving the great and absorbing themes of life and death, and their fearful consequences. Life and death are the antipodes of our existence upon the face of the earth, and constantly appeal to our consideration of their great moment and awful concern. The tongue of man, the pen of the philosophic scientist, the rapt visions of seers, the songs of the Muses, and the anthems of angels cannot bring to the contemplation of man a greater theme, more engrossing or charming than that involved in the text. Indeed, it is not possible for the mind of man to dwell upon matters of more interest and deeper importance than that of life and death. Like a shock of electricity it flashes on every wire, plays upon every-thing and ramifies all the deep gorges and labyrynthian chambers of the moral, physical and mental man. It directs the thoughts and mind to those solemn realities, and those fasci-nating conditions and relations that meet him in the present, and await him in the endless future. It is worse than useless for man to attempt to reject those premonitory thoughts that open to his view the stern decrees of God, the Irresistible, the Inevitable. Life is the normal condition of man, death is the abnormal. Man was made for life, and not for death. He was made to live and not to die. Death is the result of sin and disobedience. It is condign punishment for crime committed against the majesty of heaven and the law of God. A state of perpetual felicity, with the faculty of progression and development is the law of his being and the object of his creation.

This view is anticipated by the wonderful construction of his physical constitution. The upright bearing of his body, its symmetrical beauty and enchanting charms, the radiance of the sparkling eye and beauty of the glowing cheek, the wonders of the human foot, and the greater wonders of the human hand; the astounding miracles of the voice, the communication of thought and feeling by word, the towering mind, the massive, expansive, and versatile intellect, all present man as the masterpiece, the highest ideal of God's conception of all his earthly creations. Indeed he is the crowning architrave of heaven's architectural skill. By these high attributes of greatness he stands at the head of all earthly creations and sublunary wonders.

But the dignity of man is augmented and multiplied many times when we consider that ethereal spark and diviner subtle force which we call the soul. And this soul is the master of sovereign man.

Whatsoever the soul of man may be, as to its nature and functions and those peculiar powers enabling it to subsist apart from the body, it is the source, the foundation and spring of life. While the soul is not life itself, yet there can be no life without it. Thus the soul of man is the precious gem, the indestructible jewel "that keeps two worlds at strife"—the world of hell and the world of heaven. In fact, there is a constant and perpetual struggle between heaven and hell for this precious gem, this substantial, yet spiritual entity. Two spiritual powers—antipodal and antagonistic—assemble their aggressive and gigantic hosts in battle array upon the broad arena of every man's existence, and with jarring tread and heavy tramp of war, seek to lift the soul to heaven or cast it down to hell.

But there are many theories as to what the soul of man is, in its nature, attributes and origin. The materialistic theory is, that the soul of man is not a substance or reality, but a mere result of the combination of matter so attuned and refined as to produce results, and therefore, is not a thing with sensible properties in the sense that matter has properties. The manistic theory is substantially the same, in the final logical results, both denying the existence of spiritual substances in the Scripture sense. But the Scriptures declare that "the Lord God formed man of the dust of the ground, and breathed into his nostrils the breath of life; and man became a living soul." This "living soul" in man, was created by the breath of God, a flame kindled within by the power of the Creator. We observe, too, that it is a distinct creation from that of the body, the two creations being distinguished by two separate fiat acts of power. He first made his body "of the dust of the ground," and made his soul by "the breath of his lips," so that both body and soul are creations proper, and not the mere result of any peculiar combinations of matter, so adjusted as to produce all the phenomena and wonders of the human mind. Then man has two parts, the mind or the soul, and the body. This makes man an ideality, in eternal entity. He cannot be more than he is, he will never be less as to the nature and number of his faculties. Time or eternity, condition or place, can never change the nature of man so as to make him anything other than he is—man.

The abolition of death is the hope of man
This is the work of Christ; and Christ alone. He has abolished death, in the sense that death can do the believer no real harm. It is the abolition of that death that involves the punishment for sin and transgressions committed against God and the moral code of the

universe. This abolition of death involves the forgiveness of sins, the reconciliation of God and man, and the redemption and salvation of all who come to Jesus Christ as the Savior of the world. Christ came as God's Interpreter, a heavenly Legate with plenipotentiary powers to make plain the will and laws of God to sinful and rebellious man. He uncovers the mystery of God that could not be explained by the wisdom, research, and learning of man so as to annul the power of death and take away its terrors. He does not come to destroy natural or corporeal death, but to remove the sting of death, and release us from punishment eternal, and give us joys everlasting. Hence, "he taught them as one having authority and not as the Scribes." Death, then, is the first great foe to be overcome or destroyed. This was a work that all humanity combined could not do. It was not in the capacity of the dying to remove or destroy a power greater than itself, and there was no process or method known to mankind to remedy the defect or evade the results of sin. The sinner cannot heal himself of a spiritual malady that requires more skill and power than was in the sinner. Again, Christ has a complete knowledge of the state of man. He had the most perfect and minute comprehension of all those principles and elements that existed in man, and which had been disjointed and confused by transgressions and sins. Being man himself as well as God, he comprehends the remedy as well as the disease. To destroy death he must die himself, and to raise the dead, he himself must rise, and to break the force of the grave, he must enter its dark and cold precincts and tread the dark "valley of the shadow of death." To save man, he must become man with all his pains, his sorrows, his tears and all those death agonies through which every man must pass. "For as much then as the children are partakers of flesh and blood, he also himself likewise took part of the same, that through death, he might destroy him that had the power of death, that is, the devil; and deliver those who through fear of death were all their lifetime subject to bondage."

But what is death?

Death is the antithesis of life, the removal of the spirit from the body, the extraction of the moving and animating principle from the material machinery. It is a profound quietism and the disintegration of all of the bodily parts. This is natural death, pure and simple, This, Christ did not come to abolish in the immediate sense. But spiritual death is the death of the soul—the punishment of the spiritual and mental man, in a state of consciousness and personal identity. There is no death in the sense of annihilation. Dead men are not annihilated. Their bodies are disintegrated, and their souls are in the spirit world, but they still retain all the faculties of their being. Indeed, death cannot shake off human character or personal identity, or utterly obliterate those distinguishing features that characterize intelligent existence. Even man himself cannot devise any means to destroy himself in the sense of annihilation, because he is a stern entity, whose eternal decrees forbid his nonentity. Could an intelligent creature thus make his place a blank in creation, the will of God would be defeated, and his moral government could not be maintained. No, when the sinner lands in the state of punishment, he will still be all that he was in life and character. He will carry with him all the consciousness and vividness of memory that he ever had in this state of trial and probation. State or condition cannot change character nor mental personality. He will be himself in spite of himself, and in spite of all the efforts he may make to become nothing. He may treasure up unto himself "wrath against the day of wrath, and revelation of the righteous judgment of God," yet he cannot remove himself from the Creator, and thus evade "the day of wrath" and those awful responsibilities that belong to him as a moral being, because of his free moral agency. The elements and properties of man's being make him an everlasting entirety as a part of the permanent fixture of the universe, a real part of the most real elements—the mental part. No other being can fill his place in the eternal series and concatenations of the endless creations of God. He is an essential part of the moral universe that cannot be extracted or separated from it, and every single individual of the race must fill his own place in the mighty series of responsibility. There is a personal responsibility and moral obligation involved in human existence that cannot be escaped or evaded by shifting it upon the shoulders of others, or by sinking it in some deep and unknown part of the universe. We cannot hide our obligations any more than we can hide our sins and crimes which are written upon the tablets of the heart and wrapped up in the convolutions of the soul. Man cannot hide from God any more than he can hide from himself, and he can as soon flee from himself as he can flee from God or the moral universe of which he forms an essential part and an inextricable force. He makes one in the vast number intelligent individuals, and is a link in the great chain of being that threads the fiat acts of God, making each man a part of every other in the most minute and mutual relation. Because of the high dignity, spirituality and indestructible individualism of man his annihilation (if such were possible) would unbalance the moral sphere, and throw out of harmony the moral government of God, affecting every interest and part of moral and intelligent existence. The great chains of creation's symphonetic links would become disorganized and stripped of those consonant and responsive octachords that have for interminable ages made the universal diapason a system of wonderful and amazing harmonies, transcending the comprehension of men and angels and all the towering intellects of the universe. How, then, can man be annihilated any more than the universe can be? Is he not an important part of the great whole, made in the image of God? Nay, nay, friends, the stars may fall, and heaven and earth may pass away as they must in the coming ages, but man, the offspring of God, will hold his place in the economy of God, and the native eternity of his being. Since he has begun to be, and since he does exist, creation would be without its crown and the preponderating element in the absence of man. Man, then, is an important element in the creations of God, comprehending in his being the physical, spiritual and mental parts that belong in common to all the kingdoms and dominions of God. And because of these relations in his origin and nature, he must be an interesting object to all other intelligent creatures of the worlds of the universe.

But man is immortal. He shall live forever in some place in the universe. In the onflow of his days, four great facts surround his being. These are, place, state, development and his service or religion. These are the main and central facts of his future. The place that he shall occupy in the potency of his being is designated under the relative terms of heaven and hell—the two extremes of the moral pole. Whosoever is in heaven is not in hell, and whosoever is not in heaven is in hell. At the end of every man's physical life stands the open gate of heaven or the open gate of hell, and nothing can divert his rapid course to one or to the other. Propelled by his eternal destiny, and forced on by inexorable decrees, he traverses the dark and cold territory of death, and enters his everlasting habitation. His home is found, and his place is fixed, and he begins his eternal rounds in the infinite domains of place and space.

Man may not be confined to a small hemisphere, either in heaven, or in hell. Wide, deep and high may be the prison house of the lost—a world of darkness where no suns burn, no stars twinkle, no comets flash, no meteors blaze, and no "pale empress of the night" smiles on a darkened world—a world where no orb of fire ever sent a rippling rill of flame across its dark mountains, nor plowed those abysmal depths of interminable night. The place may be a house with steel gates and adamantine floors, with rock-ribbed mountains of impassable heights, from whose fiery summits sentinels of towering blasts forever play upon angry floods and burning seas—a place where every man is against every other man, and where envy, anger, hatred, malice, lust and pride fill every heart, and falsehood and slander ride supreme on every tongue—a place of perpetual strife and endless war, endless in duration and endless in the depth of its vileness and infamy—a place where spirits bold and daring meet in dreadful conflict and battle array with clashing sabers playing upon the bosom of the deep in the plenitude of power and the darkness of the night. But hear it, prison house of the lost, with your gates of steel and adamantine floors, where no suns burn, nor stars twinkle, where no comets flash nor meteors blaze, no "pale empress of the night" smile on a darkened world, where no orb of fire has sent a rippling rill of flame across thy dark mountains, nor plowed those abysmal depths of interminable night. Hear it, ye spirits bold and daring, with your clashing sabers playing upon the bosom of the deep in the plenitude of power and in the darkness of hell. Man is immortal, and has endless development and endless progression, whether he is in heaven or in hell. Man, then, is a gem. He belongs to those bright stars in the galaxy of God whose unfading lustre and brilliant corruscation will shine on through endless days. Christ came all the way from heaven to seek and save him. He is lost. His place is vacant in the twinkling galaxy of heaven. His value is measured by the price paid, and that price is the blood and tears and the death of the Son of God.

But death is a conqueror. He is the proud and haughty king of the ages. He reigneth over the kingdoms of the earth. His hand is on the land, and his arm is in the seas. His triumphant chariot rolls along on the declivities of the ages and through the cities and rural plains of all the people, breaking the bones of the nations, crushing out the life and vital powers and spattering the blood of the dead and dying millions on his own garments amid the shrieks and cries of weeping thousands and the lamentations of the people. His track along the ages is marked by painted sepulchers, mausoleums, sarcophagi and widespread cities of the dead. Cruel and relentless, he invades the sacred precincts of every family, greedily plucking the blooming infant from the mother's breast, and the darling child from the downy lap of ease, transporting them to the eternal city of ineffable brightness far beyond its narrow sea. Before him, thrones topple, crowned heads fall, empires quiver, scepters break, kingdoms disintegrate, and States crumble into dust. At his command warriors bow, armies flee, swords are sheathed, and belching cannon cease to play on the bloody arena of death. His quivers are filled with arrows poisoned with the venom of serpents and the pangs of asps that fly thick and fast from his bow. The winds are his horses, the zephyr his chariots, and the blushing rose and smiling lilies of the plains his boudoir. He "lurks in every flower," ripples in the curling flood, whistles in the winds, screaks in the storm, thunders in the air, and bellows in the earthquake, sweeping the zones and parallels of earth with the dense shades of Hades and the smoke and fumes of Tartarus. He has plucked crowns from kings, jewels from queens, gold plate from emperors and gems from princes and rulers. Who can stand before him and resist his power? "Who can open the doors of his face?" "He esteemeth iron as straw and brass as rotten wood." "The arrow cannot make him flee; sling-stones are turned with him unto stubble; darts are counted as stubble; he laugheth at the shaking of a spear."

See, see, he cometh over the hills, over the mountains, over the plains, through the streets, and his heavy tramp is heard on the door-sill. The latch flies, the bolts roll back and whisper sadly to the affrighted inmates, saying,

> Arise, my love, make haste away,
> Go get thee up and die.

But death, the conqueror is conquered by Jesus Christ. He opens "the doors of his face" and unhorses the proud rider, for he "hath abolished death," broken his long reign, taken away his terrors, demolished his throne, scattered his kingdom and rent his empire into pieces, and set the captives free. "If the Son therefore shall make you free, ye shall be free indeed." "Death hath no dominion over" the believer. But the abolition of death means that all the children of God shall be beyond the reach or possibility of death in that blessed place and future home. We know it is a future, and according to the Scriptures of truth it must be a place, a place of all the realities, perfections, splendors, glories and magnificences that are befitting in its wonders and elaborate arrangements for the throne of Christ, with all the equipages, powers and necessities that belong to a city of the greatest of all kings. "There God the Son forever reigns, and scatters night away." There are no "cities of the dead," nor grave-diggers, nor coffin-makers, nor black hearses, nor mournful wails of the funeral train; for death is absent—slain by "the Prince of life"—his kingdom dissolved, his scepter broken, and heaven shouts on through the ages, and fills the rolling cycles with the anthems of redemption and the glories of Messiah's triumphs. Amen! Amen!

Lucius Henry Holsey

Why We Should Love God

"On these two commandments hang all the law and the prophets."—Matt. 22:40.

The gospel of Christ is a system of divine ethics. Its philosophic and fundamental principles are few and simple, and it has its claims upon the attention and consideration of mankind, because it affects his happiness in the present and for all time to come. It is a system reared upon few pillars, yet these are but the stronger and more enduring and far-reaching because of their foundation and simplicity. It is not a mass of unintelligible enigmas whose intricacies cannot be understood or explained; but it is simple, convincing, comprehensive teaching, fitted to instruct, elevate and save the race of man. Its scope embraces the moral code of the universe in its governmental theory and practice, and is a transcript and photograph of its moral phases. The system, as such, is presented to our judgment, and appeals to our reason, and then demands our faith in its Author and in its doctrines. Faith is essential to its acceptance and fair consideration, for "without faith it is impossible to please God." It is a system that breathes "the spirit of life from God," and quickens and brings into lively play all its parts, spirit and elements of that life. It defines the moral faculties, and locates God and man in their native and true relations. As a code of morals, it is best understood when we examine its separate parts and primary principles, and observe those results that flow from its practice.

It has three great properties—morals, doctrines, and faith

We can have no proper conception of any ethical code without its elements and primary principles. These compose the bone and framework upon which sinew, flesh and skin are laid, and then the purple current of life is seen to ramify, vivify and dance through every part, diffusing light and activity and filling its spheres with God. If we would be the devotees of any system of religion, we must first partake of its spirit, become imbued with its life, learn its idioms, dogmas, and demands. The life and power of the one must be infused into the life of the other, and then the outlines of our life and character must accord with the spirit and teachings of the same, otherwise we cannot be true disciples of the system. To meet the spiritual necessities of the devotees, the system must not only be true as to its real existence, but must be true within itself. Its promises, doctrines, and predictions must rest upon truth in such a manner as to bring sure and certain realization to its followers and adherents, and thereby verify itself as true. If there is a failure here, all else is failure, intrigue and irreparable loss. This position is more apparent when we think of the stupendous fact that it may promise more than it can verify. That is, it may promise us heaven and give us hell. It may promise us life and give us death; promise good, and give us evil instead. It may pierce the heart with a thousand pangs of demons, and pour into the soul the poison of asps and the venom of serpents, and leave the soul with blasted hope and withered spirit.

For instance, Mohammedanism is a system of error mixed with truth and gilded with glittering promises that it cannot fulfill; yet it is a fact that such a thing as the system of Mohammedanism does exist, but its existence or power to be does not prove that its doctrines, dogmas and idioms are true. Yet it has the same persuasive effect upon the mind, life and civilization of its millions of votaries as the system of Christianity has upon its followers. Both obtain their hold and power over their respective followers upon the same principles of faith, theory and practice. The one is as conscious that his religion is true as the other, notwithstanding the one is false and the other true. Because of these conditions the followers of Mohammed are as devoted to their religion as the followers of Christ are devoted to theirs. If a man believes a thing to be true, when at the same time it is false, the same devotion and earnest faith is given to it as if it were true. Therefore, a system of religion does not destroy the faith and devotion of its candid believers, whether true or false within itself. How important then it is that a system of religion, presented to the world of man for his faith and practice, should be true in itself, and true in its promises, predictions and realizations. We need not enter here upon the divine originality, truth and authenticity of the Christian system. Its reasonableness, its powers, nature, and adaptations to meet the spiritual needs and the practical necessities of mankind in all ages and conditions, are a sufficient refutation of the infidel and those who doubt its truth. Mankind will seek only that that they believe to be, and such exertion depends upon faith and hope and realization. Faith is the connecting link between God and man, between heaven and earth, between the visible and invisible, between the finite and infinite. By this we see the unseen, and approach the unapproachable. It brings us to God; it brings God to us. It humanizes God without making him less God, and deifies man without making him more than man.

Christianity then is more than a name, more than a theory, more and greater than even faith and practice. It is a revolution, a transformation, and a process of redemptive restoration, by which man is evolved from and out of himself, to, and into God. This redemptive restorative process not only changes the moral status between man and God, but imparts to man a new life, a new nature, and the infusion of the Deity himself. If, then, we would be Christians, we must go farther than a mere profession, a mere assent to and practice of the formulas of the religion of Jesus. My friends, without the work of God in the soul, there can be no true, vital, spiritual and soul-saving Christianity on earth. True, we may read its history, memorize its language, repeat its dogmas, and chant its melodies and shout with its heroes, yet there are depths and heights, lengths and breadths, still farther on in the great redemptive, restorative process, which by mere formalities can never be attained. Still farther on, beyond sky-blue tops of the cloud-covered mountains and the deep gorges of repentance, are the sacred precincts of a perfect salvation. We cannot be half Christian and half alien. We must be the one or the other. In the shining phalanx of the living God, there are no mongrel progeny, half-breeds and cross-bloods, but all are shaped in the same heavenly mold, and healed by the same cleansing blood. In this earthly pilgrimage of song, there are no mutes, no unstrung harps, or silent choristers. You must sing the enchanting melodies of heaven, or the bacchanalian songs of sin, moving up to heaven, or moving down to death. There are no neutral grounds in this great warfare, but fight you must. And you must fight for God, and against the devil, or fight for the devil and against God. Two kings cannot reign upon one throne; neither can God and Satan reign in the same heart, for they are antagonistic and antipodal principles. If ever in the onward wake of the ages the world shall ever be redeemed from the thralldom of sin and darkness, it can only be accomplished by the gospel of system. Christ alone supplies all the wants and necessities of man in this and in the future state.

The Jewish people are a standing miracle and living attestation to the truth and Divine authenticity of the holy Scriptures. They are the most peculiar and most remarkable people that have ever lived upon the face of the earth. God selected them from all the idolatrous nations of the earth to serve him, and to preserve the oracles of truth as delivered to them from time to time. Amid the moral and mental darkness that covered the earth, the Israel of God had light from heaven to guide them in the way of truth and moral rectitude, and in this respect the Jew served a great end in the salvation of mankind, though this "peculiar people" has been scattered, and its polity broken into a thousand fragmentary parts. Their kings reign no longer. Their temple hill is desecrated by the Mosque of Omar and the abomination of the Mohammedans. They have been driven by the storms of persecution into every land and clime, from the cold north to the torrid south, and from the orient to the occident. The Jew lives with every nation, but mixes with none; and under all the varied conditions that have tried him through the ages, he maintains his identity and is still what he was three thousand years ago—a Jew. Though his people have been despised, rejected and slain by the hundreds and thousands, and their blood has flowed down the declivities of the ages; though aspersions, calumnies, and vile indignities have been poured in fury upon their heads, still he lives amid them all—a Jew. The Jew can trace his historical pedigree through the fleeing circles of the ages and the dispensations of the past. The storms and howling tempests have rained hailstones upon his quivering bark for three thousand years. Empires have arisen, kings have reigned, states have grown up, towered and fallen, hoary dynasties have been broken upon the wheel of time, great rivers have changed their beds and have cut their pathway through the hardest rocks, filling seas and gulfs with their drifting matter. In the wake of the ages and the march of time, the bodies of the millions have fallen, and their bleaching bones and "cities of the dead" tell the sad story of death. The tall cedars of Lebanon, and proud oaks of Bashan, have withered by the blight of age; still the Jew is the same. He has outlived the ages, outlived the ravages of war and persecutions. He has lived through flood and flame, through famines, pestilences, endemics and epidemics. Like the Gulf Stream, he flows on in his own channel without mixing with contacting elements, whether they be Japhetic or Hamitic. They are God's ancient people—the repository of the oracles of truth—and he will punish the world for the slain of his chosen Israel. In the economy of Providence he stands as a gigantic tower of strength to attest the truth and the Divine authority of Revelation. This is the standing memorial of Christianity and the miracle of the ages. Infidelity may rage and vent its keen shafts of spleen against the ramparts of God, but here is a truth whose impregnable parts stand the rage of the enemy and the assaults of hell.

"Then, one of them, which was a lawyer, asked him a question, tempting him, and saying, Master, which is the great commandment in the law? Jesus said unto him, Thou shalt love the Lord thy God with all thy heart, and with all thy soul, and with all thy mind. This is the first and great commandment. And the second is like unto it, Thou shalt love thy neighbor as thyself. On these two commandments hang all the law and the prophets."

Let us observe then, three reasons why we should love God:

Because he commands us to love him.
Because we cannot be happy without loving him.
Because he first loved us.

We should love God (1) Because he commands us to love him.

God is a sovereign. He has the undivided authority to command all creatures in earth, heaven and hell to do his biddings—to do or not to do certain things. He possesses the unquestionable right to dictate to the consciences of men and all intelligent beings. It does not affect the case whether we understand the reasons why or not. These may be given, or they may not be given. They may be positive moral commands or mere edicts of the king immortal, yet if they are from him and apply to us, we cannot disregard them without condign punishment and destruction to our happiness. As a Father, Master and Ruler, he commands. As a Father, we are his children; as a Master, we are his servants, and as a Ruler we are his subjects. Whether he speaks to us as Father, Master or Ruler we are his subjects and are bound to obey. We may not know at all times why he commands this, that, or the other. To know this is the province of the sovereign God, and not the province of his subjects. With consequences and results we have nothing to do; these belong to God alone. Christianity is a temple of truth of sublime proportion and changeless principles, whose stones have been hewn and polished by the hands of God, and placed in glorious beauty and symmetry one upon another in ascending scales and eternal harmony. "Thou shalt love the Lord thy God" is the changeless and faultless command—changeless because founded upon the equity, the justice and will of the Creator. "The law of the Lord is perfect." Nothing can be added to it or subtracted from it. There can be no review, supplement, nor second edition, nor amendments. It "is perfect" in all its parts, parcels, and ramifications. His "statutes are right" in their native and constitutional inherent qualities. True, they are the dictations of a Sovereign, yet they are none the less righteous and equitable within themselves, since they involve the "eternal fitness of things."

Thus we should love God—(2) Because we cannot be happy without loving him.

This is axiomatic. We have every evidence that the race of man was made to be happy, that the Creator originally designed that all his intelligent offspring should remain in such a state, and pursue those lines of avocation that would redound to his glory and the greatest degree of their perpetual well-being. Consequently, happiness is the natural and universal desire of the human race. This also applies to all sentient and intelligent creatures, whether they be men or angels, and it may not be going too far, when we assert that even devils and lost spirits would repent and regain their lost estate and revert to bliss, if they could. Misery and pain must be utterly at war with the feelings and desires of all intelligences, no matter in what part of the universal dominion they may live. Even the lower animals and the non-intelligent parts of creation, give evidence that show that they have the instinct of happiness impressed upon their nature. The worm of the dust wriggles beneath our tread; the wild beasts of the forest flee at the approach of man, and the finny tribes of the deep elude his presence; all have some natural means of defense and exercise a vigilance that shows their apprehension of danger. They fear death because of the pain and misery that is connected with it. If this is true respecting the non-intelligent, it is so in a larger degree among those who are "made in the image of God." Man desires happiness. It is the natural prompting of his heart and the proclivity of his being. The

Creator made him to live, and not to die; he made him to be happy, and not to be miserable.

The faculties of the mind, the attributes of the soul, the construction and ease and grace of the operations of the physical and perceptive attributes are splendidly fitted to promote his peace, ease and comfort upon the plane of his being. It has been very properly said, that "death is a foreign foe," an alien and an unlawful invader into the kingdom of life, except as man forfeited the protection of God by his rebellion and the violation of those laws and uncompromising principles upon which alone his continued prosperity depends. If we would be happy and fulfill the natural proclivities of our nature—as it was originally intended—we must obey the laws of God, "and keep his commandments." If the subjects of earthly governments cannot be happy without obedience to the laws under which they live, much less can we be happy without obedience to those laws and changeless rules that the all-wise and supreme Creator has prescribed as the norm of action laid down for us. The end of law, therefore, is the glory of God in the happiness of his creatures. One of the plainest things in the world is the fact that no intelligent being can be happy when he is violating the principles in the universe by which alone it is possible to reach the goal of bliss. The Christian system presents to the world the only foundation of substantial peace and enduring bliss, because there can be no such thing without reconciliation with God. Whether in heaven, on earth, or in any other place in illimitable space, the same principles and facts must apply with undiminishing and equal force to all localities and beings. God is God, truth is truth, love is love, and fear is fear. Time or place or conditions cannot alter or change these. Truth on earth is truth in heaven and in hell. Christianity, therefore, is not the religion of men on earth only, but is the only true God-serving and God-adoring system that can exist, because it absorbs all those great underlying principles of love, obedience, and truth upon which the government of the Almighty is founded. No, my friends, there is but one remedy in all the wide domain of God for human misery and human recovery from sin and death, and that is, "Thou shalt love the Lord thy God, with all thy heart, and with all thy soul, and with all thy mind."

It is not possible for any intelligent creature to be happy without Christianity. Let a man be placed in the most propitious condition possible in this life, yet he would be unhappy without the love of God and man. He may recline upon couches of down with ivory posts, studded and bedecked with rarest gems and precious jewels and hung with the richest damasks of the east, while frescoed walls and fluted columns ascend in awful grandeur, covered with gold and glinted with silver. Let him eat the lambs of the flock and feed upon the fat of stall-fed beasts. Let his steeps be washed in butter, and his teeth be white with milk. Let his maidens sing, and with sweetest voice and dulcet strains of harp and organ lull their enchanted lord to soft slumbers. Let him be a king upon a royal throne whose empire covers a continent with teeming millions to do his biddings. Let him be secure from fear and danger and the ramparts of his rocky castle be defended by the invincible legions of the Cæsars and the Napoleons. Let his granaries be filled, his wealth boundless, and his cattle cover a thousand hills, feeding upon the living green, richer in beauty than all the productions of the Persian looms. Let him in the splendors of courts quaff to uttermost satiety the cup of pleasure. Let obsequious millions bow the knee to honor and admire their great Lord and master. Let annalists with pen in hand and ink horn by their sides stand to record the words of wisdom and the mighty acts of the king. Yet with all this, and more, he cannot be happy without the love of God, and the power of the religion of Jesus. For amid all this marvelous wealth, honor and greatness, there is an accusing or excusing monitor—conscience—within that tells him that he is a sinner going to death and to hell. "The wicked fleeth when no man pursueth" and "are like the rough sea when it cannot rest, whose waves cast up mire and dirt." Nay, there is no place, no real substantial happiness and peace without God in the soul, Christ in the heart and life, and the whole man converted, changed, and thoroughly consecrated to God, and separated from the pollutions of the flesh, and the contaminations of the world. How can you escape or set at naught these obligations? How can you or I throw off the yoke of God and evade the momentous issues? Go, take the flight of the eagle to his lofty aerie, and build your secret chamber in the highest cleft of the granite peak, and dwell solitary and alone out of the reach of your fellows. Leave your feet in the cloud and stand upon the celestial pyramid with careless indifference as to human affairs, yet without Christ in the soul there is a burning hell within that is incompatible with peace and ease of conscience. Even in heaven, were it possible for the sinner to be carried there, he could not be happy without the love of God, because he could not enjoy the glory and pleasures of the redeemed and sanctified. There congenial spirits meet in the raptures of redeeming love to celebrate in lofty anthems the praises of God and the Lamb, saying, "Amen." Blessing and glory and wisdom and thanksgiving and honor and power and might be unto our God forever and ever, amen. And one of the elders answered, saying unto me, "What are these which are arrayed in white robes? and whence came they?" And I said unto him, "Sir, thou knowest." And he said unto me, "These are they which came out of great tribulations and have washed their robes, and made them white in the blood of the Lamb." Here are the congregated millions of congenial spirits. They "have washed their robes and made them white in the blood of the Lamb." They have passed through "great tribulations," swept through the zones of life's fiery trials, entered the city of the great king, wrapped in the shining robes of beauty and clothed in the bright habiliments of eternal salvation.

(3) We should love God because he first loved us.

"Behold what manner of love the Father hath bestowed upon us, that we should be called the sons of God." What a lofty title is this, and yet it is true—"The sons of God!" John says, "Hereby perceive we the love of God, because he laid down his life for us." But "In this was manifested the love of God toward us, because that God sent his only begotten Son into the world, that we might live through him." "For God so loved the world that he gave his only begotten Son, that whosoever believeth in him, should not perish but have everlasting life." "He first loved us," with that love that stirred his heart and moved his arm of power. But man is a sinner. He is wretched, vile and polluted, lost, ruined and broken by the fall. An outcast alien under just condemnation. A smiling heaven and a laughing paradise receded from his vision, since God, the gracious Father, was offended. Epochs and dispensations rolled on, chronicling the rise, growth and death of ages and nations. Darker and blacker grew the mental and moral night of the world, and as man multiplied sin did much more abound. Now and then a meteor flashed across the dark hemispheres, and here and there altars glowed and priests officiated. The ages, old and gray, traveled slowly down the declivities of time and space until the dying Jacob heard the rumbling of Messiah's chariot wheels, caught the whispers of his coming and the flash of his eye. When he said, "I have waited for thy salvation, O Lord," he spoke the sentiment of universal humanity. But the law must be given and the foundation of the Jewish polity of types and shadows must be laid, and its superstructure reared, and the blood of sprinkling must antedate the blood of cleansing. Jehovah descended from heaven in clouds and flaming fire. The trumpet's awful blasts and the jarring appeals of thunder announce the awful presence of God in his kingly majesty. Onward, in appalling grandeur descends his chariot of flame. Louder, longer, and louder still, swells the high trump of God. Israel looks up and the heavens are dark with sable bands and thick clouds. Lightning sparkles in fantastic and vivid glare, and play upon the burning waves of the air, as if the atmosphere in chaos trembled under the mighty tread of Deity. The legislative God descends, the earth quakes and an empire of solid granite dances beneath his feet, while wreathing columns of smoke mingled with flame are the curtains of his sanctuary. The walls of the royal sanctuary were amber flames, fanned by the swift moving wings of mighty seraphs and great archangels, attending the royal presence. And so terrible was the sight that Moses said, "I exceedingly fear and quake." "The law was given by Moses, but grace and truth came by Jesus Christ." The law could not save. Jesus alone can do that. He loved us first and pointed out his soul unto death. See him as he lays aside his crown, his kingly scepter, his robe, and the glory of heaven for you, for me, and for all the sinning race of Adam. O, come to Jesus and be saved. Why not? Hath he not loved you? Did he not give himself for you? O, ye sons of Adam, arise, stand up and flee the coming wrath of God. O, praise his name, ye his saints!

Lucius Henry Holsey

WILLIAM J. SIMMONS (1849-1890)

Introduction

Reverend William J. Simmons was President of the State University, Louisville, Kentucky, as well as a past president of the National Baptist Convention, 1885-1890.

Simmons compiled his book of biographies of prominent African Americans, *Men of Mark: Eminent, Progressive and Rising,* because he was concerned that former slaves, their children, and their children's children would grow up ignorant of the remarkable African Americans who contributed to their race and their nation. He did it so that their stories would inspire them to overcome their own hardships and the social and psychological impact two hundred years of slavery had brought them.

In his Preface to *Men of Mark: Eminent, Progressive and Rising,* Simmons states:

I desire that the book shall be a help to students, male and female, in the way of information concerning our great names.

I have noticed in my long experience as a teacher, that many of my students were woefully ignorant of the work of our great colored men—even ignorant of their names. If they knew their names, it was some indefinable something they had done—just what, they could not tell. If in a slight degree I shall here furnish the data for that class of rising men and women, I shall feel much pleased. Herein will be found many who had severe trials in making their way through schools of different grades. It is a suitable book, it is hoped, to be put into the hands of intelligent, aspiring young people everywhere, that they might see the means and manners of men's elevation, and by this be led to undertake the task of going through high schools and colleges. If the persons herein mentioned could rise to the exalted stations which they have and do now hold, what is there to prevent any young man or woman from achieving greatness? Many, yea, nearly all these came from the loins of slave fathers, and were the babes of women in bondage, and themselves felt the leaden hand of slavery on their own bodies; but whether slaves or not, they suffered with their brethren because of color. That "sum of human villainies" did not crush out the life and manhood of the race. I wish the book to show to the world—to our oppressors and even our friends—that the Negro race is still alive, and must possess more intellectual vigor than any other section of the human family, or else how could they be crushed as slaves in all these years since 1620, and yet to-day stand side by side with the best blood in America, in white institutions, grappling with abstruse problems in Euclid and difficult classics, and master them? Was ever such a thing seen in another people? Whence these lawyers, doctors, authors, editors, divines, lecturers, linguists, scientists, college presidents and such, in one quarter of a century?

Another thing I would have them notice, that the spirituality of this race was not diminished in slavery. While in bondage, it may have been somewhat objectionable, as seen in the practices of our race, it must be remembered that they copied much from their owners—they never descended to the level of brutes, and were kind, loving and faithful. They patiently waited till God broke their chains. There was more statesmanship in the Negro slaves than in their masters. Thousands firmly believed they would live to be free, but their masters could not be persuaded to voluntarily accept pay from the government, and thus save the loss they afterwards bore through the "Emancipation." They went to war and fought "the God of battles," but the slaves waited, humbly feeding the wives and children of those who went to battle to rivet their chains. To my mind, one of the most sublime points in our history is right here. We never harmed one of these helpless women and children—they testified of that themselves. And yet they tell stale lies of ravishing now, when the war is over, and freedom gained, and when the men are all home. No, God has permitted us to triumph and through Him. He implanted in us a vigorous spiritual tree, and since freedom, how has this been growing? Untrammeled, we have, out of our ignorance and penury, built thousands of churches, started thousands of schools, educated millions of children, supported thousands of ministers of the Gospel, organized societies for the care of the sick and the burying of the dead. This spirituality and love of offspring are indubitable evidences that slavery, though long and protracted, met in our race a vigorous, vital, God-like spirituality, which like the palm tree flourishes and climbs upward through opposition.

Again, I admire these men. I have faith in my people. I wish to exalt them; I want their lives snatched from obscurity to become household matter for conversation. I have made copious extracts from their speeches, sermons, addresses, correspondence and other writings, for the purpose of showing their skill in handling the English language, and to show the range of the thoughts of the American Negro. I wish also to furnish specimens of Negro eloquence, that young men might find them handy for declamations and apt quotations. It was hard to draw the line in making many selections, and I do not claim that a better selection might not be made. Indeed I am aware that many are entitled to a place here, and the reader may think I did wrong in selecting some of my subjects; but I ask no pardon for the names I present. They may be the judgment of a faulty brain, and yet there is much to admire in all. The extent of our country makes it impossible to secure all who may be "eminent, progressive and rising." I trust I have presented a representative of many classes of those who labor. The book may therefore be a suggestion for some one to do better.

Men of Mark: Eminent, Progressive and Rising

Hon. Frederick Douglass, LL. D.

Magnetic Orator—Anti-slavery Editor—Marshal of the District of Columbia—Recorder of Deeds of the District of Columbia—First Citizen of America—Eminent Patriot and Distinguished Republican.

Who can write the life of this great man and do him justice? His life is an epitome of the efforts of a noble soul to be what God intended, despite the laws, customs and prejudices. That such a soul as Douglass' could be found with the galling bonds of slavery is the blackest spot in the realm of thought and fact in the whole history of this government. But such a man as he would not remain in slavery, could not do so. Aye! it was impossible to fetter him and keep him there. He was a man. He was not going to remain bound while his legs could carry him off, and, as he facetiously remarked, he prayed for freedom, but when he made his legs pray, then he got free. He shows himself a man of works as well as faith. And these go together. But eulogy is wasted on such a man. His life speaks, and, when he is dead, his orations will keep his memory fresh, and his name will stand side by side with Webster, Summer and Clay.

Frederick Douglass was born about the year 1817, in Tuckahoe, a barren little district upon the eastern shore of Maryland, best known for the wretchedness, poverty, slovenliness and dissipation of its inhabitants. Of his mother he knew very little, having seen her only a few times in his life, as she was employed on a plantation some distance from the place where he was raised. His master was supposed to be his father.

No man perhaps has had a more varied experience than the subject of this sketch. During his early childhood he was beaten and starved, often fighting with the dogs for the bones that were thrown to them. As he grew older and could work he was given very little to eat, over-worked and much beaten. As the boy grew older still, and realized the misery and horror of his surroundings, his very soul revolted, and a determination was formed to be free or to die attempting it.

At the age of ten years he was sent to Baltimore to Mrs. Sophia Auld, as a house servant. She became very much interested in him, and immediately began teaching him his letters. He was very apt, and was soon able to read. The husband of his mistress, finding it out, was very angry and put a stop to it.

This prohibition served only to check the instruction from his mistress, but had no effect on the ambition, the craving for more light, that was within the boy, and the more obstacles he met with the stronger became his determination to overcome them. He carried his spelling book in his bosom and would snatch a minute now and then to pursue his studies. The first money he made he invested in a "Columbian Orator." In this work he read "The Fanaticism of Liberty" and the "Declaration of Independence." After reading this book he realized that there was a better life waiting for him, if he would take it, and so he ran away.

He settled in New Bedford with his wife, who, a free woman in the South, being engaged to Douglass before his escape, followed him to New York, where they were married. She was a worthy, affectionate, industrious and invaluable helpmate to the great Douglass. She ever stood side by side with him in all his struggles to establish a home, helped him and encouraged him while he climbed the ladder of knowledge and fame, together with him offered the hand of welcome and a shelter to all who were fortunate enough to escape from bondage and reach their hospitable shelter; and never, while loving mention is made of Frederick Douglass, may the name of his wife "Anna" be forgotten.

In New Bedford he sawed wood, dug cellars, shoveled coal, and did any other work by which he could turn an honest penny, having the incentive that he was working for himself and his family, and that there was no master waiting for his wages. Here several of their children were born.

He began to read the *Liberator*, for which he subscribed, and other papers, and works of the best authors. He was charmed by Scott's "Lady of the Lake," and reading it he adopted the name of "Frederick Douglass." He began to take an interest in all public matters, often speaking at the gatherings among the colored people. In 1841 he addressed a large convention at Nantucket. After this he was employed as an agent of the American Antislavery Society, which really marks the beginning of his grand struggle for the freedom and elevation of his race. He lectured all through the North, not withstanding he was in constant danger of being recaptured and sent to the far South as a slave. After a time it was deemed best that he should for a while go to England. Here he met a cordial welcome. John Bright established him in his house, and thus he was brought in contact with the best minds and made acquainted with some of England's most distinguished men. His relation of the wrongs and sufferings of his enslaved brethren excited their deepest sympathy; and their admiration for his ability was so profound, their wonder so great, that there should be any fear of such a man being returned to slavery, that they immediately subscribed the amount necessary to purchase his freedom, made him a present of his manumission papers, and sent him home to tell his people that

Slaves cannot breathe in England:
If their lungs receive our air, that moment they are free;
They touch our country, and their shackles fall.

Returning to America he settled in Rochester, New York, and established a paper called the North Star, afterwards changed to Fred Douglass' Paper, also Douglass' Monthly. These were all published in his own office, and two of his sons were the principal assistants in setting up the work, and attending to the business generally. ...

He established the *New National Era* at Washington, D. C., in 1870. This paper was edited and published principally by him and his sons, and devoted to the cause of the race and the Republican party. In 1872 he took his family to reside in the District of Columbia. In 1871 President Grant appointed him to the Territorial Legislature of the District of Columbia. In 1872 he was chosen one of the Presidential electors-at-large for the State of New York, and was the elector selected to deliver a certified statement of the votes to the president of the Senate.

He was appointed to accompany the commissioners on their trip to Santo Domingo, pending the consideration of the annexation of that island to the United States. President Grant in January, 1877, appointed him a police commissioner for the District of Columbia. In March of the same year President Hayes commissioned him United States marshal for the District of Columbia. President Garfield, in 1881, appointed him recorder of deeds for the District of Columbia. This last position he held till about May, 1886, nearly a year and a half after the ascendancy to the national administration of the Democratic party.

No man has begun where Frederick Douglass did and attained to the same giddy heights of fame. Born in a mere hovel, a creature of accident, with no mother to cherish and nurture him, no kindly hand to point out the good worthy of emulation and the evil to be shunned, no teacher to make smooth the rough and thorny paths leading to knowledge. His only compass was an abiding faith in God, and an innate consciousness of his own ability and power of perseverance.

Harriet Beecher Stowe, in her book entitled "Men of Our Times," says:

Frederick Douglass had as far to climb to get to the spot where the poorest white boy is born, as that white boy has to climb to be President of the nation, and take rank with kings and judges of the earth.

Again, in the Senate of the United States, in a recent important case under consideration, the following statement formed part of a resolution submitted by that body in reply to the President of the United States: "Without doubt Frederick Douglass is the most distinguished representative of the colored race, not only in this country, but in the world."

To-day he stands the acknowledged peer in intellect, culture and refinement of the greatest men of our age, or any age; in this country, or any country. His name has never been written on the register of any school or college, yet it will ever be written on the pages of all future history, wherever the names of the ablest men of our times appear, side by side with those of the more favored race. His relations with such men as John G. Whittier, Oliver Wendell Holmes, Wendell Phillips, William Lloyd Garrison; and such women as Lydia Maria Child, Grace Greenwood, and Harriet Beecher Stowe, have ever been cordial and pleasant. Some men who never graduate from a college have more sense in five minutes than many a conceited graduate who has all his knowledge duly accredited by a sheepskin, but is not the real possessor of an education. The trustees of Howard University honored themselves and their institution, more than they did Mr. Douglass, when they conferred upon him the title of LL. D., and when also they gave him a seat in their board.

Mr. Douglass in *His Life* written by himself, gives the following account of his visit to his old home:

The first of these events occurred four years ago, when, after a period of more than forty years, I visited and had an interview with Captain Thomas Auld at St. Michaels, Talbot county, Maryland. It will be remembered by those who have followed the thread of my story that St. Michaels was at one time the place of my home and the scene of some of my saddest experiences of slave life, and that I left there, or rather was compelled to leave there, because it was believed that I had written passes for several slaves to enable them to escape from slavery, and that prominent slaveholders in that neighborhood had, for this alleged offense, threatened to shoot me on sight, and to prevent the execution of this threat my master had sent me to Baltimore.

My return, therefore, to this place in peace, among the same people, was strange enough in itself; but that I should, when there, be formally invited by Captain Thomas Auld, then over eighty years old, to come to the side of his dying bed, evidently with a view to a friendly talk over our past relations, was a fact still more strange, and one which, until its occurrence, I could never have thought possible. To me Captain Auld had sustained the relation of master—a relation which I had held in extreme abhorrence, and which for forty years I had denounced in all bitterness of spirit and fierceness of speech. He had struck down my personality, had subjected me to his will, made property of my body and soul, reduced me to a chattel, hired me out to a noted slave breaker to be worked like a beast and flogged into submission; he had taken my hard earnings, sent me to prison, offered me for sale, broken up my Sunday-school, forbidden me to teach my fellow-slaves to read on pain of nine and thirty lashes on my bare back; he had sold my body to his brother Hugh and pocketed the price of my flesh and blood without any apparent disturbance of his conscience. I, on my part, had traveled through the length and breadth of this country and of England, holding up this conduct of his, in common with that of other slaveholders, to the reprobation of all men who would listen to my words. I had made his name and his deeds familiar to the world by my writings in four different languages; yet here we were, after four decades, once more face to face—he on his bed, aged and tremulous, drawing near the sunset of life, and I, his former slave, United States marshal of the District of Columbia, holding his hand and in friendly conversation with him in his sort of final settlement of past differences preparatory to his stepping into his grave, where all distinctions are at an end, and where the great and the small, the slave and his master, are reduced to the same level. Had I been asked in the days of slavery to visit this man, I should have regarded the invitation as one to put fetters on my ankles and handcuffs on my wrists. It would have been an invitation to the auction block and the slave whip. I had no business with this man under the old regime but to keep out of his way. But now that slavery was destroyed, and the slave and the master stood upon equal ground, I was not only willing to meet him but was very glad to do so. The conditions were favorable for remembrance of all his good deeds and generous extenuation of all his evil ones. He was to me no longer a slaveholder either in fact or in spirit, and I regarded him as I did myself, a victim of the circumstances of birth, education, law and custom.

Our courses had been determined for us, not by us. We had both been flung, by powers that did not ask our consent, upon a mighty current of life, which we could neither resist nor control. By this current he was a master, and I a slave; but now our lives were verging towards the point where differences disappeared, where even the constancy of hate breaks down, where the clouds of pride, passion and selfishness vanish before the brightness of Infinite light. At such a time and in such a place, when man is about closing his eyes on this world and ready to step into the eternal unknown, no word of reproach or bitterness should reach him or fall from his lips; and on this occasion there was to this rule no transgression on either side.

His life has been marked by a purity of purpose from its beginning. He has filled many offices of trust, yet in not one position has he ever betrayed his trust. He has been largely, deeply engaged in politics, yet has been no politician. That is, he understood and practiced none of the tricks of politicians. His work has always been honest and conscientious, because he believed in whatever cause he worked for, and did not, as most of our public men, have an eye to a personal reward. All the recompense he sought was a consciousness of having accomplished some good. Whatever has been given him in the way of office has been unsolicited by him. Some of our public men have wavered in their fidelity to the Republican party, when after long waiting they fail to see a substantial reward laid at their feet; but not so with Mr. Douglass. He believed implicitly in the Republican party and realized that being composed of human beings it might sometimes err; but he would say, "The Republican party is the deck and all outside is the sea." Another saying of his is, "I would rather be with the Republican party in defeat, than with the Democratic party in victory." By such expressions may be seen his faithful adherence to what he believed to be right.

He is generous and forgiving, almost to a fault. On the friendliest terms with Lincoln, Grant, Sumner and many of their compeers, his opinions on public matters were always heard with deference and often adopted. His clear, forcible, yet persuasive way of presenting facts, always carry conviction with it.

And now, after a long and well fought battle of seventy years, we find him still erect and strong, bearing gracefully and unassumingly the laurels he has so nobly won. No one who visits him in his beautiful home at Cedar Cottage comes away without being richer by some gem of thought, dropped by the genial host.

A few years ago Fred Douglass married a white lady, who was a clerk in his office while recorder of deeds. This was much objected to by many of his race, but on mature reflection, it has been about decided that he was no slave to take a wife as in slave times on a plantation—according to some master's wish—but that it was his own business, and he was only responsible to God. He has been invited to the President's levees and he and his wife shown every mark of consideration. His travel in foreign countries has in no way been embarrassed by this act. If any one thought he was so foolish as to not know what would be said of his marriage, they have mistaken the man. But Douglass did as he thought was right as he understood it. It showed he had the courage to brave popular opinion as he had done on other occasions.

Frederick Douglass enjoys a joke as well as any man I know. I was traveling with him recently from Atlantic City, New Jersey, to Washington. District of Columbia. We had been traveling on the territory of Maryland. Near Harve de Grace, a rather officious white gentleman was particularly attentive to Mr. Douglass, and after introducing himself to the eminent orator stood up and called out to the people in the car: "Gentlemen and ladies, this is Frederick Douglass, the greatest colored man in the United States." The people flocked around him for an introduction. One white gentleman who was a Marylander, said "Let me see, Mr. Douglass, you ran away from Maryland, did you not, somewhere in this neighborhood, I believe?" "No," said Mr. Douglass, with that grand air and good humored laugh which is his own property, "Oh, no sir, I did not run away from Maryland, I ran away from slavery."

The following is taken from his great speech in the National Convention of Colored Men held in Louisville, Kentucky, September 25, 1883.

Of course I rejoice that efforts are being made by benevolent and Christian people at the North in the interest of religion and education; but I cannot conceal from myself that much of this must seem a mockery and a delusion to the colored people there, while they are left at the mercy of anarchy and lawless violence. It is something to give the Negro religion (he could have that in time of slavery): it is more to give him justice. It is something to give him the Bible; it is more to give him the ballot. It is something to tell him that there is a place for him in the Christian's heaven; it is more to allow him a peaceful dwelling-place in this Christian country.

Benjamin Banneker

Astronomer—Philosopher—Inventor—Philanthropist

In the darkness there was light, and the fire of his intellect attracted universal attention to himself and made for him undying and imperishable fame. This remarkable genius and devoted son was born in Baltimore county, Maryland, November 9, 1731, near the village of Ellicott's Mills. It is thought that his parents were full blooded Africans, but George W. Williams, the historian, says his grandmother was a white emigrant who married a Negro whose freedom she purchased; and of the four children born to them, one was a girl who married Robert Banneker, of whom Benjamin was the only child.

His parents accumulated sufficient means to buy a few acres and build a small cabin. The son was sent to school in the neighborhood, where he learned reading, writing and arithmetic. When Benjamin reached a suitable age he was compelled to assist his aged parents in their labors, but every spare moment found him "ciphering" and storing his mind with useful knowledge. His mother was active enough to do the work of the house, and when seventy years old caught her chickens by running them down without apparent fatigue. The place of his location was thickly settled; though he was known as a boy of intelligence, yet his neighbors took but little notice of him. He was determined to acquire knowledge, and while his hands worked hard, his brain was planning and solving problems in arithmetic. His observation extended to all around him, and his memory was retentive and he lost nothing. But the little education he had acquired was all his parents, who were poor, could give him. Yet little by little he stored it all up, and in the course of time became superior to most of his white neighbors, who had more favorable opportunities and were in better circumstances than he was. His fame had spread so rapidly that they began to say to one another: "That black Ben is a smart fellow. He can make anything he sets out to; and how much he knows! I wonder where he picked it all up?"

In 1770 he made a clock which was an excellent timepiece. He had never seen a clock, as such a thing was unknown in the region in which he lived, but he had seen a watch which so attracted his attention that he aspired to make something like it. His greatest difficulty was in making the hour and minute hands correspond in their motion, but by perseverance he succeeded, though he had never read the Latin motto, "Perseverentia omnia vincet," yet he did persevere and succeeded. This was the first clock ever made in this country, and it excited much attention, especially because it was made by a Negro. Mr. Ellicott, the owner of the mills, became very much interested in the self-taught machinist, and let him have many books, among which was one on astronomy. This new supply of knowledge so interested Banneker that he thought of nothing else. This kind gentleman, who had allowed him to use his books, for some reason failed to explain the subject of the books when he gave them to him, but when he met him again he was surprised to find Banneker independent of all instruction. He had mastered all the difficult problems contained in them.

From this time the study of astronomy became the great object of his life. Soon he could calculate when the sun or moon should be eclipsed, and at what time every star would rise. In this he was so accurate that mistakes were never found. In order to pursue his studies he sold his land his parents had left him and bought an annuity on which he lived, in the little cabin of his birth. As he was never seen tilling the soil, his ignorant neighbors began to abuse him. They called him lazy when they peeped into his cabin and saw him asleep in the daytime. They were ignorant of the fact of his watching the stars all night and ciphering out his calculation. Banneker, instead of resenting all this bad feeling, endeavored to live in such a way as to demand their respect. His generous heart made him always kind and ready to oblige everybody.

A sketch of his life is found in the "History of the Negro Race in America," by the Hon. George W. Williams, from which the following extract is taken:

The following question was propounded by Banneker to Mr. George Ellicott, and was solved by Benjamin Hollowell of Alexandria:

A cooper and vintner sat down for a talk,
Both being so groggy that neither could walk.
Says cooper to vintner, "I am the first of my trade,
There is no kind of vessel but what I have made
And of any shape, sir—just what you will—
And of any size, sir, from a ton to a gill!"
"Then," says the vintner, "you are the man for me;
Make me a vessel, if we can agree.
The top and the bottom diameter define,
To bear that proportion as fifteen to nine;
Thirty-five inches are just what I crave,
No more and no less, in the depth will I have;
Just thirty-nine gallons this vessel must hold—
Then I will reward you with silver and gold—
Give me your promise, my honest old friend?"
"I'll make it tomorrow, that you may depend!"
So the next day the cooper, his work to discharge,
Soon made a new vessel, but made it too large;
He took out some staves, which made it too small,
And then cursed the vessel, the vintner and all.
He beat on his breast; "By the powers," he swore,
He never would work at his trade any more!

Now my worthy friend, find out if you can,
The vessel's dimensions and comfort the man.
(Signed) Benjamin Banneker

The answer to this question is as follows: The greater diameter of Banneker's tub must be 24.746 inches, and the lesser diameter 14.8476 inches.

In 1792, though limited in means and scanty education, he prepared an excellent almanac, which was published by Goddard & Angell of Baltimore. In the preface they expressed themselves as highly gratified with the opportunity of presenting to the public such an extraordinary effort of genius calculated by a sable son of Africa. This was the first almanac ever published in this country. Besides astronomical calculations, it contained much useful knowledge of a general nature and interesting selections of prose and verse. Professor R. T. Greener owns a copy of this almanac. Banneker sent a manuscript copy in his own handwriting to Thomas Jefferson, then secretary of state and afterwards President of the United States.

In 1803 Mr. Jefferson invited the astronomer to visit him at Monticello, but the increasing infirmities of age made it imprudent to undertake the journey. His almanacs sold well for ten years, and the income, added to his annuity, gave him a very comfortable support; and, what was a still greater satisfaction to him, was the consciousness of doing something to help the cause of his oppressed people by proving to the world that nature had endowed them with good capacities.

After 1802 he found himself too old to calculate any more almanacs, but as long as he lived he continued to be deeply interested in his various studies.

He died in 1804, in his seventy-second year; his remains were buried near the dwelling that he had occupied during his life. His mode of life was regular and retired. He was kind and generous to all around him; his head was covered with thick white hair, which gave him a venerable appearance; his dress was uniformly superfine drab broadcloth, made in the old, plain style, coat with straight collar, a long waist and a broad-brimmed hat. His color was not quite black, but decidedly Negro. In his personal appearance he is said to have borne a striking resemblance to the statue of Benjamin Franklin, at the library at Philadelphia.

Banneker's abilities have often been brought forward as an argument against the enslavement of his race, and ever since he has been quoted as a proof of the mental capacity of Africans. Surely the smoldering embers of the latent fires of their ancient greatness was awakened in him, and the thousands of camp-fires of an intellectual revival can be seen now on the highest hilltop, climbing the mountains, at its base, down the valley and in its darkest shade.

William Wells Brown
Author—Lecturer—Historian of the Negro Race—Foreign Traveler—Medical Doctor

Lexington, Kentucky, has the honor of giving to the world one of the most illustrious and earnest men, who did much in his lifetime to distinguish himself as well as to make known the virtues of the race, their origin and history, and marked for special mention a few of its eminent sons and daughters. Born of slave parents in 1816, he was in youth taken to St. Louis, Missouri, and was hired to a steamboat captain. After a year or so he was put in the printing office of Elijah P. Lovejoy. Going off on a steamboat, he escaped North. In 1834 he took to boating again, and aided many a slave to Kansas while acting as a steward. In 1843 he accepted an agency to lecture for the Anti-Slavery Society and continued his labors in connection with that mission until 1849, when he took a trip to England. When it was understood that he was going to England, the American Peace Society chose him to represent them at the Peace Congress held in Paris. The executive committee of the American Anti-Slavery Society gave him strong recommendations to distinguished people in Britain. He set sail for England, July 18, 1849; arriving at Liverpool, proceeded at once to Dublin, where he was warmly received and given a public welcome. He spent many years in Europe and had considerable attention paid him. He was an admirable public speaker, and charmed large audiences at the Peace Congress in Paris and in many gatherings in London. At this congress Victor Hugo presided and Richard Cobden, Esq., and such distinguished men paid him flattering attention. Mr. Brown is known as an author and lecturer. On one occasion he visited his native State to speak in both of the National associations for the support of temperance, and on the schools among freedmen. After holding a meeting at Louisville he started on a trip to speak at Pleasureville and was met by a colored man who told him that the meeting was five miles in the country. Following the man, they started to walk the distance, having waited a long time for a conveyance that was said to be coming for them. After some time they heard horses coming before and behind them. He was finally captured by a number of Ku-Klux and carried to a house where a man, presumably one of their party, was afflicted with the delirium tremens. The doctor's wit not forsaking him, he said he could cure the man; that he was a dealer in the black art and well acquainted with the devil. Having his doctor's case with him, he asked if he might be permitted to go into a room by himself for a while, which was granted. While in there he charged his syringe with a solution of acetate of morphia, and put the instrument in his vest pocket. Returning to the room he requested the aid of these men to hold the sick man while he made passes upon him, as if mesmerizing him; very quickly injecting the solution with his needle syringe into the man's leg, it was but a short time before he was quiet. This produced a wonderful impression upon them and saved his neck. His power having already been displayed, the leader of the band, who was called "Cap," was also suffering from a pain in his thigh. The doctor offered to cure him, if he would retire with him to the other room, which was done. While in there he injected the solution into "Cap" who soon fell asleep. All but one went away, giving him but a few hours to live, and leaving one man, who was full of whiskey, on guard. This one soon fell asleep and the woman of the house knowing that they had set four o'clock as the time to hang the doctor, kindly called the dog in, which the doctor had been wondering how to dispose of, and told him to leave, which the doctor was not long in doing. He got to town and took the morning train to Louisville, and decided never to return to that neighborhood again.

The doctor is an author of many books, among which may be mentioned "Sketches of Places and People Abroad," published in 1854; a drama entitled a "Doe Face;" the "Escape or

Leap for Freedom;" "The Black Man," published in 1863, which ran through ten editions in three years, "Clotelle," a romance founded on fact, one of the most thrilling that was ever written, the "Negro in the Rebellion," published in 1866; "The Rising Sun" in 1874, and numerous other works. In this last work he has given a sketch of the race beginning with the Ethiopians and Egyptians, describing the slave-trade of Hayti and the republic of Liberia; John Brown's raid on Harper's Ferry; proclamation of Freedom; the blacks enlisted in battle; the abolitionists and representative men of the race. His services to the race cannot be estimated. Few men have done as much by their writings as he to elevate and instruct his people. His books were very extensively read and brought quite a large sum of money, many of them running through more than ten editions.

Rev. E. K. Love

From the Ditch to the Pastorate of 5000 Christians—Editor of the Centennial Record of Georgia—Associate Editor—Honored of God

He was reared a slave and had no educational advantages before the Emancipation; he worked on the farm until 1870. He was born July 27, 1850, in Perry county, near Marion, Alabama. Being very anxious for an education he quit the farm at the time mentioned, and in 1870 entered Lincoln University, Marion, Alabama. After studying one term he reached the highest class except one in the school. He found he had learned many things imperfectly. He left this school and returned to the farm in 1872, and from that to ditching, accumulating by this means enough money to leave home again; therefore, November 17, 1872, he went to Augusta, Georgia, where he entered the Augusta Institute, under the late Rev. Joseph T. Robert, D. D., LL. D. Previous to this he was licensed to preach, and December 12, 1875, at Augusta, Georgia, he was ordained.

He was baptized into the fellowship of the Siloam Baptist church by the Rev. W. H. McIntosh, for whom he had a great attachment.

In the Augusta Institute he gained the front rank in his classes; he entered the lowest, but soon reached the head of the first class which he led until he finished school in 1877.

Under the auspices of the Home Mission Board of New York and the Georgia Mission Society; he was appointed missionary for the State of Georgia; this position he filled to the entire satisfaction of all concerned. July 1, 1879, he resigned and took charge of the First Baptist church of Thomasville, Georgia. The house of worship was repaired during his stay there, and four hundred and fifty persons baptized. October 1, 1881, he left this church and accepted the missionary position of the State of Georgia, under the auspices of the American Baptist Publication Society. This position he held for some time and gave entire satisfaction. October 1, 1885, he resigned and accepted the pastorate of the First African Baptist church at Savannah, Georgia. Since he has held that church he has baptized eight hundred and ninety-three persons. This church numbers five thousand members. He has held many positions of trust and honor among the brethren of his State, has been an assistant teacher at one time under Dr. Robert, and has taught three public schools.

He has been appointed editor of the *Centennial Record of the Negro Baptists of Georgia*, which will be read at their first centennial meeting in 1888. He is also associate editor of the

Georgia Sentinel, a Baptist paper printed at Augusta, Georgia. He is considered an eloquent speaker and deep thinker; has strong affections and is certainly persistent in pressing his views. He has the honor of holding perhaps the largest church in the United States, and perhaps in the world. To be able to do this great work is evidence conclusive of his possessing eminent power over men. His position is one that makes him as especially favored of God who has called him to this exalted station.

Rev. Richard Allen

First Bishop of the A.M.E. Church—An Eminent Preacher—A Devout Man

The growth of the A.M.E. church is a splendid tribute to the Negro genius. Of all the denominations under the name of "Methodist," white or black, it has seemed to have touched the heart of the Negro and made him a man of power. Its institutions and laws are the result of Negro genius, and is also the exhibition of his executive ability and abundant wisdom.

When Richard Allen manifested his faith in the future and declared himself no longer willing to have the body and blood of Christ prostituted by being withheld from him until his white brethren were served, he put his foot on the neck of hell-born prejudice and stamped it so hard that hell resounded with anger and a new song was given to the angels in heaven.

It was in the early days of 1816, when the times were not favorable to the expression of a dissent from anything a white man did in Church or State. And he is revered by the African Methodist Episcopal church as the founder of their faith. Says one of their scholarly writers:

> If Luther was the apostle to mind freedom, and Wesley to soul freedom, then Allen was the apostle of human freedom, or liberty of mind and body. If Luther's motto was, "The just shall live by faith;" and Wesley's, "The world is my parish;" Allen's was, "I perceive of a truth that God is no respecter of persons." The sons of Allen, through Bishop Payne, have formulated the sentiment of the three as follows: "God, our Father: Christ, our Redeemer; and Man, our Brother."

Many a time when a boy have I seen the tomb of Richard Allen in the little railing in front of the "Big Bethel" in the city of Philadelphia. This, the first church of the denomination, stands as a proud monument to the religious zeal of Richard Allen. It stands on the site of an old blacksmith shop where the first meeting was held, and as the generations pass this monument on the outside of the church, and go within the walls of "Big Bethel" they feel that Allen still lives. Often good "men's deeds are interred with their bones," but in this noble man's career we see a dignified manhood and religious zeal become the inspiration of four hundred thousand of those who follow in his footsteps. The Rev. B. W. Arnett has, in a graphic description of the times which I give here, shown how great was the cause for their separation from the white church:

> The causes which led to the organization of the African M. E. church are numerous; but a few facts will give an idea of the principal reason of our origin. After the close of the

War of the Revolution, while the world was rejoicing at the establishment of a government whose declared principles were universal, political, civil and religious liberty, and while they were singing the anthems of peace, there was another mighty conflict going on—not on the battlefield, with saber and musket, but in the churches and the social circles of the land. Prejudice, the unrelenting enemy of the oppressed and weak, was asserting its power; and from the year 1787 to 1816, the conflict continued without cessation. The colored portion of the numerous congregations of the North and South were wronged, proscribed, ostracized and compelled to sit in the back seats in the sanctuary of the Lord. The sons of toil and the daughters of oppression remained on these seats for some time, hoping that some of the members, at least, would receive a sufficient amount of grace to enable them to treat these children of sorrow with Christian courtesy. But they were doomed to disappointment; for soon bad yielded to worse, and they were sent up into the dusty galleries. There, high above the congregation, they had to serve the Lord silently—for not an amen must come down from the sable band. These and other indignities our fathers bore with Christian patience for a number of years. They were denied the communion of the Lord's Supper until all the white members had partaken. This treatment continued until forbearance ceased to be a virtue, and our fathers drew out from among them; for the watch fires of soul-freedom were burning in their bosoms. These were kindled and fed by the sentiments of the age in which they lived; for on every side could be heard the watchword of the Nation—"All men are born free and equal, and endowed by their Creator with certain inalienable rights, among which are life, liberty and the pursuit of happiness."

Allen was a man of independent character, and was converted at the age of seventeen. His influence, though a slave, was so great that his master allowed him to preach and have preachers to preach for him, as he pleased. His master was converted under his preaching, and yet I have some doubt of his conversion, as he made poor slave Richard Allen purchase his freedom. This man may have been a Christian; "God," who "moves in a mysterious way," may have done something for his soul, but he took Allen's money when he should have set him free. How they can ever harmonize God's words with their conduct will take a "general judgment" to tell. If for no other thing it were needed, it will be good for that. However, he had three able, honest men to stand by him: Rev. Absalom Jones, William White and Downs Ginnings, and they determined to erect a building for the colored people.

Says an article in the *Christian Recorder*:

This undertaking met with strong opposition from both white men in the Saint George's M. E. church and prominent colored men, while some of both classes encouraged him. Ministers of the M. E. church threatened to disown him and his followers, but with much sagacity he told them that if they turned him out otherwise than in accordance with discipline, he would seek redress. His own language is: "We are determined to seek out for ourselves, the Lord being our helper." He and his friends narrated to these brethren of the M. E. church the especial grievances suffered in their communion. He also told them: "If you deny us your name (Methodist), you cannot seal up the Scripture from us or deny us a name in heaven. We believe heaven is free for all who worship in spirit and truth."

With manly dignity and a clear indication that he knew he was cutting loose entirely from a great body of people, believing as he did on religious doctrines, he said, when told finally that he would be disowned: "This was a trial I never had to pass through, but I was confident that the great Head of the church would support us." He states that on the first day he and Absalom Jones canvassed for money with which to purchase. They raised three hundred and sixty dollars after he had been authorized by the committee. He bought a lot on Sixth street, near Lombard, the site of the present Bethel church, Philadelphia. The committee agreed to purchase a lot on Fifth street and threw the Bethel lot on his hands. Having the true grit of manhood in his moral constitution, he said: "I would rather keep it myself than forfeit the agreement I have made." This he did. He says:

As I was the first proposer for an African church, I put the first spade into the ground to dig the cellar (basement) for the same. The old blacksmith shop was made a temple in which to worship God. On canvassing the little society it was found that a majority preferred joining the Church of England, rather than force themselves upon the Methodist Episcopal society, by which they considered themselves badly treated. But Allen was a Methodist, and though but one other member of the society agreed with him, he stuck to the old church, again showing the true metal for a leader of the colored Americans.

Richard Allen was born in Philadelphia in 1760. At seventeen he united with the Methodist society in the State of Delaware. At twenty-two he commenced preaching, and R. Allen traveled through the Middle States extensively. He was ordained a deacon in 1799, by Rt. Rev. Francis Ashbury, bishop of the Methodist church. At the organization of the A.M.E. church, A. D. 1816, he was elected and ordained the first African bishop in America. The following names were enrolled in the first conference held on this occasion:

Rev. Richard Allen, Jacob Tapisco, Clayton Durham, James Champion, Thomas Webster, of Philadelphia, Pennsylvania; Daniel Coker, Richard Williams, Henry Hardin, Stephen Hill, Edward Williamson, Nicholas Gailliard, of Baltimore, Maryland; Peter Spencer, of Wilmington, Delaware; Jacob March, Edward Jackson, William Andrews, of Attleboro, Pennsylvania; Peter Cuff, Salem, New Jersey.

These men had faith in God and faith in themselves, and the splendid results of this day show that they did not miscalculate their calling. The power of this denomination is felt in the land; its leaders are courageous, bold and intelligent, and it has some of the ablest men in the country in its ranks. My personal relations with them have been of the warmest kind, and I give them credit for utilizing every man they can lay hold on, and they know how to nurse their young eaglets into strong eagles, and to put their best efforts at work for the spreading of their views.

Hon. George W. Williams, LL. D.

The Most Eminent Negro Historian in the World—Author of World Wide Reputation—
Legislator—Judge-Advocate of the Grand Army of the Republic—Novelist—Scholar—
Magnetic Orator—Editor—Soldier—Preacher—Traveler—minister to Hayti

Among the intellectual stars which shine in the zenith of the Negro world, increasing in
brightness day by day, dispensing its light to the dark corners of the world, is the Hon.
George Washington Williams. He was born at Bedford Spring, Bedford county,
Pennsylvania, on the sixteenth day of October, 1849. His mother's maiden name was Nellie
or Helen Rouse, who came of Negro and German parentage. His father was of Welsh and
Negro extraction. He was a man of large mould, standing about six feet high and weighing
from one hundred and eighty to two hundred pounds. His mother was medium in size, of
fair complexion, large dark eyes and black hair, and was a woman of rare intellectual power,
speaking German fluently, and was well up with the times in current literature. She was
noted for her dramatic and elocutionary powers, of which the son is possessed of a large
share, no doubt inherited from his mother.

When young George was about three years old, his parents moved to Newcastle,
Lawrence county, Pennsylvania, and his early education was obtained in that State and in
Massachusetts, comprising two years with a private tutor, four years in the common and
high schools, two years in an academy, and four years at Newton Center, Massachusetts.

He was enlisted in the United States volunteer army by Major George L. Sterns, and
served until the close of the war. Being only fourteen years old he ran away from home and
begged to be accepted, even against the advice of the examining surgeon. He didn't give his
own name when he enlisted, but used that of one of his half uncles. By his intelligence and
attention to the duties of a soldier, he rose rapidly from one grade to another, beginning as
private and ending the war as sergeant-major of his regiment. Having been severely
wounded he was discharged from the service, but soon re-enlisted and was detailed on the
staff of General Jackson in 1865, and accompanied him in May to Texas. While there he was
ordered to be mustered out, and he immediately enlisted in the Mexican army, where he was
at once made orderly sergeant of the First battery from the State of Tampico, and in just one
week was made assistant inspector-general of artillery, with the rank of lieutenant-colonel.
After the capture and death of Maximillian he returned to the United States and entered the
cavalry service of the regular army, serving in the Comanche campaign of 1867 with
conspicuous bravery. February, 1868, while at Fort Arbuckle, this hero was converted, and in
late autumn left the army for civil life, having been convinced as a Christian that killing
people in time of peace as a profession was not the noblest life a man could live. As soon as
he completed his six hundred miles' journey across the plains, he went to St. Louis,
Missouri.

His father was a Unitarian, and his mother a devoted member of the Lutheran church;
but the son read the New Testament and came to the conclusion that the Baptist church, in
practices and doctrines, came up to the New Testament standard. Not being acquainted with
a single person in St. Louis, save a few officers at General Sheridan's headquarters, he sallied
forth into the streets to inquire for a Baptist church. Singularly enough the first man he met

was a deacon in a church of that denomination, and on the following day, which was the Sabbath, he told his experience in the First Baptist church and was that evening baptized into the fellowship of the Baptist communion by the Rev. H. H. White.

From 1868 to 1874 he devoted himself to study, and graduated from the Newton Theological Institution, June 10, 1874, delivering an oration on "The Early Church in Africa." Here at once can be seen the tendency of Mr. Williams. He always inquires into the history of some subject connected with the race. He early developed the power of search and the love for deep investigation, and thus laid the foundation for his present and future life, which has become so widely connected with historical subjects which materialized themselves into the great histories which he has written. He was licensed to preach June 1, 1874, as the following will show:

> This is to certify that the Watertown Baptist church, having confidence in the Christian character and fitness of our brother, George W. Williams, did on the thirty-first of May, 1874, unanimously vote to give him license to preach the Gospel of Christ.
>
> In behalf of the church,
>
> William Blodgett,
>
> Church Clerk.
>
> Watertown, June 1, 1874.

His ordination to the Gospel ministry took place at Watertown, Massachusetts, June 11, 1874, under the call of the First Baptist church in Watertown.

April 4, 1874, he received a call to the Twelfth Street Baptist church in Boston. He accepted this call, and the following services were held by way of recognition of the new pastor. Sermon by Rev. Dr. George Lorimer, from 1 Corinthians chapter i, 16-17 verses. Prayer of Recognition, by Rev. R. M. Neale, D. D. Charge, Rev. D. C. Eddy. Hand of Fellowship, Rev. J. T. Beckley.

While pastor of this church he wrote the history of its struggles and labors, for the purpose of calling the attention of the charitable to its pecuniary needs. The church had done excellent work among the colored people of the West End and deserved to be sustained. It was organized in 1840, with an original membership of only about forty, who withdrew from the First Independent Baptist church. The volume contains eighty pages and was published in a popular form, by James H. Earle, No. 11 Cornhill. While pastor of this church, he preached a memorial sermon before the Robert A. Bell Post 134, Grand Army of the Republic, Sunday, May 24, 1874.

Mr. Williams applied to the Massachusetts Legislature for the position of chaplain. The request was not granted, but he made an open and plain request for that which he desired.

He served the Twelfth Street Baptist church one year as supply before he was ordained, and was pastor one year. The Divine favor that was shown him was an evidence of the fruitfulness of his ministry. His relation was terminated with that church in August, 1875, by his own voluntary resignation. He then went to the city of Washington, and the following notice is given of his purpose for visiting that city, in a speech which he delivered in the

Presbyterian church, at a meeting held for the purpose of taking steps towards establishing a journal in that city to be managed by colored men, and devoted to the interests of the colored people. The report says: "The Rev. George W. Williams delivered an eloquent address in which he stated that he proposed to establish a journal in the District of Columbia, devoted to the interests of colored people." There was no question as to the necessity of such a journal. It was offered in objection that the colored people were not a reading people, but educational statistics of the country show that within the last decade they have become a reading people. ...

He was called to take pastoral charge of the Union Baptist Church of Cincinnati, Ohio, on Thursday, February 10, 1876, which he accepted, and preached his first sermon on Sabbath, February 20, 1876. He was installed as pastor of the Union Baptist church, Thursday evening, March 2, 1876. ...

Rev. G. W. Williams resigned December 1, 1877. September 2, 1878, he was appointed internal revenue storekeeper by the Secretary of the Treasury, and served also in the Auditor's office as secretary of the four million dollar fund to build the Cincinnati Southern railroad.

He studied law in the office of Judge Alphonso Taft and the Cincinnati Law School; and was admitted to practice in the Supreme Circuit Court of the State of Ohio in the city of Columbus, June 7, 1881; and admitted in the Supreme Judicial Court at Boston, within the aforesaid Suffolk county, on the second Tuesday in September, A. D., 1883. He began his political life in Cincinnati. At first he was averse to going into politics, as he said in a speech at Hopkin's hall when addressing an enthusiastic meeting of colored Republicans:

As a rule, I believe that ministers of the Gospel should remain as far from the political arena as possible. But when the storm clouds thicken and darken our National sky, when the hand of treason is at the throat of the Nation, when the temple of justice, humanity and equality is about to be desecrated by traitors; when the Constitution is about to be eliminated and the gracious, benign amendments thereof to be rendered nugatory; when the proud institutions of America—our joy at home, and our glory among the civilized powers of the earth—are imperiled, I would be false to the race to which I am bound by the ties of consanguinity, false to the flag under which I fought, false to the great issues of this hour, false to the instincts and impulses of my better nature and deserving of the execrations of God and man, if I did not lend my pen, my voice, my soul, to the cause of the illustrious Republican party.

September, 1877, he was nominated for the Legislature from Hamilton county, Ohio. At the ratification meeting of the colored Republicans, Mr. Williams delivered an address of which the following is an extract. Said he:

My friends and fellow citizens—I appreciate the high public spirit of which this large and enthusiastic meeting is born. I am deeply touched by the manifold expressions of kindly sentiment concerning myself, and am cheered by the pledges already made to support the Republican party in the approaching canvass. I would, indeed, be an ingrate if I were insensible to the honor conferred upon me by my party and race. I did not seek the nomination, did not ask it. The party and my friends bestowed it with lavish hands, and, as I believe, with honest intentions. I said to my friends, who urged me to be a candidate for legislative honors, that I would yield to their wishes if it were certain I would serve the whole people. The nomination was made with a heartiness that led me to believe that the leaders of the Republican party, at least, honestly desired to give proper representation to the colored people; and that when a colored man, representing the people, should come to the front, they would give him their unqualified support. Then, when I turned to my people and found them almost a unit as to my nomination, there was but one thing left for me to do, and that was to accept the nomination—this unsought compliment.

I was not a stranger to every person when I came to this beautiful Queen City. I was known to quite a number of the people, either personally or through the press. From 1863 till the present moment I have identified myself with the various interests of my race and country. Upon the field of battle, under the mellow and enlightening blaze of the student's lamp, in the wide and useful field of journalism, in the sacred pulpit and in the political arena, I have striven for all that is noble, just and of good report. I was welcomed to your city by white and black men, by Democrats and Republicans, by saints and sinners. And I now call you to witness that I have labored for my people and party with zeal and faithfulness. For this you have honored me with a foremost place in your midst, a warm place in your hearts and confidence. One could scarcely be affected by a spirit of vainglory, standing where I stand to-night. I stand here, not for myself, not for the three thousand loyal colored men in this county, not for the fifteen thousand colored voters in this grand old commonwealth; but I stand here as a representative of the sovereign people. I am before you, fellow citizens, as an exponent and defender of the immortal teachings of the Republican party, the party that represents the loyal sentiment and political conscience of the American people.

During his term as a member of the Legislature, he was chairman of the committee on library, special committee on railroad terminal facilities; second member of the committee on universities and colleges, and took part in all the legislation, and secured the passage of several bills referring to police, railroad legislation and school legislation.

Mr. Williams is a man who has delivered many orations upon many topics and is still in great demand as an orator. As an author he has written two standard works, "The History of the Negro Race in America from 1819 to 1880; Negroes as Slaves, as Soldiers and as Citizens, together with a Preliminary Consideration of the Unity of the Human Family." "An Historical Sketch of Africa and an Account of the Negro Government of Sierra Leone, Africa." . . .

He does not go into society except on rare occasions and then proves himself a congenial and racy conversationalist. There is but one place in which he may be found regularly, except prevented by indisposition or inclement weather, and that is the Thursday evening prayer meeting. He is a member of the Baptist church, and during his Christian life has been an active Sunday school and Young Men's Christian Association worker, until a severe attack of pneumonia and increased literary duties admonished him to husband his strength.

Few persons have had the privilege of knowing him intimately, but those who have come in close contact with him socially have found him an intelligent and interesting gentleman. He is loyal to his friends, but pays little attention to his enemies, except they provoke and bring about war; then it may be said of him truly "Beware of the wrath of a patient man." He is the equal or the superior in general learning, information and originality of any of the representative colored men in this country. He is familiar with the classics, with several modern languages, and is well-informed upon all questions of domestic and foreign politics. He writes poetry with grace and unction and is authority on English classics. As an orator he takes first rank. He has written three novels and a tragedy; the last two productions are destined to create a profound sensation on both sides of the Atlantic and give him additional fame. Although a good lawyer, and, in the practice making a good deal of money, his real tastes are those of the scholar and literary man; and the rest of his life will be devoted to literary pursuits.

Rev. Daniel Abraham Gaddie, D. D.
From the Blacksmith Shop to the Pulpit—Temperance Advocate—Moderator of Fifty Thousand Baptists

Rev. D. A. Gaddie, one of the strong men of Kentucky, has risen from the sledge hammer and the anvil to a commanding position among men. This he has done by persevering diligence and application to business. He was born May 21, 1836, and is still hale and hearty. A man of splendid physique, a very Ajax in bravery, a Hercules in strength. He may be called a handsome man in personal appearance, and he impresses one as a safe protector in trouble. To such men we seem to fly for refuge when danger is near. In his twenty-third year he gave his heart to Christ, and commenced in earnest to serve Him who ruleth the hearts of all men.

He owes his conversion to one Robert Gardner, a white brother. He was ordained in the year 1865, and was at that time a member of Green Street church. At his ordination, Rev. Henry Adams, Rev. Richard Sneethen, Charles Edwards and Solomon Patterson took part. He was pastor of several churches in the State; among them may be mentioned Elizabethtown, Greensburg, Campbellsville, Rude's Creek, Glendale and Green Street Baptist church, of which he has charge at this writing. Elder Richard Sneethen died April 11, 1872, and the subject of this sketch was elected pastor in October of the same year. Under his wise administration of the affairs for the past fifteen years, much good has been done in the systematic organization of the work. He has added more than two thousand members to the church; fifteen hundred, perhaps, of this number were converts. He has married about five hundred couples and preached thousands of sermons and delivered many addresses. The Green Street church is one of the most faithful in the State, and under his leadership it has been trained to give, when called upon, for every object worthy of Christian benevolence.

The General Association of Kentucky Baptists has for years honored him with various offices. He has been assistant moderator for many years, but in the last session held at

Bowling Green, Kentucky, he was chosen as moderator of 50,000 colored Baptists. This was one of the largest gatherings in the State, and shows the popularity and strength of Rev. Mr. Gaddie.

He has also been very prominent in temperance work, being a strong opponent of alcoholic liquors in every shape He is eminently a friend of young preachers, and none have applied to him who do not receive abundant sympathy and material help. Herein lies his strength. For many years he has been secretary of the Ministers' and Deacons' meeting, held in the city of Louisville. He has a large office and the meetings are always held with his church. This meeting has exerted a wonderful influence upon the Baptist ministry in more ways than one, creating much social feeling and promoting brotherly love among them.

Intellectually he is a strong man, and in the subject of theology and history he is well posted, and much deference is paid to his opinion upon such subjects.

Few men in the State have more earnest supporters and well-wishers. Though he has had in lifetime many severe troubles yet he has always controlled his temper; though he has often had the power to crush enemies who are disposed to do him injustice, he has had long patience and exhibited those Christian virtues which go to make a man strong and powerful with the people, and to overthrow the machinations of them who desire to injure him.

His hand is ever ready to assist any and every enterprise calculated to benefit the people of the State. He is often elected to conventions which consider the educational and indus-trial affairs of the colored people and is therefore more prominent on account of his own advocacies of every measure which will elevate the race. Such men hasten "the good time a coming," add to the moral, religious and educational worth of the people. His life full of usefulness, piety and acts of charity, draw to him the affection of a loving people whose personal kindnesses are well known to the writer.

The Rev. D. A. Gaddie, long a central figure in the Baptist world and a man of earnest and untiring efforts in the cause of education, was given the degree of Doctor of Divinity by the State University at its annual commencement, May 17, 1887.

Rev. Lemuel Haynes, A. M.
A Distinguished Theologian.

Among the early popular preachers in the State of Connecticut was one who was born of an African father and a white mother. He enjoyed excellent advantages for improving his intellect and became a very distinguished scholar, an eloquent and forcible preacher, and maintained a reputation for over thirty years. It is said his fame was created from the preaching of a sermon from Genesis 3-4, and his discussion with the venerable Hosea Ballou. He received the degree of A. M. from Middlebury College, Vermont, and was the first of the race to receive a degree of the kind in this country. His birthplace was Hartford, Connecticut, and the date of his birth, July 18, 1753; he was also a "minute man" in 1774 at the battle of Lexington. He joined the army at Roxboro; he was a volunteer in the expedition to Ticonderoga. He lived to the age of eighty-one, and died the twenty-seventh of September, 1833. His memory is preserved, and we can with pride point to him as the first titled Negro in America. To-day we have scholarly Negroes on every hand who have earned their titles by severe intellectual labor in colleges and universities. It is refreshing also to find amalgamation on the other side of the fence. A native African and a white woman. "Holy horror!" cries somebody, "How curious they did not hang him." They were honorably married and he was popular. The black face was a thing of beauty to his wife, who saw a man with an intellectual soul and loved him. Love laughs at locks and bars and even the color of a man's skin. Both parties will cross the line.

Rev. Benjamin Tucker Tanner, A. M., D. D.

Editor of the A.M.E. Review—Twenty Years an Editor—For Many Years Editor of the Christian Recorder—Author of Ecclesiastical Works.

Without doubt, one of the brightest, grandest, noblest men in the ranks of Negro Methodism is Dr. B. T. Tanner, the veteran journalist of the colored race. His fame has extended from the lakes to the gulf, and from the Atlantic to the Pacific.

He was born of Hugh and Isabella Tanner, in Pittsburgh, Pennsylvania, and was not a slave. He spent five years in study at Avery College, Allegheny City, Pennsylvania, where he paid his expenses by working at the barber's chair. At this time of life his father was dead, and his struggles were the more severe because his widowed mother needed his care. His whole nature was independent; for he might have sweetened his life some and smoothed many a road over which he passed, but he preferred to work and win. Mr. Avery, in whose honor Avery College was named, and who was its founder, offered to pay his expenses through college, but the self-reliant young man refused it. After spending one year of the five in Avery College in the College Department, he took a three years' course in the Western Theological Seminary. His birthday being December 25, 1835, he was twenty-five years old when he received his first appointment from Bishop D. A. Payne to the Sacramento station in the California conference. The appointment was not filled on account of the distance and the money to get there. So he was "supply" for the Presbyterian church of Washington, District of Columbia, for eighteen months. This was admissible on account of the liberality of the views of each denomination, and it was a magnificent compliment to his head and heart that they invited him. While here he organized the Sabbath school for Freedmen in the navy yard, by permission of Admiral Dalghren. April, 1862, he united with the Baltimore Annual conference and was appointed to the Alexander Mission, "E" street, Washington, District of Columbia. This being the first mission possible during the war, it had to be guarded by soldiers through the kindness of provost-marshal, General Gregory.

The year 1863 found him pastor of the Georgetown, District of Columbia, church. 1866 was the date of his pastorate in "Big Baltimore" charge, and after serving to the satisfaction of all concerned he resigned the re-appointment of the charge, to become principal of the Annual Conference school at Frederickstown, Maryland. The Freedmen's Society also secured his services in organizing a common school.

His fame and talents begot for him a great name. His addresses showed thought, learning and rare gifts; so that when the general conference met in the capital of the Nation, in 1868, he was not only elected chief secretary, but editor of the church organ, the Christian Recorder, by acclamation, and this honored position was thrust upon him in succession until he had served sixteen years. This is indeed an honor. In 1870, while the lamented Dr. Henry Highland Garnet was president of Avery College, he was given the degree of A. M., a title he richly earned by diligent literary labors. Wilberforce honored him with the degree of D. D., sometime in the seventies.

In 1881 he crossed the waters, visiting England and continental Europe, and attending the Ecumenical conference. His spare time has been spent in editing books of use to his denomination. He is the author of an "Apology for African Methodism;" "The Negro's Origin; and Is He Cursed of God," "An Outline of our History and Government;" "The Negro, African and American." In the general conference of 1884 Dr. Tanner was voted a promotion to the editorship of the A.M.E. Review. This is one of the most scholarly productions of the age, and its list of writers includes all classes of thinkers and writers of all denominations, male and female. Indeed, he has the rare skill of securing the ablest articles by Negro writers. It is sent out quarterly, full of matter for brain and soul. His long experience fits him to discriminate with such rare judgment that the magazine is always nicely balanced. It is the crystallization of Negro scholarship, an epitome of Negro brains, and the doctor is as unerring in hitting the mark with his own pen as the best marksman I know. He is a member of the New England Historical Society of the M. E. church, and fills many important stations in his own church. His views are in the line of Wesley's, Richard Allen and the leading lights of their faith. The affability of the doctor, added to his general worth, makes him respected everywhere. While traveling in the old world—he was sailing on Lake Geneva, Switzerland—he was called on to preside at the dinner and was also made chairman of the committee appointed to draft resolutions complimentary to Monsieur Lemoiger, who had safely piloted the party over the Alps at Chamonix.

Dr. Arnett has said of Dr. Tanner:

> He has risen from a successful barber to be the king of Negro editors. His pen is sharper than his razor, and his editorial chair is finer than the barber chair. The church and race will long remember Dr. B. T. Tanner for the part he has taken in the reconstruction of the South and for his words of encouragement.

R. C. O. Benjamin
Lawyer—Author—Editor—Champion of the Race

R. C. O. Benjamin was born on the Island of St. Keys, March 31, 1855. Education being compulsory on the island, he was sent to school while very young, and at the age of eleven was sent to England under a private tutor, who prepared him for college. While yet a boy he entered Trinity College, Oxford, where he resided for three years, and left without taking a degree; visiting Sumatra, Java and other islands in the East Indies, then returned to England after a two years' tour. Being of a roving disposition, he soon took passage on a vessel coming to America, and arrived in the city of New York, April 13, 1869. Ten days after, the young man shipped as cabin boy on the bark Lepanto, captain, Cyrus E. Staples, and made a six months' cruise to Venezuela, Curacoa, Demerara and West Indies. Returning to New York in the fall of the same year, he concluded to abandon the sea and settled there, working at anything he could get to do. …

While at Hodgensville, Larne county, Kentucky, he borrowed some law books from ex-Congressman Reed, and studied after school hours; once a week he recited lessons to Mr. Dave Smith, now State Senator, but then county attorney. From Kentucky he went to Decatur, Alabama, and was made principal of the public school and continued to read law. Next he goes to Arkansas, to Brinkley and other points, where he taught school, and made enough money to go to Memphis, Tennessee, where he put himself under Honorable Josiah Patterson, an eminent lawyer of that city. Through his influence he was soon after admitted to the bar, January, 1880.

His success has been varied as a practitioner, and the territory over which his services have been extended aggregate twelve different States. He has also owned and edited several newspapers—the *Colored Citizen*, in Pittsburgh, Pennsylvania, and the *Chronicle*, at Evansville, Indiana. He was editor of *The Negro American*, at Birmingham, Alabama.

He is a prolific writer, always selecting such subjects as will interest the people. He has written several very valuable pamphlets, the principal ones of which are "Poetic Gems;" "The Boy Doctor;" "The Defender of Obadiah Cuff;" "The Negro Problem Solved;" "Southland;" "The Future of the Negro;" "Lectures on Africa;" and also an historical chart of the colored race.

He has the credit of being one of the best speakers in the South. He has made extensive trips in lecturing in the principal cities of the United States. In 1886 he made a tour through the principal cities of Canada and lectured to large white audiences. He is a fluent conversationalist in both the French and Spanish languages. Any one reading his paper while he was editor will find that the Negroes in Birmingham, Alabama, have had an able champion in him, and one who would never fail them. His strictures on the murders and out rages on colored people by the railroad companies, in having special gates for them to pass through, show manliness; and whatever may be his faults, he stands by the race. His future is in his own hands.

Nat Turner
Insurrectionist

He was born in Southampton county, Virginia, October 2, 1800. His master was a very wealthy man and owned many slaves. His parents were very pious people. It is natural to suppose that young Nat imbibed the characteristics of his parents, their religion, their songs, their longings and their superstitions. He was a man short in stature with a very intelligent looking forehead, and possessed an inherent quality that commanded the respect of his fellowmen. He had small eyes that shone with the brightness of diamonds whenever he spoke of the Scriptures or the wrongs of his race. He was a Baptist preacher, and was ordained by his father and other preachers from the neighboring plantations.

On account of the teachings and admonitions of his mother, he came to the conclusion that he, like Moses of old, was born to be the deliverer of his people from bondage. He nursed this belief and cherished it until it became the all-absorbing question of his soul. He possessed a trade, the carrying out of which kept him in the woods, and that was the making of wooden trays, bowls, etc. He became familiar with every tree, every nook, and every hiding place in Southampton county. He would come among his people on Sunday, preach the word of God and go back to the mountains to brood over the condition of his burdened people. At last his master saw that he was becoming too familiar with the slaves in the neighborhood, so he thought to hire him to a "nigger breaker" to have him tamed, or cowed down. But this soul was not born for that; it was not in his power to break the spirit of this heroic "black John Brown" of America and Spartacus of the Negro race. He was a man that never consented to an insult given by a white man. When his new master started out no break him, he caught him and tied his hands behind his back and left him on his face. Then he went to his old retreat—the mountains—and there remained thirty days.

Many white people reverenced and honored Nat Turner on account of his commanding influence. Strange to say, a man without the least knowledge of books commanded the admiration of all classes of men, both friends and enemies.

His plot for general uprising was laid in the month of February, 1831. He appointed a meeting to which he invited four friends, Sam Edwards, Hark Travis, Henry Porter and Nelson Williams. These five men met in a lonely glen and thus perfected their plans. But the general trouble was the getting of arms. Nat rose up and told them that the spirit had instructed him to slay his enemies with their own weapons. They at last decided on a plan, and then it was that "The Prophet Nat" arose and addressed them as follows:

Friends and Brothers: We are to commence a great work to-night. Our race is to be delivered from bondage, and God has appointed us as the men to do his bidding, and let us be worthy of our calling. I am told to slay all the whites we encounter without regard to age or sex. Remember we do not go forth for the sake of blood and carnage, but it is necessary that in the commencement of this revolution, all the whites we meet should die, until we have an army strong enough to carry on the war upon a Christian basis.

The blow was struck on the night of the twenty-first of August, 1831. They dealt death and destruction on all sides until the whole country was aroused and the planters armed themselves to baffle the determined actions of this bold emancipator. Yet this did not stop the onward march of this army. Those men, according to the directions of Nat Turner, spared neither men, women nor children. On their way to attack the first house they were joined by a slave belonging to a neighboring plantation, named Will, about six feet in height, a most desperate man, having been made so by the cruelty of his master. He hated him, and every whiteface to him was the sign of an enemy, both to himself and his race. He was overjoyed to have this opportunity to reap vengeance on those who had wronged him. He armed himself with a sharp, broad axe, under whose cruel blows many a white man fell. All night long they continued their work of death and destruction until not only the whole county of Southampton felt the stroke of that terrible blow, but the whole State of Virginia reeled on account of the boldness and persistency in action.

Soldiers were dispatched to the scene of action from different parts of the State by the shortest route as soon as it became known that the blacks were in arms against their masters. Then came the real battle. The blacks fought hand to hand with the whites. Nat saw that they were compelled to be overpowered, so he and a few others escaped and sought shelter in a near swamp where they defied the patient watching of all for two months.

At last he surrendered; loaded with heavy chains, with clothes all tattered and torn and besmeared with the blood of his victims, he was brought to Jerusalem, the county seat of Southampton county. Backed by his unfaltering trust in the Lord and by his belief in the justice of his cause, he stood before his judges like a modern Regulus, without flinching, with not a tremor in his whole body. When asked "guilty or not guilty" he answered straightway, "not guilty." He could not feel that he should die because he had sought to liberate his people from the yoke of slavery, no matter in what way he proceeded to accomplish his end. Nevertheless he was convicted and sentenced to be hanged. In a speech before he was hanged, he prophesied that when they hanged him that the sun would be darkened and the earth tremble in token of the justice of the cause in which he had been engaged. This made such an impression on the mind of the sheriff that he refused to have anything to do with the execution. They brought an old, drunken, broken down, white man forty miles to cut the rope of the trap.

Just as Nat Turner prophesied, at the time for the execution a black cloud came up from the east and veiled the sun; the earth was shaken by loud claps of thunder and the most severe storm followed, such as they had never before witnessed in that part of the country.

Thus died one of the greatest emancipators of the nineteenth century. Some called him a religious fanatic, no doubt because he was a black man. When men of other nations have arisen and used whatever means they had at their command to liberate their people, it has been called heroism; with the Negro, it is brutality. However civilized nations may judge Nat Turner, and however they may write about him, let it be remembered that he foresaw by his acts the career of John Brown. If the Negro was to blame, so was the white man. Nat Turner's insurrection was the upheaval of an honest heart to break, in any way possible, the chains which bound his people. If he was a brute, it must be remembered that his victims only suffered by a system which made him such. If he were a savage, the passions belonging to human nature were only whetted by the cruelties which he saw, and sharpened by the sufferings of his people. He planned in a few minutes, condensed in a few hours, and executed upon his victims in a short time only a tithe of the cruelties which had been heaped upon his own people. If his judgment was swift, it was no more severe than that which had been inflicted upon Negroes under his eyes. He had seen men whipped to death and brutally murdered by the overseers, and if his ideas of crime were of a crude standard, let it also be remembered that poor human nature is influenced by that with which it is surrounded.

Rev. D. A. Payne, D. D., LL. D.

Senior Bishop of the A.M.E. Church—Educator and Author—The Scholar of the Denomination

His life began in the city of Charleston, South Carolina, that city of famous men. The day was an important one in that family, when the future bishop came to visit them, February 24, 1811. His father and mother were members of the M. E. church; the father had charge of two classes, the "seekers' class" and the members' class. The mother was a woman of fine feeling, a tender, loving and faithful Christian, whom the son remembers with all the reverence of his nature. Surely she impressed her own nature to the depths of his heart.

He was early taught to read and attended school supported by an organization known as the Minor's Society, which was supported by free colored men, beginning its work as early as the year 1810. What a blessing this was; they took an interest in him and paid his tuition and book bills for two years. This society was organized to take care of orphan children and give them instruction, and the limit of such aid was two years. Young Payne received the attention of the society during this period. After leaving this school he had one year's training under Thomas Bonneau. He mastered the English branches and studied also Roman and Grecian history. He paid considerable attention to mathematics, so far as to master six books of Euclid. Greek, Latin, French and kindred studies he pursued without a teacher. He came into possession of a book named the "Self-Interpreting Bible," by Rev. John Brown, who had mastered these languages without a teacher, and Payne determined that he could do what had been done. This was a curious determination to one who had little reason to expect to attain any position of eminence in life from such a lowly station; nor did he himself have any such notion, as he had determined to become a soldier in Hayti. Rumors had come to him of the wars on that island, and he was stirred with the tales of battle and broils, and, like many young men, was lured to scenes of danger from the romance therein. He was an apprentice in the carpenter-shop of Richard Holloway, his brother-in-law, James Holloway, being the foreman.

Many a day did he ponder over his situation and long after the very things perhaps which he realized in after life. Circumscribed as he was, it is wonderful that he succeeded so admirably from such small beginnings. His warlike desires were no doubt aroused by reading the old Scottish tales which fell into his hands, and his head was full of the deeds of Wallace and Bruce.

But, like Joseph of old, he was "warned in a dream," and he changed his mind and hid forever his youthful warlike desires. At fifteen he became concerned for his soul, and was received into the class of Samuel Weston on probation, becoming a devoted seeker of the Lord Jesus Christ. Elder James O. Andrews was then in charge of the Methodist churches in the city of Charleston, and afterwards became his guide and teacher in the ways of eternal life. At fifteen he was converted, and a blessed day it was to him—a holy Sabbath day—a day of rest, when his soul found the rest it had for three years been longing. Shortly after he was impressed in a singular way to go and preach the gospel. It was on a day when at prayer he heard a voice that seemed to call him to the duty which has so faithfully marked his life.

Hands seemed to press upon his shoulders as if hurrying him forward to begin the work of an educator. He soon laid aside the plane and chisel, saw, spirit-level and the carpenter's apron, and went forth to chisel his name on the highest pinnacle of fame, and smooth down the rough places in the intellects of the young, and be guided by the spirit of Christ.

Herein also he was like Christ. He left the carpenter's bench to minister to the wants of others. He opened a school in the house of Cæsar Wright, having his children as his first scholars at fifty cents per month. This was in 1829, and during the year 1830 he had no more scholars than enough to make his pay about two dollars per month. Yet this was the embryo Wilberforce which he had in the sample before him. He soon gained popularity, and after six years had the largest and most successful school in the city.

But the thing was too good to last. Payne was having too much success. The white folks said the school must be broken up, and the bishop himself has told us that the people said Payne was playing "HELL" in Charleston. For Negroes to go to school was objectionable, and it was compared to the infernal regions in its results. This was not altogether out of place, it would seem, for as they had very little true religion, and among those people to destroy these schools, they felt the Negroes would rise in a generation and strike for freedom, and in so doing the white folks would get a through ticket to that place.

A sketch written by T. McCants Stewart says that they passed a law in the Legislature which made it impossible for Mr. Payne to remain any longer in the home of his birth and as an educator of his people. Before this time, however, Mr. Payne's life was embittered by what he saw of slavery. He himself had suffered. While never whipped under that system which Garrison rightly called "a league with death and a covenant in hell," he had suffered bonds and imprisonment. Standing on the street of Charleston, South Carolina, about fifty-six years ago, with a small walking cane in his hand, a white man snatched it from him and struck him, indignant at the idea of a "nigger" carrying a cane. Young Payne, full of fire and manhood, retaliated and was imprisoned. His soul was full of bitterness against oppression and the oppressor, because he saw husbands sold away from wives, he saw children, even nursing infants, torn cruelly from their parents. He saw the victims of the driver's lash and the auction block; he saw his people compelled to make bricks without mortar or straw. He heard their cries, "How long, O Lord, how long?" When, therefore, unjust and oppressive law forced him out of his native city, he resolved never to return again until slavery was destroyed.

In 1835 Mr. Payne sailed out of Charleston harbor with this determination. Strange to relate, he returned on the very day and date thirty years thereafter the bishop of the A.M.E. church, to plant the banner of that connection on the soil of South Carolina, and in the very city where thirty years before he had suffered imprisonment and oppression.

He landed in Philadelphia, where he taught school for several years. The same year of his arrival he entered the Lutheran Theological Seminary at Gettysburg, Pennsylvania, but was compelled by the weakness of his eyes to surrender his course. He was ordained an elder by the Lutherans in 1837, having entered the ministry the year before. While teaching and preaching in Philadelphia the old building, the Bethel of Richard Allen's day, was torn down, and Elder Payne assisted in laying the corner-stone of the present edifice. In 1840 he joined the Philadelphia conference as a local preacher. In 1843 he was traveling preacher in the same body. Bishop Morris Brown appointed him to the Israel Bethel church at Washington, District of Columbia. Here he remained for five years. He was then appointed to the Bethel church of Baltimore, Maryland, then to the Ebenezer church in the same city. The bishop rose from station to station because he preached the word of God and did right. May 7, 1852, the General conference met in New York City. A special sermon was to be preached and Elder Payne was selected the preacher. When he did so he easily carried off the prize. He was elected bishop and ruler of the representative of the younger and more progressive element. May 13, 1852, he was ordained bishop of the A.M.E. church, and beyond doubt has been a faithful steward.

Bishop Payne's name will stand in the history of the A.M.E. church as a founder of a system of education just as Aristotle and Bacon were founders of a system of logic. Garrison says Plato is philosophy and philosophy Plato. The A.M.E. church can freely say Bishop Payne is so of education, and the spirit of our education is embodied in Bishop Payne. Years ago Wilberforce University was offered the bishop as a school for our church. Certain parties stood ready to purchase the property at a higher figure than we could pay. The matter had to be decided on a certain day. Bishop Payne could not consult his colleagues and he would not permit the order to be given The bishop was without a dollar and remembered the fact that the connection was not enthusiastic over Christian education; but with a firm faith in the omnipotent arm of the Jehovah, and inspired with that courage that characterized his life, he stood in the presence of the person who was to sell. Alone with Jesus and with uplifted hands, Bishop Payne cried, "In the name of God I purchase this property for the A.M.E. church, to be consecrated by them for the sacred cause of Christian education." He lived to pay every dollar of the debt which he that day incurred. This school is truly a monument to his rare foresight and earnest zeal in the cause of education, and a great desire on his part to see the ministers of the church educated.

Dr. Tanner, in speaking of him in his apology for African Methodism, says that the Wilberforce University is preeminently the legacy he will leave to the church and the people he loves so well. Upon it he has laid himself as a willing sacrifice: of it he thinks by day and dreams by might; of it he writes, talks and works; for it he has crossed the sea. He became the president of this college in 1863 and continued till 1876, building it up into the great and powerful school which has sent out very learned men and given many titles to its clergy and scholars. Rev. B. W. Arnett, in his centennial address on the mission of Methodism, has said of Bishop Payne that he was "the apostle of an educated ministry." He was the first president of a Negro university in the western world; the first Negro to preside over the Universal Methodist family, September 17, 1881, at the Ecumenical conference held in London, England. He has been the historian of the church since 1848 and is the author of several works.

The bishop is about to publish his recollections of men and things, which has engaged his attention for the last three score years. He has recently published a book on Domestic Education. Full of years and honor, he still continues to labor for the denomination. He received the degree of LL. D. from Lincoln University in 1880, and D. D. from Wilberforce

University. He by his own exertions secured the museum to Wilberforce University, which is worth two thousand dollars; and in honor of the services which he rendered in that connection, it has been named the "Payne Museum," and, says the Wilberforce Alumnial of 1885:

Thus will his name be connected with the study of sciences, and as the young and rising generations tread the halls of the university, they will read the name of the noble author and disciple of knowledge, that in our age stands as a synonym for a Christian education, and could be transmitted from generation to generation as a worthy example of consecrated learning and a devoted love to man and God.

May his days be prolonged to do much good; but surely he will leave behind him grateful hearts and many who owe all directly to the influences which he has set in motion in the establishment of the Wilberforce University.

William J. Simmons, Geo. M. Revell & Co. 1887

JAMES T. HALEY

"Christian Truth in Slave Songs"
Rev. C. J. Ryder, D.D.

The influence of slavery in the songs of nations
The Purpose of this Paper
The oldest psalm in the whole collection of these marvelous sacred songs is the ninetieth (XC.). It was born in the heart of a man who had felt the bitter hardship of slavery. "They made their lives bitter with hard bondage," was the pitiful record of his race in Egypt. Moses, the author of this psalm, knew well of those wretched experiences of slavery. The influence of those dark days, and the thirty-eight years wandering in the wilderness, oppressed the Poet General of Israel, and he exclaimed "We are consumed by thine anger, and by thy wrath are we troubled. For all our days are passed away in thy wrath." It was the influence of slavery in the songs of the Israelite nation. You can trace the same effects in the sacred writings after each captivity. The experience of slavery colored their religious songs, as it touched their national life and molded their nation's history.

It would be a most interesting study to follow out this same line of investigation and note how the suppression of national independence, the subjugation of any people, has colored their religious thought, and found expression in their sacred songs. It is my purpose, however, only to note the fact of this influence, not to illustrate it.

The growth or development of sacred songs is an interesting study. Take some familiar hymns. We sing "Hail to the Lord's anointed," written by James Montgomery, in 1822. "Jesus shall Reign Where'er the Sun," written by Isaac Watts, in 1819. "Rescue the Perishing," by Fanny Crosby. "My Country 'tis of Thee," written by Rev. S. F. Smith, in 1832. Eighteen Christian centuries stand behind these sacred hymns. Each mighty century contributed its rich gifts to the development of the races whose blood flowed in the veins of Montgomery or Watts, or Crosby or Smith. There is evolution of Christian song. Now in studying these old slave songs, we touch hands with heathen Africa. Two hundred and fifty years of enforced bondage and thirty years of freedom are all separate those who sung these songs from barbarism. We cannot expect to find the models of expression that eighteen centuries of free Christian development have produced. We shall discover crude, weird, quaint words, and often fantastic music. But this study and analysis throws light upon race development, and proves, I think, that the great truths of the Christian faith comforted and uplifted the humble, ignorant slave just as truly as the wealthy, and intelligent, and refined.

"The best commentary on the Scripture is the Scripture," said a learned divine. So the best commentary on the Negro is the Negro. We have done almost everything with and for the Negro, except let him speak for himself. We preach at him; we hold him up as a remarkable example of total depravity, of hopeless corruption, or as rich in his religious nature. We tell of his terrible degration, or his wonderful progress, as the whim may strike us. We do everything except let him speak for himself.

This paper is a humble effort on the part of the writer to let the Negro speak for himself concerning his religious faith. These three introductory considerations just mentioned are of importance in studying the slave songs of our own bondmen.

1st. The influence of slavery in coloring their Christian songs.

2nd. The evolution of sacred songs.

3rd. The value of the Negro's views of the Negro.

Turning aside from the statistics of church growth, let us ask the question, What is there among the Negroes of the South to build up-on in Christian work? Have they correct ideas of the great fundamental truths of Christianity? What was the theology of the plantation? What are the fundamental elements in the religious thought of these freed slaves? Must we recast their conceptions of religious truth, or only seek to intellectualize that which is spiritually discerned? What are the religious conceptions of these uneducated Negroes? What was the theology of the slaves?

The answer to this question determines largely the future of our church work among the mass of colored people. The progress will be painfully slow, if we must lay the foundations of religious truth before we can build the super-structure of church work. But if we discover that they hold evangelical truth substantially correct, we have a great advantage.

"They that do His will shall know of the doctrine," we read. These poor Negroes walking never in the full day of opportunity of religious truth communed with God in the night of their oppression and wrong, and it is marvelous how wonderfully he revealed himself to them. They have no polemic literature, no dogmatic theology We learn of one old colored preacher who had a trial for heresy on his hands, because he preached against stealing chickens!

Indeed they had no literature at all as a race, but coming out from these two and a half centuries of bondage they have brought with them a whole body of Christian song. Like the Homeric plays or the Scotch ballads, these Negro songs, which came from their hearts and grew out of their religious experiences, were preserved by being repeated—handed down by word of mouth from father to son, from mother to child.

> The triumph note that Marian sung,
> The joy of uncaged birds;
> Softening with Africa's mellow tongue
> Their broken Saxon words.

Now do these plantation hymns give evidence that the great fundamental doctrines of evangelical Christianity were held by these humble people in their days of slavery? In pushing our Christian work in the South, can we assume this fact? It is not only a very interesting question in ethnology and race history, but also of great importance in our missionary enterprises to know just what these humble people learned of God's truth in the school house of slavery, having little human instruction but communing with God's Spirit. That we may discover the answer to this question, let us arrange somewhat systematically these old plantation melodies, these songs that were never written, but that burst from the hearts of the slaves when crushed under the weight of their bondage.

They could not read nor write. But let us remember that our own race is indebted for its highest poetic expression of Christian truth in the early centuries to one who could not read, Ceadmon Monk, of Whitely. He was the greatest Anglo-Saxon poet and father of English song. He gave us our first Paradise Lost, equal, in many respects, to John Milton's greatest book.

1. These slave songs teach, beyond doubt, that the slaves held to the truth of Divine Sovereignty.

We repeat in our churches the beautiful language of the Apostle's Creed: "I believe in God the Father Almighty, Maker of Heaven and Earth." So do these humble Negroes believe. This great truth bursts forth from their lips in jubilant song.

> Didn't my Lord deliver Daniel,
> D'liver Daniel, d'liver Daniel?
> Didn't my Lord deliver Daniel,
> And why not every man?

What a strange pathetic appeal to this Divine Ruler are these words in the hymn, "Keep me from sinking down:"

> I bless the Lord I'm gwine to die;
> Keep me from sinking down.
> I'm gwine to judgment by-and-bye;
> Keep me from sinking down.
> O Lord, O my Lord! O my good Lord!
> Keep me from sinking down.

It suggests to one Jean Ingelow's "Brothers and a Sermon," and the touching prayer of the old fisherman to whom the Lord Jesus came in the night season.

> O, Lord, good Lord,
> I am a broken down poor man, a fool
> To speak to thee. ...
> O Lord, our Lord,
> How great is thy compassion. Come, good Lord,
> For we will open. Come this night, good Lord;
> Stand at the door and knock.
> Only the wind knocks at my door, Oh, loud and long it knocks,
> The only thing God made that has a mind to enter in.

Yea, thus the old man spake. These were the last words of his aged mouth.

But one did knock. One came to sup with him, that humble, weak, old man; knocked at his door in the rough pauses of the laboring wind.

And when the neighbors came the morrow morn they said: "He looks as he had woke and seen the face of Christ, and with that rapturous smile held out his arms, to come to Him."

The appeal of these Negroes was to Divine Justice, not to fickle human passion, and they rejoiced in view of such a judgment day. "God, the Father Almighty," they held to, they gloried in and no mystery of suffering ever dimmed their faith. We can assume its existence and build upon it in pushing our church work among them in the Southland.

Calvinism seems to have crept in at the very basis of their doctrinal views. Original sin finds recognition in the following odd song:

Old Satan thinks he'll get us all,
Yes, my Lord;
Because in Adam we did fall,
Yes, my Lord.

Whether they hold to the federal headship of Adam, I cannot state positively. If they adopted Professor Shedd's theory that the whole race was actually, physically present in Adam and consciously sinned, it would be another argument for the unity of the human race, or else hint very strongly that Adam was slightly off color.

2. Again these slaves held to the Divinity of Christ
—crudely stated, imperfectly discerned, but tenaciously maintained. Among their plantation hymns, illustrating this, I refer to only two or three.

Just stand right still and steady yourself,
I know that my Redeemer lives.
Oh, just let me tell you about God his self,
I know that my Redeemer lives.

Or another, the refrain of which runs:

Reign, Oh, reign; Oh, reign my Savior!
Reign, Oh, reign; Oh, reign my Lord.

Or still another:

Why, He's the Lord of lords,
And the King of kings.
Why, Jesus Christ is the first and last,
No one can work like Him.

3. There is little in their songs concerning the Holy Spirit.
The Father and Son were relations that they could understand. The more mysterious

work and personality of the Holy Spirit they did not so easily grasp. But they did not doubt that God was with them and that the Lord Jesus Christ was their companion.

4. The Atonement

The atonement, the Son of God dying for them to open the way of salvation, was a truth most precious to them in their life of painful neglect or bitter persecution. Their plantation melodies are full of this truth. One, however, will illustrate the fact as well as a dozen. And what more beautiful than that with the refrain,

> I've been redeemed, I've been redeemed,
> Been washed in the blood of the Lamb.

If we turn from Theology proper to Anthropology, we find here the fundamental truths entering into their religious conceptions. They thoroughly believe in human freedom of the will, if not of the person, and in human responsibility. They sung as they swayed back and forth in their weird gatherings at night, under the old pine forests, or on a hillock in the midst of some swampy jungle, these words:

> Don't you want to be a soldier, soldier, soldier,
> Don't you want to be a soldier in the year of jubilee?
> Then you must rise and shine and give God the glory, glory,
> Rise and shine and give God the glory in the year of jubilee.

They believe that they must "work out their own salvation with fear and trembling," but they never forget that "it is God that worketh in them both to will and to do of his good pleasure."

The personality of Satan they never doubted, and his ability to tempt human souls is illustrated in many of their hymns. They sing at Tougaloo, Miss., a hymn which especially emphasizes this fact. The refrain goes,

> Old Satan, he wears de hypocrite shoe,
> If you don't mind, he slip it on you.

A warning that is not limited in its application to the Southern Negroes.

5. Convertion and Regeneration

Again, how tenaciously they hold to the doctrine of Conversion and Regeneration, the union of the Divine and human in this great change of the soul, is abundantly proved.

> Run to Jesus, shun the danger,
> I don't expect to stay much longer here.

Here is illustrated human effort, conversion, turning to Jesus. This hymn is especially interesting, for Hon. Frederick Douglass told us that these words, "Run to Jesus," sung on the plantation where he was a slave, first suggested to him the thought of escaping from slavery, "Praying with his feet," as he put it.

But carrying out the thought further, we find their idea of conversion and regeneration, and the joy of a new born soul illustrated in the following quaint hymn, "The Angels Done Changed My Name."

> I went to the hillside, I went to pray;
> I knew the angels done changed my name,
> Done changed my name for the coming day;
> I knew the angels done changed my name.
>
> I looked at my hands, my hands was new,
> I knowed the angels done changed my name;
> I looked at my feet and my feet was too,
> Thank God the angels done changed my name.

Souls that sung and felt that, knew the experiences of the great apostle, when he said, "Wherefore if any man is in Christ Jesus, he is a new creature; the old things are passed away; behold, they are become new." 2 Cor. v. 17. N. V.

But if we go a little deeper into philosophy or doctrinal analysis, we discover the familiar old doctrine of the "perseverance of the saints." Did they hold it? Did they sing it? Listen as they sing of the poor inch-worm:

> T'was inch by inch I sought the Lord,
> Jesus will come by-and-by,
> And inch by inch he blessed my soul,
> Jesus will come by-and-by.
>
> We'll inch and inch and inch along,
> Jesus will come by-and-by,
> And inch and inch till we gets home,
> Jesus will come by-and-by.
>
> Keep inching along, keep inching along;
> Jesus will come by-and-by;
> Keep inching along like the poor inch worm.
> Jesus will come by-and-by.

Now, I submit that this quaint old plantation song not only teaches the "perseverance of the saints," but aptly illustrates about the rate of progress most of us make, "Inching along like the poor inch worm."

But they believe that conversion should change their lives. It is not true that they entirely neglect ethics in their religious conceptions. Take this hymn as evidence:

You say you're aiming for the skies,
View the land, view the land;
Why don't you stop your telling lies?
Oh, view the heavenly land.

You say your Lord has set you free,
View the land, view the land;
Why don't you let your neighbors be?
Oh, view the heavenly land.

6. Their views on eschatology were also sound.

They believed in future punishment and future rewards. The former is strange. It would seem as if this whole race of Lazaruses, who received only the crumbs that fell from their rich masters' tables would feel that they experienced their share of evil in this world. But, no! they held firmly to the idea that sin must be punished and incorporated this idea into their songs. Many of their melodies illustrate this. None better, perhaps, than the one beginning:

My Lord, what a mourning, what a mourning,
When the stars begin to fall;
You'll hear the sinners mourn,
When the stars begin to fall.

But their hope in future rewards, or, better, blessings bestowed by a Heavenly Father, was bright and fadeless. We who were born in freedom can never realize how jubilant was the Christian slave in view of death. It was release. It was victory.

Heinrich Heine, the witty scholar and poet, speaking of his return to the Bible and its sources of consolation in the last years of his life, uses the following remarkable language:

"The re-awakening of my religious feelings I owe to that Holy Book, the Bible. Astonishing! that after I have whirled about all my life over all the dance-floors of philosophy, and yielded myself to all the orgies of the intellect ... without satisfaction, I now find myself on the same standpoint where poor Uncle Tom stands—on that of the Bible. I kneel down by my black brother in the same prayer! What a humiliation! ... Poor Tom, indeed, seems to have seen deeper things in the Holy Book than I. The poor Negro slave reads with his back and understands better than we do." Heine had discovered the truth that physical suffering often brings clearer spiritual vision. Paul scourged, was Paul triumphant. John in exile, was John in the Spirit. These physical hardships prepared the Apostle the better for the glories of the spiritual revelation. So these Negro slaves had no light on earth, but the glories of the Son of Righteousness burst through their gloom, and lighted and warmed and thrilled them. In view of death they broke in triumphant song as they sang of

Those bright mansions above,
Bright mansions above:
Lord, I want to live up yonder,
In bright mansions above.

Their life was full of misery here, but they looked forward with confident expectation and sang:

Wait a little while, then we'll sing the new song;
Wait a little while.
My heavenly home is bright and fair,
We will sing the new song.
No pain nor sorrow enters there,
Then we'll sing the new song.

We can understand some of the references in their songs to peculiar victories and delights in the heavenly country, only by understanding the customs that prevailed in times of slavery. Take this one: The young men of neighboring plantations were accustomed to organize and ride over the country to watch the Negroes at night. There might be some one escaping or possibly a danger of general uprising. Now the slaves must avoid these "patroles," as they called them. Even when going out at night for prayer or their revival services, they must avoid detection.

One old Negro told me that he used to hide in the smoke house to pray. A Negro woman related in a most interesting manner her experiences on her master's plantation in attending revival meetings on the river side at night, creeping out from her cabin to avoid the patrol and hounds. Now, in this heavenly country, to which these humble people looked forward, one great blessing would come to them, there would be no "patroles" nor hounds. In daylight fair and full, before the hosts of the redeemed, they could sing and pray and shout. How they gloried in this thought in their songs!

Shine, shine, I'll meet you in that morning,
O my soul's going to shine, to shine;
I'm going to sit down at a welcome table,
Shine, shine, my soul's going to shine.
I'm going to walk all about that city,
Shine, shine, my soul's going to shine.
Or, another, the refrain of which runs:

Chiluns, chiluns, we all shall be free,
Chiluns, chiluns, we all shall be free,
When the Lord shall appear.

Or that other sweet, weird song that charmed crowded audiences on both sides of the ocean, and that Mr. Gladstone himself called for whenever he heard the Jubilee singers in England. "Swing low, sweet chariot, coming for to carry me home."

> I looked over Jordan, and what did I see?
> Coming for to carry me home.
> A band of angels coming after me,
> Coming for to carry me home.

To those who were crowded in unwholesome dungeons, waiting the auction block, or were packed in the foul hole of some Mississippi steamer, to be released only as they went to the miseries of sugar plantations or rice swamps, crudely mingled with their ideas of heaven was the comfortable thought that they would be no longer harassed and annoyed and crowded, and they sung:

> For my Lord says there's room enough,
> Room enough in the heavens for you,
> My Lord says there's room enough,
> Don't stay away.

But my object is not to illustrate their hymns, but to get if possible from them their conceptions of fundamental religious truth.

One other thought. These hymns are remarkable not only for what they contain, but also for their omissions. 1st. We have in these plantation songs no mariolatry. Many Negroes belonged to Catholic masters. In Louisiana, about New Orleans, I have attended many meetings held by these Negroes. I have never heard, nor have I found anywhere in these plantation melodies, any which sung the praises of the Virgin. Such a figment of a theological brain does not have power in it. It needs the truth to take hold of humble souls and become an inspiration in their songs. 2d. We note with wonder the entire absence of all vindictiveness in these melodies. This certainly is a marvelous fact. Downtrodden, abused, sold from kindred, outraged in every way; it would seem more than human if there did not run through these songs, coming from their bleeding hearts, an undertone of vindictive satisfaction that their masters must suffer under a just God due recompense for these bitter cruelties, but you scarcely find a trace of it. There seems a hint of it in "Turn back Pharaoh's army, Hallelu!"

> When Moses smote the water,
> The children all passed over,
> And turned back Pharaoh's Pharaoh's army, Hallelu!
> And turned back Pharaoh's army, Hallelu!

> When Pharaoh crossed the water,
> The waters came together,

And drowned ole Pharaoh's army, Hallelu!
And drowned ole Pharaoh's army, Hallelu!

But this is rather the triumphant song of a black Miriam, taking the timbrel as she "sings unto the Lord, for he hath triumphed gloriously, the horse and the rider hath he thrown into the sea." This Negro song heralded the victory of God over his enemies, not over theirs. And we find them, even in the crude language of these plantation songs evidence that among these uneducated millions of Negroes there is a sound and wholesome belief in the great fundamental truths of Christianity. 1st. That God governs the world. 2d. That Christ is divine. 3d. The fact of the necessity and efficacy of the Atonement. 4th. Man's lost and ruined condition. 5th. The need and possibility of conversion and regeneration. 6th. Progress in the Christian life. 7th. Future punishment of sin and the rewards of faith and obedience. We mark also the absence of the mischievous doctrines of the Romish Church, and also all vindictive bitterness.

We can assume that these truths are in the hearts of the people whom we seek to reach as we push forward our church work. For around us there lie unreached millions of black Americans; across the ocean the uncounted millions of heathen Africa; these are to be saved under God by the Negroes of America. What a prospect! What an inspiring work! What a blessed God-given opportunity to the churches of America!

You remember that scene between Cassy and Uncle Tom, unmatched in other profane literature, when Cassy having unsuccessfully urged Uncle Tom to kill that monster Legree, determined to do it herself. With flashing eyes, her blood boiling with passion long suppressed, the abused Creole woman, robbed of womanhood, exclaims, "His time is come, and I'll have his heart's blood!"

"No, no, no," said Tom, holding his small hands which were clenched with spasmodic violence. "No, ye poor lost soul, that ye mustn't do. The dear, blessed Lord never shed no blood but his own, and that he poured out for us when we was his enemies. Lord, help us to follow his steps, and love our enemies."

"Love," said Cassy, with a fierce glare; "love such enemies! It isn't in flesh and blood."

"No, Miss, it isn't," said Tom, looking up; "but he gives it to us, and that's the victory. When we can love and pray over all, and through all, the battle's past and the victory's come, glory be to God!" And, with streaming eyes and choking voice, the black man looked up to heaven.

"And this, Oh, Africa! latest called of nations, called to the crown of thorns, the scourge, the bloody sweat, the cross of agony, this is to be thy victory; by this shalt thou reign with Christ when his kingdom shall come on earth."

"Choice Thoughts and Utterances of Wise Colored People"

Color is the sign of trouble with judge and jury.—*S. B. Wallace*

To make a contented slave you must make a thoughtless one.—*Frederick Douglass*

Don't aim to be consistent, but true. Consistency may lead to error and wrong doing.
—*G. T. Robinson*

The race must not forget the rock from whence they were hewn, nor the pit from whence they were digged.—*Wm. Still*

Remember, Christian Negroes, black as Cain, may be refined and join the angelic train.
—*Phillis Wheatley.*

If a man wants to know his own strength, he need not measure himself. He needs only to size up the fellows who are pulling against him to find out how strong he is.
—*Bishop Grant.*

We cannot go to Africa and succeed with all our ignorance and poverty. Let our big men set out to break down immorality among Negroes and white folks. Get Negroes to have more refinement and race pride, use Negro books and papers, hang Negro pictures on their walls; get up Negro industries and give deserving colored men and women employment; break down superstition and mistrust. Get Negroes to act decently both publicly and privately.
—*Athens (Ga.) Clipper*

Stay as far away from danger as possible.—*Capt. G. T. Robinson*

Flirting with the truth is the modest way of calling a man a liar without making him mad.
—*Editor Texas Gazette*

We are in favor of the saloons being closed twenty-four hours each day and seven days in each week.—*Rev. R. W. E. Ferguson.*

The captive Jews could not sing by the waters of Babylon, but the Negroes in the dark dungeon of American slavery made themselves harps, tuned then to some of the most thrilling melodies.—*E. W. Blyden*

Each race is endowed with peculiar talents, and watchful to the last degree is the great Creator over the individuality, the freedom and independence of each.—*E. W. Blyden*

There is a future before the race; a great and useful future—a future fraught with results which shall touch every phase of the world's life, and bring men into sweeter harmony with each other and with God.—*Rev. Geo. C. Rowe*

A Negro paper should pay special attention to those things which concern the race. Take politics in small doses without any shaking.—*Hon. Geo. T. Robinson*

Christian education and wealth is the colored man's only savior. Those two things acquired will do more to adjust his station in life than any two acquisitions imaginable.
—*Editor Knoxville Gleaner*

"Negroes are more religious than white folks. They are more emotional. Emotion is not a virtue, for some emotionalists are sadly wanting in all the virtues.
—*Editor Nashville Citizen*

I am exceedingly anxious that every young colored man and woman should keep a hopeful and cheerful spirit as to the future. Despite all of our disadvantages and hardships, ever since our fore-fathers set foot upon American soil as slaves, our pathway has been marked by progress. Think of it. We went into slavery pagans; we came out Christians. We went into slavery a piece of property; we came out American citizens. We went into slavery without a language; we came out speaking the proud Anglo-Saxon tongue. We went into slavery with slave chains clanking about our wrists; we came out with the American ballot in our hands.—*Prof. B. T. Washington*

There is not a single Negro in the United States on the road to practical truth, so far as his race is concerned. He feels something in him; his instincts point to it, but he cannot act out what he feels. And when he has made up his mind to remain in America, he has also made up his mind to surrender his race integrity; for he sees no chance of its preservation.
—*E. W. Blyden*

Give the women a free use of the ballot and the Upas tree of intemperance will be hewn down by the axe of prohibition.—*Mrs. M. A. McCurdy*

Influences may be set at work in your life and in mine, supported by an earnest purpose, which, like a mighty anthem, shall swell and expand, increasing in volume and sweetness as it makes its way adown the years—drawing men through the power of that Christian education which has been emphasized in us, to recognize the beauty of knowledge and wisdom, "whose ways are ways of pleasantness and all her paths are peace."—*Rev. George C. Rowe*

There is a mistaken idea that "culture" means to paint a little, sing a little, dance a little, put on haughty airs, and to quote passages from popular books. It means nothing of the kind. Culture means politeness, charity, fairness, good temper and good conduct. Culture is not a thing to make a display of; it is something to use so moderately that people do not discover all at once that you have it.—*Editor Colored American.*

While man can boast of great physical strength, skill and bull dog courage, woman carries in her weak frame a moral courage very seldom found among men. If our race is to be a great race in this great nation of races, our women must be largely instrumental in making it so.—*American Baptist.*

Reading is to the mind what eating is to the body. So to eat without giving nature time to assimilate is to rob her, first of health, then life; so to read without reflecting is to cram the intellect and paralyze the mind. In all cases, dear friends, reflect more than you read, in order to present what you read to your hearers.—*S. A. Wesson, Lincolnville, S. C.*

Let us as Negroes educate; let us survive; let us live up to our opportunities of doing good to ourselves and to others, so shall we work out a glorious destiny upon earth, and contribute our share of the good and great immorals out of every nation, that shall take their places among "the spirits of just men made perfect who are without fault before the throne."—*Rev. Wm. D. Johnson, D.D., Athens, Ga*

When I contemplate the actions of the American Negro on the battlefields of the South—at the many scenes of carnage in which he was engaged during the late War of Rebellion—with what heroism he performed deeds of valor, showing and demonstrating his ability even at the cannon's mouth, my very heart bleeds for the foul blot heaped upon the countless thousands of black men, who laid their lives upon their country's altar, for the establishment and perpetuity of this government.
—*Hon. J. A. Brown, in Ohio Legislature, March 10, 1886*

It will be a serious step for Africa, the emigrants themselves and the cause of Christianity for any great number of Negroes who do not know the primary principles of the Christian religion, and the rudiments of self-government to migrate to that dark continent. None but the very best people should go to Africa—none but wise and industrious Christians should be encouraged nor induced to go to that benighted land.—*Professor Floyd*

The exiled Negro in the Western Hemisphere, in spite of slavery, in spite of bitter prejudices, the dark passions of which he has been the victim, has come under influences which have given him the elements of a noble civilization. The seed of a spiritual, intellectual, industrial life has been planted in his bosom, which, when he is transferred to the land of his fathers, will grow up into beauty, expand into flower, and develop into fruit which the world will be glad to welcome.—*E. W. Blyden*

A potent factor for the elevation of the Negro that can be wielded to better advantage in literary and debating societies than by any other channel in the disseminating and encouragement of Negro literature among the masses, for there is no intermediate agency that will instill race pride, race confidence and race co-operation in the Negro faster than reading race books and race papers.—*Chas. V. Monk, Philadelphia*

Character possession is as essential to a people as to an individual. That is to say, the race without a greater percentage of moral worth on its side is as helpless and hopeless as the man or woman devoid of the same attribute of strength and greatness. Those nations and peoples with centuries of history behind them need not be so careful in the matter of virtuous conduct as those who have made none or but little headway on the road to civilization and race grandeur. The Afro-American youth therefore would do well to rid himself of the delusions that he can afford to follow in the wake of his dominant Caucasian companion so far as vice and immorality are involved. Japhet has reveled in success so long and maintains such a grasp on the reins of universal mastery at present, that he can with more propriety afford to take a day off than can his unfortunate brother of Hamitic descent. From pulpits, lecture stands, lyceums, tracts, books, papers, club rooms and every other medium of reaching them, our young men should be given to understand that they can ignore the claims of morality, virtue and religion only at the greatest peril. Cards, dice, drink and dissipation in numberless forms may be indulged in by the weak ones of the stronger race, but those of our weaker race who would be strong must avoid these vices as they would shun poison.—*Rev. H. T. Johnson, Editor Christian Recorder*

EMANUEL KING LOVE (1850-1900)

Introduction

Emmanuel King Love was born into slavery near Marion, in Perry County, Arkansas on July 27, 1850. In 1872, Love entered Augusta Institute in Augusta, Georgia where he became an academic success, leading all of his classes at the time of his graduation in 1877. Love was ordained to the Baptist ministry on December 12, 1875. Between 1877 and 1879, Love was a missionary in the state of Georgia. In 1885, Love became pastor at the First African Baptist Church in Savannah, Georgia, the nation's oldest continuously active African American Baptist Church. He was a popular and respected pastor, and held this position until his death in 1900. During Love's pastorate, the First African Baptist Church was probably the largest African American Baptist Church in the world.

These centennial sermons were delivered in Savannah as part of the celebrations to mark the greatest event in the history of U.S. colored Baptists. The Rev. Dr. Love's sermons created wide-spread interest as they touched on such important subjects.

They are taken from *The History of the First African Baptist Church, from its organization, January 20th, 1788, to July 1st, 1888.*

Going to Law

"Dare any of you, having a matter against another, go to law before the unjust and not before the saints?" (1 Cor. 6:1).

I am not ignorant of the fact that I have a delicate and difficult subject to handle to-night about which much has been said, written and thought. If I should carelessly speak to-night untold harm might be the result, which would be just the opposite to what I aim at and wish so much to accomplish. I am also aware that this subject is as a two-edged sword, capable of cutting both ways.

Believing it better to let two guilty men escape justice than to punish one innocent man, I proceed to discuss this subject to-night in the fear of heaven, relying upon the guidance of the Holy Spirit to assist me in so fearful an undertaking. I am outgrowing the idea that the truth should be kept from the people for fear that they will abuse it. I think the better way would be to have the whole truth and let the results be what they will. The common interpretation of this scripture will tend to make religion objectionable and church membership an unreasonable burden. The religion of Christ is based upon common-sense reasoning. We have hold of the chain of reason, the opposite end of which is centered in the eternal bosom of God. Religion requires us to live a common sense, practical life. Our Savior rebuked the Pharisees for misinterpreting the law and binding heavy burdens, and grievous to be borne, upon the people. Religion requires us to adopt a common course of justice with our fellow-men. There is as much logic in the idea of keeping the whole truth from the people for fear they will abuse it as there would be in the idea of keeping freedom from a people for fear they would abuse it. The better way would be to let the people have freedom, which is right, and then teach them the proper way to enjoy it. There is no privilege but that it has and can be abused. The principle is right, nevertheless. Water and food have made persons sick, yet it is not denied that they are good to take in. Some persons marry and do not get on well together, yet it is admitted that marrying is right. One man quits a woman upon the ground that he can not live with her, and yet another man marries her and lives happily with her.

It must be admitted also that there are exceptions to all general rules. It is so in the Bible as well as in other books. God has shown this in his dealing with the children of men. Hence the origin of miracles. The rule for entering heaven is marked through repentance toward God and faith in His son, yet none of us doubt the salvation of infants, who can not do either. The rule is that a star does not stop, and yet one stood over the manger where the young child was. It is the rule that fire will burn, yet the Hebrew children went through the fiery furnace without the smell of fire upon their clothes. It is a rule that men die, yet Enoch and Elijah were translated. It is a rule that iron sinks, yet the prophet caused it to swim. In this light we must view many scriptural precepts. It was not lawful for the disciples to enter the corn field and eat on the Sabbath, yet Christ defended them, and said he was Lord even of the Sabbath. With the foregoing remarks we can more practically discuss this much disputed subject.

I. Is it right to go to law with a brother?
We would say that it depends largely upon the character and nature of the subject in dispute. As a rule it is not right to go to law. If every body would do right we would have but little, if any, use for the courts. But from the fact that we are not predisposed to do unto all men as we would that they do unto us, God has appointed judges. The judges that sat in the gates of the city were to discern between the people. It is not good for church members to be contentious, because it does not reflect favorably upon Christianity. It would not reflect creditably upon members of the same family to be contending in the courts with each other. If brother goes to law with brother, where is the evidence that the grace of God is sufficient for all things, and that we love each other and are made perfect in one? As a rule the saints should judge points of difference between saints. As they shall take part in judging the world they might be entrusted with the matter of deciding points of difference between brethren with whom they shall be associated in deciding the destiny of the world, for the apostle says:

"Do ye not know that the saints shall judge the world? And if the world shall be judged by you, are ye unworthy to judge the smallest matters? Know ye not that we shall judge angels? How much more things that pertain to this life?" (1 Cor. 6:2, 3).

This instruction is evidently for personal differences. In cases of personal misunderstandings the church should interpose, and only the church. If a member is personally injured or aggrieved, he should, after proper gospel steps, tell it to the church. This principle is laid down by our Savior in Matthew 18:15-18, "Moreover, if thy brother shall trespass against thee go and tell him his fault between thee and him alone: if he shall hear thee, thou hast gained thy brother. But if he will not hear thee, then take with thee one or two more, that in the mouth of two or three witnesses every word may be established. And if he shall neglect to hear them, tell it unto the church: but if he neglect to hear the church, let him be unto thee as an heathen man and a publican."

In Leviticus 19:17, 18 we read, "Thou shalt not hate thy brother in thine heart: thou shalt in anywise rebuke thy neighbor, and not suffer sin upon him. Thou shalt not avenge nor bear any grudge against the children of thy people, but thou shalt love thy neighbor as thyself: I am the Lord."

As the Israelites were just emancipated from Egyptian bondage, and were freemen going to live together in a free country, it was necessary that they should know their obligation to each other as the chosen of the Lord and as fellow-citizens. We read again in Luke 17:3, 4, "Take heed to yourselves: if thy brother trespass against thee, rebuke him; and if he repent, forgive him. And if he trespass against thee seven times in a day, and seven times in a day turn again to thee, saying, I repent, thou shalt forgive him." These passages point out clearly the course to pursue in general matters.

II. Is there no circumstance under which a church member may take a case to law?

We answer, most certainly there is. To say there is not would be to most fearfully pervert the spirit of the scriptures and open a door to the dishonestly disposed for the most unmitigating frauds. Too many dishonest church members would borrow money from church members with no intention whatever to pay it, and hide behind this scripture: "Dare any of you, having a matter against another, go to law before the unjust and not before the saints." It must be considered that the Christians at Corinth were living in a heathen land and subject to heathen magistrates. We do not live in heathen lands and are not presided over by heathen rulers. We are citizens of a common country and are in honor bound to support the laws of this country. Many of our rulers are members of the Christian church, and many of their Christian lives are irreproachable. The laws of our country are based, for the most part, upon the Bible, which book is the guide to the Christian church. It must be acknowledged, therefore, that the circumstances under which the Christians at Corinth lived and the circumstances under which we live are decidedly different, and hence the exceptions to this general rule. ...

This subject has caused a great deal of trouble in the church of Christ. Many unworthy persons have taken advantage of this scripture, which the church is endeavoring to honestly obey, to be dishonest and perpetrate the most glaring frauds upon each other. For a church to insist that a member can, under no circumstances, go to law, is to license men to commit the most terrible crimes, the atrocity of which common sense and civilization will scorn. If the church continues at this, the young element will revolt and leave the church of their fathers. if men honestly owe debts, and have property out of which those debts can be paid, it is common justice that they pay them. If they will not pay those debts, the church should be no screen to protect dishonesty, and the courts should interpose to defend the rights of a citizen. If a man can pay a debt and will not pay it, and as the church cannot make him pay it, the courts should be invoked. There are numbers of church members sitting down in the church who owe debts, and upon the presumption that you dare not go to law, willfully refuse to pay them. What is the remedy? Let the member so suffering report the case to the officer whose duty it will be to labor with the debtors, and if they still refuse to pay, let the officers tell it to the church, and if they still refuse, let the church expel them, and then the suffering member can take legal steps to recover his money. This should only be done when everything else has failed. No church can consistently keep in its fellowship a dishonest member, and no person is honest who can pay a debt and will not do it. We are not bound to respect dishonest persons.

Application

I have known judges and lawyers and jurors in our courts to be preachers of the gospel. Would we call a court of that make-up "heathen," "unjust" and "unbelievers?" There is perhaps, in many instances, as much honesty and justice in the decisions of the courts as in those of the churches. As a rule, homestead is dishonest and a screen from justice. Our property ought to be subject to our debts. The church very often makes sad mistakes in its dealings with its members. This is because she is not infallible. The sweet thought is that we will get home by and by, where mistakes will be impossible. There will be no conferences nor arbitration of the courts. Jesus Christ will hug us to his holy bosom and our joy will be as pleasing as it will be eternal. Then shall we know as we are known, and having everything in common, we shall join the countless number of harpers, harping with harps, and throughout the countless ages of eternity we shall bathe our weary souls in seas of heavenly rest, and not a wave of trouble roll across our peaceful breast. Then, as we stand upon the sea of glass mingled with fire we shall make heaven's arches ring as the flightless ages of eternity roll. God help us. Amen.

Emanuel King Love

Scriptural Divorce

Introduction

There is nothing which strikes so essentially at the very root of society as the tampering with the marriage institution. If this is corrupt, society is degraded, happiness is destroyed, morality is debased, virtue is gone, civilization is crippled, Christianity is hindered, and gloom spreads her drapery over our land, the garden spot of the globe. For the family circle is the seed-bed of society, the fountain-head of civilization, the birth-place of tranquility, the cradle of prosperity, the molding-place of character, and the reservoir from which streams of joy or misery flow. As the family circle is, so will society be. Clandestine marriages and divorces seem to be the special curse of this age. It would seem that the further we get from the primeval state of man the more remote are we removed from the proper observance of the matrimonial institution. In Massachusetts for every fourteen marriages there is one divorce. In proud Maine there are 478 divorces a year. In these Southern States it is simply alarming. In the New England States there are 2,000 divorces in a single year. What must all these grass widows do? Do you believe that they will live pure? Is not this an alarming state of society? Is it not time that the church was waging war against this flood-tide of immorality? Can society rest at ease when a restless worm is eternally gnawing on its taproot? Should not the watchmen on the walls give the alarm when they see the enemy coming to destroy the city and take away the inhabitants captive? How long will it be before we will reach the point when it will not be safe for anybody's daughter to follow a man off if this thing continues? How long will it be before parents should mourn for their daughters as though they were dead when they give their hand in marriage to a man? How long will it be before there will be more grass widows than there will be young girls who have never been married? How long will it be before young men will be obliged to pick their choice from among the grass widows or wait till some more girls grow up?

"What therefore God has joined together, let not man put asunder" (Mark 10:9).

We are called upon to consider another one of those delicate subjects that gives endless trouble in the Christian church and in all this land. I can scarcely hope that this feeble effort will be wide spread and do anything like universal good; but I can and do hope that it will do good in my immediate congregation. The prevalence of divorce, clandestine marriages, and separation is simply alarming. The ignoring of the sanctity of the nuptial tie in this country is a great scandal to civilization and the cause of Christianity. The church should be aroused to throw all of her influence against this flood-tide of immorality and save this nation from this sin and shame. The marriage rite is of God, and His book alone is authority for its government. Civil government did not originate the matrimonial institution, and should not interfere with it further than His law allows. The Bible is the foundation of all just and wise laws, and no courts should presume to forego its teachings. God is the author of all of our being, and his laws should govern us all. They were given in divine wisdom, and we should not presume to improve upon them. We are not allowed to amend them. They are as everlasting as He is eternal. His own Son came to earth and denied that he had a right to change them, but that he came to explain and fulfill them. His laws should be sufficient for his children. The wisdom of men and angels combined could not produce such a book, and hence the folly in trying to make better laws than it contains, or wickedness in refusing to abide its teachings. Marriage is a religious rite, and the Bible is the book governing religious rites. Whatever the courts do in this regard that is not in accordance with that blessed book is sinful and wrong, and must work hurt to the cause of morality, Christianity and civilization. They differ only from heathens in that they know better; and hence their wrong is the more inexcusable.

I. What God hath joined together

The sacredness of the matrimonial relation is at once put forth in the fact that God joins together. He who opens and no man can shut, and shuts and no one can open, joins together man and woman as husband and wife, and puts His seal upon the union that "no man put asunder." The sacredness of the relation is further seen in that God made them at first twain. They were the only two, and, therefore, must stay together. They fell together and were driven out of the garden together. There was no other woman for Adam to take and Eve could not get another husband. It seems that if God had meant for man to have more than one wife he would have started him with more than one. He said that man should cleave unto his wife and not wives. The Bible says that woman should obey her husband, not husbands. There is nothing more wonderful and sacred than the flowing together of two human lives. Can we conceive of a thing more wonderful than that a man who is born and reared a thousand miles from Savannah, comes here on a visit, gets acquainted with one of our girls, falls in love with her, letters begin to pass between them and by and by their lives are flown into one. He lives for her and she lives for him. Their destiny is one and their interest is common. Their love is one, their joy is the same, and through the vicissitudinous cycles of time they are to live as one, for better or for worse. A union that is so sacred, so wonderful, and so sublime as this should not and can not be dissolved at will.

It is not strange, therefore, that the most stringent laws are thrown around the holy rite of matrimony. The more sacred a thing is, the more rigorous the laws concerning it, and the more severe the punishment in case of violation. The Savior described His intimacy with His church by the relation of husband and wife. The name woman means pliant, and implies that she leans upon man. If man falls she cannot stand, and if she falls she carries him with her. This is plainly shown in the fall, and in all subsequent history. Though Eve was the first to fall, she carried Adam with her. They were one in interest and in destiny, and the one could not stand after the other had fallen. Adam's only excuse to God for his sin was, "The woman whom thou gavest to be with me she gave me of the tree, and I did eat." They alike were cursed, for they were one. They went out of the garden alike and together. "Unto Adam also and to his wife did the Lord God make coats of skins and clothed them. In all of God's dealings with the children of men this fact of the union of husband and wife is recognized. The limit of the union is marked by Him. His limit is the only legal one. There is nothing on earth that is a purer picture of heaven than the family circle. There is nothing that more clearly illustrates the love of God for His church than the nuptial tie. It is not strange, therefore, that it is said that God joins them together. All true marriages are just as truly joined together by God as the church and His Son are joined together by Him. And He has just as complete control of the conjugal relation as over the union of the church and His Son. He sustains the same relation to both: God over all and blessed for evermore. The woman is said to be "the better half." See that infant boy as he comes into the world unconscious of his existence, and still every effort seems to be a struggle for his "lost piece," his "better half." The girl is the same. Every smile and graceful look seems to indicate that she is in search of something that she would be delighted to find. It is a husband with whom she wishes to cast her destiny. It is nature seeking its own. See them battling with the ins and outs of life until they come to years when the dreams of infancy are o'er and the visions of childhood are ended, and they refuse longer to remain under the parental roof. There is something without that suits them much better. It does not matter what attraction the parental home may possess, it does not matter what wealth the parents may have, nor what may be the culture and refinement the family home present, "there is a gentle voice within calls away." He goes up to a man and looks him in the face and asks him for his daughter with as much grace as a Jew would invite you into his store. Generally the father says yes. He asked once himself. How can he refuse? It is the young man's wife that God has made for him and the father has been holding her in trust simple until this young man comes for her and asks that their lives be poured into one. As a rule, it is the father's duty to surrender his guardianship just as completely as if she had died.

Their lives henceforth is to be a life. God has joined them together and he seals the union with heaven's stamp that "no man put asunder." If it be argued that all marriages are not joined together by God, I answer, neither are all persons' union with the church sanctioned by God, but they say so, and we take their word and receive them, for by their word they shall be judged. In the church we deal with hypocrites and true Christians by the same rule. We call them all brethren and sisters because we do not know any better. They are responsible to God for their internal qualification. No mistake is admissible before His righteous bar, before which, we will be tried. God has made us intelligent beings capable of making a choice, and he holds us accountable for the choice we do make. I believe it is everybody's duty to get married. I believe it is a divine duty. The God of our being, who knows every particle that goes into our make up, said it was not good for man to be alone. He made us help meets one for another. That woman's life that cannot pour into some man's life is cloddy, spongy and sticky. Lumber that can not be worked is knotty and refused, it matters not how good it may look. You very often hear persons say that the reason that they do not get married is that they can't find anybody to suit them. It is just as often true that there is nothing of genuine greatness in them to be suited. The union of husband and wife illustrates finely the union of the believer and Christ. "My beloved is mine, and I am his." "I sat down, under his shadow with great delight, and his fruit is sweet to my taste." "His left hand is under my head, and his right hand doth embrace me." "My beloved spoke, and said unto me, rise up, my love, my fair one, and come away." "I am my beloved's and his desire is toward me." "Set me as a seal upon thine heart, as a seal upon thine arm: for love is strong as death." These quotations are from the Song of Solomon that all admit to be a figure of Christ and his church. If we are Christ's by redemption and the gift of the Father, His life and our life are one, and the life which we now live is not ours, but we live by faith that is in Him. When the hearts of Christ and the believers have been joined together by the Father, then, and not until then, can we see the force and beauty in the expression of Paul: "For to me to live is Christ, and to die is gain." We come now to consider the separation.

II. Let not man put asunder

This restraint is put upon man individually and collectively. The restraining injunction is issued by the court of heaven against individuals, societies, courts and churches for anything other than God's law doth allow, and that thing is adultery or fornication. If we would come back to the old landmark the marriage institution would be purer, social order would be more sacred, and human happiness would be sublimer and the standard of morality would be raised higher. If our courts would conform to the divine law in divorce cases they would do lasting good to the cause of civilization and promote the cause of Christianity. The courts have established the following legal grounds for a divorce:

1. Inter-marriage.—That is where a man marries too near a relative—a half-sister, cousin, etc. Such a marriage the courts would declare null and void.

2. Mental Incapacity—Non compos mentis.—That is a person who is so crazed as to be unfit to discharge the marriage duties. In this case the courts would declare the nuptial relation invalid and would grant a divorce to the plaintiff, putting them asunder.

3. Impotency.—That is weakness, whether of mind or body; some disease of body or mind that makes a person incompetent to do the duties of a married life, or too disagreeable to live with. This the courts would declare sufficient grounds for divorce and the contracting parties would be set at liberty.

4. Forced Marriage.—That is where a person is forced to marry by others, by outside influence or for fear of losing life. The courts would say that the parties did not contract and hence the marriage is illegal. The parties would be declared free.

5. Pregnancy of the wife before marriage unknown to the husband at the time of marriage.—This is tantamount to adultery after marriage. This, the courts would decide a legal cause for divorce, and hence it would be granted and the parties set free. But if the man knew it when he made the contract, he would be held responsible and not be allowed a divorce.

6. Simple adultery is a legal ground for divorce by the courts.—Upon this the laws of God and of man are agreed.

7. Willful and continued desertion of either contracting party for three years.—The courts would decide the marriage vow broken and, therefore, the contract a nullity, and grant a permanent divorce, freeing the parties.

8. Conviction of either party of crime involving moral turpitude and sentenced for two years in the penitentiary.—This the courts would deem a sufficient cause for divorce. Then, again, the courts have what they term discretionary grounds for divorce. Under this head is cruel treatment and habitual intoxication. For these the courts leave themselves free to grant or refuse as they may see fit. Now have not they plausible grounds to set at naught the law of God? What can look more abominable than an earthly court sitting in judgment upon the court of heaven, reviewing its decisions, reversing and setting at naught its judgment, the lower court reviewing the higher court, men correcting God? The Supreme Law Giver has allowed but two things to put asunder what He has joined together—they are adultery and fornication. The one is unforeseen by the contracting parties, the other can't be helped. Jesus has said that if a man puts away his wife for any other cause except adultery or fornication causes her to commit adultery, and he that marries her that is put away also commits adultery. This is the gospel order and the gospel church is morally bound to support and contend for the gospel order. It does not matter, therefore, upon what ground the courts may grant a divorce the church cannot recognize it, except it is granted upon the principle laid down by our Savior and for the cause named by Him—adultery.

All other divorces are unscriptural, and the parties so obtaining them are guilty of adultery, and therefore unfit for membership in the Christian church. A married couple is bound by the law of God as long as they live, except fornication or adultery separate them. Neither is free while the other lives, unless the cause be scriptural. If the cause be scriptural, the innocent party may marry again, after a divorce is had, and remain a wholesome member of the church, but the guilty party cannot marry again and be a member of the Christian church. Though, if there is evidence of genuine repentance, the guilty party might be restored to church fellowship, but not allowed to marry again.

In cases of abandonment, or "willful continued desertion," as the courts put it, the parties might be allowed to separate and be retained as members of the church, provided they are reconciled to each other, but not be divorced from each other—not allowed to marry again, from the fact that the church cannot make laws. Her laws are made by Christ, and He has allowed only two causes for total divorce, and they are adultery and fornication. A thousand men have no more right to put asunder what God has joined together than one man has. It is no more legal, in the sight of God, for twelve men to put asunder man and wife than it is for one man to do it; and the church should regard it no more than if one man had done it.

The Apostle Paul says, in 1 Corinthians 7:10, 11—"And unto the married I command, yet not I, but the Lord, that a wife depart not from her husband: But and if she depart, let her remain unmarried, or be reconciled to her husband: And let not the husband put away his wife."

Here is no intimation of divorce, for she is told to remain unmarried.

In the twelfth and thirteenth verses, the apostle lays down the rule for the government of marriages of believers and unbelievers. He says, if a man has an unbelieving wife, and she be pleased to stay with him, he must not put her away. The same is true of a woman with an unbelieving husband.

At the fifteenth verse he seems to strike another key. He says that "If the unbelieving depart, let him depart. A brother or sister is not under bondage in such cases."

The apostle is not contradicting the general principle laid down by the Lord. Christ dealt with a general matter, and the apostle is dealing with a special matter. Christ laid down the general rule, and the apostle is applying it. We would need to consider the circumstances for which the apostle is giving this special rule, for we all know that it is one thing to lay down a general rule, and quite another to apply it.

The converted wives of pagans were subjected to many difficulties and temptations. These Christian women had learned to look upon idolatry with horror, and still the kitchen hearth was consecrated to false gods. These gods were to be worshipped by the family circle. How could a Christian woman conscientiously do this? And how could she have peace if she refused? When they sat down to a meal, libation, as worship, was poured out to some false god, "and on joyous occasions the pantomimic dance and profane song were required." What Christian could take part in such worship, so wholly repugnant to the religion of Christ? It is said that the "reign of Venus was coextensive with that of Jove." There were many heathen worships that the wife would be subjected to by marrying a heathen man that would make her life miserable. Under these circumstances the apostle wrote. Yet he does not tell her to leave him, "but if he depart, let him depart," and after he departs she is not told to remarry, but remain unmarried.

Respecting cruel treatment, it seems that this same rule would apply. If life is endangered by living together, a temporary separation may be in order, but never a remarriage. Whenever the parties became reconciled they might again resume their nuptial relation.

So with drunkenness. The wife might resort to every honorable means to cure a drunken husband, but never separate from him except it be absolutely necessary to save her life. And then she is positively forbidden to marry again. That same drunken man is her husband until he dies.

So with willful and continued desertion. If he still lives he is her husband, and the scriptures do not justify a divorce. It must be remembered that they married "for better or for worse."

I believe that either party guilty of the offense named by the Savior is bound to divorce the other when apprized of it. It is not in their province to forgive this offense, for it just as virtually dissolves the union as death. If they remain together after this both are guilty of adultery and unfit for membership in the Christian church. A man marrying a woman that is divorced, and professing Christ afterward, cannot join the Christian church so long as he lives with this divorced woman. You will see, therefore, that a divorced person is never capable of marrying again. She is forever retired from the matrimonial world. To the marriage rite she is dead, and a man has no more right to contract marriage with a divorced woman than. with a dead woman. If he does, he dies with her, and the church must regard him as dead and turn him out of her pale to mingle with the dead. The courts have what they call discretionary powers, but the church has none. The Bible is her code; to its teachings she must bow and say amen.

The cause of so many separations and divorces is because persons have gone into the matrimonial rite heedlessly—without mature thought, and, worse still, without love. Persons have been persuaded to marry by their friends who had no higher idea of marriage than to accept the advice of a foolish, deceitful friend. Many persons have married because the woman looked well, dressed well and talked well. With no higher aspiration than to get a good looking wife. Some girls have married a man to spite the other girls, or because her parents didn't want her to marry him. Some girls, I'm sorry to say, have married to get away from their parents because they were so unreasonable and cruel. They hadn't time to think of love. They were in the fire and the quickest way out was the best way to them. Some parents seem never to think that their girls are of age until they marry. Some girls have simply married a fellow because he had something; some, still, married one man and loved another. The parents objected to their choice, and hence the man married another to abuse her, and the girl married another to disobey and deceive him. It is a fearful thing to trifle with a person's love. Many parents will find it hard at the bar of God. To all of those who have gone into marriage thoughtlessly, yea, to you unfortunates, I have this word of consolation for you: You have made your bed hard, lie hard—God's word does not grant you a divorce. Try to so live that you will get over it when you die. That is the end of your suffering. You will not have to live with him as husband in heaven, for there they neither marry nor are given in marriage. But they do always behold the face of the Father, and Jesus Christ the Lord. Then it will all be over and heaven will yield you sweeter rest. It is pleasing to know that when this life of suffering, abuses and disappointments is over that we have the promise of a better life beyond—that is free from mistakes or anything that defiles a man. The hope of that heavenly home is sweet. If a single thought that I have expressed will urge you to purer lives and to think more highly of Jesus and the glorious doctrines of the cross I am satisfied. May the holy spirit impress these truths upon your hearts, for Jesus' sake. Amen."

Emanuel King Love

Loosing and Binding

Matthew 16:19—"And I will give unto thee the keys of the kingdom of heaven: and whatsoever thou shalt bind on earth shall be bound in heaven: and whatsoever thou shalt loose on earth shalt be loosed in heaven."

I appear before you to-night to discuss another one of those difficult subjects about which there is a diversity of opinion even among scholars. I do not delight in discussing difficult subjects, but it is needful for me to suggest a few thoughts from this text which I hope will be useful to you. This text is very much quoted and equally as much misunderstood. The blessed Savior's intimacy with his church is declared in the text. The Savior organized the church and left His seal of approbation upon it, with the promise that whenever they met in His name and agreed, that their meetings and doings should be clothed with divine authority, and that heaven would sanction whatever they did in His name as His representatives. This is what makes apostolic examples as binding on us as the words of our Savior. They were inspired to act as well as to say. They did what the Savior would have done, and said what He would have said. Jesus, on entering Cesarea Philippi, asked His disciples what did men think of Him. Peter said that some thought he was John the Baptist, some thought he was Elias, some thought he was Jeremias, or some of the prophets. The Savior then put the question directly to them, to which Peter answered, "Thou art Christ the Son of the living God." Upon this truth confessed by Peter the Savior promised to build His church, to which He gave Peter the keys, that he might unlock it to Jews and Gentiles. This was not to put Peter above the other disciples. As he had nearly always spoken for the crowd, being characteristic of his nature, so he represented them in the reception of the keys.

I. And I will give unto thee the keys of the kingdom of heaven

A key is an instrument for opening a door. He who has it has the privilege of entering at will. The keys referred to in the text mean authority, power, divine appointment. This authority has not been given to Peter alone, but in some respect to every minister of Jesus.

If to Peter alone was given this power and divine sanction we might justly be alarmed, unless we can find the family through which the transferring of the keys have passed from St. Peter. If we should fail in this, then we should find no open door into the kingdom. There is no evidence in the scriptures that St. Peter was promoted above his fellow-disciples. Paul withstood him to his face for he was to be blamed. This Paul would not have done had he recognized Peter as ruler. For Paul more than once taught that we should obey them that had rule over us, and that whoever resisted the rulers resisted the ordinances of God.

If St. Peter was recognized as chief of the church of the apostolic age, it is strange that none of the documents bear his signature approved as such. It is more than strange that he on no occasion issued a proclamation to the churches as such.

Every other person claiming to be chief on certain occasions has issued proclamations or documents bearing their signature as chief. The logical conclusion, therefore, must be that so far as apostolic supremacy is concerned there was none, and all of the apostles were equal.

The power was given alike to all of them. The presentation of the keys to the apostles reminds us of a husband going away and turning over the keys to his wife, to whom he entrusts all of his business. After giving her full instructions about the business, and ample directions in every part of it, he tells her that whatever she does, according to the directions given, he will approve it, for it would be as if he had done it. Or as a master going off delivers his goods into the hands of his servant, with orders and promises to approve whatever he does according to the orders given. Christ is under no promise to endorse what He has not ordered, and what the Bible does not contain He has not ordered and will not endorse. The presentation of the keys to His disciples indicates His loving intimacy with the church. Where a loving intimacy exists between two parties there also exists power of the one over the other. For intimacy breeds power, confidence and approbation. This is what makes the church the most powerful institution under heaven. She enjoys intimacy with Christ. She has His approving smiles. No other organization could have come through the bloody and fiery persecution, increasing as it marched, but the church, the Lamb's bride. Her intimacy with the King gained His favor and protection. The intimation to St. Peter here is that he would be the first to open the door of the visible kingdom—the church—to both Jews and Gentiles. This was fulfilled on the day of Pentecost, and at Cornelius' house. The kingdom evidently means the Christian church. It must be remembered that no intimation is here or elsewhere given that Christ gave Peter the keys of heaven. For in that event every one who wished to enter heaven would be obliged to consult Peter. Peter would indeed be the proper being to whom prayer would be due, since upon him would hang our chance for entering heaven; in this case it would be evident that Christ had transferred his power to Peter, and hence prayer to Christ would be improper and a violation of contract. It will be remembered, also, that Christ appeared to John many years after this with the keys of authority in his own hands, showing that he had not transferred them to any body. Our Lord has arranged it so that we can go to the throne direct and have no right or business to consult men, departed saints nor angels. We can come boldly for ourselves to a throne of grace and speak directly to the King. We have as much right to the keys of heaven as Peter had, or anybody else. We rejoice to know that God will answer our prayers as quick as He will anybody else's. That which guarantees the answer to prayer has always been the same, and that is faith. The prayer of faith has always been answered. By this means the door of heaven is opened. Whether this is the key or not, it is not important to know. It opens or it influences him to open who has the keys. In either case the result reached is the same. There need not be any miscarriage in our petitions, for we can carry them ourselves directly to the King. If we have not the keys of the kingdom of heaven, we have the keys of authority to approach His Majesty in the name of Christ, the Lord. This intimacy is encouraged by the Lord, and He is still the head of the church and hugs her to His bosom as His bride and approves her as His own.

II. Binding on earth and in heaven

This at once sets forth the seal of approbation upon the church of Christ the Lord. But this is conditioned upon the presumption that the church has complied with the contract. The word "bind" among the Jews was used to denote a thing declared—a doctrine taught. It must be remembered that "loose" and "bind" were used only among the Jews, and refers to things and not to persons. So that the Savior meant that whatever thing or censure ye inflicted upon a person, or in the church, according to the rule I have just given you, shall be ratified in heaven. Let as not forget that the Savior quotes this Jewish phrase just after he had given direction how to deal with an offending person. The language used by Christ is found only in Matthew, who is supposed to have written his gospel in Hebrew for the Jews and afterward translated it into Greek.

It will be seen that the Greek *osa* is neuter and refers to a thing, and that *desete* was used among the Jews as referring to the declaration of a doctrine or any article of restraining or granting. They generally meant that it is lawful to do or not do, as the case might, be, by "loose" and "bind." Now, then, the conclusion must be that Christ meant to teach them that whatever law they enacted or censure they inflicted according to His law He would approve of it. A sweet thought is intimated here that the doings of the church on earth are reviewed by the church in heaven. The decision of the court below is subject to the court above. If the court below meets in the name of Christ, and censures one of its members for crime or obstinacy, the court above confirms the decision of the court below and the censure is valid. Such a member is turned over to Satan to be buffeted for a season until that member shall have learned to behave and acknowledge the authority of the church. The court regards the censure as being just. Just how such a member is regarded by the court above we may not learn until we shall have been made members of that holy and infallible tribunal. If from prejudice, ill feelings, unfairness or strategy a member is turned out, the censure is unjust, the judgment of the court below is reversed. It is not "bound" in heaven, not "loosed" in the court of the righteous Judge of all the earth,

It must be noticed, also, that the apostles were inspired and therefore less likely to make mistakes. No church and no minister would presume to read the hearts of their members as Peter did Anania's and Sapphira's. That power was granted only to the pioneers of the Christian religion. It is not now used because it is not now needed. People are more capable of reasoning now, and hence we resort to reason, for the days of miracles to convince men of the power of the Christian religion are over. Where Paul found the people prepared to reason, as at Athens, no miracles were performed. The approbation of Christ upon His church is to make men fear and love the church as they would Him. It is intended to have the enemies of the cross to know that He espouses the cause of His church and will defend her. He made Paul understand that the punishment that he was inflicting upon His church was upon her Lord. "Saul, Saul, why persecuteth thou me," was the strange inquiry. He has said, "Inasmuch as ye have done it unto one of the least of these, my brethren, ye have done it unto me," and that one had better be in the sea with a millstone about his neck than to offend one of these, my little ones. Such passages should make the enemies of the cross stand in awe. If you insult the church you insult her Lord. Who can behold the wonderful accomplishments of the church without learning that she must have been supported by hands divine? Who can, after examining the victories of the church, fail to see that she was defended by an eternal arm? Who can learn the history of the church and notice her powerful enemies without feeling that a supreme being must have guided her. Criticize the church as severely as you may, but you will find fewer mistakes in her acts than in any other institution under heaven. Examine her literature and learned men and no other institution presents such an enviable front. In question of purity where is her equal? In doctrine, what institution touches her purity, justness and sublimity? In liberality and virtue she occupies the highest plane. All this shows that she is guided by the eternal eye and kept by grace through faith. As the church associates with Christ she will naturally contract His habits, imbibe His doctrines and gather strength from Him. Therefore He has promised to endorse what she does in conforming to His will. It does not mean that if the church receives an unconverted person into her fellowship that heaven accepts him. This would be inconsistent with the charter of the gospel church-regeneration.

There are many things which the church does that are not "bound" in heaven. This does not mean that if the church should owe an honest debt and "bind" not to pay it, that it will be "bound" in heaven. The Bible tells to her to "owe no man." This does not mean that should the church "bind" not to support the mission work and spread the gospel that it shall be "bound" in heaven. She is told to preach the gospel to every creature. It means that whatever the church does that is right, that the author of right will endorse it; that whatever she does that He has commanded He will approve of it. God will approve of the right in everybody and reward them accordingly. He will show her the path of life and bring her in His presence where there is fullness of joy, and set her on His right hand where there are pleasures for evermore. If the church would have the approving smiles of her Master, let her strive to do right and all will be well. His smile eclipses the frowns of all the enemies combined. It is day if He smiles upon us in the midst of ten thousand frowning worlds. In the scorns, contempts and darkness of the world, like the children of Israel in Egypt, there will be light in our house under the approving smiles of Christ, our Lord, and amid the persecutions and fierce battles of life we may sing amid the tempest, "Praise the Lord." Notice further:

III. Loosing on earth and in heaven

It is also true of this loosing. It is a seal of approbation; but it is a seal of approbation of the right, and not of the wrong. In neither case is it meant that there is a turning out of heaven. The primary meaning is that the acts of the church are endorsed by heaven. It is fair to presume, therefore, that since the church makes mistakes many of her decisions are reversed by the supreme court. Many whom the church censures do not rest under the divine censure, because the church is wrong; and many whom the church acquits still remain under the divine censure, because they are guilty. But if the church justly declares non-fellowship with a member, Christ approves it as being just. This is what is meant by "loosed" on earth and "loosed" in heaven. This further shows the intimacy between Christ and his church. Whatever she hates, He hates, and whatever she declares is wrong and unholy, He declares is wrong and unholy. It does not mean that whoever is turned out of the church is turned out of heaven. This is not what the Savior is driving at. If when they are turned out of the church they are turned out of heaven, then when they wish to make their return, they must first be taken into the church before they can be received back into heaven. This argument would place the church before heaven, and strike the deathblow to the doctrine taught by John, that we must bring forth fruit meet for repentance. The soul should first get right with its God, and then with His people. It is often the case that when God has forgiven a sin that the church is still grumbling about it. It is also true that God has forgiven many sins before the church has found them out, and hence the church in some instances works too late. The rule is nevertheless good that when the church condemns sin God approves it, and when the church accepts a true penitent God sanctions it. In neither case does the church act before God does.

Dr. P. H. Mell says on this subject: "The Savior promised the apostles to give them plenary inspiration. That he would see that they should make no mistake in any doctrines they announced, or in any gospel institution they might organize. That they should adopt (or bind) on earth what already had been decided upon in heaven, and reject (or loose) on earth what had already been rejected in heaven. This makes apostolic examples as binding on us as apostolic precepts."

Dr. J. M. Pendleton says on this subject that "we are to understand 'bind' in the sense of forbid, and 'loose' in the sense of permit, and the meaning of the passage is that what a church does in accordance with the law of Christ is approved and ratified in heaven."

Dr. DeVotie says: "It must be very clear to you that no one can be bound in heaven or on earth by a decision against Him contrary to the gospel."

Dr. Holmes says: "It is said that the words 'bind' and 'loose' were frequently used by the Jews in the sense of enjoin and permit, as applied to the teaching of their rabbis, both practical and doctrinal. That may be the sense in which 'bind' and 'loose' are used here."

Matthew Henry says: "Here is a warrant signed for the ratification of all the church's proceedings according to these rules. What was said before to Peter is here said to all the disciples, and in them to all the faithful office-bearers in the church, to the world's end."

We are to be very sure that our sentence is pronounced according to the gospel rule, or we are more censurable than those whom we attempt to censure. Or it would be true *clave erranti*—the key turning the wrong way. The keys are as a two-edged sword, which cuts those who handle it if it is turned the wrong way.

Applications

It must be very evident that the apostles did not have absolute power to 'bind' and 'loose' on earth, or there would be no need to "bind" and "loose" in heaven in ratification of what they did on earth. It must be clear from what has been said that their acts were not final, from the fact that they were to be reviewed by heaven and "bound" and "loosed" there before they were valid. The decisions of no court are final that are subject to review. The church is the highest court on earth, and therefore can be reviewed by no earthly tribunal. It must be apparent that the church is a branch of the government of heaven and is answerable alone to headquarters. It cannot be doubted that whatever the church endeavors to accomplish that is right God will see to it that she prevails. Right is immortal and will ultimately prevail.

I have been inexpressibly pleased to see that the success of the prohibitionists has been unanimously charged up to the church. She "bound" on earth, and it was "bound" in heaven. In a certain city in Georgia, where the fight against whisky was hot, a Baptist minister got on the fence and the prohibition army failed. Though the frowns of every good citizen in that community rest upon him, and though ladies, white and colored, hiss at him as he passes through the streets, he can assuage his sorrow by drinking to their health of the best whisky in that town free of charge, and in the magnanimity of his drunken soul pass their vituperation by without a rejoinder for the next two years. Then shall the Babylonian garment and the golden wedge be dug up, and Achan and his family stoned by the army of the living God, and Israel shall go up in the strength of their God and take Ai without the loss of a man. Then shall the enemies of the cross know that there is a God in Israel who pleads the cause of his church and will utterly destroy all of her enemies and build up Zion on the ruins thereof. This can but show in either case the influence of the church. The church rocked in her cradle science, dandled on her knees civilization, and from her bosom came the noble God-like spirit of liberty that has pervaded this land. She revolutionized the world and she is determined to rule it. From her rostrum comes the law that has divinity in it, before which mountains melt to flames and the king of righteousness without a rival reigns. The warp of her flag is truth, the woof is righteousness, and upon it is spangled, with divine symmetry in gorgeous beauty, the stars of holiness, peace, mercy, temperance and virtue. Under its golden fringes the blood-washed army march, cognizant of the fact that upon the flag under which they march is inscribed in golden letters "the kingdoms of this world for our God and his Christ."

"It is not disputed that the church has always been and is destined to be successful in whatever she undertakes that tends to advance the kingdom of Christ and promote the truest interest of mankind. It is to be lamented that many churches have been used by wicked designing men and some have been frightened from the path of duty by the boastful howling of the wicked. Sometimes by those who happen to be in authority. Ministers have shrunk from duty for fear of unpopularity. This will never be endorsed by heaven. We should do what we know to be right with a conscience void of offense towards God and man. Offend all the world a thousand times rather than to offend God once. That popularity that God frowns upon is eternally dangerous. Let the church do her duty and God will see to it that she is defended, guarded, protected and led. Let humility, union and love characterize all of our acts and we have nothing to fear. The Lord our God shall fight for us and we shall hold our peace. Let the church "bind" that no unrighteous man shall have rule over us, and it will be "bound" in heaven. And when we shall finish our session of "binding" and "loosing" on earth, the church on earth shall go up to join the church of the first-born in heaven, where congregations never break up and Sabbaths have no end. There we shall spend a never-ending eternity in the glorious presence of the King. And with the redeemed and sanctified we shall praise Him who died for us and by His blood purchased our pardon. To Him, the head of the church, the shepherd and bishop of our souls, be all the glory, now and forever more. Amen.

Emanuel King Love

JARED MAURICE ARTER (1850-?)

Introduction

Jared Maurice Arter was born to slave parents in 1850 in Jefferson County, West Virginia. His father died shortly before the Civil War. When Arter's family was emancipated, he and his siblings moved with their mother and her second husband to Washington, D. C., where they lived for sixteen years. Jared began his education when he was hired out to a New York family. After paying off a house they bought for their mother and family, he and his brother entered Storer College in 1873. Jared continued his education at Pennsylvania State College in 1879. After teaching for two years, he transferred to Hillsdale College in 1882 and graduated in 1885. In 1887, Jared was ordained and became a pastor and teacher at Storer College for a few years, before leaving to attend Chicago Theological Seminary from 1891 to 1894. He then worked as a teacher, pastor, or school administrator at various institutions in Virginia, West Virginia, and Kentucky for many years. Arter's story concludes by mentioning an illness requiring surgery, but does not discuss the outcome. These sermons are taken from *Echoes from a Pioneer Life* (1922).

The theme of the first sermon, *A message to the race*, is "Will you watch, pray and endeavor to teach, inculcate and lead the race of Africa in America and through them, also the race in Africa to cherish profound faith in God the Father and in His only Son, Jesus our Lord, and in the Holy Ghost as the Comforter?"

The theme of the *Baccalaureate sermon* was "A diligent and complete life of well doing."

The theme of the third sermon, A sermon delivered at the West Virginia Baptist State Convention at Beckly, W. VA., in August 1912, was, "Study, give diligence to become a Gospel minister and Christian workman approved unto God."

The concluding item is, *Extracts from an address at the celebration of fifty years of freedom of the Negro race in America, Hill Top, Fayette county, W. VA., April 9, 1913*

A Message to the Race

"Ethiopia shall soon stretch out her hands unto God." [Psalm 68:31}

The English term, "Ethiop" relating to "Ethiopia," or to its inhabitants, "Ethiopians," is derived from the Latin, "Aethiops," and two Greek words, signifying "burnt face, hence dark colored, black." Ethiopia primarily designates a country and Ethiopian an inhabitant of that country.

In the Bible we first meet with the word Ethiopia in Gen. 2:13. Here it is mentioned in connection with the second branch of the river that went out of Eden to water the garden and was parted into four heads.

The account there reads: "And the name of the second river is Gi-hon: The same is it that compasseth the whole land of Ethiopia." Here there was in Asia, a country by the name of Ethiopia. This, historians in general concede.

But the term Ethiopia both in the Old and New Testament, and in ancient and modern history, in nearly every instance, applies to a country in Africa, lying south of Egypt, including the present countries of Nubia, Abyssinia and parts of other territory.

But in a wider sense, both in ancient and modern history, the terms Ethiopia and Ethiopian and Kush, the Hebrew form of the same word, are all used to designate the African or Negro race. This is the general view advanced by commentators on the text, and this is the view firmly held by Jared.

"Ethiopia shall soon stretch out her hands unto God."

These words were uttered by David, a man after God's own heart, and Israel's greatest king. They contain a divine prophecy, promise and appeal. This prophecy, promise and appeal, given by the God of Abraham, through David the son of Jesse, is a divine and most comforting and inspiring message to Ethiopia, Kush, Africa, the Negro as a race, as a people. The Psalmist, under divine inspiration, has Jerusalem in his vision as a symbol of Israel's mission and God's promise to Abraham that in his seed should all the families of the earth be blessed. And as he looks down the line of the future, Jerusalem with her symbolisms, unfolds before his inspired soul, much of her strength, beauty, blessedness and glory. And as he steadfastly gazes upon the scenes transpiring before his keen and kindling vision, he beholds the birth, death, resurrection and ascension of the Messiah, and other glories of the Messianic dispensation. He beholds many nations and peoples moved and stirred by the infinite love of God, expressed in the unspeakable gift of his only son, and by the ineffable riches and fruition of the atoning sacrifice and efficacious life of Jesus, coming to the fountain of regeneration and the waters of eternal life. And as his prophetic and beatific vision deepens and brightens he beholds Ethiopia, Kush, Africa, the Negro race, becoming roused, stirred, and moved, through catching a sound of the good news and glad tidings of great joy which shall be to all people, for unto us a child is born, unto us a son is given. And peering deep into the souls of this people and perceiving their love of peace, music, joy and their emotional nature and responsiveness to light, and love, right and truth, he proclaims the glorious, hopeful, and inspiring divine message:

"Ethiopia shall soon stretch out her hands unto God."

We have here, then, "the sure word of prophecy," referring to a specific race, the African, the Negro race.

It would seem that the Psalmist had in mind what was and perhaps what is yet, a prevailing sentiment among the more favored and enlightened peoples of the world, that the Ethiopian or Negro race is a backward race, a race that is least expected to be stirred and inspired by highest considerations, and to move along highest lines, and to aim at and strive for that which is highest and best in life.

As God through the prophecy of Jonah and the vision of Peter sought to correct the erroneous ideas of Jonah, Peter and the Hebrew people concerning His attitude toward the heathen and Gentile world; so here it seems He would correct the erroneous notions or ideas of the more favored peoples concerning His attitude toward Ethiopia. As God is no respecter of persons in the matter of salvation, neither was He in the matter of creation. "For God is without variableness or shadow of turning, the same yesterday today and for ever."

"Ethiopia shall soon stretch out her hands unto God."

This prophecy was uttered about a thousand years before the beginning of the Christian era. But a thousand years in the sight of God is "but as yesterday or as a watch in the night," is but as a few hours when it is past. And we may see the dawning forth of the fulfillment of this prophecy in Matthew's words: "And as they came out they found a man of Cyrene, Simon by name; him they compelled to bear the cross." At first Jesus bore the cross alone, just as He trod the winepress alone and died alone, the just for the unjust. Then the Cross, in part or whole, was put upon Simon and he bore it after Jesus to show that man has to bear the cross, especially the followers of Jesus, as Jesus said: "Except a man take up his cross and follow me he can not be my disciple." By many commentators, Simon, being from Cyrene, which is in Africa, is supposed to have been an African of the Negro race, therefore shadowing the suffering, sorrow and heavy burdens which the race was destined to experience and bear, in part preparatory, and in part in the actual high mission, and lofty service of the Lord Jesus Christ. Again, in the Acts of the Apostles, we read: "Behold a man of Ethiopia, an eunuch of great authority, under Candace, Queen of Ethiopia, who had the charge of all her treasure, and had come to Jerusalem for to worship." Now this man was returning and sitting in his chariot reading Esaias the prophet. Then the Spirit said unto Philip, Go near and join thyself to this chariot. And Philip ran thither to him and heard him read the prophet Esaias and said, "Understandest thou what thou readest?" And he said, "How can I except some man should guide me?" And he desired Philip that he would come up and sit with him. The place of the Scripture which he read was this: He was led as a sheep to the slaughter; and like a lamb dumb before his shearer, so opened he not his mouth: In his humiliation his judgment was taken away. and who shall declare his generation? for his life is taken from the earth. And the eunuch answered Philip and said, I pray thee of whom speaketh the prophet this? of himself or of some other man? Then Philip opened his mouth and began at the same Scripture and preached unto him Jesus. And as they went on their way they came unto a certain water, and the eunuch said, "See, here is water, what doth hinder me to be baptized?" And Philip said, "If thou believeth with all thine heart thou mayest." And he answered and said, "I believe that Jesus Christ is the Son of God." And he commanded the chariot to stand still, and they went down both into the water, both Philip and the eunuch, and he baptized him. And when they were come up out of the water the Spirit of the Lord caught away Philip, that the eunuch saw him no more, and he went on his way rejoicing.

Thus this eunuch believed in Jesus, was converted, was baptized, and went on his way rejoicing, and in the judgment of most commentators on the Bible he is regarded as an African of the Negro race and as having been an important factor in the beginning of the fulfillment of the divine prophecy, promise and appeal.

"Ethiopia shall soon stretch out her hands unto God."

But it is of this prophecy, this divine message, in its relation and application to the Negro race in the United States of North America and through them, of its relation and application to the Ethiopian race in general, especially as found in Africa, that I wish to speak and to emphasize, in particular.

"Ethiopia shall soon stretch out her hands unto God."

We have here a divine prophecy, promise and appeal made concerning a specific people and the prophecy and promise are certain to be realized, but how rich and full the harvest shall be depends on how thoroughly aroused and how hearty the response and co-operation of Ethiopia shall be with the Holy Spirit and other means of grace.

It has been nearly 3,000 years since this prophecy was uttered, and more than nineteen centuries have rolled into eternity since the angel of the Lord announced one of the greatest events in the world's history, saying: "Fear not, for behold I bring you good tidings of great joy which shall be unto all people. For unto you is born this day in the city of David a Savior which is Christ the Lord."

Within these passing centuries God in His infinite wisdom, love and power, has been unfolding and fulfilling the prophecy and promise of the text in the life and history of Ethiopia.

The evidence of the fulfillment of this prophecy

At this point let us consider more carefully the evidences of the fulfillment of this divine prophecy and promise concerning the religious development and progress of the Negro race.

In the course of each decade, each score of years, each century, the sun of God's truth concerning the fulfillment of this prophecy has been rising higher and higher and His glorious, inspiring light has been shining brighter and brighter, and the inescapable and binding obligations of Ethiopia, Kush, Africa, the Negro, to make hearty response, and untiring endeavor to flee from darkness and to come to the waters, the fountain of life, to Jesus Christ the Lamb of God that taketh away the sins of the world, have been growing stronger and stronger.

It is true as the poet of sacred music sings:

God moves in a mysterious way,
His wonders to perform.
He plants His footsteps in the sea,
And rides upon the storm.

His purposes will ripen fast,
Unfolding every hour.
The bud may have a bitter taste,
But sweet will be the flower.

These stanzas contain rich truths that enter into the evolution of the life and history of the Negro race in the United States of America and elsewhere.

The tearing of the Negro from the soil and shores of his native land and introducing him in the dark, oppressive and corruptive life of American slavery, and holding him there with increasing rigor for nearly 250 years presents a gloomy and forlorn picture: "But every cloud has a silver lining," and "night brings out the stars."

For in the course of those long centuries of thralldom, despite privation and affliction, the slave gained valuable experience and possessions. He became trained in industry and acquired an elementary knowledge of the English language and the Christian religion—a world language and a world religion. He gained also a slight knowledge of trades and of business. And after being introduced into the richest and most favored country in the world in natural resources and advantages, and multiplying till he numbered about four millions, through the instrumentality of a great Civil War in which he in army and navy numbered about two hundred thousand, he had the exalted privilege of helping to save the Union and to assist in accomplishing his own emancipation from slavery and deliverance into freedom upon the soil.

"Ethiopia shall soon stretch out her hands unto God."
In fulfillment of this prophecy and promise since Emancipation, the truths therein involved have been unfolding in marvelous and very convincing proportions. Great statesmen and seers of large vision and ripe scholarship have declared the progress of the Negro race since Emancipation has no parallel in history.

Now, along what line has this advance, this progress been most marked? Without doubt or controversy it has been along the line of religion, of belief in Jesus Christ as the son of God; of repentance, regeneration, spirituality, of the elevation of moral taste and growth in moral and Christian character.

This is strictly in line with the prophetic promise of the text. This is giving obedience to the injunction of our Lord Jesus: "Seek ye first the kingdom of God and His righteousness," and claiming the promise that all necessary temporal blessings shall be added.

On good statistical authority it is recorded that the colored people of the United States, by 1902, had built twenty-nine thousand churches.

This is an average of 743 per year.

At the same rate by this year (1922) they have built forty-three thousand churches. But the money and energy expended in erecting these church edifices constitute the smaller part of the money and energy expended in accomplishing religious progress. In securing religious literature, fuel, janitor service, and in building parsonages, securing the services of pastors and evangelists, and in fostering Sunday School and mission work, more of life energy has gone.

Another phase of the Negro's strenuous endeavors and marked progress along religious lines is found in his hunger and struggles for education, especially, religious or Christian education.

Not only has he rushed with avidity into the industrial schools, seminaries and colleges established all over the Southland by his white friends of the North especially and of the South in his industrial, moral and Christian upbuilding, but the colored people of the country have expended millions of dollars to found, support and run industrial schools, seminaries and colleges by their own initiative and persevering efforts.

Next to the progress made in religious belief and practice, and in Christian education and provisions therefore, has been the progress made in patriotism, in loyalty to the State and country in which they have their homes and of which they are citizens.

In spite of bitter prejudice, injustice and maltreatment, whenever the country has been in danger and its welfare threatened, the Negro has always been ready and willing to volunteer his services and to play well his part.

In all the wars of the country of any note the Negro has had a part.

In the French and Indian War, and in the war with Mexico, in the Revolutionary War and in the War of 1812, in the great Civil War, in the Spanish-American War, and in the great World War, the Negro was there and played well his part.

Again, in the matter of faithfulness and loyalty in marriage and home-building as husbands and wives, fathers and mothers, the race has made very creditable and hopeful showing and progress.

When it is remembered that man's first and highest duty is to God, his second to his country, and his third to his home, and the fact is carefully noted that the greatest strides and progress of the race have been along the lofty plains of these divine institutions, and in the God appoint order, it must, to all thoughtful persons be plain and convincing that the divine prophecy of David is being beautifully fulfilled, and that the foundation that is thus being laid in the character, life and history of the race, furnish substantial grounds for firm belief and bright hopes for the future of the race.

But this progress and promising history are largely the work and result of burnt children, of those who have passed through the furnace of affliction, privation and suffering and of their immediate children, born early enough to get vivid and burning lessons concerning the sufferings and trying ordeals of their fathers and mothers.

In their afflictions the fathers and mothers gained some knowledge of the God of Israel, that he is a God of loving kindness and tender mercies and that He pitieth them that fear Him as a father pitieth his children, and is a friend to the poor and needy. They had learned to pray and spent much time in earnest, fervent prayer to Almighty God for liberty and light. And when, through the intervention of God, the chains of slavery were broken and they were ushered into freedom and the doors of opportunity swung open, divine impulse, necessity, novelty and strong desire and wise counsel led them promptly to reach out and take firm hold upon the means at hand and to move forward in the way of religious, educational, patriotic, material and economic progress, and thus to remove themselves as rapidly and as far as possible from the old life of ignorance, privation, suffering and want.

"Ethiopia shall soon stretch out her hands unto God."
The fathers and mothers and their immediate children have laid the foundation well and made commendable and hopeful progress.

But what about their children, What about the present generation? Do they give bright promise? and will they make good? The outlook for man in this world for doing his best and making most of himself, was never brighter. We must give God the glory for this bright and splendid outlook. God's claims upon the race and upon mankind for faithful service were never stronger than they are today.

Statesmen, seers and men in every legitimate line of business are coming more and more to see and believe that the lofty principles of the Bible, the divine principles enunciated and taught by our Lord Jesus are the only principles that will solve justly and rightly and truly the many real and trying problems of this life in their relation to time and eternity.

The true Christian and faithful follower of the Lord Jesus must believe this with all his heart, soul, mind and strength. Only thus can he be what he should be. Only thus can he discharge his full duty to himself, to his fellowman and his God.

The truth here expressed is one that should be pondered much, held exceedingly dear, and sought by untiring endeavor by Ethiopia, by Africa, in America to make it a genuine reality in her purpose and life.

"Ethiopia shall soon stretch out her hands unto God."

Ethiopia, Africa in America, the Negro, is now in the blazing light and stirring and impelling force of the fulfillment of this divine prophecy, promise and appeal. Hence it stands today as a divine command to the race, to Ethiopia, to Africa, saying, "Ethiopia, race of Africa, stretch forth your hands with mighty energy unto God, your creator and preserver and only hope for time and eternity."

The momentous question is: "Will Ethiopia, will the Negro as a race, as a people, respond and obey this divine prophecy, promise, appeal, this injunction? What is essential to insure obedience?

"Seek ye the Lord while He may be found, call ye upon Him while He is near." "Today is the day of salvation."

"Let the wicked forsake his way and the unrighteous man his thoughts, and let him return unto the Lord, and He will have mercy upon him and to our God, for He will abundantly pardon." The truths here revealed should be profoundly cherished and faithfully practiced.

There is much in the history of the African race in this country that is analogous to certain phases of the history of Israel.

Israel suffered slavery and oppression in Egypt and the Negro race suffered slavery and oppression in America. God delivered Israel from Egyptian slavery with a strong hand and outstretched arm, and he appealed again and again to this dark history and to the gratitude and loyalty due to this gracious and marvelous deliverance, as an incentive and motive to arouse, stir, persuade and impel them to loyal devotion and to forward and faithful movement along the lines of truth and righteousness.

And so, in the deliverance of the Colored race, the African race, from American slavery, the strong hand of God and His outstretched arm of providence were mighty in their workings, and strikingly visible. And through reason and conscience and the strength of analogy and through the bountiful benevolence and missionary spirit that prompted generous hearts of the North to pour out their millions and to send hundreds of missionaries all over the Southland to teach and to aid in building churches, schools and colleges for the education, Christianizing and uplift of the race, and the divine providence as well, which prompted the Caucasian race of the Southland to rise above prejudice and to open up and support a system of State schools for the education, uplift and betterment of the condition of the race in all of these direct and overruling divine and human providences, the mighty voice and power of God is heard and felt. Yes, verily, God has been, and is, and will continue to appeal to Ethiopia, to the Negro race in America through the sense of fear arising from the dark history of more than two hundred years of cruel slavery, and through the sense of profound gratitude, loyalty and faithful service due to the gracious and marvelous deliverance wrought for the race and the marvelous providences made for its uplift and betterment through all these means, God has been and is constantly appealing as incentives and motives to arouse, stir, persuade and impel the Negro race to loyal devotion and earnest, hearty, faithful, forward movement along the line of Christian progress, righteousness and truth. Though Israel was God's elect, God's peculiar people, and to stress how near they were to Him and how highly favored was the position they once held, Jehovah says: "The Lord's portion in His people; Jacob is the Lot of His inheritance. He found him in a desert land and in the waste howling wilderness; He led him about, He instructed him, He kept him as the apple of His eye." "So the Lord alone did lead him and there was no strange God with him. He made him ride on the high places of the earth that he might eat the increase of the fields; and He made him to suck honey out of the rock, and oil out of the flinty rock."

"But Jeshurun (Israel) waxed fat and kicked. Then he forsook God which made him, and lightly esteemed the rock of his salvation." Thus Israel in their moral blindness and sinful depravity trampled all the rich mercies of God under their feet, rebelled against His righteous laws, became steeped in iniquity and idolatry and slaves to the love of Mammon and so fell from God's grace, were carried away into captivity, and at last through the destruction of Jerusalem they became rejected and destroyed as an organized nation and church, and scattered among the various Gentile nations of the earth.

And here in this dispersion among the Gentiles without a country, and characterized in prophecy as lost and a valley of dry bones, spiritually dead, Israel, for nearly two thousand years has been allowed to suffer in various ways more severely than any other people in the world. "To whom much is given of him shall much be required." "He that knoweth the law and doeth it not shall be beaten with many stripes; but he that knoweth it not with a few."

Israel as God's elect people stand as a beacon light and blazing warning to all the world, through the direct revelations made to them, the prophecies made through them and fulfilled in them, and the history of God's dealings of mercy and severity with them.

If these people, then, the children of Abraham, of such noble heritage, and for whom God did so much in so many ways, for example, miraculously delivering them from Egyptian bondage, and schooling them at Sinai in the moral, ceremonial and civil laws and thus organizing them as an elect nation, and miraculously feeding and training them in the wilderness forty years and finally planting them as a nation in a land flowing with milk and honey, under heaven made laws and divinely chosen leaders, failed to contend against sin and successfully to resist the flesh, the world and the devil, through failure to watch and pray, to love God supremely, obey him, keep his precepts and commandments and to love their neighbor as themselves—if this people thus failed and were rejected and abolished as an organized church and nation and cast out of Jehovah's sight and buried among heathen nations to suffer for untold centuries in this life and in unmeasured intensity, and millions, perhaps, to be lost and ruined through all eternity; what right, ground or hope has any

people less favored by natural heritage, and special divine grace, and less devout and beneficent in service, and less resolute and persistent in battling against the flesh, the world and
the devil, for believing, expecting and hoping for God's special favor, if they fail to profit
by all the past; and to seize opportunity, and to yield to the quickening and illuminating
light and power of the Holy Spirit, the Living Word and the principles, examples and
precepts of Jesus, and thus prove devout, loyal, persistent and faithful soldiers and servants
of the cross? What reason, right or ground have they for believing, expecting or hoping that
God's dealing with them will be any less terrible, dreadful and severe than it was with
Israel? None whatever.

Like the Jew for the last nineteen centuries, the Negro in America, in the world for that
matter, is without a country, that is, he has no great, strong civilized nation of his own race
to enter into treaty relations with other nations, thus to invest him with increased dignity
and to furnish him greater protection of body, property and of life. Hence from every
viewpoint the Negro in America, the Negro needs to get right and stay right with God. "For
if God be for us who can be against us?" And if we be for God and remain loyal and true
to Him we need never fear; for as in the case of Elisha and his servant at Dothan, they that
will be with us as our defenders will be more than they that will be with our enemies. 2
Kings 6:16. Every consideration or reason having to do with the true progress, usefulness
and well being of the race, both in time and eternity, argues with one hundred per cent
force that the unquestionable and unfailing duty and the anchoring and eternally saving
hope of the individual members and of the race as a whole lies along the pathway of righteousness, of consecrated devotion to God, through saving belief in Jesus as the Son of God
and the world's Savior, and through persevering in His service till divinely summoned from
labor to reward.

Here lies the path of all that is truly good, eternally safe, elevated and worth while. Here
lies the royal path of life where the Negro as a race will find the least opposition from man
and the greatest encouragement. Here lies the path along which he can most rapidly and
assuredly mend his ways, rise above the dark past, acquire influence, destroy prejudice, win
the goodwill of mankind, become desirable citizens, enlist heaven's aid and enjoy heaven's
smiles, escape the snares of the devil, overcome carnal weaknesses, honor father and mother
and glorify God.

"Ethiopia shall soon stretch out her hands unto God."
Will the younger generation of the Negro race in America follow the path of religious zeal,
devotion and growth along which their fathers have trod and rise as much higher and
become as much stronger in the great principles of the religion of the triune God as the light
they have is brighter and their opportunities are greater?

It is their privilege and duty, but will they? Their own individual needs and the world's
needs demand it; but will they? The weight of their increased responsibility demand it; but
will they do it? The duty which they owe to their primitive mother land, Africa, demand it;
but will they catch the vision, foster the sentiment, rise to the height of the occasion and
please heaven and earth by making good? From the character of the reports coming in from

a large portion of the leaders of the race in the fields of the home development, public school teaching, Christian evangelism, and Christian teaching, in the higher schools and Sunday Schools, there is demand that much careful and prayerful study be given them.

These reports clearly indicate that the children in the homes of the race are showing less reverence for parents, less respect for the laws and rules of the home and are less disposed to move promptly and to do faithfully and well what they are told to do than was true of the children of the homes of the race thirty or forty years ago; besides there is less co-operation on the part of parents among themselves for the more effective training of their children.

In the work of public school instruction and government, the same declension is apparent and similar complaint is heard; that the children show less reverence for teachers and for truth and for law and rules and hence are harder to control and to bring under proper discipline than were those of a generation earlier. This in part is a natural result of the failure in the home. When we enter the higher realm of the Christian religion similar reports are heard. The complaints are that the young people of the present generation are becoming less sincere, less inclined to heed good counsel, less devout, that they do not seem to find the joy and comfort in religion that their fathers and mothers found, that they are manifesting less reverence for God, for the Gospel, for religious services and holy things, that in fact, they are becoming decidedly more worldly, more carried away with a craze for dancing, card playing, worldly pleasure and a good time in general in worldly affairs.

These reports, doubtless, should be received with much allowance. But after all is said and done there is in them enough truth to furnish alarm and to serve as timely warning. Indeed the facts of the case, the situation is a stentorian call from earth and heaven to the leaders of the race, to the fathers and mothers, teachers and Gospel ministers and the business leaders of the race, to rally and organize to stem the tide.

The call of earth and heaven is that the fathers and mothers of the different communities must organize among themselves and co-operate for the more efficient training of their children; parents must be urged with all reasonable argument and entreaty to accept and fully live up to the responsibilities of the home. Between teachers and parents there must be hearty and Christian co-operation to secure in the lives of the children the full fruits of the purpose and work of the schools.

Among parents, teachers, Gospel ministers, Sunday School workers, Y. M. C. A. and Y. W. C. A. and other Christian and community workers there should be and must be most hearty, zealous and unflagging co-operation to train up the children in every line of duty in the way they should go.

This can be done; this should be done; this must be done, if we are to catch the true vision of life's mission, to arouse and foster reasonable race consciousness, pride, affinity and unity; stem the tide, turn the life currents of the race strongly along the royal path of life, realize in a large way the fruition of the prophecy and promise of the text; and thus standing firm upon the Rock Christ Jesus and His infallible word under the guidance of the Holy Spirit, to grow in grace and into that blessed state where God shall have the first place in our life and thought, where we shall love Him supremely and our neighbor as ourself and where we shall be able to love our enemies and pray fervently for those who despitefully use us and persecute us; and thus possess good will toward all men and finally receive the well-done of heaven.

"Ethiopia shall soon stretch out her hands unto God."
Young men and young women of the race, boys and girls, young mothers and fathers, young teachers and leaders of the race, this divine prophecy, promise and appeal is to you. Will you heed it? Will you struggle to realize its promise and enjoy its fruition? Will you watch and pray and cultivate good-will and struggle to lift yourselves and the race out of the slough, the mire of despond into the lifting and saving atmosphere of divine inspiration and growth? Will you cultivate and cherish profound belief in Jesus Christ as the Son of God and the world's Savior? and strive to love God supremely and your neighbor as yourselves? Will you watch, pray and endeavor to teach, inculcate and lead the race of Africa in America and through them, also the race in Africa to cherish profound faith in God the Father and in His only Son, Jesus our Lord, and in the Holy Ghost as the Comforter? and thus become blessed yourselves and prove a blessing to the race and become a factor in fitting the race to become a blessing to the world of mankind? Will you watch and pray and endeavor to keep a loving and faithful oversight over the homes, public schools and higher schools of the race in which the children and leaders of the race are in training and over the work of the churches, as those possessing race consciousness, race pride and affinity, patriotism and Christian devotion, that under God you may become and prove to be real and important factors in leading the race in a large way to realize the prophecy, promise and appeal of the text and thus to come into the possession of the gracious favor and protection of Jehovah and to move along the royal path of life and thus to accomplish the surest and truest and only enduring progress for time and eternity?

If you will, you can. If you fail as with Israel, awful will be the calamity and suffering in time and unspeakable the woe in eternity. But you will not fail, you dare not fail, you must not fail. Let your motto be that of Joshua: "But as for me and my house we will serve the Lord," and that of Ruth 1:16-17, and that of Paul, Phil. 3:13-14.

God helping me I will.

Jared Maurice Arter

A Baccalaureate Sermon
This sermon was delivered to the graduating class of Lynchburg Theological Seminary and College in the Spring of 1895.

Text: In the morning sow thy seed and in the evening withhold not thine hand: for thou knowest not whether shall prosper either this or that or whether they both shall be alike good.—Eccl. 11:6.

Young Ladies and Young Men, Class of 1895:
These are beautiful words, beautiful in sound, in symbol, in thought, in the ideas they

picture to the mind; but they are most beautiful in the deep, rich truths which they are designed to vivify, emphasize, inculcate and impress upon the mind, heart and lives of mankind.

The message contained in these words is deeply significant; because of the infinite power of Jehovah, the author, and because of the wisdom, experience, and divine inspiration of the human personality, Solomon, through whom it pleased God to deliver the message, and because of the exalted mission of the people to whom primarily it was delivered, the Jews, God's elect nation, and because of its far-reaching and extensive application, being applicable to the children of men through all the passing centuries.

Let us think of this heavenly message, this morning, as coming directly from Almighty God, through His inspired servant, Solomon, to you and to me, but to you especially as a class just about to enter upon your commencement in life.

The divine message and injunction to you is: "In the morning sow thy seed, and in the evening withhold not thine hand: for thou knowest not whether shall prosper, either this or that, or whether they both shall be alike good."

This message is not only far-reaching and extensive; but it is comprehensive and practical. It applies to boys and girls, men and women, young and old. It applies to every species, form or element of man's complex being, his physical, mental, moral and spiritual being of life.

The author, in order to emphasize and force home the main lesson of the text—that of diligence in well-doing throughout life, makes choice, in mental conception, of the fundamental occupation and the familiar figure and essential servant, the farmer, in action, sowing his seed. The author of the text was a practical man, a careful observer. He used his eyes and his mind, he saw objects and actions and analyzed them and comprehended their meaning. He was a teacher able and experienced. He knew the occupations and the customs of the people. He knew their good qualities and their shortcomings and weaknesses.

He knew that the ideal farmer in seedtime rises and begins sowing his seed in the early morning and that he slacks not his hand in the evening but perseveres with diligence through to the close of the day.

On the other hand, he knew that there are many among farmers and those of all other callings and professions of life, who are good starters, who begin well, who will rise early and start at a rapid pace but as the sun declines towards the west they grow weary, slack their hand, become indifferent, excuse themselves on the ground of what they have done, and thus allow, in the course of days, weeks, months and years, many precious days, weeks, months and even years to be wasted, and the life in so many ways to count very much less than it should, and to fall away below the ideal.

In view of these truths, these human weaknesses and pressing needs of being instructed, aroused and stirred to diligence and perseverance in well-doing, Solomon, from his vantage ground, as king of God's people, and God's servant, takes the ideal farmer, sowing early and sowing late, sowing diligently, faithfully and sowing in hope, sowing his seed that contain life, that shall spring up, bear fruit and bring forth a harvest that shall bless him and his fellowman—he takes this ideal farmer and ideal action and holds them up before the world of mankind to arouse, stimulate and stir boys and girls, men and women to ideal service and action in every phase of life and along all the lines of duty.

Let us notice briefly some duties we owe to ourselves, to our physical, mental, moral and spiritual or religious lives.

Our bodies, individually and physically speaking, are the gift of God and are designed to be the temples of God. It is my duty and your duty to keep the body healthy, "Health is first wealth." A healthy body is the foundation of a healthy and strong development. We owe it not alone to ourselves individually, but to our families, our neighbors, the community, the State, the nation, the world.

The mind, the intellectual life, must be developed and improved. Says one, "There is nothing great in the universe but man and nothing great in man but mind;" and another "The mind is the eyesight of the soul;" another, "The mind is the atmosphere of the soul." Without vision the people perish. Man as important in prompting and stimulating him to do his best needs that enlarged vision and quickening inspiration that come from a well-trained, capacious and a well-stored mind with living, uplifting truths.

But morality or the moral life must be watched and molded with great care and fervent prayer, for the moral life is a round higher in the ladder of human development, human progress. Says one, "Morality is the vestibule of religion." "Morality is essential to good government." "What can laws do without morals?" Says Dr. Horace Mann, "Ten men have failed from defect in morals where one has failed from defect in intellect." Without enlightening the conscience and strengthening the moral sense and moral obligation you can't become good brothers and sisters, good companions, good teachers, good neighbors, good husbands and wives, good fathers and mothers, good citizens.

This brings us to consider the spiritual life, the Christian religious life, which forms the climax of human development, advance and progress. While it is the duty of each both in the morning and evening of the day and of life to watch and guard and preserve and develop the health of the body, to cultivate, enlarge and enrich the mind and to enlighten and strengthen the moral sense, yet it is the spiritual life that brings us into the family of God, links us with all that is brightest and best in eternity.

It is here man's first and highest duties lie. "Thou shalt love the Lord thy God with all thy heart, and with all thy soul and with all thy might." "And thou shalt love thy neighbor as thyself." "Seek ye first the kingdom of God and His righteousness," and we have the promise that all necessary temporal blessings shall be added.

"Bodily exercise profiteth little, but Godliness is profitable unto all things, having promise of the life that now is and of that which is to come." "Remember thy Creator in the days of thy youth."

"Believe on the Lord Jesus Christ and thou shalt be saved." It is by belief in Jesus as the Son of God that one is born unto the Kingdom of God and comes into possession of spiritual life and has communion and fellowship with the triune God and His loyal, faithful servants and is prepared to sow the good seed of which Jesus spoke that fell into good ground and brought forth some an hundred fold.

Jared Maurice Arter

Sermon Delivered at the West Virginia Baptist State Convention, August, 1912

"Study [or give diligence] to render thyself approved unto God, a workman that needeth not to be ashamed, handling aright [or rightly dividing] the word of truth" (2 Tim. 2:15).

Study, give diligence to become a Gospel minister and Christian workman approved unto God.

These words were addressed by the great apostle Paul to Timothy, his own spiritual son in the Gospel.

At the time when he uttered or wrote these words he was old in years, rich in experience, devout and consecrated in life and character, energetic in Christian service, farseeing in wisdom, heroic in courage, anchored in the hope of the Gospel and the eternity of the blessed life beyond.

I wish this morning to consider:

1. What we should study.

All study of whatever kind should be with the view and purpose of making the Gospel minister's preaching, life and work, most effective, and thus securing God's approval.

Study, give diligence.

Study books, arts, sciences.

Study self (psychology, physiology, etc.).

Study others (history, sociology, etc.).

Study things (physics, chemistry, botany, zoology).

Study God (theology, religion, spirituality).

Above all, study the plain, simple Scriptures, the inspired Word of God.

I. But we must never forget that: "The heavens declare the glory of God; and the firmament showeth His handiwork. Day unto day uttereth speech, and night unto night showeth knowledge. There is no speech nor language where their voice is not heard."

Hence God speaks to the children of men through the whole realm of nature, of the created universe as well as through His special divine revelation.

Permit me to say here that I believe in an educated and trained ministry, and in an educated and intelligent pew or laity, and that the surest and best way to have an educated and intelligent pew or laity is to have an educated and well trained ministry.

This is no reflection on that large class of uneducated and untrained ministers that have done such a large and creditable work in the Master's vineyard, only as they have through indifference and willfulness neglected education and training and in some cases have gone so far as to deny its importance.

II. Why we should study, why we should give diligence.

1. Because God commands it.

2. Because the individual minister needs it.

3. Because the Christian church needs it.

4. Because the world needs it.

God, speaking to His servant Ezekiel, said, Thou son of man, hear what I say unto thee; be not thou rebellious like that rebellious house: open thy mouth and eat that I give thee, And when I looked, said Ezekiel, behold an hand was sent unto me, and lo a roll of a book was therein; And He spread it before me; and in it was written within and without, and there was written therein lamentations and mournings and woe. Moreover he said unto me, son of man eat that thou findest, eat this roll, and go speak unto the house of Israel. So I opened my mouth and He caused me to eat that roll. And he said unto me, Son of man, cause thy belly to eat, and fill thy bowels with this roll that I give thee. Then did I eat it, and it was in my mouth as honey for sweetness. And He said unto me son of man go, get thee unto the house of Israel and speak with my words unto them.

This language makes it very plain that the minister of the Gospel is to strive to master the message he is to preach, that he is to analyze, digest and to become saturated and filled with the Word of God itself and then present it as a warm message from God to man, from God to the people.

Now just as God commanded Ezekiel to eat the roll, the word, the message, to digest it and to become saturated and filled with it and then speak to the people, so He commands you and me. Ezekiel obeyed, so must you, so must I. Obedience is the gateway to God's favor, to God's approval.

Study, give diligence. The minister of the Gospel himself needs it, in order to do his best and be his best. All through the Old Testament's sacrifices and offerings God demanded the best.

Behold to obey is better than sacrifice and to hearken than the fat of rams.

That in view of which or the purposes for which we should study, give diligence.

To become master workmen, to gain larger vision of truth. "Where there is no vision the people perish." Study, give diligence, to have the living Word kindle a flame of zeal and sacred love in our soul, to cause our light to shine bright, to become more faithful and fervent in prayer and thus to come into possession of more power with God and man, that by all means we might become instrumental in God's hands of saving some.

Jared Maurice Arter

Extracts from an Address at the Celebration of Fifty Years of Freedom of the Negro Race in America, **April 9, 1913**

Mr. President, Ladies and Gentlemen:

Fifty years ago the 22nd of September, the famous *Emancipation Proclamation* by Abraham Lincoln was issued. Fifty years ago last January 1st, that Proclamation went into legal effect. On the 9th of April fifty years ago today Gen. Robt. E. Lee, who had been the soul of the rebellion with the remnant of his army, on the field of Appomattox, surrendered to Gen. U. S. Grant.

This removed all organized resistance to the Union and marks this day in the minds of many as the day of greatest memorial significance in the deliverance of the Negro from American slavery.

This depends, however, much on conception, faith in God and the triumph of truth, and the strength of patriotic sentiment.

All the days: September 22nd, January 1st, and April 9th, are of blessed memory and deserve to have their memories cherished.

The real benefit, however, that is to be derived by us as a race, and by others through us from the celebration of one or all of these days is the development in our souls of a deeper sense of the worth and a higher appreciation of the very great privilege and blessing of liberty.

It is by contrast that we gain clearest views and receive deepest and most lasting impressions. The present sinks its roots deep in the past, and in order to know and properly value the present we must study and know much of the past. Says a great scholar: "There is no greater calamity that can befall any people than to be forgetful or ignorant of their past."

God established among the Israelites the Feast of Tabernacles to keep them mindful of their camping, marches, and trials in the wilderness. Says Patrick Henry, "I know of no way of judging the future but by the past," and looking at the blessings of liberty above slavery said, "Give me liberty or give me death." We would note and emphasize first of all the very significant truth: that from January, 1863, to the close of the war, 1865, about two hundred thousand Negro troops were enlisted in the U. S. army and navy, and that in the course of these years they fought heroically on many battlefields and in many naval contests. This circumstance furnished to the Negro a happy vantage ground. It put him in the dignified position of patriotic and loyal subject, of putting his life on the altar of his country, to help save the Union, to secure his own liberty, and that of others, and to make this country indeed and in truth "The land of the free and the home of the brave."

This patriotic and heroic service to his country, lifted the Negro much in the minds of many, softened prejudice, made many friends and paved the way for the framing and adoption of the 13th, 14th and 15th Amendments to the U. S. Constitution and the passage of the Civil Rights Bill. But with the fall of the Confederacy, April 9th, 1865, at Appomattox, nearly 4,000,000 persons of African descent in this country were legally and more or less physically free, that is, they could not be bought and sold. They belonged to themselves and had the right to contract and to receive the compensation for their services.

But under the bond and handicap of illiteracy, superstition, poverty, prejudice, jealousy, lack of homes, of confidence, of experience in business and self-direction, amid a hostile and aggressive people, were left this nearly 4,000,000 freedmen. The question naturally arose, "What will we do with the Negro?" "What must the Negro be taught to do for himself?"

Some fifty or more Freedmen's Aid Societies and active organizations by the government and the various Christian denominations were formed, and centers of distress were established at Port Royal, Fortress Monroe, Washington, New Orleans, Vicksburg, and Corinth, Miss., and Columbus, Ky., and Cairo, Ill., and elsewhere.

These centers of distress were at first under control of the treasury department. Later they were turned over to the army officials. Here the work was advanced somewhat along systematic lines by enlisting able bodied men and giving work to others. Confiscated and abandoned estates South and West were leased to superintendents or organizations and given over to the freedmen for cultivation.

The government and benevolent societies furnished the means and thus the great body of freedmen returned slowly to work. The system of control thus started rapidly grew here and there into strange little governments like that of Gen. Banks in Louisiana, with its 90,000 black subjects, is 50,000 guided laborers and its annual budget of $100,000 or more. Other systems of control like this might be mentioned that covered a wider range of territory and whose workings are given more in detail.

It was from these systems that Gen. Armstrong and Gen. Howard got their conception and caught the inspiration that led to the establishment of Hampton Institute and Howard University.

The powers of the Freedmens Bureau were enlarged in 1865, and given its final form in 1866. It continued till 1869. This bureau brought all these little systems heretofore mentioned under one central control. Gen. O. O. Howard of Maine appointed May 12, 1865, was commissioner of this new bureau and began promptly the work of his office. The bureau invited continued co-operation with benevolent societies. Nine commissioners were appointed and the object of all was:

(1) to introduce practical systems of compensated labor;

(2) to establish schools;

(3) gradually to close relief establishments and to make the destitute self supporting;

(4) to act as courts of law where there were no courts;

(5) to establish the institution of marriage among ex-slaves;

(6) to keep records;

(7) to see that freedmen were free to choose their employers and to help to make contracts for them;

(8) to sell confiscated public land for school property.

The task was gigantic.

After a year's work pushed most vigorously as it was the task seemed more difficult to grasp and solve than at the beginning. There were three things done in the first years well worth doing:

(1) it relieved a vast amount of physical suffering;

(2) it transported 7,000 fugitives from congested centers back to the farm;

(3) best of all, it inaugurated the crusade of the New England school ma'am and the outpouring of Northern benevolence.

The work of the New England school ma'am and Northern benevolence has been denominated "The Ninth Crusade." It is a most interesting story. They did their work. In that first year, it is estimated they taught 1,000,000 souls. Space forbids our going further with this interesting story of re-construction, readjustment and development.

The opposition to the Negro's development by Southern ex-slave holders and others had to be overcome. But despite it all the progress of the Negro in fifty years has no parallel in history. He has increased in numbers to 10,000,000, reduced illiteracy from ninety percent to thirty-eight per cent, growth in wealth, 337,000 farms owned in their own right, 409,717 farmed under the control as tenants, the number of acres thus controlled and owned, 38,233,933, taxable property from $600,000,000 to $800,000,000; 23462 church buildings, 23,770 church organizations.

Jared Maurice Arter, Echoes from a Pioneer Life *(1922).*

A. B. Caldwell Publishing Co., 1922.

WILLIAM H. HEARD (1850-1937)

From Slavery to the Bishopric in the A.M.E. Church, An Autobiography

Chapter 1
Birth

William Henry (Harrison) Heard was born in Elbert County, Georgia, ten miles below Elberton Court House, and three miles from Longstreet, a small town with one store and Post Office.

He was born in a log cabin. The logs were cut promiscuously from small pines, straight and crooked, and they were built like a stable or a pen of any kind. Where a log was too crooked, or left too large a hole, it was "chipped out" so as to be made to lay closer together, in the same way they built a pig pen or horse stable. The only difference, where they built a house for living was, they took the bark off the trees and chinked the cracks in winter and knocked out the chinking in summer.

In October they would chink and daub so as to make the house warm, and in May they would knock out the chinking so as to make the house cool.

During this season of the year frogs, lizards, snakes, and smaller insects would play "hide and seek" out of one crack into the other. At night you would just as liable find a snake curled up in your bed taking his rest as you were to go and take your rest.

The chimneys were built of pine sticks daubed with mud about four to five feet high, they were as good an entrance and exit as the door. The house had one door about three feet by five feet, one window about two feet by three feet, the floor was made of "puncheons"; that is: the slabs were sawed off the trees intended for sawing planks. You could count the chickens under these houses as accurately through these cracks as you could in the yard.

I was born June 25, 1850. This they called at the time "Corn plowing time." So when they designated my age, they would say: He was born in corn plowing time, in, or about the year when the stars fell," or some incident of note.

A woman who had children regularly was called a "breeder" in those days; and was allowed to go home at ten o'clock in the morning each day, again at twelve, and at three to nurse the child; for the child was reckoned as "property," and therefore valuable enough to be given this time.

My mother was a farm hand, and was considered a "breeder," so that in plowing time she worked right around her house, and plowed with an old horse by the name of "Selim." She never went away with the rest of the hands, two and three miles from the house. Not my mother only, but all women who were nursing children, were thus dealt with. The attention to the babies was given by the larger children, who looked after the smaller ones.

My father lived three miles away. He would come in on Wednesday nights after things had closed up at his home, and be back at his home by daylight Thursday mornings; come again Saturday night, and return by daylight Monday morning. He had a pass weekly from his master that gave him this permission.

The night my mother died (I was nine years of age), I lay on a pallet next to a cradle and rocked my infant brother who was just five weeks old, and gave him the bottle all night. I did this when only nine years of age myself.

Chapter 2

First and second times sold

My father, George W. Heard, was a slave of Thomas Heard, who was reputed to be his father. He was a blacksmith by trade, and while he weighed only one hundred and forty pounds, he could use a sledge hammer as steadily and actively as a man weighing two hundred pounds, and shoe as many mules as any blacksmith in the county.

After thirty years as a blacksmith, he took up the trades of a wheelwright and a carpenter, and worked at all three of these trades twenty years before he died.

He did not know figures at all, yet he could give a bill for lumber as accurately as a master mathematician.

He never belonged to the same man that my mother belonged to, but lived near enough to see her once or twice a week.

My mother was Pathenia Galloway; she and her children belonged to the Galloway estate (two boys: Wylie and George Galloway).

When the boys became of age and the estate was settled, my mother and her three children were placed upon the auction block and sold to the highest bidder. That man was Lindsay Smith, who lived at Rock Fence, in the flatwoods of Elbert County. He was a large farmer, and owned nearly one hundred Negroes. This was my first time sold.

After two or three years at Rock Fence a man by the name of John A. Trenchard, principal of the high school at Elberton, Georgia, wanted to buy a cook. He came to Lindsay Smith, who had a woman by the name of Harriet and her children to sell, but Prof. Trenchard saw us children, and asked for the woman who was the mother of these children, and was shown my mother. There were then four children, as Cordelia, my youngest sister, was born, but the difference in the sale was one thousand dollars more. He paid the difference and purchased my mother and her four children—Millie, Henry, Beverly, and Delia. We went to Elberton, my mother became the cook and two of us, large enough to do errands, became house servants; as Prof. Trenchard kept a boarding house and many of the students boarded with him.

This was my second and last time to be sold as a slave.

Prof. Trenchard was an Iowa man, and what we considered a fair master; but there were many men in Georgia very cruel as masters, for the law did not interfere with a master and his slave. It had nothing to do with his treatment of them, and there was no law in vogue as to cruelty to animals in those days.

I knew a man living just three miles from us who beat a woman belonging to him to death, and she was heavily pregnant; so he was guilty of the murder of two, instead of one person.

Many of the masters had cruel overseers and Negro drivers, who were allowed to beat the Negroes, but not to take life.

Many men and women resented this cruelty, and would fight back, but the overseers would overpower them, and the master would stand by and see this overseer or driver put one hundred lashes on their bare backs and wash them down with salt and water. The blood would run from their heads to their heels; yet many of them were never conquered. They would go to the woods and stay there for months, yes, some of them years. They would dig caves in the ground and live in them. So they would get the Negro hounds to trail them and catch them; but many of them would take a scythe and cut these hounds into pieces as they approached.

Others had "remedies" that they used that the hounds could not scent them, so they could not be trailed; for they could be within five feet of the hounds and they could not scent them.

I knew a woman who could not be conquered by her mistress, and so her master threatened to sell her to New Orleans Negro traders. She took her right hand, laid it down on a meat block and cut off three fingers, and thus made the sale impossible; but I will not recount these cruelties further.

After living at Elberton Court House two years, my mother became the mother of her last child, George Clark.

Typhoid fever broke out as an epidemic. My oldest sister and my mother died in this epidemic. Myself, Beverly, Cordelia and George Clark were left orphans. I was nine years of age, the oldest of the four. George Clark, the youngest, was five weeks old. This was about the year 1859.

When I became ten years of age I began working on the farm. A plow was made just to suit my height, and I plowed day after day. So went on until 1865.

One day in 1865 I was plowing with a mare called "Old Jane," and I looked and saw the "Yankees." I had heard before of their coming. I took out Old Jane and went to the house about three o'clock in the afternoon. I was asked why I had come home at that hour. I told them "I was afraid the Yankees would steal my horse, so I brought her home," but that was not the cause at all. Freedom had come, and I came to meet it.

Four weeks after that I was stacking hay one day, and the "boss man" came out where we were at work. He was under the influence of drink and he beat everybody. That night I took all my belongings, put them in a pocket handkerchief and "went to freedom." Thus ended slavery with me.

Chapter 3

My education

I attended Sunday School when I was ten years of age, in Elberton, Georgia, at the Methodist Episcopal Church South. We did not learn to read nor to write, as it was against the law for any person to teach any slave to read; and any slave caught writing suffered the penalty of having his forefinger cut from his right hand; yet there were some who could read and write.

In this Sunday School we were taught the Bible and Catechism, and committed much to memory by having the same repeated to us in the Sunday School, and then some member of the white family carried this out during the week; so that there were those of us who could repeat whole Psalms and chapter after chapter in the Shorter Catechism.

This was the education that came to a slave, and I for one had five years of this kind of training.

At the end of five years freedom came; but there were no teachers in the part of the county in which I lived and no schools for Negroes.

My father was a wheelwright and had a shop on the main road, not far from the town school, so I secured the services of a "Poor white" boy named Billee Adams and paid him ten cents a lesson and studied in Webster's Blue Back Spelling Book. I studied spelling, reading, and arithmetic all in this one book.

After six months the year 1865 ended and I was hired to a farmer by the name of William Henry Heard, from whom I received my name. The contract was five dollars per month and a recitation each night. I worked from "kin to cant," that is: from daylight to dark. When I came in, put up my mule, and fed him, I made my way to the dining room and waited for my teacher to finish his supper, then I recited my lesson to him. I had added another study, writing, to my curriculum, and my hour for study was twelve o'clock in the day. We were given one hour for dinner and feeding our stock. Many of the hands slept this hour. I spent it in the preparation of my lessons for the night.

Boys had no pockets in their clothes in those days, so I cut the board back from my book and carried it on my head, under my cap. It was safe unless a hard rain came up, then cap, book, and all suffered.

After we laid by the crops in June, I went to Elberton Court House and attended school six weeks under a young man named George H. Washington, from Augusta, Georgia. I studied spelling, reading, writing, arithmetic, and geography. At the end of this time I could spell words of five or six syllables, compose, and write a letter and understood the four rules of arithmetic: addition, subtraction, multiplication, and division. This was only a Summer school, and we all returned to the farm at the end of six weeks.

I kept up my studies with a farmer until Christmas. At Christmas I was hired to another farmer by the name of Clay Hulmes. He had attended the High School and was prepared to give me a great deal of help, but he was a "poor boy" and much prejudiced, but our contract was six dollars per month, board, and a lesson at night.

While I had three or four studies he would only have me recite one study each night. After six months I left him. I had broken the contract and my father felt bound to make me carry it out, so he sent me back. I stayed three days and broke it again, so they all decided that it was best that we stay apart.

By this time we had a regular school in the town taught by a lady by the name of Mrs. Hankinson. I worked at my father's shop morning and evening, and attended this school for six weeks, which so prepared me that in the Fall I began teaching school myself, and with a private teacher I carried forward my studies and was able to stand an examination and teach the three months public school, which was a great help to me financially, for we were allowed one dollar per month per scholar, and with an assistant I had one hundred or more pupils, so that I had at the close of this school term over three hundred dollars in money, and that was big money in those days, and it gave me a start in the world of economics. During this teaching I took lessons from a white man by the name of James Lofton. I studied grammar, mathematics, and history. When I learned the parts of speech in Smith's Grammar and their relation to each other, it was a revelation to me. I saw opening up along the intellectual horizon things I never dreamed of. I was a man of good memory, they said, and I got much from my studies, so that I went on teaching and in the second year I received a second grade certificate, taught the Public School and was rewarded as before.

In January, 1873, I went to Mt. Carmel, South Carolina, where I had a six months public school and a regular salary of forty dollars per month. I taught here four years and continued my studies under the township school teacher of the white school, a Mrs. Ritchie, who taught me algebra and Latin.

The State of South Carolina at that time was Republican and the University of South Carolina at that time was under State control, as it is now. There were scholarships in each county, and any boy over sixteen years of age and under twenty-one years could compete for these scholarships. Abbeyville County, in which I lived, was entitled to five. I won one of these scholarships, entered the University and received twenty dollars per month. With that I supported my family and myself. I entered as a freshman, but in 1877, when the Democrats came in power, they turned out all the Colored students. I was a sophomore in the classical department at the time.

Being a member of the Legislature from Abbeyville County, I was unseated by the Democrats and refused a school in the county because of my interest in politics.

I returned to Georgia and opened a school in the African Methodist Episcopal Church at Athens. At the end of the summer School, for that was all that we had, I entered Clarke University, spent one term there and then was persuaded to enter Atlanta University. I spent one year as a Junior in the classical department. At the end of this year I had a governmental position and so I left school until I came to Philadelphia in August, 1888. I then entered the Reformed Episcopal Seminary at Forty-first and Chestnut Streets, Philadelphia, studied Theology, Hebrew, and Greek, and took the Extension Course of Lectures at the University of Pennsylvania. Thus ended the patchwork of such an education as I have been able to pick up.

I have Honorary Degree of Doctor of Divinity (D. D.) from Allen University, also from Wilberforce University, Doctor of Laws (LL. D.) from Campbell College, Jackson, Mississippi. These titles are honorary; given to me because of the position I occupy in the Church more than from learning.

Chapter 4
In Politics

At the close of the war I was but fifteen years of age, and yet I had much to do with the politics of the county in which I lived (Elbert County).

Colonel James T. Ackerman, who was the United States Attorney General under President Ulysses S. Grant, and who lived in that county, was a staunch Republican and encouraged me much along this line. In 1872 I had just reached my majority and was the County Chairman of the Republican Party, and looked after the interests of that party together with a man by the name of Nathan Thompson, who could neither read nor write. Our tickets for the election of 1872 were printed, and distributed by the State Chairman. While our Postmaster was a Republican, yet by some Democratic move our tickets were intercepted and were not allowed to reach us. We had no railroad and got mail only every other day, so that when the mail came in on Monday, or the day before the election, no tickets came in it. So in order to have tickets the next day at the polls, I wrote tickets all night, and five hundred tickets were cast at that precinct. Had we received our tickets and distributed them at each precinct the county would have gone Republican, but as it was we lost the county.

I was a candidate for the Legislature on the Republican ticket. Grant and Colfax were the candidates for President and Vice-President.

In 1876 I was in South Carlina. It was called "The red-shirt campaign," and will never be forgotten for its bloody deeds. Yet the Republicans stood their ground and won out in many counties. I was a candidate for the Legislature on the Republican ticket, from Abbeyville County. We carried the county by over one thousand majority. I carried my precinct, Calhoun Mills, by three hundred and fifteen.

On the night before the election we gathered all the Republican voters together in a school-house near the precinct, sang and prayed, drank coffee and ate sandwiches all night.

Just at daylight we marched to the polls and stood in line until we had voted five hundred Republican votes. I was Deputy United States Marshal and had the conflict of my life, but we were three to one. Every man armed with some kind of weapon and each stood by his post. We counted our votes and left the polls about three o'clock in the morning when the Democrats undertook to capture our returns; but we were too strong for them; however, they did capture them after we had left.

On Saturday I returned to the precinct to get affidavits from the managers of the election. I was captured by the Democrats, my hands tied behind me, and carried into Elbert County, where they made a fire in an old school-house. We remained there all night. I was tied to two of these men, so if they fell asleep I could not get away.

The next morning I was carried to Ruckersville, where they all drank whisky. The South Carolina mob tried to get these Georgians to do away with me; but they did not have the courage, or they were too proud of me as a Georgian to do so.

At the fall of night they carried me to Ed Starke's, with whom I had had trouble on election day in 1872, and tried to get him to do their deed, but his father said: "There can be no killing on my place." So after supper, about eight o'clock at night, they took me down to Broad River, had a Colored man to put me across and released me.

I was thirty miles from the railroad, in Wilkes County, but, I knew my territory so that I walked that thirty miles and was at Washington-Wilkes the next morning at daylight.

I hid around until the train blew, then I went aboard and lay down as a sick man. When the conductor came around for tickets I played off that I was too sick to have bought a ticket. I had five dollars in my pockets and I paid my way to Augusta, Georgia, went across the river to Hamburg, South Carolina, and stated to the captain of the troops stationed there who I was and what position I held. He sent me to Columbia, where I made an affidavit of the vote of my precinct, which gave the State to Hayes and Wheeler, as we had a Republican majority of three hundred and fifteen. I took my seat as a member of the Legislature from Abbeyville County, and sat during that session; but at the end of the session the Democrats contested our seats and unseated us. The troops were removed and the State turned over to the Democrats.

In 1880 I was appointed railway postal clerk by the direction of Congressman Emory Speare, an independent Democrat, for whom I had canvassed, and whose election I had helped to secure. I (in my route) ran from Lula to Athens, Georgia, from Atlanta to Macon, Georgia, and from Atlanta, Georgia, to Charlotte, North Carolina, for two years. I resigned this position to enter the ministry. After this I took no great interest in politics until February, 1895, when by the assistance of Bishop Henry McNeil Turner, I was appointed by President Grover Cleveland United States Minister Resident and Consul General to Liberia, West Coast Africa, which position I held for four years.

At the same time I preached regularly and built the church at Monrovia, Liberia, from the funds received from the government, and not from the Church.

The Eliza Turner Memorial Chapel stands there today as a crowning effort and a token of my interest in the Church. ...

Chapter 6

My conversion

The word "Conversion" is used interchangeably with "Regeneration." Many of us use this word without thinking of the depth to which the meaning takes us.

I was nine years at the altar, every year seeking conversion. I had been told by many ministers during these nine years that all I had to do was to believe on the Lord. This word, believe, to me meant only to accredit things; but when I sought the Lord I accredited Him as the Omnipotent, Omnipresent, and Omniscient God; but I could not conceive that He was my Father, and, therefore, the relationship of a father was to be had by faith. So I had sought the Lord all these years without faith in Him as a Father, and myself as His child. But year after year I became more and more confident that He loved me, that He gave His Son to die for me, and that the New Birth fully established this relation, and that when I could reach that New Birth by faith in Christ as The Redeemer of the world, and of man in particular, that my relation as Son was not only established, but rejoiced in; so that at a protracted meeting in Athens, Georgia, April and May, 1879, I attended the meeting and was at the altar every night for five weeks.

One night before the services began, I reached the conclusion that open confession of my sins and acknowledgement of Christ as My Savior was the thing to do. But I lacked Faith to do this, because I had felt nothing to assure me that I was saved. So I carried out the idea by getting up in seat and undertaking to make this confession and acknowledgement.

After some time standing on my feet, being unable to speak, faith came, my mouth flew open and I shouted for joy, and then I openly acknowledged that I was a sinner and that Christ was my Savior, and that I was willing and ready to surrender all to Him.

When I did this the burden of guilt left me, and I felt that I was forgiven and the only thing I had to do was to live in fellowship with Him. And this I have tried to do all these years. Therefore I believe that I have turned my face in the right direction, and am walking in the direction prescribed in the Scriptures. And, so long as I walk therein, I am converted, or regenerated, a Son of God, a Brother of Christ, and an Heir of Heaven.

Chapter 7
The ministry
Exhorter

On May 16, 1879, I was converted. At that time I was teaching school and living with Colonel W. A. Pledger, at Athens, Georgia. He was a lawyer and I felt that to be my calling; so I had been reading Blackstone in preparation to be admitted to the bar, and to make law my profession. But, after my conversion, I felt the call to the ministry, and was so impressed that when the Quarterly Conference met in June, 1879, I applied for license to exhort, as that is the first step for a preacher in the Methodist Church.

The Rev. Peter McClain was the Presiding Elder. He was a man without literary training, yet he could read, write and preach a good gospel sermon. I had gone before my class and they had sent me to the Quarterly Conference. I was prepared educationally to stand the examination, but in those days many questions were asked to find out if the applicant had gifts, graces, and really had been called to the ministry.

I exhorted for three months. I did not preach, but exhorted; for an exhorter was not permitted to take a text, but he read a chapter, or part of a chapter and proceeded to explain the same as he understood it.

Local Preacher
At the end of three months I had gone before the Church, preached a trial sermon, and they had recommended me to be licensed as a local preacher.

My trial sermon lasted about six minutes. I had said all I knew, and I sat down. I have kept that up these forty years, that when I get through to sit down.

While I only spoke six minutes, the Church was impressed that I had been called to the ministry, so after an examination by the Quarterly Conference it recommended me for local preacher's license. I taught Sunday School, led a class, and preached whenever called upon for three months. …

Deacon
In 1881 the Annual Conference met at Atlanta, Georgia. I was examined in the first year and second year studies and ordained a Deacon by Bishop William Fisher Dickerson. I had served my first year at Johntown Mission, and at the adjournment of this conference was returned for the second year. In 1882, when the conference met, I reported Johntown Mission with fifty-three members, and it was a Circuit instead of a Mission.

Elder
When the appointments were read, I was read out for Markham Street Mission, Atlanta, Georgia. I only served this point a few months and was transferred to Aiken, South Carolina.

But before being transferred, I passed the Fourth Year Class and Bishop Dickerson ordained me an Elder at Washington, Georgia. Bishop Wesley John Gaines was chairman of the committee and examined me.

I served Aiken ten months, built a parsonage, renovated the Church, took in one hundred and sixty members at a revival, and reported the church out of debt.

Conference met this year at Georgetown, South Carolina, and I was appointed to Marion, South Carolina, but the Church at Aiken telegraphed the Bishop not to send any one else, so, in three days I was back to Aiken for the second year. We had great success, and at the conference held at Beaufort, South Carolina, I was appointed to Mt. Zion Church, Charleston, South Carolina.

When I came to Aiken, it only paid three hundred and fifty-five dollars a year, yet I resigned a government position paying me eleven hundred and fifty dollars a year. This station paid me the first year six hundred and fifty dollars; the second year, six hundred and eighty dollars, two suits of clothes each year and perquisites that amounted to two or three hundred dollars. But coming to Mt. Zion I had an appointment that would pay me one thousand dollars, house rent, fuel, and perquisites amounting to four or five hundred dollars, which took me above the salary I was receiving when I left the railway mail service.

This church was in debt to the amount of ten thousand, three hundred and fifty dollars, besides, they owed a current debt of more than fifteen hundred dollars. But in the course of six months I had met all the obligations and had gotten down to the bonded debt. I remained here three years, and at no time could my regular congregation be seated without bringing in chairs. I paid the bonded debt down to five thousand dollars, put in a pipe organ for two thousand and five hundred dollars, and renovated the church after the earthquake at a cost of one thousand eight hundred dollars. All of this was paid when I left by transfer for the Philadelphia Annual Conference. During these three years I received eleven hundred persons in the church.

Transferring from Bishop B. W. Arnett to Bishop H. M. Turner, I was appointed to Allen Chapel, Philadelphia, an appointment Bishop Levi Jenkins Coppin had held until he was elected editor of the A.M.E. Church Review. We had one of the greatest revivals that had taken place in the city of Philadelphia for many years. This revival ran for four weeks, and we took into our church alone one hundred and thirty-one persons, who I put into a class and led them with the assistance of a lady named Martha Morris, who proved to be a great leader, so that when these persons were ready for full membership, we lost not more than eight or ten out of a class of one hundred and thirty-one.

This, perhaps, was the greatest number ever received at any one time in Allen Chapel. Allen Chapel since that time has grown to be "Allen Church." We only remained there one year, and by our own choice we were moved and became Presiding Elder of the Lancaster District, and had a most successful year. But Bishop Turner removed us from this District and appointed us, to the pastorate of "Mother Bethel Church," Philadelphia. At that time the present structure was in course of erection, and so for eight months we worshipped in Horticultural Hall, on Broad Street, near Spruce, where we preached Sabbath after Sabbath, and paid one hundred dollars each Sunday for rent.

We stayed at Bethel two years, had two great revivals and took in over six hundred members. Many of the substantial members that are in Bethel today came in during this time. We finished this church at a cost of fifty-five thousand dollars and raised twenty-eight thousand during the two years' service.

No man stayed at Bethel, during these times, but two years, and even though the church was unanimous for our return, Bishop B. T. Tanner removed us and sent us to Bethel, Wilmington, Delaware. Here we remained two years, had a great revival, assisted by Doctor Benjamin F. Watson, and took in the church, during this revival, two hundred and eighty-four persons. Many of these people are there today, and make some of the leading members of that church. I took in all, four hundred and sixty persons into that church.

After serving here two years, I was appointed to Harrisburg, Pennsylvania, and finished the new church on State Street, paid the debts, kept up our monthly dues to the Building and Loan Association, and had a balance in bank to meet these dues; but the minister who followed us used up the money in bank and got behind six months in the Building and Loan Association. To save the church the Church Extension Society had to come in and assist him.

In February, 1895, I was appointed by President Grover Cleveland, United States Minister Resident and Consul General to Liberia, West Coast Africa. But we would not agree to take this appointment unless we were permitted to transfer to the Liberia Annual Conference and be given work. We were transferred and made Superintendent of the Liberia Annual Conference, which position we held for four years. We took the money out of our own pocket, purchased the land, and built the first African Methodist Episcopal Church in the city of Monrovia, Liberia. This church stands now as the Elias Turner Memorial Chapel.

Up to this time when we held conferences in Monrovia, we had to borrow a church in which to hold them, which was very inconvenient, and we were humiliated more than once by having to wait on a Sunday for a convenient hour to ordain our men; and the finances all went to the borrowed church.

After four years I left Liberia and came to America. I was appointed pastor of Zion Mission, Philadelphia, where I remained one year, renovated the church and paid for it.

At the end of that year, against my will, Bishop W. B. Derrick transferred me to the New York Conference. I was made Presiding Elder of the Long Island District, and had a year of great success; but at the end of that year I asked to be transferred to the Philadelphia Annual Conference, and was appointed to Phoenixville, Pennsylvania, where I remained a few months; yet I never enjoyed a pastorate more than I did the three or four months at Phoenixville.

In August, 1901, Rev. Doctor A. A. Whitman, pastor at Allen Temple, Atlanta, Georgia, died, so Bishop Turner appointed me to Allen Temple by transfer. I served these people for three years, increased their membership, reduced their debts, and enjoyed a pastorate such as I had not for many years. This is a great church, and is now growing to be the equal of any in Georgia.

After three years the quadrennium ended and I had been elected to the General Conference.

Chapter 8
Bishopric

I had been a member of every General Conference, at every session from 1888, at Indianapolis, Indiana, to this General Conference at Norfolk, Virginia, in 1908, twenty years.

When I was a candidate myself for the Bishopric, I had no support from "the Bench." There were two or three who did not oppose my election, but gave me no support. It was known that Bishops Turner, Gaines, Grant and Smith did all they could for my defeat, but I was elected by a large majority. No man running against me received over fifty-two votes. I received three hundred and seventy-six votes, and was elected one of the Bishops of the African Methodist Episcopal Church and assigned to West Africa.

In January, 1909, with Mrs. Heard and eight missionaries, I sailed for the West Coast of Africa. We spent a few days in Liverpool and London, England, and then started for the West Coast. After eighteen days' sailing we landed at Sierra Leone, where I held my first conference. This was indeed a great conference for a Mission field.

We left Sierra Leone for Liberia. Here we held our second conference, and our missionaries were all put to work in this field. This brought new life, and after four years' hard work the two conferences were in fine condition, meeting all the obligations incumbent upon them.

Had the war not come, and Bishop Ross been permitted to succeed me, the work would have been far in advance of what it is today.

While I did my best, and all must give me credit for having done great work from the funds at my disposal, yet Bishop Brooks has done the greatest work of any Bishop in our Missionary Fields. It will go down to his credit, and his name can never be erased from the West Coast.

After eight years' service we were called home, and I was assigned to the Eighth Episcopal District, comprising the States of Mississippi and Louisiana. The conference claims of this district, the minutes will show, were not over fifty per cent., but when I reported my fourth round of conferences, I reported ninety per cent. of dollar money, the greatest increase ever reported before, or since. The amount today, 1923, is not equal to what I reported in 1919-20. I did not only financial work, but social and spiritual work as well. The men of the district credit me as a complete success.

Leaving the Eighth District in 1920, we were assigned to the First Episcopal District. The First District reported for 1920, twenty-one thousand, seven hundred and eighty dollars and seventy-eight cents Dollar money. We are reporting for this year thirty thousand dollars, which shows our standard financially in Dollar money. We have reported for education this quadrennium more than for four quadrenniums put together, that is, the preceding four quadrenniums to this added together will not amount to the sum total to what we have raised this quadrennium for education.

We are winding up our four years with a membership of more than seven thousand above what we found at the beginning of the quadrennium. The District, to show its appreciation of the work done has just given a reception ending with a great banquet, and a purse of fifteen hundred dollars. This speaks louder than mere words and every conference of its own accord has unanimously voted for the Bishop to be returned to the district for another quadrennium.

From 1908 to 1924 in sixteen years and over this period I have lived much, took many souls into the church, and not shrank from any duty that a Bishop is called upon to fill. I go forth in the name of Him who sent me, "knowing not what may befall me and would not if I could."

William H. Heard

E. C. MORRIS (1855-?)

Introduction

E. C. Morris was born a slave on May 7, 1855 in Murray county, Georgia. He was mainly self-educated. In 1874, he converted to Christianity and began preaching. In 1877, Morris moved to Helena, Arkansas. Eventually, he earned the degree of Doctor of Divinity from the State University in Louisville, Kentucky. In 1884, Morris founded the Arkansas Baptist College. In 1894, Morris was elected President of the National Baptist Convention until 1915.

Negro Baptists—Retrospective and Prospective
This address was delivered in Boston, September 15, 1897.

Brethren of the Convention, Ladies and Gentlemen:

Again, by the providence of an all-wise God, we have been brought together in another annual meeting of our Convention, at a most opportune time and place; a time when the race is being tried in the balance of public opinion, as to its progress as citizens, and as Christian followers of the meek and lowly Nazarene, and at the place which can boast above all others, that her citizens were the first to strike the blow which felled the monster, slavery, and broke the shackles from four and a half millions of bondmen. I cannot too strongly urge upon you the importance of this meeting, for the simple reason that it represents nearly five-eighths of the Afro-American Christians on this Continent, and is, therefore, the most representative body that has or may hereafter meet to devise plans for the extension of Christ's kingdom, and the uplifting of a race of people who are only thirty-four years from a cruel bondage.

I congratulate myself upon having the honor to address the representatives of such an organization. I assure you that it is a source of supreme pleasure to me to be here, and I want to thank you, one and all, for the uniform courtesy and loyal support you have given me during the three years I have had the honor to preside over your deliberations. There may have appeared on the surface, at times, differences of opinion as to the best methods of doing the work of the Convention; but how could it have been otherwise, with such an army of leaders as we have, all endeavoring to put forth the best plans for the advancement of the race and denomination? But no matter how much we have differed in the past, we come here a grand, united army, a million six hundred thousand strong of the G. A. R. (Grand Army of the Redeemer), with our colors flying, bearing the significant declaration, "One Lord, One Faith, and One Baptism." And having firmly planted this banner in the homes of a majority of our people in the South, we are now moving on the East. And permit me to say in this connection, that when these chosen men of God, carved in ebony, shall be permitted to publish the gospel of God's dear Son to every creature, and not forced to preach it to creatures of their own race, there will be a wonderful change of belief among the white Christians of this country.

But this narrow, selfish condition is by no means the fault of the colored ministry, nor are they in any respect responsible for the fact that the Christian Churches of to-day are silent upon the wrongs heaped upon the race daily, all over the land. But rest assured that God has a remedy for all the wrongs in his Church, and in his own time and way will apply it. But, my brethren, you will bear in mind that there are notable exceptions to what I refer to here as "religious proscription;" for it is a matter of fact that there are here in Boston and other great cities of our country, those who believe in and practice the doctrine delivered at Mars Hill by the eminent Apostle to the Gentiles, that "of one blood God created all nations of men." And it is due this city to say, that when every door in the land was closed to the advocacy of universal liberty, an effectual door was opened here and the great and much-revered William Lloyd Garrison, though encountering many dangers and hardships, was finally permitted to use pen and tongue in favor of the abolition of the slave trade and of slavery. It would not perhaps be too great a speculation for me to say that that noble life which passed to its reward eighteen years ago is not dead, but he having lived to see the complete triumph of the principles for which he contended, his spirit is now associated with such noble spirits as Wendell Phillips, Charles Sumner, and our own Frederick Douglass, who are looking upon these inspiring scenes as a result of their labors and bidding us God speed.

Only one generation has passed since those of us who walk in peace here were held as chattels, and the ground upon which we walk was once made crimson with the blood of those who, like Patrick Henry, thought death preferable to bondage.

Perhaps it was the hand of an all wise Providence that ordered this meeting to this place, for it was here that the first blood for American independence was shed, and it was here that the old "Liberator," which set fire to the hearts of the loyal people of the nation to battle for the freedom of the slaves, was born. And most of you who come to this Convention are the direct beneficiaries of those contentions. You are the living testimony that the many lives sacrificed for our freedom, and the volumes of money spent for the elevation of the freedmen were not spent in vain. But I am reminded just here of a most touching statement made by a prominent gentleman representing one of the great Baptist societies of the North and East. After reviewing the relations of the two races in the South, and reminding his audience that nearly all the old abolitionists who had sacrificed, many of them, their fortunes and social pleasures, that they might enlist in the cause of freedom's cry, had been gathered home, he said: "Another king had come upon the throne which knew not Joseph." This statement for a long time lingered in my mind, and has produced the thought that if they had gone to their reward, the sons and daughters of these good and great men are here, and that the examples of the fathers are not yet erased from their memories. So we come to them, we come to the people of this nation, and say to-day: "Draw near unto us, and be not afraid; for we are (I am) the descendants of Joseph, your brother, whom ye sold. It was not you, but it was God who sent us hither."

We are representing what thirty-four years of freedom have done for a nation of people—showing to the world, what we as a wing of the great Christian army have accomplished, and our plans for future work. This Convention was organized and has been steadily at work as a separate and distinct body of Christians for seventeen years; made separate in a country for which we have done more, to the man, to build up than any other people in it, and by a people whom we have served for two hundred and fifty years. It is perhaps well for us, if not for the other race, that we have been compelled to have these separate organizations; for it is clear to my mind that had it been otherwise, the possibilities of the race, and especially that part represented by the colored Baptist, would not have been drawn out and made manifest as they have. There would not have been such a host of intelligent, self-reliant, practical leaders among us, nor would we have been able to show to the world our devotion to God's cause by pointing to the thousands of magnificent and costly church edifices and the scores of high schools and colleges built, supported, and managed by the Negro Baptists in this country.

My brethren, the forcing of these separate institutions was a blessing in disguise. Persons who have been helped and who have received alms at the beautiful gate, are too liable to remain there, if not bidden to rise up and walk. And it is by reason of the fact that we have been made to support institutions of our own that the powers of the race have been developed. The men among us who know best how to build and operate educational institutions, and to superintend missions and other Christian work, are the men who have done it.

Progress and work of colored Baptists

The progress of colored Baptists has been phenomenal, so far as the increase in numbers is concerned. They have a majority over all the other colored denominations combined. Indeed I take it that much of the time used by others in seeking prominence in the world has been by Baptists devoted to winning souls to Christ, believing that "greatness in the sight of the Lord" is far better than worldly honor and distinction. Like their white brethren of the same faith, they have shown themselves the true friends of education, and have planted schools in every Southern State, and these are rapidly multiplying until in some States they have as many as a half dozen of these Christian schools. The value of their church property, which is rated at ten million dollars, is evidence conclusive that progress has been made in the line of church building. But the greatest and most difficult task is yet to be performed. The millions of our people who are yet to be developed morally, socially, and intellectually, present a problem to the thoughtful men and women of our race which is not easy of solution. And much more of the responsibility of this great task rests upon Baptists than upon any other denomination for the simple reason that most of the colored Christians are in our churches.

Then again, the colleges and seminaries are turning out thousands of educated men and women, who are fitted by education and training to perform any of the practical duties of life; but these find, when they have finished their school days and come out to enter the public arena, that every avenue is closed against them, and, if given employment at all, it is of the most menial kind. Such a condition not only discourages those who have spent years in preparing themselves for usefulness in life, but those who may have children whom they desire to educate, are caused to inquire: "What kind of employment can they get?" To my mind there is only one alternative, and that is for the Negroes to concentrate their means, both in secular and religious matters, and operate such enterprises as will give remunerative employment to the young men and women of the race. Such a concentration of means will open the avenues in other spheres.

Our progress in literature compares favorably with that of other denominations; but perhaps the greatest progress made in this line is by the Negro Baptist press. No class of men in the denomination is more deserving of special mention and of the endorsement and support of the Convention than the editors and proprietors of the thirty-two Negro Baptist papers. They have stood up fearlessly in defense of the race and denomination, and have, at the same time, without money and without price, earnestly contended for the faith once delivered to the saints.

Special objects

One of the special objects of the Convention is to do mission work in foreign lands. This work was undertaken by colored Baptists in 1880, and has been earnestly and faithfully prosecuted ever since. It was, indeed, a great undertaking, especially in the face of the history our white brethren had made in this work. Many precious lives had been sacrificed, and many thousands of dollars had been spent by them in earnest efforts to give the Gospel to our ancestors in Africa, and yet such little results had followed. But with faith in God, and believing that he has reserved this field to be successfully entered by the colored Christians in this land (their emancipation and the removal of the fear of the African fever being almost simultaneous) the effort to give the Gospel to the heathen in Africa was made. For a while the success of our labors appeared to be great, but the Foreign Mission Board soon found that many discouragements awaited them, and for a while it looked as if all the powers of the adversary had combined against us, and that we would be compelled to abandon the work in Africa and commence operations elsewhere. But at the most critical period in this work it seemed that the finger of God pointed Rev. R. A. Jackson to go to Cape Town, South Africa, and there attempt an entrance into the Dark Continent. As soon as this fact was made known to our Board, it at once grasped the opportunity, and accepted the work as its own, and have vigorously prosecuted it from that day to the present.

You are all familiar with the perplexing conditions which confronted our Board at the time of Dr. Luke's death. But I am glad to say that nearly all those embarrassments have been removed, and through the earnest, faithful efforts of Rev. L. G. Jordan, our most efficient Corresponding Secretary, coupled with the wise and prudent management of our Foreign Mission Board, the work is in a most healthy condition. The number of missionaries has been increased from two to five during the year, and the work extended a thousand miles in the interior. A much greater interest has been created among our people in this country toward this work, and they appear to be in hearty sympathy with the Board.

The Foreign Mission Board is endeavoring to raise six thousand dollars with which to build a chapel at Cape Town, which is the principal station now held by us. The effort should meet with immediate success, for delay in the matter of building the chapel will greatly retard the work so auspiciously begun there.

It will hardly be denied that the work of giving the Gospel to the heathen in Africa lies nearer the heart of our people than any of the special objects of our Convention, and if the twelve thousand pastors can be induced to lay the matter before their churches, sufficient means will be at once given to put the work where it rightfully belongs.

I regret that I am not able to report any foreign work in any other country. Indeed, it looks a little selfish that Afro-American Christians should confine their missionary labors to Africa. But the Board hopes soon to be able to make a beginning elsewhere.

E. C. Morris

Educational Sermon
Preached before the Baptist Educational Convention at Montgomery, Ala., September, 1894.

Text:—"The light of the body is the eye: if therefore thine eye be single, thy whole body shall be full of light. But if thine eye be evil, thy whole body shall be full of darkness. If therefore the light that is in thee be darkness, how great is that darkness!"

Brethren of the Convention: I recognize in the appointment which I am about to fill, a very responsible duty. Those of you who have consulted the program for this service have seen that the Annual Sermon of the Educational Convention would be preached at this hour. It is expected, of course, that what will be said in this discourse will enable the people to see what good is to come from the Educational Convention, which has been recently organized. Just as a man whose sight has grown dim from age would adjust his glasses to behold tiny objects with accuracy, so will you doubtless draw my remarks before you to see what good there is in the Educational Convention. This organization is the youngest of our national bodies, and does not come before the people with the hope or desire of supplanting either of the older organizations among us; but it comes to do a specific work which is not assumed by either of the others. And it comes using the same words which our Heavenly Father used when darkness was brooding upon the face of the great deep. In order to remove the confusion and establish order, He said, "Let there be light." And the fact that many of the people are yet in darkness and ignorance as to the educational status of our denomination, is one of the great reasons why the leaders have launched this organization. We are anxious that the truth may be known about us as a denomination of Christians. For years the Negro Baptists of the world have been held up to the ridicule of the other denominations. Their ministers have been classed as the most ignorant of the race and their manner of worship has been called a modified form of heathenism. This grave charge has stood before the world for a generation. But I tell you to-night that the charge was never true of us as a whole, for from the days of slavery until now, the leading Baptist preachers and the intelligent and progressive element in our churches have composed the vanguard of God's great army among the Negro Christians of the world. And the only reason I assign for the ignorance of those who thus falsely charge us, is that their eyes are evil.

It is not my purpose in this discourse to give you any figures setting forth the educational status of the Negro branch of the Baptist denomination in the United States, as that matter has been looked after by our statistician, and is now a matter of history. But we do hope to at least impress you with the fact that the organization of this Convention was a pressing necessity in order to give stimulus to the educational work among us. As a body cannot be perfect without eyes, so neither is a people what they should be without a medium through which they can see and be seen. Hence we present in our first proposition, "The Educational Convention as a Means to Show the Progress and Possibilities of the Negro Baptist Denomination."

The Lord Jesus, who is and ever will be the Great Head of the Church, in that wonderful sermon on the Mount, gave the world many rules which will ever be the governing power of his Church. By noticing carefully the preceding chapter you will observe that he there introduces the law of abrogation, by first calling attention to what was said by them of old time. Then he gives to them what is to be the law in the kingdom of grace and the penalty of violating that law.

But under the paragraph from which we take our text, the blessed Master rises to what we call the loftiest pinnacle of eloquence and plunges into the very essence of his Gospel by saying, "Lay not up for yourselves treasures upon earth, where moth and rust doth corrupt, and where thieves break through and steal: But lay up for yourselves treasures in heaven, where neither moth nor rust doth corrupt, and where thieves do not break through nor steal: For where your treasure is, there will your heart be also." This beautiful context fully sets forth what is to follow. Here it is that we form the opinion from the illustration given that the Christian religion is the light of the world, that its beneficent influence is to the world what the eye is to the body. If this view of his sermon be correct, then we have within our reach the means by which every man is to enter into the kingdom of God, and should be impressed with the responsibility which devolves upon us as "the light of the world." The text brings to mind this parable: If you were passing through the crowded streets of this capital city and should see standing at some conspicuous corner a poor blind beggar with his hand extended for help, you would doubtless be moved with compassion. Perhaps the first thought would be of Bartimeus, who, when he heard the tramp of the multitude, after enquiring the cause, began to cry, "Jesus, thou Son of David, have mercy on me." They (the disciples) charged him to hold his peace, but he cried the more, "Thou Son of David, have mercy on me." When Jesus had commanded him brought to him, he asked him, "What wilt thou that I should do unto thee?" The blind man answered, "Lord that I might receive my sight?"—the very thing which the penitent are asking to-day.

Brethren, the great task resting upon the Church to-day is to convert the world to Christ and give spiritual sight to those who are blind. Indeed, you are to aid in opening the eyes of the world and help to establish that singleness of purpose and doctrine which is so beautifully portrayed in the words of Jesus when he prayed, "That they may be one, even as we are one." (John 17:22.) That these glorious results will at some day be realized, I have not the slightest doubt, but they can be sooner accomplished by organization than without it. There should be a recognized head to all of our great Baptist concerns and there should be something on which we can safely rely for truthful data concerning ourselves as a denomination and to which others may look for reliable statistics. This Educational Convention seeks to be the means by which the world may see us as a body of Christian believers, and know the truth concerning the doctrines which we preach, and that we may know our own strength and the advance which we are making against the kingdom of darkness.

It necessarily follows, that to assume this responsible position in the denomination, the purposes of the Convention should be well defined. "If therefore thine eye be single, thy whole body shall be full of light." It has been said that the eye of the soul, in a moral sense, is the intention. When we speak of a person having an evil eye, we mean that that person is jealous, envious, grudging, unstable, etc.; hence to have a single eye is to have the object of our intention single, pure and good. It is said that if there be a divided aim, if there is a cataract or skin between any of the humors, that the rays of light will never make any distinct impression on the internal seat of sight. If this be true in a natural sense, it is true also in a moral sense. If the moral eye—the intention of the soul—be single to serve God and secure heavenly treasures, it directs the whole person's actions; but if we are biased or prejudiced in our intentions, we are sure to be led aside to follow after the traditions of men rather than the commandments of God. There must be a singleness of purpose in Christian work, if we are to succeed along the lines laid out by the Savior. Every cataract should be cut off and the soul's intentions clearly set forth by these great conventions which meet annually to devise ways and means to do the work of our Master. In doing this, we will prove ourselves to be a sword rather than peace to the terrified millions about us. Such a position is necessary in order to fill the world with the true light.

You will let your minds for a moment go to the rugged slope upon the mountain side where Jesus has retired for rest, followed by his chosen disciples. And as he seats himself in a convenient place, you will observe the disciples crouching at his feet, waiting to learn of his great wisdom. You will further observe from the words of Jesus that their intentions are not single. Perhaps the various forms of religion, the desire for place or position, have clouded their minds. The upturned faces of the great multitude in the valley below has doubtless made an impression upon them, for in that multitude there must be Pharisees, Sadducees, Jews and Gentiles, and people representing all forms of religion; hence the necessity now of indoctrinating them that their minds and hearts may be set upon the truth as is embodied in the Gospel which they are to preach and teach. It seems appropriate for me to say, if indeed they have left all to follow Christ and there is no desire in them to turn back to the world, their eye is single, and, therefore, they are full of light. But if they are yet undecided and are thinking of what to-morrow will bring forth or how they will be cared for by the people, or if they are thinking upon whether it be possible to follow him and at the same time serve the world, they are full of darkness. And if they are in this latter condition, how dense is the cloud that hangs over their minds! "Ye cannot serve God and mammon." When Israel forsook God under the leadership of Ahab, and the prophet of the Lord had been driven into exile, one of the first things which the prophet of the Lord said after assembling the people was, "How long halt ye between two opinions. If God be God serve him, and if Baal be God serve him." Elijah here indicates that that singleness of purpose which had been so characteristic of Israel to serve God had departed and that the people were divided as to who was the true God, etc.

It is perhaps not out of place to make the admission that those who know the least about the Negro Baptists as a denomination, are the members of our own churches. Very many people are Baptists without being able to give an intelligent reason why they are Baptists.

The Educational Convention seeks to enlighten them and put in the minds and hearts of the great army of our followers that same knowledge, zeal and courage that is possessed by many of the leaders who have done such a marvelous work in the last twenty years. The great work of training and religiously educating the people has just begun. All of the years of the past have been spent in preparation for the campaign now before us. But the time has come to push the battle for an educated ministry as well as for an educated pew to the very last ditch. We must not rest until we have informed the people and put upon the tongue of every Baptist the names of such schools as Shaw University, Spellman Seminary, Roger Williams University, Richmond Theological Seminary, State University, Ky., Leland University, Benedict College, Bishop College, Selma University, Arkansas Baptist College, Jackson College, Guadalupe College, Hearne Academy, Howe Institute, Arkadelphia Academy, Natchez College and many others which I do not call to mind just now. These are among the many strong citadels of the denomination and their power and influence should be known by and read of by men. Our own constituency should be taught to know them and should learn to love, honor and serve them. Nor should we be content with teaching the people the names of these institutions and the great work they are doing for the cause of the race and Christianity; but they should be brought to know and put in touch with the thousands of pious Christian gentlemen who have come forth from the schools as polished shafts from the quiver, and we should seek to make place for them to work among our people. I repeat that "If thine eye be single, thy whole body shall be of light."

By way of digression, permit me to call your attention to a remark made by our blessed Savior to his disciples, when he sent them forth to preach and teach. It is this: "Behold, I send you forth as sheep in the midst of wolves: be ye therefore wise as serpents, and harmless as doves." (Matt. 10:16.) This same advice comes down to all of God's ministers to-day. The great work of convicting the world of error and converting it to truth is no less important now than it was when Christ spoke these words, and it will require much wisdom and discretion on the part of our ministry to overcome the many false religions which have gotten such a firm hold upon the people. Peter, the fisherman from Galilee, led the services on the day of Pentecost, and by the aid of the Holy Ghost was instrumental in the converting of thousands in a day. But when the church had to contend with spiritual wickedness in high places; when Governors were to be made to tremble and Kings to confess; when angry mobs were to be dispersed by simple Gospel truth clothed with superhuman eloquence. Christianity needed a Paul who was not only a classical scholar but who sat at the feet of Gamaliel in Jerusalem until he became thoroughly furnished in Biblical knowledge. This Convention aims to inspire a greater desire among the young men to prepare themselves for the high calling of the ministry.

The sad result of divided leadership
One great lesson is yet to be learned by us. It is on the proper regard for our leaders. Every preacher in our ranks has learned that every Baptist church is an independent organization and from that they have concluded, many of them, that every preacher is independent and equal in importance to every other one. Few have learned that there is an interdependence

which makes us all workers together, and that some are to lead and direct while others are to follow. The example of carrying matters to Jerusalem to receive the counsel and advice of the older and well-informed disciples has been set aside, and in many cases the courts are resorted to settle matters of the church. "If the blind lead the blind, both shall fall into the ditch." (Matt. 15:14.) There are many religions in the world and all are seeking the confidence of the people, and all claim to be the Church of Christ This, of course, cannot be true. But so zealous are the representatives of these different organizations, in pressing their views upon the minds of the people, that really intelligent professors of religion claim to be puzzled over the question of who is right and who is wrong.

We must learn to be firm, for if our doctrines are right, they should be pressed with all the power and vigor of our soul. We should convince the world that we are not reeds to be shaken by the wind. The Lord Jesus loves and honors a man who is firm and true to a principle. When the disciples of John the Baptist had delivered the message of John to Christ and departed, Jesus began to say to the multitude, "What went ye out into the wilderness to see? A reed shaken with the wind? But what went ye out for to see? A man clothed in soft raiment? Behold, they that wear soft clothing are in king's houses. But what went ye out for to see? A prophet? Yea, I say unto you, and more than a prophet. For this is he, of whom it is written, Behold, I send my messenger before thy face, which shall prepare thy way before thee." And then he proceeds to pronounce the greatest eulogium ever spoken of man. "Among them that are born of women there hath not risen a greater than John the Baptist." Above all things, be a man—one that cannot be shaken by heresies like a reed by the "wind," "Having done all to stand, stand therefore."

Brethren, the work of educating and evangelizing the world is before us and much of it devolves upon us. Jesus, that hero of Calvary who led the monster, Death, in chains, is our leader and he stands now upon the lofty summit of Gospel truth and says, "All power in heaven and in earth is given into my hands," "Go ye therefore, and teach all nations, baptizing them in the name of the Father, and of the Son, and of the Holy Ghost: teaching them to observe all things whatsoever I have commanded you: and, lo, I am with you alway, even unto the end of the world. Amen." And so long as these inspiring words can be heard, and the victorious Banner of the Cross can be seen in front of us, we should take courage and go forward, not fearing our foes, and leaving the results with God.

E. C. Morris

Infallible Proofs of the Perpetuity of Baptist Principles
This Denominational Sermon was delivered before the National Baptist Convention at Kansas City, Mo., 1898.

Text:—"These are they which came out of great tribulation." (Rev. 7:14.)

The world has never known the whole truth about the Baptists, and will, perhaps, never know it until there is a complete triumph of those principles which distinguished them as a denomination of Christian believers. Baptists are as much a phenomenon to the other religious sects and Christian professors to-day as they were in the early centuries when cruel persecutions, hunger and death haunted them day and night; when they deemed it an honor to suffer and to die for the cause of their blessed Master.

I do not fear the criticism that may follow after I tell you that the history of the Baptists covers all the time from the days of John the Baptist until now, with the possible exception of that "time and half a time" spoken of in the prophecy of this book, where the Church appears to be in obscurity, but by no means is it extinct. It is, so to speak, in the period of its infancy, like the smoldering spark beneath the heap of ashes. The Church rested upon the arm of God, gathering strength from his warm bosom, while the angry waves of the adversary rushed about her. But in the fullness of time, she came forth as bright as the morning, fair as the moon, clear as the sun, and as terrible as an army with banners, irresistible, invincible, destined to cover the whole earth.

The authenticity of the church

The regal authority by which the church exists is not questioned by any who believe the Bible to be the Book of God, for it is clearly set forth in that book that God is the founder of his church, Proofs of this may be found as far back as the days of Abraham or Moses, who looked forward to "a city which hath foundations, whose maker and builder is God," or to the time when the scepter should depart from Judah, and be given into the hand of him who would gather the people together.

But I shall not go so far back as Moses to get these infallible proofs of the authenticity of the church. I will call your attention to a more recent prophecy found in the book of Daniel (2:44), which reads: "In the days of these kings shall the God of Heaven set up a kingdom, which shall never be destroyed: and the kingdom shall not be left to other people, but it shall break in pieces and consume all these kingdoms, and it shall stand forever." The first question that arises after reading this prediction is, "Has this prophecy been fulfilled? Have the days of the kings spoken of come? And have their kingdoms been destroyed?"

By consulting Luke 3:1, 2, you will find these words, which immediately precede the preaching and baptism of John, the son of Zacharias: "Now in the fifteenth year of the reign of Tiberius Cæsar, Pontius Pilate being governor of Judæa, and Herod being tetrarch of Galilee, and his brother Philip tetrarch of Iturea and of the region of Trachonitis, and Lysanias the tetrarch of Abilene, Annas and Caiaphas being high priests, the word of God came unto John the son of Zacharias in the wilderness." This I take to be a clear enunciation of the conditions of those who, under Roman authority, held the scepter of power over both church and state. This, too, is at a time when the Roman Empire is at its zenith and challenges the admiration of the world, and at a time when those who had been entrusted with the sacred oracles of God were in absolute subjugation to Roman authority, notwithstanding the fact that the scepter (religious authority) was still held by the trembling hand of Judah. At such a time and under such conditions, John the Baptist, the greatest of Baptist preachers, appears in the wilderness of Jordan. Without any formal introduction, without a flourish of trumpets and banners, the Baptist comes forth with a voice which attracted the attention of the people of Jerusalem and of Judea and of all the region round about Jordan.

He notifies them that "the kingdom of heaven is at hand." I would not have you think for a single moment that it is my purpose to impress you that John the Baptist was the founder of the church, for he was not, and that there may be no mistake, the record says, "He was not that light, but was sent to bear witness of that light" (John 1:8). And again when John gracefully tells those who ask him, "Who art thou," that "I am the voice of one crying in the wilderness. I indeed baptize you with water unto repentance: but he that cometh after me is mightier than I, whose shoes I am not worthy to bear: he shall baptize you with the Holy Ghost and with fire." (Matt. 3:11.)

We must not pass by this inspiring scene which rushes like a sunbeam before our eyes as we approach this place. It is the most inspiring scene that heaven ever looked upon, or that ever engaged the attention of the world. May heaven listen and the world stand in breathless silence, as the record of Christ's baptism is told by the inspired writer. "Then cometh Jesus from Galilee to Jordan unto John to be baptized of him. But John forbade him, saying, I have need to be baptized of thee, and comest thou to me? And Jesus answering said unto him, Suffer it to be so now: for thus it becometh us to fulfill all righteousness. Then he suffered him. And Jesus, when he was baptized, went up straightway out of the water: and, lo, the heavens were opened unto him, and he saw the Spirit of God descending like a dove, and lighting upon him: And lo a voice from heaven, saying, This is my beloved Son, in whom I am well pleased." (Matt. 3:13-17.) So plain, unmistakable, is the evidence here given that no kind of comment is necessary.

But Jesus having waited the full time under the Levitical law before entering upon his ministry, now proceeds to call about him those whom he had chosen to be his companions and apostles, that they might be witnesses of all that he said and did, and be prepared to carry forward the work after his ascension. And when he had gone about sufficiently to cause the people to form an opinion of him, he said to his disciples, "Whom do men say that I, the Son of man am? And they said, Some say that thou art John the Baptist; some, Elias; and others, Jeremias, or one of the prophets. He saith unto them, But whom say ye that I am? And Simon Peter answered and said, Thou art the Christ, the Son of the living God. And Jesus answered and said unto him, Blessed art thou, Simon Barjona: for flesh and blood hath not revealed it unto thee, but my Father which is in heaven. And I say also unto thee, That thou art Peter, and upon this rock (the immovable faith that you have that I am the Christ) I will build my church; and the gates of hell shall not prevail against it." (Matthew 16:13-18.) The first words to engage our attention in this remarkable answer are "I will build," which expression implies that the work was to be done, and that it was done in its completeness is manifest in these words, which, like thunder, fell from the lips of that blessed Christ as he hung upon the cross—"It is finished." And after being in the grave for three days, he comes forth and says to an astonished world, "All power is given unto me in heaven and in earth. Go ye therefore, and teach all nations," etc. Hence, the church derives its authority from God, for God and Christ are one.

The glorious history of the church
This grand old church has a most glorious history. The first baptism of blood came upon

the Great Head of the Church. Having led the way through trials, persecutions, ignominious sufferings and death, the Son of God leaves this warning to those who are to follow him: "For if they do these things in a green tree, what shall be done in a dry?" And with a complete victory over death, hell and the grave, he commissions his disciples to "Go into all the world and preach the gospel to every creature," giving to them at the same time the promise, "I will be with you."

The work of the church began at Jerusalem under the immediate direction of the Holy Spirit on the day of Pentecost, and from the great outpouring of the Spirit on that day, has, as I have said, continued unto this day, and will continue to roll on until the "Gospel of the kingdom shall be preached in all the world for a witness unto all nations; and then shall the end come." None of the Protestant churches (in these, of course, I do not include Baptists) can lay claim to having had their beginning there, for it is said of the Baptists, "It may be seen that the Baptists who were formerly called Ana-Baptists, and in later times Mennonites, were the original Waldenses and have long in the history of the church received that origin and as such may be justly termed the only Christian community which has stood since the days of the apostles." (*History of Religious Denominations*, p. 42.) But as we run through the musty pages of history and look at the blood and fire through which the church has come, we are inclined to think that the road has been a dark and dreary one. But a second look will bring out the brilliancy of those glorious pages, filled with immortal deeds of those whose very names are stars on the horizon of that invincible kingdom and serve as beacon lights to cheer and encourage the weary pilgrims who are yet in the way to that unclouded glory.

The world without Christ cannot see any greater men than those who have led great armies and sat as rulers of great nations. It points with pride to such men as Napoleon, Cromwell, Hannibal, Washington and Grant; and the Christian cannot help admiring the courage, pluck and brilliancy of these great warriors and leaders. But these great men had great armies to follow them to encourage and cheer them as they went from conquest to victory. But when we come to a John, a Peter, a Paul, a Silas, who, ofttimes alone, sometimes with shackles on their limbs, with a cross before their eyes and a guillotine over the head, would profess willingness to die, if need be, for the cause of the Master; and, as we look into the face of the trembling governor and hear the testimony of the trial-king, that he is almost persuaded to be a Christian by the irresistible argument of a Christian in chains, we conclude that no just comparison can be made between these great characters as the former were great with men; the latter, great with God and man.

But one of the most glorious features of this grand old church is that her history is one unbroken chain of events and progress. It is that amazing sight which appeared to Moses in Midian, the burning bush, but not consumed. The fires of tribulation and persecution have followed the Church of God in all these years of its existence, and perhaps will follow it to the end of time. It is by reason of the principles held by the Baptists to-day and the fact that these are the same principles which characterized the earlier Christians and brought on them suffering and death, that justifies us in the claim that ours is the only Christian denomination that can lay claim to apostolic succession. In this claim we are not without evidence. It is said in the Encyclopædia of Religious Knowledge: "Their principles have subjected them to persecution from age to age and to such principles they have counted it a glory to be martyrs. Though their own blood has flown freely, they have never shed the blood of others." What was true of the early apostles is true of those who are their successors to-day.

Baptists are the pioneers of religious freedom

In 1636, according to Judge Story, a law was enacted in Rhode Island through and by them (Baptists), that conscience should be free and that men should not be punished for worshipping God in the way they are persuaded. The doctrine which is repugnant to all free people (the union of church and state) and which has, wherever it has been maintained, made the minister the vehicle of the political demagogue, has been wiped from the statute books of our country, and largely, if not altogether, this has been done through Baptist influence. And it was not accomplished without blood and tears. I have only to call up the names of Henry, Arnold, Lollard, Wycliffe, Tyndall, Milton, Bunyan, Gale, Hill, Booth, Butterworth, Carey, Ward, Fuller, Hall, Foster, Gregory, Roger Williams, and a host of others whom I need not mention, to awaken your thoughts to the cruel persecution to which Baptists were subjected even in the last three or four centuries. While some of these were not Baptists by their church connection, they believed as Baptists now believe, viz.: in baptism and liberty of conscience. The influence planted in the State of Rhode Island by the first Christian Baptist churches has permeated every State in this great Union and practically shaped the laws and policies of every local government between the two great oceans.

It is the firm unmovable stand that they (Baptists) have taken for religious freedom that has made it possible for other denominations of Christians to stand. While others may hold their episcopal orders from some great dignitary or potentate, it is nevertheless true that it is by the grace of God and the grace of the Baptists that they have been permitted to keep house outside of the Old Roman Home (the Catholic Church). It has been a war to the hilt. The old red dragon who had sought to destroy the child as soon as it was born has been continuously after the church and even now is contending against her. But the promise of Jesus inspires courage." "Lo, I am with you alway, even unto the end of the world."

Notwithstanding the beginning was small, the mustard seed has become a great tree, and the stone cut out without hands has become a great mountain and will fill the whole earth.

You have, perhaps, expected me to speak to you more particularly of the denominational work as carried on by Negro Baptists, and I shall now address myself to that feature of the work. For many years, owing to certain social conditions which have existed in this and other countries, the work of white and colored Baptists, has been carried on in separate societies and churches. This ought not to be and will not always be the case, for, as a rule, white and colored Baptists believe alike. But since they are separate, we may look at the work carried on by our own people, and in doing so we will not go beyond that period which recognizes the Negro as a man in a national sense. Immediately following the emancipation of the Negro of this country came the church and schoolhouse, and, contrary to the predic-tions of many, the Negro panted after these "as a hart panteth for the water brook," and in a very brief period he was prepared for the work of preaching the Gospel and teaching others of the race. From the first it was not known just what the Baptists were doing, for it was several years before we commenced to keep books. Those who traveled most formed the opinion that Negro Baptists were pretty well up. In view of the glorious history that our church had made, the fact that she bore the honor of being a friend to education and was the pioneer in agitating religious liberty and the first to send the Gospel to a foreign land, we came together in 1886, to count up and see what the denomination had been doing, and, to our own surprise, we had as many people in our churches as all the other denominations among our people combined; had more high schools and colleges and more children in these schools and almost two preachers to their one. The figures were astounding. We could hardly believe them, and the other folks said it was not so. And as our figures were not official, we waited quietly until after the census report of 1890 had been compiled. We found our figures not only verified, but that we had 182, 758 more than all others combined.

We are making a net increase at the rate of forty thousand a year. This is the work of colored Baptists in our own country and to these figures may be added the number in our churches in Liberia and the various mission stations in Africa and the work of the Baptists in Jamaica and other islands. In the work of Christian education we lead all the others; and not counting the magnificent colleges and seminaries built by the American Baptist Home Mission Society, we have fifty-four colleges and high schools of our own. Many of these schools will compare favorably with the best colleges in the land.

A most significant fact which tells of the indomitable energy of Negro Baptists is that while our race is only one-eighth of the entire population of the whole country, they represent three-eighths of all the Baptists and fully one-half of all the Negro Christians. So when Dr. MacArthur pays a tribute to Baptists for their rapid increase from 1870 to the present, he might have said that that increase was largely due to the ability of Negro Baptist preachers in making disciples of men.

The Baptist denomination stands for the best thought and highest ideal of a democratic form of government, and because of their unrelenting war for the absolute separation of church and state, many of them have suffered martyrdom at the hands of monarchs, kings and potentates. Our own country owes a debt of gratitude to the Baptists for the absolute liberty of conscience which it never will finish paying. We need only to refer you to the life and times of Baxter, and to Cromwell, the Speaker of whose Parliament, it is said, was a Baptist preacher, and many of the men and generals who followed him, to show the active part taken by the Baptists in the great reforms of a few centuries ago and their active participation in the American Revolutionary War, which was, indeed, fought upon these very principles for which the name Baptist stands to-day.

Honored for the suffering endured

The Son of God, as he sat upon the Mount of Olives and told of the destruction of the temple, said, "This gospel of the kingdom shall be preached in all the world for a witness unto all nations; and then shall the end come." (Matt. 24:14.)

It can be said without fear of successful contradiction that Baptists have suffered more, have sacrificed more lives on account of their loyalty to the doctrines of Jesus Christ, than any other denomination of Christians; and we are glad to be counted worthy of suffering for the cause, and, in the name of that crowned Prince who sacrificed his own life that he might save the lives of those who had fallen into the pits of eternal night. The eloquent words spoken by Paul as he stood, as it were, in sight of the guillotine, "I am now ready to be offered, and the time of my departure is at hand. I have fought a good fight, I have finished my course, I have kept the faith: henceforth there is laid up for me a crown of righteousness, which the Lord, the righteous Judge, shall give me at that day," etc., have been a source of inspiration to Christian ministers in all the time since they were uttered, and will continue to be until the consummation of all things or when the Church of God shall be called out, as it were, upon the musty hills of Zion and wave their palms, emblems of victory, before the throne and before the Lamb; and as the question is asked, "Who are these arrayed in white robes and whence came they?" the answer shall be proclaimed throughout the heavens, "These are they which came out of great tribulation, and have washed their robes, and made them white in the blood of the Lamb."

E. C. Morris

Sanctification Sermon
Sermon before the Arkansas Baptist State Convention, in 1899.

Text:—"Sanctify them through thy truth: thy word is truth." (John 17:17.)

That there is such a doctrine as Sanctification taught in the Scriptures must be admitted. And that this doctrine has been wantonly perverted and misunderstood must also be admitted. But I am charitable enough to say that many who have misunderstood and misinterpreted this doctrine have done so from honest convictions which had formed in their hearts on account of incompetent teachers. But it is not my purpose to attempt to set up an argument in answer to that class of persons who are preaching the doctrine of sinless perfection, or bodily holiness. Such an attempt would be only a waste of time in an unsuccessful effort to turn Ephraim from his idols. Indeed, if argument were needed to prove the fallacy of that contention, I would need only to refer to the statement of the Apostle Paul, found in 2 Cor. 12:9, and the reply which he claims to have received from the Lord, viz.: "My grace is sufficient." Hence, I shall present to you the doctrine of Sanctification as I find it in God's Word, and as illustrated by those who were first entrusted with the responsibility of preaching it.

The word "sanctify" means to set apart, or appoint to service. "Sanctify ye a fast, call a solemn assembly, gather the elders and all the inhabitants of the land into the house of the Lord your God, and cry unto the Lord." (Joel 1:14.) Again the same prophet says, "Blow the trumpet in Zion, sanctify a fast, call a solemn assembly." (Joel 2:15.)

Here is a call to service, a getting ready for a meeting in which to worship God; a laying aside of secular matters, that for the time, the whole being may be devoted to the service of God, and thereby turn back the calamity which was about to come upon the nation. This call to sanctification, or forming a solemn assembly, does not imply that the individuals are entirely purged from sin. But it does mean that they are to turn to God with their whole hearts, and to put themselves in absolute obedience to his commands. The wonderful prayer of the Son of God from which our text is taken was uttered perhaps on the night before his crucifixion. Those for whom this prayer was directly made had been with him for three years, and were fully decided as to their religious course; yet, they had so many imperfections that it was necessary that this remarkable prayer be made. The very wording of it implies that they were not perfect and that perfection had to be brought about by an implanting and growth of the Word. The group of disciples who are with the Son of God when these words are spoken are the same men who were gathered at his feet when he went up into the mountain away from the multitude and said to them, "If thine eye be single, thy whole body shall be full of light;" i. e., if you have gotten your whole being drawn in from the cares of the world; if you are able now to have no thought for food or raiment or even for your life, then you are full of light. But was this the case with these men who had seen not only the miracles which the Son of God had wrought, but had seen the spirit of God on him and heard the word of God proclaiming him as his only begotten Son. Nay, they were still at times filled with doubts, such as fill every believer when the clouds of the adversary rise over his head. Notwithstanding all that Christ had said and done, and this wonderful prayer in their presence, on that very night, Peter denied that he ever knew him. And after the awful tragedy on Calvary, Thomas declared that he would not believe him risen except he could put his finger in the nail prints and thrust his hand into the wounded side of the Redeemer.

Even after this, one of those discouragements which so often rush upon believers caused Peter to lead the little band back to their former occupation—that of fishing. But the Son of God was on the bank early in the morning and with a voice so tender as to awaken every thought of the past, he calls to them, "Children, have ye any meat?"

They answered him, "No."

And he said unto them, "Cast your net on the right side of the ship, and ye shall find."

The fact of their imperfection is made manifest by the divine direction which led to the great draught of fishes. Continuing, Jesus says, "Simon, son of Jonas, lovest thou me more than these?" None will doubt that Peter loved Jesus, but the desires of the flesh had not been overcome. The leaven, however, was at work and would finally leaven the whole lump.

Before leaving this remarkable prayer, let us read the nineteenth verse of the same chapter. "And for their sakes I sanctify myself, that they also might be sanctified through the truth."

Please note these words, "might be," which suggest that Sanctification is a progressive work. It begins in regeneration, which is itself a work of the Holy Spirit, and when accomplished, affects the individual in a manner above his comprehension and justifies the statement of Paul when he says, "He which hath begun a good work in you will perform it until the day of Jesus Christ. He will carry on the work begun," etc.

Sanctification, while having its root (beginning) in regeneration, implies justification and the final perseverance of the believer. For one cannot consistently be set apart to a work that is not approved of (by) him for whom he works; nor can we hope to reach the stage of perfection without persevering to the end. Hence, the ground of one's justification will determine the extent of his sanctification. "Therefore, being justified by faith we have peace with God." This justification does not rest upon our own righteousness, but upon the righteousness of the Son of God. Hence, the faith is in the fact that God was in Christ reconciling the world unto himself, "not imputing their trespasses unto them," as shown in 2 Cor. 5:19. If there were not a mighty war going on in us, why should the question be asked, "Who shall separate us from the love of Christ?" If there is a place for the evil desires to bring on a war, sin has not been entirely eradicated. The Son of God illustrates the work of the Holy Spirit in the believer in this parable, "The kingdom of heaven is like unto leaven, which a woman took, and hid in three measures of meal, until the whole was leavened." Just as the particles of leaven (yeast) worked their way until they had touched every atom of the meal, so will the Spirit, in its work of sanctification, continue to work in the believer until every superfluity of life has been touched and the whole being has been brought under its influence.

The early apostles did not understand or teach that men were perfect in the beginning of Christian life. We read in Ephesians, the fourth chapter, eleventh and fourteenth verses inclusive, "And he gave some, apostles; and some, prophets; and some, evangelists; and some, pastors and teachers; For the perfecting of the saints, for the work of the ministry, for the edifying of the body of Christ: Till we all come in the unity of the faith, and of the knowledge of the Son of God, unto a perfect man, unto the measure of the stature of the fullness of Christ." Here it is plainly taught that God has employed all the means here outlined to bring us unto that state of perfection to make us like unto Christ. Great and wonderful, indeed, is the work of sanctification! In the second epistle of Peter 1:5, 6, we are shown that regeneration only begins our Christian life.

He says, "Add to your faith virtue; and to virtue, knowledge to patience, godliness; and to godliness, brotherly kindness; and to brotherly kindness, charity." All these graces, according to the Apostle Peter, are to be acquired after one enters the Christian life. Again in the second epistle, 3:18, he says, "Grow in grace and in the knowledge of our Lord and Savior Jesus Christ." We understand by this growth that perfection is not reached in regeneration, but that we are kept by the power of God through faith unto salvation. But since there is such a doctrine as Sanctification, to what extent does it possess our being? God having begun a good work in us, will carry it on unto the day of Jesus Christ. This which is the experience of one Christian is the experience of all. "I find, then, a law that when I would do good, evil is present. For I delight in the law of God after the inward man." May that inward man control in all our lives, and the sanctifying influence of the Spirit abide in our hearts. So very often we find ourselves with Paul, saying, "O wretched man that I am; who shall deliver me from the body of this death?" It is the sinful nature that imprisons our soul, etc. Having received the sanctifying influence of the Holy Spirit in our hearts, we set about a cultivation of it with an anxious desire that we may become more and more like Christ each day. The deformity which sin has brought on us will only be lost in the regeneration of the world. Like the doctrine of baptism, sanctification implies a resurrection of the body. "It is sown a natural body, it is raised a spiritual body." (1 Cor. 15:44.) If the bodies in which we live and die are to be changed by the power of God from mortal to immortal, then they cannot be holy until that change has taken place. "But we shall all be changed." (1 Cor. 15:51.) In conclusion I would say, my brethren, that it is safe to follow that grand old doctrine set forth in the "Declaration of Principles," namely, "Sanctification is the work of the Holy Spirit, begun in regeneration and carried on in the life of the believer unto the end, or unto the perfect day."

E. C. Morris

The Brotherhood of Man Sermon

"I am Joseph your brother, whom ye sold." (Genesis 45:4.)

The text and theme which we here present comes down to us from the patriarchs of old. They present to us a rule and sentiment which should find place in the hearts of every Christian, and should direct our conduct towards our fellow-man, and especially to those who are of the household of faith wherever dispersed around the globe. The ties of blood relation are prominent in the beautiful truths presented by the Scriptures, from which my text is taken. They enable the speaker (Joseph) to rise above all privations and difficulties of the past and to forgive all the injuries inflicted, even the jealous, murderous rage of angry brothers who sought his utter destruction, and enables him to come forward and acknowledge them as his equals, notwithstanding their impoverished condition. And to remove any embarrassment which these guilty brothers might feel at a remembrance of their past conduct towards him, Joseph hastily tells them that it was God's purpose that he should be thus sent ahead of them, that he might preserve life. We cannot always understand the purposes or plans of the All wise God in his dealings with his people, nor are we at all times prepared to accept willingly the orders of his Providence or the wisdom of his counsel. But he surely knows what is best for us, for he can see the end from the beginning, and knows of every obstacle which lies in our path, from the cradle to the grave.

Joseph, who is the central figure in my text, was at an early age the fondest hope of an aged but indulgent parent, and was the brightest gem in a pious home, which fact was the cause of his brothers' hatred. But the fact that his mind was susceptible of Divine revelations which you perhaps would call dreams, added to the hatred which they had for him, and so fierce became their rage that they plotted among themselves to kill him. But the counsel of Reuben prevailed and they cast him into a pit, and as they were eating they lifted up their eyes and saw a company of Ishmaelites. They took Joseph out of the pit and sold him to these traders who were on their way to Egypt, etc. Perhaps the darkest part of the picture which I shall attempt to draw, is where an effort is made to deceive the aged father and lead him to believe that Joseph had been destroyed by some wild beast, etc. Those who traffic in human flesh lose their respect for pious, consecrated humanity and will resort to any kind of diabolism to cover up their crimes.

Slavery has existed in some form or other in nearly all ages of the past. But in some instances it proved to be a blessing in disguise, while in others it formed some of the most blood-curdling, revolting scenes in the history of the world. It has separated husband and wife, parents and children, brother and sister, and broken the cords of affection which nature and nature's God have entwined around the hearts of a happy family. But these cruel separations do not, in all cases, last forever. Sometimes they are of short duration and work for the persecuted party "a far more exceeding and eternal weight of glory." When the God-appointed time came around that the brothers of Joseph should meet with him whom they had sold, and there be humiliated by their own conduct toward him, he brings forward all the true manhood in his great soul and says, "Now therefore be not grieved, nor angry with yourselves, that ye sold me hither; for God did send me before you to preserve life."

The theme of our discourse carries us beyond blood relationship and introduces us to an unexplored field of humanity which recognizes one common Father—God, and one common brother—man.

The brotherhood of man not a new doctrine

The doctrine of the brotherhood of man is sustained both by law and by grace. But the Church has apparently gone to sleep upon this great doctrine and allowed political, economical and social questions to relegate it to the background, thereby silencing one of the most effective weapons of the Christian religion. The opponents of this heaven-appointed doctrine have endeavored to create a prejudice against it by claiming that it teaches the social equality of the races and classes, and we are forced to admit that they have, in a measure, been successful. For many so-called Christians are so very reserved in their manner of worship that they refuse to come in contact with the common people, for fear that they will have to otherwise associate with them. But, my friends, this doctrine does not teach the social equality of the races nor the classes, beyond that rule given to the world by the Son of God, which says, "Therefore, all things whatsoever ye would that men should do to you, do ye even so to them." Hence, your sociality is based upon your own choice. If you do not desire the association of men of a different race or class, you are not required to associate with them. But is there not a difference between our social and religious life? Is not every man our brother who has accepted Christ Jesus as his Savior? The Syro-Phenician woman had no legal, social or racial rights which would warrant her in approaching the Son of God, but she had a religious right, and she contended for that right. Christ is not the Savior of any particular race or class, but "whosoever will may take the water of life freely."

Class and race antipathy has been carried so far in this great Christian country of ours, that it has almost destroyed the feeling of that common brotherhood, which should permeate the soul of every Christian believer, and has shorn the Christian Church of that power and influence which it would otherwise have, if it had not repudiated this doctrine. The Apostle Peter is a notable example of those who believed that racial lines should direct in the conduct of the preaching of the Gospel of Jesus Christ. But when God had convinced him by suspending a great vessel from Heaven which enclosed all manner of four-footed beasts, creeping things and fowls of the air, he at once confessed his ignorance and went with the men who sought him. And when they had come to the house of Cornelius, Peter said, "Ye know how that it is an unlawful thing for a man that is a Jew to keep company, or come unto one of another nation; but God hath shewed me that I should not call any man common or unclean," etc., etc. Cornelius tells Peter for what purpose he calls him, etc. Peter answers and says, "Of a truth I perceive that God is no respecter of persons." While Paul waited at Athens for Silas and Timotheus, whom he had sent for, and, seeing the idolatry of the city, it caused his very soul to yearn for an opportunity to declare unto the people the Gospel of Jesus Christ. His earnest and fearless presentation of the truths of the Gospel brought out certain philosophers of the Epicureans and of the Stoics, who said to Paul what such persons will say to-day when the truth is given without compromise or apology, "May we know what this new doctrine, whereof thou speaketh, is?" After Paul's mild rebuke of their ignorant or misguided worship of the unknown God, he proceeds to tell them that God "hath made of one blood all nations of men for to dwell on all the face of the earth." The whole world is to-day indebted to Paul for the prominence he gave to this all-important doctrine at Mars Hill. We know that the doctrine is not a popular one and that none can accept and practice it, except such as are truly regenerated. But the man who has been brought into the new and living way by the birth which is from above, by contrasting his own depraved and sinful nature with the pure, immaculate character of the Son of God after meditating what that matchless Prince underwent for him, can get inspiration and courage to acknowledge every man his brother who has enlisted under the banner of the Cross, and accepted the same Christ as his Savior.

For nearly nineteen hundred years the church has been upon the field, and has been opposed by all the powers that the adversary could marshal. No opportunity has been or is overlooked, or passed, by those who are opposed to the principles of Christianity, but all are brought into play to weaken it, even to the equality of the races and the classes. But, sad to say, many church members have too often sided with the world, and especially so when this doctrine of the fatherhood of God and the brotherhood of man is presented. In the beginning only two classes were considered, Jews and Gentiles.

But with the multiplicity of religions has come a multiplicity of races and classes, and so prominent have the lines of cast been, that many Christians of the same faith cannot worship at the same altar; that God, who is no respecter of persons, is not pleased with the service which his chosen ambassadors are rendering, and he will not always chide. The commission which he gives is without regard to race, color or condition, but is that the Gospel be preached to every creature, not over the telephone or through the medium of the phonograph, but by the human voice, coming in direct contact with the people, all the people. If they are low, take their hands and lift them up. If too high, call them down. "Christ Jesus came into the world to save sinners," not white sinners, nor black sinners, nor red sinners, but sinners. The wise man Solomon who doubtless had an eye single to the division and opinions of men, where class is arrayed against class, and race against race, looked beyond the active scenes of life back to Mother Earth from whence we all were taken, and back to which we all must go, and says, "The rich and the poor meet together; the Lord is the maker of them all."

But let us not despair: the church will make to righteousness and put on her beautiful garments and her ministers will, ere long, declare that there be no North, no South, no East and no West; no black and no white, but we shall be one in Christ Jesus. And the complete fulfillment of that prophecy concerning Israel will be made manifest in his redeemed, which says. "After those days, saith the Lord, I will put my law in their inward parts, and write it in their hearts; and will be their God, and they shall be my people. And they shall teach no more every man his neighbor, and every man his brother, saying, Know the Lord: for they shall all know me, from the least of them unto the greatest of them.

When the Christians at Galatia were divided over this perplexing question, Paul said to them, "For as many of you as have been baptized into Christ have put on Christ," and, again, "There is neither Jew nor Greek, there is neither bond nor free, there is neither male nor female: for ye all are one in Christ Jesus."

What the church will do in the Twentieth century

Already the great evangelical churches are lining up for more effectual work in the coming century. And this means to me that the white man, the black man, the red man, the yellow man, all who enlist under the banner of the Cross, will form one mighty army to go mightily against the power of darkness and with the great battering ram of the Gospel pitched, as it were, upon the universal brotherhood of man, break down the strong towers of Satan until this government, as well as all the other kingdoms of the world, shall become the kingdoms of our God and his Christ, and he shall reign forever.

E. C. Morris

Origin of the Baptists

Denominational Sermon preached before the National Baptist Convention at Richmond, Va., September, 1900.

Text:—"The same was in the beginning with God." (John 1:2.)

The origin of a thing cannot be considered aside from the source from which it came. The text given in connection with the subject on which I am to speak sets up the claim that Baptists have their origin in Christ, who himself antedates the formation of the world, and that the beginning of their work in the world was made manifest with the advent of Christ and the choosing of the first disciples. This, on the face of it, is indeed a startling claim, considering, too, that there are so many other great denominations in the world, all claiming to be representatives of the Church of Christ. Hence, to define the claim which I here make, it will be necessary to prove the continued succession of those principles held by the Baptists from the days of Christ until now; that these principles are inseparable from the Church of Christ. But before coming to this, in order that you may know that the origin of the Baptists (that is, if Baptists represent the Church of Christ) was in Christ even before he came into the world, it will not be out of place to consult that prophecy which refers directly to the coming of his kingdom. In the forty-fourth verse of the second chapter of the book of Daniel we have this prophecy: "In the days of these kings shall the God of heaven set up a kingdom, which shall never be destroyed: and the kingdom shall not be left to other people, but it shall break in pieces and consume all these kingdoms, and it shall stand forever."

The commission or authority under which the churches of Christ are to operate must have its beginning (or authority) in Christ. The "Go ye into all the world, and preach the gospel to every creature," is an order of Divine appointment and has been in effect ever since it fell from the Divine lips. It did not have its origin with the establishment of the Greek Catholic Church, in the fourth century, to say nothing of those of a more recent date of organization, but had been proclaimed and pushed with vigor and determination during all the time between the ascent of the Son of God and the establishment of these later systems, and must continue to be the only authority under which the Gospel is to be preached.

You will pardon me for this quotation from one of the greatest preachers of the nineteenth century: "The covenant of grace was made before the covenant of works, for Christ Jesus, before the foundation of the world, did stand as its head and representative. And we are said to be elected according to the foreknowledge of God the Father." Perhaps the most important feature of this prophecy is that which says, "It shall not be left to other people," or, in other words, the kingdom, or the Church of God, will be of Divine and not human origin and that Christ will forever remain the Great Head of the Church or Churches; thus stamping all creeds, which claim a founder other than Christ, as human and not divine.

It is also worthy of note that the kingdom is to stand forever. Now if there has been any time since the days of Christ when this kingdom has ceased to exist, then our argument falls to the ground. Kingdoms, monarchies, and so-called churches have arisen and crumbled to the earth. Ancient Babylon, whose magnificence and glory had reached to the heavens and whose ruler defied the God of Heaven, as she reveled in her iniquity, was at last astounded by the mysterious appearance of a Divine hand writing on the wall (while Belshazzar conducted his impious feast), etc., etc., and is now the home of bats, scorpions and every kind of hateful bird and reptile. Rome, the once proud mistress of the world, whose wicked Emperor looked complacently on while the blazing fagots were pushed around the charred remains of martyred saints and mocked at the shrieks of agony as their souls went upward through the flames of persecution, has lost her glory. Jerusalem, that magnificent city in which stood the temple of God and in which Jehovah delighted to meet his saints, because she threw down the altars of God, crumbled and fell in less than half a century after the prediction made by the Son of God, that "There shall not one stone be left upon another that shall not be thrown down." But the church of God is yet standing and will continue to successfully resist all attacks that may be made in the future.

The first visible or audible token we have of the approach of the kingdom of Christ is when John the Baptist appeared in the wilderness of the Jordan. (Matt. 3:1-3.) In connection with this announcement let us examine Luke 3:1-2, and see if it accords with "the days of these kings" referred to by Daniel. "Now in the fifteenth year of the reign of Tiberius Cæsar, Pontius Pilate being the governor of Judea, and Herod being tetrarch of Galilee, and his brother Philip, tetrarch of Iturea and of the region of Trachonitis, and Lysanias the tetrarch of Abilene, Annas and Caiaphas being high priests, the word of God came unto John, the son of Zacharias, in the wilderness," etc. If these days correspond to the prophecy of Daniel— and we believe they do—it may be seen that both John and Christ were born at the time of these kings; and if this fulfillment of that prophecy is genuine, we may trace the genealogy of the Son of God from his birth to his baptism, and from his baptism to the time when he stood upon Olivet, as if reviewing the work and making a forecast of the future, and ascended to Heaven upon a cloud, leaving the promise that "I will send you another Comforter." But without any statement concerning his life from his birth to his baptism, except to say that he was subject to his parents till he was thirty years old, or the time when he was baptized by John in the river Jordan. After leaving the waters of the Jordan and circulating sufficiently among the people to give them an opportunity to form an opinion as to who he was, he asked his disciples, "Whom do men say that I, the Son of man, am? And they said, Some say that thou art John the Baptist; some, Elias; and others, Jeremias, or one of the prophets. He saith unto them, But whom say ye that I am? And Simon Peter answered and said, Thou art the Christ, the Son of the living God, And Jesus answered and said unto him, Blessed art thou, Simon Barjona: for flesh and blood hath not revealed it unto thee, but my Father which is in heaven. And I say also unto thee, that thou art Peter, and upon this rock I will build my church; and the gates of hell shall not prevail against it." (Matt. 16:13-18.)

You will please notice the statement, "I will build my church," which accords with the statement of the prophet that it should not be left to other people, and also repudiates the idea that the church existed in any recognizable form before his advent and thereby destroys the claim of Judaism. The characteristic points which set forth the Church of Christ are the doctrines which he gave the church to be observed by it. Now, it remains for us to prove that we have sacredly maintained those doctrines in all the days of the past. What are the doctrines established by Christ? There are a few of the fundamental doctrines of Christ which we desire to make prominent and which are sustained by Baptists (with all the others), such as "Salvation by Grace," "Justification by Faith," "Baptism of Believers Only," "Final Perseverance of the Saints," etc. Following these special doctrines come the ordinances of the kingdom, viz.: Baptism and the Lord's Supper, and how they are to be observed. That Christ commanded these ordinances may be seen from the following: Matt. 28:19; Mark 16:15-16; 1 Cor. 11:24-26.

For an elucidation of the doctrines we are dependent upon the Apostles who were intimately associated with the Son of God for three years. The Council of Apostles and elders held for the specific purpose of allaying the dissension which arose over the question of "Salvation," arrived at this conclusion: "But we believe that through the grace of the Lord Jesus Christ, we shall be saved," etc. (Acts 15:11, etc.) Paul in his letter to the Romans (3rd chapter, 24th verse) says, "Being justified freely by his grace through the redemption that is in Christ Jesus." Thus, it is shown that our salvation rests wholly upon the grace of God as made manifest in his Son, Jesus Christ. Peter also says, "Of which salvation the prophets have inquired and searched diligently, who prophesied of the grace that should come unto you. (1 Peter 1: 10.) Perhaps the most significant and far-reaching of these references is the one found in Ephesians 2:8: "For by grace are ye saved through faith; and that not of yourselves: it is the gift of God."

Were the early Apostles and writers who held forth these doctrines Baptists? The primary definition given to the word "Baptist," is one who believes in immersion for baptism. And if this definition is applied to Christ and his Apostles, it is clear, then, that they are all Baptists, for they were baptized of John in Jordan and did themselves baptize in the same river, those who professed faith in the Savior. (John 3:22). To sustain the contention, I quote from history the following:

"Mosheim, with all his violent prejudices against the Baptists, in relating the history of the primitive church, has given a description which will not apply to his own church, the Lutheran, nor to any sect in Christendom, except the Baptists. The churches in those early times were entirely independent, none of them subject to any foreign jurisdiction, but each one governed by its own rulers and laws. For, though churches founded by the Apostles had this peculiar difference shown them, that they were consulted in doubtful and difficult cases, yet they had no judicial authority, no sort of supremacy over the others, nor the least right to enact laws for them."

A bishop during the first and second century was the person who had the care of one Christian assembly."

"Baptism was administered in the first century without the public assemblies, in places appointed for that purpose, and was performed by the immersion of the whole body in water."

In this account, Mosheim is sustained by the Scriptures, for the Apostles, after receiving the command from the lips of the Messiah, to disciple all men and baptize them, understood that they were to immerse them, for Philip, who was of the earliest disciples, baptized the eunuch, going down into the water, and coming up out of the water after having baptized him. And Paul, who was a later disciple still, not only recognized immersion as the only mode of baptism which would set forth our death to sin, but also recognized it as being the strongest proof setting forth the resurrection of the dead. (Romans 6: 4; 1 Corinthians 15: 29-42.)

The practice of these early Apostles was kept up for many years without undergoing a change. But it had been plainly predicted that the church would go into obscurity; not that it would be extinct, but that it would be in the wilderness. Here was cited the bitter persecution by the Roman Catholics. (Rev. 12.) But it is not a question whether the individuals representing the Church of Christ lived or died, but whether the principles lived, and whether there has been a people in the world that has held to these principles during all the Christian era.

One of the best historians has said: "It may now be seen that the Baptists, who were formerly called Ana-Baptists, but in later times Mennonites, were the original Waldenses, and may, therefore, be justly termed the only Christian community which has stood since the days of Christ and the Apostles. That is to say, that the principles which the Baptists hold were held also by the Ana-Baptists and by the Mennonites." (*History of Religious Denominations of the World*, p. 42.)

Martin Luther, who is given credit of being the greatest Christian reformer, in his works expressed great surprise at finding a sect of people who held practically the very same views and principles as those which he advocated, with slight variations, at the beginning of the Reformation. These people were ready to join Luther and did co-operate with him until he attempted to introduce infant baptism. This being contrary to their principles, and not in accord with the early teachings of the disciples, they dissented, holding as Baptists now believe, that none are proper subjects for baptism except believers. These little characteristics, so to speak, are the things which caused the people to speak of Baptists as a "peculiar sect."

Now, to the foundation of this subject, Christ Jesus is the origin of the Baptists. If Christ was in the beginning with God, then the Baptists were also in the beginning, for if their origin is not in Christ, they have none; and if they have no origin, then they are like Melchisedec, without beginning of days or ending of life. If our origin is in Christ and he is the head and body of the church, he then is, indeed, the church. "Ye are indeed many members but one body." For the Baptists claim to be the only people who claim him to be the only founder or head of their churches. Others can trace their origin to some good or great man, while Baptists have no founder other than Christ; and if he is not their foundation they are without one—simple air castles to be blown about by the wind, for, indeed, they recognize no bishop or potentate on earth. Nor do they believe that any human being can be the founder of such a system of faith and practice as the one to which they subscribe their lives and fortunes. Their doctrines are all in the Bible and are, therefore, as old as the Bible. Baptists believe that John the Baptist was a man sent from God, but that Heaven only gave him the honor of introducing the Son of God, who is the embodiment of the Church—the Alpha and Omega. The figures and shadows of the Church set forth in prophecy all go to show that the Baptists represent the true intent and purpose which God had in mind before the incarnation of his Son. References made by Paul to the baptism of the children of Israel, as they were baptized in the cloud and in the sea, and which is sometimes diverted into a proof that sprinkling is baptism, can be understood by bringing that same people down to the Red Sea; and as the waters of the sea stand up as a wall on either side and the mystical cloud which has led them passes over them and stands between them and their enemy—the passing over of this cloud and the mighty walls of the sea together would effect a complete burial and justify the statement of Paul when he says, "Therefore, we are buried with him by baptism." The ordinance of baptism is inseparable from the Baptists for indeed there can be no Baptists without baptism. And if baptism was introduced before the coming of Christ into the world and Christian baptism came with his advent, the origin of the Baptists may be traced back to my text, "The same was in the beginning with God."

Christ is not only the foundation of the Church and the beginning of Christian history, but he is the object to which all the ancient and sacred history pointed before his incarnation. Was Christ a Baptist? is a question which can be answered by asking, Was he baptized? If he was baptized, he was a Baptist or else baptism will not make one a Baptist. If he was a Baptist, then the Baptists originated in him, for he is the first and the last, the beginning and the ending of all things.

We conclude by saying that nothing is more clearly set forth than the eternity of the Son of God, and the eternity of his church. In speaking of this, Solomon says, "The Lord possessed me in the beginning of his way, before his works of old. I was set up from everlasting, from the beginning, or ever the earth was. When there were no depths, I was brought forth; when there were no fountains abounding with water. Before the mountains were settled, before the hills was I brought forth; while as yet he had not made the earth, nor the fields, nor the highest part of the dust of the world. When he prepared the heavens, I was there: when he set a compass upon the face of the depth. Then I was by him, as one brought up with him: and I was daily his delight, rejoicing always before him; rejoicing in the habitable part of his earth; and my delights were with the sons of men." (Prov. 8:22-31.)

Paul, the great Apostle to the Gentiles, recognizes this eternal existence when he says, "According as he has chosen us in him before the foundation of the world." The origin of the Baptists was in Christ, Christ was in the beginning with God. Far beyond the granite hills of time, nestling in the varied colors reflected in the foundation walls of jasper, sapphire, chalcedony, emerald, sardonyx, crysolyte, and the topaz, were the everlasting principles which characterize the Church of Christ, the mysterious analysis of the Word made flesh "and dwelt among us, and we beheld his glory." Notwithstanding the exalted place I have endeavored to give the churches of Christ in this discourse, John says, "It doth not yet appear what we shall be." But we shall be like unto his own glorious body, for we shall be with him, and shall see him as he is. Amen.

E. C. Morris

BOOKER T. WASHINGTON (1856-1915)

Introduction

"For the combination of shrewd common sense, fine executive ability, ready speech, genial acceptance of conditions, optimistic faith in the future of his race and self-sacrificing zeal in their behalf, Booker T. Washington stands easily first among the nine million Negroes of America," according to Silas Xavier Floyd.

Booker Taliaferro Washington was an American political leader, educator and author. He was one of the dominant figures in African American history in the United States from 1890 to 1915.

Washington was born into slavery to a white slave owner [father], and a slave [mother] in Franklin County, Virginia. He eventually learned to read and write while working at manual labor jobs. At the age of sixteen, he went to Hampton, Virginia to Hampton Normal and Agricultural Institute, now Hampton University, to train as a teacher. In 1881, he was named as the first leader of the Tuskegee Institute in Alabama. He was granted an honorary Masters of Arts degree from Harvard University in 1896 and an honorary Doctorate degree from Dartmouth College in 1901. Washington played a very prominent role in black politics.

Washington received national prominence for his famous Atlanta Address of 1895, attracting the attention of politicians and the public as a popular spokesperson for African American citizens. Although labeled by some activists as an "accommodator"; his work, in cooperating with white people and enlisting the support of wealthy philanthropists, helped raise funds to establish and operate hundreds of small community schools and institutions of higher education for the betterment of black persons throughout the South.

In addition to the substantial contributions in the field of education, Dr. Washington did much to improve the overall friendship and working relationship between the races in the United States. His autobiography, *Up From Slavery*, has been widely read since it was first published in 1901.

Up from Slavery
Chapter 1
A slave among slaves

I was born a slave on a plantation in Franklin County, Virginia. I am not quite sure of the exact place or exact date of my birth, but at any rate I suspect I must have been born somewhere and at some time. As nearly as I have been able to learn, I was born near a cross-roads post-office called Hale's Ford, and the year was 1858 or 1859. I do not know the month or the day. The earliest impressions I can now recall are of the plantation and the slave quarters—the latter being the part of the plantation where the slaves had their cabins.

My life had its beginning in the midst of the most miserable, desolate, and discouraging surroundings. This was so, however, not because my owners were especially cruel, for they were not, as compared with many others. I was born in a typical log cabin, about fourteen by sixteen feet square. In this cabin I lived with my mother and a brother and sister till after the Civil War, when we were all declared free.

Of my ancestry I know almost nothing. In the slave quarters, and even later, I heard whispered conversations among the colored people of the tortures which the slaves, including, no doubt, my ancestors on my mother's side, suffered in the middle passage of the slave ship while being conveyed from Africa to America. I have been unsuccessful in securing any information that would throw any accurate light upon the history of my family beyond my mother. She, I remember, had a half-brother and a half-sister. In the days of slavery not very much attention was given to family history and family records—that is, black family records. My mother, I suppose, attracted the attention of a purchaser who was afterward my owner and hers. Her addition to the slave family attracted about as much attention as the purchase of a new horse or cow. Of my father I know even less than of my mother. I do not even know his name. I have heard reports to the effect that he was a white man who lived on one of the near-by plantations. Whoever he was, I never heard of his taking the least interest in me or providing in any way for my rearing. But I do not find especial fault with him. He was simply another unfortunate victim of the institution which the Nation unhappily had engrafted upon it at that time.

The cabin was not only our living-place, but was also used as the kitchen for the plantation. My mother was the plantation cook. The cabin was without glass windows; it had only openings in the side which let in the light, and also the cold, chilly air of winter. There was a door to the cabin—that is, something that was called a door—but the uncertain hinges by which it was hung, and the large cracks in it, to say nothing of the fact that it was too small, made the room a very uncomfortable one. In addition to these openings there was, in the lower right-hand corner of the room, the "cat-hole,"—a contrivance which almost every mansion or cabin in Virginia possessed during the ante-bellum period. The "cat-hole" was a square opening, about seven by eight inches, provided for the purpose of letting the cat pass in and out of the house at will during the night. In the case of our particular cabin I could never understand the necessity for this convenience, since there were at least a half-dozen other places in the cabin that would have accommodated the cats. There was no wooden floor in our cabin, the naked earth being used as a floor.

In the center of the earthen floor there was a large, deep opening covered with boards, which was used as a place in which to store sweet potatoes during the winter. An impression of this potato-hole is very distinctly engraved upon my memory, because I recall that during the process of putting the potatoes in or taking them out I would often come into possession of one or two, which I roasted and thoroughly enjoyed. There was no cooking-stove on our plantation, and all the cooking for the whites and slaves my mother had to do over an open fireplace, mostly in pots and "skillets." While the poorly built cabin caused us to suffer with cold in the winter, the heat from the open fireplace in summer was equally trying.

The early years of my life, which were spent in the little cabin, were not very different from those of thousands of other slaves. My mother, of course, had little time in which to give attention to the training of her children during the day. She snatched a few moments for our care in the early morning before her work began, and at night after the day's work was done. One of my earliest recollections is that of my mother cooking a chicken late at night, and awakening her children for the purpose of feeding them. How or where she got it I do not know. I presume, however, it was procured from our owner's farm. Some people may call this theft. If such a thing were to happen now, I should condemn it as theft myself. But taking place at the time it did, and for the reason that it did, no one could ever make me believe that my mother was guilty of thieving. She was simply a victim of the system of slavery. I cannot remember having slept in a bed until after our family was declared free by the Emancipation Proclamation. Three children—John, my older brother, Amanda, my sister, and myself—had a pallet on the dirt floor, or, to be more correct, we slept in and on a bundle of filthy rags laid upon the dirt floor.

I was asked not long ago to tell something about the sports and pastimes that I engaged in during my youth. Until that question was asked it had never occurred to me that there was no period of my life that was devoted to play. From the time that I can remember anything, almost every day of my life has been occupied in some kind of labor; though I think I would now be a more useful man if I had had time for sports. During the period that I spent in slavery I was not large enough to be of much service, still I was occupied most of the time in cleaning the yards, carrying water to the men in the fields, or going to the mill, to which I used to take the corn, once a week, to be ground. The mill was about three miles from the plantation. This work I always dreaded. The heavy bag of corn would be thrown across the back of the horse, and the corn divided about evenly on each side; but in some way, almost without exception, on these trips, the corn would so shift as to become unbalanced and would fall off the horse, and often I would fall with it. As I was not strong enough to reload the corn upon the horse, I would have to wait, sometimes for many hours, till a chance passer-by came along who would help me out of my trouble. The hours while waiting for some one were usually spent in crying. The time consumed in this way made me late in reaching the mill, and by the time I got my corn ground and reached home it would be far into the night. The road was a lonely one, and often led through dense forests. I was always frightened. The woods were said to be full of soldiers who had deserted from the army, and I had been told that the first thing a deserter did to a Negro boy when he found him alone was to cut off his ears. Besides, when I was late in getting home I knew I would always get a severe scolding or a flogging.

I had no schooling whatever while I was a slave, though I remember on several occasions I went as far as the schoolhouse door with one of my young mistresses to carry her books. The picture of several dozen boys and girls in a schoolroom engaged in study made a deep impression upon me, and I had the feeling that to get into a schoolhouse and study in this way would be about the same as getting into paradise.

So far as I can now recall, the first knowledge that I got of the fact that we were slaves, and that freedom of the slaves was being discussed, was early one morning before day, when I was awakened by my mother kneeling over her children and fervently praying that Lincoln and his armies might be successful, and that one day she and her children might be free. In this connection I have never been able to understand how the slaves throughout the South, completely ignorant as were the masses so far as books or newspapers were concerned, were able to keep themselves so accurately and completely informed about the great National questions that were agitating the country. From the time that Garrison, Lovejoy, and others began to agitate for freedom, the slaves throughout the South kept in close touch with the progress of the movement. Though I was a mere child during the preparation for the Civil War and during the war itself, I now recall the many late-at-night whispered discussions that I heard my mother and the other slaves on the plantation indulge in. These discussions showed that they understood the situation, and that they kept themselves informed of events by what was termed the "grape-vine" telegraph.

During the campaign when Lincoln was first a candidate for the Presidency, the slaves on our far-off plantation, miles from any railroad or large city or daily newspaper, knew what the issues involved were. When war was begun between the North and the South, every slave on our plantation felt and knew that, though other issues were discussed, the primal one was that of slavery. Even the most ignorant members of my race on the remote plantations felt in their hearts, with a certainty that admitted of no doubt, that the freedom of the slaves would be the one great result of the war, if the Northern armies conquered. Every success of the Federal armies and every defeat of the Confederate forces was watched with the keenest and most intense interest. Often the slaves got knowledge of the results of great battles before the white people received it. This news was usually gotten from the colored man who was sent to the post-office for the mail. In our case the post-office was about three miles from the plantation and the mail came once or twice a week. The man who was sent to the office would linger about the place long enough to get the drift of the conversation from the group of white people who naturally congregated there, after receiving their mail, to discuss the latest news. The mail-carrier on his way back to our master's house would as naturally retail the news that he had secured among the slaves, and in this way they often heard of important events before the white people at the "big house," as the master's house was called.

I cannot remember a single instance during my childhood or early boyhood when our entire family sat down to the table together, and God's blessing was asked, and the family ate a meal in a civilized manner. On the plantation in Virginia, and even later, meals were gotten by the children very much as dumb animals get theirs. It was a piece of bread here and a scrap of meat there. It was a cup of milk at one time and some potatoes at another. Sometimes a portion of our family would eat out of the skillet or pot, while some one else would eat from a tin plate held on the knees, and often using nothing but the hands with which to hold the food. When I had grown to sufficient size, I was required to go to the "big house" at meal-times to fan the flies from the table by means of a large set of paper fans operated by a pulley. Naturally much of the conversation of the white people turned upon the subject of freedom and the war, and I absorbed a good deal of it. I remember that at one time I saw two of my young mistresses and some lady visitors eating ginger-cakes, in the yard. At that time those cakes seemed to me to be absolutely the most tempting and desirable things that I had ever seen; and I then and there resolved that, if I ever got free, the height of my ambition would be reached if I could get to the point where I could secure and eat ginger-cakes in the way that I saw those ladies doing.

Of course as the war was prolonged the white people, in many cases, often found it difficult to secure food for themselves. I think the slaves felt the deprivation less than the whites, because the usual diet for the slaves was corn bread and pork, and these could be raised on the plantation; but coffee, tea, sugar, and other articles which the whites had been accustomed to use could not be raised on the plantation, and the conditions brought about by the war frequently made it impossible to secure these things. The whites were often in great straits. Parched corn was used for coffee, and a kind of black molasses was used instead of sugar. Many times nothing was used to sweeten the so-called tea and coffee.

The first pair of shoes that I recall wearing were wooden ones. They had rough leather on the top, but the bottoms, which were about an inch thick, were of wood. When I walked they made a fearful noise, and besides this they were very inconvenient since there was no yielding to the natural pressure of the foot. In wearing them one presented an exceedingly awkward appearance. The most trying ordeal that I was forced to endure as a slave boy, however, was the wearing of a flax shirt. In the portion of Virginia where I lived it was common to use flax as part of the clothing for the slaves. That part of the flax from which our clothing was made was largely the refuse, which of course was the cheapest and roughest part. I can scarcely imagine any torture, except, perhaps, the pulling of a tooth, that is equal to that caused by putting on a new flax shirt for the first time. It is almost equal to the feeling that one would experience if he had a dozen or more chestnut burrs, or a hundred small pin-points, in contact with his flesh. Even to this day I can recall accurately the tortures that I underwent when putting on one of these garments. The fact that my flesh was soft and tender added to the pain. But I had no choice. I had to wear the flax shirt or none; and had it been left to me to choose, I should have chosen to wear no covering.

In connection with the flax shirt, my brother John, who is several years older than I am, performed one of the most generous acts that I ever heard of one slave relative doing for another. On several occasions when I was being forced to wear a new flax shirt, he gener-ously agreed to put it on in my stead and wear it for several days, till it was "broken in." Until I had grown to be quite a youth this single garment was all that I wore.

One may get the idea, from what I have said, that there was bitter feeling toward the white people on the part of my race, because of the fact that most of the white population was away fighting in a war which would result in keeping the Negro in slavery if the South was successful. In the case of the slaves on our place this was not true, and it was not true of any large portion of the slave population in the South where the Negro was treated with anything like decency. During the Civil War one of my young masters was killed, and two were severely wounded. I recall the feeling of sorrow which existed among the slaves when they heard of the death of "Mars' Billy." It was no sham sorrow, but real. Some of the slaves had nursed "Mars' Billy"; others had played with him when he was a child. "Mars' Billy" had begged for mercy in the case of others when the overseer or master was thrashing them. The sorrow in the slave quarter was only second to that in the "big house." When the two young masters were brought home wounded the sympathy of the slaves was shown in many ways. They were just as anxious to assist in the nursing as the family relatives of the wounded. Some of the slaves would even beg for the privilege of sitting up at night to nurse their wounded masters. This tenderness and sympathy on the part of those held in bondage was a result of their kindly and generous nature. In order to defend and protect the women and children who were left on the plantations when the white males went to war, the slaves would have laid down their lives. The slave who was selected to sleep in the "big house" during the absence of the males was considered to have the place of honor. Any one attempting to harm "young Mistress" or "old Mistress" during the night would have had to cross the dead body of the slave to do so. I do not know how many have noticed it, but I think that it will be found to be true that there are few instances, either in slavery or freedom, in which a member of my race has been known to betray a specific trust.

As a rule, not only did the members of my race entertain no feelings of bitterness against the whites before and during the war, but there are many instances of Negroes tenderly caring for their former masters and mistresses who for some reason have become poor and dependent since the war. I know of instances where the former masters of slaves have for years been supplied with money by their former slaves to keep them from suffering. I have known of still other cases in which the former slaves have assisted in the education of the descendants of their former owners. I know of a case on a large plantation in the South in which a young white man, the son of the former owner of the estate, has become so reduced in purse and self-control by reason of drink that he is a pitiable creature; and yet, notwithstanding the poverty of the colored people themselves on this plantation, they have for years supplied this young white man with the necessities of life. One sends him a little coffee or sugar, another a little meat, and so on. Nothing that the colored people possess is too good for the son of "old Mars' Tom," who will perhaps never be permitted to suffer while any remain on the place who knew directly or indirectly of "old Mars' Tom."

I have said that there are few instances of a member of my race betraying a specific trust. One of the best illustrations of this which I know of is in the case of an ex-slave from Virginia whom I met not long ago in a little town in the state of Ohio. I found that this man had made a contract with his master, two or three years previous to the Emancipation Proclamation, to the effect that the slave was to be permitted to buy himself, by paying so much per year for his body; and while he was paying for himself, he was to be permitted to labor where and for whom he pleased. Finding that he could secure better wages in Ohio, he went there. When freedom came, he was still in debt to his master some three hundred dollars. Notwithstanding that the Emancipation Proclamation freed him from any obligation to his master, this black man walked the greater portion of the distance back to where his old master lived in Virginia, and placed the last dollar, with interest, in his hands. In talking to me about this, the man told me that he knew that he did not have to pay the debt, but that he had given his word to his master, and his word he had never broken. He felt that he could not enjoy his freedom till he had fulfilled his promise.

From some things that I have said one may get the idea that some of the slaves did not want freedom. This is not true. I have never seen one who did not want to be free, or one who would return to slavery.

I pity from the bottom of my heart any nation or body of people that is so unfortunate as to get entangled in the net of slavery. I have long since ceased to cherish any spirit of bitterness against the Southern white people on account of the enslavement of my race. No one section of our country was wholly responsible for its introduction, and, besides, it was recognized and protected for years by the General Government. Having once got its tentacles fastened on to the economic and social life of the Republic, it was no easy matter for the country to relieve itself of the institution. Then, when we rid ourselves of prejudice, or racial feeling, and look facts in the face, we must acknowledge that, notwithstanding the cruelty and moral wrong of slavery, the ten million Negroes inhabiting this country, who themselves or whose ancestors went through the school of American slavery, are in a stronger and more hopeful condition, materially, intellectually, morally, and religiously, than is true of an equal number of black people in any other portion of the globe. This is so to such an extent that Negroes in this country, who themselves or whose forefathers went through the school of slavery, are constantly returning to Africa as missionaries to enlighten those who remained in the fatherland. This I say, not to justify slavery—on the other hand, I condemn it as an institution, as we all know that in America it was established for selfish and financial reasons, and not from a missionary motive—but to call attention to a fact, and to show how Providence so often uses men and institutions to accomplish a purpose. When persons ask me in these days how, in the midst of what sometimes seem hopelessly discouraging conditions, I can have such faith in the future of my race in this country, I remind them of the wilderness through which and out of which, a good Providence has already led us.

Ever since I have been old enough to think for myself, I have entertained the idea that, notwithstanding the cruel wrongs inflicted upon us, the black man got nearly as much out of slavery as the white man did. The hurtful influences of the institution were not by any means confined to the Negro. This was fully illustrated by the life upon our own plantation. The whole machinery of slavery was so constructed as to cause labor, as a rule, to be looked upon as a badge of degradation, of inferiority. Hence labor was something that both races on the slave plantation sought to escape. The slave system on our place, in a large measure, took the spirit of self-reliance and self-help out of the white people. My old master had many boys and girls, but not one, so far as I know, ever mastered a single trade or special line of productive industry. The girls were not taught to cook, sew, or to take care of the house. All of this was left to the slaves. The slaves, of course, had little personal interest in the life of the plantation, and their ignorance prevented them from learning how to do things in the most improved and thorough manner. As a result of the system, fences were out of repair, gates were hanging half off the hinges, doors creaked, window-panes were out, plastering had fallen but was not replaced, weeds grew in the yard. As a rule, there was food for whites and blacks, but inside the house, and on the dining room table, there was wanting that delicacy and refinement of touch and finish which can make a home the most convenient, comfortable, and attractive place in the world. Withal there was a waste of food and other materials which was sad. When freedom came, the slaves were almost as well fitted to begin life anew as the master, except in the matter of book-learning and ownership of property. The slave owner and his sons had mastered no special industry. They unconsciously had imbibed the feeling that manual labor was not the proper thing for them. On the other hand, the slaves, in many cases, had mastered some handicraft, and none were ashamed, and few unwilling, to labor.

Finally the war closed, and the day of freedom came. It was a momentous and eventful day to all upon our plantation. We had been expecting it. Freedom was in the air, and had been for months. Deserting soldiers returning to their homes were to be seen every day. Others who had been discharged, or whose regiments had been paroled, were constantly passing near our place. The "grape-vine telegraph" was kept busy night and day. The news and mutterings of great events were swiftly carried from one plantation to another. In the fear of "Yankee" invasions, the silverware and other valuables were taken from the "big house," buried in the woods, and guarded by trusted slaves. Woe be to any one who would have attempted to disturb the buried treasure. The slaves would give the Yankee soldiers food, drink, clothing—anything but that which had been specifically entrusted to their care and honor. As the great day drew nearer, there was more singing in the slave quarters than usual. It was bolder, had more ring, and lasted later into the night. Most of the verses of the plantation songs had some reference to freedom. True, they had sung those same verses before, but they had been careful to explain that the "freedom" in these songs referred to the next world, and had no connection with life in this world. Now they gradually threw off the mask, and were not afraid to let it be known that the "freedom" in their songs meant freedom of the body in this world. The night before the eventful day, word was sent to the slave quarters to the effect that something unusual was going to take place at the "big house" the next morning. There was little, if any, sleep that night. All was excitement and expectancy. Early the next morning word was sent to all the slaves, old and young, to gather at the house. In company with my mother, brother, and sister, and a large number of other slaves, I went to the master's house. All of our master's family were either standing or seated on the veranda of the house, where they could see what was to take place and hear what was said. There was a feeling of deep interest, or perhaps sadness, on their faces, but not bitterness. As I now recall the impression they made upon me, they did not at the moment seem to be sad because of the loss of property, but rather because of parting with those whom they had reared and who were in many ways very close to them. The most distinct thing that I now recall in connection with the scene was that some man who seemed to be a stranger (a United States officer, I presume) made a little speech and then read a rather long paper—the Emancipation Proclamation, I think. After the reading we were told that we were all free, and could go when and where we pleased. My mother, who was standing by my side, leaned over and kissed her children, while tears of joy ran down her cheeks. She explained to us what it all meant, that this was the day for which she had been so long praying, but fearing that she would never live to see.

For some minutes there was great rejoicing, and thanksgiving, and wild scenes of ecstasy. But there was no feeling of bitterness. In fact, there was pity among the slaves for our former owners. The wild rejoicing on the part of the emancipated colored people lasted but for a brief period, for I noticed that by the time they returned to their cabins there was a change in their feelings. The great responsibility of being free, of having charge of themselves, of having to think and plan for themselves and their children, seemed to take possession of them. It was very much like suddenly turning a youth of ten or twelve years out into the world to provide for himself. In a few hours the great questions with which the

Anglo-Saxon race had been grappling for centuries had been thrown upon these people to be solved. These were the questions of a home, a living, the rearing of children, education, citizenship, and the establishment and support of churches. Was it any wonder that within a few hours the wild rejoicing ceased and a feeling of deep gloom seemed to pervade the slave quarters? To some it seemed that, now that they were in actual possession of it, freedom was a more serious thing than they had expected to find it. Some of the slaves were seventy or eighty years old; their best days were gone. They had no strength with which to earn a living in a strange place and among strange people, even if they had been sure where to find a new place of abode. To this class the problem seemed especially hard. Besides, deep down in their hearts there was a strange and peculiar attachment to "old Marster" and "old Missus," and to their children, which they found it hard to think of breaking off. With these they had spent in some cases nearly a half-century, and it was no light thing to think of parting. Gradually, one by one, stealthily at first, the older slaves began to wander from the slave quarters back to the "big house" to have a whispered conversation with their former owners as to the future. ...

Chapter 9
Anxious days and sleepless nights

The coming of Christmas, that first year of our residence in Alabama, gave us an opportunity to get a farther insight into the real life of the people. The first thing that reminded us that Christmas had arrived was the "foreday" visits of scores of children rapping at our doors, asking for "Chris'mus gifts! Chris'mus gifts!" Between the hours of two o'clock and five o'clock in the morning I presume that we must have had a half-hundred such calls. This custom prevails throughout this portion of the South to-day.

During the days of slavery it was a custom quite generally observed throughout all the Southern states to give the colored people a week of holiday at Christmas, or to allow the holiday to continue as long as the "yule log" lasted. The male members of the race, and often the female members, were expected to get drunk. We found that for a whole week the colored people in and around Tuskegee dropped work the day before Christmas, and that it was difficult to get any one to perform any service from the time they stopped work until after the New Year. Persons who at other times did not use strong drink thought it quite the proper thing to indulge in it rather freely during the Christmas week. There was a widespread hilarity, and a free use of guns, pistols, and gunpowder generally. The sacredness of the season seemed to have been almost wholly lost sight of.

During this first Christmas vacation I went some distance from the town to visit the people on one of the large plantations. In their poverty and ignorance it was pathetic to see their attempts to get joy out of the season that in most parts of the country is so sacred and so dear to the heart. In one cabin I noticed that all that the five children had to remind them of the coming of Christ was a single bunch of firecrackers, which they had divided among them. In another cabin, where there were at least a half-dozen persons, they had only ten cents' worth of ginger-cakes, which had been bought in the store the day before. In another family they had only a few pieces of sugarcane. In still another cabin I found nothing but a new jug of cheap, mean whiskey, which the husband and wife were making free use of, notwithstanding the fact that the husband was one of the local ministers. In a few instances I found that the people had gotten hold of some bright-colored cards that had been designed for advertising purposes, and were making the most of those. In other homes some member of the family had bought a new pistol. In the majority of cases there was nothing to be seen in the cabin to remind one of the coming of the Savior, except that the people had ceased work in the fields and were lounging about their homes. At night, during Christmas week, they usually had what they called a "frolic," in some cabin on the plantation. This meant a kind of rough dance where there was likely to be a good deal of whiskey used, and where there might be some shooting or cutting with razors.

While I was making this Christmas visit I met an old colored man who was one of the numerous local preachers, who tried to convince me, from the experience Adam had in the Garden of Eden, that God had cursed all labor, and that, therefore, it was a sin for any man to work. For that reason this man sought to do as little work as possible. He seemed at that time to be supremely happy, because he was living, as he expressed it, through one week that was free from sin.

In the school we made a special effort to teach our students the meaning of Christmas, and to give them lessons in its proper observance. In this we have been successful to a degree that makes me feel safe in saying that the season now has a new meaning, not only through all that immediate region, but, in a measure, wherever our graduates have gone.

At the present time one of the most satisfactory features of the Christmas and Thanksgiving seasons at Tuskegee is the unselfish and beautiful way in which our graduates and students spend their time in administering to the comfort and happiness of others, especially the unfortunate. Not long ago some of our young men spent a holiday in rebuilding a cabin for a helpless colored woman who is about seventy-five years old. At another time I remember that I made it known in chapel, one night, that a very poor student was suffering from cold, because he needed a coat. The next morning two coats were sent to my office for him.

I have referred to the disposition on the part of the white people in the town of Tuskegee and vicinity to help the school. From the first, I resolved to make the school a real part of the community in which it was located. I was determined that no one should have the feeling that it was a foreign institution, dropped down in the midst of the people, for which they had no responsibility and in which they had no interest. I noticed that the very fact that they had been asked to contribute toward the purchase of the land made them begin to feel as if it was going to be their school, to a large degree. I noted that just in proportion as we made the white people feel that the institution was a part of the life of the community, and that, while we wanted to make friends in Boston, for example, we also wanted to make white friends in Tuskegee, and that we wanted to make the school of real service to all the people, their attitude toward the school became favorable.

Perhaps I might add right here, what I hope to demonstrate later, that, so far as I know, the Tuskegee school at the present time has no warmer and more enthusiastic friends anywhere than it has among the white citizens of Tuskegee and throughout the state of

Alabama and the entire South. From the first, I have advised our people in the South to make friends in every straightforward, manly way with their next-door neighbor, whether he be a black man or a white man. I have also advised them, where no principle is at stake, to consult the interests of their local communities, and to advise with their friends in regard to their voting.

For several months the work of securing the money with which to pay for the farm went on without ceasing. At the end of three months enough was secured to repay the loan of two hundred and fifty dollars to General Marshall, and within two months more we had secured the entire five hundred dollars and had received a deed of the one hundred acres of land. This gave us a great deal of satisfaction. It was not only a source of satisfaction to secure a permanent location for the school, but it was equally satisfactory to know that the greater part of the money with which it was paid for had been gotten from the white and colored people in the town of Tuskegee. The most of this money was obtained by holding festivals and concerts, and from small individual donations.

Our next effort was in the direction of increasing the cultivation of the land, so as to secure some return from it, and at the same time give the students training in agriculture. All the industries at Tuskegee have been started in natural and logical order, growing out of the needs of a community settlement. We began with farming, because we wanted something to eat.

Many of the students, also, were able to remain in school but a few weeks at a time, because they had so little money with which to pay their board. Thus another object which made it desirable to get an industrial system started was in order to make it available as a means of helping the students to earn money enough so that they might be able to remain in school during the nine months' session of the school year.

The first animal that the school came into possession of was an old blind horse given us by one of the white citizens of Tuskegee. Perhaps I may add here that at the present time the school owns over two hundred horses, colts, mules, cows, calves, and oxen, and about seven hundred hogs and pigs, as well as a large number of sheep and goats.

The school was constantly growing in numbers, so much so that, after we had got the farm paid for, the cultivation of the land begun, and the old cabins which we had found on the place somewhat repaired, we turned our attention toward providing a large substantial building. After having given a good deal of thought to the subject, we finally had the plans drawn for a building that was estimated to cost about six thousand dollars. This seemed to us a tremendous sum, but we knew that the school must go backward or forward, and that our work would mean little unless we could get hold of the students in their home life.

One incident which occurred about this time gave me a great deal of satisfaction as well as surprise. When it became known in the town that we were discussing the plans for a new, large building, a Southern white man who was operating a sawmill not far from Tuskegee came to me and said that he would gladly put all the lumber necessary to erect the building on the grounds, with no other guarantee for payment than my word that it would be paid for when we secured some money. I told the man frankly that at the time we did not have in our hands one dollar of the money needed. Notwithstanding this, he insisted on being allowed to put the lumber on the grounds. After we had secured some portion of the money we permitted him to do this.

Miss Davidson again began the work of securing in various ways small contributions for the new building from the white and colored people in and near Tuskegee. I think I never saw a community of people so happy over anything as were the colored people over the prospect of this new building. One day, when we were holding a meeting to secure funds for its erection, an old, ante-bellum colored man came a distance of twelve miles and brought in his ox-cart a large hog. When the meeting was in progress, he rose in the midst of the company and said that he had no money which he could give, but that he had raised two fine hogs, and that he had brought one of them as a contribution toward the expenses of the building. He closed his announcement by saying: "Any nigger that's got any love for his race, or any respect for himself, will bring a hog to the next meeting." Quite a number of men in the community also volunteered to give several days' work, each, toward the erection of the building.

After we had secured all the help that we could in Tuskegee, Miss Davidson decided to go North for the purpose of securing additional funds. For weeks she visited individuals and spoke in churches and before Sunday schools and other organizations. She found this work quite trying, and often embarrassing. The school was not known, but she was not long in winning her way into the confidence of the best people in the North.

The first gift from any Northern person was received from a New York lady whom Miss Davidson met on the boat that was bringing her North. They fell into a conversation, and the Northern lady became so much interested in the effort being made at Tuskegee that before they parted Miss Davidson was handed a check for fifty dollars. For some time before our marriage, and also after it, Miss Davidson kept up the work of securing money in the North and in the South by interesting people by personal visits and through correspondence. At the same time she kept in close touch with the work at Tuskegee, as lady principal and classroom teacher. In addition to this, she worked among the older people in and near Tuskegee, and taught a Sunday school class in the town. She was never very strong, but never seemed happy unless she was giving all of her strength to the cause which she loved. Often, at night, after spending the day in going from door to door trying to interest persons in the work at Tuskegee, she would be so exhausted that she could not undress herself. A lady upon whom she called, in Boston, afterward told me that at one time when Miss Davidson called to see her and sent up her card the lady was detained a little before she could see Miss Davidson, and when she entered the parlor she found Miss Davidson so exhausted that she had fallen asleep.

While putting up our first building, which was named Porter Hall, after Mr. A. H. Porter, of Brooklyn, N. Y., who gave a generous sum toward its erection, the need for money became acute. I had given one of our creditors a promise that upon a certain day he should be paid four hundred dollars. On the morning of that day we did not have a dollar. The mail arrived at the school at ten o'clock, and in this mail there was a check sent by Miss Davidson for exactly four hundred dollars. I could relate many instances of almost the same character. This four hundred dollars was given by two ladies in Boston. Two years later, when the work at Tuskegee had grown considerably, and when we were in the midst of a season when we were so much in need of money that the future looked doubtful and gloomy, the same two Boston ladies sent us six thousand dollars. Words cannot describe our surprise, or the encouragement that the gift brought to us. Perhaps I might add here that for fourteen years these same friends have sent us six thousand dollars each year.

As soon as the plans were drawn for the new building, the students began digging out the earth where the foundations were to be laid, working after the regular classes were over. They had not fully outgrown the idea that it was hardly the proper thing for them to use their hands, since they had come there, as one of them expressed it, "to be educated, and not to work." Gradually, though, I noted with satisfaction that a sentiment in favor of work was gaining ground. After a few weeks of hard work the foundations were ready, and a day was appointed for the laying of the corner-stone.

When it is considered that the laying of this corner-stone took place in the heart of the South, in the "Black Belt," in the center of that part of our country that was most devoted to slavery; that at that time slavery had been abolished only about sixteen years; that only sixteen years before that no Negro could be taught from books without the teacher receiving the condemnation of the law or of public sentiment—when all this is considered, the scene that was witnessed on that spring day at Tuskegee was a remarkable one. I believe there are few places in the world where it could have taken place.

The principal address was delivered by the Hon. Waddy Thompson, the Superintendent of Education for the county. About the corner-stone were gathered the teachers, the students, their parents and friends, the county officials—who were white—and all the leading white men in that vicinity, together with many of the black men and women whom these same white people but a few years before had held a title to as property. The members of both races were anxious to exercise the privilege of placing under the corner-stone some memento.

Before the building was completed we passed through some very trying seasons. More than once our hearts were made to bleed, as it were, because bills were falling due that we did not have the money to meet. Perhaps no one who has not gone through the experience, month after month, of trying to erect buildings and provide equipment for a school when no one knew where the money was to come from, can properly appreciate the difficulties under which we labored. During the first years at Tuskegee I recall that night after night I would roll and toss on my bed, without sleep, because of the anxiety and uncertainty which we were in regarding money. I knew that, in a large degree, we were trying an experiment—that of testing whether or not it was possible for Negroes to build up and control the affairs of a large educational institution. I knew that if we failed it would injure the whole race. I knew that the presumption was against us. I knew that in the case of white people beginning such an enterprise it would be taken for granted that they were going to succeed, but in our case I felt that people would be surprised if we succeeded. All this made a burden which pressed down on us, sometimes, it seemed, at the rate of a thousand pounds to the square inch.

In all our difficulties and anxieties, however, I never went to a white or a black person in the town of Tuskegee for any assistance that was in their power to render, without being helped according to their means. More than a dozen times, when bills figuring up into the hundreds of dollars were falling due, I applied to the white men of Tuskegee for small loans, often borrowing small amounts from as many as a half-dozen persons, to meet our obligations. One thing I was determined to do from the first, and that was to keep the credit of the school high; and this, I think I can say without boasting, we have done all through these years.

I shall always remember a bit of advice given me by Mr. George W. Campbell, the white man to whom I have referred as the one who induced General Armstrong to send me to Tuskegee. Soon after I entered upon the work Mr. Campbell said to me, in his fatherly way: "Washington, always remember that credit is capital."

At one time when we were in the greatest distress for money that we ever experienced, I placed the situation frankly before General Armstrong. Without hesitation he gave me his personal check for all the money which he had saved for his own use. This was not the only time that General Armstrong helped Tuskegee in this way. I do not think I have ever made this fact public before.

During the summer of 1882, at the end of the first year's work of the school, I was married to Miss Fannie N. Smith, of Malden, W. Va. We began keeping house in Tuskegee early in the fall. This made a home for our teachers, who now had been increased to four in number. My wife was also a graduate of the Hampton Institute. After earnest and constant work in the interests of the school, together with her housekeeping duties, my wife passed away in May, 1884. One child, Portia M. Washington, was born during our marriage.

From the first, my wife most earnestly devoted her thoughts and time to the work of the school, and was completely one with me in every interest and ambition. She passed away, however, before she had an opportunity of seeing what the school was designed to be. ...

Chapter 13

Two thousand miles for a five-minute speech

Soon after the opening of our boarding department, quite a number of students who evidently were worthy, but who were so poor that they did not have any money to pay even the small charges at the school, began applying for admission. This class was composed of both men and women. It was a great trial to refuse admission to these applicants, and in 1884 we established a night-school to accommodate a few of them.

The night-school was organized on a plan similar to the one which I had helped to establish at Hampton. At first it was composed of about a dozen students. They were admitted to the night-school only when they had no money with which to pay any part of their board in the regular day-school. It was further required that they must work for ten hours during the day at some trade or industry, and study academic branches for two hours during the evening. This was the requirement for the first one or two years of their stay. They were to be paid something above the cost of their board, with the understanding that all of their earnings, except a very small part, were to be reserved in the school's treasury, to be used for paying their board in the regular day-school after they had entered that department. The night-school, started in this manner, has grown until there are at present four hundred and fifty-seven students enrolled in it alone.

There could hardly be a more severe test of a student's worth than this branch of the Institute's work. It is largely because it furnishes such a good opportunity to test the backbone of a student that I place such high value upon our night-school. Any one who is willing to work ten hours a day at the brick-yard, or in the laundry, through one or two years, in order that he or she may have the privilege of studying academic branches for two hours in the evening, has enough bottom to warrant being further educated.

After the student has left the night-school he enters the day-school, where he takes academic branches four days in a week, and works at his trade two days. Besides this he usually works at his trade during the three summer months. As a rule, after a student has succeeded in going through the night-school test, he finds a way to finish the regular course in industrial and academic training. No student, no matter how much money he may be able to command, is permitted to go through school without doing manual labor. In fact, the industrial work is now as popular as the academic branches. Some of the most successful men and women who have graduated from the institution obtained their start in the night-school.

While a great deal of stress is laid upon the industrial side of the work at Tuskegee, we do not neglect or overlook in any degree the religious and spiritual side. The school is strictly undenominational, but it is thoroughly Christian, and the spiritual training of the students is not neglected. Our preaching service, prayer-meetings, Sunday-school, Christian Endeavor Society, Young Men's Christian Association, and various missionary organizations, testify to this.

In 1885, Miss Olivia Davidson, to whom I have already referred as being largely responsible for the success of the school during its early history, and I were married. During our married life she continued to divide her time and strength between our home and the work for the school. She not only continued to work in the school at Tuskegee, but also kept up her habit of going North to secure funds. In 1889 she died, after four years of happy married life and eight years of hard and happy work for the school. She literally wore herself out in her never ceasing efforts in behalf of the work that she so dearly loved. During our married life there were born to us two bright beautiful boys, Booker Taliaferro and Ernest Davidson. The older of these, Booker, has already mastered the brickmaker's trade at Tuskegee.

I have often been asked how I began the practice of public speaking. In answer I would say that I never planned to give any large part of my life to speaking in public. I have always had more of an ambition to do things than merely to talk about doing them. It seems that when I went North with General Armstrong to speak at the series of public meetings to which I have referred, the President of the National Educational Association, the Hon. Thomas W. Bicknell, was present at one of those meetings and heard me speak. A few days afterward he sent me an invitation to deliver an address at the next meeting of the Educational Association. This meeting was to be held in Madison, Wis. I accepted the invitation. This was, in a sense, the beginning of my public-speaking career.

One the evening that I spoke before the Association there must have been not far from four thousand persons present. Without my knowing it, there were a large number of people present from Alabama, and some from the town of Tuskegee. These white people afterward frankly told me that they went to this meeting expecting to hear the South roundly abused, but were pleasantly surprised to find that there was no word of abuse in my address. On the contrary, the South was given credit for all the praiseworthy things that it had done. A white lady who was teacher in a college in Tuskegee wrote back to the local paper that she was gratified, as well as surprised, to note the credit which I gave the white people of Tuskegee for their help in getting the school started. This address at Madison was the first that I had delivered that in any large measure dealt with the general problem of the races. Those who heard it seemed to be pleased with what I said and with the general position that I took.

When I first came to Tuskegee, I determined that I would make it my home, that I would take as much pride in the right actions of the people of the town as any white man could do, and that I would, at the same time, deplore the wrong-doing of the people as much as any white man. I determined never to say anything in a public address in the North that I would not be willing to say in the South. I early learned that it is a hard matter to convert an individual by abusing him, and that this is more often accomplished by giving credit for all the praiseworthy actions performed than by calling attention alone to all the evil done.

While pursuing this policy I have not failed, at the proper time and in the proper manner, to call attention, in no uncertain terms, to the wrongs which any part of the South has been guilty of. I have found that there is a large element in the South that is quick to respond to straightforward, honest criticism of any wrong policy. As a rule, the place to criticize the South, when criticism is necessary, is in the South—not in Boston. A Boston man who came to Alabama to criticize Boston would not effect so much good, I think, as one who had his word of criticism to say in Boston.

In this address at Madison I took the ground that the policy to be pursued with reference to the races was, by every honorable means, to bring them together and to encourage the cultivation of friendly relations, instead of doing that which would embitter. I further contended that, in relation to his vote, the Negro should more and more consider the interests of the community in which he lived, rather than seek alone to please some one who lived a thousand miles away from him and from his interests.

In this address I said that the whole future of the Negro rested largely upon the question as to whether or not he should make himself, through his skill, intelligence, and character, of such undeniable value to the community in which he lived that the community could not dispense with his presence. I said that any individual who learned to do something better than anybody else—learned to do a common thing in an uncommon manner—had solved his problem, regardless of the color of his skin, and that in proportion as the Negro learned to produce what other people wanted and must have, in the same proportion would he be respected.

I spoke of an instance where one of our graduates had produced two hundred and sixty-six bushels of sweet potatoes from an acre of ground, in a community where the average production had been only forty-nine bushels to the acre. He had been able to do this by reason of his knowledge of the chemistry of the soil and by his knowledge of improved methods of agriculture. The white farmers in the neighborhood respected him, and came to him for ideas regarding the raising of sweet potatoes. These white farmers honored and respected him because he, by his skill and knowledge, had added something to the wealth and the comfort of the community in which he lived. I explained that my theory of education for the Negro would not, for example, confine him for all time to farm life—to the production of the best and the most sweet potatoes—but that, if he succeeded in this line of industry, he could lay the foundations upon which his children and grandchildren could grow to higher and more important things in life.

Such, in brief, were some of the views I advocated in this first address dealing with the broad question of the relations of the two races, and since that time I have not found any reason for changing my views on any important point.

In my early life I used to cherish a feeling of ill will toward any one who spoke in bitter terms against the Negro, or who advocated measures that tended to oppress the black man or take from him opportunities for growth in the most complete manner. Now, whenever I hear any one advocating measures that are meant to curtail the development of another, I pity the individual who would do this. I know that the one who makes this mistake does so because of his own lack of opportunity for the highest kind of growth. I pity him because I know that he is trying to stop the progress of the world, and because I know that in time the development and the ceaseless advance of humanity will make him ashamed of his weak and narrow position. One might as well try to stop the progress of a mighty railroad train by throwing his body across the track, as to try to stop the growth of the world in the direction of giving mankind more intelligence, more culture, more skill, more liberty, and in the direction of extending more sympathy and more brotherly kindness.

The address which I delivered at Madison, before the National Educational Association, gave me a rather wide introduction in the North, and soon after that opportunities began offering themselves for me to address audiences there.

I was anxious, however, that the way might also be opened for me to speak directly to a representative Southern white audience. A partial opportunity of this kind, one that seemed to me might serve as an entering wedge, presented itself in 1893, when the international meeting of Christian Workers was held at Atlanta, Ga. When this invitation came to me, I had engagements in Boston that seemed to make it impossible for me to speak in Atlanta. Still, after looking over my list of dates and places carefully, I found that I could take a train from Boston that would get me into Atlanta about thirty minutes before my address was to be delivered, and that I could remain in that city about sixty minutes before taking another train for Boston. My invitation to speak in Atlanta stipulated that I was to confine my address to five minutes. The question, then, was whether or not I could put enough into a five-minute address to make it worth while for me to make such a trip.

I knew that the audience would be largely composed of the most influential class of white men and women, and that it would be a rare opportunity for me to let them know what we were trying to do at Tuskegee, as well as to speak to them about the relations of the races. So I decided to make the trip. I spoke for five minutes to an audience of two thousand people, composed mostly of Southern and Northern whites. What I said seemed to be received with favor and enthusiasm. The Atlanta papers of the next day commented in friendly terms on my address, and a good deal was said about it in different parts of the country. I felt that I had in some degree accomplished my object—that of getting a hearing from the dominant class of the South.

The demands made upon me for public addresses continued to increase, coming in about equal numbers from my own people and from Northern whites. I gave as much time to these addresses as I could spare from the immediate work at Tuskegee. Most of the addresses in the North were made for the direct purpose of getting funds with which to support the school. Those delivered before the colored people had for their main object the impressing upon them of the importance of industrial and technical education in addition to academic and religious training.

I now come to that one of the incidents in my life which seems to have excited the greatest amount of interest, and which perhaps went further than anything else in giving me a reputation that in a sense might be called National. I refer to the address which I delivered at the opening of the Atlanta Cotton states and International Exposition, at Atlanta, Ga., September 18, 1895.

So much has been said and written about this incident, and so many questions have been asked me concerning the address, that perhaps I may be excused for taking up the matter with some detail. The five-minute address in Atlanta, which I came from Boston to deliver, was possibly the prime cause for an opportunity being given me to make the second address there. In the spring of 1895 I received a telegram from prominent citizens in Atlanta asking me to accompany a committee from that city to Washington for the purpose of appearing before a committee of Congress in the interest of securing Government help for the Exposition. The committee was composed of about twenty-five of the most prominent and most influential white men of Georgia. All the members of this committee were white men except Bishop Grant, Bishop Gaines, and myself. The Mayor and several other city and state officials spoke before the committee. They were followed by the two colored bishops. My name was the last on the list of speakers. I had never before appeared before such a committee, nor had I ever delivered any address in the capital of the Nation. I had many misgivings as to what I ought to say, and as to the impression that my address would make. While I cannot recall in detail what I said, I remember that I tried to impress upon the committee, with all the earnestness and plainness of any language that I could command, that if Congress wanted to do something which would assist in ridding the South of the race question and making friends between the two races, it should, in every proper way, encourage the material and intellectual growth of both races. I said that the Atlanta Exposition would present an opportunity for both races to show what advance they had made since freedom, and would at the same time afford encouragement to them to make still greater progress.

I tried to emphasize the fact that while the Negro should not be deprived by unfair means of the franchise, political agitation alone would not save him, and that back of the ballot he must have property, industry, skill, economy, intelligence, and character, and that no race without these elements could permanently succeed. I said that in granting the appropriation Congress could do something that would prove to be of real and lasting value to both races, and that it was the first great opportunity of the kind that had been presented since the close of the Civil War.

I spoke for fifteen or twenty minutes, and was surprised at the close of my address to receive the hearty congratulations of the Georgia committee and of the members of Congress who were present. The Committee was unanimous in making a favorable report, and in a few days the bill passed Congress. With the passing of this bill the success of the Atlanta Exposition was assured.

Soon after this trip to Washington the directors of the Exposition decided that it would be a fitting recognition of the colored race to erect a large and attractive building which should be devoted wholly to showing the progress of the Negro since freedom. It was further decided to have the building designed and erected wholly by Negro mechanics. This plan was carried out. In design, beauty, and general finish the Negro Building was equal to the others on the grounds.

After it was decided to have a separate Negro exhibit, the question arose as to who should take charge of it. The officials of the Exposition were anxious that I should assume this responsibility, but I declined to do so, on the plea that the work at Tuskegee at that time demanded my time and strength. Largely at my suggestion, Mr. I. Garland Penn, of Lynchburg, Va., was selected to be at the head of the Negro department. I gave him all the aid that I could. The Negro exhibit, as a whole, was large and creditable. The two exhibits in this department which attracted the greatest amount of attention were those from the Hampton Institute and the Tuskegee Institute. The people who seemed to be the most surprised, as well as pleased, at what they saw in the Negro Building were the Southern white people.

As the day for the opening of the Exposition drew near, the Board of Directors began preparing the program for the opening exercises. In the discussion from day to day of the various features of this program, the question came up as to the advisability of putting a member of the Negro race on for one of the opening addresses, since the Negroes had been asked to take such a prominent part in the Exposition. It was argued, further, that such recognition would mark the good feeling prevailing between the two races. Of course there were those who were opposed to any such recognition of the rights of the Negro, but the Board of Directors, composed of men who represented the best and most progressive element in the South, had their way, and voted to invite a black man to speak on the opening day. The next thing was to decide upon the person who was thus to represent the Negro race. After the question had been canvassed for several days, the directors voted unanimously to ask me to deliver one of the opening-day addresses, and in a few days after that I received the official invitation.

The receiving of this invitation brought to me a sense of responsibility that it would be hard for any one not placed in my position to appreciate. What were my feelings when this invitation came to me? I remembered that I had been a slave; that my early years had been spent in the lowest depths of poverty and ignorance, and that I had had little opportunity to prepare me for such a responsibility as this. It was only a few years before that time that any white man in the audience might have claimed me as his slave; and it was easily possible that some of my former owners might be present to hear me speak.

I knew, too, that this was the first time in the entire history of the Negro that a member of my race had been asked to speak from the same platform with white Southern men and women on any important National occasion. I was asked now to speak to an audience composed of the wealth and culture of the white South, the representatives of my former masters. I knew, too, that while the greater part of my audience would be composed of Southern people, yet there would be present a large number of Northern whites, as well as a great many men and women of my own race.

I was determined to say nothing that I did not feel from the bottom of my heart to be true and right. When the invitation came to me, there was not one word of intimation as to what I should say or as to what I should omit. In this I felt that the Board of Directors had paid a tribute to me. They knew that by one sentence I could have blasted, in a large degree, the success of the Exposition. I was also painfully conscious of the fact that, while I must be true to my own race in my utterances, I had it in my power to make such an ill-timed address as would result in preventing any similar invitation being extended to a black man again for years to come. I was equally determined to be true to the North, as well as to the best element of the white South, in what I had to say.

The papers, North and South, had taken up the discussion of my coming speech, and as the time for it drew near this discussion became more and more widespread. Not a few of the Southern white papers were unfriendly to the idea of my speaking. From my own race I received many suggestions as to what I ought to say. I prepared myself as best I could for the address, but as the eighteenth of September drew nearer, the heavier my heart became, and the more I feared that my effort would prove a failure and a disappointment.

The invitation had come at a time when I was very busy with my school work, as it was the beginning of our school year. After preparing my address, I went through it, as I usually do with all those utterances which I consider particularly important, with Mrs. Washington, and she approved of what I intended to say. On the sixteenth of September, the day before I was to start for Atlanta, so many of the Tuskegee teachers expressed a desire to hear my address that I consented to read it to them in a body. When I had done so, and had heard their criticisms and comments, I felt somewhat relieved, since they seemed to think well of what I had to say.

On the morning of September 17, together with Mrs. Washington and my three children, I started for Atlanta. I felt a good deal as I suppose a man feels when he is on his way to the gallows. In passing through the town of Tuskegee I met a white farmer who lived some distance out in the country. In a jesting manner this man said: "Washington, you have spoken before the Northern white people, the Negroes in the South, and to us country white people in the South; but in Atlanta, to-morrow, you will have before you the Northern whites, the Southern whites, and the Negroes all together. I am afraid that you have got yourself into a tight place." This farmer diagnosed the situation correctly, but his frank words did not add anything to my comfort.

In the course of the journey from Tuskegee to Atlanta both colored and white people came to the train to point me out, and discussed with perfect freedom, in my hearing, what was going to take place the next day. We were met by a committee in Atlanta. Almost the first thing that I heard when I got off the train in that city was an expression something like this from an old colored man near by: "Dat's de man of my race what's gwine to make a speech at de Exposition to-morrow. I'se sho' gwine to hear him."

Atlanta was literally packed, at the time, with people from all parts of this country, and with representatives of foreign governments, as well as with military and civic organizations. The afternoon papers had forecasts of the next day's proceedings in flaring headlines. All this tended to add to my burden. I did not sleep much that night. The next morning, before day, I went carefully over what I intended to say. I also kneeled down and asked God's blessing upon my effort. Right here, perhaps, I ought to add that I make it a rule never to go before an audience, on any occasion, without asking the blessing of God upon what I want to say.

I always make it a rule to make especial preparation for each separate address. No two audiences are exactly alike. It is my aim to reach and talk to the heart of each individual audience, taking it into my confidence very much as I would a person. When I am speaking to an audience, I care little for how what I am saying is going to sound in the newspapers, or to another audience, or to an individual. At the time, the audience before me absorbs all my sympathy, thought, and energy.

Early in the morning a committee called to escort me to my place in the procession which was to march to the Exposition grounds. In this procession were prominent colored citizens in carriages, as well as several Negro military organizations. I noted that the Exposition officials seemed to go out of their way to see that all of the colored people in the procession were properly placed and properly treated. The procession was about three hours in reaching the Exposition grounds, and during all of this time the sun was shining down upon us disagreeably hot. When we reached the grounds, the heat, together with my nervous anxiety, made me feel as if I were about ready to collapse, and to feel that my address was not going to be a success. When I entered the audience-room, I found it packed with humanity from bottom to top, and there were thousands outside who could not get in.

The room was very large, and well suited to public speaking. When I entered the room, there were vigorous cheers from the colored portion of the audience, and faint cheers from some of the white people. I had been told, while I had been in Atlanta, that while many white people were going to be present to hear me speak, simply out of curiosity, and that others who would be present would be in full sympathy with me, there was a still larger element of the audience which would consist of those who were going to be present for the purpose of hearing me make a fool of myself, or, at least, of hearing me say some foolish thing, so that they could say to the officials who had invited me to speak, "I told you so!"

One of the trustees of the Tuskegee Institute, as well as my personal friend, Mr. William H. Baldwin, Jr. was at the time General Manager of the Southern Railroad, and happened to be in Atlanta on that day. He was so nervous about the kind of reception that I would have, and the effect that my speech would produce, that he could not persuade himself to go into the building, but walked back and forth in the grounds outside until the opening exercises were over.

Chapter 14

The Atlanta exposition address

The Atlanta Exposition, at which I had been asked to make an address as a representative of the Negro race, as stated in the last chapter, was opened with a short address from

Governor Bullock. After other interesting exercises, including an invocation from Bishop Nelson, of Georgia, a dedicatory ode by Albert Howell, Jr., and addresses by the President of the Exposition and Mrs. Joseph Thompson, the President of the Woman's Board, Governor Bullock introduced me with the words, "We have with us to-day a representative of Negro enterprise and Negro civilization."

When I arose to speak, there was considerable cheering, especially from the colored people. As I remember it now, the thing that was uppermost in my mind was the desire to say something that would cement the friendship of the races and bring about hearty cooperation between them. So far as my outward surroundings were concerned, the only thing that I recall distinctly now is that when I got up, I saw thousands of eyes looking intently into my face. The following is the address which I delivered:

Mr. President and gentlemen of the board of directors and citizens.

One-third of the population of the South is of the Negro race. No enterprise seeking the material, civil, or moral welfare of this section can disregard this element of our population and reach the highest success. I but convey to you, Mr. President and Directors, the sentiment of the masses of my race when I say that in no way have the value and manhood of the American Negro been more fittingly and generously recognized than by the managers of this magnificent Exposition at every stage of its progress. It is a recognition that will do more to cement the friendship of the two races than any occurrence since the dawn of our freedom.

Not only this, but the opportunity here afforded will awaken among us a new era of industrial progress. Ignorant and inexperienced, it is not strange that in the first years of our new life we began at the top instead of at the bottom; that a seat in Congress or the state legislature was more sought than real estate or industrial skill; that the political convention of stump speaking had more attraction than starting a dairy farm or truck garden.

A ship lost at sea for many days suddenly sighted a friendly vessel. From the mast of the unfortunate vessel was seen a signal, "Water, water; we die of thirst!" The answer from the friendly vessel at once came back, "Cast down your bucket where you are." A second time the signal, "Water, water; send us water!" ran up from the distressed vessel, and was answered, "Cast down your bucket where you are." And a third and fourth signal for water was answered, "Cast down your bucket where you are." The captain of the distressed vessel, at last heeding the injunction, cast down his bucket, and it came up full of fresh, sparkling water from the mouth of the Amazon River. To those of my race who depend on bettering their condition in a foreign land or who underestimate the importance of cultivating friendly relations with the Southern white man, who is their next-door neighbor, I would say: "Cast down your bucket where you are"—cast it down in making friends in every manly way of the people of all races by whom we are surrounded.

Cast it down in agriculture, mechanics, in commerce, in domestic service, and in the professions. And in this connection it is well to bear in mind that whatever other sins the South may be called to bear, when it comes to business, pure and simple, it is in the South that the Negro is given a man's chance in the commercial world, and in nothing is this

Exposition more eloquent than in emphasizing this chance. Our greatest danger is that in the great leap from slavery to freedom we may overlook the fact that the masses of us are to live by the productions of our hands, and fail to keep in mind that we shall prosper in proportion as we learn to dignify and glorify common labor and put brains and skill into the common occupations of life; shall prosper in proportion as we learn to draw the line between the superficial and the substantial, the ornamental gewgaws of life and the useful. No race can prosper till it learns that there is as much dignity in tilling a field as in writing a poem. It is at the bottom of life we must begin, and not at the top. Nor should we permit our grievances to overshadow our opportunities.

To those of the white race who look to the incoming of those of foreign birth and strange tongue and habits for the prosperity of the South, were I permitted I would repeat what I say to my own race, "Cast down your bucket where you are." Cast it down among the eight millions of Negroes whose habits you know, whose fidelity and love you have tested in days when to have proved treacherous meant the ruin of your firesides. Cast down your bucket among these people who have, without strikes and labor wars, tilled your fields, cleared your forests, builded your railroads and cities, and brought forth treasures from the bowels of the earth, and helped make possible this magnificent representation of the progress of the South. Casting down your bucket among my people, helping and encouraging them as you are doing on these grounds, and to education of head, hand, and heart, you will find that they will buy your surplus land, make blossom the waste places in your fields, and run your factories. While doing this, you can be sure in the future, as in the past, that you and your families will be surrounded by the most patient, faithful, law-abiding, and unresentful people that the world has seen. As we have proved our loyalty to you in the past, in nursing your children, watching by the sick-bed of your mothers and fathers, and often following them with tear-dimmed eyes to their graves, so in the future, in our humble way, we shall stand by you with a devotion that no foreigner can approach, ready to lay down our lives, if need be, in defense of yours, interlacing our industrial, commercial, civil, and religious life with yours in a way that shall make the interests of both races one. In all things that are purely social we can be as separate as the fingers, yet one as the hand in all things essential to mutual progress.

There is no defense or security for any of us except in the highest intelligence and development of all. If anywhere there are efforts tending to curtail the fullest growth of the Negro, let these efforts be turned into stimulating, encouraging, and making him the most useful and intelligent citizen. Effort or means so invested will pay a thousand per cent. interest. These efforts will be twice blessed—"blessing him that gives and him that takes."

There is no escape through law of man or God from the inevitable: -

The laws of changeless justice bind
Oppressor with oppressed;
And close as sin and suffering joined
We march to fate abreast.

Nearly sixteen millions of hands will aid you in pulling the load upward, or they will pull against you the load downward. We shall constitute one-third and more of the ignorance and crime of the South, or one-third its intelligence and progress; we shall contribute one-third to the business and industrial prosperity of the South, or we shall prove a veritable body of death, stagnating, depressing, retarding every effort to advance the body politic.

Gentlemen of the Exposition, as we present to you our humble effort at an exhibition of our progress, you must not expect overmuch. Starting thirty years ago with ownership here and there in a few quilts and pumpkins and chickens (gathered from miscellaneous sources), remember the path that has led from these to the inventions and production of agricultural implements, buggies, steam-engines, newspapers, books, statuary, carving, paintings, the management of drug-stores and banks, has not been trodden without contact with thorns and thistles. While we take pride in what we exhibit as a result of our independent efforts, we do not for a moment forget that our part in this exhibition would fall far short of your expectations but for the constant help that has come to our educational life, not only from the Southern states, but especially from Northern philanthropists, who have made their gifts a constant stream of blessing and encouragement.

The wisest among my race understand that the agitation of questions of social equality is the extremist folly, and that progress in the enjoyment of all the privileges that will come to us must be the result of severe and constant struggle rather than of artificial forcing. No race that has anything to contribute to the markets of the world is long in any degree ostracized. It is important and right that all privileges of the law be ours, but it is vastly more important that we be prepared for the exercises of these privileges. The opportunity to earn a dollar in a factory just now is worth infinitely more than the opportunity to spend a dollar in an opera-house.

In conclusion, may I repeat that nothing in thirty years has given us more hope and encouragement, and drawn us so near to you of the white race, as this opportunity offered by the Exposition; and here bending, as it were, over the altar that represents the results of the struggles of your race and mine, both starting practically empty-handed three decades ago, I pledge that in your effort to work out the great and intricate problem which God has laid at the doors of the South, you shall have at all times the patient, sympathetic help of my race; only let this be constantly in mind, that, while from representations in these buildings of the product of field, of forest, of mine, of factory, letters, and art, much good will come, yet far above and beyond material benefits will be that higher good, that, let us pray God, will come, in a blotting out of sectional differences and racial animosities and suspicions, in a determination to administer absolute justice, in a willing obedience among all classes to the mandates of law. This, this, coupled with our material prosperity, will bring into our beloved South a new heaven and a new earth.

The first thing that I remember, after I had finished speaking, was that Governor Bullock rushed across the platform and took me by the hand, and that others did the same. I received so many and such hearty congratulations that I found it difficult to get out of the building. I did not appreciate to any degree, however, the impression which my address seemed to have made, until the next morning, when I went into the business part of the city. As soon as I was recognized, I was surprised to find myself pointed out and surrounded by a crowd of men who wished to shake hands with me. This was kept up on every street on to which I went, to an extent which embarrassed me so much that I went back to my boarding-place. The next morning I returned to Tuskegee. At the station in Atlanta, and at almost all of the stations at which the train stopped between that city and Tuskegee, I found a crowd of people anxious to shake hands with me.

The papers in all parts of the United States published the address in full, and for months afterward there were complimentary editorial references to it. Mr. Clark Howell, the editor of the Atlanta Constitution, telegraphed to a New York paper, among other words, the following, "I do not exaggerate when I say that Professor Booker T. Washington's address yesterday was one of the most notable speeches, both as to character and as to the warmth of its reception, ever delivered to a Southern audience. The address was a revelation. The whole speech is a platform upon which blacks and whites can stand with full justice to each other."

The Boston Transcript said editorially: "The speech of Booker T. Washington at the Atlanta Exposition, this week, seems to have dwarfed all the other proceedings and the Exposition itself. The sensation that it has caused in the press has never been equaled."

I very soon began receiving all kinds of propositions from lecture bureaus, and editors of magazines and papers, to take the lecture platform, and to write articles. One lecture bureau offered me fifty thousand dollars, or two hundred dollars a night and expenses, if I would place my services at its disposal for a given period. To all these communications I replied that my life-work was at Tuskegee; and that whenever I spoke it must be in the interests of the Tuskegee school and my race, and that I would enter into no arrangements that seemed to place a mere commercial value upon my services.

Some days after its delivery I sent a copy of my address to the President of the United States, the Hon. Grover Cleveland. I received from him the following autograph reply: -

Gray Gables, Buzzard's Bay, Mass.,
October 6, 1895
Booker T. Washington, Esq.:
My dear Sir: I thank you for sending me a copy of your address delivered at the Atlanta Exposition.
I thank you with much enthusiasm for making the address. I have read it with intense interest, and I think the Exposition would be fully justified if it did not do more than furnish the opportunity for its delivery. Your words cannot fail to delight and encourage all who wish well for your race; and if our colored fellow-citizens do not from your utterances gather new hope and form new determinations to gain every valuable advantage offered them by their citizenship, it will be strange indeed.
Yours very truly,
Grover Cleveland.

Later I met Mr. Cleveland, for the first time, when, as President, he visited the Atlanta Exposition. At the request of myself and others he consented to spend an hour in the Negro

Building, for the purpose of inspecting the Negro exhibit and of giving the colored people in attendance an opportunity to shake hands with him. As soon as I met Mr. Cleveland I became impressed with his simplicity, greatness, and rugged honesty. I have met him many times since then, both at public functions and at his private residence in Princeton, and the more I see of him the more I admire him. When he visited the Negro Building in Atlanta he seemed to give himself up wholly, for that hour, to the colored people. He seemed to be as careful to shake hands with some old colored "auntie" clad partially in rags, and to take as much pleasure in doing so, as if he were greeting some millionaire. Many of the colored people took advantage of the occasion to get him to write his name in a book or on a slip of paper. He was as careful and patient in doing this as if he were putting his signature to some great state document.

Mr. Cleveland has not only shown his friendship for me in many personal ways, but has always consented to do anything I have asked of him for our school. This he has done, whether it was to make a personal donation or to use his influence in securing the donations of others. Judging from my personal acquaintance with Mr. Cleveland, I do not believe that he is conscious of possessing any color prejudice. He is too great for that. In my contact with people I find that, as a rule, it is only the little, narrow people who live for themselves, who never read good books, who do not travel, who never open up their souls in a way to permit them to come into contact with other souls—with the great outside world. No man whose vision is bounded by color can come into contact with what is highest and best in the world. In meeting men, in many places, I have found that the happiest people are those who do the most for others; the most miserable are those who do the least. I have also found that few things, if any, are capable of making one so blind and narrow as race prejudice. I often say to our students, in the course of my talks to them on Sunday evenings in the chapel, that the longer I live and the more experience I have of the world, the more I am convinced that, after all, the one thing that is most worth living for—and dying for, if need be—is the opportunity of making some one else more happy and more useful.

The colored people and the colored newspapers at first seemed to be greatly pleased with the character of my Atlanta address, as well as with its reception. But after the first burst of enthusiasm began to die away, and the colored people began reading the speech in cold type, some of them seemed to feel that they had been hypnotized. They seemed to feel that I had been too liberal in my remarks toward the Southern whites, and that I had not spoken out strongly enough for what they termed the "rights" of the race. For a while there was a reaction, so far as a certain element of my own race was concerned, but later these reactionary ones seemed to have been won over to my way of believing and acting.

While speaking of changes in public sentiment, I recall that about ten years after the school at Tuskegee was established, I had an experience that I shall never forget. Dr. Lyman Abbott, then the pastor of Plymouth Church, and also editor of the Outlook (then the Christian Union), asked me to write a letter for his paper giving my opinion of the exact condition, mental and moral, of the colored ministers in the South, as based upon my observations. I wrote the letter, giving the exact facts as I conceived them to be. The picture painted was a rather black one—or, since I am black, shall I say "white"? It could not be otherwise with a race but a few years out of slavery, a race which had not had time or opportunity to produce a competent ministry.

What I said soon reached every Negro minister in the country, I think, and the letters of condemnation which I received from them were not few. I think that for a year after the publication of this article every association and every conference or religious body of any kind, of my race, that met, did not fail before adjourning to pass a resolution condemning me, or calling upon me to retract or modify what I had said. Many of these organizations went so far in their resolutions as to advise parents to cease sending their children to Tuskegee. One association even appointed a "missionary" whose duty it was to warn the people against sending their children to Tuskegee. This missionary had a son in the school, and I noticed that, whatever the "missionary" might have said or done with regard to others, he was careful not to take his son away from the institution. Many or the colored papers, especially those that were the organs of religious bodies, joined in the general chorus of condemnation or demands for retraction.

During the whole time of the excitement, and through all the criticism, I did not utter a word of explanation or retraction. I knew that I was right, and that time and the sober second thought of the people would vindicate me. It was not long before the bishops and other church leaders began to make a careful investigation of the conditions of the ministry, and they found out that I was right. In fact, the oldest and most influential bishop in one branch of the Methodist Church said that my words were far too mild. Very soon public sentiment began making itself felt, in demanding a purifying of the ministry. While this is not yet complete by any means, I think I may say, without egotism, and I have been told by many of our most influential ministers, that my words had much to do with starting a demand for the placing of a higher type of men in the pulpit. I have had the satisfaction of having many who once condemned me thank me heartily for my frank words.

The change of the attitude of the Negro ministry, so far as regards myself, is so complete that at the present time I have no warmer friends among any class than I have among the clergymen. The improvement in the character and life of the Negro ministers is one of the most gratifying evidences of the progress of the race. My experience with them as well as other events in my life, convince me that the thing to do, when one feels sure that he has said or done the right thing, and is condemned, is to stand still and keep quiet. If he is right, time will show it.

In the midst of the discussion which was going on concerning my Atlanta speech, I received the letter which I give below, from Dr. Gilman, the President of Johns Hopkins University, who had been made chairman of the judges of award in connection with the Atlanta Exposition: -

Johns Hopkins University, Baltimore,
President's Office, September 30, 1895.
Dear Mr. Washington:
Would it be agreeable to you to be one of the Judges of Award in the Department of

Education at Atlanta? If so, I shall be glad to place your name upon the list. A line by telegraph will be welcomed.

Yours very truly,

D. C. Gilman

I think I was even more surprised to receive this invitation than I had been to receive the invitation to speak at the opening of the Exposition. It was to be a part of my duty, as one of the jurors, to pass not only upon the exhibits of the colored schools, but also upon those of the white schools. I accepted the position, and spent a month in Atlanta in performance of the duties which it entailed. The board of jurors was a large one, consisting in all of sixty members. It was about equally divided between Southern white people and Northern white people. Among them were college presidents, leading scientists and men of letters, and specialists in many subjects. When the group of jurors to which I was assigned met for organization, Mr. Thomas Nelson Page, who was one of the number, moved that I be made secretary of that division, and the motion was unanimously adopted. Nearly half of our division were Southern people. In performing my duties in the inspection of the exhibits of white schools I was in every case treated with respect, and at the close of our labors I parted from my associates with regret.

I am often asked to express myself more freely than I do upon the political condition and the political future of my race. These recollections of my experience in Atlanta give me the opportunity to do so briefly. My own belief is, although I have never before said so in so many words, that the time will come when the Negro in the South will be accorded all the political rights which his ability, character, and material possessions entitle him to. I think, though, that the opportunity to freely exercise such political rights will not come in any large degree through outside or artificial forcing, but will be accorded to the Negro by the Southern white people themselves, and that they will protect him in the exercise of those rights. Just as soon as the South gets over the old feeling that it is being forced by "foreigners," or "aliens," to do something which it does not want to do, I believe that the change in the direction that I have indicated is going to begin. In fact, there are indications that it is already beginning in a slight degree.

Let me illustrate my meaning. Suppose that some months before the opening of the Atlanta Exposition there had been a general demand from the press and public platform outside the South that a Negro be given a place on the opening program, and that a Negro be placed upon the board of jurors of award. Would any such recognition of the race have taken place? I do not think so. The Atlanta officials went as far as they did because they felt it to be a pleasure, as well as a duty, to reward what they considered merit in the Negro race. Say what we will, there is something in human nature which we cannot blot out, which makes one man, in the end, recognize and reward merit in another, regardless of color or race.

I believe it is the duty of the Negro—as the greater part of the race is already doing—to deport himself modestly in regard to political claims, depending upon the slow but sure influences that proceed from the possession of property, intelligence, and high character for the full recognition of his political rights. I think that the according of the full exercise of political rights is going to be a matter of natural, slow growth, not an over-night, gourd-vine affair. I do not believe that the Negro should cease voting, for a man cannot learn the exercise of self-government by ceasing to vote any more than a boy can learn to swim by keeping out of the water, but I do believe that in his voting he should more and more be influenced by those of intelligence and character who are his next-door neighbors.

I know colored men who, through the encouragement, help, and advice of Southern white people, have accumulated thousands of dollars' worth of property, but who, at the same time, would never think of going to those same persons for advice concerning the casting of their ballots. This, it seems to me, is unwise and unreasonable, and should cease. In saying this I do not mean that the Negro should buckle, or not vote from principle, for the instant he ceases to vote from principle he loses the confidence and respect of the Southern white man even.

I do not believe that any state should make a law that permits an ignorant and poverty-stricken white man to vote, and prevents a black man in the same condition from voting. Such a law is not only unjust, but it will react, as all unjust laws do, in time; for the effect of such a law is to encourage the Negro to secure education and property, and at the same time it encourages the white man to remain in ignorance and poverty. I believe that in time, through the operation of intelligence and friendly race relations, all cheating at the ballot-box in the South will cease. It will become apparent that the white man who begins by cheating a Negro out of his ballot soon learns to cheat a white man out of his, and that the man who does this ends his career of dishonesty by the theft of property or by some equally serious crime. In my opinion, the time will come when the South will encourage all of its citizens to vote. It will see that it pays better, from every standpoint, to have healthy, vigorous life than to have that political stagnation which always results when one-half of the population has no share and no interest in the Government.

As a rule, I believe in universal, free suffrage, but I believe that in the South we are confronted with peculiar conditions that justify the protection of the ballot in many of the states, for a while at least, either by an educational test, a property test, or by both combined; but whatever tests are required, they should be made to apply with equal and exact justice to both races. ...

Chapter 17
Last words

Before going to Europe some events came into my life which were great surprises to me. In fact, my whole life has largely been one of surprises. I believe that any man's life will be filled with constant, unexpected encouragements of this kind if he makes up his mind to do his level best each day of his life—that is, tries to make each day reach as nearly as possible the high-water mark of pure, unselfish, useful living. I pity the man, black or white, who has never experienced the joy and satisfaction that come to one by reason of an effort to assist in making some one else more useful and more happy.

Six months before he died, and nearly a year after he had been stricken with paralysis, General Armstrong expressed a wish to visit Tuskegee again before he passed away.

Notwithstanding the fact that he had lost the use of his limbs to such an extent that he was practically helpless, his wish was gratified, and he was brought to Tuskegee. The owners of the Tuskegee Railroad, white men living in the town, offered to run a special train, without cost, out to the main station—Chehaw, five miles away—to meet him. He arrived on the school grounds about nine o'clock in the evening. Some one had suggested that we give the General a "pine-knot torchlight reception." This plan was carried out, and the moment that his carriage entered the school grounds he began passing between two lines of lighted and waving "fat pine" wood knots held by over a thousand students and teachers. The whole thing was so novel and surprising that the General was completely overcome with happiness. He remained a guest in my home for nearly two months, and, although almost wholly without the use of voice or limb he spent nearly every hour in devising ways and means to help the South. Time and time again he said to me, during this visit, that it was not only the duty of the country to assist in elevating the Negro of the South, but the poor white man as well. At the end of his visit I resolved anew to devote myself more earnestly than ever to the cause which was so near his heart. I said that if a man in his condition was willing to think, work, and act, I should not be wanting in furthering in every possible way the wish of his heart.

The death of General Armstrong, a few weeks later, gave me the privilege of getting acquainted with one of the finest, most unselfish, and most attractive men that I have ever come in contact with. I refer to the Rev. Dr. Hollis B. Frissell, now the Principal of the Hampton Institute, and General Armstrong's successor. Under the clear, strong, and almost perfect leadership of Dr. Frissell, Hampton has had a career of prosperity and usefulness that is all that the General could have wished for. It seems to be the constant effort of Dr. Frissell to hide his own great personality behind that of General Armstrong—to make himself of "no reputation" for the sake of the cause.

More than once I have been asked what was the greatest surprise that ever came to me. I have little hesitation in answering that question. It was the following letter, which came to me one Sunday morning when I was sitting on the veranda of my home at Tuskegee, surrounded by my wife and three children: -

> Harvard University, Cambridge, May 28, 1896.
> President Booker T. Washington,
> My dear Sir:
> Harvard University desires to confer on you at the approaching Commencement an honorary degree; but it is our custom to confer degrees only on gentlemen who are present. Our Commencement occurs this year on June 24, and your presence would be desirable from about noon till about five o'clock in the afternoon. Would it be possible for you to be in Cambridge on that day?
> Believe me, with great regard,
> Very truly yours,
> Charles W. Eliot.

This was a recognition that had never in the slightest manner entered into my mind, and it was hard for me to realize that I was to be honored by a degree from the oldest and most renowned university in America. As I sat upon my veranda, with this letter in my hand, tears came into my eyes. My whole former life—my life as a slave on the plantation, my work in the coal-mine, the times when I was without food and clothing, when I made my bed under a sidewalk, my struggles for an education, the trying days I had had at Tuskegee, days when I did not know where to turn for a dollar to continue the work there, the ostracism and sometimes oppression of my race,—all this passed before me and nearly overcame me.

I had never sought or cared for what the world calls fame. I have always looked upon fame as something to be used in accomplishing good. I have often said to my friends that if I can use whatever prominence may have come to me as an instrument with which to do good, I am content to have it. I care for it only as a means to be used for doing good, just as wealth may be used. The more I come into contact with wealthy people, the more I believe that they are growing in the direction of looking upon their money simply as an instrument which God has placed in their hand for doing good with. I never go to the office of Mr. John D. Rockefeller, who more than once has been generous to Tuskegee, without being reminded of this. The close, careful, and minute investigation that he always makes in order to be sure that every dollar that he gives will do the most good—an investigation that is just as searching as if he were investing money in a business enterprise—convinces me that the growth in this direction is most encouraging.

At nine o'clock, on the morning of June 24, I met President Eliot, the Board of Overseers of Harvard University, and the other guests, at the designated place on the university grounds, for the purpose of being escorted to Sanders Theatre, where the Commencement exercises were to be held and degrees conferred. Among others invited to be present for the purpose of receiving a degree at this time were General Nelson A. Miles, Dr. Bell, the inventor of the Bell telephone, Bishop Vincent, and the Rev. Minot J. Savage. We were placed in line immediately behind the president and the Board of Overseers, and directly afterward the Governor of Massachusetts, escorted by the Lancers, arrived and took his place in the line of march by the side of President Eliot. In the line there were also various other officers and professors, clad in cap and gown. In this order we marched to Sanders Theatre, where, after the usual Commencement exercises, came the conferring of the honorary degrees. This, it seems, is always considered the most interesting feature at Harvard. It is not known, until the individuals appear, upon whom the honorary degrees are to be conferred, and those receiving these honors are cheered by the students and others in proportion to their popularity. During the conferring of the degrees excitement and enthusiasm are at the highest pitch.

When my name was called, I rose, and President Eliot, in beautiful and strong English, conferred upon me the degree of Master of Arts. After these exercises were over, those who had received honorary degrees were invited to lunch with the President. After the lunch we were formed in line again, and were escorted by the Marshal of the day, who that year happened to be Bishop William Lawrence, through the grounds, where, at different points, those who had been honored were called by name and received the Harvard yell. This march ended at Memorial Hall, where the alumni dinner was served. To see over a thousand strong men, representing all that is best in State, Church, business, and education, with the glow and enthusiasm of college loyalty and college pride,—which has, I think, a peculiar Harvard flavor,—is a sight that does not easily fade from memory.

Among the speakers after dinner were President Eliot, Governor Roger Wolcott, General Miles, Dr. Minot J. Savage, the Hon. Henry Cabot Lodge, and myself. When I was called upon, I said, among other things: -

It would in some measure relieve my embarrassment if I could, even in a slight degree, feel myself worthy of the great honor which you do me to-day. Why you have called me from the Black Belt of the South, from among my humble people, to share in the honors of this occasion, is not for me to explain; and yet it may not be inappropriate for me to suggest that it seems to me that one of the most vital questions that touch our American life is how to bring the strong, wealthy, and learned into helpful touch with the poorest, most ignorant, and humblest, and at the same time make one appreciate the vitalizing, strengthening influence of the other. How shall we make the mansions on yon Beacon Street feel and see the need of the spirits in the lowliest cabin in Alabama cotton fields or Louisiana sugar-bottoms? This problem Harvard University is solving, not by bringing itself down, but by bringing the masses up.

If my life in the past has meant anything in the lifting up of my people and the bringing about of better relations between your race and mine, I assure you from this day it will mean doubly more. In the economy of God there is but one standard by which an individual can succeed—there is but one for a race. This country demands that every race shall measure itself by the American standard. By it a race must rise or fall, succeed or fail, and in the last analysis mere sentiment counts for little. During the next half-century and more, my race must continue passing through the severe American crucible. We are to be tested in our patience, our forbearance, our perseverance, our power to endure wrong, to withstand temptations, to economize, to acquire and use skill; in our ability to compete, to succeed in commerce, to disregard the superficial for the real, the appearance for the substance, to be great and yet small, learned and yet simple, high and yet the servant of all.

As this was the first time that a New England university had conferred an honorary degree upon a Negro, it was the occasion of much newspaper comment throughout the country. A correspondent of a New York paper said: -

When the name of Booker T. Washington was called, and he arose to acknowledge and accept, there was such an outburst of applause as greeted no other name except that of the popular soldier patriot, General Miles. The applause was not studied and stiff, sympathetic and condoling; it was enthusiasm and admiration. Every part of the audience from pit to gallery joined in, and a glow covered the cheeks of those around me, proving sincere appreciation of the rising struggle of an ex-slave and the work he has accomplished for his race.

A Boston paper said, editorially: -

In conferring the honorary degree of Master of Arts upon the Principal of Tuskegee Institute, Harvard University has honored itself as well as the object of this distinction. The work which Professor Booker T. Washington has accomplished for the education, good citizenship, and popular enlightenment in his chosen field of labor in the South entitles him to rank with our national benefactors. The university which can claim him on its list of sons, whether in regular course or honoris causa, may be proud.

It has been mentioned that Mr. Washington is the first of his race to receive an honorary degree from a New England university. This, in itself, is a distinction. But the degree was not conferred because Mr. Washington is a colored man, or because he was born in slavery, but because he has shown, by his work for the elevation of the people of the Black Belt of the South, a genius and a broad humanity which count for greatness in any man, whether his skin be white or black.

Another Boston paper said: -

It is Harvard which, first among New England colleges, confers an honorary degree upon a black man. No one who has followed the history of Tuskegee and its work can fail to admire the courage, persistence, and splendid common sense of Booker T. Washington. Well may Harvard honor the ex-slave, the value of whose services, alike to his race and country, only the future can estimate.

The correspondent of the New York Times wrote: -

All the speeches were enthusiastically received, but the colored man carried off the oratorical honors, and the applause which broke out when he had finished was vociferous and long-continued.

Soon after I began work at Tuskegee I formed a resolution, in the secret of my heart, that I would try to build up a school that would be of so much service to the country that the President of the United States would one day come to see it. This was, I confess, rather a bold resolution, and for a number of years I kept it hidden in my own thoughts, not daring to share it with any one.

In November, 1897, I made the first move in this direction, and that was in securing a visit from a member of President McKinley's Cabinet, the Hon. James Wilson, Secretary of Agriculture. He came to deliver an address at the formal opening of the Slater-Armstrong Agricultural Building, our first large building to be used for the purpose of giving training to our students in agriculture and kindred branches.

In the fall of 1898 I heard that President McKinley was likely to visit Atlanta, Georgia, for the purpose of taking part in the Peace Jubilee exercises to be held there to commemorate the successful close of the Spanish-American war. At this time I had been hard at work, together with our teachers, for eighteen years, trying to build up a school that we thought would be of service to the Nation, and I determined to make a direct effort to secure a visit from the President and his Cabinet. I went to Washington, and I was not long in the city before I found my way to the White House. When I got there I found the waiting rooms full of people, and my heart began to sink, for I feared there would not be much chance of my seeing the President that day, if at all. But, at any rate, I got an opportunity to see Mr. J. Addison Porter, the secretary to the President, and explained to him my mission. Mr. Porter kindly sent my card directly to the President, and in a few minutes word came from Mr. McKinley that he would see me.

How any man can see so many people of all kinds, with all kinds of errands, and do so much hard work, and still keep himself calm, patient, and fresh for each visitor in the way that President McKinley does, I cannot understand. When I saw the President he kindly thanked me for the work which we were doing at Tuskegee for the interests of the country. I then told him, briefly, the object of my visit. I impressed upon him the fact that a visit from the Chief Executive of the Nation would not only encourage our students and teachers, but would help the entire race. He seemed interested, but did not make a promise to go to Tuskegee, for the reason that his plans about going to Atlanta were not then fully made; but he asked me to call the matter to his attention a few weeks later.

By the middle of the following month the President had definitely decided to attend the Peace Jubilee at Atlanta. I went to Washington again and saw him, with a view of getting him to extend his trip to Tuskegee. On this second visit Mr. Charles W. Hare, a prominent white citizen of Tuskegee, kindly volunteered to accompany me, to reinforce my invitation with one from the white people of Tuskegee and the vicinity.

Just previous to my going to Washington the second time, the country had been excited, and the colored people greatly depressed, because of several severe race riots which had occurred at different points in the South. As soon as I saw the President, I perceived that his heart was greatly burdened by reason of these race disturbances. Although there were many people waiting to see him, he detained me for some time, discussing the condition and prospects of the race. He remarked several times that he was determined to show his interest and faith in the race, not merely in words, but by acts. When I told him that I thought that at that time scarcely anything would go farther in giving hope and encouragement to the race than the fact that the President of the Nation would be willing to travel one hundred and forty miles out of his way to spend a day at a Negro institution, he seemed deeply impressed.

While I was with the President, a white citizen of Atlanta, a Democrat and an ex-slave-holder, came into the room, and the President asked his opinion as to the wisdom of his going to Tuskegee. Without hesitation the Atlanta man replied that it was the proper thing for him to do. This opinion was reinforced by that friend of the race, Dr. J. L. M. Curry. The President promised that he would visit our school on the 16th of December.

When it became known that the President was going to visit our school, the white citizens of the town of Tuskegee—a mile distant from the school—were as much pleased as were our students and teachers. The white people of the town, including both men and women, began arranging to decorate the town, and to form themselves into committees for the purpose of cooperating with the officers of our school in order that the distinguished visitor might have a fitting reception. I think I never realized before this how much the white people of Tuskegee and vicinity thought of our institution. During the days when we were preparing for the President's reception, dozens of these people came to me and said that, while they did not want to push themselves into prominence, if there was anything they could do to help, or to relieve me personally, I had but to intimate it and they would be only too glad to assist. In fact, the thing that touched me almost as deeply as the visit of the President itself was the deep pride which all classes of citizens in Alabama seemed to take in our work.

The morning of December 16th brought to the little city of Tuskegee such a crowd as it had never seen before. With the President came Mrs. McKinley and all of the Cabinet officers but one; and most of them brought their wives or some members of their families. Several prominent generals came, including General Shafter and General Joseph Wheeler, who were recently returned from the Spanish-American war. There was also a host of newspaper correspondents. The Alabama Legislature was in session at Montgomery at this time. This body passed a resolution to adjourn for the purpose of visiting Tuskegee. Just before the arrival of the President's party the Legislature arrived, headed by the governor and other state officials.

The citizens of Tuskegee had decorated the town from the station to the school in a generous manner. In order to economize in the matter of time, we arranged to have the whole school pass in review before the President. Each student carried a stalk of sugar-cane with some open bolls of cotton fastened to the end of it. Following the students the work of all departments of the school passed in review, displayed on "floats" drawn by horses, mules, and oxen. On these floats we tried to exhibit not only the present work of the school, but to show the contrasts between the old methods of doing things and the new. As an example, we showed the old method of dairying in contrast with the improved methods, the old methods of tilling the soil in contrast with the new, the old methods of cooking and house-keeping in contrast with the new. These floats consumed an hour and a half of time in passing.

In his address in our large, new chapel, which the students had recently completed, the President said, among other things: -

To meet you under such pleasant auspices and to have the opportunity of a personal observation of your work is indeed most gratifying. The Tuskegee Normal and Industrial Institute is ideal in its conception, and has already a large and growing reputation in the country, and is not unknown abroad. I congratulate all who are associated in this under-taking for the good work which it is doing in the education of its students to lead lives of honor and usefulness, thus exalting the race for which it was established.

Nowhere, I think, could a more delightful location have been chosen for this unique educational experiment, which has attracted the attention and won the support even of conservative philanthropists in all sections of the country.

To speak of Tuskegee without paying special tribute to Booker T. Washington's genius and perseverance would be impossible. The inception of this noble enterprise was his, and he deserves high credit for it. His was the enthusiasm and enterprise which made its steady progress possible and established in the institution its present high standard of accom-plishment. He has won a worthy reputation as one of the great leaders of his race, widely known and much respected at home and abroad as an accomplished educator, a great orator, and a true philanthropist.

The Hon. John D. Long, the Secretary of the Navy, said in part: -

I cannot make a speech to-day. My heart is too full—full of hope, admiration, and pride for my countrymen of both sections and both colors. I am filled with gratitude and admiration for your work, and from this time forward I shall have absolute confidence in your progress and in the solution of the problem in which you are engaged.

The problem, I say, has been solved. A picture has been presented to-day which should be put upon canvas with the pictures of Washington and Lincoln, and transmitted to future time and generations—a picture which the press of the country should spread broadcast over the land, a most dramatic picture, and that picture is this: The President of the United States standing on this platform; on one side the Governor of Alabama, on the other, completing the trinity, a representative of a race only a few years ago in bondage, the colored President of the Tuskegee Normal and Industrial Institute.

God bless the President under whose majesty such a scene as that is presented to the American people. God bless the state of Alabama, which is showing that it can deal with this problem for itself. God bless the orator, philanthropist, and disciple of the Great Master— who, if he were on earth, would be doing the same work—Booker T. Washington.

Postmaster General Smith closed the address which he made with these words:

We have witnessed many spectacles within the last few days. We have seen the magnificent grandeur and the magnificent achievements of one of the great metropolitan cities of the South. We have seen heroes of the war pass by in procession. We have seen floral parades. But I am sure my colleagues will agree with me in saying that we have witnessed no spectacle more impressive and more encouraging, more inspiring for our future, than that which we have witnessed here this morning.

Some days after the President returned to Washington I received the letter which follows: -

Executive Mansion, Washington, Dec. 23, 1899.
Dear Sir:
By this mail I take pleasure in sending you engrossed copies of the souvenir of the visit of the President to your institution. These sheets bear the autographs of the President and the members of the Cabinet who accompanied him on the trip. Let me take this opportunity of congratulating you most heartily and sincerely upon the great success of the exercises provided for and entertainment furnished us under your auspices during our visit to Tuskegee. Every feature of the program was perfectly executed and was viewed or participated in with the heartiest satisfaction by every visitor present. The unique exhibition which you gave of your pupils engaged in their industrial vocations was not only artistic but thoroughly impressive. The tribute paid by the President and his Cabinet to your work was none too high, and forms a most encouraging augury, I think, for the future prosperity of your institution. I cannot close

without assuring you that the modesty shown by yourself in the exercises was most favorably commented upon by all the members of our party.

With best wishes for the continued advance of your most useful and patriotic undertaking, kind personal regards, and the compliments of the season, believe me, always,

Very sincerely yours,

John Addison Porter,

Secretary to the President.

Twenty years have now passed since I made the first humble effort at Tuskegee, in a broken-down shanty and an old hen-house, without owning a dollar's worth of property, and with but one teacher and thirty students. At the present time the institution owns twenty-three hundred acres of land, one thousand of which are under cultivation each year, entirely by student labor. There are now upon the grounds, counting large and small, sixty-six buildings; and all except four of these have been almost wholly erected by the labor of our students. While the students are at work upon the land and in erecting buildings, they are taught, by competent instructors, the latest methods of agriculture and the trades connected with building.

There are in constant operation at the school, in connection with thorough academic and religious training, thirty industrial departments. All of these teach industries at which our men and women can find immediate employment as soon as they leave the institution. The only difficulty now is that the demand for our graduates from both white and black people in the South is so great that we cannot supply more than one-half the persons for whom applications come to us. Neither have we the buildings nor the money for current expenses to enable us to admit to the school more than one-half the young men and women who apply to us for admission.

In our industrial teaching we keep three things in mind: first, that the student shall be so educated that he shall be enabled to meet conditions as they exist now, in the part of the South where he lives—in a word, to be able to do the thing which the world wants done; second, that every student who graduates from the school shall have enough skill coupled with intelligence and moral character, to enable him to make a living for himself and others; third, to send every graduate out feeling and knowing that labor is dignified and beautiful— to make each one love labor instead of trying to escape it. In addition to the agricultural training which we give to young men, and the training given to our girls in all the usual domestic employments, we now train a number of girls in agriculture each year. These girls are taught gardening, fruit-growing, dairying, bee-culture, and poultry-raising.

While the institution is in no sense denominational, we have a department known as the Phelps Hall Bible Training School, in which a number of students are prepared for the ministry and other forms of Christian work, especially work in the country districts. What is equally important, each one of these students works half of each day at some industry, in order to get skill and the love of work, so that when he goes out from the institution he is prepared to set the people with whom he goes to labor a proper example in the matter of industry.

The value of our property is now over $700,000. If we add to this our endowment fund, which at present is $1,000,000, the value of the total property is now $1,700,000. Aside from the need for more buildings and for money for current expenses, the endowment fund should be increased to at least $3,000,000. The annual current expenses are now about $150,000. The greater part of this I collect each year by going from door to door and from house to house. All of our property is free from mortgage, and is deeded to an undenominational board of trustees who have the control of the institution.

From thirty students the number has grown to fourteen hundred, coming from twenty-seven states and territories, from Africa, Cuba, Porto Rico, Jamaica, and other foreign countries. In our departments there are one hundred and ten officers and instructors; and if we add the families of our instructors, we have a constant population upon our grounds of not far from seventeen hundred people.

I have often been asked how we keep so large a body of people together, and at the same time keep them out of mischief. There are two answers: that the men and women who come to us for an education are in earnest; and that everybody is kept busy. The following outline of our daily work will testify to this: -

5 A.M., rising bell; 5.50 A.M., warning breakfast bell; 6 A.M., breakfast bell; 6.20 A.M., breakfast over; 6.20 to 6.50 A.M., rooms are cleaned; 6.50, work bell; 7.30, morning study hour; 8.20, morning school bell; 8.25, inspection of young men's toilet in ranks; 8.40, devotional exercises in chapel; 8.55, "five minutes with the daily news;" 9 A.M., class work begins; 12, class work closes; 12.15 P.M., dinner; 1 P.M., work bell; 1.30 P.M., class work begins; 3.30 P.M., class work ends; 5.30 P.M., bell to "knock off" work; 6 P.M., supper; 7.10 P.M., evening prayers; 7.30 P.M., evening study hour; 8.45 P.M., evening study hour closes; 9.20 P.M., warning retiring bell; 9.30 P.M., retiring bell.

We try to keep constantly in mind the fact that the worth of the school is to be judged by its graduates. Counting those who have finished the full course, together with those who have taken enough training to enable them to do reasonably good work, we can safely say that at least six thousand men and women from Tuskegee are now at work in different parts of the South; men and women who, by their own example or by direct effort, are showing the masses of our race how to improve their material, educational, and moral and religious life. What is equally important, they are exhibiting a degree of common sense and self-control which is causing better relations to exist between the races, and is causing the Southern white man to learn to believe in the value of educating the men and women of my race. Aside from this, there is the influence that is constantly being exerted through the mothers' meeting and the plantation work conducted by Mrs. Washington.

Wherever our graduates go, the changes which soon begin to appear in the buying of land, improving homes, saving money, in education, and in high moral character are remarkable. Whole communities are fast being revolutionized through the instrumentality of these men and women.

Ten years ago I organized at Tuskegee the first Negro Conference. This is an annual gathering which now brings to the school eight or nine hundred representative men and women of the race, who come to spend a day in finding out what the actual industrial, mental, and moral conditions of the people are, and in forming plans for improvement. Out from this central Negro Conference at Tuskegee have grown numerous state and local conferences which are doing the same kind of work. As a result of the influence of these gatherings, one delegate reported at the last annual meeting that ten families in his community had bought and paid for homes. On the day following the annual Negro Conference, there is held the "Workers' Conference." This is composed of officers and teachers who are engaged in educational work in the larger institutions in the South. The Negro Conference furnishes a rare opportunity for these workers to study the real condition of the rank and file of the people.

In the summer of 1900, with the assistance of such prominent colored men as Mr. T. Thomas Fortune, who has always upheld my hands in every effort, I organized the National Negro Business League, which held its first meeting in Boston, and brought together for the first time a large number of the colored men who are engaged in various lines of trade or business in different parts of the United States. Thirty states were represented at our first meeting. Out of this national meeting grew state and local business leagues.

In addition to looking after the executive side of the work at Tuskegee, and raising the greater part of the money for the support of the school, I cannot seem to escape the duty of answering at least a part of the calls which come to me unsought to address Southern white audiences and audiences of my own race, as well as frequent gatherings in the North. As to how much of my time is spent in this way, the following clipping from a Buffalo (N.Y.) paper will tell. This has reference to an occasion when I spoke before the National Educational Association in that city.

Booker T. Washington, the foremost educator among the colored people of the world, was a very busy man from the time he arrived in the city the other night from the West and registered at the Iroquois. He had hardly removed the stains of travel when it was time to partake of supper. Then he held a public levee in the parlors of the Iroquois until eight o'clock. During that time he was greeted by over two hundred eminent teachers and educators from all parts of the United States. Shortly after eight o'clock he was driven in a carriage to Music Hall, and in one hour and a half he made two ringing addresses, to as many as five thousand people, on Negro education. Then Mr. Washington was taken in charge by a delegation of colored citizens, headed by the Rev. Mr. Watkins, and hustled off to a small informal reception, arranged in honor of the visitor by the people of his race.

Nor can I, in addition to making these addresses, escape the duty of calling the attention of the South and of the country in general, through the medium of the press, to matters that pertain to the interests of both races. This, for example, I have done in regard to the evil habit of lynching. When the Louisiana State Constitutional Convention was in session, I wrote an open letter to that body pleading for justice for the race. In all such efforts I have received warm and hearty support from the Southern newspapers, as well as from those in all other parts of the country.

Despite superficial and temporary signs which might lead one to entertain a contrary opinion, there was never a time when I felt more hopeful for the race than I do at the present. The great human law that in the end recognizes and rewards merit is everlasting and universal. The outside world does not know, neither can it appreciate, the struggle that is constantly going on in the hearts of both the Southern white people and their former slaves to free themselves from racial prejudice; and while both races are thus struggling they should have the sympathy, the support, and the forbearance of the rest of the world.

As I write the closing words of this autobiography I find myself—not by design—in the city of Richmond, Virginia: the city which only a few decades ago was the capital of the Southern Confederacy, and where, about twenty-five years ago, because of my poverty I slept night after night under a sidewalk.

This time I am in Richmond as the guest of the colored people of the city; and came at their request to deliver an address last night to both races in the Academy of Music, the largest and finest audience room in the city. This was the first time that the colored people had ever been permitted to use this hall. The day before I came, the City Council passed a vote to attend the meeting in a body to hear me speak. The state Legislature, including the House of Delegates and the Senate, also passed a unanimous vote to attend in a body. In the presence of hundreds of colored people, many distinguished white citizens, the City Council, the state Legislature, and state officials, I delivered my message, which was one of hope and cheer; and from the bottom of my heart I thanked both races for this welcome back to the state that gave me birth.

Booker T. Washington

The Awakening of the Negro

When a mere boy, I saw a young colored man, who had spent several years in school, sitting in a common cabin in the South, studying a French grammar. I noted the poverty, the untidiness, the want of system and thrift, that existed about the cabin, notwithstanding his knowledge of French and other academic subjects. Another time, when riding on the outer edges of a town in the South, I heard the sound of a piano coming from a cabin of the same kind. Contriving some excuse, I entered, and began a conversation with the young colored woman who was playing, and who had recently returned from a boarding-school, where she had been studying instrumental music among other things. Despite the fact that her parents were living in a rented cabin, eating poorly cooked food, surrounded with poverty, and having almost none of the conveniences of life, she had persuaded them to rent a piano for four or five dollars per month. Many such instances as these, in connection with my own struggles, impressed upon me the importance of making a study of our needs as a race, and applying the remedy accordingly.

Some one may be tempted to ask, Has not the Negro boy or girl as good a right to study a French grammar and instrumental music as the white youth? I answer, Yes, but in the present condition of the Negro race in this country there is need of something more. Perhaps I may be forgiven for the seeming egotism if I mention the expansion of my own life partly as an example of what I mean. My earliest recollection is of a small one-room log hut on a large slave plantation in Virginia. After the close of the war, while working in the coal-mines of West Virginia for the support of my mother, I heart in some accidental way of the Hampton Institute. When I learned that it was an institution where a black boy could study, could have a chance to work for his board, and at the same time be taught how to work and to realize the dignity of labor, I resolved to go there. Bidding my mother good-by, I started out one morning to find my way to Hampton, though I was almost penniless and had no definite idea where Hampton was. By walking, begging rides, and paying for a portion of the journey on the steam-cars, I finally succeeded in reaching the city of Richmond, Virginia. I was without money or friends. I slept under a sidewalk, and by working on a vessel next day I earned money to continue my way to the institute, where I arrived with a surplus of fifty cents. At Hampton I found the opportunity—in the way of buildings, teachers, and industries provided by the generous—to get training in the class-room and by practical touch with industrial life, to learn thrift, economy, and push. I was surrounded by an atmosphere of business, Christian influence, and a spirit of self-help that seemed to have awakened every faculty in me, and caused me for the first time to realize what it meant to be a man instead of a piece of property.

While there I resolved that when I had finished the course of training I would go into the far South, into the Black Belt of the South, and give my life to providing the same kind of opportunity for self-reliance and self-awakening that I had found provided for me at Hampton. My work began at Tuskegee, Alabama, in 1881, in a small shanty and church, with one teacher and thirty students, without a dollar's worth of property. The spirit of work and of industrial thrift, with aid from the State and generosity from the North, has enabled us to develop an institution of eight hundred students gathered from nineteen States, with seventy-nine instructors, fourteen hundred acres of land, and thirty buildings, including large and small; in all, property valued at $280,000. Twenty-five industries have been organized, and the whole work is carried on at an annual cost of about $80,000 in cash; two fifths of the annual expense so far has gone into permanent plant.

What is the object of all this outlay? First, it must be borne in mind that we have in the South a peculiar and unprecedented state of things. It is of the utmost importance that our energy be given to meeting conditions that exist right about us rather than conditions that existed centuries ago or that exist in countries a thousand miles away. What are the cardinal needs among the seven millions of colored people in the South, most of whom are to be found on the plantations? Roughly, these needs may be stated as food, clothing, shelter, education, proper habits, and a settlement of race relations. The seven millions of colored people of the South cannot be reached directly by any missionary agency, but they can be reached by sending out among them strong selected young men and women, with the proper training of head, hand, and heart, who will live among these masses and show them how to lift themselves up.

The problem that the Tuskegee Institute keeps before itself constantly is how to prepare these leaders. From the outset, in connection with religious and academic training, it has emphasized industrial or hand training as a means of finding the way out of present condi-tions. First, we have found the industrial teaching useful in giving the student a chance to work out a portion of his expenses while in school. Second, the school furnishes labor that has an economic value, and at the same time gives the student a chance to acquire knowledge and skill while performing the labor. Most of all, we find the industrial system valuable in teaching economy, thrift, and the dignity of labor, and in giving moral backbone to students. The fact that a student goes out into the world conscious of his power to build a house or a wagon, or to make a harness, gives him a certain confidence and moral independence that he would not possess without such training.

A more detailed example of our methods at Tuskegee may be of interest. For example, we cultivate by student labor six hundred and fifty acres of land. The object is not only to cultivate the land in a way to make it pay our boarding department, but at the same time to teach the students, in addition to the practical work, something of the chemistry of the soil, the best methods of drainage, dairying, the cultivation of fruit, the care of livestock and tools, and scores of other lessons needed by a people whose main dependence is on agriculture. Notwithstanding that eighty-five per cent of the colored people in the South live by agriculture in some form, aside from what has been done by Hampton, Tuskegee, and one or two other institutions practically nothing has been attempted in the direction of teaching them about the very industry from which the masses of our people must get their subsistence. Friends have recently provided means for the erection of a large new chapel at Tuskegee. Our students have made the bricks for this chapel. A large part of the timber is sawed by students at our own sawmill, the plans are drawn by our teacher of architecture and mechanical drawing, and students do the brick-masonry, plastering, painting, carpentry work, tinning, slating, and make most of the furniture. Practically, the whole chapel will be built and furnished by student labor; in the end the school will have the building for permanent use, and the students will have a knowledge of the trades employed in its construction. In this way all but three of the thirty buildings on the grounds have been erected. While the young men do the kinds of work I have mentioned, the young women to a large extent make, mend, and launder the clothing of the young men, and thus are taught important industries.

One of the objections sometimes urged against industrial education for the Negro is that it aims merely to teach him to work on the same plan that he was made to follow when in slavery. This is far from being the object at Tuskegee. At the head of each of the twenty-five industrial departments we have an intelligent and competent instructor, just as we have in our history classes, so that the student is taught not only practical brick-masonry, for example, but also the underlying principles of that industry, the mathematics and the mechanical and architectural drawing. Or he is taught how to become master of the forces of nature so that, instead of cultivating corn in the old way, he can use a corn cultivator, that lays off the furrows, drops the corn into them, and covers it, and in this way he can do more work than three men by the old process of corn-planting; at the same time much of the toil is eliminated and labor is dignified. In a word, the constant aim is to show the student how to put brains into every process of labor; how to bring his knowledge of mathematics and the sciences into farming, carpentry, forging, foundry work; how to dispense as soon as possible with the old form of ante-bellum labor. In the erection of the chapel just referred to, instead of letting the money which was given us go into outside hands, we make it accomplish three objects: first, it provides the chapel; second, it gives the students a chance to get a practical knowledge of the trades connected with building; and third, it enables them to earn something toward the payment of board while receiving academic and industrial training.

Having been fortified at Tuskegee by education of mind, skill of hand, Christian character, ideas of thrift, economy, and push, and a spirit of independence, the student is sent out to become a center of influence and light in showing the masses of our people in the Black Belt of the South how to lift themselves up. How can this be done? I give but one or two examples. Ten years ago a young colored man came to the institute from one of the large plantation districts; he studied in the class-room a portion of the time, and received practical and theoretical training on the farm the remainder of the time. Having finished his course at Tuskegee, he returned to his plantation home, which was in a county where the colored people outnumber the whites six to one, as is true of many of the counties in the Black Belt of the South. He found the Negroes in debt. Ever since the war they had been mortgaging their crops for the food on which to live while the crops were growing. The majority of them were living from hand to mouth on rented land, in small, one-room log cabins, and attempting to pay a rate of interest on their advances that ranged from fifteen to forty per cent per annum. The school had been taught in a wreck of a log cabin, with no apparatus, and had never been in session longer than three months out of twelve. With as many as eight or ten persons of all ages and conditions and of both sexes huddled together in one cabin year after year, and with a minister whose only aim was to work upon the emotions of the people, one can imagine something of the moral and religious state of the community.

But the remedy. In spite of the evil, the Negro got the habit of work from slavery. The rank and file of the race, especially those on the Southern plantations, work hard, but the trouble is, what they earn gets away from them in high rents, crop mortgages, whiskey, snuff, cheap jewelry, and the like. The young man just referred to had been trained at Tuskegee, as most of our graduates are, to meet just this condition of things. He took the three months' public school as a nucleus for his work. Then he organized the older people into a club, or conference, that held meetings every week. In these meetings he taught the people in a plain, simple manner how to save their money, how to farm in a better way, how to sacrifice,—to live on bread and potatoes, if need be, till they could get out of debt, and begin the buying of lands.

Soon a large proportion of the people were in condition to make contracts for the buying of homes (land is very cheap in the South), and to live without mortgaging their crops. Not only this: under the guidance and leadership of this teacher, the first year that he was among them they learned how, by contributions in money and labor, to build a neat, comfortable schoolhouse that replaced the wreck of a log cabin formerly used. The following year the weekly meetings were continued, and two months were added to the original three months of school. The next year two more months were added. The improvement has gone on, until now these people have every year an eight months' school.

I wish my readers could have the chance that I have had of going into this community. I wish they could look into the faces of the people and see them beaming with hope and delight. I wish they could see the two or three room cottages that have taken the place of the usual one-room cabin, the well-cultivated farms, and the religious life of the people that now means something more than the name. The teacher has a good cottage and a well-kept farm that serve as models. In a word, a complete revolution has been wrought in the industrial, educational, and religious life of this whole community by reason of the fact that they have had this leader, this guide and object-lesson, to show them how to take the money and effort that had hitherto been scattered to the wind in mortgages and high rents, in whiskey and gewgaws, and concentrate them in the direction of their own uplifting. One community on its feet presents an object-lesson for the adjoining communities, and soon improvements show themselves in other places.

Another student who received academic and industrial training at Tuskegee established himself, three years ago, as a blacksmith and wheelwright in a community, and, in addition to the influence of his successful business enterprise, he is fast making the same kind of changes in the life of the people about him that I have just recounted. It would be easy for me to fill many pages describing the influence of the Tuskegee graduates in every part of the South. We keep it constantly in the minds of our students and graduates that the industrial or material condition of the masses of our people must be improved, as well as the intellectual, before there can be any permanent change in their moral and religious life. We find it a pretty hard thing to make a good Christian of a hungry man. No matter how much our people "get happy" and "shout" in church, if they go home at night from church hungry, they are tempted to find something before morning. This is a principle of human nature, and is not confined to the Negro.

The Negro has within him immense power for self-uplifting, but for years it will be necessary to guide and stimulate him. The recognition of this power led us to organize, five years ago, what is now known as the Tuskegee Negro Conference,—a gathering that meets every February, and is composed of about eight hundred representative colored men and women from all sections of the Black Belt. They come in ox-carts, mule-carts, buggies, on muleback and horseback, on foot, by railroad: some traveling all night in order to be present. The matters considered at the conferences are those that the colored people have it within their own power to control: such as the evils of the mortgage system, the one-room cabin, buying on credit, the importance of owning a home and of putting money in the bank, how to build schoolhouses and prolong the school term, and how to improve their moral and religious condition.

As a single example of the results, one delegate reported that since the conferences were started five years ago eleven people in his neighborhood had bought homes, fourteen had got out of debt, and a number had stopped mortgaging their crops. Moreover, a schoolhouse had been built by the people themselves, and the school term had been extended from three to six months; and with a look of triumph he exclaimed, "We is done stopped libin' in de ashes!"

Besides this Negro Conference for the masses of the people, we now have a gathering at the same time known as the Workers' Conference, composed of the officers and instructors in the leading colored schools of the South. After listening to the story of the conditions and needs from the people themselves, the Workers' Conference finds much food for thought and discussion.

Nothing else so soon brings about right relations between the two races in the South as the industrial progress of the Negro. Friction between the races will pass away in proportion as the black man, by reason of his skill, intelligence, and character, can produce something that the white man wants or respects in the commercial world. This is another reason why at Tuskegee we push the industrial training. We find that as every year we put into a Southern community colored men who can start a brick-yard, a sawmill, a tin-shop, or a printing-office,—men who produce something that makes the white man partly dependent upon the Negro, instead of all the dependence being on the other side,—a change takes place in the relations of the races.

Let us go on for a few more years knitting our business and industrial relations into those of the white man, till a black man gets a mortgage on a white man's house that he can foreclose at will. The white man on whose house the mortgage rests will not try to prevent that Negro from voting when he goes to the polls. It is through the dairy farm, the truck garden, the trades, and commercial life, largely, that the Negro is to find his way to the enjoyment of all his rights. Whether he will or not, a white man respects a Negro who owns a two-story brick house.

What is the permanent value of the Tuskegee system of training to the South in a broader sense? In connection with this, it is well to bear in mind that slavery taught the white man that labor with the hands was something fit for the Negro only, and something for the white man to come into contact with just as little as possible. It is true that there was a large class of poor white people who labored with the hands, but they did it because they were not able to secure Negroes to work for them; and these poor whites were constantly trying to imitate the slave-holding class in escaping labor, and they too regarded it as anything but elevating. The Negro in turn looked down upon the poor whites with a certain contempt because they had to work. The Negro, it is to be borne in mind, worked under constant protest, because he felt that his labor was being unjustly required, and he spent almost as much effort in planning how to escape work as in learning how to work. Labor with him was a badge of degradation. The white man was held up before him as the highest type of civilization, but the Negro noted that this highest type of civilization himself did no labor; hence he argued that the less work he did, the more nearly he would be like a white man. Then, in addition to these influences, the slave system discouraged labor-saving machinery. To use labor-saving machinery intelligence was required, and intelligence and slavery were not on friendly terms; hence the Negro always associated labor with toil, drudgery, something to be escaped. When the Negro first became free, his idea of education was that it was something that would soon put him in the same position as regards work that his recent master had occupied. Out of these conditions grew the Southern habit of putting off till to-morrow and the day after the duty that should be done promptly to-day. The leaky house was not repaired while the sun shone, for then the rain did not come through. While the rain was falling, no one cared to expose himself to stop the leak. The plough, on the same principle, was left where the last furrow was run, to rot and rust in the field during the winter. There was no need to repair the wooden chimney that was exposed to the fire, because water could be thrown on it when it was on fire. There was no need to trouble about the payment of a debt to-day, for it could just as well be paid next week or next year. Besides these conditions, the whole South, at the close of the war, was without proper food, clothing, and shelter,—was in need of habits of thrift and economy and of something laid up for a rainy day.

To me it seemed perfectly plain that here was a condition of things that could not be met by the ordinary process of education. At Tuskegee we became convinced that the thing to do was to make a careful systematic study of the condition and needs of the South, especially the Black Belt, and to bend our efforts in the direction of meeting these needs, whether we were following a well-beaten track, or were hewing out a new path to meet conditions probably without a parallel in the world. After fourteen years of experience and observation, what is the result? Gradually but surely, we find that all through the South the disposition to look upon labor as a disgrace is on the wane, and the parents who themselves sought to escape work are so anxious to give their children training in intelligent labor that every institution which gives training in the handicrafts is crowded, and many (among them Tuskegee) have to refuse admission to hundreds of applicants. The influence of the Tuskegee system is shown again by the fact that almost every little school at the remotest cross-roads is anxious to be known as an industrial school, or, as some of the colored people call it, an "industrus" school.

The social lines that were once sharply drawn between those who labored with the hand and those who did not are disappearing. Those who formerly sought to escape labor, now when they see that brains and skill rob labor of the toil and drudgery once associated with it, instead of trying to avoid it are willing to pay to be taught how to engage in it. The South is beginning to see labor raised up, dignified and beautified, and in this sees its salvation. In proportion as the love of labor grows, the large idle class which has long been one of the curses of the South disappears. As its members become absorbed in occupations, they have less time to attend to everybody else's business, and more time for their own.

The South is still an undeveloped and unsettled country, and for the next half century and more the greater part of the energy of the masses will be needed to develop its material opportunities. Any force that brings the rank and file of the people to a greater love of industry is therefore especially valuable. This result industrial education is surely bringing about. It stimulates production and increases trade,—trade between the races,—and in this new and engrossing relation both forget the past. The white man respects the vote of the colored man who does $10,000 worth of business, and the more business the colored man has, the more careful he is how he votes.

Immediately after the war, there was a large class of Southern people who feared that the opening of the free schools to the freedmen and the poor whites—the education of the head alone—would result merely in increasing the class who sought to escape labor, and that the South would soon be overrun by the idle and vicious. But as the results of industrial combined with academic training begin to show themselves in hundreds of communities that have been lifted up through the medium of the Tuskegee system, these former prejudices against education are being removed. Many of those who a few years ago opposed general education are now among its warmest advocates.

This industrial training, emphasizing as it does the idea of economic production, is gradually bringing the South to the point where it is feeding itself. Before the war, and long after it, the South made what little profit was received from the cotton crop, and sent its earnings out of the South to purchase food supplies,—meat, bread, canned vegetables, and the like; but the improved methods of agriculture are fast changing this habit. With the newer methods of labor, which teach promptness and system, and emphasize the worth of the beautiful,—the moral value of the well-painted house, and the fence with every paling and nail in its place,—we are bringing to bear upon the South an influence that is making it a new country in industry, education, and religion.

Booker T. Washington, Atlantic Monthly, *(1896)*

THE ABSTRACT OF PRINCIPLES, 1858

Introduction

The Abstract of Principles is the first official confession of Faith which Southern Baptists endorsed. When the original charter of the Southern Baptist Theological Seminary was adopted in 1858 it contained the following statement which continues as a part of the "fundamental laws."

"Every professor of the institution shall be a member of a regular Baptist Church; and all persons accepting professorships in this Seminary shall be considered, by such acceptance, as engaging to teach in accordance with, and not contrary to, the Abstract of Principles hereinafter laid down, a departure from which principles on his part shall be grounds for his resignation or removal by the Trustees."

The Abstract of Principles

I. The Scriptures.

The Scriptures of the Old and New Testament were given by inspiration of God, and are the only sufficient, certain and authoritative rule of all saving knowledge, faith and obedience.

II. God.

There is but one God, the Maker, Preserver and Ruler of all things, having in and of himself, all perfections, and being infinite in them all; and to Him all creatures owe the highest love, reverence and obedience.

III. The Trinity.

God is revealed to us as Father, Son and Holy Spirit each with distinct personal attributes, but without division of nature, essence or being.

IV. Providence.

God from eternity, decrees or permits all things that come to pass, and perpetually upholds, directs and governs all creatures and all events; yet so as not to destroy the free will and responsibility of intelligent creatures.

V. Election.

Election is God's eternal choice of some persons unto everlasting life—not because of foreseen merit in them, but of his mere mercy in Christ—in consequence of which choice they are called, justified and glorified.

VI. The Fall of Man.

God originally created man in His own image, and free from sin; but, through the temptation of Satan, he transgressed the command of God, and fell from his original holiness and righteousness; whereby his posterity inherit a nature corrupt and wholly opposed to God and His law, are under condemnation, and as soon as they are capable of moral action, become actual transgressors.

VII. The Mediator.
Jesus Christ, the only begotten Son of God, is the divinely appointed mediator between God and man. Having taken upon Himself human nature, yet without sin, He perfectly fulfilled the Law, suffered and died upon the cross for the salvation of sinners. He was buried, and rose again the third day, and ascended to His Father, at whose hand He ever liveth to make intercession for His people. He is the only Mediator, the Prophet, Priest and King of the Church, and Sovereign of the Universe.

VIII. Regeneration.
Regeneration is a change of heart, wrought by the Holy Spirit, who quickeneth the dead in trespasses and sins enlightening their minds spiritually and savingly to understand the Word of God, and renewing their whole nature, so that they love and practice holiness. It is a work of God's free and special grace alone.

IX. Repentance.
Repentance is an evangelical grace, wherein a person being, by the Holy Spirit, made sensible of the manifold evil of his sin, humbleth himself for it, with godly sorrow, detestation of it, and self-abhorrence, with a purpose and endeavor to walk before God so as to please Him in all things.

X. Faith.
Saving faith is the belief, on God's authority, of whatsoever is revealed in His Word concerning Christ; accepting and resting upon Him alone for justification and eternal life. It is wrought in the heart by the Holy Spirit, and is accompanied by all other saving graces, and leads to a life of holiness.

XI. Justification.
Justification is God's gracious and full acquittal of sinners, who believe in Christ, from all sin, through the satisfaction that Christ has made; not for anything wrought in them or done by them; but on account of the obedience and satisfaction of Christ, they receiving and resting on Him and His righteousness by faith.

XII. Sanctification.
Those who have been regenerated are also sanctified, by God's word and Spirit dwelling in them. This sanctification is progressive through the supply of Divine strength, which all saints seek to obtain, pressing after a heavenly life in cordial obedience to all Christ's commands.

XIII. Perseverance of the Saints.
Those whom God hath accepted in the Beloved, and sanctified by His Spirit, will never

totally nor finally fall away from the state of grace, but shall certainly persevere to the end; and though they may fall, through neglect and temptation, into sin, whereby they grieve the Spirit, impair their graces and comforts, bring reproach on the Church, and temporal judgments on themselves, yet they shall be renewed again unto repentance, and be kept by the power of God through faith unto salvation.

XIV. The Church.

The Lord Jesus is the Head of the Church, which is composed of all his true disciples, and in Him is invested supremely all power for its government. According to his commandment, Christians are to associate themselves into particular societies or churches; and to each of these churches he hath given needful authority for administering that order, discipline and worship which he hath appointed. The regular officers of a Church are Bishops, or Elders, and Deacons.

XV. Baptism.

Baptism is an ordinance of the Lord Jesus, obligatory upon every believer, wherein he is immersed in water in the name of the Father, and of the Son, and of the Holy Spirit, as a sign of his fellowship with the death and resurrection of Christ, of remission of sins, and of his giving himself up to God, to live and walk in newness of life. It is prerequisite to church fellowship, and to participation in the Lord's Supper.

XVI. The Lord's Supper.

The Lord's Supper is an ordinance of Jesus Christ, to be administered with the elements of bread and wine, and to be observed by his churches till the end of the world. It is in no sense a sacrifice, but is designed to commemorate his death, to confirm the faith and other graces of Christians, and to be a bond, pledge and renewal of their communion with him, and of their church fellowship.

XVII. The Lord's Day.

The Lord's Day is a Christian institution for regular observance, and should be employed in exercises of worship and spiritual devotion, both public and private, resting from worldly employments and amusements, works of necessity and mercy only excepted.

XVIII. Liberty of Conscience.

God alone is Lord of the conscience; and He hath left it free from the doctrines and commandments of men, which are in anything contrary to His word, or not contained in it. Civil magistrates being ordained of God, subjection in all lawful thing commanded by them ought to be yielded by us in the Lord, not only for wrath, but also for conscience sake.

XIX. The Resurrection.

The bodies of men after death return to dust, but their spirits return immediately to God— the righteous to rest with Him; the wicked to be reserved under darkness to the judgment. At the last day, the bodies of all the dead, both just and unjust, will be raised.

XX. The Judgment.

God hath appointed a day, wherein he will judge the world by Jesus Christ, when every one shall receive according to his deeds; the wicked shall go into everlasting punishment; the righteous, into everlasting life.

JOHN EDWARD BRUCE (1856-1924)

Introduction

John Edward Bruce, also known as Bruce Grit was a journalist, historian, writer, orator, and Pan African nationalist.

He was born in Piscataway, Maryland, to enslaved parents Robert and Martha Allen (Clark) Bruce. This self-educated man married Florence A. Bishop of Cleveland, Ohio on September 10, 1885.

In 1911 he founded the Negro Society for Historical Research in Yonkers, New York with Arthur Schomburg.

His belief in an independent national destiny led him in the period around 1919 to embrace Marcus Garvey's Pan African nationalism. As a member of Garvey's Universal Negro Improvement Association, he wrote for the movement's *Negro World* and the *Daily Negro Times*.

The Blood Red Record

A Review of the Horrible Lynchings and Burning of Negroes by Civilized White Men in the United States, 1901

> I tremble for my country when I remember that God is just.
> Thomas Jefferson.
> If you injure a harmless person, the evil will fall back upon you like light dust thrown against the Wind.
> Buddhist Proverb.

...

What shall we say of a nation of more than 76,000,000 people, with courts of law, school-houses on every hilltop, churches on almost every other corner in the cities, towns and villages of this great country, with a powerful and influential press, which goes into paroxysms when an American citizen is murdered in a foreign land—that quietly and complacently winks at the foul and disgraceful saturnalia of crime within their own borders, when the victim of these crimes are Negroes? What shall we say of the Christian ministers of the white race who seem to lack the moral courage to denounce from their pulpits this species of lawlessness and barbarism, which is no longer confined to the South—in obedience to a cowardly public sentiment which threatens their living and closes their mouths as tightly as though they were dumb men? What shall we say and think of those in authority in State and nation whose silence or apathy, or both, discovers a desire to compromise with law-breakers, whose next step will be the lynching and roasting of white men to save court expenses?

It would seem that we in this country are fast approaching the period when every man will again be a law unto himself, when hip-pockets will be made deeper and larger, when courts will be a superfluity and the law only a memory.

The blood-thirstiness of the white men of America, who lynch and roast Negroes at the stake, is the saddest imaginable commentary on the boasted civilization and humanity of the proud white race. A race that can quietly look on and see a human being, black or white, consigned to the deadly flames and writhe in agony and anguish for any crime, howsoever brutal or fiendish, is not far from barbarism.

It won't do to attempt to justify the crime of lynching by saying that the victim of the mob's fury was a "burly Negro brute."

The crime cannot be justified while white men, guilty of similar crimes against women, are given the benefit of the doubt and a trial by a jury of their peers.

Two wrongs have never yet made one right; justice was never yet evolved from passion, and vengeance is not justice. ...

An observant man cannot fail to see, if he looks about him, that prejudice against the Negro in the North results from friction—contact—where they comgregated in great numbers, and that while at the South its results, very largely from the fact that in freedom he has disappointed the prophets of evil—his late masters, who declared that he would relapse into barbarism, if left to himself, that he was indolent, shiftless, ignorant, and that his normal natural condition was subordination to the dominant race. The census of 1890 shows that this indolent, shiftless, ignorant Negro, after two hundred and forty-seven years of servitude to the crafty, industrious and intelligent Christian white men of the South who failed to impart to him any of their virtues of which they now boast, but who did inoculate him with all their vices—emerged from slavery almost as ignorant and as barbarous as when he was forced into it, and after thirty-eight years of freedom has done what the white race never could have done under like conditions. He has reduced his illiteracy forty per cent and accumulated property to the value of more than $199,000,000. He has done a great many more things, which are to his credit, and which we will not stop here to enumerate.

The great Wendell Phillips, in his lecture on the "Lost Arts," referring to the conceit of the average American says: "We seem to imagine that whether knowledge will die with us or not, it certainly began with us, We have a pitying estimate, a tender pity, for the narrowness, ignorance and darkness of by-gone ages. We seem to ourselves, not only to monopolize, but to have began the era of light. In other words, we are all running over with a fourth day of July spirit of self-content. I am often reminded of the German whom the English poet, Coleridge, met at Frankfort. He always took off his hat with profound respect when he ventured to speak of himself. It seems to me the American people might be painted in the chronic attitude of taking off its hat to itself."

"Prejudice against color," says Lewis, "never existed in Great Britain, France Spain, Portugal, the Italian States. Prussia, Austria, Russia or in any part of the world where colored person have not been held as slaves. Indeed, in many countries where multitudes of Africans and their descendants have been long held as slaves, no prejudice against color has ever existed. This is the case in Turkey, Brazil and Persia, In Brazil, where there were more than 2,000,000 slaves, some of the highest offices of State were filled by black men. Some of the most distinguished officers in the Brazilian army are Blacks and Mulattos." ...

Terrorism reigned throughout the South; intimidation and murder were common happenings, and, when after about 50,000 Negroes had been slaughtered by the thugs, bullies and midnight assassins who had received their baptism of freedom and been made citizens at the same time the Negro was—they raised the cry "no Negro domination ," and appealed to the passions and prejudices of the whites of the South to refuse to permit Negroes to vote, or if they voted to refuse to count their votes as cast. The Negro in the meantime resorted to every legitimate means to conserve his citizenship rights by appeal to the National Congress and the administration at Washington. Finding that Northern sentiment was favorable to the Negro and majority rule when legally constituted, the wily Southern diplomatists sent missionaries to the North who were eloquent and persuasive, who explained the situation at banquets gotten up in their honor and before bodies of learned men—students of sociology and thinkers, who thought great thoughts on the irrepressible problem, and who were content to swallow at one gulp the sublimated rot of these cunning and crafty word-mongers, who privately boasted of their ability to twist the gullible Yankee around their fingers and make him believe that the moon is made of green cheese and silver bullion. They told the Yankee that they had suckled at the breasts of black mammies," that they were the only white men on this continent who thoroughly understood and sympathized with the Negro; that the Negroes were lazy, shiftless, docile, faithful, the best laborers in the world and the best managed; that without them the South would soon become bankrupt. But they omitted to account in any satisfactory manner for the ignorance of the Negro; they did not tell the Yankee that it was necessary to keep him ignorant in order to control him and to make their thousands out of his unrequited labor. But, like the man out of whom Jesus cast the devils, they cried: "Let us alone." Let us manage the Negroes in our own way. There is a new South, and, if we are permitted to control it, it will again blossom as the rose, etc., etc. Democratic majorities increased in the South and Democratic mendacity and scoundrelism made themselves manifest wherever the Negro republican or the white republican attempted to exercise their constitutional rights. The latter was shot or lynched or burned at the stake; the former was ostracized socially and politically. Congressional investigation of these iniquities resulted in the formulation of a new charge against the Negro—that of rape—although in all the years of his servitude as a slave this charge was never brought against the Negro except in one or two instances, notably in North Carolina in 1835, when the Negro was not the guilty party, and in two other States of the South. The characteristics of a race are the result of growth—custom, habit. As a slave, the Negro was deferential, courteous, tractable, docile. The slavish feeling forbade his making advances to white women. The fear of the lash or the auction block made him the most circumspect domestic that ever obeyed an order. If there is anything in heredity, how comes it that the children and grandchildren of the Negroes of the ante-bellum period have developed in freedom the lustful passion for white women which our enemies now say is a distinctively Negro crime or characteristic? Who believes this libel uttered against the Negro? Of 117 Negroes lynched, shot or burned in 1900, only eighteen were charged or suspected of the crime of rape. We must look farther for the cause of lynching than that alleged against the Negro, for there is a deeper significance and meaning for all this deviltry than appears on the surface. There are about 12,000,000 Negroes in this country; necessarily there are some murderers among them, some ravishers of women, but not more of either class than among an equal number of whites. Criminals, black or white, should be punished, but punished by law. Lynch law is a vicious thing, and it has become so popular at the South that the North and West, not to be out-done, have imported the custom and are assisting the South to make this nation a disgrace in the eyes of the world.

History tells us that at a time when it was easily in the power of the Negroes to have massacred nearly every white person at the South they were kindly and obedient, even to those who had lashed them as slaves, and sold their wives and children into distant servitude. Did any one ever hear of a Negro raping a white woman during the four years' bloody war when the masters of the South were fighting to rivet the chains about the limbs of the faithful slaves who protected and fed their wives and children? No other race in the hour of its sudden freedom ever behaved with such magnanimity towards its former masters as ours did. The voice of history cannot be gainsaid. The facts it records cannot be rubbed out.

The antagonism to the Negro is political; primarily the demand for his disfranchisement proceeds from those who owe him most—the white man of the South. The conspiracy to thus blacken the character of the Negro by white men at the South may succeed, but its success will be followed by consequences more damaging to the white race in that section than it can now conceive of. The more they conspire against us, the more clearly and plainly will they discover to the world the malignity and malevolence which is at the bottom of their desperate and cowardly efforts to eliminate the Negro from participation in government and to reduce him to the condition of a political pariah in the government, which he, in common with the loyal white men of the Union, helped to make possible by his valor and his courage in every war of the Republic.

The charge of rape is exceedingly diaphanous when applied to the Negro as the cause of white opposition to him in those communities where he is most in evidence and most ambitious to enjoy, in common with white men, his constitutional rights and prerogatives. The bitterness engendered by the desire of the Negro to come into his rights as a citizen is responsible for many of the brutal crimes which impel "respectable white citizens," North and South, to commit the crime of lynching, thus trenching upon the power and authority of courts which the people of all races are taxed to maintain, in the belief that they are the bulwarks of our safety—the Palladium of our liberties.

William Penn, in his "Reflections and Maxims," thus tells us what he conceives justice to be. We commend it to the fiery and untamed barbarians, who, upon hearsay or suspicion, take that which they cannot give: "Believe nothing against another, but upon good authority; nor report what may hurt another, unless it be a greater hurt to others to conceal it."

We conclude these reflections by reproducing a letter written by Hon. W.E. Chandler, of New Hampshire:

United States Senate, Washington, D.C., April 30, 1888.
My Dear Mr. Bruce:
The Republican party can never abandon its efforts to enforce the fifteenth amendment. That was an outcome of the War for the Union and one of the terms of the

settlement made by the North with the South. To allow it to become permanently a dead-letter would be cowardly and disgraceful. A deliberate determination to surrender it would be the destruction of the Republican party.

There is an eclipse of faith just now in the minds of some Republicans. Our business men are indifferent to the sentiment of devotion to human rights, at least, where the persons concerned are black. But there will come, I am sure, a revival of fidelity and courage. The continued adherence of the colored men to the Republican party, which gave them liberty and suffrage, will necessitate the renewed championship by that party of the political equality of the proscribed race. The present unnatural and dangerous condition of affairs at the South, where the black man is deprived of his constitutional rights is a constant menace against the peace and prosperity of the white people. Justice and obedience to the Constitution can alone avert the danger. I think the colored as well as the white Republican at the South should keep up his courage and look for the coming of the morning.

Faithfully your friend,

W. E. Chander

The Republican party, we are told by this eminent authority, "can never abandon its efforts to enforce the fifteenth amendment." Well, if it hasn't abandoned it, it has, at least, suspended its efforts in that direction, and its indifference or apathy, or both, to the just demands of the Negro for protection in the exercise of the rights which it voluntarily conferred to him, as it did upon the white men of the South, is the cause of the trouble in that section between the races, and of the growing spirit of lawlessness in other parts of the country, of which Negroes are victims. What Mr. Justice Taney is alleged to have said respecting the rights of Negroes, viz., "that black men have no rights which white men are bound to respect," is a true to-day in this country as when it was first uttered. Negroes are lynched and burned because the white men who do these things know or believe, at least, that no serious consequences to them will follow, they are prepared for the spasmodic outbursts of indignation which are usually heard when a Negro is thus punished. They know the press and the pulpit will condemn them in a vague and meaningless way, and that in a week or a month the circumstance will be forgotten. They do not misunderstand the popular estimate in which the Negro is held by the white race, or its feeling with respect to his social and political status. Very few white men, North or South, regard the Negro as their equal, and fewer still are willing to acknowledge him as a man and a brother. The knowledge thus possessed by the mobs of the true estimate in which the Negro is held emboldens them to commit the cowardly and brutal deeds which shock even the so-called "heathen nations" of the world.

The difference in the estimate of the white men of the South and the white men of the North, regarding the Negro, is that the former is frank, outspoken in the conviction that the Negro is fundamentally inferior to the white man, and, therefore, can never be his equal, while the white men of the North, who almost believe the same thing patronize him and in a half-hearted manner call him brother . Yet when this black brother is burned at the stake by his white Southern brother, his white Northern brother does not take on nearly so much, nor express himself with half the vigor, earnestness and bitterness that he does when Christian missionaries are massacred in China or when the serfs of Russia are brutally whipped with the knout in the salt mines of Siberia, or when the American brethren are murdered by the hundred for Christ's sake by the unspeakable Turk. These dear Northern brethren of ours make themselves perniciously active in enlisting government aid, in urging the sending of war vessels to these foreign lands to impress the foreign barbarians, who murder helpless Americans, with the idea that this government will not permit any outrages upon its citizens abroad. And yet its black citizens at home are subjected to all sorts of indignities and outrages, and no voice is raised in their defense, no concerted effort made to prevent a repetition of the brutalities that make their lives miserable in the house of their brethren. Why? Because the party which gave them their rights, while it may not have quite abandoned its efforts to enforce the law for their protection, have for reasons, largely commercial, at least, suspended the work which first called it into being. It is no longer the party of human rights. Ship subsidies, expansion, the development of the commerce of the nation, the building of a great navy, the organization of a standing army, are any or all of them of far greater importance than the protection of the lives and property of Negroes, who wear the empty and meaningless title, American citizens?

The danger to the Republic is not past as long as this condition of insecurity and lawlessness is permitted to exist in any part of this land. As has been well said, the correct and equitable solution of the problem cannot be much longer adjourned. The gravity of the situation which now confronts this nation affects not only the civic and political rights of the Negro, but of the white man as well. "The wise man adapts himself to circumstances, as water shapes itself to the vessel that contains it," says a Chinese proverb. Under the American system of government, the Negro, being a citizen, must perforce advance with the nation that made him a citizen. He is not a black citizen merely; he is an American citizen , as well, and whatever benefits, or privileges, or rights are enjoyed by his white fellow-citizens, must , of necessity, be accorded to him. He does not ask for more than this, and he will not be satisfied with less . The solution of the problem which seems to perturb the white man very greatly is comprehended in these words of the lowly Nazarene:

"As ye would that men should do unto you do ye even so unto them."

If the American white man has the courage and the manliness to live up to this rule of conduct and right-living, he will have made good his boast of being of the "superior race," and we shall hear less of lynching and all the other iniquities which disgrace his civilization and belittle his manhood and his humanity.

John Edward Bruce (Bruce Grit)

CHARLES T. WALKER (1858-1921)

Introduction

Charles T. Walker, D.D., has been called "The Black Spurgeon", due to his exceptional preaching gifts. He was Pastor Mt. Olivet Baptist Church, New York City.

Life of Charles T. Walker by Silas Xavier Floyd
Introduction

There is no species of literary composition more difficult that the writing of a good biography. Biographers are under a great temptation at times to create, or at least to magnify, the virtues of their subjects; and the temptation is not less on other occasions to deny, or greatly to minify, their vices. The biographies of Holy Scripture are models of biographical literary production. Inspired writers neither extenuate the defects nor magnify the excellencies of their subjects; extenuating nothing on the one hand, they do not, on the other, set down aught in malice. The excellence of the inspired writings in this regard differentiates them from the uninspired writings of any country or century.

But while to biographize is a confessedly difficult task, it is at the same time universally admitted to be a form of literary production of great value, when properly executed. A biography is generally understood to be the history of the life, actions and character of a particular person; it is that form of history proper whose subject is described in the facts and events of his individual experience. Carlyle, in his "Sartor Resartus," says: "Biography is by nature the most universally profitable, universally pleasant of all things." He also elsewhere says: "There is no heroic poem in the world but is at bottom a biography, the life of a man." He has frequently expressed the idea that history is biography that the history of any nation is the story of the lives of its great men. In a profound sense this statement is literally true. We thus see that peculiar ability is required accurately to write the life of any representative man. His forbears for many generations ought to be accurately known; his environment, in all its essential characteristics, ought to be thoroughly mastered. The times partly make men, and men partly make their time; each acts and reacts upon the other. Neither can be exhaustively described independent of the other.

The difficulty of writing good biographies is so great that comparatively few great biographies have been written. All the world is familiar with the unique biography of Johnson by Boswell. It has excited hearty laughter, while it has imparted valuable information. Lockhart's Life of Scott and Lady Holland's Life of Sydney Smith, fill almost a unique place in biographical literature. G. Otto Trevelyan's Life of Lord Macaulay and Hallam Tennyson's Life of his father are among the more recent and valuable illustrations of the biographical literature of modern times.

The word biography comes from two Greek words, bios, life, and graphein, to write. In order that there should be a good biography, it is necessary, therefore, that there should be a life nobly lived, and a writer competent to describe it in fitting terms. In the biography of Rev. Charles T. Walker, D. D., by Rev. Silas X. Floyd, D. D., both these conditions are excellently met. By his careful literary training, his wide experience as a writer, and his intimate knowledge of the history of Dr. Walker, Dr. Floyd is eminently fitted to write a readable account of Dr. Walker's life and work. He has been associated in newspaper, pastoral and evangelistic work with Dr. Walker for the past twenty years. When Dr. Walker was business manager of the Augusta Sentinel, Dr. Floyd was its editor; and when Dr. Walker resigned the pastorate of the Tabernacle Baptist Church in Augusta, Ga., Dr. Floyd became his successor. He thus has had unusual opportunities to study Dr. Walker's public and private life day by day for nearly a quarter of a century. Dr. Floyd is a graduate of Atlanta University, Georgia, from which institution he received the degree of A. M., three years after his graduation. For three years he was employed by the International Sunday School Convention as one of its Field Workers in the South. He is at present in the employ of the American Baptist Publication Society as a Missionary for Georgia and Alabama. The degree of "Doctor of Divinity" was conferred upon him by Morris Brown College, Atlanta, Ga., June 4, 1902.

There is probably no other Negro in the United States, and perhaps no other in the world, who is a better subject for a biography than Charles T. Walker. Many will affirm that Booker T. Washington is the most prominent representative of his race in America; doubtless, in his special department of effort for his people, he is the representative Negro. But all intelligent men, black or white, familiar with the facts, will say that Dr. Walker is the ablest Negro preacher and pastor in the United States. His racial characteristics are so strongly emphasized that the most bitter opponent of his race cannot attribute his acknowledged ability as thinker, writer and preacher to any interfusion of white blood in his veins. He is a Negro in every drop of his blood. Dr. Walker had careful training as a preparation for the work of the gospel ministry. Too many men, both white and black, rush into the ministry with quite inadequate preparation. The time has come when the apostolic injunction, "Lay hands suddenly on no man," must be literally obeyed. This injunction is especially important in its relation to preachers and pastors of Negro churches. They are the natural and powerful leaders of their people. This is a transition period for the millions of the Negro race in America. Tremendously important racial problems are now demanding solution. Whites and blacks, both North and South, must have great patience with one another in the presence of these pulsing problems. Right solutions will eventually come; and all men must remember that no question is settled truly until it is settled rightly.

Dr. Walker has been an earnest student ever since his school days. He has traveled widely, read extensively, and thought profoundly. In all these respects he has set a good example to all preachers and pastors. There is no standing still in professional life. If a man does not advance, he must retrograde; if he does not grow up, he must grow down. Every preacher is like a man on a bicycle—he must go on constantly or go off speedily.

Dr. Walker's ministry in New York has been remarkable for pulpit power and for practical results. His ministry in this city is a distinct accession to the pulpit force of the entire church, irrespective of denominational divisions and creedal distinctions. Perhaps in the entire history of the city no pastor of any church ever had so many accessions to the membership of his church in the same length of time as Dr. Walker has had.

A great future still awaits his ministerial labors. Marvelous possibilities are before his race in America. Booker Washington, Dr. Walker, and a few great Negroes, are wisely training their people for a noble future; they are teaching their people that the time for pitying them, and coddling them, as well as for abusing, not to say lynching, them has passed, never to return. They must take their place as men and women among the men and women of the hour. They are to be neither babied nor bullied; neither petted nor pampered; they ought only to expect and demand simple justice; on their behalf these great leaders demand nothing more, and they will be satisfied with nothing less. To deny them simple justice would be an unspeakable reproach to the dominant race in America. Dr. Walker's greatest days as preacher and pastor are still in the future. That he and his race may worthily perform their whole duty, and grandly attain their high destiny is the sincere desire of every true man, earnest patriot, and devout Christian.

This volume ought to be widely circulated and generally studied. It will give genuine inspiration to all men, white or black, who are struggling for higher and better things for time and eternity. Its general circulation will greatly help the Negro toward the realization of his laudable ambitions as a man, a citizen and a churchman.

Robert Stuart MaCarthur

To the young men of the Negro race in America.

Preface

For the combination of shrewd common sense, fine executive ability, ready speech, genial acceptance of conditions, optimistic faith in the future of his race and self-sacrificing zeal in their behalf, Booker T. Washington stands easily first among the nine million Negroes of America. The greatest claim that has yet been made by the Negro in English Literature, according to the most competent critics, has been made by Paul Laurence Dunbar, who, for the first time in our language, has given literary interpretation of a very artistic completeness to what passes in the hearts and minds of a lowly people. The greatest claim that has been made by the Negro in the field of scholarship has been made by W. E. Burghardt DuBois, Ph. D., the eminent sociologist. But not more certain is it that Washington stands first in the list of Negro educators, and Dunbar first in the list of Negro poets and literary men, and DuBois first among scholars, than that the Rev. Charles T. Walker, D. D., who is popularly called "The Black Spurgeon," stands first among eminent and successful Negro preachers.

Dr. Walker's father died the day before Dr Walker was born His mother died when he was only eight years old. The first seven years of his life he was a slave. Becoming an orphan one year after emancipation, the years of his youth and young manhood were years of great hardship and privation. In this respect, his early life resembled that of other distinguished men of humble origin who have been a power in the world, and whose names have an honorable place on the pages of history. The prophetic reference to Christ, "Though thou be little among the thousands of Judah, yet out of thee shall he come forth unto me that is to be ruler in Israel," has been paralleled in human lives by a host of men whose names and deeds are recorded in history, sacred and profane. From the anointing of the Bethlehemite shepherd boy as King of Israel to the present time, history has furnished innumerable illustrations of the providential selection of men from obscure localities and unpretentious surroundings for great responsibilities and important fields of influence. Again and again, in the history of our own country, we have had memorable examples of men who have left an undying influence, whose early life was without friends, and whose heritage was void of patrimony. Abraham Lincoln, James A. Garfield, Benjamin Franklin, Frederick Douglass, George W. Childs, Henry Wilson, Stephen Girard, Horace Greeley, and a host of others were such men.

One of the most profitable uses of history is the narrative of such lives. Having this in mind, it is safe to say that there is no species of writing of more value than biography. It inspires the young to nobler purposes, develops higher resolves, and proves an incentive to the laudable imitation of men who in prominent positions have proved true to principle and duty. It is in this spirit and with this thought in mind, that I undertake to write the story of the life of Dr. Walker. I confess to a great degree of admiration for the man; I glory in his career; I thought that the story of his life ought to be told; I believe that the telling of his life story will do much to encourage, inspire and incite to new endeavor thousands of young colored men all over the land, who need to be encouraged and inspired, and who, because of the peculiar environments of American civilization, find so little to incite them to high resolves, honest endeavors and upright lives. If, therefore, the story of Dr. Walker's life as told by me shall encourage, inspire or incite one single human being, I shall have my reward.

Silas Xavier Floyd, Augusta, Ga., February 1, 1902

Chapter 1
Parentage and birth

It has long been a mooted question as to which State in the Union produces the best class of Negroes. Though there are no scientific data form which to draw definite conclusions, it is very generally agreed that the best Negroes—the most intellectual, most industrious, wealthiest, and the best behaved Negroes—come either from Virginia or Georgia. If that be true, then, if one is so fortunate as to be a native Georgian with Virginia ancestors, or vice versa, he ought to be considered a Negro of superior birth, to say the least. Viewed in this light, Charles Thomas Walker was born to superiority. In 1773, a family of Negroes was brought from Virginia to Burke County, Georgia, by the grandfather of the late Col. A. C. Walker, who was a prominent Georgia planter and politician and who for many years was a member of the Georgia legislature. In 1880, Col. Walker, writing of the Negro Walkers who had descended from the family brought to Georgia by his grandfather, said: "As slaves, they were noted for their admirable qualities, and as freedmen they have sustained their reputation."

Charles Thomas Walker was the fourth in descent from this family. His father was a man of the name of Thomas Walker, and was one of three brothers. Thomas Walker was his master's coachman—a position which only the best and most trustworthy slaves were allowed to hold, and a position which the slaves themselves always considered as a place of honor. The fact, also, that he was a deacon in the church of which he was a member attests the esteem in which he was held by the other slaves. Two of Charles T. Walker's uncles, Joseph T. Walker and Nathan Walker, were both Baptist ministers. The Franklin Covenant Baptist Church, about five miles from Hephzibah, Ga., and only a short distance from the Burke County line, was organized for the colored people in 1848. In 1852 or 1853, this church, though its membership was made up of slaves, raised the necessary amount and purchased the freedom of the Rev. Joseph T. Walker, at that time their pastor, in order that he might devote himself entirely to his church work and to the preaching of the gospel in the counties of Richmond, Jefferson and Burke. In this work, Rev. Joseph T. Walker continued until the close of the war. The Rev. Nathan Walker, though a licensed preacher before the war, was not ordained to the ministry until 1866, when he succeeded his brother as pastor of the Franklin Covenant Baptist Church.

In 1848, Thomas Walker was married to a young woman of the name of Hannah Walker. To them eleven children were born—six females and five males. On the 5th day of February, 1858, near Hephzibah, Richmond County, Ga., about sixteen miles southwest of Augusta, their youngest child—Charles Thomas Walker—was born. Thomas Walker, the father, was buried the day before Charles was born, having died of pneumonia. Mrs. Hannah Walker survived her husband eight years, dying in Augusta, Ga., in 1866. It is related of her that she was a woman of unusual piety and strength of character, being a devout member of the Franklin Covenant Baptist Church, of which her husband was a deacon. She had high hopes and fond expectations for her youngest child, and longed to live to see him make a great and good man of himself, and especially so, because of the sad death of his father which occurred only two days before the child was born. God willed otherwise, and took her home to be with him and to watch from the "high and uplifted" battlements of glory the career of her son.

The following tribute to Mrs. Hannah Walker is taken from "Under the Stars and Bars; or Memories of Four Years' Service with the Confederate Army." This book was written by Mr. Walter A. Clark, Treasurer of Richmond County, Ga. Mr. Clark was a prominent officer in the Confederate Army; he is a graduate of Emory College (Georgia), and a literary man of great merit; he is a nephew of the late Col. Walker, already quoted in this book, was reared along with the black Walkers and knows whereof he speaks. His tribute to Mrs. Walker is no less a credit to the memory of the deceased than it is a testimony of the goodness of heart and magnificent manhood of the writer.

"My heart prompts me to pay its earnest tribute to one whose memory the sketch above recalls—dear old Aunt Hannah. How her name brings back to my heart and life to-day the glamour of the old, old days that will never come again—days when to me a barefoot boy, life seemed a long and happy holiday! I can see her now, her head crowned with a checkered handkerchief, her arms bare to the elbows, her spectacles set primly on her nose, while from her kindly eyes there shone the light of a pure white soul within! She was only an humble slave, and yet her love for me was scarcely less than that my father and mother bore me; and when, on a summer's day in 1861, my brother and myself left the old homestead to take our humble places under a new born flag, there was not a dry eye on the whole plantation, old Aunt Hannah wept in grief as pure and deep as if the clods were falling on an own child.

"Long years have come and gone since she was laid away in the narrow house appointed for all the living. No marble headstone marks the spot, yet I am sure the humble mound that lies above her sleeping dust covers a heart as honest and as faithful, as patient and as gentle, as kindly and as true, as any that rests beneath the proudest monument that art could fashion or affection buy. She reared a large family of children, the Rev. Charles T. Walker, "The Black Spurgeon," among them, and transmitted to them all a character for honesty and virtue marked even in those, the better days of the Republic.

"Wisely or other wisely, in the order of Providence, or in the order of Napoleon's 'heavier battalions,' we have in this good year of our Lord (1900) not only a New South, but a new type of Aunt Hannah. The old is, I fear, a lost Pleiad, whose light will shine no more on land or sea or sky."

The Walker family produced a number of able and successful preachers—some say more, some say less. As already shown two of Dr. Walker's uncles—Joseph T. Walker and Nathan Walker—were ministers. The latter is still living, venerated and honored at the good old age of 85. He was one of the founders of the Walker Baptist Association, and was for more than twenty years its moderator, retiring about ten years ago on account of the infirmities of old age. The Association was named in honor of the Rev. Joseph T. Walker. The Walker Baptist Institute at Augusta, named also for the Rev. Joseph T. Walker, was founded by this Association and has been for many years supported by it. In all respects the Walker Baptist Association is to-day the leading Association in Georgia. An older brother of Dr. Walker, the Rev. Peter Walker, now retired on account of age, was, in his day, a man of great force and power in the pulpit. A nephew of Dr. Walker, the Rev. Prof. Joseph A. Walker, son of Rev. Peter Walker, was up to the time of his death, about eight years ago, the honored and successful Principal of Walker Baptist Institute. Besides these, there are two first cousins of Dr. Walker who are among Georgia's most distinguished clergymen—the Rev. W. G. Johnson, D. D., Pastor of the First Baptist Church, Macon, Ga., who is Secretary of the Walker Baptist Association, Chairman of the Board of Trustees of the Walker Baptist Institute, and a member of the Board of Trustees of the Atlanta Baptist College; and the Rev. R. J. Johnson, Pastor of the First Baptist Church, Millen, Ga., and Treasurer of the Board of Trustees of the Walker Baptist Institute. Other cousins in the ministry are the Rev. Samuel C. Walker, Augusta, Ga., Rev. A. J. Walker, Millen, Ga., Rev. T. W. Walker, Wrightsville, Ga., Rev. Solomon Walker, Savannah, Ga., Rev. Matthew Walker, Savannah, Ga., an elder in the C. M. E. Church, and Rev. Nathan Wilkerson, Waynesboro, Ga. In addition to these, there are many of this family who were once in the ministry of earth, but who have long since gone to join the ministry on high.

Descended from a generation of preachers, Dr. Walker towers above them all like Saul among his brethren. So great is his fame and so celebrated has he made the name of Walker that the other members of the family find it a passport in many places for them to make it known that they belong to the generation of Walkers. ...

Chapter 9

A colored man abroad

Mention has already been made of the fact that while Dr. Walker was traveling abroad he wrote weekly letters to the Augusta Sentinel, which were compiled on his return and published in book form, under the name and style of "A Colored Man Abroad." Extracts from that publication will serve not only to show Dr. Walker's literary style, but will also be of interest, instruction and entertainment to the reader.

Dr. Walker's letters from the Holy Land were written for the most part from notes taken on the ground, somewhat as one would keep a diary or a sailor's log. The second day out from New York, he paid the following tribute to the sea.

"The sea is a revelation of the omnipotence of the Almighty! It carries with perfect ease upon its bosom the greatest ships that circumnavigate the globe. It is the home of numerous animals, small and great, as well as the pathway of Jehovah. It is also the tomb of hundreds of thousands of human beings; for the sea has wrecked hundreds of vessels and sailing craft, and holds entombed the bodies of countless shipwrecked people. As we look at the sea, we are reminded of the grand old words of Byron:

Roll on, thou deep and dark blue ocean, roll,
Ten thousand fleets sweep over thee in vain;
Man marks the earth with ruin,—his control
Stops with the shore,—upon the watery plain
The wrecks are all thy deed, nor doth remain
A shadow of man's ravage, save his own,
When for a moment, like a drop of rain,
He sinks into thy depth with bubbling groan.
Without a grave, unknelled, uncoffined and unknown.

In the following words, Dr. Walker describes his first Sabbath at sea.

It is Sunday morning. The day is calm, and the sun is shining brightly. Divine services were held in the chapel at 10:30 a. m., conducted by the captain, who read the Episcopal service. A Sabbath at sea is a sad day to those who love the house of God. No church bell is heard calling the people to their respective places of worship. No soul-inspiring anthems are sung. No heartfelt prayers are heard ascending like sweet incense from the altar of praise. We miss the pulpit ministration and the Christian greeting that come from the gentle throbbing of loving and affectionate hearts. We miss the Sunday school, where the little folks are singing their many beautiful songs, expressive of our dear Savior's life and love. In place of all this, we observe men drinking and carousing and engaged in all kinds of frivolity; we see many women and girls reading novels, but not one perusing the Bible. Give me no more Sabbaths in mid-ocean.

The first Sunday in London, Dr. Walker visited Spurgeon's church. Following is his description of Spurgeon's Tabernacle.

"Spurgeon's Tabernacle is the greatest church on earth, and its pastor is undoubtedly the grandest preacher in the universe. Eternity alone can tell the good this man of God is doing. Seven thousand people hear him twice on each Lord's Day. He has a Baptist College, perfect in its every appointment, a missionary society, a tract society, a place for the poor, an orphan home, a mission station conducted by the young men of his congregation, a printing press, and everything else in the line of an active, live and progressive church. Here the 'rich and the poor meet together; and the Lord is the maker of them all.' The doctrine of the fatherhood of God and the universal brotherhood of man is taught with all the earnestness of which this good man is capable. In this Tabernacle, you will find men and women who are worth thousands and ten thousands of pounds sterling out in the streets and alleys of London, bringing the poor, the wayward, the blasphemer, the halt and the blind to hear Spurgeon preach. We heard him on the Sabbath, occupying a seat near him. What a privilege! Two rows of galleries extend all round the edifice. Just below the pastor's stand, there is a gallery for orphan children from the home and those who manage the home. The people are rushing for seats—thousands are already seated, having been admitted because they held quarterly tickets. At five minutes before eleven o'clock, the signal bell is tapped, announcing to all persons who have not secured seats to get them anywhere they can find them, as the holders of tickets have no claim on seats after the tap of the bell. Mr. Spurgeon comes in, followed by his assistant pastor and deacons who take seats near him. He then opens the service with a short, earnest, eloquent prayer that moves many to tears. No organ is used; the chorister stands near the pastor, and the multitude rises and sings a soul-inspiring hymn. The pastor then reads, with exposition, the Scripture lesson. He announces this morning that he will preach the annual missionary sermon. When he begins preaching, seven thousand pairs of eyes are looking steadfastly upon him. He leads the vast audience step by step as he unfolds to them the word of God. Every hearer's heart burns within him. It is a grand sight. I wept as I looked on such a vast throng of people seated in breathless silence, catching the words as they fell from the mouth of God's prophet."

In the month of May, 1891, Dr. Walker spent five days on the Mediterranean Sea en route to Alexandria. While on this sea, famous for its storms, he encountered a storm which he said must have been similar to the one that Paul wrote about in the 27th chapter of the Acts. Following is Dr. Walker's picture o a storm on the Mediterranean Sea.

"The sea had been turbulent all night. The fury of the sea continued until noon to-day, when it reached its climax. For nearly an hour the waves united and lashed the steamer in a fearful manner, as if chastening it for disobeying some sea law. We closely watched the treacherous water during the contest. The ship at first seemed to think itself invincible, and had a perfect right to move in its own chosen route, despite the ocean's objection. It was then that the hottest part of the contest took place. The ocean gave one command, and, at that summons, dashing, foaming, giant waves came from every direction to reinforce those already at the scene of battle. When they had combined their forces, they struck the steamer a few times; she cracked, reeled, bowed, tossed herself to and fro, shook up the passengers, made them sick, and put some to bed. Each time the vessel attempted to move out of her tracks she only lifted herself up and came back in the same place. The man on the bridge turned the wheel, but the steamer shook her head. The wind blew, the tempest raged, the captain came from his room, ascended the bridge, took charge of affairs, called up the sailors, gave orders to turn the wheel and let her drive, but she could not go. The sea continued to assert its rights, and when the crew confessed that they were defeated and at the mercy of the waves, they cast anchor, stood still, and waited on the sea to obtain a permit to move forward. The Mediterranean seemed to recognize that the whole crew were baffled, confused and beseeching mercy; so she called in her waves, sent them back to their several stations, each bearing a spray of snowy whiteness as an emblem of the victory they had won. And now all is serene on the water."

Speaking of the people of Syria and other Eastern countries, Dr. Walker wrote the following about the present manners and customs of the East.

"The manners and customs of these people are about the same as in the days of Moses, Abraham, Isaac and Jacob. Men work for years to pay for their wives; lead their flocks as David did; dwell in tents; plow oxen as did Elijah; water their fields; sow grain among thorns and rocks; wear the same kind of costumes with the old-time sandals on their feet; use donkeys and camels as beasts of burden—all as in the days of yore. The majority of the Mohammedans and Arabs have no chairs, tables, knives and forks, with no bedsteads in their houses. They eat with their fingers, stretch out on the floor or ground, sleep by the roadside, just as Jacob did when he had his vision. The Mohammedans believe that a person who goes crazy becomes holy. The Turkish government does not allow its subjects to embrace Christianity. To ask a Mohammedan to change his religion is to endanger one's life."

Following is Dr. Walker's notion of the testimony of the mountains.

"Having made a study of the mountains in this country, they seem to me to wear an air of dignity at once charming and attractive. Lofty, stately, queenly, they look like silent but impressive heralds, standing as reminiscences of the far away past and as landmarks, preserving and perpetuating the history of notable events. Immovable and unchangeable, like their Creator, they have stood while the mighty have fallen; they have witnessed the enthronement and dethronement of kings; the captivity and extermination of nations, and to-day they are almost the only places in Palestine that the searcher after truth may feel safe in pointing out the identical location of Scriptural occurrences. Too lofty and unchangeable for tradition, they are the true historians of past centuries and for ages to come Sinai, Moriah, Carmel, Ebal, Gerizim, Tabor, Beatitudes, Zion and the Mount of Olives will bear witness to the Scriptures in a manner that will be obvious and convincing to the most skeptical mind. Well may Jehovah liken his church to the mountains. And why should not the snow decorate the mountains; the clouds circle about them; the sun linger and play upon their summits; the moon and the stars gaze smilingly upon them, while the lightnings race and prance up and down like electricity from a galvanic battery? Why not the sea crowd the mountain's base, bathe its feet, and perpetually sing sweet anthems to its praise? 'How beautiful upon the mountains are the feet of them that publisheth peace, that say unto Zion, Thy God reigneth.'

Here is Dr. Walker's idea of how some people are heedlessly drifting on life's ocean.

"I have been thinking how humanity is drifting on life's ocean. For seven days on the Atlantic, our steamer never stopped. The passengers ate, slept, walked, talked, got sick, some died—but we sailed on. The ship passed other vessels; it was often cloudy; the winds blew; the rains fell; storms and gales were often encountered; the ship caught on fire—but we sailed on. Men gambled, drank whiskey and champagne, cursed and spent their hours in frivolity—and so they sailed on, apparently little dreaming that they were rapidly sailing to that eternal shore from whence no traveler returns."

In view of the recent sad assassination of President McKinley, how like prophecy and solemn warning will the following words, which were written ten years ago, seem. At last, the American congress, at the dictation of President Roosevelt, is turning its attention to this great question which ten years ago Dr. Walker declared must be given some attention. Following is the extract, "Anarchy—a Warning."

"In the first-class saloon, there are seventy-six passengers; in the second, sixty; and in the steerage there are about eight hundred—nearly all emigrants. Some are Jews from Russia, fleeing from persecution; others are Belgians, Swedes, Germans, Italians, Irishmen, Welshmen and Scotchmen, all going to our home of freedom—America. Many of them are very immoral, and utterly oblivious of modesty. As a rule, they are a dirty lot, some actually nauseating; and hundreds of them have not washed either their hands or faces on this voyage, so far. Yet these very people come to America to supercede the Negro, and to boss him! These immigrants have extended to them the rights of citizenship in every particular, and yet these inalienable rights are denied the colored man who has helped to make America what it is. Many of these foreigners are of the very worst element in their own country. They are ignorant, treacherous, uncivilized, and many of them heathen. They have no respect for the Sabbath; they have no respect for the law; they have no regard for Christianity; they are antagonistic to the principles of liberty as laid down in the Declaration of Independence of the United States. Mark this prediction: So sure as we live, America is fast getting a Jumbo on her hands. She is nestling a Vesuvius in her bosom that may remain dormant for a long period; but when the volcanic eruption breaks forth, seventy times seven streams of lava will be shot out at one time, and the main pillars that support and uphold the whole fabric of our American institutions will be undermined, uprooted, and partially, if not wholly, destroyed. Chicago and New Orleans should be held in remembrance by our whole people, East, West, North and South. The outrages perpetrated by these villains in those cities were comparable to the firing of the first gun on Fort Sumter. Let the American congress spend some time in legislating against these holy terrors, instead of needlessly discussing schemes to deport the poor unfortunate Negro."

Chapter 12

As an evangelist

Mention has been made in a preceding chapter of the fact that Dr. Walker has been very successful in the field of evangelistic work. In speaking of his work as an evangelist, let it be understood at the outset that the only limitation that has been put upon his efforts in evangelism has been due to the fact that all along he has been a stated pastor and has only given such time to evangelistic campaigns as he could spare from an unusually busy pastorate. Yet even with this limitation he has been very successful in evangelistic work, though he has not been able, for the reason stated, to accept scores of invitations from great cities to serve the Lord by conducting revival services.

He has the calling, the spirit, the gift, the courage, the directness, the sympathy, the faith, the fervor, and the flexibility of the true evangelist. What gives him his greatest preaching power is the enthusiastic warmth and impulsiveness of his speech both in matter and manner. Another thing that adds to the attractiveness of his meetings is the singing. Unlike most of the world's greatest preachers, he is a great singer. It has been often said of him that he can out-preach any man, and then, without stopping, put in and out-sing any man. It is beyond the power of man to describe an audience of four or five thousand colored people engaged in a service of song. In addition to the Gospel Hymns and Revival Songs, the colored people always use the old time Negro Spirituals, sometimes called Plantation Songs, and in the rendition of these last the colored people are inimitable. With Dr. Walker leading the singing in stentorian notes and the multitude joining in, its worth a day's journey of any man's life to witness the sight. To be understood, to be appreciated, it must be seen and heard.

At sometime or other, during the past twenty years, revival services have been held by Dr. Walker in every important city in Georgia without exception. It will be unnecessary to speak of each meeting. The first "big meetings" that gave him anything like a national standing as a recognized leading revivalist were held in Kansas City, Mo. The papers gave large space daily to the accounts of his meetings. This was in 1892, soon after his return from the Holy Land. During the progress of these meetings, invitations came to him to go to St. Louis, San Francisco, and Chicago to continue the good work. As much as he desired to do so, he was compelled to return to his church at Augusta, after five weeks of hard work, in which many hundreds were saved. In 1894, Dr. Walker was invited to New York City to take part in the great religious campaign inaugurated there during that year. The meetings were held during March and April. He remained for three weeks. He spoke at the Antioch Baptist Church, 352 W. 35th Street; St. Mark's M. E. Church, 139 W. 48th Street; Niblo's Garden, Broadway, near Prince Street; the Academy of Music, Metropolitan Hall, near Macy's, and at other points under assignment of the Metropolitan Association. He was associated with such men as the Rev. A. C. Dixon, the Rev. Ernest Lyon, the Rev. Granville Hunt, Mr. Arthur Crane, Leonard Weaver, Mr. Theodore Bjorksten, Mr. and Mrs. George C. Stebbins, the Rev. D. J. Burrell, and others. The following is taken from the New York Tribune concerning those meetings:

"The most unique figure in the present evangelistic campaign is, without a doubt, the Rev. Dr. Walker, of Georgia, who is better known as the 'Black Spurgeon.' This preacher has been working principally among the members of his own race in the course of his stay in New York, and has made many converts of the attendants at the meetings in Antioch Baptist Church and in St. Mark's M. E. Church. Dr. Walker is a man who would attract attention anywhere. He has strong features and his voice, although deep, has a remarkably winning intonation. His manner is eloquent, and in preaching Christ he follows closely the life of the Master, and illustrates his remarks by vivid descriptive phrases."

The column from which this is taken is headed "The Black Spurgeon's Work—Many Negroes Uplifted by His Eloquent Words—Part Which Dr. Walker is Taking in the Evangelical Services—His Attractive Personality."

The New York Sun said:

"'The Black Spurgeon' met with great success in his work in this city. He is a large and powerful man, with a deep voice, but what gives him his greatest preaching power is the earnestness he displays in matter and manner. Dr. Walker aroused a religious feeling which is finding expression in daily meetings. In St. Mark's, three meetings are held each day. The special aim of the revival has been to bring the young into the church, and to reclaim backsliders."

The New York Times, the New York Press, the New York Independent and other papers spoke of the "Black Spurgeon" and his work in New York at this time.

The following account of one of the Metropolitan noon-day meetings is taken from Sabbath Reading, a religious paper:

"'showers of Blessing,' was the opening hymn at a Metropolitan meeting a few days ago; and the reports of this and other meetings indicate that showers of blessing have indeed been falling. After several hymns had been sung, the Rev. Mr. Hunt led in prayer; Mr. Spencer sang touchingly the hymn, "My Son, Give Me Thine Heart." Mr. Arthur Crane then spoke a short while. Miss Anna Parks rendered a solo on a cornet, 'When the Sea Gives up its Dead.' Dr. Walker, of Augusta, Ga., who is called the 'Black Spurgeon,' was introduced. He spoke in a voice tremulous with emotion and enthusiasm, and the audience gave him their close attention, that not a word might be lost. Opening the Bible, he read the first seven verses from Luke 5. 'There are four things to learn from this lesson,' he said; 'first, failure; second, faith; third, fullness; fourth, fellowship. These disciples had had a night of fruitless toil Jesus was not with them. They were fishermen and were plying their usual vocation on the lake, but they hadn't met with success. That was failure. In the morning, Jesus came along with a great crowd of people, and he asked Peter to lend him his ship for a pulpit, so that he might preach to the people. Peter did so, and to reward him for his courtesy, Jesus told him to launch out. Now, that seemed a foolish thing to do, because Peter and the others had been fishing all night, and hadn't caught one fish, and Jesus knew it; but he wanted to teach them a lesson of faith and obedience, as well as to reward them.

It's just like Jesus. He always does reward us right away, and he is continually paying us for what we do. The disciples took Jesus at his word. That was faith. And you know the story, how they let down the nets and drew in so many that the nets broke. That was fullness. Jesus always honors faith, even when it is mixed with ignorance and superstition. Seeing their companions at a distance with their empty boat, the disciples called them to come and share the fish with them. That was fellowship. The Lord intends that each of us shall share our joys with others. While this mighty tidal wave of religion is sweeping over the country, this is a good time for you to come to God and bring your friends with you. Jesus blesses us so that we might bless others. As he is exemplified in our conduct, so shall we win souls. Are there none here to-day who wish this Christ to come into their souls to be their own, their personal Savior?' Several raised their hands for prayer, and the speaker said, 'Thank God.'"

Since 1894, Dr. Walker has held successful meetings in Galveston, Texas; Houston, Texas; Kansas City, St. Louis, Boston, Philadelphia, Nashville, Louisville and Atlanta. The last great meeting in Atlanta was held in April, 1897. The meetings commenced in Friendship Baptist Church, W. Mitchell St., of which the Rev. E. R. Carter, D. D., is the pastor. The interest increased so rapidly, and the number that came was so large that the meetings had to be transferred to the auditorium in Exposition Park, which before that had been made famous by meetings held by Sam Jones, and later by D. L. Moody. He crowded the great hall, with a seating capacity of nearly 8,000 souls, from the start. There probably has never been just such a meeting on the American continent as the one held in Atlanta at that time. It was attended by the white people as well as by the black people. At more than one service there were more than a thousand whites present—some of them representing the wealth and culture and refinement of Atlanta. Ministers, lawyers, members of the city council, the mayor and his wife, the merchants and bankers—all came out to hear the "Black Spurgeon." And the white people were just as eager, and some of them just as emotional in their worship as were the colored people. Many whites stood for prayer along with colored people; many were bathed in tears during the preaching; many of them testified for Jesus in the testimonial meetings; many were helped; some were saved. At the close of each meeting, the most prominent people would not think of leaving the building before shaking hands with the great preacher. Speaking of this meeting, the Atlanta Constitution said:

"The Negroes of Atlanta are stirred up over the wonderful religious revival that has been going on in the Friendship Baptist Church for the past two weeks. The success of the meeting has been unparalleled, and more religious enthusiasm has been aroused in the two weeks that the meetings have been running than has been felt in this city in years. The meetings are being conducted by the Rev. Charles T. Walker, 'the colored Spurgeon.' He is assisted by Rev. E. R. Carter, the regular pastor. Every night, thousands are turned away from the church on W. Mitchell St., and the building is always crowded with people long before the hour of service. Rev. Walker is proving as great a drawing card among the colored people as Sam Jones did among the whites. He attracts fully as large crowds and his preaching is drawing fully as many people into the church as Sam Jones' meeting—if not more. Dr. Walker is pastor of the Tabernacle Baptist Church at Augusta, and is regarded as one of the leading colored preachers in the country. He attracts large crowds by his preaching wherever he goes, and his meetings are always attended by wonderful outbursts of religious enthusiasm."

In 1899, Dr. Walker again held meetings in Kansas City. The following is taken from the Kansas City Star, April, 1899:

"Many a white man would be glad to have the eloquence, the command of language and the power of thought that Rev. Dr. C. T. Walker, the 'Black Spurgeon,' displayed in his sermon to a great crowd of colored people in the Second Baptist Church, Tenth and Campbell Sts., last night. He is one of the best colored speakers ever heard in Kansas City.

"The Rev. Walker's home is in Augusta, Ga. He is so well thought of by the prominent people of his city that when the mayor died yesterday, he received several telegrams asking him to come and attend the funeral. He may return home to-day, but may decide to remain longer.

"Every seat in the large auditorium of the new colored church was occupied when he ascended the pulpit steps last night, and long rows of black faces looked down at him from the balcony.

"Dr. Walker is a man of perhaps forty or more. He is of medium size; although his face is as black as a stove pipe, he says he never drinks coffee because it is deleterious to the complexion. His features are prominent, he has a sharp mustache and a short head. His voice is not exceedingly strong, but clear and well modulated.

"His sermons are sententious and epigrammatic. They abound in original and striking observations, and his gestures, though not graceful, are spontaneous.

"'Men talk a great deal of the perplexing problems that confront humanity to-day,' he said. 'But if men would put the Bible into practice, there will be no problems. That book is statesmanship as well as religion, and it not only teaches the fatherhood of God, but the universal brotherhood of man.'

"The subject of his sermon was 'Christ the supreme object of worship.' In referring to God's plan of salvation, he said: So many say they failed to understand the plan and sometimes wondered why the Almighty did not take man into his confidence just a little bit in arranging it. But it wouldn't have done. In this day, when there are so many trusts and combines, salvation would have been bought up and cornered and monopolized until only the rich could get at it, if man had had anything to do with it. As some rhymester has said:

If religion was a thing that money could buy,
The rich would live and the poor would die.

"One of the characteristics of 'the Black Spurgeon's' style is his fund of illustrative anecdotes. He used one of these to show that man cannot read the Bible without feeling instinctively that Christ was divine, relating a conversation supposed to have taken place between Napoleon and Gen. Bertrand on the Island of St. Helena. When the latter expressed his opinion that Christ was only a man, Napoleon stopped him, and said: 'No, General Bertrand, I know men. But I never knew one like Christ. He had that in Him that no man ever had. He was divine. His army—soldiers of the cross—are now marching on through ages to victory. But who, general, think you, is marshalling any forces for me? In a year or two I shall die and be no more, and my name will be forgotten. But his name will live forever.'

"'Col. Ingersoll and Gen. Lew Wallace were once taking a ride together,' the speaker said, 'when Wallace informed his companion that he intended to write a book tearing the mask from the face of Christ and showing Him to have been but human. Ingersoll told him that he was the very man to write such a book and commended the idea.' 'When Gen. Wallace prepared to write the book,' said the preacher, 'he first set about reading the New Testament carefully as a prerequisite. Before he had finished it, he convinced himself of his own error and wrote Ben Hur instead.'

"'Over and over again,' continued the speaker, 'I have read of the Pharisee who, after recounting his virtues, thanked God that he was not like other men. And I have often wondered who this Pharisee was like. He was not like God, and he was not like the publican—he must have been like the devil.'

"Dr. Walker dealt sanctification a blow in declaring that such a thing as perfection was impossible to man. Man was intended to grow unceasingly into Christian strength.

"'The Lord's our judge,' he said, 'the Lord is our King; the Lord is our law-giver—the judicial. The executive and legislative combined in one.'

"But it is his pictures of the hereafter, of the hosts of saints marching up to glory, that the Black Spurgeon excels. Then it is that his voice is raised and his body sways back and forth as he adds stroke after stroke to the grand scene, and marshals phalanx after phalanx of moral heroes in Miltonic array, moving on with steady tread, glittering, triumphant, to the gates of heaven. In the course of a bit of description of this kind, near the close of his sermon, shouts went up from every quarter of the church and the audience was worked up to a high pitch of religious frenzy and exaltation.

"'I hear the tread of the feet of the great host,' he said, 'tramp, tramp, tramp, they come. Like the angel whose wings John, in his vision saw released, they are not retarded by polar snows nor equatorial heat.'

"'On they come—tramp tramp, tramp, shoulder to shoulder, wheel to wheel, charger to charger; onward they march—company after company, cavalcade after cavalcade, thousands upon thousands and millions upon millions, marching, marching, marching, on through the ages and forever. The church of God is going home to Zion. Ah! friends many are waiting there for you! That mother that lies buried beneath the sod, that little son or daughter, that sister, that brother—they are waiting and calling for you. Be of good courage, they say. They are not far away; they see your struggles; they know your temptations.'

"Then when the emotion of the audience began to find vent in shouts, the speaker lowered his voice and shifted to another line of attack, gradually working upon the feelings of his hearers again until he was again compelled to let up."

It is not necessary to prolong this chapter. The record of service done in the Master's Vineyard by Dr. Walker is one to be proud of. He has led more than 8,000 persons to Christ, has baptized and received into the membership of the church more than 3,500, and has not missed preaching the glorious Gospel of the blessed Christ but four Sundays in twenty-four years—twice on account of sickness, and twice on account of being at sea. ...

Chapter 16

Extracts from sermons

Wednesday, June 6, 1888, by appointment of the Missionary Baptist State Convention of Georgia, the Rev. Mr. Walker preached the opening sermon in honor of the one hundredth anniversary of the founding of the Negro Baptist Church in Georgia. The centennial exercises were conducted on a grand scale, running through ten days, and the fact that he was selected to preach the opening sermon shows the esteem in which he was held by his brethren. Following are some extracts from the sermon preached by the great leader and preacher at that time:

What Hath God Wrought

"According to this time it shall be said, What hath God wrought."—Numbers 23:23.

"We stand to-day upon an eminence from which we may take a retrospective view of a one hundred years' journey. This is a glorious day. We have come to celebrate the progress and triumphs of a century. We are here to speak of the vicissitudes through which we have passed, the conflicts we have encountered, the obstacles we have overcome, the success already attained, and the victories yet to be achieved. We are here to pass up and down the line of march from 1788 to 1888. Old fathers, worn and weary with burdens and cares of long and useful lives, their heads whitened by the frosts of many winters, infirm and super-annuated, have come up to shake hands with the century, to bid God-speed to their brethren, and, like Simeon of old, to exclaim, 'Lord, now lettest thou thy servant depart in peace, for mine eyes have seen thy salvation.' Young men have come to get inspiration from a review of the work of the fathers and to return to their various fields stimulated, electrified and encouraged.

"We shall discuss, first, what God has wrought in the permanent establishment of His church. The founder of the true church is Jesus Christ. He is the Son of Abraham, according to the flesh, and He is also the Son of God. Two natures and three offices mysteriously meet his person. He is the foundation of the true church, the chief corner stone, the lawgiver in Zion. He has given us a kingdom which cannot be moved. He began in Asia to ride in the gospel chariot. He sent out twelve small boats at first. On the day of Pentecost, 3,000 were added to the number. In 1630, He sent Roger Williams to America. In the spirit of his Master, he planted churches in New England, and the stone continued to roll until it reached the sunny South. In 1788, the oppressed, rejected and enslaved brother in black, for the first time in Georgia, lifted the Baptist flag under the leadership of Andrew Bryan. The handful of corn was sown not on the high, wild and rocky mountains, but on the seaboard; but the wind carried the seed to every part of Georgia and the barren rocks and sandy deserts became gardens of the Lord. From that handful of corn have sprung more than 1,500 churches, 500 ordained preachers, and 166,429 communicants. The little one has become a thousand. In the entire United States there are to-day more than 1,250,000 colored Baptists. I make bold to say here and now that the progress of the Baptists in this country has been due to the earnest, faithful and simple preaching of Christ crucified. The fathers in their preaching did not preach philosophy, nor did they strive to reach the people with rhetorical strains of eloquence, but they strove to reach the people by preaching the plain, old-fashioned, simple truths of the gospel. The gospel declared in its truth and simplicity will make Baptists.

"Third, we shall discuss what God has wrought for our race during this century. For our race, this century was one of hardship, oppression, persecution and sore trial. We were slaves; we had no moral training; no intellectual advantages during the greater part of this century and the two preceding; we were run by bloodhounds; sometimes whipped to death; we were sold from the auction block, husbands and fathers being separated from wives and children at the behest of some white man; we had to get a ticket to go to church; we had to get permission from some white man before we could join the church; we were outcasts. But all that has been changed. God was against slavery, and in his own time and way He removed the foul blot from the national escutcheon. Emancipated without a dollar, without education, without friends and without competent leaders, like Hagar and Ishmael, we were turned out to die. But despite all obstacles, the Negro in Georgia has to-day $10,000,000 worth of property and has proven himself worthy of citizenship. We have thousands of children in our public schools. Our men will be found in the law, in the practice of medicine, in legislative halls, among teachers and professors, on the list of authors, skilled musicians, journalists, theologians and business men. God has wrought wonderfully among us. God is still opening the way for greater progress. The cry is loud and long all along the line for consecrated crated workers. The harvest truly is white but the laborers are few.

"A last thing, we would urge upon you by way of application. We need more earnestness and simplicity in proclaiming the gospel. Our fathers were men of one book. They received power from on high by constant prayerfulness, and proclaimed earnestly and plainly what they understood. They felt like Paul, 'Though I preach the gospel, I have nothing to glory of; necessity is laid upon me; yea, woe is me if I preach not the gospel. The gospel is the intervention of Jesus Christ to save lost men. It is heaven's appointed remedy for man's malady; and the directions for taking the medicine must be so plain that the fool may take it assured of the fact that he will be healed. The gospel is a ship loaded with the bread of life, and must be brought so near the landing that the hungry can reach forth and take the bread of life. The gospel is the announcement of reconciliation between God and the sinner, a message of mercy, the history of the advent of Christ, His life, miracles, death, burial, resurrection, ascension and intercession. The gospel is the Messiah's conquering, triumphal car. There is power and magnetism about it. It is the power of God unto salvation to every one that believeth. It must be preached in its purity, in its simplicity, and with blood-earnestness. Man has been honored of God in being chosen to carry this holy message. Beginning a new century in the history of our denomination, let us carry this message with the same earnestness as did our fathers. Discourage inactivity, coldness, in difference, formalism in our preaching, and denounce spasmodic religion among our hearers. Contend earnestly for those principles which have been the very life of Baptists. The gospel must go, like the sun shining in his strength, scattering all clouds from the face of the world, until the moon and the stars shall be lost in its effulgence."

Go Forward

The following extract is from a sermon preached by Dr. Walker before the Walker Baptist Association at Summerville, near Augusta, Ga., in September, 1899. Following the sermon, he raised a cash collection of $342.00 for the Walker Baptist Institute from poor country farmers.

"And the Lord said unto Moses, Wherefore criest thou unto me? Speak unto the children of Israel, that they go forward."—Exodus 14:15.

"For more than 400 years the Israelites had been slaves in Egypt. God's time for deliverance had come. Moses, his servant, is sent as ambassador to the court of Egypt with divine credentials to represent the court of heaven. Pharaoh refuses to obey the mandates of the mighty

God, and ten or more plagues are sent upon the land. The cruel ruler decides to let Israel go. The mighty host, about three million strong, began their march. The pillar of cloud by day and the pillar of fire by night led them; they start out on the wilderness route, a distance of over four hundred miles. They rallied at Rameses, and marched out in wide columns.

"The Israelites were on foot. They were pursued by Pharaoh with 600 chosen chariots, and all the chariots of Egypt, and captains over each of them. The very flower of the Egyptian army hotly pursued the people of God; and, as Israel came to the Red Sea, at a point where it was probably ten miles wide, they saw mountains on either side, the sea in front of them, and the Egyptian army behind them. Many of the Israelites became faint-hearted and murmured against Moses. He said unto them: 'stand still, see the salvation of God, for the Egyptians you have seen to-day you will see no more forever.' Moses seemed to have been praying to God secretly, for there is no record of his public prayer. Yet the Lord said unto him, 'Wherefore criest thou unto me? Speak unto the children that they go forward.' Man's extremity is God's opportunity. The last of man is the first of God—God takes up where man leaves off. Prayer, diligence and effort go together. There is a time to pray, and then a time to act, to move. God seemed to say, 'You have prayed—now obey orders. Go forward.' The leaders moved off to the edge of the sea; the mighty waters divided—the Eternal God cut a pathway for the moving caravan. It was in the morning watch, or between 2 o'clock in the morning and sunrise. The king of day soon dispelled the darkness, and all day long the tramp, tramp of the footsteps of the Israelites was heard passing between the giant mountains of water. The angel, who had guarded them and led them, changed his position from front to rear, and got between the Israelites and the Egyptians. The Eternal God fully protects his people. As the last column of Israel passed, the Egyptian host came in. They traveled for a while as safely as did the Israelites, until the last chariot had left the bank, and when they were all out in the sea, and all Israel on the other side, Moses stretched out his rod over the sea, the waters came together and deluged the Egyptian army, while the Israelites saw the dead bodies of the Egyptians washed against the banks.

"I would have you notice that

"(1) Diligence and action must accompany prayer. Jesus taught his disciples to watch and pray. We are to pray for guidance, for direction, for strength, for conformity to God's will, for clean hearts, for the renewal of the Spirit, for the coming and extension of God's kingdom, and then watch and seize the opportunities for work under the guidance of the Holy Spirit. Joshua prayed, and then rallied his men while the sun stood still on Gibeon and the moon stood in the valley of Ajalon. God stopped the sun and moon; Israel did the fighting. A Quaker going along the Valley Forge road, heard some one in the thick brush praying. He turned aside to see who it was; he found a man in deep supplication, face suffused with tears, calling upon God for help. It was General Washington, praying for the success of the American army. He prayed for it, and then rose up and fought for it, and was victorious.

"(2) In order to go there must be reconciliation with God. The Lord is pledged to those who have become reconciled to him through Christ. Elijah built an altar, filled up the trenches, put the sacrifice upon the altar, got everything ready, and then prayed for fire. He was heard, for he was reconciled to God. Abraham was called from Mesopotamia to wander along the banks of the Euphrates; he left all he possessed for what was promised. He was reconciled to God. The language of the Christian is:

> My God is reconciled;
> I hear his pardoning voice;
> I can no longer fear;
> With confidence I now draw near,
> And Abba, Father, Abba, cry.

"(3) They were not ordered to the right hand nor to the left, but to go forward. The road to victory is often through seas, through the fire, over mountains, through floods and through flames. We must go through the world's wild forest of tribulation, through the den of lions, over the mountains of leopards, through the fiery furnace, but we must go.

"(4) The guarding angel went from front to rear and stood between Israel and the Egyptian army—so did the cloud. They passed over and saw their enemies destroyed. When you obey God, he secures and protects you. The angels encamp around to deliver. Cæsar said to his boatmen: 'You can't sink, for you carry great Cæsar.' But the child of God can sing with boldness and assurance:

> How can I die while Jesus lives
> As my Eternal God?
> Who holds the earth's huge pillars up
> And spreads the heavens abroad.
>
> How can I sink with such a prop
> Who rose and left the dead?
> Pardon and peace my soul receives
> From my exalted head.

Infallible Proofs of the Resurrection

The following is an extract from an Easter Sermon delivered by Dr. Walker at Mt. Olivet Baptist Church, April 7, 1901. The sermon was published in pamphlet form at the request of the church:

"To whom also he shewed himself alive after his passion by many infallible proofs, being seen of them forty days, and speaking of the things pertaining to the kingdom of God."—Acts 1:3.

"The presence of the two angels in shining white from the glory world, and the empty grave were evidences of Christ's resurrection, but not infallible proofs. Technically speaking, they would be considered circumstantial evidence, but our text declares there were many infallible proofs of his resurrection.

"The infallible proofs of his resurrection are to be found in his appearances at different times in various places, to different people.

"First he appeared to Mary Magdalene. She recognized his voice, and said, 'Rabboni,' which means, 'My Master, my Teacher.' She recognized his loving voice and turned to grasp his hands, but he said, 'Touch me not, for I have not yet ascended to my God, and to your God; but tell Peter and my disciples I have gone before them into Galilee; there shall they see me.' Then he appeared to two disciples on the way to Emmaus, 7½ miles from Jerusalem, talking sadly, as they journeyed, on the crucifixion, and of their disappointment. Then Jesus, as he journeyed with them, began to speak of the fulfillment of the prophecy, and to rebuke them for their unbelief of the Scriptures; when their eyes became open, they found it was their Lord. The same evening he appeared to ten of them shut up in a room for fear of the Jews. Thomas being absent. Eight days after that time he appeared to eleven, Thomas being present. Paul states that he was seen of Peter. He met the disciples at the Sea of Tiberius. And then he was seen of the twelve, as he gave the marching order from Olivet's brow. He was seen of five hundred of the brethren at once. He was seen of James. Then Paul says, last of all, 'He was seen of me also, as of one born out of due time.'

"Christ's resurrection occurred at the time of year when nature was being revived from the effects of bleak winter; spring had burst forth in greenness and beauty, the birds were singing their cheerful lays—nature was vocal with His praise; earth was putting on her spring costume, representing a resurrection of all nature from the death and grave of the winter. So our Lord chose that season of the year to come out from the tomb when all nature was teaching the lesson of the resurrection.

"Christ's resurrection proved several things. It proved that he was the real Christ, the Holy One. They had said he was a deceiver. He had said that he would lay down his life and take it up again. Real divinity, which had never died, resurrected humanity. Here the Godhead sustained manhood and revived humanity. They killed his manhood, but divinity was untouched; and on the third day Divinity restored humanity to life.

"It settled the atonement, made it efficacious and gave power to the gospel. If Christ had remained in the grave the claims of justice would have been unsatisfied; reconciliation between God and the sinner would not have been effected; heaven and earth could not have been united. Paul says: 'If Christ be not risen, our faith is vain; we are yet in our sins, and we are found false witnesses.' God sealed him as the world's Redeemer in his resurrection.

"It is a greater attestation of heaven's approval than the voice at his baptism, transfiguration, and prayer for special glorification. He proved his right to leadership. He dignified and exalted humanity. He reinstated man to favor with God. He founded his kingdom on the impregnable rock of truth, and the kingdoms of this world must become the kingdoms of our Lord and his Christ.

"His resurrection was necessary for our justification. For if he had not risen, man could not be justified with God, for our faith must rest upon a crucified, buried and risen Redeemer.

"His resurrection was necessary for the payment of the price of our redemption. It was to be a victory over sin, for he was to put away sin in the flesh and establish the reign of righteousness. It was to be a victory over the world; he was to have power in heaven and in earth, and hence must conquer the earth and subdue it; and his resurrection proved his power over nature, over disease, over death and over the grave.

"It was also a victory over Satan, for Satan was styled the prince of this world. The earth he claimed as his territory. He said to Jesus on the Mount of Temptation, that the world with all of its glory belonged to him, and he promised it to Christ if Christ would fall down and worship him. Christ chose to win the world by entering into conflict with Satan and overcoming him by his divine power.

"Ten years ago I stood on holy ground at the sepulcher where it is believed that our Lord was laid. And it seemed on that morning that I could hear again the message of the angels, 'He is not here, he is risen as he said; come, see the place where the Lord lay.' I bowed down on my knees and said, 'Thank God this is an empty tomb; the Lord is risen indeed.'

His resurrection was not only the stupendous manifestation of his power, but it was the exceeding greatness of his power. The Scripture gives us many exhibitions of the greatness of Christ's power. We have an exhibition of it in his first miracle, wrought at Cana of Galilee, when he turned the water into wine; there was a wonderful demonstration of power in stilling the tempest on the Sea of Galilee, when nature heard him and obeyed—the raging, surging billows calmed down at the voice of him who said, 'Peace, be still.' His giving sight to the blind, casting out devils, healing diseases, raising Lazarus, the widow's son of Nain, and the ruler's daughter, all were wonderful demonstrations of the power of the Christ. But the exceeding greatness of his power was not even seen in his causing darkness at high noon, while on Calvary, but it was the resurrecting of himself from the grave. O, thou living Christ, thou resurrected Jesus, live on to die no more! The exceeding greatness of thy power was seen in the resurrection of thyself from the dead!" . . .

Chapter 17
Extracts from orations and addresses
In this chapter will be found some extracts from orations and addresses delivered at different times and in different places by Dr. Walker. It has not been thought advisable to publish these addresses in full in this volume. For one thing, it would make the book too large for present purposes, and for another thing, it is proposed to issue later on a separate volume of his speeches and addresses, and also a volume of his sermons. These extracts will, nevertheless, serve to illustrate the lucid style of Dr. Walker and give some idea of the scope of the subjects treated by him from time to time.

Tuesday evening, Oct. 8, 1901, public memorial services were held in Mt. Olivet Baptist Church, New York City, by the Saloonmen's Protective Union No. I, a benevolent association, in honor of the late President McKinley. Dr. Walker accepted the invitation to deliver the principal address. More than 2,000 people were present at the exercises. He delivered the following:

Eulogy on President McKinley
"It was said of Franklin when he died that the genius that had freed America and poured a flood of light over Europe had returned to the bosom of divinity. We are here this evening

to honor the memory of our late President, who reunited the American nation, was the advance agent of protection and prosperity, universally beloved and deservedly popular. It is highly appropriate that the colored citizens of the metropolis of America should, in common with all other American citizens, pay honor to the noble-hearted, high-minded, Christian chief executive of the nation. who so recently passed to the great beyond.

"President McKinley came from the common people, and was always in sympathy with the masses. It was often said that he kept his ear close to the ground, listening for the voice of the people. It may be as truly said that he kept his ear open to hear the command of his Maker, for he had triumphant Christian faith.

"Mr. McKinley came to the executive chair at a crucial period of the nation's existence. Hard times, strikes, unrest, scarcity of money, were problems with which he was confronted. The war with Spain was soon waged; grave problems had to be faced and solved, and all these he disposed of in a statesmanlike manner.

"It has been claimed by many colored people that Mr. McKinley was not specially friendly to the Negro, and that colored men did not receive much recognition under his administration. Such a statement is made either because of ignorance of the truth or from misconception. I am one of those who believe the colored man should not stop to worry about position and office under any administration. That is a secondary consideration. Equal rights before the law, protection to life and property, the right to exist, the right to vote, the right to earn a living, the right to be a man, the right to be a freedman and a freeman, the right to expect equal and exact justice irrespective of creed, color or condition, is a greater privilege than being an officeholder. And yet, Mr. McKinley was the representative of a party which had enacted every piece of constructive legislation that we know anything about for the advancement of the colored people. Under his administration practical recognition was given to more colored citizens than under any other president. He appointed twelve men in the diplomatic and consular service. A colored man was appointed as Register of the Treasury, a colored man was appointed as Recorder of Deeds for the District of Columbia, a colored man was appointed United States Stamp Agent; colored men were appointed collectors of internal revenue in several States; collectors of ports, postmasters, collectors of census returns, land office registers, receivers of public moneys, and scores of minor Federal appointments throughout the country were given to colored men. Two distinguished colorel men were appointed paymasters in the U. S. V. during the Spanish-American War. In that same war, there were 260 colored commissioned officers and 15,000 enlisted men. In the 48th and 49th regiments, the President appointed 24 Negro captains, 50 Negro first lieutenants, 48 second lieutenants, with 2,688 enlisted men. It is estimated that, under Mr. McKinley's administration, colored men drew $8,477,000.

"Not only did the President show his interest in the race by these and other appointments, but by his visits to several of our Southern schools, such as Tuskegee, the Georgia State Industrial College, and the Prairie View Normal School in Texas. At each of these schools he made excellent speeches, in which he spoke handsomely of the military prowess and patriotism of 'the brave black boys,' as well as of the industrial and educational progress of the Negro.

"There is uneasiness in some sections concerning the attitude of Mr. McKinley's successor toward our race. We have no cause to fear President Roosevelt. His past record entitles him to the confidence, love and respect of this American nation. He has a public record in times of peace and war of which this American nation should be proud. I have but to refer to him as Police Commissioner of New York City, as Assistant Secretary of the Navy, as Civil Service Commissioner, where he made it possible for a larger number of intelligent and worthy colored men to hold permanent positions than has been made possible by any other man in the nation. His administration as Governor of the Empire State was on of fairness and impartiality. He will always be remembered as leading the Rough Riders up San Juan Heights, through the high grass, cutting the barb-wire fences, repulsing the Spanish soldiers, capturing the block house, planting Old Glory on the ramparts of Santiago, hastening the surrender of General Toral to General Shafter, and thereby freeing oppressed, suffering, bleeding Cuba.

"While Mr. McKinley made a great record as a soldier, statesman and president, he stands out conspicuously in the galaxy of presidents for his triumphant Christian faith. He said on one occasion, 'A religious spirit helps every man. It is at once a comfort and an inspiration, and makes one stronger, wiser and better in every relation of life. There is no substitute for it. It may be assailed by its enemies, as it has been, but they offer nothing in its place. It has stood the test of centuries, and has never failed to bless mankind.' He was shot by a ruthless assassin, Sept. 6, 1901. The conduct of the president at that tragic moment was like that of the Lord. In the shadow of death, as he had done in the executive mansion, he protested against mob violence, and said, referring to the murderer, 'Let no harm be done him.' Our dear dead President was again like our Christ when he said, just before yielding up the ghost, 'Good by: all, good bye; it is God's way; let his will be done, not ours.' His last prayer was one of submission and resignation to the will of the great God in whom he had so long trusted. And then, while standing on the interlacing margin of eternity, he repeated the Lord's prayer and chanted 'Nearer, my God, to thee, nearer to thee.' And lifting up his eyes on the land afar off, he beheld the King in his beauty, and fell on that long and tranquil sleep, hanging up his garments in the wardrobe of nations to rest until the archangel's trump shall disturb the long disordered creation, and soul and body shall be reunited.

"The race of which we are members feels proud of the part played by James B. Parker in preventing the assassin from firing the third shot, though prejudice has prevented his receiving his due meed of praise. But let us not despair. Mr. McKinley is not dead to this American nation. He is still joined to us by the past, and by the still more glorious anticipations of the future. Heaven has discussed the sins of America as Lincoln, Garfield and McKinley, our martyred Presidents, have walked the golden streets, arm in arm. Too long have we winked at crime, lawlessness and anarchy. And we must yet learn that the highest citizen is not safe so long as the life of the lowest citizen is not protected."

From Dr. Walker's celebrated "Reply to Hannibal Thomas," which he has delivered in many American cities, next will be given two or three short extracts.

Reply to Hannibal Thomas

"Allow me to state that the author of 'The American Negro' has given us a book that will pass as a well-written, and in some respects, scholarly production. He has given important and interesting historical information and some advice that no sensible Negro will object to. On the other hand, he has made such sweeping charges against his own race—false charges, slanderous charges, malicious charges—as to entitle him to pass alongside of Judas Iscariot, Benedict Arnold and Aaron Burr, the trinity of traitors.

"In his chapter on 'Characteristic Traits,' Mr. Thomas charges that the Negro represents an illiterate race, in which cowardice, ignorance and idleness are rife. In reply, I ask that Mr. Thomas read the history of the wars of this country from colonial times to the present days. Let him acquaint himself with the 54th Massachusetts regiment in the late Civil War; let him inform himself of the deportment of Negro soldiers at Cold Harbor, Fort Pillow, Fort Donelson, Fort Wagner, Port Royal, Port Hudson, Petersburg and Palmetto Ranch. Let him learn something about San Juan Hill and El Caney. Then ask him about this charge. It will fall of its own weight. As to ignorance among the colored race, it may be stated that they have decreased their illiteracy by nearly one-half since emancipation; they have given $13,000,000 towards their own education; they have 17,000 graduates; 500 doctors; 400 lawyers; 1,000 authors; 5 banks; 6 magazines, and 500 newspapers. At the close of the war, there were not more than 75 Negro teachers in the United States. To-day, we have more than 30,000 men and women of the race engaged in teaching school. There are yet many ignorant Negroes, just as there are still many ignorant whites, and the whites had a start on us of 250 years. As to idleness, there is a great deal of idleness among colored people—that is true; but you will find a smaller number of idlers, loafers, beggars and tramps among colored people in proportion to their numbers than among any other race. His criticism on Northern teachers who entered the South immediately after the war to lift up the recently emancipated Negro is unwarranted, as well as is the slap at Northern philanthropists for making contributions out of their princely munificence toward removing illiteracy among Southern Negroes. Their money was wisely spent, as can be clearly seen in the thousands of men and women who have been trained at these mission schools. The great men and women who went from the North to teach the despised Negro did the best work of their lives. Hampton Institute would have done good for the race if it had not educated any other man except Booker T. Washington; for he has inspired his entire race, and is to-day doing for the race what a thousand Hannibal Thomases could not do. Hannibal Thomas is pessimistic; Booker T. Washington is optimistic. Hannibal Thomas is grumbling; Booker Washington is working.

"With regard to Negro men seeking to marry white women, it is untrue of the masses. Nearly all of our men are satisfied to marry the women of the race to which they belong. We have women as good and as pure and as beautiful as any other race; and, as to variety, we excel them.

"I state it as my opinion that the solution of the so-called Negro Problem does not depend upon emigration, amalgamation nor colonization. The Negro must learn that character, industry, education and money are the essential prerequisites for intelligent citizenship. Let the American white man decide to lend a helping hand to his struggling black brother on life's highway; give him justice, equal and exact justice, North and South, East and West."

At the famous Golden Rule Meeting held at Calvary Baptist Church, West 57th Street, New York City, March 26, 1901, Dr. Walker represented the Negro race. The object of the Golden Rule Society is to do away with race prejudice and religious intolerance as far as possible. Jews, the followers of Confucius, and Protestants took part in the meeting. Rabbi Schulman and Rabbi Silverman represented the Jews, Wu Ting-fang, the Chinese minister to this country, represented Confucianism, and Dr. R. S. MacArthur, the pastor of Calvary Baptist Church, and one of the very ablest pulpit orators and lecturers in the world, Gen. T. L. James, Dr. R. Heber Newton, Edwin Markham, the poet, and Dr. Walker were among the prominent Protestants on the program. Dr. Walker was the only colored speaker and was next to the last on the list of partic-ipants. More than three thousand people were packed into Calvary's great auditorium. The audience had already been kept for nearly two hours when it came his time to speak, many hundreds having been compelled to stand during that long time. There was some interest, at least the interest of curiosity, to see and hear the colored man, and it was thought by a few that there was some misgiving on the part of the promoters of the meeting, because no one knew just what he would say or just what course he would take. An ill-timed word, an ill-considered expression on his part, might have cast a dampness over the meeting—might, in fact, have destroyed the very purpose for which the meeting was called. But he discussed his subject, "The Golden Rule as an Individual Motto," without one single mention of the Race Question in an offensive and undignified way. He made his mark, and won a great place for Negro leaders on that memorable night. Of the ten or twelve speeches made that night, the metropolitan press the next morning united in saying that the honors of the evening were carried off by Mr. Wu Ting-fang and Dr. Walker. As Wu Ting-fang was the honored guest of the occasion, it seemed courteous to couple his name with that of the man who made the best speech of the evening and won the greatest applause. Dr. Walker caught the crowd at the outset by announcing that if any one doubted the sincerity of the promoters of the Golden Rule Meeting, their doubts would be dispelled so soon as they saw him on the platform to make an address; for, said he, so far as he knew, his race identity had never been questioned. This sally provoked great laughter and applause, because Mr. Walker is a very dark-skinned Negro, and the audience saw at once the wit and humor of his statement and appreciated it.

The Golden Rule as an Individual Motto

"All men are the workmanship of the same Almighty Father. God made of one blood all nations to dwell on the face of the earth. All are alike subjected to sin and infirmity; all are responsible begins, and all alike are hastening to an eternity of righteous retribution. All men are members of the same social family. No man, therefore, can injure his fellowman without injuring himself. We build up ourselves and increase our happiness in proportion as we labor for the welfare of others. With the Golden Rule as an individual motto, will come the recognition of the Fatherhood of God and the universal brotherhood of man; and when this doctrine of the unity of the human family shall be believed and accepted by each individual, then man's inhumanity to man will cease; there will no longer be that monstrous indifference, when the question is asked, 'Where is Abel thy brother?' that replies, 'Am I my brother's keeper?' Yes, we are our brother's keeper, and this motto will not only connect man with his Creator, but will also connect man with man.

"This motto will include justice and fair play. Many of the courts of our land known as temples of justice are misnamed; they are but temples of injustice. Justice should hold an even balance. Justice should make no inquiry as to racial identity. Justice should have no kin people. With this motto adopted by every individual, each man will have an equal chance in the race of life: equal and exact justice will be given to all; a healthy public sentiment will be created in favor of law and order; law itself is weak and helpless unless upheld and supported by public sentiment.

"We should adopt the Golden Rule as an individual motto, for it will produce an era of peace and good-will among men; it will become the prophetic music of the ages. The Golden Rule will cause us to see humanity not only as it is, but humanity as it shall be. Not Lazarus, the beggar at the rich man's gate, full of sores—a mass of corruption and putrefying sores; but Lazarus in Abraham's bosom; humanity redeemed; humanity regenerated, re-organized, reanimated, reconstructed and relighted with heavenly glory. This motto will prepare us for the grand reunion of the human family in the last day. The sons of Noah who separated in the Plain of Shinar will one day hold a reunion. I believe in the theory of the unity of the human family, and that it is the order of divine Providence that these long separated brethren must meet again. Shem went into Asia, Japhet into Europe, and Ham into Africa. At the reunion, Shem will be represented in the person of the despised Chinaman and Japanese; Japhet in the person of the proud and cultured Caucasian, and Ham in the person of the despised, rejected and oppressed Negro. And I promise you that the sons of Ham will make a creditable showing when the reunion takes place."

At Carnegie Hall, New York City, on Sunday evening, May 27th, 1900, Dr. Walker shook the country by an able and patriotic address on the so-called Race Question. The hall was packed from pit to dome by an audience of fully 8,000 souls, white and black. The speech, which he called "An Appeal to Cæsar," was a review of the Conference on the Race Question held a short time before that at Montgomery, Ala., and in which such men as Bourke Cochran, John Temple Graves, Dr. H. B. Frissell, Governor MacCorkel and others participated, and was also a reply to some strictures heaped upon the race in Carnegie Lyceum the Sunday before by A. Rev. Henry Frank. The newspapers in the metropolis and throughout the country published extracts from Dr. Walker's address, and the speech won the orator much fame, as well as the title, "the defender of his race." Following are extracts from:

An Appeal to Caesar
"It is my desire to speak to you on this occasion concerning a race of people greatly misrep-resented, despised, oppressed and hated; a race peculiarly situated and everywhere spoken against. I appear in behalf of a people born in tribulation and disciplined in the hard school

of slavery; opposed and persecuted, as it has been, by some of the brightest minds that ever spoke or wielded a pen, and yet defended by some of the ablest, purest and noblest men and women the earth has ever known; among the latter may be mentioned Charles Summer. Horace Greeley, William Lloyd Garrison, Wendell Phillips, Henry Ward Beecher, Mrs. Harriet Beecher Stowe, Dr. Nathan Bishop, Mrs. Benedict and a host of others.

"From this great hall on last Sunday the news went out to the world that one Henry Frank, in preaching the gospel of the Lowly Nazarene, stated in the prelude to his discourse that the Negro should again be reduced to the slavery of ante-bellum days.

"I have now given you a hasty survey of Mr. Frank's utterances and also some of the unfavorable criticism of the gentlemen who were among the participants at the recent Montgomery Conference. Now let me give you the colored man's side. First, the Negro is an American citizen; he is a member of the body politic; he has been in this country almost as long as anybody else. The amendment to the constitution did not make us men. God made us men before man made us citizens. The amendment was only a recognition of the God-given rights of the colored man. Second, the emancipation of the colored race was the overruling providence of God. Slavery was wrong, and the time had come in the Providence of the mighty God that the battalions of the righteous army of God should march against the giant walls of slavery, and slavery fell like Dagon before the ark. Although Mr. Lincoln wrote the immortal proclamation liberating 4,000,000 human beings, which was the central act of his administration and the most glorious event of the nineteenth century, yet the hand that wrote the proclamation was guided by the bruised and pierced hand of the incarnate Christ. The 15th amendment to the Constitution of the United States, under which the colored man acquired the right to vote, was placed there after the nation had been baptized in blood, and it will require a second baptism of blood to remove it. Third, the colored man's right to citizenship cannot be denied on any ground—human or divine. Citizenship is due the Negro as a reward for his meritorious service on the battlefield. As early as 1770, Crispus Attucks, during the Boston massacre, led in the bloody drama which opened up a new and thrilling chapter in American history. He attacked the main guard of the ministerial army and went down in his own blood before the terrible fire, the first man to give his life for American independence. He is known in history as a soldier, patriot and martyr. And from that day down to the records of yesterday, the Negro has fought, bled and died for this country, and his bones have been left to bleach on a thousand battlefields. What has the Negro done to be maligned, maliciously assailed and inhumanly persecuted as he is?

"The Negro only asks for simple justice—that is all. He would have an equal chance in the race of life. He wants better opportunities. He wants to be admitted to the industrial and mechanical trades. He wants a chance to earn a living. He is striving to be honest, industrious, intelligent, economical and self-reliant. He wants his manhood recognized and encouraged rather than choked and stifled. He wants his white brother to dethrone prejudice and enthrone reason; remove hatred and place love in its stead."

The following extract is from a lecture by Dr. Walker delivered in many cities during the past year. The subject of the lecture was:

The colored men for the twentieth century

"True education is the development of power; its mission is to prepare men and women for the duties of life. There should be round, full, symmetrical development. A cultured brain and a corrupt heart frequently produces a demon, while a good heart without an enlightened brain may produce a sentimentalist. That education which isolates and walls off from the masses is a curse. We are blessed to be a blessing; nature receives to impart.

"We must be mechanics, skilled in industrial arts, a noble band of professional men, of business men. Men must prepare for the pulpit. We demand skill and ability in our professional men, and our churches must demand moral and intellectual strength on the part of those who fill the pulpit. An ignorant man in the pulpit is more dangerous than a quack doctor in a family. The man who preaches the gospel deals with immortal souls, and it is highly important that he be 'a workman that needeth not to be ashamed, rightly dividing the word of truth.'

"I do not believe in special education for the colored man. He needs the same kind of education as other people. He has proven his susceptibility to the highest intellectual attainment, and, while he needs industrial training, he should strive to secure the highest possible development along all lines. Every mind was made for growth and development and its nature is sinned against when it is doomed to ignorance. It is better to have a dead body hung to one than a dead mind.

"Our spiritual development must be commensurate with our intellectual advancement. There will be a series of conflicts between wickedness and righteousness, between virtue and vice, between truth and error; if we would join the crusade of virtue against vice, the army of righteousness against wickedness, there must be spiritual progress.

"The colored man is a bona fide American citizen; he is no Afro-American; he is a full-fledged American citizen; this country is his home, and the American flag is his flag. He is a part of the history of this great nation; a part of the body politic—bone of her bone, flesh of her flesh—her near kinsman, the brother of Shem and Japheth. Our forefathers felled the timbers, cleared the forests, bedewed the soil with their sweat, tears and blood, built up the country and perpetuated its history. They fought in all the wars from the Revolutionary struggle until this time, and even now are represented in the Philippines by our brave soldier boys. It is high time that we were claiming this as our home. Most that has been said and written concerning emigration has been written by foreigners who came to this country to find a home, and now, guilty of base ingratitude, they are talking of emigration or colonization for others.

"The twentieth century will demand that class of young men who will support the dignity of their nature. Men who will use aright their powers and capacities; men who will respect the women of their race, who will feel proud of them and their accomplishments.

"The new century is coming laden with treasuries, new gifts of heaven, hopes, aspirations, golden purposes, rings and bracelets for the adornment of personal character. The twentieth century is coming with new trials, new joys, new opportunities and increased responsibilities. The new century is coming as the bearer of glad tidings, ambassador of peace—herald of the great king.

"Let the men of the twentieth century arise, prepare to face the problems of life, to play the men for their people and for the cities of our God.

We live in deeds, not years; in thoughts, not breaths;
In feelings, no figures on a dial;
We should count time by heart throbs. He most lives
Who thinks most, feels noblest, acts the best.

Chapter 22
Conclusion

Of the countless gifts which God bestows upon man, the rarest. the most divine, is an ability to take supreme interest in human welfare. If any pious soul will accurately ascertain what it is in the character of the Man Christ Jesus, the contemplation of which fills his heart with rapture and his eyes with tears, that pious soul will know what is here meant by the expression "supreme interest in human welfare." Most of us, alarmed at the dangers which beset our lives, distracted with cares, blinded with desires to secure our own safety, are absorbed in schemes of personal advantage. Only a few men go apart, ascend the heights, survey the scene with serene, unselfish eye, and make discoveries which those engaged in their own selfish pursuits could never arrive at. But for such, the race of mankind would long ago have extirpated itself in its mad, blind strife. But for such, it never would have been discovered that no individual can be safe in welfare while any other individual is not.

In summing up the life story of Dr. Walker, I ask myself what it is that has given this man of God such a place in the affection, regard and sincere esteem of those who know and love and honor him. Is it mere intellectual ability? Great as is his intellectual strength, there are many men in his same calling of greater intellect. but they are not known and loved as he is. Is it official station? He holds no office except that of an humble minister of the gospel. Is it wealth? Dr. Walker is a poor man. In his case, I believe that the secret lies in active Christian charity, or what might be called the magnetism of simple goodness. I need not say that Dr. Walker's heart is as large as his brain—that love for humanity is an inwrought element of his nature. It is manifested in a kindness and regard that keep a silent record in many hearts; in a hand ever open and ready to help; in one of the kindest faces ever worn by man, the expression of which is: "A meeting of gentle lights without a name."

How wide, how manifold is the circle of interests which he has touched! How many, many minds has he instructed with practical wisdom! How many lives has he stimulated to wholesome energy! How many young men gratefully acknowledge him as their teacher and guide! How many aged people, how many orphans have looked up to him for succor! How many precious souls have been saved for truth, for righteousness, for God! His pen never idle, his lips never still his feet never weary, what a blessing he has been to his day and generation! In his eyes, the noblest career is that which is given up to others' wants. The successful life is that which is worn cut in conflict with wrong and woe. The only ambition worth following is the ambition to alleviate human misery and leave the world better—a little better for one's having lived in it.

And this, verily, is the greatness which the world at last acknowledges, confesses, honors—the greatness of goodness. Those who read this story of Dr. Walker's life ought, therefore, to be encouraged, not discouraged, because the greatness of goodness is a communicable power for the goodness of mankind and, unlike intellectual power, unlike official station, unlike wealth, may be attained by all. Let the reader, then, drink from this story inspiration for his best endeavors, while he thanks God that the achievement in Dr. Walker's case has been so large and so effective. The real forces of the world are not those which science chiefly delights to celebrate, but those other inward spiritual forces, such as righteousness, justice and truth, which lie behind the more visible energies, giving them all the real power that they possess, and guiding them, not blindly, but intelligently, to rational and beneficent ends.

Silas Xavier Floyd, 1902

IDA B. WELLS-BARNETT (1862-1931)

Introduction

Ida B. Wells-Barnett was born in Holly Springs, Mississippi, months before the signing of the Emancipation Proclamation.

She was the oldest of eight children. When her parents died in 1880 as a result of a yellow fever plague in Holly Springs, Wells took it upon herself to become a teacher in Holly Springs in order to support her younger siblings.

In spite of hardship, Wells was able to complete her studies at Rust College and in 1888 became a teacher in Memphis, Tennessee.

While living in Memphis, Wells became an editor and co-owner of a local black newspaper called "The Free Speech and Headlight." She wrote her editorials under the pen-name "Iola."

When a respected black store owner and friend of Barnett was lynched in 1892, Wells used her paper to attack the evils of lynching and encouraged the black townsmen of Memphis to go west.

While attending an editor's convention in New York, Wells received word not to return to Memphis because her life would be in danger. Wells took her cause to England to gain support and earned a reputation as a fiery orator and courageous leader of her people.

Upon returning to the United States, she settled in Chicago and formed the Women's Era Club, the first civic organization for African-American women. The name was later changed to the Ida B. Wells Club in honor of its founder.

She never forgot her crusade against lynching, and, in 1895 Wells published "A Red Record," which recorded race lynching in America.

At the beginning of the 20th century the racial strife in the country was disturbing. Lynching and race riots abounded across the nation.

In 1909, Barnett was asked to be a member of the "Committee of 40." This committee established the groundwork for the organization now known as the NAACP, the oldest civil rights organization in the country.

Wells-Barnett continued her tireless crusade for equal rights for African-Americans until her death in 1931. One of her mottos stated: "One had better die fighting against injustice than die like a dog or a rat in a trap."

Lynch Law in America

Our country's national crime is lynching. It is not the creature of an hour, the sudden outburst of uncontrolled fury, or the unspeakable brutality of an insane mob. It represents the cool, calculating deliberation of intelligent people who openly avow that there is an "unwritten law" that justifies them in putting human beings to death without complaint under oath, without trial by jury, without opportunity to make defense, and without right of appeal. The "unwritten law" first found excuse with the rough, rugged, and determined man who left the civilized centers of eastern States to seek for quick returns in the goldfields of the far West. Following in uncertain pursuit of continually eluding fortune, they dared the savagery of the Indians, the hardships of mountain travel, and the constant terror of border State outlaws.

Naturally, they felt slight toleration for traitors in their own ranks. It was enough to fight the enemies from without; woe to the foe within! Far removed from and entirely without protection of the courts of civilized life, these fortune-seekers made laws to meet their varying emergencies. The thief who stole a horse, the bully who "jumped" a claim, was a common enemy. If caught he was promptly tried, and if found guilty was hanged to the tree under which the court convened. Those were busy days of busy men. They had no time to give the prisoner a bill of exception or stay of execution. The only way a man had to secure a stay of execution was to behave himself. Judge Lynch was original in methods but exceedingly effective in procedure. He made the charge, impaneled the jurors, and directed the execution. When the court adjourned, the prisoner was dead. Thus lynch law held sway in the far West until civilization spread into the Territories and the orderly processes of law took its place. The emergency no longer existing, lynching gradually disappeared from the West. But the spirit of mob procedure seemed to have fastened itself upon the lawless classes, and the grim process that at first was invoked to declare justice was made the excuse to wreak vengeance and cover crime.

It next appeared in the South, where centuries of Anglo-Saxon civilization had made effective all the safeguards of court procedure. No emergency called for lynch law. It asserted its sway in defiance of law and in favor of anarchy. There it has flourished ever since, marking the thirty years of its existence with the inhuman butchery of more than ten thousand men, women, and children by shooting, drowning, hanging, and burning them alive. Not only this, but so potent is the force of example that the lynching mania has spread throughout the North and middle West. It is now no uncommon thing to read of lynchings north of Mason and Dixon's line, and those most responsible for this fashion gleefully point to these instances and assert that the North is no better than the South. This is the work of the "unwritten law" about which so much is said, and in whose behest butchery is made a pastime and national savagery condoned. The first statute of this "unwritten law" was written in the blood of thousands of brave men who thought that a government that was good enough to create a citizenship was strong enough to protect it. Under the authority of a national law that gave every citizen the right to vote, the newly-made citizens chose to exercise their suffrage. But the reign of the national law was short-lived and illusionary. Hardly had the sentences dried upon the statute-books before one Southern State after another raised the cry against "Negro domination" and proclaimed there was an "unwritten law" that justified any means to resist it. The method then inaugurated was the outrages by the "red-shirt" bands of Louisiana, South Carolina, and other Southern States, which were succeeded by the Ku-Klux Klans. These advocates of the "unwritten law" boldly avowed their purpose to intimidate, suppress, and nullify the Negro's right to vote. In support of its plans the Ku-Klux Klans, the "red-shirt" and similar organizations proceeded to beat, exile, and kill Negroes until the purpose of their organization was accomplished and the supremacy of the "unwritten law" was effected. Thus lynchings began in the South, rapidly spreading into the various States until the national law was nullified and the reign of the "unwritten law" was supreme.

Men were taken from their homes by "red-shirt" bands and stripped, beaten, and exiled; others were assassinated when their political prominence made them obnoxious to their political opponents; while the Ku-Klux barbarism of election days, reveling in the butchery of thousands of colored voters, furnished records in Congressional investigations that are a disgrace to civilization. The alleged menace of universal suffrage having been avoided by the absolute suppression of the Negro vote, the spirit of mob murder should have been satisfied and the butchery of Negroes should have ceased. But men, women, and children were the victims of murder by individuals and murder by mobs, just as they had been when killed at the demands of the "unwritten law" to prevent "Negro domination." Negroes were killed for disputing over terms of contracts with their employers. If a few barns were burned some colored man was killed to stop it.

If a colored man resented the imposition of a white man and the two came to blows, the colored man had to die, either at the hands of the white man then and there or later at the hands of a mob that speedily gathered. If he showed a spirit of courageous manhood he was hanged for his pains, and the killing was justified by the declaration that he was a "saucy nigger." Colored women have been murdered because they refused to tell the mobs where relatives could be found for "lynching bees." Boys of fourteen years have been lynched by white representatives of American civilization. In fact, for all kinds of offenses—and, for no offenses—from murders to misdemeanors, men and women are put to death without judge or jury; so that, although the political excuse was no longer necessary, the wholesale murder of human beings went on just the same.

A new name was given to the killings and a new excuse was invented for so doing. Again the aid of the "unwritten law" is invoked, and again it comes to the rescue. During the last ten years a new statute has been added to the "unwritten law." This statute proclaims that for certain crimes or alleged crimes no Negro shall be allowed a trial; that no white woman shall be compelled to charge an assault under oath or to submit any such charge to the investigation of a court of law. The result is that many men have been put to death whose innocence was afterward established; and to-day, under this reign of the "unwritten law," no colored man, no matter what his reputation, is safe from lynching if a white woman, no matter what her standing or motive, cares to charge him with insult or assault. It is considered a sufficient excuse and reasonable justification to put a prisoner to death under this "unwritten law" for the frequently repeated charge that these lynching horrors are necessary to prevent crimes against women. The sentiment of the country has been appealed to, in describing the isolated condition of white families in thickly populated Negro districts; and the charge is made that these homes are in as great danger as if they were surrounded by wild beasts. And the world has accepted this theory without let or hindrance. In many cases there has been open expression that the fate meted out to the victim was only what he deserved.

In many other instances there has been a silence that says more forcibly than words can proclaim it that it is right and proper that a human being should be seized by a mob and burned to death upon the unsworn and the uncorroborated charge of his accuser. No matter that our laws presume every man innocent until he is proved guilty; no matter that it leaves a certain class of individuals completely at the mercy of another class; no matter that it encourages those criminally disposed to blacken their faces and commit any crime in the calendar so long as they can throw suspicion on some Negro, as is frequently done, and then lead a mob to take his life; no matter that mobs make a farce of the law and a mockery of justice; no matter that hundreds of boys are being hardened in crime and schooled in vice by the repetition of such scenes before their eyes—if a white woman declares herself insulted or assaulted, some life must pay the penalty, with all the horrors of the Spanish Inquisition and all the barbarism of the Middle Ages. The world looks on and says it is well. Not only are two hundred men and women put to death annually, on the average, in this country by mobs, but these lives are taken with the greatest publicity. In many instances the leading citizens aid and abet by their presence when they do not participate, and the leading journals inflame the public mind to the lynching point with scare-head articles and offers of rewards. Whenever a burning is advertised to take place, the railroads run excursions, photographs are taken, and the same jubilee is indulged in that characterized the public hangings of one hundred years ago. There is, however, this difference: in those old days the multitude that stood by was permitted only to guy or jeer. The nineteenth century lynching mob cuts off ears, toes, and fingers, strips off flesh, and distributes portions of the body as souvenirs among the crowd. If the leaders of the mob are so minded, coal-oil is poured over the body and the victim is then roasted to death. This has been done in Texarkana and Paris, Tex., in Bardswell, Ky., and in Newman, Ga.

In Paris the officers of the law delivered the prisoner to the mob. The mayor gave the school children a holiday and the railroads ran excursion trains so that the people might see a human being burned to death. In Texarkana, the year before, men and boys amused themselves by cutting off strips of flesh and thrusting knives into their helpless victim. At Newman, Ga., of the present year, the mob tried every conceivable torture to compel the victim to cry out and confess, before they set fire to the faggots that burned him. But their trouble was all in vain—he never uttered a cry, and they could not make him confess. This condition of affairs were brutal enough and horrible enough if it were true that lynchings occurred only because of the commission of crimes against women—as is constantly declared by ministers, editors, lawyers, teachers, statesmen, and even by women themselves. It has been to the interest of those who did the lynching to blacken the good name of the helpless and defenseless victims of their hate. For this reason they publish at every possible opportunity this excuse for lynching, hoping thereby not only to palliate their own crime but at the same time to prove the Negro a moral monster and unworthy of the respect and sympathy of the civilized world. But this alleged reason adds to the deliberate injustice of the mob's work. Instead of lynchings being caused by assaults upon women, the statistics show that not one-third of the victims of lynchings are even charged with such crimes. The Chicago Tribune, which publishes annually lynching statistics, is authority for the following: In 1892, when lynching reached high-water mark, there were 241 persons lynched.

Of this number, 160 were of Negro descent. Four of them were lynched in New York, Ohio, and Kansas; the remainder were murdered in the South. Five of this number were females.

Quite a number of the one-third alleged cases of assault that have been personally investigated by the writer have shown that there was no foundation in fact for the charges; yet the claim is not made that there were no real culprits among them. The Negro has been too long associated with the white man not to have copied his vices as well as his virtues. But the Negro resents and utterly repudiates the efforts to blacken his good name by asserting that assaults upon women are peculiar to his race. The Negro has suffered far more from the commission of this crime against the women of his race by white men than the white race has ever suffered through his crimes. Very scant notice is taken of the matter when this is the condition of affairs. What becomes a crime deserving capital punishment when the tables are turned is a matter of small moment when the Negro woman is the accusing party.

But since the world has accepted this false and unjust statement, and the burden of proof has been placed upon the Negro to vindicate his race, he is taking steps to do so. The Anti-Lynching Bureau of the National Afro-American Council is arranging to have every lynching investigated and publish the facts to the world, as has been done in the case of Sam Hose, who was burned alive last April at Newman, Ga. The detective's report showed that Hose killed Cranford, his employer, in self-defense, and that, while a mob was organizing to hunt Hose to punish him for killing a white man, not till twenty-four hours after the murder was the charge of rape, embellished with psychological and physical impossibilities, circulated. That gave an impetus to the hunt, and the Atlanta Constitution's reward of $500 keyed the mob to the necessary burning and roasting pitch. Of five hundred newspaper clippings of that horrible affair, nine-tenths of them assumed Hose's guilt—simply because his murderers said so, and because it is the fashion to believe the Negro peculiarly addicted to this species of crime. All the Negro asks is justice—a fair and impartial trial in the courts of the country. That given, he will abide the result.

But this question affects the entire American nation, and from several points of view: First, on the ground of consistency. Our watchword has been "the land of the free and the home of the brave." Brave men do not gather by thousands to torture and murder a single individual, so gagged and bound he cannot make even feeble resistance or defense. Neither do brave men or women stand by and see such things done without compunction of conscience, nor read of them without protest. Our nation has been active and outspoken in its endeavors to right the wrongs of the Armenian Christian, the Russian Jew, the Irish Home Ruler, the native women of India, the Siberian exile, and the Cuban patriot. Surely it should be the nation's duty to correct its own evils!

Second, on the ground of economy. To those who fail to be convinced from any other point of view touching this momentous question, a consideration of the economic phase might not be amiss. It is generally known that mobs in Louisiana, Colorado, Wyoming, and other States have lynched subjects of other countries. When their different governments demanded satisfaction, our country was forced to confess her inability to protect said subjects in the several States because of our State-rights doctrines, or in turn demand punishment of the lynchers. This confession, while humiliating in the extreme, was not satisfactory; and, while the United States cannot protect, she can pay. This she has done, and it is certain will have to do again in the case of the recent lynching of Italians in Louisiana.

The United States already has paid in indemnities for lynching nearly a half million dollars, as follows:

Paid China for Rock Springs (Wyo.) massacre: $147,748.74
Paid China for outrages on Pacific Coast: $276,619.75
Paid Italy for massacre of Italian prisoners at New Orleans: $24,330.90
Paid Italy for lynchings at Walsenburg, Col: $10,000.00
Paid Great Britain for outrages on James Bain and Frederick Dawson: $2,800.00

Third, for the honor of Anglo-Saxon civilization. No scoffer at our boasted American civilization could say anything more harsh of it than does the American white man himself who says he is unable to protect the honor of his women without resort to such brutal, inhuman, and degrading exhibitions as characterize "lynching bees." The cannibals of the South Sea Islands roast human beings alive to satisfy hunger. The red Indian of the Western plains tied his prisoner to the stake, tortured him, and danced in fiendish glee while his victim writhed in the flames. His savage, untutored mind suggested no better way than that of wreaking vengeance upon those who had wronged him. These people knew nothing about Christianity and did not profess to follow its teachings; but such primary laws as they had they lived up to. No nation, savage or civilized, save only the United States of America, has confessed its inability to protect its women save by hanging, shooting, and burning alleged offenders.

Finally, for love of country. No American travels abroad without blushing for shame for his country on this subject. And whatever the excuse that passes current in the United States, it avails nothing abroad. With all the powers of government in control; with all laws made by white men, administered by white judges, jurors, prosecuting attorneys, and sheriffs; with every office of the executive department filled by white men—no excuse can be offered for exchanging the orderly administration of justice for barbarous lynchings and "unwritten laws." Our country should be placed speedily above the plane of confessing herself a failure at self-government. This cannot be until Americans of every section, of broadest patriotism and best and wisest citizenship, not only see the defect in our country's armor but take the necessary steps to remedy it. Although lynchings have steadily increased in number and barbarity during the last twenty years, there has been no single effort put forth by the many moral and philanthropic forces of the country to put a stop to this wholesale slaughter. Indeed, the silence and seeming condemnation grow more marked as the years go by.

A few months ago the conscience of this country was shocked because, after a two-weeks trial, a French judicial tribunal pronounced Captain Dreyfus guilty. And yet, in our own land and under our own flag, the writer can give day and detail of one thousand men, women, and children who during the last six years were put to death without trial before any tribunal on earth. Humiliating indeed, but altogether unanswerable, was the reply of the French press to our protest: "Stop your lynchings at home before you send your protests abroad."

Ida B. Wells-Barnett, Chicago, 1900

LENA MASON (1864-?)

Introduction

Mrs. Lena Mason was born in Quincy, Illinois on May 8, 1864. Her parents, Reida and Vaughn Doclin, were devout Christians and Lena became a Christian as a young child. She attended the Douglass High School of Hannibal, Missouri as well as Professor Knott's School in Chicago.

During the first three years of her ministry she preached to whites exclusively. Later her congregations were mixed. She was a member of the Colored Conference. She preached in nearly every state in the nation. She was lauded for her speaking ability and it was said "the preachers are few who can excel her in preaching". A contemporary, Rev. C.L. Leonard, pastor of the Central German M. E. Church, said of her,

I desire to express my highest appreciation of Mrs. Mason's church and effective evangelical work in my church and in many others. Mrs. Mason is now making a tour of the South, and by her lectures and sermons is doing a work among the colored people that will bear good fruit in the future. One only needs to hear Mrs. Mason lecture and preach to understand how it is that one never tires listening to her.

Her poem *A Negro In It*, written in response to the assassination of President William McKinley in 1901, also demonstrates her commitment to the civil rights for African Americans.

A Negro in It

In the last civil war,
The white folks, they began it,
But before it could close,
The Negro had to be in it.

At the battle of San Juan hill,
The rough-riders they began it;
But before victory could be won
The Negro had to be in it.

The Negro shot the Spaniard from the tree,
And never did regret it;
The rough-riders would have been dead to-day
Had the Negro not been in it.

To Buffalo, McKinley went,
To welcome people in it;

The prayer was prayed, the speech made,
The Negro, he was in it.

September sixth, in Music Hall,
With thousands, thousands in it,
McKinley fell, from the assassin's ball,
And the Negro, he got in it.

He knocked the murderer to the floor,
He struck his nose, the blood did flow;
He held him fast, all nearby saw,
When for the right, the Negro in it.

J. B. Parker is his name,
He from the state of Georgia came;
He worked in Buffalo, for his bread,
And there he saw McKinley dead.

They bought his clothes for souvenirs,
And may they ever tell it,
That when the President was shot
A brave Negro was in it.

He saved him from the third ball,
That would have taken life with it;
He held the foreigner fast and tight,
The Negro sure was in it.

McKinley now in heaven rests,
Where he will ne'er regret it;
And well he knows, that in all his joys
There was a Negro in it.

White man, stop lynching and burning
This black race, trying to thin it,
For if you go to heaven or hell
You will find some Negroes in it.

Parker knocked the assassin down,
And to beat him, he began it;
In order to save the President's life,
Yes, the Negro truly was in it.

You may try to shut the Negro out,
The courts, they have begun it;
But when we meet at the judgment bar
God will tell you the Negro is in it.

Pay them to swear a lie in court,
Both whites and blacks will do it;
Truth will shine, to the end of time,
And you will find the Negro in it.

Lena Mason

GEORGE WASHINGTON CARVER (1864-1943)

Introduction

George Washington Carver was a world-famous chemist who made important agricultural discoveries and inventions. His research on peanuts, sweet potatoes, and other products helped poor southern farmers vary their crops and improve their diets.

George Washington Carver was born on a farm near Diamond, Missouri, in Newton County about 1865. His mother, Mary, was owned by Moses and Susan Carver. His father, a slave on a neighboring farm, died before George was born. When George was just a few months old, he and his mother were kidnapped from the Carver farm by a band of men who roamed Missouri during the Civil War era. These outlaws hoped to sell George and his mother elsewhere. Young George was recovered by a neighbor and returned to the Carvers, but his mother was not. George and his older brother, Jim, were raised by Moses and Susan Carver.

In 1896, George Washington Carver left Iowa to take a job with Booker T. Washington at Tuskegee Institute in Alabama. There he conducted agricultural research and taught students until his death. Carver's research and instruction helped poor southern farmers, both white and black, change their farming practices and improve their diets. He stressed the importance of planting peanuts to upgrade the quality of the soil, which had been depleted from years of planting cotton. Carver found many practical uses for peanuts, sweet potatoes, and other agricultural products. He also created and tested many recipes in his laboratory. Carver's ideas and discoveries helped farmers improve their lives. His work also helped revitalize the depressed southern economy. He developed 118 derivative products from sweet potatoes and 300 from peanuts—including, peanut butter. Thanks to his efforts, by 1940, peanuts were the second largest cash crop in the South.

In the mid-1930s when the polio virus struck in America, Carver offered a treatment of peanut-oil massages that he believed helped many people, especially children, gain relief from the painful and paralyzing effects of polio. As word of Carver's treatment spread, people flocked to the Tuskegee campus for Carver's "cure."

Carver died on January 5, 1943, at Tuskegee Institute. He is buried on that campus near the grave of Booker T. Washington. The George Washington Carver National Monument in Diamond was created soon after his death. Established by legislation sponsored by Senator Harry S. Truman, it was the first national memorial to an African American. It shows Carver as a boy and stands on the farm where Carver was born.

Own Brief History of His Life (c. 1897)

As nearly as I can trace my history, I was about two weeks old when the war closed. My parents were both slaves. Father was killed shortly after my birth while hauling wood to town on an ox wagon.

I had three sisters and one brother. Two sisters and my brother, I know to be dead only as history tells me, yet I do not doubt it, as they are buried in the family burying ground.

My sister, mother and myself were kuckluckled, and sold in Arkansas, and there are now so many conflicting reports concerning them, I dare not say if they are dead or alive. Mr. Carver, the gentleman who owned my mother, sent a man for us, but only I was brought back, nearly dead with whooping cough, with the report that mother and sister was dead, although some say they saw them afterwards going north with the soldiers.

My home was near Neosho, Newton County, Missouri, where I remained until I was about 9 years old. My body was very feeble and it was a constant warfare between life and death to see who would gain the mastery.

From a child, I had an inordinate desire for knowledge, and especially music, painting, flowers, and the sciences, algebra being one of my favorite studies.

Day after day I spent in the woods alone in order to collect my floral beauties, and put them in my little garden I had hidden in brush not far from the house, as it was considered foolishness in the neighborhood to waste time on flowers.

And many are the tears I had shed because I would break the roots or flowers of some of my pets while removing them from the ground, and strange to say all sorts of vegetation seemed to thrive under my touch until I was styled the plant doctor, and plants from all over the country would be brought to me for treatment.

At this time I had never heard of botany and could scarcely read. Rocks had an equal fascination for me and many are the basketful that I have been compelled to remove from the outside chimney corner of the old log house, with the injunction to throw them downhill, I obeyed but picked up the choicest ones and hid them in another place, and somehow the same chimney corner would, in a few days or weeks, be running over again to suffer the same fate. I have some of the specimens in my collection now and consider them the choices of the lot. Mr. and Mrs. Carver were very kind to me and I thank them so much for my home training. They encouraged me to secure knowledge, helping me all they could, but this was quite limited. As we lived in the country, no colored schools were available. So I was permitted to go 8 miles to a school at town (Neosho). This simply sharpened my appetite for more knowledge. I managed to secure all my meager wardrobe from home, and when they heard from me I was cooking for a wealthy family in Ft. Scott, Kansas, for my board, clothes, and school privileges.

Of course, they were indignant and set for me to come home at once to die, as the family doctor had told them I would never live to see 21 years of age, I trusted to God and pressed on (I had been a Christian since about 8 years old). Sunshine and shadow were profusely intermingled such as naturally befall a defenseless orphan by those who wish to prey upon them. My health began improving and I remained here for two or three years. From here to Olathe, Kansas to school. From there to Paola Normal School. From there to Minneapolis, Kansas, where I remained in school about 7 years finishing high school, and in addition some Latin and Greek. From here to Kansas City, entered a business college of shorthand and typewriting. I was here to have a position in the union telegraph office as stenographer and typewriter, but the thirst for knowledge gained the mastery and I sought to enter Highland College at Highland, Kansas. Was refused on account of my color. I went from here to the Western part of Kansas where I saw the subject of my famous yucca and cactus painting that went to the World's Fair. I drifted from here to Winterset, Iowa, began as head cook in a large hotel. Many thanks here for the acquaintance of Mr. & Mrs. Dr. Milholland, who insisted upon me going to an art school, and chose Simpson College for me.

The opening of school found me at Simpson attempting to run a laundry for my support and batching to economize. For quite one month, I lived on prayer, beef suet and cornmeal, and quite often being without the suet and meal. Modesty prevented me telling my condition to strangers.

The news soon spread that I did laundry work and really needed it, so from that time on favors not only rained but poured on me. I cannot speak too highly of the faculty, students and in fact, the town generally. They all seemed to take pride in seeing if he or she might not do more for me than someone else.

But I wish to especially mention the names of Miss Etta M. Budd, my art teacher, Mrs. W. A. Liston & family and Rev. A. D. Field & family. Aside from their substantiate help at Simpson, were the means of my attendance at Ames. (Please fix this to suit).

I think you know my career at Ames and will fix it better than I. I will simply mention a few things. I received the prize offered for the best herbarium in cryptogamy. I would like to have said more about you Mrs. Liston & Miss Budd, but I feared you would not put it in about yourself, and I did not want one without all.

I received a letter from Mrs. Liston and she gave me an idea that it was not to be a book or anything of the kind this is only a fragmentary list.

I knit, I crochet, and make all my hose, mittens, etc., while I was in school.

If this is not sufficient, please let me know, and if it ever comes out in print, I would like to see it.

God Bless you all,

Geo. W. Carver

George Washington Carver Quotations
Education is the key to unlock the golden door of freedom.
George Washington Carver

Fear of something is at the root of hate for others, and hate within will eventually destroy the hater.
George Washington Carver

I didn't make these discoveries. God has only worked through me to reveal to His children some of His wonderful providence.
George Washington Carver

How far you go in life depends on your being tender with the young, compassionate with the aged, sympathetic with the striving and tolerant of the weak and strong. Because someday in your life you will have been all of these.
George Washington Carver

I love to think of nature as an unlimited broadcasting station, through which God speaks to us every hour, if we will only tune in.
George Washington Carver

Ninety-nine percent of the failures come from people who have the habit of making excuses.
George Washington Carver

Our creator is the same and never changes despite the names given Him by people here and in all parts of the world. Even if we gave Him no name at all, He would still be there, within us, waiting to give us good on this earth.
George Washington Carver

Reading about nature is fine, but if a person walks in the woods and listens carefully, he can learn more than what is in books, for they speak with the voice of God.
George Washington Carver

Since new developments are the products of a creative mind, we must therefore stimulate and encourage that type of mind in every way possible.
George Washington Carver

We have become ninety-nine percent money mad. The method of living at home modestly and within our income, laying a little by systematically for the proverbial rainy day which is due to come, can almost be listed among the lost arts.
George Washington Carver

When our thoughts—which bring actions—are filled with hate against anyone, Negro or white, we are in a living hell. That is as real as hell will ever be.
George Washington Carver

When you do the common things in life in an uncommon way, you will command the attention of the world.
George Washington Carver

Where there is no vision, there is no hope.
George Washington Carver

It is not the style of clothes one wears, neither the kind of automobile one drives, nor the amount of money one has in the bank, that counts. These mean nothing. It is simply service that measures success.
George Washington Carver

Learn to do common things uncommonly well; we must always keep in mind that anything that helps fill the dinner pail is valuable.
George Washington Carver

There is no short cut to achievement. Life requires thorough preparation—veneer isn't worth anything.
George Washington Carver

Christian Faith
I never have to grope for methods. The method is revealed at the moment I am inspired to create something new. Without God to draw aside the curtain I would be helpless.
George Washington Carver

W. W. EVERTS

Introduction

Produced by W. W. Everts in 1866 while serving as pastor of First Baptist Church in Chicago, IL, this *Compend of Christian Doctrines Held by Baptists* is a well-balanced catechism and contains several unusual features.

The series of questions on the family and beatitudes are without precedent in Baptist catechisms.

Church successionism finds expression in the catechetical format, (III. 30) when the question is asked, "What is the age of the Baptist?"

According to the answer, Baptists do not claim any human founder but trace their origin directly to the age and teaching of the Apostles; thus, Baptists are "older than Protestantism or Papacy".

The theology of Everts' catechism is Calvinistic in its emphasis.

Compend of Christian Doctrines Held by Baptists

Chapter 1

Being and Law of God

Q. (1) How is God made known to us?

A. Through nature, intuition, and special revelation Ps. 19:1; Rom. 1:20.

Q. (2) How is the necessity of special revelation shown'?

A. By the failure of natural religion to determine a standard of truth and duty, or provide a way of pardon and salvation. Rom. 1; 2:1-25; 1 Cor. 1:21; Luke 10:21.

Q. (3) How are the Scriptures of the Old and New Testaments shown to be a special revelation from God?

A. By inspiration, miracle, prophecies, unity, exalted character and beneficent influence. 2 Tim. 3:16; Acts 1:16; Luke 16:29; Heb. 10:7; 2 Pet. 1:21; John 17:17; Ps. 12:6, 119:140, 19:7-10.

Q. (4) How are we assured of the substantial correctness of the canon of Scriptures?

A. By the carefulness of the Hebrews in guarding the Old, and of the Church in guarding both Old and New Testaments; by comparison of ancient catalogues and manuscripts; and by the concurring testimony of all competent witnesses.

Q. (5) What is the significance of the titles of the sacred writings?

A. They are called the Scriptures, from their distinction above all human writings: Bible, as the book of books; Old and New Testaments, as embracing the will and promise of God in two dispensations; and the Word of God, as the grand summary of divine revelation.

Q. (6) How should the Scriptures be received?

A. As a treasure of heavenly truth, a standard of faith and practice, available to all without the mediation of priest of council. Deut. 11:18-21; Josh. 1:8, Isa. 8:20; Ps. 119:10, 19; 2 Tim. 3:16; 1 Pet. 2:12; Deut. 5:5; Gal. 1:8, 9; Ex. 20:8-11; Rom. 15:4.

Q. (7) What do the Scriptures principally teach?

A. The attributes, providence and will of God, and the relations and duties of man. Deut. 31:12; Job 11:7-11; Ps. 48; Luke 10:25, 26.

Q. (8) What is God?

A. A Spirit—infinite, eternal, and unchangeable in being, power, wisdom, truth, justice, goodness and holiness. John 4:24; 1 Kings 8:27; Jer. 2:24; Ps. 90:2; Mal. 3:6; Gen. 17:1; Rom. 16:27; 1 Tim. 6:1-17; Jer. 10:10; John 17:3; Isa. 44:21; Ps 99:9; Rev. 5:4.

Q. (9) Are there more Gods than one?

A. There is only one — the living and true God, whose name is Jehovah; revealed to us in the personal and relative distinctions of Father, Son, and Holy Spirit, the same in essence, equal in power and glory. Deut. 4:35; 6:4; Isa. 44:6; 1 John 5:7; Matt. 3:16; 27:11, 12.

Q. (10) What is the chief end of man?

A. To glorify God and enjoy his favor forever. Rom. 14:8; Ps. 71:22; 86:11, 12.

Q. (11) How may we glorify God and enjoy his favor?

A. By loving him and keeping his commandments. 1 Cor. 10:31; John 14:15.

Q. (12) What is the authorized summary of God's law?

A. The ten commandments recorded in twentieth chapter of Exodus. repeat the commandments in short).

Q. (13) What is the first commandment of the Decalogue?

A. Thou shalt have no other gods before me.

Q. (14) What does this commandment comprehend?

A. Supreme homage to the living and true God, forbidding the worship of any other being or any object.

Q. (15) What is the second commandment?

A. Thou shalt not make to thyself any graven image, nor the likeness of anything in heaven or earth, to bow down and worship it.

Q. (16) What does this commandment comprehend?

A. Spiritual homage, forbidding the worship of images and symbols of God, as confusing the sense of his presence and sovereignty.

Q. (17) What is the third commandment?

A. Thou shalt not take the name of the Lord thy God in vain, for the Lord will not hold him guiltless that taketh his name in vain.

Q. (18) What does this commandment comprehend?

A. Reverent use of names, attributes, ordinances, word and works of God; forbidding all profane conversation, thoughtless utterance of divine titles, or the careless observance of religion.

Q. (19) What is the fourth commandment?

A. Remember that thou keep holy the Sabbath day.

Q. (20) What does this commandment comprehend?

A. The observance of a seventh part of time (the first day of the week, according to apostolic order) as a holy day, to be devoted to religious worship and duties; forbidding all profanation of that day by secular business the pursuit of pleasure, vacant idleness, or indifference to religion.

Q. (21) What is the fifth commandment?

A. Honor thy father and thy mother, that thy days may be long in the land.

Q. (22) What does this commandment comprehend?

A. Reverence to parents and guardians; forbidding all rude behavior towards them, or any superiors in age or office.

Q. (23) What is the sixth commandment?

A. Thou shalt do no murder.

Q. (24) What does this commandment comprehend?

A. Careful preservation of our own and the life of others; forbidding all temper or conduct that leads to its destruction.

Q. (25) What is the seventh commandment?

A. Thou shalt not commit adultery.

Q. (26) What does this commandment comprehend?

A. Purity of heart, speech and conduct: forbidding unchaste thoughts words and actions.

Q. (27) What is the eighth commandment?

A. Thou shalt not steal.

Q. (28) What does this commandment comprehend?

A. Security of possessions; forbidding unauthorized appropriation of them, either by stealth, violence or fraud.

Q. (29) What is the ninth commandment?

A. Thou shall not bear false-witness against thy neighbor.

Q. (30) What does this commandment comprehend?

A. Universal truthfulness; forbidding especially whatever causelessly injures the reputation of others.

Q. (31) What is the tenth commandment?

A. Thou shalt not covet anything that is thy neighbor's.

Q. (32) What does this commandment comprehend?

A. Contentment in our own condition and circumstances; forbidding inordinate desire for the possessions, offices, or advantages of others.

Q. (33) What do the first four precepts of the Decalogue embrace?

A. Duties of God, summed up in the first great commandment -"Thou shalt love the Lord thy God with all thy soul, mind and strength." Matt. 22:37.

Q. (34) What do the remaining six precepts embrace?

A. Duties to men, summed up in the second great commandment. "Thou shalt love thy neighbor as thyself." Matt. 22:39.

Chapter 2

Salvation of Man

Q. (1) Do any perfectly keep the law of God?

A. "There is none righteous; no, not one." Fed. 7:20; Rom. 3:10.

Q. (2) In what state were our first parents created?

A. In a holy and happy state. Gen. 1:27.

Q. (3) How did they lose that holy and happy state?

A. By hearkening to Satan (one of the fallen angels) and disobeying God. Gen. 2:15-17, and iii.

Q. (4) How are all mankind made sinners?

A. By inheriting sinful nature, yielding to temptation, and transgressing God's law. Rom. 5:14; Gen. 3:20; Rom. 5:12; 1 Cor. 15:22.

Q. (5) What is sin?

A. Disobedience, or want of conformity to God's law. 1 John 3:4; Deut. 9:7; Rev. 15:9.

Q. (6) What is the penalty of sin?

A. Death of the body and of the soul. Ezek. 18:4; Rom. 6:23; Ps. 19:17.

Q. (7) How may we be saved from that penalty?

A. By the regeneration of the soul and the resurrection of the body to everlasting life, through Jesus Christ, our Lord. Rom. 6:4-8; Gal. 4:4, 5.

Q. (8) Who is the Savior of the world?

A. Jesus—in mysterious union of human and divine nature, declared to be Son of Man and Son of God. Matt. 1:23; Heb. 1:8; 1 John 5:20; 1 Tim. 3:16; Col. 2:9.

Q. (9) What has Jesus done to save us?

A. In our nature He lived a holy life, died for our sins on the cross, and rose for our justification. Rom. 5:8; 1 Tim. 1:15.

Q. (10) What offices does he execute in becoming the Savior of men?

A. Those of Mediator, Prophet, Priest and King; and only such as accept Him in these offices avail themselves of His salvation. 1 Tim. 2:5; Heb. 8:6; Deut. 18:15, 16; Acts 3:22; Ps. cx: 4; Heb. 4:15; Isa. 6:1-5; John 12:41.

Q. (11) How does Christ execute the office of Prophet?

A. By revealing to us through his Word and Spirit, the will and promise of God. John 15:15; 14:26, and 20:31; 2 Cor. 5:19.

Q. (12) How does Christ execute the office of Priest?

A. By once offering up himself a sacrifice to satisfy divine justice and reconcile us to God, and by making continual intercession for us.

Q. (13) How does Christ execute the office of King?

A. By subduing us to himself, by ruling and defending us, and by restraining and conquering all his and our foes. Ps. cx; 3; Isa. xxxiii: 22; Ps. lxxxix: 18 and lxxxi: 10; 1 Cor. 15:25.

Q. (14) How does Christ execute the office of Mediator?

A. By pleading with the Father his own death and righteousness for our pardon and peace.

Q. (15) How is Christ a Redeemer?

A. By paying, as the price of man's redemption, his own righteousness and sufferings. Heb. 9:12.

Q. (16) How does Christ make atonement?

A. By obedience and sufferings in man's stead, thereby securing to him the righteousness, and freeing him from the penalty of the law. Gal. 4:4, 5; Acts 4:12.

Q. (17) Wherein appears the humiliation of Christ?

A. In being born, and in that lowly condition, made under the law, suffering the miseries of this life, the frown of his Father, and the cursed death of the cross; in being buried, and continuing for a period under the power of death. Phil. 2:6, 7; Luke 1: 35; Phil. 2:8; Matt. 27:46 and 12:40.

Q. (18) Wherein appears the exaltation of Christ?

A. In his rising from the dead, ascending to heaven, sitting at the right hand of God the Father, and in coming to judge the world at the Last day. 1 Cor. 15:4; Luke 24:51; Col. 3:1; Acts 17:31.

Q. (19) How is this salvation made sure?

A. By the regenerating power of the Holy Spirit, leading to faith, repentance and obedience to the Lord Jesus Christ. Eph. 2:8; 2 Cor. 7:10; 1 John 2:3. Heb. 9:26 and 7:27.

Q. (20) What are the principal evidences of the acceptance of this salvation?

A. Love to Christ and his church, hatred of sin, purity of life, and abounding charity—leading to hatred of sin, forgiveness of enemies, habitual beneficence and zeal in good works. 1 Pet. 2:7; 1 John 3:14; Matt. 5:10, 44, 45.

Q. (21) What are good works'?

A. Works of charity, philanthropy and piety, done through love to God, and an indispensable fruit of it. 2 Cor. 9:8-14; 2 Tim. 6:18, 19; James 1:27.

Q. (22) What are the decrees of God?

A. The prescribed plan of creation and providence, according to which all events take place. Eph. 1:11 and 3:11; Rom. 9:18; Acts 4:28; Rev. 4:11; Ps. ciii: 19.

Q. (23) What is God's providence?

A. That supervision and over-ruling of the order and operations of nature and the affairs of the world that insures his will in all things. Ps. cxix: 6.8, lxv: 8-13; xxxv: 5; civ: 14-28; xxxvi: 6; cxiv: 15, 16; Luke 12:6, 7.

Q. (24) What is the doctrine of election?

A. Election is the gracious purpose of God, according to which he re- generates, sanctifies and saves sinners. John xv:16; Eph. v:11, 12; Rom. 8:29; 1 Pet. 1:2; 2 Thes. 2:13.

Q. (25) What is regeneration?

A. The work of God's spirit convincing man of sin and helplessness disposing him to right-eousness, and enabling him to reform his life and embrace the Lord Jesus Christ as his Savior. John 3:3, 5,7, 8; Matt. 18:13.

Q. (26) What is justification?

A. Pardoning the believer and accepting him as righteous through the name and right-eousness of Christ. Rom. 3:24 and 5:1; Gal. 2:16; 1 Cor. 5:11; Tit. 3:7.

Q. (27) How are we assured of the perseverance of the believer to everlasting life?

A. By the tendency of his renewed nature to perfect and defend itself by circumstances, companionship and habit, and especially by the promised agency of the Holy Spirit to complete in the believer the work of salvation. 1 John 3:9; Job 17:9; Phil. 1:6; John 8:31 and 2:19; Rom. 8:28.

Q. (28) What is sanctification?

A. The progressive conformity of the believer to the divine law, through the Word and Spirit of God. 2 Cor. 6:17; 1 Cor. 6:11; Heb. 1:10; Eph. 5:26, 27.

Q. (29) What does sanctification embrace?

A. Primarily, consecration of heart; and secondarily, of mind and body. 1 Cor. 6:15-19 and 9:27; Rom. 2:1.

Q. (30) How does the importance of consecration of heart appear?

A. It is more particularly enjoined in the Scriptures: the heart leaves its impress upon the character and life, and in judging men God looks at the heart. Prov. 4:23 and 3:5; Matt. 22:37; Jer. 17:9, 10; Matt. 5:28.

Q. (31) How does the importance of consecration of mind appear?

A. In elevation of mind man rises above animal races, and is endowed with immortality; and through its improved capacity truth and duty are apprehended, and being and destiny ennobled. Isa. 26:13; Acts 20:19; Rom. 7:25; Phil. 4:7; Heb. 13:16.

Q. (32) How does the importance of consecration of the body appear?

A. It is the most wonderful of the material works of God—is claimed as his abode and temple, and its true condition is essential to the greatest virtue, happiness and progress of the race, while its abuse betrays insensibility to the goodness and contempt for the authority of the Creator. Rom. 8:13; 1 Cor. 6:13, 15, 19; Eph. 5:23; Col. 2:11; 1 Thes. 5:1,2,3; Phil, 3:21.

Q. (33) What do the Scriptures specially enjoin as a means of attaining exalted spiritual life?

A. Prayer. Ps. cxiv: 18, 19; Matt. 7:7, 8, 9; Luke 11:13; James 1: 5; John 14:13, 14.

Q. (34) What is acceptable prayer?

A. Offering up desires to God for things agreeable to his will, in the name of Christ, with confession of sins and acknowledgement of his mercies. James 5:16; Mark 11:24; Matt. 5:44.

Q. (35) What is our guide in prayer?

A. The Scriptures generally, and the Lord's Prayer particularly.

Q. (36) What does the address of the Lord's Prayer teach?

A. It teaches that we should come to God in reverence and endearing confidence, as children to a father, praying with and for each other.

Q. (37) What does the first petition ask?

A. That God will dispose all to hallow his name and declare his glory.

Q. (38) What does the second petition ask?

A. That opposing rule and rival authority may be put down, and the kingdom of God established in the earth.

Q. (39) What does the third petition ask?

A. That men may know, do, and submit to God's will on earth, as angels do in heaven.

Q. (40) What does the fourth petition ask?

A. Food for the body, mind and heart.

Q. (41) What does the fifth petition ask?

A. Forgiveness of all our sins, of thought, and deed, through the plenitude of God's mercy, as we forgive those trespassing against us.

Q. (42) What does the sixth petition ask?

A. That God would by his providence shield us from temptation, or succor us in it, and deliver us from it.

Q. (43) What does the close of the Lord's Prayer teach?

A. That we should praise God in Prayer, and seek ever all our supply from the sufficiency of his power and goodness.

Q. (44) What blessings does Christ pronounce upon exalted spiritual life?

A. The Beatitudes, recorded in Matthew V.

Q. (45) What is the first beatitude?

A. "Blessed are the poor in spirit, for theirs is the kingdom of heaven."

Q. (46) Who are the poor in spirit?

A. Those humbly estimating their own attainments, sensible of their imperfections, and penitent for their faults.

Q. (47) How do they possess the kingdom of heaven?

A. fly sharing its power, protection and promise.

Q. (48) What is the second beatitude?

A. "Blessed are they that mourn, for they shall be comforted."

Q. (49) How is this blessing bestowed?

A. By alleviating, terminating and sanctifying sorrow, and crowning it with heavenly hope.

Q. (50) What is the third beatitude?

A. "Blessed are the meek, for they shall inherit the earth

Q. (51) Who are the meek?

A. Not the haughty or vindictive, but the gentle, patient and forbearing.

Q. (52) How do they inherit the earth?

A. By conciliating favor and friends, they gain property and power, the most valued possessions of earth.

Q. (53) What is the fourth beatitude?

A. "Blessed are they which do hunger and thirst after righteousness,
for they shall be filled."

Q. (54) How is this promise verified?

A. In the sanctification of individuals seeking after holiness, and in certain progress of truth and righteousness in the earth, filling the heart of the church with joy.

Q. (55) What is the fifth beatitude?

A. "Blessed are the merciful, for they shall obtain mercy."

Q. (56) How is the blessing realized?

A. Through sympathy awakened in the hearts of men toward the merciful; and by the gracious providence of God over them.

Q. (57) What is the sixth beatitude?

A. "Blessed are the pure in heart, for they shall see God."

Q. (58) How is this promise fulfilled?

A. By clearer perception of truth, duty, divine character and providence; and by a nearer approach to the presence of God in heaven.

Q. (59) What is the seventh beatitude?

A. "Blessed are the peace-makers, for they shall be called the children of God."

Q. (60) Why are peace-makers called the children of God?

A. Because all strifes of earth arise from undutifulness to God, and only by renewed filial devotion in the heart of the race can the peace of the world be restored.

Q. (61) What is the eighth beatitude?

A. "Blessed are they which are persecuted for righteousness' sake, for theirs is the kingdom of heaven."

Q. (62) How do they possess the kingdom of heaven?

A. They suffer in its cause, are promised its succor, and will enjoy its triumph.

Q. (63) What is the ninth beatitude?

A. "Blessed are ye when men shall revile you and persecute you, and shall say all manner of evil against you, falsely, for my sake."

Q. (64) How is this blessing assured?

A. Because slander leaves no stain on the soul; righteousness of character ultimately manifests itself as the light, and the last judgment will correct and compensate for the false-judgements of earth..

Q. (65) How is a future life proved?

A. It is proved by the instinct of immortality in man, by natural religion, and by divine revelation. 2 Tim. 1:10; Rom. 2:17; 1 Cor. 15:53.

Q. (66) How are we assured of the resurrection of the dead?

A. Obviously, the power that creates man can raise him from the dead. Renewal of spring from the death of winter and frequent exaltation of being from a lower to a higher grade, through apparent death, illustrate the possibility of a resurrection. The foregoing doctrine of a future life implicates it, and the testimony of Scripture renders it certain.

Q. (67) How is a future general judgment proved?

A. It is proved by the present unequal distribution of rewards and punishments, the instinctive and irrepressible craving of man for universal and impartial justice, and the explicit declaration of Holy Scripture.

Q. (68) What will be the reward of the righteous?

A. More intimate enjoyment of God, and companionship of glorified and happy spirits in progressive exaltation of being and destiny. 1 Cor. 6:2; Rom. 8:33, 34; Matt. 25:34-40; 2 Tim. 4:8.

Q. (69) What will be the punishment of the wicked?

A. Separation from the favoring presence of God, and abandonment to sinful and miserable character and companionship. Matt. 7:22, 23; xxv. 25, 40, 41.

Q. (70) How is the future punishment of the wicked proved?

A. By instinctive apprehension of mankind; by natural religion and the traditions of ages; and by the explicit testimony of divine revelation. 2 Pet. 3:7; Feel. 3:17; Acts 24:25; 2 Cor. 5:11.

Q. (71) What do the Scriptures teach of a spiritual world?

A. That as science proves that there is an endless gradation of being, from man to nothing, so there are orders of being rising in gradation from men toward the Supreme Being — some fallen from their exalted state, and others remaining in their original purity and glory. Heb. 12:22, 23; 2 Pet. 2:4; Jude vi; Rev. 7:11.

Chapter 3

Positive institutions

Q. (1) What is a positive institution?

A. One not resting merely on deductions of reason or supposed fitness of things, but upon positive enactment. Lev. i-viii.

Q. (2) What positive institutions are enjoined or recognized and guarded by Christianity?

A. Baptism, Lord's Supper, Church, Sabbath, Family and State.

Baptism

Q. (3) What is Christian Baptism?

A. The immersion of the believer in water, in the name of the Father,

Son and Holy Spirit. Mark 3:16; Acts 8:38.

Q. (4) What is the doctrine of Baptism?

A. It is the symbol of regeneration and new birth—of Christian profession, obedience, and of resurrection of the dead. Gal. 3:26; Col. 2:11, 12; Rom. 6:3-8; John 14:15 and 15:14; Luke 6:46; 1 Sam. 15:16-23.

Q. (5) How is it proved that other modes of using water are not Baptism?

A. From the terms and symbolic import of the law, and from the concurring testimony of the best scholars. Rom. 6:4, 5; Matt. 3:16; Acts 8:36-39 and 2:41; Col. 2:12.

Q. (6) How is it proved that Baptism is limited to believers?

A. It is limited to them in the Commission, in scriptural examples of its observance, and in the voluntary character of the Christian profession. Matt. 16:16; Acts 2:37, 38, 41. and 10:47.

Q (7) Why may not "Infant Baptism" be enforced as a positive law?

A. While positive law must rest at once on certain precept and example as well as clear inference, "Infant Baptism," having neither of these supports, can not properly be regarded as a law of the New Testament.

Lord's Supper

Q. (8) What is the Lord's Supper?

A. Partaking of bread and wine by the church, in commemoration of the sufferings and death of Christ for the salvation of the world. Luke 22:14-20; I ?r. 11:23-26 and 10:16.

Q. (9) Who are the proper subjects of this fellowship?

A. Believers, walking in the prescribed order and discipline of the church. Acts 2:39-41.

Q. (10) Why may not all claiming discipleship be invited to the communion?

A. Because a ceremonial fellowship should be limited to ceremonial order; the Lord's Supper should be approached only in the Lord's way; and in the primitive church none but baptized believers partook of the supper. 1 Cor. 12:13; Eph. 4:4, 5.

Q. (11) What analogies support the limitation of church fellowship?

A. As immunities of citizens are awarded to attested citizenship, and connubial fellowship only to authenticated marriage, so church communion should be awarded only to church institution—ceremonial fellowship to ceremonial order.

Q. (12) Is this ordinance designed to be a test of Christian fellowship?

A. It was not established for this purpose, but to be a perpetual remembrance of Christ's suffering and death. Luke 22:14-20; 1 Cor. 10:16 and 11:23-26.

Q. (13) Is it practically a measure of Christian fellowship?

A. It is not, as often those intercommuning evince little increase of this fellowship, while those not intercommuning are united by closer affinities of faith, experience and practice.

Church

Q. (14) What is the church of Christ?

A. His "calling" or followers taken collectively, or any number of them personally associated for his worship and glory. 1 Cor. 1: 2; Rev. 2:7; Col. 1:18-24.

Q. (15) What is the government of the church?

A. A rule of teaching, example and persuasion, enforced only by admonition, rebuke or disfellowship.

Q. (16) Where is the government of a church vested?

A. In the sense of the membership, acting freely under the law of Christ. Matt. 18:17.

Q. (17) Why should wider ecclesiastical jurisdiction be distrusted?

A. Because unauthorized in the Scriptures; discrediting the freedom and enterprise of the church; and insidiously leading to hierarchy and anti-Christ.

Q. (18) What are the principal dangers of church governments?

A. Encroachments from without by ecclesiastical association or council, or aggression from within by pretension of individuals or schism of parties.

Q. (19) What is the advantage of true church government?

A. It is the weakest with a worldly, and the strongest with a spiritual community. It declines or disappears when no longer answering its purpose, while enlarged and usurped jurisdiction may become more powerful and firm in the decline of spiritual life and liberty.

Q. (20) What is the superiority of the Church over other societies?

A. It is more easily available to all ages, lands, and classes; it is based upon higher principles and character; combines more versatile and spiritual ministries; and is exempt from evils of exclusiveness, partiality and corruption, incident to prevailing orders of association.

Q. (21) Why should all be subject to the church in its essential character?

A. Because it is the organ of public religious conscience—the executive of the kingdom of heaven; and provides the exact discipline and companionship necessary to spiritual life and achievement.

Q. (22) What is the ministry of the church?

A. The co-operation of the membership with necessary official service.

Q. (23) What officers are distinguished in the church?

A. Proclaimers or evangelists, pastors and deacons. Eph. 4:2, 12.

Q. (24) What is the office of evangelist?

A. it embraces primarily missions, but may include all general supervision and ministry required by the church.

Q. (25) What is the scope of the pastoral office?

A. It is limited to the service and care of a particular congregation or church. Eph. 4:II; 1 Tim. 3:1—7.

Q. (26) What is the deaconship?

A. It supplements the pastoral office, assuming the less public and more secular care of the congregation. Acts 6:1-6; 1 Tim. 3:8-13.

Q. (27) What is the meaning of titles of the Christian minister?

A. He is called deacon, as devoted to service; elder, as receiving office originally and naturally confided to the experience of years; bishop as entrusted with supervision; and pastor, as assuming the tender care of the shepherd.

Q. (28) Why should no gradation be established in the pastoral office?

A. Because none is recognized in i? Scriptures; names of of the adduced to sustain such gradation are fallaciously applied; and such gradation is the natural stepping-stone to papacy and Anti-Christ.

Q. (29) What are the origin and significance of principal denominational titles?

A. The ecclesiastical order rising in the ascendancy of ancient Rome, is called the Romish church; the order arising in the ascendancy of Greek cities and civilization, the Greek church; the various order of those protesting against corruptions of Christianity is called Protestantism; the followers of Luther are called Lutherans; those magnifying an order of government by elders, Presbyterians; those maintaining rule by diocesan bishops (episcopio), Episcopalians; those following Wesley, in his method of life and discipline, Methodists; those insisting on the independence of the congregation, Independents or Congregationists; those retaining the primitive baptisms are called Baptists.

Q. (30) What is the age of the Baptists?

A. While other denominations may boast uninspired founders and modern institutional and historical development, Baptists can trace their origin directly, and only to the age and teachings of the Apostles. They claim, therefore, to be older than prevailing sects and national establishments—older than Protestantism or Papacy.

Q. (31) What are the principles and practices of Baptists?

A. Exaltation of the Scriptures as the only rule of faith and practice; voluntary Christian profession, symbolized by baptism of believers; orderly observance of the Lord's Supper; covenant meeting,. as a circumspect approach to the Lord's Supper; prayer meeting, as of more certain authority and no less importance than the more imposing order of public worship; congregational government; careful instruction of the rising generation in the family and Sabbath school and zealous devotion to the spread of the gospel at home and abroad.

Q. (32) What is the missionary organization of Baptists?

A. The individual church acting freely in the diffusion of Christian knowledge through its own locality; any number of churches combining for the spread of the gospel through a particular district; the churches of a State associating for its spiritual culture; and various national associations for education, general benevolence, and home and foreign missions.

Q. (33) What is the social influence of Baptists?

A. Discrediting artificial and hereditary distinctions and monopolies, pledged alike by tradition and principle against persecution for conscience sake, they cherish the broadest philanthropy, assert the equal rights of all, and are foremost champions of soul-liberty.

Q. (34) Who are responsible for the disfellowship of sects?

A. Chiefly those holding error, and those holding truth in uncharitable temper.

Q. (35) What are the principal obstacles to the re-union and fellowship of the church?

A. Weak piety, sectarian spirit, and organized error proselyting succeeding generations to unscriptural doctrines and observance.

Sabbath

Q. (36) What is the law of the Sabbath?

A. Consecration of the seventh part of time to religious worship and duty. Ex. 20:8-12 and xxxi: 13-17.

Q. (37) How was this law originally enforced?

A. As periods are distinguished in the works of the Creator, so periods are fixed to the labors of the creature. As material creation was followed by spiritual repose and promise, so secular cares of the week should be followed by the spiritual rest of a Sabbath. As the Creator regarded with complacency the completion and glory of his works, so man is summoned by the recurring Sabbath to worship and adore Jehovah, made glorious by those works. Gen. 2:3; Deut. v:14; Jer. 21:22; Isa. lvi: 2-7 and lviii: 13, 14. lviii: 13, 14.

Q. (38) Why was the Sabbath changed from the seventh to the first day of the week?

A. To commemorate, in connection with its rest, the "new creation" by Christ, and the restored and perfected spiritual order of the world promised through him. Mark 2:28 and 16:1-4; John 20:19, 26; Acts 20:7.

Q. (39) How should the Christian Sabbath be observed?

A. By scrupulously guarding its sanctity in private and public religious worship and duty. Gen. 2:3; Isa. lviii: 13, 14; Heb. 16:25; Matt. 28:1-8.

Family

Q. (40) What social order is prescribed in the Scriptures?

A. The Family, the State and the Church.

Q. (41) Can other associations be of equal authority with these?

A. Arising from particular occasions, and without special warrant, other associations may pass away; but the family, the state and the church, founded upon permanent, necessity and divine appointment are of universal and perpetual obligation.

Q. (42) How is the divine authority of the family shown?

A. It was instituted in the garden, guarded by Moses, and reaffirmed with more spiritual sanctions by Christ, while the universal experience of mankind proved it to be a necessary foundation of happiness, social virtue and true civilization. Gen. 2:18, 21, 22; Matt. 19:4-9; Heb. 13:4; Prov. 18:22; Eph. v:22, 25, 28.

Q. (43) How is this institution guarded?

A. By numerical equality of the sexes; by civil enactments; and by divine retributions against all departure from its order.

Q. (44) Who are eligible to family order?

A. Those of suitable age and congeniality of mind, with mutual esteem and an affection transcending every other earthly love.

Q. (45) What do those entering the family order mutually pledge?

A. That, leaving all others, they will be faithful to each other, assisting each other's duties, lightening each other's cares, and promoting each other's happiness to the end of life. Gen. 2:18, 24; Matt. 19:5-9; Eph. 5:31.

Q. (46) Where is the final authority in family government vested?

A. In man, as the superior in office. Eph. v:22, 23.

Q. (47) What is woman's ascendancy in the family?

A. An empire of the heart—a rule of love.

Q. (48) What duties do parents owe their offspring?

A. Material support, impartial government, religious instruction, pure example, and continued sympathy, providence and prayer for their present and everlasting welfare. Gen. 18:18, 19; Deut. xxxi: 11-13; xxxii: 46, and 6:7-9; 1 Sam. 3:11-13; Prov. 22:6; 19:7; Rom. 5:8.

Q. (49) What do children owe their parents?

A. Filial obedience and reverence, with sympathy and care for them in old age. Ex. 20:12; Col. 3:20; Prov. 23:22 and 30:17; Deut. 17:16.

State

Q. (50) What is a State?

A. A form of civil government.

Q. (51) What is the end of civil government?

A. To protect individual liberty, and promote public welfare.

Q. (52) What is liberty?

A. Freedom of person and pursuit, as inviolate in peasant as in prince.

Q. (53) How is liberty shown to be a religious as well as civil right?

A. Because it is a natural and inalienable endowment of man; is essential to his highest culture, virtue and happiness; and also to the duties he owes to God and man.

Q. (54) What are the limits of freedom?

A. Man is free to do right—not wrong. The will of Heaven is the true freedom of earth and only by rigid enforcement of law and order are the rights of any secure. 1 Pet. 2:19.

Q. (55) How does it appear that existing government is an ordinance God?

A. Because any government is better than anarchy; existing government always approximates the character of the governed; while revolution, without preparation of the people, results in anarchy, demoralization and fiercer despotism. 1 Pet. 2:13-15; Rom. 13:1-7.

Q. (56) Is the obligation to uphold free government especially binding?

A. It is: because, proceeding from the people, it may by the suffrage be progressively and perfectly conformed to public justice and the rights of all; resistance to its authority, therefore, is a crime against the peace of nations and the Supreme Governor.

Q. (57) How may the jurisdiction of unjust government by thrown off?

A. Only by a right of revolution—a right so exceptional as to be defined by no human or divine law. If a State may at will secede from a Republic, a province may from an empire, a city from a common-wealth, and there are no "powers ordained of God," and binding the conscience.

Q. (58) What are the chief dangers to a free government?

A. Popular ignorance, party prejudice, and practical atheism. No government can be beneficent whose citizens are in antagonism with the laws of God. The wisest constitution, in the hands of a wicked nation, may be perverted to "sublime mechanics of depravity."

Q. (59) Should the State be supported?

A. By obedience to its authority, prayers for its magistracy, and promotion of its constitutional reform.

W. W. Everts, D.D.

W. E. BURGHARDT DU BOIS (1868-1963)

Introduction

William Edward Burghardt Du Bois was an American civil rights activist, leader, Pan-Africanist, sociologist, educator, historian, writer, editor, poet, and scholar. He became a naturalized citizen of Ghana in 1963 at the age of 95.

David Levering Lewis, his biographer, wrote, "In the course of his long, turbulent career, W.E.B. Du Bois attempted virtually every possible solution to the problem of twentieth-century racism—scholarship, propaganda, integration, cultural and economic separatism, politics, international communism, expatriation, third world solidarity." (*W.E.B. Du Bois: The Fight for Equality and the American Century 1919-1963*)

Du Bois' book, *The Suppression of the African Slave Trade to the United States of America, 1638-1870*, was acclaimed by Rev. J. Q. Johnson, D.D., as "Probably the best book [written in the nineteen century by an African American] from the standpoint of scientific, historical investigation."

Suppression of the African Slave Trade to the United States of America, 1638-1870

Chapter 12
The Essentials in the Struggle

How the Question Arose

We have followed a chapter of history which is of peculiar interest to the sociologist. Here was a rich new land, the wealth of which was to be had in return for ordinary manual labor. Had the country been conceived of as existing primarily for the benefit of its actual inhabitants, it might have waited for natural increase or immigration to supply the needed hands; but both Europe and the earlier colonists themselves regarded this land as existing chiefly for the benefit of Europe, and as designed to be exploited, as rapidly and ruthlessly as possible, of the boundless wealth of its resources. This was the primary excuse for the rise of the African slave-trade to America.

Every experiment of such a kind, however, where the moral standard of a people is lowered for the sake of a material advantage, is dangerous in just such proportion as that advantage is great. In this case it was great. For at least a century, in the West Indies and the southern United States, agriculture flourished, trade increased, and the English manufactures were nourished, in just such proportion as Americans stole Negroes and worked them to death. This advantage, to be sure, became much smaller in later times, and at one critical period was, at least in the Southern states, almost nil; but energetic efforts were wanting, and before the nation was aware, slavery had seized a new and well-nigh immovable footing in the Cotton Kingdom.

The colonists averred with perfect truth that they did not commence this fatal traffic, but that it was imposed upon them from without. Nevertheless, all too soon did they lay aside scruples against it and hasten to share its material benefits. Even those who braved the rough Atlantic for the highest moral motives fell early victims to the allurements of this system. Thus, throughout colonial history, in spite of many honest attempts to stop the further pursuit of the slave-trade, we notice back of nearly all such attempts a certain moral apathy, an indisposition to attack the evil with the sharp weapons which its nature demanded. Consequently, there developed steadily, irresistibly, a vast social problem, which required two centuries and a half for a nation of trained European stock and boasted moral fiber to solve.

The Moral Movement

For the solution of this problem there were, roughly speaking, three classes of efforts made during this time—moral, political, and economic: that is to say, efforts which sought directly to raise the moral standard of the nation; efforts which sought to stop the trade by legal enactment; efforts which sought to neutralize the economic advantages of the slave-trade. There is always a certain glamour about the idea of a nation rising up to crush an evil simply because it is wrong. Unfortunately, this can seldom be realized in real life; for the very existence of the evil usually argues a moral weakness in the very place where extraordinary moral strength is called for. This was the case in the early history of the colonies; and experience proved that an appeal to moral rectitude was unheard in Carolina when rice had become a great crop, and in Massachusetts when the rum-slave-traffic was paying a profit of 100%. That the various abolition societies and anti-slavery movements did heroic work in rousing the national conscience is certainly true; unfortunately, however, these movements were weakest at the most critical times. When, in 1774 and 1804, the material advantages of the slave-trade and the institution of slavery were least, it seemed possible that moral suasion might accomplish the abolition of both. A fatal spirit of temporizing, however, seized the nation at these points; and although the slave-trade was, largely for political reasons, forbidden, slavery was left untouched. Beyond this point, as years rolled by, it was found well-nigh impossible to rouse the moral sense of the nation. Even in the matter of enforcing its own laws and cooperating with the civilized world, a lethargy seized the country, and it did not awake until slavery was about to destroy it. Even then, after a long and earnest crusade, the national sense of right did not rise to the entire abolition of slavery. It was only a peculiar and almost fortuitous commingling of moral, political, and economic motives that eventually crushed African slavery and its handmaid, the slave-trade in America.

The Political Movement

The political effort to limit the slave-trade were the outcome partly of moral reprobation of the trade, partly of motives of expediency. This legislation was never such as wise and powerful rulers may make for a nation, with the ulterior purpose of calling in the respect which the nation has for law to aid in raising its standard of right. The colonial and national laws on the slave-trade merely registered, from time to time, the average public opinion concerning this traffic, and are therefore to be regarded as negative signs rather than as positive efforts. These signs were, from one point of view, evidences of moral awakening; they indicated slow, steady development of the idea that to steal even Negroes was wrong. From another point of view, these laws showed the fear of servile insurrection and the desire to ward off danger from the State; again, they often indicated a desire to appear well before the civilized world, and to rid the "land of the free" of the paradox of slavery. Representing such motives, the laws varied all the way from mere regulating acts to absolute prohibitions. On the whole, these acts were poorly conceived, loosely drawn, and wretchedly enforced. The systematic violation of the provisions of many of them led to a widespread belief that enforcement was, in the nature of the case, impossible; and thus, instead of marking ground already won, they were too often sources of distinct moral deterioration. Certainly the carnival of lawlessness that succeeded the Act of 1807, and that which preceded final suppression in 1861, were glaring examples of the failure of the efforts to suppress the slave-trade by mere law.

The Economic Movement
Economic measures against the trade were those which from the beginning had the best chance of success, but which were least tried. They included tariff measures; efforts to encourage the immigration of free laborers and the emigration of the slaves; measures for changing the character of Southern industry; and finally, plans to restore the economic balance which slavery destroyed, by raising the condition of the slave to that of complete freedom and responsibility. Like the political efforts, these rested in part on a moral basis; and, as legal enactments, they were also themselves often political measures. They differed, however, from purely moral and political efforts, in having as a main motive the economic gain which a substitution for free slave labor promised.

The simplest form of such efforts was the revenue duty on slaves that existed in all the colonies. This developed into the prohibitive tariff, and into measures encouraging immigration or industrial improvements. The colonization movement was another form of these efforts; it was inadequately conceived, and not altogether sincere, but it had a sound, although in this case, impracticable, economic basis. The on great measure which finally stopped the slave-trade forever was, naturally, the abolition of slavery, i.e., the giving to the Negro the right to sell his labor at a price consistent with his own welfare. The abolition of slavery itself, while due in part to direct moral appeal and political sagacity, was largely the result of the economic collapse of the large-farming slave system.

The Lesson for Americans
It may be doubted if ever before such political mistakes as the slavery compromises of the Constitutional Convention had such serious results, and yet, by a succession of unexpected accidents, still left a nation in position to work out its destiny. No American can study the connection of slavery with United States history, and not devoutly pray that his country may never have a similar social problem to solve, until it shows more capacity for such work than it has shown in the past. It is neither profitable nor in accordance with scientific truth to consider that whatever the constitutional fathers did right, or that slavery was a plague sent

from God and fated to be eliminated in due time. We must face the fact that this problem arose principally from the cupidity and carelessness of our ancestors. It was the plain duty of the colonies to crush the trade and the system in its infancy: they preferred to enrich themselves on its profits. It was the plain duty of the Constitutional Convention, in founding a new nation, to compromise with a threatening social evil only in case its settlement would thereby be postponed to a more favorable time: this was not the case in the slavery and the slave-trade compromises; there never was a time in the history of America when the system had a slighter economic, political, and moral justification than in 1787; and yet with this real, existent, growing evil before their eyes, a bargain largely of dollars and cents was allowed to open the highway that led straight to the Civil War. Moreover, it was due to no wisdom and foresight on the part of the fathers that fortuitous circumstances made the result of that war what it was, nor was it due to exceptional philanthropy on the part of their descendants that that result included the abolition of slavery.

With the faith of the nation broken at the very outset, the system of slavery untouched, and twenty years' respite given to the slave-trade to feed and foster it, there began, with 1787, that system of bargaining, truckling, and compromising with a moral, political, and economic monstrosity, which makes the history of our dealing with slavery in the first half of the nineteenth century so discreditable to a great people. Each generation sought to shift its load upon the next, and the burden rolled on, until a generation came which was both too weak and too strong to bear it longer. One cannot, to be sure, demand of whole nations exceptional moral foresight and heroism; but a certain hard common-sense in facing the complicated phenomena of political life must be expected in every progressive people. In some respects we as a nation seem to lack this; we have the somewhat inchoate idea that we are not destined to be harassed with great social questions, and that even if we are, and fail to answer them, the fault is with the question and not with us. Consequently we often congratulate ourselves more on getting rid of a problem than on solving it. Such an attitude is dangerous; we have and shall have, as other peoples have had, critical, momentous, and pressing questions to answer. The riddle of the Sphinx may be postponed, it may be evasively answered now; sometime it must be fully answered.

It behooves the United States, therefore, in the interest both of scientific truth and of future social reform, carefully to study such chapters of her history as that of the suppression of the slave-trade. The most obvious question which this study suggest is: How far in a State can a recognized moral wrong safely be compromised? And although this chapter of history can give us no definite answer suited to the ever-varying aspects of political life, yet it would seem to warn any nation from allowing, through carelessness and moral cowardice, any social evil to grow. No persons would have seen the Civil War with more surprise and horror than the Revolutionists of 1776; yet from the small and apparently dying institution of their day arose the walled and castled Slave-Power. From this we may conclude that it behooves nations as well as men to do things at the very moment when they ought to be done.

W. E. Burghardt Du Bois

WILLIAM J. SEYMOUR (1870-1922)

Introduction

William Joseph Seymour was an African American minister, and an initiator of the Pentecostal religious movement.

Born the son of freed slaves in Centerville, Louisiana, Seymour developed a belief in *glossolalia* ("speaking in tongues") as a confirmation of the gifts of the Holy Spirit. As a consequence of teaching this, he was asked to leave the Los Angeles parish where he had formerly ministered. Looking for a place to continue his work, he found a run-down building in downtown Los Angeles located on Azusa Street, and preached his doctrinal beliefs there.

The result was the Azusa Street Revival. Seymour not only rejected the existing racial barriers in favor of "unity in Christ", he also rejected the then almost-universal barriers to women in any form of church leadership. These revival meetings took place between 1906 and 1909, and became the subject of intense investigation by more mainstream Protestants. Some left feeling that Seymour's views were heresy, while others accepted his teachings and returned to their own congregations to expound them. The resulting movement became widely known as "Pentecostalism", likening it to the manifestations of the Holy Spirit recorded as occurring in the first two chapters of Acts.

Most of the current charismatic groups can claim some lineage linking them to the Azusa Street Revival and William Seymour.

Although many instances of *glossolalia* occurred prior to 1906, the Azusa Street Revival led by William J. Seymour is the watershed of the Pentecostal movement in the U.S and worldwide. Beginning April 9, 1906 in Los Angeles, California at the home of Edward Lee who claimed the infilling of the Holy Spirit as of such date. William J. Seymour claimed that he was overcome with the Holy Spirit on April 12, 1906. On April 18, 1906, the *Los Angeles Times* ran a front page story on the revival, "Weird Babel of Tongues, New Sect of fanatics is breaking loose, Wild scene last night on Azusa Street, gurgle of wordless talk by a sister".

William Seymour died of a heart attack in 1922

Many of the sermons that William Seymour preached at the Azusa Street mission were recorded by a stenographer and then published in the *Apostolic Faith* newspaper. Examples of Seymour's preaching follow.

River of Living Water

In the fourth chapter of John, the words come, "Jesus answered and said unto her, If thou knewest the gift of God and who it is that saith to thee Give me to drink, thou wouldest have asked of Him and He would have given thee living water." Praise God for the living waters today that flow freely, for it comes from God to every hungry and thirsty heart. Jesus said, "He that believeth on me, as the scripture hath said, out of his inmost being shall flow rivers of living waters." Then we are able to go in the mighty name of Jesus to the ends of the earth and water dry places, deserts and solitary places until these parched, sad, lonely hearts are made to rejoice in the God of their salvation. We want the rivers today. Hallelujah! Glory to God in the highest.

In Jesus Christ we get forgiveness of sin, and we get sanctification of our spirit, soul and body, and upon that we get the gift of the Holy Ghost that Jesus promised to His disciples, the promise of the Father. All this we get through the atonement. Hallelujah!

The prophet said that He had borne our griefs and carried our sorrows. He was wounded for our transgressions, bruised for our iniquities, the chastisement of our peace was upon Him and with His stripes we are healed. So we get healing, health, salvation, joy, life—everything in Jesus. Glory to God!

There are many wells today, but they are dry. There are many hungry souls today that are empty. But let us come to Jesus and take Him at His Word and we will find wells of salvation, and be able to draw waters out of the well of salvation, for Jesus is that well.

At this time Jesus was weary from a long journey, and He sat on the well in Samaria, and a woman came to draw water. He asked her for a drink. She answered, "How is it that thou being a Jew askest drink of me who am a woman of Samaria, for the Jews have no dealings with the Samaritans?" Jesus said, "If thou knewest the gift of God, and who it is that saith to thee, give me to drink, thou wouldest have asked of Him and He would have given thee living water."

O, how sweet it was to see Jesus, the Lamb of God that takes away the sin of the world, that great sacrifice that God had given to a lost, dying and benighted world, sitting on the well and talking with the woman; so gentle, so meek and so kind that it gave her an appetite to talk further with Him, until He got into her secret and uncovered her life. Then she was pricked in her heart, confessed her sins and received pardon, cleansing from fornication and adultery, was washed from stain and guilt of sin and was made a child of God, and above all, received the well of salvation in her heart. It was so sweet and joyful and good. Her heart was so filled with love that she felt she could take in a whole lost world. So she ran away with a well of salvation and left the old water pot on the well. How true it is in this day, when we get the baptism with the Holy Spirit, we have something to tell, and it is that the blood of Jesus Christ cleanseth from all sin. The baptism with the Holy Ghost gives us power to testify to a risen, resurrected Savior. Our affections are in Jesus Christ, the Lamb of God that takes away the sin of the world. How I worship Him today! How I praise Him for the all-cleansing blood.

Jesus' promises are true and sure. The woman said to Him, after He had uncovered her secret, "Sir I perceive that Thou art a prophet." Yes, He was a prophet. He was that great prophet that Moses said the Lord would raise up. He is here today. Will we be taught of that prophet? Will we hear Him? Let us accept Him in all His fullness.

He said, "He that believeth on me, the works that I do shall he do also, and greater works than these shall ye do, because I go unto my Father." These disciples to whom He was speaking, had been saved, sanctified, anointed with the Holy Spirit, their hearts had been opened to understand the scriptures, and yet Jesus said, "Tarry ye in the city of Jerusalem, until ye be endued with power from on high." "John truly baptized with water, but ye shall be baptized with the Holy Ghost not many days hence." So the same commission comes to us. We find that they obeyed His commission and were all filled with the Holy Ghost on the day of Pentecost, and Peter standing up, said, "This is that which was spoken by the prophet Joel." Dear loved ones, we preach the same sermon. "This is that which was spoken by the prophet Joel, and it shall come to pass in the last days, saith God, I will pour out my Spirit upon all flesh, and your sons and your daughters shall prophesy, and your young men shall see visions, and your old men shall dream dreams; and on my servants and on my handmaidens I will pour out in those days of my Spirit, and they shall prophesy ... The promise is unto you, and to your children, and to all that are afar off, even as many as the Lord our God shall call." That means until now and to last until Jesus comes.

There are so many people today like the woman. They are controlled by the fathers. Our salvation is not in some father or human instruments. It is sad to see people so blinded, worshiping the creature more than the Creator. Listen to what the woman said, "Our fathers worshiped in this mountain, and ye say Jerusalem is the place where men ought to worship." So many today are worshiping in the mountains, big churches, stone and frame buildings. But Jesus teaches that salvation is not in these stone structures—not in the mountains—not in the hills, but in God. For God is a Spirit. Jesus said unto her, "Woman, believe Me, the hour cometh and now is, when ye shall neither in this mountain nor yet at Jerusalem worship the Father." So many people today are controlled by men. Their salvation reaches out no further than the boundary line of human creeds, but praise God for freedom in the Spirit. There are depths and heights and breadths that we can reach through the power of the blessed Spirit. "Eye hath not seen, nor ear heard, neither have entered into the hearts of man the things that God hath prepared for them that love Him."

The Jews were the religious leaders at this time, and people had no more light upon salvation than the Jews gave them. The Jews were God's chosen people to evangelize the world. He had entrusted them to give all nations the true knowledge of God, but they went into traditions and doctrines of men, and were blinded and in the dark. Jesus came as the light of the world, and He is that light. "If we walk in the light as He is in the light, we have fellowship one with another, and the blood of Jesus Christ His Son cleanseth us from all sin." Let us honor the Spirit, for Jesus has sent Him to teach and lead us into all truth.

Above all, let us honor the blood of Jesus Christ every moment of our lives, and we will be sweet in our souls. We will be able to talk of this common salvation to everyone that we meet. god will let His anointing rest upon us in telling them of this precious truth. This truth belongs to God. We have no right to tax anyone for the truth, because God has entrusted us with it to tell it. Freely we receive, freely we give. So the gospel is preached freely, and God will bless it and spread it Himself, and we have experienced that He does. We have found Him to be true to His promise all the way. We have tried Him and proved Him. His promises are sure.

William J. Seymour

Sanctified on the Cross
"I pray not that Thou shouldest take them out of the world, but that Thou shouldest keep them from the evil. They are not of the world even as I am not of the world. Sanctify them

through Thy truth, Thy word is truth." Jesus is still praying this prayer today for every believer to come and be sanctified. Glory to God! Sanctification makes us one with the Lord Jesus (Heb. 2:11).

Sanctification makes us holy as Jesus is. Then the prayer of Jesus is answered, and we become one with Him, even as He is one with the Father. Bless His holy name.

He says again in 1 Thess. 4:3, "For this is the will of God even your sanctification." So it is His will for every soul to be saved from all sin, actual and original. We get our actual sins cleansed away through the blood of Jesus Christ at the cross; but our original sin we got cleansed on the cross. It must be a real death to the old man. Romans 6:6, 7, "Knowing this that our old man is crucified with Him, that the body of sin might be destroyed, that henceforth we should not serve sin: for he that is dead is freed from sin." So it takes the death of the old man in order that Christ might be sanctified in us. It is not sufficient to have the old man stunned or knocked down, for he will rise again.

God is calling His people to true holiness in these days. We thank God for the blessed light that He is giving us. He says in 2 Tim. 2:21, "If a man therefore purge himself from these, he shall be a vessel unto honor, sanctified and meet for the Master's use." He means for us to be purged from uncleanness and all kinds of sin. Then we shall be a vessel unto honor, sanctified and meet for the Master's use, and prepared unto every good work. Sanctification makes us holy and destroys the breed of sin, the love of sin and carnality. It makes us pure and whiter than snow. Bless His holy name!

The Lord Jesus says, "Blessed are the pure in heart." Sanctification makes us pure in heart. Any man that is saved and sanctified can feel the fire burning in his heart, when he calls on the name of Jesus. O may God help men and women everywhere to lead a holy life, free from sin, for the Holy Spirit seeks to lead you out of sin into the marvelous light of the Son of God.

The Word says, "Follow peace with all men and holiness without which no man shall see the Lord." So, beloved, when we get Jesus Christ our King of Peace in our hearts, we have the almighty Christ, the everlasting Father, the Prince of Peace. "Thou wilt keep him in perfect peace whose mind is stayed on Thee, because He trusteth in Thee." We shall have wisdom, righteousness and power, for God is righteous in all His ways and holy in all His acts. This holiness means perfect love in our hearts, perfect love that casteth out fear.

Brother Paul says in order to become holy and live a holy life, we should abstain from all appearance of evil. Then the apostle adds, "And the very God of peace sanctify you wholly, and I pray God your whole spirit and soul and body be preserved blameless unto the coming of our Lord Jesus Christ" (1 Thess. 5:23). "To the end He may establish your hearts unblameable in holiness before God, even our Father, at the coming of our Lord Jesus Christ with all His saints" (1 Thess. 3:13). Bless His holy name. O beloved, after you have received the light, it is holiness or hell. God is calling for men and women in these days that will live a holy life free from sin. We should remain before God until His all cleansing blood makes us holy—body, soul and spirit.

William J. Seymour

The Doctrines and Discipline of the Azusa Street Apostolic Faith Mission

The Apostolic Faith: A Doctrinal Overview

The Apostolic Faith stands for the restoration of the faith once delivered to the saints, the old-time religion of camp meetings, revivals, missions, street mission work and Christian unity everywhere.

According to God's word (John 17:20,21).

Teaching on repentance (Mark 1:14,15).

Godly sorrow for sins (Examples: Matt. 9:13; 2 Cor. 7:9,11; Acts 3:19; Acts 17:30).

Confession of sin (Luke 15:21; Luke 18:13).

Restitution and faith in Jesus Christ (Ezek. 33:15; Luke 19:18).

Jesus died for our sins and arose for our justification (Romans 4:25).

The first work of grace. Justification is that act of God's free grace by which we receive remission of sins (Rom. 3:25; Acts 10:42,43; Rom. 5:1,10; John 3:3,14; 2 Cor. 5:17).

The second work of grace. The Holy Ghost calls the second work the "second benefit." The margin reads "second grace." And the Syriac reads that you might receive the grace "doubly" (2 Cor. 1:15).

Sanctification is the second work of grace and is that act of God's grace by which He makes us holy in doctrine and life (John 17:15, 17; Heb. 13:12;2:11; Heb. 12:14). Jesus opened the Bible to his disciples before He went back to heaven (Luke 24:24-50). He taught His doctrine to them well before He went to Heaven so when we get sanctified Jesus will teach us the Bible also, bless the Lord.

Sanctification is cleansing to make holy. The disciples were sanctified before the day of Pentecost. By careful study of scripture, you will find it is so now. "Ye are clean through the word which I have spoken unto you" and Jesus had breathed on them the Holy Ghost (John 15:3; John 13-10; John 20:21,22). You know that they could not receive the Spirit if they were not all clean. Jesus cleansed and got all doubt out of His church before He went back to glory. The disciples had the grace of the Spirit before the day of Pentecost. The disciples had an infilling of the Spirit before the day of Pentecost. For Jesus had cleansed the sanctuary and they had the witness in their hearts that He was their risen Lord and Savior and they were continually in the temple praising and blessing God (Luke 24:51,53).

The baptism in the Holy Ghost and fire means to be flooded with the love of God and power for service, and a love for the truth as it is in God's word. So when we receive it we have the same signs to follow as the disciples received on the day of Pentecost. For the Holy Spirit gives us a sound mind, faith, love and power (2 Tim. 1:7). This is the standard Jesus gave to the church.

The greatest evidence of the Holy Spirit abiding in the believer is what Jesus Christ promised He would do. Jesus promised He would teach us all things, and bring all things to your remembrance whatsoever I have said so He means what He says. (John 14:17-26; John 16:7-15). So when He comes He does that in the believer, for He does it for me.

Seeking healing. We must believe, with great joy, that God is able to heal "I am the Lord that healeth thee" (Exodus 15:26; Jas. 5:14; Psalm 103:3; 2 Kings 20:5; Matt. 8:16,17; Mark

16:16-18). "Behold I am the Lord, the God of all flesh; is there anything too hard for Me?" (Jer. 32:27; Luke 24:52,53).

God, Spirit and Word go together. They are the two witnesses spoken of in Zech. 4:3-14 and Rev. 11:3. When these two witnesses are not recognized all kinds of confusion will be manifested in the church.

Too many have confused the grace of sanctification with the endowment of power or the baptism with the Holy Ghost. Others have taken "the anointing" which we receive after we are sanctified for the baptism and failed to reach the glory and power of a true Pentecost (John 20:21-24; Acts 2:3,4).

We read in the second chapter of Colossians, "Beware lest any man spoil you through philosophy and vain deceit, after the tradition of men, after the rudiments of the world, and not after Christ." This chapter tells us about Christ blotting out the handwriting of ordinances that were against us and contrary to us, and I am glad He did nail these ordinances to the cross with Him. He took them out of the way, nailing it to His cross. Bless the Lord. These were the old Jewish ordinances of divers washings, Sabbath days, new moons, circumcision and the Passover supper, and so on. But Jesus has ordinances in His church. Bless His dear Name.

Three ordinances Christ Himself instituted in His Church. First, He commands His ministers to baptize in water in the name of the Father and the Son and the Holy Ghost and it was practiced by the apostles (Matt. 28:19; Acts 32:38; Acts 22:16; Acts 8:12,17). The eunuch was baptized (Acts 8:35). The Apostle Paul was baptized. So many cases we can find in Acts where it was practiced after John the Baptist had died.

We believe in water baptism. Our mode is immersion only, and single, in the name of the Father, and of the Son, and of the Holy Ghost. Matt. 28:19,20; 2 Cor. 13:13; and as much light as the Holy Ghost will reveal to us by His word.

Second, foot washing is an ordinance that Jesus Himself instituted in His church and we, His followers, should observe it. For He has commanded us to observe all things that He has commanded us to teach. So we find we will have to recognize these three ordinances.

We believe in the feet washing; we believe it to be an ordinance. Jesus said, in the John 13-17, "Ye call me Master and Lord, and ye say well, for so I am. If I then, your Lord and Master, have washed your feet, ye also ought to wash one another's feet for I have given you an example, that ye should do as I have done to you. Verily, verily I say unto you, the servant is not greater than his Lord: neither is he that is sent greater than he that sent him. If ye know these things, happy are ye if ye do them.

We believe in the ordinance of the Lord's supper, as it is set forth in 1 Cor. 11:2, 23-34 and Matt. 26: 26-29. We believe in taking unfermented wine and unleavened bread.

We the ministers, must be the husband of one wife (1 Tim. 3:2; Titus 1:6-9). We do not believe in unscriptural marriage (Rom. 7:2-4; 1 Cor. 7:39).

In Matt. 19:3-9, Matt. 5:32 and Mark 10:5-11, Jesus restored marriage back to the Edenic standard. Many are confused over the meaning of these passages. If either the husband or wife have defied themselves in the sins mentioned Jesus does not give either recognition as being legally married, while the first husband or wife is still living. They must repent to God and be reconciled to each other "for as Christ forgives so must we forgive" (1 Cor. 7:11). If a man or woman marry and either one has a living husband or wife their continuing to live together as a committing of fornication or adultery and the party who has a living husband or wife should be put away by the other, leaving the man or woman who has no living companion free to marry again to some one who is also free (1 Cor. 7:2; Matt. 19:9).

We do not believe in making a hobby of this doctrine of divorce, but we believe in the truth be comparing scripture with scripture, that no one in this work can marry the second husband or the second wife, while the first one is living (Rom. 7:2,3,4; 1 Cor. 7:10,11; 1 Cor. 7:39; 1 Tim. 3:9; Matt. 5:32; Luke 16:18; Mark 2-12).

Bishop Hurst says, in his *Church History*, that the gift of tongues has appeared in communities under powerful religious stimulus, as among the Cornisards, early Quakers, Lasare in Sweden in 1841-43, in the Irish Revival in 1859, and in the Catholic Apostolic (Irvingite) Church (Vol. 1, page 90).

I can say, through the power of the Spirit, that wherever God can get a people that will come together in one accord and one mind in the Word of God, the baptism of the Holy Ghost will fall upon them, like as at Cornelius' house (Acts 10:45,46). It means, to be in one accord, as the word says in Acts 2:42,47.

The blood of Jesus will never blot out any sin between man and man they can make right; but if we can't make wrongs right, the blood graciously covers (Matt. 5:24; Matt. 6:15; Matt. 18:35; 1 John 1:7-9).

Dear loved ones, God's promises are true. We read in Exodus 12:3, God commanded Moses to take a lamb for a house and a house for a lamb when He was about to bring the children out of Egypt. Bless His holy Name, amen! They were to kill the lamb and take its blood and sprinkle it over the door overhead and the sides to save them from the destroyer. But in the very house they were instructed to eat the body. The blood saved them from the destroyer, but the body of the lamb saved them from disease and sickness. Glory to His Name! May we obey God's word and voice and we shall be saved through Jesus from sins and feast on His perfect body. Jesus is founder of His church, the Christian church, by His own precious blood. Hallelujah! So, Jesus is the Christian Passover. When the Jews eat the Passover they remember God bringing them out of Egypt and point to His coming. So we eat the Christian Passover and remember Calvary, how Jesus died and saved us, and we look forward to His coming again.

Moses' lamb was a type of Christ, the true Lamb, so Christ is our Lamb, bringing health to our imperfect body. Moses was founder of the Jewish church, by God, through the paschal lamb by the blood and body of the lamb. But Jesus is the Lamb of God, the founder of the Christian church.

William J. Seymour, The Doctrines and Discipline of the Azusa
Street Apostolic Faith Mission, Los Angeles, California. *1915*

JAMES WELDON JOHNSON (1871-1938)

Introduction

James Weldon Johnson was a leading American author, poet, early civil rights activist, and prominent figure in the Harlem Renaissance. Johnson is best remembered for his writing, which includes novels, poems, and collections of folklore. He was also one of the first African-American professors at New York University.

Johnson was born in Jacksonville, Florida. As a youth, he attended the preparatory school, then college division of Atlanta University (now called Clark Atlanta University), from which he graduated in 1896. He was the first African American accepted to the Florida bar and became a member of Phi Beta Sigma Fraternity, Inc..

He served as principal of Stanton, a school for African American students in Jacksonville, until 1902, when he resigned and moved to New York City to work in musical theater with his brother, J. Rosamond Johnson. In 1906 he became a diplomat, serving as consul to Venezuela and Nicaragua. During his work in the foreign service, Johnson became a published poet, with work printed in the magazine *The Century Magazine* and in *The Independent.*

Johnson's first major literary success was *The Autobiography of an Ex-Colored Man* (1912), a fictional account of a light-skinned black man's attempts to survive and succeed in the early 20th Century that is designed to read like an autobiography. Initially released anonymously, the book was republished by Johnson under his own name in 1927.

While serving the NAACP from 1920 through 1931 — starting as an organizer and becoming the first black male secretary in the organization's history — he continued to write and edit in a variety of genres. In 1922, he edited *The Book of American Negro Poetry*, which the Academy of American Poets calls "a major contribution to the history of African-American literature." One of the works for which he is best remembered today, *God's Trombones: Seven Negro Sermons in Verse*, was published in 1927 and celebrates the tradition of the folk preacher.

Johnson composed the lyrics of *Lift Ev'ry Voice and Sing*, for which his brother J. Rosamond Johnson composed the music, during the years at Stanton. This song, originally composed in 1900 to celebrate the birthday of Abraham Lincoln, is commonly known as the "Negro (or Black) National Anthem." The song was entered into the Congressional Record as the official African American National Hymn following the success of a 1990 rendition by singer Melba Moore.

James Weldon Johnson died in 1938 while on vacation in Wiscasset, Maine, when the car he was driving was hit by a train.

God's Trombones: Seven Negro Sermons in Verse
Preface

A good deal has been written on the folk creations of the American Negro: his music, sacred and secular; his plantation tales, and his dances; but that there are folk sermons, as well, is a fact that has passed unnoticed. I remember hearing in my boyhood sermons that were current, sermons that passed with only slight modifications from preacher to preacher and from locality to locality. Such sermons were, "The Valley of Dry Bones," which was based on the vision of the prophet in the 37th chapter of Ezekiel; the "Train Sermon," in which both God and the devil were pictured as running trains, one loaded with saints, that pulled up in heaven, and the other with sinners, that dumped its load in hell; the "Heavenly March," which gave in detail the journey of the faithful from earth, on up through the pearly gates to the great white throne. Then there was a stereotyped sermon which had no definite subject, and which was quite generally preached; it began with the Creation, went on to the fall of man, rambled through the trials and tribulations of the Hebrew Children, came down to the redemption by Christ, and ended with the Judgment Day and a warning and an exhortation to sinners. This was the framework of a sermon that allowed the individual preacher the widest latitude that could be desired for all his arts and powers. There was one Negro sermon that in its day was a classic, and widely known to the public. Thousands of people, white and black, flocked to the church of John Jasper in Richmond, Virginia, to hear him preach his famous sermon proving that the earth is flat and the sun does move. John Jasper's sermon was imitated and adapted by many lesser preachers.

I heard only a few months ago in Harlem an up-to-date version of the "Train Sermon." The preacher styled himself "Son of Thunder"—a sobriquet adopted by many of the old-time preachers—and phrased his subject, "The Black Diamond Express, running between here and hell, making thirteen stops and arriving in hell ahead of time."

The old-time Negro preacher has not yet been given the niche in which he properly belongs. He has been portrayed only as a semi-comic figure. He had, it is true, his comic aspects, but on the whole he was an important figure, and at bottom a vital factor. It was through him that the people of diverse languages and customs who were brought here from diverse parts of Africa and thrown into slavery were given their first sense of unity and solidarity. He was the first shepherd of this bewildered flock. His power for good or ill was very great. It was the old-time preacher who for generations was the mainspring of hope and inspiration for the Negro in America. It was also he who instilled into the Negro the narcotic doctrine epitomized in the Spiritual, "You May Have All Dis World, But Give Me Jesus." This power of the old-time preacher, somewhat lessened and changed in his successors, is still a vital force; in fact, it is still the greatest single influence among the colored people of the United States. The Negro today is, perhaps, the most priest-governed group in the country.

The history of the Negro preacher reaches back to Colonial days. Before the Revolutionary War, when slavery had not yet taken on its more grim and heartless economic aspects, there were famed black preachers who preached to both whites and blacks. George Liele was preaching to whites and blacks at Augusta, Ga., as far back as 1773, and Andrew Bryan at Savannah a few years later.

The most famous of these earliest preachers was Black Harry, who during the Revolutionary period accompanied Bishop Asbury as a drawing card and preached from the same platform with other founders of the Methodist Church. Of him, John Ledman in his History of the Rise of Methodism in America says, "The truth was that Harry was a more popular speaker than Mr. Asbury or almost anyone else in his day." In the two or three decades before the Civil War Negro preachers in the North, many of them well-educated and cultured, were courageous spokesmen against slavery and all its evils.

The effect on the Negro of the establishment of separate and independent places of worship can hardly be estimated. Some idea of how far this effect reached may be gained by a comparison between the social and religious trends of the Negroes of the Old South and of the Negroes of French Louisiana and the West Indies, where they were within and directly under the Roman Catholic Church and the Church of England. The old-time preacher brought about the establishment of these independent places of worship and thereby provided the first sphere in which race leadership might develop and function. These scattered and often clandestine groups have grown into the strongest and richest organization among colored Americans. Another thought—except for these separate places of worship there never would have been any Spirituals.

The old-time preacher was generally a man far above the average in intelligence; he was, not infrequently, a man of positive genius. The earliest of these preachers must have virtually committed many parts of the Bible to memory through hearing the scriptures read or preached from in the white churches which the slaves attended. They were the first of the slaves to learn to read, and their reading was confined to the Bible, and specifically to the more dramatic passages of the Old Testament. A text served mainly as a starting point and often had no relation to the development of the sermon. Nor would the old-time preacher balk at any text within the lids of the Bible. There is the story of one who after reading a rather cryptic passage took off his spectacles, closed the Bible with a bang and by way of preface said, "Brothers and sisters, this morning—I intend to explain the unexplainable—find out the indefinable—ponder over the imponderable—and unscrew the inscrutable."

The old-time Negro preacher of parts was above all an orator, and in good measure an actor. He knew the secret of oratory, that at bottom it is a progression of rhythmic words more than it is anything else. Indeed, I have witnessed congregations moved to ecstasy by the rhythmic intoning of sheer incoherencies. He was a master of all the modes of eloquence. He often possessed a voice that was a marvelous instrument, a voice he could modulate from a sepulchral whisper to a crashing thunder clap. His discourse was generally kept at a high pitch of fervency, but occasionally he dropped into colloquialisms and, less often, into humor. He preached a personal and anthropomorphic God, a sure-enough heaven and a red-hot hell. His imagination was bold and unfettered. He had the power to sweep his hearers before him; and so himself was often swept away. At such times his language was not prose but poetry. It was from memories of such preachers there grew the idea of this book of poems.

In a general way, these poems were suggested by the rather vague memories of sermons I heard preached in my childhood; but the immediate stimulus for setting them down came quite definitely at a comparatively recent date. I was speaking on a Sunday in Kansas City, addressing meetings in various colored churches. When I had finished my fourth talk it was after nine o'clock at night, but the committee told me there was still another meeting to address. I demurred, making the quotation about the willingness of the spirit and the weakness of the flesh, for I was dead tired. I also protested the lateness of the hour, but I was informed that for the meeting at this church we were in good time. When we reached the church an "exhorter" was just concluding a dull sermon. After his there were two other short sermons. These sermons proved to be preliminaries, mere curtain-raisers for a famed visiting preacher. At last he arose. He was a dark-brown man, handsome in his gigantic proportions. He appeared to be a bit self-conscious, perhaps impressed by the presence of the "distinguished visitor" on the platform, and started in to preach a formal sermon from a formal text. The congregation sat apathetic and dozing. He sensed that he was losing his audience and his opportunity. Suddenly he closed the Bible, stepped out from behind the pulpit and began to preach. He started intoning the old folk-sermon that begins with the creation of the world and ends with Judgment Day. He was at once a changed man, free, at ease and masterful. The change in the congregation was instantaneous. An electric current ran through the crowd. It was in a moment alive and quivering; and all the while the preacher held it in the palm of his hand. He was wonderful in the way he employed his conscious and unconscious art. He strode the pulpit up and down in what was actually a very rhythmic dance, and he brought into play the full gamut of his wonderful voice, a voice—what shall I say?—not of an organ or a trumpet, but rather of a trombone, the instrument possessing above all others the power to express the wide and varied range of emotions encompassed by the human voice—and with greater amplitude.

He intoned, he moaned, he pleaded—he blared, he crashed, he thundered. I sat fascinated; and more, I was, perhaps against my will, deeply moved; the emotional effect upon me was irresistible. Before he had finished I took a slip of paper and somewhat surreptitiously jotted down some ideas for the first poem, "The Creation."

At first thought, Negro dialect would appear to be the precise medium for these old-time sermons; however, as the reader will see, the poems are not written in dialect. My reason for not using the dialect is double. First, although the dialect is the exact instrument for voicing certain traditional phases of Negro life, it is, and perhaps by that very exactness, a quite limited instrument. Indeed, it is an instrument with but two complete stops, pathos and humor. This limitation is not due to any defect of the dialect as dialect, but to the mould of convention in which Negro dialect in the United States has been set, to the fixing effects of its long association with the Negro only as a happy-go-lucky or a forlorn figure. The Aframerican poet might in time be able to break this mould of convention and write poetry in dialect without feeling that his first line will put the reader in a frame of mind which demands that the poem be either funny or sad, but I doubt that he will make the effort to do it; he does not consider it worth the while. In fact, practically no poetry is being written in dialect by the colored poets of today. These poets have thrown aside dialect and discarded most of the material and subject matter that went into dialect poetry. The passing of dialect as a medium for Negro poetry will be an actual loss, for in it many beautiful things can be done, and done best; however, in my opinion, traditional Negro dialect as a form for Aframerican poets is absolutely dead. The Negro poet in the United States, for poetry which he wishes to give a distinctively racial tone and color, needs now an instrument of greater range than dialect; that is, if he is to do more than sound the small notes of sentimentality. I said something on this point in *The Book of American Negro Poetry,* and because I cannot say it better, I quote: "What the colored poet in the United States needs to do is something like what Synge did for the Irish; he needs to find a form that will express the racial spirit by symbols from within rather than by symbols from without—such as the mere mutilation of English spelling and pronunciation. He needs a form that is freer and larger than dialect, but which will still hold the racial flavor; a form expressing the imagery, the idioms, the peculiar turns of thought and the distinctive humor and pathos, too, of the Negro, but which will also be capable of voicing the deepest and highest emotions and aspirations and allow of the widest range of subjects and the widest scope of treatment." The form of "The Creation," the first poem of this group, was a first experiment by me in this direction.

The second part of my reason for not writing these poems in dialect is the weightier. The old-time Negro preachers, though they actually used dialect in their ordinary intercourse, stepped out from its narrow confines when they preached. They were all saturated with the sublime phraseology of the Hebrew prophets and steeped in the idioms of King James English, so when they preached and warmed to their work they spoke another language, a language far removed from traditional Negro dialect. It was really a fusion of Negro idioms with Bible English; and in this there may have been, after all, some kinship with the innate grandiloquence of their old African tongues. To place in the mouths of the talented old-time Negro preachers a language that is a literary imitation of Mississippi cotton-field dialect is sheer burlesque.

Gross exaggeration of the use of big words by these preachers, in fact by Negroes in general, has been commonly made; the laugh being at the exhibition of ignorance involved. What is the basis of this fondness for big words? Is the predilection due, as is supposed, to ignorance desiring to parade itself as knowledge? Not at all. The old-time Negro preacher loved the sonorous, mouth-filling, ear-filling phrase because it gratified a highly developed sense of sound and rhythm in himself and his hearers.

I claim no more for these poems than that I have written them after the manner of the primitive sermons. In the writing of them I have, naturally, felt the influence of the Spirituals. There is, of course, no way of recreating the atmosphere—the fervor of the congregation, the amens and hallelujahs, the undertone of singing which was often a soft accompaniment to parts of the sermon; nor the personality of the preacher—his physical magnetism, his gestures and gesticulations, his changes of tempo, his pauses for effect, and, more than all, his tones of voice. These poems would better be intoned than read; especially does this apply to "Listen, Lord," "The Crucifixion," and "The Judgment Day." But the intoning practiced by the old-time preacher is a thing next to impossible to describe; it must be heard, and it is extremely difficult to imitate even when heard. The finest, and perhaps the only demonstration ever given to a New York public, was the intoning of the dream in

Ridgely Torrence's Rider of Dreams by Opal Cooper of the Negro Players at the Madison Square Theatre in 1917. Those who were fortunate enough to hear him can never, I know, forget the thrill of it. This intoning is always a matter of crescendo and diminuendo in the intensity—a rising and falling between plain speaking and wild chanting. And often a startling effect is gained by breaking off suddenly at the highest point of intensity and dropping into the monotone of ordinary speech.

The tempos of the preacher I have endeavored to indicate by the line arrangement of the poems, and a certain sort of pause that is marked by a quick intaking and an audible expulsion of the breath I have indicated by dashes. There is a decided syncopation of speech—the crowding in of many syllables or the lengthening out of a few to fill one metrical foot, the sensing of which must be left to the reader's ear. The rhythmical stress of this syncopation is partly obtained by a marked silent fraction of a beat; frequently this silent fraction is filled in by a hand clap.

The old-time Negro preacher is rapidly passing. I have here tried sincerely to fix something of him.

James Weldon Johnson , New York City, 1927

Listen Lord—A Prayer

O Lord, we come this morning
Knee-bowed and body-bent
Before thy throne of grace.
O Lord—this morning—
Bow our hearts beneath our knees,
And our knees in some lonesome valley.
We come this morning—
Like empty pitchers to a full fountain,
With no merits of our own.
O Lord—open up a window of heaven,
And lean out far over the battlements of glory,
And listen this morning.

Lord, have mercy on proud and dying sinners—
Sinners hanging over the mouth of hell,
Who seem to love their distance well.
Lord—ride by this morning—
Mount your milk-white horse,

And ride-a this morning—
And in your ride, ride by old hell,
Ride by the dingy gates of hell,
And stop poor sinners in their headlong plunge.

And now, O Lord, this man of God,
Who breaks the bread of life this morning—
Shadow him in the hollow of thy hand,
And keep him out of the gunshot of the devil.
Take him, Lord—this morning—
Wash him with hyssop inside and out,
Hang him up and drain him dry of sin.
Pin his ear to the wisdom-post,
And make his words sledge hammers of truth—
Beating on the iron heart of sin.
Lord God, this morning—
Put his eye to the telescope of eternity,
And let him look upon the paper walls of time.
Lord, turpentine his imagination,
Put perpetual motion in his arms,
Fill him full of the dynamite of thy power,
Anoint him all over with the oil of thy salvation,
And set his tongue on fire.

And now, O Lord—
When I've done drunk my last cup of sorrow—
When I've been called everything but a child of God—
When I'm done traveling up the rough side of the mountain—
O—Mary's Baby—

When I start down the steep and slippery steps of death—
When this old world begins to rock beneath my feet—
Lower me to my dusty grave in peace
To wait for that great gittin' up morning—Amen.
                              James Weldon Johnson

The Creation
And God stepped out on space,
And he looked around and said:
I'm lonely—
I'll make me a world.

And far as the eye of God could see
Darkness covered everything,
Blacker than a hundred midnights
Down in a cypress swamp.

Then God smiled,
And the light broke,
And the darkness rolled up on one side,
And the light stood shining on the other,
And God said: That's good!

Then God reached out and took the light in his hands,
And God rolled the light around in his hands

Until he made the sun;
And he set that sun a-blazing in the heavens.
And the light that was left from making the sun
God gathered it up in a shining ball
And flung it against the darkness,
Spangling the night with the moon and stars.
Then down between
The darkness and the light
He hurled the world;
And God said: That's good!

Then God himself stepped down—
And the sun was on his right hand,
And the moon was on his left;
The stars were clustered about his head,
And the earth was under his feet.
And God walked, and where he trod
His footsteps hollowed the valleys out
And bulged the mountains up.

Then he stopped and looked and saw
That the earth was hot and barren.
So God stepped over to the edge of the world
And he spat out the seven seas—
He batted his eyes, and the lightnings flashed—
He clapped his hands, and the thunders rolled—
And the waters above the earth came down,
The cooling waters came down.

Then the green grass sprouted,
And the little red flowers blossomed,
The pine tree pointed his finger to the sky,
And the oak spread out his arms,

The lakes cuddled down in the hollows of the ground,
And the rivers ran down to the sea;
And God smiled again,
And the rainbow appeared,
And curled itself around his shoulder.

Then God raised his arm and he waved his hand
Over the sea and over the land,
And he said: Bring forth! Bring forth!
And quicker than God could drop his hand,
Fishes and fowls
And beasts and birds
Swam the rivers and the seas,
Roamed the forests and the woods,
And split the air with their wings.
And God said: That's good!

Then God walked around,
And God looked around
On all that he had made.
He looked at his sun,
And he looked at his moon,
And he looked at his little stars;
He looked on his world
With all its living things,
And God said: I'm lonely still.
Then God sat down—
On the side of a hill where he could think;
By a deep, wide river he sat down;
With his head in his hands,
God thought and thought,
Till he thought: I'll make me a man!

Up from the bed of the river
God scooped the clay;
And by the bank of the river
He kneeled him down;
And there the great God Almighty
Who lit the sun and fixed it in the sky,
Who flung the stars to the most far corner of the night,
Who rounded the earth in the middle of his hand;
This Great God,

Like a mammy bending over her baby,
Kneeled down in the dust
Toiling over a lump of clay
Till he shaped it in his own image;

Then into it he blew the breath of life,
And man became a living soul.
Amen. Amen.

James Weldon Johnson

The Prodigal Son

Young man—
Young man—
Your arm's too short to box with God.

But Jesus spake in a parable, and he said:
A certain man had two sons.
Jesus didn't give this man a name,
But his name is God Almighty.
And Jesus didn't call these sons by name,
But ev'ry young man,
Ev'rywhere,
Is one of these two sons.

And the younger son said to his father,
He said: Father, divide up the property,
And give me my portion now.

And the father with tears in his eyes said: Son,
Don't leave your father's house.
But the boy was stubborn in his head,
And haughty in his heart,
And he took his share of his father's goods,
And went into a far-off country.

There comes a time,
There comes a time
When ev'ry young man looks out from his father's house,
Longing for that far-off country.

And the young man journeyed on his way,
And he said to himself as he traveled along:

This sure is an easy road,
Nothing like the rough furrows behind my father's plow.

Young man—
Young man—
Smooth and easy is the road
That leads to hell and destruction.
Down grade all the way,
The further you travel, the faster you go.
No need to trudge and sweat and toil,
Just slip and slide and slip and slide
Till you bang up against hell's iron gate.

And the younger son kept traveling along,
Till at night-time he came to a city.

And the city was bright in the night-time like day,
The streets all crowded with people,
Brass bands and string bands a-playing,
And ev'rywhere the young man turned
There was singing and laughing and dancing.
And he stopped a passer-by and he said:
Tell me what city is this?
And the passer-by laughed and said: Don't you know?
This is Babylon, Babylon,
That great city of Babylon.
Come on, my friend, and go along with me.
And the young man joined the crowd.

Young man—
Young man—
You're never lonesome in Babylon.
You can always join a crowd in Babylon.
Young man—
Young man—
You can never be alone in Babylon,
Alone with your Jesus in Babylon.
You can never find a place, a lonesome place,
A lonesome place to go down on your knees,
And talk with your God, in Babylon.
You're always in a crowd in Babylon.

And the young man went with his new-found friend,
And bought himself some brand new clothes,
And he spent his days in the drinking dens,
Swallowing the fires of hell.
And he spent his nights in the gambling dens,

Throwing dice with the devil for his soul.
And he met up with the women of Babylon.
Oh, the women of Babylon!
Dressed in yellow and purple and scarlet,
Loaded with rings and earrings and bracelets,
Their lips like a honeycomb dripping with honey,
Perfumed and sweet-smelling like a jasmine flower;
And the jasmine smell of the Babylon women
Got in his nostrils and went to his head,
And he wasted his substance in riotous living,
In the evening, in the black and dark of night,
With the sweet-sinning women of Babylon.
And they stripped him of his money,
And they stripped him of his clothes,
And they left him broke and ragged
In the streets of Babylon.

Then the young man joined another crowd—
The beggars and lepers of Babylon.
And he went to feeding swine,
And he was hungrier than the hogs;
He got down on his belly in the mire and mud
And ate the husks with the hogs.
And not a hog was too low to turn up his nose
At the man in the mire of Babylon.

Then the young man came to himself—
He came to himself and said:
In my father's house are many mansions,
Ev'ry servant in his house has bread to eat,
Ev'ry servant in his house has a place to sleep;
I will arise and go to my father.

And his father saw him afar off,
And he ran up the road to meet him.
He put clean clothes upon his back,

And a golden chain around his neck,
He made a feast and killed the fatted calf,
And invited the neighbors in.

Oh-o-oh, sinner,
When you're mingling with the crowd in Babylon—
Drinking the wine of Babylon—
Running with the women of Babylon—
You forget about God, and you laugh at Death.
Today you've got the strength of a bull in your neck
And the strength of a bear in your arms,
But some o' these days, some o' these days,
You'll have a hand-to-hand struggle with bony Death,
And Death is bound to win.

Young man, come away from Babylon,
That hell-border city of Babylon.
Leave the dancing and gambling of Babylon,
The wine and whiskey of Babylon,
The hot-mouthed women of Babylon;
Fall down on your knees,
And say in your heart:
I will arise and go to my Father.

James Weldon Johnson

Go Down Death—A Funeral Sermon

Weep not, weep not,
She is not dead;
She's resting in the bosom of Jesus.
Heart-broken husband—weep no more;
Grief-stricken son—weep no more;
Left-lonesome daughter—weep no more;
She's only just gone home.

Day before yesterday morning,
God was looking down from his great, high heaven
Looking down on all his children,
And his eye fell on Sister Caroline,
Tossing on her bed of pain.
And God's big heart was touched with pity,
With the everlasting pity.

And God sat back on his throne,
And he commanded that tall, bright angel standing at his right hand:
Call me Death!
And that tall, bright angel cried in a voice
That broke like a clap of thunder:
Call Death!—Call Death!
And the echo sounded down the streets of heaven
Till it reached away back to that shadowy place,
Where Death waits with his pale, white horses.

And Death heard the summons,
And he leaped on his fastest horse,
Pale as a sheet in the moonlight.
Up the golden street Death galloped,
And the hoofs of his horse struck fire from the gold,
But they didn't make no sound.
Up Death rode to the Great White Throne,
And waited for God's command.

And God said: Go down, Death, go down,
Go down to Savannah, Georgia,
Down in Yamacraw,
And find Sister Caroline.
She's borne the burden and heat of the day,
She's labored long in my vineyard,
And she's tired—
She's weary—
Go down, Death, and bring her to me.

And Death didn't say a word,
But he loosed the reins on his pale, white horse,
And he clamped the spurs to his bloodless sides,
And out and down he rode,
Through heaven's pearly gates,
Past suns and moons and stars;
On Death rode,
And the foam from his horse was like a comet in the sky;
On Death rode,
Leaving the lightning's flash behind;
Straight on down he came.

While we were watching round her bed,
She turned her eyes and looked away,
She saw what we couldn't see;
She saw Old Death. She saw Old Death
Coming like a falling star.
But Death didn't frighten Sister Caroline;
He looked to her like a welcome friend.
And she whispered to us: I'm going home,
And she smiled and closed her eyes.

And Death took her up like a baby,
And she lay in his icy arms,
But she didn't feel no chill.
And Death began to ride again—
Up beyond the evening star,
Out beyond the morning star,
Into the glittering light of glory,
On to the Great White Throne.
And there he laid Sister Caroline
On the loving breast of Jesus.

And Jesus took his own hand and wiped away her tears,
And he smoothed the furrows from her face,
And the angels sang a little song,
And Jesus rocked her in his arms,
And kept a-saying: Take your rest,
Take your rest, take your rest.

Weep not—weep not,
She is not dead;
She's resting in the bosom of Jesus.
                    James Weldon Johnson

Noah Built the Ark

In the cool of the day—
God was walking—
Around in the Garden of Eden.
And except for the beasts, eating in the fields,
And except for the birds, flying through the trees,
The garden looked like it was deserted.
And God called out and said: Adam,
Adam, where art thou?

And Adam, with Eve behind his back,
Came out from where he was hiding.

And God said: Adam,
What hast thou done?
Thou hast eaten of the tree!
And Adam,
With his head hung down,
Blamed it on the woman.

For after God made the first man Adam,
He breathed a sleep upon him;
Then he took out of Adam one of his ribs,
And out of that rib made woman.
And God put the man and woman together
In the beautiful Garden of Eden,
With nothing to do the whole day long
But play all around in the garden.
And God called Adam before him,
And he said to him:
Listen now, Adam,
Of all the fruit in the garden you can eat,
Except of the tree of knowledge;
For the day thou eatest of that tree,
Thou shalt surely die.

Then pretty soon along came Satan.
Old Satan came like a snake in the grass
To try out his tricks on the woman.
I imagine I can see Old Satan now
A-sidling up to the woman.
I imagine the first word Satan said was:
Eve, you're surely good looking.
I imagine he brought her a present, too,—
And, if there was such a thing in those ancient days,
He brought her a looking-glass.

And Eve and Satan got friendly—
Then Eve got to walking on shaky ground;
Don't ever get friendly with Satan.—
And they started to talk about the garden,
And Satan said: Tell me, how do you like

The fruit on the nice, tall, blooming tree
Standing in the middle of the garden?
And Eve said:
That's the forbidden fruit,
Which if we eat we die.

And Satan laughed a devilish little laugh,
And he said to the woman: God's fooling you, Eve;
That's the sweetest fruit in the garden.
I know you can eat that forbidden fruit,
And I know that you will not die.

And Eve looked at the forbidden fruit,
And it was red and ripe and juicy.
And Eve took a taste, and she offered it to Adam,
And Adam wasn't able to refuse;
So he took a bite, and they both sat down
And ate the forbidden fruit.—
Back there, six thousand years ago,
Man first fell by woman—
Lord, and he's doing the same today.

And that's how sin got into this world.
And man, as he multiplied on the earth,
Increased in wickedness and sin.
He went on down from sin to sin,
From wickedness to wickedness,
Murder and lust and violence,
All kinds of fornications,
Till the earth was corrupt and rotten with flesh,
An abomination in God's sight.

And God was angry at the sins of men.
And God got sorry that he ever made man.
And he said: I will destroy him.
I'll bring down judgment on him with a flood.
I'll destroy ev'rything on the face of the earth,
Man, beasts and birds, and creeping things.
And he did—
Ev'rything but the fishes.

But Noah was a just and righteous man.
Noah walked and talked with God.
And, one day, God said to Noah,
He said: Noah, build thee an ark.
Build it out of gopher wood.
Build it good and strong.
Pitch it within and pitch it without.
And build it according to the measurements
That I will give to thee.
Build it for you and all your house,
And to save the seeds of life on earth;
For I'm going to send down a mighty flood
To destroy this wicked world.

And Noah commenced to work on the ark.
And he worked for about one hundred years.
And ev'ry day the crowd came round
To make fun of Old Man Noah.
And they laughed and they said: Tell us, old man,
Where do you expect to sail that boat
Up here amongst the hills?

But Noah kept on a-working.
And ev'ry once in a while Old Noah would stop,
He'd lay down his hammer and lay down his saw,
And take his staff in hand;
And with his long, white beard a-flying in the wind,
And the gospel light a-gleaming from his eye,
Old Noah would preach God's word:

Sinners, oh, sinners,
Repent, for the judgment is at hand.
Sinners, oh, sinners,
Repent, for the time is drawing nigh.
God's wrath is gathering in the sky.
God's a-going to rain down rain on rain.
God's a-going to loosen up the bottom of the deep,
And drown this wicked world.
Sinners, repent while yet there's time
For God to change his mind.

Some smart young fellow said: This old man's
Got water on the brain.
And the crowd all laughed—Lord, but didn't they laugh;
And they paid no mind to Noah,
But kept on sinning just the same.

One bright and sunny morning,
Not a cloud nowhere to be seen,
God said to Noah: Get in the ark!
And Noah and his folks all got in the ark,
And all the animals, two by two,
A he and a she marched in.
Then God said: Noah, Bar the door!
And Noah barred the door.

And a little black spot begun to spread,
Like a bottle of ink spilling over the sky;
And the thunder rolled like a rumbling drum;
And the lightning jumped from pole to pole;
And it rained down rain, rain, rain,
Great God, but didn't it rain!
For forty days and forty nights
Waters poured down and waters gushed up;
And the dry land turned to sea.
And the old ark-a she begun to ride;
The old ark-a she begun to rock;
Sinners came a-running down to the ark;
Sinners came a-swimming all round the ark;
Sinners pleaded and sinners prayed—
Sinners wept and sinners wailed—
But Noah'd done barred the door.

And the trees and the hills and the mountain tops
Slipped underneath the waters.
And the old ark sailed that lonely sea—
For twelve long months she sailed that sea,
A sea without a shore.

Then the waters begun to settle down,
And the ark touched bottom on the tallest peak
Of old Mount Ararat.
The dove brought Noah the olive leaf,

And Noah when he saw that the grass was green,
Opened up the ark, and they all climbed down,
The folks, and the animals, two by two,
Down from the mount to the valley.
And Noah wept and fell on his face
And hugged and kissed the dry ground.

And then—

God hung out his rainbow cross the sky,
And he said to Noah: That's my sign!
No more will I judge the world by flood—
Next time I'll rain down fire.

James Weldon Johnson

The Crucifixion

Jesus, my gentle Jesus,
Walking in the dark of the Garden—
The Garden of Gethsemane,
Saying to the three disciples:
Sorrow is in my soul—
Even unto death;
Tarry ye here a little while,
And watch with me.

Jesus, my burdened Jesus,
Praying in the dark of the Garden—
The Garden of Gethsemane.
Saying: Father,
Oh, Father,
This bitter cup,
This bitter cup,
Let it pass from me.

Jesus, my sorrowing Jesus,
The sweat like drops of blood upon his brow,
Talking with his Father,
While the three disciples slept,
Saying: Father,
Oh, Father,
Not as I will,

Not as I will,
But let thy will be done.

Oh, look at black-hearted Judas—
Sneaking through the dark of the Garden—
Leading his crucifying mob.
Oh, God!
Strike him down!
Why don't you strike him down,
Before he plants his traitor's kiss
Upon my Jesus' cheek?

And they take my blameless Jesus,
And they drag him to the Governor,
To the mighty Roman Governor.
Great Pilate seated in his hall,—
Great Pilate on his judgment seat,
Said: In this man I find no fault.
I find no fault in him.
And Pilate washed his hands.
But they cried out, saying:
Crucify him!—
Crucify him!—
Crucify him!—
His blood be on our heads.
And they beat my loving Jesus,
They spit on my precious Jesus;
They dressed him up in a purple robe,
They put a crown of thorns upon his head,
And they pressed it down—
Oh, they pressed it down—
And they mocked my sweet King Jesus.

Up Golgotha's rugged road
I see my Jesus go.
I see him sink beneath the load,
I see my drooping Jesus sink.
And then they laid hold on Simon,
Black Simon, yes, black Simon;
They put the cross on Simon,
And Simon bore the cross.

On Calvary, on Calvary,
They crucified my Jesus.
They nailed him to the cruel tree,
And the hammer!
The hammer!
The hammer!
Rang through Jerusalem's streets.
The hammer!
The hammer!
The hammer!
Rang through Jerusalem's streets.

Jesus, my lamb-like Jesus,
Shivering as the nails go through his hands;
Jesus, my lamb-like Jesus,
Shivering as the nails go through his feet.
Jesus, my darling Jesus,
Groaning as the Roman spear plunged in his side;
Jesus, my darling Jesus,
Groaning as the blood came spurting from his wound.
Oh, look how they done my Jesus.

Mary,
Weeping Mary,
Sees her poor little Jesus on the cross.
Mary,
Weeping Mary,
Sees her sweet, baby Jesus on the cruel cross,
Hanging between two thieves.
And Jesus, my lonesome Jesus,
Called out once more to his Father,
Saying:
My God,
My God,
Why hast thou forsaken me?
And he drooped his head and died.

And the veil of the temple was split in two,
The midday sun refused to shine,

The thunder rumbled and the lightning wrote
An unknown language in the sky.

What a day! Lord, what a day!
When my blessed Jesus died.

Oh, I tremble, yes, I tremble,
It causes me to tremble, tremble,
When I think how Jesus died;
Died on the steeps of Calvary,
How Jesus died for sinners,
Sinners like you and me.
                    James Weldon Johnson

Let My People Go

And God called Moses from the burning bush,
He called in a still, small voice,
And he said: Moses—Moses—
And Moses listened,
And he answered and said:
Lord, here am I.

And the voice in the bush said: Moses,
Draw not nigh, take off your shoes,
For you're standing on holy ground.
And Moses stopped where he stood,
And Moses took off his shoes,
And Moses looked at the burning bush,
And he heard the voice,
But he saw no man.

Then God again spoke to Moses,
And he spoke in a voice of thunder:
I am the Lord God Almighty,
I am the God of thy fathers,
I am the God of Abraham,
Of Isaac and of Jacob.
And Moses hid his face.

And God said to Moses:
I've seen the awful suffering
Of my people down in Egypt.
I've watched their hard oppressors,
Their overseers and drivers;
The groans of my people have filled my ears

And I can't stand it no longer;
So I'm come down to deliver them
Out of the land of Egypt,
And I will bring them out of that land
Into the land of Canaan;
Therefore, Moses, go down,
Go down into Egypt,
And tell Old Pharaoh
To let my people go.

And Moses said: Lord, who am I
To make a speech before Pharaoh?
For, Lord, you know I'm slow of tongue.
But God said: I will be thy mouth and I will be thy tongue;
Therefore, Moses, go down,
Go down yonder into Egypt land,
And tell Old Pharaoh
To let my people go.
And Moses with his rod in hand
Went down and said to Pharaoh:
Thus saith the Lord God of Israel,
Let my people go.

And Pharaoh looked at Moses,
He stopped still and looked at Moses;
And he said to Moses: Who is this Lord?
I know all the gods of Egypt,
But I know no God of Israel;
So go back, Moses, and tell your God,
I will not let this people go.

Poor Old Pharaoh,
He knows all the knowledge of Egypt,
Yet never knew—
He never knew
The one and the living God.
Poor Old Pharaoh,
He's got all the power of Egypt,
And he's going to try
To test his strength
With the might of the great Jehovah,
With the might of the Lord God of Hosts,

The Lord mighty in battle.
And God, sitting high up in his heaven,
Laughed at poor Old Pharaoh.
And Pharaoh called the overseers,
And Pharaoh called the drivers,
And he said: Put heavier burdens still
On the backs of the Hebrew Children.
Then the people chode with Moses,
And they cried out: Look here, Moses,
You've been to Pharaoh, but look and see
What Pharaoh's done to us now.
And Moses was troubled in mind.

But God said: Go again, Moses,
You and your brother, Aaron,
And say once more to Pharaoh,
Thus saith the Lord God of the Hebrews,
Let my people go.
And Moses and Aaron with their rods in hand
Worked many signs and wonders.
But Pharaoh called for his magic men,
And they worked wonders, too.
So Pharaohs' heart was hardened,
And he would not,
No, he would not
Let God's people go.

And God rained down plagues on Egypt,
Plagues of frogs and lice and locusts,
Plagues of blood and boils and darkness,
And other plagues besides.
But ev'ry time God moved the plague
Old Pharaoh's heart was hardened,
And he would not,
No, he would not
Let God's people go.
And Moses was troubled in mind.

Then the Lord said: Listen, Moses,
The God of Israel will not be mocked,
Just one more witness of my power
I'll give hard-hearted Pharaoh.

This very night about midnight,
I'll pass over Egypt land,
In my righteous wrath will I pass over,
And smite their first-born dead.

And God that night passed over.
And a cry went up out of Egypt.
And Pharaoh rose in the middle of the night
And he sent in a hurry for Moses;
And he said: Go forth from among my people,
You and all the Hebrew Children;
Take your goods and take your flocks,
And get away from the land of Egypt.

And, right then, Moses led them out,
With all their goods and all their flocks;
And God went on before,
A guiding pillar of cloud by day,
And a pillar of fire by night.
And they journeyed on in the wilderness,
And came down to the Red Sea.

In the morning,
Oh, in the morning,
They missed the Hebrew Children.
Four hundred years,
Four hundred years
They'd held them down in Egypt land.
Held them under the driver's lash,
Working without money and without price.
And it might have been Pharaoh's wife that said:
Pharaoh—look what you've done.
You let those Hebrew Children go,
And who's going to serve us now?
Who's going to make our bricks and mortar?
Who's going to plant and plow our corn?
Who's going to get up in the chill of the morning?
And who's going to work in the blazing sun?
Pharaoh, tell me that!

And Pharaoh called his generals,
And the generals called the captains,

And the captains called the soldiers.
And they hitched up all the chariots,
Six hundred chosen chariots of war,
And twenty-four hundred horses.
And the chariots all were full of men,
With swords and shields
And shiny spears
And battle bows and arrows.
And Pharaoh and his army
Pursued the Hebrew Children
To the edge of the Red Sea.

Now, the Children of Israel, looking back,
Saw Pharaoh's army coming.
And the rumble of the chariots was like a thunder storm,
And the whirring of the wheels was like a rushing wind,
And the dust from the horses made a cloud that darked the day,
And the glittering of the spears was like lightnings in the night.

And the Children of Israel all lost faith,
The children of Israel all lost hope;
Deep Red Sea in front of them
And Pharaoh's host behind.
And they mumbled and grumbled among themselves:
Were there no graves in Egypt?
And they wailed aloud to Moses and said:
Slavery in Egypt was better than to come
To die here in this wilderness.

But Moses said:
Stand still! Stand still!
And see the Lord's salvation.
For the Lord God of Israel
Will not forsake his people.
The Lord will break the chariots,
The Lord will break the horsemen,
He'll break great Egypt's sword and shield,
The battle bows and arrows;
This day he'll make proud Pharaoh know
Who is the God of Israel.

And Moses lifted up his rod
Over the Red Sea;
And God with a blast of his nostrils
Blew the waters apart,
And the waves rolled back and stood up in a pile,
And left a path through the middle of the sea
Dry as the sands of the desert.
And the Children of Israel all crossed over
On to the other side.

When Pharaoh saw them crossing dry,
He dashed on in behind them—
Old Pharaoh got about half way cross,
And God unlashed the waters,
And the waves rushed back together,
And Pharaoh and all his army got lost,
And all his host got drownded.
And Moses sang and Miriam danced,
And the people shouted for joy,
And God led the Hebrew Children on
Till they reached the promised land.

Listen!—Listen!
All you sons of Pharaoh.
Who do you think can hold God's people
When the Lord God himself has said,
Let my people go?

James Weldon Johnson

The Judgment Day

In that great day,
People, in that great day,
God's a-going to rain down fire.
God's a-going to sit in the middle of the air
To judge the quick and the dead.

Early one of these mornings,
God's a-going to call for Gabriel,
That tall, bright angel, Gabriel;
And God's a-going to say to him: Gabriel,
Blow your silver trumpet,
And wake the living nations.

And Gabriel's going to ask him: Lord,
How loud must I blow it?

And God's a-going to tell him: Gabriel,
Blow it calm and easy.
Then putting one foot on the mountain top,
And the other in the middle of the sea,
Gabriel's going to stand and blow his horn,
To wake the living nations.

Then God's a-going to say to him: Gabriel,
Once more blow your silver trumpet,
And wake the nations underground.

And Gabriel's going to ask him: Lord
How loud must I blow it?
And God's a-going to tell him: Gabriel,
Like seven peals of thunder.
Then the tall, bright angel, Gabriel,
Will put one foot on the battlements of heaven
And the other on the steps of hell,
And blow that silver trumpet
Till he shakes old hell's foundations.

And I feel Old Earth a-shuddering—
And I see the graves a-bursting—
And I hear a sound,
A blood-chilling sound.
What sound is that I hear?
It's the clicking together of the dry bones,
Bone to bone—the dry bones.
And I see coming out of the bursting graves,
And marching up from the valley of death,
The army of the dead.

And the living and the dead in the twinkling of an eye
Are caught up in the middle of the air,
Before God's judgment bar.

Oh-o-oh, sinner,
Where will you stand,
In that great day when God's a-going to rain down fire?

Oh, you gambling man—where will you stand?
You whore-mongering man—where will you stand?
Liars and backsliders—where will you stand,
In that great day when God's a-going to rain down fire?

And God will divide the sheep from the goats,
The one on the right, the other on the left.
And to them on the right God's a-going to say:
Enter into my kingdom.
And those who've come through great tribulations,
And washed their robes in the blood of the Lamb,
They will enter in—
Clothed in spotless white,
With starry crowns upon their heads,
And silver slippers on their feet,
And harps within their hands;—
And two by two they'll walk
Up and down the golden street,
Feasting on the milk and honey
Singing new songs of Zion,
Chattering with the angels
All around the Great White Throne.

And to them on the left God's a-going to say:
Depart from me into everlasting darkness,
Down into the bottomless pit.
And the wicked like lumps of lead will start to fall,
Headlong for seven days and nights they'll fall,
Plumb into the big, black, red-hot mouth of hell,
Belching out fire and brimstone.
And their cries like howling, yelping dogs,
Will go up with the fire and smoke from hell,
But God will stop his ears.

Too late, sinner! Too late!
Good-bye, sinner! Good-bye!
In hell, sinner! In hell!
Beyond the reach of the love of God.

And I hear a voice, crying, crying:
Time shall be no more!
Time shall be no more!

Time shall be no more!
And the sun will go out like a candle in the wind,
The moon will turn to dripping blood,
The stars will fall like cinders,
And the sea will burn like tar;
And the earth shall melt away and be dissolved,
And the sky will roll up like a scroll.
With a wave of his hand God will blot out time,
And start the wheel of eternity.

Sinner, oh, sinner,
Where will you stand
In that great day when God's a-going to rain down fire?

James Weldon Johnson

O Black and Unknown Bards

O black and unknown bards of long ago,
How came your lips to touch the sacred fire?
How, in your darkness, did you come to know
The power and beauty of the minstrel's lyre?
Who first from midst his bonds lifted his eyes?
Who first from out the still watch, lone and long,
Feeling the ancient faith of prophets rise
Within his dark-kept soul, burst into song?

Heart of what slave poured out such melody
As "Steal away to Jesus"? On its strains
His spirit must have nightly floated free,
Though still about his hands he felt his chains.
Who heard great "Jordan roll"? Whose starward eye
Saw chariot "swing low"? And who was he
That breathed that comforting, melodic sigh,
"Nobody knows de trouble I see"?

What merely living clod, what captive thing,
Could up toward God through all its darkness grope,
And find within its deadened heart to sing
These songs of sorrow, love and faith, and hope?
How did it catch that subtle undertone,
That note in music heard not with the ears?
How sound the elusive reed so seldom blown,
Which stirs the soul or melts the heart to tears.

Not that great German master in his dream
Of harmonies that thundered amongst the stars
At the creation, ever heard a theme
Nobler than "Go down, Moses." Mark its bars
How like a mighty trumpet-call they stir
The blood. Such are the notes that men have sung
Going to valorous deeds; such tones there were
That helped make history when Time was young.

There is a wide, wide wonder in it all,
That from degraded rest and servile toil
The fiery spirit of the seer should call
These simple children of the sun and soil.
O black slave singers, gone, forgot, unfamed,
You—you alone, of all the long, long line
Of those who've sung untaught, unknown, unnamed,
Have stretched out upward, seeking the divine.

You sang not deeds of heroes or of kings;
No chant of bloody war, no exulting pean
Of arms-won triumphs; but your humble strings
You touched in chord with music empyrean.
You sang far better than you knew; the songs
That for your listeners' hungry hearts sufficed
Still live,—but more than this to you belongs:
You sang a race from wood and stone to Christ.

James Weldon Johnson

Fifty Years

(1863-1913)

On the Fiftieth Anniversary of the Signing of the Emancipation Proclamation.

O brothers mine, to-day we stand
Where half a century sweeps our ken,
Since God, through Lincoln's ready hand,
Struck off our bonds and made us men.

Just fifty years—a winter's day—
As runs the history of a race;
Yet, as we look back o'er the way,
How distant seems our starting place!
Look farther back! Three centuries!

To where a naked, shivering score,
Snatched from their haunts across the seas,
Stood, wild-eyed, on Virginia's shore.

This land is ours by right of birth,
This land is ours by right of toil;
We helped to turn its virgin earth,
Our sweat is in its fruitful soil.

Where once the tangled forest stood,—
Where flourished once rank weed and thorn,—
Behold the path-traced, peaceful wood,
The cotton white, the yellow corn.
To gain these fruits that have been earned,
To hold these fields that have been won,
Our arms have strained, our backs have burned,
Bent bare beneath a ruthless sun.

That Banner which is now the type
Of victory on field and flood—
Remember, its first crimson stripe
Was dyed by Attucks' willing blood.

And never yet has come the cry—
When that fair flag has been assailed—
For men to do, for men to die,
That we have faltered or have failed.

We've helped to bear it, rent and torn,
Through many a hot-breath'd battle breeze
Held in our hands, it has been borne
And planted far across the seas.

And never yet,—O haughty Land,
Let us, at least, for this be praised—
Has one black, treason-guided hand
Ever against that flag been raised.

Then should we speak but servile words,
Or shall we hang our heads in shame?
Stand back of new-come foreign hordes,
And fear our heritage to claim?

No! stand erect and without fear,
And for our foes let this suffice—
We've bought a rightful sonship here,
And we have more than paid the price.

And yet, my brothers, well I know
The tethered feet, the pinioned wings,
The spirit bowed beneath the blow,
The heart grown faint from wounds and stings;

The staggering force of brutish might,
That strikes and leaves us stunned and dazed;
The long, vain waiting through the night
To hear some voice for justice raised.

Full well I know the hour when hope
Sinks dead, and 'round us everywhere
Hangs stifling darkness, and we grope
With hands uplifted in despair.

Courage! Look out, beyond, and see
The far horizon's beckoning span!
Faith in your God-known destiny!
We are a part of some great plan.

Because the tongues of Garrison
And Phillips now are cold in death,
Think you their work can be undone?
Or quenched the fires lit by their breath?

Think you that John Brown's spirit stops?
That Lovejoy was but idly slain?
Or do you think those precious drops
From Lincoln's heart were shed in vain?

That for which millions prayed and sighed,
That for which tens of thousands fought,
For which so many freely died,
God cannot let it come to naught.

James Weldon Johnson

BLACK AMERICAN POETRY COLLECTION, 1922

Compiled by James W. Johnson

Introduction

Campbell, James Edwin

Was born at Pomeroy, Ohio, in the early sixties. His early life was somewhat shrouded in mystery; he never referred to it even to his closest associates. He was educated in the public schools of his native city. Later he spent a while at Miami College. In the late eighties and early nineties he was engaged in newspaper work in Chicago. He wrote regularly on the various dailies of that city. He was also one of a group that issued the *Four O'Clock Magazine*, a literary publication which flourished for several years. He died, perhaps, twenty years ago. He was the author of *Echoes from The Cabin* and *Elsewhere*, a volume of poems.

Carmichael, Waverley Turner

A young man who had never been out of his native state of Alabama until several years ago when he entered one of the summer courses at Harvard University. His education to that time had been very limited and he had endured poverty and hard work. His verses came to the attention of one of the Harvard professors. He has since published a volume, From the Heart of a Folk. He served with the 367th Regiment, "The Buffaloes," during the World War and saw active service in France. At present he is employed as a postal clerk in Boston, Mass.

Cotter, Joseph S., Jr., (1895-1919)

Born at Louisville, Kentucky, in the room in which Paul Laurence Dunbar first read his dialect poems in the South. He was precocious as a child, having read a number of books before he was six years old. All through his boyhood he had the advantage and inspiration of the full library of poetic books belonging to his father, himself a poet of considerable talent. Young Cotter attended Fisk University but left in his second year because he had developed tuberculosis. A volume of verse, *The Band of Gideon*, and a number of unpublished poems were written during the six years in which he was an invalid.

Du Bois, W. E. Burghardt, (1868-1963)

Born at Great Barrington, Mass., 1868. Educated at Fisk University, Harvard University and the University of Berlin. For a number of years professor of economics and history at Atlanta University. Author of the *Suppression of the Slave Trade, The Philadelphia Negro, The Souls of Black Folk, John Brown, Darkwater*, etc. He was the editor of *The Crisis*.

Hill, Leslie Pinckney

Born at Lynchburg, Va., 1880. He was educated in the public schools at Lynchburg and at Harvard University. On graduation he became a teacher of English and methods at

Tuskegee. Author of the *Wings of Oppression*, a volume of verse. He is principal of the Cheyney Training School for Teachers at Cheyney, Pa.

Jamison, Roscoe C., (1888-1918)
Born at Winchester, Tenn., 1888; died 1918. He was a graduate of Fisk University.

Johnson, Fenton
Born at Chicago, 1888. He was educated in the public schools and at the University of Chicago and Northwestern University. The author of *A Little Dreaming, Songs of the Soil* and *Visions of the Dusk*. He has devoted much time to journalism and the editing of a magazine.

Jones, Edward Smyth
Attracted national attention about ten years ago by walking some hundreds of miles from his home in the South to Harvard University. Arriving there, he was arrested on a charge of vagrancy. While in jail, he wrote a poem, *Harvard Square*. The poem created a sentiment that led to his quick release. He is the author of *The Sylvan Cabin*.

Rogers, Alex
Born at Nashville, Tenn., 1876. Educated in the public schools of that city. For many years a writer of words for popular songs. He wrote many of the songs for the musical comedies in which Williams and Walker appeared. He is the author of *The Jonah Man, Nobody* and other songs made popular by Mr. Bert Williams.
Shackelford, Theodore Henry
Author of *Mammy's Cracklin' Bread and Other Poems*, and *My Country and Other Poems*.

When Ol' Sis' Judy Pray
James Edwin Campbell

When ol' Sis' Judy pray,
De teahs come stealin' down my cheek,
De voice ur God widin me speak';
I see myse'f so po' an' weak,
Down on my knees de cross I seek,
When ol' Sis' Judy pray.

When ol' Sis' Judy pray,
De thun'ers ur Mount Sin-a-i
Comes rushin' down f'um up on high—
De Debbil tu'n his back an' fly
While sinnahs loud fur pa'don cry,
When ol' Sis' Judy pray.

When ol' Sis' Judy pray,
Ha'd sinnahs trimble in dey seat
Ter hyuh huh voice in sorro 'peat;
(While all de chu'ch des sob an' weep)
"O Shepa'd, dese, dy po' los' sheep!"
When ol' Sis' Judy pray.

When ol' Sis' Judy pray,
De whole house hit des rock an' moan
Ter see huh teahs an' hyuh huh groan;
Dar's somepin' in Sis' Judy's tone
Dat melt all ha'ts dough med ur stone
When ol' Sis' Judy pray.

When ol' Sis' Judy pray,
Salvation's light comes pourin' down—
Hit fill de chu'ch an' all de town—
Why, angels' robes go rustlin' 'roun',
An' hebben on de Yurf am foun',
When ol' Sis' Judy pray.

When ol' Sis' Judy pray,
My soul go sweepin' up on wings,
An' loud de chu'ch wid "Glory!" rings,
An' wide de gates ur Jahsper swings
Twel you hyuh ha'ps wid golding strings,
When ol' Sis' Judy pray.

A Litany of Atlanta
W. E. Burghardt Du Bois

Done at Atlanta, in the Day of Death, 1906
O Silent God, Thou whose voice afar in mist and mystery hath left our ears
an-hungered in these fearful days—
Hear us, good Lord!

Listen to us, Thy children: our faces dark with doubt are made a mockery
in Thy sanctuary. With uplifted hands we front Thy heaven, O God, crying:
We beseech Thee to hear us, good Lord!

We are not better than our fellows, Lord, we are but weak and human men.
When our devils do deviltry, curse Thou the doer and the deed: curse them

as we curse them, do to them all and more than ever they have done to
innocence and weakness, to womanhood and home.
Have mercy upon us, miserable sinners!

And yet whose is the deeper guilt? Who made these devils? Who nursed them
in crime and fed them on injustice? Who ravished and debauched their
mothers and their grandmothers? Who bought and sold their crime, and waxed
fat and rich on public iniquity?
Thou knowest, good God!

Is this Thy justice, O Father, that guile be easier than innocence, and
the innocent crucified for the guilt of the untouched guilty?
Justice, O judge of men!

Wherefore do we pray? Is not the God of the fathers dead? Have not seers
seen in Heaven's halls Thine hearsed and lifeless form stark amidst the
black and rolling smoke of sin, where all along bow bitter forms of
endless dead?
Awake, Thou that sleepest!

Thou art not dead, but flown afar, up hills of endless light, thru blazing
corridors of suns, where worlds do swing of good and gentle men, of women
strong and free—far from the cozenage, black hypocrisy and chaste
prostitution of this shameful speck of dust!
Turn again, O Lord, leave us not to perish in our sin!

From lust of body and lust of blood
Great God, deliver us!

From lust of power and lust of gold,
Great God, deliver us!

From the leagued lying of despot and of brute,
Great God, deliver us!

A city lay in travail, God our Lord, and from her loins sprang twin Murder
and Black Hate. Red was the midnight; clang, crack and cry of death and
fury filled the air and trembled underneath the stars when church spires
pointed silently to Thee. And all this was to sate the greed of greedy men
who hide behind the veil of vengeance!
Bend us Thine ear, O Lord!

In the pale, still morning we looked upon the deed. We stopped our ears
and held our leaping hands, but they—did they not wag their heads and
leer and cry with bloody jaws: Cease from Crime! The word was
mockery, for thus they train a hundred crimes while we do cure one.
Turn again our captivity, O Lord!

Behold this maimed and broken thing; dear God, it was an humble black man
who toiled and sweat to save a bit from the pittance paid him. They told
him: Work and Rise. He worked. Did this man sin? Nay, but some one
told how some one said another did—one whom he had never seen nor known.
Yet for that man's crime this man lieth maimed and murdered, his wife
naked to shame, his children, to poverty and evil.
Hear us, O Heavenly Father!

Doth not this justice of hell stink in Thy nostrils, O God? How long shall
the mounting flood of innocent blood roar in Thine ears and pound in our
hearts for vengeance? Pile the pale frenzy of blood-crazed brutes who do
such deeds high on Thine altar, Jehovah Jireh, and burn it in hell forever
and forever!
Forgive us, good Lord; we know not what we say!

Bewildered we are, and passion-tost, mad with the madness of a mobbed and
mocked and murdered people; straining at the armposts of Thy Throne, we
raise our shackled hands and charge Thee, God, by the bones of our stolen
fathers, by the tears of our dead mothers, by the very blood of Thy
crucified Christ: What meaneth this? Tell us the Plan; give us the
Sign!
Keep not thou silence, O God!

Sit no longer blind, Lord God, deaf to our prayer and dumb to our dumb
suffering. Surely Thou too art not white, O Lord, a pale, bloodless,
heartless thing?
Ah! Christ of all the Pities!

Forgive the thought! Forgive these wild, blasphemous words. Thou art still
the God of our black fathers, and in Thy soul's soul sit some soft
darkenings of the evening, some shadowings of the velvet night.

But whisper—speak—call, great God, for Thy silence is white terror to
our hearts! The way, O God, show us the way and point us the path.

Whither? North is greed and South is blood; within, the coward, and
without, the liar. Whither? To death?
Amen! Welcome dark sleep!

Whither? To life? But not this life, dear God, not this. Let the cup pass
from us, tempt us not beyond our strength, for there is that clamoring and
clawing within, to whose voice we would not listen, yet shudder lest we
must, and it is red, Ah! God! It is a red and awful shape.
Selah!

In yonder East trembles a star.
Vengeance is mine; I mill repay, saith the Lord!
Thy will, O Lord, be done!
Kyrie Eleison!

Lord, we have done these pleading, wavering words.
We beseech Thee to hear us, good Lord!

We bow our heads and hearken soft to the sobbing of women and little
children.

We beseech Thee to hear us, good Lord!
Our voices sink in silence and in night.
Hear us, good Lord!

In night, O God of a godless land!
Amen!

In silence, O Silent God.
Selah!

The Teacher
Leslie Pinckney Hill

Lord, who am I to teach the way
To little children day by day,
So prone myself to go astray?

I teach them knowledge, but I know
How faint they flicker and how low
The candles of my knowledge glow.

I teach them power to will and do,
But only now to learn anew
My own great weakness through and through.

I teach them love for all mankind
And all God's creatures, but I find
My love comes lagging far behind.

Lord, if their guide I still must be,
Oh let the little children see
The teacher leaning hard on Thee.

A Song of Thanks
Edward Smyth Jones

For the sun that shone at the dawn of spring,
For the flowers which bloom and the birds that sing,
For the verdant robe of the gray old earth,
For her coffers filled with their countless worth,
For the flocks which feed on a thousand hills,
For the rippling streams which turn the mills,
For the lowing herds in the lovely vale,
For the songs of gladness on the gale,—
From the Gulf and the Lakes to the Oceans' banks,—
Lord God of Hosts, we give Thee thanks!

For the farmer reaping his whitened fields,
For the bounty which the rich soil yields,
For the cooling dews and refreshing rains,
For the sun which ripens the golden grains,
For the bearded wheat and the fattened swine,
For the stallèd ox and the fruitful vine,
For the tubers large and cotton white,
For the kid and the lambkin frisk and blithe,
For the swan which floats near the river-banks,—
Lord God of Hosts, we give Thee thanks!

For the pumpkin sweet and the yellow yam,
For the corn and beans and the sugared ham,
For the plum and the peach and the apple red,
For the dear old press where the wine is tread,
For the cock which crows at the breaking dawn,

And the proud old "turk" of the farmer's barn,
For the fish which swim in the babbling brooks,
For the game which hide in the shady nooks,—
From the Gulf and the Lakes to the Oceans' banks—
Lord God of Hosts, we give Thee thanks!

For the sturdy oaks and the stately pines,
For the lead and the coal from the deep, dark mines,
For the silver ores of a thousand fold,
For the diamond bright and the yellow gold,
For the river boat and the flying train,
For the fleecy sail of the rolling main,
For the velvet sponge and the glossy pearl,
For the flag of peace which we now unfurl,—
From the Gulf and the Lakes to the Oceans' banks,—
Lord God of Hosts, we give Thee thanks!

For the lowly cot and the mansion fair,
For the peace and plenty together share,
For the Hand which guides us from above,
For Thy tender mercies, abiding love,
For the blessed home with its children gay,
For returnings of Thanksgiving Day,
For the bearing toils and the sharing cares,
We lift up our hearts in our songs and our prayers,—
From the Gulf and the Lakes to the Oceans' banks,—
Lord God of Hosts, we give Thee thanks!

Children of the Sun

Fenton Johnson

We are children of the sun,
Rising sun!
Weaving Southern destiny,
Waiting for the mighty hour
When our Shiloh shall appear
With the flaming sword of right,
With the steel of brotherhood,
And emboss in crimson die
Liberty! Fraternity!

We are the star-dust folk,
Striving folk!
Sorrow songs have lulled to rest;
Seething passions wrought through wrongs,
Led us where the moon rays dip
In the night of dull despair,
Showed us where the star gleams shine,
And the mystic symbols glow—
Liberty! Fraternity!

We have come through cloud and mist,
Mighty men!
Dusk has kissed our sleep-born eyes,
Reared for us a mystic throne
In the splendor of the skies,
That shall always be for us,
Children of the Nazarene,
Children who shall ever sing
Liberty! Fraternity!

The New Day

Fenton Johnson

From a vision red with war I awoke and saw the Prince
of Peace hovering over No Man's Land.
Loud the whistles blew and the thunder of cannon was
drowned by the happy shouting of the people.
From the Sinai that faces Armageddon I heard this chant
from the throats of white-robed angels:

Blow your trumpets, little children!
From the East and from the West,
From the cities in the valley,
From God's dwelling on the mountain,
Blow your blast that Peace might know
She is Queen of God's great army.
With the crying blood of millions
We have written deep her name
In the Book of all the Ages;
With the lilies in the valley,
With the roses by the Mersey,
With the golden flower of Jersey

We have crowned her smooth young temples.
Where her footsteps cease to falter
Golden grain will greet the morning,
Where her chariot descends
Shall be broken down the altars
Of the gods of dark disturbance.
Nevermore shall men know suffering,
Nevermore shall women wailing
Shake to grief the God of Heaven.
From the East and from the West,
From the cities in the valley,
From God's dwelling on the mountain,
Little children, blow your trumpets!

From Ethiopia, groaning 'neath her heavy burdens, I
heard the music of the old slave songs.
I heard the wail of warriors, dusk brown, who grimly
fought the fight of others in the trenches of Mars.
I heard the plea of blood-stained men of dusk and the
crimson in my veins leapt furiously.

Forget not, O my brothers, how we fought
In No Man's Land that peace might come again!
Forget not, O my brothers, how we gave
Red blood to save the freedom of the world!
We were not free, our tawny hands were tied;
But Belgium's plight and Serbia's woes we shared
Each rise of sun or setting of the moon.
So when the bugle blast had called us forth
We went not like the surly brute of yore
But, as the Spartan, proud to give the world
The freedom that we never knew nor shared.
These chains, O brothers mine, have weighed us down
As Samson in the temple of the gods;
Unloosen them and let us breathe the air
That makes the goldenrod the flower of Christ.
For we have been with thee in No Man's Land,
Through lake of fire and down to Hell itself;
And now we ask of thee our liberty,
Our freedom in the land of Stars and Stripes.

A Prayer

Joseph S. Cotter, Jr.

As I lie in bed,
Flat on my back;
There passes across my ceiling
An endless panorama of things—
Quick steps of gay-voiced children,
Adolescence in its wondering silences,
Maid and man on moonlit summer's eve,
Women in the holy glow of Motherhood,
Old men gazing silently thru the twilight
Into the beyond.
O God, give me words to make my dream-children live.

And What Shall You Say?

Joseph S. Cotter, Jr.

Brother, come!
And let us go unto our God.
And when we stand before Him
I shall say—
"Lord, I do not hate,
I am hated.
I scourge no one,
I am scourged.
I covet no lands,
My lands are coveted.
I mock no peoples,
My people are mocked."
And, brother, what shall you say?

The Band of Gideon

Fenton Johnson

The band of Gideon roam the sky,
The howling wind is their war-cry,
The thunder's roll is their trump's peal,
And the lightning's flash their vengeful steel.
Each black cloud
Is a fiery steed.
And they cry aloud

With each strong deed,
"The sword of the Lord and Gideon."

And men below rear temples high
And mock their God with reasons why,
And live in arrogance, sin and shame,
And rape their souls for the world's good name.
Each black cloud
Is a fiery steed.
And they cry aloud
With each strong deed,
"The sword of the Lord and Gideon."

The band of Gideon roam the sky
And view the earth with baleful eye;
In holy wrath they scourge the land
With earth-quake, storm and burning brand.
Each black cloud
Is a fiery steed.
And they cry aloud
With each strong deed,
"The sword of the Lord and Gideon."

The lightnings flash and the thunders roll,
And "Lord have mercy on my soul,"
Cry men as they fall on the stricken sod,
In agony searching for their God.
 Each black cloud
 Is a fiery steed.
 And they cry aloud
 With each strong deed,
"The sword of the Lord and Gideon."

And men repent and then forget
That heavenly wrath they ever met,
The band of Gideon yet will come
And strike their tongues of blasphemy dumb.
 Each black cloud
 Is a fiery steed.
 And they cry aloud
 With each strong deed,
"The sword of the Lord and Gideon."

Supplication
Joseph S. Cotter, Jr.

I am so tired and weary,
So tired of the endless fight,
So weary of waiting the dawn
And finding endless night.

That I ask but rest and quiet—
Rest for days that are gone,
And quiet for the little space
That I must journey on.

The Negro Soldiers
Roscoe C. Jamison

These truly are the Brave,
These men who cast aside
Old memories, to walk the blood-stained pave
Of Sacrifice, joining the solemn tide
That moves away, to suffer and to die
For Freedom—when their own is yet denied!
O Pride! O Prejudice! When they pass by,
Hail them, the Brave, for you now crucified!
These truly are the Free,
These souls that grandly rise
Above base dreams of vengeance for their wrongs,
Who march to war with visions in their eyes
Of Peace through Brotherhood, lifting glad songs,
Aforetime, while they front the firing line.
Stand and behold! They take the field to-day,
Shedding their blood like Him now held divine,
That those who mock might find a better way!

Why Adam Sinned
Alex Rogers

"I heeard da ole folks talkin' in our house da other night
'Bout Adam in da scripchuh long ago.
Da lady folks all 'bused him, sed, he knowed it wus'n right
An' 'cose da men folks dey all sed, "Dat's so."

I felt sorry fuh Mistuh Adam, an' I felt like puttin' in,
'Cause I knows mo' dan dey do, all 'bout whut made Adam sin:

Adam nevuh had no Mammy, fuh to take him on her knee
An' teach him right fum wrong an' show him
Things he ought to see.
I knows down in my heart—he'd-a let dat apple be
But Adam nevuh had no dear old Ma-am-my.

He nevuh knowed no chilehood roun' da ole log cabin do',
He nevuh knowed no pickaninny life.
He started in a great big grown up man, an' whut is mo',
He nevuh had da right kind uf a wife.
Jes s'pose he'd had a Mammy when dat temptin' did begin
An' she'd a come an' tole him
"Son, don' eat dat—dat's a sin."

But, Adam nevuh had no Mammy fuh to take him on her knee
An' teach him right fum wrong an' show him
Things he ought to see.
I knows down in my heart he'd a let dat apple be,
But Adam nevuh had no dear old Ma-am-my.

Keep Me, Jesus, Keep Me
Waverley Turner Carmichael

Keep me 'neath Thy mighty wing,
Keep me, Jesus, keep me;
Help me praise Thy Holy name,
Keep me, Jesus, keep me.
O my Lamb, come, my Lamb,
O my good Lamb,
Save me, Jesus, save me.

Hear me as I cry to Thee;
Keep me, Jesus, keep me;
May I that bright glory see;
Keep me, Jesus, keep me.
O my Lamb, my good Lamb,
O my good Lamb,
Keep me, Jesus, keep me.

Sonnet
Alice Dunbar-Nelson

I had no thought of violets of late,
The wild, shy kind that spring beneath your feet
In wistful April days, when lovers mate
And wander through the fields in raptures sweet.
The thought of violets meant florists' shops,
And bows and pins, and perfumed papers fine;
And garish lights, and mincing little fops
And cabarets and songs, and deadening wine.
So far from sweet real things my thoughts had strayed,
I had forgot wide fields, and clear brown streams;
The perfect loveliness that God has made,—
Wild violets shy and Heaven-mounting dreams.
And now—unwittingly, you've made me dream
Of violets, and my soul's forgotten gleam.

The Big Bell in Zion
Theodore Henry Shackelford

Come, children, hear the joyful sound,
Ding, Dong, Ding.
Go spread the glad news all around,
Ding, Dong, Ding.

Chorus
Oh, the big bell's tollin' up in Zion,
The big bell's tollin' up in Zion,
The big bell's tollin' up in Zion,
Ding, Dong, Ding.

I've been abused and tossed about,
Ding, Dong, Ding.
But glory to the Lamb, I shout!
Ding, Dong, Ding.

My bruthah jus' sent word to me,
Ding, Dong, Ding.
That he'd done set his own self free.
Ding, Dong, Ding.

Ole massa said he could not go,
Ding, Dong, Ding.
But he's done reached Ohio sho'.
Ding, Dong, Ding.

Ise gwine to be real nice an' meek,
Ding, Dong, Ding.
Den I'll run away myself nex' week.
Ding, Dong, Ding.

Chorus

Oh, the big bell's tollin' up in Zion,
The big bell's tollin' up in Zion,
The big bell's tollin' up in Zion,
Ding, Dong Ding.

PAUL LAURENCE DUNBAR (1872-1905)

Introduction

Poet Paul Laurence Dunbar was born on June 27, 1872 in Dayton, Ohio. While Dunbar was not the first African American poet and writer, he was the first to achieve a national reputation and to be accepted by both white and black audiences.

Growing up in Dayton, Dunbar often attended predominantly white schools. Consequently many of his friends were white, and most of them continued their friendship with Dunbar to the end of his short life. Before their successful flight attempt at Kitty Hawk, the Wright brothers were among Dunbar's friends. They not only operated a bicycle shop but also a successful printing business. Orville helped Paul print a newspaper for black readers known as the *Dayton Tattler*, near the end of 1890. They were only able to print three issues before the project had to be abandoned because it was not economically feasible. No doubt Dunbar learned an important lesson from this early experience: it would be difficult to further his writing ambitions by targeting black readers only.

Dunbar was a prolific writer of poetry (in both dialect verse and literary English), short stories, and plays. He also collaborated with the African American composer Will Marion Cook in writing musicals. Due to the economics of his day he targeted mainly white audiences and had a large readership among them. He was also popular and well-respected among black readers.

The Strength of Gideon is located on the plantation. The devotion of a black house servant is pathetically misplaced. There is a sense of loss over Gideon's refusal to take his freedom. The girl he loves, Martha, chooses freedom over love.

The Strength of Gideon

Old Mam' Henry, and her word may be taken, said that it was "De powerfulles' sehmont she ever had hyeahd in all huh bo'n days." That was saying a good deal, for the old woman had lived many years on the Stone place and had heard many sermons from preachers, white and black. She was a judge, too.

It really must have been a powerful sermon that Brother Lucius preached, for Aunt Doshy Scott had fallen in a trance in the middle of the aisle, while "Merlatter Mag," who was famed all over the place for having white folk's religion and never "waking up," had broken through her reserve and shouted all over the camp ground.

Several times Cassie had shown signs of giving way, but because she was frail some of the solicitous sisters held her with self-congratulatory care, relieving each other now and then, that each might have a turn in the rejoicings. But as the preacher waded out deeper and deeper into the spiritual stream, Cassie's efforts to make her feelings known became more and more decided. He told them how the spears of the Midianites had "clashed upon de shiels of de Gideonites, an' aftah while, wid de powah of de Lawd behin' him, de man Gideon triumphed mightily," and swaying then and wailing in the dark woods, with grim branches waving in the breath of their own excitement, they could hear above the tumult the clamor of the fight, the clashing of the spears, and the ringing of the shields. They could see the conqueror coming home in triumph. Then when he cried, "A-who, I say, a-who is in Gideon's ahmy to-day?" and the wailing chorus took up the note, "A-who!" it was too much even for frail Cassie, and, deserted by the solicitous sisters, in the words of Mam' Henry, "she broke a-loose, and faihly tuk de place."

Gideon had certainly triumphed, and when a little boy baby came to Cassie two or three days later, she named him Gideon in honor of the great Hebrew warrior whose story had so wrought upon her. All the plantation knew the spiritual significance of the name, and from the day of his birth the child was as one set apart to a holy mission on earth.

Say what you will of the influences which the circumstances surrounding birth have upon a child, upon this one at least the effect was unmistakable. Even as a baby he seemed to realize the weight of responsibility which had been laid upon his little black shoulders, and there was a complacent dignity in the very way in which he drew upon the sweets of his dirty sugar-teat when the maternal breast was far off bending over the sheaves of the field.

He was a child early destined to sacrifice and self-effacement, and as he grew older and other youngsters came to fill Cassie's cabin, he took up his lot with the meekness of an infantile Moses. Like a Moses he was, too, leading his little flock to the promised land, when he grew to the age at which, barefooted and one-shifted, he led or carried his little brothers and sisters about the quarters. But the "promised land" never took him into the direction of the stables, where the other pickaninnies worried the horses, or into the region of the hen-coops, where egg-sucking was a common crime.

No boy ever rolled or tumbled in the dirt with a heartier glee than did Gideon, but no warrior, not even his illustrious prototype himself, ever kept sterner discipline in his ranks when his followers seemed prone to overstep the bounds of right. At a very early age his shrill voice could be heard calling in admonitory tones, caught from his mother's very lips, "You 'Nelius, don' you let me ketch you th'owin' at ol' mis' guinea-hens no mo'; you hyeah me?" or "Hi'am, you come offen de top er dat shed 'fo' you fall an' brek yo' naik all to pieces."

It was a common sight in the evening to see him sitting upon the low rail fence which ran before the quarters, his shift blowing in the wind, and his black legs lean and bony against the whitewashed rails, as he swayed to and fro, rocking and singing one of his numerous brothers to sleep, and always his song was of war and victory, albeit crooned in a low, soothing voice. Sometimes it was "Turn Back Pharaoh's Army," at others "Jinin' Gideon's Band." The latter was a favorite, for he seemed to have a proprietary interest in it, although, despite the martial inspiration of his name, "Gideon's band" to him meant an aggregation of people with horns and fiddles.

Steve, who was Cassie's man, declared that he had never seen such a child, and, being quite as religious as Cassie herself, early began to talk Scripture and religion to the boy. He was aided in this when his master, Dudley Stone, a man of the faith, began a little Sunday class for the religiously inclined of the quarters, where the old familiar stories were told in simple language to the slaves and explained. At these meetings Gideon became a shining light. No one listened more eagerly to the teacher's words, or more readily answered his questions at review. No one was wider-mouthed or whiter-eyed. His admonitions to his family now took on a different complexion, and he could be heard calling across a lot to a mischievous sister, "Bettah tek keer daih, Lucy Jane, Gawd's a-watchin' you; bettah tek keer."

The appointed man is always marked, and so Gideon was by always receiving his full name. No one ever shortened his scriptural appellation into Gid. He was always Gideon from the time he bore the name out of the heat of camp-meeting fervor until his master discovered his worthiness and filled Cassie's breast with pride by taking him into the house to learn "mannahs and 'po'tment."

As a house servant he was beyond reproach, and next to his religion his Mas' Dudley and Miss Ellen claimed his devotion and fidelity. The young mistress and young master learned to depend fearlessly upon his faithfulness.

It was good to hear old Dudley Stone going through the house in a mock fury, crying, "Well, I never saw such a house; it seems as if there isn't a soul in it that can do without Gideon. Here I've got him up here to wait on me, and it's Gideon here and Gideon there, and every time I turn around some of you have sneaked him off. Gideon, come here!" And the black boy smiled and came.

But all his days were not days devoted to men's service, for there came a time when love claimed him for her own, when the clouds took on a new color, when the sough of the wind was music in his ears, and he saw heaven in Martha's eyes. It all came about in this way.

Gideon was young when he got religion and joined the church, and he grew up strong in the faith. Almost by the time he had become a valuable house servant he had grown to be an invaluable servant of the Lord. He had a good, clear voice that could lead a hymn out of all the labyrinthian wanderings of an ignorant congregation, even when he had to improvise both words and music; and he was a mighty man of prayer. It was thus he met Martha. Martha was brown and buxom and comely, and her rich contralto voice was loud and high on the sisters' side in meeting time. It was the voices that did it at first. There was no hymn or "spiritual" that Gideon could start to which Martha could not sing an easy blending second, and never did she open a tune that Gideon did not swing into it with a wonderfully sweet, flowing, natural bass. Often he did not know the piece, but that did not matter, he sang anyway. Perhaps when they were out he would go to her and ask, "Sis' Martha, what was that hymn you stahrted to-day?" and she would probably answer, "Oh, dat was jes' one o' my mammy's ol' songs."

"Well, it sholy was mighty pretty. Indeed it was."

"Oh, thanky, Brothah Gidjon, thanky."

Then a little later they began to walk back to the master's house together, for Martha, too, was one of the favored ones, and served, not in the field, but in the big house.

The old women looked on and conversed in whispers about the pair, for they were wise, and what their old eyes saw, they saw.

"Oomph," said Mam' Henry, for she commented on everything, "dem too is jes' natchelly singin' demse'ves togeddah."

"Dey's lak de mo'nin' stahs," interjected Aunt Sophy.

"How 'bout dat?" sniffed the older woman, for she objected to any one's alluding to subjects she did not understand.

"Why, Mam' Henry, ain' you nevah hyeahd tell o' de mo'nin' stahs whut sung deyse'ves togeddah?"

"No, I ain', an' I been livin' a mighty sight longah'n you, too. I knows all 'bout when de stahs fell, but dey ain' nevah done no singin' dat I knows 'bout."

"Do heish, Mam' Henry, you sho' su'prises me. W'y, dat ain' happenin's, dat's Scripter."

"Look hyeah, gal, don't you tell me dat's Scripter, an' me been a-settin' undah de Scripter fu' nigh onto sixty yeah."

"Well, Mam' Henry, I may 'a' been mistook, but sho' I took hit fu' Scripter. Mebbe de preachah I hyeahd was jes' inlinin'."

"Well, wheddah hit's Scripter er not, dey's one t'ing su'tain, I tell you,—dem two is singin' deyse'ves togeddah."

"Hit's a fac', an' I believe it."

"An' it's a mighty good thing, too. Brothah Gidjon is de nicest house dahky dat I ever hyeahd tell on. Dey jes' de same diffunce 'twixt him an' de othah house-boys as dey is 'tween real quality an' strainers—he got mannahs, but he ain't got aihs."

"Heish, ain't you right!"

"An' while de res' of dem ain' thinkin' 'bout nothin' but dancin' an' ca'in' on, he makin' his peace, callin', an' 'lection sho'."

"I tell you, Mam' Henry, dey ain' nothin' like a spichul named chile."

"Humph! g'long, gal; 'tain't in de name; de biggest devil I evah knowed was named Moses Aaron. 'Tain't in de name, hit's all in de man hisse'f."

But notwithstanding what the gossips said of him, Gideon went on his way, and knew not that the one great power of earth had taken hold of him until they gave the great party down in the quarters, and he saw Martha in all her glory. Then love spoke to him with no uncertain sound.

It was a dancing-party, and because neither he nor Martha dared countenance dancing, they had strolled away together under the pines that lined the white road, whiter now in the soft moonlight. He had never known the pine-cones smell so sweet before in all his life. She had never known just how the moonlight flecked the road before. This was lovers' lane to them. He didn't understand why his heart kept throbbing so furiously, for they were walking slowly, and when a shadow thrown across the road from a by-standing bush frightened her into pressing close up to him, he could not have told why his arm stole round her waist and drew her slim form up to him, or why his lips found hers, as eye looked into eye. For their simple hearts love's mystery was too deep, as it is for wiser ones.

Some few stammering words came to his lips, and she answered the best she could. Then why did the moonlight flood them so, and why were the heavens so full of stars? Out yonder in the black hedge a mocking-bird was singing, and he was translating—oh, so poorly—the song of their hearts. They forgot the dance, they forgot all but their love.

"An' you won't ma'y nobody else but me, Martha?"

"You know I won't, Gidjon."

"But I mus' wait de yeah out?"

"Yes, an' den don't you think Mas' Stone'll let us have a little cabin of ouah own jest outside de quahtahs?"

"Won't it be blessid? Won't it be blessid?" he cried, and then the kindly moon went under a cloud for a moment and came out smiling, for he had peeped through and had seen what passed. Then they walked back hand in hand to the dance along the transfigured road, and they found that the first part of the estivities were over, and all the people had sat down to supper. Every one laughed when they went in. Martha held back and perspired with embarrassment. But even though he saw some of the older heads whispering in a corner, Gideon was not ashamed. A new light was in his eyes, and a new boldness had come to him. He led Martha up to the grinning group, and said in his best singing voice, "Whut you laughin' at? Yes, I's popped de question, an' she says 'Yes,' an' long 'bout a yeah f'om now you kin all 'spec' a' invitation." This was a formal announcement. A shout arose from the happy-go-lucky people, who sorrowed alike in each other's sorrows, and joyed in each other's joys. They sat down at a table, and their health was drunk in cups of cider and persimmon beer.

Over in the corner Mam' Henry mumbled over her pipe, "Wha'd I tell you? wha'd I tell you?" and Aunt Sophy replied, "Hit's de pa'able of de mo'nin' stahs."

"Don't talk to me 'bout no mo'nin' stahs," the mammy snorted; "Gawd jes' fitted dey voices togeddah, an' den j'ined dey hea'ts. De mo'nin' stahs ain't got nothin' to do wid it."

"Mam' Henry," said Aunt Sophy, impressively, "you's a' oldah ooman den I is, an' I ain' sputin' hit; but I say dey done 'filled Scripter 'bout de mo'nin' stahs; dey's done sung deyse'ves togeddah."

The old woman sniffed.

The next Sunday at meeting some one got the start of Gideon, and began a new hymn. It ran:

At de ma'ige of de Lamb, oh Lawd,
  God done gin His 'sent.
Dey dressed de Lamb all up in white,
  God done gin His 'sent.
Oh, wasn't dat a happy day,
Oh, wasn't dat a happy day, Good Lawd,
Oh, wasn't dat a happy day,
  De ma'ige of de Lamb!

The wailing minor of the beginning broke into a joyous chorus at the end, and Gideon wept and laughed in turn, for it was his wedding-song. The young man had a confidential chat with his master the next morning, and the happy secret was revealed.

"What, you scamp!" said Dudley Stone. "Why, you've got even more sense than I gave you credit for; you've picked out the finest girl on the plantation, and the one best suited to you. You couldn't have done better if the match had been made for you. I reckon this must be one of the marriages that are made in heaven. Marry her, yes, and with a preacher. I don't see why you want to wait a year."

Gideon told him his hopes of a near cabin.

"Better still," his master went on; "with you two joined and up near the big house, I'll feel as safe for the folks as if an army was camped around, and, Gideon, my boy,"—he put his arms on the black man's shoulders,—"if I should slip away some day—"

The slave looked up, startled.

"I mean if I should die—I'm not going to run off, don't be alarmed—I want you to help your young Mas' Dud look after his mother and Miss Ellen; you hear? Now that's the one promise I ask of you,—come what may, look after the women folks." And the man promised and went away smiling.

His year of engagement, the happiest time of a young man's life, began on golden wings. There came rumors of war, and the wings of the glad-hued year drooped sadly. Sadly they drooped, and seemed to fold, when one day, between the rumors and predictions of strife, Dudley Stone, the old master, slipped quietly away out into the unknown.

There were wife, daughter, son, and faithful slaves about his bed, and they wept for him sincere tears, for he had been a good husband and father and a kind master. But he smiled, and, conscious to the last, whispered to them a cheery good-bye. Then, turning to Gideon, who stood there bowed with grief, he raised one weak finger, and his lips made the word, "Remember!"

They laid him where they had laid one generation after another of the Stones and it seemed as if a pall of sorrow had fallen upon the whole place. Then, still grieving, they turned their long-distracted attention to the things that had been going on around, and lo! The ominous mutterings were loud, and the cloud of war was black above them.

It was on an April morning when the storm broke, and the plantation, master and man, stood dumb with consternation, for they had hoped, they had believed, it would pass. And now there was the buzz of men who talked in secret corners. There were hurried saddlings and feverish rides to town. Somewhere in the quarters was whispered the forbidden word "freedom," and it was taken up and dropped breathlessly from the ends of a hundred tongues. Some of the older ones scouted it, but from some who held young children to their breasts there were deep-souled prayers in the dead of night. Over the meetings in the woods or in the log church a strange reserve brooded, and even the prayers took on a guarded tone. Even from the fullness of their hearts, which longed for liberty, no open word that could offend the mistress or the young master went up to the Almighty. He might know their hearts, but no tongue in meeting gave vent to what was in them, and even Gideon sang no more of the gospel army. He was sad because of this new trouble coming hard upon the heels of the old, and Martha was grieved because he was.

Finally the trips into town budded into something, and on a memorable evening when the sun looked peacefully through the pines, young Dudley Stone rode into the yard dressed in a suit of gray, and on his shoulders were the straps of office. The servants gathered around him with a sort of awe and followed him until he alighted at the porch. Only Mam' Henry, who had been nurse to both him and his sister, dared follow him in. It was a sad scene within, but such a one as any Southern home where there were sons might have shown that awful year. The mother tried to be brave, but her old hands shook, and her tears fell upon her son's brown head, tears of grief at parting, but through which shone the fire of a noble pride. The young Ellen hung about his neck with sobs and caresses.

"Would you have me stay?" he asked her.

"No! no! I know where your place is, but oh, my brother!"

"Ellen," said the mother in a trembling voice, "you are the sister of a soldier now."

The girl dried her tears and drew herself up. "We won't burden your heart, Dudley, with our tears, but we will weight you down with our love and prayers."

It was not so easy with Mam' Henry. Without protest, she took him to her bosom and rocked to and fro, wailing "My baby! my baby!" and the tears that fell from the young man's eyes upon her gray old head cost his manhood nothing.

Gideon was behind the door when his master called him. His sleeve was traveling down from his eyes as he emerged.

"Gideon," said his master, pointing to his uniform, "you know what this means?"

"Yes, suh."

"I wish I could take you along with me. But—"

"Mas' Dud," Gideon threw out his arms in supplication.

"You remember father's charge to you, take care of the women-folks." He took the servant's hand, and, black man and white, they looked into each other's eyes, and the compact was made. Then Gideon gulped and said "Yes, suh" again.

Another boy held the master's horse and rode away behind him when he vaulted into the saddle, and the man of battle-song and warrior name went back to mind the women-folks.

Then began the disintegration of the plantation's population. First Yellow Bob slipped away, and no one pursued him. A few blamed him, but they soon followed as the year rolled away. More were missing every time a Union camp lay near, and great tales were told of the chances for young Negroes who would go as body-servants to the Yankee officers. Gideon heard all and was silent.

Then as the time of his marriage drew near he felt a greater strength, for there was one who would be with him to help him keep his promise and his faith.

The spirit of freedom had grown strong in Martha as the days passed, and when her lover went to see her she had strange things to say. Was he going to stay? Was he going to be a slave when freedom and a livelihood lay right within his grasp? Would he keep her a slave? Yes, he would do it all—all.

She asked him to wait.

Another year began, and one day they brought Dudley Stone home to lay beside his father. Then most of the remaining Negroes went. There was no master now. The two bereaved women wept, and Gideon forgot that he wore the garb of manhood and wept with them.

Martha came to him.

"Gidjon," she said, "I's waited a long while now. Mos' eve'ybody else is gone. Ain't you goin'?"

"No."

"But, Gidjon, I wants to be free. I know how good dey've been to us; but, oh, I wants to own myse'f. They're talkin' 'bout settin' us free every hour."

"I can wait."

"They's a camp right near here."

"I promised."

"The of'cers wants body-servants, Gidjon—"

"Go, Martha, if you want to, but I stay."

She went away from him, but she or some one else got word to young Captain Jack Griswold of the near camp that there was an excellent servant on the plantation who only needed a little persuading, and he came up to see him.

"Look here," he said, "I want a body-servant. I'll give you ten dollars a month."

"I've got to stay here."

"But, you fool, what have you to gain by staying here?"

"I'm goin' to stay."

"Why, you'll be free in a little while, anyway."

"All right."

"Of all fools," said the Captain. "I'll give you fifteen dollars."

"I do' want it."

"Well, your girl's going, anyway. I don't blame her for leaving such a fool as you are."

Gideon turned and looked at him.

"The camp is going to be moved up on this plantation, and there will be a requisition for this house for officers' quarters, so I'll see you again," and Captain Griswold went his way.

Martha going! Martha going! Gideon could not believe it. He would not. He saw her, and she confirmed it. She was going as an aid to the nurses. He gasped, and went back to mind the women-folks.

They did move the camp up nearer, and Captain Griswold came to see Gideon again, but he could get no word from him, save "I'm goin' to stay," and he went away in disgust, entirely unable to understand such obstinacy, as he called it.

But the slave had his moments alone, when the agony tore at his breast and rended him. Should he stay? The others were going. He would soon be free. Every one had said so, even his mistress one day. Then Martha was going. "Martha! Martha!" his heart called.

The day came when the soldiers were to leave, and he went out sadly to watch them go. All the plantation, that had been white with tents, was dark again, and everywhere were moving, blue-coated figures.

Once more his tempter came to him. "I'll make it twenty dollars," he said, but Gideon shook his head. Then they started. The drums tapped. Away they went, the flag kissing the breeze. Martha stole up to say good-bye to him. Her eyes were overflowing, and she clung to him.

"Come, Gidjon," she plead, "fu' my sake. Oh, my God, won't you come with us—it's freedom." He kissed her, but shook his head.

"Hunt me up when you do come," she said, crying bitterly, "fu' I do love you, Gidjon, but I must go. Out yonder is freedom," and she was gone with them.

He drew out a pace after the troops, and then, turning, looked back at the house. He went a step farther, and then a woman's gentle voice called him, "Gideon!" He stopped. He crushed his cap in his hands, and the tears came into his eyes. Then he answered, "Yes, Mis' Ellen, I's a-comin'."

He stood and watched the dusty column until the last blue leg swung out of sight and over the gray hills the last drum-tap died away, and then turned and retraced his steps toward the house.

Gideon had triumphed mightily.

Paul Laurence Dunbar

MARY MCLEOD BETHUNE (1875-1955)

Introduction

In the New Deal era, educator and activist Mary McLeod Bethune was called the "First Lady of the Struggle" for her influence on the Roosevelt administration on civil rights issues. In 1904, Bethune founded a small school for black girls in Florida that she quickly built into a thriving college-prep and vocational training program. In 1923, she merged the school with Cookman College to create the first fully accredited black institution of higher learning in the state.

Bethune was born to former slaves in 1875. One of seventeen children, she grew up picking cotton in Sumter County, South Carolina. Her parents owned a five-acre parcel of land, and her mother continued to work for the family that once owned her. Though her parents and siblings were illiterate, Bethune knew as a child that she wanted to escape "the dense darkness and ignorance" in which she found herself. Her ambition to read was only fueled by a white girl who once commanded her to put down a book, saying, "You can't read."

Bethune was one of the first youngsters to sign up for a new mission school for black children built near her home. She recalled, "That first morning on my way to school I kept the thought uppermost, 'put that down—you can't read,' and I felt that I was on my way to read." Bethune was not only on her way to read, she was on her way to a lifelong career devoted to educating a people only a generation or two away from slavery.

"What Does American Democracy Mean to Me?"

Democracy is for me, and for 12 million black Americans, a goal towards which our nation is marching. It is a dream and an ideal in whose ultimate realization we have a deep and abiding faith. For me, it is based on Christianity, in which we confidently entrust our destiny as a people. Under God's guidance in this great democracy, we are rising out of the darkness of slavery into the light of freedom. Here my race has been afforded the opportunity to advance from a people 80 percent illiterate to a people 80 percent literate; from abject poverty to the ownership and operation of a million farms and 750,000 homes; from total disfranchisement to participation in government; from the status of chattels to recognized contributors to the American culture.

As we have been extended a measure of democracy, we have brought to the nation rich gifts. We have helped to build America with our labor, strengthened it with our faith and enriched it with our song. We have given you Paul Lawrence Dunbar, Booker T. Washington, Marian Anderson and George Washington Carver. But even these are only the first fruits of a rich harvest, which will be reaped when new and wider fields are opened to us.

The democratic doors of equal opportunity have not been opened wide to Negroes. In the Deep South, Negro youth is offered only one-fifteenth of the educational opportunity of the average American child. The great masses of Negro workers are depressed and unprotected in the lowest levels of agriculture and domestic service, while the black workers in industry are barred from certain unions and generally assigned to the more laborious and poorly paid work. Their housing and living conditions are sordid and unhealthy. They live too often in terror of the lynch mob; are deprived too often of the Constitutional right of suffrage; and are humiliated too often by the denial of civil liberties. We do not believe that justice and common decency will allow these conditions to continue.

Our faith in visions of fundamental change as mutual respect and understanding between our races come in the path of spiritual awakening. Certainly there have been times when we may have delayed this mutual understanding by being slow to assume a fuller share of our national responsibility because of the denial of full equality. And yet, we have always been loyal when the ideals of American democracy have been attacked. We have given our blood in its defense-from Crispus Attucks on Boston Commons to the battlefields of France. We have fought for the democratic principles of equality under the law, equality of opportunity, equality at the ballot box, for the guarantees of life, liberty and the pursuit of happiness. We have fought to preserve one nation, conceived in liberty and dedicated to the proposition that all men are created equal. Yes, we have fought for America with all her imperfections, not so much for what she is, but for what we know she can be.

Perhaps the greatest battle is before us, the fight for a new America: fearless, free, united, morally re-armed, in which 12 million Negroes, shoulder to shoulder with their fellow Americans, will strive that this nation under God will have a new birth of freedom, and that government of the people, for the people and by the people shall not perish from the earth. This dream, this idea, this aspiration, this is what American democracy means   to me.

Mary McLeod Bethune, America's Town Meeting of the Air,
New York City, November 23, 1939

CARTER GODWIN WOODSON (1875-1950)

Introduction

"Those who have no record of what their forebears have accomplished lose the inspiration which comes from the teaching of biography and history."

These are the words of Dr. Carter Godwin Woodson, distinguished Black author, editor, publisher, and historian (December 1875—April 1950). Carter G. Woodson believed that Blacks should know their past in order to participate intelligently in the affairs of their country. He strongly believed that Black history—which others have tried so diligently to erase—is a firm foundation for young Black Americans to build on in order to become productive citizens of our society.

Known as the "Father of Black History," Carter G. Woodson holds an outstanding position in early 20th century American history. Woodson authored numerous scholarly books on the positive contributions of Blacks to the development of America. He also published many magazine articles analyzing the contributions and role of Black Americans. He reached out to schools and the general public through the establishment of several key organizations and founded *Negro History Week* (precursor to *Black History Month*). His message was that Blacks should be proud of their heritage and that other Americans should also understand it.

Carter G. Woodson was born in New Canton, Buckingham County, Virginia, to former slaves Anne Eliza (Riddle) and James Henry Woodson. Although his parents could neither read nor write, Carter G. Woodson credits his father for influencing the course of his life. His father, he later wrote, insisted that "learning to accept insult, to compromise on principle, to mislead your fellow man, or to betray your people, is to lose your soul."

His father supported the family on his earnings as a carpenter. As one of a large and poor family, young Carter G. Woodson was brought up without the "ordinary comforts of life." He was not able to attend school during much of its five-month term because helping on the farm took priority over a formal education. Determined not to be defeated by this setback, Carter was able "largely by self-instruction to master the fundamentals of common school subjects by the time he was seventeen." Ambitious for more education, Carter and his brother Robert Henry moved to Huntington, West Virginia, where they hoped to attend the Douglass High School. However, Carter was forced to earn his living as a miner in Fayette County coal fields and was able to devote only a few months each year to his schooling. In 1895, a twenty-year-old Carter entered Douglass High School, where he received his diploma in less than two years.

From 1897 to 1900, Carter G. Woodson began teaching in Winona, Fayette County. In 1900, he returned to Huntington to become the principal of Douglass H.S.; he finally received his Bachelor of Literature degree from Berea College, Kentucky. From 1903 to 1907, he was a school supervisor in the Philippines. Later he traveled throughout Europe and Asia and studied at the Sorbonne University in Paris. In 1908, he received his M.A. from the University of Chicago, and in 1912, he received his Ph.D. in history from Harvard University.

During his lifetime, Dr. Woodson developed an important philosophy of history. History, he insisted, was not the mere gathering of facts. The object of historical study is to arrive at a reasonable interpretation of the facts. History is more than political and military records of peoples and nations. It must include some description of the social conditions of the period being studied.

Woodson's work endures in the institutions and activities he founded and promoted. In 1915, he and several friends in Chicago established the Association for the Study of Negro Life and History. The following year, the *Journal of Negro History* appeared, one of the oldest learned journals in the United States. In 1926, he developed *Negro History Week* and in 1937 published the first issue of the *Negro History Bulletin*.

Dr. Woodson often said that he hoped the time would come when *Negro History Week* would be unnecessary; when all Americans would willingly recognize the contributions of Black Americans as a legitimate and integral part of the history of this country. Dr. Woodson's concept has given a profound sense of dignity to all Black Americans.

Summary of *The History of the Negro Church*

In his classic *The History of the Negro Church*, Carter G. Woodson traces the influence of the black church in America from colonial times through the early years of the twentieth century. Beginning with early church movements in the North and efforts to minister to slaves in the South, the author describes the origins of religious instruction for a race that he characterizes as "neglected" among an unenlightened colonial population. Woodson describes the numerous sectarian movements that arose over the slave controversy, and details the establishment of the Colored Methodist Episcopal, African Methodist Episcopal, and African Methodist Episcopal Zion Churches.

Following the Civil War, the church took on a new, more important role in the black community. Church organizations and benefactors both domestic and foreign helped establish schools and churches to educate the newly freed blacks. Woodson argues that the church served as a Chamber of Commerce, educational facility, and a social center. Additionally, the ministry was one of the highest stations to which a black leader could aspire; the visibility and education available to the clergy was notable in a community that was often denied opportunity. To emphasize this fact, Woodson includes numerous short biographies of church leaders who were instrumental in the development of various denominations or were significant members of the religious community.

The History of the Negro Church
Preface

The importance of the church in the life of the Negro justifies the publication of this brief account of the development of the institution. For many years the various denominations have been writing treatises bearing on their own particular work, but hitherto there has been no effort to study the achievements of all of these groups as parts of the same institution and to show the evolution of it from the earliest period to the present time. This is the objective of this volume.

Whether or not the author has done this task well is a question which the public must decide. This work does not represent what he desired to make it. Many facts of the past could not be obtained for the reason that several denominations have failed to keep records and facts known to persons now active in the church could not be collected because of indifference or the failure to understand the motives of the author. Not a few church officers and ministers, however, gladly co-operated with the author in giving and seeking information concerning their denominations. Among these were Mr. Charles H. Wesley, Prof. J. A. Booker, and Dr. Walter H. Brooks. For their valuable assistance the author feels deeply grateful.

Carter G. Woodson, Washington, D. C., September, 1921.

Chapter 1
Early Missionaries and the Negro

One of the causes of the discovery of America was the translation into action of the desire of European zealots to extend the Catholic religion into other parts. Columbus, we are told, was decidedly missionary in his efforts and felt that he could not make a more significant contribution to the church than to open new fields for Christian endeavor. His final success in securing the equipment adequate to the adventure upon the high seas was to some extent determined by the Christian motives impelling the sovereigns of Spain to finance the expedition for the reason that it might afford an opportunity for promoting the cause of Christ. Some of the French who came to the new world to establish their claims by further discovery and exploration, moreover, were either actuated by similar motives or welcomed the co-operation of earnest workers thus interested.

The first persons proselyted by the Spanish and French missionaries were Indians. There was not any particular thought of the Negro. It may seem a little strange just now to think of persons having to be converted to faith in the possibility of the salvation of the Negro, but there were among the colonists thousands who had never considered the Negro as belonging to the pale of Christianity. Negroes had been generally designated as infidels; but, in the estimation of their self-styled superiors, they were not considered the most desirable of this class supposedly arrayed against Christianity. There were few Christians who did not look forward to the ultimate conversion of those infidels approaching the Caucasian type, but hardly any desired to make an effort in the direction of proselyting Negroes.

When, however, that portion of this Latin element primarily interested in the exploitation of the Western Hemisphere failed to find in the Indians the substantial labor supply necessary to their enterprises and at the suggestion of men like las Casas imported Negroes for this purpose, the missionaries came face to face with the question as to whether this new sort of heathen should receive the same consideration as that given the Indians. Because of the unwritten law that a Christian could not be held a slave, the exploiting class opposed any such proselyting; for, should the slaves be liberated upon being converted, their plans for development would fail for lack of a labor supply subject to their orders as bondmen. The sovereigns of Europe, once inclined to adopt a sort of humanitarian policy toward the Negroes, at first objected to their importation into the new world; and when under the pressure of the interests of the various countries they yielded on this point, it was stipulated that such slaves should have first embraced Christianity. Later, when further concessions to the capitalists were necessary, it was provided in the royal decrees of Spain and of France that Africans enslaved in America should merely be early indoctrinated in the principles of the Christian religion.

These decrees, although having the force of law, soon fell into desuetude. There was not among these planters any sentiment in favor of such humanitarian treatment of the slaves. Unlike the missionaries, the planters were not interested in religion and they felt that too much enlightenment of the slaves might inspire them with the hope of attaining the status of freemen. The laws, therefore, were nominally accepted as just and the functionaries in the colonies in reporting to their home countries on the state of the plantations made it appear that they were generally complied with. As there was no such thing as an inspection of these commercial outposts, moreover, no one in Europe could easily determine exactly what attitude these men had toward carrying out the will of the home countries with respect to the Christianization of the bondmen. From time to time, therefore, the humanitarian world heard few protests like that of Alfonso Sandoval in Cuba and the two Capucin monks who were imprisoned in Havana because of their inveighing against the failure on the part of the planters to provide for the religious instruction of the slaves. Being in the minority, these upright pioneers too often had their voices hushed in persecution, as it happened in the case of the two monks.

It appears, however, that efforts in behalf of Negroes elsewhere were not in vain; for the Negroes in Latin America were not only proselyted thereafter but were given recognition among the clergy. Such was the experience of Francisco Xavier de Luna Victoria, son of a freedman, a Panama charcoal burner, whose chief ambition was to educate this young man for the priesthood. He easily became a priest and after having served acceptably in this capacity a number of years was chosen Bishop of Panama in 1751 and administered this office eight years. He was later called to take charge of the See of Trujillo, Peru.

In what is now the United States the Spanish and French missionaries had very little contact with the Negroes during the early period, as they were found in large numbers along the Atlantic coast only. In the West Indies, however, the Latin policy decidedly dominated during the early colonial period, and when the unwritten law that a Christian could not be held a slave was by special statutes and royal decrees annulled, the planters eventually yielded in their objection to the religious instruction of the slaves and generally complied with the orders of the home country to this effect.

Maryland was the only Atlantic colony in which the Catholics had the opportunity to make an appeal to a large group of Negroes. After some opposition the people of that colony early met the test of preaching the gospel to all regardless of color. The first priests and missionaries operating in Maryland regarded it their duty to enlighten the slaves; and, as the instruction of the communicants of the church became more systematic to make their preparation adequate to the proper understanding of the church doctrine, some sort of instruction of the Negroes attached to these establishments was provided in keeping with the sentiment expressed in the first ordinances of the Spanish and French sovereigns and later in the Black Code governing the bondmen in. the colonies controlled by the Latins.

Although the attitude of the Catholic pioneers was not altogether encouraging to the movement for the evangelization of the Negroes, still less assistance came from the Protestants settling the English colonies. Few, if any, of the pioneers from Great Britain had the missionary spirit of some of the Latins. As the English were primarily interested in founding new homes in America, they thought of the Negroes not as objects of Christian philanthropy but rather as tools with which they might reach that end. It is not surprising then that with the introduction of slavery as an economic factor in the development of the English colonies little care was taken of their spiritual needs, and especially so when they were confronted with the unwritten law that a Christian could not be held a slave.

Owing to the more noble example set by the Latins, however, and the desirable results early obtained by their missionaries, the English planters permitted some sort of religious instruction of the bondmen, after providing by royal decrees and special statutes in the colonies that conversion to Christianity would not work manumission. Feeling, however, that the nearer the blacks were kept to the state of brutes that the more useful they would be as laborers, the masters generally neglected them.

The exceptions to this rule were the efforts of various clergymen in coöperation with the Society for the Propagation of the Gospel in Foreign Parts. This organization was established in London in 1701 to do missionary work among the heathen, especially the Indians and the Negroes. Its function was to prepare the objects of its philanthropy for a proper understanding of the church doctrine and the relation of man to God. This body operated through the branches of the established church, the ministrations of which were first limited to a few places in Virginia, New York Maryland, and the cities of Boston and Philadelphia. From the very beginning this society felt that the conversion of the Negroes was as important as that of bringing the whites or the Indians into the church and such distinguished churchmen as Bishops Lowth, Fleetwood, Williams, Sanderson, Butler, and Wilson, persistently urged this duty upon their subordinates. In 1727 Bishop Gibson sent out two forceful pastoral letters outlining this duty of the missionaries, Bishop Secker preached a soul-stirring sermon thereupon in 1741, and in 1784 Bishop Porteus published an extensive plan for the more effectual conversion of the slaves, contending that "despicable as they are in the eyes of man they are, nevertheless, the creatures of God."

The first successful worker in this field was the Rev. Samuel Thomas of Goose Creek Parish in the colony of South Carolina. The records show that he was thus engaged as early as 1695 and that ten years later he reported 20 black communicants who, with several others, well understood the English language. By 1705 he had brought under his instruction as many as 1,000 slaves, "many of whom," said he, "could read the Bible distinctly and great numbers of them were engaged in learning the scriptures." When these blacks approached the communion table, however, some white persons seriously objected, inquiring whether it was possible that slaves should go to heaven anyway. But having the coöperation of a number of liberal slaveholders in that section and working in collaboration with Mrs. Haig, Mrs. Edwards, and the Rev. E. Taylor, who baptized a number of them, the missionaries in that colony prepared the way for the Christianization of the Negro slaves.

Becoming interested in the thorough indoctrination of these slaves, Mr. Taylor planned for their instruction, encouraging the slaveholders to teach the blacks at least to the extent of learning the Lord's Prayer. Manifesting such interest in these unfortunate blacks, their friends easily induced them to attend church in such large numbers that they could not be accommodated. "So far as the missionaries were permitted," says one, "they did all that was possible for their evangelization, and while so many professed Christians among the whites were lukewarm, it pleased God to raise to himself devout servants among the heathen, whose faithfulness was commended by the Masters themselves." In some of the congregations the Negroes constituted one-half of the communicants.

This interest in proselyting the Negroes was extended into other parts. In 1723, Rev. Mr. Guy of St. Andrew's Parish reported that he had baptized a Negro man and woman. About the same time Rev. Mr. Hunt, in charge of St. John's Parish, had among his communicants a slave, "a sensible Negro who can read and write and come to church, a catechumen under probation for baptism, which he desires."

A new stage in the progress of this movement was reached in 1743 when there was established at Charleston, South Carolina, a special school to train Negroes for participation in this missionary work. This school was opened by Commissary Garden and placed in charge of Harry and Andrew, two young men of color, who had been thoroughly instructed in the rudiments of education and in the doctrines of the church. It not only served as the training school for missionary workers, but directed its attention also to the special needs of adults who studied therein during the evenings. From this school there were sent out from year to year numbers of youths to undertake this work in various parts of the colony of South Carolina. After having accomplished so much good for about a generation, however, the school was, in 1763, closed for various reasons, one of them being that one of the instructors died and the other proved inefficient.

Farther upward in the colony of North Carolina, the same difficulties were encountered. There the motive was the fear that, should the slaves be converted, they would, according to the unwritten law of Christendom, become free. Some planters, however, were very soon thereafter persuaded to let these missionaries continue their work. "By much importunity," says an annalist, Mr. Ranford of Chowan, "in 1712 we prevailed upon Mr. Martin to let him baptize three of his Negroes, two women and a boy. All the arguments I could make use of," said he, "would scarce effect it till Bishop Fleetwood's sermon in 1711 turned ye scale." These workers then soon found it possible to instruct and baptize more than forty Negroes in one year, and not long thereafter some workers reported as many as 15 to 24 in one month, 40 to 50 in six months and 60 to 70 in a year. Rev. Mr. Newman, proclaiming the new day of the Gospel in that colony, reported in 1723 that he had baptized two Negroes who could say the Creed, the Lord's Prayer, the Ten Commandments and gave good sureties for their fuller information. According to the report of Rev. C. Hall, the number of conversions there among the Negroes for eight years was 355, including 112 adults; and "at Edenton the blacks generally were induced to attend service at all these stations where they behaved with great decorum."

In the middle colonies the work was given additional impetus by the mission of Dr. Thomas Bray. The Bishop of London sent this gentleman to the colony of Maryland for the purpose of devising plans to convert adult Negroes and educate their children. Having also the influential support of M. D'Alone, the private secretary of King William, who gave for its maintenance a fund, the proceeds of which were to be used to employ catechists, the Thomas Bray Mission decidedly encouraged these missionaries. The catechists appointed, however, failed; but the work was well extended throughout Maryland, into neighboring colonies, and even into the settlements of Georgia, through certain persons assuming the title of Dr. Bray's Associates. Traveling in North Carolina, Rev. Mr. Stewart, a missionary, found there a school maintained by Dr. Bray's Associates for the education of Indians and Negroes. They were supporting such a school in Georgia in 1751; Page 11

but in 1766 the Rev. S. Frink, a missionary trying to secure a hearing in Augusta, found that he could neither convert the Indians nor the whites, who seemed to be as destitute of religion as the former; but he succeeded in converting some Negroes.

In Pennsylvania the missionary movement among the Negroes found apparently less obstacles. There are records showing the baptism of Negroes as early is 1712. One Mr. Yates, a worker at Chester, was commended by the Rev. G. Ross "for his endeavors to train up the Negroes in the knowledge of religion." Mr. Ross himself had on one occasion at Philadelphia baptized as many as twelve adult Negroes, who were examined before the congregation and answered to the admiration of all who heard them "The like sight had never been seen before in that church." Giving account of his efforts in Sussex County in 1723, Rev. Mr. Beckett said that many Negroes constantly attended his services, while Rev. Mr. Bartow about the same time baptized a Negro at West Chester. Rev. Richard Locke christened eight Negroes in one family at Lancaster in 1747 and another Negro there the following year. In 1774 the Rev. Mr. Jenney observed a great and daily increase of Negroes in this city, "who with joy attend upon the catechist for instruction." He had baptized several but was unable to add to his other duties.

The Society, ever ready to lend a helping hand to such an enterprise, appointed the Rev. W. Sturgeon as catechist for the Negroes in Philadelphia. At the same time the Rev. Mr. Neal of Dover was meeting with equally good results, having baptized as many as 162 Negroes within eight months. Now and then, however, as in the case of Rev. Mr. Pugh, a missionary at Appoquinimmick, Pennsylvania, the missionaries received very few Negroes, because their masters here, as elsewhere, were prejudiced against their being Christians.

The Society did not operate extensively in the State of New Jersey. The Rev. Mr. Lindsay mentions his baptizing a Negro at Allerton in 1736. The missions of New Brunswick reported a large number of Negroes as having become attached to their churches, but this favorable situation was not the rule throughout the State. The missionary spirit was not wanting, however, and the accession of Negroes to the churches followed later in spite of local opposition and the general apathy as to the indoctrination of the blacks.

In those colonies further north where the Negroes were not found in large numbers, little opposition to their indoctrination was experienced; and their evangelization proceeded without interruption, whereas in most southern colonies the proselyting of the Negroes was largely restricted to what the ministers and missionaries could do during their spare time. There was in New York a special provision for the employment of 16 clergymen and 13 lay teachers for the conversion of free Indians and Negro slaves. Elias Neau, a worker in these ranks, established in New York City in 1704 a catechizing school for Negro slaves. After several years of imprisonment in France because of his Protestant faith he had come to New York as a trader. Upon witnessing, however, the neglected condition of the blacks, who, according to his words, "were without God in the world and of whose souls there was no manner of care taken," he proposed the appointment of a catechist to undertake their instruction. Finally being prevailed upon to accept the position himself, he obtained a license from the Governor, resigned his position as elder in the French church, and conformed to the established church of England. At first he served from house to house but very soon secured a regular place of instruction, after being commended by the Society to Mr. Vesey, as a constant communicant of the church and a most zealous and prudent servant of Christ in proselyting the Negroes and Indians to the Christian religion whereby he did great service to God and his church. There was a further expression of confidence in him in a bill to be offered to Parliament "for the more effectual conversion of the Negroes and other servants in the plantations, to compel owners of slaves to cause their children to be baptized within three months after their birth and to permit them, when come to years of discretion, to be instructed in the Christian religion on our Lord's Day by the missionaries under whose ministry they live."

Neau's school suffered considerably in the Negro riot in that city in 1712, when it was closed by local authority and an investigation of his operations ordered. Upon learning, however, that the slaves primarily concerned in this rising were not connected with his school but had probably engaged in this enterprise because of their neglected condition, the city permitted him to continue his operations as a teacher, feeling that Christian knowledge would not necessarily be a means of more cunning and aptitude to wickedness. The Governor and the Council, the Mayor, the Recorder, and Chief Justice informed the Society that Neau had "performed his work to the great advancement of religion and particular benefit of the free Indians, Negro slaves and other heathen in these parts, with indefatigable zeal and application."

Neau died in 1722; but his work was continued by Huddlestone, Whitmore, Colgan, Auchmutty, and Charlton. The last mentioned had undertaken the instruction of the blacks while at New Windsor and found it practical and convenient to throw into one class his white and black catechumens. Mr. Auchmutty served from 1747 to 1764 and finally reported that there was among the Negroes an ever-increasing desire for instruction and not one single black "that had been admitted by him to the holy communion had turned out bad or been in any way a disgrace to our holy profession. "

This good work done in the city of New York extended into other parts of the colony. We hear of Rev. Mr. Stoupe in 1737 baptizing four black children at New Rochelle. At New Windsor, Rev. Charles Taylor, a school-master, kept a night school for the instruction of the Negroes. Rev. J. Sayre, of Newburgh, promoted the education of the two races in four of the churches under his charge. In 1714 Rev. T. Barclay, an earnest worker among the slaves in Albany, reported a great forwardness among them to embrace Christianity and a readiness to receive instruction, although there was much opposition among some of the masters.

Sixty years later Schenectady reported among its members eleven Negroes who were sober and serious communicants.

These missionaries met with some opposition in New England among the Puritans, who had no serious objection to seeing the Negroes saved but did not care to see them incorporated into the church, which then being connected with the state would grant them political as well as religious equality. There had been an academic interest in the conversion of the Negroes. John Eliot had no particular objection to slavery but regretted that it precluded the possibility of their instruction in the Christian doctrine and worked a loss of their souls. Cotton Mather, taking the task of evangelization seriously, drew up a set of rules by which masters should be governed in the instruction of their slaves. He had much fear of the prodigious wickedness of deriding, neglecting and opposing all due means of bringing the poor Negroes unto God. He did not believe that Almighty God made so many thousand reasonable creatures for nothing but "only to serve the lusts of epicures or the gains of mammonists." In the protest of Jonathan Sewell set forth in his Selling of Joseph, there was an attack on slavery because the servants differed from those of Abraham, who commanded his children and his household that they should keep the way of the Lord. In this they were standing upon the high ground taken by Richard Baxter, an authority among the Puritans, who, denouncing the use of the slaves as beasts for their mere commodity, said, that their masters who "betray or destroy or neglect their souls are fitter to be called incarnate devils than Christians though they be no Christian whom they so abuse."

The opposition there, however, was not apparent everywhere among the ministers of other sects. From Bristol, Rev. J. Usher of the Society for the Propagation of the Gospel in Foreign Parts, wrote in 1730 that several Negroes desired baptism and were able to "render a very good account of the hope that was in them," but he was forbidden by their masters to comply with the request. Yet he reported the same year that among others he had in his congregation "about 30 Negroes and Indians," most of whom joined "in the public service very decently." At Newton, where greater opposition was encountered, J. Beach seemed to have baptized by 1733 many Indians and a few Negroes. Dr. Cutler, a missionary at Boston wrote to the Society in 1737 that among those he had admitted to his church were four Negro slaves. Endeavoring to do more than to effect nominal conversions, Dr. Johnson, while at Stratford, gave catechetical lectures during the summer months of 1751, attended by "many Negroes and some Indians, as well as whites, about 70 or 80 in all." And said he: "As far as I can find, where the Dissenters have baptized two, if not three or four, Negroes or Indians, I have four or five communicants." Dr. Macsparran conducted at Narragansett a class of 70 Indians and Negroes whom he frequently catechized and instructed before the regular service. J. Honyman, of Newport, had in his congregation more than 100 Negroes who "constantly attended the Public Worship."

The real interest in the evangelization of the Negroes in the English colonies, however, was manifested not by those in authority but by the Quakers, who, being friends of all humanity, would not neglect the Negroes. In accepting these persons of color on a basis of equality, however, the Quakers, in denouncing the nakedness of the religion of the other colonists at the same time, alienated their affections and easily brought down upon them the wrath of the public functionaries in these plantations. Believing that such influence would not be salutary in slaveholding communities, many of them, as they did in Virginia, prohibited the Quakers from taking the Negroes to their meetings. Such opposition was but natural when we find that their leader, George Fox, was advocating the instruction of Negroes in 1672 and boldly entreating his coworkers to instruct and teach the Indians and Negroes in 1679 how that "Christ by the grace of God tasted death for every man." When George Keith in 1693 began to promote the religious training of the slaves as preparation for emancipation and William Penn actually advocated the abolition of the system to commit the whole sect to a definite scheme to return the Negroes to Africa to Christianize that continent, such opposition easily developed wherever the Friends operated.

These people, however, would not be deterred from carrying out their purpose. The results which followed show that they were not frustrated in the execution of their plans. John Woolman, one of the fathers of the Quakers in America, always bore testimony against slavery and repeatedly urged that the blacks be given religious instruction. We hear later of their efforts in towns and in the colonies of Virginia and North Carolina to teach Negroes to read and write. Such Negroes as were accessible in the settlements of the North came under the influence of Quakers of the type of John Hepburn, William Burling, Elihu Coleman, Ralph Sandiford, and Anthony Benezet, who established a number of successful missions operating among the Negroes. As the Quakers were, because of their anti-slavery tendencies, the owners of few slaves and were denied access to those of others, what they did for the evangelization of the whole group was little when one considers the benighted darkness in which most Negro slaves in America lived. The faith of the Quakers, their religious procedure, and peculiar customs, moreover, could not be easily understood and appreciated by the Negroes in their undeveloped state.

Generally speaking, then, one should say that the Negroes were neglected. The few missionaries among them stood like shining lights after a great darkness. They, moreover, faced numerous handicaps, among which might be mentioned the conflicts of views, and especially that of the established church with the Catholics and later with the evangelical sects. There were also the difficulties resulting from dealing with a backward pioneering people, the scarcity of workers, and the lack of funds to sustain those who volunteered for this service.

Some difficulty resulted too from the differences of opinion as to what tenets of religion should be taught the Negro and how they should be presented. Should the Negroes be first instructed in the rudiments of education and then taught the doctrines of the church or should the missionaries start with the Negro intellect as he found it on his arrival from Africa and undertake to inculcate doctrines which only the European mind could comprehend? There was, of course, in the interest of those devoted to exploitation, a tendency to make the religious instruction of the Negroes as nearly nominal as possible only to remove the stigma attached to those who neglected the religious life of their servants. Such limited instruction, however, as the slaves received when given only a few moments on Sunday proved to be tantamount to no instruction at all; for missionaries easily observed in the end that Christianity was a rather difficult religion for an undeveloped mind to grasp.

As long as these efforts were restricted to the Anglican clergy, moreover, there could be little question among the British as to the advisability of the procedure. When, however, upon the expansion of the territory of the Catholics and other sects the Negroes came under the influence of different sorts of religion promoted by men of a new thought and new method, some conflict necessarily arose. There was another handicap in that the Anglican clergymen in America during the seventeenth and eighteenth centuries were not of the highest order. Their establishments were maintained by a tax on the colonists in keeping with the customs and laws of England, so that their income was assured, whether or not they wielded an influence for good among the people. The colonial clergy, therefore, too often became corrupt in this independent economic position. They spent much of their time at games and various sports, tarried at the cup and looked upon the wine when it was red, in fact, became so interested in the enjoyment of the things inviting in this world that they had in some cases little time to devote to the elevation of the whites, to say nothing about the elevation of the Negroes. They did not feel disposed to undertake this work themselves and in adhering to their rights as representatives of the established church precluded the possibility of a more general evangelization of the Negroes by the other sects. One might expect from a country, the religious affairs of which were thus administered, a number of protests from those thus served. There was such a general lack of culture among these backward colonists, however, that no such complaint followed. Interest in religion must come from the promoters of religion. If the clergymen themselves did not manifest interest in this work, it was out of the question to expect others to do so.

Another difficulty was the lack of workers. The colonies were not rapidly becoming densely populated and it was not then an easy matter to induce young clergymen to try their fortunes in the wilderness of the western world for such remuneration as the colonists in their scattered and undeveloped economic state were able to give. As many of the white settlements, therefore, were neglected, it would naturally follow that the Negroes suffered likewise. Some of these workers volunteering to toil in this field as missionaries were, of course, supported by funds raised for that purpose; but the difficulty in raising money for missions is still a problem of the church. At that time the people were generally more disinclined to contribute to such causes than they are to-day. That was the age of commercial expansion and available funds were drawn into that field, much at the expense of the higher things of life. The intelligent Christians, therefore, with a clear understanding of the Bible and the doctrines derived there from were not legion even among the whites prior to the American Revolution. The slaves with the handicap of bondage, of course, could not constitute exceptions to this rule.

Chapter 2
The Dawn of the New Day

The new thought at work in the minds of the American people during the second half of the eighteenth century, especially after the Seven Years' War, aroused further interest in the uplift of the groups far down. By this time the colonists had become more conscious of their unique position in America, more appreciative of their worth in the development of the new world, and more cognizant of the necessity to take care of themselves by development from within rather than addition from without. How to rehabilitate the weakened forces and how to minister to those who had been neglected became a matter of concern to all forward-looking men of that time.

The clergy thereafter considered the Negro more seriously even in those parts where slaves were found in large numbers. Among those directing attention to the spiritual needs of the race were Rev. Thomas Bacon and Rev. Jonathan Boucher of the Anglican Church. The former undertook to arouse his people through a series of sermons addressed to masters and slaves about the year 1750. He said: "We should make this reading and studying the Holy Scriptures and the reading and explaining of them to our children and servants or the catechizing and instructing them in the principles of the Christian religion a stated duty. If the grown up slaves from confirmed habits of vice are hard to be reclaimed, the children surely are in our power and may be trained up in the way they should go, with rational hopes that when they are old, they will not depart from it." In 1763 Jonathan Boucher boldly said: "It certainly is not a necessary circumstance essential to the condition of the slave that he be not indoctrinated; yet this is the general and almost universal lot of the slaves." He said, moreover: "You may unfetter them from the chains of ignorance, you may emancipate them from the bondage of sin, the worse slavery to which they could be subjected; and by thus setting at liberty those that are bruised though they still continue to be your slaves, they shall be delivered from the bondage of corruption into the glorious liberty of the children of God."

The accomplishment of the task of more thoroughly proselyting the Negroes, however, belongs to the record of other sects than the Anglican Church. Even if the Negroes had been given the invitation to take a part in the propagation of the gospel as promoted by the first sects in control, the organization of these bodies, the philosophical foundation of their doctrines, and the controversial atmosphere in which their protagonists lived in this conflict of creeds, made it impossible for persons of such limited mental development as the slaves were permitted to experience, to participate. The Latin ceremonies of the Catholic church and the ritualistic conformity required by the Anglicans too often baffled the Negro's understanding, leaving him, even when he had made a profession of faith, in a position of being compelled to accept the spiritual blessings largely on the recommendation of the missionary proffering them. The simplicity of the Quakers set forth as an attack on the forms and ceremonies of the more aristocratic churches equally taxed the undeveloped intellect of certain Negroes who often wondered how matters so mysterious could be reduced to such an ordinary formula.

During the latter part of the seventeenth century and throughout the eighteenth, there were rising to power in the United States two sects, which, because of their evangelical appeal to the untutored mind, made such inroads upon the Negro population as to take over in a few years thereafter the direction of the spiritual development of most of the Negroes throughout the United States. These were the Methodists and Baptists. They, together with the Scotch-Irish Presbyterians, imbibed more freely than other denominations the social-compact philosophy of John Locke and emphasized the doctrines of Coke, Milton, and Blackstone as a means to justify the struggle for an enlargement of the domain of political liberty, primarily for the purpose of securing religious freedom denied them by the adherents of the Anglican Church.

Neither the Baptists nor the Methodists, however, were at first especially interested in the Negro. Whitefield in Georgia advocated the introduction of slaves and rum for the economic improvement of the colony. He even owned slaves himself, although Wesley, Coke, and Asbury opposed the institution and advocated emancipation as a means to thorough evangelization. The work of the Methodists in behalf of the Negroes, moreover, was still less directed toward their liberation in the West Indies than on the continent, doubtless because of the fact that in that section there did not develop the struggle for the rights of man as an attack upon the British government as it happened in the colonies along the Atlantic. But it is said that out of the 352,404 signatures to memorials sent by Dissenters to Parliament praying for the abolition of slavery, 229,426 were the names of Methodists.

The missionaries, however, seemed to be trying to steer between Scylla and Charybdis. They were forbidden to hold slaves but they were required to promote the moral and religious improvement of the slaves without in the least degree, in public or private, interfering with their civil condition. One who served for twenty years in the West Indies said: "For half a century from the commencement of Methodism the slaves never expected freedom, and the missionaries never taught them to expect it; and when the agitation of later years unavoidably affected them more or less, as they learned chiefly through the violent speeches of their own masters or overseers what was going on in their favor in England; it was missionary influence that moderated their passions, kept them in the steady course of duty, and prevented them from sinning against God by offending against the laws of man. Whatever outbreaks or insurrections at any time occurred, no Methodist slave was ever proved guilty of incendiarism or rebellion for more than seventy years, namely, from 1760 to 1833. An extensive examination of their correspondence throughout that lengthened period, and an acquaintance with their general character and history, enables me confidently to affirm that a more humble, laborious, zealous, and unoffending class of Christian missionaries were never employed by any section of the church than those sent out by the British conference to the West India Isles. They were eminently men of one business, unconnected with any political party, though often strongly suspected by the jealousies so rife in slaveholding communities. A curious instance of this jealousy occurred in regard to one who was firmly believed to be a correspondent of the Anti-Slavery Society in England. "I did not know," said Fowell Buxton, in the House of Commons, "that such a man was in existence, till I heard that he was to be hung for corresponding with me."

In what is now the United States, on the contrary, there developed among the Baptists and Methodists a number of traveling missionaries, seemingly like the apostles of old, who in preaching to blacks and whites alike won most Negroes by attacking all evils, among which was slavery. Freeborn Garretson, one of the earliest Methodist missionaries, said to his countrymen that it was revealed to him that "it is not right for you to keep your fellow creatures in bondage; you must let the oppressed go free." He said in 1776: "It was God, not man, that taught me the impropriety of holding slaves: and I shall never be able to praise him enough for it. My very heart has bled, since that, for slaveholders, especially those who make a profession of religion; for I believe it to be a crying sin."

Bishop Asbury recorded in his Journal in 1776: "I met the class and then the black people, some of whose unhappy masters forbid their coming for religious instruction. How will the sons of oppression answer for their conduct when the great proprietor of all shall call them to account?" In 1780 he records that he spoke to some select friends about slave keeping but they could not bear it. He said: "This I know. God will plead the cause of the oppressed though it gives offense to say so here. ... I am grieved for slavery and the manner of keeping these poor people. "

With these missionaries attacking slavery, the church as an organization had to take some position. In 1780 the church required traveling preachers to set their slaves free, declaring at the same time that slavery is contrary to the laws of God, man and nature, and hurtful to society; contrary to the dictates of conscience and pure religion, and doing that which we would not that others should do to us and ours. In 1784 the conference took steps for the abolition of slavery, viewing it as "contrary to the golden laws of God, on which hang all the law and the prophets; and the inalienable rights of mankind, as well as every principle of the Revolution, to hold in the deepest abasement in a more abject slavery, than is, perhaps, to be found in any part of the world, except America, so many souls that are all capable of the image of God." Every slaveholding member of their society was required to liberate his bondmen within twelve months. A record was to be kept of all slaves belonging to masters within the respective circuits and further records of their manumissions. Any person who would not comply with these regulations would have liberty quietly to withdraw from the society within twelve months, and, if he did not, he would be excluded at that time.

Persons thus withdrawing should not partake of the Lord's Supper and those holding slaves would be excluded from this same privilege.

The Methodists who had taken this advanced position on slavery in 1784, however, soon found that they were ahead of the majority of the local members. Much agitation had been caused by this discussion in the State of Virginia and in 1785 there came several petitions asking for a suspension of the resolution passed in 1784 and it was so ordered in 1785 in the words: "It is recommended to all our brethren to suspend the execution of the minute on slavery till the deliberations of a future conference; and that an equal space of time be allowed to all our members for consideration when the minute shall be put in force." The conference declared, however, that it held in deepest abhorrence the practice of slavery and would not cease to seek its destruction by all wise and prudent means. These rules of 1784 were thereafter never put in effect but in 1796 the conference took the position of requiring the Methodists to be exceedingly cautious what persons they admitted to official stations in the church; "and in case of future admission to official stations, to require such security of those who hold slaves for the emancipation of them immediately, or gradually, as the laws of the States respectively and the circumstances of the case will admit." A traveling preacher becoming the owner of a slave forfeited his ministerial position. No slaveholder should be received in the society until the preacher who has oversight of the circuit had spoken to him freely and faithfully upon the subject of slavery. Every member who sold a slave should immediately after full proof be excluded from the society, and if any member purchased a slave, the quarterly meeting should determine the number of years in which the slave so purchased would work out the price of his purchase. The preachers and other members of the society were requested to consider the subject of Negro slavery with deep attention and to impart to the General Conference through the medium of yearly conferences, or otherwise, any important thought upon the subject. The annual conferences were directed to draw up addresses for the gradual emancipation of the slaves to the legislatures of those States in which no general laws had been passed for that purpose.

Locally the Baptists were winning more Negroes than the Methodists by their attack on slavery during these years, but because of the lack of organized effort the Baptists did not exert as much antislavery influence as the early Methodists. Through their conferences they often influenced the local churches to do more against slavery than they would have done for fear that they might lose their status among their brethren. As the Baptist church emphasized above all things local self government, each church being a law unto itself, it did not as a national body persistently attack slavery. The Baptists reached their most advanced position as an anti-slavery body in 1789 when they took action to the effect "that slavery is a violent depredation of the rights of nature and inconsistent with a republican government, and therefore, recommend it to our brethren, to make use of their local missions to extirpate this horrid evil from the land; and pray Almighty God that our honorable legislature may have it in their power to proclaim the great jubilee consistent with the principles of good policy. "

From this position most Baptists gradually receded. Yet, although not working as an organized body, the Baptists in certain parts of the country were unusually outspoken and effective in waging war on slavery. As there were a number of disputes, owing to the fact that the denomination as a body was far from unanimity on this subject, some dissension in the ranks followed. Those who believed in the abolition of slavery by immediate means styled themselves the Emancipating Baptists or the Emancipating Society in contradistinction to the remaining Calvinistic Baptists who desired to be silent on the question.

The most outspoken of the former was David Barrow.

In 1778, Mr. Barrow received an invitation to preach at the house of a gentleman who lived on Nansemond River, near the mouth of James River. A ministering brother accompanied him. They were informed on their arrival, that they might expect rough usage, and so it happened. A gang of well-dressed men came up to the stage, which had been erected under some trees, as soon as the hymn was given out, and sang one of their obscene songs. They then undertook to plunge both of the preachers. Mr. Barrow was plunged twice. They pressed him into the mud, held him long under the water, and came near drowning him. In the midst of their mocking, they asked him if he believed? and throughout treated him with the most barbarous insolence and outrage. His companion they plunged but once. The whole assembly was shocked, the women shrieked, but no one durst interfere; for about twenty stout fellows were engaged in this horrid measure. They insulted and abused the gentleman who invited them to preach, and every one who spoke a word in their favor. Before these persecuted men could change their clothes, they were dragged from the house, and driven off by these outrageous churchmen. But three or four of them died in a few weeks, in a distracted manner, and one of them wished himself in hell before he had joined the company, &c.

In Mr. Barrow's piece against slavery, we find the following note: "To see a man (a Christian) in the most serious period of all his life—making his last will and testament—and in the most solemn manner addressing the Judge of all the earth—In the name of God, Amen.—Hearken to him—he will very shortly appear before the Judge, where kings and slaves have equal thrones!—He proceeds:

"Item. I give and bequeath to my Son —, a Negro man named —, a Negro woman named —, with five of her youngest children.

"Item. I give and bequeath to my daughter —, a Negro man named —, also a Negro woman named —, with her three children.

"Item. All my other slaves, whether men, women or children, with all my stock of horses, cattle, sheep, and hogs, I direct to be sold to the highest bidder, and the monies arising there from (after paying my just debts) to be equally divided between my two above-named children!!!

"The above specimen is not exaggerated; the like of it often turns up. And what can a real lover of the rights of man say in vindication thereof?

"Suppose for a moment, that the testator, or if the owner, dies intestate (which is often the case), was ever so humane a person, who can vouch for their heirs and successors? This consideration, if nothing else, ought to make all slaveholders take heed what they do, 'for they must give an account of themselves to God.'"

He was a native of Virginia, where he commenced his ministry in 1771, passing through the period of much insolence and persecution of the rude countrymen then denying the liberal sects religious freedom. He early became attached to the antislavery school and consequently emancipated his own slaves in Virginia without at first having so very much to say against the institution. After distinguishing himself in the State of Virginia for his unusual piety and great ability, he moved to Kentucky in 1798 and settled in Montgomery County. When the antislavery dispute became very ardent soon thereafter, he carried his opposition to the extent of alienating the support of his coworkers, who, sitting as an advisory council, expelled him from the ministry for preaching emancipation, and preferred similar charges against him that his local church at Mount Sterling might act accordingly. After having taken this drastic step, however, the Association at its next session voted to rescind this action; but Barrow had then joined with the emancipators and did not desire to return. Among those whom he found sufficiently companionable in the new work which he had undertaken were Rev. Donald Holmes, Carter Tarrant, Jacob Grigg, George Smith, and numerous other ministers, some of whom were native Americans and others native Europeans.

These emancipators began by inquiring: "Can any person whose practice is friendly to perpetual slavery be admitted a member of this meeting?" They thought not. They inquired, moreover: "Is there any case in which persons holding slaves may be admitted to membership into the church of Christ?" They said: "No, except in the case of holding young slaves with a view to their future emancipation when they reach the age of responsibility, in the case of persons who have purchased slaves in their ignorance and desire to leave it to the church to say when they may be free, in the case of women whose husbands are opposed to emancipation, in the case of a widow who has it not in her power to liberate them, and in the case when the slaves are idiots or too old to maintain themselves." Another query was: "Shall members in union with us be at liberty in any case to purchase slaves?" The answer was negative, except it was with a view to ransom them in such a way as the church might approve. These emancipators in Kentucky constituted themselves some years later an organized body and finally became known as the "Baptized Licking-Locust Association." In the course of time, however, feeling that that mode of association or the consolidation of churches was unscriptural and ought to be laid aside, they changed their organization to that of an abolition society.

It is interesting to note the attitude of the Presbyterians toward the amelioration of the condition of the Negroes. In 1774 when abolition was agitated in connection with the struggle for the rights of man, the Presbyterians were early requested to take action. A representation from Dr. Ezra Stiles and Rev. Samuel Hopkins respecting the sending of two natives of Africa on a mission to propagate Christianity in that land, brought before that body a discussion of all aspects of Negro slavery. In this debate a committee was requested to bring in a report on Negro slavery. The Assembly concurred in the proposal to send the missionaries to Africa, but deferred further consideration of slavery.

The first action taken on the subject came, after delay from year to year, in 1787. The committee on overtures brought in a report to the effect that the "Creator of the world having made of one flesh all the children of men, it becomes them as members of the same family, to consult and promote each other's happiness. It is more especially the duty of those who maintain the rights of humanity, and who acknowledge and teach the obligations of Christianity, to use such means as are in their power to extend the blessings of equal freedom to every part of the human race." Convinced of these truths, and sensible that the rights of human nature are too well understood to admit of debate, the Synod recommended in the warmest terms to every member of their body, and to all the churches and families under their care, to do everything in their power consistent with the rights of civil society, to promote the abolition of slavery, and the instruction of Negroes, whether bond or free.

After some consideration, however, the Synod reached the conclusion of expressing very much interest in the principles in favor of universal liberty that prevailed in America and also in that of the abolition of slavery. Yet inasmuch as it would be difficult to change slaves from a servile state to a participation in all the privileges of society without proper education and previous habits of industry, it recommended to all persons holding slaves to give them such education as might prepare them for the better enjoyment of freedom, and recommended further that in those cases in which the masters found the slaves disposed to make just improvement of the privilege they should give them "sufficient time and sufficient means for procuring their liberty at a moderate rate."

There was some agitation of the question in 1793, when a memorial was addressed to the General Assembly by Warner Mifflin, a member of the Society of Friends; but no action of importance was taken again until 1795, when there arose the question as to whether the church should uphold communion with slaveholders. After due deliberation the General Assembly passed a resolution referring the memorialists to the action that the Assembly had already taken with reference to slavery in 1787 and 1793. As it seemed that the Presbytery of Transylvania was primarily concerned in this affair, Mr. Rice and Dr. Muir, ministers, and Mr. Robert Patterson, an elder, all of that section, were appointed a committee to draft the following pacifist letter to that Assembly, which determined for generations thereafter the policy of the Presbyterians with reference to slavery:

> To our brethren, members of the Presbyterian Church, under the care of Transylvania Presbytery.
>
> Dear Friends and Brethren—The General Assembly of the Presbyterian Church hear with concern from your Commissioners, that differences of opinion with respect to holding Christian communion with those possessed of slaves, agitate the minds of some among you, and threaten divisions which may have the most ruinous tendency. The subject of slavery has repeatedly claimed the attention of the General Assembly, and the Commissioners from the Presbytery of Transylvania are furnished with attested copies of these decisions, to be read by the Presbytery when it shall appear to them proper, together with a copy of this letter, to the several Churches under their care.
>
> The General Assembly have taken every step which they deemed expedient or wise, to encourage emancipation, and to render the state of those who are in slavery as mild and tolerable as possible.
>
> Forbearance and peace are frequently inculcated and enjoined in the New Testament. "Blessed are the peacemakers." "Let no one do anything through strife and vainglory." "Let such esteem others better than himself." The followers of Jesus ought conscientiously to walk worthy of their vocations, "with all lowliness, and meekness, with long-suffering, forbearing one another, endeavoring to keep the unity of the Spirit in the bond of peace." If every difference of opinion were to keep men at a distance, they could subsist in no state of society, either civil or religious. The General Assembly would impress this upon the minds of their brethren, and urge them to follow peace, and the things which make for peace.
>
> The General Assembly commend our dear friends and brethren to the grace of God, praying that the peace of God, which passeth all understanding may possess their hearts and minds.

Chapter 3
Pioneer Negro Preachers

The new stage reached in the development of religious freedom in America in securing toleration for the evangelical denominations, meant the increasing importance of the Negro in the church. Given access to the people in all parts of the country by virtue of this new boon resulting from the struggle for the rights of man, the Methodists, Baptists and Presbyterians soon became imbued with the idea of an equality of the Negro in the church although they did not always militantly denounce slavery. Negroes were accepted in these congregations on this basis and when exhibiting the power of expounding the scriptures were sometimes heard with unusual interest. Such elevation of the blacks by these more liberal denominations, of course, incurred the displeasure and opposition of the aristocratic churchmen to the extent that these liberal denominations could not grant the Negroes as much freedom of participation in the church work as they were disposed to do.

In those cases in which Negroes were permitted to preach, they found themselves confronting not only the opposition of the more aristocratic sects but violating laws of long standing, prohibiting Negro ministers from exercising their gifts. When their ministrations were of a local order, and they did not seemingly stir up their fellow men to oppose the established order of things, not so much attention was paid to their operations. When, however, these Negroes of unusual power preached with such force as to excite not only the blacks but the whites, steps were generally taken to silence these speakers heralding the coming of a new day. This opposition on the part of the whites apparently grew more strenuous upon the attainment of independence. As British subjects, they had more feeling of toleration for the rise of the Negro in the church than they had after the colonies became independent. While struggling for liberty themselves, even for religious freedom, these Americans were not willing to grant others what they themselves desired. The attitude of most Americans then, unlike that of some of the British, seemed to be that the good things of this life were intended as special boons for a particular race.

The efforts to establish the early churches of South Carolina and Georgia are cases in evidence. The first Negro Baptist Church in America, according to Dr. W. H. Brooks, was founded by one Mr. Palmer at Silver Bluff across the river from Augusta, Georgia, in the colony of South Carolina, some time between the years 1773 and 1775. This group was fortunate in having the kind master, George Galphin, who became a patron of this congregation. He permitted David George to be ordained for this special work after having formerly allowed George Liele to preach there during these early years. Upon the evacuation of Savannah by the Americans in 1778, the Silver Bluff Church was driven into exile. Called upon to decide whether they would support the American or British cause, friend separated from friend and sometimes master from slave. When Galphin, a patriot, abandoned his slaves in his flight for refuge from the British, David George and fifty of these slaves went over to the British in Savannah where they were freed. David George returned to South Carolina and resided for a time in Charleston, from which he went, in 1782, to Nova Scotia, where he abode for ten years, preaching to Baptist congregations at Shelburne, Birchtown, Ragged Island, and in St. John, New Brunswick. Because of the inhospitable climate, the Negro slaves who had escaped with their loyal masters crossing the Canadian border to these points in Nova Scotia, went in 1792 to Sierra Leone where they constituted themselves a colony, with David George the founder of their first Baptist Church. After peace was made in 1783, the Silver Bluff Church was revived under the direction of the Rev. Jesse Peter who, unlike George Liele in having departed with his master when the British evacuated Savannah in 1782, remained as a slave here in South Carolina to carry forward the work across the river from Augusta in South Carolina.

According to Dr. Walter H. Brooks, a portion of this Silver Bluff Church brought into Savannah, Georgia, at the time of the departure of certain Americans to join the British in 1778, took shape as an organized body under George Liele, who had been the servant of a British officer. It is highly probable that David George and Jesse Peter, who had served these people at Silver Bluff, did not have sufficient influence to secure a permit to preach to them in Savannah, although they did unite with the church there. Out of this effort of George Liele developed what Dr. Brooks considers the first Negro Baptist Church in the city of Savannah, which flourished during the British occupancy from 1779 to the year 1782. The oldest Negro Baptist Church in this country, however, was that of the Silver Bluff Church which, in another meeting place and under a new name, became established at Augusta, having existed from the year 1773 to 1793 before the time of Andrew Bryan's organizing efforts in Savannah.

The struggles of George Liele and Andrew Bryan throw additional light on these early efforts. George Liele was born in Virginia about the year 1750, but soon moved with his master, Henry Sharpe, to Burke County, Georgia, a few years before the Revolutionary War. As his master was a deacon of the Baptist church of which Matthew Moore was pastor, George, upon hearing this minister preach from time to time when accompanying his owner, became converted and soon thereafter was baptized by this clergyman. Not long thereafter upon discovering that he had unusual ministerial gifts, this church permitted him to preach upon the plantations along the Savannah river and sometimes to the congregation of the white church to which he belonged. As his master was much more liberal than most of his kind, Liele was permitted to extend his operations down the Savannah river as far as Brampton, Savannah, and Yamacraw, where he preached to the slaves.

His ministerial work became so important that his master finally liberated him that he might serve without interference; but his work was interrupted by the Revolutionary War, during which his master was killed. Upon the death of his master, moreover, some of the heirs to the estate, not being satisfied with the manumission of George Liele, had him thrown into prison, hoping to re-enslave him; but Colonel Kirkland, of the British Army, then in control of Savannah, came to his rescue by securing his release from prison. When the British evacuated that city, George Liele went with them to Jamaica, indenturing himself to Colonel Kirkland as a servant for the amount of money necessary to pay his transportation.

Before leaving Savannah, however, fortune brought it to pass that the vessel in which he embarked was detained for some weeks near Tybee Island, not far from the mouth of the Savannah river. While waiting there he came to the city of Savannah and baptized Andrew Bryan and his wife Hannah, Kate Hogg, and Hagar Simpson, who became the founders of the first African Baptist Church in Savannah.

When George Liele landed at Kingston he was, upon the recommendation of Colonel Kirkland to General Campbell, the Governor of Jamaica, employed to work out the money for which he had been indentured. Upon discharging the debt he obtained for himself and family a certificate of manumission and was free in 1784 to begin his work as a preacher. He preached first in a private home to a small congregation and then organized a church with four men who had emigrated from the American colonies. Delivering with power a message of such telling effect as the first dissenter to undertake the establishment of a liberal sect in the midst of communicants of the established church of England, he soon found his meetings interrupted and himself cruelly persecuted. Frequently memorialized for a grant of religious freedom, however, the Jamaica Assembly finally permitted George Liele to proceed with his work. Within a few years he had a following of about 500 communicants, and with the help of a number of inspired deacons and elders extended the work far into the rural districts. In addition to his ministerial work he administered the affairs of these various groups, taught a free school, and conducted a business at which he earned his living.

At first this work was largely inspirational, stirring up the people here and there; and many thought that it would be a movement of short duration: but becoming convinced that this was the real way of salvation and life, persons adhering to this new creed contributed sufficiently to its support to give it a standing in the community. Within a few years we hear of the purchase for a sum of nearly 155 pounds of about three acres of land at the east end of Kingston, on which they built a church. When success had crowned his efforts in Jamaica, he took steps toward the establishment of an edifice at Spanish Town, which was completed a few years later. The records show too that he interested in his cause some men of influence like Mr. Steven A. Cook, a member of the Jamaica Assembly, who solicited funds for him in England. Of him Mr. Cook bears this testimony: "He is a very industrious man, decent, humble in his manners, and, I think, a good man." Contemporaries speak of his family life as pleasant. He had a wife and four children, three boys and a girl. He was not a well educated man, but he found time to read some good literature.

The unusual tact of George Liele was the key to his success. He seemed to know how to handle men diplomatically, but some of his policy may be subject to criticism. Unlike so many Baptist and Methodist missionaries who came forward preaching freedom of body and mind and soul to all men and thereby stirring up the slaves in certain parts, George Liele would not receive any slaves who did not have permission of their owners, and instead of directing attention to their wrongs, conveyed to them the mere message of Christ. His influence among the masters and overseers became unusual, and the membership of his church rapidly increased. No literature was used and no instruction given until it had at first been shown to the members of the legislature, the magistrates, and the justices to secure their permission beforehand. One of the masters, speaking of the wholesome influence of Liele's preaching, said that he did not need to employ an assistant nor to make use of the whip whether he was at home or elsewhere, as his slaves were industrious and obedient, and lived together in unity, brotherly love, and peace.

The next pioneer preacher of worth among the Negroes was Andrew Bryan, George Liele's successor in Georgia. Andrew Bryan was born a slave in 1737 at Goose Creek, South Carolina, about sixteen miles from Charleston. He was later brought to Savannah, Georgia, where, as stated above, he came under the influence of the preaching of George Liele. He at first commenced by public exhortations and prayer meetings at Brampton. Nine months after the departure of George Liele, Bryan began to preach to congregations of black and white people at Savannah. Moved by his convincing message, his master and other whites encouraged him in his chosen field, inasmuch as the influence he had upon slaves was salutary. He was thereafter permitted to erect on the land of Mr. Edward Davis at Yamacraw a rough wooden building of which his group was soon artfully dispossessed. As his ministrations were opposed by others who did not like this simple faith, unusual persecution soon followed. Bryan's adherents were not permitted to hold frequent meetings, and in trying to evade this regulation by assembling in the swamps, they ran the risk of rigid discipline. With the aid of his brother Sampson, Andrew Bryan, however, gradually held this group together. At first it was small; but finally sufficiently large to receive the attention of the Rev. Thomas Burt in 1785, and that of the Rev. Abraham Marshall of Kioke in 1788. The latter then baptized forty-five additional members of this congregation, and on January 20, 1788, organized them as a church and ordained Andrew Bryan as a minister with full authority to preach the gospel and to administer the ordinances of the Baptist church.

This recognition of Bryan as a minister, however, did not solve all of his problems. The greater his influence among the slaves, the more the masters were inclined to believe that his work could result only in that of servile insurrection. It became more difficult, therefore, for slaves to attend his meetings; the patrols whipped them sometimes even when they had passes, and finally a large number of the members were arrested and severely punished. The culmination was that Andrew Bryan, their pastor himself, and his brother, Sampson Bryan, one of the first deacons, were "inhumanly cut and their backs were so lacerated that their blood ran down to the earth as they, with uplifted hands, cried unto the Lord; but Bryan, in the midst of his torture, declared that he rejoiced not only to be whipped but would freely suffer death for the cause of Jesus Christ." Accused of sinister plans, Andrew Bryan and his brother Sampson were, upon the complaint of their traducers, imprisoned and dispossessed of their meeting house. Lorenzo Dow, an eccentric itinerant preacher appearing in Savannah about this time, preached at Bryan's church to show not only his compassion for Bryan's waiting congregation, but his disapproval of the persecution to which this apostle was subjected.

Jonathan Bryan, the master of Andrew and Sampson, insisting that they were the victims of prejudice and wickedness, however, secured for them a hearing. They came before the Justices of the Inferior Court of Chatham County, Henry Osborne, James Haversham, and James Montague, who, finding no criminal intent in their efforts, ordered that they be released. They were then permitted by their master to resume worship in the barn on his plantation, but persecution followed them even there, where they were surrounded by spies and eavesdroppers. This continued until one of the eavesdroppers, upon listening to what was going on among these communicants at Andrew Bryan's private home, heard this man of God earnestly praying for the men who had so mercilessly used him. This enlisted so much sympathy among the people kindly disposed that the chief justice of the court, before whom they had been brought, granted them permission to continue their worship of God at any time between sunrise and sunset. They held meetings at Brampton about two years, during which they made a number of influential friends among the whites, who, along with the communicants of this group, assisted Bryan in raising funds to purchase a lot upon which to begin the erection of a church in 1794. The first African church stood for years on this lot on what is now known as Mill Street, running to Indian Street Lane in Savannah.

Andrew Bryan faced another crisis upon the death of Jonathan Bryan, his master. He succeeded, however, in emerging as a free man, the heirs of the estate having given him an opportunity to purchase his freedom for fifty pounds. Fortune prospered him thereafter to the extent that he soon bought in Yamacraw a lot on which he built a residence not far from the place of worship. Upon the final division of the Bryan estate it developed that the church building was still controlled by that family, but the worship of these communicants continued there under the supervision of the whites without serious interruption. The membership had then reached 700.

Bryan soon obtained a position of influence in spite of all of his difficulties, as is evidenced by his own testimony in addressing his coworker, Dr. Rippon, in 1800. He said: "With much pleasure inform you, dear sir, that I enjoy good health, and am strong in body, at the age of sixty-three years, and am blessed with a pious wife, whose freedom I have obtained, and an only daughter and child, who is married to a free man, though she, and consequently under our laws, her seven children, five sons and two daughters, are slaves. By a kind Providence I am well provided for, as to worldly comforts (though I have had very little given me as a minister), having a house and lot in this city, besides the land on which several buildings stand, for which I receive a small rent, and a fifty-acre tract of land, with all necessary buildings, four miles in the country, and eight slaves; for whose education and happiness I am enabled through mercy to provide."

As this congregation continued to increase, Andrew Bryan secured the services of his brother as an assistant pastor. He planned, moreover, to divide the church whenever the membership became too large for him to serve it efficiently. This was what led to the organization of the Second African Baptist Church of Savannah, with Henry Francis, a slave of Colonel Leroy Hamilton, as pastor. As the head of this congregation, Francis manifested power of remarkable leadership, and soon thereafter purchased his freedom to devote all of his time to his congregation. Bryan's church was further divided upon reaching the stage of having an unwieldy number, when there emerged from it the Third African Baptist Church. Bryan's church, moreover, became in the course of time the beacon light in the Negro religious life of Georgia. From this center went other workers into the inviting fields of that State, as to Augusta, where a flourishing Baptist church was established. This condition obtained until the Negro preacher became circumscribed during the thirties and forties by laws intended to prevent such disturbances as were caused by Nat Turner in Southampton County, Virginia. Andrew Bryan, however, did not live to see this. He passed away in 1812, respected by all who knew him and loved by his numerous followers. The position which he finally attained in the esteem and the respect of the community is well illustrated by the honor shown him by the following resolutions of the Savannah Baptist Association (white) on the occasion of his death:

"The Association is sensibly affected by the death of the Rev. Andrew Bryan, a man of color, and pastor of the First Colored Church in Savannah. This son of Africa, after suffering inexpressible persecutions in the cause of his divine Master, was at length permitted to discharge the duties of the ministry among his colored friends in peace and quiet, hundreds of whom, through his instrumentality, were brought to a knowledge of the truth as 'it is in

Jesus.' He closed his extensively useful and amazingly luminous course in the lively exercise of faith and in the joyful hope of a happy immortality."

In those parts of the South where the pro-slavery sentiment was not developed so early as in Georgia, the Baptists were able to give their Negro communicants more consideration. After this denomination had won toleration in Virginia, its leaders experienced much less difficulty in proselyting Negroes than in the case of other communicants. From 1770 to 1790 Negro preachers, thanks to the pioneer work of a man of color, Rev. Mr. Moses, were in charge of congregations in Charles City, Petersburg, Williamsburg, and Allen's Creek, in Lunenburg County. In 1801 Gowan Pamphlet of that State was the pastor of a progressive Baptist church in Williamsburg, some members of which could read, write and keep accounts. William Lemon was about this time chosen by a white congregation to serve at the Pettsworth or Gloucester church in that State.

In Portsmouth, Virginia, a Negro Baptist preacher attained unusual distinction. There the blacks and whites belonging to the same Baptist church experienced very little difficulty in their acceptance of each other on the basis of religious equality. They were constituted a church by the Association held in Isle of Wight County in 1789, and after the service of a number of pioneer ministers the church called one Thomas Armistead. The church fell into bad hands a few years thereafter and suffered a decline under one Frost, a Baptist preacher, who in the propagation of the doctrines of free will caused unusual excitement. This did not subside until he, according to the contemporaries, was stricken by the hand of God. While looking out for another pastor there came to this community, in 1795, from Northampton County, a black preacher whose name was Josiah Bishop. He preached with such fervor and with such success that the whites as well as the blacks hung, as it were, upon his words. He easily rallied the scattered forces of the church, revived their spirits, and lifted high the banner of the gospel. So impressed was the congregation with his work that the church gave Josiah Bishop the money with which to purchase his freedom and soon thereafter bought his wife and his eldest son.

It is said that his preaching was much admired by both saints and sinners wherever he went. "As a stranger," say Lemuel Burkett and Jesse Reed in their Concise History of the Kehukee Baptist Association, "few received equal degree of liberality with him." They were, therefore, advised, "that whereas the black brethren in the church seemed anxious for a vote in the conference that it would be best to consider the black people as a wing of the body, and Josiah Bishop to take over sight of them, as this church, at that time, fellowshiped a number of Negroes. The black people at first seemed pleased with the proposition, but soon repented and came and told the deacons they were afraid that matters might turn up disagreeable to them and dishonoring to God, and said that they would be subordinate to the white brethren, if they would let them continue as they were, which was consented to." Josiah Bishop, of course, could not long remain as the pastor of a mixed church in the slave-holding colony of Virginia. After toiling successfully for a short period in that city, he moved to Baltimore, where he helped to promote the cause of the rising Baptists in that city. When his work was well done there, he moved to the city of New York, where during 1810 and 1811 he served as the pastor of the Abyssinian Baptist Church.

Pioneering in this same field in 1792 was the famous "Uncle Jack," a full-blooded African, recognized by the whites as a forceful preacher of the gospel in the Baptist Church. For some years he preached from plantation to plantation, moving so many to repentance that the white citizens in appreciation of his worth had him licensed to preach and raised a fund with which they purchased his freedom. They bought him a small farm in Virginia, where for more than 40 years he continued his ministry as an instrument in the conversion of a large number of white people.

Contemporaneous with Uncle Jack was Henry Evans, a free Negro of Virginia. On his way to Charleston, South Carolina, to work at the trade of shoemaking, Evans happened to stop at Fayetteville, North Carolina. Having been licensed as a local preacher in the Methodist Church, he tarried there to work among the people, whose deplorable condition excited his sympathy. At first he worked at his trade and preached on Sunday. The town council, feeling that he was a public danger, ordered him to refrain from preaching. Whereupon he began to hold secret meetings. His preaching became so effective, however, and so many white persons attended his meetings, that the official opposition yielded sufficiently to have a regular Methodist Church organized there in 1790. The edifice was so constructed as to provide quarters for Evans, who remained there until his death in 1810, although a white minister was in actual charge of the church.

From the Methodists there emerged another such preacher, Black Harry, who, accompanying Mr. Asbury, learned from him to preach more forcefully than Asbury himself. According to a contemporary, Harry was "small, very black, keen-eyed, possessing great volubility of tongue; and, although illiterate so that he could not read," was one of the most popular preachers of that age. Upon hearing Harry preach, Dr. Benjamin Rush pronounced him the greatest orator in America. Desiring Harry to accompany him in 1782, Bishop Asbury made the request, saying that the way to have a very large congregation was to give out that Harry was to preach, as more would come to hear Harry than to hear Bishop Asbury. On one occasion in Wilmington, Delaware, where the cause of the Methodist was unpopular, a large number of persons came out of curiosity to hear Bishop Asbury. But, as the auditorium was already taxed to its fullest capacity, they could only hear from the outside. At the conclusion of the exercises, they said, without having seen the speaker: "If all Methodist preachers can preach like the Bishop, we should like to be constant hearers." Someone present replied: "That was not the Bishop, but the Bishop's servant that you heard." This, to be sure, had the desired effect, for these inquirers concluded: "If such be the servant, what must the master be?" "The truth was," says John Ledman in his History of the rise of Methodism in America, "that Harry was a more popular speaker than Mr. Asbury or almost any one else in his day." In this same capacity Harry accompanied and preached with not only Mr. Asbury but with Garretson, Watcote, and Dr. Coke.

"After he had moved on the tide of popularity for a number of years," says John Ledman, "he fell by wine, one of the strong enemies of both ministers and people. And now, alas! this popular preacher was a drunken ragpicker in the streets of Philadelphia. But we will not leave him here. One evening Harry started down the Neck, below Southwark, determined to remain there until his backslidings were healed. Under a tree he wrestled with God in prayer.

Sometime that night God restored to him the joys of his salvation. From this time Harry continued faithful; though he could not stand before the people with that pleasing confidence as a public speaker that he had before his fall. About the year 1810 Harry finished his course; and, it is believed, made a good end. An unusually large number of people, both white and colored, followed his body to its last resting place, in a free burying ground in Kensington."

Among the pioneer Negro preachers one of the most interesting was John Stewart. He was born of free parents in Powhatan County, Virginia, where he received some religious training and attended a school during the winter, thus securing to him so much mental development by the time of reaching maturity that he could make a living much more easily than some of his fellows. This early training, however, did not seem to restrain him from certain temptations of this life; for, in going away from home to make his career, he fell a victim to bad habits, becoming a dissolute drunkard, drifting here and there. Finally he came to Marietta, Ohio, where under the influence of the gospel as it was preached Among his lowly people in that center, he was converted and united with the Methodist Episcopal Church. He then became a man of very regular habits and devoted much of his time to meditation and prayer. On a certain occasion he said, "I heard a voice like a woman's singing and praising the Lord, while straight from the northern sky, which was filled with a great radiance, came a man's voice, saying, 'You must declare my counsel faithfully,' and I found myself standing on my feet speaking as to a congregation." He felt that this was a call to preach, but at first resisted the influence, hoping to escape there from. Having fallen sick not long thereafter, however, he looked upon this as a punishment and responded to the voices that he heard, overcoming his fears. Having his mind thoroughly made up, he set off then to preach the gospel, steering, as he said, "my course sometimes by the road, sometimes through the cities, until I came to Goshen, where I found the Delaware Indians."

He preached and sang among these people for A short period, and finally returned to Marietta. He was again summoned by the voices in the night impelling him to make another pilgrimage. This time he drifted into a settlement of whites, to whom he preached with much success, moving many of them to repentance and organizing them as a church. He then proceeded to Upper Sandusky, the home of the Wyandot Indians, who, having never received the gospel, although the Roman Catholics had unsuccessfully tried to evangelize them, had fallen back into a worse state of heathenism and especially drunkenness, resulting from the vices imported by traders. Here he had the opposition of William Walker, the government agent, who did not take well to his message, but on being converted very soon thereafter, Walker gave Stewart less trouble in reaching the Indians. Another great hindrance, however, was the coming of the other white traders, who prospered by the liquor traffic that they carried on with these Indians. At first they tried to show that Stewart was not properly authorized as a minister and should be denied the right to preach; but having then the support of William Walker, the zealous missionary succeeded in delivering his message. Some of the Indians, too, felt that the gospel which he preached was not intended for the Indians but for the white man, although Stewart endeavored to show that this boon was for all nations and for all people. He persisted in holding his position, and in the end success crowned his efforts in bringing about the conversion of all of the prominent chiefs of this tribe.

It is said that because of this success his enemies contrived to discourage him. They prepared for an unusually great celebration in accordance with the festive ideas of the Indians, trying to bring them back to their old habits. Becoming discouraged, John Stewart preached his farewell sermon and returned to Marietta. But he came back to Upper Sandusky after an absence of a few months and devoted the rest of his life to work among the Wyandot Indians. Fortunately be was then filled with enthusiasm and the word which he preached did not return void. As his mission was then a success, he appealed for help to the higher conference, then meeting at Urbana, in March, 1817. J. B. Finley was chosen to work in this field. Stewart had planned for a thorough elevation of these people, including industrial training, which centered around the erection of a sawmill and the purchase of a farm upon which he taught agriculture. A log structure was soon built for school purposes, and there soon followed Miss Harriet Stubbs, who volunteered to teach the Indians. Subsequent reports show that the work was in good condition in 1822. The religion of Jesus Christ was flourishing and everywhere the Indians were living upright lives. At this time, however, Stewart's health had failed him, as he had well run his course, having been exposed to all sorts of hardships. He passed away on the 17th of December, his hand in that of his wife. His last words, addressed to the sorrowing people about his bed, were: "Oh, be faithful."

Lemuel Haynes, another pioneer preacher, was born July 18, 1753, at West Hartford, Connecticut. His father was a man of unmingled African extraction and his mother a white woman of respectable New England ancestry. As he was a natural son, the mother abandoned him in infancy, but he fortunately found asylum at the home of one Haynes, whose name he took and with whom he lived until at the age of five months, when he was bound out to David Rose of Granville, Massachusetts, where Lemuel grew to manhood.

Lemuel was given the rudimentary training in the backwoods schools of the community, in which he learned to read and write. These meager advantages led him to seek an extension of his knowledge through the reading of good books. As these were scarce, he had to be content with the Bible, the Psalter, the writings of Watts and Doddridge, and Young's Night Thoughts. Before his education could be completed, however, Lemuel, having been prostrated with grief because of the loss of the wife of his kind master, entered the continental army, first as a minute man in 1774 and then as a regular soldier after the battle of Lexington.

Returning from the war, Lemuel engaged in agriculture; but he had early been given a pious trend and soon decided to study theology in anticipation of the designs of Providence concerning him. For some time he had been accustomed to read the Bible and sermons of others on the occasions of conducting family prayers in the home of David Rose. From this exercise he mustered sufficient courage to read one of his own sermons, and finally to preach before the local congregations, which marveled at the power of his words. To prepare himself thoroughly to preach, Haynes once planned to attend Dartmouth College, but shrank from it. After studying privately under Daniel Farrand of Canaan, Connecticut, and

William Bradford of Wintonbury, Haynes spent a short period teaching a school for whites. He was licensed to preach in the Congregational Church in 1780 and was ordained soon thereafter, beginning his ministry at Middle Granville, where he labored five years. Here Bessie Babbit, a white woman of considerable education and piety, offered him her heart and they were married in 1783.

From this small charge Haynes was called to Torrington, Connecticut. A leading citizen was much displeased that the church should have a "nigger minister," and to show his lack of respect for the new incumbent this man went into the church and sat with his hat on. "He had not preached far," said the man, "when I thought I saw the whitest man I ever knew in that pulpit, and I tossed my hat under the pew." Haynes was then called to take charge of the Congregational Church in West Rutland. Here his usefulness was appreciated and his efforts were extended to other towns through his revivals, one of the most successful of which he conducted in Pittsfield. Having developed such power, he was employed, in 1804, by the Connecticut Missionary Society to labor in the destitute sections of Vermont. In 1809 he was appointed to a similar service by the Vermont Missionary Society. In 1814 he preached extensively in Connecticut, appearing before crowded houses, having in his audience on one occasion President Dwight of Yale.

With such standing in the church Haynes was expected to manifest interest in the great questions at issue in New England. One of these was the Stoddardian principle of admitting moral persons without credible evidences of grace, to the Lord's Supper, and the half-way covenant by which parents though not admitted to the Lord's Supper were encouraged to offer their children in baptism. In this debate Haynes, with his eloquence and logic, vanquished the famous Hosea Ballou by his powerful sermon based on the text Ye shall not surely die. There was also a difference of opinion with respect to the operations of the Holy Spirit, but Haynes stood with Edwards and Whitefield. Being thus active in dispelling clouds of doubt, he brought many back to a more righteous conduct.

Becoming involved in the partisan strife which characterized the rise of political parties after Washington's inauguration, Haynes alienated the affections of some of his communicants by his bold advocacy of the principle conducive to a strong national government as administered in the beginning by George Washington, whose policies Haynes admired. He then left West Rutland and preached a while in Manchester, Vermont, until 1822, when he accepted a call to Granville, New York. There he spent usefully the last eleven years of his life.

In spite of the fact that Lemuel Haynes was working altogether among white people, however, he was successful wherever he was stationed. His eloquence and Christian nobility won him much attention. "He always showed himself a man of a feeling heart, sensibly affected by human suffering," says Cooley, his biographer. "At home he was industrious, his family government was parental. He was the embodiment of piety and honesty." Churches and associations were strengthened by his labors. Their membership increased and the influence of the gospel was extended. So lived and died one of the noblest of the New England Congregational ministers of a century ago. Of illegitimate birth, and of no advantageous circumstances of family, rank or station, he became one of the choicest instruments of Christ. His face betrayed his race and blood, and his life revealed his Lord.

There served as a pioneer worker for the Presbyterians John Gloucester, who founded the first African Presbyterian Church in Philadelphia in 1807. According to Gillett's History of the Presbyterian Church in the United States, this church owed its existence, and for many years its continued support, largely to the "Evangelical Society of Philadelphia," organized upon the recommendation and influence of Dr. Alexander. "Its first pastor, although never installed," says Gillett, "was John Gloucester, a slave of Dr. Blackburn of Tennessee. He had attracted the attention of the latter, under whose preaching he was converted, by his piety and natural gifts, and by him was purchased, and encouraged to study with a view to the ministry. After having been licensed and ordained by the Union Presbytery, he was, in 1818, received from that body by the Philadelphia Presbytery, and, under the patronage of the 'Evangelical Society,' continued in charge of the African Church until his death in 1822. The house of worship, located on the corner of Shippen and Seventh Streets, was completed in 1811."

"Mr. Gloucester first commenced his missionary efforts by preaching in private houses," continues Gillett, "but these were soon found insufficient to accommodate his congregations. A schoolhouse was procured near the site of the future edifice; but in clear weather he preached in the open air. Possessed of a strong and musical voice, he would take his stand on the corner of Shippen and Seventh Streets, and while singing a hymn would gather around him many besides his regular hearers, and hold their attention till he was prepared to commence his exercises. Possessed of a stout, athletic frame, and characterized by prudence, forbearance, and a fervent piety, he labored with unremitting zeal, securing the confidence and respect of his brethren of the Presbytery, and building up the congregation which he had gathered. His freedom was granted him by Dr. Blackburn, and by his own application he secured the means in England and this country to purchase his family. He is said to have been a man of strong mind, mighty of prayer, and of such fervor and energy in wrestling supplication that persons sometimes fell under his power, convicted of sin."

To this class of Negro preachers in the South belongs John Chavis, mentioned in another connection below. Chavis was a full-blooded Negro of dark brown color, born probably near Oxford, Granville County, North Carolina, about 1763. From a youth he impressed the public as a man of unusual power and was, therefore, sent by his friends to Princeton to see if a Negro could take a collegiate education. Some have said that he was never a regularly enrolled student at Princeton. The records, however, show that he was under the direction of Dr. Witherspoon, who was soon convinced that the experiment "would issue favorably." In keeping with the course of study of that time, he was chiefly interested in the classics. In these fields he easily took rank as a good Latin and a fair Greek scholar. Exactly how much work he did in the field of theology is not known, but as the line drawn between theology and classical studies at that time was not very definite, he could easily lay a foundation for work in the ministry, and especially so if his instruction were under the direction of one man, who would shape his course of study in keeping with his practical needs rather than in conformity with the formal training of the school.

Whether Chavis was sent to Princeton to make a minister of him or not, however, he very soon bestirred himself in that direction. From Princeton he went to Lexington, Virginia, to preach. In the records of the Presbyterians for 1801, Chavis is referred to as "a black man of prudence and piety." "For his better direction in the discharge of duties which are attended with many circumstances of delicacy and difficulty" some prudential instructions were issued to him by the General Assembly, "governing himself by which the knowledge of religion among the Negroes might be made more and more to strengthen the order of the society." The annals of the year 1801 report him in the service of the Hanover Presbytery as a "riding missionary under the direction of the General Assembly." He was very soon stationed in Lexington as a recognized preacher of official status working among his own people. In 1805, however, he returned to his native State, where as a result of the close relations existing between the whites and blacks and his power as an expounder of the gospel, he preached to large congregations of both races.

Referring to his career, Paul C. Cameron, a son of Judge Duncan of North Carolina, said: "In my boyhood life at my father's home I often saw John Chavis, a venerable old Negro man, recognized as a freeman and as a preacher or clergyman of the Presbyterian Church. As such he was received by my father and treated with kindness and consideration, and respected as a man of education, good sense and most estimable character." Mr. George Wortham, a lawyer of Granville County, said: "I have heard him read and explain the Scriptures to my father's family repeatedly. His English was remarkably pure, containing no 'Negroisms'; his manner was impressive, his explanations clear and concise, and his views, as I then thought and still think, entirely orthodox. He was said to have been an acceptable preacher, his sermons abounding in strong common sense views and happy illustrations, without any effort at oratory or sensational appeals to the passions of his hearers."

In North Carolina the disastrous result of the reaction against the Negroes handicapped Chavis in his work. As a result of the fear of servile insurrection among the slaves after Nat Turner's uprising, the exercise of the gift of preaching was prohibited to Negroes in North Carolina. Chavis thereafter devoted himself to teaching, maintaining classical schools for white persons in Granville, Wake, and Chatham counties. He was patronized by the most aristocratic white people of that State. In the end he counted among his former students W. P. Mangum, afterward United States Senator; P. H. Mangum, his brother; Archibald and John Henderson, sons of Chief Justice Henderson; Charles Manly, later Governor of that commonwealth, and Dr. James L. Wortham of Oxford, North Carolina. ...

Chapter 8
Preachers of Versatile Genius

The situation in the North was then more encouraging, though far from being ideal. During the critical period through which the Negroes were passing between 1830 and the Civil War the Negro minister had to divide his attention so as to take care of all of the varying interests of an oppressed race. Among the poor it has never been considered exceptional for a minister to work at some occupation to increase the meager income which he receives from his parishioners. We have already observed above that Andrew Bryan made himself independent as a planter, that Richard Allen at first earned his living as a teamster, and that Andrew Marshall with much business acumen maintained himself in a local express business. During the critical period from 1830 to 1860, however, the Negro minister was not only compelled sometimes thus to support himself, but often had to devote part of his time to the problems of education, abolition, colonization and the Underground Railroad.

Education for the Negro was both a test and a challenge. Few persons believed that the Negro was capable of the mental development known to the white man. The challenge to them, then, was: Show that your race has possibilities in the intellectual world, bring forth proof to uproot the argument that your race is the inferior of the other peoples. To make the challenge more concrete, can a Negro master the grammar, language, and literature of Latin, Greek, and Hebrew? Can he learn to think? Can he understand the significant things of life as expounded by mathematicians, scientists, and philosophers? A few Negroes had demonstrated here and there unusual ability in these fields; but they were not generally known or their achievements were accounted for by their racial connection with the white race in this country or with some Arabic stock of Africa, known to be Caucasian rather than Negroid.

The greater impetus to education among Negro ministers, however, came not so much from the desire to meet this requirement as from the need of it in promoting the work of the church. It is true that the whites were subjecting the blacks to a mental test, but it required very little logic to show that the contention as to Negro inferiority was a case of making desire father to the thought. The independent church movement had to depend on education; and the Negroes themselves, as they made progress, required of their ministry the service of instructors to bring the people to a higher standard of thought. Acquiring an education then was not always an easy task. Negroes had no advanced schools of their own and they were generally refused in most of those of the North. Until the rise of the Union Literary Institute in Indiana, Oberlin and Wilberforce in Ohio, Ashmun Institute in Pennsylvania, and Oneida Institute in New York, the Negro had to break his way into whatever institution of learning he entered. Negroes who were ignorant themselves could not always appreciate what the struggle for educational opportunities actually meant.

The Negro ministers, moreover, were at the same time in the midst of a life and death struggle. During the thirties and forties the questions involving the Negroes engaged the attention of almost everybody. The Negro ministers, the then best developed leaders among their people, could not be silent. Inasmuch as men had to be won to the support of the cause, these apostles to the lowly had to appear before the other race in the North as spokesmen of an oppressed people. Preaching was important enough, but there could be no preaching without the liberty to preach. Except in a few such cases as that of William Douglass, the rector of St. Thomas Church, Philadelphia, and that of Peter Williams, the rector of St. Phillips', in New York City, where the proslavery church hierarchy hushed the Negro ministers loyally speaking for their people, the Negro clergyman spoke out fearlessly for the emancipation of his race and its elevation to citizenship.

As the American Colonization Society went only half way in carrying out this program in that it advocated the emancipation of the Negroes for deportation to Africa, merely to rid the country of freemen belonging to another than the Caucasian race, the Negro ministers were generally opposed to that organization. They fearlessly attacked the promoters of the cause, saying, "Here we were born, here we fought for the independence of this country, and here we intend to die and be buried in the soil hallowed by the blood of our fathers shed in defense of this country." When, however, the increasing intelligence of the Negroes made their humiliation in this country less and less durable, the Negro ministers became divided among themselves on this important question; for a few of the leaders of that day began to advocate colonization in some other country than Africa.

In the meantime, moreover, almost every Negro minister was otherwise engaged in spiriting away fugitives from the slaveholding States through the North into Canada. They were in touch with men in other centers, found out what was going on, learned what was the trend of things, and planned to act accordingly. And well might they be so engaged; for not a few of these ministers were fugitives themselves, and whether or not their freedom had such origin, all Negroes in the North were, after the passage of that unconstitutional drastic Fugitive Slave Law of 1850, in danger of being apprehended and enslaved without what civilized countries regard as due process of law. Some of the ministers themselves had to move for safety into Canada during this crisis, carrying in some cases practically all of their congregations with them.

The Negro minister easily learned also the power of the press. Much time which they would have under other circumstances devoted to the edification of their flocks they had to spend in raising funds to purchase printing plants and in editing the publications issuing there from. They could deliver their message to their congregations, they could occasionally address thus groups of the other race; but their message needed a wider circulation in a more enduring form. There were, therefore, during this crisis few Negro ministers of literary attainments who did not either undertake to edit a newspaper or to contribute thereto. If they had a message worth while, the abolition papers would generally delight in publishing it. If they refused and the message was a burning one, the Negroes would establish an organ of their own.

To bring out this idea of the minister of divided interests serving his people in many ways, no career is more illuminating than that of Bishop Daniel A. Payne. Having been much better trained than most of his coworkers, he emphasized education as a necessary foundation for thorough work in the ministry. Taking this position, he made himself at first more of a teacher than a preacher, devoting most of his time to actual classroom instruction, hoping to raise the standard of the ministry in the African Methodist Episcopal Church, with which he finally cast his lot after being graduated at the Lutheran Seminary at Gettysburg. Taking this position, he had arrayed against him all the enemies of culture. One writer charged him with branding the ministry with infamy and with reckless slander on the general character of his own denomination. There was great fear that there might follow discord and dissolution between the ignorant and the intelligent portion of the church. Preaching to his congregation, the ignorant minister would often boast of having not rubbed his head against the college walls, whereupon the congregation would respond: "Amen." Sometimes one would say: "I did not write out my sermon." With equal fervor the audience would cry out: "Praise ye the Lord." Working zealously, however, Bishop Payne committed the denomination to the policy of thorough education for the ministry, a position from which the African Methodist Episcopal Church has never departed, and to which it owes not a few of the advantages that it now enjoys in having so many intelligent men in its ministry.

While Bishop Payne as a churchman did not become altogether involved in the anti-slavery movement, so many distinguished men in the church did. John N. Marrs of the African Methodist Episcopal Zion Church was more of an anti-slavery lecturer than a preacher. Thomas James of the same denomination was equally as effective as an anti-slavery lecturer. He was much readier to fight than to preach when he thought of the enormities of slavery. Another Zionite, Dempsey Kennedy, a pioneer preacher of remarkable skill in stirring up audiences, rendered as much service as an abolitionist as he did as a minister.

One of the best examples of this type is Charles Bennett Ray, born in Falmouth, Massachusetts, December 28, 1807. He was educated at the Wesleyan Academy of Wilbraham, Massachusetts, and later at Wesleyan University, Middletown, Connecticut. After studying theology he became a Congregational minister. For twenty years he was the pastor of the Bethesda Church in New York City, where many learned to wait upon his ministry. He is better known to fame, however, by the work which he did outside of his chosen field in connection with the anti-slavery movement, the Underground Railroad, and The Colored American, which he creditably edited from 1839 to 1843.

Ray aided the cause of liberty by lending practical aid which men in high places often had neither the time nor the patience to give, using his home as a mecca for the meetings of such men as Lewis Tappan, Simeon S. Josselyn, Gerit Smith, the land philanthropist, and James Sturge, the celebrated English philanthropist, interested in the abolition of slavery. In coöperation with wealthy abolitionists he assisted many a slave to the light of freedom, especially through the aid of Henry Ward Beecher of the Plymouth Church in Brooklyn. Ray found himself cooperating also with the group of radical free people of color meeting in Philadelphia and in other cities of the North from 1830 until the Civil War. When one reads of his participation in this work with James Forten, a business man, and Charles B. Purvis, another layman, he is inclined to forget that Charles B. Ray was a minister, as his name appears in the records of practically all of these conventions of the free people of color and his work stands out as an important factor contributing to the success with which these aggressive Negroes kept their case before the world and gradually hastened the dawn of their freedom. In all of his various employments, however, Ray did not lose interest in and did not necessarily neglect his mission to promote the moral uplift of his fellows. A contemporary, William Wells Brown, paying him a tribute as a terse, vigorous writer and an able and eloquent speaker, well informed upon all subjects of the day, says also that he was "blameless in his family relations, guided by the highest moral rectitude, a true friend of everything that tends to better the moral, social, religious and political condition of man."

In the class with Ray should be mentioned Henry Highland Garnett, another minister of the Presbyterian Church, devoting most of his time to the many movements which attracted the attention of his colaborers. Having escaped from Maryland to the North in 1822, Garnett experienced sufficient mental development to ask for admission to the Canaan Academy, where he, along with Alexander Crummell and others, caused the school to be broken up by a mob arraying itself against the idea of permitting persons of color to enjoy such privileges in that community. Proceeding, however, to the Oneida Institute in New York, he succeeded in laying a foundation for his work under the noble-hearted friend of man, Beriah Green. Here Garnett attained the reputation of an accomplished man, an able and eloquent debater and a good writer. He soon developed into a preacher of power of the evangelical type, whose discourses showed much thought and careful study. He had complete command of his voice and used it with skill, never failing to fill the largest hall. Soon there was a demand for him as a preacher. He was sent as a missionary to the Island of Jamaica. He later spent some time in Washington as the pastor of the Presbyterian Church and served at another time at the Shiloh Church in New York City.

Garnett, however, was soon more than a preacher. From the time he made his first public appearance in New York City in 1837 he secured for himself a standing among first-class orators. In 1843 he delivered before the National Convention of Colored Americans at Buffalo, New York, one of the most remarkable addresses ever uttered by man. His contemporary says: "None but those who heard that speech have the slightest idea of the tremendous influence which he exercised over the assembly." For forty years thereafter he was an advocate of the rights of his race, a forcible and daring speaker wherever he had an opportunity to present his cause. Visiting England in 1850, he was well received as an orator. Garnett, moreover, served much of his time as an educator, having been President of Avery College, where he passed as a man of learning.

In this group of enterprising clergymen of this period should be mentioned Alexander Crummell, although his more important service to the race belongs to the two generations following the Civil War. Crummell was a native of New York, but a descendant of a Timanee chief in West Africa. Early in his career he attended a Quaker school with Thomas S. Sidney and Henry Highland Garnett in New York, and later experienced with the latter, as mentioned above, the humiliation of seeing the Academy of Canaan, New Hampshire, broken up because of the admission of Negroes. Crummell then studied three years under Beriah Green at the Oneida Institute. Having then the aspiration to enter the ministry of the Episcopal Church, he applied for admission to the General Theological Seminary of the Protestant Episcopal Church of New York, which, in keeping with its hostile attitude toward the Negro, refused to accept him.

Thus barred from entering upon his life's work, Crummell could not then influence the public to the same extent as Negro leaders laboring in the more inviting fields. Presenting his case to the clergy in Boston in 1842, he was ordained deacon by Bishop Griswold. After studying two years under Dr. A. H. Vinton of Providence, Rhode Island, Crummell was ordained priest by Bishop Lee of Delaware at St. Paul's Church in Philadelphia, and engaged to work in a barren field. Here poverty and ill health overtook him and rendered his circumstances all but intolerable. To earn livelihood he conducted for four men a private school, which, after having a promising beginning, proved inadequate to his support.

He then went to England, where he was well received as a preacher and given the opportunity to prosecute further his studies at Queen's College, Cambridge University, from which he obtained the degree of Bachelor of Arts in 1853. Crummell then began his career as a missionary and educator, working in Liberia and Sierra Leone for about twenty years. He returned to the United States in 1873 and entered upon his work as an Episcopal priest in Washington, where, as the rector of St. Mary's, and as the founder of the American Negro Academy, he experienced the culmination of his usefulness as a scholar, a clergyman, and a champion of the rights of his people.

Among these workers should be mentioned also James W. C. Pennington, another minister of the Presbyterian Church. Pennington was born a slave on a farm in Maryland and there became a blacksmith by trade. Upon reaching maturity he escaped to the North, where he early embraced the opportunities for learning. He developed into an unusually bright scholar in Greek, Latin, and German; and soon manifested an inclination for the study of theology, in which he showed much proficiency. Impressed with his worth as an educated man well trained for the ministry, the Presbyterians ordained him to preach and stationed him at Hartford, Connecticut, where he served some years. He later became the pastor of the Shiloh Church in New York City.

While Dr. Pennington did not drift so far from the ministry as many of his colaborers, he was at once in demand for work in various other fields. He went to Europe three times in the capacity of a lecturer. His second visit was the occasion on which he remained for four years, preaching, lecturing and attending the Peace Congresses held at Paris, Brussels, and London. While at Paris in 1849 he was invited to conduct divine services at the Protestant Church, which on that occasion was visited by the American and English delegates. His sermon was an elegant production, left a marked impression upon his hearers, and above all made a more logical case for the Negro. While in Germany the degree of Doctor of Divinity was conferred upon him by the University of Heidelberg. Returning to this country, he labored zealously and successfully for the education and the moral, social, and religious elevation of the race, until he went to Jamaica, where he died.

Rev. E. Payson Rogers, another Presbyterian preacher stationed as pastor of a church at Newark, New Jersey, divided his time between writing and preaching. He was a man of education, research, and literary ability. Although not a fluent and easy speaker, he was logical and spoke with a degree of refinement seldom observed. Possessing the inclination to write verse to express the thought and feeling of a struggling people, he wrote a poem on the Missouri Compromise which he read in many of the New England cities and towns in 1856. This poem contained brilliant thought and amusing suggestions. Anxious to benefit his race, he visited Africa in 1861, where he was attacked by a fever and died in a few days.

J. Theodore Holly was another minister of versatile genius. He acquired a good education through studious habits and contact with men of culture. Although he became a clergyman of the Protestant Episcopal Church and was for several years pastor at New Haven, where he sustained the reputation of being an interesting and eloquent preacher, he set about to establish what he called Negro nationality. He was not primarily interested in African colonization, but believed that the redemption of Africa could be effected through Haitian emigration. In the Anglo-African, a magazine published in 1859, he contributed a dissertation setting forth these facts. Impressed with the idea that Haiti might be used as an asylum for free persons of color, he raised a colony in keeping with the resolution passed by the Convention of Free Persons of Color in Rochester in 1853 and sailed for Haiti in 1861. As the location which he selected was infelicitous, most of those who went with him, including his own family, died, and he returned to the United States, where he finally rendered greater service and from which he was later commissioned as Bishop of the Protestant Episcopal Church in Haiti.

One of the most interesting men of this type was Leonard A. Grimes, a Baptist minister, born in Leesburg, Loudoun County, Virginia, in 1815. Although he was a man of free parentage he was subjected to all of the disabilities that his race had to endure in the South except that of an actual slave. He spent his youth working at the butcher's trade and at an apothecary's establishment in Washington but subsequently hired himself out to a slaveholder whose confidence he gained. In accompanying his employer in his travels in the remote parts of the South he had an opportunity to see slavery in its worst form and to reach a decision that he would make every effort possible to destroy the evil. Returning to Washington very soon thereafter, he began to express an interest in the operations of the Underground Railroad, in connection with which he rendered valuable service. Upon being appealed to by a free man of color with a slave wife and seven children, he aided them to escape to Canada. Suspicion, however, fell upon Grimes and he was soon thereafter apprehended, tried, found guilty, and sent to the State penitentiary at Richmond for two years.

Upon the expiration of his imprisonment Grimes returned to Washington and soon then went to New Bedford, Massachusetts, where he resided two years. He next went to Boston. Having early in his career been impressed with the thought that he was called to the ministry, he had spent much of his time in this work while engaged as an agent of the Underground Railroad. Finding a group of persons in Boston at that time in need of a pastor, he entered upon the task of serving them in that capacity. This congregation was known as the Twelfth Baptist Church, of which he was the pastor for more than twenty-five years, ministering to some of the best persons of color in that city in such a way as to make his work a monument to which Bostonians still point with pride. As a preacher he was a man of power, though not an easy speaker. He manifested great amiability of character and always had a pleasant word for those with whom be came into contact. Although primarily engaged in the work of the ministry during the great crisis in this country, he never abandoned entirely the anti-slavery cause, in spite of the fact that many of his denomination were trying to defend that institution. He passed away in 1873, after having experienced some of the freedom for which he struggled.

Among the prominent Negro ministers who lived through this critical period no one exhibited more versatility than Samuel R. Ward. Impressed with the superior gifts with which he was endowed, Gerrit Smith enabled him to secure a liberal education. Ward then entered upon the ministry in the Presbyterian Church. For several years he was settled over a white church at South Butler, New York, where, according to William Wells Brown, Ward "preached with great acceptance and was highly respected." Coming to the aid of his race during the trying days of the abolition agitation, Ward took the platform and from 1840 to the passage of the Fugitive Slave Law of 1850 preached or lectured in every church, hall, or schoolhouse in Western and Central New York. "Standing about six feet in height, possessing a strong voice, and energetic in his gestures, Ward," says his biographer, "always impressed his highly finished and logical speeches upon his hearers."

Ward became more of a platform orator than a preacher. His aim seemed to be not so much to preach the gospel of heaven as to preach the gospel of this world that men calling themselves Christians might learn to respect the natural and political rights of their fellows. In the interest of this cause he traveled through much of this country, visited England in 1852, and then went to Jamaica, where he finally resided until he died at an early age. Referring to the death of R. B. Elliot, Frederick Douglass, Ward's most famous contemporary, remarked: "I have known but one other black man to be compared with Elliot, and that was Samuel R. Ward, who, like Elliot, died in the midst of his years. The thought of both men makes me sad. We are not over rich with such men, and we may well mourn when one such has fallen."

No better example of the varying interests of the Negro can be mentioned than that of Hiram R. Revells, who after the Civil War became one of the two Negroes who have served in the United States Senate. Revells was born a free man at Fayetteville, North Carolina, in 1822. There he passed his boyhood and then went to Indiana, because the laws of North Carolina in 1835 forbade the establishment of schools for persons of color. He had experienced some educational development by private instruction and was prepared to profit by the advanced training received in a Quaker school in Indiana. He then moved to Darke County, Ohio, where he remained for some time. He was subsequently graduated at Knox College, Galesburg, Illinois. Revells then entered the ministry as a preacher of the African Methodist Church at the age of twenty-five, holding his first charge in Indiana. He filled important posts in Missouri, Maryland, Kentucky, and Kansas, but did not succeed so well in St. Louis, where the church developed into a turmoil, resulting in the resignation of the pastor.

Upon the outbreak of the war, Revells directed his attention to other matters. He assisted in raising the first Negro regiment in Maryland and the first one in Missouri. He then returned to Mississippi in 1864, settling at Vicksburg and later at Jackson, where he had charge of congregations. He also assisted in the extension of the work of the African Methodist Episcopal Church in other parts and in establishing a school system. His health having failed, however, he returned to the North after the close of hostilities and remained there eighteen months, at the expiration of which he again came to Natchez, Mississippi, where he preached regularly to large audiences. Entering politics, he was appointed alderman by General Ames, who was then military governor there. In 1869 he was elected to the State Senate and the following year to the United States Senate.

Chapter 9
The Civil War and the Church

The outbreak of the Civil War was also an outbreak in the church. The versatile minister then proclaimed war and sometimes donned the uniform. One half of the nation had preached that God hath made of one blood all nations that dwell upon the face of the earth; the other half insisted that the plan of the Creator was a caste system by which one element of the population should be made hewers of wood and drawers of water for the other. The ordeal of battle was then on, and it was believed that the exhibition of the greater force on one of the two sides would determine the will of God. Men of both sections fought for what they believed to be right. Sermons resounded with the ring of freedom, the Bible was quoted to strengthen the belief in a just war, and songs of a militant tone made the welkin ring with that enthusiasm with which the Christian boy was inspired to give his life as a sacrifice, fighting for freedom or defending his section from the invasion of the ruthless foe. God was here; God was there; in fact, he was, as the participants would have it, fighting the battles of all.

Negroes realized that the Christianity of America was being subjected to a test. They had entered the church themselves but only with the belief that this liberal doctrine of the power of God to free a man's soul from sin meant also that such power would eventually be adequate to free the body. They had borne the burden in the heat of the day, even walked through the flames of that fiery ordeal of death; but they had never lost faith in God. Here and there an old hero in the midst of his martyrdom had prophesied upon his dying bed that God would deliver his people from the hands of the oppressors; a heroine of vision had dreamed that her Maker had poured healing oils upon her lacerated back, assuaged her excruciating pain, and made her free. Patience had been the watchword of the Negro. God was moving in a mysterious way to perform wonders which in the near future would make all things plain. Stand still, therefore, and see the salvation of the Lord.

Would these dreams come true? Evidently they would, the Negroes thought, when they heard of churchmen denouncing slavery in no uncertain terms, memorializing the State legislatures and Congress for its abolition, and assuring the nation of their heartiest support in the suppression of the rebellion occasioned by the effort to save the tottering institution. The Negroes could not fail to see the hand of God in the declaration of these churchmen that our national sorrows and calamities had resulted from our forgetfulness of God and the oppression of our fellowmen. Chastened by the affliction of the Civil War, many like the Methodists hoped that the nation might humbly repent of its sins, lay aside its haughty pride, honor God in all her future legislation, and render justice to all who had been wronged. They honored Lincoln for his proclamation of freedom and rejoiced in the enactment of the measures designed to reach this end. And so impressed with this militant service of the church, Lincoln had to say in reply to this denomination: "The Methodist Episcopal Church, not less devoted than the best, is, by its greater numbers the most important of all. It is no fault in others that the Methodist Church sends more soldiers to the field, more nurses to the hospitals, more prayers to Heaven, than any. God bless the Methodist Church! Bless all the Churches! And blessed be God, who, in this our great trial, giveth us the churches!"

Because of this militant attitude of the church, the Negroes thought more of fighting for freedom than they did of saving souls. The slaves breathed the spirit of the song:

Oh, freedom! Freedom over me!
Before I'd be a slave,
I'd be buried in my grave
And go home to my Lord and be free!"

Negroes known to be pious gladly donned the uniform and some ministers of the gospel abandoned their charges to recruit men to fight for the cause. The friends of the Negroes, moreover, were militantly arrayed against their former brethren in the South. The abolition churches of the North received the anathemas of the churches of the South and vice versa. The war was religious as well as political, causing wounds which having not yet been healed even unto this day seriously affect church work among Negroes in the South.

The Civil War as a social and political upheaval made necessary some readjustments in the church. The Negroes in the South were no longer bondmen to be circumscribed in keeping with the regulations of a slave commonwealth and the Negroes in the North might then exercise more liberty without the fear of incurring the displeasure of those having the impression that the Negroes should in religious as well as in other matters be subject to men who enjoy a superior social position. It was then, moreover, a different question from what it was before. Prior to the Civil War one had inquired as to what should be done for the Negro. It was then a question as to what the Negro would do for himself. Things for which he had long asked theretofore were thereafter readily given or taken.

For example, during the period intervening between the separation of the northern and southern wings of the church in 1844 and the Civil War, the Negro members of the Methodist Episcopal Church in the North asked for separate conferences, a more general recognition of their local preachers, and a larger participation in the affairs of the church. The reason given was that the African Methodists, holding up to these Negro communicants the contempt with which they had been treated by their white superiors, caused large numbers of Negro Methodists to join the independent African churches. The policy of the Methodist Church was not to grant such recognition, deciding, as it did in 1848, that such separate conferences were inexpedient. Some encouragement was given the employment of Negro local preachers. In 1852, in reply to an urgent request of this sort from the Negro Methodists of the Philadelphia and New Jersey conferences, where they were losing many to the African Methodists, a sort of annual meeting of the Negro Methodist pastors was allowed, if the bishop of the diocese concerned found it practicable. The Methodist Church held this position, however, despite the fact that on this account it lost not less than one-fourth of the membership of its churches from the year 1844 to the time when the annual conference of the Negro pastors was provided for in 1866. These white Methodists, however, consecrated Francis Burns for the service as Bishop of Africa in 1858 and in 1866 thus elevated to the episcopacy John W. Roberts, another man of color. As the appeal for the Negro conference was still more urgent this time not only from the Negroes of the Philadelphia and New Jersey conferences but from that of Baltimore, the General Conference had to take more definite action than merely to say that such a step was inexpedient.

The reasons for this action were many and complicated. In the first place, even after the secession of those in the South, there were in the Methodist Episcopal Church a number of members who, wishing to get rid of the Negroes, thought that a refusal to grant this request would alienate their affections to the extent that they would secede as the other African Methodists had done. Some of these communicants actually encouraged the Negroes in saying that, should the blacks go out and establish themselves independently of the whites, the latter would have more respect for them because of this exhibition of their self-reliance. To impress this on the Negro, some white Methodists went so far as to invite to their pulpits the ministers of the African Methodist Churches, whereas the Negro ministers in the Methodist Church itself were ignored. When this method of trying to convince the Negro that he was an intruder failed, the busy-bodies would often say that the white management of the Methodist Church was merely using the Negro members as tools.

Some then thought that, because of love for the Negroes, the Methodist Church did not want to see them go. Others believed that a majority felt that the Negroes should have their own choice whether for separate organization or to unite with one of the African Methodist Churches but that, should such action be taken, the public would get the impression that the Methodists had organized another Negro church to break the other two down. It was thought wise, moreover, to defer action of such far-reaching effects until the Negro question then so intensely agitated should approach nearer a definite settlement. A Negro national church, furthermore, could not minister to the wants of all Negroes inasmuch as the one proposed, like the other two already in the field, could not have prior to emancipation operated among the Negro Methodists in the South. The Methodist Church was neutral, if anything, during the Civil War period. It did not try to get rid of its Negro membership and it made no particular effort to increase it. Wherever one of the two African Methodist Churches was in a position to minister to the spiritual needs of the Negroes, the Methodists made no effort to proselyte such Negroes, although Negroes desiring admission to the Methodist churches were not refused.

This question was further agitated and had to be given serious consideration in 1864. The conference after discussing the memorials from the Negro membership took the position that it must retain oversight of the Negroes to give them efficient supervision. The conference, however, encouraged colored pastorates for colored people wherever practicable. It authorized the organization of mission conferences. These separate conferences, however, were not to impair the existing rights of the colored members nor yet to forbid the transfer of white ministers to such conferences where it might be deemed practicable and necessary. The Negroes in the Methodist Church had at last received some right to share in the management of their own pastorates, which, however, were still subject to the supervision of the white bishops. The African Methodists still made inroads on the Negro membership, therefore, because they could point with pride to men in authority in their church and the Negro members of the white connection usually conceded their point as well taken in that they received the bishops of the African Methodists in their homes and churches and gave them every possible consideration.

Some less numerous Negro communicants of white denominations were at this time severing their connection with their former coworkers. In 1865 the Negro members of the white Primitive Baptist Churches of the South organized at Columbia, Tennessee, the Colored Primitive Baptists in America. In 1866 the African Union First Colored Methodist Protestant Church of America and elsewhere was established by merging the African Union Church with the First Colored Methodist Protestant Church. In 1869 the General Assembly of the Cumberland Presbyterian Church organized its Negro membership as the Colored Cumberland Presbyterian Church.

The Methodist Episcopal Church, South, with a much larger number of Negro members than all of these denominations easily solved the problem of Negro membership, as the Cumberland Presbyterians had done. While the Methodists in the North reluctantly loosed their hold on the Negro membership by granting the people of color active participation in their affairs through an annual conference, the Methodist Church, South, almost voluntarily agreed to organize its Negro constituency as a separate organization known as the Colored Methodist Episcopal Church. Whether the southern Methodists did this to eliminate the Negroes or because they thought that the Negroes in their new status as freemen could do their own work better than white men, is a much mooted question. It is clear that many of the slaveholding type of Christians would want to get rid of the Negro members since they could no longer determine their faith and how it should be exercised. The only reason there was for the Negro to belong to the same church as that of his master was to control the exercise of his religious belief. As this was no longer necessary, the Negroes, so far as one element was concerned, could then easily go.

Desiring to attach to this branch of the Methodist Church the stigma of their having been once connected with their oppressors, some Negroes themselves have referred to these Colored Methodists as "seceders" and "a Democratic Rebel concern" intended to lead the Negroes back into slavery.

Such statements are most uncharitable and they not only do the Negroes concerned an injustice but question the good motives of a number of benevolent southern men who took this step, feeling that it was the best way for the Negroes to develop their religious life after emancipation. There were many masters who believed that, since the Negroes had finally become free, they should have every encouragement to learn how to take care of themselves.

It would be most uncharitable, moreover, to suffer any stigma to attach to the Colored Methodists on this account. The Negroes who constituted this church went with the southern wing of that denomination at the time of its secession because they were compelled so to do. The independent African Methodists were by law and public opinion prohibited from extensive proselyting in the South and prior to the Civil War they had with the exception of their establishments in the liberal border States hardly touched the large body of the black population south of the Mason and Dixon line. The free Negroes in the South were, as in the case of Morris Brown and his followers in 1822, cut off from their brethren in the North and the slaves were compelled to worship according to the rigid regulations set forth above and in the same churches to which their masters belonged.

The separation of the Negro membership from the Methodist Episcopal Church, South, came after the Civil War. In 1866 the conference meeting that year in New Orleans made provision for the organization of the Negro members in separate congregations and for district and annual conferences, if the Negroes so desired. It was further provided on this occasion that if it were acceptable to the Negroes and it met the approval of the bishops of the church, the freedmen might have a general conference like that of the Methodist Episcopal Church, South, according to the regulations of which the Negro deacons, elders, and bishops, if necessary, should be ordained to conduct this work among their own people. It was further determined that should the time arrive when the Negro members should be so set apart, all the property intended for the use of such members, held by the trustees of the Methodist Episcopal Church, South, should be transferred to duly qualified trustees of the new organization.

At the next conference of the Methodist Episcopal Church, South, meeting in Memphis in 1870, it was reported that the Negro membership had organized five annual conferences and unanimously desired to be organized as a distinct body. The Memphis Conference thereupon agreed to comply with this request. Delegates were then elected to the first general conference which assembled in Jackson, Tennessee, December 15, 1870. From the Methodist Episcopal Church, South, there were sent as representatives Bishops Robert Paine and H. N. McTyeire; and as ministers, A. L. P. Green, Samuel Watson, Thomas Taylor, Edmund W. Sehon, Thomas Whitehead, and B. J. Morgan. The prominent delegates from the five annual conferences of the Negro members were Richard Samuels, Solon Graham, Anderson Jackson, R. T. Thiergood, L. H. Holsey, I. H. Anderson, R. H. Vanderhorst, W. H. Miles, W. P. Churchill, Isaac Lane, John W. Lane, Job Grouch, F. Ambrose, and William Jones.

After having had read to this body the action of the conference it was suggested that a committee be appointed to find a new name for this proposed body. The name proposed was the Colored Methodist Episcopal Church in America, which was unanimously accepted. The body then proceeded to elect bishops. W. H. Miles was elected on the first ballot. Afterward R. H. Vanderhorst was also chosen. Bishops Paine and McTyiere then consecrated them the first two bishops of the Colored Methodist Episcopal Church in America. Three additional bishops, L. H. Holsey, J. A. Beebe, and Isaac Lane, were elected and ordained in March, 1873.

The large body of Negroes, however, were attracted after the war not by the Methodist Church but by the Baptist. The freedom, which even prior to emancipation meant so much in the growth of the Baptists, was thereafter a still greater cause for their expansion. It was easier than ever for a man to become a prominent figure in the Baptist Church. While the Methodists were hesitating as to what recognition should be allowed the Negroes or whether they should be set apart as a separate body, the Negro Baptists were realizing upon their new freedom which made possible the enjoyment of greater democracy in the church. Every man was to be equal to every other man and no power without had authority to interfere.

This situation in the Baptist Church appealed very strongly to the then recently enfranchised Negro in the reconstructed States. As the white man of the South had over emphasized politics and the professions to the extent that these avenues in that section were over manned, the Negro in his undeveloped state accordingly made the same mistake in trying to escape drudgery. A rather hard row to hoe, or an unusually heavy burden was too often abandoned on hearing a call to the ministry, and the devotee thus impressed had practically no difficulty in securing a hearing in this locally democratic Baptist Church. The grade of intellect possessed by the novice in this ministerial service had little to do with his acceptability; for there were all sorts of degrees of mental development among the freedmen and every man preferred to follow the one who saw the spiritual world from his own particular angle and explained its mysteries in the dialect and in the manner in which he could understand it. If in delivering the gospel message the verb might not every time agree with the subject, that had little to do with the power to start a soul on the way to glory.

Operating on this basis, local churches sprang up here and there as Baptist preachers, a law unto themselves, went abroad seeking a following. Out of some of these efforts came several good results. Many of the churches thus established have in our day developed into beacon lights. And so was it true of some of those churches which branched off from or drew out of the old Baptist Churches of long standing established years before the Civil War. There were not so many such African Baptist churches in the South during that period. Because of fear of servile insurrection the whites would not permit many Negro churches to have an independent existence. The pressure once removed, however, groups of Negroes long waiting for religious freedom found adequate opportunity for exercising it in the organization of numerous Baptist churches. This was not in all cases abruptly effected, for the Negroes had no church buildings of their own and could not easily purchase them; but in their poverty they made unusual sacrifices to meet this emergency and whites liberally inclined assisted them in the rapid promotion of this work. Yet this movement did not reach its climax until some years later; for the lure of politics presented another field of so much interest to the Negroes that even the preachers of long standing too often abandoned their posts altogether. After the Reconstruction, moreover, when the Negro in the South had been removed from politics, a much larger number of bankrupt leaders entered the ministry or devised schemes to make use of the various churches.

An impetus toward improvement came from mutual associations. The Baptist churches were not obligated to unite to form associations and when formed did not necessarily have to be bound by the action of these annual meetings; but immediately after the war Negro Baptist churches, which in the South had formerly been coolly received by white bodies and were not permitted to form associations of their own, readily united for mutual benefit in the exercise of their new freedom. In those meetings the uninformed heard of the urgent need to educate the masses, the duty of the ministry to elevate the laity, and the call upon all to Christianize the heathen. The periodical visits of white churchmen, interested either in the Negro or in exploiting them, brought new light as to what was going on in the other bodies conducted by men of higher attainments.

As the Negro Baptists, however, did not soon effect more potential organizations than the district Baptist Associations then composed of a few churches, they never had a national policy; and their local democracy would have furnished no machinery to carry out such a policy, if they had adopted one. To the State groups, then, must the reader look for the signs of progress and thanks to the genius of the Negro, such evidence was not long wanting.

The Negro Baptists of North Carolina organized the first State Convention in 1866. Alabama and Virginia followed in 1867, and very soon thereafter came Arkansas, Kentucky, and finally all of the States in the South. Immediately thereafter they began to affiliate with larger national bodies. The first of these larger groups was the Northwestern and Southern Baptist Convention, organized in 1864. In 1866 there was held an important convention in Richmond, when it was determined to consolidate all of the general interests of the Negro Baptists, the Missionary, the Northwestern and Southern conventions as one large body, to be called the Consolidated American Baptist Missionary Convention.

Some years later these Baptists sent six missionaries to Africa. These were J. H. Pressly, W. W. Colley together with their wives, J. J. Coles and H. McKinney. The National

Convention was organized in 1880, out of a protest against the attitude of certain whites toward the Negroes and they have since continued as a separate body having a publishing house of their own rather than patronize the American Baptist Publication Society.

This convention operated largely in the South and tended to decline. In 1873 the West revived its organization under the name of the Baptist Association of the Western States and Territories, while the northern churches adhered to another organization called the New England Missionary Convention, organized in 1875. In the course of time these two bodies so expanded as to embrace the whole country, yet in 1880 certain Baptists here and there formed a national body to do work in foreign lands, designating it the Baptist Foreign Mission Convention of the United States. The feeling, however, that there should be a concentration of the efforts of all Baptists directed through one national body to a particular point of attack led to a more significant national meeting of the Negro Baptists held in St. Louis in 1886. The work of the Baptist Foreign Mission Convention was later so modified that all of the national and international church work of the denomination was unified through the organization of the National Baptist Convention.

That these Baptists despite their excess of liberty succeeded as well as they did, was due in a measure to the fact that they exercised the good judgment in not immediately getting too far from their friends. The Negroes used the same polity, the same literature, and sometimes the same national agencies as the white Baptists. The southern Baptists were then less interested in these communicants whom, some say, they gladly got rid of when they could no longer dictate their spiritual development as the master did that of the slave; but the northern Baptists felt obligated to send their missionaries among the freedmen. These apostles to the lowly brought words of good cheer, expounded the gospel, established new churches, and distributed books for the enlightenment of the masses. Among some of these lowly people these men were received as apostles of old, welcomed to a new harvest which had long been waiting, for the laborers among the lowly were few. ...

Chapter 15

The Negro Church of To-day

Because of many undesirable situations here and there in the church comparatively few young men have, during the last decade or so, aspired to this work. Some young Negroes have learned to look upon the calling as a necessary nuisance. Except in church schools where the preparation for the ministry is an objective, it has often been unusual to find one Negro student out of a hundred aspiring to the ministry, and too often those who have such aspirations represent the inferior intellect of the group, as it happened in the church during the middle ages. So rapidly did the ministry fall into discredit in many quarters a few years ago that most women of promise would not dare to engage themselves to men who thought of becoming clergymen; and, if the marital connection happened to be effected before the lot of the bride was known, it was in many cases considered a calamity. Because Negroes now realize how limited the opportunity for the race is in politics and some of the professions, however, the ministry will doubtless continue, as it has since the Reconstruction, a sort of avenue through which the ambitious youth must pass to secure a hearing and become a man of influence among his people. This does not mean that irreligious men will masquerade as spiritual advisers but that, inasmuch as the church as an institution is considered a welfare agency as well as a spiritual body to edify souls, some Negroes, interested in the social uplift of the race, are learning to accomplish this task by accepting leadership in the church.

Negroes see in the ministry, moreover, a new mission. The world, having now gone mad after the trifles of this life, is sadly in need of a redeemer to save men from themselves. In the contest between selfishness and godliness the former has been victor in the soul of the American and European. There are those like Bishop John Hurst believing that the Negro church must play the role of keeping the fire burning on the altar until the day when men again become reverent, and that the Negro's liberal interpretation of the Christian religion, based upon the brotherhood of man and the fatherhood of God, must gain ascendancy and be accepted by a regenerated world of to-morrow.

As a preparation to this end the afflictions of the Negro have adequately developed self-control in the race. The watchword of the Negro church has been patience while waiting on the Lord. The Negro has learned not to avenge his own wrongs, believing that God will adjust matters in the end. The Negro agrees with Professor Joseph A. Booker, that he that taketh up the sword shall perish by the sword. Even during these days, when we learn much about the lawless, the behavior of the Negroes is no exception to the rule. An investigation shows that the Negroes never do any more than to defend themselves in keeping with the first law of nature. White persons who once found it possible to intimidate the whole group by shooting or lynching one or two now face persons of color bent upon defending their homes. At heart, however, the Negro is conservatively Christian and looks forward to that favorable turn in the affairs of man when the wrongs of the oppressed shall be righted without the shedding of blood.

The Negro church is criticized by a few radical members of the race as a hindrance to the immediate achievement of the aims of the race, in that the white race in the exercise of foresight encourages and even subsidizes the Negro ministry in carrying out this conservative program. This will tend, it is said, to keep the Negro down, whereas the white people themselves do not actually believe in such doctrine; for their own actions show that they use it as a means to an end. This, however, is hardly a fair criticism of the Negro church of to-day. No force from without can claim control of this institution, and certainly no one can bridle its fearless speakers who stand for the Negro of to-day. The Negro churchmen, moreover, are not any more conservative than other leaders of the people. They may be more generally effective because of their greater influence. That the Negro church is conservative is due to teaching and to tradition, and it is fortunate that Providence has had it so. Acting as a conservative force among the Negroes, the church has been a sort of balance wheel. It has not been unprogressive but rather wise in its generation in not rushing forward to a radical position in advance of public opinion. In other words, the Negro church has known how far it can safely instruct its people to go in righting their own wrongs, and this conservatism has no doubt saved the Negro from the fate of other oppressed groups who have suffered extermination because of the failure to handle their case more diplomatically.

This does not mean, however, that the Negro church of to-day is not alive to the sufferings of the race and is not critical of the attitude of the so-called Christian elements in this country. Some Negro ministers like Dr. F. J. Grimké are decidedly outspoken, even to the extent of being classed with the militant Reds now being deported. Dr. Pezavia O'Connell, a gentleman of scholarship and character, has all but suffered professional martyrdom because he has always fearlessly championed the cause of the Negro. Inasmuch as such an advanced position does not always harmonize with the faith of his communicants, he has been proscribed in certain circles. R. W. Bagnall, George Frazier Miller, and Byron Gunner have actually preached the use of force and encouraged resistance to the mobs to the extent that some Negroes have probably addressed themselves vindictively to the task of retribution. Through the Negro churches, and these alone, have the Negroes been able to effect anything like a cooperative movement to counteract the evil influences of such combinations against the race as the revived Ku Klux Klan.

The church then is no longer the voice of one man crying in the wilderness, but a spiritual organization at last becoming alive to the needs of a people handicapped by social distinctions of which the race must gradually free itself to do here in this life that which will assure the larger life to come. To attain this the earth must be made habitable for civilized people. Funds are daily raised in Negro churches to fight segregation, and an innocent Negro in danger of suffering injustice at the hands of the local oppressor may appeal with success to the communicants with whom he has frequented a common altar. The National Association for the Advancement of Colored People would be unable to carry out its program without the aid of the Negro church.

Although Negroes are not now attracted to the church as much as formerly, the census reports still show that there are more Negroes in the ministry than in any other profession. The only really close competitor of the Negro in this profession is the southern white man. While the educated white men of the North are taking up scientific pursuits and business, the southern whites are carrying out their designs on the ministry, in keeping with the well-laid plans by which they have succeeded in getting partial control of the northern press. During recent years so many southern white students have crowded northern schools of theology that, in keeping with the spirit of Beelzebub, some of these institutions now deny Negroes admission. The pulpits of the North are being gradually taken over by the apostles indoctrinated by the medieval agents of race hate.

Since the Negro ministry is still the largest factor in the life of this race, it naturally conflicts with the propaganda of the ministry preaching caste. These representatives of the master and slave classes must, in the capacity of spokesmen of widely differing groups, work out the solution of the problems of the church in the United States; for either the one or the other must dictate the religious program of the economically mad North. The North cares little about priest-craft. The struggle there for dollars and cents and for opportunities to spend them in riotous living is too keen to spare time for such matters as Christian living and the remote hereafter. The South, on the other hand, has never lost its bearing. In spite of riots here and there and lynchings almost anywhere, that section still considers itself a Christian land and, in its way, has lifted high the name of Christ without being influenced by his life. The North, then, if it ever awakes from its lethargy, will probably accept either the principles of Jesus of Nazareth as they have been preached and practiced by the Negroes, or the Anglo-Saxon-chosen-people-of-God faith for which many misguided white communicants have jeopardized their own lives and have taken those of Negroes unwilling to worship at the shrine of race prejudice.

The white people of this country are not interested in the real mission of Christ. In the North the church has surrendered to the materialistic system and developed into an agency seeking to assuage the pains of those suffering from the very economic evils which the institution has not the courage to attack. In the southern portion of the United States, the white churches have degenerated into perfunctory machines engaged in the service of deceiving the multitude with the doctrine that the Anglo-Saxon, being superior to other races by divine ordination, may justly oppress them to maintain its supremacy and that the principles of Jesus are exemplified in the lives of these newly chosen people of God when they permit their so-called inferiors to eat the crumbs let fall by those whom their idol god has carefully selected as the honor guests at the feast. If the humble Nazarene appeared there disturbing the present caste system, he would be speedily lynched as he was in Palestine.

In spite of the Negroes' logical preaching of the fatherhood of God and the brotherhood of man, however, the North now seems inclined to accept the faith of the South. Science has long since uprooted the theory that one race can be superior to another, but the northern churches are loath to act accordingly. The same churches, which prior to emancipation, championed the cause of the Negro, are to-day working indirectly to promote racial distinctions. The southern white man, wiser in his generation than most of his competitors, easily realized that he could not legally re-enslave the Negro, but early devised a scheme to convert the North to the doctrine of segregation, educational distinctions, and the elimination of the Negroes from the body politic, to make it improbable, if not impossible, for the Negroes to attain the status of white men. The Christian spirit of the North at first rebelled against the very idea; but, already pledged to the policy of the economic proscription of Negroes through trades unions, that section, once bristling with churches dominated by abolitionists, soon yielded to the temptation of sacrificing the principles of Jesus for dollars and cents. The Negro of to-day, therefore, is hated as much by the northern religious devotee as by the southern enthusiast at the shrine of race prejudice.

Evidence as to such conditions obtaining is not wanting. In the midst of the changing order involving all but the annihilation of the Negro, the race has repeatedly appealed to the "Christian" element of the North only to have a deaf ear turned to its petition. Inasmuch as the northern ministers are influenced by rich laymen whose businesses have so many ramifications in the South, they refrain from such criticism or interference in behalf of the Negro, since it might mean economic loss. Negroes at first secured from northern churches large sums of money to establish adequate private schools and colleges throughout the South, but before these institutions could be developed these funds were diverted to the support of industrial education which the South openly interpreted to signify that no Negro must be encouraged to become the equal of any white man, and that education for him must mean something entirely different from that training provided for the Caucasian. The northern white man, more interested in developing men to produce cotton and tobacco than in the training of a race to think for itself, again bowed to mammon. Churches which once annually raised sums for the maintenance of various Negro schools have now, as a majority, restricted their contributions to Hampton and Tuskegee, where, it is believed, the ultimate distinctions of the whites and blacks can, by the process of safeguarded education, be best effected. Practically all of the so-called Christian philanthropists have followed their example.

The Negro church, however, finds itself facing still another problem. During recent years Negroes have manifested more interest in the redemption of Africa, Negro churches have long since contributed to missions and the periodical return of the apostle to the lowly far away has been awaited with the anticipation of unwonted joy; but it is only recently that the church has begun to make sacrifices for the cause. Whereas a few years ago a congregation felt that it had done its duty in raising a missionary collection of ten or fifteen dollars, that same group is to-day supporting one or two missionaries in Africa. The raising of funds for this purpose and the administration of it have been of late so well extended as noted above, that the national church organizations have had to assign this work to boards, whose business is to supply the missionaries at the various posts and extend their operations by establishing schools where they have sufficiently well established the work to require systematic training.

In spite of their well-laid plans, however, the Negro church finds itself handicapped in reaching the Africans. Controlled as that continent is by the capitalistic powers of Europe, they have much apprehension as to the sort of gospel the Negro missionary may preach in Africa, lest the natives be stirred up to the point of self-assertion. They desire that missionaries to Africa, like race leaders in the United States, be "hand-picked." In other words, the missionary movement must bow to mammon. To the heathen, then, must go those who have served only as forerunners of foreign conquests involving the discomfiture, the oppression, and in many cases the annihilation of the very people whom they professed to be saving.

Following in their wake, a certain American "Christian" organization financed by "philanthropists" recently sent to Africa Thomas J. Jones who, in behalf of his race, sought to carry out this policy. The effect of this mission was soon apparent. After having nobly served in Africa and India, Max Yergan, in International Young Men's Christian Association Secretary, appointed to serve permanently in Africa, recently toured the United States for a mission fund which the Negroes freely contributed that through him some portion of Africa might be redeemed. This man in Africa having ingratiated himself into the favor of the capitalistic government there, however, according to Yergan's statement, influenced the administration to refuse him the permit to work among his own people. The same meddler, according to a complaint made by the colored branch of the Young Men's Christian Association, all but made himself the dictator of the appointments of that department and other Negro welfare agencies sent abroad during the World War. His business now seems to be that of furnishing the world with "hand-picked" Negro leaders to damn even the natives in Africa. The white church then, has not only failed to preach the social gospel of Jesus, but is preventing the Negroes from carrying that message to their own people. In other words, the principles of the humble Nazarene must be crushed out to make money and perpetuate caste.

This and other handicaps, however, have not prevented the progress of the church. Probably the most promising aspect is that Negro ministers of to-day measure up to a higher standard than formerly. They are not diverted from their course by politics and the like. Here and there, of course, are some of little promise, who in a poverty-stricken condition accept almost any bribe offered them by political bosses, but fortunately this number is known to be rapidly decreasing. During the last generation there has developed among Negroes the feeling that the political embroglio is an unclean sphere which the minister should not enter. The increasing duties of the Negro preachers, moreover, have recently so multiplied that they have no time for such service. Experience has shown that even in the case of those who have gone into politics in self-defense that they have accomplished little good or that some layman could have handled the matter more successfully.

We have recently had two striking cases in evidence. Bishop Alexander Walters, after having rendered valuable service to the cause as an educator and minister in Kentucky, California, and Tennessee, became the ranking bishop of the African Methodist Episcopal Zion Church. He then decided that his people had been so long duped by the grafters and tricksters masquerading as the successors of Lincoln and Grant, that he would use his influence to have the Negroes divide their vote by supporting Woodrow Wilson in 1912. Dr. J. Milton Waldron, an influential Baptist minister of Washington, feeling that it would mean a new day for the Negro to have this democratic college president of many promises elevated to the headship of the nation by the aid of the Negro vote, did likewise. Disappointed in the end, however, by the hypocrisy of Wilson, who, in his heart hated Negroes, these churchmen saw themselves painfully humiliated among their people, who, in return for the large number of votes which they gave Wilson, received nothing but segregation in the civil service, elimination from public office, and conscription to do forced labor in the World War, while he was promising that the Negroes should have justice and have it abundantly.

The Negro churchmen of to-day realize, as most leaders of the race do, that the hope of the blacks lies not in politics from without but in race uplift from within in the form of social amelioration and economic development. Neither Democrats nor Republicans are interested in the Negro except so far as the race may be used to enable them to got into office. Their platform promises have Page 313

been not something to stand on but to get into office on. This does not in any sense, however, mean that the Negro minister has lost interest in public matters of concern to every citizen, but rather that he has learned the possibilities in the political world. He will in no sense withdraw from the contest in behalf of the rights of his people. His method of attack will be different. Carrying out this reconstructed policy for the rehabilitation of the race, the Negro minister, like a majority of the thinking members of this group to-day, will welcome the assistance and coöperation of the white man, but will not suffer himself to be used as a tool in connection with forces from without the circles of the race, pretending to be interested in the solution of its problems.

Carter Godwin Woodson

MARCUS GARVEY (1887-1940)

Introduction

Marcus Mosiah Garvey was a publisher, journalist, entrepreneur, Black nationalist, and founder of the Universal Negro Improvement Association and African Communities League (UNIA-ACL).

Garvey, born in St. Ann's Bay, Saint Ann, Jamaica, is best remembered as an important proponent of the Back-to-Africa movement, which encouraged those of African descent to return to their ancestral homelands. This movement inspired other movements ranging from the Nation of Islam to the Rastafari movement, which proclaimed him a prophet. Garvey said he wanted those of African ancestry to "redeem" Africa and for the European colonial powers to leave it.

In 1914 Garvey organized the Universal Negro Improvement Association and its coordinating body, the African Communities League. In 1920 the organization held its first convention in New York. The convention opened with a parade down Harlem's Lenox Avenue. That evening, before a crowd of 25,000, Garvey outlined his plan to build an African nation-state. In New York City his ideas attracted popular support, and thousands enrolled in the UNIA. He began publishing the newspaper The Negro World and toured the United States preaching black nationalism.

The Tragedy of White Injustice

(1)
Lying and stealing is the whiteman's game;
For rights of God nor man he has no shame
(A practice of his throughout the whole world)
At all, great thunderbolts he has hurled;
He has stolen everywhere-land and sea;
A buccaneer and pirate he must be,
Killing all, as he roams from place to place,
Leaving disease, mongrels-moral disgrace-
(2)
The world's history of him is replete,
From his javelin-bolt to new-built fleet:
Hosts he has robbed and crushed below;
Of friend and neighbor he has made a foe.
From our men and women he made the slave,
Then boastingly he calls himself a brave;
Cowardly, he steals on his trusting prey,
Killing in the dark, then shouts he hoo ray!

(3)
Not to go back to time pre-historic,
Only when men in Nature used to frolic,
And you will find his big, long murder-list,
Showing the plunderings of his mailed fist;
Africa, Asia and America
Tell the tale in a mournful replica
How tribesmen, Indians and Zulus fell
Fleeing the murdering bandit pell mell.
(4)
American Indian tribes were free,
Sporting, dancing, and happy as could be;
Asia's hordes lived then a life their own,
To civilization they would have grown;
Africa's millions laughed with the sun,
In the cycle of man a course to run;
In stepped the white man, bloody and grim,
The light of these people's freedom to dim.
(5)
Coolies of Asiatics they quickly made,
In Africa's blacks they built a world trade,
The Red Indians they killed with the gun,
All else of men and beasts they put to run;
Blood of murderer Cain is on their head,
Of man and beast they mean to kill dead;
A world of their own is their greatest aim,
For which Yellow and Black are well to blame.
(6)
Out of cold old Europe these white men came,
From caves, dens, and holes, without any fame,
Eating their dead's flesh and sucking their blood,
Relics of the Mediterranean flood;
Literature, science and art they stole,
After Africa had measured each pole,
Asia taught them what great learning was,
Now they frown upon what the Coolie does.
(7)
They have stolen, murdered, on their way here,
Leaving desolation and waste everywhere;
Now they boastingly tell what they have done,
Seeing not the bloody crown they have won;
Millions of Blacks died in America,

Coolies, peons, serfs, too, in Asia;
Upon these dead bones Empires they builded,
Parceling out crowns and coronets gilded.
(8)
Trifling with God's Holy Name and Law,
Mixing Christ's religion that had no flaw,
They have dared to tell us what is right,
In language of death-bullets, gas and might
Only with their brute force they hold us down,
Men of color, Yellow, Red, Black and Brown:
Not a fair chance give they our men to rise,
Christian liars we see in their eyes.
(9)
With the Bible they go to foreign lands,
Taking Christ and stealth in different hands;
Making of God a mockery on earth,
When of the Holy One there is no dearth:
They say to us: "You, sirs, are the heathen,
"We your brethren-Christian fellowman,
"We come to tell the story of our God";
When we believe, they give to us the rod.
(10)
After our confidence they have thus won,
From our dear land and treasure we must run;
Story of the Bible no more they tell,
For our souls redeemed we could go to hell.
Oil, coal and rubber, silver and gold,
They have found in wealth of our lands untold;
Thus, they claim the name of our country, all,
Of us they make then their real foot-ball.
(11)
If in the land we happen to tarry,
Most of us then become sad and sorry,
For a white man's country they say it is,
And with shot, gas and shell, they prove it his:
What can we do who love the Gracious Lord,
But fight, pray, watch and wait His Holy word:
His second coming we know to be true,
Then, He will greet the white man with his due-
(12)
This Christ they killed on Calvary's Cross.
After this Person around they did toss:

White men the Savior did crucify,
For eyes not blue, but blood of Negro tie;
Now they worship Him in their churches great,
And of the Holy Ghost they daily prate;
"One God" they say, enough for all mankind,
When in slavery the Blacks they entwined.
(13)
Their churches lines of demarcation draw;
In the name of Christ there is no such law,
Yet Black and White they have separated,
A Jim Crow God the preachers operated,
Then to Heaven they think they will all go,
When their consciences ought to tell them NO.
God is no respecter of persons great,
So each man must abide his final fate.
(14)
We'd like to see the white man converted,
And to right and justice be devoted;
Continuing in land-values to lie and steal,
Will bring destruction down upon his heel.
All that the other races want, I see,
Is the right to liberty and be free;
This the selfish white man doesn't want to give;
He alone, he thinks, has the right to live.
(15)
There shall be a bloody mix-up everywhere;
Of the white man's plunder we are aware:
Men of color the great cause understand,
Unite they must, to protect their own land.
No fool's stand on argument must we make;
Between Heaven and earth an oath we take:
"Our lands to deliver from foreign foes,
Caring not of trials and maudlin woes."
(16)
The privilege of men to protect home
Was established before the days of Rome.
Many gallant races fought and died,
Alien hordes in triumph thus defied.
Carthage did not crush Ancient Greece
For their believing in the Golden Fleece.
No other race shall kill the sturdy Blacks
If on their tribal gods we turn our backs.

(17)

From Marathon, Tours, Blenheim and the Marne
A braver courage in man has been born;
Africans died at Thermopylae's Pass,
Standing firm for Persia-men of Brass.
The Black Archers of Ethiopia stood
At Marathon, proving their stern manhood;
Senegalese held their own at Verdun,
Even though their praises are not now sung.

(18)

In the Americas' modern warfare
The Blacks have ever borne their share;
With Cortez, Washington, too, and the rest,
We did for the others our truthful best;
At St. Domingo we struck a clear blow
To show which way the wind may one day go.
Toussaint L'Ouverture was our leader then,
At the time when we were only half-men.

(19)

Italians, Menelik put to chase,
Beating a retreat in uneven haste;
So down the line of history we come,
Black, courtly, courageous and handsome.
No fear have we today of any great men
From Napoleon back to Genghis Khan;
All we ask of men is "Give a square deal,"
Returning to others same right we feel.

(20)

With a past brilliant, noble and grand,
Black men march to the future hand in hand;
We have suffered long from the white man's greed,
Perforce he must change his unholy creed.
Stealing, bullying and lying to all
Will drag him to ignominious fall;
For men are wise-yes, no longer are fools,
To have grafters make of them still cheap tools.

(21)

Each race should be proud and stick to its own,
And the best of what they are should be shown;
This is no shallow song of hate to sing,
But over Blacks there should be no white king.
Every man on his own foothold should stand,

Claiming a nation and a Fatherland!
White, Yellow and Black should make their own laws,
And force no one-sided justice with flaws.
(22)
Man will bear so much of imposition,
Till he starts a righteous inquisition.
History teaches this as a true fact,
Upon this premise all men do act.
Sooner or later each people take their stand
To fight against the strong, oppressive hand;
This is God's plan, raising man to power,
As over sin and greed He makes him tower.
(23)
This trite lesson the white man has Dot learnt,
Waiting until he gets his fingers burnt.
Millenniums ago, when white men slept,
The great torch of light Asia kept.
Africa at various periods shone
Above them all as the bright noonday sun;
Coming from the darkened cave and hut,
The white man opened the gate that was shut.
(24)
Gradually light bore down upon him,
This ancient savage who was once dim;
When he commenced to see and move around,
He found the book of knowledge on the ground;
Centuries of wonder and achievements
Were cast before him in God's compliments;
But, like the rest, he has now fallen flat,
And must in the Lord's cycle yield for that.
(25)
We shall always be our brother's keeper,
Is the injunction of the Redeemer;
Love and tolerance we must ever show,
If in Grace Divine we would truly grow;
This is the way clear to God's great kingdom-
Not by the death-traps of Argonne or Somme,
When the terrible white man learns this much,
He will save even the African Dutch.
(26)
South Africa has a grave problem now
In reducing the Negro to the plow;

White men are to live in their lazy case
While the patience of the goodly natives tease;
They make new laws to have Africa white
Precipitating righteous and ready fight:
Around the world they speak of being so just,
Yet, in fact, no lone white man can you trust.
(27)
In Australia the same they have done,
And so, wherever man's confidence won:
This they call the religion of the Christ,
And upon their willing slave try to foist.
Only a part of the world can you fool,
And easily reduce to your foot-stool;
The other one-half is always awake,
And from it you cannot liberty take.
(28)
"And now valiant Black men of the west
Must ably rise to lead and save the rest":
This is the ringing call Africa sounds,
As throughout the Godly world it resounds;
Clansmen! black, educated, virile and true!
Let us prove too that we are loyal blue.
We must win in the blessed fight of love,
Trusting on the Maker of men above.
(29)
The Christian world is yet to be saved!
Man, since the risen Christ has not behaved!
Wanton, reckless, wicked, he still remains,
Causing grief, sorrow, tears and human pains!
Can we show the Godly light to anyone
Seeking for earnest truth while marching on?
If so, friend, let us tell you now and here,
For love, freedom, justice let's all prepare!
(30)
God in His Glorious Might is coming,
Wonderful signs He is ever showing,
Unrest, earthquakes, hurricanes, floods and storms
Are but revelations of Heavenly Forms:
The proud white scientist thinks he is wise
But the Black man's God comes in true disguise,
God is sure in the rumbling earthquake,
When He is ready, the whole world will shake.

(31)

The Armageddon is gathering now;
The sign is on every oppressed man's brow:
The whites who think they are ever so smart
Do not know other men can play their part:
When the opportune time is almost here
Black, Yellow and Brown will be everywhere,
In union of cause they'll stand together
And storms of the bully boldly weather.

(32)

Their gases and shots, and their rays of death,
Shall only be child's play-a dream of Seth,
For out of the clear, sleeping minds of ages,
Wonders shall be written on history's pages:
Our buried arts and sciences then shall rise,
To show how for centuries we were wise:
Silent tongues we kept, by God's true command,
Until of us, action, He did demand.

(33)

Under the canopy of Nature's law
We shall unitedly and bravely draw.
On the plains of God's green Amphitheatre,
Swords, in rhythm with Divine Meter:
Jehovah's Day will have surely come,
With Angelic strains and Seraphic hum:
The Guides of Heaven will direct the way,
Keeping us from wandering far astray.

(34)

Like around the high walls of Jericho,
March we, as Rio speeds through Mexico:
Trumpets loud will the Guiding Angels blow.
As scatter the enemy to-and-fro:
Heaven will have given us a battle cry:
"Oh Brave Soldiers you shall never die":
Rally to the command of Heaven's King,
As Cherubim to Him your tidings bring.

(35)

See the deadly clash of arms! Watch! They fall!
There is stillness!-It is the funeral pall!
A sad requiem now is to be sung!
Not by Angels. but in their human tongue!
The cruel masters of yesterday are done!

From the fields of battle they have run!
A brand new world of justice is to be!
"You shall be a true brother unto me!"
(36)
This is a forecast of God's wrath:
White man, will you turn from the evil path?
There is still hope for you, among the good:
If you will seek the bigger-brotherhood:
Stop your tricks, frauds, lying and stealing,
And settle down to fair and square dealing;
If not, prepare yourself for gloomy hell,
As God announces the sorrowing knell.
(37)
Your lies, to us called diplomacy,
Are known by us, a brazen phantasy;
You imprison men for crimes not so great,
While on your silly wisdom you do prate.
The masses are soberly watching you;
They know that you are false and so untrue.
The laborers of your race you oppress,
As well as black and other men you distress.
(38)
If you were wise you'd read between the lines
Of feudal isms and others of old times.
Men have fought against ugly royal gods,
Burying them 'neath European sods.
Such to heartless masters the people do,
From Syracuse to bloody Waterloo;
Wonderful lessons for any sober man,
Who worships not idols or the god Pan.
(39)
In the vicious order of things today,
The poor, suffering black man has no say;
The plot is set for one 'gainst the other,
With organization they mustn't bother.
"If one should show his head as a leader,
Whom we cannot use, the rest to pilfer,
We shall discredit him before his own,
And make of him a notorious clown."
(40)
"In Africa we have plans to match him,
While the native Chiefs of their lands we trim;

The Blacks schooled in England are too smart,
On the I BETTER THAN YOU scheme we'll start,
And have them thinking away from the rest;
This philosophy for them is best-
Easier then we can rob the good lands
And make ourselves rich without soiled hands."
(41)
"We will so keep from them the' NEGRO WORLD'
That no news they'll have of a flag unfurled;
Should they smuggle copies in, and we fail,
We will send the sly agents all to jail."
This is the white man's plan across the sea.
Isn't this wily and vicious as can be?
In other lands they have things arranged
Differently, yet they have never changed.
(42)
In America they have Colored to tell
What they know of the rest, whose rights they sell;
The Blacks they do try to keep always down,
But in time they will reap what they have sown.
No Negro's good life is safe in the STATES
If he tries to be honest with his mates;
In politics he must sell at the polls,
To suit the white man in his many roles.
(43)
The West Indian whites are tricky, too;
They have schemes curved like the horse's shoe:
There is only one opening for the black-
Three other sides are close up to his back;
Hence he never gets a chance to look in
Whilst staring at the world of mortal sin.
Yes, this is the game they play everywhere,
Leaving the Negro to gloom and despair.
(44)
And now, white man, can we reason with you,
For each race in the world to give it due?
Africa for Africans is most right;
Asia for Asiatics is light;
To Europe for the Europeans,
America for the Americans:
This is the doctrine of the goodly Klan,
Now fighting for the alien ban.

(45)
Blacks do not hate you because you are white;
We believe in giving to all men right;
Some we do keep for ourselves to protect,
Knowing it as a virtue to select.
We are willing to be friends of mankind,
Pulling all together with none behind,
Growing in sane goodness and fellowship,
Choosing but the Almighty to worship.
(46)
Let Justice prevail, at home and abroad;
Cease over the weak your burdens to lord;
You're but mortal man, like the rest of us-
Of this happy truth we need make no fuss.
All Nature's kindly gifts are justly ours-
Suns, oceans, trees, to pretty flowers-
So we need not doubt the marvelous fact
That God has given to each man his tract.
(47)
The common thief now steals a crust of bread,
The law comes down upon his hungry head;
The haughty land robber steals continents,
With men, oil, gold, rubber and all contents.
The first you say is a hopeless convic',
While the latter escapes the law by trick;
That grave, one-sided justice will not do-
The poor call for consideration, too.
(48)
The rich white man starts the unholy war,
Then from the line of action he keeps far;
He pushes to the front sons of the poor,
There to do battle, die, suffer galore,
As the guns rage, liberty loans they raise,
And in glorious tones sing freedom's praise.
This is the method to gain them more wealth,
Then, after vict'ry they practice great stealth.
(49)
Those who make wars should first go to the front,
And of gas, shot and shell bear there the brunt:
In first lines of action they are all due,
If to their country and people they are true:
When this is demanded in right of all,

There will be no more deadly cannon ball:
The downtrodden poor whites and blacks should join
And prevent rich whites our rights to purloin.
(50)
Weeping mothers, tricked in patriotism,
Send their sons to fight for liberalism:
Into most far off lands they go with pride,
Thinking right and God be on their side:
When they get into the bloody trenches,
They find of lies they had awful drenches:
The people they were all supposed to kill,
Like themselves, had gotten of lies their fill.
(51)
In the private club and drawing room,
White schemes are hatched for the nation's doom:
Speculators, grafters, bankers-all,
With politicians join to hasten the fall,
By stealing rights from other citizens,
As if they weren't fit or true denizens:
How awful is this daring story
That we tell to men young and hoary.
(52)
Crooked lawyers, friends and politicians,
Corrupt the morals of the good nations:
Between them and others, fly plots they make,
Innocent citizens' money to take;
From banks they find out your real account,
Then have you indicted on legal count:
Large fees they charge, to have you surely broke,
Then, to prison you go-what a sad joke!
(53)
The white man controls cable and wireless,
Connections by ships with force and duress:
He keeps black races of the world apart,
So to his schemes they may not be smart:
"There shall be no Black Star Line Ships," he says,
"For that will interfere with our crooked ways:
"I'll disrupt their business and all their plans,
"So they might not connect with foreign lands."
(54)
Black women are raped by the lordly white,
In colonies, the shame ne'er reaching light:

In other countries abuses are given,
Shocking to morality and God's Heaven.
Hybrids and mongrels are the open result,
Which the whites give us as shameful insult:
How can they justify this? None can tell;
Yet, crimes of the blacks are rung with a bell.
(55)
White men newspapers subsidize and own,
For to keep them on their racial throne:
Editors are slaves to fool the public,
Reporters tell the lie and pull the trick;
The papers support only what they want,
Yet truth, fair play, and justice, daily flaunt:
They make criminals out of honest men,
And force judges to send them to the Pen.
(56)
Capitalists buy up all blank space
To advertise and hold the leading place
For to influence public opinion
And o'er Chief-editors show dominion.
The average man is not wise to the scheme,
He, the reformer, must now redeem;
This isn't a smooth or very easy job,
For, you, of your honor and name, they'll rob.
(57)
The bankers employ men to shoot and kill,
When we interfere with their august will;
They take the savings of deaf, dumb and poor,
Gamble with it here and on foreign shore:
In oil, gold, rum, rubber they speculate,
Then bring their foreign troubles upon the State:
Friends in Government they control at will;
War they make, for others, our sons to kill.
(58)
The many foundations of researches,
And the foreign missions and their churches,
Are organized to catch the mild converts
Who don't understand the way of perverts.
Our wealth when discovered by researchers,
In lands of the Native occupiers
Is surveyed and marked to the river's rim
Till they dislodge a Premprey or Abd-El-Krim.

(59)

It is not freedom from prison we seek;
It is freedom from the big thieves we meet:
All life is now a soulless prison cell,
A wild suspense between heaven and hell:
Selfish, wicked whites have made it so;
To the Author and Finisher we'll go,
Carrying our sad cares and many wrongs
To Him in prayers and holy songs.

(60)

This is the game that is played all around,
Which is sure one day to each race rebound:
The world is gone mad with the money craze,
Leaving the poor man in a gloomy haze:
There must be world reorganization,
To save the masses from exploitation-,
The cry is for greater democracy.
A salvation from man's hypocrisy.

(61)

Out in this heartless, bitter oasis
There's now very little of human bliss;
The cold capitalists and money sharks
Have made life unsafe, like ocean barks.
The once dear, lovely Garden of Eden
Has become the sphere of men uneven;
The good God created but an equal pair,
Now man has robbed others of their share.

(62)

Shall there be freedom of liberal thought?
No; the white man has all agencies bought-
Press, pulpit, law and every other thing-
Hence o'er public opinion he reigns king.
This is indisputable, glaring fact;
You may find it out with a little tact.
College tutors and presidents are paid,
So that in universities schemes are laid.

(63)

Cleopatra, Empress Josephine,
Were black mongrels like of the Philippine:
Mixtures from black and other races they,
Yet "true" the white man's history will not say
To those who seek the light of pure knowledge

In the inquiring world, school or college.
Napoleon fell for a Negro woman;
So did the Caesars, and the Great Roman.
(64)
Anthony lost his imperial crown
To escape Cleo's fascinating -frown.
This truth the New Negro knows very well,
And to his brothers in darkness he'll tell.
No one can imprison the brain of man-
That was never intended in God's plan;
You may persecute, starve, even debase-
That will not kill truth nor virtue efface.
(65)
The white man now enjoys his "Vanity Fair";
He thinks of self and not of others care-
Fratricidal course, that to hell doth lead-
This is poison upon which the gentry feed.
Blacks should study physics, chemistry, more,
While the gold God all such sinners adore;
This is no idle prattle talk to you;
It has made the banners red, white and blue.
(66)
Out of the clear of God's Eternity
Shall rise a kingdom of Black Fraternity;
There shall be conquests o'er militant forces;
For as man proposes, God disposes.
Signs of retribution are on every hand:
Be ready, black men, like Gideon's band.
They may scoff and mock at you today,
But get you ready for the awful fray.
(67)
In the fair movement of God's Abounding Grace
There is a promised hope for the Negro race;
In the sublimest truth of prophecy,
God is to raise. them to earthly majesty,
Princes shall come out of Egypt so grand,
The noble black man's home and Motherland,
The Psalmist spoke in holy language clear,
As Almighty God's triune will declare.
(68)
In their conceit they see not their ruin;
You soldiers of trust, be up and doing!

Remember Belshazzar's last joyous feast,
And Daniel's vision of the Great Beast!
"Weighed in the balances and found wanting"
Is the Tekel to which they are pointing.
This interpretation of the Prophet
Black men shall never in their dreams forget.
(69)
The resplendent rays of the morning sun
Shall kiss the Negro's life again begun;
The music of God's rhythmic natural law
Shall stir Afric's soul without Divine flaw.
The perfume from Nature's rosy hilltops
Shall fall on us spiritual dewdrops.
Celestial beings shall know us well,
For, by goodness, in death, with them we'll dwell.
(70)
And how sad a finis!
With battleship, artillery and gun
White men have put all God's creatures to run;
Heaven and earth they have often defied.,
Taking no heed of the rebels that died.
God can't be mocked in this daring way,
So the evil ones shall sure have their day.
"You may rob, you may kill, for great fame,"
So says the white man, for this is his game.

Marcus Garvey

VERNON JOHNS (1892-1965)

Introduction

Vernon Johns was an American minister, and inspirational civil rights leader. He worked tirelessly in the struggle for Civil Rights for African American's since the 1920's. He was Martin Luther King, Jr.'s predecessor as pastor at Dexter Avenue Baptist Church in Montgomery, Alabama, and a mentor of Ralph Abernathy, Wyatt Walker, and many others in the Southern Christian Leadership Conference's circle. The father of the American Civil Rights Movement, he laid the foundation on which King and others would build. In 1948 Johns accepted the post of minister at Dexter Avenue Baptist Church in Montgomery Alabama.

Born in Darlington Heights, Virginia, in Prince Edward County, he was educated at Union University, Oberlin College, and Virginia Seminary, with later studies in the University of Chicago. He was ordained to the Baptist ministry in 1918. After teaching homiletics and New Testament interpretation in the Virginia Theological Seminary for one year, in 1920 he became pastor of the Court Street Church of Lynchburg—one of the old colored Churches of the South, organized many years before the Civil War. Johns served as pastor of the Dexter Avenue Baptist Church from 1947 to 1952.

Transfigured Moments

Then answered Peter, and said unto Jesus, Lord, it is good for us to be here: if thou wilt, let us make here three tabernacles; one for thee, and one for Moses, and one for Elijah. Matthew 17:4

Peter, James and John, who had already gone with the Master to the death bed in the house of Jairus, and would very soon come closer to his agony in Gethsemane than the other disciples, were now with him in "a place apart", somewhere on the slopes of Hermon. Strange things were happening there: things difficult for people to believe until they have felt the unfathomed mystery of life, and learned that "there are more things in heaven and earth than we have dreamed in our philosophy." As the Divine man prayed that night, on the snow-capped mountain, with the weight of humanity's sin and humanity's hope upon his heart, his disciples beheld his body suddenly overcast with an unfamiliar luster. His pure soul had overflowed and clothed his figure with a wonderful radiance. His face shone as the sun, and his garments became glistening white such "as no fuller on earth could white them"; the glory of Jesus, already attested by a few fine and sensitive souls, was now apparent to the very eyes of men. And Moses and Elijah, venerable pioneers of law and prophecy, had come through the intervening mystery which separates the living from the dead, and were talking with Jesus, within sight and hearing of the disciples. Then a voice broke forth from the luminous clouds: "This is my beloved son: hear ye him!"

Any one acquainted with Simon Peter will not be surprised if he speaks now. He is the type of man who can be depended on to say what others must need think and feel, but dare not utter. He was a valuable man to Jesus: a rock foundation man, for this very reason he revealed his thoughts and made it possible for Jesus to give them direction. Bishop

McConnell says that Peter asked many foolish questions, but those questions brought from Jesus very wise answers. It would be difficult for us to sojourn with Simon and dodge sensitive questions; covering up grave issues that so nearly concern us, and trying to hide them from ourselves as though they did not exist. The blundering genius for expression, which was the virtue of Simon Peter, would save us from the folly of applying ostrich wisdom to vital problems. If we had the courage to talk frankly concerning our problems, there would be less occasion to fight about them. In grave moral and social situations where the spokesmen of Jesus, so-called, keep dependably mute, Simon Peter would certainly have something to say or at least ask some embarrassing questions. Peter was a true disciple of the one who came to earth "That thoughts out of many hearts might be revealed."

So on the Mount of Transfiguration, while experiencing was rife, James reflected deeply, John thrilled with awe, and Peter spoke! Peter felt the tides running high in his soul: and he said so: "Lord it is good to be here." When Peter has a weighty idea or a generous impulse, it is likely to get expression. No matter what celebrities are present, no matter how delicate the situation, no matter if he breaks down short of the goal which he sets for himself; at least his Master may count on him to give honest expression to the best that he knows and feels. This is the man whom Jesus commissions to feed his sheep and lambs. This is the foundation man, on whose God-inspired utterance the Kingdom will be built against which the gates of hell shall not prevail. One of the biographers of Jesus felt it necessary to apologize for Peter's speech during the Transfiguration. "He knew not what to say, for he was sore afraid." There are always disciples, more cautious, but less valuable than Peter, who guard their words very zealously in tense situations, and for fear they may say something indiscreet will almost certainly be silent. They talk most when there is but little need to say anything, and the topic of their conversation is not likely to be material which will spread fire in the earth or set a father against his son, or make a man's enemies those of his own household. There are things "that Babbitt will not talk about". No apology was really needed for what Peter said. Who can doubt that it was good to be there, high upon Hermon, in those Transfigured Moments! The experience was so rich and lasting that it went to record, many years later, in three of the Gospels and one New Testament epistle: and the glory which shone that night, in "a mountain place apart", lingers after two thousand years on every continent and over every sea.

It is good to be the possessor of some mountain-top experience.
Now to know life on the heights, is to suffer an impoverishing incompleteness. To be sure, there is better opportunity for practical pursuits in the valley regions, and life is easier and safer there: but views are possible from the mountain-top which are not to be had in the vale. A missionary in the Balkans once took a small boy, who lived at the base of a mountain, on a journey up its side. When they gained the summit, the little climber looked this way and that, and then said with astonishment: "My! What a wonderful world. I never dreamed it was so large."

Horizons broaden when we stand on the heights. There is always the danger that we will make of life too much of a dead-level existence; that we will make of life a slavish following of the water courses; a monotonous tread of beaten paths; a matter of absorbing, spiritless, deadening routine. There is the danger that we will drop our lives into the passing current to be kept steadily going we hardly know where or why. Crowded in the throngs that traverse the common ways, we proceed through life with much motion and little vision.

The late President Wilson, in a wonderful essay, spoke of the man who allows his duties to rise about him like a flood. Such a man goes on through the years "swimming with sturdy stroke, his eyes level with the surface, never seeing any clouds or any passing ships." We can pay such regular tribute to motion that all valid sense of direction is lost; so that all our hurrying activities may prove but the rush to ruin. In view of this, it is good for us, occasionally at least, to clamber up from the levels of our set habits of thought, our artificial actions and our settled prejudices to some loftier plane which affords a more commanding view than we have from the crowded thoroughfare, the low familiar ways. From some mountain eminence let us have occasionally a quiet look upon life, to reflect what it means and whither it is carrying us. The luminaries of humanity were familiar with elevated ground. Moses, Elijah, Mohammed and Jesus all had mountain traditions. It is said by a well-known Old Testament interpreter that the religious history of the Hebrew people is inseparable from the topography of their country. The mountains round about Jerusalem are tied up with the vision of God and the vision of life, which Israel gave to mankind.

Who of all the contemporaries of Jesus, busy in marketplace fields and thoroughfares, dreamed that the next great strides of history would take their direction from the visions of one who was praying in the midst of three unheralded fishermen, far above sea level and the level of life! So it was. So it may ever be. How many people in high and lofty moments, when they have taken the time and pains to climb above the dingy, foggy levels of incorporated thinking and living, have struck out for themselves and others new and better courses! "I thought on my ways, and turned my feet . . ." "And he taketh them up into an exceeding high mountain." These passages belong to the experience of epoch makers. On the heights is the location for moral discovery. It is a slower process and requires stouter gear to do the mountain road than to run along the shining speedways of the valley. But woe to the world when there are no visitors on the heights!

It is good to be present when the ordinary is transformed
when the dull plain garments of a peasant becoming shining white, and the obscure "mountain place, apart", comes into the gaze of centuries. It is good to see the commonplace illumined and the glory of the common people revealed. On the Mount of Transfiguration there is no representative of wealth, social rank or official position. The place could boast in the way of population only four poor men, members of a despised race, and of the remnant of a subjected and broken nation. But it is here, instead of Jerusalem or Rome, that the voice of God is heard. It is here, instead of Mount Moriah, where the mighty temple stands, that the cloud of glory hovers. Out there where a carpenter and three fishermen kept vigil with the promise of a new day, God is a living Reality and life is charged with meaning and radiance. Out there in a deserted place, the meek and lowly are enhaoled.

There is no recounting the instances where the things that are excellent have blossomed in unexpected places. "He giveth power to the faint; and to them that have not might He increaseth strength." A man who is not a prophet, neither a prophet's son, is called by the Lord from following the sheep, to prophesy to the House of Israel. In the heyday of Egyptian civilization, God visits the wilderness of Midian and commissions a shepherd for the most significant work of the age:

"In the fifteenth year of the reign of Tiberius Caesar, Pontius Pilate being governor of Judaea, and Herod tetrarch of Galilee, and his brother Philip tetrarch of Iturea and the region of Trachonitis, and Lysanias the tetrarch of Abilene; in the high priesthood of Annas and Caiphas, the word of the Lord came to John the son of Zacharias, in the wilderness."

"Who is this man that is answering Douglas in your State?" wrote prominent statesman of the East, to the editor of a Chicago paper, concerning the unheralded Lincoln. "Do you realize that his knowledge of the most important question before the American people is complete and profound; that his logic is unanswerable and his style inimitable?" It is the illumination of the commonplace, the transfiguring of the ordinary, the glistening radiance of a peasant's seamless robe!

There are two ways in which this transfiguring of the ordinary is specially needed. The lowly ones of earth need to experience this transformation. The great majority of our lives must be lived apart from any elaborate or jeweled settings; must plod along without any spectacular achievements. We ordinary people, then, must learn how to set the scraggy bushes of the wilderness ablaze with glory and make the paths that we tread, under the pressure of duty, like Holy Ground. In the humblest routine, we must discover our task as a part of the transforming enterprise of the Heavenly Father. The laborer that toils on a country road must know himself as the builder of a highway to a Christian civilization. The cobbler may be a mere cobbler, or he may transform his occupation and be a foundation man in the Kingdom of Christ. Make tents if we must, but we will illumine the old task with a radiant new heart, and, with our tent making, make a shining new earth. If toil be confined to the same old field, keep a land of promise shining in the distance and call down angels to sing until the drab turns golden. "My garden is very small," said an old German, "but it's wondrous high." Let us light up the commonplace and make the ordinary radiant. Let us make seamless peasant garments shine like the sun.

Again, those who think themselves the favored ones of earth need a transforming vision of life among the lowly. There is no warrant in the theory and practice of Jesus for dull and frigid doctrines of "lesser breeds within the law." If the life of Jesus means anything, it means implicit faith in the universal capacity of man for the highest character and worth. To this end, the doors of the kingdom of the best are thrown open to all the points of the compass that men may "come from the North and the South, the East and the West to sit down with Abraham and Isaac, in the Kingdom of God."

A low theory, a despicable view of a given group must usually be thrown ahead like a barrage before we can follow with the outrage and mistreatment of that group. We make them hydra-headed in theory so that we may be inhuman in our practice toward them. The validity for such judgment crops out unaware at times, as when masters avow their slaves' inability to learn and at the same time penalize them if caught with a book. Humanity that has climbed to places of social and economic authority must learn how to trace the rainbow tint over the life of the lowly, and to interpret the swelling and ferment at the bottom of society as a healthy and beautiful essay of one's fellowmen in the direction of fuller life. It is a heart strangely unChrist-like that cannot thrill with joy when the least of men begin to pull in the direction of the stars.

It is good to be in the presence of persons who can kindle us for fine, heroic living.
The population on the Mount of Transfiguration was very small, but it was tremendously significant. Jesus, Moses and Elijah! In the presence of personality like this, men can kindle their torches and go forth in life as bearers of light and heat. Humanity needs the contagion of lofty spirits. Humanity needs contact with persons who are aglow with the good life. All too frequently our righteousness is sufficiently meager to go to waste: it is not vital enough to communicate itself. Mr. Roosevelt's criticism of his progressive party was that it meant well, but meant it feebly. That is often the trouble with our righteousness. It lacks intensity. It does not make itself felt. We are trying to grind great mills with a quart of water; we would set great masses of cold and slimy material aglow with a wet match. We have our hands full of half-way measures. We scrap a part of our navies. We enthrone Justice in places where there is no serious objection to it. We practice brotherhood within carefully restricted areas. We forgive other people's enemies. We carry a Bible but not a cross. Instead of the Second Mile, we go a few yards of the first and then wonder that Christian goals are not realized. "O fools and slow of heart to believe all that the prophets have spoken!" When we lift ourselves, at least from the ruin and entanglements of our diluted and piecemeal righteousness, it will be under the leadership of persons for whom righteousness was a consuming and holy fire, instead of a mere lukewarm and foggy something. It is such leadership, such righteous dynamics as this that we find in the presence of Jesus and Moses and Elijah. "We beheld his glory, glory as of the only begotten of the Father, full of grace and truth. And of his fullness we have all received." You can kindle at a flame like that! It is the full receptacle that overflows, spreading its content to neighboring borders. It is a flame vital enough not to be extinguished by a slight jostle at which men can kindle. " I have come to set a fire in the earth."

We need power for renunciation
In the service of social progress, justice and brotherhood there are views and possessions of which one must have power to let go. Nothing short of power will work the transformation. But we are apt to hang on to our self-love, our vantage points, our place with the strong, our purpose of self-advancement. And we get no strength for the demands laid upon us from the weaklings on our level.. But here on the mountain-top is personality in which the power of renunciation rises to white heat!

"By faith, Moses when he was come to years, refused to be called the son of Pharaoh's daughter, choosing rather to suffer affliction with the people of God than to enjoy the pleasures of sin for a season; esteeming the reproach of Christ greater riches than the treasure of Egypt."

When this ancient Hero exchanged a princely existence at court for exile in Midian, and defied the oppressor in the interest of the oppressed, he lighted a flame a t which humanity through thousands of years has kindled power of heroic renunciation. It is good to sit in the presence of Moses if one is to live the life of heroic self-denial.

And there is a power on the Mount of Transfiguration which kindles tongues and sends forth in evil times for the service of justice. Ahab the king has lifted his bloody hand against a weak subject. He has killed Naboth and taken his patch of land to fill out a nook in one of the royal estates. It is a dastardly act, but Naboth is weak and Ahab mighty, so the voices of justice are not heard. Tyranny broods restfully over the face of the nation. Murder and robbery issue from the very sea of law; and all is well. Thank God, here comes a loud, clear note of discord in the evil harmony! Ahab has gone down to his ill-gotten vineyard and Elijah meets him there. No one can stand with Elijah in that garden without feeling the thrill of manhood: it is a fine place to kindle holy courage. Mighty is Ahab in Israel, but mighty also is Elijah in the service of truth. The Tisbite, in his camel's hair, rubs against the purple of a king mighty in war and peace. He does not wait for royal permission. One listening to that conversation without seeing the participants would have mistaken peasant for king and king for peasant.

"Hast thou killed and also taken possession? Has thou found me, O mine enemy?" And Elijah answered, "I have found thee; and thus saith the Lord, in the spot where dogs licked the blood of Naboth, shall dogs lick thy blood."

The courage of Elijah is a glowing flame at which humanity has kindled power to shake the foundations of a thousand despotisms! And how Jesus could kindle people for courageous, loving and lofty living! Here is Zacchaeus hovering at zero! His malady is not emotional, passionate weakness, but cold-blooded guile. He is a professional trader in the political misfortunes of his nation. His business is to sell the helplessness of his own race to the Roman overlord, and he has made the business pay. With Zacchaeus "business is business." The trouble with Zacchaeus is that he has never been shown a pattern of selfishness as large as his own selfishness. There have been little sputters of righteousness here and there, but nothing dramatic in that line. Zacchaeus feels some serious lack in connection with his own life and method, but he has never seen character the opposite of his own that was sufficiently large or radiant to be attractive. In the flaming proximity of Jesus the lost son of Israel finds himself. His frigidity thaws up: a new found sense of justice and generosity blazes out: "Half of my goods I give to the poor, and if I have wronged any man by false accusation I will restore unto him fourfold". At the flaming soul of Jesus the frigid soul of Zacchaeus is set aglow.

Here is a woman who is a victim of a great primal emotion. Her name has dishonorable associations; her respect is buried deep beneath the ashes of excess. Each day finds her more shameless and deeper lost; each person passing throws a few more ashes upon the tiny spark of virtue left amid the embers. A lustful suggestion from this man, a contemptuous look from that women, and the dim inner vision of something wholesome and pure fades rapidly toward extinction. But Jesus comes along! In the atmosphere about him every slumbering impulse of love and purity begins to quicken. He discovers the faint spark in the ashes and embers and warms it to life. He is so pure himself that this poor woman, sunk to the depths, feels the contagion of his character pulling her toward the stars. A touch of shame mounts the throne in her cheek where a calloused indifference had sat: it turns to penitence and then to hope. "Can I become a worthy person in spite of all that is?" her heart is asking the Master. And the Master, who understands the language of hearts and listens for it, answers:

"Verily, I say unto you, wherever this gospel is preached in all the earth, your name and character shall attend it like the fragrance of precious ointment."

Again, the strength of a Personality, radiant with truth and love, had lifted a life from shame to sainthood.

Jesus kindled the consciousness of human brotherhood in the most self-conscious and provincial of all races. His character was so dramatically free from all class and national and racial hatreds and prejudices that no follower could long mistake him. To mistake him would have been to cease following!

"There is no difference between Jew and Greek, barbarian, Scythian, bond or free, but all are one in Christ Jesus."

"I perceive that God is no respecter of persons, but in every nation they that fear God and work righteousness are acceptable with him."

"Out of one blood hath God created all nations to swell upon the face of the earth."

This is the language of men who had kindled their lives at the feet of Jesus for the wise and noble adventure in human brotherhood.

It is good to be present when the great, distant peaks of history join hands to point the way of life: when seers, standing in different ages and places, one on Sinai another on Carmel and another on Olivet come together to speak to us out of the wisdom of the ages concerning the way and the meaning of life. All this is the privilege of those who frequent the heights! Up there we can read history with our eyes instead of our prejudices. Up there we do not hear the clamor of time-servers and self-servers: and as we look down from the heights, it is too far to descry the hue of faces or the peculiarity of skulls, all we can see is the forms of men, toiling or contending in the valleys—swayed by the same hopes and fears, the same joys and sorrows. The whole creation groaning in travail and pain together and waiting for deliverance; one in need, one in destiny. "If drunk with sight of Power" we incline to boastings and vauntings, the seers on the heights say to us out of the wealth of the ages:

"Not by might; not by power; but by My Spirit saith the Lord."

And they have wide inductions from the debris of many civilizations as warrant for the utterance. On the heights, too, there is hope for the world! Too often, history strikes us as a medley of blind and futile ramblings. "A tale told by an idiot amid great sound and fury, signifying nothing."

But on the mountain-top, perspective is possible; above the confusion of the plains, the visitant beholds Moses in one age, Elijah in another, Jesus, Luther and Lincoln, each in another; all joining hands across the Ages and moving humanity in the direction of that "one far off, divine event to which the whole creation moves."

"It is good for us to be here."

Vernon Johns, 1925

WALTER COACHMAN (1899-1978)

Introduction

In the following entry Walter Coachman described his life to the Federal Writers' Project in 1939. South Carolina, where he lived, was a cotton state in America's Deep South; in Walter's day the population here was forty percent black. Coachman was a Baptist pastor, of Manning Grove, Holiness Church.

Originally, America's black population had been brought to South Carolina by force, to work as slaves on the cotton plantations. By the early 20th Century, slavery was long abolished, but Walter's parents, like many poor blacks, remained tied to land they didn't own, dependent on a local white farmer. They were sharecroppers, taking, as the name suggests, a share of the crop. It was a hard life.

The whites in the South weren't all rich plantation owners, far from it. But most, rich and poor, were determined to keep alive the racist hierarchy of the old slave days. State laws—the so-called "Jim Crow' laws—segregated blacks from white, keeping them apart. According to the American Constitution, blacks could vote. But State laws blocked that right with requirements for literacy or land-ownership that blacks could rarely meet. Whites often deluded themselves that the blacks accepted their situation. The reality was, they had no choice. Because behind the force of the law, was the threat of violence. The Ku Klux Klan, a white supremacist movement, had grown in strength. Everyone knew the penalty for stepping out of line.

I Am a Negro

A mere whimsy of fate made me black and you white. It might easily have been the other way around. You were born with the blessing of Providence. Hands were extended to help you the day you were born, and you may go as far as your capabilities permit. But me? The cards were stacked against me the day I came into the world. I can go just so far—no further.

I was born the twelfth son in a family of thirteen children. My father was as black as the ace of spades, and killed himself working for old man Whitelaw on the twelve horse plantation just outside Bennetsville.

I realized early in life that I was a Negro, and that it was the lot of our people to get the bum end of everything, all things said to the contrary. My father worked hard, made good crops, and was always in the hole at the end of the year.

My mother was a woman of most forceful character even if she was colored. She fought tooth and toe-nail to see that us children got some education. I went to a one-room Negro school about three miles from where we lived. I learned to read, write and figure. I was, and still am, interested in figuring! When I was twelve, I had gone through the fifth grade. I began to figure against old man Whitelaw. My mother was in full accord. Pappy always said it was a sin to take advantage of people. It was against the Bible. Pappy was a good, Christian Negro. He was too meek to suit my mother. I remember my first experience in looking out for number one. My father had me hitch up the two horse wagon and haul the corn in. Two loads to Mr., Whitelaw's barn, and one to ours. I made the mistake of occasionally hauling two loads to our barn and one to old man Whitelaw's. Honest? Of course, it was honest! Didn't Whitelaw charge my father twelve dollars an acre for corn land? I wasn't exactly a fool even as a child.

Later, I checked up on the cotton and found the biggest part in Mr. Whitelaw's cotton house. It was waiting there to be ginned. I slipped in there one night and made a rough estimate between the value of that cotton, and the cost of fertilizer and the value of the land, and I came out two bales to the good. That cotton was ginned at Whaley's gin down below Bennetsville. I hauled it away in the night! Pappy came out pretty good the next year.

When I was eighteen, I left home and went to Columbia to go to Allen University. I hadn't been there long when my father began to go in the hole again, and I had to shift around to pay my tuition. I got a job with Mrs. Reynolds, a widow lady who loved flowers and had a wonderful garden. She didn't have much money. In fact I soon found out while working around the flowers and garden that she was really up against it. She had given me the yard work to help me stay in school. There was an acre lot next to her house that belonged to her, so one day after studying the situation thoroughly I suggested that she turn it into a flower and plant garden, and sell plants, bulbs and flowers. I told her I would put in every minute I wasn't in school to make it go over. She fell in for the plan right off, and I certainly put out on that bare acre.

I was working hard at my classes, studying theology, and every moment I could spare I slipped away to work in the garden. It soon showed the result of intensive cultivation, and it wasn't long before it became a showplace in Columbia. People would stop their cars along the street and just sit and look. I painted a sign or two stating that we had plants of all kinds for sale. I planted plenty tomato, pepper, and egg-plant seed, and sold every plant.

It wasn't long before Mrs. Reynolds was busy all day long driving about filling orders. I did all the dirty work, and she did the talking, advertising, and selling. It was a glorious partnership, because Mrs. Reynolds was the finest woman God ever let breath, and she gave me a fair share of the profit. When she died in Columbia hospital, it nearly killed me. I was about twenty-two then, and graduating from school. I hoped so much that she would come to the graduating exercises, because I was class poet, and I meant to show off for her.

I shall never forget that cold, blustery day in the cemetery. As they lowered her casket, something in me went down with her. I stayed there until everyone had left, and then I got down on my knees and cried. All I could say was: "Goodbye, Miss Alice." My eyes were so filled up I couldn't hardly see. If only God would put more white people like her on earth. Why, I used to sometime spend the night in the house with her. Do you think she was afraid? I never slept a wink, because I was watching over Miss Alice. Her niece stayed with her most of the time, but occasionally she would go home on the week-end. She went to school in Columbia, and stayed with Miss Alice because it was cheaper than boarding or staying at the dormitory. It was when she went home that I used to stay with Miss Alice. Did I ever get the idea I was as good as Miss Alice? Certainly not. I am a Negro, and I'm not ashamed of it. I know, and I have to teach and preach that we are entitled to economic equality but never social equality. If God hadn't intended for us to always be two separate races, he'd made us alike.

I remember the day the grocery man came to the house. He shouted to me in the yard: "Hey, nigger, gimme a hand with these groceries."

Miss Alice gave him a look fit to kill him and said: "There are no niggers working here, Mr. Blake. I shall appreciate your not addressing my help as nigger."

That was Miss Alice all over. She wouldn't stand running over. Why, I'da died for Miss Alice. I used to wonder late in the night when I stayed in the house to look after her, what I would do if some danger really threatened. I was like most young fellows I guess—a little scary. But I believe I would have faced death easily to protect that good woman. I owe my education to her, and a lot more besides. She taught me how to conduct myself around decent white people, and I've never forgotten her teachings.

Only the other day I was over in Columbia addressing the colored Bible Class of the Methodist Church South when I came down Hampton Street to find a little colored boy and a white boy fighting. A group of whites had gathered and was shouting encouragement to the white child. On the other side had grouped a bunch of Negroes, and they were pulling for the colored boy. The white boy was much larger, and the little colored boy crying pitifully and taking an awful beating. The Negroes saw the unfairness of it all, and the tenseness between the two warring groups could be felt. Now, I had learned from Miss Alice that diplomacy would always get you further than simply being pig-headed because you were right, so I quietly eased in and when the children separated, I grasped the colored child by the hand and walked on down the street with him, talking softly to soothe him. I didn't look back, and I didn't speak to anyone except the child.

Suppose I had been outspoken? It would have been striking a match to dynamite. I try to impress on my people the necessity for diplomacy in their dealings with their white brothers. I know that we will never work out our problems in any other way. Kindness and thoughtfulness will do much towards improving the feelings between us. I know we are downtrodden. But you know, Miss Alice showed me that we can work things out peacefully if we only will. The real trouble after all is lack of consideration. I can understand the feelings of the Jews. They have to fight tooth and toe-nail for everything. It is the same way with the Negro. You know, and I know there are plenty white people in the south who think that a Negro should live on nothing and go ragged. They think that is enough for him. It hurts me deeply to see my people going about in the cold winter time with no shoes. I hate to see them living in nasty hovels. They are human, and they are entitled to humans treatment.

In the last few years, I think the Negro has forgiven a lot because he sees so many poor white people living on his level. He sees the poor, scrawny little mill woman with her weazened baby trudging to the relief office to get something to eat. Only the other day, an old colored mammy who has raised ten children of her own, told me she has been taking care of a poor girl's baby. The mother wasn't married, and she died just after the baby was born. Her people would have nothing to do with her, and she was actually lying in one of those mill-village shanties alone with her child. The old mammy told me that when she heard about it, it made her sick all over. She said she told the people around the neighborhood thatnif they wouldn't do something for that poor girl, she would. That girl was actually lying in a dirty bed and there wasn't a thing to eat in the house. Mammy took the child and nursed that girl until she died. The county buried her, and the Dept. Welfare took the child.

I tell you, I don't know what we're coming to. I try to find solace in the Bible, and also an explanation for the terrible times we are having. But one thing is certain, we've got to get back to God and his teachings. There is so much greed and hatred in the lives and hearts of men. The rich people in America look like they don't care anything about anyone but themselves. Even the colored race sticks together better than the white people. I cant understand it all. I have noticed that when a Greek or Italian comes to this country he gets help right off. The same with a Jew. People say you never see a Jew working. They work, but they work their heads, and they stand by one another.

It is very seldom that the county has to bury a Negro. We have our burial societies. We tide our members over when they get in the tight. When Negroes go to the relief, it is because there are so many to help that the fairly well-to-do Negroes have their hands full and can't help but so many. But it is certainly different with the white people.. I saw a poor white boy go in a store the other day and ask for work. The manager wasn't even kind to him, but told him to go to the WPA and get work. If that had been a Greek boy, the manager would have given him something to do to help him until he could get on his feet. Now I've got four children. I'm forty-one and my wife is thirty. We determined to help our children, and stick by them to the last ditch. My oldest is a boy 17. He goes to School in Bennetsville, and is interested in electricity. I'm going to help him in every way I can. I have told him what its all about, and me and his mammy are sacrificing to keep him in school. Our other three children are going to grammar school. I don't make very much now that times are so hard with my people. I have four churches scattered throughout Marlboro County, and I preach at each one once a month. In this way, I make more than just one church.

I am buying a little farm, if I ever get it paid for. We are living there, and my wife works the garden, and looks after the chickens. The children do the heavy outdoor work such as cutting wood, milking, etc.

I have very little time at home, because I have to go from church to church, and in the meantime, I'm busy on my sermons. Then too, I put on revival meetings here and there. I save a lot of people, but I don't make much. I wont average over eight or nine dollars a Sunday. You see that has to be stretched over the week. I thank God I'm doing as well as I am. I have a car or at least a piece of one, and my congregation pays my oil and gas bill. If they didn't I couldn't get around. I am doing everything I can to set an example for my children. I shall continue to teach them that courtesy, kindness and consideration for the feelings of others will carry them far, and I shall impress on them the necessity for upholding the ideals of their race. I want them to become men and women worthy of the best treatment any Negro can hope to receive, and I want them to win the respect of white people, and do all in their power to promote better understanding between the two races. If they do not fulfill my hopes, it wont be my fault, because I shall do everything to make them fine men and women.

Walter Coachman

MARTIN LUTHER KING JR. (1929-1968)

Introduction

Dr. Martin Luther King, Jr. was a famous leader of the American civil rights movement, a political activist, and a Baptist minister. In 1964, King became the youngest man to be awarded the Nobel Peace Prize (for his work as a peacemaker, promoting nonviolence and equal treatment for different races). On April 4, 1968, Dr. King was assassinated in Memphis, Tennessee. In 1977, he was posthumously awarded the Presidential Medal of Freedom by Jimmy Carter. In 1986, Martin Luther King Day was established as a United States holiday, only the fourth Federal holiday to honor an individual (the other three being in honor of Jesus of Nazareth, George Washington, and Christopher Columbus). In 2004, King was posthumously awarded the Congressional Gold Medal. He was known as a great public speaker. Dr. King often called for personal responsibility in fostering world peace. King's most influential and well-known public address is the "I Have A Dream" speech, delivered on the steps of the Lincoln Memorial in Washington, D.C..

Early life

Martin Luther King, Jr. was born on April 20, 1929 in Atlanta, Georgia. He was the son of the Reverend Michael Luther King, Sr. and Alberta Williams King. King entered Morehouse College at the age of fifteen, as he skipped his ninth and twelfth high school grades without formally graduating. In 1948 he graduated from Morehouse with a B.A. degree in sociology, and enrolled in Crozer Theological Seminary in Chester, Pennsylvania. In 1951 King began doctoral studies in Systematic Theology at Boston University, and received his Ph.D. in 1955.

Civil rights activism

In 1953, at the age of twenty-four, King became pastor of the Dexter Avenue Baptist Church, in Montgomery, Alabama. On December 1, 1955, Rosa Parks was arrested for refusing to comply with the Jim Crow laws that required her to give up her seat to a white man. The Montgomery Bus Boycott, led by King, soon followed. The boycott lasted for 381 days, the situation becoming so tense that King's house was bombed. King was arrested during this campaign, which ended with a United States Supreme Court decision outlawing racial segregation on all public transport.

King was instrumental in the founding of the Southern Christian Leadership Conference (SCLC) in 1957, a group created to harness the moral authority and organizing power of black churches to conduct non-violent protests in the service of civil rights reform. King continued to dominate the organization. King was an adherent of the philosophies of nonviolent civil disobedience used successfully in India by Mahatma Gandhi, and he applied this philosophy to the protests organized by the SCLC.

The FBI began wiretapping King in 1961, fearing that communists were trying to infiltrate the Civil Rights Movement, but when no such evidence emerged, the bureau used the incidental details caught on tape over six years in attempts to force King out of the preeminent leadership position.

King correctly recognized that organized, nonviolent protest against the racist system of southern segregation known as Jim Crow laws would lead to extensive media coverage of the struggle for black equality and voting rights. Indeed, journalistic accounts and televised footage of the daily deprivation and indignities suffered by southern blacks, and of segregationist violence and harassment of civil rights workers and marchers, produced a wave of sympathetic public opinion that made the Civil Rights Movement the single most important issue in American politics in the early 1960s.

King organized and led marches for blacks' right to vote, desegregation, labor rights and other basic civil rights. Most of these rights were successfully enacted into United States law with the passage of the Civil Rights Act of 1964 and the Voting Rights Act of 1965.

King and the SCLC applied the principles of nonviolent protest with great success by strategically choosing the method of protest and the places in which protests were carried out in often dramatic stand-offs with segregationist authorities. Sometimes these confrontations turned violent. King and the SCLC were instrumental in the unsuccessful protest movement in Albany, in 1961 and 1962, where divisions within the black community and the canny, low-key response by local government defeated efforts; in the Birmingham protests in the summer of 1963; and in the protest in St. Augustine, Florida, in 1964. King and the SCLC joined forces with SNCC in Selma, Alabama, in December 1964, where SNCC had been working on voter registration for a number of months. His 1964 book Why We Can't Wait elaborated this idea further, presenting it as an application of the common law regarding settlement of unpaid labor.

The March on Washington

King is perhaps most famous for his "I Have a Dream" speech, given in front of the Lincoln Memorial during the 1963 March on Washington for Jobs and Freedom. King, representing SCLC, was among the leaders of the so-called "Big Six" civil rights organizations who were instrumental in the organization of the March on Washington for Jobs and Freedom in 1963. The other leaders and organizations comprising the Big Six were: Roy Wilkins, NAACP; Whitney Young, Jr., Urban League; A. Philip Randolph, Brotherhood of Sleeping Car Porters; John Lewis, SNCC; and James Farmer of the Congress of Racial Equality (CORE). For King, this role was another which courted controversy, as he was one of the key figures who acceded to the wishes of President John F. Kennedy in changing the focus of the march. Kennedy initially opposed the march outright, because he was concerned it would negatively impact the drive for passage of civil rights legislation, but the organizers were firm that the march would proceed.

The march originally was conceived as an event to dramatize the desperate condition of blacks in the South and a very public opportunity to place organizers' concerns and grievances squarely before the seat of power in the nation's capital. Organizers intended to excoriate and then challenge the federal government for its failure to safeguard the civil rights and physical safety of civil rights workers and blacks, generally, in the South. However, the group acquiesced to presidential pressure and influence, and the event ultimately took on a far less strident tone.

As a result, some civil rights activists felt it presented an inaccurate, sanitized pageant of racial harmony; Malcolm X called it the "Farce on Washington," and members of the Nation of Islam who attended the march faced a temporary suspension.

The march did, however, make specific demands: an end to racial segregation in public school; meaningful civil rights legislation, including a law prohibiting racial discrimination in employment; protection of civil rights workers from police brutality; a $2 minimum wage for all workers; and self-government for the District of Columbia, then governed by congressional committee.

Despite tensions, the march was a resounding success. More than a quarter of a million people of diverse ethnicities attended the event, sprawling from the steps of the Lincoln Memorial onto the National Mall and around the reflecting pool. At the time, it was the largest gathering of protesters in Washington's history. King's I Have a Dream speech electrified the crowd. It is regarded, along with Abraham Lincoln's Gettysburg Address, as one of the finest speeches in the history of American oratory. President Kennedy, himself opposed to the march, met King afterwards with enthusiasm—repeating King's line back to him; "I have a dream", while nodding with approval.

Throughout his career of service, King wrote and spoke frequently, drawing on his long experience as a preacher. His "Letter from Birmingham Jail", written in 1963, is a passionate statement of his crusade for justice. On October 14, 1964, King became the youngest recipient of the Nobel Peace Prize, which was awarded to him for leading non-violent resistance to end racial prejudice in the United States.

Stance on compensation

On the several occasions Martin Luther King Jr. expressed a view that black Americans, as well as other disadvantaged Americans, should be compensated for historical wrongs. Speaking to Alex Haley in 1965, he said that granting black Americans only equality could not realistically close the economic gap between them and whites. King said that he did not seek a full restitution of wages lost to slavery, which he believed impossible, but proposed a government compensatory program of US $50 billion over ten years to all disadvantaged groups. He posited that "the money spent would be more than amply justified by the benefits that would accrue to the nation through a spectacular decline in school dropouts, family breakups, crime rates, illegitimacy, swollen relief rolls, rioting and other social evils." His 1964 book *Why We Can't Wait* elaborated this idea further, presenting it as an application of the common law regarding settlement of unpaid labor. ...

Further challenges

Starting in 1965, King began to express doubts about the United States' role in the Vietnam War. On April 4, 1967—exactly one year before his death—King spoke out strongly against the US's role in the war, insisting that the US was in Vietnam "to occupy it as an American colony" and calling the US government "the greatest purveyor of violence in the world today." But he also argued that the country needed larger and broader moral changes:

"A true revolution of values will soon look uneasily on the glaring contrast of poverty and wealth. With righteous indignation, it will look across the seas and see individual capitalists of the West investing huge sums of money in Asia, Africa and South America, only to take the profits out with no concern for the social betterment of the countries, and say: 'This is not just.'"

King also stated in his "Beyond Vietnam" speech that "True compassion is more than flinging a coin to a beggar; it comes to see that an edifice which produces beggars needs restructuring." From Vietnam to South Africa to Latin America, King said, the U.S. was "on the wrong side of a world revolution." King questioned "our alliance with the landed gentry of Latin America," and asked why the U.S. was suppressing revolutions "of the shirtless and barefoot people" in the Third World, instead of supporting them.

In 1968, King and the SCLC organized the "Poor People's Campaign" to address issues of economic justice. ... The campaign culminated in a march on Washington, D.C. demanding economic aid to the poorest communities of the United States. He crisscrossed the country to assemble "a multiracial army of the poor" that would descend on Washington—engaging in nonviolent civil disobedience at the Capitol, if need be—until Congress enacted a poor people's bill of rights. Reader's Digest warned of an "insurrection."

King's economic bill of rights called for massive government jobs programs to rebuild America's cities. He saw a crying need to confront a Congress that had demonstrated its "hostility to the poor"—appropriating "military funds with alacrity and generosity," but providing "poverty funds with miserliness." His vision was for change that was more revolutionary than mere reform: he cited systematic flaws of racism, poverty, militarism and materialism, and that "reconstruction of society itself is the real issue to be faced."

In April 3, 1968, at Mason Temple (Church of God in Christ, Inc.—World Headquarters) King prophetically told a euphoric crowd during his "I've Been to the Mountaintop" speech:

It really doesn't matter what happens now.... some began to... talk about the threats that were out—what would happen to me from some of our sick white brothers.... Like anybody, I would like to live a long life. Longevity has its place, but I'm not concerned about that now. I just want to do God's will. And He's allowed me to go up to the mountain! And I've looked over, and I've seen the Promised Land. I may not get there with you. But I want you to know tonight, that we, as a people, will get to the Promised Land. And so I'm happy tonight. I'm not worried about anything. I'm not fearing any man. Mine eyes have seen the Glory of the coming of the Lord!

He was assassinated the following day.

Assassination

The Lorraine Motel, where Rev. King was assassinated, now the site of the National Civil Rights Museum Martin Luther King's tomb, located on the grounds of the King Center. In late March, 1968, Dr. King went to Memphis, Tennessee in support of the black garbage workers of AFSCME Local 1733, who had been on strike since March 12 for higher wages and better treatment: for example, African American workers, paid $1.70 per hour, were not paid when sent home because of inclement weather (unlike white workers).

On April 3, Dr. King returned to Memphis and addressed a rally, delivering his "I've been to the Mountaintop" address.

King was assassinated at 6:01 p.m. April 4, 1968, on the balcony of the Lorraine Motel in Memphis, Tennessee. Friends inside the motel room heard the shots and ran to the balcony to find King shot in the throat. He was pronounced dead at St. Joseph's Hospital at 7:05 p.m. The assassination led to a nationwide wave of riots in more than 60 cities. Five days later, President Lyndon B. Johnson declared a national day of mourning for the lost civil rights leader. A crowd of 300,000 attended his funeral that same day.

Awards and recognition

From the Gallery of 20th century martyrs at Westminster Abbey- Mother Elizabeth of Russia, Rev. Martin Luther King, Archbishop Oscar Romero, Pastor Dietrich Bonhoeffer. Besides winning the 1964 Nobel Peace Prize, in 1965 the American Jewish Committee presented King with the American Liberties Medallion for his "exceptional advancement of the principles of human liberty." Reverend King said in his acceptance remarks, "Freedom is one thing. You have it all or you are not free."

In 1966, the Planned Parenthood Federation of America awarded Dr. King the Margaret Sanger Award for "his courageous resistance to bigotry and his lifelong dedication to the advancement of social justice and human dignity."

In 1971, Dr. King was awarded the Grammy Award for Best Spoken Word Recording for his Why I Oppose the War in Vietnam.

In 1977, the Presidential Medal of Freedom was awarded posthumously to King by Jimmy Carter.

King is the second most admired person in the 20th century, according to a Gallup poll.

King was voted 6th in the Person of the Century poll by TIME.

King was elected the third Greatest American of all time by the American public in a contest conducted by the Discovery Channel and AOL.

Wikipedia

Sermon Collection

Rediscovering Lost Values (28 November, 1954)

… The trouble isn't so much that we don't know enough, but it's as if we aren't good enough. The trouble isn't so much that our scientific genius lags behind, but our moral genius lags behind. The great problem facing modern man is that, that the means by which we live have outdistanced the spiritual ends for which we live. So we find ourselves caught in a messed-up world. The problem is with man himself and man's soul. We haven't learned how to be just and honest and kind and true and loving. And that is the basis of our problem. The real problem is that through our scientific genius we've made of the world a neighborhood, but through our moral and spiritual genius we've failed to make of it a brotherhood. And the great danger facing us today is not so much the atomic bomb that was created by physical science. Not so much that atomic bomb that you can put in an aeroplane and drop on the heads of hundreds and thousands of people—as dangerous as that is. But the real danger confronting civilization today is that atomic bomb which lies in the hearts and souls of men, capable of exploding into the vilest of hate and into the most damaging selfishness—that's the atomic bomb that we've got to fear today. Problem is with the men. Within the heart and the souls of men. (Lord) That is the real basis of our problem.

… Our world hinges on moral foundations. God has made it so. God has made the universe to be based on a moral law. So long as man disobeys it he is revolting against God. That's what we need in the world today: people who will stand for right and goodness. It's not enough to know the intricacies of zoology and biology, but we must know the intricacies of law. It is not enough to know that two and two makes four, but we've got to know somehow that it's right to be honest and just with our brothers. It's not enough to know all about our philosophical and mathematical disciplines, but we've got to know the simple disciplines of being honest and loving and just with all humanity. If we don't learn it, we will destroy ourselves by the misuse of our own powers.

Martin Luther King Jr. © The Estate of Martin Luther King, Jr.

Paul's Letter to American Christians (4 November, 1956)
This sermon was delivered at Dexter Avenue Baptist Church, Montgomery, Alabama, on 4 November 1956.

I would like to share with you an imaginary letter from the pen of the Apostle Paul. The postmark reveals that it comes from the city of Ephesus…

You have made tremendous strides in the area of scientific and technological development. But America, as I look at you from afar, I wonder whether your moral and spiritual progress has been commensurate with your scientific progress. It seems to me that your moral progress lags behind your scientific progress. Your poet Thoreau used to talk about "improved means to an unimproved end." How often this is true. You have allowed the material means by which you live to outdistance the spiritual ends for which you live. You have allowed your mentality to outrun your morality. … So America, I would urge you to keep your moral advances abreast with your scientific advances. …

Let me rush on to say something about the church. Americans, I must remind you, as I have said to so many others, that the church is the Body of Christ. So when the church is true to its nature it knows neither division nor disunity. But I am disturbed about what you are doing to the Body of Christ. They tell me that in America you have within Protestantism more than two hundred and fifty six denominations. The tragedy is not so much that you have such a multiplicity of denominations, but that most of them are warring against each other with a claim to absolute truth. This narrow sectarianism is destroying the unity of the Body of Christ. You must come to see that God is neither a Baptist nor a Methodist; He is neither a Presbyterian nor a Episcopalian. God is bigger than all of our denominations. If you are to be true witnesses for Christ, you must come to see that America.

In your struggle for justice, let your oppressor know that you are not attempting to defeat or humiliate him, or even to pay him back for injustices that he has heaped upon you. Let him know that you are merely seeking justice for him as well as yourself. Let him know that the festering sore of segregation debilitates the white man as well as the Negro. With this attitude you will be able to keep your struggle on high Christian standards.

Martin Luther King Jr. © The Estate of Martin Luther King, Jr.

Eulogy for the Young Victims of the Sixteenth Street Baptist Church Bombing (18 September, 1963)

This eulogy was given in Birmingham, Alabama at the funeral service for three of the children—Addie Mae Collins, Carol Denise McNair, and Cynthia Diane Wesley—who were killed in the bombing of the Sixteenth Street Baptist Church in Birmingham, Alabama, which was used as a meeting-place for civil rights leaders such as Martin Luther King Jr.. A separate service was held for the fourth victim, Carole Robertson.

This afternoon we gather in the quiet of this sanctuary to pay our last tribute of respect to these beautiful children of God. They entered the stage of history just a few years ago, and in the brief years that they were privileged to act on this mortal stage, they played their parts exceedingly well. Now the curtain falls; they move through the exit; the drama of their earthly life comes to a close. They are now committed back to that eternity from which they came.

These children—unoffending, innocent, and beautiful—were the victims of one of the most vicious and tragic crimes ever perpetrated against humanity. And yet they died nobly. They are the martyred heroines of a holy crusade for freedom and human dignity. And so this afternoon in a real sense they have something to say to each of us in their death. They have something to say to every minister of the gospel who has remained silent behind the safe security of stained-glass windows. They have something to say to every politician who has fed his constituents with the stale bread of hatred and the spoiled meat of racism. They have something to say to a federal government that has compromised with the undemocratic practices of southern Dixiecrats and the blatant hypocrisy of right-wing northern Republicans. They have something to say to every Negro who has passively accepted the evil system of segregation and who has stood on the sidelines in a mighty struggle for justice. They say to each of us, black and white alike, that we must substitute courage for caution. They say to us that we must be concerned not merely about who murdered them, but about the system, the way of life, the philosophy which produced the murderers. Their death says to us that we must work passionately and unrelentingly for the realization of the American dream. And so my friends, they did not die in vain. God still has a way of wringing good out of evil. And history has proven over and over again that unmerited suffering is redemptive. The innocent blood of these little girls may well serve as a redemptive force that will bring new light to this dark city.

Martin Luther King Jr. © The Estate of Martin Luther King, Jr.

A Knock at Midnight (1963)

Although this parable is concerned with the power of persistent prayer, it may also serve as a basis for our thought concerning many contemporary problems and the role of the church in grappling with them. It is midnight in the parable; it is also midnight in our world, and the darkness is so deep that we can hardly see which way to turn.

It is midnight within the social order. On the international horizon nations are engaged in a colossal and bitter contest for supremacy. Two world wars have been fought within a generation, and the clouds of another war are dangerously low. Man now has atomic and nuclear weapons that could within seconds completely destroy the major cities of the world. … Will these circumstances and weapons bring the annihilation of the human race?

This midnight in man's external collective is paralleled by midnight in his internal individual life. It is midnight within the psychological order. Everywhere paralyzing fears harrow people by day and haunt them by night. Deep clouds of anxiety and depression are suspended in our mental skies. More people are emotionally disturbed today than at any other time of human history. The psychopathic wards of our hospitals are crowded, and the most popular psychologists today are the psychoanalysts. Bestsellers in psychology are books such as Man Against Himself, The Neurotic Personality of Our Times, and Modern Man in Search of a Soul. Bestsellers in religion are such books as Peace of Mind and Peace of Soul. The popular clergyman preaches soothing sermons on "How to Be Happy" and "How to Relax." Some have been tempted to revise Jesus' command to read, "Go ye into all the world, keep your blood pressure down, and, lo, I will make you a well-adjusted personality." All of this is indicative that it is midnight within the inner lives of men and women.

It is also midnight within the moral order. At midnight colors lose their distinctiveness and become a sullen shade of gray. Moral principles have lost their distinctiveness. For modern man, absolute right and wrong are a matter of what the majority is doing. Right and wrong are relative to likes and dislikes and the customs of a particular community. We have unconsciously applied Einstein's theory of relativity, which properly described the physical universe, to the moral and ethical realm.

Martin Luther King Jr. © The Estate of Martin Luther King, Jr.

The American Dream (4 July, 1965)
This sermon was delivered at Ebenezer Baptist Church, Atlanta, Georgia, on 4 July 1965.

… It is marvelous and great that we do have a dream, that we have a nation with a dream; and to forever challenge us; to forever give us a sense of urgency; to forever stand in the midst of the "isness" of our terrible injustices; to remind us of the "oughtness" of our noble capacity for justice and love and brotherhood. This morning I would like to deal with some of the challenges that we face today in our nation as a result of the American dream. First, I want to reiterate the fact that we are challenged more than ever before to respect the dignity and the worth of all human personality. We are challenged to really believe that all men are created equal. And don't misunderstand that. It does not mean that all men are created equal in terms of native endowment, in terms of intellectual capacity—it doesn't mean that. There are certain bright stars in the human firmament in every field. ... It does not mean that every philosopher is equal to Plato, Aristotle, Immanuel Kant, and Friedrich Hegel. It doesn't mean that. There are individuals who do excel and rise to the heights of genius in their areas and in their fields. What it does mean is that all men are equal in intrinsic worth. (Yes)

You see, the founding fathers were really influenced by the Bible. The whole concept of the imago dei, as it is expressed in Latin, the "image of God," is the idea that all men have something within them that God injected. Not that they have substantial unity with God, but that every man has a capacity to have fellowship with God. And this gives him a uniqueness, it gives him worth, it gives him dignity. And we must never forget this as a nation: there are no gradations in the image of God. Every man from a treble white to a bass black is significant on God's keyboard, precisely because every man is made in the image of God. One day we will learn that. (Yes) We will know one day that God made us to live together as brothers and to respect the dignity and worth of every man.

Martin Luther King Jr. © The Estate of Martin Luther King, Jr.

Guidelines for a Constructive Church (5 June, 1966)
This sermon was delivered at Ebenezer Baptist Church, Atlanta, Georgia, on 5 June 1966.

... I say to you this morning that the acceptable year of the Lord can be this year. (Yes) And the church is called to preach it.

The acceptable year of the Lord is any year (Amen) when men decide to do right.

The acceptable year of the Lord is any year when men will stop lying and cheating. (Amen, Make it plain)

The acceptable year of the Lord is that year when women will start using the telephone for constructive purposes (Yes) and not to spread malicious gossip and false rumors on their neighbors. (Right)

The acceptable year of the Lord is any year (Any year) when men will stop throwing away the precious lives that God has given them in riotous living. (Make it plain)

The acceptable year of the Lord (Yes) is that year when people in Alabama (Make it plain) will stop killing civil rights workers and people who are simply engaged in the process of seeking their constitutional rights. (Make it plain)

The acceptable year of the Lord (Yes) is that year when men will learn to live together as brothers. (Yes, sir)

The acceptable year of the Lord (Yes) is that year when men will keep their theology abreast with their technology.

The acceptable year of the Lord is that year when men will keep the ends for which they live abreast with the means by which they live. (Yes)

The acceptable year of the Lord is that year (That year) when men will keep their morality abreast with their mentality.

The acceptable year of the Lord is that year (Yes) when all of the leaders of the world will sit down at the conference table (Make it plain) and realize that unless mankind puts an end to war, war will put an end to mankind. (Yes)

The acceptable year of the Lord is that year when men will beat their swords into plowshares, (Yes) and their spears into pruning hooks: and nations will not rise up against nations, neither will they study war anymore. (Yes)

The acceptable year of the Lord is that year (That year) when men will allow justice to roll down like waters, and righteousness like a mighty stream. (Yes)

Martin Luther King © The Estate of Martin Luther King, Jr.

The Three Dimensions of a Complete Life (9 April, 1967)

This sermon was delivered at New Covenant Baptist Church, Chicago, Illinois, on 9 April 1967.

I want to use as the subject from which to preach: "The Three Dimensions of a Complete Life." (All right) You know, they used to tell us in Hollywood that in order for a movie to be complete, it had to be three-dimensional. Well, this morning I want to seek to get over to each of us that if life itself is to be complete, (Yes) it must be three-dimensional. ...

You may not be able to define God in philosophical terms. Men through the ages have tried to talk about him. (Yes) Plato said that he was the Architectonic Good. Aristotle called him the Unmoved Mover. Hegel called him the Absolute Whole. Then there was a man named Paul Tillich who called him Being-Itself. We don't need to know all of these high-sounding terms. (Yes) Maybe we have to know him and discover him another way. ... Go out this morning. Love yourself, and that means rational and healthy self-interest. You are commanded to do that. That's the length of life. Then follow that: Love your neighbor as you love yourself. You are commanded to do that. That's the breadth of life. And I'm going to take my seat now by letting you know that there's a first and even greater commandment: "Love the Lord thy God with all thy heart, (Yeah) with all thy soul, with all thy strength." I think the psychologist would just say with all thy personality. And when you do that, you've got the breadth of life. And when you get all three of these together, you can walk and never get weary. You can look up and see the morning stars singing together, and the sons of God shouting for joy. When you get all of these working together in your very life, judgment will roll down like waters, and righteousness like a mighty stream. When you get all the three of these together, the lamb will lie down with the lion. When you get all three of these together, you look up and every valley will be exalted, and every hill and mountain will be made low; the rough places will be made plain, and the crooked places straight; and the glory of the Lord shall be revealed and all flesh will see it together.

Martin Luther King © The Estate of Martin Luther King, Jr.

Unfulfilled Dreams (3 March, 1968)

This sermon was delivered at Ebenezer Baptist Church, Atlanta, Georgia, on 3 March 1968.

... If your heart isn't right, fix it up today; get God to fix it up. (Go ahead) Get somebody to be able to say about you, "He may not have reached the highest height, (Preach it) he may not have realized all of his dreams, but he tried." (Yes) Isn't that a wonderful thing for somebody to say about you? "He tried to be a good man. (Yes) He tried to be a just man. He tried to be an honest man. (Yes) His heart was in the right place." (Yes) And I can hear a voice saying, crying out through the eternities, "I accept you. (Preach it) You are a recipient of my grace because it was in your heart. . .

It will be dark sometimes, and it will be dismal and trying, and tribulations will come. But if you have faith in the God that I'm talking about this morning, it doesn't matter. (Yes) For you can stand up amid the storms. And I say it to you out of experience this morning, yes, I've seen the lightning flash. (Yes, sir) I've heard the thunder roll. (Yes) I've felt sin-breakers dashing, trying to conquer my soul. But I heard the voice of Jesus, saying still to fight on. He promised never to leave me, (Yes, sir) never to leave me alone. (Thank you, Jesus) No, never alone. No, never alone. He promised never to leave me. Never to leave me alone. (Glory to God)

And when you get this faith, you can walk with your feet solid to the ground and your head to the air, and you fear no man. (Go ahead) And you fear nothing that comes before you. (Yes, sir) Because you know that God is even in Crete. (Amen) If you ascend to the heavens, God is there. If you descend to hell, God is even there. If you take the wings of the morning and fly out to the uttermost parts of the sea, even God is there. Everywhere we turn we find him. We can never escape him.

Martin Luther King © The Estate of Martin Luther King, Jr.

Remaining Awake Through a Great Revolution (31 March, 1968)
This sermon was delivered at the National Cathedral, Washington, D.C., on 31 March 1968. Congressional Record, 9 April 1968.

. . . Whenever anything new comes into history it brings with it new challenges and new opportunities. And I would like to deal with the challenges that we face today as a result of this triple revolution that is taking place in the world today.

First, we are challenged to develop a world perspective. No individual can live alone, no nation can live alone, and anyone who feels that he can live alone is sleeping through a revolution. The world in which we live is geographically one. The challenge that we face today is to make it one in terms of brotherhood.. . .

Secondly, we are challenged to eradicate the last vestiges of racial injustice from our nation. I must say this morning that racial injustice is still the black man's burden and the white man's shame.

It is an unhappy truth that racism is a way of life for the vast majority of white Americans, spoken and unspoken, acknowledged and denied, subtle and sometimes not so subtle—the disease of racism permeates and poisons a whole body politic. And I can see nothing more urgent than for America to work passionately and unrelentingly—to get rid of the disease of racism.

Something positive must be done. Everyone must share in the guilt as individuals and as institutions. The government must certainly share the guilt; individuals must share the guilt;

even the church must share the guilt. ...

There is another thing closely related to racism that I would like to mention as another challenge. We are challenged to rid our nation and the world of poverty. Like a monstrous octopus, poverty spreads its nagging, prehensile tentacles into hamlets and villages all over our world. Two-thirds of the people of the world go to bed hungry tonight. They are ill-housed; they are ill-nourished; they are shabbily clad. I've seen it in Latin America; I've seen it in Africa; I've seen this poverty in Asia.

Thank God for John, who centuries ago out on a lonely, obscure island called Patmos caught vision of a new Jerusalem descending out of heaven from God, who heard a voice saying, "Behold, I make all things new; former things are passed away."

God grant that we will be participants in this newness and this magnificent development.

Martin Luther King© The Estate of Martin Luther King, Jr.

The Drum Major Instinct (4 April, 1968)
This sermon was delivered at Ebenezer Baptist Church, Atlanta, Georgia, on 4 February 1968.

... We all have the drum major instinct. We all want to be important, to surpass others, to achieve distinction, to lead the parade. Alfred Adler, the great psychoanalyst, contends that this is the dominant impulse. Sigmund Freud used to contend that sex was the dominant impulse, and Adler came with a new argument saying that this quest for recognition, this desire for attention, this desire for distinction is the basic impulse, the basic drive of human life, this drum major instinct. And you know, we begin early to ask life to put us first. Our first cry as a baby was a bid for attention. And all through childhood the drum major impulse or instinct is a major obsession. Children ask life to grant them first place. They are a little bundle of ego. And they have innately the drum major impulse or the drum major instinct.

... You see people over and over again with the drum major instinct taking them over. And they just live their lives trying to outdo the Joneses. (Amen) They got to get this coat because this particular coat is a little better and a little better-looking than Mary's coat. And I got to drive this car because it's something about this car that makes my car a little better than my neighbor's car. (Amen) I know a man who used to live in a thirty-five-thousand-dollar house. And other people started building thirty-five-thousand-dollar houses, so he built a seventy-five-thousand-dollar house. And then somebody else built a seventy-five-thousand-dollar house, and he built a hundred-thousand-dollar house. And I don't know where he's going to end up if he's going to live his life trying to keep up with the Joneses. There comes a time that the drum major instinct can become destructive. (Make it plain) And that's where I want to move now. I want to move to the point of saying that if this instinct is not harnessed, it becomes a very dangerous, pernicious instinct. For instance, if it isn't harnessed, it causes one's personality to become distorted. ...

Martin Luther King © The Estate of Martin Luther King, Jr.

SPEECH COLLECTION

The Negro and the Constitution (May 1944)
Introduction

Negroes were first brought to America in 1620 when England legalized slavery both in England and the colonies and America; the institution grew and thrived for about 150 years upon the backs of these black men. The empire of King Cotton was built and the southland maintained a status of life and hospitality distinctly its own and not anywhere else.

On January 1, 1863 the proclamation emancipating the slaves which had been decreed by President Lincoln in September took effect, millions of Negroes faced a rising sun of a new day begun. Did they have habits of thrift or principles of honesty and integrity? Only a few! For their teachings and duties had been but two activities, love of Master, right or wrong, good or bad, and loyalty to work. What was to be the place for such men in the reconstruction of the south?

America gave its full pledge of freedom seventy-five years ago. Slavery has been a strange paradox in a nation founded on the principles that all men are created free and equal. Finally after tumult and war, the nation in 1865 took a new stand, freedom for all people. The new order was backed by amendments to the national constitution making it the fundamental law that thenceforth there should be no discrimination anywhere in the "land of the free" on account of race, color or previous condition of servitude.

"The Negro and the Constitution"

We cannot have an enlightened democracy with one great group living in ignorance. We cannot have a healthy nation with one tenth of the people ill-nourished, sick, harboring germs of disease which recognize no color lines, obey no Jim Crow laws. We cannot have a nation orderly and sound with one group so ground down and thwarted that it is almost forced into unsocial attitudes and crime. We cannot be truly Christian people so long as we flaunt the central teachings of Jesus: brotherly love and the Golden Rule. We cannot come to full prosperity with one great group so ill-delayed that it cannot buy goods. So as we gird ourselves to defend democracy from foreign attack, let us see to it that increasingly at home we give fair play and free opportunity for all people.

Today thirteen million black sons and daughters of our forefathers continue the fight for the translation of the 13th, 14th, and 15th amendments from writing on the printed page to an actuality. We believe with them that "if freedom is good for any it is good for all," that we may conquer southern armies by the sword, but it is another thing to conquer southern hate, that if the franchise is given to Negroes, they will be vigilant and defend even with their arms, the ark of federal liberty from treason and destruction by her enemies.

The spirit of Lincoln still lives; that spirit born of the teachings of the Nazarene, who promised mercy to the merciful, who lifted the lowly, strengthened the weak, ate with publicans, and made the captives free. In the light of this divine example, the doctrines of demagogues shiver in their chaff. Already closer understanding links Saxon and Freedman in mutual sympathy.

America experiences a new birth of freedom in her sons and daughters; she incarnates the spirit of her martyred chief. Their loyalty is repledged; their devotion renewed to the work He left unfinished. My heart throbs anew in the hope that inspired by the example of Lincoln, imbued with the spirit of Christ, they will cast down the last barrier to perfect freedom. And I with my brother of blackest hue possessing at last my rightful heritage and holding my head erect, may stand beside the Saxon, a Negro, and yet a man!

Martin Luther King © The Estate of Martin Luther King, Jr.

I Have A Dream (28 August 1963)
Introduction
As far as black Americans were concerned, the nation's response to Brown was agonizingly slow, and neither state legislatures nor the Congress seemed willing to help their cause along. Finally, President John F. Kennedy recognized that only a strong civil rights bill would put teeth into the drive to secure equal protection of the laws for African Americans. On June 11, 1963, he proposed such a bill to Congress, asking for legislation that would provide "the kind of equality of treatment which we would want for ourselves." Southern representatives in Congress managed to block the bill in committee, and civil rights leaders sought some way to build political momentum behind the measure.

A. Philip Randolph, a labor leader and longtime civil rights activist, called for a massive march on Washington to dramatize the issue. He welcomed the participation of white groups as well as black in order to demonstrate the multiracial backing for civil rights. The various elements of the civil rights movement, many of which had been wary of one another, agreed to participate. The National Association for the Advancement of Colored People, the Congress of Racial Equality, the Southern Christian Leadership Conference, the Student Non-violent Coordinating Committee and the Urban League all managed to bury their differences and work together. The leaders even agreed to tone down the rhetoric of some of the more militant activists for the sake of unity, and they worked closely with the Kennedy administration, which hoped the march would, in fact, lead to passage of the civil rights bill.

On August 28, 1963, under a nearly cloudless sky, more than 250,000 people, a fifth of them white, gathered near the Lincoln Memorial in Washington to rally for "jobs and freedom." The roster of speakers included speakers from nearly every segment of society—labor leaders like Walter Reuther, clergy, film stars such as Sidney Poitier and Marlon Brando and folksingers such as Joan Baez. Each of the speakers was allotted fifteen minutes, but the day belonged to the young and charismatic leader of the Southern Christian Leadership Conference.

Dr. Martin Luther King Jr. had originally prepared a short and somewhat formal recitation of the sufferings of African Americans attempting to realize their freedom in a society chained by discrimination. He was about to sit down when gospel singer Mahalia Jackson called out, "Tell them about your dream, Martin! Tell them about the dream!" Encouraged by shouts from the audience, King drew upon some of his past talks, and the result became the landmark statement of civil rights in America—a dream of all people, of all races and colors and backgrounds, sharing in an America marked by freedom and democracy.

"I Have A Dream"

I am happy to join with you today in what will go down in history as the greatest demonstration for freedom in the history of our nation.

Five score years ago, a great American, in whose symbolic shadow we stand today, signed the Emancipation Proclamation. This momentous decree came as a great beacon light of hope to millions of Negro slaves who had been seared in the flames of withering injustice. It came as a joyous daybreak to end the long night of their captivity.

But 100 years later, the Negro still is not free. One hundred years later, the life of the Negro is still sadly crippled by the manacles of segregation and the chains of discrimination. One hundred years later, the Negro lives on a lonely island of poverty in the midst of a vast ocean of material prosperity. One hundred years later, the Negro is still languished in the corners of American society and finds himself an exile in his own land. And so we've come here today to dramatize a shameful condition.

In a sense we've come to our nation's capital to cash a check. When the architects of our republic wrote the magnificent words of the Constitution and the Declaration of Independence, they were signing a promissory note to which every American was to fall heir. This note was a promise that all men—yes, black men as well as white men—would be guaranteed the unalienable rights of life, liberty, and the pursuit of happiness.

It is obvious today that America has defaulted on this promissory note insofar as her citizens of color are concerned. Instead of honoring this sacred obligation, America has given the Negro people a bad check, a check that has come back marked "insufficient funds."

But we refuse to believe that the bank of justice is bankrupt. We refuse to believe that there are insufficient funds in the great vaults of opportunity of this nation. And so we've come to cash this check, a check that will give us upon demand the riches of freedom and security of justice. We have also come to his hallowed spot to remind America of the fierce urgency of now. This is no time to engage in the luxury of cooling off or to take the tranquilizing drug of gradualism. Now is the time to make real the promises of democracy. Now is the time to rise from the dark and desolate valley of segregation to the sunlit path of racial justice. Now is the time to lift our nation from the quicksands of racial injustice to the solid rock of brotherhood. Now is the time to make justice a reality for all of God's children.

It would be fatal for the nation to overlook the urgency of the moment. This sweltering summer of the Negro's legitimate discontent will not pass until there is an invigorating autumn of freedom and equality. Nineteen sixty-three is not an end but a beginning. Those who hoped that the Negro needed to blow off steam and will now be content will have a rude awakening if the nation returns to business as usual. There will be neither rest nor tranquility in America until the Negro is granted his citizenship rights. The whirlwinds of revolt will continue to shake the foundations of our nation until the bright day of justice emerges.

But there is something that I must say to my people who stand on the warm threshold which leads into the palace of justice. In the process of gaining our rightful place we must not be guilty of wrongful deeds. Let us not seek to satisfy our thirst for freedom by drinking from the cup of bitterness and hatred. We must forever conduct our struggle on the high plane of dignity and discipline. We must not allow our creative protest to degenerate into physical violence. Again and again we must rise to the majestic heights of meeting physical force with soul force. The marvelous new militancy which has engulfed the Negro community must not lead us to a distrust of all white people, for many of our white brothers, as evidenced by their presence here today, have come to realize that their destiny is tied up with our destiny. And they have come to realize that their freedom is inextricably bound to our freedom. We cannot walk alone.

And as we walk, we must make the pledge that we shall always march ahead. We cannot turn back. There are those who are asking the devotees of civil rights, "When will you be satisfied?" We can never be satisfied as long as the Negro is the victim of the unspeakable horrors of police brutality. We can never be satisfied as long as our bodies, heavy with the fatigue of travel, cannot gain lodging in the motels of the highways and the hotels of the cities. We cannot be satisfied as long as the Negro's basic mobility is from a smaller ghetto to a larger one. We can never be satisfied as long as our children are stripped of their selfhood and robbed of their dignity by signs stating "for whites only." We cannot be satisfied as long as a Negro in Mississippi cannot vote and a Negro in New York believes he has nothing for which to vote. No, no we are not satisfied and we will not be satisfied until justice rolls down like waters and righteousness like a mighty stream.

I am not unmindful that some of you have come here out of great trials and tribulations. Some of you have come fresh from narrow jail cells. Some of you have come from areas where your quest for freedom left you battered by storms of persecution and staggered by the winds of police brutality. You have been the veterans of creative suffering. Continue to work with the faith that unearned suffering is redemptive.

Go back to Mississippi, go back to Alabama, go back to South Carolina, go back to Georgia, go back to Louisiana, go back to the slums and ghettos of our northern cities, knowing that somehow this situation can and will be changed.

Let us not wallow in the valley of despair. I say to you today my friends—so even though we face the difficulties of today and tomorrow, I still have a dream. It is a dream deeply rooted in the American dream.

I have a dream that one day this nation will rise up and live out the true meaning of its creed: "We hold these truths to be self-evident, that all men are created equal."

I have a dream that one day on the red hills of Georgia the sons of former slaves and the sons of former slave owners will be able to sit down together at the table of brotherhood.

I have a dream that one day even the state of Mississippi, a state sweltering with the heat of injustice, sweltering with the heat of oppression, will be transformed into an oasis of freedom and justice.

I have a dream that my four little children will one day live in a nation where they will not be judged by the color of their skin but by the content of their character.

I have a dream today.

I have a dream that one day down in Alabama, with its vicious racists, with its governor having his lips dripping with the words of interposition and nullification—one day right there in Alabama little black boys and black girls will be able to join hands with little white boys and white girls as sisters and brothers.

I have a dream today.

I have a dream that one day every valley shall be exalted, and every hill and mountain shall be made low, the rough places will be made plain, and the crooked places will be made straight, and the glory of the Lord shall be revealed and all flesh shall see it together.

This is our hope. This is the faith that I go back to the South with. With this faith we will be able to hew out of the mountain of despair a stone of hope. With this faith we will be able to transform the jangling discords of our nation into a beautiful symphony of brotherhood. With this faith we will be able to work together, to pray together, to struggle together, to go to jail together, to stand up for freedom together, knowing that we will be free one day.

This will be the day, this will be the day when all of God's children will be able to sing with new meaning "My country 'tis of thee, sweet land of liberty, of thee I sing. Land where my father's died, land of the Pilgrim's pride, from every mountainside, let freedom ring!"

And if America is to be a great nation, this must become true. And so let freedom ring from the prodigious hilltops of New Hampshire. Let freedom ring from the mighty mountains of New York. Let freedom ring from the heightening Alleghenies of Pennsylvania.

Let freedom ring from the snow-capped Rockies of Colorado. Let freedom ring from the curvaceous slopes of California.

But not only that; let freedom ring from Stone Mountain of Georgia.

Let freedom ring from Lookout Mountain of Tennessee.

Let freedom ring from every hill and molehill of Mississippi—from every mountainside.

Let freedom ring. And when this happens, and when we allow freedom ring—when we let it ring from every village and every hamlet, from every state and every city, we will be able to speed up that day when all of God's children—black men and white men, Jews and Gentiles, Protestants and Catholics—will be able to join hands and sing in the words of the old Negro spiritual: "Free at last! Free at last! Thank God Almighty, we are free at last!"

Distribution statement: Accepted as part of the Douglass Archives of American Public Address (http://douglass.speech.nwu.edu) on May 26, 1999. Prepared by D. Oetting (http://nonce.com/oetting).

Address Delivered in Acceptance of the Nobel Peace Prize (19 December, 1964)

This address was delivered in acceptance of the Nobel Peace Prize in Oslo.

Your Majesty, Your Royal Highness, Mr. President, excellencies, ladies and gentlemen: I accept the Nobel Prize for Peace at a moment when twenty-two million Negroes of the United States are engaged in a creative battle to end the long night of racial injustice. I accept this award on behalf of a civil rights movement which is moving with determination and a majestic scorn for risk and danger to establish a reign of freedom and a rule of justice.

I am mindful that only yesterday in Birmingham, Alabama, our children, crying out for brotherhood, were answered with fire hoses, snarling dogs, and even death. I am mindful that only yesterday in Philadelphia, Mississippi, young people seeking to secure the right to vote were brutalized and murdered. I am mindful that debilitating and grinding poverty afflicts my people and chains them to the lowest rung of the economic ladder. Therefore, I must ask why this prize is awarded to a movement which is beleaguered and committed to unrelenting struggle, and to a movement which has not yet won the very peace and brotherhood which is the essence of the Nobel Prize. After contemplation, I conclude that this award, which I receive on behalf of that movement, is a profound recognition that nonviolence is the answer to the crucial political and moral questions of our time: the need for man to overcome oppression and violence without resorting to violence and oppression.

Civilization and violence are antithetical concepts. Negroes of the United States, following the people of India, have demonstrated that nonviolence is not sterile passivity, but a powerful moral force which makes for social transformation. Sooner or later, all the peoples of the world will have to discover a way to live together in peace, and thereby transform this pending cosmic elegy into a creative psalm of brotherhood. If this is to be achieved, man must evolve for all human conflict a method which rejects revenge, aggression, and retaliation. The foundation of such a method is love. The torturous road which has led from Montgomery, Alabama, to Oslo bears witness to this truth, and this is a road over which millions of Negroes are traveling to find a new sense of dignity.

Martin Luther King Jr. © The Estate of Martin Luther King, Jr.

Beyond Vietnam: A Time to Break Silence (4 April 1967)
This speech was given by Dr. Martin Luther King, Jr., on April 4, 1967, at a meeting of Clergy and Laity Concerned at Riverside Church in New York City.

I come to this magnificent house of worship tonight because my conscience leaves me no other choice. I join with you in this meeting because I am in deepest agreement with the aims and work of the organization which has brought us together: Clergy and Laymen Concerned about Vietnam. The recent statement of your executive committee are the sentiments of my own heart and I found myself in full accord when I read its opening lines: "A time comes when silence is betrayal." That time has come for us in relation to Vietnam. The truth of these words is beyond doubt but the mission to which they call us is a most difficult one. Even when pressed by the demands of inner truth, men do not easily assume the task of opposing their government's policy, especially in time of war. Nor does the human spirit move without great difficulty against all the apathy of conformist thought within one's own bosom and in the surrounding world. Moreover when the issues at hand seem as perplexed as they often do in the case of this dreadful conflict we are always on the verge of being mesmerized by uncertainty; but we must move on. Some of us who have already begun to break the silence of the night have found that the calling to speak is often a vocation of agony, but we must speak.

The Importance of Vietnam
I have seven major reasons for bringing Vietnam into the field of my moral vision. There is

at the outset a very obvious and almost facile connection between the war in Vietnam and the struggle I, and others, have been waging in America.

Strange Liberators
And as I ponder the madness of Vietnam and search within myself for ways to understand and respond to compassion my mind goes constantly to the people of that peninsula. I speak now not of the soldiers of each side, not of the junta in Saigon, but simply of the people who have been living under the curse of war for almost three continuous decades now. I think of them too because it is clear to me that there will be no meaningful solution there until some attempt is made to know them and hear their broken cries.

Martin Luther King Jr. © The Estate of Martin Luther King, Jr.

I've Been to the Mountaintop (3 April 1968)
This was Dr. King's last sermon. He delivered it, on the eve of his assassination, at [the Bishop Charles] Mason Temple in Memphis, Tennessee, on April 3, 1968. Mason Temple is the headquarters of the Church of God in Christ, the largest African American Pentecostal denomination in the United States.

The issue is injustice. The issue is the refusal of Memphis to be fair and honest in its dealings with its public servants, who happen to be sanitation workers. Now, we've got to keep attention on that. That's always the problem with a little violence. You know what happened the other day, and the press dealt only with the window-breaking. I read the articles. They very seldom got around to mentioning the fact that one thousand, three hundred sanitation workers were on strike, and that Memphis is not being fair to them, and that Mayor Loeb is in dire need of a doctor. They didn't get around to that. ...

And they were telling me, now it doesn't matter now. It really doesn't matter what happens now. I left Atlanta this morning, and as we got started on the plane, there were six of us, the pilot said over the public address system, "We are sorry for the delay, but we have Dr. Martin Luther King on the plane. And to be sure that all of the bags were checked, and to be sure that nothing would be wrong with the plane, we had to check out everything carefully. And we've had the plane protected and guarded all night."

And then I got into Memphis. And some began to say that threats, or talk about the threats that were out. What would happen to me from some of our sick white brothers?

Well, I don't know what will happen now. We've got some difficult days ahead. But it doesn't matter with me now. Because I've been to the mountaintop. And I don't mind. Like anybody, I would like to live a long life. Longevity has its place. But I'm not concerned about that now. I just want to do God's will. And He's allowed me to go up to the mountain. And I've looked over. And I've seen the promised land. I may not get there with you. But I want you to know tonight, that we, as a people will get to the promised land. And I'm happy, tonight. I'm not worried about anything. I'm not fearing any man. Mine eyes have seen the glory of the coming of the Lord.

Martin Luther King Jr. © The Estate of Martin Luther King, Jr.

LETTER COLLECTION

Letter from a Birmingham Jail (April 16, 1963)

I am in Birmingham because injustice is here. …

I'm grateful to God that, through the Negro church, the dimension of nonviolence entered our struggle.

Was not Jesus an extremist for love—"Love your enemies, bless them that curse you, pray for them that despitefully use you." Was not Amos an extremist for justice—"Let justice roll down like waters and righteousness like a mighty stream." Was not Paul an extremist for the gospel of Jesus Christ—"I bear in my body the marks of the Lord Jesus." Was not Martin Luther an extremist—"Here I stand; I can do none other so help me God." Was not John Bunyan an extremist—"I will stay in jail to the end of my days before I make a butchery of my conscience." Was not Abraham Lincoln an extremist—"This nation cannot survive half slave and half free." Was not Thomas Jefferson an extremist—"We hold these truths to be self-evident, that all men are created equal." …

There was a time when the church was very powerful. It was during that period when the early Christians rejoiced when they were deemed worthy to suffer for what they believed. In those days the church was not merely a thermometer that recorded the ideas and principles of popular opinion; it was a thermostat that transformed the mores of society. Whenever the early Christians entered a town the power structure got disturbed and immediately sought to convict them for being "disturbers of the peace" and "outside agitators." But they went on with the conviction that they were "a colony of heaven," and had to obey God rather than man. …

We will win our freedom because the sacred heritage of our nation and the eternal will of God are embodied in our echoing demands.

One day the South will know that when these disinherited children of God sat down at lunch counters they were in reality standing up for the best in the American dream and the most sacred values in our Judaeo-Christian heritage, and thusly, carrying our whole nation back to those great wells of democracy which were dug deep by the founding fathers in the formulation of the Constitution and the Declaration of Independence.

Martin Luther King © The Estate of Martin Luther King, Jr.

QUOTATION COLLECTION

We cannot be truly Christian people so long as we flaunt the central teachings of Jesus: brotherly love and the Golden Rule.
Martin Luther King Jr.

My heart throbs anew in the hope that inspired by the example of Lincoln, imbued with the spirit of Christ, they will cast down the last barrier to perfect freedom.
Martin Luther King Jr.

In the end, we will remember not the words of our enemies, but the silence of our friends.
Martin Luther King Jr.

It is quite easy for me to think of a God of love mainly because I grew up in a family where love was central and where lovely relationships were ever present.
Martin Luther King Jr.

My parents would always tell me that I should not hate the white man, but that it was my duty as a Christian to love him.
Martin Luther King Jr.

Human salvation lies in the hands of the creatively maladjusted.
Martin Luther King Jr.

I submit that an individual who breaks a law that conscience tells him is unjust, and who willingly accepts the penalty of imprisonment in order to arouse the conscience of the community over its injustice, is in reality expressing the highest respect for the law.
Martin Luther King Jr.

It may be true that the law cannot make a man love me, but it can stop him from lynching me, and I think that's pretty important.
Martin Luther King Jr.

Like an unchecked cancer, hate corrodes the personality and eats away its vital unity. Hate destroys a man's sense of values and his objectivity. It causes him to describe the beautiful as ugly and the ugly as beautiful, and to confuse the true with the false and the false with the true.
Martin Luther King Jr.

Returning violence for violence multiplies violence, adding deeper darkness to a night already devoid of stars... Hate cannot drive out hate: only love can do that.
Martin Luther King Jr.

Segregation is the adultery of an illicit intercourse between injustice and immorality.
Martin Luther King Jr.

Ten thousand fools proclaim themselves into obscurity, while one wise man forgets himself into immortality.
Martin Luther King Jr.

The hope of a secure and livable world lies with disciplined nonconformists who are dedicated to justice, peace and brotherhood.
Martin Luther King Jr.

Nonviolence is the answer to the crucial political and moral questions of our time; the need for mankind to overcome oppression and violence without resorting to oppression and

violence. Mankind must evolve for all human conflict a method which rejects revenge, aggression, and retaliation. The foundation of such a method is love.
Martin Luther King Jr.

Injustice anywhere is a threat to justice everywhere.
Martin Luther King Jr.

The church was not merely a thermometer that recorded the ideas and principles of popular opinion; it was a thermostat that transformed the mores of society.
Martin Luther King Jr.

I submit to you that if a man hasn't discovered something he will die for, he isn't fit to live.
Martin Luther King Jr.

...And I've looked over, and I've seen the promised land. I may not get there with you, but I want you to know tonight that we as a people will get to the promised land. So I'm happy tonight. I'm not worried about anything. I'm not fearing any man.
Martin Luther King Jr., Speech in Memphis, April 3, 1968, the day before King was assassinated

I just want to do God's will. And he's allowed me to go to the mountain. And I've looked over, and I've seen the promised land! I may not get there with you, but I want you to know tonight that we as a people will get to the promised land.
Martin Luther King Jr., Speech in Memphis, April 3, 1968, the day before King was assassinated

Nothing in all the world is more dangerous than sincere ignorance and conscientious stupidity.
Martin Luther King Jr.

Our scientific power has outrun our spiritual power. We have guided missiles and misguided men.
Martin Luther King Jr.

The ultimate measure of a man is not where he stands in moments of comfort and convenience, but where he stands at times of challenge and controversy.
Martin Luther King Jr.

If you will protest courageously, and yet with dignity and Christian love, when the history books are written in future generations, the historians will have to pause and say, "There lived a great people—a black people—who injected new meaning and dignity into the veins of civilization."
Martin Luther King Jr.

The question is not whether we will be extremist but what kind of extremist will we be.
Martin Luther King Jr.

We are not makers of history. We are made by history.
Martin Luther King Jr.

There can be no deep disappointment where there is not deep love.
Martin Luther King Jr.

We will have to repent in this generation not merely for the hateful words and actions of the bad people but for the appalling silence of the good people.
Martin Luther King Jr.

I decided early to give my life to something eternal and absolute. Not to these little gods that are here today and gone tomorrow, but to God who is the same yesterday, today, and forever.
Martin Luther King Jr.

Discrimination is a hellhound that gnaws at Negroes in every waking moment of their lives to remind them that the lie of their inferiority is accepted as truth in the society dominating them.
Martin Luther King Jr.

A riot is the language of the unheard.
Martin Luther King Jr.

Shallow understanding from people of good will is more frustrating than absolute misunderstanding from people of ill will.
Martin Luther King Jr.

If physical death is the price that I must pay to free my white brothers and sisters from a permanent death of the spirit, then nothing can be more redemptive.
Martin Luther King Jr.

All men are caught in an inescapable network of mutuality.
Martin Luther King Jr.

Man must evolve for all human conflict a method which rejects revenge, aggression and retaliation. The foundation of such a method is love.
Martin Luther King Jr.

Our lives begin to end the day we become silent about things that matter.
Martin Luther King Jr.

Hate cannot drive out hate: only love can do that.
Martin Luther King Jr.

We must learn to live together as brothers or perish together as fools.
Martin Luther King Jr.

When you are right you cannot be too radical; when you are wrong, you cannot be too conservative.
Martin Luther King Jr.

All progress is precarious, and the solution of one problem brings us face to face with another problem.
Martin Luther King Jr.

The good neighbor looks beyond the external accidents and discerns those inner qualities that make all men human and, therefore, brothers.
Martin Luther King Jr.

I believe that unarmed truth and unconditional love will have the final word in reality. That is why right, temporarily defeated, is stronger than evil triumphant.
Martin Luther King Jr.

Somehow this madness must cease. We must stop now. I speak as a child of God and brother to the suffering poor of Vietnam.
Martin Luther King, Jr.

A nation that continues year after year to spend more money on military defense than on programs of social uplift is approaching spiritual death.
Martin Luther King, Jr.

Man was born into barbarism when killing his fellow man was a normal condition of existence. He became endowed with a conscience. And he has now reached the day when violence toward another human being must become as abhorrent as eating another's flesh.
Martin Luther King, Jr.

The curse of poverty has no justification in our age.
Martin Luther King, Jr.

The time has come for us to civilize ourselves by the total, direct and immediate abolition of poverty.
Martin Luther King, Jr.

The slums are the handiwork of a vicious system of the white society; Negroes live in them, but they do not make them, any more than a prisoner makes a prison.
Martin Luther King, Jr.

Darkness cannot drive out darkness; only light can do that.
Martin Luther King, Jr.

Success, recognition, and conformity are the bywords of the modern world where everyone seems to crave the anesthetizing security of being identified with the majority.
Martin Luther King, Jr.

We must combine the toughness of the serpent and the softness of the dove, a tough mind and a tender heart.
Martin Luther King, Jr.

The church must be reminded that it is not the master or the servant of the state, but rather the conscience of the state.
Martin Luther King, Jr.

Power at its best is love implementing the demands of justice. Justice at its best is love correcting everything that stands against love.
Martin Luther King, Jr.

Man is man because he is free to operate within the framework of his destiny. He is free to deliberate, to make decisions, and to choose between alternatives. He is distinguished from animals by his freedom to do evil or to do good and to walk the high road of beauty or tread the low road of ugly degeneracy.
Martin Luther King, Jr.

Nonviolent action, the Negro saw, was the way to supplement, not replace, the progress of change. It was the way to divest himself of passivity without arraying himself in vindictive force.
Martin Luther King, Jr.

Even though I have never had an abrupt conversion experience, religion has been real to me and closely knitted to life. In fact the two cannot be separated; religion for me is life.
Martin Luther King, Jr.

APPENDIXES

CORETTA SCOTT KING (1927-2006)

Introduction

Coretta Scott King was the wife of the assassinated civil rights activist Martin Luther King, Jr., and a noted community leader in her own right.

How We Open Our Hearts to God

Throughout the epic freedom struggle of African Americans, our great sustainer of hope has been the power of prayer. We prayed for deliverance in a dozen African languages, chained to the holds of slave ships, on the auction block, in the fields of oppression, and under the lash. We prayed when we "followed the drinking gourd" on the Underground Railroad. We prayed when our families were torn asunder by the slave traders. We prayed when our homes and churches were burned and bombed and when our people were lynched by racist mobs. So many times it seemed our prayer went unanswered, but we kept faith that one day our unearned suffering would prove to be redemptive. ...

My parents made sure that prayer would be a regular part of my life, and it has been to this very day. Prayer is how we open our hearts to God, how we make that vital connection that empowers us to overcome overwhelming obstacles and become instruments of God's will. And despite the pain and suffering that I have experienced and that comes to all of our lives, I am more convinced than ever before that prayer gives us strength and hope, a sense of divine companionship, as we struggle for justice and righteousness.

Prayer was a wellspring of strength and inspiration during the Civil Rights Movement. Throughout the movement, we prayed for greater human understanding. We prayed for the safety of our compatriots in the freedom struggle. We prayed for victory in our nonviolent protests, for brotherhood and sisterhood among people of all races, for reconciliation and the fulfillment of the Beloved Community.

For my husband, Martin Luther King, Jr. prayer was a daily source of courage and strength that gave him the ability to carry on in even the darkest hours of our struggle. With his head in his hands, Martin bowed over the kitchen table and prayed aloud to God: "Lord, I am taking a stand for what I believe is right. The people are looking to me for leadership, and if I stand before them without strength and courage, they will falter. I am at the end of my powers. I have nothing left. I have nothing left. I have come to the point where I can't face it alone."

Coretta Scott King, Standing in the Need of Prayer *from the Schomburg Center, with grateful acknowledgement to The Free Press, a division of Simon & Schuster.*

MARTIN LUTHER KING III (1957-)

Introduction

Luther King III (born in Montgomery, Alabama) is the son of Martin Luther King, Jr. and Coretta Scott King.

King attended Morehouse College, the same school his father attended. He graduated with a Bachelor of Arts in Political Science. King served as an elected commissioner of Fulton County, Georgia, from 1987 to 1993.

In 1997, King was unanimously elected to head the Southern Christian Leadership Conference (SCLC), a civil rights organization founded by his father. King left the SCLC in January 2004 to take over the King Center for Nonviolent Social Change from his brother, Dexter Scott King.

Wikipedia

"I Have A Dream" 40 Years Later

This is an except from Luther King III's address at the 40th Anniversary of The Great March on Washington.

I was only five years old the day my father gave his "I Have a Dream" speech before more than 200.000 participants in the March on Washington on August 28, 1963. Even though my daddy was famous, when I was five, my mother, Coretta Scott King, went out of her way to provide my sister Yolanda and me with "normal" childhoods.

I have no first-hand knowledge of [that great day], but I do know that my father was more than a dreamer and that redeeming the bad check that America had given African Americans was his number one dream.

The glorious dream my father shared with us on August 28, 1963 was not just an exercise in eloquent speechmaking. We need to remember that Martin Luther King, Jr. was first and foremost a minister of action who didn't just talk that beautiful talk. He walked the walk, unbent and unbowed, from Montgomery, Alabama to Memphis, Tennessee, from civil rights to human rights. Be assured that he intended his dream as a challenge to the nation he loved, a challenge we must accept to rise up and live out the true meaning of our creed and make America a beloved community.

Forty years later, we have lots of work to do to create the beloved community of his dream, for despite the progress we have made during the last four decades, people of color are still being denied a fair share of employment and educational opportunities in our society. They still experience incidents of racial violence. Forty years later we have yet to end racial oppression in the criminal justice system. We have yet to end selective prosecution and discrimination in sentencing. And we must abolish racial profiling and the death penalty. Forty years later, we must challenge racial injustice against people of color; we must support social and economic decency for people of all races. Right now in America, 15 million of our white brothers and sisters live below the poverty line. That is an injustice that must also be rectified if we are serious about building the beloved community that my father fought for.

Forty four million Americans have no health insurance, and many millions more have health insurance that doesn't cover serious illnesses. We yet need to establish a health insurance system that covers every person and every illness. Nothing less is acceptable for a great democracy.

© Martin Luther King, III.

GLOSSARY OF AFRICAN AMERICAN TERMS

Abolitionism

An active movement to end slavery in the U.S. North before the Civil War.

Abolitionist

Person who advocated or supported the end of slavery.

Affirmative action

A term coined during the Kennedy Administration (1961-63). A range of programs designed to overcome the effects of past discrimination and to provide equal opportunity for historically discriminated against groups, especially African Americans and women.

African American

An American of African ancestry.

African Free School

School for African Americans founded in 1787 by the New York Manumission Society.

Antebellum

Historical period in the United States, immediately preceding the Civil War.

Bigotry

Prejudice and/or discrimination against one or all members of a particular group based on negative perceptions of their beliefs and practices or on negative group stereotypes.

Black

Belonging to an ethnic group of African ancestry.

Black codes

Laws enacted after the Civil War to keep African Americans as a cheap work force.

Black nationalism

A philosophy advocated by some African-American leaders, such as Malcolm X (1925-1965), calling for self-determination for African-Americans.

Brown v. Board of Education of Topeka (1954)

U.S. Supreme Court decision that prohibited segregation in public schools and unanimously declared that "separate facilities are inherently unequal."

Bus boycott

See Montgomery Bus Boycott

Busing

The transportation of children by bus to schools outside the neighborhoods in which they live to achieve racial integration.

Civil Rights Act of 1964

National legislation that prohibits discrimination in voting, employment, public accommodations and facilities, and public schools, and provides for enforcement of desegregation.

Civil rights movement

The use of boycotts, sit-ins, marches, and other forms of nonviolent protest in the 1950s and 1960s to demand equal treatment under the law and an end to racial prejudice.

Civil War

The war (1861-1865) between the northern U.S. states, which remained in the Union, and the southern states, which seceded and formed the Confederacy. The victory of the North ended slavery and preserved the Union.

Color-blind

Used in this sense to describe a society that does not form opinions or take actions based on the color of people's skin.

Congress of Racial Equality (CORE)

A mainstream civil rights organization founded in 1942.

Degrade

To lower someone in status or role.

Discrimination

Discrimination is the denial of justice and fair treatment in many arenas, including employment, housing and political rights.

Emancipation

Refers to the Emancipation Proclamation issued by President Abraham Lincoln on January 1, 1863, which freed all slaves in states that had seceded from the Union.

Enslave Make a slave of; bring into servitude.

Equal opportunity

The principle that no person should be discriminated against because of race, gender, religion, or other inherent attributes.

Ethnic awareness

Acknowledgment of ethnic heritage with respect and pride.

Fifteenth Amendment

Ratified in 1870, this amendment gave African American men the right to vote.

"Fill up the jails"

A strategy by civil rights organizations to put pressure on local authorities by getting arrested in large numbers for acts of civil disobedience in Southern cities.

Free men of color

African Americans who were legally free through manumission, self-purchase, or by being born to a free black mother.

Freedman

Before 1865, a freedman was any person of African or partial African descent who was not a slave because he or she was able to purchase his or her freedom, or, granted freedom upon his or her master's death, or, the child of a free woman. After the Civil War, the term "freedmen" included all people of African or partial African descent living in the United States.

Freedom riders

Nonviolent black and white protesters who traveled by bus through the American South in 1961 to challenge race-based separation of facilities at bus and rail terminals. In November of that year the U.S. Interstate Commerce Commission prohibited segregated public accommodations.

Freedom Rides

Bus rides through the South organized in the 1960s by CORE to convince the federal government to enforce desegregation laws.

Gerrymandering

The distorted drawing of electoral lines to give an unfair advantage to one group. The word comes from a combination of salamander and Elbridge Gerry (I 744-1814), a Revolutionary era governor of Massachusetts and signer of the Declaration of Independence.

Gibbet

A structure used to hang someone. The bodies of lynching victims were sometimes left hanging from gibbets for many days as examples of what could happen to people who did not behave as members of conservative white hate groups thought they should.

Gullah

A Creole language that combines African words and sentence structure with English.

Harlem Renaissance, 1917-1936

The Harlem Renaissance was a flowering of African American art, literature, music and culture in the United States led primarily by the African American community based in Harlem, New York City after World War I.

Hearing

A preliminary examination in a criminal procedure.

Howard University

The nation's largest historically black university. Initially conceived by the First Congregational Society of Washington, DC, it was chartered by Congress in 1867.

Indentured servant

Person placed under contract to work over a period of time, usually seven years; prevalent during the 17th to 19th centuries.

Jim Crow

The term "Jim Crow" comes from the name of a character in an old minstrel show. The name "Jim Crow" was given to the day-to-day legal segregation of blacks from whites before the civil rights movement. So laws restricting African Americans to the back of a bus or creating separate restrooms, drinking fountains or eating facilities were known as "Jim Crow" laws.

Jim Crow laws

Laws passed in Southern states to separate whites and blacks in public and private facilities.

Ku Klux Klan (KKK)

A white Southern vigilante group created during Reconstruction and responsible for lynching and intimidating blacks and sympathetic whites.

Literacy tests

Tests that citizens had to pass to register to vote. Literacy tests were used in the South to prevent African-Americans from voting during the segregation era. The Voting Rights Act of 1965 banned their use.

Lynching

The term is derived from the "vigilante justice" practiced by Captain William Lynch and his neighbors in Pittsylvania County, Virginia, in the late 18th century. In the 19th century, lynching—usually associated with hanging but also including tar and feathering, burning and other methods of killing—became increasingly directed against African Americans. In the last 16 years of the 19th century, there were some 2,500 reported lynchings. The quest for federal laws against lynching was among the first crusades of the NAACP in the early decades of the 20th century.

Manumission Legal

Release of a person from slavery. Owners freed slaves as a reward for meritorious or faithful service.

Manumit

To manumit means to free from slavery, to emancipate. Masters occasionally granted manumissions in their wills, especially to their mistresses and children.

March on Washington in 1963

This was one of the largest demonstrations in support of civil rights and justice for African Americans and other minorities. Led by Dr. Martin Luther King, Jr., the gathering at the Lincoln Memorial of over 250,000 civil rights activists and ordinary citizens made clear the pressing need for legislation to overcome discrimination and make the law serve all people equally. Dr. King's "I Have a Dream" speech became the rallying cry in the struggle for civil rights.

Master

Colonist/owner who had control over slaves.

Million Man March

A gathering of upwards of one million African-American men that took place in Washington, D.C., on October 16, 1995. Participants came to the rally to pledge themselves to self-reliance, self-improvement, and respect for women, and to demonstrate unity and a commitment to support each other. The initiative for the event came from Louis Farrakhan, Leader of the Black Muslim Nation of Islam.

Montgomery Bus Boycott

Boycott of the public bus system in Montgomery, Alabama, in protest of the general requirement in the southern United States that African-Americans sit in the back of buses. The boycott lasted 381 days from December 1955 until December 1956, when the U.S. Supreme Court upheld a lower court decision that such segregation violated the Fourteenth Amendment of the U.S. Constitution.

Mulatoo

Person having one African American parent and one white parent. Many mulattos were children of white masters and the black slave women they owned.

Mustees

Any person of partial Native American and partial European descent.

National Association for the Advancement of Colored People (NAACP)

Interracial organization founded in 1909 to advocate and fight for civil rights of African Americans and against racial injustice.

National Association for the Advancement of Colored People (NAACP)

Founded in 1909, it is the oldest civil rights organization in the United States. Its Supreme Court victory in the Brown v. Board of Education decision mandated school desegregation.

National Colored Women's League of Washington, D. C.

Early organization formed by African American in Washington, D. C. to improve the image of the African American woman.

National Federation of Afro-American Women

An early organization formed by African American women in 12 states to improve the image of the African American woman.

Negro

Sociological term referring to any person whose ancestors are of African descent.

Negro-American

Term, generally accepted about 1934 when it was used as the title of a book, *Negro American, What Now?* by James Weldon Johnson.

"Passed over" or "passing"

Refers to a light skinned Black person assuming a white identity. In African-American culture occurred during slavery and after the Civil War until the mid-twentieth century as individuals chose to forsake their race and family to become white in an effort to escape widespread prejudice and discrimination.

Poll tax

Tax that citizens had to pay to vote. It was often used in the South to prevent African-Americans from voting. The 24th Amendment to the U.S. Constitution, ratified in 1964, barred the poll tax in federal elections.

Prejudice, prejudging

Making a decision about a person or group of people without sufficient knowledge. Prejudicial thinking is based on stereotypes.

Puritans

English religious and political reformers who fled their native land in search of religious freedom, and who settled and colonized New England in the 17th century.

Quadroon

Person having one-quarter African ancestry.

Racial preference

The practice of granting advantageous treatment to a person or group based on considerations of race.

Racism

Prejudice and/or discrimination based on the myth of race. Racists believe that some groups are born superior to others, and in the name of protecting their race from "contamination," they justify the domination and destruction of races they consider to be inferior to their own.

Railroad

See "Underground Railroad"

Reconstruction

Reconstruction began with the end of the Civil War in 1865, and its goal was to rebuild the South as homes, schools, hospitals, and farms had been destroyed by battle, neglect, and Sherman's March.

Restoration

When Reconstruction ended in 1877, conservative whites began to do things that, in effect, restored the South to its pre-war condition by returning African-Americans to their pre-war condition. Without federal troops, black people had no protection from this corruption.

Revolutionary War

The War of Independence, 1775-1783, fought by the American colonies against Great Britain.

Segregation

The imposition of separation or isolation on a race or class from the rest of the population.

Segregation laws

Laws that separated African Americans from the rest of the population based on race; also know as "Jim Crow" laws.

"Separate but equal"

Doctrine first established, and later overturned, by the U.S. Supreme Court allowing states to maintain segregated facilities for blacks and whites as long as they provided equal service.

Sit-ins

A nonviolent strategy used by civil rights groups to challenge Jim Crow laws by demanding equal treatment and the end to segregated facilities.

Slave codes

Laws enacted to curtail the rights of slaves and free men of color.

Slave narrative

The first black literary prose genre in the United States, featuring accounts of the horrors and abuse suffered by slaves at the hands of their master and the conditions under which they live.

South

A region of the United States comprising the states of Alabama, Arkansas, Florida, Georgia, Kentucky, Louisiana, Mississippi, Missouri, North Carolina, South Carolina, Tennessee, Virginia, and West Virginia, as well as eastern Texas.

Southern Christian Leadership Conference (SCLC)

A civil rights organization formed in 1957 by Southern ministers and led by the Rev. Martin Luther King Jr. The SCLC is committed to the principle of nonviolence.

Southern states

See "South"

Stereotype

An oversimplified generalization about a person or group of people without regard for individual differences.

"Talented tenth"

A term coined by W. E. B. Du Bois to describe the small percentage of educated and upper middle class Negroes who were high achievers in the face of racial prejudice.

Thirteenth Amendment

Ratified in 1865, this amendment abolished slavery.

Underground Railroad

For the 240 years from the first African slave until 1860, slaves ran and some escaped to freedom. In 1850, the value of a trained slave was around $2500—an enormous sum at a time more than ten times the average person's annual earnings. Thus, slaves were chased by their masters or bounty hunters. Because intelligence agencies placed single men and women in domestic jobs in cities like Syracuse and towns as Geneva, the transportation of slaves to freedom obviously had to be done under the utmost secret of conditions. The transport worked much like a railroad and so it was called The Underground Railroad.

White Citizens' Council

A white hate group formed in Mississippi to maintain segregation following the Supreme Court's Brown decision.

Whites

Term used to describe people with fair colored skin.

Yeoman

The owner of a small farm who tends his own fields.